$14⁹⁵

3rd EDITION

1915-1965
American Premium

RECORD GUIDE

78's, 45's and LP's

IDENTIFICATION AND VALUES

By L.R. DOCKS

BOOKS AMERICANA
INC

ISBN 0-89689-054-6

ACKNOWLEDGEMENTS

Special thanks must be given to my wife, Pam, for her encouragement and indispensable assistance in compiling and revising this reference work, for the many hours she spent putting together and revising the index, and for her tolerant understanding during those periods when I was holed up in the "shellac shack," virtually incommunicado, compensating for earlier procrastination, getting everything ready to send to the publisher.

I am indebted also to the following for furnishing records for photography and for contribution of data: Werner Benecke (whose contribution to a more accurate second and third edition is especially appreciated), George Blacker, Dan Campbell, Fred Chambers, Rex Clark, Scott Cleveland, F. Curran, Lou Curtiss, Ron Evry, Mike Gietzen, Don Gray, Doug Gregory, Steve Gronda, E.J. Henke, The John Edwards Memorial Foundation (and Linda Painter, Editor of its J.E.M.F. Quarterly), Glenn Keck, Bob Mays, William C. (Bill) Menor, Jerry Nieporte, Charlie O'Haver, Dan Stevens, Keith Titterington.

My appreciation must also be expressed to Elaine Cary for her able typing services furnished on short notice, and to Dan Alexander, President of Books Americana, Inc., for his patience each time this book and its revisions took shape.

INTRODUCTION

There is nothing "official" about this or any other price guide. It, like other books on collectibles, reflects the opinions of the author, based upon lengthy experience buying selling and trading records, consulting countless auction lists, sales lists, record publications, discographies, record company promotional literature, and collectors' want lists. Undoubtedly, many errors and omissions will be noted by knowledgeable collectors; it is hoped that these will be brought to my attention by writing to L.R. DOCKS, P.O. Box 32924, San Antonio, Texas 78216.

Here, in a single volume, are listed thousands of desirable records in the most widely collected categories: Jazz, Dance Bands, Celebrity, Blues, Rhythm and Blues, Country and Western, Hillbilly, Rockabilly, and Rock and Roll. Included are 78s, 45s, EPs, and LPs. Emphasis is given to categories heretofore neglected and/or inadequately treated, such as early jazz, blues and country 78s.

As in previous editions, the majority of records listed are unfamiliar to non-collectors. Indeed, many are so obscure as to be unfamiliar even to sophisticated collectors. Quick now: Who were Dubin's Dandies? Very few of the records listed are top-selling hits. This book is intended to be a guide to scarce, sought-after, and otherwise desirable discs that *ought to be* recognized as collectible. It is not meant to afford readers a "nostalgia trip," by listing thousands of familiar old favorites, complete with titles. Those treasured (when was the last time they were dug out of the cellar and played?) records by Bing Crosby, Al Jolson, Glenn Miller, et al., even if they are indeed "originals," are probably not discs that are saleable to a knowledgeable collector, and certainly not at more than a nominal sum. Common sense ought to suggest that records which sold in the largest quantities remain relatively common and inexpensive today. But common sense sometimes seems uncommon: "I have an original "White Christmas" by Bing Crosby; what will you give me for it?" Oh, well! I don't really expect to get many calls offering me a store stock of 8000 series Okeh records.

Readers of previous editions will note, however, the inclusion this time of many more relatively common and inexpensive records, i.e. records valued at two to five dollars, by the more familiar artists, and on commonly found labels such as red Columbia. They may well ask, "Has Docks sold out?" The answer is a resounding "no." Well, maybe not so resounding. This seeming concession is only slightly in response to popular (and publisher, to whom Kay Kyser fans owe their gratitude) demand. The real purpose is to create a sense of relative scarcity and desirability between very common and scarcer records, and to avoid having to answer numerous inquiries about why certain common records aren't listed and whether the correspondent has unearthed a heretofore unknown rarity. I know that I can't foreclose all such inquiries, even from those who do read this introduction. But at least I shouldn't get any more letters from owners of Gene Autry red label *Columbia* records who think that they are unlisted rarities.

What kinds of records are regarded as desirable by knowledgeable collectors? Records in the categories mentioned above, regarded as excellent examples of their idiom; or records which are historically important, as for example records featuring the early work of a future star; or records issued on rare or interesting labels. There are certainly other factors; sometimes there's no accounting for taste. Many of the records listed herein were issued in special series or on labels aimed at limited markets. "Race" series and labels, aimed at the Negro, and hillbilly series (styled "Songs From Dixie" series or the like) aimed at the white, rural folk never attained the levels of distribution of the more popular, acceptable, and civilized music of polite society. So, the music that was denigrated, isolated and segregated in its own time is today the music that is most appreciated and prized.

DEFINITIONS, SYMBOLS and TERMS

Following are brief explanations of some of the terms and symbols used by record collectors and dealers. Some of them are forthright and succinct. Others, attempting to define the various styles and idioms of music, are somewhat amorphous, if not downright evasive. Music appeals to the emotions and senses, and does not invite verbal analysis. Most people know jazz (or blues, or country/western music) when they hear it. "It Don't Mean A Thing If It Ain't Got That Swing" is better than any dictionary definition. If you have a record you're not familiar with—for example, "Four Or Five Times" by McKinney's Cotton Pickers, play it. You'll probably know what category it falls into without reading any definition. Or, just consult the Complete Artist Index at the end of this book, starting at page 341.

BLUES: Webster's New Collegiate Dictionary defines blues as "a song of lamentation characterized by 12-bar phrases, 3-line stanzas in which the words of the second stanza repeat those of the first, and continual occurence of blue notes in melody and harmony." A bit of overdubbing: The songs relate to the troubles, hardships and common experiences of blacks (and poor whites). Some blues are country style with accompaniments usually consisting of stringed or even makeshift instruments; some blues are urbanized, closer to jazz, with wind instruments often accompanying the vocalist. If all this seems meaningless, play a blues record; it—even just 12 bars of it—will be worth a thousand words.

BOOTLEG: An unauthorized issue of a previously unreleased performance in derogation of the rights of the real owner of the tape of master and the artist. The term also is used in reference to an unauthorized copy or reissue of a previously issued record. Where the unauthorized copy closely resembles the original record in label design, the more correct term is "REPRODUCTION," or "COUNTERFEIT." Since the practice of bootlegging or reproducing rare and valuable 45rpm records of the 1950's has become widespread, collectors are advised to exercise caution when expending large sums on records of that period. There is no substitute for personal familiarity with the subtle characteristics of the original records: such things as the distinctness of the lettering, the texture of the paper used for the label, the appearance of the grooves, master numbers in the wax, the thickness of the pressing, etc.

CONTEMPORANEOUS ISSUES: Contemporaneous issues of the same performance on two or more labels was common in the 1920s

and 1930s. This was the result of contractual arrangement, corporate affiliation, or the ownership of several labels by the same company. The most frequently encountered grouping comprises Banner, Conqueror, Melotone, Oriole, Perfect, Romeo, and sometimes Vocalion. Many recordings of the 1930s for the American Record Company were issued at the same time on several if not all of the labels mentioned. The song titles, the artists' names, the typography, and even the catalog number of the record on many, would be identical on each label. Other examples from the 1930s are Champion and Decca; Bluebird, Electradisk, Montgomery Ward, and Timely Tunes (all RCA Victor products). In the 1920s, the following label affiliations commonly occurred: Cameo, Lincoln, Romeo; Harmony, Diva, Velvet-Tone (and later, about 1930, Clarion); Perfect and Pathe-Actuelle; Gennett. Champion, Challenge, Claxtonola, Herschel Gold Seal, Silvertone, Superior, Supertone; Harmograph, Paramount, Black Swan; Arto, Bell, Cleartone, Globe, Grey Gull, Radiex, Brunswick, Vocalion; Banner, Cameo, Jewel, Oriole, Regal, Romeo. The practice also existed in the 1950s; for example Sun and Flip labels. It should be noted that the affiliated labels may not have been issued at *exactly* the same time; technically, one might be regarded as the original issue. Collectors of 1950s records are far more particular in this regard than are collectors of vintage 78s. It should also be noted that the real name of the artist was not always used on all of the affiliated labels; the use of pseudonyms was extensive. The purpose was often to evade exclusive recording artist contractual restrictions, or to avoid making royalty payments to artists. Several examples: Performances by Irving Mills' groups were variously credited as by Jimmy Bracken's Toe Ticklers, Dixie Jazz Band, Kentucky Grasshoppers, The Lumberjacks and The Whoopee Makers on Banner, Jewell, Oriole, Regal and Romeo. The Wolverine Orchestra on Gennett became The Jazz Harmonizers on Claxtonola. Bradley Kincaid on Gennett became Dan Hughey on Champion. If this isn't confusing enough, one pseudonym, such as Dixie Jazz Band on Oriole, might conceal the true identity of a dozen or more bands, whose performances appeared on other labels perhaps under different pseudonyms! Records listed in this volume are listed according to the label credits, without regard to pseudonyms. The real name behind pseudonyms should be sought in the various discographies listed in the Bibliography. Those wishing the delve further into the complexities of label affiliation and the corporate evolution of record companies should consult "From Tin Foil to Stereo," by Read and Welch, and "The American Record Label Book" by Brian Rust, both listed in the Bibliography.

COUNTRY/WESTERN/HILLBILLY MUSIC: Webster's New Collegiate Dictionary defines this music as "derived from or imitating the folk style of the southern U.S. or of the Western cowboy." At least this definition seems to exclude much of the watered-down Nashville product. Is it broad enough to include Jimmie Rodgers, Bob Wills, Ernest Stoneman, Fiddlin' John Carson, et al?

DISCOGRAPHY: A compilation of data concerning the recorded work of an artist including recordings issued and unissued, recording dates, personnels, locations, master numbers. Of course, discographies can vary as to completeness and accuracy. Discographies of a single artist usually are found in record collectors' publications. The term many also refer to books such as the outstanding works by Brian Rust in the areas of Jazz, Dance Bands, and Entertainment. These attempt to list all records by all artists, to the extent that their recordings fall within the subject field. Label discographies are numerical listings of particular labels, according to catalog number. Some offer only record numbers and song titles. See, for example, Roger Kinkle's four-volume work, listed in the Bibliography. Kinkle offers numerical listings of nine major labels of the 1920s, 1930s, and 1940s, which listings are often useful, even though abbreviation of titles and artists' names is often cause for puzzlement. Ken Clee's four-volume collection consists of 45 rpm labels of the 1950s and later; it is also listed in the Bibliography. Other label discographies are more thorough, offering, in addition to song titles and record numbers, master numbers, release dates, production figures, and more. See, for example, Dan Mahoney's "The Columbia 13000/14000-D Series," also listed in the Bibliography. Label discographies are often found in record collectors' publications.

"D.J. COPY" refers to Disc Jockey, or Promotional records, which are issued to radio stations. The label color often differs from that of the regular issue, and usually bears the statement "Promotional Copy—Not For Sale" or words of similar import. The pressing quality of some D.J. copies is higher than that of the regular issue. Some are pressed from translucent colored vinyl rather than black.

"E.P." refers to Extended Play records. These are usually 45rpm records containing four or more songs, issued in a stiff cardboard jacket similar to those for LPs. Some EPs were issued in series of two and three, together containing the contents of an LP issued concurrently. Records issued in the early 1930s having extended playing time, such as some Clarion and Hit of the Week records, are not distinguished herein by the abbreviation "E.P."

JAZZ: Webster's New Collegiate Dictionary defines jazz as "American music developed . . from ragtime and blues and characterized by syncopated rhythms, contrapuntal ensemble playing, and . . . improvisation often with special melodic features (as blue notes) peculiar to the individual interpretation of the player," or "popular dance music influenced by jazz and played in a loud rhythmic manner." You'll know it when you hear it. The second part of the definition is particularly noteworthy. Many records of jazz interest are ordinary fox trots having one or more "hot" solos by a jazz musician or some unknown stepping out of character and assuming that role. There are jazz records by the orchestras of Jan Garber and Guy Lombardo, believe it or not. Conversely, not every record whose label suggests the presence of hot music should be believed. The Missouri Jazz Band (often encountered on Banner and Regal discs of the 1920s) rarely produced anything sounding like jazz, and probably weren't from Missouri, either. Take a few weeks off and study Rust's "Jazz Records, 1897-1942."

"JUNKING" The practice of record collector of visiting fleas markets, garage sales, and secondhand stores in quest of records.

"L.P." The abbreviation of "Long Play," which refers to a record utilizing a finer groove, and therefore containing more playing time, than a single 45 or 78 rpm record of equivalent diameter. Most LPs have several or more songs on each side, but may instead have a single extended performance. Most modern LPs are 12-inches in diameter; issues from the early 1950s are 10-inches in diameter. Playing speed is 33⅓rpm. Some early LPs issued by Edison in the 1920s contained as much as 20 minutes playing time on each side—at 80rpm! These were failures, technically and commercially, and the records are quite scarce today. Musically, they contain little of interest to most collectors. In the early 1930s, RCA Victor issued 10-inch 33⅓ rpm records called "Program Transcriptions." These too were technically inadequate and failed to sell well. Some of these scarce discs do have interesting musical content, and are listed herein. See photo in label section under RCA Victor.

PICTURE RECORD This is a record displaying a picture over its entire surface, including the portion normally occupied by a label. The picture, which may be of the artist or a fanciful device (See Vogue picture record, in label listing), are printed on paper which is laminated between the clear plastic or vinyl which constitutes the playing surface. The current mania for picture records may be unprecedented, but the basic idea is not new. Vogue picture records attained respectable sales levels briefly in the late 1940s. Picture records were commercially issued in the early 1930s, most successfully by RCA Victor; but even these are quite scarce. (See Fig. 1).

Figure 1

PICTURE SLEEVE A record sleeve of a 45rpm record having no center hole exposing the record, but rather having a picture usually of the artist or group. Some picture sleeves are more highly valued than the subject record.

PROMOTIONAL COPY (See D.J. COPY)

"RACE" RECORDS Records of the 1920s and 1930s produced for the Negro market, utilizing primarily Negro talent. Musical content is usually blues, jazz, or gospel. Certain labels were almost entirely "race" oriented (Black Swan and Black Patti) and were even owned and managed by blacks. Usually, however, race records were issued by the larger labels in special series bearing a special numerical sequence or even a variation in label design to distinguish the race records from the popular white-oriented series. (Hillbilly records were similarly distinguished.)

Examples are the Victor 38000 series, the Vocalion 1000 series, the Brunswick 7000 series (employing the distinctive "lightning" label design in addition to the special number series), the Columbia 13000-D and 14000-D series, and the Okeh 8000 series. While this musical segregation persisted well into the 1950s, the labels which were then the strongholds of black talent (Federal, DeLuxe, Vee Jay, Jubilee, to name just a few) became "rhythm and blues" labels rather than race labels. Few white radio stations would play them.

"R & B" (Abbreviation for "rhythm and blues") the music of the 1950s by and essentially for the Negro market, which evolved from blues, jazz, and jump blues. This music was a major force in the emergence of rock and roll and rockabilly.

"RED PLASTIC" (or other colored plastic) "RED WAX," etc. Records which are made of other than the usual black material. The most frequent variation from black is translucent red vinyl. Many 45 rpm records from the 1950s issued in this form are highly prized. Other records were made of translucent green, blue or orange vinyl. Still others were made of opaque colored plastic, in the style of children's records. Where a record occurs in both black and colored form, the colored version usually commands a substantial premium over the black. In the 1920s, some 78s were made of other than black material. Perfect and early Vocalion records were a brownish-orange; Pathe-Actuelle was mottled. In the early 1930s, Columbia attempted to spur lagging sales with its "Royal Blue" issues, which today are a favorite of collectors.

REISSUE: A re-release of a previously issued record by the owner of the performance or under license from such owner. A reissue may be on the original label, with the same catalog number, or with a different catalog number.

Figure 2   Figure 3

The label design may also have changed between the time of the original or the reissue may be on an entirely different label than the original issue. (See Figs. 2 & 3) (Veteran collectors may note that some of the "reissues" are "alternate takes" issued for the first time years after recording.)

RHYTHM & BLUES (See "R & B")

ROCKABILLY: Rock and roll sung by a hillbilly-sounding singer; up-tempo country music. Other elements are a "slappin' bass," "hot" guitar and/or piano, and echo effects. Back-up voices or horns detract from desirability, according to rockabilly purists. The style is defined by early Elvis Presley records, as well as by such artists as Jerry Lee Lewis, Carl Perkins, and more obscure rockers such as Sonny Fisher and Pat Cupp.

ROCK AND ROLL: Popular, usually up-tempo, hard-driving music with solid rhythm, often having frantic vocals, wailing saxophones, hot piano, and elements of hillbilly boogie and jump blues and rhythm and blues from which it evolved. Although rock and roll is identified with the 1950s, and such artists as Chuck Berry, Elvis Presley, and Bill Haley, rock and roll was actually being performed several years earlier by rhythm and blues artists such as Jackie Brenston and The Dominoes.

78 RPM; 78s: The playing speed of most pre-1950 single records. Actually, many early 78 rpm records were intended to be played at 80 rpm, or some other speed, but these are treated herein as 78s without distinction.

TEST PRESSING: A record pressed to give the artist and/or record company executive a chance to hear and judge the merits of a recording and its suitability for issue commercially. The record may be pressed on one side or on both sides. The label is usually plain white with the information handwritten, often cryptically, or printed (See Fig. 4). The edge of the disc may be somewhat jagged and irregular, rather than smooth. Not pressed for sale to the public, any test pressing is scarce. But not every test pressing is valuable or highly collectible. Let the next one you find be a previously unissued jazz, blues, or rockabilly performance, or an "alternate take" of an issued performance; and let me know about it!

Figure 4

ORGANIZATION OF THIS BOOK

The main listing of this book is divided into four sections:

1. Jazz, Dance Bands, Big Bands, Swing, Personality; primarily 78 rpm records, 1915 to about 1950
2. Blues; primarily 78s 1920s—early 1950s
3. Country/Western, hillbilly, old-time singing, string bands, fiddling; primarily 78rpm; 1920s—early 1950s
4. Rhythm & Blues, Blues, Rock & Roll, Rockabilly, etc.; primarily 45 rpm, EPs and LPs, with selected 78s; 1950s and early 1960s.

The inclusion of a given artist in a particular section is often a matter of arbitrary choice. For example, many records by blues artists are found in the Jazz, etc., section due to the fact that their accompaniment is of jazz interest. Some artists are found in more than one section. Where recordings were made in the 1930s and also in the 1950s, that artist might appear in both sections: for example, Lonnie Johnson. An index of all artists listed in this book, following the listings, on page 341, will enable readers to find all listed records by an artist even when that artist appears in more than one section.

Within each category, the listings are alphabetical by artist. The listings for each artist are presented alphabetically by label, and by catalog number, from lowest to highest, within each label. This may not reflect the chronological order of issue. For example Bluebirds are listed before Victors; but the Victors are almost always earlier issues than the Bluebirds. And the Gennett 3000 numbers are later than the 5000 numbers. The true order of recording and issue is left to the discographies. The intention here is to provide ease of usage.

Some listings embrace a number of issues on the same label:

Bluebird, most other issues 2.00-4.00

Such a listing, while consisting of records of

minimal scarcity and value, may well include some discs so common that they are viturally unsaleable to any real record collector.

Catalog number prefixes and suffixes (numbers or letters) common to all or most issues on a label or series are usually omitted. Thus, RCA Victor 47-6604 is listed as RCA Victor 6604. The prefix "47-" (or "20-" in the case of 78s) appears on the majority of RCA Victor 45rpm records. Also omitted are the ubiquitous suffixes "-A" and "-B" (and variants such as "-L" and "-R" on Edison). Prefixes and suffixes do serve to distinguish between seemingly overlapping numerical series on Columbia records, and are therefore included.

All listings reflect the names as credited on the actual records, without regard to whether such names are actual or pseudonyms. Cross-references are kept to a minimum, it being assumed that interested collectors will seek any further information about pseudonyms (and any other matters beyond the scope of this reference, such as personnels, recording dates, additional recordings, reissues) from the discographies and other sources listed in the Bibliography.

WHERE TO BUY, SELL OR TRADE RECORDS

Every record collector, whether novice or veteran, obtains at least some of his discs by "junking." (See definition on page v.) The more avid the collector, the more time, effort and expense he devotes to junking; and this is often true even though the resultant finds aren't worth the trouble—either for their musical enjoyment or their value. But there's always the possibility of that great find: King Oliver on Gennett; Charlie Spand on Paramount; Hank Williams on Sterling; Elvis Presley on Sun; or maybe a whole box of "goodies." And getting up before daybreak to get first pick at the flea market or an estate sale, certainly increases your chances!

Most collectors are not content to leave the acquisition of their wants to the fortuities of junking. The best source of collectible records is other collectors and dealers (in many instances the same persons). Often, a knowledgeable collector is easier to deal with than a casual or one-time vendor of records. I've seen common, middle-of-the-road records at flea markets priced at $5.00 each, accompanied by a warning against handling the treasures! To get in contact with other collectors and/or dealers, begin in any case with record collectors publications. (See Publications listing, page 339.)

Some leading record publications are largely marketplaces for selling, buying and trading records. It is advisable to utilize those most appropriate to your interests. If you specialize in Rockabilly, you'll find little of interest in *Vintage Jazz Mart; Goldmine* contains little for the collector of Edison discs. Once you've gotten familiar with the appropriate publications, and the terms and conditions of transacting business with advertisers, you might consider advertising your wants, as well as contacting other advertisers, particularly those who invite "want lists."

Record collectors' conventions are becoming more numerous, but are still to be found only in a relatively few cities. The publications referred to above usually give notice of these. The crowds often present at these conventions attest to the high level of enthusiasm record collectors have for their hobby. Nowhere was this more evident than at the record flea-market (termed a "bizarre ritual" in *Goldmine,* November, 1980) which until recently was held in the parking lot of Capitol Records in Hollywood, California; it began in the middle of the night, and would actually break up by late morning!

In a number of cities, there are stores specializing in collectors' records. Unfortunately, the majority of these shops do not advertise in record collector publications. I have visited such shops in Bloomington, Indiana, Chicago, Detroit, Fort Worth, Glendale, California, Salt Lake City, San Diego and Santa Monica, California, and elsewhere.

VALUATION OF RECORDS

The prices herein are estimations of what records might reasonably be expected to bring in transactions between knowledgeable buyers and sellers. Most estimations are stated as a range i.e. $10.00 to $15.00, rather than a specific figure. This method of pricing recognizes the partial validity of the widely held contention that it is impossible at this time, given the fluid and formative state of the market, to assign definite values to records.

Although most of the really desirable records are bought and sold by mail, often at auction, the prices herein are not intended to reflect the highest sale prices or winning bids. A given record might bring $10.00 in one auction and $4.00 in the next. Indeed, in the same auction, the array of bids often demonstrates a wide disparity in bidders' estimations of value; and auction bidders are generally fairly knowledgeable. Widely differing prices on the same record are also found when comparing set sale lists or minimum bid figures in auction lists. Certainly these dealers in records must also be regarded as fairly knowledgeable. So, what is any record really worth? The only sure answer is, whatever you can get for it.

The casual seller of records, such as the flea market or garage sale vendor, who has no real knowledge or appreciation of records, who does not intelligently and selectively acquire records, who does not properly organize and preserve them, and who does not seek, by appropriate advertising, knowledgeable collectors as customers, will have difficulty realizing even a small fraction of the prices quoted herein for the better records. There is nothing unfair about this situation. One not disposed to invest the time, effort and expense (beyond the cost of a price guide) necessary to deal with some expertise should perhaps be in another business. I have seen several such record vendors, compelled by economic realities, make just that decision.

GRADING OF RECORDS

The condition of a record is of paramount importance. A new, apparently (who can be certain?) unplayed copy might be worth many times the price of a worn "junk-shop" copy. Indeed, a very worn copy may not be saleable at all.

The prices quoted herein are for records in excellent condition. "Excellent" is more or less a term or art, being part of the standard grading code following, which has been in use for many years:

"NEW" or "N": New; apparently unplayed and of course showing no signs of wear.

"EXCELLENT" or "E": Showing only slight wear; playing surfaces still retain much of their original shine. Surface noise is minimal.

"VERY GOOD" or "V": Somewhat more worn than an "excellent" record, slight grayness appearing in the grooves, especially in louder passages. Still a fairly clean and acceptable copy. Surface and extraneous noise is noticeable, but does not overwhelm the music.

"GOOD" or "G": A misnomer, a "good" record is really not so good. It shows considerable wear and usage, grayness in the grooves, random mars and light abrasions from an undoubted sleeveless existence. Surface noise is prominent enough to impair enjoyment of music.

"FAIR" ("F") and "POOR" ("P") indicate the lowest grades of the condition code. Since only the rarest records would be saleable in these grades, they appear infrequently.

Plus and minus signs are often suffixed to above grades to indicate a somewhat better or worse grade, when appropriate.

Another grading code is often employed by persons and publications concerned with the music of the 1950s and 1960s, which are primarily 45s, EPs, and LPs: "Mint" or "M" is used in place of "New" or "N"; "Very Good" or "VG" corresponds more closely to "Excellent" ("E") than to the older system's "Very Good" ("V"); "Good" or "G" is roughly equivalent to the older system's "Very Good" ("V").

In addition to the wear factor, defects and impairments can drastically affect the value and saleability of a record. Some of these, affecting the playing surface, are cracks, digs, and warps. A crack usually renders a record practically worthless; even the value of a rarity is generally reduced to a nominal sum by the presence of a crack. This is true even if the crack is "tight" and negotiable by a needle. There are exceptions, such as "lamination cracks" which affect only one side of a laminated record (having a cardboard core between the playing surfaces) such as Columbia or Okeh: these cracks severely affect, but do not necessarily destroy, the record's value. With most defects, how much the value of the record is reduced is a matter of degree. Is that scratch inaudible, or does it make the tone-arm jump half an inch? Does that dig allow the needle to negotiate the groove, or does the affected passage repeat? Other defects, such as the label or stickers on the label, do not affect play, but only appearance; but this can be very important. In short, the acknowledgement of defects is an essential part of the grading process.

Most auction lists and price lists will contain an explanation of the grading system and symbols used. But it is important that the system, whichever is used, be applied fairly and objectively. Often it is not; overgrading has become commonplace in the collectors' record market. A reputable dealer will make adjustments or refunds if a record proves to be erroneously graded.

TRENDS AND FADS
IN RECORD COLLECTING

Record collecting has undergone great change over the decades. Prior to 1935, most record collectors favored classical and operatic records. In the 1930s and 1940s, jazz and blues records (particularly blues records with jazz accompaniments) became the primary area of interst. Prior to the era of the LP as a vehicle for reissuing, the original 78s, commanded prices higher than they do now (particularly if the decline in the value of the dollar is taken into account). The extensive reissuing of jazz has undoubtedly affected the market for the original 78s, although there are many collectors who insist upon owning the original discs. Furthermore, many of the old-time collectors lose interest or relinquish their 78s in favor of LP reissues.

Interest in early country and western records developed considerably later than did the mania for jazz. The reissuing of this music has also lagged far behind, and still has a long way to go to reach the point, which might be said of jazz, where most significant performances have been reissued. Contrary to the situation with jazz 78s, the demand for these records (and consequently their values) has yet to peak, much less decline. The expected appearance of a country-western discography is certain to heighten interest in this field of collecting.

Seemingly the most active category of record collecting is the music of th 1950s and 1960s, including Rock and Roll, Rhythm and Blues, Rockabilly, and Blues. In the early 1960s, Rhythm and Blues records, particularly vocal groups, were already being collected seriously with obscure discs of only a few years earlier commanding respectable premiums. Interest spread to single-artist Rhythm and Blues, Blues, Rockabilly, and Rock and Roll obscurities. Certain artists such as Elvis Presley, The Beatles, The Beach Boys, and The Four Seasons, have a following bordering on fanaticism, with some collectors seeking any tangible object relating to the artist, recorded or otherwise (see comment preceding Elvis Presley listing). Notable among many of the newer crop of collectors is their penchant for acquiring, displaying and preserving visual, graphic art souvenirs of recording artists, relegating the audio aspect to secondary importance. Thus, many albums remain sealed, and Elvis' Sun records find homes on collector's walls. The jacket of an album is more important than the record in some cases (see The Beatles and Frank Ifield, in listings); picture sleeves can be worth more than the subject record; picture records find a market at exhorbitant prices. Not too long ago, there were only the colored wax freaks to wonder at!

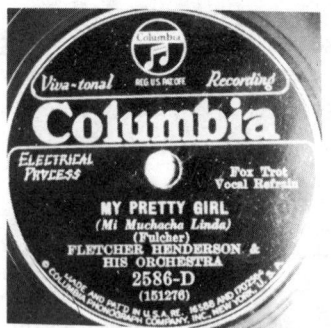 

Figure 5   Figure 6

Figure 7

Figure 8   Figure 9

RECORD LABELS

What's on a record label? Referring to figure 5, you'll find the name of the label (Columbia) and logo; the song title in English and Spanish ("Mi Muchacha Linda"); composer/lyricist credits (Fulcher); the name of the artist/group/orchestra (Fletcher Henderson & His Orchestra); the record catalog number (2586-D) the master number 151276; the type of music and whether vocal or instrumental (Fox Trot, Vocal Refrain"); copyright, patent or trademark registration numbers or dates; the name and address of the manufacturer. Labels may also contain a picture of the artist (see fig. 7); the suggested retail price; and occasionally a release date (see Gennett, fig. 8); "11-25" at 3 o'clock position indicates November, 1925); or a designation "Race Record); (see fig. 9). A common feature is a slogan referring to the use of electrical recording processes: "Electrically Recorded," "Electrical Process,"

"Super Electrical Recorded," "Viva-Tonal Recording," "Electrobeam," "Orthophonic Recording," "Truetone," and others. Starting in the early 1930s, an admonition against use for radio broadcast was commonly used (see fig. 6).

Information usually not found on record labels includes the date of recording, or release of the record. There are exceptions, such as Gennett (see fig. 8), Champion, and Mercury, and there are other instances where the date of release appears cryptically, such as the mid-1930s Banner, Melotone, Oriole, Perfect and Romeo issues. A knowledge of when various record labels were issued, and their rate of usage of master numbers and catalog numbers, will make possible a reasonable close estimation of recording and issue dates. Referring to a discography will provide the best information. Normally, dates appearing on the label relate to copyright, patent and trademark registration, and have little relation to the recording or issue date. For example, the 1921 copyright date on Regal records might appear on a record recorded and issued several (or more) years later.

Personnels usually don't appear on record labels until the late 1930s when they began to be used on some original jazz and swing issues, principally by Columbia and Victor (which even had a special "Swing Classic" series).

Reissues for collectors are likely to have personnels, recording dates, the name and number of the original issue label, and may even credit the name of the artist differently than did the original issues. These reissues often were sold in album sets; Brunswick, Columbia and RCA Victor engaged in considerable such reissuing in the late 1930s and 1940s. Few collectors' reissues will be found listed in this reference because of their minimal value; but they do contain many great, classic performances of vintage jazz which are practically unobtainable as original issues.

The record labels themselves are often colorful and interesting, as a perusual of pages 1 through 45 will (or perhaps already has) confirmed. The song titles are amusing relics of other times and cultures. Perhaps it isn't such a bad idea to decorate your wall with interesting labels and titles.

Certain labels have a more than usual attraction, or even a mystique which leads some collectors to collect by label, rather than by artist or type of music. Most collectors are guilty (is this the correct word?) of this tendency perhaps only to the extent of having favorite labels. But some collectors seek to obtain every issue on a certain label, regardless of artist or musical content. The label most commonly collected in this manner is the "SUN" label which in the 1950s assumed a major role in producing first-class rockabilly and rock and roll with such artists as Elvis Presley, Carl Perkins and Jerry Lee Lewis. Of course, not everything issued on that label was great and worthy of collecting, but sometimes it seems that way. In any event, substantial sums have been paid on occasion for scarce but musically mediocre Sun records in order to fill a numerical gap. Other labels of the 1950s collected in this manner include Atlantic, Federal, and Vee Jay; and probably any of the Rhythm and Blues Labels you can think of has its specialists. Among the 78rpm labels, some of the most popular among label collectors are the Vogue picture record, Columbia 14000-D (Race) series, Victor 23000 and 38000 series, Gennett, Paramount, and Okeh 8000 series. Few collectors of the early 78s really are in earnest, however, about obtaining a complete numerical run as are "Sun" collectors. Incidentally, for the enlightenment, amusement and perhaps frustration of "Sun" collectors, I offer the following photo of a "Sun" record from the early 1900s (having no relationship, of course, to the 1950s-1960s Memphis product):

There are a relatively small number of collectors who strive to obtain as many different labels as they can, often without regard to musical content. Auction lists of vintage 78s occasionally offer a "rare and unusual label" section. A scarce label such as Autograph may bring several dollars even though the pipe-organ solo it offers is of no musical interest to the bidders. Other scarce labels (early 78s) include Blu-Disc, Black Patti, Black Swan, Buddy, Connorized, Claxtonola, Edison (thin), Electradisk, Everybody's, Gennett (Electrobeam), Harmograph, Herschel Gold Seal, Herwin, Hudson, Hy-Tone, Meritt, Mitchell, National (Iowa City label), New Flexo, Nordskog, Odeon (U.S. issue), Parlophone (U.S. issue), Q.R.S., Rich-Tone, Stark, Superior, Sunshine, Timely Tunes, Up-To-Date. Some of these are so scarce that photographs for this book have only recently come to hand; two or three are lacking yet! Some scarce 1950s labels include After Hours, Blue Lake, Chance, Club-51, Drexel, Great Lakes, Jax, J-V-B, Luna, Meteor, Parrot, Recorded in Hollywood, Red Robin, S.R.C., Sabre, States, Tin Pan Alley, United. These are by no means all of the scarce labels. Particularly in the 1950s, a local or regional label might have been in existence for only one or two issues; the labels preceding are better known or of longer duration, but still scarce.

Knowledge of record labels is helpful in the intelligent acquisition of records, whether such acquisition consists of bidding in auctions by mail or just "junking" in local second-hand stores. If you know your labels, you're not likely to bid $50.00 on BIX & HIS RHYTHM JUGGLERS on English Brunswick only to find out later that original issue is on Gennett. And you won't buy Chess (LP) 1433 by The Flamingos with an orange label if you require originals only (see Chess photos). Errors in "junking" purchases usually involve no great financial loss if it turns out that the supposed $20.00 record you've gotten for .25 proves to be third pressing. But label knowledge can be handy when time is of the essence, for example, when on your weekly visit to the Salvation Army Thrift Store you find that a local radio station has just donated its record library, but another record sharpshooter is also there, shuffling vinyl. Of course, it's always a relief to find that he had beaten you to a choice copy of "The Chipmunk Song," leaving you to settle for all that unheard-of junk on labels such as Chess, Parrot and Red Robin. Or maybe *you'd* prefer "The Chipmunk Song."

PRESENTATION OF LABELS (PHOTOGRAPHS)

Labels are presented in the photo section following in alphabetical order, without regard to vintage. 78s, 45s, EPs, and LPs are all illustrated in the following section. For a given label, more than one speed or type of record may be shown. In such case, 78s are shown first, followed by 45s, EPs, and finally LPs. It is intended that the reader use this section to identify most of the important, interesting and rare labels and significant variations thereof. Photos of a number of worthwhile labels could not be obtained in time for publication, and it is hoped that a fourth edition of this book will contain additional photographs. Of course, it is not intended that every record label mentioned in the listings, much less every known record label, be represented.

In the 1950s, records were often issued in both 78 and 45 rpm form. Where the label design and/or logo is similar on the two speeds, only one is usually illustrated.

In the case of major, long-lived labels such as Okeh or Victor, significant changes in label design are shown in chronological order. Also, special "race" and hillbilly series, distinguishable by number series and/or label variation, are often illustrated and identified. See, for example, the Brunswick 7000-7233 series and the Brunswick 100 series, both having the "lightning" label.

Accompanying the photos are approximate issue dates, e.g. "late 1920s." Where a label is primarily a "race" or rhythm and blues label, this is indicated.

For further information on pre-1943 labels, see Rust's "American Record Label Book," listed in the Bibliography. No comparable work dealing with post-war labels is available. Ken Clee's "The Directory of American 45 R.P.M. Records" (also listed in the Bibliography) is a discography. Those seeking illustrated essays on post-war labels will find them piecemeal in current and back issues of record collectors' publications.

1

AARDELL
Late 1950s (45)

ABBOTT
Early 1950s (78)

ABCO
Rhythm & Blues (78)
Mid 1950s

ABNER
Late 1950s (78)

ABC PARAMOUNT
Late 1950s (78)

ABC PARAMOUNT
Late 1950s (78)

ABC PARAMOUNT
Late 1950s Early 1960s (45)

ACE
Ca. 1950 (78)

ACE
Ca. 1950 (78)

ACE
Mid-Late 1950s (45)

ACE
Mid to Late 1950s

ACT IV
Ca 1960 (78)

ACTUELLE
Ca. 1920 (78)

ADMIRAL
Late 1950s (45)

AFTER HOURS
Early 1950s (45)

AJAX
(Canadian) "Race" (78)
Early-Mid 1920s

ALADDIN
Rhythm & Blues, Jazz (78)
Late 1940s

ALADDIN
Rhythm and Blues (78)
Early 1950s

ALADDIN
Rhythm and Blues (78)
Mid 1950s

ALBEN
Ca. 1950 (78)

ALERT
Late 1940s (78)

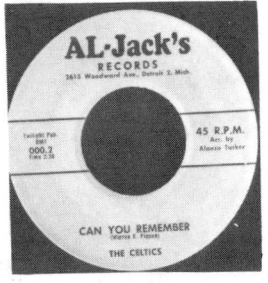
AL-JACK'S
Late 1950s (45)

ALLEN
Rhythm and Blues (45)
Mid 1950s

ALL STAR
Rhythm and Blues (45)
Late 1950s

ALL STAR
Rhythm and Blues (45)
Mid 1950s

ALLSTAR
Late 1950s (45)

AL'S
Ca. 1960 (45)

AMERICAN MUSIC
1940s (78)

**AMERICAN RECORD
COMPANY**
Ca. 1916 (78)

**AMERICAN RECORD
CORP.**
Ca. 1930 (78)

AMMOR
Early 1940s (78)

ANDEX
Ca. 1960 (45)

ANDIE
Early 1960s (45)

ANNA
Rhythm and Blues (78)
Late 1959-60

ANNA
Rhythm and Blues (45)
Late 1959-60s

ANTHEM
Ca. 1960 (45)

ANTLER
Ca. 1960 (45)

THE ANTONES
Country and Western (78)
Late 1940s

APEX
Mid 1920s (78)
Canadian

APEX
Late 1950s (45)

APOLLO
Mid 1950s (45)

APOLLO
Late 1940s (78)

APOLLO
Rhythm and Blues (78)
Early 1950s

APOLLO
Rhythm and Blues (78)
Mid 1950s

ARC
Late 1950s (45)

ARC
Late 1950s (45)

ARCADE
Late 1950s (45)

ARCADIA
Ca. 1950 (78)

ARCTIC
Late 1950s (45)

ARGO
Late 1950s (78)

3

ARGO
Late 1950s (78)

ARGO
Late 1950s (45)

ARISTOCRAT
Rhythm and Blues (78)
Late 1940s

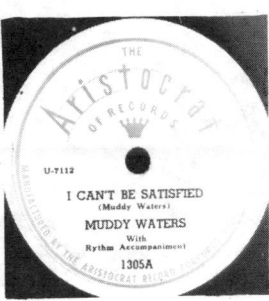

ARISTOCRAT
Rhythm and Blues (78)
Late 1940s

ARTISTIC
Late 1950s (78)

ARTO
Early 1920s (78)

ARVEE
Ca. 1960 (45)

ARWIN
Late 1950s (78)

ASCH
1940s (78)

ATCO
Late 1950s (78)

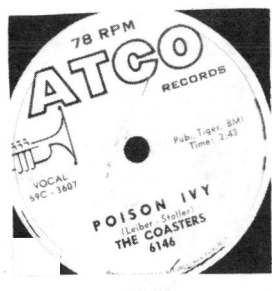

ATCO
Rhythm and Blues (78)
Late 1950s

ATHENS
Late 1950s (45)

ATLANTIC
Rhythm and Blues
Early 1950s

ATLANTIC
Rhythm and Blues (E.P.)
Mid 1950s

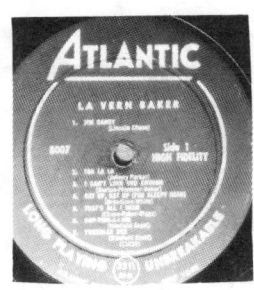

ATLANTIC
Rhythm and Blues (LP)
Mid 1950s

ATLANTIC
Rhythm and Blues (LP)
Later Pressing

ATLANTIC
Rhythm and Blues (45)
1950s

ATLAS
Late 1940s (78)

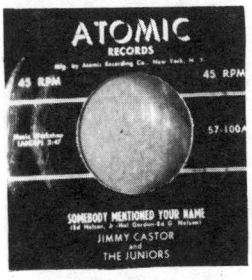

ATOMIC
Mid 1950s (45)

ATOMIC-H
Mid 1950s (45)

AUTOGRAPH
Ca. 1924 (78)

AYO
Late 1940s (78)

AZALEA
Late 1950s (45)

BACK BEAT
Mid 1950s (78)

BACK BEAT
Mid 1950s (45)

4

B & S
Ca. 1950   (78)

BAND BOX
Early 1960s

BANDERA
Rhythm and Blues   (45)
Late 1950s

BANNER
Early 1930s   (78)

BATON
Late 1950s   (45)

BAYOU
Rhythm and Blues   (45)
Mid 1950s

BAY-TONE
Late 1950s   (45)

BEA & BABY
Rhythm and Blues   (45)
Ca. 1960

BEACON
Late 1940s   (78)

BELL
Early 1920s   (78)

BELL
Mid 1920s (78)

BERNARDO
Ca. 1929   (78)

BIG
Early 1960s   (45)

BIG HOWDY
Late 1950s   (45)

BIG TOWN
Rhythm and Blues (78)
Mid 1950s

BIG TOWN
Mid 1950s (45)

BILTMORE
1940s   (78)
(A reissue label for
jazz collectors)

BINGO
Ca. 1960s   (45)

BLACK PATTI
Ca. 1927   (78)
("race" record)

BLACK SWAN
"Race"   (78)
Early 1920s

BLACK SWAN
"Race"   (78)
Early 1920s

BLACK SWAN
"Race"   (78)
Early 1920s

BLACK AND WHITE
Blues and Jazz   (78)
Late 1940s

BLAZE
Early 1960s   (45)

BLAZON
Late 1940s   (78)

BLUE BIRD
Early 1920s (78)
(Unrelated to more familiar
RCA Victor product)

BLUE BIRD
Mid 1930s (78)

BLUEBIRD
Late 1930s (78)

BLUEBIRD
Late 1930s-41 (78)

BLUE BONNET
Country and Western (78)
Late 1940s

BLUE-CHIP
Late 1950s (45)

BLUES & RHYTHM
Ca. 1950 (78)

**BLUES BOYS·
KINGDOM** (45)
Rhythm and Blues

BOBBIN
Rhythm and Blues (45)
Late 1950s

BO-KAY
Late 1950s (45)

BOULEVARD
Mid 1950s (45)

BRAX
Ca. 1960 (45)

BRENT
Rhythm and Blues (45)
Mid 1960s

BROADWAY
Mid 1920s (78)

BROADWAY
Late 1920s (78)

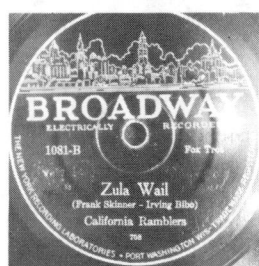

BROADWAY
Popular Series (78)
Late 1920s

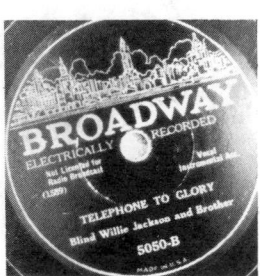

BROADWAY
"Race" (78)
5000 series

BROADWAY
8000 series (78)
Country and Western
Late 1920s

BRONZE
Ca. 1940 (78)

BRUCE
Late 1950s (45)

BRUNSWICK
Mid 1920s (78)

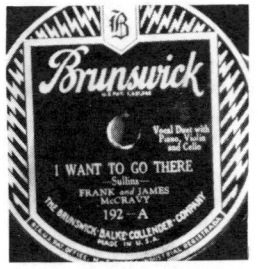

BRUNSWICK
100 series - Hillybilly (78)
Late 1920s

BRUNSWICK
7000 series - "Race" (78)
Late 1920s

BRUNSWICK
Ca. 1931 (78)

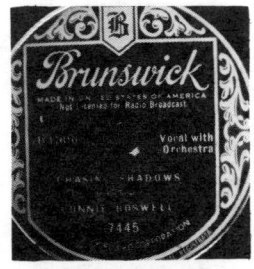

BRUNSWICK
Mid 1930s (78)

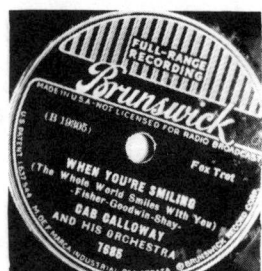

BRUNSWICK
Late 1930s (78)

BRUNSWICK
1940s-Early 1950s (78)
(collector's reissue series)

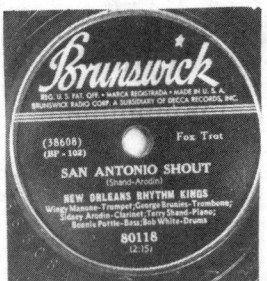

BRUNSWICK
Late 1940s (78)
Early 1950s

BRUNSWICK
Late 1950s (78)

BRUNSWICK
Late 1950s (45)

BRYTE
Late 1950s (45)

BUDDY
Ca. 1925 (78)

BULLET
Blues (78)
Late 1940s

BULLSEYE
Late 1950s (45)

CADDY
Late 1950s (45)

CADENCE
Late 1920s (78)

CADENCE
Late 1950s (45)

CALVERT
Early 1960s (45)

CAMEO
Early 1960s (78)

CAMEO
Late 1920s (78)

CAMEO
Late 1950s (78)

CAMEO
Late 1950s (45)

CAMEO
Early 1960s (45)

CANDIX
Early 1960s (45)

CAPITOL
1950s (78)

CAPITOL
Late 1950s (78)

CAPITOL
Ca. 1969 (45)
special commemorative
record

CAPITOL
Late 1950s (45)

CAPITOL
Mid 1960s (45)

CAPITOL
Late 1950s (L.P.)

CAPITOL
7-inch (L.P.)
Mid 1960s

CAPROCK
Country and Western (45)
Late 1950s

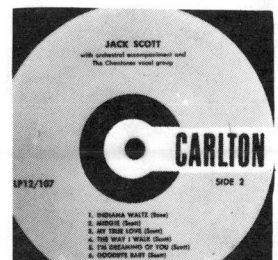

CARLTON
Late 1950s (L.P.)

CASA GRANDE
Late 1950s (45)

CASH
Rhythm and Blues (45)
Mid 1950s

CASINO
Late 1950s (45)

CAT
Late 1950s (78)

CAT
Late 1950s (45)

CAVA-TONE
Ca. 1950 (78)

CENTRAL
Late 1950s (45)

CENTRAL
Late 1950s (45)

CHALLENGE
Mid 1920s (78)

CHALLENGE
Late 1950s (78)

CHALLENGE
Late 1950s (45)

CHAMPION
Mid 1920s (78)
Early 1930s

CHAMPION
Mid 1930s (78)

CHAMPION
Ca. 1960 (45)

CHANCE
Rhythm and Blues (78)
Early 1950s

CHANCE
Rhythm and Blues (78)
Mid 1950s

CHANCE
Rhythm and Blues (45)
Mid 1950s

CHANCELLOR
Late 1950s (78)

CHANT
Early 1960s (45)

**CHAPPELLE AND
STINNETTE**
Ca. 1921 (78)

CHART
Late 1950s (45)

CHAUTAUQUA
Ca. 1922 (78)

CHECKER
Rhythm and Blues (78)
Early 1950s

CHECKER
Rhythm and Blues (45)
Mid 1950s

CHECKER
Rhythm and Blues (78)
Late 1950s

CHECKER
Rhythm and Blues (L.P.)
Late 1950s

CHECK-MATE
Early 1960s (45)

CHERRY
Ca. 1960 (45)

CHESS
Rhythm and Blues (78)
Early 1950s

CHESS
Rhythm and Blues (78)
Late 1950s

CHESS
Rhythm and Blues (78)
Late 1950s

CHESS
Rhythm and Blues (45)
Mid 1950s

CHESS
Late 1950s (45)

CHESS
Rhythm and Blues (78)
Late 1950s

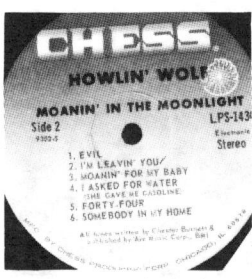

CHESS
Rhythm and Blues (L.P.)
Later Pressing

CHIEF
Mid 1950s (45)

CHIEF
Late 1950s (45)

**CHOCK FULL
OF HITS**
Late 1950s (45)

CHOICE
Ca. 1960 (45)

CIMARRON
Early 1960s (45)

CINDY
Ca. 1960 (78)

CIRECO
Ca. 1948 (78)

CLARION
Ca. 1910 (78)

CLARION
Early 1930s (78)

CLARION
Early 1930s (78)
"Double Track"
record

CLASS
Late 1950s (78)

CLAXTONOLA
Mid 1920s (78)

9

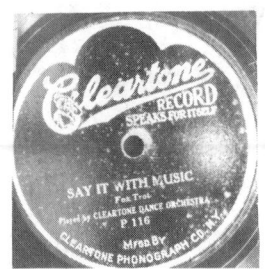

CLEARTONE
Early 1920s (78)

CLEARTONE
Early 1920s (78)

CLIF
Mid 1950s (45)

CLIMAX
Ca. 1910 (78)

CLOVER
Ca. 1925 (78)

CLUB 51
Mid 1950s (45)

CLUB
Late 1950s (45)

COBRA
Late 1950s (78)

COBRA
Rhythm and Blues (45)
Late 1950s

COBRA
Early 1960s (45)

COLONIAL
Ca. 1950 (78)

COLONIAL
Late 1950s (78)

COLONIAL
Late 1950s (45)

COLONIAL
Late 1950s (45)

COLONY
Ca. 1950 (78)

COLPIX
Ca. 1960 (45)

COLUMBIA
Ca. 1906 (78)

COLUMBIA
Advertising Record
Ca. 1915 (78)

COLUMBIA
Personal
Ca. 1915 (78)

COLUMBIA
Early 1920s (78)

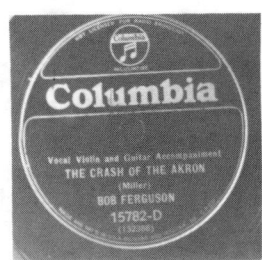

COLUMBIA
Mid 1920s (78)

COLUMBIA
14000-D Series is "Race" (78)
15000-D Series is Country
and Western Late 20s

COLUMBIA
Picture Label (78)
Late 1920s

COLUMBIA
Spanish Series
Ca. 1930 (78)

COLUMBIA
Folk Series
Ca. 1933 (78)

10

COLUMBIA
Mid 1930s (78)

COLUMBIA
Mid 1930s (78)

COLUMBIA
1939-1950s (78)

COLUMBIA
Sacred Series
Ca. 1950 (78)

COLUMBIA
Personal
Ca. 1924 (78)

COLUMBIA
Early 1950s (45)

COLUMBIA
Late 1950s (78)

COLUMBIA
Late 1950s (78)

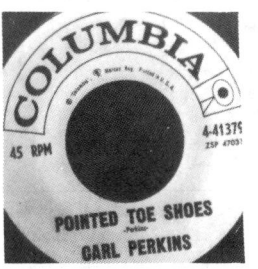
COLUMBIA
Early 1960s (45)

COMBO
Mid 1950s (78)

COMBO
Mid 1950s (45)

COMBO
Mid 1950s (45)

COMMODORE
Jazz (78)
Late 1930s Early 1940s

CONNORIZED
Ca. 1922 (78)

CONQUEROR
Late 1920s (78)

CONQUEROR
Early 1930s (78)

CONQUEROR
Late 1930s-1940 (78)

CONTINENTAL
1940s (78)

CONTINENTAL
Ca. 1947 (78)

CORAL
Late 1950s (78)

CORAL
Late 1950s (45)

CORAL
Late 1950s (L.P.)

CORMAC
Ca. 1950 (78)

CORMAC
Ca. 1950 (78)

CORT
Ca. 1915 (78)

COSMO
Ca. 1950 (78)

COVER
Late 1950s (45)

COWTOWN
Ca. 1950 (78)

COWTOWN
Late 1950s (45)

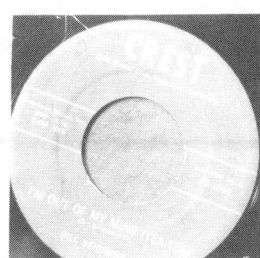
CREST
Late 1950s (45)

CREST
Early 1960s (45)

CROWN
Early 1930s (78)

CROWN
Canadian
Ca. 1928 (78)

CRYSTAL
Ca. 1950 (78)

CRYSTALETTE
Early 1950s (78)

CUB
Late 1950s (45)
Early 1960s

CULLMAN
Ca. 1960 (45)

D
Late 1950s (45)

DAMON
Mid 1950s (45)

DC
Rhythm and Blues (45)
Late 1950s

DALE
Late 1950s (45)

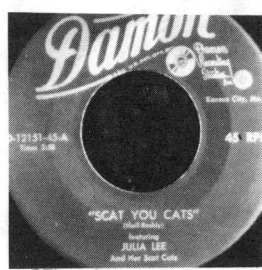
DAMON
Mid 1950s (45)

DARL
Mid 1950s (45)

DARSA
Late 1950s (45)

DART
Early 1960s (45)

DAVIS
Late 1940s (78)

DAVIS
Late 1950s (45)

DAWN
Late 1950s (45)

DAWN
Ca. 1960 (45)

D B C
Ca. 1960 (45)

12

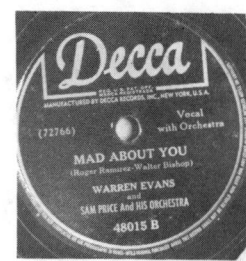
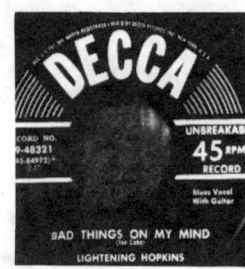

DECCA
7000 series - "Race" (78)
Mid 1930s

DECCA
"Race" series
Ca. 1938 (78)

DECCA
Ca. 1941 (78)

DECCA
Late 1940s (78)

DECCA
Mid 1950s (45)

DECCA
Late 1950s (78)

DECCA
Late 1950s (45)

DEL-CO
Late 1950s (45)

DEL-FI
Late 1950s (45)

DELTA
Mid 1950s (45)

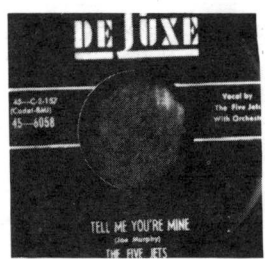

DELTA
Ca. 1960 (45)

DELTONE
Early 1960s (45)

DE-LUXE
Late 1940s (78)

DeLUXE
Rhythm and Blues (78)
Mid 1950s

DeLUXE
Mid 1950s (45)

DEMON
Late 1950s (78)

DERBY
Mid 1950s (45)

DIADON
Ca. 1960 (45)

DIAL
Late 1940s (78)

DIAL
Ca. 1960 (45)

DIAMOND
Ca. 1950 (78)

DIG
Late 1950s (45)

DIR
Late 1950s (45)

DITTO
Late 1950s (45)

DIVA
Late 1920s (78)

DIXIE
Late 1950s (45)

DOKE
Late 1950s (45)

DOMINO
Mid 1920s (78)

DOMINO
Late 1920s (78)

DOMINO
Late 1950s (45)

DONA
Late 1950s (45)

DON TAN
Ca. 1960 (45)

DOOTONE
Late 1950s (78)

DOOTONE
Late 1950s (78)

DOT
Early 1950s (78)

DOT
Mid 1950s (78)

DOT
Mid 1950s (45)

DOT
Late 1950s (78)

DOVE
Late 1950s (45)

DOWN BEAT
Rhythm and Blues (78)
Late 1940s

DOWN TOWN
Late 1940s (78)

DRAG RACE
Mid-1950s (78)

DREW-BLAN
Early 1960s (45)

DRUMFIRE
Ca. 1960 (45)

DRUMMOND
Mid 1950s (45)

D TOWN
Ca. 1960 (45)

DUB
Late 1950s (45)

DUCHESS
Early 1960s (45)

DUKE
Mid 1950-Early 1960s (45)

DUNCAN
Ca. 1959 (45)

DUOPHONE
(English) Ca. 1929 (78)

DUPLEX
Late 1950s (78)

DURIUM JUNIOR
Early 1930s (78)
paper record, 4" diam

DYNAMIC
Ca. 1964 (45)

E & M
Early 1960s (45)

EAGLE
Ca. 1908 (78)

EAGLE
Early 1960s (45)

EAST-WEST
Late 1950s (45)

EBB
Rhythm and Blues (45)
Mid-late 1950s

ECHO
Ca. 1950 (78)

ECHO
Late 1950s (45)

EDDIE'S
Late 1940s (78)

EDISON
1920s thick (78)

EDISON
Special Pressing (thick) (78)
1924

EDISON
1929 thin (78)

**EDISON
INTERNATIONAL**
Late 1950s (45)

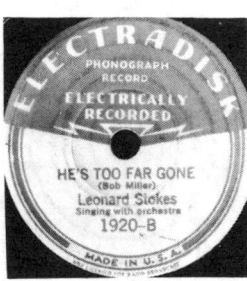

ELECTRADISK
Early 1930s (78)

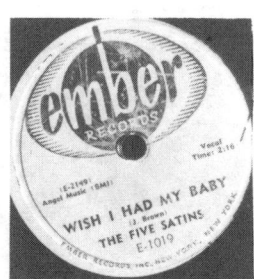

EMBER
Late 1950s (78)

EMBER
Late 1950s (45)

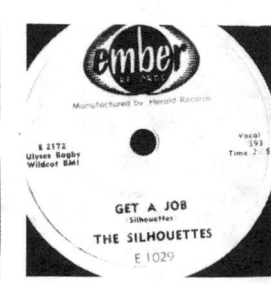

EMBER
Ca. 1960 (78)

EMBER
Late 1950s (45)

EMERSON
Ca. 1918 (78)

EMERSON
Ca. 1922 (78)

EMERSON
Mid 1920s (78)

ENCINO
Mid 1950s (45)

END
Late 1950s (78)

END
Late 1950s (45)

ENSIGN
Ca. 1960 (45)

ENTERPRISE
Ca. 1950 (78)

ERA
Late 1950s (45)

ESSEX
Mid 1950s (78)

ESSEX
Mid 1950s (45)

EVEREST
Ca. 1960 (45)

EVERLAST
Late 1950s (45)

EVERYBODY'S
Mid 1920s (78)

EVERSTATE
Ca. 1948 (78)

EXCELLO
Mid 1950s (78)

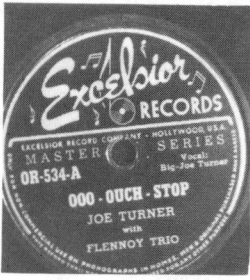

EXCELSIOR
Late 1940s (78)

EXCELSIOR
Late 1940s (78)

EXCLUSIVE
Late 1950s (78)

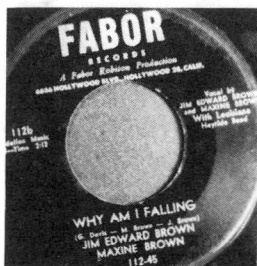

FABOR
Late 1950s (45)

FALCON
Late 1950s (45)

FARGO
Ca. 1950 (78)

FASCINATION
Mid 1950s (45)

FASCINATION
Late 1950s (45)

FASCINATION
Late 1950s (45)

FEATURE
Mid 1950s (45)

FEATURE
Late 1950s (45)

FEDERAL
Ca. 1923 (78)

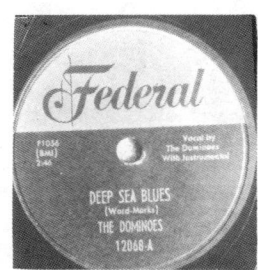

FEDERAL
Mid 1950s (78)

16

FEDERAL
Mid 1950s (45)

FEDERAL
Mid 1950s (L.P.)

FEDERAL
Late 1950s (78)

FEDERAL
Late 1950s (45)

FELSTED
Late 1950s (45)

FERNWOOD
Late 1950s (45)

FIDELITY
Early 1950s (78)

FIRE
Ca. 1960 (78)

FIRE
Early 1960s (45)

FLAIR
Rhythm and Blues (78)
Mid 1950s

FLAIR
Mid 1950s (45)

FLAIR-X
Late 1950s (45)

FLASH
Late 1950s (78)

FLASH
Late 1950s (45)

FLIP
Mid 1950s (78)

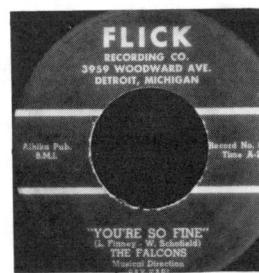

FLIP
Mid 1950s (78)

FLIP
Mid 1950s (45)

FLIP
Late 1950s (78)

FLIP
Late 1950s (45)

FLICK
Late 1950s (45)

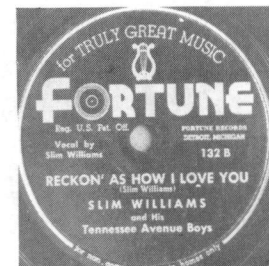
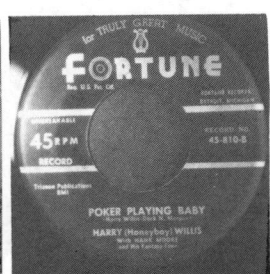

F M
Early 1950s (78)

FONSCA
Ca. 1960 (45)

FORD
Mid-1950s (78)

FORTUNE
Early 1950s (78)

FORTUNE
Mid 1950s (45)

4 STAR
1950s (78)

FOX
Late 1950s (45)

FOX MOVIETONE
Mid-1930s (78)

FRATERNITY
Late 1950s (78)

FRATERNITY
Late 1950s (45)

FREEDOM
Ca. 1950 (78)

FREEDOM
Ca. 1950 (78)

FREEDOM
Late 1950s (45)

FURY
Late 1950s (45)

FURY
Ca. 1960 (45)

G & G
Late 1940s (78)

GAMETIME
Late 1950s (45)

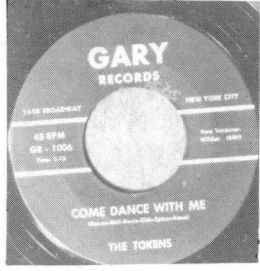

GARY
Late 1950s (45)

GATEWAY
Late 1950s (45)

GEE
Mid 1950s (45)

GEE
Late 1950s (78)

GEE
Late 1950s (78)

GEE
Ca. 1960 (45)

GEM
Ca. 1950 (78)

GEM
Mid 1950s (45)

GENERAL
Ca. 1940 (78)

GENNETT
Mid 1920s (78)

GENNETT
Late 1920s (78)

GENNETT
1940s (78)

GILBERT
Mid 1950s (45)

GILT-EDGE
Late 1940s (78)

GILT-EDGE
(DJ issue (Early 1950s (45)

GINA
Ca. 1960 (45)

GLOBAL
Early 1960s (45)

GLOBE
Ca. 1922 (78)

GLOBE
Mid 1920s (78)

GLOBE
Late 1940s (78)

GOLDBAND
Late 1950s (45)

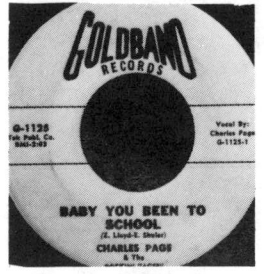

GOLDBAND
Late 1950s (45)

GOLDEN
Mid-1920s (78)

GOLDEN CREST
Early 1960s (45)

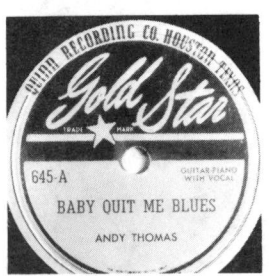

GOLD STAR
Late 1940s (78)

GONE
Mid 1950s (45)

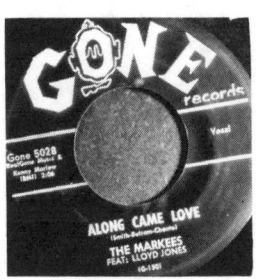

GONE
Late 1950s (45)

GOOD
Late 1950s (45)

**GOOD TIME
JAZZ**
Mid 1950s (78)

GOTHAM
Late 1940s to (78)
Early 1950s

GOTHAM
Early 1950s (45)

GRAND
Mid 1950s (45)

GREYCLIFF
Ca. 1960 (45)

GREY GULL
Mid-1920s (78)

GREY GULL
1920s (78)

GREY GULL
Ca. 1929 (78)

GROOVE
Late 1950s (45)

GROOVE
Mid 1950s (45)

GROOVE
Late 1950s (45)

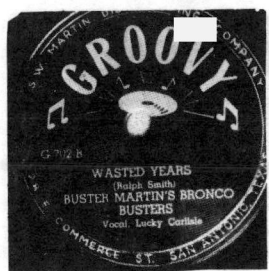

GROOVY
Late 1940s (78)

GUARDSMAN
(English) Ca. 1917 (78)

GULF
Late 1940s (78)

GUYDEN
Late 1950s (78)

GUYDEN
Late 1950s (45)

H.R.S.
Late 1940s (78)

HALL-WAY
Ca. 1960 (45)

HAMILTON
Late 1950s (45)

HANOVER
Ca. 1960 (45)

HARLEM
Late 1940s (78)

HARLEM
Late 1950s (78)

HARLEM
Ca. 1960 (45)

HARMOGRAPH
Early 1920s (78)

HARMOGRAPH
Early 1920s (78)

HARMONY
1925 to Early 1930s (78)

HARMONY DISC
Ca. 1906 (78)

HART
Late 1950s (45)

HARVEY
Early 1960s (45)

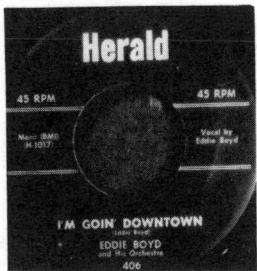

HERALD
Rhythm and Blues (45)
Mid 1950s

HERALD
Mid 1950s (45)

HERALD
Mid 1950s (45)

HERALD
Mid 1950s (78)

HERALD
Late 1950s
(45)

**HERSCHEL
GOLD SEAL**
Late 1920s (78)

20

HERWIN
Late 1920s (78)

HI
Late 1950s (45)

HICKORY
Late 1950s (45)

HIS MASTER'S VOICE
(Canadian) Ca. 1924 (78)

HIT MAKER
Late 1950s (45)

HIT OF THE WEEK
Paper Record (78)
Early 1930s

HOLIDAY
Late 1950s (45)

HOLIDAY INN
Early 1960s (45)

HOLLYWOOD
Mid-1920s (78)

HOLLYWOOD
Mid 1950s (45)

**HOLLYWOOD
HOT SHOTS**
Ca. 1940 (78)

HOMESTEAD
Late 1920s (78)

**HOT JAZZ CLUB
OF AMERICA**
1940s (78)
(Collectors reissue series)

HOT RECORD SOCIETY
Ca. 1939 (78)
(Collectors Series)

HUB
Late 1940s

HUDSON
Mid 1950s (78)

HULL
Late 1950s (45)

HUMMING BIRD
Ca. 1950 (78)

HUMMING BIRD
Early 1950s (45)

HUNTER
Late 1960s (45)

HYTONE
Early 1920s (78)

HY-TONE
Late 1950s (45)

IMPERIAL
Ca. 1950 (78)
(country series)

IMPERIAL
Early 1950s (78)

IMPERIAL
Mid 1950s (45)

21

IMPERIAL
Late 1950s (78)

IMPERIAL
Late 1950s (45)

IMPERIAL
Late 1950s (45)

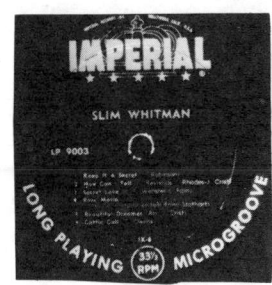
IMPERIAL
Late 1950s (LP)

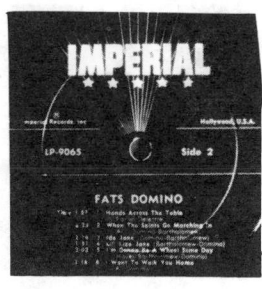
IMPERIAL (LP)
Late 1950s to Early 1960s

IMPRA
Late 1950s (45)

INTRO
Early 1950s (78)

INTRO
Country and Western (45)
Late 1950s

IRAGEN
1930s (78)

IRMA
Late 1950s (78)

IVORY
Early 1960s (45)

JACKPOT
Ca. 1960 (45)

JACKSON
Mid 1950s (45)

JAGUAR
Mid 1950s (45)

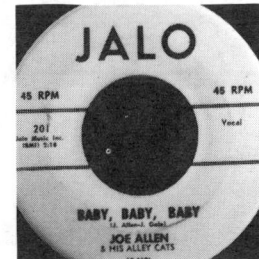
JALO
Late 1950s (45)

JALYNNE
Early 1950s (45)

JAMIE
Late 1950s (78)

JAMIE
Late 1950s (45)

JAMIE
Late 1950s (45)

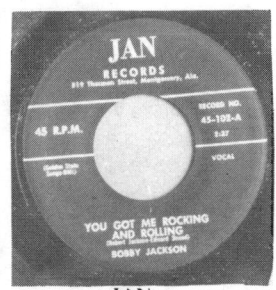
JAN
Late 1950s (45)

JAN
Late 1950s (45)

JAX
Ca. 1950   78)

JAX
Early 1950s (45)

JAX
Early 1950s (45)

JAY-DEE
Mid 1950s (78)

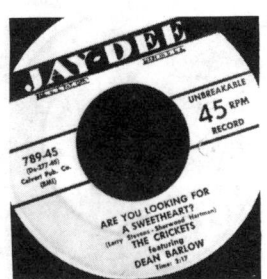

JAY-DEE
Mid 1950s (45)

JAY WING
Late 1950s (45)

JAZZ MAN
Late 1940s (78)

JAZZ MAN
Late 1940s (78)

J-B
Mid 1950s (45)

JEWEL
Late 1920s (78)

JEWEL
Mid 1960s (45)

JIN
Late 1950s (45)

JIN
Late 1950s (45)

JIN
Late 1950s (45)

J.O.B.
Early 1950s (78)

J.O.B.
Late 1950s (45)

JOE DAVIS
Late 1940s (78)

JOHNSON
Ca. 1960 (45)

JOZ (JOSIE)
Late 1950s (78)

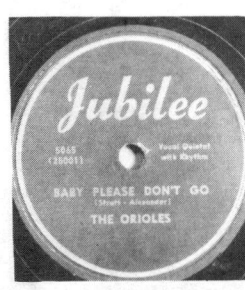

JOZ (JOSIE)
Late 1950s (45)

JUBILEE
Rhythm and Blues (78)
Early 1950s

JUBILEE
Early 1950s (45)

JUBILEE
Mid 1950s (78)

JUBILEE
Mid 1950s (45)

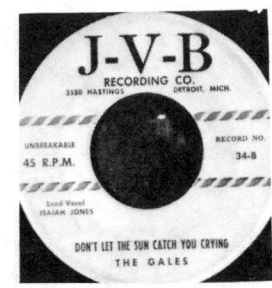

JUDD
Ca. 1960 (45)

JUMP
Ca. 1950 (78)

JUKE BOX
Late 1940s (78)

JVB
Rhythm and Blues (45)
Late 1950s

JVB
Late 1950s (45)

JVB
Rhythm & Blues   (78)
Late 1950s

K K K
Mid 1920s   (78)

KRC
Late 1950s   (45)

K-ARK
Late 1950s   (45)

KEEN
Late 1950s   (78)

KEEN
Late 1950s   (78)

KENT
Ca. 1960 (45)

KENTUCKY
Early 1950s   (78)

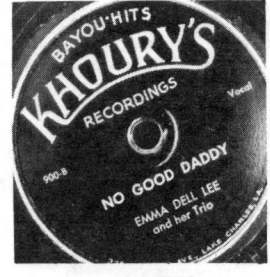

KHOURY'S
1950s   (78)

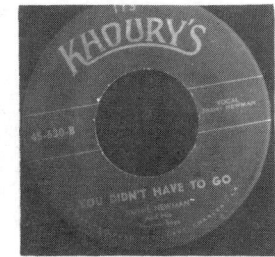

KHOURY'S
Mid 1950s   (45)

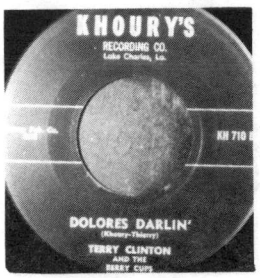

KHOURY'S
Late 1950s   (45)

KICK
Late 1950s   (45)

KICKS
Late 1950s   (45)

KING
Late 1940s   (78)

KING
Late 1950s   (78)

KING
Late 1950s   (45)

KING
Late 1950s (LP - 33rpm)

KLIFF
Late 1950s   (45)

KLIK
Mid 1950s   (45)

KOOL
Early 1960s   (45)

KUDO
Late 1950s   (45)

LAMP
Mid 1950s   (45)

LASSO
Early 1950s   (78)

LAURIE
Late 1950s   (45)

LAURIE
Early 1960s   (45)

LE CAM
Early 1960s (45)

LEE
Early 1950s (78)

LEE
Late 1950s (45)

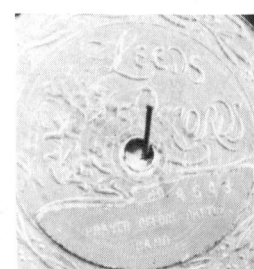

LEEDS
Ca. 1910 (78)

LEGRAND
Ca. 1960 (45)

LESLEY
Late 1950s (45)

LIBERTY
Late 1950s (78)

LIBERTY
Late 1950s (45)

LIGHTNING
Mid 1950s (45)

LIN
Late 1950s (78)

LIN
Late 1950s (45)

LIN
Ca. 1960 (45)

LITTLE WONDER
Ca. 1918 (78)

LLOYDS
Late 1950s (45)

LODE
Late 1950s (45)

LODE
Late 1950s (45)

LONDON
Early 1950s (78)

LONGHORN
Early 1960s (45)

LUCKY
MMid 1950s (45)

LUCKY
Ca. 1960 (45)

LUCKY FOUR
Ca. 1960 (45)

LUCKY SEVEN
Ca. 1950 (45)

LUCKY STRIKE
Mid 1920s (78)
(Canadian)

LUDWIG
Late 1950s (45)

LUNA
Mid 1950s (45)

LUNIVERSE
Late 1950s (78)

LUNIVERSE
Late 1950s (45)

LUNIVERSE
Late 1950s (78)

LUNIVERSE
Late 1950s (45)

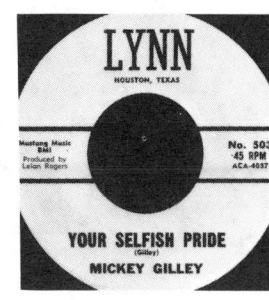

LYNN
Early 1960s (45)

LYRIC
Ca. 1919 (78)

LYRIC
Ca. 1920 (78)

LYRIC
Early 1950s (78)

LYRIC
1960 (45)

MGM
Late 1950s (78)

MGM
Late 1950s (45)

MGM
Mid 1950s (L.P.)

MACY'S
Ca. 1950 (78)

MADISON
1920s (78)

MAIL CALL
Early 1960s (45)

MAJESTIC
Late 1940s (78)

MAJOR
Late 1950s (45)

MANHATTAN
Ca. 1910 (78)

MANOR
Late 1940s (78)

MARATHON
Ca. 1950 (78)

MARTIN
Ca. 1950 (78)

MAR-VEL
Late 1950s (45)

MASTER
Late 1930s (78)

MASTER
Late 1940s (78)

MASTER
Ca. 1960 (45)

MASTERTONE
Early 1920s (78)

MAXSA
Mid 1920s (78)

MELADEE
Late 1950s (45)

MEDALLION
Ca. 1919 (78)

MEDALLION
Ca. 1920 (78)

MEDIA
Mid 1950s (78)

MELBA
Late 1950s (45)

MELODY
Ca. 1923 (78)

MELODY
Ca. 1950 (78)

MELODISC
Early 1920s (78)

MELOTONE
Early 1930s (78)

MELOTONE
1930s (78)

MEMO
Early 1950s (78)

MERCER
Ca. 1950 (78)

MERCURY
8000 Series (78)
Rhythm and Blues
Early 1950s

MERCURY
Mid 1950s (45)

MERCURY
Late 1950s (78)

MERCURY
Late 1950s (45)

MERCURY
Late 1950s (45)

MERCURY
Late 1950s (L.P.)

MERIDIAN
Ca. 1960 (45)

MERITT
Ca. 1927 (78)

METEOR
Ca. 1918 (78)

METEOR
Mid 1950s (78)

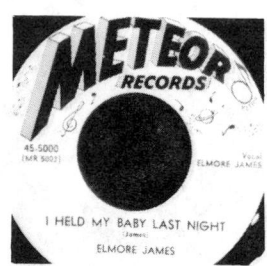

METEOR
Mid 1950s (45)

METEOR
Late 1950s (45)

METRO
Late 1950s (45)

METRO-GOLDWYN-AYER
Ca. 1929 (78)

MICROPHONE
Mid 1920s (78)
(Canadian)

MILTONE
(Label Design Varies) (78)
Late 1940s

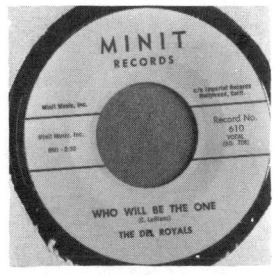

MINIT
Ca. 1960 (45)

MINOR
Late 1950s (45)

MITCHELL
Mid 1920s (78)

MODE
Late 1950s (45)

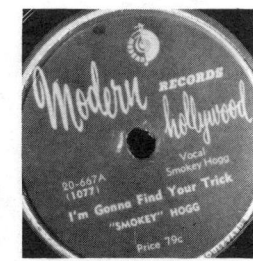

MODERN (HOLLYWOOD) (78)
1950s

MODERN
Mid 1950s (45)

MODERN (MUSIC)
Late 1940s (78)

MODERN (MUSIC)
Late 1940s (78)

MOHAWK
Ca. 1960 (45)

MONEY
Late 1950s (45)

MONTEL
Ca. 1960 (45)

MONTGOMERY WARD
Mid 1930s (78)

MONTGOMERY WARD
Late 1930s (78)

MONUMENT
Early 1960s (45)

MOOD
(Mid 1950s (78)

MOTOWN
Ca. 1960 (45)

MOVIN'
Ca. 1960 (45)

MOULDIE FYGGE
Late 1940s (78)
(collectors series)

MUSE
Early 1920s (78)

MUSIC CITY
Late 1950s (45)

MUSIC CITY
Late 1950s   (45)

MUSIC CITY
Ca. 1960   (45)

MUSICNOTE
Ca. 1960   (45)

MUSICRAFT
Late 1940s   (78)

NRC
1960   (45)

NADSCO
Early 1920s   (78)

NASCO
Late 1950s   (78)

NATIONAL
Mid 1920s   (78)

NATIONAL
Late 1940s   (78)

**NATIONAL MUSIC
LOVERS**   (45)
Mid 1920s

NATURAL
Ca. 1950   (78)

NEW COMFORT
Mid 1920s   (78)

NEW FLEXO
Ca. 1925   (78)

NEW PHONIC
Ca. 1927   (78)

NIKE
Late 1950s   (45)

NORDSKOG
Early 1920s   (78)

NORMAN
Late 1950s   (45)

NORTHERN
Late 1950s   (45)

NORTH STAR
Mid 1950s   (78)

NOR-VA-JAK
Late 1950s   (45)

NOTE
Mid 1950s   (45)

NUCRAFT
Ca. 1950   (78)

OT
Ca. 1950   (78)

ODEON
(American) Ca. 1930   (78)

OKEH
Mid 1920s   (78)

OKEH
Early 1920s (78)
(race series)

OKEH
Mid 1920s (78)
(race series)

OKEH
Late 1920s (78)

OKEH
Ca. 1930 (78)

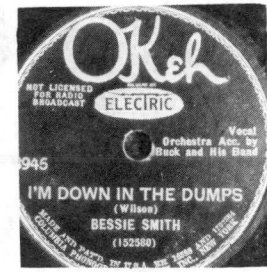

OKEH
Note: 8000 Series is 'race'
45000 Series is Hillbilly
Early 1930s (78)

OKEH
1940-1942 (78)

OKEH
Late 1950s (45)

OKLAHOMA
Late 1950s (45)

OLD SWING MASTER
Late 1940s (78)

OLD TOWN
Mid 1950s (45)

OLD TOWN
Late 1950s (78)

OLD TOWN
Late 1950s (45)

OLIMPIC
Ca. 1960 (45)

ONYX
Late 1950s (45)

ONYX
Late 1950s (45)

OPERA
Ca. 1950 (78)

OPERAPHONE
Ca. 1919 (78)

ORIOLE
Early-Mid 1920s (78)

ORIOLE
Late 1920s (78)
Early 1930s

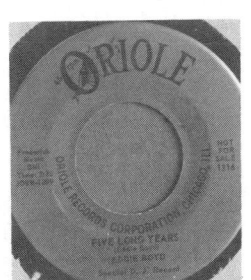

ORIOLE
Ca. 1960 (45)

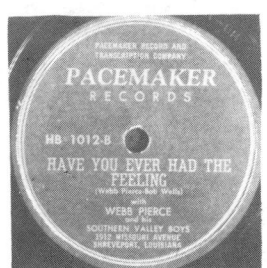

PACEMAKER
Ca. 1950 (78)

PACIFIC
Late 1940s (78)

PARADISE
Late 1940s (78)

PARAMOUNT
Early 1920s (78)

PARAMOUNT
Race Series (78)
12-13000 Series
Late 1920s

PARAMOUNT
Hillbilly 3000 series (78)
Late 1920s

PARIS
Late 1950s (45)

PARK
Late 1950s (45)

PARKWAY
Ca. 1960 (45)

PARLOPHONE
Late 1920s (78)

PARLOPHONE
Late 1920s (78)
(English)

PARROT
Mid 1950s (45)

PATHE
Late Teens-Early 1920s (78)

PATHE ACTUELLE
Mid-Late 1920s (78)

PATSY CLINE
Late 1950s (EP)

PEACOCK
Mid 1950s (78)

PEACOCK
Late 1950s (45)

PEARL
Late 1950s (45)

PENTHOUSE
Late 1950s (45)

PERFECT
Ca. 1922 (78)

PERFECT
(STAR SERIES)
Mid-Late 1920s (78)

PERFECT
Mid-Late 1920s (78)

PERFECT
Early 1930s (78)

PERFECT
Early 1930s (78)

PERFECT
Ca. 1937 (78)

PERSONAL RECORD
Ca. 1927 (78)

PERSONAL
Late 1920s (78)

PERSONAL RECORDING
Ca. 1928 (78)

PERSONALITY
Late 1940s (78)

PETITE
Late 1950s (45)

PHAMOUS
Ca. 1950 (78)

PHANTASIE
Early 1920s (78)

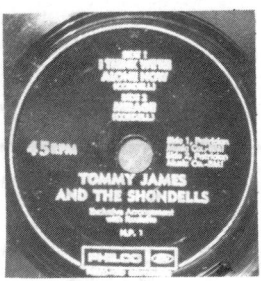

PHILCO
"Hip Pocket" (45)
record: 3⅞" diam. Ca. 1968

PHILLES
Early 1960s (45)

PHILLIPS
Late 1950s (78)

PHILLIPS
Late 1950s (78)

PHILO
Late 1940s (78)

PHONO-CUT RECORD
Ca. 1919 (78)

PIC 1
Ca. 1960 (45)

PICTURE
Late 1950s (45)

PILGRIM
Late 1950s (45)

PILGRIM
Late 1950s (78)

PILGRIM
Mid 1950s (78)

PINK
Late 1950s (45)

PLUS
Late 1950s (45)

POLK
Ca. 1930 (78)

POPLAR
Ca. 1960 (45)

PREMIUM
Late 1940s ((78)

PREMIUM
Late 1950s (45)

PRESTAGE
Mid 1950s (45)

PRINCESS
Early 1960s (45)

PROFILE
Late 1950s (45)

PIBLIX
Ca. 1930 (78)

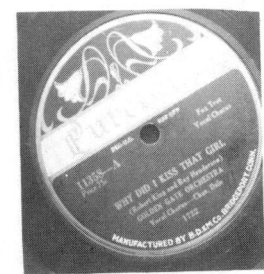

PURETONE
Mid 1920s (78)

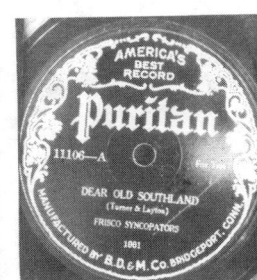

PURITAN
Early 1920s (78)

32

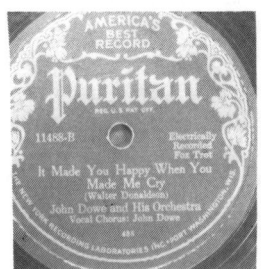

PURITAN
Mid 1920s (78)

PURITAN
Mid 1920s (78)

PURITAN
Ca. 1927 (78)

Q. R. S.
7000 "Race Series" (78)
9000 Series is Hillbilly

Q. R. S.
Late 1920s (78)

QUE
Late 1950s (45)

QUEEN
Late 1940s (78)

R AND B
Late 1950s (45)

RCA VICTOR
Program Transcription
Early 1930s (L.P.)

RCA VICTOR
Mid 1950s (78)

RCA VICTOR
Early 1950s (45)

RCA VICTOR
Early 1950s (45)

RCA VICTOR
Late 1950s (78)

RCA VICTOR
Mid 1950s (45)

RCA VICTOR
Ca. 1956-59 (L.P.)

RCA VICTOR
Ca. 1960-1963 (L.P.)

RCA VICTOR
Late 1950s (33⅓)
(7-inch record)

RPM
Early 1950s (45)

RPM
Early 1950s (78)

RPM
Late 1950s (45)

RADIEX
Ca. 1925 (78)

RADIEX
Mid 1920s (78)

RADIO
Ca. 1960 (45)

RADIO ARTIST
Ca. 1950 (78)

RAINBOW
Early 1950s (45)

33

RAMA
Mid 1950s (78)

RAMA
Mid 1950s (45)

RAMA
Rhythm and Blues (45)
Late 1950s

RAYS
Mid 1950s (45)

RECORTE
Late 1950s (45)

RED ROBIN
Rhythm and Blues (45)
Mid 1950s

RED TOP
Late 1950s (45)

RED TOP
Late 1950s (45)

REELFOOT
Late 1950s (45)

REGAL
Late 1920s (78)

REGAL
Early 1920s to Early 1930s

REGAL
Late 1940s (78)

REGENT
Late 1940s (78)

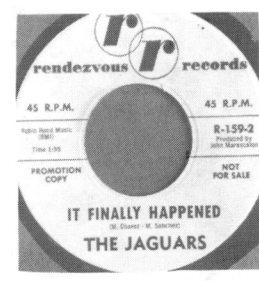
RENDEZVOUS RECORDS
Ca. 1960 (45)

RENNER
Early 1960 (45)

REPUBLIC
Ca. 1950 (78)

REPUBLIC
Mid 1950s (45)

REPUBLIC
Ca. 1960 (45)

RESERVE
Late 1950s (45)

RESONA
Mid 1920s (78)

REV
Late 1950s (45)

REX
Ca. 1918 (78)

REX
Ca. 1960 (45)

RHUMBOOGIE
Late 1940s (78)

RHYTHM
Early 1950s (78)

RHYTHM
Mid 1950s (45)

RIC
Rhythm and Blues(45)
Ca. 1960

RIC
Early 1960s (45)

RICH-TONE
Ca. 1922 (78)

ROCKIN'
Mid 1950s (45)

ROME
Ca. 1960 (45)

ROMEO
Late 1920s (78)

ROMEO
Ca. 1930s (78)

ROMEO
Ca. 1932 (78)

ROMEO
Early 1930s (78)

ROMEO
Ca. 1937 (78)

RON
Late 1950s (78)

RON
Late 1950s (45)

ROOST
Ca. 1950 (78)

ROULETTE
Late 1950s (78)

ROULETTE
Late 1950s (78)

ROULETTE
Late 1950s (45)

ROULETTE
Late 1950s (78)

ROULETTE
Late 1950s (45)

ROULETTE
Ca. 1960 (L.P.)

ROYAL ROOST
Mid 1950s (45)

ROYALTY
Late 1940s (78)

RUDDER RECORDS
Ca. 1950 (78)

RUST
Ca. 1960 (45)

S D
Late 1940s (78)

S D
Late 1940s (78)

S & G
Mid 1950s (45)

S.R.C.
Late 1950s (45)

SABRINA
Ca. 1960 (45)

SABRINA

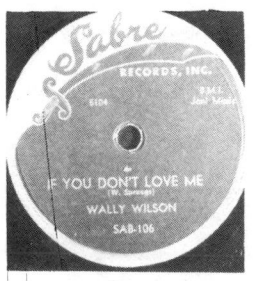

SABRE
Early 1950s (78)

SABRE
Mid 1950s (45)

SAGE
Late 1950s (78)

SAGE
Late 1950s (45)

SANDY
Late 1950s (45)

SAPPHIRE
Mid 1950s (45)

SARG
Late 1950s (45)

SATIN
Ca. 1960 (45)

SAVOY
Ca. 1930 (78)

SAVOY
reissue Ca. 1950 (78)

SAVOY
Rhythm and Blues (78)
Ca. 1950

SAVOY
Rhythm and Blues
Late 1950s

SCARLET
Ca. 1960 (45)

SCEPTER
Early 1960s (45)

SCOOP
Ca. 1950 (78)

SCORE
Late 1940s (78)

SCOTTIE
Early 1960s (45)

SCOTTY'S
Late 1940s (78)

SEE BEE
Early 1920s (78)

SELECTIVE
Ca. 1950 (78)

SELMA
Late 1950s (45)

SESSION
Jazz (78)
1940s

SEVEN ELEVEN
Mid 1950s (78)

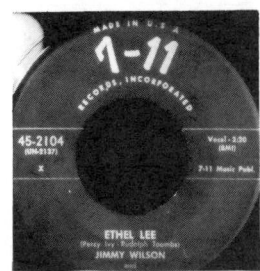

SEVEN ELEVEN
Mid 1950s (45)

SHADE
Late 1950s (45)

SHAN-TODD
Ca. 1960 (45)

SHARP
Early 1960s (45)

SHELL
Ca. 1960 (45)

SHOWTIME
Mid 1950s (45)

SIGMA NU
Ca. 1924 (78)

SIGNATURE
Late 1940s (78)

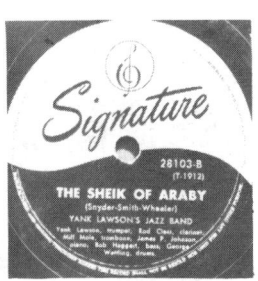

SIGNATURE
Late 1940s (78)

SILHOUETTE
Late 1950s (45)

SILVERTONE
Ca. 1916 (78)

SILVERTONE
Ca. 1920 (78)

SILVERTONE
Mid 1920s (78)

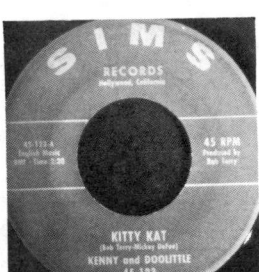

SIMS
Late 1950s (45)

SINGULAR
Late 1950s (45)

SIR
Late 1950s (45)

SITTIN' IN WITH
Ca. 1950 (78)

SITTIN' IN WITH
Early 1950s (45)

SKYLA
Ca. 1960 (45)

SKYLARK
Mid 1950s (78)

SLIM WILLET
Ca. 1956 (78)

SMASH
Ca. 1960 (45)

SMOKE
Late 1950s (45)

SOLO
Ca. 1950 (78)

SONORA
Late 1940s (78)

SOUND
Late 1950 (45)

SOUND TEX
Early 1960s (45)

SPANGLE
Late 1950s (45)

SPARK
Mid 1950s (78)

SPARK
Mid 1950s (45)

SPARK
Rhythm and Blues (45)
Mid 1950s

SPARKELL
Late 1950s (45)

SPARTAN
Early 1960s (45)

SPECIAL EDITIONS
1940s (78)

SPECIALTY
Ca. 1950 (78)

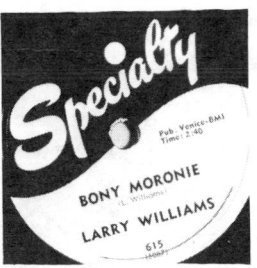

SPECIALTY
1950s (78)

SPECIALTY
1950s (45)

SPEED
Early 1950s (78)

SPEED
Late 1950s (45)

SPINNING
Late 1950s (45)

SPIRE
Late 1950s (78)

SPOTLIGHT
Late 1950s (45)

STACY
Ca. 1960 (45)

STAFF
Mid 1950s (45)

STARCK
Mid 1920s (78)

STAR X
Late 1950s (45)

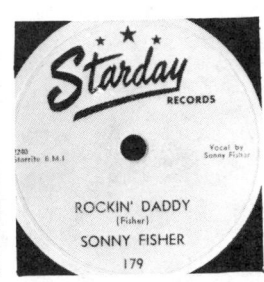

STAR DAY
Mid 1950s (78)

STARDAY
Late 1950s (45)

STARDAY
Late 1950s (45)

STARDAY
Early 1960s (45)

STAR RECORD
Ca. 1915 (78)

STARR
Ca. 1917 (78)

STAR GENNETT
Early 1920s (78)

STARRETT
Ca. 1960 (45)

STATES
Mid 1950s (78)

STATES
Mid 1950s (45)

STATUE
Early 1960s (45)

STERLING
Late 1940s (78)

STERLING
Late 1950s (45)

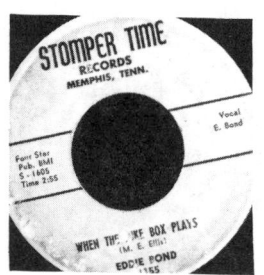

STOMPER TIME
Late 1950s (45)

STORM
Ca. 1960 (45)

SUE
Late 1950s (45)

SUGAR HILL
Mid 1950s (45)

SUMMIT
Late 1950s (45)

SUN
Mid 1950s (78)

SUN
Mid 1950s (45)

SUN
Late 1950s (33)

SUN (DJ COPY)
Mid 1960s (45)

SUNBEAM
Late 1950s (45)

SUNDOWN
Late 1950s (45)

SUNRISE
Ca. 1929 (78)

SUNRISE
Ca. 1933 (78)

SUNSET
Mid 1920s (78)

SUPER DISC
Late 1940s (78)

SUPERIOR
Ca. 1930 (78)

SUPERIOR
Ca. 1950 (78)

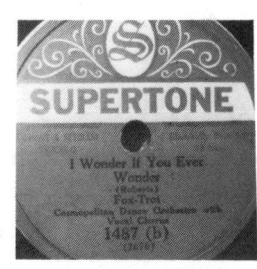

SUPERTONE
Ca. 1925 (78)

SUPERTONE
Late 1920s (78)

SUPERTONE
Late 1920s (78)

SUPREME
Ca. 1950s (78)

SUPREME
Early 1960s (45)

SURE
Late 1950s (45)

SURF
Late 1950s (45)

SWAN
Late 1950s (45)

SWAN
Early 1960s (45)

SWING
Late 1940s (78)

SWING BEAT
Late 1940s (78)

SWINGIN'
Early 1960s (45)

SWING TIME
Early 1950s (78)

SWING TIME
Early 1950s (45)

SYMPHONOLA
Ca. 1919 (78)

TNT
Early 1950s (78)

TNT
Late 1950s (78)

TNT
Mid 1950s (45)

TNT
Late 1950s (45)

TNT
Late 1950s (45)

TNT
Late 1950s (45)

TALENT
1950s (78)

TALENT
Early 1960s (45)

TALENT SCOUT
Ca. 1959 (45)

TALLY
Ca. 1960 (45)

TAMLA
Ca. 1960 (45)

TAMPA
Late 1950s (78)

TAMPA
Late 1950s (45)

TARA
Ca. 1959 (45)

TEE GEE
Late 1950s (45)

TEEN
Mid 1950s (78)

TEENAGE
Mid 1950s (45)

TEEN LIFE
Late 1950s

TELL
Late 1940s (78)

TEMPO
Early 1950s (78)

TENDER
Late 1950s (45)

TENNESSEE
Early 1950s (78)

TENNESSEE
Mid 1950s (78)

TENNESSEE
Mid 1950s (45)

TERRACE
Late 1950s (45)

TETRA
Late 1950s (78)

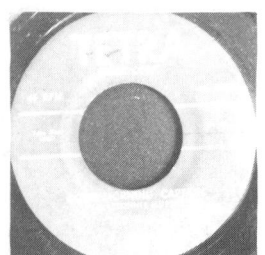

TETRA
Late 1950s (45)

TEX-TALENT
Early 1950s (78)

THANKS!
Ca. 1960 (45)

TIFFANY
Early 1950s (78)

TILT
Early 1960s (45)

TIME
Late 1950s (45)

TIMELY
Mid 1950s (45)

TIMELY TUNES
Early 1930s (78)

TIN PAN ALLEY
Late 1950s (45)

TIP TOP
Late 1950s (45)

TITAN
Late 1950s (45)

TONE
Late 1950s (45)

TOP HAT
Late 1940s (78)

TOP HAT
Ca. 1950 (78)

TOP RANK
Ca. 1960 (45)

TOP TEN
Early 1960s (45)

TORCH
Ca. 1950 (78)

TOWN & COUNTRY
Late 1940s (78)

TOWN & COUNTRY
Late 1940s (78)

TREAT
Mid 1950s (78)

TREL
Ca. 1960 (45)

TREMONT
Mid 1920s (78)

TREND
Ca. 1960 (45)

TRESS
Late 1950s (45)

TRI ESS
Early 1960s (45)

TRIANGLE
Early 1920s (78)

TRIDELT
Early 1960s (45)

TRILON
Late 1940s (78)

TRIUMPH
Ca. 1960 (45)

TROPHY
Late 1950s (45)

TRUMPET
Mid 1950s (78)

TRUMPET
Mid 1950s (45)

TURF
Late 1950s (45)

20th CENTURY
Mid 1950s (45)

20th FOX
Late 1950s (45)

TWIN STAR
Late 1950s (45)

TWIRL
Ca. 1960 (45)

U.H.C.A.
Late 1930s (78)
(Collectors Series)

U.S.A.
Early 1960s (45)

ULTRA
Late 1950s (45)

UNITED
Mid 1950s (78)

UNITED
Rhythm and Blues (45)
Mid 1950s

UNITED
Rhythm and Blues (45)
Mid 1950s

UNITY
Ca. 1925 (78)

UNIVERSAL ARTIST
Ca. 1960 (45)

UNIVERSAL-FOX
Ca. 1950 (78)

UNIVERSITY
Late 1940s (78)

UP-TO-DATE
Ca. 1924 (78)

VADEN
Late 1950s (45)

VADEN
Late 1950s (45)

VALLEY
Late 1950s (45)

**VALLEY'S
MEADOWLARK**
Late 1950s (45)

VALOR
Ca. 1960 (45)

VANDAN
Late 1950s (45)

VAN DYKE
Ca. 1929 (78)

43

VAN-ES
Ca. 1950 (78)

VARIETY
Mid 1920s (78)

VARIETY
Late 1930s (78)

VARSITY
Ca. 1940 (78)

V-DISC
Ca. 1947 (12-inch) (78)
(Issued for armed forces.)

VEE
Late 1950s (45)

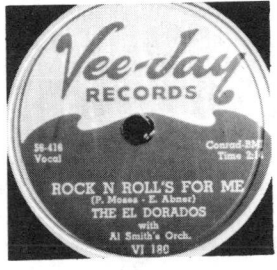

VEE-JAY
Mid 1950s (78)

VEE-JAY
Late 1950s (LP)

VEE-JAY
Early 1960s (45)

VEL-TONE
Late 1950s (45)

VELTONE
Early 1950s (45)

VELVET-TONE
Late 1920s (78)

VELVET TONE
Ca. 1932 (78)

VENUS
Late 1950s (45)

VESTA
Late 1950s (45)

VICEROY
Late 1950s (45)

VICTOR
Ca. 1915 (78)

VICTOR
1915-Early 1920s (78)

VICTOR
Mid 1920s (78)

VICTOR
Special Record Late 1920s

VICTOR
"Hot Dance" 38,000 (78)
Series 1929-1930

VICTOR
(V-38500 series)
Ca. 1929 (78)

VICTOR
Ca. 1932 (78)
(Canadian)

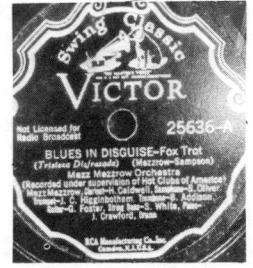

VICTOR
"SWING CLASSIC" (78)
Mid 1930s

VICTOR
Late 1930s (78)

44

VICTOR
1940s (78)
(Collectors' reissue series)

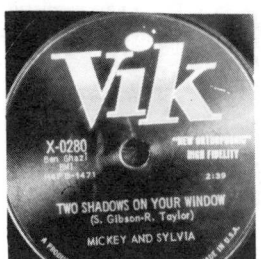

VIK
Late 1950s (78)

VIK
Mid 1950s (45)

VIN
Ca. 1960 (78)

VIN
Ca. 1960 (45)

VITA
Rhythm and Blues (78)
Late 1950s

VITA
Late 1950s (45)

VOCALION
Mid 1920s (78)

VOCALION
1000 Series "Race" (78)

VOCALION
Early 1930s (78)

VOCALION
Mid 1930s (78)

VOCALION
Ca. 1937 (78)

VOCALION
Late 1930s (78)

VOGUE
Picture Disc (78)
Late 1940s - (Pictures vary)

VOGUE Picture Disc
(Another issue)

VOGUE Picture Disc
Ca. 1947 (another issue)
representative of the series

VULCAN
1920s (78)

VULCAN
Late 1950s (45)

WALDORF
Late 1950s (EP)

WAR CONN
Early 1960s (45)

WARNER BROS.
Early 1960s (45)

WARRIOR
1959-1960 (45)

WASCO
Early 1950s (78)

WAYSIDE
Late 1950s (45)

WELLS
Late 1950s (45)

WESTPORT
Late 1950s (45)

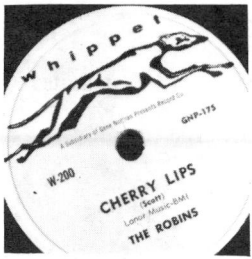

WHIPPET
Late 1950s (78)

WHIRLIN DISC
Late 1950s (45)

WHITE ROCK
Late 1950s (45)

WIGGS, INC.
Ca. 1950 (78)

WILDCAT
Early 1960s (45)

WING
Late 1950s (45)

WINLEY
Late 1950s (45)

WIZARD
Early 1960s (45)

WONDER
Late 1950s (45)

"X"
Mid 1950s (78)

X-TRA
Late 1950s (45)

XYZ
Late 1950s (45)

"Y"
Late 1950s (45)

YOUR COPY
Late 1950s (45)

YUCCA
Late 1950s (45)

ZYNN
Early 1960s (45)

JAZZ, BIG BANDS, DANCE BANDS, PERSONALITY

1915 to 1950 (approximately)

All records in this section are ten-inch 78 rpm unless otherwise indicated.

IRVING AARONSON & HIS COMMANDERS:

Columbia 2946-D *Pardon My Southern Accent*..	7.00 -	10.00
Columbia 2980-D *Flirtation Walk*............	7.00 -	10.00
Columbia 2981-D *Let's Be Thankful*..........	7.00 -	10.00
Columbia 3037-D *An Evening In June*........	7.00 -	10.00
Columbia 3043-D *Commanderism*............	7.00 -	10.00
Edison 51685 *Don't Wake Me Up*..........	4.00 -	7.00
Victor 20002, 20034, 20059, 20063, 20083, 20094, 20095, 20100, 20117, 20473, 21451, 21778, 21834, 21867............................	2.00 -	3.00
Victor 20385 *Everything's Peaches*............	5.00 -	8.00
Victor 21260 *Let's Misbehave*...............	5.00 -	8.00
Victor 21745 *Let's Do It*...................	5.00 -	8.00
Victor 21888 *Outside*......................	5.00 -	8.00
Vocalion 2535 *That's How Rhythm Was Born*..	7.00 -	10.00
Vocalion 2536 *The Day You Came Along*......	5.00 -	8.00
Vocalion 2570, 2571.........................	3.00 -	5.00
Vocalion 25004 *Shadows on the Swanee*.......	7.00 -	10.00
Vocalion 25005 *I've Gotta Get Up And Go To Work*	7.00 -	10.00

LARRY ABBOTT & HIS ORCHESTRA:

Okeh 41044 *I'm More Than Satisfied*.........	15.00 -	20.00

IRWIN ABRAMS & HIS (HOTEL MANAGER/KNICKERBOCKER GRILL) ORCHESTRA:

Banner, most titles........................	2.00 -	3.00
Domino, most titles........................	2.00 -	3.00
Edison 51633 *The Co-Ed*...................	8.00 -	12.00
Edison 51625, 52106, 52107, 52114...........	3.00 -	5.00
Edison 52148 *Dream Kisses*.................	5.00 -	8.00
Edison 52168 *Moon of Japan*................	5.00 -	8.00
Okeh 40783, 40864, 40869, 40918, 40948......	4.00 -	6.00
Okeh 40798 *Shanghai Dream Man*............	5.00 -	8.00
Okeh 40846 *Magnolia*......................	7.00 -	10.00

BERNARD ADDISON & HIS RHYTHM:

Bluebird 6144 *Lovely Liza Lee*...............	6.00 -	10.00
6174 *Toledo Shuffle*......................	6.00 -	10.00

ADRIAN & HIS ORCHESTRA/TAP ROOM GANG; ADRIAN'S RAMBLERS:

Brunswick 6786 *Get Goin'*..................	8.00 -	12.00
6877 *Why Don't You Practice What You Preach?*	8.00 -	12.00
6889 *I Wish I Were Twins*..................	8.00 -	12.00
Columbia 2785-D *Happy As The Day Is Long*..	15.00 -	20.00
Victor 25072 *Weather Man*..................	5.00 -	8.00
Victor 25085 *Nagasaki*.....................	5.00 -	8.00
Victor 25208 *Honeysuckle Rose*..............	5.00 -	8.00

ALABAMA CREOLE BAND:

Claxtonola 40397 *Choo Choo*...............	7.00 -	10.00

ALABAMA FUZZY WUZZIES:

Champion 15415 *Congo Stomp*...............	75.00 -	100.00

ALABAMA HARMONY BOYS:

Champion 15398 *Chicken Supper Strut*.......	75.00 -	100.00
Silvertone 5139 *Sweet Patootie*..............	75.00 -	100.00

ALABAMA JAZZ PIRATES:

Bell 1182 *Canned Heat Blues*...............	90.00 -	130.00

ALABAMA JUG BAND:

Decca 7000 *My Gal Sal*....................	8.00 -	12.00
Decca 7001 *Gulf Coast Blues*...............	8.00 -	12.00
Decca 7041 *Somebody Stole My Gal*.........	8.00 -	12.00
Decca 7042 *Crazy Blues*....................	8.00 -	12.00

ALABAMA RASCALS:

Titles, issued contemporeously on Banner, Melotone, Oriole, Perfect, Romeo: *Dirty Dozen's Cousins; Endurance Stomp; Georgia Grind; Jockey Stomp; Rukus Juice Shuffle; Stomp That Thing*.....	30.00 -	40.00

ALABAMA RED JACKETS:

Champion 15228 *You Can't Cry Over My Shoulder*	7.00 -	10.00
Champion 15229 *I'm Gonna Meet My Sweetie Now*	7.00 -	10.00

ALABAMA RED PEPPERS:

Titles, issued contemporaneously on Cameo, Lincoln, Romeo: *The Drag; Eccentric; The New Twister; Red Head Blues; Riverboat Shuffle*........	6.00 -	10.00

ALABAMA SERENADERS:

Champion 15140 *Alabama Stomp*............	10.00 -	15.00
Champion 15213 *There Ain't No Maybe In My Baby's Eyes*..............................	7.00 -	10.00
Champion 15238 *Underneath the Weeping Willow*	7.00 -	10.00
Champion 15239 *What Do I Care What Somebody Said?*.................................	7.00 -	10.00
Champion 15271 *South Wind*...............	7.00 -	10.00
Champion 15292 *I'm In Love Again*..........	7.00 -	10.00

ALABAMA WASHBOARD STOMPERS:

Vocalion 1546 *I Want A Little Girl*...........	15.00 -	25.00
Vocalion 1587 *Who Stole The Lock?*.........	15.00 -	25.00
Vocalion 1626 *I Surrender, Dear*............	15.00 -	25.00
Vocalion 1630 *Corinne Corinna*.............	15.00 -	25.00
Vocalion 1635 *I Need Lovin'*................	15.00 -	25.00
Vocalion 1684 *Can't We Talk It Over?*........	15.00 -	25.00
Vocalion 1689 *If All The World Was Made Of Glass*	15.00 -	25.00
Vocalion 1697 *Pepper Steak*................	15.00 -	25.00

DON ALBERT & HIS ORCHESTRA:

Vocalion 3401 *True Blue Lou*...............	*8.00 -*	*12.00*
Vocalion 3411 *The Sheik of Araby*...........	*8.00 -*	*12.00*
Vocalion 3423 *On The Sunny Side Of The Street*	*8.00 -*	*12.00*
Vocalion 3491 *Liza*.......................	*8.00 -*	*12.00*

JACK ALBIN'S ORCHESTRA; JACK ALBIN & HIS HOTEL PENNSYLVANIA MUSIC:

Crown 3002, 3006, 3012, 3013, 3029, 3047, 3069, 3089, 3091, 3098..........................	4.00 -	7.00
Edison 51811 *Wasn't It Nice?*...............	7.00 -	10.00
Edison 51829 *Hugs And Kisses*..............	10.00 -	15.00
Edison 51831 *The Two Of Us*...............	10.00 -	15.00
Edison 51851 *Cover Me Up With Sunshine*.....	10.00 -	15.00
Edison 51852 *I Found A Million Dollar Baby*...	10.00 -	15.00

VAN ALEXANDER & HIS ORCHESTRA:

Bluebird, various titles.....................	2.00 -	3.00
Varsity, various titles......................	2.00 -	3.00

HENRY ALLEN (JR.) & HIS (NEW YORK) OR-CHESTRA; HENRY ALLEN-COLEMAN HAWKINS & THEIR ORCHESTRA:

Titles, issued contemporaneously on Banner, Melotone, Oriole, Perfect, Romeo: *"Aintcha Got Music?", "Believe I, Beloved;" "Dark Clouds," "Don't Let Your Love Go Wrong," "How's About Tomorrow Night?", "I Never Slept A Wink Last Night," "It's Written All Over Your Face," "I Wish I Were Twins," "My Galveston Gal," "Pardon My Southern Accent," "The River's Takin' Care Of Me," "Rug Cutter Swing," "Shadows On The Swanee," "Smooth Sailing," "Stringin' Along On A Shoe String," "There's A House In Harlem For Sale," "Whose Honey Are You?," "Why Don't You Practice What You Preach?," "You're Gonna Lose Your Gal"*...................	7.00 -	12.00
Victor 23006 *Patrol Wagon Blues*............	20.00 -	30.00
Victor 23338 *Singing Pretty Songs*..........	35.00 -	50.00
Victor 38073 *It Should Be You*.............	20.00 -	50.00
Victor 38080 *Feeling Drowsy*...............	20.00 -	30.00
Victor 38121 *Dancing Dave*.................	25.00 -	40.00
Victor 38140 *Sugar Hill Function*............	25.00 -	40.00
Vocalion 2956 *Get Rhythm In Your Feet*......	8.00 -	12.00

Vocalion 2965 *Rosetta*...............	8.00 -	12.00
Vocalion 2997 *I Wished On The Moon*.......	8.00 -	12.00
Vocalion 2998 *Dinah Lou*...............	8.00 -	12.00
Vocalion 3097 *Red Sails In The Sunset*.......	7.00 -	10.00
Vocalion 3098 *On Treasure Island*.......	7.00 -	10.00
Vocalion 3214 *I'll Bet You Tell That To All The Girls*	7.00 -	10.00
Vocalion 3215 *Every Minute Of The Hour*.....	7.00 -	10.00
Vocalion 3244 *Would You?*...............	7.00 -	10.00
Vocalion 3245 *Nothing's Blue But The Sky*.....	8.00 -	12.00
Vocalion 3261 *Take My Heart*............	7.00 -	10.00
Vocalion 3262 *You're Not The King*.......	7.00 -	10.00
Vocalion 3292 *Am I Asking Too Much?*.......	7.00 -	10.00
Vocalion 3302 *Algiers Stomp*............	7.00 -	10.00
Vocalion 3305 *Out Where The Blues Begin*.....	7.00 -	10.00
Vocalion 3306 *Picture Me Without You*.......	7.00 -	10.00
Vocalion 3339 *Whatcha Gonna Do When There Ain't No Swing?*...............	7.00 -	10.00
Vocalion 3340 *Lost In My Dreams*............	7.00 -	10.00
Vocalion 3377 *Did You Mean It?*............	7.00 -	10.00
Vocalion 3389 *Here's Love In Your Eye*.......	7.00 -	10.00
Vocalion 3422 *Let's Put Our Heads Together*...	7.00 -	10.00
Vocalion 3432 *He Ain't Got Rhythm*.........	8.00 -	12.00
Vocalion 3490 *There's A Kitchen Up In Heaven*	7.00 -	10.00
Vocalion 3524 *I Was Born To Swing*.......	7.00 -	10.00
Vocalion 3564 *Sticks And Stones*.........	7.00 -	10.00
Vocalion 3574 *Meet Me In The Moonlight*.....	7.00 -	10.00
Vocalion 3594 *The Merry-Go-Round Broke Down*	7.00 -	10.00
Vocalion 3607 *Till The Clock Strikes Three*.....	7.00 -	10.00
Vocalion 3690 *Can I Forget You?*............	7.00 -	10.00
Vocalion 3704 *Have You Ever Been In Love*...	7.00 -	10.00

ALL STAR BAND:

Victor 26144 *The Blues*...............	2.00 -	3.00

ALL STAR CALIFORNIANS:

Melotone 12000 *Cheerful Little Earful*........	15.00 -	25.00
Melotone 12002 *Never Swat A Fly*...........	5.00 -	8.00

ALL STAR COLLEGIANS:

Perfect 15509, 15535...................	2.00 -	3.00
Perfect 15550 *Now's The Time To Fall In Love*.	5.00 -	8.00

ALL-STAR ORCHESTRA:

Victor 21149 *Chloe*...............	4.00 -	7.00
Victor 21326 *I Must Be Dreaming*...........	8.00 -	12.00
Victor 21212 *My Melancholy Baby*..........	4.00 -	7.00
Victor 21423 *Add A Little Wiggle*............	7.00 -	10.00
Victor 21605 *I'm More Than Satisfied*........	7.00 -	10.00
Victor 22054, 22073, 22104, 22106, 22197.....	4.00 -	8.00

ALL-STAR RHYTHM BOYS:

Titles issued contemporaneously on Clarion, Diva, Velvet Tone: *Pardon Me, Pretty Baby; Sensation*	7.00 -	12.00

OVIE ALSTON & HIS ORCHESTRA:

Vocalion 4448 *Junk Man's Serenade*...........	5.00 -	8.00
Vocalion 4462 *How Much Do You Mean To Me?*	5.00 -	8.00
Vocalion 4500 *Home Cookin' Mama*...........	5.00 -	8.00
Vocalion 4577 *Spare-Ribs and Spaghetti*.......	5.00 -	8.00

DANNY ALTIER & HIS ORCHESTRA:

Vocalion 15740 *My Gal Sal*.................	40.00 -	60.00

THE AMBASSADORS:

Vocalion 14620, 14668, 14686, 14810, 14823, 14851, 14907, 14916, 14928, 15131.....	2.00 -	4.00
Vocalion 15156 *Military Mike*...............	5.00 -	8.00
Vocalion 15752 *Me and the Man in the Moon*..	5.00 -	8.00
Vocalion 15793 *You've Never Been Blue*.....	5.00 -	8.00

ALBERT AMMONS (AND HIS RHYTHM KINGS):

Blue Note 2 *Boogie Woogie Stomp*...........	5.00 -	8.00
Blue Note 4 *Chicago In Mind*............	5.00 -	8.00
Blue Note 21 *Suitcase Blues*............	5.00 -	8.00
Decca 749 *Boogie Woogie Stomp*...........	7.00 -	10.00
Decca 975 *Early Mornin' Blues*............	7.00 -	10.00
Solo Art 12000 *Monday Struggle*............	10.00 -	15.00
Solo Art 12001 *Boogie Woogie*............	10.00 -	15.00
Solo Art 12003 *St. Louis Blues*............	10.00 -	15.00
Vocalion 4608 *Shout For Joy*............	5.00 -	8.00

AMOS 'N' ANDY (See CORRELL and GOSDEN)

EDDIE "ROCHESTER" ANDERSON:

Columbia 35442, 36185...................	4.00 -	7.00

IVIE ANDERSON & HER BOYS FROM DIXIE:

Variety 591 *All God's Chillun Got Rhythm*.....	7.00 -	10.00

WALTER ANDERSON & HIS GOLDEN PHEASANT HOODLUMS

Titles, issued contemporaneously on Bell, Challenge, Gennett: *After I've Called You Sweetheart; Alabama Stomp; Melancholy; Mokus; Rain; What's We Do For Dough?*...............	15.00 -	20.00

THE ANDREWS SISTERS:

Decca 1496 *Just a Simple Melody*............	5.00 -	8.00
Decca 1562 *Bei Mir Bist du Schoen*...........	5.00 -	8.00
Decca 1691, 1703, 1744, 1859, 1875, 1912, 1974, 2016, 2082, 2214, 2290, 2414............	3.00 -	5.00
Decca, most other titles...................	2.00 -	3.00

ANONYMOUS (Records on which no artist credit is given. In most cases, the identity of the artist is known. The following have been recognized as collectible. No effort has been made to list "test pressings.")

Brunswick *"Mood Accompaniment Library"* most dance band selections...................	2.00 -	3.00
Grey Gull 1701 *Battleship Kate*...............	5.00 -	10.00
Grey Gull 1702 *Jimtown Blues*...............	5.00 -	10.00
Grey Gull 1706 *Lead Pipe Blues*...............	5.00 -	10.00
Grey Gull 1710 *Coal Black Blues*...............	15.00 -	20.00
Grey Gull 1718 *Close Fit Blues*...............	15.00 -	25.00
Grey Gull 1724 *Baby, Won't You Please Come Home?*...............	15.00 -	25.00
Grey Gull 7028 *Sure Enough Blues*...........	5.00 -	8.00
Grey Gull 7029 *Mississippi Mud Blues*...........	5.00 -	8.00
Grey Gull 7037 *Jimtown Blues*...............	5.00 -	10.00
Little Wonder 20 *Back To The Carolina You Love*	15.00 -	20.00
(Note: The unidentified baritone on the above is Al Jolson.)		
Radiex 1701 *Battleship Kate*.................	5.00 -	10.00
Radiex 1706 *Sweat Blues*.................	5.00 -	10.00
Radiex 7037 *Jimtown Blues*.................	5.00 -	10.00

ARCADIAN SERENADERS:

Okeh 40272 *Fidgety Feet*.................	15.00 -	20.00
Okeh 40378 *San Sue Strut*.................	15.00 -	20.00
Okeh 40440 *Who Can Your Regular Be Blues*..	15.00 -	20.00
Okeh 40503 *The Co-Ed*.................	15.00 -	20.00
Okeh 40517 *Angry*.................	15.00 -	20.00
Okeh 40538 *Carry It On Down*...............	15.00 -	20.00
Okeh 40562 *Yes Sir, Boss*...............	15.00 -	20.00

ARCADIA PEACOCK ORCHESTRA OF ST. LOUIS:

Okeh 40044 *Dream Boat*...............	7.00 -	10.00
Okeh 40052 *Ain't You Ashamed?*...............	7.00 -	10.00
Okeh 40254 *Where's My Sweetie Hiding?*......	5.00 -	8.00
Okeh 40264 *Ah! Ah! Archie*...............	8.00 -	12.00
Okeh 40272 *Dog on the Piano*...............	15.00 -	20.00
Okeh 40372 *Waiting for the Moon*............	10.00 -	15.00

ARKANSAS/ARKANSAW TRAVELERS:

Titles, issued contemporaneously on Diva, Harmony, Velvet Tone: *Birmingham Breakdown; Boneyard Shuffle; I Ain't Got Nobody; Ja Da; Sensation; Stompin' Fool; That's No Bargain; Washboard Blues*...............	8.00 -	12.00
Red Head Blues...............	12.00 -	15.00
Okeh 40124 *Georgia Blues*...............	5.00 -	8.00
Okeh 40183 *Any Way The Wind Blows*.......	5.00 -	8.00
Okeh 40236 *Copenhagen*...............	7.00 -	10.00
Okeh 40267 *Homebound*...............	7.00 -	10.00
Okeh 40277 *I'll See You In My Dreams*.......	5.00 -	8.00
Okeh 40426 *Row, Row, Rosie*...............	7.00 -	10.00
Okeh 40438 *Indian Nights*...............	5.00 -	8.00

Okeh 40640 *Breezin' Along With The Breeze*...	5.00 -	8.00
Okeh 40641 *I'm Walking Around In Circles*....	5.00 -	8.00
Okeh 40674 *Ting-a-ling, The Bells'll Ring*......	7.00 -	10.00
Okeh 40700 *Give Me a Ukelele*.............	5.00 -	8.00
Okeh 40724 *Take in the Sun, Hang Out the Moon*	5.00 -	8.00
Okeh 40727 *Brown Sugar*.................	5.00 -	8.00

ARKANSAS TRIO:

Edison 51373 *Boll Weevil Blues*.............	5.00 -	8.00

FRED ARMSTRONG & HIS SYNCOPATORS:

Timely Tunes C-1578 *When I Can't Be With You*	25.00 -	40.00
Timely Tunes C-1587 *Sugar Blues*............	15.00 -	20.00

LIL ARMSTRONG & HER SWING BAND/ORCHESTRA:

Decca 1059, 1092, 1182, 1272, 1299, 1388, 1502	4.00 -	7.00

LOUIS ARMSTRONG & HIS HOT FIVE/SAVOY BALLROOM FIVE/OR-CHESTRA/SEBASTIAN NEW COTTON CLUB ORCHESTRA:

Bluebird 5086 *Mahogany Hall Stomp*..........	4.00 -	6.00
Bluebird 5173 *Hustlin' and Bustlin' For Baby*...	4.00 -	6.00
Bluebird 5280 *St. Louis Blues*.............	4.00 -	6.00
Bluebird 5363 *Laughin' Louie*...............	7.00 -	10.00
Bluebird 5408 *Dusky Stevedore*.............	4.00 -	6.00
Bluebird 5409 *Mighty River*...............	4.00 -	6.00
Bluebird 6501 *Mississippi Basin*............	4.00 -	6.00
Bluebird 6590 *Some Sweet Day*.............	4.00 -	6.00
Bluebird 6644 *That's My Home*.............	4.00 -	6.00
Bluebird 6771 *High Society*...............	4.00 -	6.00
Bluebird 6910 *I've Got the World on a String*...	4.00 -	6.00
Bluebird 7506 *Sittin' in the Dark*...........	4.00 -	6.00
Bluebird 7787 *Honey, Do!*................	5.00 -	8.00
Bluebird 10225 *Swing, You Cats*.............	4.00 -	7.00
Bluebird 10236 *That's My Home*............	4.00 -	6.00
Columbia 2754-D *Star Dust*.............	7.00 -	12.00
Columbia 2606-D *All Of Me*..............	7.00 -	12.00
Columbia 2631-D *The New Tiger Rag*........	7.00 -	12.00
Columbia 2646-D *Keepin' Out Of Mischief Now.*	7.00 -	12.00
Columbia 2688-D *Rockin' Chair*.............	7.00 -	12.00
Columbia 2709-D *Body And Soul*............	7.00 -	12.00
Columbia 2727-D *After You've Gone*.........	7.00 -	12.00
Decca 579 *Got A Bran' New Suit*.............	5.00 -	10.00
Decca 580 *You Are My Lucky Star*...........	5.00 -	10.00
Decca 622 *Old Man Mose*...............	5.00 -	10.00
Decca 623 *I'm Shooting High*.............	5.00 -	10.00
Decca 648 *Red Sails In The Sunset*.........	5.00 -	10.00
Decca 666 *Thanks A Million*..............	5.00 -	10.00
Decca 672 *Shoe Shine Boy*...............	5.00 -	10.00
Decca 685 *Rhythm Saved The World*.........	5.00 -	10.00
Decca 698 *I'm Putting All My Eggs In One Basket*	8.00 -	12.00
Decca 797 *Somebody Stole My Break*..........	5.00 -	10.00
Decca 824 *Mahogany Hall Stomp*.............	5.00 -	8.00
Decca 835 *Lyin' To Myself*................	5.00 -	8.00
Decca 866 *Swing That Music*..............	5.00 -	8.00
Decca 906 *Dipper Mouth Blues*.............	5.00 -	8.00
Decca 914 *On A Cocoanut Island*..............	4.00 -	6.00
Decca 949 *Hurdy-Gurdy Man*...............	5.00 -	8.00
Decca 1049 *When Ruben Swings The Cuban*...	5.00 -	10.00
Decca 1245 *Carry Me Back To Old Virginny*...	7.00 -	10.00
Decca 1347 *Public Melody Number One*.......	5.00 -	10.00
Decca 1353 *Cuban Pete*..................	5.00 -	8.00
Decca 1360 *The Old Folks At Home*..........	7.00 -	10.00
Decca 1369 *Yours And Mine*...............	5.00 -	8.00
Decca 1408 *Alexander's Ragtime Band*.........	5.00 -	8.00
Decca 1495 *In The Shade Of The Old Apple Tree*	7.00 -	10.00
Decca 1560 *On The Sunny Side Of The Street*..	5.00 -	8.00
Decca 1635 *Jubilee*..................	5.00 -	8.00
Decca 1636 *Satchel Mouth Swing*..........	5.00 -	8.00
Decca 1653 *The Trumpet Player's Lament*......	5.00 -	8.00
Decca 1661 *Struttin' With Some Barbecue*.....	5.00 -	8.00
(Original issues of early Deccas have shaded letters in logo)		
Decca (most later numbers).............	3.00 -	6.00

Decca 3011 *Bye and Bye*.................	5.00 -	8.00
Decca 3151 *W.P.A.* (with THE MILLS BROTHERS)	20.00 -	30.00
Okeh 8261 *Gut Bucket Blues*................	40.00 -	60.00
Okeh 8299 *Oriental Strut*................	40.00 -	60.00
Okeh 8300 *Heebie Jeebies*................	30.00 -	50.00
Okeh 8318 *Georgia Grind*................	30.00 -	50.00
Okeh 8320 *Cornet Chop Suey*..............	30.00 -	50.00
Okeh 8343 *I'm Gonna Gitcha*..............	30.00 -	50.00
Okeh 8357 *Dropping Shucks*...............	30.00 -	50.00
Okeh 8379 *Sweet Little Papa*..............	30.00 -	50.00
Okeh 8396 *The King Of The Zulus*...........	30.00 -	50.00
Okeh 8423 *Big Butter And Egg Man*.........	30.00 -	50.00
Okeh 8436 *Jazz Lips*...................	30.00 -	50.00
Okeh 8447 *Irish Black Bottom*..............	30.00 -	50.00
Okeh 8474 *Wild Man Blues*...............	30.00 -	50.00
Okeh 8482 *Willie The Weeper*.............	30.00 -	50.00
Okeh 8496 *Keyhole Blues*................	30.00 -	50.00
Okeh 8503 *Potatoe Head Blues*.............	30.00 -	50.00
Okeh 8519 *Weary Blues*..................	30.00 -	50.00
Okeh 8535 *Savoy Blues*..................	30.00 -	50.00
Okeh 8551 *Got No Blues*.................	30.00 -	50.00
Okeh 8566 *Struttin' With Some Barbecue*......	30.00 -	50.00
Okeh 8597 *West End Blues*................	20.00 -	40.00
Okeh 8609 *Sugar Foot Strut*..............	20.00 -	40.00
Okeh 8631 *Knee Drops*..................	20.00 -	40.00
Okeh 8641 *Squeeze Me*..................	20.00 -	40.00
Okeh 8649 *Tight Like This*...............	20.00 -	40.00
Okeh 8657 *Save It, Pretty Mama*............	20.00 -	40.00
Okeh 8669 *No-One Else But You*............	20.00 -	40.00
Okeh 8680 *Beau-Koo Jack*................	20.00 -	40.00
Okeh 8690 *Basin Street Blues*.............	20.00 -	40.00
Okeh 8703 *Knockin' A Jug*................	30.00 -	50.00
Okeh 8714 *Ain't Misbehavin'*..............	15.00 -	25.00
Okeh 8729 *Some Of These Days*.............	15.00 -	25.00
Okeh 8756 *Rockin' Chair*................	15.00 -	25.00
Okeh 8774 *Bessie Couldn't Help It*..........	15.00 -	25.00
Okeh 8800 *Dinah*.....................	15.00 -	25.00
Okeh 41078 *Fireworks*..................	15.00 -	25.00
Okeh 41157 *Knee Drops*.................	8.00 -	12.00
Okeh 41180 *Save It, Pretty Mama*...........	8.00 -	12.00
Okeh 41204 *No-One Else But You*...........	12.00 -	15.00
Okeh 41241 *Basin Street Blues*.............	12.00 -	15.00
Okeh 41276 *Black And Blue*..............	12.00 -	15.00
Okeh 41281 *Sweet Savannah Sue*...........	15.00 -	20.00
Okeh 41298 *Some Of These Days*...........	15.00 -	20.00
Okeh 41350 *After You've Gone*.............	15.00 -	20.00
Okeh 41375 *Song Of The Islands*...........	10.00 -	15.00
Okeh 41415 *My Sweet*..................	15.00 -	20.00
Okeh 41423 *Exactly Like You*.............	15.00 -	20.00
Okeh 41442 *I'm A Ding Dong Daddy*.........	15.00 -	20.00
Okeh 41448 *Confessin'*..................	15.00 -	20.00
Okeh 41454 *Weather Bird*................	20.00 -	25.00
Okeh 41463 *You're Lucky To Me*...........	12.00 -	16.00
Okeh 41468 *Body And Soul*...............	12.00 -	16.00
Okeh 41478 *You're Drivin' Me Crazy*........	12.00 -	16.00
Okeh 41486 *Shine*....................	12.00 -	16.00
Okeh 41497 *Walkin' My Baby Back Home*.....	12.00 -	16.00
Okeh 41498 *Blue Again*.................	12.00 -	16.00
Okeh 41501 *Them There Eyes*.............	12.00 -	16.00
Okeh 41504 *When It's Sleepy Time Down South*	12.00 -	16.00
Okeh 41530 *Star Dust*..................	12.00 -	16.00
Okeh 41534 *Chinatown, My Chinatown*.......	12.00 -	16.00
Okeh 41538 *The Lonesome Road*...........	12.00 -	16.00
Okeh 41541 *Lazy River*.................	12.00 -	16.00
Okeh 41550 *Kickin' The Gong Around*.......	12.00 -	16.00
Okeh 41552 *All Of Me*.................	12.00 -	16.00
Okeh 41557 *The New Tiger Rag*............	12.00 -	16.00
Okeh 41560 *Keepin' Out of Mischief Now*.....	12.00 -	16.00
Victor 24200 *That's My Home*.............	8.00 -	12.00
Victor 24204 *I Hate To Leave You Now*.......	8.00 -	12.00
Victor 24323 *High Society*...............	8.00 -	12.00

Victor 24233 *I Gotta Right To Sing The Blues*..	8.00 -	12.00
Victor 24245 *Sittin' In The Dark*.............	8.00 -	12.00
Victor 24257 *Some Sweet Day*...............	8.00 -	12.00
Victor 24320 *St. Louis Blues*...............	8.00 -	12.00
Victor 24321 *Mississippi Basin*..............	8.00 -	12.00
Victor 24334 *There's A Cabin in the Pines*.....	8.00 -	12.00
Victor 24351 *Basin Street Blues*.............	8.00 -	12.00
Victor 24369 *Snowball*................	8.00 -	12.00
Victor 24425 *Don't Play Me Cheap*........	8.00 -	12.00
Victor 3608A (12 inch) Medley of Armstrong Hits	7.00 -	10.00
Vocalion 3008 *Basin Street Blues*...........	4.00 -	7.00
Vocalion 3009 *Tiger Rag*...................	4.00 -	7.00
Vocalion 3025 *Dallas Blues*...............	5.00 -	8.00
Vocalion 3026 *The Lonesome Road*..........	5.00 -	8.00
Vocalion 3039 *Chinatown, My Chinatown*.....	5.00 -	8.00
Vocalion 3040 *Exactly Like You*.............	4.00 -	7.00
Vocalion 3055 *Mahogany Hall Stomp*.........	4.00 -	7.00
Vocalion 3059 *Confessin'*................	4.00 -	7.00
Vocalion 3072 *Body And Soul*.............	5.00 -	8.00
Vocalion 3073 *Georgia On My Mind*.........	5.00 -	8.00
Vocalion 3085 *Beau Koo Jack*.............	5.00 -	8.00
Vocalion 3102 *I Ain't Go Nobody*............	5.00 -	8.00
Vocalion 3114 *Lazy River*................	5.00 -	8.00
Vocalion 3115 *Black And Blue*.............	5.00 -	8.00
Vocalion 3124 *The New Tiger Rag*............	5.00 -	8.00
Vocalion 3125 *Home*...................	5.00 -	8.00
Vocalion 3135 *All Of Me*................	5.00 -	8.00
Vocalion 3136 *Sweet Savannah Sue*..........	5.00 -	8.00
Vocalion 3137 *Keyhole Blues*.............	5.00 -	8.00
Vocalion 3148 *Sugar Foot Strut*............	5.00 -	8.00
Vocalion 3172 *Wrap Your Troubles In Dreams*..	5.00 -	8.00
Vocalion 3180 *You're Lucky To Me*...........	10.00 -	15.00
Vocalion 3181 *Keepin' Out Of Mischief Now*...	5.00 -	8.00
Vocalion 3193 *Gully Low Blues*.............	5.00 -	8.00
Vocalion 3194 *The Peanut Vendor*............	4.00 -	7.00
Vocalion 3202 *When You're Smiling*..........	5.00 -	8.00
Vocalion 3203 *When It's Sleepy Time Down South*	5.00 -	8.00
Vocalion 3204 *West End Blues*.............	4.00 -	7.00
Vocalion 3205 *That Rhythm man*............	5.00 -	8.00
Vocalion 3216 *You're Driving Me Crazy*......	5.00 -	8.00
Vocalion 3217 *Savoy Blues*...............	4.00 -	7.00
Vocalion 3237 *Hotter Than That*............	4.00 -	7.00
Vocalion 3301 *I'm In The Market For You*.....	5.00 -	8.00
Vocalion 3303 *Tight Like This*.............	4.00 -	7.00
Vocalion 3337 *Them There Eyes*............	4.00 -	7.00
Vocalion 3370 *Indian Cradle Song*..........	4.00 -	7.00
Vocalion 3381 *Save It Pretty Mama*..........	4.00 -	7.00
Vocalion 3643 *After You've Gone*............	4.00 -	7.00

GUS ARNHEIM & HIS (AMBASSADOR HOTEL/COCOANUT GROVE) ORCHESTRA:

Brunswick 6683, 6693, 6729, 6734, 6751, 6765..	3.00 -	5.00
Brunswick 7900 *The Image Of You*..........	7.00 -	10.00
Brunswick 7904 *Exactly Like You*............	7.00 -	10.00
Brunswick 7919 *So Rare*..................	7.00 -	10.00
Brunswick 7922 *High, Wide and Handsome*.....	7.00 -	10.00
Brunswick 7933 *All You Want To Do Is Dance*.	7.00 -	10.00
Brunswick 7937 *On With The Dance*........	7.00 -	10.00
Okeh 41037 *If I Can't Have You*............	5.00 -	8.00
Okeh 41057 *Feelin' Good*................	5.00 -	8.00
Okeh 41208 *Glad Rag Doll*................	5.00 -	8.00
Victor L-16011 Medley of Popular Selections....	7.00 -	10.00
(Preceding is long-playing "Program Transcription")		
Victor 22054 *Lovable and Sweet*.............	4.00 -	6.00
Victor 22384 *Dancing to Save Your Sole*......	5.00 -	8.00
Victor 22470 *I've Gotta Yen For You*........	5.00 -	8.00
Victor 22561 *Fool Me Some More*........	5.00 -	8.00
Victor 22580 *Them There Eyes*............	5.00 -	8.00
Victor 22618 *I Surrender, Dear*...........	5.00 -	8.00
Victor 22691 *I'm Gonna Get You*.........	7.00 -	10.00
Victor 22700 *One More Time*............	7.00 -	10.00

Victor 22851 *There's Nothing Too Good For My Baby*	8.00 -	12.00
Victor 24061 *Evening*..................	5.00 -	8.00
Victor 24234 *Love Is a Dream*...........	5.00 -	8.00
Victor 24235 *Love in the Moonlight*..........	5.00 -	8.00

BILLY "PETE" ARTZ & HIS HENRY AND GEORGE ORCHESTRA:

Titles, issued contemporaneously on Banner, Conqueror, Oriole, Perfect, and Romeo: *I'm All Dressed Up with a Broken Heart; Never; Parkin' in the Moonlight; There's a Time and Place for Everything*	7.00 -	10.00

PAUL ASH & HIS MERRY MAD MUSICAL GANG/ORCHESTRA:

Clarion 5104-C *I Got Rhythm*...............	7.00 -	10.00
Columbia 1066-D *Ain't That a Grand and Glorious Feeling?*........................	5.00 -	8.00
Columbia 1349-D *My Pet*.................	5.00 -	8.00
Columbia 1616-D *Salty*.................	5.00 -	8.00
Columbia 2796-D *Shadows on the Swanee*......	5.00 -	8.00
Columbia 2798-D *Louisville Lady*............	5.00 -	8.00
Harmony 1234-H *I Got Rhythm*............	7.00 -	10.00
Variety 649 *Raggin' The Scale*............	5.00 -	8.00

FRED ASTAIRE:

Brunswick 7486 *Cheek To Cheek*...........	5.00 -	8.00
Brunswick 7608 *Let's Face the Music and Dance*	5.00 -	8.00
Brunswick 7609 *I'm Putting All My Eggs In One Basket*	5.00 -	8.00
Brunswick 7610 *I'd Rather Lead a Band*......	5.00 -	8.00
Brunswick 7716 *A Fine Romance*............	5.00 -	8.00
Brunswick 7717 *Pick Yourself Up*...........	5.00 -	8.00
Brunswick 7718 *Never Gonna Dance*........	5.00 -	8.00
Brunswick 7855 *Beginner's Luck*............	5.00 -	8.00
Brunswick 7856 *Slap That Bass*............	5.00 -	8.00
Brunswick 7857 *Let's Call the Whole Thing Off*.	5.00 -	8.00
Brunswick 7982 *A Foggy Day*..............	5.00 -	8.00
Brunswick 7983 *Nice Work If You Can Get It*...	5.00 -	8.00
Brunswick 8189 *Change Partners*...........	5.00 -	8.00
Brunswick 8190 *The Yam Step Explained*......	5.00 -	8.00
Columbia 3164-D *They Can't Take That Away From Me*	5.00 -	8.00
Columbia 3165-D *They All Laughed*..........	5.00 -	8.00
Columbia 3166-D *Shall We Dance?*............	5.00 -	8.00
Columbia 35517, 35815, 35852............	3.00 -	5.00

ATLANTA MERRYMAKERS:

Madison 1935 *Black Stomp*..................	7.00 -	10.00
Madison 50015 *Sweet Little Sis*.............	7.00 -	10.00
Madison 50024 *Sweet Little Sis*.............	7.00 -	10.00

ATLANTA SYNCOPATORS:

Grey Gull 1888 *That Wicked Stomp*...........	10.00 -	15.00
Madison 50008 *That Wicked Stomp*...........	10.00 -	15.00
Madison 50009 *Step On It*..............	8.00 -	12.00
Madison 50015 *Lead Pipe Blues*............	7.00 -	10.00
Radiex 5008 *That Wicked Stomp*............	10.00 -	15.00
Radiex 5015 *Beale Street Blues*...........	7.00 -	10.00
Van Dyke 508 *That Wicked Stomp*...........	10.00 -	15.00

FRANK AUBURN & HIS ORCHESTRA:

Clarion 5179-C *I'm Tickled Pink With a Blue-Eyed Baby*	7.00 -	10.00
Clarion 5180-C *A Peach of a Pair*..........	7.00 -	10.00
Clarion 5212-C *Would You Like To Take a Walk?*	5.00 -	8.00
Clarion 5273-C *Rockin' Chair*.............	7.00 -	10.00
Clarion 5277-C *When I Take My Sugar To Tea*.	7.00 -	10.00
Clarion 5283-C *I'm Crazy 'Bout My Baby*......	7.00 -	10.00
Clarion 5286-C *You'll Be Mine in Apple Blossom Time*	7.00 -	10.00
Clarion 5335-C *Faithfully Yours*.............	4.00 -	7.00
Clarion 5340-C *I Found a Million Dollar Baby*..	7.00 -	10.00
Clarion 5356-C *Hikin' Down the Highway*......	5.00 -	8.00
Clarion 5369-C *Me!*..................	5.00 -	8.00
Clarion 5450-C *Goodnight, Moon*............	4.00 -	7.00

Clarion 5451-C *One Little Quarrel*	4.00 -	7.00
Clarion 5455-C *Between the Devil and the Deep Blue Sea*	7.00 -	10.00
Clarion 11001-C *Little Girl*	8.00 -	12.00
(Above is a "double track" record)		
Harmony 1138-H *Kickin' a Hole in the Sky*	7.00 -	10.00
Harmony 1200-H *Why Am I So Romantic?*	4.00 -	7.00
Harmony 1202-H *Good Evenin'*	4.00 -	7.00
Harmony 1234-H *It's a Great Life*	7.00 -	10.00
Harmony 1240-H *My Ideal*	4.00 -	7.00
Harmony 1249-H *Cheerful Little Earful*	5.00 -	8.00
Harmony 1269-H *I'm So Afraid of You*	5.00 -	8.00
Harmony 1306-H *Rockin' Chair*	7.00 -	10.00
Harmony 1327-H *My Cradle Sweetheart*	4.00 -	7.00
Harmony 1331-H *In the Merry Month of Maybe*	7.00 -	10.00
Harmony 1344-H *Hikin' Down the Highway*	5.00 -	8.00
Harmony 1357-H *Give Me Your Affection, Honey*	5.00 -	8.00
Harmony 1412-H *Between the Devil and the Deep Blue Sea*	7.00 -	10.00
Harmony 6001-H *Sunny Skies*	8.00 -	12.00
(Above is a "double track" record.)		
Velvet Tone 2333-V *Got the Bench-Got the Park*	4.00 -	7.00
Velvet Tone 2339-V *Rockin' Chair*	7.00 -	10.00
Velvet Tone 2343-V *When I Take My Sugar To Tea*	7.00 -	10.00
Velvet Tone 2349-V *I'm Crazy 'Bout My Baby*	7.00 -	10.00
Velvet Tone 2352-V *You'll Be Mine in Apple Blossom Time*	7.00 -	10.00
Velvet Tone 2404-V *In the Merry Month of Maybe*	7.00 -	10.00
Velvet Tone 2420-V *The Hour of Parting*	5.00 -	8.00
Velvet Tone 2433-V *Give Me Your Affection, Honey*	5.00 -	8.00
Velvet Tone 2510-V *Goodnight, Moon*	4.00 -	7.00
Velvet Tone 2511-V *One Little Quarrel*	4.00 -	7.00
Velvet Tone 2515-V *Between the Devil and the Deep Blue Sea*	7.00 -	10.00
Velvet Tone 10001-V *Sunny Skies*	8.00 -	12.00
(Above is a "double track" record.)		

GEORGE AULD & HIS ORCHESTRA:

Varsity 8152, 8159, 8163, 8199, 8212	3.00 -	5.00

AUSTIN & HIS MUSICAL AMBASSADORS:

Paramount 12359 *Don't Forget To Mess Around*	10.00 -	15.00

GENE AUSTIN:

Titles, issued contemporaneously on Banner, Conqueror, Melotone, Oriole, Perfect, Romeo: *Blue Kentucky Moon; Easter Parade; Everything I Have Is Yours; A Faded Summer Love; A Ghost of a Chance; Goodnight, Sweetheart; Guilty; If I Didn't Have You; In a Dream; Just a Little Home for the Old Folks; A Little Street Where Old Friends Meet; The Lonesome Road; When I Was a Boy From the Mountains*	4.00 -	8.00
Titles, issued contemporaneously on Banner, Conqueror, Melotone, Oriole, Perfect, Romeo: *Build a Little Home; Did You Ever See a Dream Walking?*	7.00 -	10.00
Titles, issued contemporaneously on Banner, Conqueror, Melotone, Oriole, Perfect, Romeo: *Dear Old Southland; I'm Sorry, Dear; Jail House Blues; Lies*	10.00 -	15.00
Decca 904 *When I'm With You*	5.00 -	8.00
Decca 926 *I Cried For You*	5.00 -	8.00
Decca 1578 *Marie*	5.00 -	8.00
Decca 1656 *Dear Old Southland*	8.00 -	12.00
Decca 1832, 3102, 3939, 4175, 4333, 4354	3.00 -	5.00
Hit-of-the-Week L-3 *Now That You're Gone*	5.00 -	8.00
Victor 19585, 19599, 19625, 19637, 19677, 19656, 19857, 19864, 19899, 19928, 19950, 19968, 20030, 20044, 20084, 20143, 20371, 20397, 20411, 20561, 20568, 20569, 20730, 20964, 20977, 21015, 21098, 21329, 21334, 21374, 21454, 21545, 21564, 21714, 21779, 21798, 21833, 21856, 21893, 21915, 21916, 21952, 22033, 22068	3.00 -	6.00

Victor 22128, 22223	3.00 -	6.00
Victor 22299 *After You've Gone*	7.00 -	10.00
Victor 22341, 22416, 22451, 22490, 22518, 22527, 22539, 22601, 22635, 22687	4.00 -	7.00
Victor 22739 *Without That Gal!*	7.00 -	10.00
Victor 22806 *Love Letters in the Sand*	5.00 -	8.00
Victor 24663 *All I Do Is Dream of You*	10.00 -	15.00
Victor 24725 *Blue Sky Avenue*	5.00 -	8.00

LOVIE AUSTIN & HER (BLUES) SERENADERS:

Paramount 12255 *Steppin' On The Blues*	30.00 -	40.00
Paramount 12277 *Peepin' Blues*	30.00 -	40.00
Paramount 12278 *Charleston Mad*	30.00 -	40.00
Paramount 12283 *Heebie Jeebies*	30.00 -	40.00
Paramount 12300 *Rampart Street Blues*	25.00 -	35.00
Paramount 12313 *Too Sweet For Words*	75.00 -	100.00
Paramount 12361 *Frog Tongue Stomp*	75.00 -	100.00
Paramount 12380 *Chicago Mess Around*	75.00 -	100.00
Paramount 12391 *In The Alley Blues*	75.00 -	100.00

AUSTIN'S SERENADERS:

Broadway 1018 *Jackass Blues*	75.00 -	100.00

THE AVALONIANS:

Vocalion 15577 *Zulu Wail*	8.00 -	12.00

CHARLES AVERY:

Paramount 12896 *Dearborn Street Breakdown*	80.00 -	100.00

JOHN AYRES' ORCHESTRA:

Parlophone PNY-34084 *What's The Use Of Cryin', Baby?*	25.00 -	35.00
PNY-34085 *When You're Feelin' Blue*	25.00 -	35.00

BABS & HER BROTHERS:

Decca 505 *Let's Swing It*	7.00 -	10.00
Decca 518 *Double Trouble*	7.00 -	10.00
Decca 634 *A Little Bit Independent*	7.00 -	10.00
Decca 635 *Yankee Doodle Never Went To Town*	7.00 -	10.00

BABY ARISTOCRATS BAND:

Gennett 6198 *Darktown Shuffle*	15.00 -	20.00

BABY ROSE MARIE:

Brunswick 6570 *My Bluebird's Singing The Blues*	7.00 -	10.00
Victor 22960 *Take A Picture Of The Moon*	15.00 -	20.00
Victor 24196 *In the Dim, Dim Dawning*	7.00 -	10.00

THE BADGERS:

Broadway 1055 *I Gotta Get Myself Somebody To Love*	5.00 -	8.00
Broadway 1058 *It All Depends On You*	5.00 -	8.00
Broadway 1339, 1378	3.00 -	5.00
Broadway 1379 *Exactly Like You*	5.00 -	8.00
Broadway 1409 *If I Could Be With You One Hour Tonight*	8.00 -	12.00
Paramount 20820 *Exactly Like You*	5.00 -	8.00

MOE BAER & HIS WARDMAN PARK ORCHESTRA:

Vocalion 15760 *Susianna*	5.00 -	8.00

BAILEY'S DIXIE DUDES:

Gennett 5562 *I Want to See My Tennessee*	5.00 -	8.00
Gennett 5577 *I'm Satisfied*	5.00 -	8.00
Gennett 5606 *Go 'Long, Mule*	5.00 -	8.00

BAILEY'S LUCKY SEVEN

Gennett 3008, 3009, 3011, 3015, 3086, 3088, 3093, 3094, 3114, 3135, 3140, 3175, 3191, 3192, 3198, 3204, 3224, 3225, 3243, 3249, 5532, 5540, 5648, 5710	7.00 -	10.00
Gennett 4795, 4815, 4831, 4855, 4857, 4868, 4872, 4874, 4887, 4903, 4908, 4909, 4910, 4922, 4929 4933, 4934, 4935, 4969, 4975, 4979, 4980, 5001, 5004, 5005, 5013, 5016, 5017, 5022, 5030, 5049, 5057, 5076, 5078, 5110, 5145, 5153, 5154, 5183, 5186, 5197, 5232, 5241, 5243, 5249, 5258, 5264, 5290, 5300, 5301, 5308, 5324, 5325, 5344, 5349, 5350, 5357, 5363	4.00 -	7.00
Gennett 5364, 5407, 5424, 5432, 5433, 5452, 5463, 5471	5.00 -	8.00

THE BAILEY SWING GROUP

Juke Box 506 *Eccentric Rag*	3.00 -	6.00

BUSTER BAILEY & HIS RHYTHM BUSTERS/SEVEN CHOCOLATE DANDIES

Variety 668 *Dizzy Debutante*	8.00 -	12.00
Varsity 8333 *The Blue Room*	5.00 -	8.00
Varsity 8337 *April in Paris*	7.00 -	10.00
Varsity 8358 *Fable of a Rose*	7.00 -	10.00
Varsity 8365 *Eccentric Rag*	5.00 -	8.00
Vocalion 2887 *Call of the Delta*	15.00 -	20.00
Vocalion 3846 *Afternoon in Africa*	8.00 -	12.00
Vocalion 4089 *Sloe Jam Fizz*	5.00 -	8.00
Vocalion 4564 *Man With a Horn Goes Berserk*	8.00 -	12.00
Vocalion 5510 *Chained to a Dream*	7.00 -	10.00

JENE BAILEY'S ORCHESTRA

Gennett 5681 *All Aboard for Heaven*	7.00 -	10.00

MILDRED BAILEY

Brunswick 6558, 6587, 6655, 6680	6.00 -	10.00
6184 *Wrap Your Troubles In Dreams*	8.00 -	12.00
6190 *Blues In My Heart*	8.00 -	12.00
Victor 22874, 22880, 22891, 22942, 24117, 24137	5.00 -	8.00
Vocalion 3056, 3057, 3367, 3378, 3449, 3456, 3508, 3553, 3615, 3626, 3931, 3932	6.00 -	10.00
Vocalion (most others)	3.00 -	5.00

WILLIAM BAILEY

Banner 1563 *Squeeze Me*	15.00 -	25.00

MAYNARD BAIRD & HIS ORCHESTRA/ SOUTHERN SERENADERS

Vocalion 1615 *Postage Stamp*	30.00 -	50.00
Vocalion 15834 *Sorry*	30.00 -	50.00

SMITH BALLEW & HIS ORCHESTRA

Columbia 2350-D, 2406-D	5.00 -	8.00
Okeh 41384, 41394, 41429, 41464	5.00 -	8.00

THE BALTIMORE BELLHOPS

Columbia 2449-D *Hot And Anxious*	15.00 -	20.00

BILLY BANKS & HIS ORCHESTRA

Titles, issued contemporaneously on Banner, Oriole, Perfect, Romeo: *Bald-Headed Mama; Bugle Call Rag; Margie; Oh Peter; Spider Crawl; Who's Sorry Now?*	10.00 -	20.00
Victor 23399 *Mighty Sweet*	30.00 -	40.00
Victor 24027 *The Scat Song*	8.00 -	12.00
Victor 24148 *It Don't Mean A Thing*	8.00 -	12.00

BARBARY COAST ORCHESTRA

Personal Record 72-P *Washboard Blues*	8.00 -	12.00
Personal Record 94-P *Weary Blues*	8.00 -	12.00

BARBECUE JOE & HIS HOT DOGS

Champion 16127 *Up The Country Blues*	50.00 -	75.00
Champion 16153 *Tin Roof Blues*	50.00 -	75.00
Champion 16192 *Shake That Thing*	50.00 -	75.00
Champion 4005, 40055	8.00 -	12.00
Gennett 7320 *Weary Blues*	50.00 -	75.00
Champion 40005, 40055	8.00 -	12.00
Gennett 7320 *Weary Blues*	50.00 -	75.00

BARBECUE PETE:

Champion 15904 *Avenue Strut*	35.00 -	50.00

EDDIE BAREFIELD & HIS QUINTETTE:

Sonora 104 *After Hours*	*5.00 -*	*8.00*

TOM BARKER & HIS ORCHESTRA:

Parlophone PNY-34084 *Happy Feet*	10.00 -	15.00
Parlophone PNY-34085 *I Like To Do Things For You*	10.00 -	15.00
Parlophone PNY-34119 *What's The Use?*	10.00 -	15.00
Parlophone PNY-34120 *Hittin' The Bottle*	10.00 -	15.00

BILLIE BARNES:

Broadway 5063 *Dearborn Street Breakdown*	75.00 -	100.00

FAYE BARNES:

Paramount 12209 *The Gouge Of Armour Avenue*	15.00 -	20.00

WALTER BARNES & HIS ROYAL CREOLIANS:

Brunswick 4187 *How Long How Long Blues*	25.00 -	40.00
Brunswick 4244 *It's Tight Like That*	40.00 -	60.00
Brunswick 4480 *Birmingham Bertha*	25.00 -	40.00
Brunswick 7072 *Third Rail*	40.00 -	60.00

CHARLIE BARNET & HIS (GLEN ISLAND CASINO) ORCHESTRA:

Titles, isued contemporaneously on Banner, Conqueror, Melotone, Oriole, Perfect, Romeo: *Baby, Take a Bow; Buckin' The Wind; Butterfingers; Cross Patch; Emaline; I Lost Another Sweetheart; I'm No Angel; Infatuation; I Want You, I Need You; My First Thrill; The Swing Waltz; This Is Our Last Night Together; Too Good To Be True; What Is Sweeter?*	5.00 -	10.00
Bluebird 5814 *I'm Keeping Those Keepsakes*	5.00 -	8.00
Bluebird 5815 *Nagasaki*	5.00 -	8.00
Bluebird 5816 *Growlin'*	5.00 -	8.00
Bluebird 6432 *Long Ago And Far Away*	5.00 -	8.00
Bluebird 6433 *But Definitely*	5.00 -	8.00
Bluebird 6448 *Empty Saddles*	5.00 -	8.00
Bluebird 6487 *Always*	5.00 -	8.00
Bluebird 6488 *A Star Fell Out of Heaven*	5.00 -	8.00
Bluebird 6504 *Make-Believe Ballroom*	5.00 -	8.00
Bluebird 6593 *The Milkman's Matinee*	4.00 -	6.00
Bluebird 6594 *It's Love I'm After*	5.00 -	8.00
Bluebird 6605 *Did You Mean It?*	5.00 -	8.00
Bluebird 6619 *Rainbow on the River*	5.00 -	8.00
Bluebird 6967 *A Sailboat in the Moonlight*	4.00 -	7.00
Bluebird 6973 *The First Time I Saw You*	4.00 -	7.00
Bluebird 6975 *In Your Own Little Way*	5.00 -	8.00
Bluebird, most higher numbers	2.00 -	4.00
Capitol 843 *All The Things You Are*		
Variety 627 *Shame on You*	7.00 -	10.00
Variety 633 *Surrealism*	7.00 -	10.00
Vocalion 3835 Overheard in a Cocktail Lounge	7.00 -	10.00

BARREL HOUSE FIVE (ORCHESTRA):

Paramount 12851 *Hot Lovin*	50.00 -	70.00
Paramount 12875 *Endurance Stomp*	50.00 -	70.00
Paramount 12942 *Scufflin' Blues*	50.00 -	70.00
QRS 7019 *Endurance Stomp*	60.00 -	90.00
QRS 7057 *Nobody's Business*	60.00 -	90.00
QRS 7059 *Hot Lovin'*	60.00 -	90.00

DICK BARRIE & HIS ORCHESTRA:

Vocalion 4193, 4209, 4271, 4285, 4334, 4348, 4366, 4397, 4409, 4421	2.00 -	4.00

BLUE BARRON & HIS ORCHESTRA:

Bluebird 7419, 7429, 7456, 7540, 7542, 7554, 7605, 7608, 7620, 7709, 7711, 7736, 7856, 7872, 7886	3.00 -	5.00
Bluebird, higher numbers	2.00 -	3.00
MGM, most issues	2.00 -	3.00
Vocalion 3772 *Yours and Mine*	7.00 -	10.00

RAYMOND BARROW:

Paramount 12803 *Walking Blues*	40.00 -	60.00

ALEX BARTHA & HIS HOTEL TRAYMORE ORCHESTRA:

Victor 24056, 24059	7.00 -	10.00

SLIM BARLETT & HIS ORCHESTRA:

Superior 2692 *Asphalt Walk*	50.00 -	75.00

COUNT BASIE & HIS ORCHESTRA: COUNT BASIE'S KANSAS CITY SEVEN:

Columbia 35231 *Riff Interlude*	4.00 -	7.00
Columbia 35338 *Hollywood Jump*	4.00 -	7.00
Columbia 35357 *Ham 'n' Eggs*	3.00 -	5.00
Columbia 35448 *Louisiana*	4.00 -	7.00
Columbia 35500 *Somebody Stole My Gal*	4.00 -	6.00
Columbia 36601, 36647, 36675, 36685, 36709, 36710, 36711, 36712, 36766, 36795, 36831, 36845, 36889, 36946, 36990, 37070, 37093	2.00 -	4.00
Decca 1121 *Pennies From Heaven*	7.00 -	10.00
Decca 1141 *Honeysuckle Rose*	7.00 -	10.00
Decca 1228 *The Glory Of Love*	7.00 -	10.00
Decca 1252 *Exactly Like You*	7.00 -	10.00
Decca 1363 *One O'Clock Jump*	7.00 -	10.00
Decca 1379 *Smarty (You Know It All)*	7.00 -	10.00
Decca 1446 *Good Morning Blues*	7.00 -	10.00

Decca 1538 *Let Me Dream*.................. 7.00 - 10.00
Decca 1581 *I Keep Remembering*............. 7.00 - 10.00
Decca 1682 *Blues In The Dark*............... 5.00 - 8.00
Decca 1728 *Every Tub*...................... 5.00 - 8.00
Decca 1770 *Don't You Miss Your Baby?*....... 5.00 - 8.00
Decca 1880 *Swinging The Blues*.............. 4.00 - 7.00
Decca 1965 *Doggin' Around*................. 4.00 - 7.00
Decca 2004 *London Bridge Is Falling Down*.... 5.00 - 8.00
Decca 2030 *Texas Shuffle*.................. 4.00 - 7.00
Decca 2249 *Sing For Your Supper*............ 5.00 - 8.00
Decca 2284 *The Blues I Like To Hear*........ 5.00 - 8.00
Decca (other)............................. 3.00 - 6.00
Okeh 5623, 5629, 5732, 5773, 5862, 5884, 5897,
    5922, 5963, 6010, 6047.................. 3.00 - 6.00
Okeh (other)............................. 3.00 - 5.00
Vocalion 4734, 4747, 4748, 4784, 4860, 4886, 4967,
    5036, 5085, 5118, 5169............... 4.00 - 7.00

PHIL BAXTER & HIS ORCHESTRA:
Okeh 40522 *Something Tells Me*............. 15.00 - 20.00
Okeh 40637 *If I Had You And You Had Me*.... 15.00 - 20.00
Victor V-40160 *I Ain't Got No Gal Now*...... 20.00 - 30.00
Victor V-40204 *Honey Child*................ 15.00 - 25.00

JOHNNY BAYERSDORFFER & HIS JAZ-
    ZOLA NOVELTY ORCHESTRA:
Okeh 40133 *The Waffle Man's Call*.......... 30.00 - 40.00

BERLYN BAYLOR'S ORCHESTRA:
Gennett 6457 *Clarinet Marmalade*........... 15.00 - 20.00

BEALE STREET WASHBOARD BAND:
Vocalion 1403 *Forty And Tight*.............. 50.00 - 75.00

IRENE BEASLEY:
Victor 21467 *Choo Choo Train*.............. 7.00 - 10.00
Victor 21639 *Missin' My Pal*............... 7.00 - 10.00
Victor 40092 *Baby's Back Today*............ 7.00 - 10.00
Victor 40125 *Sometimes I Wonder*........... 7.00 - 10.00
Victor 40173 *You'll Come Back To Me Someday* 7.00 - 10.00

JOSEPHINE BEATTY, ACCOMPANIED BY
    THE RED ONION JAZZ BABIES:
Buddy 8024 *Early Every Morn*.............. 100.00 - 150.00
Buddy 8025 *Everybody Loves My Baby*....... 100.00 - 150.00
Gennett 3049 *Everybody Loves My Baby*..... 100.00 - 150.00
Gennett 3044 *Early Every Morn*............. 100.00 - 150.00
Gennett 5594 *Texas Moaner Blues*........... 100.00 - 150.00
Silvertone 4030 *Early Every Morn*........... 100.00 - 150.00
Silvertone 4033 *Texas Moaner Blues*......... 100.00 - 150.00

SIDNEY BECHET & HIS NEW ORLEANS
    FEETWARMERS/ORCHESTRA: SIDNEY
    BECHET'S BLUE NOTE
    QUARTET/QUINTET:
Bluebird 8509 *Sidney's Blues*.............. 5.00 - 8.00
Bluebird 10623 *Indian Summer*.............. 5.00 - 8.00
Blue Note 6 *Summertime*.................. 5.00 - 8.00
Blue Note 13 *Lonesome Blues*.............. 5.00 - 8.00
Blue Note 502 *Bechet's Steady Rider*........ 5.00 - 8.00
Victor 26640, 26663, 26746, 27204, 27240, 27337,
    27386, 27485, 27447, 27574, 27600, 27663,
    27707, 27904.......................... 3.00 - 5.00
Vocalion 4537 *Jungle Drums*............... 5.00 - 8.00
Vocalion 4575 *What A Dream*............... 5.00 - 8.00

NOAH BEERY:
Brunswick 4828 *One Little Drink*............ 5.00 - 10.00

BIX BEIDERBECKE (& HIS
    GANG/ORCHESTRA):
Okeh 40916 *In A Mist*..................... 20.00 - 30.00
Okeh 40923 *At The Jazz Band Ball*.......... 20.00 - 30.00
Okeh 41001 *Sorry*........................ 15.00 - 20.00
Okeh 41030 *Somebody Stole My Gal*........ 20.00 - 30.00
Okeh 41088 *Ol' Man River*................. 20.00 - 30.00
Okeh 41173 *Rhythm King*.................. 20.00 - 30.00
Special Edition 5013-S *Margie*.............. 7.00 - 10.00
Victor 23008 *I Don't Mind Walking In The Rain* 10.00 - 15.00
Victor 23018 *Deep Down South*............ 15.00 - 20.00

LEON BELASCO & HIS ORCHESTRA:
Vocalion 7863 *Jammin'*.................... 10.00 - 15.00
Vocalion 7872 *Wake Up and Live*........... 10.00 - 15.00

ANNA BELL:
QRS 7007 *Hopeless Blues*................. 50.00 - 75.00
QRS 7008 *Kitchen Woman Blues*........... 50.00 - 75.00
QRS 7009 *Shake It, Black Bottom*.......... 50.00 - 75.00

GEORGE BELSHAW & HIS KFAB
    ORCHESTRA:
Brunswick 4365 *Sweet Liza*................ 10.00 - 15.00

BENNETT'S SWAMPLANDERS:
Columbia 14557-D *Big Ben*................. 25.00 - 40.00
Columbia 14662-D *Jet Black Blues*.......... 25.00 - 40.00

BEN'S BAD BOYS:
Victor 21971 *Wang Wang Blues*............. 8.00 - 12.00

BENNY BENSON'S ORCHESTRA:
Champion 15886 *'Tain't No Sin*............. 12.00 - 16.00
Champion 15932 *Honeysuckle Rose*.......... 12.00 - 16.00

BENSON ORCHESTRA OF CHICAGO:
Victor 19470 *Copenhagen*................. 5.00 - 8.00
Victor 19688 *Riverboat Shuffle*............. 5.00 - 8.00

BUNNY BERIGAN & HIS
    BOYS/ORCHESTRA:
Brunswick 7784 *That Foolish Feeling*......... 8.00 - 12.00
Brunswick 7823 *Who's Afraid Of Love?*....... 7.00 - 10.00
Brunswick 7832 *The Gonna Goo*............. 8.00 - 12.00
Brunswick 7847 *Big Boy Blue*.............. 8.00 - 12.00
Brunswick 7858 *Dixieland Shuffle*........... 8.00 - 12.00
Elite 5005, 5006, 5019, 5020.............. 4.00 - 7.00
Victor.................................... 3.00 - 5.00
Vocalion 3178 *I'd Rather Lead A Band*....... 10.00 - 15.00
Vocalion 3179 *Swing, Mister Charlie*........ 10.00 - 15.00
Vocalion 3224 *A Melody From The Sky*....... 8.00 - 12.00
Vocalion 3225 *I Can't Get Started*.......... 8.00 - 12.00
Vocalion 3254 *If I Had My Way*............. 8.00 - 12.00
Vocalion 15875, 15884, 15887, 15891......... 5.00 - 10.00

BEN BERNIE & HIS HOTEL ROOSEVELT
    ORCHESTRA:
Brunswick 3042, 3082, 3126, 3143, 4943....... 4.00 - 7.00
Brunswick 4020 *When Polly Walks Through The*
    Hollyhocks............................. 5.00 - 8.00
Brunswick 4042 *Cannon Ball Rag*........... 7.00 - 10.00
Brunswick 4767 *You Brought a New Kind of Love*
    To Me................................. 5.00 - 8.00
Brunswick 6165 *This Is The Missus*.......... 5.00 - 8.00
Brunswick, most other issues............... 2.00 - 4.00
Columbia 2804-D *Marching Along Together*.... 5.00 - 8.00
Columbia 2809-D *The Duke Is On A Bat Again*. 5.00 - 8.00
Columbia 2820-D *This Is Romance*.......... 5.00 - 8.00
Columbia 2824-D *Shanghai Lil*............. 5.00 - 8.00
Columbia 2836-D *So This Is Susie?*.......... 5.00 - 8.00
Decca 874 *Long Ago and Far Away*.......... 5.00 - 8.00
Decca 877 *Am I Asking Too Much?*.......... 5.00 - 8.00
Decca 878 *When Did You Leave Heaven?*..... 3.00 - 5.00
Vocalion, most issues...................... 3.00 - 5.00

CHU BERRY & HIS STOMPY STEVEDORES
Commodore 516, 541, 1502, 1508........... 3.00 - 5.00
Variety 532 *Too Marvelous For Words*........ 8.00 - 12.00
Variety 587 *Limehouse Blues*.............. 7.00 - 10.00
Variety 657 *My Secret Love Affair*.......... 7.00 - 10.00

VIC BERTON & HIS ORCHESTRA:
Columbia 3074-D *Devil's Kitchen*........... 10.00 - 15.00
Columbia 3092-D *Imitations of You*......... 10.00 - 15.000
Vocalion 2915 *Dardanella*................. 10.00 - 15.00
Vocalion 2944 *Lonesome and Sorry*......... 10.00 - 15.00
Vocalion 2964 *A Smile Will Go A Long, Long Way* 10.00 - 15.00
Vocalion 2974 *Blue*...................... 10.00 - 15.00

JIMMY BERTRAND'S WASHBOARD
    WIZARDS:
Vocalion 1035 *Little Bits*................. 20.00 - 30.00
Vocalion 1060 *47th Street Stomp*........... 50.00 - 75.00

Vocalion 1099 *I'm Goin' Huntin'*.............. 50.00 - 75.00
Vocalion 1100 *The Blues Stampede*.......... 50.00 - 75.00
Vocalion 1280 *I Won't Give You Some*....... 50.00 - 75.00

DON BESTOR & HIS ORCHESTRA:
Victor 24253 *Forty-Second Street*............. 7.00 - 10.00
Victor 24505 *Armful of Trouble*.............. 15.00 - 20.00
Victor 24556, 24596, 24658 .... 4.00 - 7.00

HENRY BIAGINI & HIS ORCHESTRA:
Titles, on Banner, Melotone, Oriole, Perfect, Romeo:
Go Into Your Dance; The Little Things You Used
To Do.................. 5.00 - 8.00

THE BIG ACES:
Okeh 41136 *Cherry*...................... 12.00 - 18.00

BARNEY BIGARD & HIS OR-
CHESTRA/JAZZOPATORS:
Bluebird 10981, 11098, 11581 .... 3.00 - 5.00
Variety 515, 525, 564, 596, 626, 655 .... 6.00 - 10.00
Vocalion 03809, 03813, 03820, 03828, 03834, 03842,
03985 .... 6.00 - 10.00

JACK BINNEY & HIS ORCHESTRA:
Parlophone PNY-34096 *Freshman Hop*........ 15.00 - 20.00

BIRMINGHAM BLUETETTE:
Herwin 92019 *Old Man Blues*............... 50.00 - 70.00

THE BIRMINGHAM FIVE:
Champion 15008, 15015, 15018, 15028, 15046,
15049, 15050............. 5.00 - 10.00

BIRMINGHAM JUG BAND:
Okeh 8856 *German Blues*.................. 75.00 - 100.00
Okeh 8866 *Kickin' Mules Blues*.............. 75.00 - 100.00
Okeh 8895 *Birmingham Blues*............... 75.00 - 100.00
Okeh 8908 *Wild Cat Squall*................. 75.00 - 100.00

BIRMINGHAM SERENADERS:
Decca 7052 *Black Gal Blues*............... 10.00 - 15.00
Decca 7060 *Milk Cow Blues*............... 10.00 - 15.00

BLACKBIRDS OF PARADISE:
Black Patti 8053 *Razor Edge*............. 100.00 - 150.00
Gennett 6210 *Tishomingo Blues*............ 90.00 - 120.00
Gennett 6211 *Muddy Water*................ 90.00 - 120.00

BLACK DIAMOND ORCHESTRA:
Gennett 6442 *I've Got Somebody Now*....... 10.00 - 20.00

BLACK DIAMOND SERENADERS:
Pathe 36503 *Toe-To-Toe*.................... *5.00 - 8.00*
Pathe 36511 *Ace In The Hole*............... 5.00 - 8.00
Perfect 14684 *Sally's Not The Same Old Sally*.... 5.00 - 8.00
Perfect 14692 *Ace In The Hole*............. *5.00 - 8.00*

THE BLACK DOMINOES:
Gennett 5263, 5347................... 4.00 - 7.00

BLACK KIDS OF HARMONY:
Silvertone 3831 *So's Your Old Man*.......... 8.00 - 12.00

THE BLACK PIRATES:
Broadway 1230, 1374................. 4.00 - 7.00

BLACK SWAN DANCE ORCHESTRA:
Black Swan 2014 *Pretty Ways*.............. 10.00 - 15.00

EUBIE BLAKE (& HIS ORCHESTRA); EUBIE
BLAKE TRIO:
Crown 3086 *When Your Lover Has Gone*...... 10.00 - 15.00
Crown 3090 *I'm No Account Any More*....... 10.00 - 15.00
Crown 3105 *It Looks Like Love*............. 10.00 - 15.00
Crown 3111 *One More Time*............... 10.00 - 15.00
Crown 3130 *Nobody's Sweetheart*........... 10.00 - 15.00
Crown 3193 *River Stay 'Way From My Door*... 10.00 - 15.00
Crown 3197 *Sweet Georgia Brown*........... 10.00 - 15.00
Emerson 10434, 10450................. 5.00 - 8.00
Pathe 20336, 20358................. 7.00 - 10.00
Victor 22735 *My Blue Days Blew Over*........ 10.00 - 15.00
Victor 22737 *Thumpin And Bumpin*......... 10.00 - 15.00

JACK BLAND & HIS RHYTHMAKERS
Titles, issued contemporaneously on Banner,
Melotone, Oriole, Perfect, Romeo: *It's Gonna Be*
You; A Shine On Your Shoes; Someone Stole
Gabriel's Horn; Who Stole The Lock........ 15.00 - 20.00

RUBE BLOOM & HIS BAYOU BOYS:
Columbia 2103-D *The Man From The South*... 10.00 - 15.00
Columbia 2186-D *Bessie Couldn't Help it*....... 10.00 - 15.00
Columbia 2218-D *On Revival Day*........... 10.00 - 15.00

THE BLU-DISC ORCH.:
Blu-Disc 1005 *I Want To Be Happy*.......... 20.00 - 30.00
Blu-Disc 1006 *It Had To Be You*........... 20.00 - 30.00

THE BLUEBIRDS:
Vocalion 15652 *Let's Misbehave*............. 7.00 - 10.00

BLUE GRASS FOOT WARMERS:
Harmony 206-H *Senorita Mine*............... 8.00 - 12.00
Harmony 248-H *Old Folks Shuffle*............ 8.00 - 12.00
(Same titles also appear on Diva, Velvet Tone.)

BLUE JAY BOYS:
Decca 7224 *Endurance Stomp*.............. 10.00 - 15.00
Decca 7225 *Some Do And Some Don't*....... 10.00 - 15.00
Decca 7240 *My Baby*.................. 10.00 - 15.00

BLUE MOON MELODY BOYS:
Champion 15429 *Louisiana*.................. 8.00 - 12.00

BLUE RHYTHM BAND/BOYS:
Brunswick 6143 *Blue Flame*.................. 30.00 - 40.00
Brunswick 6199 *Snake Hips*.................. 30.00 - 40.00

BLUE RHYTHM ORCHESTRA:
Pathe-Actuelle 36350 *Santa Claus Blues*....... 30.00 - 50.00
Pathe-Actuelle 36364 *Keep Your Temper*....... 30.00 - 40.00
Perfect 14531 *Santa Claus Blues*............. 30.00 - 40.00
Perfect 14545 *Keep Your Temper*............. 30.00 - 40.00

BLUE RIBBON BOYS:
Titles, issued contemporaneously on Banner, Con-
queror, Regal, Romeo: *Black And Tan Fantasy;*
Futuristic Jungleism; Low Down On The Bayou;
Poor Minnie The Moocher; Star Dust; Sugar
Blues..................... 7.00 - 12.00

BLUE RIBBON SYNCOPATORS:
Columbia 14215-D *Memphis Sprawler*......... 30.00 - 40.00
Columbia 14235-D *Whale Dip*.............. 30.00 - 40.00

THE BLUES CHASERS:
Perfect 14428 *Sweet Georgia Brown*........... 5.00 - 8.00
Perfect 14432 *Charleston*.................... 5.00 - 8.00

BLYTHE'S BLUE BOYS:
Champion 15344 *There'll Come A Day*........ 75.00 - 100.00
Champion 15528 *My Baby*................ 75.00 - 100.00
Champion 15551 *Pleasure Mad*............. 75.00 - 100.00
Champion 15570 *Tell Me, Cutie*............. 75.00 - 100.00
Champion 15615 *Endurance Stomp*.......... 75.00 - 100.00
Champion 15676 *Oriental Man*............. 75.00 - 100.00
Champion 40023 *Oriental Man*............. 10.00 - 20.00
Champion 40025 *Endurance Stomp*.......... 10.00 - 20.00
Champion 40062 *Tack It Down*............. 10.00 - 20.00
Champion 40115 *Tell Me, Cutie*............. 10.00 - 20.00

BLYTHE'S SINFUL FIVE;
Paramount 12346 *Pump Tillie Pump*.......... 35.00 - 50.00

BLYTHE'S WASHBOARD
BAND/RAGAMUFFINS:
Paramount 12368 *Bohunkus Blues*............ 60.00 - 90.00
Paramount 12428 *Ape Man*................. 60.00 - 90.00

JAMES/JIMMIE/JIMMY BLYTHE (&
BURTON/& HIS RAGAMUFFINS); JIMMIE
BLYTHE'S OWLS/WASHBOARD
WIZARDS:
Champion 16451 *Bow To Your Papa*.......... 35.00 - 50.00
Gennett 6502 *Dustin' The Keys*.............. 40.00 - 60.00
Paramount 12207 *Chicago Stomp*........... 25.00 - 35.00
Paramount 12304 *Jimmie Blues*............. 25.00 - 35.00
Paramount 12370 *Mr. Freddie Blues*.......... 60.00 - 90.00
Paramount 12376 *Messin Around*........... 60.00 - 90.00
Vocalion 1135 *Weary Way Blues*............ 50.00 - 75.00
Vocalion 1136 *Have Mercy!*............... 50.00 - 75.00
Vocalion 1180 *Oriental Man*.............. 50.00 - 75.00
Vocalion 1181 *Alley Rat*................. 20.00 - 30.00

BOBBY'S REVELERS:

Silvertone 3551 *Heebie Jeebies*	35.00 -	50.00
Silvertone 3552 *Mojo Blues*	35.00 -	50.00

BOGAN'S BIRMINGHAM BUSTERS:

Titles, issued contemporaneously on Banner, Melotone, Oriole, Perfect, Romeo: *Everything Is Rhythm Now; She Caught The Boat*	15.00 -	20.00
Vocalion 03540 *She Caught The Boat*	15.00 -	20.00
Vocalion 03570 *The Sheik of Araby*	15.00 -	20.00

TOMMY BOHN PENN-SIRENS ORCHESTRA:

Odeon ONY-36047 *You've Got That Thing*	10.00 -	15.00
Okeh 41372 *Amos 'n' Andy*	10.00 -	15.00
Okeh 41374 *You've Got That Thing*	10.00 -	15.00

BOLTON AND CIPRIANI'S WESTCHESTER BILTMORE ORCHESTRA:

Columbia Personal 93-P *You'll Do It Someday*	10.00 -	15.00

PETE BONTSEMA & HIS HOTEL TULLER ORCHESTRA OF DETROIT:

Gennett 20016 *Salt Your Sugar*	7.00 -	10.00

BOOKER ORCHESTRA:

Gennett 6375 *Salty Dog*	30.00 -	50.00

BOOTS AND HIS BUDDIES:

Bluebird 6063 *Rose Room*	7.00 -	10.00
Bluebird 6081 *Riffs*	7.00 -	10.00
Bluebird 6132 *Anytime*	5.00 -	8.00
Bluebird 6301 *Georgia*	8.00 -	12.00
Bluebird 6307 *Coquette*	6.00 -	10.00
Bluebird 6333 *The Vamp*	7.00 -	10.00
Bluebird 6357 *Sweet Girl*	6.00 -	10.00
Bluebird 6862 *Jealous*	8.00 -	12.00
Bluebird 6880 *Haunting Memories*	8.00 -	12.00
Bluebird 6921 *Swanee River Blues*	10.00 -	15.00
Bluebird 6968 *Sleepy Gal*	6.00 -	10.00
Bluebird 7005 *San Antonio Tamales*	10.00 -	15.00
Bluebird 7187 *Blues of Avalon*	7.00 -	10.00
Bluebird 7217 *The Goo*	7.00 -	10.00
Bluebird 7236 *The Sad*	6.00 -	10.00
Bluebird 7241 *Ain't Misbehavin'*	7.00 -	10.00
Bluebird 7245 *The Happy*	7.00 -	10.00
Bluebird 7269 *The Somebody*	7.00 -	10.00
Bluebird 7556 *Deep South*	8.00 -	12.00
Bluebird 7596 *True Blue Lou*	7.00 -	10.00
Bluebird 7669 *Lonely Moments*	7.00 -	10.00
Bluebird 7944 *A Salute To Harlem*	10.00 -	15.00
Bluebird 10036 *East Commerce Stomp*	7.00 -	10.00
Bluebird 10043 *Sweet Girl*	5.00 -	8.00
Bluebird 10044 *San Antonio Tamales*	5.00 -	8.00
Bluebird 10106 *Boots Stomp*	7.00 -	10.00
Bluebird 10113 *Lonesome Road Stomp*	7.00 -	10.00

THE BOSTONIANS:

Banner 7246 *My Blackbirds Are Bluebirds Now*	5.00 -	8.00
Domino 4216 *My Blackbirds Are Bluebirds Now*	5.00 -	8.00
Regal 8654 *My Blackbirds Are Bluebirds Now*	5.00 -	8.00
Vocalion 15275 *So Does Your Old Mandarin*	5.00 -	8.00
Vocalion 15298 *I've Found a New Baby*	7.00 -	10.00

THE BOSWELL SISTERS:

Brunswick 6083, 6109, 6151, 6170, 6173, 6218, 6231, 6257, 6271, 6291, 6302, 6335, 6360, 6395, 6418, 6442, 6470, 6483, 6545, 6596, 6625, 6650, 6733, 6798	6.00 -	10.00
Brunswick 6847, 6929, 6951, 7302, 7348, 7412, 7454, 7467	4.00 -	7.00
Decca 574, 671, 709	4.00 -	6.00
Victor 19639 *Nights When I'm Lonely*	15.00 -	20.00

CONNIE BOSWELL:

Brunswick 6162, 6210, 6223, 6267, 6297, 6405, 6483	6.00 -	10.00
Brunswick 6552, 6592, 6603, 6632, 6640, 6754, 6862, 6871, 6921, 6962, 7303, 7354, 7363, 7445, 7457	4.00 -	7.00
Victor 19639 *I'm Gonna Cry*	15.00 -	20.00

JIMMY BRACKEN'S TOE TICKLERS:

Titles, issued contemporaneously on Banner, Conqueror, Domino, Regal: *After You've Gone; Icky*

Blues; It's So Good; It's Tight Like That; Making Friends; Four Or Five Times; Shirt Tail Stomp; Tiger Rag; Twelfth Street Rag | 8.00 - | 15.00 |

PERRY BRADFORD & HIS GANG; PERRY BRADFORD'S JAZZ PHOOLS:

Titles, issued contemporaneously on Claxtonola, Harmograph, Paramount, Puritan: *Day Break Blues; Fade Away Blues*	10.00 -	15.00
Additional titles: *Charleston, South Carolina; Hoola Boola Dance*	15.00 -	25.00
Columbia 14142-D *So's Your Old Man*	7.00 -	10.00
Okeh 8324 *So's Your Old Man*	10.00 -	15.00
Okeh 8416 *Kansas City Blues*	20.00 -	30.00
Okeh 8450 *Lucy Long*	25.00 -	35.00
Vocalion 15165 *Lucy Long*	60.00 -	90.00

WILL BRADLEY AND HIS ORCHESTRA:

Columbia 35333, 35354, 35399, 35414, 35464, 35470, 35485, 35530, 35542, 35543, 35545, 35566, 35597, 35607, 35645	3.00 -	6.00
Columbia, most others	2.00 -	4.00
Signature 15048, 15049, 15111, 15134	2.00 -	4.00
Vocalion 5130, 5182, 5210, 5237, 5262	3.00 -	6.00

TINY BRADSHAW & HIS ORCHESTRA:

Decca 194, 236, 317, 456	6.00 -	10.00

ARDELL/ARDELLA/ARDELLE ("SHELLEY") BRAGG (& HER TEXAS BLUE BLOWERS):

Paramount 12398 *Pig Meat Blues*	25.00 -	40.00
Paramount 12410 *Bird Nest Blues*	25.00 -	40.00
Paramount 12429 *That's Alright*	25.00 -	40.00
Paramount 12458 *Wolf man*	25.00 -	40.00

J.H. BRAGG AND HIS RHYTHM FIVE:

Vocalion 03060 *Ethiopian Stomp*	10.00 -	15.00
Vocalion 03174 *Frisky Honey*	10.00 -	15.00

BRASHEAR'S CALIFORNIA ORCHESTRA:

Black Swan 2078 *Stuttering*	12.00 -	16.00
Black Swan 10074 *Stuttering*	12.00 -	16.00
Black Swan 10079 *Carolina Shout*	12.00 -	16.00

(A.) BRILLHARDT'S ORCHESTRA:

Pathe-Actuelle 36430 *The Girl Friend*	8.00 -	12.00
Pathe-Actuelle 36438 *Hello, Aloha! How Are You?*	8.00 -	12.00
Pathe Actuelle 36450 *State Street Shuffle*	10.00 -	15.00
Perfect 14611 *The Girlfriend*	8.00 -	12.00
14619 *Hello, Aloha! How Are You*	8.00 -	12.00
14631 *State Street Shuffle*	10.00 -	15.00

MATT BRITT & HIS ORCHESTRA:

Victor 21760 *Goose Creek-Stomp*	12.00 -	16.00
Victor 22933 *Learning*	7.00 -	10.00
Victor 22956 *Down The Old Back Road*	7.00 -	10.00
Victor V-40012 *Sadness Will Be Gladness*	10.00 -	15.00

BROADWAY BELL-HOPS:

Diva 2504-G *There's A Cradle In Caroline*	30.00 -	50.00
Harmony 504-H *There's A Cradle In Caroline*	30.00 -	50.00
Velvet Tone 1504-V *There's A Cradle In Caroline*	30.00 -	50.00

BROADWAY DANCE ORCHESTRA:

Edison 51302 *An Orange Grove In California*	8.00 -	12.00
Edison 51303 *Old Fashioned Love*	8.00 -	12.00
Edison 51412 *Sally Lou*	10.00 -	15.00
Edison 51420 *Eliza*	8.00 -	12.00
Edison 51421 *Doodle-Doo-Doo*	5.00 -	8.00

BROADWAY PICKERS:

Broadway 5069 *Salty Dog*	75.00 -	100.00

BROADWAY RASTUS:

Paramount 12764 *Rock My Soul*	40.00 -	50.00

IRVING BRODSKY & HIS ORCHESTRA:

Harmony 1021-H *If You Believed In Me*	7.00 -	10.00
Harmony 1041-H *The End of the Lonesome Trail*	7.00 -	10.00

HARVEY BROOKS' QUALITY FOUR:

Hollywood 1008 *Mistreating Daddy*	50.00 -	80.00
Hollywood 1021 *Nobody's Sweetheart*	50.00 -	80.00
Hollywood 1022 *Down On The Farm*	50.00 -	80.00

BROWN-MORRIS ORCHESTRA:
Diva 2521-G, 2528-G....................	6.00 -	10.00
Harmony 521-H, 528-H....................	6.00 -	10.00
Velvet Tone 1521-V, 1528-V..............	6.00 -	10.00

BROWN AND TERRY'S JAZZOLA BOYS:
Okeh 8006 *Hesitating Blues*...................	8.00 -	12.00
Okeh 8014 *All By Myself*.....................	7.00 -	10.00
Okeh 8017 *Saxophone Blues*..................	7.00 -	10.00
Okeh 8018 *Aunt Hagar's Blues*...............	7.00 -	10.00
Okeh 8021 *Jump Steady Blues*...............	8.00 -	12.00

BILL BROWN & HIS BROWNIES:
Brunswick 7003 *Bill Brown Blues*.............	15.00 -	30.00
Brunswick 7142 *Zonky*.......................	15.00 -	30.00
Vocalion 1128 *Bill Brown Blues*..............	15.00 -	30.00

FRANK BROWN & HIS TOOTERS:
Parlophone PNY-34154 *Ring Dem Bells*........	15.00 -	20.00
Parlophone PNY-34156 *Three Little Words*.....	15.00 -	20.00

HENRY BROWN:
Brunswick 7086 *Stomp 'Em Down To The Bricks*	40.00 -	60.00
Paramount 12825 *Twenty-First Street Stomp*....	50.00 -	75.00
Paramount 12934 *Blues Stomp*................	50.00 -	75.00
Paramount 12988 *Eastern Chimes BLues*.......	50.00 -	75.00

LES BROWN & HIS (DUKE UNIVERSITY)
BLUE DEVILS/ORCHESTRA:
Bluebird 7796, 7812, 7858, 7869.............	4.00 -	6.00
Bluebird, most others......................	3.00 -	5.00
Decca 991 *Swing For Sale*...................	7.00 -	10.00
Decca 1231 *Swamp Fire*.....................	4.00 -	7.00
Decca 1238 *Rigamorole*.....................	5.00 -	8.00
Decca 1296 *Ramona*........................	5.00 -	8.00
Decca 1323 *Lazy River*.....................	5.00 -	8.00
Decca 2045, 3155, 3167.....................	3.00 -	5.00
Okeh, most issues..........................	3.00 -	5.00

RUSSELL BROWN & HIS ORCHESTRA:
Parlophone PNY-34088 *Washin' The Blues From*		
My Soul.................................	15.00 -	20.00
PNY-34089 *Washin' The Blues From My Soul*..	15.00 -	20.00
PNY-34090 *Absence Makes The Heart Grow Fonder*	8.00 -	15.00
PNY-34091 *I Remember You From Somewhere*.	8.00 -	15.00
PNY-34130 *Little Sunshine*..................	8.00 -	15.00
PNY-34133 *When The Organ Played At Twilight*	8.00 -	15.00

TED BROWNAGLE AND HIS ORCHESTRA:
Victor 20262 *Arcadia Shuffle*...............	10.00 -	15.00

SAM BROWNE & HIS ORCHESTRA:
Superior 2693 *Hard Times Stomp*............	30.00 -	50.00

BROWNLEE'S ORCHESTRA OF NEW
ORLEANS:
Okeh 40337 *Dirty Rag*.....................	35.00 -	50.00

ALBERT BRUNIES & HIS HALFWAY HOUSE
ORCHESTRA:
Columbia 1959-D *Just Pretending*............	12.00 -	16.00

MERRITT BRUNIES & HIS FRIARS INN
ORCHESTRA:
Autograph (unnumbered) *Up Jumped The Devil*.	75.00 -	100.00
Autograph 610 *Angry*......................	75.00 -	100.00
Autograph 624 *Clarinet Marmalade*..........	75.00 -	100.00
Okeh 40526 *Sugar Foot Stomp*..............	20.00 -	30.00
Okeh 40576 *I'm As Blue As The Blue Grass of*		
Kentucky...............................	15.00 -	20.00
Okeh 40579 *Flamin' Mamie*..................	15.00 -	20.00
Okeh 40593 *Someone's Stolen My Sweet Baby*..	15.00 -	20.00
Okeh 40618 *Up Jumped The Devil*............	15.00 -	20.00

LAURA BRYANT:
Paramount 12870 *Saturday Night Jag*........	60.00 -	100.00
QRS 7055 *Dentist Chair Blues*...............	50.00 -	75.00

WILLIE BRYANT & HIS ORCHESTRA:
Bluebird 6361, 6362, 6374, 6435, 6436........	5.00 -	10.00
Decca 1772, 1881..........................	5.00 -	8.00
Victor 24847, 24858, 25038, 25045, 25129, 25160	6.00 -	10.00

THE BUBBLING-OVER FIVE:
Okeh 8737 *Get Up Off That Jazzophone*.......	25.00 -	40.00

BUCK AND BUBBLES:
Columbia 2873-D *Rhythm For Sale*..........	10.00 -	15.00

THE BUCKTOWN FIVE:
Gennett 5405 *Mobile Blues*..................	40.00 -	60.00
Gennett 5418 *Buddy's Habits*................	40.00 -	60.00
Gennett 5419 *Steady Roll Blues*.............	40.00 -	60.00
Gennett 5518 *Hot Mittens*..................	40.00 -	60.00

THE BUFFALODIANS:
Banner 1776 *Baby Face*....................	5.00 -	8.00
Banner 1778 *How Many Times*..............	5.00 -	8.00
Columbia 665-D *Deep Henderson*............	7.00 -	10.00
Columbia 723-D *Wouldja?*...................	7.00 -	10.00

CHICK BULLOCK (& HIS LEVEE
LOUNGERS):

Titles, selected from this artist's large output contemporaneously issued on Banner, Conqueror, Melotone, Oriole, Perfect, Romeo: *And Still No Luck With You; Any Time, Any Day, Any Where; Chasing Shadows; Extra! (All About That Gal of Mine); I Can't Get Mississippi Off My Mind; I Know You're Lying, But I Love It; I'm Hummin', I'm Whistlin', I'm Singin'; Keepin' Out Of Mischief Now; I'm Gonna Sit Right Down And Write Myself A Letter; My Melancholy Baby; Sing A New Song; Stop The Sun, Stop The Moon; What's Good For The Goose; With Plenty Of Money And You; You Oughta Be In Pictures; You Rascal, You*......

....	4.00 -	7.00
Additional Titles: *Frankie and Johnnie; I Can't Dance*		
(I Got Ants In My Pants); Swingy Little Thingy	8.00 -	12.00
Vocalion 15882 *Low Down Upon The Harlem River*	10.00 -	15.00

BILLY BUNCH & HIS SMOKY RHYTHM:
Bluebird 10305 *Three Little Maids*............	6.00 -	10.00

FRANK BUNCH & HIS FUZZY WUZZIES:
Gennett 6278 *Fuzzy Wuzzy*.................	75.00 -	100.00
Gennett 6293 *Fourth Avenue Stomp*..........	75.00 -	100.00
Herwin 92044 *Congo Stomp*.................	75.00 -	100.00

SONNY BURKE AND HIS ORCHESTRA:
Okeh 5139, 5813, 5873, 5955, 5989...........	4.00 -	7.00
Vocalion 5356, 5397, 5459..................	4.00 -	7.00

JOHNNY BURRIS AND HIS ORCHESTRA:
Gennett 6850 *So Comfy*.....................	15.00 -	20.00

SAMMY BURRIS & HIS NIGHT OWLS:
Vocalion 03917 *Blue Baby*...................	10.00 -	15.00
Vocalion 03980 *Reefer Man's Dream*..........	10.00 -	15.00

(EZRA) BUZZINGTON'S RUBE BAND/RUSTIC
REVELERS:
Broadway 1081 *Magnolia*....................	7.00 -	10.00

EMILIO CACERES TRIO:
Victor 25710, 25719, 26109...................	5.00 -	8.00

CAHN-CHAPLIN ORCHESTRA:
Champion 40113 *Christopher Columbus*........	10.00 -	15.00

LOU CALABRESE & HIS HOT SHOTS:
Gennett 6421 *Lip-Stick*....................	10.00 -	15.00

CALIFORNIA POPPIES:
Sunset 506/507 *What A Wonderful Time*.......	80.00 -	120.00

CALIFORNIA RAMBLERS:

This orchestra appeared on a very large number of records during the 1920s and 1930s, under its own name and pseudonyms (principally THE GOLDEN GATE ORCHESTRA). The records, even those of general interest to collectors, do not generally command sizable premiums. Following is a selected listing only:

Bluebird 6076, 6077, 6078, 6082, 6083, 6145, 6146,		
6156, 6173, 6189, 6190, 6238, 6239, 6240...	4.00 -	7.00
Broadway 1081 *Magnolia*...................	7.00 -	10.00
Columbia 9-D, 15-D, 39-D, 43-D, 49-D, 67-D, 91-D,		
92-D, 103-D, 105-D, 127-D, 153-D, 171-D, 179-D,		
199-D, 218-D, 223-D......................	4.00 -	8.00
Columbia 236-D, 268-D, 278-D, 293-D, 340-D,		
380-D, 419-D, 449-D, 522-D, 527-D, 610-D,		

638-D, 647-D, 669-D, 704-D, 758-D, 800-D, 834-D, 883-D, 992-D, 1038-D, 1148-D, 1227-D, 1275-D, 1314-D, 1411-D, 1504-D, 1574-D, 1642-D, 2208-D..................... 4.00 - 8.00
Edison (thin) 11000 and 14000 series......... 10.00 - 15.00
Edison (thick) 52602 *Wedding Of The Painted Doll* 10.00 - 15.00
Edison 52610 *I Get The Blues When It Rains...* 10.00 - 15.00
Edison 52622 *Painting The Clouds With Sunshine* 10.00 - 15.00
Edison 52629 *Tip-Toe Through The Tulips With Me* 10.00 - 15.00
Edison 52638 *Song Of The Blues*............ 10.00 - 15.00

CALIFORNIA VAGABONDS:
Gennett 6140 *I'm Back In Love Again*......... 8.00 - 12.00
Gennett 6170 *S-L-U-E Foot*.................. 8.00 - 15.00
Gennett 6172 *Yes She Do—No She Don't*...... 8.00 - 15.00
Gennett 6426 *Waitin' For Katy*.............. 8.00 - 15.00

BOB CALL:
Brunswick 7137 *Thirty-One Blues*............ 50.00 - 75.00

BLANCHE CALLOWAY (& HER JOY BOYS/BAND)
Titles, issued contemporaneously on Banner, Melotone, Perfect, Oriole, Romeo: *Catch On; Growlin' Dan; I Need Lovin'; What's A Poor Girl Gonna Do?*.................... 7.00 - 10.00
Okeh 8279 *Lazy Woman's Blues*.............. 30.00 - 40.00
Victor 22640 *Casey Jones Blues*............. 15.00 - 20.00
Victor 22641 *I Need Lovin'*................. 8.00 - 12.00
Victor 22659 *Loveless Love*................. 8.00 - 12.00
Victor 22661 *Sugar Blues*................... 8.00 - 12.00
Victor 22717 *It's Right Here For You*........ 8.00 - 12.00
Victor 22738 *It Looks Like Susie*............ 8.00 - 12.00
Victor 22736 *Make Me Know It*............... 15.00 - 20.00
Victor 22862 *Last Dollar*................... 8.00 - 12.00
Victor 22866 *I Got What It Takes*............ 8.00 - 12.00
Victor 22896 *Blue Memories*................. 8.00 - 12.00
Vocalion 3112 *Louisiana Liza*............... 7.00 - 10.00
Vocalion 3113 *Line-A-Jive*................. 7.00 - 10.00

CAB CALLOWAY & HIS ORCHESTRA:
Banner 0835, 0847, 32116, 32152, 32185, 32227, 32237, 32295, 32323, 32340, 32378, 32483, 32511, 32540, 32563, 32624, 32642....... 6.00 - 10.00
Brunswick 6020, 6074, 6105, 6141, 6196, 6209, 6214, 6272, 6292, 6321, 6340, 6400, 6435, 6450, 6460, 6473............... 5.00 - 10.00
Brunswick 6992, 7386, 7411, 7504, 7530, 7638, 7639, 7677, 7685, 7748, 7756............. 4.00 - 7.00
Cameo 0435, 0447....................... 7.00 - 10.00
Conqueror 7769, 7817..................... 7.00 - 10.00
Domino 4656, 4686....................... 7.00 - 10.00
Jewel 6094, 6185, 6224, 6243............. 7.00 - 10.00
Melotone 12487, 12488, 12489, 12554, 12583, 12609, 12695................. 6.00 - 10.00
Oriole 2094, 2185, 2224, 2243, 2274, 2299, 2302, 2317, 2326, 2361, 2382, 2421, 2495, 2522, 2607, 2626, 2640, 2659, 2699, 2727, 2766, 2823, 2824, 2908.................... 5.00 - 10.00
Perfect 15366, 15376, 15412, 15442, 15457, 15474, 15490, 15494, 15500, 15507, 15531, 15541, 15551, 15572, 15623, 15635, 15659, 15704, 15715, 15727, 15770, 15791, 15825, 15853, 15841, 15872, 15873.............. 5.00 - 10.00
Regal 10152, 10173, 10230, 10279, 10327...... 7.00 - 10.00
Romeo 1460, 1482, 1548, 1587, 1609, 1642, 1671, 1677, 1685, 1698, 1731, 1751, 1766, 1794, 1868, 1888, 1933, 1980, 1997, 2013, 2139....... 5.00 - 10.00
Variety 501, 535, 593, 612, 643, 644, 651, 662.. 5.00 - 8.00
Victor 24414, 24451, 24511, 24557, 24592, 24659, 24690.................... 7.00 - 10.00
Vocalion 3787, 3788, 3789, 3796, 3807, 3825, 3970, 3995, 4019, 4045.............. 4.00 - 7.00

ERMINE CALLOWAY:
Edison (thin) 14024 *Do Something*.......... 10.00 - 15.00

Edison 14071 *S Nice, Like This*............. 10.00 - 15.00
Edison (thick) 52519 *Good Little, Bad Little You* 8.00 - 12.00
Edison 52567 *I Want To Be Bad*............. 8.00 - 12.00
Edison 52570 *Do Something*................ 8.00 - 12.00
Edison 52617 *When We Get Together In The Moonlight*.................. 8.00 - 12.00

BUDDY CAMPBELL & HIS ORCHESTRA:
Okeh 41503 *Let's Get Friendly*.............. 8.00 - 15.00
Okeh 41507 *When Yuba Plays The Rumba On The Tuba*................. 8.00 - 15.00
Okeh 41511 *My Sweet Tooth Says 'I Wanna'*... 8.00 - 15.00
Okeh 41524 *Little Mary Brown*.............. 8.00 - 15.00
Okeh 41527 *Charlie Cadet*................. 8.00 - 15.00
Okeh 41532 *Last Dollar*................... 8.00 - 12.00
Okeh 41540 *I Wonder Who's Under The Moon*. 8.00 - 12.00
Okeh 41543 *Bend Down, Sister*............. 8.00 - 15.00

JOHNNIE CAMPBELL'S ORCHESTRA:
New Flexo 301 *Jimtown Blues*.............. 20.00 - 40.00
New Flexo 302 *Somebody Loves Me*.......... 20.00 - 40.00
New Flexo 303 *The Only, Only One*......... 20.00 - 40.00
New Flexo 304 *Tin Roof Blues*............. 20.00 - 40.00
New Flexo 305 *Where's My Sweetie Hiding?*... 20.00 - 40.00
New Flexo 307 *Charleston Cabin*........... 20.00 - 40.00
New Flexo 308 *No Wonder*................. 20.00 - 40.00

THE CAMPUS CUT-UPS:
Edison 11049 *Farewell Blues*............... 10.00 - 15.00
Edison 11050 *Ballin' The Jack*............. 10.00 - 15.00
Edison 14044 *Campus Rush*................ 10.00 - 15.00
Edison (thick) 52591 *Wabash Blues*.......... 8.00 - 12.00
Edison 52616 *Ballin' The Jack*............. 8.00 - 12.00
Edison 52649 *Campus Rush*................ 8.00 - 12.00

JOE CANDULLO & HIS (EVERGLADES) ORCHESTRA:
Banner 1784, 1796, 1800, 1814, 1815, 1839.... 3.00 - 6.00
Banner 7169 *A Jazz Holiday*............... 5.00 - 10.00
Banner 7192 *Deep Hollow*................. 5.00 - 10.00
Banner 7217, 7218, 7220.................. 3.00 - 6.00
Buddy 8052 *Spanish Mama*................ 10.00 - 20.00
Buddy 8069 *Black Bottom*................. 10.00 - 20.00
Buddy 8070 *Messin' Around*............... 10.00 - 20.00
Cameo 1048, 1061....................... 3.00 - 6.00
Domino 3751, 3772, 3783, 3787, 3956, 4201.... 3.00 - 6.00
Edison 51826 *Bass Ale Blues*.............. 8.00 - 12.00
Edison 51836 *Scatter Your Smiles*........... 7.00 - 10.00
Edison 51848 *The Birth Of The Blues*........ 10.00 - 15.00
Edison 51852 *Brown Sugar*................ 10.00 - 15.00
Edison 51912 *Windy City Stomp*............ 10.00 - 15.00
Gennett 3316, 3311, 3351, 3352, 3358, 3385, 3392 5.00 - 8.00
Gennett 3402 *Bobadilla*.................. 7.00 - 12.00
Gennett 3405 *Tomboy Sue*................ 7.00 - 12.00
Gennett 3406 *Lonely Eyes*................ 7.00 - 12.00
Harmony 150-H, 208-H, 211-H, 235-H, 260-H, 286-H, 361-H.................. 3.00 - 6.00
Herwin 55004 *Black Bottom*............... 10.00 - 20.00
Pathe-Actuelle 36462, 36540, 36693.......... 5.00 - 8.00
Perfect 14643, 14721, 14874............... 5.00 - 8.00
Regal 8089, 8109, 8150, 8310, 8637.......... 3.00 - 6.00
Velvet-Tone 1150-V, 1208-V, 1211-V, 1235-V, 1260-V, 1286-V, 1361-V............. 3.00 - 6.00

CANDY AND COCO:
Vocalion 2833 *Kingfish Blues*.............. 15.00 - 20.00
Vocalion 2849 *China Boy*................. 15.00 - 20.00

CANNON'S JUG STOMPERS:
Bluebird 5030 *Minglewood Blues*........... 20.00 - 30.00
Bluebird 5287 *Big Railroad Blues*.......... 20.00 - 30.00
Bluebird 5389 *Bugle Call Rag*............. 20.00 - 30.00
Bluebird 5413 *Goin' To Germany*........... 20.00 - 30.00
Victor 21267 *Minglewood Blues*............ 50.00 - 80.00
Victor 21351 *Springdale Blues*............ 50.00 - 80.00
Victor 23262 *Money Never Runs Out*........ 75.00 - 100.00
Victor 23272 *Wolf River Blues*............ 75.00 - 100.00

Victor 38006 *Pig Ankle Strut*...............	50.00 -	80.00
Victor 38515 *Feather Bed*..................	50.00 -	80.00
Victor 38523 *Viola Lee Blues*.............	50.00 -	80.00
Victor 38539 *Ripley Blues*...............	50.00 -	80.00
Victor 38566 *Hollywood Rag*.............	50.00 -	80.00
Victor 38585 *Goin To Germany*...........	50.00 -	80.00
Victor 38593 *Last Chance Blues*.........	50.00 -	80.00
Victor 38611 *Walk Right In*.............	50.00 -	80.00
Victor 38629 *Jonestown Blues*............	50.00 -	80.00

EDDIE CANTOR:

Aeolian Vocalion 1220 *The Modern Maiden's Prayer*	10.00 -	15.00
1228 *Down In Bordeo Isle*..............	12.00 -	18.00
1233 *Dixie Volunteers*..................	12.00 -	18.00
Columbia 56-D *If You Do What You Do*......	7.00 -	10.00
Columbia 120-D, 140-D, 182-D, 196-D, 213-D,		
234-D, 256-D, 277-D, 283-D............	4.00 -	7.00
Columbia 364-D, 397-D, 415-D, 457-D........	5.00 -	8.00
Columbia 2723-D *What a Perfect Combination*..	8.00 -	12.00
Columbia A-3624, A-3682, A-3754, A-3784, A-3906,		
A-3934, A-3964....................	3.00 -	6.00
Columbia 35325, 35428...............	2.00 -	4.00
Emerson 1071, 1094, 10102, 10105, 10119, 10134,		
10200, 10212, 10263, 10292, 10301, 10327,		
10349, 10352, 10397................	4.00 -	8.00
Melotone 13183, 13184...............	5.00 -	8.00
Pathe 22163, 22201, 22260, 22318........	4.00 -	8.00
Victor 18342, 21831, 21982, 22189, 24330.....	4.00 -	7.00

CAPTIVATORS (DIRECTION OF RED NICHOLS):

Brunswick 4308, 4321, 4591................	4.00 -	8.00
Melotone 12005, 12049..................	4.00 -	8.00

EDDIE CARLEW'S BABY ARISTOCRATS ORCHESTRA:

Gennett 6184 *Indiana Mud*.................	15.00 -	25.00

BILL CARLSEN & HIS ORCHESTRA:

Broadway 1359 *Milenburg Joys*.............	10.00 -	20.00
1365 *Baby, Won't You Please Come Home?*..	10.00 -	20.00
Paramount 20797 *Clarinet Marmalade*........	10.00 -	20.00

ROY CARLSON'S DANCE ORCHESTRA:

Banner 0504 *Hummin' With Love*...........	5.00 -	8.00
Banner 0511, 0516, 0542, 0559..........	3.00 -	5.00
Banner 0563 *I Can't Blame The Boys For Loving*		
You......................	5.00 -	8.00
Banner 0567 *We'll Be Married In June*........	5.00 -	8.00
Banner 0573 *Whenever I Think of You*........	5.00 -	8.00
Banner 0584 *Just a Lone Hill Billy*...........	5.00 -	8.00
Banner 0694 *I'll Keep On Loving You*........	5.00 -	8.00
Banner 6417, 6423, 6437, 6443, 6444, 6445, 6446,		
6450, 6471, 6478, 6503............	3.00 -	5.00
Banner 6504 *Send Love Through The Breeze*...	5.00 -	8.00
Banner 6505, 6512, 6518, 6539..........	3.00 -	6.00
Banner 6542 *Sweet Kentucky Sue*..........	5.00 -	8.00
Banner 6552 *Would You Believe Me?*........	5.00 -	8.00
Cameo 0111 *Hummin' With Love*...........	5.00 -	8.00
0173 *Whenever I Think of You*.........	5.00 -	8.00
Oriole 1829 *Whenever I Think of You*.......	5.00 -	8.00
Romeo 1244 *Dearest Adorable*.............	5.00 -	8.00

RUSS CARLSON & HIS ORCHESTRA:

Crown 3147 *Minnie The Moocher*...........	7.00 -	10.00
Crown 3163 *It's The Girl*..................	5.00 -	8.00
3301 *I Know You're Lying, But I Love It*....	7.00 -	10.00
3367 *Thou Shalt Not*..................	5.00 -	8.00

BUD CARLTON'S ORCHESTRA:

Crown (Canadian) 81234 *A Little Kiss Each Morning*	5.00 -	8.00
81308 *Rainy Weather Rose*..............	7.00 -	10.00
81469 *Syncopated Jamboree*.............	10.00 -	15.00

HOAGY CARMICHAEL & HIS ORCHESTRA/ PALS: CARMICHAEL'S COLLEGIANS:

Gennett 6311 *Stardust*....................	15.00 -	25.00
6474 *Walkin' The Dog*..................	15.00 -	25.00
Victor L-16009 (long-playing "Program Transcrip-		

tion") Dance Medley of Hoagy Carmichael		
Compositions......................	10.00 -	15.00
Victor 22864 *Bessie Couldn't Help It*..........	15.00 -	20.00
23013 *One Night In Havana*...............	15.00 -	20.00
23034 *Lazy River*....................	12.00 -	15.00
24119 *After Twelve O'Clock*.............	5.00 -	8.00
24123 *Mighty River*..................	5.00 -	8.00
24182 *Sing It Way Down Low*...........	5.00 -	8.00
24402 *Lazy Bones*....................	5.00 -	8.00
24484 *Stardust*......................	7.00 -	10.00
24505 *One Morning In May*..............	15.00 -	20.00
24627 *Moon Country*..................	8.00 -	12.00
V-38139 *Barnacle Bill The Sailor*.........	20.00 -	30.00

CAROLINA CLUB ORCHESTRA:

Melotone 12110, 12177.....................	4.00 -	7.00
Okeh 41199, 41226, 41237, 41277, 41309.....	5.00 -	8.00
41326 *He's So Unusual*.................	9.00 -	12.00
41332, 41337, 41356, 41358............	5.00 -	8.00
41360 *Under A Texas Moon*...........	7.00 -	10.00
41408, 41409.....................	5.00 -	8.00
Pathe-Actuelle 036181.................	3.00 -	6.00
Perfect 14362.....................	3.00 -	6.00

CAROLINA COLLEGIANS:

Banner 6316 *Wedding Bells*..............	5.00 -	8.00
6319 *Before The Rain*...............	5.00 -	8.00

CAROLINA COTTON PICKERS:

Vocalion 03527 *Let's Get Together*............	15.00 -	20.00
03539 *Western Swing*.................	15.00 -	20.00
03580 *Off And On Blues*................	15.00 -	20.00

CAROLINA DANDIES:

Victor 22776 *Come Easy, Go Easy Love*.......	7.00 -	10.00

ROY CARROLL & HIS SANDS POINT ORCHESTRA:

Clarion 5252-C, 5253-C, 5255-C, 5262-C, 5263-C	4.00 -	7.00
Clarion 5321-C *Moonlight Savings Time*........	7.00 -	10.00
5337-C *Two Little, Blue Little Eyes*.......	5.00 -	8.00
5338-C *Let's Get Friendly*..............	7.00 -	10.00
5343-C *High and Low*...............	7.00 -	10.00
5351-C *On The Beach With You*........	7.00 -	10.00
5357-C *I Can't Write The Words*........	5.00 -	8.00
5393-C *Waitin' For A Call From You*.......	4.00 -	
Clarion 5406-C 5407-C, 5455-C..........	4.00 -	7.00
Clarion 5420-C *Bend Down, Sister*..........	7.00 -	10.00
5442-C *Chances Are*.................	10.00 -	15.00
Harmony 1253-H *Overnight*.............	5.00 -	8.00
1261-H *Little Did I Know*.............	5.00 -	8.00
1271-H *Royal Garden Blues*...........	7.00 -	10.00
Harmony 1289-H, 1297-H...............	4.00 -	7.00
Harmony 1322-H *Roll On, Mississippi, Roll On*.	7.00 -	10.00
1328-H *Love Is Like That*.............	5.00 -	8.00
1329-H *One More Time*...............	7.00 -	10.00
1334-H *Dancing in the Dark*...........	7.00 -	10.00
1340-H *Without That Gal!*.............	7.00 -	10.00
1345-H *I Can't Write The Words*........	5.00 -	8.00
1379-H *Waiting For A Call From You*......	5.00 -	8.00
1397-H *Bend Down, Sister*............	7.00 -	10.00
Harmony 1403-H *Chances Are*.............	10.00 -	15.00
Harmony 1406-H, 1407-H, 1412-H.........	4.00 -	7.00
Velvet Tone 2328-V, 2329-V, 2506-V, 2507-V,		
2515-V	4.00 -	7.00
Velvet Tone 2387-V *Moonlight Savings Time*...	7.00 -	10.00
2401-V *Love Is Like That*.............	5.00 -	8.00
2402-V *One More Time*...............	7.00 -	10.00
2407-V *High And Low*...............	7.00 -	10.00
2415-V *On the Beach With You*........	7.00 -	10.00
2421-V *I Can't Write the Words*........	5.00 -	8.00
2457-V *Waitin' for a call from You*........	5.00 -	8.00
2480-V *Bend Down, Sister*............	7.00 -	10.00
2502-V *Chances Are*.................	10.00 -	15.00

BENNY CARTER & HIS ORCHESTRA:

Columbia 2898-D *Devil's Holiday*.............	15.00 -	20.00

Crown 3321 *Tell All Your Day Dreams To Me* ..   20.00 -   30.00
Okeh 41567 *Blue Lou* ....   15.00 -   20.00
Vocalion 2870 *Everybody Shuffle* ....   10.00 -   15.00
    2898 *Shoot The Works* ....   10.00 -   15.00
    4984, 5112, 5224, 4294, 5399 ....   5.00 -   8.00

KING CARTER & HIS ROYAL ORCHESTRA:
Columbia 2439-D *Minnie The Moocher* ....   15.00 -   20.00
    2504-D *Blue Rhythm* ....   15.00 -   20.00
    2638-D *Low Down On The Bayou* ....   15.00 -   20.00

MARGARET CARTER:
Pathe-Actuelle 7511 *I Want Plenty Grease In My Fry-
    ing Pan* ....   15.00 -   20.00
Perfect 111 *I Want Plenty Grease In My Frying Pan*   15.00 -   20.00

CASA LOMA ORCHESTRA:
Brunswick 6085 *When I Take My Sugar To Tea*   7.00 -   10.00
    6092 *White Jazz* ....   7.00 -   10.00
    6100 *Alexander's Ragtime Band* ....   5.00 -   10.00
    6124 *I Wanna Sing About You* ....   7.00 -   10.00
    6150 *Do The New York* ....   7.00 -   10.00
    6153 *It's The Girl* ....   7.00 -   10.00
    6187 *Blue Kentucky Moon* ....   7.00 -   10.00
    6201 *Time On My Hands* ....   7.00 -   10.00
    6242 *Maniac's Ball* ....   7.00 -   10.00
    6252 *Rain On The Roof* ....   7.00 -   10.00
    6256 *One Of Us Was Wrong* ....   7.00 -   10.00
    6263 *You're Still In My Heart* ....   7.00 -   10.00
    6289 *Smoke Rings* ....   5.00 -   8.00
    6311 *Lazy Day* ....   7.00 -   10.00
    6318 *All Of A Sudden* ....   7.00 -   10.00
    6337 *Indiana* ....   7.00 -   10.00
    6397 *After Tonight* ....   7.00 -   10.00
    6402 *Mighty River* ....   7.00 -   10.00
    6463 *Rhythm Man* ....   7.00 -   10.00
    6486 *New Orleans* ....   7.00 -   10.00
    6494 *Why Can't This Go On Forever* ....   7.00 -   10.00
    6513 *Blue Parade* ....   7.00 -   10.00
    6584 *Love Is The Thing* ....   7.00 -   10.00
    6588 *Wild Goose Chase* ....   7.00 -   10.00
    6602 *For You* ....   7.00 -   10.00
    6681 *Mississippi Basin* ....   7.00 -   10.00
    6626 *That's How Rhythm Was Born* .....   7.00 -   10.00
    6628 *Music From Across The Sea* ......   7.00 -   10.00
    6642 *This Is Romance* ....   7.00 -   10.00
    6647 *Savage Serenade* ....   7.00 -   10.00
    6660 *Sweet Madness* ....   7.00 -   10.00
    6666 *And So, Goodbye* ....   7.00 -   10.00
    6679 *Heat Wave* ....   7.00 -   10.00
    6708 *You're Gonna Lose Your Gal* .....   7.00 -   10.00
    6726 *Dixie Lee* ....   7.00 -   10.00
    6738 *Shadows Of Love* ....   7.00 -   10.00
    6764 *That's Love* ....   7.00 -   10.00
    6775 *A Hundred Years From Today* ......   7.00 -   10.00
    6791 *Infatuation* ....   7.00 -   10.00
    6800 *Ol' Man River* ....   7.00 -   10.00
    6858 *This House Is Haunted* ....   7.00 -   10.00
    6870 *Ridin' Around In The Rain* ......   7.00 -   10.00
    6886 *Limehouse Blues* ....   7.00 -   10.00
    6910 *Spellbound* ....   7.00 -   10.00
    6922 *Milenberg Joys* ....   7.00 -   10.00
    6927 *Long May We Love* ....   7.00 -   10.00
    6932 *Jungle Fever* ....   7.00 -   10.00
    6937 *You Ain't Been Living Right* ......   7.00 -   10.00
    6945 *Pardon My Southern Accent* ......   7.00 -   10.00
    6954 *Two Cigarettes In The Dark* ......   7.00 -   10.00
    6964 *Out In The Cold Again* ....   7.00 -   10.00
    6983 *How Can You Face Me?* ....   7.00 -   10.00
    7321 *Nocturne* ....   7.00 -   10.00
    7325 *Linger Awhile* ....   7.00 -   10.00
    7427 *Corrine Corrina* ....   7.00 -   10.00
    7532 *Avalon* ....   7.00 -   10.00
(Some of above Brunswicks are as *Glen Gray & The*

    Casa Loma Orchestra)
Brunswick 20108 (12-inch) *Washboard Blues* .....   10.00 -   15.00
Brunswick paper advertising record, unnumbered:
    Limehouse Blues ....   25.00 -   40.00
Columbia 2884-D *San Sue Strut* ....   7.00 -   10.00
Okeh 41339 *Happy Days Are Here Again* ....   7.00 -   10.00
    41373 *Sweeping The Clouds Away* ....   7.00 -   10.00
    41403 *Alexander's Ragtime Band* ....   7.00 -   10.00
    41477 *Overnight* ....   7.00 -   10.00
    41492 *Casa Loma Stomp* ....   7.00 -   10.00

**CASTLE FARMS SERENADERS/
ENTERTAINERS:**
Titles, issued contemporously on Broadway, Para-
    mount: *Chill Blues; High On A Hilltop; Ol' Man
    River; Silver Moon; 'Taint So, Honey, 'Taint So*   8.00 -   12.00

SID CATLETT QUARTETTE/SEXTETTE/TRIO:
Delta, Session ....   3.00 -   6.00

BOB CAUSER & HIS CORNELLIANS:
Melotone 12848 *Puddin' Head Jones* ....   7.00 -   10.00
Perfect 15858 *Puddin' Head Jones* ....   7.00 -   10.00

**CELESTIN'S ORIGINAL TUXEDO JAZZ
ORCHESTRA:**
Columbia 636-D *Station Calls* ....   15.00 -   20.00
    14200-D *I'm Satisfied You Love Me* ....   15.00 -   20.00
    14220-D *Papa's Got The Jim-Jams* ....   15.00 -   20.00
    14259-D *As You Like It* ....   15.00 -   20.00
    14323-D *It's Jam Up* ....   15.00 -   20.00
    14396-D *The Sweetheart of T.K.O.* ....   15.00 -   20.00

THE CELLAR BOYS:
Vocalion 1503 *Barrel House Stomp* ....   50.00 -   80.00

CHALLENGE DANCE ORCHESTRA:
Challenge 210 *Don't Sing Aloha When I Go* .....   10.00 -   20.00
    809 *Sweetheart* ....

**CHARLIE CHAPLIN CONDUCTING ABE
LYMAN'S AMBASSADOR ORCHESTRA:**
Brunswick 2912 *Sing a Song* ....   7.00 -   10.00

JUANITA STINNETTE CHAPPELLE:
Chappelle & Stinnette 5003, 5004, 5005, 5006 ...   5.00 -   10.00
Victor 21062 *Florence* ....   15.00 -   20.00

THE CHARLESTON CHASERS:
Columbia 446-D *Red Hot Henry Brown* ....   5.00 -   8.00
Columbia 861-D *After You've Gone* ....   8.00 -   12.00
    909-D *Davenport Blues* ....   8.00 -   12.00
    911-D *One Sweet Letter From You* ....   8.00 -   12.00
    1076-D *Delirium* ....   15.00 -   20.00
    1229-D *Five Pennies* ....   7.00 -   10.00
    1335-D *My Melancholy Baby* ....   7.00 -   10.00
    1539-D *Farewell Blues* ....   8.00 -   12.00
    1891-D *Ain't Misbehavin* ....   8.00 -   12.00
    1925-D *Lovable And Sweet* ....   8.00 -   12.00
    1989-D *Turn On The Heat* ....   12.00 -   16.00
    2133-D *Sing, You Sinners* ....   8.00 -   12.00
    2219-D *Here Comes Emily Brown* ....   12.00 -   16.00
    2309-D *You're Lucky To Me* ....   8.00 -   12.00
    2415-D *Basin Street Blues* ....   15.00 -   25.00

CHARLESTON MELODY SYNCOPATORS:
Dandy 5073 *Always Got The Blues* ....   10.00 -   15.00

THE CHARLESTON SEVEN:
Edison 51446 *Nashville Nightingale* ....   10.00 -   15.00

FRED CHESS & THE MERRYMAKERS:
Supertone 9381 *My Sugar And Me* ....   8.00 -   12.00

CHICAGO BLACK SWANS:
Titles, issued contemporaneously on Banner,
    Melodone, Oriole, Perfect, Romeo, Vocalion:
    *Don't Tear My Clothes No. 2; You Drink Too
    Much* ....   7.00 -   10.00

CHICAGO BLUES DANCE ORCHESTRA:
Columbia A-3923 *Blue Grass Blues* ....   12.00 -   18.00

THE CHICAGO FOOTWARMERS:
Okeh 8533 *Ballin' The Jack* ....   40.00 -   60.00
    8548 *Oriental Man* ....   40.00 -   60.00

8599 *Get 'Em Again Blues*	40.00 -	60.00
8613 *Brown Bottom Bess*	40.00 -	60.00
8675 *Goin' To Town*	15.00 -	25.00
8792 *Sweep 'Em Clean*	50.00 -	75.00

CHICAGO HOT FIVE:

Victor 23285 *Star Dust*	15.00 -	25.00
23300 *Wake 'Em Up*	15.00 -	25.00
23326 *Oh! What A Thrill*	15.00 -	25.00

CHICAGO HOTTENTOTS:

Vocalion 1008 *All Night Shags*	25.00 -	35.00

THE CHICAGO LOOPERS:

Pathe-Actuelle 36729 *Three Blind Mice*	40.00 -	60.00
Perfect 14910 *Clorinda*	40.00 -	60.00

CHICAGO RHYTHM KINGS:

Bluebird 6371 *Little Sanwich Wagon*	10.00 -	15.00
6412 *Stompin' At The Savoy*	5.00 -	8.00
Brunswick 4001 *I've Found A New Baby*	30.00 -	40.00
Vocalion 03208 *You Battle Head Beetle Head*	10.00 -	15.00

THE CHICAGO STOMPERS:

Champion 16297 *Wild Man Stomp*	40.00 -	60.00

THE CHICKASAW SYNCOPATORS:

Columbia 14301-D *Memphis Rag*	20.00 -	30.00

IVORY CHITTISON AND BANJO JOE;

Vocalion 25011 *Unlucky Blues*	15.00 -	20.00

THE CHOCOLATE DANDIES:

Columbia 2543-D *Bugle Call Rag*	15.00 -	25.00
2875-D *I Never Knew*	15.00 -	25.00
Okeh 8668 *Birmingham Break-Down*	20.00 -	25.00
41568 *Once Upon A Time*	20.00 -	25.00
Vacalion 1610 *Loveless Love*	75.00 -	100.00
1616 *That's My Stuff*	50.00 -	75.00
1646 *Levee Low Down*	15.00 -	20.00

CHOO CHOO JAZZERS:

Ajex 17038 *Snuggle Up A Bit*	8.00 -	12.00

BUDDY CHRISTIAN'S CREOLE FIVE/JAZZ RIPPERS:

Okeh 8311 *Sunset Blues*	50.00 -	75.00
8342 *Sugar House Stomp*	60.00 -	90.00
Pathe-Actuelle 8518 *South Rampart Street Blues*	50.00 -	75.00
Perfect 118 *South Rampart Street Blues*	50.00 -	75.00

LILIE DELK CHRISTIAN:

Okeh 8317 *Sweet Georgia Brown*	6.00 -	10.00
8356 *Baby O'Mine*	20.00 -	30.00
8475 *Ain't She Sweet?*	12.00 -	16.00
8536 *My Blue Heaven*	20.00 -	30.00
8596 *Too Busy*	20.00 -	35.00
8607 *You're A Real Sweetheart*	20.00 -	35.00
8650 *I Can't Give You Anything But Love*	20.00 -	35.00
8660 *I Must Have That Man*	20.00 -	35.00

CHUBB-STEINBERG ORCHESTRA (OF CINCINNATI):

Gennett 3058 *Mandy, Make Up Your Mind*	10.00 -	15.00
5663 *Because They All Love You*	10.00 -	15.00
Okeh 40106 *From One Till Two*	15.00 -	20.00
40107 *Blue Evening Blues*	15.00 -	20.00

CINCINNATI JUG BAND:

Paramount 12743 *Newport Blues*	40.00 -	60.00

SUNNY CLAPP & HIS BAND O' SUNSHINE:

Harmony 899-H *Remember I Love You*	7.00 -	10.00
Victor 22682 *Treat Me Like A Baby*	7.00 -	10.00
22684 *When My Baby Smiles At Me*	7.00 -	10.00
22777 *Reflections of You*	5.00 -	8.00
V-40152 *Down On Biscayne Bay*	8.00 -	12.00

CLARINET JOE & HIS HOT FOOTERS:

Harmony 8-H *Rabbit Foot Blues*	4.00 -	7.00

DON CLARK & HIS LOS ANGELES BILTMORE HOTEL ORCHESTRA:

Columbia 824-D *I've Got The Girl!*	15.00 -	25.00

JIM CLARKE:

Vocalion 1536 *Fat Fanny Stomp*	60.00 -	90.00

SONNY CLAY'S PLANTATION ORCHESTRA;

SONNY CLAY & HIS ORCHESTRA:

Vocalion 1000 *Plantation Blues*	30.00 -	50.00
1050 *California Stomp*	30.00 -	50.00
15078 *Jambled Blues*	40.00 -	60.00
15641 *Devil's Serenade*	50.00 -	80.00

CLAYTON, JACKSON AND DURANTE:

Columbia 1860-D *So I Ups To Him*	5.00 -	8.00

JOHNNY CLESI'S AREOLIANS:

Gennett 3380 *Ain't I Got Rosie?*	15.00 -	25.00
6033 *Brotherly Love*	15.00 -	25.00
Herschel Gold Seal 2010 *Ain't I Got Rosie?*	15.00 -	25.00

CLIFFORD'S LOUISVILLE JUG BAND:

Okeh 8221 *Dancing Blues*	40.00 -	60.00
8238 *Struttin' The Blues*	40.00 -	60.00
8248 *Mammy O'Mine Blues*	40.00 -	60.00
8269 *Get It Fixed Blues*	40.00 -	60.00

CLINE'S COLLEGIANS:

DAL-571/572 *Chicadore Stomp*	75.00 -	100.00
(Note: Above is a test pressing.)		
Brunswick 4162 Peruna	15.00 -	20.00

LARRY CLINTON AND HIS ORCHESTRA: LARRY CLINTON'S BLUEBIRD ORCHESTRA:

Bluebird, most issues	2.00 -	4.00
Decca, most issues	2.00 -	3.00
Victor, most issues	2.00 -	5.00

CLOVERDALE COUNTRY CLUB ORCHESTSRA:

Okeh 41519, 41520, 41523, 41528, 41531, 41535, 41539, 41542, 41544, 41555, 41564	4.00 -	7.00
41551 *Chances Are*	10.00 -	15.00

CLUB ALABAM' ORCHESTRA:

Domino 354, 355, 356, 366, 368, 369, 370, 371	6.00 -	10.00
415 *How Come You Do Me Like You Do?*	8.00 -	12.00
426 *One Of These Days*	8.00 -	12.00
430 *My Dream Man*	8.00 -	12.00

CLUB AMBASSADORS ORCHESTRA:

Brunswick 7096 *Apex Blues*	30.00 -	40.00

CLUB WIGWAM ORCHESTRA:

Domino 3458 *Alabamy Bound*	10.00 -	15.00

JACK COAKLEY'S (FLEXO RECORDING) ORCHESTRA:

Flexo 103 *It Seems To Be Spring*	20.00 -	30.00
117 *Wabash Blues*	20.00 -	30.00
130 *Walkin' My Baby Back Home*	20.00 -	30.00
131 *Reaching For The Moon*	20.00 -	30.00

E. C. COBB & HIS CORN EATERS:
Victor 38023 *Transatlantic Stomp*.............. 20.00 - 30.00

J. C. JUNIE COBB & HIS GRAINS OF CORN:
JUNIE COBB'S HOMETOWN BAND:
Paramount 12382 *East Coast Trot*............ 80.00 - 120.00
Vocalion 1204 *Endurance Stomp*.............. 25.00 - 40.00
  1263 *Shake That Jelly Roll*.............. 30.00 - 50.00
  1269 *Smoke Shop Drag*.................... 40.00 - 60.00
  1449 *Once Or Twice*..................... 20.00 - 25.00

OLIVER COBB:
Paramount 13002 *Cornet Pleading Blues*....... 70.00 - 90.00

GEORGE M. COHAN:
Victor 60042, 60043, 60044, 60045, 60049, 60052,
  70039 .... 5.00 - 10.00

E.L. COLEMAN:
Okeh 8216 *Steel String Blues*................ 15.00 - 20.00

ROY COLLINS' DANCE ORCHESTRA:
Challenge 933 *Papa's Mama's Blue*............ 5.00 - 8.00
Oriole 1044 *There's Always Somebody Lookin' For*
  Somebody................................ 5.00 - 8.00
  1488 *Shake Off The Blues*............... 5.00 - 8.00
  1541 *Papa's Mama's Blue*................ 5.00 - 8.00

RUSS COLUMBO:
Brunswick 6972 *When You're In Love*......... 7.00 - 10.00
Victor 22801, 22802, 22826, 22861, 22867, 22903,
  22909, 22976, 24045, 24076, 24077, 24194,
  24195 .... 4.00 - 7.00

EDDIE CONDON & HIS FOOTWARMERS/
ORCHESTRA:
Brunswick 6743 *Home Cooking*................ 8.00 - 12.00
Okah 41142 *I'm Sorry I Made You Cry*........ 15.00 - 20.00

CONNIE'S INN ORCHESTRA:
Crown 3180 *You Rascal, You*................. 15.00 - 25.00
  3194 *Sugar Foot Stomp*.................. 15.00 - 25.00
  3212 *Milenberg Joys*.................... 15.00 - 25.00
Melotone 12145 *I'm Crazy 'Bout My Baby*..... 15.00 - 20.00
  12216 *The House Of David Blues*......... 15.00 - 20.00
  12239 *Sugar Foot Stomp*................. 15.00 - 20.00
  12340 *Goodbye Blues*.................... 15.00 - 20.00
Victor 22698 *Moan, You Moaners*............. 8.00 - 12.00
  22721 *Singing The Blues*................ 8.00 - 12.00

LOU CONNOR'S COLLEGIANS:
Oriole 1156, 1171, 1172..................... 5.00 - 8.00
  1483 *It's Tight Like That*.............. 8.00 - 12.00

COOK & HIS DREAMLAND ORCHESTRA:
COOK'S DREAMLAND ORCHESTRA:
"DOC" COOK & HIS 14 DOCTORS OF
SYNCOPATION:
Columbia 727-D *Spanish Mama*................ 20.00 - 25.00
  813-D *High Fever*....................... 20.00 - 25.00
  862-D *Sidewalk Blues*................... 20.00 - 25.00
  1070-D *Willie The Weeper*............... 20.00 - 25.00
  1298-D *Alligator Crawl*................. 20.00 - 25.00
  1430-D *Hum And Strum*................... 15.00 - 20.00
Gennett 5360 *So This Is Venice*............. 15.00 - 30.00
  5373 *Moanful Man*....................... 20.00 - 30.00
  5374 *Scissor Grinder Joe*............... 30.00 - 50.00
Silvertone 4044 *Scissor Grinder Joe*........ 25.00 - 35.00
  4045 *Moanful Man*....................... 20.00 - 30.00

COOKIE'S GINGERSNAPS:
Okeh 8369 *High Fever*....................... 35.00 - 50.00
  8390 *Messin' Around*.................... 60.00 - 90.00
  40675 *Love Found You For Me*............ 30.00 - 50.00

COON-SANDERS (ORIGINAL NIGHTHAWK)
ORCHESTRA:
Victor 20461 *High Fever*.................... 25.00 - 35.00
  21397 *Hallucinations*................... 10.00 - 15.00
  22077, 22089, 22342...................... 5.00 - 10.00
  22300 *Harlem Madness*................... 10.00 - 15.00
  22939, 22950, 22951, 22969, 22971, 22979... 4.00 - 8.00
  38083 *Louder and Funnier*............... 15.00 - 20.00
Victor (others)............................. 4.00 - 6.00

AL COOPER & HIS (ORIGINAL) SAVOY
SULTANS:
Decca 2526 *Jumpin' At The Savoy*............ 5.00 - 8.00
  2608 Stitches.......................... *5.00 - 8.00*
  2819 Love Gave Me You.................. *5.00 - 8.00*
  2930 Jumpin' The Blues................. *5.00 - 8.00*
  3142 Frenzy............................ 5.00 - 8.00
  3274 *Sophisticated Jump*................ 5.00 - 8.00
  7499 *Rhythm Doctor Man*................. 5.00 - 8.00
  7525 *Gettin' In The Groove*............. 5.00 - 8.00
  7549 *Looney*............................ 5.00 - 8.00
  8540 *Norfolk Ferry*..................... 5.00 - 8.00
  8545 *Second Balcony Jump*............... 5.00 - 8.00
  8598 *Fis For Your Supper*............... 5.00 - 8.00
  8615 *'At's In There*.................... 5.00 - 8.00

ROBERT COOPER:
Bluebird 5459 *West Dallas Drag*............. 15.00 - 20.00
  5947 *West Dallas Drag—No. 2*............ 15.00 - 25.00

ANDREW COPELAND:
Black Swan 14124 *Buzz Mirandy*.............. 12.00 - 16.00

CORNELL & HIS ORCHESTRA:
Okeh 41386 *Accordion Joe*................... 10.00 - 15.00
  41395 *I Was Made To Love You*........... 10.00 - 15.00

(CHARLES) CORRELL AND (FREEMAN)
GOSDEN (AMOS 'N' ANDY):
Victor 20032, 20093, 20375, 20788, 21608, 22119,
  22234, 22393............................. 4.00 - 8.00

COTTON CLUB ORCHESTRA:
Columbia 287-D *Down And Out Blues*.......... 8.00 - 12.00
  374-D *Riverboat Shuffle*................ 10.00 - 15.00
  14113-D *Everybody Stomp*................ 10.00 - 15.00

THE COTTON PICKERS:
Brunswick 2292, 2338, 2380, 2382, 2404, 2418, 2436,
  2461 .... 3.00 - 5.00
  2486, 2490, 2507, 2532................... 4.00 - 6.00
  2766, 2818, 2879, 2937, 2981, 3001....... 5.00 - 10.00
  4325 *Rampart Street Blues*.............. *7.00 - 12.00*
  4404 *Sweet Ida Joy*..................... 7.00 - 12.00
  4440 *St. Louis Gal*..................... 7.00 - 12.00
  4446 *Moanin' Low*....................... 7.00 - 12.00
  4447 *Shoo Shoo Boogie Boo*.............. 7.00 - 12.00
Cameo 9207 *Hot Heels*....................... 7.00 - 10.00
Cameo 9048 *Railroad Man*.................... 8.00 - 12.00
Gennett 6380 *What'll You Do?*............... 10.00 - 15.00
  6396 *After Awhile*...................... 10.00 - 15.00
Lincoln 3077 *Railroad Man*.................. 8.00 - 12.00
Romeo 852 *Railroad Man*..................... 8.00 - 12.00

WALLIE COULTER & HIS BAND:
Gennett 6369 *Hollywood Shuffle*............. 35.00 - 50.00

DEL COURTNEY AND HIS ORCHESTRA:
Vocalion 4850, 4864, 4985, 4992, 5046, 5061, 5088,
  5127, 5212, 5279, 5291, 5306, 5332, 5354, 5608,
  5616 .... 3.00 - 5.00

IDA COX (Accompanied by Lovie Austin's Blues
Serenaders; Her Five Blue Spells, et al.):
Paramount 12022 *Come Right In*.............. 10.00 - 15.00
  12044 *Weary Way Blues*.................. 20.00 - 30.00
  12045 *Bama Bound Blues*................. 12.00 - 16.00
  12053 *Blue Monday Blues*................ 12.00 - 16.00
  12056 *Chicago Bound Blues*.............. 12.00 - 16.00
  12063 *I've Got The Blues For Rampart Street*. 20.00 - 30.00
  12064 *Moanin' Groanin' Blues*........... 20.00 - 30.00
  12085 *Worried Mama Blues*............... 20.00 - 30.00

12086	Confidential Blues.....................	20.00 -	30.00
12087	Mail Man Blues......................	20.00 -	30.00
12094	Down The Road Bound Blues........	12.00 -	16.00
12097	Mean Papa, Turn Your Key..........	20.00 -	30.00
12202	Chicago Monkey Man Blues...........	15.00 -	20.00
12212	Last Time Blues.....................	15.00 -	20.00
12210	Kentucky Man Blues..................	15.00 -	20.00
12228	Cherry Picking Blues.................	15.00 -	20.00
12237	Worried In Mind Blues...............	25.00 -	40.00
12251	Mississippi River Blues..............	25.00 -	40.00
12258	Misery Blues........................	25.00 -	40.00
12263	Georgia Hound Blues.................	25.00 -	40.00
12275	Mister Man.........................	20.00 -	30.00
12282	Someday Blues.......................	20.00 -	30.00
12291	Black Crepe Blues...................	25.00 -	40.00
12298	Southern Woman's Blues..............	25.00 -	40.00
12307	Lonesome Blues......................	25.00 -	40.00
12318	Coffin Blues........................	60.00 -	80.00
12325	One Time Woman Blues...............	30.00 -	40.00
12334	I Ain't Got Nobody..................	30.00 -	40.00
12344	Trouble Trouble Blues................	30.00 -	40.00
12353	Night And Day Blues.................	30.00 -	40.00
12381	Don't Blame Me.....................	30.00 -	40.00
12488	'Fore Day Creep.....................	20.00 -	30.00
12502	Mercy Blues........................	20.00 -	30.00
12513	Pleading Blues......................	20.00 -	30.00
12540	Mojo Hand Blues....................	30.00 -	45.00
12556	Seven Day Blues.....................	20.00 -	30.00
12582	Midnight Hour Blues.................	20.00 -	30.00
12664	Bone Orchard Blues..................	40.00 -	60.00
12667	Broadcasting Blues...................	30.00 -	45.00
12690	Fogyism............................	30.00 -	45.00
12727	Separated Blues.....................	35.00 -	50.00
12965	Jail House Blues....................	50.00 -	80.00
Vocalion 05298, 05336..................		6.00 -	10.00

JACK CRAWFORD & HIS BOYS/ ORCHESTRA:

Champion 15383	Down South................	10.00 -	20.00
15384	The Best Things In Life Are Free.....	10.00 -	20.00
15400	Together We Two....................	10.00 -	20.00
15404	For My Baby........................	10.00 -	20.00
15418	One More Night.....................	10.00 -	20.00
15422	Beautiful...........................	10.00 -	20.00
15439	Dear On A Night Like This...........	10.00 -	20.00
Victor 20847, 20901, 20944, 21173, 21217.....		3.00 -	6.00

WILTON CRAWLEY (& HIS ORCHESTRA/ THE WASHBOARD RHYTHM KINGS):

Bluebird 5827	She's Got What I Need.........	10.00 -	15.00
Okeh 8479	Crawley Blues.................	8.00 -	12.00
8492	Geechie River Blues.................	8.00 -	12.00
8539	Love Will Drive Me Crazy............	7.00 -	10.00
8555	She's Nothing But Nice..............	7.00 -	10.00
8589	I'm Forever Changing Sweetheart......	8.00 -	12.00
8619	Shadow Of The Blues................	8.00 -	12.00
8718	My Perfect Thrill...................	10.00 -	15.00
Victor 23292	Big Time Woman................	70.00 -	100.00
23344	New Crawley Blues..................	70.00 -	100.00
38094	Snake Hip Dance....................	20.00 -	30.00
38116	She's Got What I Need..............	30.00 -	40.00
38136	You Oughta See My Gal..............	30.00 -	40.00

CHAS. CREATH'S JAZZ-O-MANIACS:

Okeh 8201	Pleasure Mad..................	15.00 -	25.00
8210	King Porter Stomp..................	15.00 -	25.00
8217	My Daddy Rocks Me.................	15.00 -	25.00
8257	Grandpa's Spell.....................	15.00 -	25.00
8280	Market Street Stomp.................	15.00 -	25.00
8477	Crazy Quilt........................	25.00 -	40.00

BING CROSBY:

Bluebird 7102, 7118..................		4.00 -	7.00
Brunswick 6090	Out Of Nowhere...........	7.00 -	10.00
6120	Were You Sincere?..................	7.00 -	10.00
6140	At Your Command...................	7.00 -	10.00

6169	Star Dust...........................	7.00 -	10.00
6179	I Apologize.........................	7.00 -	10.00
6200	Now That You're Gone..............	7.00 -	10.00
6203	Goodnight Sweetheart................	7.00 -	10.00
6226	Where The Blue Of The Night........	7.00 -	10.00
6240	Can't We Talk It Over?..............	7.00 -	10.00
6248	I Found You........................	7.00 -	10.00
6259	How Long Will It Last?..............	7.00 -	10.00
6268	Love, You Funny Thing..............	7.00 -	10.00
6276	Shadows On The Window.............	7.00 -	10.00
6285	Paradise............................	7.00 -	10.00
6306	Lazy Day...........................	7.00 -	10.00
6320	Sweet Georgia Brown................	7.00 -	10.00
6329	Cabin In The Cotton................	7.00 -	10.00
6351	Some Of These Days.................	7.00 -	10.00
6394	Please.............................	7.00 -	10.00
6406	Here Lies Love......................	7.00 -	10.00
6414	Brother, Can You Spare A Dime?......	7.00 -	10.00
6427	I'll Follow You.....................	7.00 -	10.00
6454	Just An Echo In The Valley..........	7.00 -	10.00
6464	Street Of Dreams....................	7.00 -	10.00
6472	Young And Healty...................	7.00 -	10.00
6477	You're Beautiful Tonight, My Dear.....	7.00 -	10.00
6480	Try A Little Tenderness..............	7.00 -	10.00
6485	Shine..............................	7.00 -	10.00
6491	You've Got Me Crying Again.........	7.00 -	10.00
6525	Someone Stold Gabriel's Horn........	7.00 -	10.00
6594	Learn To Croon.....................	7.00 -	10.00
6599	I've Got To Sing A Torch Song.......	7.00 -	10.00
6601	Down The Old Ox Road..............	7.00 -	10.00
6610	There's A Cabin In The Pines........	7.00 -	10.00
6623	I Would If I Could But I Can't.......	7.00 -	10.00
6643	Black Moonlight.....................	7.00 -	10.00
6644	The Day You Came Along............	5.00 -	8.00
6663	Home On The Range.................	5.00 -	8.00
6694	Beautiful Girl.......................	5.00 -	8.00
6695	Temptation.........................	5.00 -	8.00
6696	Our Big Love Scene.................	5.00 -	8.00
6724	Did You Ever See A Dream Walking?..	5.00 -	8.00
6594	Little Dutch Mill...................	5.00 -	8.00
6852	Love Thy Neighbor..................	5.00 -	8.00
6853	She Reminds Me Of You.............	5.00 -	8.00
6854	One In A Blue Moon................	5.00 -	8.00
6936	Straight From The Shoulder..........	5.00 -	8.00
6953	Give Me A Heart To Sing To.......	5.00 -	8.00

(Note: Many of the foregoing titles were issued contemporaneously and/or reissued within several years of initial release on Banner, Brunswick, Conqueror, Melotone, Oriole, Perfect and Romeo.)

Brunswick 20105 (12-inch)	St. Louis Blues......	10.00 -	15.00
20109 (12-inch)	Lawd, You Made The Night Too Long...............................	10.00 -	15.00
Columbia 1773-D	My Kinda Love.............	8.00 -	12.00
1851-D	I Kiss Your Hand, Madame.........	8.00 -	12.00
2001-D	Can't We Be Friends?..............	8.00 -	12.00
Decca 100	I Love You Truly...............	5.00 -	8.00
101	Let Me Call You Sweetheart...........	5.00 -	8.00
179	The Very Thought Of You............	5.00 -	8.00
245	Two Cigarettes In The Dark..........	5.00 -	8.00
309	With Every Breath I Take............	5.00 -	8.00
310	June In January.....................	5.00 -	8.00
391	It's Easy To Remember...............	5.00 -	8.00
392	Down By The River.................	5.00 -	8.00
543	I Wished On The Moon..............	5.00 -	8.00
547	From The Top Of Your Head.........	5.00 -	8.00
548	Takes Two To Make A Bargain........	5.00 -	8.00
616	Red Sails In The Sunset.............	5.00 -	8.00
617	On Treasure Island.................	5.00 -	8.00
621	Adeste Fidelis......................	5.00 -	8.00
631	Sailor, Beware......................	5.00 -	8.00
756	Lovely Lady........................	5.00 -	8.00
757	The Touch Of Your Lips.............	5.00 -	8.00

791	*Robins And Roses*...............	5.00 -	8.00
806	*I Got Plenty O'Nuttin'*.............	5.00 -	8.00
870	*Empty Saddles*..................	5.00 -	8.00
871	*I Can't Seem To Escape From You*.....	5.00 -	8.00
905	*The House Jack Built For Jill*..........	5.00 -	8.00

Victor 22701 *Wrap Your Troubles In Dreams*... 5.00 - 8.00
Troubles In Dreams" were widely, although il-
legally, distributed, and are not valuable rarities
as some would assume.

Decca, most other issues on Blue label Decca.... 2.00 - 3.00
Note: recordings on which Bing makes mistakes and
curses, such as "Blue Serenade" and "Wrap Your

**BOB CROSBY (& HIS BOB CATS/
ORCHESTRA):**

Decca 112	*It's My Night To Howl*..........	5.00 -	8.00
478	*The Dixieland Band*..................	5.00 -	8.00
502	*And Then Some*.....................	5.00 -	8.00
508	*I'm In The Mood For Love*.............	5.00 -	8.00
544	*Tender Is The Night*................	5.00 -	8.00
614	*On Treasure Island*..................	5.00 -	8.00
615	*I Found A Dream*....................	5.00 -	8.00
629	*A Little Bit Independent*..............	5.00 -	8.00
633	*Eeny Meeny Miney Mo*................	5.00 -	8.00
727	*What's The Name Of That Song?*.......	5.00 -	8.00
728	*I Don't Want To Make History*........	5.00 -	8.00
753	*Christopher Columbus*...............	5.00 -	8.00
759	*You're Toots To Me*................	5.00 -	8.00

Decca 836, 841, 896, 903, 930, 1094, 1170, 1196,
1346, 1370, 1539, 1552, 1555, 1556, 1566, 1576,
1580, 1593....................... 4.00 - 6.00

CROSSTOWN RAMBLERS:
Champion 15030 *River Bottom Glide*.......... 15.00 - 20.00

BERNIE CUMMINS AND HIS ORCHESTRA:
Columbia 2827-D, 2828-D, 2830-D, 2838-D, 2844-D,
2848-D, 2874-D........................ 5.00 - 8.00

Gennett 3395	*Home Folks Blues*.............	7.00 -	10.00
5466	*St. Louis Blues*.................	7.00 -	10.00
5468	*Jiminy Gee*....................	7.00 -	10.00
5546	*Keep On Dancing*..............	7.00 -	10.00
5555	*That's Georgia*................	7.00 -	10.00
5641	*Poplar Street Blues*............	7.00 -	10.00

Victor 22110, 22295, 22331, 22351, 22355, 22408,
22409, 22425, 22525................. 3.00 - 5.00
Victor 24053 *Deep Sea Low Down*........... 5.00 - 8.00

JOE CURRAN & HIS ORCHESTRA:

Parlophone PHY-34012	*Thank You Father*.....	10.00 -	15.00
PNY-41231	*Louise*....................	10.00 -	15.00
PNY-41232	*That's A Plenty*.............	10.00 -	15.00
PNY-41254	*Hittin' The Ceilin'*..........	10.00 -	15.00
PNY-41282	*Just You—Just Me*..........	10.00 -	15.00
PNY-41301	*Love Ain't Nothin' But The Blues*	10.00 -	15.00
PNY-41310	*Sophomore Prom*.............	10.00 -	15.00
PNY-41313	*Turn On The Heat*...........	10.00 -	15.00

DALLAS JAMBOREE JUG BAND:
Vocalion 03092 *Dusting the Frets*............. 40.00 - 60.00

JACK DALTON & THE 7 BLUE BABIES:
Edison 52508 *I Love To Bumpity Bump On A
Bumpity*.............................. 7.00 - 10.00

52516	*Where Did You Get That Name*......	7.00 -	10.00
52528	*Outside*.........................	7.00 -	10.00
52556	*If I Give Up The Saxophone*.........	7.00 -	10.00
52583	*She's A Good Girl*................	7.00 -	10.00
52621	*I Don't Work For A Living*..........	7.00 -	10.00

Edison (thin), last three titles above.......... 10.00 - 15.00

THE DANCING CHAMPIONS:
Champion 15183 *Don't Take That Black Bottom
Away*.............................. 8.00 - 12.00

15184	*I Still Believe In You*............	7.00 -	10.00
15185	*A Little Music In The Moonlight*.....	7.00 -	10.00

THE DANCING STEVEDORES:

Silvertone 3054	*Panama*....................	10.00 -	15.00
3056	*Stretch It, Boy*.................	10.00 -	15.00

PUTNEY DANDRIDGE & HIS ORCHESTRA:

Vocalion 2935	*You're A Heavenly Thing*.......	7.00 -	10.00
2982	*Chasing Shadows*................	7.00 -	10.00
3006	*Isn't This A Lovely Day?*.........	7.00 -	10.00
3007	*I'm In The Mood For Love*........	7.00 -	10.00
3024	*Nagosaki*.....................	7.00 -	10.00
3082	*Double Trouble*.................	7.00 -	10.00
3083	*Eeny Meeny Miney Mo*............	7.00 -	10.00
3122	*A Little Bit Independent*.........	7.00 -	10.00
3123	*You Took My Breath Away*........	7.00 -	10.00
3189	*Dinner For One, Please James*.....	7.00 -	10.00
3190	*Honeysuckle Rose*...............	7.00 -	10.00
3252	*It's A Sin To Tell A Lie*..........	7.00 -	10.00
3269	*Ol' Man River*.................	7.00 -	10.00
3277	*Cross Patch*...................	7.00 -	10.00
3287	*Mary Had A Little Lamb*..........	7.00 -	10.00
3291	*Here Comes Your Pappy*..........	7.00 -	10.00
3304	*You Turned The Tables On Me*........	7.00 -	10.00
3315	*It's The Gypsy In Me*............	7.00 -	10.00
3351	*You Do The Darndest Things, Baby*....	7.00 -	10.00
3352	*The Skeleton In The Closet*........	7.00 -	10.00
3399	*I'm In A Dancing Mood*..........	7.00 -	10.00
3409	*Gee! But You're Swell*...........	7.00 -	10.00

**JACK DANFORD AND HIS BEN FRANKLIN
HOTEL ORCHESTRA:**
Phonograph Recording Co. of San Francisco (un-
numbered) *Alabama Stomp*.............. 40.00 - 60.00

DOT DARE:
Diva, Harmony, Velvet Tone................. 4.00 - 7.00

DOC DAUGHERTY & HIS ORCHESTRA:
Victor 23040, 40119.................... 6.00 - 10.00
40111 *Ninety In The Shade*............ 15.00 - 20.00

DAVE'S HARLEM HIGHLIGHTS:

Timely Tunes 1576	*Rockin' Chair*.............	20.00 -	30.00
1577	*Loveless Love*.............	15.00 -	25.00
1587	*Somebody Stole My Gal*.....	25.00 -	40.00
1588	*St. Louis Blues*...........	25.00 -	40.00

**CHARLES (COW COW) DAVENPORT:
CHARLIE DAVENPORT:**

Broadway 5046	*Chimes Blues*.............	40.00 -	60.00
Gennett 6829	*Givin' It Away*............	40.00 -	60.00
6838	*Chimes Blues*.............	40.00 -	60.00
6869	*Atlanta Rag*.............	40.00 -	60.00
Paramount 12439	*Jim Crow Blues*.........	30.00 -	50.00
12452	*Stealin' Blues*...........	30.00 -	50.00
Vocalion 1198	*Cow Cow Blues*..........	30.00 -	40.00
1227	*Alabama Mistreater*.......	30.00 -	40.00
1282	*Back In The Alley*........	30.00 -	40.00
1291	*Texas Shout*.............	30.00 -	40.00
1434	*Mama Don't Allow No Easy Riders*....	30.00 -	40.00

**(COW COW) DAVENPORT AND (IVA/IVY)
SMITH:**

Gennett 7231	*Alabammy Mistreated*..........	40.00 -	60.00
Superior 2763	*Alabammy Mistreated*..........	50.00 -	75.00
Vocalion 1253	*Alabama Strut*..............	30.00 -	40.00

**COW COW DAVENPORT AND SAM
THEARD:**
Vocalion 1408 *That'll Get It*.............. 30.00 - 40.00

JED DAVENPORT:
Vocalion 1440 *How Long How Long Blues*..... 15.00 - 20.00

**JED DAVENPORT & HIS BEALE STREET
JUG BAND:**

Vocalion 1478	*The Dirty Dozen*.............	30.00 -	50.00
1504	*Jug Blues*.................	30.00 -	50.00
1513	*Save Me Some*.............	30.00 -	50.00

JACK DAVIES' KENTUCKIANS:
Champion 16607 *Sick O'Licks*............... 15.00 - 20.00

**CARL DAVIS WITH THE DALLAS
JAMBOREE JUG BAND:**
Vocalion 03132 *Flying Crow Blues*........... 15.00 - 25.00

CHARLIE DAVIS AND HIS ORCHESTRA:
Vocalion 15701 *The Drag*..................... 10.00 - 15.00
15702 *Just Like A Melody Out Of The Sky*... 10.00 - 15.00
JASPER DAVIS & HIS ORCHESTRA:
Harmony 944-H *Georgia Gigolo*............. 15.00 - 20.00
JOHNNIE DAVIS & HIS ORCHESTRA:
Decca 256, 257, 271, 272................. 7.00 - 10.00
JULIA DAVIS:
Paramount 12248 *Black Hand Blues*.......... 20.00 - 30.00
MADLYN DAVIS (& HER HOT SHOTS):
Paramount 12498 *Climbing Mountain Blues*.... 30.00 - 40.00
12528 *Hurry Sundown Blues*.............. 30.00 - 40.00
12615 *Winter Blues*..................... 40.00 - 60.00
12755 *Death Bell Blues*................. 40.00 - 60.00
PAUL DAVIS & HIS ORCHESTRA:
Champion 16524 *Underneath The Harlem Moon* 15.00 - 25.00
RED HOT SHAKIN' DAVIS:
Paramount 12703 *It's Red Hot*............. 25.00 - 35.00
WILMER DAVIS:
Vocalion 3342 *Gut Struggle*.................. 20.00 - 30.00
THE DEAN & HIS KIDS:
Vocalion 3342 *Spreadin' Knowledge Around*.... 8.00 - 12.00
**EDDIE DEAS AND HIS BOSTON
  BROWNIES:**
Victor 22841 *Jes' Shufflin'*.................. 10.00 - 15.00
22844 *Little Mary Brown*................. 10.00 - 15.00
DEAUVILLE DOZEN:
Pathe-Actuelle 36338 *Pep*.................. 5.00 - 8.00
Perfect 14519 *Pep*........................ 5.00 - 8.00
DEAUVILLE SYNCOPATORS:
Parlophone PNY-34144 *Satan's Holiday*....... 10.00 - 15.00
PNY-34149 *I Got Rhythm*................. 10.00 - 15.00
PNY-34155 *I'm Tickled Pink With A Blue-Eyed
  Baby*.................................. 10.00 - 15.00
PNY-34157 *Cheerful LIttle Earful*.......... 10.00 - 15.00
PNY-34172 *Would You Like To Take A Walk?* 10.00 - 15.00
PNY-34186 *The Last One Left On The Corner* 10.00 - 15.00
PNY-34199 *Just A Crazy Song*............. 10.00 - 15.00
**JOHNNNY DE DROIT & HIS NEW
  ORLEANS JAZZ ORCHESTRA:**
Okeh 40090 *The Swing*.................... 15.00 - 25.00
40150 *Number Two Blues*................. 15.00 - 25.00
40192 *Brown Eyes*...................... 15.00 - 25.00
40240 *Panama*.......................... 15.00 - 25.00
40285 *Lucky Kentucky*................... 15.00 - 25.00
DEEP RIVER ORCHESTRA:
Pathe-Actuelle 36574, 36575, 36635, 36679, 36690 5.00 - 8.00
Perfect 14755, 14756, 14816, 14871.......... 5.00 - 8.00
VOLTAIRE DE FAUT:
Autograph 623 *Wolverine Blues*.............. 125.00 - 200.00
MAUD DE FORREST:
Black Swan 14143 *Roamin' Blues*............ 12.00 - 16.00
Paramount 12147 *Roamin' Blues*............ 10.00 - 15.00
12148 *Cruel Papa Blues*................. 10.00 - 15.00
BOB DEIKMAN AND HIS ORCHESTRA:
Gennett 3196 *Spanish Shawl*................ 10.00 - 15.00
3236 *Shanghai Honeymoon*............... 10.00 - 15.00
6339 *Roll Up The Carpets* .... 10.00 - 15.00
EDDIE DE LANGE AND HIS ORCHESTRA:
Bluebird, most issues...................... 3.00 - 5.00
**DEL DELBRIDGE AND HIS CAPITOL
  THEATRE ORCHESTRA:**
Brunswick 4393 *Do Something*.............. 5.00 - 8.00
**HAL DENMAN AND HIS CAROLINA
  COTTON PICKERS:**
Champion 16221 *She Loves Me Just The Same.* 7.00 - 10.00
16266 *I Can't Get Enough Of You*......... 7.00 - 10.00
16274 *When I Take My Sugar To Tea*...... 7.00 - 10.00
DEPPE'S SERENADERS:
Gennett 20012 *Falling*.................... 15.00 - 20.00
LOUIS DEPPE:

Gennett 20021 *Southland*.................. 12.00 - 16.00
20022 *Isabel*.......................... 12.00 - 16.00
DEVINE'S WISCONSIN ROOF ORCHESTRA:
Broadway 1123 *Black Maria*................ 10.00 - 20.00
1140 *Tiger Rag*........................ 10.00 - 20.00
1141 *Riverboat Blues*................... 10.00 - 20.00
Paramount 20582 *Tiger Rag*............... 10.00 - 20.00
20583 *Singapore Sorrows*................ 10.00 - 20.00
20651 *Farewell Blues*................... 10.00 - 20.00
FRED DEXTER'S PENNSYLVANIANS:
Gennett 7256 *What's The Use?*.............. 10.00 - 15.00
HARRY DIAL'S BLUSICIANS:
Queen 4164 *I Like What I Like Like I Like It..* 7.00 - 10.00
Vocalion 1515 *Don't Give It Away*.......... 50.00 - 75.00
1567 *I Like What I Like Like I Like It*.... 50.00 - 75.00
1594 *Poison*.......................... 100.00 - 150.00
**CARROLL DICKERSON'S SAVOY
  ORCHESTRA:**
Brunswick 3990 *Missouri Squabble*........... 15.00 - 20.00
DUKE DIGGS & HIS ORCHESTRA:
Supertone 9487 *Nightmare*................ 60.00 - 80.00
9653 *After You've Gone*................. 60.00 - 80.00
THE DIXIE BOYS:
Champion 15227 *I've Found A New Baby*..... 50.00 - 75.00
THE DIXIE DAISIES:
Titles, issued contemporaneously on Cameo, Lincoln,
  Romeo: *Baby; Bugle Call Rag*............ 10.00 - 15.00
Additional titles: *Eyes of Blue, You're My Waterloo;
  I'm Just Wondering Who; Japanese Dream..* 7.00 - 10.00
Cameo 1168 *Stompin' Fool*................. 8.00 - 12.00
THE DIXIE DEVILS:
Van Dyke 71804 *In Harlem's Araby*.......... 10.00 - 15.00
71805 *Miss Golden Brown*................ 10.00 - 15.00
DIXIE FOUR:
Paramount 12661 *St. Louis Man*............. 50.00 - 75.00
12674 *Five O'Clock Stamp*............... 50.00 - 75.00
DIXIE JAZZ BAND:
Challenge 628, 929, 952, 995............... 5.00 - 10.00
958 *Icky Blues*........................ 8.00 - 12.00
999 *Makin' Friends*.................... 8.00 - 12.00
Conqueror 7189......................... 5.00 - 10.00
Jewel 5002, 5067........................ 5.00 - 10.00
5145, 5171............................. 7.00 - 12.00
5263, 5292, 5405, 5412, 5446, 5488, 5521, 5677 5.00 - 10.00
5547 *Icky Blues*....................... 8.00 - 12.00
5569 *Makin' Friends*................... 8.00 - 12.00
5575 *Sweet Liza*....................... 8.00 - 12.00
5748 *Twelfth Street Rag*................ 8.00 - 12.00
5685 *It's So Good*..................... 10.00 - 15.00
5729 *The Way He Loves Is Just Too Bad*.... 12.00 - 16.00
5730 *Broadway Rhythm*................. 15.00 - 25.00
Oriole 269 *My Lovie Lee*.................. 10.00 - 15.00
271 *How Could You Leave Me Now?*....... 10.00 - 15.00
291 *Copenhagen*...................... 10.00 - 15.00
315 *Hot Sax*.......................... 15.00 - 20.00
347 *West Texas Blues*.................. 15.00 - 20.00
Oriole 413, 443, 445, 464, 475, 521, 674, 682, 685,
  688, 705, 723......................... 5.00 - 10.00
Oriole 748, 762, 799, 804, 819, 828, 829, 926, 927,
  956, 960, 963, 977, 1022, 1046, 1071, 1171, 1172,
  1275, 1313, 1343, 1348, 1360, 1363, 1368, 1371,
  1387, 1396, 1416, 1474, 1612, 1663........ 5.00 - 8.00
565 *Wait Till You See My Baby Do The
  Charleston* .... 10.00 - 15.00
717 *Old Folks' Shuffle*................. 15.00 - 20.00
880 *I'm In Love Again*.................. 8.00 - 12.00
883 *Rosy Cheeks*...................... 8.00 - 12.00
952 *Memphis Blues*.................... 8.00 - 12.00
984 *Tiger Rag*........................ 8.00 - 12.00
1100 *Sorry*........................... 8.00 - 12.00
1515 *Icky Blues*....................... 8.00 - 12.00

1537 *Makin' Friends*....................	8.00 -	12.00
1540 *Sweet Liza*.......................	8.00 -	12.00
1624 *Twelfth Street Rag*................	8.00 -	12.00
1668 *It's So Good*.....................	10.00 -	15.00
1726 *The Way He Love Is Just Too Bad*.....	12.00 -	16.00
1728 *Broadway Rhythm*.................	15.00 -	25.00
1730 *Doin' The Voom Voom*............	12.00 -	16.00
Regal 8874 *Flaming Youth*...............	15.00 -	20.00

DIXIE JAZZERS WASHBOARD BAND:

Pathe-Actuelle 7536 *Memphis Shake*......	30.00 -	40.00
7539 *Kansas City Shuffle*...............	30.00 -	40.00
Perfect 136 *Memphis Shake*.............	30.00 -	40.00
139 *Kansas City Shuffle*.................	30.00 -	40.00

DIXIE JAZZ HOUNDS:

Domino 306 *Hula Lou*..................	10.00 -	15.00
308 *Lots O'Mama*....................	10.00 -	15.00
328 *31st Street Blues*................	15.00 -	20.00
329 *Waitin' Around*..................	15.00 -	20.00

DIXIELAND JUG BLOWERS:

Victor 20403 *Florida Blues*.............	20.00 -	30.00
20415 *Memphis Shake*.................	15.00 -	20.00
20420 *Don't Give All The Lord Away*......	20.00 -	30.00
20480 *Carpet Alley*...................	20.00 -	30.00
20649 *Hen Party Blues*................	25.00 -	35.00
20770 *When I Stopped Runnin', I Was At Home*	25.00 -	40.00
20854 *I Never Did Want You*............	25.00 -	40.00
20954 *Southern Shout*.................	25.00 -	40.00
21126 *Garden Of Joy Blues*............	25.00 -	40.00
21472 *Banjoreno*	25.00 -	40.00

DIXIELAND THUMPERS:

Paramount 12525 *Weary Way Blues*...........	100.00 -	175.00
12595 *Oriental Man*....................	100.00 -	175.00

DIXIE RHYTHM KINGS:

Brunswick 7115 *Congo Love Song*...........	30.00 -	50.00
7127 *Easy Rider*.....................	30.00 -	50.00

THE DIXIE SERENADERS:

Champion 16341 *River, Stay 'Way From My Door*	30.00 -	50.00

THE DIXIE STOMPERS:

Titles, issued contemporaneously on Diva, Harmony, Velvet Tone: *Ain't She Sweet?; Alabama Stomp; Baltimore; Black Horse Stomp; Black Maria; Brotherly Love; Chinese Blues; Clap Hands!; Here Comes Charley!; Cornfed; Dynamite; Feelin' Good; Florida Stomp; Get It Fixed; Hard-To-Get-Gertie; Have It Ready; Hi-Diddle-Diddle; I Found A New Baby; I'm Feelin' Devilish; Jackass Blues; Nervous Charlie Stomp; Off To Buffalo; Oh, Baby; Panama; Snag It; Spanish Shawl; St. Louis Blues; St. Louis Shuffle; Tampeekoe; Variety Stomp; Wabash Blues; The Wang Wang Blues*	8.00 -	15.00

DIXIE WASHBOARD BAND:

Banner 1781 *I've Found A New Baby*........	15.00 -	20.00
Columbia 14128-D *Livin' High*..........	10.00 -	15.00
14141-D *My Own Blues*.................	12.00 -	16.00
14172-D *King Of The Zulus*.............	15.00 -	20.00
14188-D *Gimme Blues*.................	15.00 -	20.00
14239-D *Cushion Foot Stomp*...........	15.00 -	20.00
Regal 8093 *Boodle Am*.................	15.00 -	20.00

DIXON'S CHICAGO SERENADERS:

Black Patti 8010 *Monte Carlo Joys*........	60.00 -	90.00

DIXON'S JAZZ DUO/MANIACS:

Paramount 12385 *Headache Blues*...........	20.00 -	30.00
12405 *Tiger Rag*.....................	20.00 -	30.00
12446 *Crazy Quilt*....................	20.00 -	30.00

VANCE DIXON & HIS PENCILS:

Columbia 14608-D *Hot Peanuts*..........	20.00 -	30.00
14673-D *Who Stole The Lock?*..........	20.00 -	30.00
Okeh 8891 *Who Stole The Lock?*.........	20.00 -	30.00

DIXON AND CHANNEY:

Paramount 12471 *Sweet Patunia*............	50.00 -	75.00

JOHNNY DODDS: JOHNNY DODDS' BLACK

BOTTOM STOMPERS/ORCHESTRA/TRIO/ WASHBOARD BAND; JOHNNY DODDS & HIS CHICAGO BOYS:

Brunswick 3567 *Wild Man Blues*............	15.00 -	20.00
3568 *After You've Gone*..............	15.00 -	25.00
3574 *Clarinet Wobble*...............	15.00 -	25.00
3565 *The New St. Louis Blues*.........	15.00 -	25.00
3997 *Joe Turner Blues*..............	15.00 -	25.00
7015 *The New St. Louis Blues*.........	20.00 -	30.00
7016 *San*.........................	20.00 -	30.00
Decca 1676, 2111, 7413...............	6.00 -	10.00
Victor 21552 *Bull Fiddle Blues*.........	15.00 -	20.00
21554 *Blue Clarinet Stomp*...........	15.00 -	20.00
23396 *Goober Dance*................	50.00 -	75.00
38004 *Bucktown Stomp*..............	20.00 -	30.00
38038 *Pencil Papa*.................	25.00 -	40.00
38541 *My Little Isabel*..............	25.00 -	40.00
Vocalion 1128 *Melancholy*.............	25.00 -	40.00
1148 *After You've Gone*..............	25.00 -	40.00
15632 *Weary Blues*.................	50.00 -	75.00

DODDS AND PARHAM:

Paramount 12471 *Oh Daddy*............	50.00 -	75.00
12483 *19th Street Blues*..............	60.00 -	90.00

CLYDE DOERR AND HIS ORCHESTRA:

Edison 51988 *Ain't She Sweet?*.........	7.00 -	10.00
52065 *Dew-Dew-Dewy Day*...........	5.00 -	8.00

PAT DOLLOHAN AND HIS ORCHESTRA:

Gennett 6711 *My Supressed Desire*.......	7.00 -	10.00
6784 *True Blue*....................	10.00 -	15.00

AL DONOHUE AND HIS ORCHESTRA:

Decca 559, 604, 608, 626, 630, 665, 673, 981, 989	3.00 -	5.00
Okeh, most issues...................	3.00 -	5.00
Vocalion, most issues.................	3.00 -	5.00

D'ORSAY DANCE ORCHESTRA:

Clarion 5394-C *Little Mary Brown*.........	7.00 -	10.00
Clarion 5440-C, 5450-C, 5466-C.........	4.00 -	7.00
Harmony 1380-H, *Little Mary Brown*.......	7.00 -	10.00
Harmony 1409-H, 1419-H..............	4.00 -	7.00
Velvet Tone 2458-V, *Little Mary Brown*......	7.00 -	10.00
Velvet Tone 2510-V, 2526-V.............	4.00 -	7.00

THE DORSEY BROTHERS' ORCHESTRA: THE DORSEY BROTHERS AND THEIR ORCHESTRA:

Brunswick 6409, 6537, 6624, 6722, 6938.......	7.00 -	10.00
Columbia 2581-D *Ooh! That Kiss*............	8.00 -	12.00
2589-D *Why Did It Have To Be Me?*........	8.00 -	12.00
Decca 115, 116, 117, 118, 195, 196, 206, 207, 208, 258, 259, 260, 283, 291, 296, 297, 311, 314, 318, 319, 320, 321, 335, 340, 348, 357, 358, 367, 368, 370, 371, 469, 476, 482, 515, 516, 519, 520, 559, 560, 561, 1503 (12-inch).................	3.00 -	7.00
Okeh 40995 *Mary Ann*..................	6.00 -	12.00
41007 *The Yale Blues*................	6.00 -	12.00
41032 *My Melancholy Baby*............	6.00 -	12.00
41050 *Dixie Dawn*..................	6.00 -	12.00
41065 *Evening Star*.................	6.00 -	12.00
41124 *Out Of The Dawn*.............	6.00 -	12.00
41151 *Cross Roads*.................	6.00 -	12.00
41158 *She's Funny That Way*.........	6.00 -	12.00
41181 *The Spell Of The Blues*........	20.00 -	30.00
41188 *My Kinda Love*...............	20.00 -	30.00
41210 *Mean To Me*.................	8.00 -	12.00
41220 *I'll Never Ask For More*........	8.00 -	12.00
41259 *Am I Blue?*..................	8.00 -	12.00
41260 *Breakaway*..................	8.00 -	12.00
41272 *Singin' In The Rain*...........	8.00 -	12.00
41279 *Maybe—Who Knows?*..........	8.00 -	12.00

JIM/JIMMY DORSEY (AND HIS ORCHESTRA):

Brunswick 6352 *Oodles of Noodles*.........	7.00 -	10.00
Decca 570, 571, 602, 607, 655...........	4.00 -	7.00

Decca 762,764, 768, 776, 782, 808, 873, 901.... 4.00 - 7.00
Decca 939 *Rap Tap On Wood*............ 5.00 - 8.00
  940 *Swingin' The Jinx Away*............. 5.00 - 8.00
Decca 941, 950, 951, 1040, 1086, 1187, 1200, 1203,
  1204, 1256, 1301, 1377, 1378, 1508, 1651, 1652,
  1660, 1671, 1723, 1724, 1745, 1746, 1784, 1799,
  1809, 1834, 1860, 1921, 1939............ 3.00 - 6.00
Decca, most other issues................ 3.00 - 5.00
MGM, most issues.................... 2.00 - 3.00

TOM DORSEY (& HIS NOVELTY ORCHESTRA); TOMMY DORSEY & HIS CLAMBAKE SEVEN/ORCHESTRA:
Okeh 41178 *It's Right Here For You*......... 10.00 - 15.00
  41422 *You Can't Cheat A Cheater*........ 10.00 - 15.00
Victor 25144, 25145, 25158, 25159, 25172, 25173,
  25183, 25191, 25201, 25206, 25216, 25217,
  25214, 25220, 25246, 25256, 25284, 25291,
  25292, 25335, 25341, 35349, 25352, 25476,
  25482............................. 4.00 - 7.00
Victor 25314, 15320, 25363, 25446, 25447, 25467,
  25484, 25496, 25508, 25509, 25513, 25516,
  25519, 25523, 25532, 25534, 25539, 25544,
  25549, 25553, 25556, 25557, 25568, 25570,
  25573, 25577, 25581, 25591, 25596, 25600,
  25603, 25605, 25607, 25610, 25620, 25623,
  25625, 25630, 25635, 25647, 25648, 25649,
  25652, 25657, 25663, 25673, 25676, 25686,
  25692, 25693, 25694, 25695,.......... 3.00 - 6.00
(Note: Foregoing issues, if first pressings, have the "scroll" label.)
Victor 25703, 25741, 25750, 25763, 25768, 25774,
  25780, 25795, 25799, 25803, 25813, 25815,
  25821, 25824, 25828, 25832, 25848, 25856,
  25862, 25866, 25899, 26005, 26016, 26030.. 3.00 - 6.00
Victor, most other issues................ 2.00 - 4.00

MIKE DOTY AND HIS ORCHESTRA:
Bluebird 5251 *Puddin' Head Jones*............ 5.00 - 8.00
  5252 *Lenox Avenue*.................... 5.00 - 8.00
  5253 *My Galveston Gal*................. 5.00 - 8.00
  5277 *You're My Thrill*................. 5.00 - 8.00

DOWN HOME SERENADERS:
Champion 15399 *Cootie Stomp*............. 75.00 - 100.00

GEORGE DREW & HIS ORCHESTRA:
Superior 2829 *Hard Luck*................ 20.00 - 30.00

LEO DREYER AND HIS ORCHESTRA:
Crown 3404 *Fit As A Fiddle*............. 5.00 - 8.00
Edison 52466 *Pompanola*................ 10.00 - 15.00

EDDIE DROESCH AND HIS ORCHESTRA:
Clarion 5407-C *Last Dollar*............. 5.00 - 10.00
Harmony 1388-H *Last Dollar*............. 5.00 - 10.00
Velvet Tone 2467-V *Last Dollar*.......... 5.00 - 10.00

GEORGE DRUCK'S SWEETS BALLROOM ORCHESTRA:
Flexo (unnumbered) *Tiger Rag*........... 20.00 - 30.00

DUBIN'S DANDIES:
Banner 0505, 0510, 0513, 0533, 0537, 0784.... 3.00 - 5.00
  0557 *Stay In The Sunshine And Smile*....... 5.00 - 8.00
  0564 *You Know Better Than That*......... 5.00 - 8.00
  0569 *In Harlem's Araby*................. 8.00 - 12.00
  0570 *When The Moon Shines Down On Sunshine and Me*................. 5.00 - 8.00
  0572 *Angel Eyes*..................... 5.00 - 8.00
  0804 *Syncopated Jamboree*............. 10.00 - 15.00
  6425 *Hoodoo Voodoo Man*............. 5.00 - 8.00
Banner 6426, 6439, 6440, 6447, 4449, 6451... 3.00 - 5.00
  6452 *Whoopee-in' Up*................. 5.00 - 8.00
  6468, 6470, 6472, 6473, 6479.......... 3.00 - 5.00
  6477 *You're Gonna Regret*............. 5.00 - 8.00
  6506, 6511, 6513................... 3.00 - 5.00
Banner 6507 *In My Wedding Gown*........ 5.00 - 8.00
  6516 *That's What Love Did To Me*........ 5.00 - 8.00

  6537 *Any Old Time*................... 5.00 - 8.00
Cameo 0169 *In Harlem's Araby*.......... 8.00 - 12.00
  0404 *Syncopated Jamboree*............ 10.00 - 15.00
Oriole 1824 *In Harlem's Araby*........... 8.00 - 12.00
  1825 *When The Moon Shines Down on Sunshine and Me*......... 5.00 - 8.00
  2007 *I've Got My Mind On You*......... 5.00 - 8.00
  2059 *Syncopated Jamboree*............ 10.00 - 15.00
Romeo 1153 *Can You Fry An Egg?*......... 3.00 - 5.00
  1177 *Stay In The Sunshine and Smile*....... 5.00 - 8.00
  1187 *In Harlem's Araby*................. 8.00 - 12.00
  1243 *She Stole My Heart*............... 5.00 - 8.00

EDDIE DUCHIN AND HIS (CENTRAL PARK CASINO) ORCHESTRA:
Brunswick 6425, 6431, 6439, 6445, 6458, 6476, 6481,
  6488.......................... 3.00 - 5.00
Brunswick 8155 *Between the Devil and the Deep Blue Sea*................. 5.00 - 8.00
Brunswick, most other issues............ 2.00 - 4.00
Columbia 2625-D *Can't We Talk It Over?*...... 5.00 - 8.00
  2626-D *By The Fireside*............... 5.00 - 8.00
  2677-D *You're Blase*................. 5.00 - 8.00
  2680-D *The Clouds Will Soon Roll By*...... 5.00 - 8.00
Columbia, most other issues............ 2.00 - 4.00
Victor 24274, 24275, 24280, 24325, 24326, 24327,
  24376, 24377, 24380, 24441, 24447, 24461,
  24477, 24479, 24492, 24510, 24512, 24518,
  24576.......................... 3.00 - 5.00
Victor 24579 *As Long As I Live*......... 5.00 - 8.00
Victor, most other issues............... 2.00 - 5.00

ROBERTA DUDLEY:
Nordskog 3007 *Krooked Blues*............ 125.00 - 200.00
Sunshine 3001 *Krooked Blues*........... 125.00 - 200.00
(Sunshine label is pasted over Nordskog label.)

HERVE DUERSON:
Gennett 7009 *Avenue Strut*............. 35.00 - 50.00
  7191 *Easy Drag*.................... 35.00 - 50.00

LOUIS DUMAINE'S JAZZOLA EIGHT:
Victor 20580 *Red Onion Drag*........... 20.00 - 30.00
  20723 *Pretty Audrey*................ 20.00 - 30.00

SONNY DUNHAM AND HIS ORCHESTRA:
Bluebird 11124, 11148, 11200, 11214, 11239, 11253,
  11305, 11337, 11504, 11514.......... 3.00 - 5.00
Varsity 8205, 8227, 8234.............. 4.00 - 7.00
Vogue R-774 *Save Me A Dream*.......... 10.00 - 15.00
  R-775 *Clementine*.................. 10.00 - 15.00

BLIND WILLIE DUNN: BLIND WILLIE DUNN'S GIN BOTTLE FOUR:
Okey 8633 *Church Street Sobbin' Blues*........ 10.00 - 15.00
  8689 *Jet Black Blues*.............. 50.00 - 75.00

JOHNNY DUNN (& HIS BAND/JAZZ BAND): DUNN'S ORIGINAL JAZZ HOUNDS:
Columbia 124-D *Dunn's Cornet Blues*......... 7.00 - 10.00
Columbia A-3541, A-3579, A-3729, A-3839, A-3878,
  A-3893.......................... 4.00 - 7.00
  13004-D *Jazzin' Babies Blues*............. 9.00 - 12.00
  14306-D *Buffalo Blues*............... 30.00 - 40.00
  14358-D *Ham and Eggs*.............. 30.00 - 40.00
Vocalion 1176 *Original Bugle Blues*........ 50.00 - 80.00

JIMMY DURANTE: JIMMY DURANTE'S JAZZ BAND:
Brunswick 6774 *Inka Dinka Doo*......... 5.00 - 8.00
Gennett 9045 *Why Cry Blues*........... 7.00 - 10.00
(See also: CLAYTON, JACKSON AND DURANTE)

BURT EARLE with ANGLO-AMERICAN ORCHESTRA:
Pathe 30124 *King Chanticleer*............

CHARLIE EATON:
Herwin 93017 *Bucket of Blood*........... 60.00 - 80.00

GEORGE EDKHARDT JR. AND HIS (CAFE

EDDIE   66   **ELLINGTON**

LAFAYETTE) ORCHESTRA:
Vocalion 15738, 15796, 15803, 15806 . . . .   4.00 -   8.00

EDDIE'S HOT SHOTS:
Victor 38046 *That's A Serious Thing* . . . .   20.00 -   30.00

EDDIE AND SUGAR LOU'S HOTEL TYLER
ORCHESTRA:
Vocalion 1445 *K. W. K. H. Blues* . . . .   50.00 -   80.00
   1455 *There'll Be Some Changes Made* . . . . . .   50.00 -   80.00
   1514 *Eddie And Sugar Lou Stomp* . . . .   50.00 -   80.00
   1714 *Sympathetic Blues* . . . .   60.00 -   90.00
   1723 *Cruel Mama Blues* . . . .   60.00 -   90.00

EDGEWATER CROWS:
Titles, issued contemporaneously on Banner, Melotone, Oriole, Perfect Romeo: *No Bonus Blues; Swinging Rhythm Around* . . . .   15.00 -   20.00

EDDIE EDINBOROUGH & HIS NEW
ORLEANS WILDCATS/WASHBOARD
BAND:
Columbia 14613-D *Wild Cat's Ball* . . . .   25.00 -   35.00
   14629-D *Brown Baby* . . . .   25.00 -   35.00
Vocalion 1701 *Dream Sweetheart* . . . .   25.00 -   35.00
   1702 *Nobody's Sweetheart* . . . .   25.00 -   35.00

CLIFF EDWARDS:
Pathe-Actuelle 025159, 025160, 025163, 025164, 025167, 025169, 025173, 25198, 25199, 25200, 25203, 25204, 25206 . . . .   4.00 -   7.00
Perfect 11593, 11594, 11597, 11598, 11601, 11603, 11607, 11632, 11633, 11634, 11637, 11638, 11640 . . . .   4.00 -   7.00

DAVID EDWARDS & HIS BOYS:
Okey 41492 *Just A Crazy Song* . . . .   7.00 -   10.00

JOAN EDWARDS WITH THE VOGUE
RECORDING ORCHESTRA:
Vogue R-761 *More Than You Know* . . . .   10.00 -   15.00
   R-767 *This Is Always* . . . .   10.00 -   15.00
   R-782 *Maybe You'll Be There* . . . .   12.00 -   18.00

BOB EFFROS:
Brunswick 4620 *Tin Ear* . . . .   10.00 -   15.00

ROY ELDRIDGE & HIS ORCHESTRA:
Vocalion 3458, 3479, 3577 . . . .   5.00 -   10.00

ELGAR'S CREOLE ORCHESTRA:
Vocalion 15477 *Cafe Capers* . . . .   35.00 -   50.00
   15478 *Brotherly Love* . . . .   35.00 -   50.00

FRED ELIZALDE'S CINDERELLA ROOF
ORCHESTRA:
Hollywood 1012 *Boneyard Shuffle* . . . .   25.00 -   35.00
   1013 *Melancholy Weeps* . . . .   25.00 -   35.00
   1014 *Tonight's My Night With Baby* . . . .   25.00 -   35.00
   1015 *Tickling Julie* . . . .   25.00 -   35.00

DUKE ELLINGTON (& HIS ORCHESTRA/
COTTON CLUB ORCHESTRA/KENTUCKY
CLUB ORCHESTRA/WASHINGTONIANS):
Blu-Disc 1004 *Rose Marie* . . . .   20.00 -   30.00
Bluebird 6269, 6280, 6305, 6306, 6335, 6396, 6415, 6430 . . . .   5.00 -   8.00
   6450 *Old Man Blues* . . . .   10.00 -   15.00
   6531, 6565, 6614, 6727, 6728, 7182 . . . . . .   5.00 -   8.00
   10242, 10243, 10245 . . . .   4.00 -   7.00
Brunswick 3480 *Birmingham Breakdown* . . . . . .   10.00 -   15.00
   3987 *Tishomingo Blues* . . . .   10.00 -   15.00
   4110 *Louisiana* . . . .   10.00 -   15.00
   4122 *The Mooche* . . . .   10.00 -   15.00
   6093 *Creole Rhapsody* . . . .   10.00 -   15.00
   6265, 6288, 6317, 6355, 6374, 6404, 6432, 6516, 6527, 6571, 6600, 6607, 6638, 6646 . . . . .   6.00 -   10.00
   6987, 7310, 7440, 7461, 7514, 7526, 7546, 7547, 7625, 7627, 7650, 7667, 7710, 7734, 7752, 7989, 7990, 7994, 8004, 8029, 8044, 8063, 8083, 8093, 8099, 8108, 8131, 8168, 8169, 8174, 8186, 8200, 8204, 8221, 8231, 8256, 8293, 8297, 8306, 8344, 8365, 8380, 8405, 8411 . . . .   4.00 -   10.00

Buddy 8010 *If You Can't Hold The Man You Love*   40.00 -   60.00
   8063 *Animal Crackers* . . . .   40.00 -   60.00
Columbia 953-D *Hop Head* . . . .   15.00 -   20.00
   1076-D *Down In Our Alley Blues* . . . .   15.00 -   20.00
Gennett 3291 *Wanna Go Back Again Blues* . . .   35.00 -   50.00
   3342 *Animal Crackers* . . . .   35.00 -   50.00
Okeh 8521 *Black And Tan Fantasy* . . . .   *15.00 -   20.00*
   8602 Diga Diga Doo . . . .   15.00 -   20.00
   8636 Black Beauty . . . .   15.00 -   20.00
   8662 Misty Mornin' . . . .   15.00 -   20.00
   40955 Black And Tan Fantasy . . . .   15.00 -   20.00
   41013 Jubilee Stomp . . . .   15.00 -   20.00
Pathe-Actuelle 7504 *Georgia Grind* . . . .   50.00 -   75.00
   36333 *Trombone Blues* . . . .   30.00 -   50.00
Perfect 104 *Georgia Grind* . . . .   50.00 -   75.00
   14514 *Trombone Blues* . . . .   30.00 -   50.00
Victor L-16006* *Mood Indigo Plus 2* . . . .   20.00 -   30.00
   L-16007* *East St. Louis Toodle-Oo Plus 2* . . .   20.00 -   30.00
(*These are long-playing "Program Transcriptions")

Victor 21137 *Creole Love Call* . . . .   15.00 -   20.00
   21284 *Washington Wobble* . . . .   15.00 -   20.00
   21490 *The Blues I Love To Sing* . . . .   15.00 -   20.00
   21580 *Black Beauty* . . . .   15.00 -   20.00
   21703 *Got Everything But You* . . . .   15.00 -   20.00
   22528 *Three Little Words* . . . .   5.00 -   8.00
   22586 *What Good Am I Without You* . . . . . .   10.00 -   15.00
   22587 *Mood Indigo* . . . .   6.00 -   9.00
   22603 *Blue Again* . . . .   6.00 -   9.00
   22614 *Keep A Song In Your Soul* . . . .   10.00 -   15.00
   22743 *Limehouse Blues* . . . .   7.00 -   10.00
   22791 *It's Glory* . . . .   10.00 -   15.00
   22800 *The Mystery Song* . . . .   7.00 -   10.00
   22938 *Bugle Call Rag* . . . .   10.00 -   15.00
   23016 *Hittin' The Bottle* . . . .   20.00 -   30.00
   23017 *You're Lucky To Me* . . . .   20.00 -   30.00
   23022 *Jungle Nights In Harlem* . . . .   20.00 -   30.00
   23036 *Sam And Delilah* . . . .   15.00 -   20.00
   23041 *Shout 'Em, Aunt Tillie* . . . .   20.00 -   30.00
   24431 *Rude Interlude* . . . .   10.00 -   15.00
   24501 *Daybreak Express* . . . .   6.00 -   10.00
   24617 *Cocktails For Two* . . . .   6.00 -   10.00
   24622 *Ebony Rhapsody* . . . .   8.00 -   12.00
   24651 *My Old Flame* . . . .   8.00 -   12.00
   24755 *Delta Serenade* . . . .   8.00 -   12.00
   38007 *Bandanna Babies* . . . .   12.00 -   16.00
   38008 *Diga Diga Doo* . . . .   12.00 -   16.00
   38034 *The Mooche* . . . .   20.00 -   30.00
   38025 *Flaming Youth* . . . .   15.00 -   25.00
   38036 *Saturday Night Function* . . . .   15.00 -   25.00
   38045 *Japanese Dream* . . . .   15.00 -   25.00
   38053 *Stevedore Stomp* . . . .   15.00 -   25.00
   38058 *Saratoga Swing* . . . .   15.00 -   25.00
   38065 *Hot Feet* . . . .   20.00 -   25.00
   38079 *Cotton Club Stomp* . . . .   20.00 -   25.00
   38089 *Swanee Shuffle* . . . .   20.00 -   25.00
   38092 *The Duke Steps Out* . . . .   20.00 -   30.00
   38115 *Breakfast Dance* . . . .   20.00 -   30.00
   38129 *Jazz Lips* . . . .   20.00 -   30.00

38143 *Sweet Jazz O'Mine*	20.00 -	30.00
Vocalion 1064 *Birmingham Breakdown*	40.00 -	50.00
1077 *Immigration Blues*	50.00 -	70.00
1086 *New Orleans Low-Down*	60.00 -	80.00
1153 *Red Hot Band*	60.00 -	80.00

GAY ELLIS:

Diva, Harmony, Velvet-Tone	4.00 -	8.00

SEGER ELLIS:

Brunswick 6022, 6050, 6076, 6078, 6135	5.00 -	8.00
Columbia 2362-D *Cheerful Little Earful*	5.00 -	8.00
Okeh 41024, 41047, 41077, 41160, 41165, 41190, 41221, 41222, 41224, 41225, 41289, 41321, 41396, 41413, 41417, 41424, 41447	4.00 -	7.00
41441, 41443, 41452, 41467, 41473, 41479	7.00 -	10.00
41255 *To Be In Love*	15.00 -	25.00
41290 *True Blue Lou*	10.00 -	15.00
41291 *Ain't Misbehavin'*	15.00 -	25.00

THE EMPERORS:

Harmony 362-H *Clarinet Marmalade*	7.00 -	10.00
383-H *Go, Joe, Go*	7.00 -	10.00

PEGGY ENGLISH:

Vocalion 15093 *Charleston Baby O'Mine*	5.00 -	8.00
15118 *You Can't Shush Katy*	5.00 -	8.00
15132 *Sweet Man*	5.00 -	8.00
15381 *How Many Times?*	5.00 -	8.00
15504 *High-High-High Up In The Hills*	10.00 -	15.00

SHARLIE ENGLISH:

Paramount 12610 *Transom Blues*	30.00 -	40.00
12644 *Broke Woman Blues*	30.00 -	40.00

EQUINOX ORCHESTRA OF PRINCETON, NEW JERSEY:

Personal Record 115-P *China Boy*	10.00 -	15.00

WALLY ERICKSON'S COLISEUM ORCHESTRA:

Gennett 3068 *The Meanest Kind of Blues*	10.00 -	15.00
3069 *The Call Of The South*	10.00 -	15.00
Vocalion 15778 *Hard Luck*	30.00 -	50.00

ERWING BROTHERS' ORCHESTRA:

Vocalion 2564 *The Erwing Blues*	15.00 -	20.00

ESSEX CLUB ORCHESTRA:

Vocalion 15170 *A Little Bit Bad*	5.00 -	8.00
Vocalion 15221, 15224, 15230	3.00 -	5.00
Vocalion 15423, 15424	4.00 -	7.00

RUTH ETTING:

Titles, issued contemporaneously on Banner, Conqueror, Melotone, Oriole, Perfect, Romeo: *All Of Me; Can't We Talk It Over; Happy-Go-Lucky You; Have You Forgotten?; Hey! Young Fella; How Can I Go On Without You; If I Didn't Have You; I'll Follow You; I'll Never Be The Same; I'll Never Have To Dream Again; It Was So Beautiful; Just One More Chance; Lazy Day; Let Me Call You Sweetheart; Linger A Little While Longer in the Twilight; Love Letters In the Sand; Nevertheless; Some Day We'll Meet Again; Take Me In Your Arms Again; That's What Heaven Means to Me; Try a Little Tenderness; Without That Gal; With Summer Coming On; You've Got Me Crying Again.*

	7.00 -	10.00
Brunswick 6657 *Close Your Eyes*	5.00 -	8.00
6671 *What Is Sweeter*	5.00 -	8.00
6697 *Build A Little Home*	5.00 -	8.00
6719 *Everything I Have Is Yours*	5.00 -	8.00
6761 *Keep Romance Alive*	5.00 -	8.00
6769 *Smoke Gets In Your Eyes*	5.00 -	8.00
6892 *Easy Come, Easy Go*	5.00 -	8.00
6914 *Were Your Ears Burning?*	5.00 -	8.00
7646 *It's Been So Long*	5.00 -	8.00
Columbia 580-D *Let's Talk About My Sweetie*	5.00 -	8.00
Columbia, 633-D, 644-D, 692-D	4.00 -	7.00
675-D *What A Man!*	5.00 -	8.00

722-D *Her Beaus Are Only Rainbows*	5.00 -	8.00
764-D *Stars*	5.00 -	8.00
Columbia 827-D, 865-D, 908-D, 924-D, 979-D	4.00 -	8.00
Columbia 995-D, 1288-D, 1312-D	3.00 -	6.00
Columbia 1052-D, 1075-D, 1104-D	4.00 -	7.00
Columbia 1113-D *Shaking the Blues Away*	5.00 -	8.00
Columbia 1196-D, 1208-D, 1352-D	4.00 -	7.00
Columbia 1237-D *The Varsity Drag*	5.00 -	8.00
Columbia 1393-D, 1420-D, 1454-D, 1563-D, 1595-D	4.00 -	7.00
Columbia 1680-D, 1707-D, 1733-D, 1801-D	4.00 -	8.00
Columbia 1762-D *Button Up Your Overcoat*	7.00 -	10.00
Columbia 1830-D, 1883-D	4.00 -	8.00
Columbia 1958-D *Ain't Misbehavin'*	5.00 -	8.00
1998-D *The Right Kind Of Man*	5.00 -	8.00
2038-D *A Place To Call Home*	5.00 -	8.00
2073-D *Crying For The Carolines*	5.00 -	8.00
2146-D *Ten Cents A Dance*	4.00 -	7.00
2172-D *Let Me Sing And I'm Happy*	5.00 -	8.00
2199-D *Exactly Like You*	5.00 -	8.00
2216-D *Dancing With Tears In My Eyes*	5.00 -	8.00
2280-D *The Kiss Waltz*	5.00 -	8.00
2300-D *If I Could Be With You*	7.00 -	10.00
2307-D *Just A Little Closer*	7.00 -	10.00
2318-D *Laughing At Life*	7.00 -	10.00
2377-D *Reaching For The Moon*	7.00 -	10.00
2398-D *You're The One I Care For*	7.00 -	10.00
2445-D *Were You Sincere?*	7.00 -	10.00
2454-D *Out Of Nowhere*	8.00 -	12.00
2470-D *Moonlight Saving Time*	*8.00 -*	*12.00*
2505-D *I'm Falling In Love*	7.00 -	10.00
2529-D *Guilty*	8.00 -	12.00
2557-D *Goodnight, Sweetheart*	7.00 -	10.00
2580-D *Cuban Love Song*	7.00 -	10.00
2630-D *When We're Alone*	7.00 -	10.00
2660-D *The Voice in the Old Village Choir*	7.00 -	10.00
2681-D *Holding My Honey's Hand*	8.00 -	12.00
2954-D *Talkin' To Myself*	10.00 -	15.00
2955-D *Out In The Cold Again*	10.00 -	15.00
2979-D *A Needle In A Haystack*	10.00 -	15.00
2985-D *Am I To Blame?*	10.00 -	15.00
3014-D *March Winds and April Showers*	10.00 -	15.00
3031-D *It's Easy To Remember*	10.00 -	15.00
3070-D *I Wished on the Moon*	10.00 -	15.00
3085-D *Ten Cents A Dance*	10.00 -	15.00
Decca 1084 *There's Something in the Air*	5.00 -	8.00
1107 *Goodnight, My Love*	5.00 -	8.00
1212 *It's Swell Of You*	5.00 -	8.00
1259 *On A Little Dream Ranch*	5.00 -	8.00

EDITH EVANS:

Brunswick 4291 *My Kinda Love*	7.00 -	10.00

ROY EVANS:

Columbia 1559-D, 1934-D, 2198-D, 2257-D, 2338-D, 2469-D	3.00 -	7.00
Crown 3154 *One More Time*	7.00 -	10.00

EVERETT'S SERENADERS:

Dandy 5118 *I Wonder Where My Baby Is Tonight*

ELIOT EVERETT AND HIS ORCHESTRA:

Victor 22921 *Blue Danube Blues*	5.00 -	8.00
24080 *In a Little Blue Canoe With You*	5.00 -	8.00
24085 *Little Nell*	5.00 -	8.00

WILL EZELL:

Paramount 12549 *Barrel House Man*	40.00 -	70.00
12688 *Mixed Up Rag*	40.00 -	70.00
12729 *Crawlin' Spider Blues*	40.00 -	70.00
12753 *Barrel House Woman*	40.00 -	70.00
12773 *Bucket of Blood*	40.00 -	70.00
12855 *Pitchin' Boogie*	40.00 -	70.00
12914 *Freakish Mistreater Blues*	40.00 -	70.00

SAMMY FAIN:

Harmony 904-H *The Things That Were Made For Love*	5.00 -	8.00

(Fallon, continued)

943-H *What A Day!*	7.00 -	10.00
961-H *Why Can't You*	7.00 -	10.00
Harmony 993-H, 1014-H, 1163-H, 1179-H	5.00 -	8.00
Velvet Tone 1943-V *To Be In Love*	7.00 -	10.00

OWEN FALLON AND HIS CALIFORNIANS:

Melotone 12199 *Under Your Window Tonight*	8.00 -	12.00
12212 *Take It From Me (I'm Takin' To You)*	5.00 -	8.00
12337 *I Know You're Lying, But I Love It*	5.00 -	8.00
12409 *Sleep (Come On And Take Me)*	5.00 -	8.00
Sunset *1135 Darktown Shuffle*	15.00 -	20.00
1152 *I Love My Baby*	7.00 -	10.00

WILLIE FARMER AND HIS ORCHESTRA:

Bluebird 7024, 7026, 7036, 7170, 7171, 7181, 7183, 7519, 7527, 7685, 7687, 7698, 7722, 7724, 7735, 7795, 7799, 7813	3.00 -	6.00

ALICE FAYE:

Titles, issued contemporaneously on Banner, Brunswick, Melotone, Oriole, Perfect, Romeo: *According To The Moonlight; I Love To Ride The Horses; I'm Shootin' High; I've Got My Fingers Crossed; My Future Star; Oh, I Didn't Know; Spreadin' Rhythm Around; Yes To You* ..... 5.00 - 10.00

Brunswick 7821, 7825, 7860, 7876	4.00 -	7.00

CARL FENTON & HIS ORCHESTRA:

Brunswick 3519 *Delirium*	5.00 -	8.00
4421 *What A Day!*	15.00 -	20.00
QRS 1023 *St. James Infirmary*	15.00 -	20.00

JERRY FENWYCK AND HIS ORCHESTRA:

Clarion 5282-C *Little Joe*	4.00 -	6.00
5305-C *That Little Boy Of Mine*	4.00 -	6.00
5352-C *How The Time Can Fly*	5.00 -	8.00
5360-C *Take It From Me*	7.00 -	10.00
5364-C *Do The New York*	7.00 -	10.00
5398-C *A Faded Summer Love*	5.00 -	8.00
5408-C *You Didn't Know The Music*	5.00 -	8.00
5415-C *Now's The Time To Fall In Love*	8.00 -	12.00
5420-C *By The Sycamore Tree*	7.00 -	10.00
5421-C *I Wouldn't Change You For The World*	5.00 -	8.00
5442-C *All Of Me*	7.00 -	10.00
11500-C *You Call It Madness*	5.00 -	8.00
11503-C *Who's Your Little Who-Zis!*	8.00 -	12.00

Note: 11503-C is a five-minute record having two cuts of the tune — one instrumental, the other vocal.)

Harmony 1301-H *Little Joe*	4.00 -	6.00
1314-H *That Little Boy of Mine*	4.00 -	6.00
1341-H *How The Time Can Fly*	5.00 -	8.00
1348-H *Take It From Me*	7.00 -	10.00
1352-H *Do The New York*	7.00 -	10.00
1384-H *A Faded Summer Love*	5.00 -	8.00
1389-H *You Didn't Know The Music*	5.00 -	8.00
1394-H *Now's The Time To Fall In Love*	8.00 -	12.00
1397-H *By The Sycamore Tree*	7.00 -	10.00
1398-H *I Wouldn't Change You For The World*	5.00 -	8.00
1403-H *All Of Me*	7.00 -	10.00
6500-H *You Call It Madness*	5.00 -	8.00
Velvet Tone 2348-V *Little Joe*	4.00 -	6.00
2371-V *Out Of Nowhere*	5.00 -	8.00
2373-V *That Little Boy Of Mine*	4.00 -	6.00
2416-V *How The Time Can Fly*	5.00 -	8.00
2424-V *Take It From Me*	7.00 -	10.00
2461-V *Lies*	5.00 -	8.00
2462-V *A Faded Summer Love*	5.00 -	8.00
2468-V *You Didn't Know The Music*	5.00 -	8.00
2475-V *Now's The Time To Fall In Love*	8.00 -	12.00
2480-V *By The Sycamore Tree*	7.00 -	10.00
2481-V *I Wouldn't Change You For the World*	5.00 -	8.00
2502-V *All Of Me*	7.00 -	10.00
10500-V *When The Rest of the Crowd Goes Home*	5.00 -	8.00

ARTHUR FIELDS AND HIS ASSASSINATORS/NOODLERS:

Banner 6314 *Let's Get Together*	5.00 -	8.00
6315 *Geraldine*	5.00 -	8.00

6317 *What Do You Think Of My Baby*	5.00 -	8.00
Edison (thin) *Sophomore Prom*	10.00 -	15.00
14075 *Piccolo Pete*	10.00 -	15.00
Edison (thick) 52123 *Is It Possible?*	7.00 -	10.00
52180 *Look In The Mirror*	7.00 -	10.00
52264 *She's A Great, Great Girl*	10.00 -	15.00
52535 *She Only Laughs At Me*	5.00 -	8.00
52553 *I Faw Down An' Go 'Boom*	5.00 -	8.00

BUDDY FIELDS AND HIS ORCHESTRA:

Romeo 1052, 1053, 1069, 1070, 1084	3.00 -	5.00
Romeo 1068 *Lovable and Sweet*	5.00 -	8.00

ERNIE FIELDS & HIS ORCHESTRA:

Vocalion 5073 *Lard Stomp*	5.00 -	8.00
5157 *High Jivin'*	5.00 -	8.00
5240 *I'm Living In A Great Big Way*	5.00 -	8.00
5344 *Blues At Midnight*	5.00 -	8.00

SHEP FIELDS AND HIS ORCHESTRA/ RIPPLING RHYTHM:

Bluebird, most issues	2.00 -	5.00
Musicraft, most issues	2.00 -	3.00
Victor, most issues	2.00 -	3.00
Vogue R-712 *Atlanta, Ga.*	10.00 -	15.00
R-715 *I Can't Begin To Tell You*	10.00 -	15.00
R-764 *Whattaya Gonna Do*	10.00 -	15.00
R-765 *What Is Love*	10.00 -	15.00

LLOYD FINLAY AND HIS ORCHESTRA:

Victor 19643 *You'll Want Me Back Someday*	10.00 -	15.00
19644 *Fido Blues*	7.00 -	12.00
19696 *Ride 'Em, Cowboy*	10.00 -	15.00

BOB FINLEY AND HIS ORCHESTRA:

Cameo 9101 *Doin' The Campus Crawl*	7.00 -	10.00
9103 *Nobody's Baby But Mine*	7.00 -	10.00
9105 *Audition Blues*	10.00 -	15.00
Romeo 903 *Doin' The Campus Crawl*	7.00 -	10.00
905 *Nobody's Baby But Mine*	7.00 -	10.00
907 *Audition Blues*	10.00 -	15.00

DOUGLAS FINNELL AND HIS ROYAL STOMPERS:

Brunswick 7123 *Sweet Sweet Mama*	40.00 -	60.00

ETHEL FINNIE:

Ajax 17015 *Don't You Quit Me, Daddy*	10.00 -	15.00
17027 *Hula Blues*	15.00 -	20.00
Emerson 10846 *Heart-Breakin' Joe*	15.00 -	20.00

FINZEL'S ARCADIA ORCHESTRA OF DETROIT:

Okeh 4735, 4743, 4758, 4759	4.00 -	7.00
Okeh 4847 *Farewell Blues*	7.00 -	10.00
Okeh 4858, 4859, 4861, 4985, 4999	5.00 -	10.00
Okeh 40148 *Lots O' Mama*	7.00 -	10.00
40161 *Dicty Blues*	8.00 -	12.00
40298 *Laff It Off*	8.00 -	12.00
40301 *Big Bad Bill*	8.00 -	12.00
40304 *I Can't Stop Babying You*	8.00 -	12.00

TED FIORITO AND HIS (EDGEWATER BEACH HOTEL) ORCHESTRA:

Brunswick 6422, 6478, 6479, 6493, 6503, 6505, 6526, 6555, 6556, 5686, 6598, 6627, 6670, 6705, 6706, 6736, 6746, 6859, 6860, 6863, 6902, 6919, 6924, 6928, 7311, 7315, 7327, 7364, 7379, 7380, 7392, 7399, 7446, 7451, 7452, 7478, 7489	3.00 -	6.00
Columbia 1967-D *Then You've Never Been Blue*	5.00 -	8.00
Decca 677, 678, 679, 694, 697, 746, 771, 777, 784, 793, 894, 909, 910, 925, 935, 936, 954, 1176, 1193, 1257, 1258, 1450, 1452, 1453, 1561, 1567, 1591	3.00 -	5.00
Decca, most other issues	2.00 -	3.00

MARK FISHER AND HIS EDGEWATER BEACH HOTEL ORCHESTRA:

Columbia 2749-D *Black-Eyed Susan Brown*	7.00 -	10.00

ELLA FITZGERALD & HER SAVOY EIGHT:

Decca 1061, 1062, 1148, 1302, 1339, 1596, 1669	4.00 -	7.00

FIVE BIRMINGHAM BABIES:

Pathe-Actuelle 036129, 036130, 036142, 036168, 036169, 036218, 036228, 036235, 036236, 036274, 036296, 36349, 36350, 36352, 36432, 36451, 36454, 36467 .... 5.00 - 8.00

Perfect 14310, 14311, 14323, 14349, 14350, 14399, 14409, 14416, 14417, 14455, 14477, 14521, 14530, 14531, 14533, 14613, 14632, 14635, 14648 .... 5.00 - 8.00

FIVE HARMANIACS: FIVE HARMONIACS:
Brunswick 3664 *Carolina Bound* .... 12.00 - 16.00
7002 *Sleepy Blues* .... 15.00 - 20.00
Edison 51902 *Rippin' In Off* .... 20.00 - 30.00
Gennett 6033 *What Did Romie-O-Juliet* .... 30.00 - 50.00
Victor 20293 *Coney Island Washboard* .... 8.00 - 12.00
20507 *What Makes My Baby Cry?* .... 15.00 - 20.00

FIVE HOT CHOCOLATES:
Radiex 952 *Baby Knows How* .... 10.00 - 15.00
Van Dyke 71767 *Baby Knows How* .... 10.00 - 15.00
71775 *Alabama Shuffle* .... 15.00 - 25.00
71786 *Memphis Stomp* .... 15.00 - 25.00

FIVE LITTLE CHOCOLATE DANDIES:
Okeh 8627 *Paducah* .... 12.00 - 15.00

FIVE MUSICAL BLACKBIRDS:
Pathe-Actuelle 7508 *18th Street Strut* .... 25.00 - 40.00
36404 *Hot Coffee* .... 25.00 - 40.00
Perfect 108 *18th Street Strut* .... 25.00 - 40.00
14585 *Hot Coffee* .... 25.00 - 40.00

FIVE RHYTHM KINGS:
Victor 23269 *Minnie The Moocher* .... 20.00 - 30.00

FLEETWOOD ORCHESTRA:
Vocalion 15152, 15422, 15462, 15466, 15470, 15516 3.00 - 6.00

JAY C. FLIPPEN (& HIS HOT COMBINATION):
Pathe-Actuelle 32218, 32223, 32229, 32260 ..... 5.00 - 8.00
Perfect 12297, 12302, 12308, 12339 .... 5.00 - 8.00

TROY FLOYD & HIS PLAZA HOTEL/ SHADOWLAND ORCHESTRA:
Okeh 8571 *Shadowland Blues* .... 25.00 - 40.00
8719 *Dreamland Blues* .... 25.00 - 40.00

BILL FOLEY'S KEYSTONE SERENADERS:
Vocalion 15122 *Everything Is Hotsy Totsy Now.* 5.00 - 8.00
Vocalion 15123, 15124 .... 3.00 - 5.00

FOOR-ROBINSON CAROLINA CLUB ORCHESTRA:
Okeh 40466 *Collegiate* .... 10.00 - 15.00

LOUIS FORBSTEIN'S ROYAL SYNCOPATORS:
Okeh 40379 *Deep Elm* .... 15.00 - 20.00
40392 *Someday We'll Meet Again* .... 15.00 - 20.00
41417 *Down And Out Blues* .... 15.00 - 20.00

FORD AND FORD:
Paramount 12244 *I'm Three Times Seven* ...... 30.00 - 40.00

REGINALD FORESYTHE, THE NEW MUSIC OF:
Columbia 3012-D *Dodging A Divorce* .... 10.00 - 15.00
3060-D *Melancholy Clown* .... 10.00 - 15.00

DEACON FORSTER & HIS BOYS:
Champion 15656 *Black And Blue Rhapsody* .... 20.00 - 30.00

GENE FOSDICK'S HOOSIERS:
Vocalion 14496 *'Way Down Yonder In New Orleans* 5.00 - 8.00
14535 *Farewell Blues* .... 5.00 - 8.00
14585 *Railroad Man* .... 5.00 - 8.00

FOUR ACES AND THE JOKER: (Some Brunswicks by JABBO SMITH and are so labelled; see JABBO SMITH):

THE FOUR SPADES:
Columbia 14028-D *Squabblin' Blues* .... 7.00 - 10.00

LEMUEL FOWLER; FOWLER'S FAVORITES/WASHBOARD WONDERS:
Columbia A-3959 *Blues Mixture* .... 5.00 - 8.00
14084-D *Chitterlin' Strut* .... 10.00 - 15.00

14096-D *Pig Foot Shuffle* .... 10.00 - 15.00
14101-D *Express Train Blues* .... 10.00 - 15.00
14111-D *Salty Dog* .... 10.00 - 15.00
14155-D *Jelly Roll Blues* .... 10.00 - 15.00
14230-D *Percolatin' Blues* .... 10.00 - 15.00

WILLIAM FRANCIS AND RICHARD SOWELL:
Vocalion 1090 *John Henry Blues* .... 15.00 - 20.00

ARNOLD FRANK & HIS ORCHESTRA/ ROGERS CAFE ORCHESTRA:
Okeh 40896, 41086 .... 4.00 - 7.00

FRANKIE & HER JAZZ DEVILS;
Pathe-Actuelle 7507 *Those Creeping Sneaking Blues* 12.00 - 16.00
Perfect 107 *Those Creeping Sneaking Blues* ..... 12.00 - 16.00

FRANKIE AND JOHNNIE ORCHESTRA:
Bluebird 6470 *Swing Fever* .... 8.00 - 12.00
6499 *Stompin'* .... 8.00 - 12.00
6564 *I'm Looking For Someone To Love* ..... 8.00 - 12.00
6760 *Frankie And Johnnie Swing* .... 8.00 - 12.00

FRANKIE FRANKO & HIS LOUISIANIANS:
Melotone 12009 *Somebody Stole My Gal* ...... 30.00 - 40.00

EDDIE FRAZIER AND HIS PLANTATION ORCHESTRA:
Sunset 1100 *Cheatin' On Me* .... 15.00 - 25.00

JAKE FRAZIER:
Ajax 17117 *Jake's Weary Blues* .... 15.00 - 25.00

BUD FREEMAN & HIS ORCHESTRA:
Okeh 41168 *Craze-O-Logy* .... 15.00 - 25.00

JAY/JERRY FREEMAN AND HIS ORCHESTRA:
Titles, issued contemporaneously on Banner, Melotone, Oriole, Perfect, Romeo: *Alabama Barbecue; Copper-Colored Gal; Getting Away With Murder; I'm At The Mercy Of Love; Mr. Ghost Goes To Town; A Moment In The Dark; My Newest Excitement; That's What You Mean To Me* .... 4.00 - 7.00
Additional titles issued on Banner, Mellotone, Oriole, Perfect, Romeo: *Sugar Foot Stomp; Night Ride* 5.00 - 8.00
Bluebird 5231, 5232, 5233 .... 4.00 - 7.00
Variety 511 *Poor Robinson Crusoe* .... 7.00 - 10.00

FRENCH'S STRING BAND:
Columbia 14387-D *Sunshine Special* .... 30.00 - 50.00

FRIARS SOCIETY ORCHESTRA:
Gennett 4966 *Farewell Blues* .... 15.00 - 25.00
4967 *Bugle Call Blues* .... 15.00 - 25.00
4968 *Panama* .... 15.00 - 20.00
5009 *Eccentric* .... 15.00 - 20.00

BEN FRIEDMAN'S PARAMOUNT HOTEL ORCHESTRA:
Timely Tunes 1580 *The One-Man Band* .... 10.00 - 15.00
1583 *Some Of These Days* .... 10.00 - 15.00
1584 *Swamp Ghosts* .... 10.00 - 15.00
1588 *Roll On Mississippi, Roll On* .... 25.00 - 40.00

FRISCO SYNCOPATORS:
Claxtonola 40244 *Buddy's Habits* .... 7.00 - 12.00
40264 *Arkansas Mule* .... 7.00 - 12.00
Puritan 11244 *Buddy's Habits* .... 7.00 - 12.00
11271 *Sweet Harry* .... 7.00 - 12.00
11291 *Forgetful Blues* .... 7.00 - 12.00
Triangle 11384 *I Can't Get The One I Want* .... 7.00 - 12.00

FRANK FROEBA & HIS SWING BAND:
Columbia 3110-D *The Music Goes 'Round and Around* .... 9.00 - 12.00
3131-D *Just To Be In Caroline* .... 10.00 - 15.00
3151-D *Organ Grinder's Swing* .... 12.00 - 16.00
3152-D *It All Begins And Ends With You* .... 12.00 - 16.00

(CHARLIE) FRY & HIS MILLION DOLLAR PIER ORCHESTRA; FRY'S MILLION-DOLLAR PIER ORCHESTRA:
Edison 51406, 51416, 51435, 51574 .... 5.00 - 10.00

Pathe-Actuelle 036122 *Where The Dreamy Wabash Flows* .... 7.00 - 10.00
Perfect 14303 *Where The Dreamy Wabash Flows* 7.00 - 10.00

CHARLES FULCHER & HIS ORCHESTRA; FULCHER'S DANCE TRIO:
Columbia 316-D *The Georgia Stomp* .... 8.00 - 12.00
551-D *My Pretty Girl* .... 7.00 - 10.00
726-D *Blue Georgia Moon* .... 7.00 - 10.00
1267-D *After That* .... 7.00 - 10.00
1706-D *Hey! Hey!* .... 8.00 - 12.00
1734-D *Atlanta Gal* .... 7.00 - 10.00
Okeh 4889 *The Eskimo Song* .... 10.00 - 15.00

BOB FULLER:
Ajax 17088 *Crossword Puzzle Blues* .... 10.00 - 15.00
17091 *Spread Yo' Stuff* .... 10.00 - 15.00
17117 *Growin' Old Blues* .... 15.00 - 25.00
Brunswick 7006 *I Ain't Got Nobody* .... 10.00 - 15.00
Banner, Columbia, Diva, Domino, Harmony, Velvet Tone .... 5.00 - 8.00

SLIM GAILLARD AND HIS FLAT FOOT FLOOGIE BOYS:
Okeh, most issues .... 3.00 - 5.00
Vocalion, most issues .... 3.00 - 7.00

ALBERT GALE AND HIS ORCHESTRA:
Vocalion 03514 *Horses and Numbers* .... 15.00 - 20.00

GALVESTON SERENADERS:
Champion 15266 *Twin Blues* .... 30.00 - 40.00
15285 *Monte Carlo Joys* .... 30.00 - 40.00

JAY GARBER & HIS (GREATER COLUMBIA RECORDING) ORCHESTRA:
Brunswick, most issues .... 2.00 - 5.00
Columbia 1306-D *Since My Best Gal Turned Me Down* .... 5.00 - 8.00
1334-D *Back In Your Own Back Yard* .... 7.00 - 10.00
1372-D *She's a Great, Great Girl* .... 5.00 - 8.00
1615-D *Louisiana* .... 7.00 - 10.00
1642-D *Tin Ear* .... 5.00 - 8.00
1823-D *'Way Down Yonder in New Orleans* .. 5.00 - 8.00
2115-D *Puttin' On The Ritz* .... 8.00 - 12.00
Columbia, most other issues .... 2.00 - 5.00
Decca, most issues .... 2.00 - 4.00
Okeh, most issues .... 2.00 - 3.00
Victor 20322 *How Could Red Riding Hood?* .... 15.00 - 25.00
24885 *Love and a Dime* .... 5.00 - 8.00
Victor, most other issues .... 3.00 - 6.00
Vocalion, most issues .... 2.00 - 4.00

LOUIS "KING" GARCIA AND HIS SWING BAND:
Bluebird 6302 *Love Is Like A Cigarette* .... 4.00 - 7.00)
6303 *Christopher Columbus* .... 5.00 - 8.00
6357 *Swing, Mr. Charlie* .... 6.00 - 10.00

FRED GARDNER'S TEXAS UNIVERSITY TROUBADOURS:
Okeh 41440 *Papa's Gone* .... 15.00 - 25.00
41458 *No Trumps* .... 15.00 - 25.00

JACK GARDNER'S ORCHESTRA:
Okeh 40245 *Ponjola* .... 7.00 - 10.00
40465 *Too Late Now* .... 7.00 - 10.00
40339 *Who'd A Thunk It?* .... 10.00 - 15.00
40495 *Hitch Up The Horses* .... 10.00 - 15.00
40501 *Ida, I Do* .... 10.00 - 15.00
40518 *Hot Aire* .... 15.00 - 20.00
40555 *Japp-a-Jazz* .... 10.00 - 15.00
40572 *You'll Never Know The Difference* ... 10.00 - 15.00

JUDY GARLAND:
Decca 848 *Stompin' At The Savoy* .... 7.00 - 10.00
1432 *All God's Chillun Got Rhythm* ...... 7.00 - 10.00
1463 *You Can't Have Everything* .... 7.00 - 10.00
1796 *Sleep, My Baby, Sleep* .... 5.00 - 8.00
Decca (blue label), most others .... 2.00 - 5.00

BLIND LEROY GARNETT:

Paramount 12879 *Louisiana Glide* .... 40.00 - 60.00

SID GARRY:
Melotone 12069 *At Last I'm Happy* .... 12.00 - 16.00

TOM GATES & HIS ORCHESTRA:
Champion 15305 *The Bucket's Got A Hole In It* ... 15.00 - 20.00
15307 *Wabash Blues* .... 15.00 - 20.00
Gennett 6184 *The Bucket's Got A Hole In It* ... 15.00 - 20.00
6198 *Wabash Blues* .... 15.00 - 20.00

HENRI GENDRON'S STRAND ROOF ORCHESTRA:
Banner 1490 *Prince of Wails* .... 10.00 - 15.00

GEORGIA COTTON PICKERS:
Diva 6064-G *Cotton Pickers' Shuffle* .... 15.00 - 20.00
Harmony 1090-H *Cotton Pickers' Shuffle* ..... 15.00 - 20.00
1127-H *Louisiana Bo Bo* .... 15.00 - 20.00

GEORGIA JUMPERS:
Columbia 14603-D *California Blues* .... 10.00 - 15.00
14620-D *The Big Feet Rag* .... 10.00 - 15.00

GEORGIA MELODIANS:
Edison 51336 *Wop Blues* .... 7.00 - 12.00
51338 *Wait'll You See My Gal* .... 7.00 - 12.00
51346 *Savannah* .... 7.00 - 12.00
51347 *Tea Pot Dome Blues* .... 7.00 - 12.00
51359 *How You Gonna Keep Kool?* .... 7.00 - 12.00
51378 *Why Did You Do It?* .... 7.00 - 12.00
51394 *Red Hot Mama* .... 7.00 - 12.00
51412 *San* .... 10.00 - 15.00
51419 *Everybody Loves My Baby* .... 7.00 - 12.00
51420 *Do Wacka Doo* .... 8.00 - 12.00
51425 *I'm Satisfied Beside That Sweetie O'Mine* 7.00 - 12.00
51437 *I'm Bound For Tennessee* .... 10.00 - 15.00
51438 *My Mammy's Blues* .... 10.00 - 15.00
51588 *Give Us The Charleston* .... 10.00 - 15.00
51598 *She's Drivin' Me Wild* .... 10.00 - 15.00
51678 *Charleston Ball* .... 10.00 - 15.00
51730 *Rhythm Of The Day* .... 10.00 - 15.00

THE GEORGIANS:
Columbia .... 4.00 - 7.00

GEORGIA STRUTTERS:
Harmony 231-H *Georgia Grind* .... 10.00 - 15.00
311-H *Original Black Bottom Dance* ...... 10.00 - 15.00
468-H *It's Right Here For You* .... 15.00 - 25.00

GEORGIA WASHBOARD STOMPERS:
Bluebird 5027 *Wake 'Em Up* .... 8.00 - 12.00
5088 *Happy As The Day Is Long* .... 8.00 - 12.00
5089 *My Pretty Girl* .... 8.00 - 12.00
5092 *Bug A-Boo* .... 8.00 - 12.00
5127 *Dinah* .... 8.00 - 12.00
Decca 7002 *Everybody Loves My Baby* .... 8.00 - 12.00
7004 *I Can't Dance (I Got Ants In My Pants)* 8.00 - 12.00
7005 *Limehouse Blues* .... 8.00 - 12.00
7006 *After You've Gone* .... 8.00 - 12.00
7094 *You're An Angel* .... 8.00 - 12.00
7095 *Lulu's Back In Town* .... 8.00 - 12.00
7096 *Every Little Moment* .... 8.00 - 12.00
7097 *The Lady In Red* .... 8.00 - 12.00

GEORGE GERSHWIN:
Columbia 809-D, 812-D .... 5.00 - 8.00

TOM GERUNOVITCH & HIS ROOF GARDEN ORCHESTRA:
Brunswick 4050 *My Gal Sal* .... 7.00 - 10.00
4115, 4179, 4429, 4755 .... 4.00 - 6.00

THE GET-HAPPY BAND:
Columbia 14091-D *Harlem's Araby* .... 10.00 - 15.00
14099-D *Puddin' Pappa* .... 10.00 - 15.00

IRENE GIBBONS (& JAZZ BAND); IRENE GIBBONS & CLARENCE WILLIAMS' JAZZ BAND:
Columbia A-3834, A-3922 .... 4.00 - 7.00
14296-D *Longing* .... 5.00 - 8.00
14362-D *I'm Busy And You Can't Come In* .. 25.00 - 40.00

CLEO GIBSON:
Okeh 8700 *Nothing But Blues*.............. 15.00 - 20.00
GENE GIFFORD & HIS ORCHESTRA:
Victor 25041, 25065..................... 6.00 - 10.00
EMERSON GILL & HIS (BAMBOO GARDEN/ CASTLE OF PARIS) ORCHESTRA:
Columbia 1355-D, 1396-D, 1408-D.......... 3.00 - 6.00
　2416-D *I've Got Five Dollars*............ 5.00 - 8.00
Okeh 40065 *On Saturday Night*........... 8.00 - 12.00
　40066 *Days Of Yesterday*................ 7.00 - 10.00
　40313 *My Name Will Always Be Chickie*..... 8.00 - 12.00
　40315 *That's My Gal*.................... 8.00 - 12.00
　43069 *Birmingham Bound*................ 8.00 - 12.00
　40577 *It Must Be Love*.................. 8.00 - 12.00
　40590 *Say It Again*.................... 8.00 - 12.00
　45094 *The Rhythm Rag*.................. 10.00 - 15.00
　40615 *Lo-Nah*....................... 10.00 - 15.00
ART GILLHAM:
Columbia 2265-D, 2291-D, 2331-D .... 4.00 - 7.00
MAX GILMORE AND HIS BOYS:
Superior 2565 *I'll Sing A Love Song*.......... 8.00 - 12.00
JOSEPH GISH AND HIS ORACHESTRA;
New Flexo 311 *Milenberg Joys*.............
PERCY GLASCOE:
Columbia 14088-D *Stomp 'Em Down*......... 6.00 - 9.00
JACK GLASSNER AND HIS COLONIAL INN ORCHESTRA:
Okeh 40559 *Hot Coffee*.................. 5.00 - 8.00
　40644 *Tonight's My Night With Baby*....... 7.00 - 10.00
AL GOERING'S COLLEGIANS:
Vocalion 15337, 15374, 15409, 15495........ 4.00 - 7.00
LOU GOLD AND HIS ORCHESTRA:
Harmony 851-H *It's Tight Like That*....... 5.00 - 8.00
　950-H *He's A Good Man To Have Around*... 5.00 - 8.00
　1052-H *Piccolo Pete*................... 5.00 - 8.00
(Note: Same titles were also issued on Velvet Tone and Diva.)
Oriole 2007 *Nobody Cares If I'm Blue*........ 5.00 - 8.00
GOLDEN GATE (DANCE) ORCHESTRA:
　(See comments on CALIFORNIA RAMBLERS)
Banner 1999 *Magnolia*.................... 7.00 - 10.00
　6007 *Zulu Wail*...................... 7.00 - 10.00
　6048 *Beale Street Blues*............... 7.00 - 10.00
　6049 *Delirium*...................... 7.00 - 10.00
　6050 *Someday, Sweetheart*............. 7.00 - 10.00
　6082 *Jelly Roll Blues*................. 7.00 - 10.00
Broadway 11404 *Manda*................. 30.00 - 40.00
Domino 3971, 3973..................... 5.00 - 10.00
Edison 51387 *Sing A Little Song*.......... 7.00 - 10.00
　51388 *Lucille*..................... 7.00 - 10.00
　51443 *Southern Rose*................ 7.00 - 10.00
　51491 *Oh! Mabel*.................... 8.00 - 12.00
　51538 *On The Oregon Trail*............. 8.00 - 12.00
　51542 *Charleston*................... 8.00 - 12.00
　51551 *Everything Is Hosty-Totsy Now*....... 8.00 - 12.00
　51562 *Cheatin' On Me*................ 8.00 - 12.00
　51580 *Collegiate* .... 8.00 - 12.00
　51590 *Manhattan*................... 8.00 - 12.00
　51591 *Look Who's Here*................ 8.00 - 12.00
　51622 *Sweet Man*................... 8.00 - 12.00
　51633 *Freshie*..................... 8.00 - 12.00
　51661 *Five Foot Two, Eyes Of Blue*....... 8.00 - 12.00
　51725 *Here Comes Malinda*............ 10.00 - 15.00
　51737 *Shake*...................... 10.00 - 15.00
　51746 *Static Strut*.................. 10.00 - 15.00
　51762 *Hard-To-Get Gertie*............. 10.00 - 15.00
　51768 *I Wonder What's Become Of Joe?*..... 10.00 - 15.00
　51797 *To Be With You*................ 8.00 - 12.00
　51799 *When The Red Red Robin Comes Bob, Bob Bobbin' Along*.................... 8.00 - 12.00

51814 *Looking At The World Thru Rose Colored Glasses* .... 8.00 - 12.00
51820 *Up And At 'Em*................. 8.00 - 12.00
51822 *How Many Times?*............... 8.00 - 12.00
51824 *You Need Someone To Lvoe*........ 8.00 - 12.00
51851 *Lay Me Down To Sleep In Carolina*... 8.00 - 12.00
51860 *Pretty Cinderella*............... 8.00 - 12.00
51862 *All Alone Monday*............... 8.00 - 12.00
51897 *Stockholm Stomp*............... 15.00 - 20.00
51960 *Lonely Eyes*................... 8.00 - 12.00
51970 *Look At The World And Smile*....... 8.00 - 12.00
51975 *Crazy Words — Crazy Tune*......... 10.00 - 15.00
52014 *Yes She Do - No She Don't*......... 10.00 - 15.00
52043 *Beedle-Um Bo*................. 10.00 - 15.00
52075 *Miss Annabelle Lee*............. 10.00 - 15.00
52097 *You Don't Like It — Not Much*...... 10.00 - 15.00
52101 *Dawning*..................... 10.00 - 15.00
51205 *Blue River*................... 10.00 - 15.00
52109 *Clementine*................... 10.00 - 15.00
52162 *Tell Me, Little Daisy*............. 10.00 - 15.00
52164 *Make My Cot Where The Cot-Cot-Cotton Grows*......................... 10.00 - 15.00
52181 *The Pay Off*................... 15.00 - 20.00
52206 *Third Rail*.................... 15.00 - 20.00
52366 *Dream House*.................. 7.00 - 10.00
52390 *Vaniteaser*.................... 10.00 - 15.00
52399 *'Cause I Feel Low Down*........... 15.00 - 20.00
52416 *Get Out And Get Under The Moon*... 10.00 - 15.00
52437 *There's A Rainbow 'Round My Shoulder* 10.00 - 15.00
52444 *You're The Cream In My Coffee*...... 10.00 - 15.00
52477 *Along Came Sweetness*............ 10.00 - 15.00
52480 *To Know You Is To Love You*....... 10.00 - 15.00
52486 *Glad Rag Doll*.................. 10.00 - 15.00
52506 *Sweethearts On Parade*........... 10.00 - 15.00
52513 *Button Up Your Overcoat*.......... 15.00 - 20.00
52515 *I Loved You Then*............... 6.00 - 10.00
52535 *Guess Who?*................... 10.00 - 15.00
52542 *When I'm Walking With My Sweetness* 10.00 - 15.00
52547 *A Precious Little Thing Called Love*... 10.00 - 15.00
52550 *My Suppressed Desire*............. 10.00 - 15.00
52553 *The One I Love Loves Me*.......... 5.00 - 8.00
52561 *Avalon Town*................... 10.00 - 15.00
52562 *Lover Come Back*................ 10.00 - 15.00
52568 *That's Living*.................. 10.00 - 15.00
52580 *Honey* .... 10.00 - 15.00
52590 *Huggable, Kissable You*........... 10.00 - 15.00
Paramount 20349, 20352, 20353, 20380, 20389, 20394, 20395, 20405..................... 5.00 - 10.00
Pathe-Actuelle 036121, 036128, 036130, 036167, 036260, 036266, 36304, 36307, 36315, 36318, 36319, 36361, 36441, 36497, 36509, 36540, 36543, 36554, 36590, 36613, 36650, 36656, 36693, 36707, 36716.................. 5.00 - 10.00
Pathe-Actelle 36724 *For My Baby*.......... 40.00 - 60.00
Perfect 14302, 14309, 14311, 15348, 14386, 14412, 14416, 14441, 14447, 14457, 14485, 14488, 14496, 14499, 14500, 14542, 14622, 14678, 14690, 14721, 14724, 14735, 14771, 14794, 14831, 14834, 14874, 14888, 14897.............. 5.00 - 10.00
Perfect 14905 *For My Baby*............... 40.00 - 60.00
Puritan 11352, 11353, 11380, 11389, 11394, 11395, 11405............................ 5.00 - 8.00
Regal 8334, 8377, 8413................... 7.00 - 10.00
Triangle 11462......................... 5.00 - 8.00
GOLDEN GATE SERENADERS:
Gennett 6487 *On! Baby*................ 8.00 - 12.00
　6488 *He's Worth His Weight In Gold*........ 8.00 - 12.00
ERNIE GOLDEN & HIS HOTEL McALPIN ORCHESTRA:
Banner 6226 *Doin' The Raccoon*............ 5.00 - 8.00
　6227 *Come On, Baby*.................. 5.00 - 8.00

6271 *Makin' Whoopee*	5.00 -	8.00
Brunswick 2999, 3302, 3359	3.00 -	6.00
Cameo 0358 *Dirty Hot*	7.00 -	10.00
Edison 51658 *Sleepy Time Gal*	7.00 -	10.00
51944 *Oriental Moonlight*	10.00 -	15.00
52109 *The Varsity Drag*	10.00 -	15.00

JEAN GOLDKETTE AND HIS ORCHESTRA:

Victor 19308, 19313, 19327, 19345, 19600, 19664, 19947, 19965, 19975, 20031, 20033, 20256, 20257, 20268	3.00 -	6.00
Victor 20270 *Idolizing*	5.00 -	8.00
20273 *Sunday*	5.00 -	8.00
20300 *Just One More Kiss*	7.00 -	10.00
20466 *I'm Looking Over a Four Leaf Clover*	7.00 -	10.00
20469 *Proud of a Baby Like You*	15.00 -	20.00
20471 *Hoosier Sweetheart*	5.00 -	8.00
20472 *Look At The World and Smile*	5.00 -	8.00
20491 *A Lane in Spain*	5.00 -	8.00
20493 *Sunny Disposish*	10.00 -	15.00
20588 *My Pretty Girl*	7.00 -	10.00
20675 *I'm Gonna Meet My Sweetie Now*	5.00 -	8.00
20926 *Slow River*	5.00 -	8.00
20961 *Blue River*	5.00 -	8.00
20994 *Clementine*	5.00 -	8.00
Victor 21150, 21166, 21527, 21565	4.00 -	7.00
Victor 21590 *That's Just My Way Of Forgetting You*	5.00 -	8.00
21800 *Sweethearts On Parade*	5.00 -	8.00
21804 *Withered Roses*	5.00 -	8.00
21805 *My Blackbirds Are Bluebirds Now*	7.00 -	10.00
Victor 21853, 21871, 21889, 22027, 22123	4.00 -	7.00
Victor 22077 *Birmingham Bertha*	7.00 -	10.00
25354 *Slow River*	5.00 -	8.00
Victor (unnumbered) *In My Merry Oldsmobile*		*100 up*

(Note: Above is a special pressing, having the tune rendered as a fox-trot on one side, as a waltz on the other.)

BENNY GOODMAN: BENNY (BENNIE) GOODMAN'S BOYS (WITH JIM AND GLENN); BENNY GOODMAN AND HIS (MUSIC HALL) ORCHESTRA:

Brunswick 3975 *Shirt Tail Stomp*	10.00 -	15.00
4013 *Jungle Blues*	10.00 -	15.00
4968 *After A While*	15.00 -	20.00
7644 *Bugle Call Rag*	4.00 -	6.00
Capitol, most issues	2.00 -	4.00
Columbia 2542-D *Not That I Care*	15.00 -	25.00
2835-D *Ain'tcha Glad?*	15.00 -	25.00
2845-D *Dr. Heckle and Mr. Jibe*	15.00 -	25.00
2856-D *Your Mother's Son-in-Law*	15.00 -	25.00
2687-D *Riffin' The Scotch*	15.00 -	25.00
2871-D *Love Me Or Leave Me*	15.00 -	25.00
2892-D *Junk Man*	15.00 -	25.00
2927-D *Breakfast Ball*	15.00 -	25.00
2947-D *Take My Word*	15.00 -	15.00
2958-D *Bugle Call Rag*	12.00 -	16.00
2988-D *Like A Bolt From The Blue*	15.00 -	20.00
3003-D *Blue Moon*	15.00 -	20.00
3011-D *Music Hall Rag*	15.00 -	20.00
3015-D *Night Wind*	15.00 -	20.00
3018-D *Singing A Happy Song*	15.00 -	20.00
3022-D *Down Home Rag*	15.00 -	20.00
Columbia 35201, 35210, 35211, 35230, 35241, 35254, 35289, 35308, 35313, 35331, 35374, 35391, 35396, 35420, 35461, 35472, 35487	4.00 -	7.00
Columbia, most others on red label	2.00 -	5.00
Melotone 12023 *He's Not Worth Your Tears*	15.00 -	20.00
12024 *Overnight*	15.00 -	20.00
12079 *Falling In Love Again*	15.00 -	20.00
12100 *99 Out Of A Hundred Wanna Be Loved*	15.00 -	20.00
12120 *We Can Live On Love*	15.00 -	20.00
12138 *I Wanna Be Around My Baby All The Time*	15.00 -	20.00

12149 *It Looks Like Love*	15.00 -	20.00
12205 *Slow But Sure*	15.00 -	20.00
12208 *Pardon Me, Pretty Baby*	15.00 -	20.00
Victor 25009 *Hunkadola*	5.00 -	8.00
25011 *Hooray For Love*	5.00 -	8.00
25021 *Restless*	5.00 -	8.00
25024 *Japanese Sandman*	5.00 -	8.00
25081 *Ballad In Blue*	6.00 -	10.00
25090 *King Porter*	4.00 -	7.00
Victor 25115, 25136, 25145	4.00 -	6.00
Victor 25193 *No Other One*	5.00 -	8.00
25195 *Eeeny Meeny Miney Mo*	5.00 -	8.00
Victor 25215, 25245, 25247, 25258	4.00 -	6.00
Victor 25263 *Madhouse*	5.00 -	8.00
Victor 25279, 25290, 25316, 25320, 25329, 25333	4.00 -	6.00
Victor 25340 *Sing Me A Swing Song*	5.00 -	8.00
25345, *Nobody's Sweetheart*	4.00 -	6.00
25350 House Hop	5.00 -	8.00
Victor 25351, 25355, 25363, 25387, 25391, 25398, 25406, 25411, 25434, 25445	3.00 -	6.00
25461, *Goodnight My Love* (vocal Ella Fitzgerald) /*Take Another Guess* (vocal, Ella Fitzgerald)	15.00 -	20.00
25461 *Goodnight My Love* (vocal, Frances Hunt) /*Tain't No Use*	8.00 -	12.00
25469 *Did You Mean It?*/*Tain't No Use*	15.00 -	20.00
Victor 25467, 25473, 25481, 25497	3.00 -	6.00
Victor 25486 *Smoke Dreams*	5.00 -	8.00
25492 *Swing Low, Sweet Chariot*	5.00 -	8.00
Victor 25500, 25505, 25510, 25521, 25529, 25531	3.00 -	6.00
Victor 25621, 25627, 25634	4.00 -	7.00
Victor 25644, 26660, 25678, 25683, 25705, 25708, 25711, 25717, 25720, 25725, 25726, 25727, 25751	3.00 -	6.00

(Note: The foregoing, up to number 25683, if original pressings, are of the "scroll" label or scroll label "Swing Classic" label.)

Victor 25808 *Pop-Corn Man/oooh-OO-BOOM*	250.00	up

(Note: The rare coupling above should be distinguished from the common issue, below, which does not have the song "Pop-Corn Man".)

Victor 25808 *Always and Always/oooOO-Oh-Boom!*	4.00 -	6.00
Victor 25814, 25822, 25827	3.00 -	5.00
Victor 25840 *Feelin' High and Happy*	5.00 -	8.00
35846 *It's The Dreamer In Me*	5.00 -	8.00
25867 *Don't Wake Up My Heart*	5.00 -	8.00
Victor 25871, 25880	3.00 -	6.00
Victor 25878 *What Goes On Here In My Heart*	5.00 -	8.00
26000 *I've Got a Date With A Dream*	5.00 -	8.00
26021 *When I Go A Dreamin'*	5.00 -	8.00
Victor 26044, 26060	3.00 -	5.00
Victor 26053 *You're Lovely, Madame*	5.00 -	8.00
26071 *I Have Eyes*	5.00 -	8.00
26082 *I Had To Do It*	5.00 -	8.00
Victor 26087, 26090, 26095	3.00 -	5.00
Victor 26099 *Sing For Your Supper*	5.00 -	8.00
26107 *Smoke House Rhythm*	4.00 -	7.00
26110 *I Must See Annie Tonight*	4.00 -	7.00
Victor 26125, 25130, 26134, 26139, 26166, 26170, 26230, 26240, 26263	3.00 -	5.00
Victor 26159 *Good For Nothin' But Love*	5.00 -	8.00
26175 *Cuckoo in the Clock*	5.00 -	8.00
26187 *Estrellita*	4.00 -	7.00
26211 *The Lady's In Love With You*	4.00 -	7.00
Vocalion 15656 *A Jazz Holiday*	35.00 -	50.00
Vocalion 15795 *That's A Plenty*	40.00 -	50.00

LILLIAN GOODNER:

Ajax 17018 *Ramblin' Blues*	10.00 -	15.00
17020 *Chicago Blues*	10.00 -	15.00
17028 *Four-Flushin' Papa*	10.00 -	15.00

GOODY'S GOOD TIMERS:

Pathe-Actuelle 36902 *Diga Diga Doo*	10.00 -	15.00

36924 *'Cause I'm In Love*..............	10.00 -	15.00
Perfect 15083 *Diga Diga Doo*............	10.00 -	15.00
15105 *'Cause I'm In Love*..............	10.00 -	15.00

THE GOOFUS FIVE (AND THEIR ORCHESTRA):

Okeh 40179 *Them Ramblin' Blues*............	5.00 -	8.00
40208 *Go, Emmaline*...................	5.00 -	8.00
40233 *Go 'Long, Mule*.................	5.00 -	8.00
40244 *Everybody Loves My Baby*......	7.00 -	10.00
40261 *Oh! Mabel*..................	5.00 -	8.00
40292 *Alabamy Bound*.................	7.00 -	10.00
40314 *Hot Tamale Molly*............	7.00 -	10.00
40340 *I Had Someone Else Before I Had You*.	7.00 -	10.00
40423 *Yes, Sir! That's My Baby*.......	7.00 -	10.00
40442 *I'm Gonna Charleston Back To Charleston*	8.00 -	12.00
40464 *Loud Speakin' Papa*............	7.00 -	10.00
40500 *Clap Hands! Here Comes Charlie*......	7.00 -	10.00
40534 *That Certain Party*.............	7.00 -	10.00
40624 *I Wonder What's Become of Joe?*....	7.00 -	10.00
40644 *You Gotta Know How To Love*......	7.00 -	10.00
40649 *Where'd You Get Those Eyes*......	7.00 -	10.00
40661 *Mary Lou*....................	7.00 -	10.00
46087 *Crazy Quilt*....................	7.00 -	10.00
40690 *Heebie Jeebies*.................	7.00 -	10.00
40739 *I've Got The Girl*...............	8.00 -	12.00
40767 *Farewell Blues*.................	8.00 -	12.00
40809 *Muddy Water*..................	7.00 -	10.00
40817 *Arkansas Blues*.................	8.00 -	12.00
40821 *The Whisper Song*.............	7.00 -	10.00
40841 *Vo-Do-Do-De-O Blues*..........	8.00 -	12.00
40886 *Clementine*..................	8.00 -	12.00
40997 *Nothin' Does-Does Like To Used To Do-Do-Do*.	8.00 -	12.00
41069 *Ready For The River*..........	8.00 -	12.00
41110 *Right Or Wrong*..............	6.00 -	10.00
41113 *Vaniteaser*....................	6.00 -	10.00
41138 *My Blackbirds Are Bluebirds Now*....	7.00 -	10.00
41169 *Sweetheart of All My Dreams*.......	7.00 -	10.00
41177 *Rambling Wreck From Georgia Tech*..	7.00 -	10.00
41220 *Deep Night*..................	8.00 -	12.00

EDDIE GORDON'S BAND:

Odeon ONY-36008 *March Of The Hoodlums*...	12.00 -	18.00
ONY-41153 *Wild Oat Joe*................	12.00 -	18.00
ONY-41204 *No One Else But You*.......	12.00 -	18.00
ONY-41273 *Birmingham Bertha*........	12.00 -	18.00
Parlophone PNY-41320 *Chant Of The Jungle*...	12.00 -	18.00

RALPH GORDON & HIS ORCHESTRA:

Victor 26033, 26041	4.00 -	6.00

GRAY GORDON AND HIS TIC-TOC RHYTHM:

Bluebird, most issues..................	2.00 -	5.00
Victor, most issues..................	2.00 -	4.00

JIMMIE GORDON (AND HIS VIP VOP BAND):

Decca 7322, 7334, 7373, 7409, 7474, 7490, 7519, 7536, 7555, 7592, 7611, 7624, 7661, 7702, 7764, 7794	3.00 -	6.00

REX GORDON AND HIS ACES:

Champion 15701 *She's Got Great Ideas*........	15.00 -	20.00

ROSS GORMAN & HIS (EARL CARROLL) ORCHESTRA/FIRE EATERS/VIRGINIANS:

Columbia 435-D, 460-D, 495-D	3.00 -	5.00
Columbia 498-D *Rhythm of the Day*........	7.00 -	10.00
516-D *Sleepy Time Gal*...........	7.00 -	10.00
Columbia 563-D, 576-D, 615-D, 631-D..	3.00 -	6.00
Edison 51866 *Idolizing*..............	7.00 -	10.00
51896 *You're Burning Me Up*............	10.00 -	15.00
51905 *Come Day, Go Day*.............	10.00 -	15.00
51944 *High, High, High Up In The Hills*.....	10.00 -	15.00
Gennett 6057 *She Looks Like Helen Brown*....	10.00 -	15.00
6118 *Phantom Blues*..............	15.00 -	20.00
6132 *Pardon The Glove*.............	15.00 -	20.00

Harmony 322-H *Sidewalk Blues*..............	7.00 -	10.00
Harmony 350-H, 379-H..............	3.00 -	5.00
Harmony 372-H *She Looks Like Helen Brown*..	7.00 -	10.00
403-H *My Wife's In Europe Today*.........	7.00 -	10.00
427-H *Phantom Blues*..............	7.00 -	10.00
(Note: Harmony issues also appear on Diva, Velvet Tone)		

THE GOTHAM NIGHTINGALES:

Okeh 40291 *Keep Smiling at Trouble*..........	5.00 -	8.00
40679 *Bobadilla*..................	5.00 -	8.00
40686 *She Belongs To Me*.............	5.00 -	8.00

THE GOTHAM STOMPERS:

Variety 541 *Did Anyone Ever Tell You*.......	8.00 -	12.00
629 *My Honey's Lovin' Arms*.......	8.00 -	12.00

GOWAN'S RHAPSODY MAKERS:

Gennett 3408 *I'll Fly To Hawaii*..........	15.00 -	20.00
6039 *Sunny Hawaii*..............	15.00 -	20.00

PORTER GRAINGER:

Ajax 17039 *In Harlem's Araby*..........	20.00 -	30.00

GLEN GRAY & HIS CASA LOMA ORCHESTRA: (See also THE CASA LOMA ORCH.)

Decca 192 *I'm In Love*..................	7.00 -	10.00
193 *You're A Builder-Upper*.............	7.00 -	10.00
199 *Chinatown, My Chinatown*........	7.00 -	10.00
200 *Nagosaki*	7.00 -	10.00
286 *Stompin' Around*............	7.00 -	10.00
287 *Maybe I'm Wrong Again*........	7.00 -	10.00
298 *Two In A Dream*...............	7.00 -	10.00
312 *Blue Moon*..................	6.00 -	10.00
334 *You Took Advantage Of Me*..........	6.00 -	10.00
339 *In My Country That Means Love*.......	6.00 -	10.00
349 *The Night Is Young*............	6.00 -	10.00
352 *Fare Thee Well, Annabelle*.............	6.00 -	10.00
375 *Ain't It Just Too Bad?*.............	6.00 -	10.00
379 *Who's Sorry Now?*.............	6.00 -	10.00
386 *My Heart Is An Open Book*..........	6.00 -	10.00
387 *My Dance*..................	6.00 -	10.00
405 *You're Walking In My Sleep*........	6.00 -	10.00
430 *Once Upon A Midnight*.............	6.00 -	10.00
463 *Chant Of The Jungle*............	6.00 -	10.00
552 *Without A Word Of Warning*..........	6.00 -	10.00
553 *The Devis Is Afraid Of Music*........	6.00 -	10.00
603 *Yankee Doddle Never Went To Town*...	6.00 -	10.00
652 *With All My Heart*.............	6.00 -	10.00
688 *Moonburn*..................	6.00 -	10.00
696 *I'd Rather Lead A Band*............	6.00 -	10.00
869 *Bugle Call Rag*.............	5.00 -	8.00
986 *Shades Of Hades*.............	5.00 -	8.00
1048 *Jungle Jitters*..............	5.00 -	8.00
1126 *You're Laughing At Me*...........	5.00 -	8.00
1129 *Swing High, Swing Low*..........	5.00 -	8.00
1158 *Too Marvelous For Words*..........	5.00 -	8.00
1159 *A Study In Brown*.................	5.00 -	8.00
1179 *I'd Be A Fool Again*...............	5.00 -	8.00
1180 *Was It Rain?*.................	5.00 -	8.00
1211 *Never In A Million Years*........	5.00 -	8.00
1246 *One, Two Three Little Hours*.......	5.00 -	8.00
1312 *Zig-Zag*.....................	5.00 -	8.00
1368 *Yours And Mine*.............	5.00 -	8.00
1396 *Swing Low, Sweet Chariot*..........	5.00 -	8.00
1412 *Casa Loma Stomp*.............	5.00 -	8.00
1473 *Smoke Rings*...............	5.00 -	8.00
Decca 1519, 1520, 1530, 1540, 1541, 1575, 1596, 1607, 1608, 1634, 1650, 1672, 1679, 1725, 1755, 1783, 1864	4.00 -	7.00
Decca (higher numbers)..............	3.00 -	6.00
Victor L-16023 *Dardanella* and 2 other tunes...	15.00 -	20.00
(above is long-playing "Program Transcription")		
Victor 24222 *Hey! Young Fella*..............	7.00 -	10.00
24224 *Sittin' By The Fire With You*.........	8.00 -	12.00

24254 *Black-Eyed Susan Brown*	8.00 -	12.00
24256 *Casa Loma Stomp*	8.00 -	12.00

KITTY GRAY & HER WAMPUS CATS:

Vocalion 03869 *Swingology*	8.00 -	12.00
03992 *I Can't Dance (I Got Ants In My Pants)*	8.00 -	12.00
04014 *Weeping Willow Swing*	8.00 -	12.00
04121 *My Baby's Ways*	8.00 -	12.00
04629 *I'm Yours To Command*	8.00 -	12.00

RUSSELL GRAY & HIS ORCHESTRA:

Okeh 40486 *Ain't That A Grand And Glorious Feeling*	7.00 -	10.00
40938 *Sugar*	10.00 -	15.00

GREEN BROTHERS' NOVELTY BAND:

Edison 51321 *New Orleans Wiggle*	5.00 -	8.00
51425 *Some Other Day*	7.00 -	12.00
51437 *Back Where the Daffodils Grow*	10.00 -	15.00
51493 *Those Panama Mamas*	5.00 -	8.00
51497 *Fascinating Rhythm*	5.00 -	8.00
51876 *That's What God Made Mothers For*	7.00 -	10.00
52072 *Say It With a Red, Red Rose*	8.00 -	12.00
52410 *I Wanna Be Loved By You*	7.00 -	10.00

GREEN PARROT INN ORCHESTRA:

Champion 15322 *At Sundown*	8.00 -	15.00
15326 *One O'Clock Baby*	7.00 -	10.00
15345 *Is It Possible?*	7.00 -	10.00

BOB GREEN'S DANCE ORCHESTRA:

Oriole 722 *Tuck In Kentucky and Smile*	5.00 -	8.00
1313 *Ready For The River*	8.00 -	12.00
1580 *Why Can't It Be Me?*	5.00 -	8.00
1598 *Sure Enough Blues*	5.00 -	8.00

JOHNNY GREEN AND HIS ORCHESTRA:

Brunswick 6797 *Live and Love Tonight*	10.00 -	15.00
6855 *Easy Come, Easy Go*	10.00 -	15.00
Brunswick 7441, 7455, 7521, 7522, 7661, 7662, 7716	3.00 -	5.00
Brunswick 7487 *Isn't This a Lovely Day?*	5.00 -	8.00
7497 *Fruitas*	5.00 -	8.00
Columbia 2940-D, 2943-D, 2959-D, 2999-D, 3002-D, 3022-D, 3024-D, 3028-D, 3029-D	4.00 -	8.00

GREENWICH VILLAGE ORCHESTRA:

Titles, issued contemporaneously on Broadway, Claxtonola, Harmograph, Paramount, Pennington, Puritan, Triangle: *House of David Blues; Ringside Blues*	10.00 -	15.00

SONNY GREER & THE D'C'ns / HIS MEMPHIS MEN:

Blu-Disc 1003 *Oh! How I Love My Darling*	125.00 -	250.00
Columbia 1868-D *Saturday Night Function*	10.00 -	15.00
2833-D *Saturday Night Function*	7.00 -	10.00

EARL GRESH AND HIS GANGPLANT ORCHESTRA; EARL GRESH'S ORCHESTRA:

Columbia 424-D, 469-D	4.00 -	7.00
672-D *Ace In The Hole*	7.00 -	10.00
Columbia 693-D, 841-D, 1031-D	4.00 -	7.00
Pathe-Actuelle 36636 *White Ghose Shivers*	7.00 -	10.00
Perfect 14818 *White Ghost Shivers*	7.00 -	10.00

JIMMIE GRIER & HIS (COCOANUT GROVE) ORCHESTRA:

Brunswick 6597, 7306, 7307, 7308, 7355, 7381, 7383,

7505, 7519	3.00 -	5.00
Brunswick 7528 *Bugle Call Rag*	5.00 -	8.00
Brunswick 7619, 7622, 7679, 7683, 7733, 7760, 7790, 7802, 7887, 7901, 7908	3.00 -	5.00
Decca 1474, 1475, 1486, 1497	3.00 -	6.00
Decca 1797, 1812, 1813	3.00 -	5.00
Victor 22970, 22971	3.00 -	6.00
Victor 24174 *Here Lies Love*	4.00 -	7.0
24175 *Second-Hand Heart*	5.00 -	8.00

GORDON GRIMES & HIS ORCHESTRA:

Champion 15290 *Yes She Do—No She Don't*	8.00 -	15.00
15293 *I'm Back In Love Again*	8.00 -	15.00
15322 *S-L-U-E Foot*	8.00 -	15.00
15456 *In The Sing-Song Sycamore Tree*	8.00 -	15.00
15495 *Oh! Baby*	8.00 -	15.00
15496 *Delores*	8.00 -	15.00

TOM GRISELLE AND HIS ORCHESTRA:

Gennett 3081 *Stop, You're Tickling Me*	8.00 -	12.00

FERDIE GROFE AND HIS ORCHESTRA:

Columbia 2851-D *Cinderella's Fella*	5.00 -	8.00
2858-D *Inka Dinka Doo*	5.00 -	8.00

WALTER GROSS:

Bluebird 10795, 10937	4.00 -	6.00

ELMER GROSSO AND HIS ORCHESTRA:

Champion 16154 *You're Driving Me Crazy*	7.00 -	10.00
16176 *Cheerful Little Earful*	7.00 -	10.00
Gennett 7184 *Sing, You Sinners*	7.00 -	10.00

FRANK GUARENTE AND HIS ORCHESTRA:

Harmony 787-H *Sweethearts on Parade*	5.00 -	8.00
830-H *When Polly Walks Through the Hollyhocks*	5.00 -	8.00

THE GULF COAST SEVEN:

Columbia A-3916 *Daybreak Blues*	8.00 -	12.00
A-3978 *Memphis, Tennessee*	8.00 -	12.00
14107-D *Santa Claus Blues*	10.00 -	15.00
14373-D *Daylight Savin' Blues*	10.00 -	15.00

GULF COAST TRIO:

Buddy 8041 *Grand Opera Blues*	15.00 -	25.00

JOE GUMIN AND HIS ORCHESTRA:

Broadway 1430 *Tie a Little String Around Your Finger*	7.00 -	10.00
Columbia 2571-D *I'll Think of You*	7.00 -	10.00

JIMMIE GUNN AND HIS ORCHESTRA:

Bluebird 6469 *My Blue Heaven*	7.00 -	10.00
6500 *I've Found a New Baby*	7.00 -	10.00
6508 *Slats Shuffle*	7.00 -	10.00
6578 *The Operator Special*	7.00 -	10.00

MICKEY GUY AND HIS ROSE-TREE CAFE ORCHESTRA; MICKEY GUY'S HOTTENTOTS:

Okeh 40462 *Rose-Tree Strut*	10.00 -	15.00
40588 *In Your Green Hat*	10.00 -	15.00
Pathe-Actuelle 36433 *Rhythm Rag*	7.00 -	10.00
36478 *Two-Ton Tessie*	7.00 -	10.00
Perfect 14614 *Philadelphia*	7.00 -	10.00
14659 *Two-Ton Tessie*	7.00 -	10.00

GUYON'S PARADISE ORCHESTRA:

Okeh 4732, 4737, 4742	3.00 -	5.00
Okeh 4862 *Louisville Lou*	5.00 -	8.00
Okeh 4866, 4999	5.00 -	8.00

BOBBY HACKETT AND HIS ORCHESTRA:

Okeh 4047, 4142, 4499, 4565, 4806, 4877, 5198, 5375, 5493, 5620	4.00 -	7.00
Vocalion 4047, 4152, 4499, 4565, 4806, 4877, 5198, 5375, 5493, 5620	4.00 -	7.00

(W. G.) HAENSCHEN'S (BANJO) ORCHESTRA SAINT LOUIS:

Personal Record 60781 *Country Club Melody*	10.00 -	20.00
M61068 *Honky Tonk*	10.00 -	20.00
M61070 *Maple Leaf Rag*	10.00 -	20.00
M61071 *Admiration*	10.00 -	20.00

(Note: Other records by this band, if they exist, would probably be of equal interest to collectors.)

CASS HAGAN AND HIS (HOTEL MANAGER/ PARK CENTRAL HOTEL) ORCHESTRA:

Columbia 966-D *Sometimes I'm Happy*	5.00 -	8.00
1033-D *Melancholy Charlie*	7.00 -	10.00
1089-D *Havana*	7.00 -	10.00
1114-D *The Varsity Drag*	7.00 -	10.00
1138-D *Manhattan Mary*	5.00 -	8.00
1176-D *My Lady*	4.00 -	6.00
1222-D *Dear, On a Night Like This*	4.00 -	6.00
1301-D *My Ohio Home*	7.00 -	10.00
1334-D *Golden Gate*	7.00 -	10.00
Edison 51959 *It All Depends On You*	10.00 -	15.00
52012 *Lily*	10.00 -	15.00

BILL HAID & HIS CUBS/THIEVES OF SLEEP:

Broadway 1187, 1188, 1200, 1201, 1205, 1206, 1207, 1211, 1217, 1220, 1229, 1235, 1237	6.00 -	10.00
Paramount 20628, 20630, 20643, 20644, 20646, 20647, 20648, 20652, 20658, 20660, 20661, 20676, 20678	6.00 -	10.00

HAITIAN ORCHESTRA:

Varsity 8360, 8363, 8364, 8399, 8405	4.00 -	5.00

HALFWAY HOUSE (DANCE) ORCHESTRA:

Columbia 476-D *Maple Leaf Rag*	12.00 -	16.00
541-D *New Orleans Shuffle*	12.00 -	16.00
681-D *Since You're Gone*	15.00 -	20.00
1041-D *Snookum*	15.00 -	20.00
1263-D *When I'm Blue*	15.00 -	20.00
1542-D *Tell Me Who*	15.00 -	20.00
Okeh 40318 *Pussy Cat Rag*	25.00 -	40.00

ADELAIDE HALL:

Brunswick 4031, 6362, 6376, 6518	7.00 -	10.00

FRED "SUGAR" HALL AND HIS (ROSELAND) ORCHESTRA/SUGAR BABIES; FRED HALL'S JAZZ BAND:

Banner 6264 *Missouri Squabble*	5.00 -	8.00
6269 *Louder and Funnier*	5.00 -	8.00
7248 *West End Blues*	7.00 -	10.00
Emerson 3007 *Say It Again*	7.00 -	10.00
3021 *After I Say I'm Sorry*	7.00 -	10.00
3082 *Here Comes Fatima*	7.00 -	10.00
3089 *The Spinx*	5.00 -	8.00
3094 *Tell Me Tonight*	7.00 -	10.00
3112 *The Birth of the Blues*	7.00 -	10.00
Harmony 13-H *Say Arabella*	5.00 -	8.00
Okeh 40410 *Look Who's Here!*	8.00 -	12.00
40437 *Dallas Blues*	8.00 -	12.00
40442 *She's Driving Me Wild*	8.00 -	12.00
40482 *Melancholy Lou*	8.00 -	12.00
40496 *I Ain't Got Nobody*	8.00 -	12.00
40891 *Is It Possible?*	5.00 -	8.00
40986 *Plenty Of Sunshine*	5.00 -	8.00
41008 *It's Balogney*	5.00 -	8.00
41026 *Waitin' For Katy*	5.00 -	8.00
41055 *Chilly Pom-Pom-Pee*	5.00 -	8.00
41112 *Butternut*	5.00 -	8.00
41123 *It Goes Like This*	5.00 -	8.00
41152 *Come On, Baby*	5.00 -	8.00
41183 *She Only Laughs At Me*	5.00 -	8.00
41239 *Here's That Party Now In Person*	5.00 -	8.00
41269 *It Ain't No Fault Of Mine*	5.00 -	8.00
41310 *Sophomore Prom*	5.00 -	8.00
41317 *Piccolo Pete*	8.00 -	12.00
41369 *Harmonica Harry*	8.00 -	12.00
41425 *When I Look To The West*	7.00 -	10.00

GEORGE HALL AND HIS (HOTEL TAFT) ORCHESTRA:

Bluebird, most issues	3.00 -	6.00
Okeh, most issues	3.00 -	5.00
Vocalion, most issues	3.00 -	5.00

MAL HALLETT AND HIS ORCHESTRA:

Titles, issued contemporaneously on Banner, Conqueror, Melotone, Oriole, Perfect, Romeo: *An Earful Of Music; Okay, Toots; When My Ship Comes In; Your Head On My Shoulder*	4.00 -	7.00
Columbia 917-D, 967-D, 996-D, 1287-D, 1341-D	3.00 -	6.00
Decca 1163 *Big Boy Blue*	5.00 -	8.00
Decca 1167, 1281, 1282, 1384	4.00 -	7.00
Edison (thin) 14080 *Boomerang*	15.00 -	20.00
Okeh 40573 *Whose Who Are You*	4.00 -	7.00
Pathe-Actuelle 36435, 36437	3.00 -	5.00
Perfect 14616, 14618	3.00 -	5.00
Vocalion 3235 *The Glory Of Love*	5.00 -	8.00
3236 *Swing Fever*	5.00 -	8.00
Vocalion 3268, 3278	3.00 -	5.00

PAUL HAMILTON AND HIS ORCHESTRA:

Vocalion 2662 *She Reminds Me Of You*	10.00 -	15.00
2708 *I've Had My Moments*	10.00 -	15.00
2721 *Easy Come, Easy Go*	10.00 -	15.00

FRED HAMM AND HIS ORCHESTRA:

Victor 19672 *Stomp Off, Let's Go*	5.00 -	8.00
Victor 19737, 19915, 20023	3.00 -	6.00

CHARLES W. HAMP:

Columbia 1816-D *Pretty Little Thing*	4.00 -	7.00
Okeh 41308 *Sweethearts' Holiday*	5.00 -	8.00

JOHNNY HAMP'S KENTUCKY SERENADERS; JOHNNY HAMP AND HIS ORCHESTRA:

Bluebird 6745, 6746, 6748	3.00 -	6.00
Victor 20101, 20105, 20241, 20829, 21323, 22650, 22722, 22727, 22730	3.00 -	6.00
Victor 22636 *All On Account Of Your Kisses*	5.00 -	8.00
Victor 24000 *Hummin' To Myself*	5.00 -	8.00

LIONEL HAMPTON & HIS ORCHESTRA:

Victor 25527, 25535, 25575, 25586, 25592, 25601, 25658, 25666, 25674, 25682, 25699	4.00 -	7.00
Victor, most other issues	3.00 -	5.00

HOGAN HANCOCK AND HIS ORCHESTRA:

Gennett 6413 *So Long*	8.00 -	12.00

AL HANDLER AND HIS (ALAMO CAFE) ORCHESTRA:

Columbia 713-D *Cryin For The Moon*	7.00 -	10.00
Columbia 883-D, 866-D, 1047-D, 1126-D	3.00 -	6.00

KATHERINE HANDY:

Paramount 12011 *Loveless Love*	15.00 -	20.00

(W. C.) HANDY'S MEMPHIS BLUES BAND: HANDY'S ORCHESTRA (OF MEMPHIS):

Banner 1036 *St. Louis Blues*	10.00 -	15.00
1053 *She's A Mean Job*	10.00 -	15.00
Black Swan 2053 *Yellow Dog Blues*	15.00 -	20.00
2054 *Muscle Shoals Blues*	15.00 -	20.00
Columbia A-2417, A-2481, A-2419, A-2420, A-2421	5.00 -	8.00
Lyratone 4211 *Beale Street Blues*	20.00 -	30.00
4212 *Yellow Dog Blues*	20.00 -	30.00
Okeh 4789 *Aunt Hagar's Blues*	15.00 -	20.00
4880 *Gulf Coast Blues*	15.00 -	20.00
4886 *Florida Blues*	15.00 -	20.00
4896 *Memphis Blues*	15.00 -	20.00
8046 *Louisville Blues*	15.00 -	20.00
8059 *Down-Hearted Blues*	15.00 -	20.00
8066 *Mama's Got The Blues*	15.00 -	20.00
8110 *Darktown Revelle*	15.00 -	20.00
Paramount 20098 *St. Louis Blues*	15.00 -	20.00
20012 *She's A Mean Job*	15.00 -	20.00
Varsity 8261, 8163	5.00 -	7.00

(MISS) ANNETTE HANSHAW (AND HER SIZZLIN' SYNCOPATORS):

Titles, issued contemporaneously on Banner, Conqueror, Melotone, Oriole, Perfect, Romeo, include: *Don't Blame Me; Give Me Liberty Or Give Me Love; Fit As A Fiddle; I Cover The Waterfront; Love Me Tonight; Moon Song; Say It Isn't So*	7.00 -	12.00

Clarion 5017-C *I Want A Good Man*	10.00 -	15.00
5037-C *The Way I Feel Today*........	10.00 -	15.00
5093-C *Yes Indeedy*	10.00 -	15.00
5101-C *Now I Know*................	10.00 -	15.00
5216-C *Crying To The Moon*...........	10.00 -	15.00
5217-C *I'll Lock You In My Arms*.........	10.00 -	15.00
5248-C *Walkin' My Baby Back Home*......	10.00 -	15.00
5249-C *Would You Like To Take A Walk?*...	10.00 -	15.00
5327-C *Moonlight Saving Time*...........	10.00 -	15.00
5390-C *I Don't Know Why*..............	10.00 -	15.00
Columbia 1769-D *Lover, Come Back To Me*....	7.00 -	10.00
1812-D *Big City Blues*..................	7.00 -	10.00
Diva 2915-G *The One in the World*........	5.00 -	8.00
2940-G *Am I Blue?*..................	5.00 -	8.00
2981-G *True Blue Lou*................	5.00 -	8.00
3012-G *Tip-Toe Thru The Tulips With Me*...	5.00 -	8.00
3066-G *Aren't We All?*................	7.00 -	10.00
3106-G *I'm Following You*............	5.00 -	8.00
3196-G *Nobody Cares If I'm Blue*........	7.00 -	10.00
Harmony 1324-H *Ho Hum!*...............	10.00 -	15.00
1376-H *Guilty*.......................	10.00 -	15.00
Okeh 41292 *Moanin' Low*...............	7.00 -	10.00
41327 *If I Can't Have You*...........	7.00 -	10.00
41351 *I Have To Have You*	7.00 -	10.00
41370 *When A Woman Loves A Man*......	10.00 -	15.00
41397 *With You*..................	7.00 -	10.00
Pathe-Actuelle 32207 *Black Bottom*	7.00 -	10.00
32211 *Six Feet Of Papa*..............	7.00 -	10.00
32213 *Don't Take That Black Bottom Away*..	7.00 -	10.00
Pathe-Actuelle 32217, 32222, 32226, 32230, 32240,		
32244, 32250, 32255, 32259, 32267, 32283 .	5.00 -	8.00
Pathe-Actuelle 32235 *Here Or There*.........	7.00 -	10.00
32275 *Under The Moon*..............	7.00 -	10.00
Pathe-Actuelle 32309, 32314, 32320, 32332....	5.00 -	8.00
Pathe-Actuelle 32293 *It Was Only A Sun Shower*	7.00 -	10.00
32340 *I Just Roll Along*..............	7.00 -	10.00
32348 *Lila*	7.00 -	10.00
32358 *Ready For The River*............	7.00 -	10.00
32365 *Get Out And Get Under The Moon*...	7.00 -	10.00
36664 *I'm Somebody's Somebody Now*.......	7.00 -	10.00
Perfect 12286 *Black Bottom*	7.00 -	10.00
12290 *Falling In Love With You*..........	7.00 -	10.00
12292 *Cherie, I Love You*............	7.00 -	10.00
Perfect 12296, 12301, 12305, 12309, 12319, 12323,		
12329, 12334, 12338, 12346, 12362......	5.00 -	8.00
Perfect 12314 *Here Or There*.............	7.00 -	10.00
12354 *Ain't That A Grand And Glorious Feeling*	7.00 -	10.00
12372 *Who's That Knocking At My Door?*...	7.00 -	10.00
12419 *I Just Roll Along*..............	7.00 -	10.00
12427 *'Cause I Feel Low Down*..........	7.00 -	10.00
12437 *Ready For The River*............	7.00 -	10.00
12444 *We Love It*..................	7.00 -	10.00
14845 *I Like What You Like*...........	7.00 -	10.00
Velvet Tone 1706-V *I Must Have That Man!*...	5.00 -	8.00
1734-V *That's Just My Way of Forgetting You*	5.00 -	8.00
1766-V *My Blackbirds Are Bluebirds Now*....	5.00 -	8.00
1785-V *My Inspiration Is You*...........	7.00 -	10.00
1792-V *I Wanna Be Loved By You*.......	7.00 -	10.00
1832-V *In a Great Big Way*.............	7.00 -	10.00
1859-V *Mean To Me*................	7.00 -	10.00
1910-V *My Sin*....................	5.00 -	8.00
1915-V *The One In The World*.........	5.00 -	8.00
1940-V *Daddy Won't You Please Come Home*	5.00 -	8.00
1981-V *Here We Are*................	5.00 -	8.00
2012-V *What Wouldn't I Do For That Man*..	5.00 -	8.00
2066-V *If I Had a Talking Picture of You*....	7.00 -	10.00
2106-V *Happy Days Are Here Again*.......	5.00 -	8.00
2155-V *I've Got "It"*	7.00 -	10.00
2178-V *My Future Just Passed*...........	7.00 -	10.00
2196-V *Nobody Cares If I'm Blue*..........	7.00 -	10.00
2274-V *Crying To The Moon*............	10.00 -	15.00
2289-V *Wasting My Love On You*.........	10.00 -	15.00

2314-V *Ever Since Time Began*............	10.00 -	15.00
2315-V *Would You Like To Talk a Walk*....	10.00 -	15.00
2393-V *Ho Hum!*......................	10.00 -	15.00
2454-V *Guilty*.......................	10.00 -	15.00
Vocalion 2735 *Let's Fall In Love*...........	10.00 -	15.00
THE HAPPY HARMONISTS:		
Gennett 5286 *Home Brew Blues*..........	20.00 -	30.00
5402 *Baptistown Crawl*...............	20.00 -	30.00
LIL HARDAWAY'S ORCHESTRA; DIAMOND		
LIL HARDAWAY & HER GEMS OF		
RHYTHM:		
Vocalion 1252 *Milenberg Joys*.................	50.00 -	70.00
Decca 7293, 7241, 7247, 7276................	4.00 -	6.00
(LATE PRESIDENT) WARREN G. HARDING:		
Victor 35718 *Address at Washington/Hoboken*..	5.00 -	8.00
GLENN HARDMAN & HIS HAMMOND		
FIVE:		
Columbia 35263, 25341................	5.00 -	10.00
Vocalion 4971 *Exactly Like You*............	7.00 -	10.00
MARLOW HARDY & HIS ALABAMIANS:		
Columbia 2034-D *Song of The Bayou*..........	8.00 -	12.00
BOB HARING AND HIS ORCHESTRA:		
Banner 32162 *Ho Hum!*.................	5.00 -	8.00
Brunswick 4281, 4283, 4472, 4545, 4608.....	3.00 -	6.00
Cameo 893, 1065, 8279.................	4.00 -	7.00
Oriole 2222 *When I Take My Sugar To Tea*....	5.00 -	8.00
Romeo 810 *How About Me?*..............	5.00 -	8.00
EARL HARLAN AND HIS ORCHESTRA:		
Banner 32806, 32924................	6.00 -	10.00
Melotone 12417, 12739, 12840, 12848, 12867...	6.00 -	10.00
Oriole 2798, 2812	5.00 -	8.00
Perfect 15789, 15852, 15862.........	6.00 -	10.00
Romeo 2095, 2171, 2185.............	6.00 -	10.00
THE HARLEM FOOTWARMERS:		
Columbia 14670-D *Sweet Chariot*.............	25.00 -	35.00
Okeh 8720 *Jungle Jamboree*.................	25.00 -	35.00
8746 *Syncopated Shuffle*...............	25.00 -	35.00
8760 *Lazy Duke*...................	25.00 -	35.00
8836 *Big House Blues*................	25.00 -	35.00
8840 *Mood Indigo*..................	25.00 -	35.00
8869 *Old Man Blues*.................	25.00 -	35.00
HARLEM HAMFATS:		
Decca 7182, 7196, 7205, 7206, 7218, 7229, 7245,		
7251, 7266, 7274, 7310, 7362, 7283, 7299, 7312,		
7326, 7339, 7351, 7367, 7382, 7395, 7406, 7439,		
7484	5.00 -	8.00
7454, 7466, 7530, 7761.............	5.00 -	8.00
Vocalion 04813, 04828, 04870, 04925, 05136, 05179,		
05233, 05287..........................	7.00 -	10.00
HARLEM HARLEY & HIS WASHBOARD		
BAND:		
Decca 7492, 7505.....................	6.00 -	10.00
HARLEM HOT CHOCOLATES:		
Hit of the Week 1045 *Sing, You Sinners*.......	10.00 -	15.00
1046 *St. James Infirmary*.................	10.00 -	15.00
HARLEM HOT SHOTS:		
Titles, issued contemporaneously on Banner,		
Melotone, Oriole, Perfect, Romeo: *Dust Off That*		
Old Pianna; Love Is Just Around The Corner;		
House Rent Party Day; March Winds And April		
Showers	7.00 -	12.00
Bluebird 5481 *Somebody Stole My Gal*........	5.00 -	8.00
Electradisk 1931 *St. Louis Blues*.............	15.00 -	20.00
Oriole 2284 *Black and Tan Fantasy*..........	8.00 -	12.00
HARLEM HOUSE RENT STOMPERS:		
Brunswick 7210 *Gravel Pit Stomp*............	25.00 -	35.00
HARLEM STOMPERS:		
Decca 7600, 7616..................	4.00 -	6.0
HARLEM TRIO:		
Herwin 93012 *St. Louis Blues*............	25.00 -	35.00
Okeh 8072, 8158, 8189, 40220.........	5.00 -	7.00

DAVE HARMAN & HIS ORCHESTRA:
Edison 51458, 51479, 51510.............. 5.00 -   7.00
HARMANIAC FIVE:
Paramount 20476 *Harmaniac Blues*......... 15.00 - 25.00
THE HARMONIANS:
Harmony 1308-H, 1310-H, 1311-H.......... 5.00 - 10.00
HARMONICA TIM:
Clarion 5194-C *Harmonica Blues*.............. 10.00 - 15.00
5195-C *Mean Low Blues*........... 10.00 - 15.00
Velvet Tone 7123-V *Mean Low Blues*........ 10.00 - 15.00
ACE HARRIS & HIS SUNSET ROYAL
  ORCHESTRA:
Voalion 3864, 3935.................... 5.00 -   8.00
HARRIS BROTHERS TEXANS:
Brunswick 4644 *Gut Bucket Shuffle*.......... 20.00 - 30.00
6047 *The South's Been A Mother To Me*.... 15.00 - 25.00
Vocalion 15747 *The Pay-Off*.......... 25.00 - 40.00
HELEN HARRIS ACCOMPANIED BY
  SKILLET DICK & HIS FRYING PANS:
Champion 15881 *Don't Say Goodbye*......... 35.00 - 50.00
PHIL HARRIS & HIS (COCOANUT GROVE)
  ORCHESTRA:
Columbia 2761-D, 2766-D............... 5.00 - 10.00
Vocalion 3447, 3466, 3488, 3533, 3565, 3583... 5.00 - 10.00
HARRY'S HAPPY FOUR:
Okeh 8229 *Swinging The Swing*.............. 15.00 - 20.00
8266 *Western Melody*.............. 15.00 - 20.00
HARRY'S RECKLESS FIVE:
Broadway 1355 *Wailing Blues*............. 40.00 - 60.00
BOB HARTMAN & HIS ORCHESTRA:
Broadway 1501 *Charley Cadet*............... 10.00 - 15.00
GEORGIA HARVEY:
Black Swan 14119 *Castaway*................. 12.00 - 15.00
14135 *That Sweet Something, Dear*... 12.00 - 15.00
COLEMAN HAWKINS AND HIS ALL-STAR
  OCTET/ORCHESTRA/RHYTHM:
Apollo 751, 752, 753................. 3.00 -   5.00
Bluebird 10253, 10477, 10523, 10693, 10770.... 3.00 -   5.00
Capitol, most issues.................. 3.00 -   5.00
Mercury, most issues.................. 2.00 -   4.00
Okeh 6284, 6347..................... 4.00 -   7.00
ERSKINE HAWKINS AND HIS 'BAMA
  STATE COLLEGIANS:
Bluebird, most issues................. 3.00 -   5.00
Victor, most issues................... 2.00 -   4.00
Vocalion 3280 *I Can't Escape From You*....... 7.00 - 10.00
3289 *It Was A Sad Night in Harlem*.......... 7.00 - 10.00
3318 *Big John's Special*................. 7.00 - 10.00
3336 *A Swingy Little Rhythm*.......... 7.00 - 10.00
3545 *Uproar Shout*................. 7.00 - 10.00
3567 *Dear Old Southland*................. 5.00 -   8.00
3668 *Red Cap*..................... 7.00 - 10.00
3689 *I'll See You In My Dreams*........ 7.00 - 10.00
4007 *Lost in the Shuffle*............... 7.00 - 10.00
4072 *Who's Sorry Now?*............. 7.00 - 10.00
BILL HAWLEY:
Victor 21383 *Delores*.................... 7.00 - 10.00
CLIFFORD HAYES' LOUISVILLE
  STOMPERS:
Victor 20955 *Blue Guitar Stomp*........... 8.00 - 12.00
21489 *Bare-Foot Stomp*.......... 40.00 - 60.00
21583 *Blue Harmony*.......... 15.00 - 20.00
21584 *The Petter's Stomp*.......... 15.00 - 20.00
23346 *Tenor Guitar Fiend*.......... 50.00 - 80.00
23407 *Automobile Blues*.......... 60.00 - 90.00
38011 *Clef Club Stomp*.......... 20.00 - 30.00
38022 *Old Chord's Stomp*.......... 20.00 - 30.00
38529 *You're Ticklin' Me*.......... 40.00 - 60.00
38557 *Hey! Am I Blue*.......... 40.00 - 60.00
EDGAR HAYES AND HIS ORCHESTRA;
EDGAR HAYES QUINTET:

Decca 1338 *Caravan* .... 5.00 -   8.00
1382 *Satan Takes a Holiday* .... 5.00 -   8.00
1416 *Stomping at the Renny*........... 5.00 -   8.00
1444 *So Rare*......................... 5.00 -   8.00
1509 *I Know Now*...................... 5.00 -   8.00
1527 *Queen Isabella*.................. 5.00 -   8.00
Decca 1665 *Swingin' in the Promised Land*..... 5.00 -   8.00
1684 *Blue Skies*..................... 5.00 -   8.00
1748 *Fugitive from a Harem*............ 5.00 -   8.00
1882 *Star Dust*...................... 3.00 -   5.00
1940 *Meet The Band*.................. 5.00 -   8.00
2048 *Shindig*....................... 5.00 -   8.00
2193 *Help Me*....................... 5.00 -   8.00
NAP HAYES:
Okeh 45231 *Somethin' Doin'.*............ 15.00 - 20.00
JOE HAYMES & HIS ORCHESTRA:
Banner, Bluebird, Conqueror, Melotone, Oriole,
  Perfect, Romeo, ... 3.00 -   6.00
Columbia 2704-D, 2716-D, 2739-D, 2781-D, 2784-D 8.00 - 12.00
Victor 24007, 24038, 24040, 24055, 24123, 24152,
  25353 .... 5.00 -   8.00
Vocalion 3307, 3335, 3369................ 6.00 -   8.00
LENNIE HAYTON'S BLUE FOUR:
Vocalion 15750 *Old-Fashioned Girl*......... 10.00 - 15.00
MONK HAZEL & HIS BIENVILLE ROOF
  ORCHESTRA:
Brunswick 4181 *High Society*............... 15.00 - 20.00
4182 *Git-Wit-It*.................... 15.00 - 20.00
LUCILLE HEGAMIN (AND HER BLUE
  FLAME SYNCOPATORS/JAZZ ARTISTS):
Arto 9045, 9053, 9058, 9063, 9068, 9069, 9074, 9105,
  9119, 9129, 9169 .... 5.00 - 10.00
Banner 1014, 1048, 1072, 1093; Bell......... 5.00 - 10.00
Black Swan 2032 *Arkansas Blues*............ 15.00 - 20.00
2049 *He May Be Your Man*............... 15.00 - 20.00
Cameo, most issues.................. 4.00 -   8.00
Columbia 14164-D *Senorita Mine*........... 7.00 - 10.00
Globe 7045, 7053, 7058, 7063, 7068, 7074, 7105,
  7119, 7129, 7169 .... 5.00 - 10.00
Claxtonola, Harmograph, Paramount......... 8.00 - 12.00
Famous, Muse, Puritan, Regal............... 5.00 -   8.00

HORACE HEIDT AND HIS MUSICAL
  KNIGHTS/ORCHESTRA:
Brunswick, most issues.................... 3.00 -   5.00
Columbia, most issues.................... 2.00 -   3.00
Victor 20608 *Hello Cutie!*.................. 5.00 -   8.00
21310 *Golden Gate*.................. 5.00 -   8.00
21311 *Get 'Em in a Rumble Seat*.......... 5.00 -   8.00
21312 *Every Evening*.................. 5.00 -   8.00
Victor 21335, 21568, 21956, 21957, 22195, 22222 3.00 -   6.00
BUD HELMS & HIS BAND:
Champion 15285 *Pee Wee Blues*............. 30.00 - 50.00
15364 *Hot Lips*...................... 15.00 - 20.00
BERTHA HENDERSON:
Paramount 12511 *Six Thirty Blues*.......... 30.00 - 45.00
Okeh 8265 *Jamboree Blues*.............. 15.00 - 20.00
CATHERINE HENDERSON:

Diva 6040-G *Keep It To Yourself*............ 8.00 - 12.00
  6050-G *What If We Do?*............ 8.00 - 12.00
Okeh 8240 *Four Thirty Blues*............ 6.00 - 10.00
Velvet Tone 7066-V *What If We Do?*............ 8.00 - 12.00
  7076-V *Keep It To Yourself*............ 8.00 - 12.00

EDMONIA HENDERSON:
Paramount 12084 *Black Man Blues*........... 20.00 - 30.00
  12095 *Brownskin Man*................. 20.00 - 30.00
  12097 *If You Sheik On Your Mama*....... 20.00 - 30.00
  12203 *Hateful Blues*.................. 20.00 - 30.00
  12239 *Jelly Roll Blues*.............. 40.00 - 50.00
Vocalion 1015 *Nobody Else Will Do*... 40.00 - 50.00
  1043 *Dead Man Blues*.............. 40.00 - 60.00

FLETCHER HENDERSON & HIS (CONNIE INN) ORCHESTRA/SAWIN'SIX; F.H. HENDERSON (JR.); HENDERSON'S (CLUB ALABAM'/DANCE) ORCHESTRA/HOT SIX/ SIX WONDER BOYS:
Titles, issued contemporaneously on Broadway, Claxtonola, Famous, Harmograph, Puritan, Triangle: *Beale Street Mama; Down Hearted Blues; My Sweetie Went Away; When You Walked Out* 10.00 - 15.00
Ajax 17016 *Bull Blues*............ 20.00 - 30.00
  17017 *Chattanooga*................. 20.00 - 30.00
  17022 *Mistreatin' Daddy*............ 20.00 - 30.00
  17023 *House Rent Ball*............ 20.00 - 30.00
  17029 *Just Blues*............ 20.00 - 30.00
  17030 *I'm Crazy Over You*........... 20.00 - 30.00
  17109 *Everybody Loves My Baby*......... 35.00 - 50.00
  17113 *Alabama Bound*............ 20.00 - 25.00
  17114 *I'll See You In My Dreams*...... 20.00 - 25.00
  17123 *Why Couldn't It Be Poor Little Me?*... 20.00 - 25.00
Apex 8194, 8205, 8218, 8230, 8233, 8280...... 7.00 - 10.00
  8300 *Everybody Loves My Baby*.......... 35.00 - 50.00
  8309 *Alabamy Bound*............ 10.00 - 15.00
  8311 *I'll See You In My Dreams*...... 10.00 - 15.00
  8316 *Why Couldn't It Be Poor Little Me?*.... 10.00 - 15.00
  8419 *Sleepy Time Gal*............ 10.00 - 15.00
Banner 1361, 1364, 1372, 1373, 1383, 1388, 1508, 1654............ 7.00 - 10.00
  1457, 1470, 1471, 1475, 1476............ 10.00 - 15.00
  1488, 1639, 6128............ 10.00 - 15.00
Black Swan 2022 *My Oriental Rose*......... 15.00 - 20.00
  2026 *The Unknown Blues*......... 20.00 - 30.00
  2076 *Love Days*......... 15.00 - 20.00
  2079 *Blue*......... 15.00 - 20.00
  2116 *Chime Blues*......... 30.00 - 40.00
  10072 *Love Days*......... 15.00 - 20.00
  10075 *Blue*......... 15.00 - 20.00
  10083 *Dumbell*......... 10.00 - 15.00
Bluebird 5682 *Hocus Pocus*......... 8.00 - 12.00
  6515, 10246............ 4.00 - 7.00
Brunswick 2592 *War Horse Mama*......... 7.00 - 10.00
  3406 *Clarinet Marmalade*......... 8.00 - 12.00
  3460 *Stockholm Stomp*......... 8.00 - 12.00
  3521 *Sensation*......... 8.00 - 12.00
  4119 *Hop Off*......... 10.00 - 15.00
Cameo 9033 *Old Black Jack Joe's Blues*......... 10.00 - 15.00
  9174 *Freeze and Melt*......... 15.00 - 20.00
  9175 *Raisin' The Roof*......... 15.00 - 20.00
Columbia 126-D *Somebody Stole My Gal*...... 10.00 - 15.00
  164-D *Muscle Shoals Blues*......... 10.00 - 15.00
  202-D *That's Georgia*......... 10.00 - 15.00
  209-D *He's The Hottest Man In Town*....... 10.00 - 15.00
  228-D *Manda*......... 15.00 - 20.00
  249-D *The Meanest Kind Of Blues*......... 15.00 - 20.00
  292-D *Play Me Slow*......... 15.00 - 20.00
  383-D *Money Blues*......... 15.00 - 20.00
  395-D *Sugar Foot Stomp*......... 15.00 - 20.00
  509-D *Carolina Stomp*......... 15.00 - 20.00
  532-D *Pensacola*......... 15.00 - 20.00

  654-D *The Stampede*.............. 15.00 - 20.00
  817-D *The Chant*.............. 15.00 - 20.00
  854-D *Sweet Thing*.............. 15.00 - 20.00
  970-D *Rocky Mountain Blues*.............. 15.00 - 20.00
  1002-D *P.D.Q. Blues*.............. 15.00 - 20.00
  1059-D *Whiteman Stomp*.............. 15.00 - 20.00
  1543-D *King Porter Stomp*.............. 15.00 - 20.00
  1913-D *Blazin*.............. 15.00 - 20.00
  2329-D *Somebody Loves Me*.............. 15.00 - 20.00
  2352-D *Keep A Song In Your Soul*.............. 15.00 - 20.00
  2414-D *Sweet And Hot*.............. 15.00 - 20.00
  2513-D *Clarinet Marmalade*.............. 15.00 - 20.00
  2559-D *Sugar*.............. 15.00 - 20.00
  2565-D *Singin' The Blues*.............. 15.00 - 20.00
  2586-D *My Gal Sal*.............. 15.00 - 20.00
  2615-D *Business in F*.............. 15.00 - 20.00
  2732-D *Honeysuckle Rose*.............. 15.00 - 20.00
  2825-D *Nagasaki*.............. 15.00 - 20.00
  A-3951 *Gulf Coast Blues*.............. 10.00 - 15.00
  A-3995 *Dicty Blues*.............. 10.00 - 15.00
  14392-D *Easy Money*.............. 15.00 - 20.00
Crown 3093 *After You've Gone*.............. 15.00 - 20.00
  3107 *Tiger Rag*.............. 15.00 - 20.00
Decca 157 *Limehouse Blues*.............. 8.00 - 12.00
  158 *Shanghai Shuffle*.............. 8.00 - 12.00
  213 *Tidal Wave*.............. 8.00 - 12.00
  214 *Big John's Special*.............. 8.00 - 12.00
  342 *Rug Cutter's Swing*.............. 8.00 - 12.00
  555 *Hotter Than 'Ell*.............. 8.00 - 12.00
Edison 51276 *Shake Your Feet*.............. 10.00 - 15.00
  51277 *Linger Awhile*.............. 10.00 - 15.00
Emerson 10713 *Mamma's Gonna Slow You Down* 15.00 - 20.00
  10714 *Steppin' Out*.............. 15.00 - 20.00
  10744 *Ghost Of The Blues*.............. 15.00 - 20.00
Gennett 3285 *When Spring Comes Peeping Through* 15.00 - 20.00
  3286 *Honeybunch*.............. 15.00 - 20.00
Lincoln 3062 *Old Black Joe's Blues*.............. 10.00 - 15.00
  3201 *Freeze and Melt*.............. 15.00 - 20.00
  3202 *Raisin'The Roof*.............. 15.00 - 20.00
Paramount 12143 *Chimes Blues*.............. 15.00 - 20.00
  12486 *Off To Buffalo*.............. 20.00 - 30.00
  20367 *Prince of Wails*.............. 30.00 - 40.00
Pathe-Actuelle 036027, 036042, 036069, 036083, 036084, 036090, 036213, 036214............. 6.00 - 12.00
  036156, 036266............. 10.00 - 12.00
  036157 *Shanghai Shuffle*............. 15.00 - 20.00
Perfect 14208, 14223, 14250, 14264, 14265, 14271 6.00 - 10.00
  14337, 14447............. 10.00 - 12.00
  14338 *Shanghai Shuffle*............. 15.00 - 20.00
Regal 8441, 8442, 9658, 9673, 9682, 9668, 9680, 9681, 9683, 9684, 9739, 9767, 9789, 9803, 9961 7.00 - 10.00
  8455, 9753, 9770, 9775............. 10.00 - 15.00
Romeo 837 *Old Black Joe's Blues*.............. 10.00 - 15.00
  976 *Freeze and Melt*.............. 15.00 - 20.00
  977 *Raisin' the Roof*.............. 15.00 - 20.00
Victor 20944 *St. Louis Shuffle*.............. 12.00 - 16.00
  22775 *Malinda's Wedding Day*.............. 12.00 - 16.00
  22786 *Oh, It Looks Like Rain*.............. 12.00 - 16.00
  22955 *Strangers*.............. 15.00 - 20.00
  24008 *Poor Old Joe*.............. 15.00 - 20.00
  24699 *Harlem Madness*.............. 10.00 - 15.00
  25298, 25317, 25334, 25339, 25373, 25375, 25379 5.00 - 8.00
Vocalion 1065 *Clarinet Marmalade*.............. 20.00 - 30.00
  1079 *Some Of These Days*.............. 50.00 - 75.00
  1092 *Fidgety Feet*.............. 20.00 - 30.00
  2527 *Yeah Man!*.............. 15.00 - 25.00
  2583 *Queer Notions*.............. 15.00 - 25.00
  3211 *Christopher Columbus*.............. 7.00 - 10.00
  3213 *Stealin' Apples*.............. 7.00 - 10.00
  3485 *Slumming On Park Avenue*.............. 7.00 - 10.00
  3487 *It's Wearin' Me Down*.............. 7.00 - 10.00

3511	Back In Your Own Backyard	7.00 -	10.00
3534	Stampede	7.00 -	10.00
3627	If You Should Ever Leave	7.00 -	10.00
3641	All God's Children Got Rhythm	7.00 -	10.00
3713	Worried Over You	7.00 -	10.00
3760	What's Your Story	7.00 -	10.00
3850	If It's The Last Thing I Do	7.00 -	10.00
4125	Sing You Sinners	7.00 -	10.00
4154	Saving Myself For You	5.00 -	8.00
4167	There's Rain In My Eyes	5.00 -	8.00
4180	Moten Stomp	7.00 -	10.00
14636	Gulf Coast Blues	8.00 -	12.00
14654	Dicty Blues	8.00 -	12.00
14726	Charleston Crazy	8.00 -	12.00
14740	Potomac River Blues	8.00 -	12.00
14759	Lots O'Mama	8.00 -	12.00
14788	Chicago Blues	8.00 -	12.00
14800	Tea Pot Dome Blues	8.00 -	12.00
14828	Strutter's Drag	8.00 -	12.00
14838	Do That Thing	8.00 -	12.00
14880	A New Kind Of Man	8.00 -	12.00
14892	Forsaken Blues	8.00 -	12.00
14926	Copenhagen	20.00 -	30.00
14935	Shanghai Shuffle	20.00 -	30.00
15030	Memphis Bound	30.00 -	40.00
15174	Hay Foot, Straw Foot	30.00 -	40.00
15204	Dinah	30.00 -	40.00
15205	Let Me Introduce You To My Rosie	30.00 -	40.00
15497	Clarinet Marmalade	15.00 -	25.00
15532	Stockholm Stomp	15.00 -	25.00

HORACE HENDERSON & HIS ORCHESTRA:
Okeh 5433, 5518, 5579, 5606, 5632, 5748, 5841, 5900, 5953, 5978, 6026 .... 4.00 - 6.00
Vocalion 5433, 5518, 5579, 5606 .... 4.00 - 6.00

HENNY HENDRICKSON'S LOUISVILLE SERENADERS:
Victor 22749 On The Beach With You .... 8.00 - 12.00
22750 Without That Gal! .... 8.00 - 12.00

TAL HENRY AND HIS NORTH CAROLINIANS/ORCHESTRA:
Bluebird 5364, 5365, 5366 .... 4.00 - 7.00
Victor 21404 Some Little Someone .... 5.00 - 8.00
21471 Lonesome .... 5.00 - 8.00
21573 Louise, I Love You .... 5.00 - 8.00
V-40034 When Shadows Fall .... 10.00 - 15.00
V-40035 Found My Gal .... 10.00 - 15.00
V-40133 Shame On You .... 10.00 - 15.00

RAY HERBECK AND HIS MUSIC WITH ROMANCE:
Okeh, most issues .... 2.00 - 4.00
Vocalion, most issues .... 2.00 - 4.00

JULES HERBUVEAUX AND HIS PALMER HOUSE VICTORIANS:
Vocalion 15380 Where'd You Get Those Eyes? .... 5.00 - 8.00
15402 Mandy .... 5.00 - 8.00
15403 Someone Is Losin' Susan .... 5.00 - 8.00
15426 Havin' Lots Of Fun .... 5.00 - 8.00

JOE HERLIHY & HIS ORCHESTRA:
Edison 52059 Cornfed .... 10.00 - 15.00
52076 State and Madison .... 15.00 - 20.00
52098 Bye-Bye, Pretty Baby .... 10.00 - 15.00
52100 Rolling Around In Roses .... 10.00 - 15.00

WOODY HERMAN & HIS ORCHESTRA:
Columbia, most issues .... 2.00 - 5.00
Decca 1056 The Goose Hangs High .... 8.00 - 12.00
1057 I Can't Pretend .... 7.00 - 10.00
1064 Old 'Fashioned Swing .... 7.00 - 10.00
1079 Mr. Ghost Goes To Town .... 7.00 - 10.00
1288 Dupree Blues .... 7.00 - 10.00
1307 Trouble In Mind .... 7.00 - 10.00
1385 Stardust On The Moon .... 7.00 - 10.00
1397 Double Or Nothing .... 7.00 - 10.00
1523, 1535, 1570, 1583 .... 5.00 - 8.00
1801, 1839, 1879, 1900 .... 4.00 - 7.00
Decca, blue label, most other issues .... 3.00 - 5.00

MILT HERTH (TRIO):
Decca, blue label, most issues .... 3.00 - 5.00

HERWIN HOT SHOTS:
Herwin 93015 Salty Dog .... 75.00 - 100.00

EDDIE HEYWOOD/AND HIS JAZZ SIX ORCHESTRA:
Decca, most issues .... 2.00 - 3.00
Okeh 8094 The Mixed Up Blues .... 15.00 - 20.00
8402 Trombone Moanin' Blues .... 40.00 - 60.00

BILLY HICKS & HIS SIZZLIN' SIX
Variety 601 Fade Out .... 8.00 - 12.00

RAMONA HICKS:
Bluebird 8173, 8200, 8233 .... 5.00 - 8.00

J. C. HIGGINBOTHAM & HIS SIX HICKS; J. C. HIGGINBOTHAM QUINTET:
Okeh 8772 Higginbotham Blues .... 25.00 - 35.00
Session 10013, 12016 .... 7.00 - 10.00

THE HIGH STEPPERS:
Crown 3184 You Can't Stop Me From Loving You .... 7.00 - 10.00
3298 Lawd, You Made The Night Too Long .... 7.00 - 10.00
3300 Keepin' Out of Mischief Now .... 7.00 - 10.00
3394 Please .... 7.00 - 10.00

HIGHTOWER'S NIGHT HAWKS:
Black Patti 8045 Boar Hog Blues .... 150.00 - 250.00

ALEX HILL/AND HIS HOLLYWOOD SEPIANS/ORCHESTRA:
Vocalion 1270 Tack Head Blues .... 75.00 - 100.00
1465 Southbound .... 75.00 - 100.00
1493 Dyin' With The Blues .... 50.00 - 70.00
2826 Ain't In Nice? .... 20.00 - 30.00
2848 Song of the Plow .... 20.00 - 30.00

JUD HILL'S BLUE DEVILS/CLUB MOROCCO ORCHESTRA:
Gennett 3180, 3186, 3200, 3211, 3218, 3230 .... 4.00 - 8.00

SAM HILL & HIS ORCHESTRA:
Oriole 245 One Of These Days .... 10.00 - 15.00
290 My Dream Man .... 10.00 - 15.00
303 Everybody Loves My Baby .... 10.00 - 15.00
304 How Come You Do Me Like You Do .... 10.00 - 15.00
341 I'll See You In My Dreams .... 10.00 - 15.00
347 Alabama Bound .... 10.00 - 15.00
348 Why Couldn't It Be Poor Little Me? .... 10.00 - 15.00
365 Swannee Butterfly .... 10.00 - 15.00
437 Naughty Man .... 10.00 - 15.00

TEDDY HILL & HIS (NBC) ORCHESTRA:
Titles, issued contemporaneously on Banner, Conqueror, Melotone, Oriole, Perfect, Romeo: Got Me Doin' Things; Here Comes Cookie; When The Robin Sings His Song Again .... 10.00 - 15.00
Bluebird 6897 The Love Bug Will Bite You .... 8.00 - 12.00
6898 My Marie .... 8.00 - 12.00
6908 Big Boy Blue .... 8.00 - 12.00
6941 China Boy .... 8.00 - 12.00

6943 *A Study In Brown*	7.00 -	10.00
6954 *I Know Now*	7.00 -	10.00
6988 *King Porter Stomp*	10.00 -	15.00
6989 *Blue Rhythm Fantasy*	10.00 -	15.00
7013 *Yours And Mine*	10.00 -	15.00
Vocalion 3247 *Blue Rhythm Fantasy*	10.00 -	15.00
3294 *Uptown Rhapsody*	10.00 -	15.00

TINY HILL AND HIS ORCHESTRA:

Mercury, most issues	2.00 -	3.00
Okeh, most issues	2.00 -	4.00
Vocalion, most issues	2.00 -	4.00

HILL TOP INN ORCHESTRA:

Champion 15031 *Choose Your Pal*	15.00 -	20.00
15203 *Brotherly Love*	15.00 -	25.00

RICHARD HIMBER & HIS ESSEX HOUSE/
RHYTHMIC PYRAMIDS RITZ-CARLTON)
ORCHESTRA; RICHARD HIMBER'S
SEVEN STYLISTS:

Bluebird 5418, 5419, 5421	5.00 -	8.00
Victor 24661, 24662, 24670, 24672, 24680, 24745, 24750, 24756, 24757, 24764, 24811, 24823, 24824, 24829, 24868, 24869, 24886, 25036, 25037, 25042, 25049, 25073, 25074, 25077, 25119, 25122, 25124, 25128, 25132, 25161, 25179, 25189, 26101, 26148	3.00 -	6.00
25235, 25239, 25243, 25293, 25298. 25299, 25365, 25392, 25443, 25457, 25738, 25754	4.00 -	8.00
Vocalion 2526, 2537, 2538, 2551, 2560, 2572, 2588, 2589, 25008	5.00 -	10.00

EARL HINES & HIS ORCHESTRA:

Bluebird 6744 *Blue Nights*	7.00 -	10.00
Bluebird 7040 *Beau-Koo Jack*	7.00 -	10.00
7768 *Good Little, Bad Little You*	7.00 -	10.00
10555 *Glad Rag Doll*	7.00 -	10.00
Brunswick 6345 *Blue Drag*	8.00 -	12.00
6379 *Sensational Mood*	8.00 -	12.00
6403 *Love Me Tonight*	8.00 -	12.00
6541 *Rosetta*	8.00 -	12.00
6710 *Bubbling Over*	8.00 -	12.00
6771 *Harlem Lament*	8.00 -	12.00
6872 *Blue*	8.00 -	12.00
6960 *Just To Be In Caroline*	8.00 -	12.00
Columbia 2800-D *Fifty-Seven Varieties*	10.00 -	15.00
Decca 182 *That's A Plenty*	7.00 -	10.00
183 *Cavernism*	7.00 -	10.00
218 *Maple Leaf Rag*	7.00 -	10.00
337 *Copenhagen*	7.00 -	10.00
389 *Rhythm Lullaby*	7.00 -	10.00
577 *Wolverine Blues*	7.00 -	10.00
654 *Japanese Sandman*	7.00 -	10.00
714 *Bubbling Over*	7.00 -	10.00
Okeh 8832 *A Monday Date*	25.00 -	35.00
8653 *Fifty-Seven Varieties*	25.00 -	35.00
41175 *Fifty-Seven Varieties*	25.00 -	35.00
QRS 7036 *Off Time Blues*	90.00 -	120.00
7037 *A Monday Date*	90.00 -	120.00
7038 *Chimes In Blues*	90.00 -	120.00
7039 *Panther Rag*	90.00 -	120.00
Victor 22683 *Sister Kate*	15.00 -	20.00
22842 *Sweet Ella May*	20.00 -	30.00
38042 *Chicago Rhythm*	20.00 -	30.00
38043 *Beau-Koo Jack*	20.00 -	30.00
38048 *Have You Ever Felt That Way?*	20.00 -	30.00
38096 *Grand Piano Blues*	30.00 -	40.00
Vocalion 3379 *Madhouse*	7.00 -	10.00
3392 *Swingin' Down*	7.00 -	10.00
3467 *Rhythm Sundae*	7.00 -	10.00
3501 *Flany Doodle Swing*	7.00 -	10.00
3586 *Honeysuckle Rose*	7.00 -	10.00
4008 *Please Be Kind*	7.00 -	10.00
4032 *Dominick Swing*	7.00 -	10.00

4143 *Tippin' At The Terrace*	7.00 -	10.00
4272 *Jack Climbed A Beanstalk*	7.00 -	10.00

HITCH'S HAPPY HARMONISTS:

Gennett 3066 *Boneyard Shuffle*	15.00 -	25.00
5633 *Cataract Rag Blues*	20.00 -	30.00

LES HITE & HIS ORCHESTRA:

Bluebird 11109, 11210; Hit 7001, 7002	4.00 -	6.00
Varsity 8373, 8391, 8396	4.00 -	6.00

RICHARD HITTER'S BLUE
KNIGHTS/CABINEERS:

Everybody's 1062 *Eccentric*	30.00 -	50.00
1063 *Riverboat Shuffle*	30.00 -	50.00
Gennett 3149 *Stomp Off, Let's Go*	20.00 -	30.00

ART HODES' ART HODES' COLUMBIA
QUINTET:

Jazz Records 1001, 1002, 1003, 1004, 1005, 1009	5.00 -	8.00
Solo Art 12005	5.00 -	8.00

JOHNNY HODGES & HIS ORCHESTRA:

Variety 546, 586	7.00 -	10.00
Vocalion 3948, 4046, 4115, 4213, 4242, 4309, 4335, 4351, 4386, 4573, 4622, 4710, 4849, 4917, 4941, 5100, 5170, 5330, 5353, 5533, 5940	4.00 -	8.00

HARVEY HOFFMAN & HIS ORCHESTRA:

Champion 15263 *Original Black Bottom Dance*	30.00 -	50.00
15266 *All That I Has Is Gone*	30.00 -	50.00

HOKUM TRIO:

Tittles, issued contemporaneously on Clarion, Diva, Velvet Tone: *He Wouldn't Stop Doing It; I'm Havin' My Fun; You're Bound to Look Like a Monkey; You've Had Your Way*	15.00 -	20.00

BILLIE HOLIDAY & HER ORCHESTRA:

Conqueror 9097, 9457, 9458	4.00 -	6.00
Harmony 1075 *Wherever You Are*	5.00 -	8.00
Okeh 3276, 3288, 3333, 3334, 3431, 3440, 3520, 3543, 3593, 3605, 3701, 3748, 3947, 4029, 4126, 4151, 4208, 4238, 4396, 4457, 4631, 4786, 4834, 5021, 5129, 5302, 5377, 5481, 5609, 5719	3.00 -	6.00
5806 *Practice Makes Perfect*	5.00 -	10.00
5831 *I'm All For You*	7.00 -	10.00
5991 *Time On My Hands*	7.00 -	10.00
6064 *St. Louis Blues*	5.00 -	8.00
6134 *Let's Do It*	5.00 -	8.00
6214 *All Of Me*	5.00 -	8.00
6270 *Solitude*	7.00 -	10.00
6369 *Love Me Or Leave Me*	5.00 -	8.00
6451 *Gloomy Sunday*	5.00 -	8.00
Vocalion 3276 *Did I Remember?*	8.00 -	12.00
3288 *Billie's Blues*	8.00 -	12.00
3333 *A Fine Romance*	8.00 -	12.00
3334 *Let's Call A Heart A Heart*	8.00 -	12.00
3431 *One Never Knows, Does One?*	8.00 -	12.00
3440 *If My Heart Could Only Talk*	8.00 -	12.00
3520 *Let's Call The Whole Thing Off*	8.00 -	12.00
3543 *Where Is The Sun?*	8.00 -	12.00
3593 *Without Your Love*	8.00 -	12.00
3605 *A Sailboat In The Moonlight*	8.00 -	12.00
3701 *Getting Some Fun Out Of Life*	8.00 -	12.00
3748 *He's Funny That Way*	8.00 -	12.00
3947 *Now They Call It Swing*	8.00 -	12.00
4029 *When A Woman Loves A Man*	8.00 -	12.00
4126 *You Go To My Hear*	8.00 -	12.00
4156 *If I Were You*	8.00 -	12.00
4208 *Having Myself A Time*	8.00 -	12.00
4238 *I Wish I Had You!*	5.00 -	8.00
4396 *I've Got A Date With A Dream*	7.00 -	10.00
4457 *The Very Thought Of You*	5.00 -	8.00
4631 *Dream Of Life*	7.00 -	10.00
4786 *Under A Blue Jungle Moon*	7.00 -	10.00
4834 *You're Too Lovely To Last*	7.00 -	10.00
5021 *Them There Eyes*	7.00 -	10.00
5129 *Swing, Brother Swing*	7.00 -	10.00

5302 *You're Just A No-Account*	7.00 -	10.00
5377 *Night And Day*	5.00 -	8.00
5481 *Body and Soul*	5.00 -	8.00
5609 *Falling In Love Again*		
5719 *Tell Me More*	5.00 -	8.00

HOLLYWOOD DANCE ORCHESTRA:

Banner 0503, 0506, 0509, 0517	4.00 -	6.00
Banner 0539 *I'm Following You*	5.00 -	8.00
0563 *Hello Baby*	5.00 -	8.00
0564 *I Have To Have You*	5.00 -	8.00
0573 *I've Got To Have You*	5.00 -	8.00
Banner 6097, 6453, 6455, 6515, 6544, 6552, 7158	3.00 -	6.00
Cameo 0173 *I've Got to Have You*	5.00 -	8.00
Domino 4318, 4453	3.00 -	6.00
Domino 4609 *In Memory Of You*	5.00 -	8.00
Oriole 1792 *I'm Following You*	5.00 -	8.00
1829 *I've Got To Have You*	5.00 -	8.00
Regal 8894, 8927	3.00 -	6.00

HOLLYWOOD SHUFFLERS:

Vocalion 15837 *Low Down Rhythm*	40.00 -	60.00
15841 *Bigger and Better Than Ever*	35.00 -	50.00

HOLLYWOOD SYNCOPATORS:

Nordskog 3013 *Pacific Coast Blues*	15.00 -	20.00

THE HOME TOWNERS:

Cameo 0224 *What's The Use?*	7.00 -	10.00
9130 *Let's Get Together*	5.00 -	8.00
9131 *What D'Ya Think of My Baby?*	5.00 -	8.00
Jewel 5883 *Headin' South*	7.00 -	10.00
Oriole 1883 *Headin' South*	7.00 -	10.00

HONEY SWAMP STOMPERS:

Harmony 856-H *Wipin' The Pan*	5.00 -	8.00

CLAUDE HOPKINS AND HIS ORCHESTRA:

Ammor 114, 115, 116	4.00 -	8.00
Brunswick 6750 *Washington Squabble*	7.00 -	10.00
6864 *My Gal Sal*	7.00 -	10.00
6981 *I Can't Dance*	7.00 -	10.00
6916 *Everybody Shuffle*	8.00 -	12.00
Columbia 2665-D *Mad Moments*	10.00 -	15.00
2674-D *Mush Mouth*	10.00 -	15.00
2741-D *California, Here I Come*	10.00 -	15.00
2747-D *He's A Son of the South*	10.00 -	15.00
2880-D *Ain't Misbehavin*	10.00 -	15.00
2904-D *Marie*	10.00 -	15.00
Decca 184 *King Porter Stomp*	7.00 -	10.00
185 *Just You, Just Me*	7.00 -	10.00
270 *Walkin' The Dog*	7.00 -	10.00
353 *Do You Ever Think Of Me?*	7.00 -	10.00
374 *Love In Bloom*	7.00 -	10.00
441 *Chasing All The Blues Away*	7.00 -	10.00
674 *Monkey Business*	5.00 -	8.00
1153 *Sunday*	7.00 -	10.00
1286 *Church Street Sobbin' Blues*	7.00 -	10.00
1316 *My Kinda Love*	7.00 -	10.00

HORSEY'S HOT FIVE:

Gennett 6722 *Weeping Blues*	35.00 -	50.00

THE HOT AIR MEN:

Columbia 2092-D *Navy Blues*	8.00 -	11.00
2175-D *Red Hot Chicago*	8..00 -	11.00

HOT AND HEAVY:

Pathe-Actuelle 7510 *Memphis Rag*	20.00 -	30.00
Perfect 110 *Memphis Rag*	20.00 -	30.00

THE HOT DOGS:

Silvertone 3560 *Hot Mustard*	80.00 -	100.00
3572 *Carolina Shuffle*	20.00 -	40.00
3574 *Steady Roll*	80.00 -	100.00

THE HOTSY TOTSY GANG:

Brunswick 4014, *Doin' The New Low Down*	8.00 -	12.00
4044 *Don't Mess Around With Me*	10.00 -	15.00
4112 *I Couldn't If I Wanted To*	8.00 -	12.00
4122 *Since You Went Away*	8.00 -	12.00
4200 *Futuristic Rhythm*	10.00 -	15.00

THE HOTTENTOTS:

Paramount 12539 *Lots O'Mama*	10.00 -	15.00
Supertone 9447 *Chicago Rhythm*	25.00 -	35.00
Vocalion 15161 *Down And Out Blues*	15.00 -	20.00
15209 *Pensacola*	15.00 -	20.00

THE HOUR OF CHARM ALL GIRL ORCHESTRA:

Vogue R-725 *Alice Blue Gown*	10.00 -	15.00
Vogue R-726 *Blue Skies*	10.00 -	15.00
(Note: The above two records comprise *Vogue* album no. V100, "A Study In Blue".)		
Vogue R-733 *Seville*	10.00 -	15.00

BOB HOWARD & HIS ORCHESTRA:

Decca 343 *Throwin' Stones At The Sun*	8.00 -	12.00
347 *It's Unbelievable*	8.00 -	12.00
400 *Pardon My Love*	8.00 -	12.00
407 *Breakin' The Ice*	8.00 -	12.00
439 *I'll Never Change*	8.00 -	12.00
460 *A Porter's Love Song*	7.00 -	10.00
484 *Corrine Corrina*	7.00 -	10.00
504 *If The Moon Turns Green*	7.00 -	10.00
513 *In A Little Gypsy Tea Room*	7.00 -	10.00
524 *I'm Painting The Town Red*	7.00 -	10.00
598 *It's Written In The Stars*	5.00 -	8.00
627 *Give Me A Break, Baby*	5.00 -	8.00
689 *You Hit The Spot*	7.00 -	10.00
720 *Spreadin' Rhythm Around*	7.00 -	10.00
722 *Much Too Much*	7.00 -	10.00
839 *Let's Not Fall In Love*	7.00 -	10.00
862 *Public Weakness No. 1*	7.00 -	10.00
Decca 917, 927, 983, 1195, 1205, 1293, 1306	3.00 -	5.00

GORDON HOWARD & HIS MULTNOMAH CHIEFTAINS:

Gennett 6381 *Wob-A-Ly Walk*	8.00 -	12.00
6395 *Golden Gate*	8.00 -	12.00

PAUL HOWARD'S QUALITY SERENADERS:

Bluebird 5804 *Stuff*	7.00 -	10.00
Victor 22660 *New Kinda Blues*	20.00 -	30.00
23354 *California Swing*	60.00 -	80.00
23420 *Gettin' Ready Blues*	60.00 -	80.00
38068 *The Ramble*	20.00 -	30.00
38070 *Charlie's Idea*	20.00 -	30.00
38122 *Quality Shout*	30.00 -	40.00

BERT HOWELL:

Paramount 13063 *You're Driving Me Crazy*	15.00 -	20.00
Victor 21062 *Bye Bye Florence*	15.00 -	20.00

HUDSON-DE LANGE ORCHESTRA; WILL HUDSON & HIS ORCHESTRA/SEVEN SWINGSTERS:

Brunswick 7598, 7618, 7656, 7667, 7700, 7708, 7715, 7727, 7743, 7785, 7795, 7809, 7828, 7991, 7996, 7998, 8002, 8007, 8016, 8023, 8040, 8049, 8071, 8077, 8081, 8090, 8113, 8147, 8156, 8164, 8177, 8191, 8195, 8213, 8222	3.00 -	6.00
Master 103, 112, 125, 132, 138	4.00 -	7.00

PHIL HUGHES AND HIS HIGH HATTERS:

Clarion 5304-C *Just A Crazy Song*	7.00 -	10.00
5342-C *Treat Me Like A Baby*	5.00 -	8.00
5365-C *It's A Long Time Between Kisses*	5.00 -	8.00
Harmony 1313-H *Just A Crazy Song*	7.00 -	10.00
1333-H *Look in the Looking Glass*	5.00 -	8.00
1353-H *It's a Long Time Between Kisses*	5.00 -	8.00
Velvet Tone 2370-V *Just a Crazy Song*	7.00 -	10.00
2406-V *Treat Me Like a Baby*	5.00 -	8.00
2429-V *It's a Long Time Between Kisses*	5.00 -	8.00

HUNTER'S SERENADERS:

Vocalion 1621 *Sensational Mood*	35.00 -	50.00

CHARLEY HUNTER'S ORCHESTRA:

Broadway 5023 *Bottomland*	30.00 -	40.00

INA RAY HUTTON & HER MELODEARS:

Victor 24692 *How's About Tomorrow Night?*	7.00 -	10.00
Vocalion 2801 *Georgia's Gorgeous Gal*	7.00 -	10.00

2816 *Wild Party*	7.00 -	10.00

JOHN HYMAN'S BAYOU STOMPERS:

Victor 20593 *Alligator Blues*	20.00 -	30.00

BERTHA IDAHO:

Columbia 14437-D *Move It On Out Of Here*	15.00 -	20.00

IDEAL SERENADERS:

Columbia 1131-D *Dawning*	5.00 -	8.00

IMPERIAL DANCE ORCHESTRA:

Banner 0514, 0532, 0747, 7165	3.00 -	6.00
Banner 7192 *Ready For The River*	7.00 -	10.00
Domino 4449 *Miss Wonderful*	5.00 -	8.00
4469 *I'm Following You*	5.00 -	8.00
Domino 4479, 4485	3.00 -	6.00
Domino 4646 *Just A Little Dance, Mamselle*	7.00 -	10.00
Oriole 1883 *Sing You Sinners*	7.00 -	10.00
Regal 8893 *Miss Wonderful*	5.00 -	8.00
8914 *I'm Following You*	5.00 -	8.00
Regal 8924, 8930	3.00 -	6.00

INDIANA FIVE: (See ORIGINAL INDIANA FIVE)

Emerson, most issues	7.00 -	10.00

INDIANA SYNCOPATERS:

LaBelle 1418 *Bees Knees*	10.00 -	20.00

THE INK SPOTS:

Decca 817, 883, 1036, 1154, 1236, 1251	4.00 -	8.00
Victor 24851 *Your Feet's Too Big*	15.00 -	25.00
24876 *Swing Gate, Swing*	15.00 -	25.00

INTERSTATE BLUE JACKETS:

Champion 15053 *Spanish Shawl*	10.00 -	15.00
15064 *Shanghai Honeymoon*	10.00 -	15.00
15304 *Indiana Mud*	15.00 -	25.00

IPANA TROUBADOURS:

Columbia 503-D *Paddlin' Madeline Home*	5.00 -	8.00
528-D *Jig Walk*	5.00 -	8.00
1009-D *Side By Side*	5.00 -	8.00
1463-D *Nagasaki*	8.00 -	12.00
1638-D *Glorianna*	15.00 -	20.00
1694-D *Rose Of Mandalay*	20.00 -	30.00
1717-D *Mississippi*	5.00 -	8.00
1881-D *There Was Nothing Else To Do*	5.00 -	8.00
1920-D *Hang On To Me*	5.00 -	8.00
1982-D *True Blue Lou*	5.00 -	8.00
2006-D *My Sweeter Than Sweet*	5.00 -	8.00
2117-D *Kickin' A Hole in the Sky*	7.00 -	10.00
2174-D *Whippoorwill*	5.00 -	8.00
2220-D *Sing*	5.00 -	8.00
2317-D *Three Little Words*	5.00 -	8.00
2368-D *I'm So Afraid Of You*	5.00 -	8.00
2486-D *On The Beach With You*	5.00 -	8.00
Columbia 3585-X *Just a Little Glimpse of Paradise*	10.00 -	15.00

(Note: Above is part of a Spanish series, lacking the vocal present in the performance issued for U.S. market and issued as by "Trovadores Ipana." Other similar issues probably exist, and would possibly be of interest to collectors.)

KITTY IRVIN:

Gennett 2592 *Copenhagen*	20.00 -	30.00

VIC IRWIN & HIS ORCHESTRA:

Banner 32327, 32331; Oriole 2386, 2387	5.00 -	10.00
Perfect 15547; Romeo 1757, 1760	5.00 -	10.00

JACK'S FAST-STEPPIN' BELLHOPS:

Champion 15088 *Honey Bunch*	15.00 -	20.00

JACKSON & HIS SOUTHERN STOMPERS:

Marathon (7-inch record) 227 *Dusky Stevedore*	75.00 -	100.00

ALEX JACKSON'S PLANTATION ORCHESTRA:

Gennett 6249 *Jackass Blues*	30.00 -	50.00
6296 *Missouri Squabble*	25.00 -	40.00

DEWEY JACKSON'S PEACOCK ORCHESTRA:

Vocalion 1039 *Go 'Won To Town*	50.00 -	75.00

1040 *She's Cryin' For Me*	60.00 -	90.00

EARL JACKSON'S MUSICAL CHAMPIONS:

Melotone 12080 *Is That Religion?*	10.00 -	15.00
12093 *Rockin' Chair*	7.00 -	10.00
12164 *Red Devil*	7.00 -	10.00
Perfect 15468 *Star Dust*	7.00 -	10.00
15481 *Black and Tan Fantasy*	7.00 -	10.00

FRISKY FOOT JACKSON & HIS THUMPERS:

Champion 15696 *Good Time Mama*	60.00 -	80.00
15929 *Mississippi Stomp*	60.00 -	80.00
40043 *Good Time Mama*	15.00 -	20.00

LITTLE JOE JACKSON & HIS BOYS:

Bell 1174 *Fourth Avenue Stomp*	75.00 -	100.00

MARY JACKSON:

Pathe-Actuelle 032013, Perfect 12097 *All The Time*	8.00 -	10.00

MIKE JACKSON:

Victor 20181 *Just Too Bad*	10.00 -	15.00
20482 *Alabama Mama*	8.00 -	12.00

PRESTON JACKSON & HIS UPTOWN BAND:

Paramount 12400 *Harmony Blues*	75.00 -	100.00
12411 *Trombone Man*	75.00 -	100.00

SLIM JACKSON TRIO:

Cameo 705 *Freakish Blues*	7.00 -	10.00

SMOKE JACKSON & HIS RED ONIONS:

Champion 15714 *It's Tight Like That*	40.00 -	50.00
15905 *Wailin' Blues*	40.00 -	50.00

JACKSONVILLE HARMONY TRIO:

Victor 20960 *Jacksonville Blues*	10.00 -	15.00
21204 *I Wonder*	10.00 -	15.00

BUD JACOBSON'S JUNGLE KINGS:

Signature 103, 106, 903, 904	3.00 -	6.00

JAFFE'S COLLEGIANS:

Okeh 40561 *Sweet and Low Down*	7.00 -	10.00

JAMAICA JAZZERS:

Okeh 40117 *West Indies Blues*	20.00 -	30.00

BILLY JAMES' DANCE ORCHESTRA:

Oriole 271 *Hard Hearted Hannah*	7.00 -	10.00
Oriole 521, 829	4.00 -	7.00
Oriole 1008 *Swanee's Calling Me*	5.00 -	8.00
1250 *Straight Back Home*	5.00 -	8.00
1284 *I Wanna Go Back To Indiana*	5.00 -	8.00

CORKY JAMES & HIS BLACKBIRDS:

Bell 1182 *Bugahoma Blues*	90.00 -	130.00

HARRY JAMES & HIS ORCHESTRA; HARRY JAMES & THE BOOGIE WOOGIE TRIO:

Brunswick 8035 *When We're Alone*	7.00 -	10.00
8038 *(I Can Dream) Can't I?)*	7.00 -	10.00
8055 *One O'Clock Jump*	7.00 -	10.00
8067 *Texas Chatter*	7.00 -	10.00
8136 *Out Of Nowhere*	5.00 -	8.00
8178 *Wrap Your Troubles In Dreams*	5.00 -	8.00
8318 *Boo-Woo*	7.00 -	10.00
8326 *Blame It On My Last Affair*	5.00 -	8.00
8327 *Ciribiribin*	5.00 -	8.00
8337 *Two O'Clock Jump*	5.00 -	8.00
8350 *Home James*	7.00 -	10.00
8355 *Got No Time*	5.00 -	8.00
8366 *King Porter Stomp*	5.00 -	8.00
8395 *I Can't Afford To Dream*	5.00 -	8.00
8406 *I Found A New Baby*	7.00 -	10.00
8443 *From The Bottom Of My Heart*	15.00 -	25.00
Columbia 35209 *It's Funny To Everyone But Me*	7.00 -	10.00
35227 *Here Comes The Night*	7.00 -	10.00
35242 *My Buddy*	7.00 -	10.00
35261 *Who Told You I Cared?*	7.00 -	10.00
Columbia, most other issues	2.00 -	5.00

JEANETTE JAMES:

Paramount 12451 *What's That Thing?*	50.00 -	75.00
12470 *Midnight Stomp*	50.00 -	75.00

JELLY JAMES & HIS FEWSICIANS:

Gennett 6045 *Georgia Bo Bo*	50.00 -	75.00

MADELYN JAMES:
Brunswick 7155 *Long Time Blues*............ 25.00 - 40.00
ART JARRETT:
Columbia 2672-D, 2691-D.................. 5.00 - 8.00
FRANKIE "HALF-PINE" JAXON (& HIS HOT SHOTS):
Black Patti 8048 *Willie The Weeper*........ 35.00 - 50.00
Decca 7286, 7304, 7345, 7360, 7482, 7523, 7548,
  7619, 7638, 7733, 7742, 7786, 7795, 7806... 4.00 - 8.00
Gennett 6214 *Can't You Wait Till You Get Home?* 20.00 - 30.00
  6244 *She's Got "It"*..................... 20.00 - 30.00
Vocalion 1226 *Down at Jasper's Bar-Be-Que.*. 15.00 - 25.00
  1257 *Fan It*........................... 15.00 - 25.00
  1285 *Let's Knock a Jug*................ 15.00 - 25.00
  1424 *Take It Easy*.................... 15.00 - 25.00
  1472 *Down Home in Kentucky*........... 20.00 - 30.00
  1539 *Jive Man Blues*.................. 15.00 - 20.00
  1583 *Scuddlin*........................ 15.00 - 20.00
  2553 *My Baby's Hot*................... 10.00 - 15.00
  2603 *Fifteen Cents*................... 10.00 - 15.00
JAZZ-O-HARMONISTS:
Claxtonola 40336 *Copenhagen*............. 50.00 - 75.00
  40339 *Riverboat Shuffle*.............. 50.00 - 75.00
  40375 *Sensation*..................... 50.00 - 75.00
THE JAZZ MASTERS:
Black Swan 2109 *Bees Knees*.............. 7.00 - 10.00
THE JAZZ-O-MONISTS:
Edison 51157 *Snakes Hips*................ 8.00 - 12.00
  51161 *Funny Feet*.................... 8.00 - 12.00
  51165 *Long-Lost Mama*................ 8.00 - 12.00
  51168 *The Cat's Whiskers*............ 8.00 - 12.00
  51171 *I Ain't Never Had Nobody Crazy Over Me* 8.00 - 12.00
  51172 *Henpecked Blues*............... 8.00 - 12.00
  51229 *I've Got the 'Yes We Have No Bananas Blues'* 8.00 - 12.00
  51247 *Darktown Reveille*............. 10.00 - 15.00
  51302 *I'm Goin' South*............... 8.00 - 12.00
  51303 *If I Stay Away Too Long From Carolina* 8.00 - 12.00
THE JAZZOPATORS:
Grey Gull 1797 *Don't Know and Don't Care*... 7.00 - 10.00
  1816 *Everybody Dance*................ 7.00 - 10.00
  1819 *Blue Ridge Blues*............... 7.00 - 10.00
Van Dyke *Sweet Little Sis*............... 5.00 - 8.00
SPEED JEFFRIES & HIS NIGHT OWLS:
Superior 2648 *Georgia Grind*............. 60.00 - 90.00
  2670 *Kentucky Blues*................. 60.00 - 90.00
  2728 *Stomp Your Stuff*............... 60.00 - 90.00
  2738 *Sic 'Em, Tige*.................. 60.00 - 90.00
  2755 *Tiger Moon*..................... 60.00 - 90.00
  2797 *Richmond Stomp*................. 60.00 - 90.00
THE JELLY WHIPPERS:
Herwin 92018 *S.O.B. Blues*.............. 50.00 - 75.00
FREDDY JENKINS & HIS HARLEM SEVEN:
Bluebird 6129 *Old Fashioned Love*........ 7.00 - 10.00
  6193 *Swingin' 'Em Down*............. 7.00 - 10.00
JACK JENNEY & HIS ORCHESTRA:
Vocalion 3972, 4130, 4803, 5304, 5407, 5494, 5535, 5545 .... 4.00 - 8.00
JETER-PILLARS CLUB PLANTATION ORCHESTRA:
Vocalion 3715 *Lazy Rhythm*.............. 10.00 - 15.00
  3973 *Make Believe*.................. 10.00 - 15.00
THE JIM-DANDIES:
Harmony 55-H *Shake That Thing*.......... 5.00 - 9.00
JIMMIE'S BLUE MELODY BOYS:
Vocalion 1439 *Love Me*................. 30.00 - 40.00
JIMMIE'S JOYS:
Golden 1858 *No No Nora*................ 35.00 - 50.00
  1865 *Bugle Call Rag*................ 35.00 - 50.00
JOE'S HOT BABIES:
Paramount 12783 *Beans and Greens*........ 30.00 - 50.00

JOE & HIS RHYTHM ORCHESTRA:
Bluebird 6447 *Confessin'*............... 8.00 - 12.00
THE JOHNSON BOYS:
Okeh 8708 *Violin Blues*................ 15.00 - 20.00
JOHNSON'S JAZZERS:
Columbia 14247-D *Can I Get It Now?*....... 15.00 - 20.00
JOHNSON'S PLANTATION SERENADERS:
Silvertone 5024 *A Blues Serenade*........ 8.00 - 12.00
BERT JOHNSON:
Brunswick 7136 *Nasty But Nice*.......... 30.00 - 50.00
BILL JOHNSON'S LOUISIANA JUG BAND:
Brunswick 7067 *Don't Drink It In Here*..... 40.00 - 60.00
BLANCHE JOHNSON:
Herwin 92016 *Galveston Blues*........... 75.00 - 100.00
BUNK JOHNSON & HIS BAND:
American Music 101..................... 5.00 - 10.00
American Music (12-inch) 251, 253, 255.... 5.00 - 10.00
Jazz Information 12, 14................. 5.00 - 10.00
Jazz Man 8, 9, 10...................... 5.00 - 10.00
V-Disc (12-inch) 630, 658.............. 5.00 - 10.00
CAROLINE JOHNSON:
Buddy 8033 *Mama's Losin' a Mighty Good Chance* 25.00 - 35.00
  8034 *Ain't Got Nobody To Grind My Coffee.* 25.00 - 35.00
Gennett 3307 *Mama's Losin' a Might Good Chance* 20.00 - 30.00
Pathe-Actuelle 7503 *Georgia Grind*....... 15.00 - 20.00
Perfect 103 *Georgia Grind*.............. 15.00 - 20.00
CHARLIE JOHNSON'S (ORIGINAL) (PARADISE) ORCHESTRA/TEN: CHARLIE JOHNSON & HIS (PARADISE) BAND/ ORCHESTRA:
Bluebird 10248 *Walk That Thing*.......... 7.00 - 10.00
Emerson 10854 *Don't Forget You'll Regret Day By Day*. 30.00 - 50.00
  10856 *Meddlin' With The Blues*........ 40.00 - 60.00
Victor 20551 *Paradise Wobble*........... 25.00 - 35.00
  20653 *Don't You Leave Me Here*....... 25.00 - 35.00
  21247 *You Ain't The One*............ 25.00 - 35.00
  21491 *Charleston is the Best Dance After All.* 25.00 - 35.00
  21712 *Walk That Thing*.............. 25.00 - 35.00
  38059 *Hot Bones and Rice.*.......... 25.00 - 35.00
EDDIE JOHNSON'S CRACKERJACKS:
Victor 23329 *The Duck's Yas Yas Yas*...... 60.00 - 90.00
GRAVEYARD JOHNSON & HIS GANG:
Supertone 9369 *Good Times Mama*.......... 90.00 - 120.00
  9431 *Original Stomp*................ 90.00 - 120.00
  9432 *Shake Your Shimmy*............. 90.00 - 120.00
HAVEN JOHNSON & HIS ORCHESTRA:
Vocalion 3457 *There Is No Moon*.......... 8.00 - 12.00
HENRY JOHNSON'S BOYS:
Gennett 6156 *Blue Hawaii*.............. 40.00 - 60.00
  6168 *Ash Can Stomp*................ 60.00 - 90.00
Herwin 92024 *Hawaiian Harmony Blues*..... 40.00 - 60.00
  92025 *Neck Bones and Beans*........
J. C. JOHNSON & HIS FIVE HOT SPARKS:
QRS 7064 *Red Hot Hottentot*............ 80.00 - 120.00
JAMES P. JOHNSON; JAMES P. JOHNSON'S HARMONY EIGHT; JIMMIE JOHNSON'S JAZZ BOYS; JIMMIE/ JIMMY JOHNSON & HIS BAND/ ORCHESTRA:
Black Swan 2026 *The Harlem Strut*........ 25.00 - 35.00
Brunswick 4712 *Crying for the Carolines*.... 15.00 - 20.00
  4762 *You've Got To Be Modernistic*.... 15.00 - 20.00
Cleartone P-96 *Carolina Shout*.......... 15.00 - 20.00
Columbia A-3950 *Weeping Blues*.......... 7.00 - 10.00
  2248-D *Go Harlem*.................. 15.00 - 25.00
  14204-D *Snowy Morning Blues*......... 8.00 - 12.00
  14334-D *Chicago Blues*.............. 20.00 - 30.00
  14417-D *Fare Thee Honey Blues*....... 20.00 - 30.00
  14502-D *I've Found a New Baby*........ 20.00 - 30.00
  14668-D *A Porter's Love Song*......... 30.00 - 50.00

Okeh 4495 *Carolina Shout*	15.00 -	20.00
4504 *Dear Old Southland*	15.00 -	20.00
4937 *Toddlin'*	15.00 -	20.00
8770 *Riffs*	20.00 -	30.00
Paramount 12144 *The Harlem Strut*	25.00 -	35.00
Victor 19123 *Bleeding Hearted Blues*	5.00 -	8.00
38099 *You Don't Understand*	35.00 -	50.00
Vocalion 4768 *Harlem Woogie*	8.00 -	12.00
4903 *Back Water Blues*	8.00 -	12.00

JOHNNY JOHNSON & HIS (POST LODGE) ORCHESTRA/STATLER PENNSYLVANIANS:

Cameo 477 *WOP Blues*	5.00 -	8.00
Victor 21113 *Thou Swell*	7.00 -	10.00
22468 *On Revival Day*	5.00 -	8.00
22493 *What's The Use*	5.00 -	8.00
22564 *I'm A Ding Dong Daddy*	5.00 -	8.00
Vocalion 2811, 2847	4.00 -	7.00

PETE JOHNSON (AND HIS BOOGIE WOOGIE BOYS):

Solo Art 12004 *How Long How Long*	7.00 -	10.00
12005 *Pete's Blues*	7.00 -	10.00
12006 *B & O Blues*	7.00 -	10.00
12010 *Shuffle Boogie*	7.00 -	10.00
Vocalion 4997 *Cherry Red*	5.00 -	8.00

ROY JOHNSON'S HAPPY PALS:

Okeh 8723 *Savoy Rhythm*	35.00 -	50.00

MERLE JOHNSTON & HIS CECO COURIERS:

Columbia 1968-D, 2114-D	4.00 -	7.00

THE JOLLY THREE:

Vocalion 03955 *Ain't Got a Dime Blues*	15.00 -	20.00

AL JOLSON:

Brunswick 2567, 2569, 2582, 2595, 2611, 2650, 2671, 2743, 2763, 3013, 3014, 3183, 3196, 3222, 3719, 3775, 3867, 3912, 4033	3.00 -	6.00
Brunswick 4400, 4401, 4402, 4721, 4722	5.00 -	10.00
Brunswick 6500 *You Are Too Beautiful*	10.00 -	15.00
6502 *April Showers*	15.00 -	20.00
Columbia A-1356 *That Little German Band*	8.00 -	12.00
A-1374 *Pullman Porter's Parade*	8.00 -	12.00
A-1621 *Back To The Carolina You Love*	8.00 -	12.00
A-1671 *Sister Susie's Sewing Shirts For Soldiers*	8.00 -	12.00
Columbia A-1956, A-1976, A-2007, A-2021	5.00 -	8.00
Columbia, most other issues	4.00 -	7.00
Victor 17037 *That Haunting Melody*	7.00 -	10.00
17068 *Brass Band Ephram Jones*	8.00 -	12.00
17075 *Snap Your Fingers*	7.00 -	10.00
17081 *Ragging The Baby To Sleep*	7.00 -	10.00
17119 *That Lovin' Traumerei*	10.00 -	15.00
17915 *Asleep In The Deep*	5.00 -	8.00

(Note: See ANONYMOUS listing, *Little Wonder* 20.)

BOBBY JONES & HIS ORCHESTRA:

Buddy 8001 *Leaky Roof Blues*	15.00 -	25.00
Champion 15177 *Blowin' the Blues Away*	5.00 -	8.00
15294 *Wherever You Go—Whatever You Do*	7.00 -	10.00

CLARENCE M. JONES:

Titles, on Autograph (unnumbered) are: *Modulation; Trot Along; Hula Lou; Maybe*	15.00 -	20.00
Okeh 8404 *The Arm Breaker*	15.00 -	25.00
Paramount 12716 *'Mid the Pyramids*	25.00 -	40.00
12747 *Hold It Boy Blues*	25.00 -	40.00

HANK JONES & HIS GINGER:

Champion 15338 *Neck Bones and Beans*	40.00 -	60.00
15437 *Ash Can Stomp*	60.00 -	90.00
15509 *Down Home Special*	40.00 -	60.00

ISHAM JONES & HIS ORCHESTRA; ISHAM JONES' JUNIORS:

Brunswick 4868, 4907, 4914, 4985	4.00 -	7.00
6000 numbers	4.00 -	7.00
Decca 170, 220, 262, 300, 443, 493, 569, 662, 754,		

770, 834, 1022	4.00 -	7.00
Victor 24098, 24099, 24294, 24409, 24421, 24496, 24519, 24649, 24695, 24701	5.00 -	10.00

PIGGY JONES & HIS ORCHESTRA:

Gennett 3104, 3109	4.00 -	7.00

RICHARD M. JONES: RICHARD M. JONES' (THREE) JAZZ MEN/WIZARDS; JONES' CHICAGO COSMOPOLITANS; RICHARD M. JONES & HIS JAZZ WIZARDS:

Bluebird 6569 *Trouble In Mind*	10.00 -	15.00
Decca 7051 *Blue Reefer Blues*	*12.00 -*	*18.00*
7064 *Muggin' The Blues*	10.00 -	15.00
7115 *Joe Louis Chant*	10.00 -	15.00
Gennett 5174 *Jazzin' Babies' Blues*	15.00 -	20.00
Okeh 8260 *29th and Dearborn*	25.00 -	35.00
8290 *New Orleans Shags*	25.00 -	35.00
8349 *Mushmouth Blues*	35.00 -	50.00
8390 *Baby O'Mine*	75.00 -	100.00
8431 *Dusty Bottom Blues*	40.00 -	60.00
Paramount 12705 *Hot and Ready*	50.00 -	80.00
Session 12-006, 12-007	6.00 -	10.00
Victor 20812 *Hollywood Shuffle*	20.00 -	30.00
20859 *Smoked Meat Blues*	25.00 -	35.00
21203 *Boar Hog Blues*	25.00 -	35.00
21345 *African Hunch*	25.00 -	35.00
38040 *Tickle Britches Blues*	20.00 -	30.00

WILLIE JONES & HIS ORCHESTRA:

Gennett 6326 *Michigan Stomp*	25.00 -	40.00
6370 *Ragamuffin Stomp*	25.00 -	40.00

JONES AND COLLINS ASTORIA HOT EIGHT:

Bluebird 10952 *Damp Weather*	7.00 -	10.00
Victor 38576 *Astoria Strut*	30.00 -	50.00

JONES' PARAMOUNT CHARLESTON FOUR:

Paramount 12279 *Old Steady Roll*	20.00 -	30.00

JONES-SMITH INCORPORATED:

Vocalion 3441 *Shoe-Shine Boy*	10.00 -	15.00
3459 *Lady Be Good*	10.00 -	15.00

JOE JORDAN'S TEN SHARPS AND FLATS:

Banner 1821 *Morocco Blues*	15.00 -	20.00
Columbia 14144-D *Senegalese Stomp*	20.00 -	30.00
Domino 3791 *Morocco Blues*	15.00 -	20.00
Regal 8129 *Old Folks Shuffle*	15.00 -	20.00

TAFT JORDAN AND THE MOB:

Titles, issued contemporadaneously on Banner, Conqueror, Melotone, Oriole, Perfect, Romeo: *Devil In The Moon; If The Moon Turns Green; Louisiana Fairy Tale; Night Wind*	7.00 -	10.00

JIMMIE/JIMMY JOY'S (BAKER ST. ANTHONY HOTEL) ORCHESTRA:

Brunswick 3905 *From Monday On*	7.00 -	10.00
3959 *I Got Worry*	7.00 -	10.00
3960 *Today Is Today*	7.00 -	10.00
4640 *Harmonica Harry*	8.00 -	12.00
Okeh 40251 *Milenberg Joys*	25.00 -	40.00
40329 *Clarinet Marmalade Blues*	25.00 -	40.00
40381 *China Girl*	25.00 -	40.00
40388 *Riverboat Shuffle*	25.00 -	40.00
40420 *Wild Jazz*	25.00 -	40.00
40484 *Springtime Is Love Time*	15.00 -	20.00
40494 *Fallin' Down*	25.00 -	40.00
40504 *Everybody Stomp*	25.00 -	40.00
40539 *St. Louis Blues*	25.00 -	40.00
40627 *Stomp It, Mr. Kelly*	25.00 -	40.00

THE JUNGLE BAND:

Brunswick 3956 *Tiger Rag*	8.00 -	10.00
4238 *Tiger Rag*	10.00 -	15.00
4309 *Paducah*	10.00 -	15.00
4345 *Doin' The Voom Voom*	10.00 -	15.00
4450 *Dog Bottom*	10.00 -	15.00
4492 *Jungle Jamboree*	10.00 -	15.00

4760 *Sweet Mama*...........	10.00 -	15.00
4776 *Maori*...............	10.00 -	15.00
4783 *Double Check Stomp*.........	10.00 -	15.00
4889 *Wall Street Wail*...........	10.00 -	15.00
4936 *St. Louis Blues*...........	10.00 -	15.00
4952 *Runnin' Wild*...........	10.00 -	15.00
6003 *Wang Wang Blues*.........	8.00 -	12.00
6038 *Rockin' In Rhythm*.........	8.00 -	10.00
6732 *Rockin' Chair*............	5.00 -	8.00

JUNGLE KINGS:

Paramount 12654 *Friars Point Shuffle*........	75.00 -	100.00

JUNGLE TOWN STOMPERS:

Okeh 8686 *Slow As Molasses*..............	20.00 -	30.00

ART KAHN & HIS ORCHESTRA:

Columbia 16-D *Sobbin' Blues*...........	7.00 -	10.00
45-D *Bahama*................	7.00 -	10.00
104-D *Blue Evening Blues*........	7.00 -	10.00
221-D *Off And Gone*..........	7.00 -	10.00
310-D *Lucky Kentucky*...........	7.00 -	10.00
624-D *Hobo's Prayer*...........	7.00 -	10.00
Meltone 12090 *I'm Happy When You're Happy*.	15.00 -	20.00
Okeh 40857 *When Day Is Done*.......	7.00 -	10.00
Titles, issued contemporaneously on Banner, Meltone, Oriole, Perfect Romeo: *The Gold-diggers' Song; Pettin' in the Park*..........	7.00 -	10.00

ROGER WOLFE KAHN & HIS ORCHESTRA:

Brunswick 4374, 4479, 4571, 4583, 4600, 4614, 4699, 4742, 4750, 4811, 4826............	4.00 -	6.00
Columbia 2653-D, 2662-D, 2695-D, 2697-D.....	5.00 -	8.00
2722-D *It Don't Mean a Thing*.....	7.00 -	10.00
2726-D *Fit As A Fiddle*........	7.00 -	10.00
Victor 20466, 20493, 20634, 21425......	4.00 -	8.00
21326 *She's a Great, Great Girl*.........	8.00 -	12.00

ELMER KAISER & HIS BALLROOM ORCHESTRA:

Autograph (unnumbered) *Monkey Business*.....	20.00 -	30.00

CHARLES KALEY:

Columbia 910-D *Alabama Stomp*............	7.00 -	10.00

HELEN KANE:

Victor 22397, 22407, 22470, 22520...........	4.00 -	7.00

KANSAS CITY FIVE/FOUR:

Ajax 17072 *Louisville Blues*..........	25.00 -	35.00
17078 *Believe Me, Hot Mama*............	25.00 -	35.00
17128 *Dark Gal Blues*.........	25.00 -	35.00
Pathe-Actuelle 036175 *Get Yourself a Monkey Man*	20.00 -	30.00
36335 *Get It Fixed*...........	20.00 -	30.00
Perfect 14356 *Get Yourself a Monkey Man*....	20.00 -	30.00
14377 *Louisville Blues*...............	20.00 -	30.00
14516 *Dark Gal Blues*...........	20.00 -	30.00

KANSAS CITY FRANK (AND HIS FOOTWARMERS):

Brunswick 7062 *Jelly Roll Stomp*............	40.00 -	60.00
Paramount 12898 *Wailing Blues*...........	60.00 -	90.00
14026 *Blue Slug*..............	4.00 -	7.00

KANSAS CITY (TIN ROOF) STOMPERS:

Brunswick 7066 *Aunt Jemima Stomp*........	35.00 -	50.00
7091 *Shanghai Honeymoon*..............	35.00 -	50.00

GENE KARDOS & HIS ORCHESTRA:

Titles, issued contemporaneously on Banner, Conqueror, Melotone, Oriole, Perfect, Romeo: *Did You Ever See a Dream Walking?; Good Morning, Glory; Many Moons Ago; You're Such a Comfort To Me*...........	5.00 -	8.00
Victor 22790, 22792, 22840, 22843, 22865, 22897, 22899, 22918, 22957, 24006, 24081.......	4.00 -	6.00

ART KARLE & HIS BOYS:

Vocalion 3146 *Moon Over Miami*............	8.00 -	12.00
3147 *Lights Out*................	8.00 -	12.00

BETTY KASHMAN:

Okey 8942 *Hoochee Miss Lou*...............	7.00 -	10.00

ART KASSEL'S IN THE AIR: ART KASSEL &

HIS ORCHESTRA:

Bluebird, most issues.................	2.00 -	5.00
Columbia 2636-D, 2643-D..................	4.00 -	7.00
Columbia 2682-D *Hell's Bells*............	7.00 -	10.00
2687-D *Rain, Rain, Go Away*............	7.00 -	10.00
Columbia 2742-D, 2743-D, 2745-D..........	4.00 -	8.00
Columbia 2765-D *Chant of the Swamp*.......	8.00 -	12.00
Victor 21884, 21885...............	4.00 -	7.00
Vogue R-714 *Doodle Doo Doo*.........	10.00 -	15.00
R-723 *Wave To Me My Lady*.........	10.00 -	15.00
R-734 *A Little Consideration*........	10.00 -	15.00
R-770 *The Whiffenpoof Song*........	10.00 -	15.00
R-771 *Jeannine*..................	12.00 -	18.00
R-780 *Touch Me Not*..........	12.00 -	18.00
R-781 *Sooner Or Later*..........	12.00 -	18.00
R-785 *The Echo Said No*........	15.00 -	20.00

AL KATZ AND HIS KITTENS:

Victor 20081 *Ace in the Hole*...............	5.00 -	8.00

IRVING KAUFMAN:

Okeh 41230, 41412....................	5.00 -	8.00

JACK KAUFMAN & THE 7 BLUE BABIES:

Edison 52209 *The Grass Grows Greener*.......	10.00 -	15.00
52298 *What's The Color Of A Yellow Horse?*.	10.00 -	15.00
52323 *Since She Learned To Ride A Horse*...	10.00 -	15.00
52364 *That's My Weakness Now*...........	15.00 -	20.00
52405 *Nagasaki*............	15.00 -	20.00

SWING AND SWAY WITH SAMMY KAYE; SAMMY KAYE AND HIS ORCHESTRA:

Titles, issued contemporaneously on Banner, Conqueror, Melotone, Oriole, Perfect, Romeo: *After you; Alibi Baby; Avalon; Cry, Baby, Cry; The Dipsy Doodle; Dreamy Eyes; Good Mornin'; Have You Met Miss Jones?; If I Can Count On You; If You Were Someone Else; Indiana; It Looks Like Rain In Cherry Blossom Lane; Josephine; Moonlight On The Highway; My Buddy; Night and Day; Rosalie; Somebody Loves Me; So You Won't Sing; A Strange Loneliness; Swing Is Here To Stay; True Confession; We'll Ride The Tide Together; What Makes You So Sweet?*.	3.00 -	6.00
Victor, most issues.................	2.00 -	3.00
Vocalion, most issues................	3.00 -	6.00

JOE KAYSER AND HIS NOVELTY ORCHESTRA:

Gennett Personal (unnumbered)

LLOYD KEATING AND HIS MUSIC/ORCHESTRA:

Clarion 5045-C *I Love You So Much*..........	4.00 -	7.00
5103-C *I'll Be Blue*.................	5.00 -	8.00
5186-C *You're Driving Me Crazy*..........	7.00 -	10.00
5322-C *Wrap Your Troubles in Dreams*......	7.00 -	10.00
5328-C *Sweet and Hot*...........	7.00 -	10.00
5334-C *Under Your Window Tonight*.......	7.00 -	10.00
5339-C *Sing A Little Jingle*.............	7.00 -	10.00
5350-C *I'm Keepin' Company*..........	7.00 -	10.00
5355-C *Let's Drink a Drink to the Future*....	7.00 -	10.00
5362-C *My Sweet Tooth Says I Wanna*......	7.00 -	10.00
5368-C *There's No Depression In Love*.......	7.00 -	10.00
5379-C *I Apologize*...........	5.00 -	8.00
5386-C *Can't You See*...........	5.00 -	8.00
5407-C *You Try Somebody Else*.........	5.00 -	10.00
11002-C *Love Letters in the Sand*.........	7.00 -	10.00

(Note: 11002-C is a "double track" record, with instrumental and vocal versions of the same title occupying the same playing surface.)

Diva 3052-G *Low Down Rhythm*............	5.00 -	8.00
Diva 3118-G *Sing You Sinners*...............	5.00 -	8.00
Harmony 1143-H *Strike Up The Band!*.......	7.00 -	10.00
1145-H *Looking At You Across The Breakfast Table*......................	7.00 -	10.00

1181-H *I Love You So Much*...............	5.00 -	8.00
1233-H *I'll Be Blue*......................	5.00 -	8.00
1246-H *I'm Tickled Pink With A Blue-Eyed Baby*	7.00 -	10.00
1252-H *I Hate Myself*..................	5.00 -	8.00
1274-H *Keep A Song In Your Soul*......	7.00 -	10.00
1290-H *Sweet And Hot*................	7.00 -	10.00
1323-H *Wrap Your Troubles In Dreams*......	7.00 -	10.00
1326-H *Under Your Window Tonight*.......	7.00 -	10.00
1339-H *I'm Keepin' Company*...........	7.00 -	10.00
1343-H *Let's Drink a Drink To The Future*...	7.00 -	10.00
1350-H *My Sweet Tooth Says I Wanna*......	7.00 -	10.00
1356-H *There's A Time And Place For Everything*	7.00 -	10.00
1366-H *I Apologize*...................	5.00 -	8.00
1372-H *Can't You See*.................	5.00 -	8.00
1388-H *You Try Somebody Else*.........	7.00 -	10.00
6501-H *An Evening In Caroline*..........	7.00 -	10.00
6502-H *Ooh! That Kiss*...............	7.00 -	10.00
Velvet Tone 2394-V *Sweet And Hot*......	7.00 -	10.00
2388-V *Wrap Your Troubles In Dreams*......	7.00 -	10.00
2398-V *Under Your Window Tonight*.......	7.00 -	10.00
2414-V *I'm Keepin' Company*...........	7.00 -	10.00
2419-V *Let's Drink a Drink to the Future*....	7.00 -	10.00
2426-V *My Sweet Tooth Says I Wanna*......	7.00 -	10.00
Velvet Tone 2432-V *There's No Depression In Love*	7.00 -	10.00
2442-V *I Apologize*..................	5.00 -	8.00
2450-V *Can't You See*................	5.00 -	10.00
2467-V *You Try Somebody Else*...........	5.00 -	10.00
10501-V *An Evening In Caroline*..........	7.00 -	10.00
10502-V *Oooh! That Kiss*.............	7.00 -	10.00

EDDIE KELLY'S WASHBOARD BAND:

Bluebird 7127 *Come On 'Round To My House*..	15.00 -	20.00
7134 *Corina, I'm Goin' Away*.............	15.00 -	20.00
7148 *Shim Shaming*..................	10.00 -	15.00
7204 *Blues in the Rain*.................	15.00 -	20.00
7277 *Goin' Back To Alabama*...........	15.00 -	20.00

HAL KEMP AND HIS ORCHESTRA (from THE UNIVERSITY OF NORTH CAROLINA):

Brunswick 3486 *Brown Sugar*...........	5.00 -	8.00
3536 *Go, Joe, Go*....................	5.00 -	8.00
Brunswick 3792, 3841, 3863..........	4.00 -	7.00
Brunswick 3937 *I Don't Care*...........	5.00 -	8.00
3954 *Oh, Baby!*.....................	5.00 -	8.00
4078 *High Up On A Hill Top*...........	5.00 -	8.00
4151 *My Troubles Are Over*............	5.00 -	8.00
4212 *My Lucky Star*.................	5.00 -	8.00
4307 *That's What I Call Heaven*........	5.00 -	8.00
4327 *That's You, Baby*...............	5.00 -	8.00
4388 *To Be In Love*..................	5.00 -	8.00
4424 *In The Hush Of The Night*.........	5.00 -	8.00
4580 *I Gotta Have You*...............	7.00 -	10.00
4612 *A Little Kiss Each Morning*........	7.00 -	10.00
4676 *Navy Blues*....................	7.00 -	10.00
4805 *Washin' The Blues From My Soul*.....	7.00 -	10.00
4807 *If I Had A Girl Like You*...........	7.00 -	10.00
4988 *Fraternity Blues*................	8.00 -	12.00
4992 *Them There Eyes*...............	7.00 -	10.00
Brunswick 6055 *Would You Like To Take A Walk?*	5.00 -	8.00
6056 *I Want You For Myself*............	5.00 -	8.00
6071 *Little Joe*.....................	5.00 -	8.00
6108 *Moonlight Saving Time*...........	7.00 -	10.00
6110 *Whistles*......................	7.00 -	10.00
6130 *I'm Keepin' Company*............	7.00 -	10.00
Brunswick 6416, 6419, 6436, 6437, 6452, 6471, 6487, 6492, 6528, 6532, 6568, 6574, 6582, 6583, 6598, 6605, 6609, 6613, 6616, 6636, 6648, 6656, 6703, 6707, 6790...............	4.00 -	8.00
Brunswick 6587 *Hold My Hand*...........	7.00 -	10.00
Brunswick 6925, 6943, 6947, 6974, 6985, 7315, 7317, 7319, 7322, 7334, 7343, 7351, 7357, 7360, 7369, 7370, 7385, 7388, 7404, 7413, 7429, 7434, 7437,		

7458, 7493, 7503, 7509, 7517, 7552, 7553, 7565, 7566, 7578, 7587, 7589, 7600, 7601, 7626, 7630, 7634, 7636, 7668, 7681, 7707, 7711, 7720, 7730, 7745, 7749, 7766, 7769, 7775, 7783, 7812, 7830, 7854, 7865, 7883.....................	3.00 -	6.00
Victor, most issues..................	2.00 -	5.00

JOE KENNEDY & HIS RHYTHM ORCHESTRA:

Bluebird 6062 *Double Trouble*...............	8.00 -	12.00
6080 *Rosetta*......................	8.00 -	12.00
6102 *I Never Knew*..................	8.00 -	12.00
6233 *Rhythm Is Our Business*..........	8.00 -	12.00
6245 *You Can Depend On Me*..........	7.00 -	10.00

KEN KENNY & HIS ORCHESTRA:

Champion 40100 *Let Yourself Go*...........	7.00 -	10.00
40101 *Misty Islands Of The Highlands*.......	7.00 -	10.00
40107 *What's The Name Of That Song?*.....	7.00 -	10.00

THE KENTUCKY BLOWERS:

Gennett 5517, 5602..................	5.00 -	7.00

KENTUCKY GRASSHOPPERS:

Banner 6295 *Four Or Five Times*...........	8.00 -	15.00
6323 *Icky Blues*....................	8.00 -	15.00
6355 *Tiger Rag*....................	8.00 -	15.00
6358 *Sweet Liza*....................	8.00 -	15.00
6360 *Makin' Friends*................	8.00 -	15.00
Conqueror 7303 *Icky Blues*............	8.00 -	15.00

KENTUCKY HOT HOPPERS:

Pathe-Auctuelle 36841 *Red Head Blues*.......	7.00 -	10.00
Perfect 15022 *Red Head Blues*..........	7.00 -	10.00

KENTUCKY JAZZ BABIES:

Victor 38616 *Old Folks Shake*...........	40.00 -	60.00

KENTUCKY JUG BAND:

Vocalion 1564 *Walkin' Cane Stomp*..........	35.00 -	50.00

FREDDIE KEPPARD'S JAZZ CARDINALS:

Paramount 12399 *Stock Yards Strut*..........	75.00 -	100.00

CHARLIE KERR'S ORCHESTRA; KERR'S FAMOUS PLAYERS:

Edison 51147, 51164, 51167, 51194..........	5.00 -	10.00
Gennett 3219......................	5.00 -	10.00

KING BRADY'S CLARINET BAND:

Gennett 6393 *Lazybones Blues*..............	30.00 -	40.00

KIND DAVID'S JUG BAND:

Okeh 8861 *Georgia Bo Bo*.............	50.00 -	75.00
8901 *Sweet Potatoe Blues*.............	50.00 -	75.00
8913 *Rising Sun Blues*...............	50.00 -	75.00

KING GEORGE (AND QUEEN MARY) OF ENGLAND:

Victor 19072 *Empire Day Messages*..........	3.00 -	6.00
22338 *At the opening of the five-power naval conference*	5.00 -	8.00

KING MUTT AND HIS TENNESSEE THUMPERS:

Gennett 6796 *Nut House Stomp*.............	125.00 -	175.00
6844 *Good Time Mama*..............	125.00 -	175.00

CHUCK KING & HIS KENTUCKIANS:

Champion 15456 *Isabella (Tell Your Fella)*......	10.00 -	20.00
Champion 15458 *Caroline*............	10.00 -	20.00
15459 *Green River Blues*.............	10.00 -	20.00

FRANCES KING:

Okeh 40854 *She's Got It*...............	7.00 -	10.00

HENRY KING AND HIS ORCHESTRA:

Columbia 2941-D, 2945-D, 2949-D, 2950-D, 2991-D, 2992-D, 2998-D, 3005-D, 3010-D, 3036-D, 3042-D, 3049-D....................	3.00 -	6.00
Decca, most issues....................	2.00 -	4.00
Victor, most issues....................	3.00 -	5.00
Vocalion 2550, 2561, 2562, 2573, 2579, 2580...	3.00 -	6.00

TEMPO KING AND HIS KINGS OF TEMPO:

Titles, issued contemporaneously on Banner, Conqueror, Melotone, Oriole, Perfect, Romeo: *Alligator Crawl; All Over Nothing At All; Am*

I Dreaming?; Don't You Know Or Don't You Care?; The Folks Who Live On The Hill; High, Wide and Handsome; I Can Always Dream; I'm Gonna Put You In Your Place; On With The Dance; The One Rose; Riding On The Old Ferris Wheel; You've Got Me Under Your Thumb. ... 4.00 - 7.00

Bluebird 6553, 6534, 6335, 6560, 6563, 6575, 6637, 6642, 6643, 6684, 6687, 6688, 6721, 6725, 6758, 6768, 6770, 6880 ...... 4.00 - 7.00

THE KING'S JESTERS (AND LOUISE):
Bluebird 5149, 5184, 6517 ...... 4.00 - 8.00
Vogue R-708 *I Surrender, Dear* ...... 10.00 - 15.00
R-716 *Mean To Me* ...... 10.00 - 15.00
R-750 *Who's Got A Tent For Rent* ...... 12.00 - 16.00
R-751 *Humphrey, The Sweet Singing Pig* ..... 12.00 - 16.00
R-766 *Sepulveda* ...... 12.00 - 16.00

KIRBY'S KINGS OF JAZZ:
Bell 589 *Oh! Daisy* ...... 10.00 - 20.00
591 *Green River Blues* ...... 10.00 - 20.00
592 *Isabella (Tell Your Fella)* ...... 10.00 - 20.00
598 *Caroline* ...... 10.00 - 20.00

JOHN KIRBY & HIS ONYX CLUB BOYS/ORCHESTRA:
Decca 2216 *Undecided* ...... 5.00 - 8.00
2367 *Pastel Blue* ...... 5.00 - 8.00
Okeh 4624, 4653, 4890, 5048, 5187, 5520, 5542, 5570, 5605, 5632, 5661, 5705, 5761, 5805 ... 4.00 - 7.00
Vocalion 4624, 4653, 4890, 5048, 5187, 5520, 5542, 5570 ...... 4.00 - 7.00

ANDY KIRK & HIS TWELVE CLOUDS OF JOY:
Brunswick 4653 *Casey Jones Special* ...... 15.00 - 20.00
4694 *Blue Clarinet Stomp* ...... 15.00 - 20.00
4803 *I Lost My Gal From Memphis* ...... 15.00 - 20.00
4863 *Once Or Twice* ...... 15.00 - 20.00
4878 *Snag It* ...... 15.00 - 20.00
4893 *Froggy Bottom* ...... 15.00 - 20.00
4981 *Honey, Just For You* ...... 15.00 - 20.00
6027 *Saturday* ...... 15.00 - 20.00
6129 *Dallas Blues* ...... 15.00 - 20.00
Decca 729 *Froggy Bottom* ...... 5.00 - 8.00
744 *All The Jive I Gone* ...... 5.00 - 8.00
772 *Blue Illusion* ...... 5.00 - 8.00
809 *Walkin' And Swingin'* ...... 5.00 - 8.00
853 *Moten Swing* ...... 5.00 - 8.00
931 *Steppin' Pretty* ...... 7.00 - 10.00
1046 *Bearcat Shuffle* ...... 7.00 - 10.00
1085 *The Lady Who Swings The Band* ...... 7.00 - 10.00
1146 *Fifty-Second Street* ...... 5.00 - 8.00
1208 *Puddin' Head Serenade* ...... 5.00 - 8.00
1261 *In The Groove* ...... 5.00 - 8.00
1303 *Wednesday Night Hop* ...... 5.00 - 8.00
1349 *Skies Are Blue* ...... 5.00 - 8.00
1422 *Better Luck Next Time* ...... 5.00 - 8.00
1477 *With Love In My Heart* ...... 5.00 - 8.00
1531 *Downstream* ...... 5.00 - 8.00
1579 *A Mellow Bit OF Rhythm* ...... 5.00 - 8.00
1606 *The Big Dipper* ...... 5.00 - 8.00
1663 *Poor Butterfly* ...... 5.00 - 8.00
Decca (higher numbers) ...... 3.00 - 6.00

MANNIE KLEIN/KLINE & HIS ORCHESTRA:
Brunswick 7605 *Ringside Table For Two* ...... 7.00 - 10.00
7606 *Hot Spell* ...... 7.00 - 10.00

THE KNICKERBOCKERS:
Columbia 2067-D, 2129-D, 2502-D ...... 5.00 - 10.00

KOLSTER DANCE ORCHESTRA:
Columbia 2072-D *Do Ya Love Me?* ...... 7.00 - 10.00

JERRY KRUGER (AND HER ORCHESTRA):
Variety 666 *The Bed Song* ...... 8.00 - 12.00
Vocalion 3799 *So You Won't Sing* ...... 8.00 - 12.00
4927 *Rain, Rain, Go Away* ...... 8.00 - 12.00

GENE KRUPA AND HIS ORCHESTRA/GENE KRUPA'S SWING BAND:
Brunswick 8123, 8124, 8139, 8161, 8166, 8188, 8198, 8205, 8211, 8246, 8249, 8253, 8274, 8280, 8282, 8289, 8296, 8335, 8340, 8346, 8361, 8387, 8400, 8412, 8448, 8451 ...... 4.00 - 8.00
Columbia 35205, 35218, 35237, 35262, 35304, 35324, 35336, 35361, 35366, 35387, 35408, 35415, 35423, 35429, 25444 ...... 4.00 - 8.00
Columbia, most higher numbers ...... 2.00 - 4.00
Okeh, most issues ...... 3.00 - 5.00
Victor 25263, 25276 ...... 4.00 - 7.00

KXYZ NOVELTY BAND:
Bluebird 5831 *The Sheik Of Araby* ...... 7.00 - 10.00
5832 *I Never Knew* ...... 7.00 - 10.00
5852 *Bugle Call Rag* ...... 7.00 - 10.00
5868 *Indiana* ...... 7.00 - 10.00

BILLY KYLE & HIS SWING CLUB BAND:
Variety 531 *Big Boy Blue* ...... 8.00 - 12.00
574 *Havin' A Ball* ...... 8.00 - 12.00
617 *Can I Forget You?* ...... 7.00 - 10.00
659 *Girl Of My Dreams* ...... 7.00 - 10.00
Vocalion 3778 *All You Want To Do Is Dance* .. 7.00 - 10.00
3815 *Margie* ...... 7.00 - 10.00
3843 *Handle My Heart With Care* ...... 7.00 - 10.00

KAY KYSER AND HIS ORCHESTRA:
Brunswick 7449, 7453, 7465, 7470, 7541, 7555, 7647, 7648, 7682, 7701, 7755, 7759, 7793, 7805, 7819, 7826, 7836, 7846 ...... 3.00 - 6.00
Brunswick 7881, 7891, 8114, 8120, 8126, 8143, 8149, 8165, 8170, 8181, 8185, 8193, 8197, 8201, 8209, 8210, 8215, 8222, 8225, 8228, 8234, 8244, 8258, 8263, 8267, 8279, 8295, 8301, 8308, 8312, 8317, 8320, 8324, 8328, 8338, 8853, 8368, 8377, 8381, 8385, 8392, 8415, 8439, 8440, 8446, 8456 ... 3.00 - 6.00
Columbia, most issues ...... 2.00 - 4.00
Victor V-40028 *Broken Dreams of Yesterday* ... 8.00 - 12.00
V-40222 *Rainy Weather* ...... 10.00 - 15.00
V-40258 *Collegiate Fanny* ...... 10.00 - 15.00

LADA'S LOUISIANA LADS:
Sunset 1149 *Everybody Stomp* ...... 20.00 - 30.00
1151 *Everything's Gonna Be All Right* ...... 20.00 - 30.00

LADD'S BLACK ACES:
Gennett 4762, 4794, 4806, 4809, 4843, 4856, 4869, 4886, 4938, 4995, 5018, 5023, 5035, 5060, 5075, 5125, 5127, 5142, 5150, 5164, 5187, 5272, 5366, 5422, 5521 ...... 5.00 - 10.00
Superior 2748 *When It's Sleepy Time Down South* 30.00 - 50.00
2771 *St. Louis Blues* ...... 30.00 - 50.00

TOMMY LADNIER & HIS ORCHESTRA:
Bluebird 10086, 10089 ...... 3.00 - 5.00

SLIM LAMAR & HIS SOUTHERNERS; SLIM LAMAR'S ORCHESTRA:
Victor 21710, 40005, 40049 ...... 6.00 - 10.00
40093 *That's A Plenty* ...... 15.00 - 20.00
40130 *You Never Did That Before* ...... 10.00 - 15.00
40146 *Memphis Kick-Up* ...... 15.00 - 20.00

DOROTHY LAMOUR:
Brunswick 7829, 7838, 7017, 8132, 8154, 8291, 8304 4.00 - 8.00

LAMPE'S ORCHESTRA FROM THE TRIANON BALLROOM; DELL LAMPE & HIS ORCHESTRA:
Autograph (unnumbered) *Trianon (A New Dance)* 15.00 - 20.00
604 *Prince Of Wails* ...... 30.00 - 40.00
628 *Lady Of The Nile* ...... 20.00 - 30.00
629 *Candied Sweets* ...... 20.00 - 30.00
Crown 3409 *Street Of Dreams* ...... 5.00 - 8.00
3426 *My River Home* ...... 5.00 - 8.00
3441 *Darkness on the Delta* ...... 5.00 - 8.00
Victor 24005 *Spring is Here Again* ...... 5.00 - 8.00
24020 *Scattin' The Skeeter Scott* ...... 7.00 - 10.00

MIKE LANDAU & HIS OAKLAND TERRACE ORCHESTRA:

Edison 52538 *Sugar Is Back In Town*......... 7.00 - 10.00

ART LANDRY'S CALL OF THE NORTH ORCHESTRA/SYNCOPATIN' SIX; ART LANDRY AND HIS ORCHESTRA:

Gennett 5053, 5170, 5171, 5184, 5189, 5222, 5255 4.00 - 7.00
Victor 19850, 19858, 19866, 19984, 20023, 20126,
20142, 20598, 20644...................... 3.00 - 6.00

EDDIE LANG; ED LANG & HIS ORCHESTRA:

Brunswick 6254 *Pickin' My Way*............. 7.00 - 10.00
Okeh 8696 *Freeze An' Melt*.................. 15.00 - 20.00
40807 *Eddie's Twister*................. 8.00 - 12.00
40936 *Melody Man's Dream*...... 8.00 - 12.00
40989 *A Little Love, A Little Kiss*..... 8.00 - 12.00
41134 *Add a Little Wiggle*............. 8.00 - 12.00
41253 *Freeze An' Melt*................. 15.00 - 20.00
41344 *Walkin' The Dog*............... 15.00 - 20.00
41410 *Bugle Call Rag*.................. 20.00 - 25.00

LANGE-McKAY ORCHESTRA AT CASTLE FARMS:

Gennett 5584 *Leaky Roof Blues*............. 10.00 - 15.00

HENRY LANGE AND HIS (BAKER HOTEL) ORCHESTRA:

Brunswick 4161 *I Want You More*........... 7.00 - 10.00
4478 *China Boy*..................... 15.00 - 20.00
Champion 16294 *Moonlight Saving Time*....... 15.00 - 20.00
16332 *Mood Indigo*..................... 15.00 - 20.00
Gennett 6263 *Hot Lips*..................... 15.00 - 20.00
20389 *Sweet*.................... 15.00 - 20.00

FRANCES LANGFORD:

Nasty Man, issued contemporaneously on Banner,
Melotone, Oriole, Perfect, Romeo:.......... 5.00 - 8.00
Bluebird 5016 *Moon Song*................. 5.00 - 8.00
Columbia 2696-D *I Can't Believe It's True*...... 5.00 - 8.00
Victor 24191 *When Mother Played The Organ*.. 5.00 - 8.00

LANIN'S RED HEADS; LANIN'S SOUTHERN SERENADERS (See SAM LANIN)

HOWARD LANIN AND HIS BENJAMIN FRANKLIN HOTEL ORCHESTRA:

Victor 19711 *On A Night Like This*........... 5.00 - 8.00
19797 *Melancholy Lou*.................... 5.00 - 8.00

SAM LANIN & HIS ORCHESTRA/FAMOUS PLAYERS (AND SINGERS); LANIN'S RED HEADS; SAM LANIN'S DANCE ORCHESTRA/TROUBADOURS; LANIN'S SOUTHERN SERENADERS:

Arto 9097 *Memphis Blues*.................. 7.00 - 10.00
Banner 0688 *Exactly Like You*.............. 5.00 - 8.00
Banner 1015, 1100, 1182, 1500, 1517, 1541, 1564,
1567, 1601, 1617, 1622, 1644, 1655, 1711, 1800,
1883, 1886........................ 4.00 - 7.00
Banner 6261 *Happy Days And Lonely Nights*... 5.00 - 8.00
6328 *He, She And Me*............. 5.00 - 8.00
6388 *Do Something!*................. 5.00 - 8.00
6445 *Wishing And Waiting For Love*....... 5.00 - 8.00
32219 *Little Girl*................. 5.00 - 8.00
Cameo 8225 *My Pet*................. 5.00 - 8.00
8227 *Sweet Sue - Just You*........... 5.00 - 8.00
8228 *Who Wouldn't Be Blue?*......... 5.00 - 8.00
8245 *Ready For The River*........... 5.00 - 8.00
8348 *Don't Be Like That*............. 5.00 - 8.00
9008 *Adorable Dora*.................... 5.00 - 8.00
Champion 16039 *Hullabaloo*............... 10.00 - 15.00
Columbia 279-D, 285-D, 324-D............ 3.00 - 5.00
Columbia 327-D *King Porter Stomp*........ 10.00 - 15.00
376-D *Flag That Train*............. 7.00 - 10.00
Columbia 396-D, 414-D, 438-D............ 3.00 - 6.00
Columbia 447-D *Desdemona*............. 7.00 - 10.00
483-D *Five Foot Two, Eyes Of Blue*....... 7.00 - 10.00
Conqueror 7810 *Little Girl*................. 5.00 - 8.00

Diva 3083-G *Crying For The Carolinas*....... 7.00 - 10.00
Emerson 10496 *Arkansas Blues*.............. 7.00 - 10.00
Harmony 1029-H, 1036-H................ 3.00 - 5.00
Harmony 1083-H *Crying For The Carolinas*.... 7.00 - 10.00
1084-H *When I'm Housekeeping For You*.... 10.00 - 15.00
1107-H *Hangin' On The Garden Gate*....... 5.00 - 8.00
1109-H *Keepin' Myself For You*........... 5.00 - 8.00
1139-H *The Free And Easy*............. 5.00 - 8.00
1165-H *Be Careful With Those Eyes*......... 5.00 - 8.00
1265-H *You're Simply Delish*............. 7.00 - 10.00
Odeon ONY-36112 *Seems To Me*............. 8.00 - 12.00
ONY-36113 *Rollin' Down The River*....... 8.00 - 12.00
ONY-36189 *Please Don't Talk About Me When
I'm Gone*.............................. 8.00 - 12.00
ONY-36190 *I Surrender, Dear*............ 8.00 - 12.00
ONY-36195 *The One-Man Band*.......... 8.00 - 12.00
Okeh 40111, 40170, 40754, 40810, 40833, 40855,
40863, 40914, 40933, 40937, 41038, 41063,
41097, 41121, 41159...................... 3.00 - 6.00
Okeh 41188 *If I Had You*................. 20.00 - 30.00
41228 *If I'm Crazy Over You*............ 20.00 - 30.00
Okeh 41383 *Cooking Breakfast For The One I Love* 10.00 - 15.00
41385 *Mona*............................... 7.00 - 10.00
Pathe-Actuelle 036184 *Forsaken Blues*......... 5.00 - 8.00
Pathe-Actuelle 036202, 036203, 026219, 36342,
36343, 36344.......................... 4.00 - 7.00
Pathe-Actuelle 36357 *Spanish Shawl*......... 5.00 - 8.00
36363 *No Man's Mama*................ 5.00 - 8.00
Pathe-Actuelle 36512, 36545, 36547.......... 4.00 - 7.00
Pathe-Actuelle 36797 *My Pet*............... 5.00 - 8.00
36798 *Get Out And Get Under The Moon*... 5.00 - 8.00
36802 *Sweet Sue - Just You*............. 5.00 - 8.00
36804 *Who Wouldn't Be Blue?*............ 5.00 - 8.00
Perfect 14365 *Forsaken Blues*............. 5.00 - 8.00
Perfect 14330, 14383, 14384, 14440, 14486, 14523,
14524, 14525.......................... 4.00 - 7.00
Perfect 14538 *Spanish Shawl*............... 5.00 - 8.00
14544 *No Man's Mama*.................... 5.00 - 8.00
Perfect 14693, 14726, 14728............. 4.00 - 7.00
Perfect 14978 *My Pet*................... 5.00 - 8.00
14979 *Get Out And Get Under The Moon*... 5.00 - 8.00
14983 *Sweet Sue- Just You*............. 5.00 - 8.00
14985 *Who Wouldn't Be Blue?*............ 5.00 - 8.00
15486 *Little Girl*..................... 5.00 - 8.00
Regal 8413 *The Varsity Drag*............. 7.00 - 10.00
8600 *Two Lips*..................... 4.00 - 7.00
8671 *Me And The Man In The Moon*....... 5.00 - 8.00
8701 *Happy Days And Lonely Nights*....... 5.00 - 8.00
8817 *Wishing and Waiting For Love*....... 5.00 - 8.00
Romeo 948 *That's Her Now!*............. 5.00 - 8.00
Supertone 9458 *I'm In Seventh Heaven*........ 7.00 - 10.00
9550 *Hang On To Me*................. 7.00 - 10.00
9576 *Miss Wonderful*................. 7.00 - 10.00
9580 *Lady Luck*..................... 7.00 - 10.00
9744 *Hullabaloo*..................... 10.00 - 15.00

LA PALINA BROADCASTERS:

Conqueror 7412 *Little By Little*............. 5.00 - 8.00
Domino 4405 *Little By Little*............. 5.00 - 8.00
4408 *Sweetheart, We Need Each Other*...... 5.00 - 8.00
Pathe-Actuelle 37022 *Sweetness*............. 5.00 - 8.00
37024 *Piccolo Pete*.................... 5.00 - 8.00
37037 *Little By Little*................. 5.00 - 8.00
37043 *Sweetheart, We Need Each Other*..... 5.00 - 8.00
Perfect 15203 *Sweetness*................ 5.00 - 8.00
15205 *Piccolo Pete*.................... 5.00 - 8.00
15218 *Little By Little*................. 5.00 - 8.00
15224 *Sweetheart, We Need Each Other*..... 5.00 - 8.00

HAL LASKA AND HIS ORCHESTRA:

Parlophone PNY-34034 *Romance*............ 5.00 - 8.00
PNY-34038 *Sweeping The Clouds Away
(instrumental)*........................ 15.00 - 20.00

PNY-34039 *Any Time's The Time To Fall In Love*		
(instrumental)	15.00 -	20.00
PNY-34040 *Sweeping The Clouds Away*	10.00 -	15.00
PNY-34041 *Any Time's The Time To Fall In Love*	15.00 -	20.00
PNY-34064 *When The Little Red Roses Get The*		
Blues	15.00 -	20.00
PNY-34070 *Exactly Like You*	10.00 -	15.00
PNY-34072 *Dust*	10.00 -	15.00
PNY-34073 *Leave It That Way*	10.00 -	15.00
PNY-34074 *On The Sunny Side of the Street*	10.00 -	15.00
PNY-34161 *Put On Your Old Grey Bonnet*	7.00 -	10.00
PNY-34162 *Alexander's Ragtime Band*	7.00 -	10.00
PNY-34164 *Overnight*	7.00 -	10.00
PNY-34165 *Little Did I Know*	7.00 -	10.00

HARLAN LATTIMORE & HIS CONNIE'S INN ORCHESTRA:

Columbia 2675-D *Chant of the Weed*	12.00 -	15.00
2678-D *Reefer Man*	12.00 -	15.00

LA VEEDA DANCE ORCHESTRA:

Columbia 1549-D *Strut Yo' Stuff*	15.00 -	20.00

THELMA LA VIZZO:

Paramount 12206 *Trouble In Mind Blues*	25.00 -	40.00
12250 *The Stomps*	50.00 -	75.00

GERTRUDE LAWRENCE:

Columbia 512-D, 513-D, 514-D	4.00 -	8.00
Victor 20331	4.00 -	8.00

SARA LAWRENCE:

Oriole 894 *Don't Love Me*	7.00 -	10.00

DAVE LAWSON'S ORCHESTRA:

Challenge 365 *Me and My Shadow*	15.00 -	20.00
Champion 15326 *Me and My Shadow*	15.00 -	20.00

YANK LAWSON'S JAZZ BAND:

Signature	4.00 -	7.00

LAZY LEVEE LOUNGERS:

Columbia 2243-D *Shout, Sister, Shout*	10.00 -	15.00

LEE'S BLACK DIAMONDS:

Broadway 1294 *Piggly Wiggly Blues*	35.00 -	50.00

BARON LEE & THE BLUE RHYTHM BAND:

Titles, issued contemporaneously on Banner, Melotone, Oriole, Perfect, Romeo: *Cabin In The Cotton; The Crawl; Doin' The Shake; Heatwaves; Jazz Cocktail; Mighty Sweet; Minnie The Moocher's Wedding Day; Old Yazoo; Reefer Man; Rhythm Spasm; The Scat Song; Sentimental Gentleman From Georgia; Smoke Rings; White Lightning; Wild Waves; You Gave Me Everything But Love*	10.00 -	15.00

GEORGE E. LEE & HIS (NOVELTY SINGING) ORCHESTRA:

Brunswick 4684 *Ruff Scufflin'*	25.00 -	35.00
7132 *Paseo Strut*	35.00 -	50.00
Merritt 2206 *Down Home Syncopated Blues*	200.00 -	300.00

JULIA LEE:

Brunswick 4761 *He's Tall and Dark and Handsome*	25.00 -	35.00

MANDY LEE:

Titles, issued contemporaneously on Banner, Conqueror, Domino, Regal: *Crap Shootin' Pappa, Mama Done Caught Your Dice; Harlem Blues; Someone's Been Lovin' My Baby*	7.00 -	10.00
Pathe-Actuelle 7509, Perfect 109 *Wandering Papa Blues*	10.00 -	15.00

MARGUERITE LEE:

Vocalion 1150 *You Will Always Live in Our Memory*	35.00 -	50.00

RUTH LEE:

Nordskog 3008 *Maybe Someday*	100.00 -	150.00
Sunshine 3002 *Maybe Someday*	100.00 -	150.00
(Sunshine 3002 label is pasted over Nordskog label)		

WINTHROP LEE & HIS ORCHESTRA:

Parlophone PNY-34124 *Loveless Love*	15.00 -	25.00
PNY-34148 *Daniel's Blues*	15.00 -	25.00

BOBBIE LEECAN; BOBBIE LEECAN'S NEED-MORE BAND:

Victor 20251 *Black Cat Bone Blues*	25.00 -	35.00
20660 *Midnight Susie*	25.00 -	35.00
20768 *Blue Harmonica*	25.00 -	35.00
20853 *Apaloosa Blues*	25.00 -	35.00
20958 *Royal Palm Blues*	25.00 -	35.00

CHESTER LEIGHTON AND HIS SOPHOMORES:

Clarion 5125-C *Cheerful Little Earful*	7.00 -	10.00
5177-C *Someone Sang a Sweeter Song To Mary*	5.00 -	8.00
5180-C *A Peach of a Pair*	5.00 -	8.00
5186-C *The Little Things in Life*	5.00 -	8.00
5276-C *If You Should Ever Need Me*	5.00 -	8.00
5277-C *When I Take My Sugar To Tea*	7.00 -	10.00
5319-C *Star Dust*	7.00 -	10.00
5337-C *Love Is Like That*	5.00 -	8.00
5351-C *On The Beach With You*	7.00 -	10.00
5353-C *Just One More Chance*	7.00 -	10.00
5363-C *The Kiss That You've Forgotten*	5.00 -	8.00
Harmony 1233-H *A Peach of a Pair*	5.00 -	8.00
1242-H *My Love For You*	5.00 -	8.00
1248-H *Satan's Holiday*	8.00 -	12.00
1251-H *Someone Sang a Sweeter Song To Mary*	5.00 -	8.00
1307-H *When I Take My Sugar To Tea*	7.00 -	10.00
1328-H *Love Is Like That*	5.00 -	8.00
1340-H *Without That Gal!*	7.00 -	10.00
1342-H *Makin' Faces at the Man in the Moon*	7.00 -	10.00
1351-H *The Kiss That You've Forgotten*	5.00 -	8.00
Velvet Tone 2343-V *When I Take My Sugar To Tea*	7.00 -	10.00
2342-V *If You Should Ever Need Me*	5.00 -	8.00
2401-V *Love Is Like That*	5.00 -	8.00
2415-V *On The Beach With You*	7.00 -	10.00
2417-V *Just One More Chance*	7.00 -	10.00
2427-V *The Kiss That You've Forgotten*	5.00 -	8.00

HAROLD LEM & HIS ORCHESTRA:

Okeh 41465 *I Got Rhythm*	8.00 -	12.00

LENOX DANCE ORCHESTRA:

Perfect 14394 *Me Neenyah*	7.00 -	10.00

HARLAN LEONARD & HIS ROCKETS:

Bluebird	3.00 -	5.00

LEROY'S DALLAS BAND

Columbia 14402-D *Tampa Shout*	30.00 -	40.00

LEW LESLIE'S BLACKBIRD'S ORCHESTRA:

Brunswick 4030 *Bandanna Babies*	10.00 -	15.00

NATE LESLIE & HIS ORCHESTRA:

Vocalion 3584 *Shake Yo' Bones*	7.00 -	10.00

LEVEE LOUNGERS:

Pahte-Actuelle 36679, 36883	5.00 -	8.00
Perfect 14680, 15064	5.00 -	8.00

LEVEE SERENADERS:

Vocalion 1154 *Midnight Mama*	75.00 -	100.00

LEVEE SYNCOPATORS:

Titles, issued contemporaneously on Gray Gull, Radiex, Van Dyke: *The Rackett; The Harlem Stomp Down*	15.00 -	20.00

ALFRED LEWIS:

Vocalion 1498 *Friday Moan Blues*	25.00 -	35.00

MEADE LUX LEWIS:

Blue Note	3.00 -	6.00
Decca 819 *Yancey Special*	8.00 -	12.00
Paramount 12896 *Honky Train Blues*	90.00 -	120.00
Solo Art 12002, 12003, 12004	7.00 -	10.00
Victor 25541 *Honky Tonk Train Blues*	8.00 -	12.00
Vocalion 4606 *Boogie Woogie Prayer*	5.00 -	8.00
4608 *Bear Cat Crawl*	5.00 -	8.00

NOAH LEWIS; NOAH LEWIS'S JUG BAND:

Bluebird 5675 *Ticket Agent Blues*	50.00 -	75.00
Victor 23266 *New Minglewood Blues*	90.00 -	120.00
23336 *Like I Want To Be*	75.00 -	100.00
38681 *Chickasaw Special*	50.00 -	75.00

SAMMY LEWIS (AND HIS BAMVILLE SYNCOPATORS):

Okeh 8285 *Just Too Late*	7.00 -	10.00

Vocalion 1029 *Hateful Papa Blues*.............	15.00 -	20.00
1030 *Arkansas Shout*...................	15.00 -	20.00

TED LEWIS & HIS BAND:

Columbia 1-S *Popular Favorites (medley)*.......	2.00 -	3.00
Columbia 48-D, 52-D, 82-D, 122-D, 157-D, 170-D, 195-D, 227-D, 241-D, 255-D, 274-D, 295-D, 311-D, 406-D, 416-D, 439-D, 478-D, 504-D, 543-D, 565-D, 585-D, 600-D, 620-D......	3.00 -	6.00
Columbia 667-D *Where'd You Get Those Eyes?*.	7.00 -	10.00
Columbia 670-D, 697-D, 770-D, 826-D, 844-D, 895-D	4.00 -	7.00
Columbia 922-D *When My Baby Smiles At Me*.	5.00 -	8.00
Columbia 988-D, 1017-D, 1050-D, 1084-D, 1207-D, 1242-D, 1296-D, 1313-D, 1346-D, 1391-D, 1428-D, 1485-D......	4.00 -	8.00
Columbia 1525-D *A Jazz Holiday*..........	7.00 -	10.00
1573-D *Clarinet Marmalade*...........	7.00 -	10.00
1656-D *She's Funny That Way*.........	5.00 -	8.00
1709-D *Glad Rag Doll*...............	5.00 -	8.00
1789-D *Limehouse Blues*.............	5.00 -	8.00
1854-D *Maybe Who Knows?*.........	5.00 -	8.00
1882-D *I'm The Medicine Man For The Blues*	5.00 -	8.00
1916-D *Lewisada Blues*..............	7.00 -	10.00
1957-D *Lonely Troubadour*...........	5.00 -	8.00
1999-D *Lady Luck*..................	5.00 -	8.00
2029-D *Farewell Blues*..............	8.00 -	12.00
2088-D *Harmonica Harry*............	8.00 -	12.00
2113-D *Aunt Hagar's Blues*..........	8.00 -	12.00
2144-D *Singing a Vagabond Song*.........	8.00 -	12.00
2181-D *Dinah*....................	10.00 -	15.00
2217-D *Sobbin' Blues*...............	10.00 -	15.00
2246-D *The World Is Waiting For The Sunrise*	10.00 -	15.00
2311-D *Laughing At Life*............	10.00 -	15.00
2336-D *Somebody Stole My Gal*.........	10.00 -	15.00
2378-D *Headin' For Better Times*.......	15.00 -	20.00
2408-D *At Last I'm Happy*...........	10.00 -	15.00
2428-D *Egyptian Ella*..............	15.00 -	20.00
2452-D *Ho Hum!*...................	15.00 -	20.00
2467-D *Dip Your Brush in the Sunshine*.....	15.00 -	20.00
2492-D *I'm All Dressed Up with a Broken Heart*	15.00 -	20.00
2527-D *Royal Garden Blues*............	15.00 -	20.00
2560-D *An Evening In Caroline*........	15.00 -	20.00
2635-D *Somebody Loves You*..........	15.00 -	20.00
2652-D *A Shanty in Old Shanty Town*.......	15.00 -	20.00
2728-D *Play, Fiddle, Play*............	8.00 -	12.00
2748-D *Buy American!*...............	10.00 -	15.00
2753-D *There's A New Day Coming*......	10.00 -	15.00
2758-D *All Aboard For Dreamland, Baby*....	10.00 -	15.00
2774-D *Stormy Weather*..............	10.00 -	15.00
2775-D *The Gold-Diggers' Song*...........	15.00 -	20.00
2777-D *In a Garden In Old Kalua*........	7.00 -	10.00
2786-D *Rhythm*....................	15.00 -	20.00
2799-D *Here You Come With Love*......	10.00 -	15.00
2807-D *Ten Thousand Years Ago*..........	12.00 -	18.00

(Note: Most of the foregoing, after number 1656-D, were issued with the special Ted Lewis picture label, and some earlier numbers were repressed with that special label.)

Columbia A-2798, A-2844, A-2895...........	2.00 -	4.00
Columbia A-2908, A-2927, A-2945, A-2998, A-3306, A-3329, A-3351, A-3400, A-3411, A-3421, A-3434, A-3453.................	3.00 -	5.00
Columbia A-3464, A-3473, A-3499, A-3538, A-3590, A-3647, A-3662, A-3676, A-3709, A-3730, A-3738.................	3.00 -	5.00
Columbia A-3790, A-3813................	4.00 -	7.00
Columbia A-3814, A-3957................	3.00 -	5.00
Columbia A-3879, A-3892, A-3972...........	4.00 -	8.00
Decca 106, 107, 239, 240, 241, 242...........	4.00 -	7.00
Decca, most other issues.................	2.00 -	5.00

JOIE LICHTER'S STRAND SYMPHONISTS:

Paramount 20289, 20428, 20439...........	10.00 -	15.00

Puritan 11428, 11439..................	10.00 -	15.00

LOUIS LILIENFELD & HIS HOTEL BILTMORE ORCHESTRA:

Edison 52128, 52176, 52216, 52237, 52289...	5.00 -	8.00
52241 *Let A Smile Be Your Umbrella*.......	10.00 -	15.00
52272 *Forever And Ever*..............	10.00 -	15.00

LILL'S HOT SHOTS:

Vocalion 1037 *Drop That Sack*.............	75.00 -	100.00

DONALD LINDLEY (& HIS BOYS):

Columbia 546-D, 1443-D...............	5.00 -	8.00
Edison 51771 *Hot As A Summer's Day*........	10.00 -	15.00

JACK LINX & HIS (BIRMINGHAM) SOCIETY SERENADERS:

Okeh 40188 *Doodle Doo Doo*...............	8.00 -	12.00
40192 *How Come You Do Me Like You Do?*.	15.00 -	20.00
40365 *Sweet Georgia Brown*............	10.00 -	15.00
40429 *She's My Sheba, I'm Her Sheik*.......	10.00 -	15.00
40439 *When Eyes Of Blue Are Fooling You*..	10.00 -	15.00
40458 *Don't You Try To High-Hat Me*......	10.00 -	15.00
40587 *Nobody's Rose*...............	10.00 -	15.00
40602 *Fallen Arches*...............	15.00 -	20.00
40619 *Tiger Rag*..................	15.00 -	20.00
40803 *Beale Street Blues*.............	15.00 -	20.00
41014 *Pardon The Glove*.............	15.00 -	20.00

THE LITTLE ACES:

Okeh 41136 *Four Or Five Times*............	15.00 -	20.00

THE LITTLE CHOCOLATE DANDIES:

Okeh 8728 *Six or Seven Times*.............	15.00 -	20.00

LITTLE'S COLLEGIANS:

Superior 2817 *Clarinet Marmalade*...........	20.00 -	30.00

THE LITTLE RAMBLERS:

Bluebird 6043, 6045, 6077, 6130, 6131, 6144, 6189, 6191, 6192, 6193, 6220, 6232, 6237.......	5.00 -	8.00
Columbia 175-D, 203-D, 217-D, 248-D, 346-D, 403-D, 423-D, 524-D, 535-D, 628-D, 679-D, 719-D, 1103-D.................	5.00 -	10.00

LITTLE JACK LITTLE & HIS ORCHESTRA:

Bluebird 5056, 5065................	4.00 -	6.00
Columbia 2895-D, 2900-D, 2969-D, 2978-D, 2984-D, 2993-D, 3006-D, 3009-D, 3068-D, 3069-D, 3095-D, 3107-D, 3108-D.................	4.00 -	6.00

ED LLOYD AND HIS ORCHESTRA (SEE ED LOYD)

PAUL LOCH & HIS ORCHESTRA:

Parlophone PNY-34059 *I Was Made To Love You*	10.00 -	20.00
PNY-34063 *Accordion Joe*...............	10.00 -	20.00
PNY-34065 *Collegiate Love*............	10.00 -	20.00

LOCKE BROTHERS RHYTHM ORCHESTRA:

Bluebird 6287 *Don't You Tear My Clothes*.....	10.00 -	15.00
6288 *Sills Stomp*....................	10.00 -	15.00
6297 *Elephant Stomp*...............	10.00 -	15.00
6316 *Some Of These Days*............	10.00 -	15.00
6332 *China Boy*..................	10.00 -	15.00

GUY LOMBARDO & HIS ROYAL CANADIANS:

Columbia 1395-D, 1451-D, 1721-D, 2578-D.....	5.00 -	8.00
Gennett 5416 *So This Is Venice*.............	30.00 -	40.00
5417 *Cotton Picker's Ball*..............	30.00 -	40.00
Personal Record 140-P *She'll Come Along*......	15.00 -	20.00

FRED LONGSHAW:

Columbia 14080-D.................	5.00 -	8.00

ERNEST LOOMIS' ORCHESTRA:

Victor 20755 *Sweet Someone*................	8.00 -	12.00

VINCENT LOPEZ & HIS (CASA LOPEZ/HOTEL PENNSYLVANIA) ORCHESTRA:

Brunswick 20065, 20066 (both 12-inch records)..	4.00 -	7.00
Okeh 40478, 40552, 40586.............	4.00 -	7.00

LOU & HIS GINGER SNAPS:

Banner 6536 *Broadway Rhythm*.............	15.00 -	20.00
6540 *The Way He Loves Is Just Too Bad*....	10.00 -	15.00

Cameo 9319 *Broadway Rhythm*. . . . . 15.00 - 20.00
  9320 *The Way He Loves Is Just Too Bad*. . . . 10.00 - 15.00

LOUIS' HARLEM STOMPERS:
Columbia 2615-D *Casa Loma Stomp*. . . . . 15.00 - 20.00

LOUISIANA JOE AND SLIM:
Champion 50063 *Crossin' Beale Street*. . . . . 10.00 - 15.00

LOUISIANA RHYTHM KINGS:
Brunswick 4706 *Oh, Lady Be Good*. . . . . 8.00 - 12.00
  4845 *Swanee*. . . . . 8.00 - 12.00
  4908 *Karavan*. . . . . 8.00 - 12.00
  4923 *Lazy Daddy*. . . . . 8.00 - 12.00
  4938 *Pretty Baby*. . . . . 8.00 - 12.00
  4953 *Squeeze Me*. . . . . 8.00 - 12.00
Vocalion 15657 *Nobody's Sweetheart*. . . . . 15.00 - 20.00
  15710 *I Can't Give You Anything But Love*. . 20.00 - 30.00
  15716 *Dusky Stevedore*. . . . . 15.00 - 20.00
  15729 *Skinner's Sock*. . . . . 15.00 - 20.00
  15779 *Futuristic Rhythm*. . . . . 25.00 - 35.00
  15784 *That's A Plenty*. . . . . 25.00 - 35.00
  15810 *I'm Walking Through Clover*. . . . . . . 30.00 - 40.00
  15815 *Last Cent*. . . . . 30.00 - 40.00
  15828 *Ballin' The Jack*. . . . . 30.00 - 40.00
  15833 *Waiting at the End of the Road*. . . . . . 30.00 - 40.00
  15841 *Little By Little*. . . . . 35.00 - 50.00

LOUISIANA RHYTHMAKERS:
Titles, issued contemporaneously on Banner, Melotone, Oriole, Perfect, Romeo; *Casa Loma Stomp; Clarinet Marmalade; Runnin' Wild; Twelfth Street Rag*. . . . . 7.00 - 12.00

LOUISIANA STOMPERS:
Paramount 12550 *Hop Off*. . . . . 35.00 - 50.00

LOUISIANA SUGAR BABES:
Bluebird 10260 *Thou Swell*. . . . . 5.00 - 8.00
Victor 21346 *Persian Rug*. . . . . 5.00 - 8.00
  21348 *Willow Tree*. . . . . 5.00 - 8.00

LOUISVILLE RHYTHM KINGS:
Okeh 41189 *Let's Sit and Talk About You*. . . . . 20.00 - 30.00

LOUISVILLE WASHBOARD BAND:
Domino 3671 *Shake That Thing*. . . . . 40.00 - 60.00
  3755 *I've Found a New Baby*. . . . . 15.00 - 20.00
Oriole 650 *Boodle Am*. . . . . 15.00 - 20.00
  674 *I've Found a New Baby*. . . . . 15.00 - 20.00

BERT LOWN & HIS LOUNGERS/OR-
CHESTRA/HOTEL BILTMORE
ORCHESTRA:
Titles, issued contemporaneously on Banner, Cameo, Conqueror, Perfect, Oriole, Regal, Romeo: *Blue Is The Night; I Love You, Believe Me; I Never Dreamt; Keepin' Myself For You; The One I Love Just Can't Be Bothered With Me; The Perfect Song; Strike Up The Band*. . . . . 5.00 - 8.00
Bluebird 5067, 5068, 5087, 5099, 5100. . . . . 4.00 - 7.00
  5088 *We'll Have a Honeymoon Some Day*. . . 8.00 - 12.00
Columbia 2258-D, 2292-D. . . . . 5.00 - 8.00
Harmony 852-H, 853-H, 863-H, 892-H, 920-H, 1088-H, 1111-H. . . . . 5.00 - 10.00
  974-H *The Jazz Me Blues*. . . . . 10.00 - 15.00
Victor 22541, 22568, 22582, 22583, 22602, 22603, 22612, 22623, 22563, 22654, 22689, 22696, 22715, 22738, 22740, 22744, 22787, 22795, 22804, 22805, 22810, 22908, 22927, 24086, 24087, 24116. . . . . 4.00 - 7.00

ED LOYD AND HIS ORCHESTRA:
Odeon ONY-36060 *The Free And Easy (instrumental)*. . . . . 15.00 - 20.00
  ONY-36061 *The Free And Easy*. . . . . 10.00 - 15.00
  ONY-36065 *You Brought a New Kind of Love To Me*. . . . . 10.00 - 15.00
  ONY-36080 *Reminiscing*. . . . . 10.00 - 15.00
  ONY-36081 *Nobody Cares If I'm Blue*. . . . . 10.00 - 15.00
  ONY-36089 *You For Me*. . . . . 10.00 - 15.00

ONY-36090 *Ro-Ro Rolling Along*. . . . . 10.00 - 15.00
ONY-36113 *Just a Little Closer*. . . . . 10.00 - 15.00
ONY-36123 *Hullabaloo*. . . . . 10.00 - 15.00
ONY-36124 *My One Ambition Is You*. . . . . 10.00 - 15.00
ONY-36132 *I'm Doin' That Thing*. . . . . 10.00 - 15.00
ONY-36133 *Don't Tell Her*. . . . . 10.00 - 15.00
ONY-36147 *I'll Still Belong To You*. . . . . 10.00 - 15.00
ONY-36150 *Sweet Jennie Lee*. . . . . 10.00 - 15.00
ONY-36161 *Morning, Noon and Night*. . . . . . . 10.00 - 15.00
Oden ONY-36172 *Fall In Love With Me*. . . . . . 10.00 - 15.00
ONY-36176 *Where Have You Been?*. . . . . 10.00 - 15.00
ONY-36177 *He's My Secret Passion*. . . . . 10.00 - 15.00
ONY-36182 *It Must Be True*. . . . . 10.00 - 15.00
ONY-36185 *Sing Song Girl*. . . . . 10.00 - 15.00
ONY-36186 *Hello! Beautiful*. . . . . 10.00 - 15.00
ONY-36193 *All On Account Of Your Kisses*. . 12.00 - 18.00
Okeh 41250 *I Get The Blues When It Rains*. . . 7.00 - 10.00
  41259 *The One In The World*. . . . . 7.00 - 10.00
  41294 *Lovable and Sweet*. . . . . 5.00 - 8.00
  41295 *I'm Doing What I'm Doing For Love*. . 5.00 - 8.00
  41312 *Wouldn't It Be Wonderful?*. . . . . 5.00 - 8.00
  41319 *Lonely Troubadour*. . . . . 5.00 - 8.00
  41338 *A Little Kiss Each Morning*. . . . . 5.00 - 8.00
  41348 *If You Were The Only Girl In The World* 5.00 - 8.00
  41353 *What Do I Care?*. . . . . 5.00 - 8.00
  41354 *Put A Little Salt On The Bluebird's Tail* 5.00 - 8.00
  41367 *Singing a Vagabond Song*. . . . . 5.00 - 8.00
  41368 *Beside an Open Fireplace*. . . . . 5.00 - 8.00
  41407 *You Brought A New Kind of Love To Me* 7.00 - 10.00
  41392 *The Free and Easy*. . . . . 7.00 - 10.00
  41428 *I'm Needin' You*. . . . . 7.00 - 10.00
  41435 *I've Got My Eye On You*. . . . . 7.00 - 10.00

LUCKY TEN ENTERTAINERS:
Domino 3992 *Dew Dew Dewy Day*. . . . . 5.00 - 8.00
  3996 *Sing Me a Baby Sone*. . . . . 5.00 - 8.00
Regal 8352 *Dew Dew Dewy Day*. . . . . 5.00 - 8.00
  8355 *Sing Me a Baby Song*. . . . . 5.00 - 8.00

THE LUMBERJACKS:
Cameo 8352 *Black Beauty*. . . . . 5.00 - 8.00
  8356 *Spanish Dream*. . . . . 5.00 - 8.00
  9007 *Oh, Boy! It's A Pleasure*. . . . . 5.00 - 8.00
  9020 *I Found My Sunshine in the Rain*. . . . . 5.00 - 8.00
  9030 *Whoopee Stomp*. . . . . 10.00 - 15.00
  9041 *Blue Little You*. . . . . 7.00 - 10.00
  9045 *Let Me Be Alone With You*. . . . . 5.00 - 8.00
  9084 *I've Never Been Loved By Anyone Like You* 5.00 - 8.00
  9147 *Would You Be Happy?*. . . . . 5.00 - 8.00
Lincoln 3000 *Spanish Dream*. . . . . 5.00 - 8.00
  3036 *Oh, Boy! It's a Pleasure*. . . . . 5.00 - 8.00
  3049 *I Found My Sunshine in the Rain*. . . . . 5.00 - 8.00
  3059 *Whoopee Stomp*. . . . . 10.00 - 15.00
  3070 *Blue Little You*. . . . . 7.00 - 10.00
  3074 *Let Me Be Alone With You*. . . . . 5.00 - 8.00
  3111 *I've Never Been Loved By Anyone Like You* 5.00 - 8.00
  3174 *Would You Be Happy?*. . . . . 5.00 - 8.00
Romeo 775 *Black Beauty*. . . . . 5.00 - 8.00
  779 *Spanish Dream*. . . . . 5.00 - 8.00
  811 *Oh, Boy! It's a Pleasure*. . . . . 5.00 - 8.00
  824 *I Found My Sunshine in the Rain*. . . . . 5.00 - 8.00
  834 *Whoopee Stomp*. . . . . 10.00 - 15.00
  845 *Blue Little You*. . . . . 7.00 - 10.00
  849 *Let Me Be Alone With You*. . . . . 5.00 - 8.00
  886 *I've Never Been Loved By Anyone Like You* 5.00 - 8.00
  949 *Would You Be Happy?*. . . . . 5.00 - 8.00

GUY LUMPKIN:
QRS 7078 *Decatur Street Rag*. . . . . 50.00 - 75.00

JIMMIE LUNCEFORD & HIS CHICASAW
SYNCOPATORS/ORCHESTRA:
Bluebird 5330 *Sweet Rhythm*. . . . . 8.00 - 12.00
  5713 *White Heat*. 4.00 - 6.00
  6133 *Breakfast Ball*. . . . . 5.00 - 8.00

Decca 129 *Sophisticated Lady*	5.00 -	8.00	
130 *Nana*	7.00 -	10.00	
131 *Mood Indigo*	7.00 -	10.00	
299 *Solitude*	5.00 -	8.00	
369 *Stardust*	5.00 -	8.00	
415 *Because You're You*	5.00 -	8.00	
453 *Since My Best Gal Turned Me Down*	5.00 -	8.00	
503 *Four Or Five Times*	5.00 -	8.00	
572 *Rhythm In My Nursery Rhymes*	5.00 -	8.00	
576 *Thunder*	5.00 -	8.00	
628 *Charmaine*	5.00 -	8.00	
639 *Bird Of Paradise*	5.00 -	8.00	
668 *Swanee River*	5.00 -	8.00	
682 *I'm Nuts About Screwy Music*	5.00 -	8.00	
712 *My Blue Heaven*	5.00 -	8.00	
765 *Hittin' The Bottle*	5.00 -	8.00	
788 *The Best Things In Life Are Free*	5.00 -	8.00	
805 *The Melody Man*	5.00 -	8.00	
908 *Organ Grinder's Song*	5.00 -	8.00	
915 *Me And The Moon*	5.00 -	8.00	
960 *Living From Day To Day*	5.00 -	8.00	
980 *Harlem Shout*	5.00 -	8.00	
1035 *Running A Temperature*	5.00 -	8.00	
1128 *He Ain't Got Rhythm*	5.00 -	8.00	
1219 *Honest And Truly*	5.00 -	8.00	
1229 *Linger Awhile*	5.00 -	8.00	
1318 *I'll See You In My Dreams*	5.00 -	8.00	
1340 *For Dancer's Only*	5.00 -	8.00	
1355 *Honey, Keep Your Mind On Me*	5.00 -	8.00	
1364 *Ragging The Scale*	5.00 -	8.00	
1506 *Hell's Bells*	5.00 -	8.00	
1569 *Annie Laurie*	5.00 -	8.00	
1617 *Margie*	5.00 -	8.00	
1659 *Pigeon Walk*	5.00 -	8.00	
1734 *Teasin' Tessie Brown*	5.00 -	8.00	
1808 *My Melancholy Baby*	5.00 -	8.000	
1927 *Down By The Old Mill Stream*	5.00 -	8.00	
Victor 24522 *Jazznocracy*	8.00 -	12.00	
24586 *White Heat*	10.00 -	15.00	
24601 *Breakfast Ball*	10.00 -	15.00	
24669 *Swingin' Uptown*	10.00 -	15.00	
38141 *In Dat Mornin'*	25.00 -	35.00	

Vocalion 4582, 4595, 4667, 4712, 4754, 4831, 4875,
4979, 5033, 5116, 5156, 5276 .... 5.00 - 7.00

**JIMMY LUVERTE & HIS SOCIETY
TROUBADOURS:**

Vocalion 03559 *You Think She Ain't*	15.00 -	20.00	
03602 *Music Box Blues*	15.00 -	20.00	

**ABE LYMAN & HIS CALIFORNIA
ORCHESTRA; ABE LYMAN'S SHARPS &
FLATS; ABE LYMAN'S CALIFORNIA
(AMBASSADOR HOTEL) ORCHESTRA:**

Bluebird, most issues	2.00 -	5.00	
Brunswick 2980 *Everybody Stomp*	4.00 -	7.00	
3241 *Ace In The Hole*	5.00 -	8.09	
3316 *Twelfth Street Rag*	5.00 -	8.00	
3964 *Weary Weasel*	7.00 -	10.00	
4155 *A Jazz Holiday*	7.00 -	10.00	
4912 *Hullabaloo*	7.00 -	10.00	
4924 *Never Swat a Fly*	7.00 -	10.00	
6314 *Farewell Blues*	7.00 -	10.00	
6325 *Milenberg Joys*	7.00 -	10.00	
6380 *Riddle Me This*	5.00 -	8.00	
6637 *Weary Blues*	7.00 -	10.00	
Brunswick 6637, 6674, 6756	4.00 -	7.00	
Brunswick (12-inch) 20063 *"Good News" medley*	7.00 -	10.00	
20103 (12") *"The Laugh Parade" medley*	7.00 -	10.00	
20122 (12") *"Stormy Weather"*	10.00 -	15.00	
Brunswick, most others	3.00 -	5.00	
Columbia, most issues	2.00 -	4.00	

Decca 1098, 1104, 1105, 1119, 1120, 1127, 1130,

1225, 1226, 1235	3.00 -	6.00	

AL LYNCH AND HIS ORCHESTRA:

Banner 7107 *Light The Way To Somebody's Heart*	7.00 -	10.00	
7109 *Put Your Loving Arms Around Me*	7.00 -	10.00	
Challenge 615 *Light The Way To Somebody's Heart*	7.00 -	10.00	
616 *Put Your Loving Arms Around Me*	7.00 -	10.00	

AL LYNN'S MUSIC MASTERS:

Edison 51952, 52041, 52148	5.00 -	8.00	
52004, *There Ain't No Maybe In My Baby's Eyes*	8.00 -	12.00	
52086 *Me and My Shadow*	8.00 -	12.00	
52099 *Marvelous*	8.00 -	12.00	
52101 *Who Gives You All Your Kisses?*	10.00 -	15.00	
52226 *Anything To Make You Happy*	7.00 -	10.00	
52227 *Symphonic Raps*	10.00 -	15.00	
52270 *Lauretta*	15.00 -	25.00	
52399 *Lonely Little Bluebird*	15.00 -	20.00	

GLEN LYTE'S ORCHESTRA:

Broadway 1459 *When I Take My Sugar To Tea*	7.00 -	10.00	

JIMMY LYTELL:

Pathe-Actuelle 36568 *Old Folks Shuffle*	10.00 -	15.00	
36584 *Messin' Around*	10.00 -	15.00	
36607 *Pardon The Glove*	10.00 -	15.00	
36665 *Zulu Wail*	10.00 -	15.00	
36717 *Headin' For Harlem*	10.00 -	15.00	
36741 *Stockholm Stomp*	10.00 -	15.00	
36775 *Missouri Squabble*	10.00 -	15.00	
36824 *Yellow Dog Blues*	10.00 -	15.00	
Perfect 14749 *Old Folks Shuffle*	10.00 -	15.00	
14765 *Messin' Around*	10.00 -	15.00	
14788 *Pardon The Glove*	10.00 -	15.00	
14846 *Zulu Wail*	10.00 -	15.00	
14898 *Headin' For Harlem*	10.00 -	15.00	
14922 *Stockholm Stomp*	10.00 -	15.00	
14956 *Missouri Squabble*	10.00 -	15.00	
15005 *Yellow Dog Blues*	10.00 -	15.00	

BABY MACK:

Okeh 8313 *What Kind Of Man Is You?*	20.00 -	30.00	

CHARLES E. MACK:

Columbia 50061-D (12-inch record) *Our Child*	7.00 -	10.00	

**ENRIC MADRIGUERA AND HIS
ORCHESTRA:**

Vogue R-760 *So It Goes*	10.00 -	15.00	
R-776 *Mujercita*	10.00 -	15.00	
R-777 *La Rumbita Tropical*	10.00 -	15.00	
R-778 *Guilty of Love*	10.00 -	15.00	
R-779 *A Man, A Moon, and a Maid*	10.00 -	15.00	

SHERRY MAGEE & HIS DIXIELANDERS:

Okeh 5436 *Satanic Blues*	5.00 -	8.00	
Vocalion 5281 *Shake It and Break It*	7.00 -	10.00	
5436 *Bluin' The Blues*	7.00 -	10.00	

MAJESTIC DANCE ORCHESTRA:

Banner 0537 *Love Me In My Dreams*	3.00 -	5.00	
0561 *My Way Right Back To Arkansas*	5.00 -	8.00	
0596 *I've Seen My Baby*	5.00 -	8.00	
0851 *You're Simply Delish*	7.00 -	10.00	
Cameo 0139 *I'm Following You*	5.00 -	8.00	
0196 *I've Seen My Baby*	5.00 -	8.00	
0451 *You're Simply Delish*	7.00 -	10.00	
Domino 4449 *Somebody Mightly Like You*	5.00 -	8.00	
Oriole 928 *Magnolia*	5.00 -	8.00	
933 *Zulu Wail*	5.00 -	8.00	
980 *Delirium*	10.00 -	15.00	
990 *Farewell Blues*	8.00 -	12.00	
Pathe-Actuelle 37004 *Am I Blue?*	5.00 -	8.00	
Perfect 15185 *Am I Blue?*	5.00 -	8.00	
15244 *Somebody Mighty Like You*	5.00 -	8.00	
Regal 8893 *Somebody Mighty Like You*	5.00 -	8.00	
8960 *My Love Parade*	5.00 -	8.00	
Romeo 1129 *Somebody Mighty Like You*	5.00 -	8.00	

MAJOR & HIS ORCHESTRA:

Hollywood 1028 *Blue Evening Blues*	50.00 -	75.00	

MANHATTAN DANCE ORCHESTRA:

National Music Lovers 1099 *I Can't Get the One I Want* .... 5.00 - 8.00

MARION MANN WITH BOB HAGGART'S ORCHESTRA:

Vogue R-731 *You Took Advantage of Me* ...... 12.00 - 18.00
R-758 *Long, Strong, and Consecutive* .... 12.00 - 18.00

SAM MANNING & HIS COLE JAZZ ORCHESTRA/BLUE HOT SYNCOPATORS:

Columbia 14110-D *Bingo* .... 7.00 - 10.00
Okeh 8302 *Keep Your Hand Off That* .... 10.00 - 15.00

JOE MANNONE'S HARMONY KINGS; JOE "WINGY" MANNONE & HIS CLUB ROYALE ORCHESTRA; WINGY MANNONE & HIS ORCHESTRA:

Bluebird 6359, 6360, 6375, 6393, 6411, 6472, 6473, 6483, 6536, 6537, 6549, 6605, 6606, 6616, 6618, 6804, 6806, 6816, 7002, 7003, 7014, 7197, 7198, 7214, 7389, 7391, 7395 .... 4.00 - 8.00
Bluebird (others) .... 3.00 - 5.00
Brunswick 6911 *No Calling Card* .... 8.00 - 12.00
6940 *Send Me* .... 8.00 - 12.00
Columbia 1044-D *Up The Country Blues* .... 30.00 - 40.00
1482-D *Cat's Head* .... 30.00 - 40.00
Okeh 41569 *She's Crying For Me* .... 12.00 - 15.00
41570 *Royal Garden Blues* .... 12.00 - 15.00
41573 *Nickel In The Slot* .... 8.00 - 12.00
Special Edition 5011-S *Never Had No Lovin* .... 10.00 - 15.00
Vocalion 15728 *Fare Thee Well* .... 35.00 - 50.00
15797 *Isn't There a Little Love?* .... 35.00 - 50.00
Vocalion 2913 *I Believe In Miracles* .... 7.00 - 10.00
2914 *Fare Thee Well, Annabelle* .... 7.00 - 10.00
2933 *You're An Angel* .... 7.00 - 10.00
2934 *Let's Spill The Beans* .... 7.00 - 10.00
2963 *Black Coffee* .... 7.00 - 10.00
2972 *Lulu's Back In Town* .... 7.00 - 10.00
2989 *Love And Kisses* .... 8.00 - 12.00
2990 *Let's Swing It* .... 8.00 - 12.00
3023 *From The Top Of Your Head* .... *7.00 - 10.00*
3058 *I'm Gonna Sit Right Down And Write Myself A Letter* .... 7.00 - 10.00
3070 *You Are My Lucky Star* .... 10.00 - 15.00
3071 *I've Got A Note* .... 10.00 - 15.00
3134 *The Music Goes 'Round And 'Round* ... 7.00 - 10.00
3135 *I've Got My Fingers Crossed* .... 7.00 - 10.00
3158 *The Broken Record* .... 7.00 - 10.00
3159 *Old Man Mose* .... 7.00 - 10.00
3171 *Nickel In The Slot* .... 7.00 - 10.00
3191 *Is It True What They Say About Dixie?* . 7.00 - 10.00
3192 *Shoe-Shine Boy* .... 7.00 - 10.00

EDDIE MAPP:

QRS 7078 *Riding The Blues* .... 50.00 - 75.00

PAUL MARES & HIS FRIARS SOCIETY ORCHESTRA:

Okeh 41574 *Nagasaki* .... 15.00 - 20.00
41575 *Reincarnation* .... 15.00 - 20.00

THE MARIGOLD ENTERTAINERS:

Vocalion 15800 *Jealous* .... 15.00 - 20.00

THE MARINERS:

Okeh 41433 *Happy Feet* .... 7.00 - 10.00
41449 *I Don't Mind Walkin' in the Rain* ..... 7.00 - 10.00

MIKE MARKEL & HIS ORCHESTRA; MARKEL'S ORCHESTRA; MARKELS' ORCHESTRA; MARKEL'S SOCIETY ORCHESTRA:

Brunswick 3091 *Flamin' Mamie* .... 5.00 - 8.00
3189 *Lulu Belle* .... 5.00 - 8.00
3263 *Precious* .... 5.00 - 8.00
Columbia 617-D *Black Horse Stomp* .... 5.00 - 8.00
Edison 51752 *Tonight's My Night With Baby* ... 7.00 - 10.00
51800 *Baby Face* .... 7.00 - 10.00

Okeh 4580 *Lonesome Mama Blues* .... 5.00 - 8.00
4610 *Black Eyed Blues* .... 5.00 - 8.00
4656 *Blued Eyed Blues* .... 5.00 - 8.00
4967 *Stavin' Change* .... 5.00 - 8.00
40045 *31st Street Blues* .... 5.00 - 8.00
40625 *Deep Henderson* .... 7.00 - 10.00
40686 *For My Sweetheart* .... 7.00 - 10.00

GERALD MARKS AND HIS ORCHESTRA:

Columbia 1432-D *If I Can't Have You* .... 5.00 - 8.00

EARL MARLOW AND HIS ORCHESTRA:

Parlophone PNY-34018 *Wrapped in a Red, Red Rose* 7.00 - 10.00
PNY-34019 *Put a Little Salt on the Bluebird's Tail* 7.00 - 10.00
PNY-34022 *What Do I Care?* .... 7.00 - 10.00
PNY-34025 *There's Danger in Your Eyes, Cherie* 7.00 - 10.00
PNY-34026 *Singing a Vagabond Song* ...... 7.00 - 10.00
PNY-34058 *Living in the Sunlight, Loving in the Moonlight* .... 10.00 - 15.00
PNY-34059 *You Brought a New Kind Of Love To Me* .... 10.00 - 15.00
PNY-34074 *Nobody Cares If I'm Blue* .... 10.00 - 15.00
PNY-34075 *Mysterious Mose* .... 10.00 - 15.00
PNY-34082 *I'm Needin' You* .... 10.00 - 15.00
PNY-34083 *Ro-Ro-Rolling Along* .... 10.00 - 15.00
PNY-34105 *This Love* .... 4.00 - 7.00
PNY-34106 *I've Got My Eye On You* .... 10.00 - 15.00
PNY-34115 *Dixiana* .... 10.00 - 15.00
PNY-34116 *My One Ambition Is You* .... 10.00 - 15.00
PNY-34124 *I'm Doing That Thing* .... 10.00 - 15.00
PNY-34125 *A Big Bouquet For You* .... 7.00 - 10.00
PNY-34126 *Don't Tell Her* .... 7.00 - 10.00
PNY-34139 *I Am The Words* .... 7.00 - 10.00
PNY-34140 *I Still Belong To You* .... 7.00 - 10.00
PNY-34142 *Sweet Jennie Lee* .... 12.00 - 18.00
PNY-34143 *Roamin' Thru' The Roses* .... 10.00 - 15.00
PNY-34167 *Reaching For The Moon* .... 4.00 - 7.00
PNY-34168 *Fall In Love With Me* .... 5.00 - 8.00
PNY-34169 *He's My Secret Passion* .... 5.00 - 8.00
PNY-34170 *Lady, Play Your Mandolin* ...... 5.00 - 8.00
PNY-34174 *It Must Be True* .... 7.00 - 10.00
PNY-34176 *Hello! Beautiful* .... 10.00 - 15.00
PNY-34177 *Walkin' My Baby Back Home* ...... 10.00 - 15.00
PNY-34178 *Sing Song Girl* .... 10.00 - 15.00
PNY-34179 *Wabash Moon* .... 4.00 - 7.00
PNY-34184 *All On Account Of Your Kisses* .. 12.00 - 18.00

RUDY MARLOW AND HIS ORCHESTRA:

Harmony 1062-H *Dixie Jamboree* .... 7.00 - 10.00
1063-H *He's So Unusual* .... 7.00 - 10.00
1088-H *Do Ya Love Me?* .... 7.00 - 10.00
1119-H *Thank Your Father* .... 5.00 - 8.00
1137-H *Get Happy* .... 5.00 - 8.00
1162-H *Dark Night* .... 4.00 - 7.00
1232-H *Three Little Words* .... 5.00 - 8.00
(Note: Some of above also issued on Velvet Tone)

JOE MARSALA & HIS DELTA FOUR; JOE MARSALA'S CHICAGOANS:

General 1717, 3001 .... 5.00 - 10.00
Variety 565 .... 5.00 - 10.00

GILBERT MARSH & HIS ORCHESTRA:

Parlophone PNY-34038 *Navy Blues* .... 15.00 - 20.00
PNY-34039 *Lucky Little Devil* .... 15.00 - 20.00
PNY-34040 *Navy Blues* .... 10.00 - 15.00
PNY-34041 *Lucky Little Devil* .... 10.00 - 15.00

FATTY MARTIN'S ORCHESTRA:

Victor 19700 *Jimtown Blues* .... 10.00 - 15.00

FREDDIE MARTIN & HIS ORCHESTRA:

Brunswick 6407, 6408 .... 4.00 - 6.00
Columbia 2703-D, 2708-D, 3770-D .... 5.00 - 8.00

MARY MARTIN:

Brunswick 8282 .... 5.00 - 10.00
V-Disc (12-inch) 542 .... 5.00 - 10.00

SARA MARTIN'S JUG BAND:

Okeh 8188 *Blue Devil Blues*............... 20.00 - 30.00

JELLY ROLL MARTON & HIS ORCHESTRA:

Muddy Water Blues issued contemporaneously on
Famous 3245, Harmograph 834, National 12251,
Paramount 12050 and 20251, Puritan 11251. 80.00 - 100.00

**FRANK MARVIN: (See also country-western
listing)**

Brunswick 400, 4949.................... 4.00 - 8.00

JOHNNY MARVIN:

Columbia 2655-D, 15750-D............... 5.00 - 10.00

Edison 51709 *The Memphis Blues*........... 7.00 - 10.00

Melotone 12610...................... 5.00 - 7.00

Victor 20386, 20714, 20731, 20832, 21650..... 3.00 - 5.00

21376 *Angel*...................... 8.00 - 12.00

21435 *My Pet*.................... 8.00 - 12.00

23691, 23708, 23728............... 5.00 - 10.00

ALBERT MASON'S ORCHESTRA:

Parlophone PNY-34069 *Girl Trouble*......... 10.00 - 15.00

PNY-34104 *Rollin' Down the River*...... 10.00 - 15.00

PNY-34105 *Seems To Me*............ 10.00 - 15.00

PNY-34114 *I Wonder How It Feels*...... 10.00 - 15.00

PNY-34174 *Keep a Song In Your Soul*..... 10.00 - 15.00

PNY-34185 *The One Man Band*.......... 10.00 - 15.00

PNY-34187 *Got the Bench-Got the Park*..... 10.00 - 15.00

JERRY MASON'S CALIFORNIANS:

Harmony 1242-H *Can This Be Love?*......... 5.00 - 8.00

MASON-DIXON ORCHESTRA:

Columbia 1861-D *What A Day!*.............. 12.00 - 15.00

MASTER MELODY MAKERS:

National Music Lovers 1133 *Then I'll Be Happy.* 7.00 - 10.00

FRANKIE MASTERS & HIS ORCHESTRA:

Victor 21102, 21217, 21565, 21602........... 4.00 - 7.00

Vocalion, most issues.................. 3.00 - 5.00

Vogue R-724 *Everybody Knew But Me*....... 10.00 - 15.00

R-735 *Welcome To My Dreams*........... 10.00 - 15.00

R-772 *All By Myself*................. 12.00 - 18.00

FRANK MATER:

Diva 2759-G *Doin' The Raccoon*......... 5.00 - 8.00

Harmony 759-H *Doin' The Raccoon*....... 5.00 - 8.00

Harmony 808-H *Let's Do It.*........... 7.00 - 10.00

811-H *The Song I Love*............ 7.00 - 10.00

825-H *Makin' Whoopee*................. 7.00 - 10.00

**CHARLES A MATSON'S CREOLE
SERENADERS: MATSON'S LUCKY
SEVEN:**

Edison 51222 *Tain't Nobody's Business If I Do* 15.00 - 20.00

51224 *I Just Want A Daddy*............. 15.00 - 20.00

Lawdy, Lawdy Blues issued contemporeanously on
Claxtonola, Paramount, Pruitan.......... 15.00 - 20.00

EMMETT MATTHEWS & HIS ORCHESTRA:

Vocalion 3226 *I'll Stand By*............. 7.00 - 10.00

3228 *Take A Good Look At Mine*........ 7.00 - 10.00

3371 *Bojangles of Harlem*............ 7.00 - 10.00

3332 *You Come To My Rescue*.......... 7.00 - 10.00

**GEORGE MATTHEWS & THE CAROLINA
NIGHT HAWKS:**

Gennett 6183 *Oh Miss Hannah!*............ 15.00 - 20.00

**NORRIDGE MAYHAMS & HIS BARBECUE
BOYS:**

*Sloppy Drunk Woman; Wrap Your Troubles In
Dreams;* issued contemporaneously on Banner,
Melotone, Oriole, Perfect, Romeo....... 10.00 - 15.00

Vocalion 03429 *Ash Haulin' Blues*........... 10.00 - 15.00

03465 *If I Had My Way*............. 10.00 - 15.00

03498 *Sloppy Drunk Woman*............ 10.00 - 15.00

TED MAYS AND HIS BAND:

Bluebird 7193 *Gee, It Must Be Love*......... 7.00 - 10.00

7206 *Take It On Home To Grandma*....... 7.00 - 10.00

7237 *Married Man Blues*.............. 7.00 - 10.00

THE McALPINEERS:

Edison 52237, 52239, 52385............... 5.00 - 10.00

52266 *Rhapsody In Rhythm*.......... 10.00 - 15.00

52371 *I'm On The Crest Of a Wave*....... 10.00 - 15.00

52411 *High Up on a Hill-Top*............ 10.00 - 15.00

**GEORGE McCLENNON; GEORGE McCLEN-
NON'S JAZZ BAND/DEVILS:**

Okeh 8143 *Dark Alley Blues*.................. 20.00 - 30.00

8150 *New Orleans Wiggle*............. 25.00 - 35.00

8236 *Home Alone Blues*............. 30.00 - 40.00

8314 *Cut Throat Blues*............ 30.00 - 40.00

8337 *Everybody But Me*............ 30.00 - 40.00

8397 *Pig Foot Blues*............... 30.00 - 40.00

8406 *Disaster*.................... 40.00 - 60.00

**CLYDE McCOY & HIS (DRAKE HOTEL)
ORCHESTRA:**

Columbia 2389-D *Sugar Blues*................. 5.00 - 8.00

2453-D *It Looks Like Love*.............. 5.00 - 8.00

2466-D *Black And Tan Fantasy*.......... 5.00 - 8.00

2531-D *I Found A New Baby*............ 8.00 - 12.00

2597-D *Creole Love Call*............. 5.00 - 8.00

2794-D *Smoke Rings*.............. 5.00 - 8.00

2801-D *Some Of These Days*.......... 5.00 - 8.00

2808-D *Nobody's Sweetheart*............ 8.00 - 12.00

2865-D *Palooka*.................... 7.00 - 10.00

2866-D *Little Women*................. 5.00 - 8.00

2874-D *Business on the Q.T.*.............. 5.00 - 8.00

Decca 381, 382, 422, 461, 509, 566, 620, 681, 758,
833, 1109, 1152, 1230, 1297, 1766, 1788, 1917,
2149, 2217, 2630, 2737, 2995, 3074, 3581, 3633 2.00 - 5.00

Vogue R-707 *Sugar Blues*.................... 7.00 - 12.00

R-722 *Tear It Down*................. 10.00 - 15.00

R-752 *There's Good Blues Tonight*.......... 8.00 - 12.00

R-753 *Way Down Yonder In New Orleans*... 10.00 - 15.00

**RANDOLPH McCURTAIN'S COLLEGE
RAMBLERS:**

Okeh Ramblers' 1 *Low Down Brown*.......... 15.00 - 25.00

**EARL McDONALD'S ORIGINAL
LOUISVILLE JUG BAND:**

Columbia 14206-D *Under the Chicken Tree*..... 30.00 - 40.00

14226-D *Rocking Chair Blues*.............. 30.00 - 40.00

14255-D *She's In The Graveyard Now*....... 30.00 - 40.00

14371-D *Casey Bill*................... 30.00 - 40.00

DICK McDONOUGH & HIS ORCHESTRA:

Titles, issued contemporaneously on Banner,
Melotone, Oriole, Perfect, Romeo: *Afterglow; All
God's Chillun Got Rhythm; The Big Apple; Dar-
danella; Dear Old Southland; The Gonna Goo;
He Ain't Got Rhythm; I'm in a Dancing Mood;
It Ain't Right; Love, What Are You Doing To
My Heart; The Mood That I'm In; Now Or
Never; When The Moon Hangs High; With Thee
I Swing; You and I Know*................ 5.00 - 10.00

HOWARD McGHEE:

Dial 1005, 1007, 1010, 1011, 1027............ 5.00 - 7.00

BOB McGOWAN & HIS ORCHESTRA:

Gennett 6709 *Me and the Man In the Moon*... 8.00 - 12.00

6754 *As Long As We're In Love*........... 5.00 - 8.00

JIMMY McHUGH'S BOSTONIANS:

Harmony 795-H *Baby*.................... 10.00 - 15.00

823-H *Let's Sit and Talk About You*........ 10.00 - 15.00

836-H *The Whoopee Stomp*................ 10.00 - 15.00

MARION McKAY & HIS ORCHESTRA:

Gennett 5615 *Doo Wacka Doo*.............. 6.00 - 10.00

6294 *My Blue Heaven*.................. 6.00 - 10.00

**RED McKENZIE; McKENZIE'S CANDY KIDS;
RED McKENZIE & HIS MUSIC
BOX/RHYTHM KINGS; RED McKENZIE
WITH THE SPIRITS OF RHYTHM:**

Titles, issued contemporaneously on Banner,
Melotone, Oriole, Perfect, Romeo: *Georgianna;
Farewell My Love*.................... 7.00 - 10.00

Columbia 2556-D *Just Friends*..............	5.00 -	8.00
2587-D *I'm Sorry, Dear*..............	5.00 -	8.00
2620-D *Can't We Talk It Over?*..........	5.00 -	8.00
2645-D *Dream Sweetheart*..............	5.00 -	8.00
Decca 186 *From Monday On*..............	7.00 -	10.00
243 *It's All Forgotten Now*..............	7.00 -	10.00
302 *As Long As I Live*..............	7.00 -	10.00
507 *Let's Swing It*..............	7.00 -	10.00
521 *Double Trouble*..............	7.00 -	10.00
587 *Every Now And Then*..............	7.00 -	10.00
609 *Georgia Rockin' Chair*..............	7.00 -	10.00
667 *I'm Building Up To An Awful Letdown*..	8.00 -	12.00
721 *Don't Count Your Kisses (Before You're Kissed)*..............	8.00 -	12.00
734 *When Love Has Gone*..............	8.00 -	12.00
790 *I Can't Get Started With You*..............	8.00 -	12.00
Okeh 40893 *There'll Be Some Changes Made*...	20.00 -	30.00
41071 *From Monday On*..............	20.00 -	30.00
Variety 520 *Sweet Lorraine*..............	8.00 -	12.00
589 *I Cried For You*..............	10.00 -	15.00
Vocalion 2534 *It's The Talk Of The Town*.....	8.00 -	12.00
3875 *Farewell, My Love*..............	7.00 -	10.00
3898 *You're Out Of This World*..............	7.00 -	10.00
14977 *Panama*..............	10.00 -	15.00
14978 *Stretch It, Boy*..............	10.00 -	15.00
15088 *The Morning After Blues*..............	10.00 -	15.00
15166 *Hot Honey*..............	10.00 -	15.00
15539 *Nervous Puppies*..............	10.00 -	15.00

McKENZIE & CONDON'S CHICAGOANS:

Okeh 40971 *Nobody's Sweetheart*..............	15.00 -	20.00
41011 *China Boy*..............	15.00 -	20.00

RAY McKINLEY'S JAZZ BAND:

Decca 1019, 1020..............	3.00 -	6.00

McKINNEY'S COTTON PICKERS:

Victor 21583 *Four Or Five Times*..............	15.00 -	20.00
21611 *Milenberg Joys*..............	15.00 -	20.00
21730 *Cherry*..............	15.00 -	20.00
22511 *Hullabaloo*..............	15.00 -	20.00
22628 *She's My Secret Passion*..............	8.00 -	12.00
22640 *Talk To Me*..............	15.00 -	20.00
22683 *I Want Your Love*..............	15.00 -	20.00
22736 *Wherever There's a Will, Baby*..............	15.00 -	20.00
22811 *Wrap Your Troubles In Dreams*.......	15.00 -	20.00
22932 *Rocky Road*..............	20.00 -	30.00
23000 *Okay, Baby*..............	10.00 -	15.00
23012 *Just a Shade Corn*..............	15.00 -	20.00
23020 *Never Swat a Fly*..............	15.00 -	20.00
23024 *I Miss a Little Miss*..............	15.00 -	20.00
23031 *Hello!*..............	15.00 -	20.00
23035 *To Whom It May Concern*..............	15.00 -	20.00
38000 *Nobody's Sweetheart*..............	10.00 -	15.00
38013 *It's Tight Like That*..............	10.00 -	15.00
38025 *Put It There*..............	15.00 -	20.00
38051 *Do Something*..............	15.00 -	20.00
38052 *Sellin' That Stuff*..............	15.00 -	20.00
38061 *I've Found a New Baby*..............	15.00 -	20.00
38097 *Plain Dirt*..............	15.00 -	25.00
38102 *Miss Hannah*..............	15.00 -	25.00
38112 *Travelin' All Alone*..............	15.00 -	25.00
38118 *Zonky*..............	8.00 -	12.00
38133 *I'd Love It*..............	20.00 -	30.00
38142 *I'll Make Fun For You*..............	20.00 -	30.00

McLAUGHLIN'S MELODIANS:

Pathe-Actuelle 36515 *Play, Gypsies*..........	5.00 -	8.00
36517 *I Never Knew What The Moonlight Could Do*..............	7.00 -	10.00
36518 *Someone Is Losin' Susan*..............	7.00 -	10.00
36524 *Broken-Hearted Sue*..............	7.00 -	10.00
Perfect 14696 *Play, Gypsies, Dance, Gypsies*....	5.00 -	8.00
14698 *I Never Knew What The Moonlight Could Do*..............	7.00 -	10.00

14699 *Someone Is Losin' Susan*..............	7.00 -	10.00
14705 *Broken-Hearted Sue*..............	7.00 -	10.00

CONNIE McLEAN & HIS RHYTHM ORCHESTRA; CONNIE McLEAN'S RHYTHM BOYS:

Bluebird 6474, 6482, 6485..............	4.00 -	7.00
Decca 7175, 7176, 7189..............	4.00 -	7.00

McMURRAY'S CALIFORNIA THUMPERS:

Gennett 4904 *Haunting Blues*..............	7.00 -	10.00
4943 *Oogie Oogie Wa Wa*..............	7.00 -	10.00

JIMMY McPARTLAND'S SQUIRRELS:

Hot Record Society 1003, 1004..............	5.00 -	8.00

JAY McSHANN (AND HIS ORCHESTRA/QUARTET):

Decca 4387, 4418, 8559, 8570, 8583, 8595, 8607, 8623, 8635..............	4.00 -	7.00
Supreme 1540 *McShann's Bounce*..............	4.00 -	7.00

THE MELODY FOUR:

Victor 23289 *I'm Crazy 'Bout My Baby*........	20.00 -	25.00

MELODY KINGS DANCE ORCHESTRA:

His Master's Voice (Canadian) 216450 *Limehouse Blues*..............	7.00 -	10.00

THE MELODY SHEIKS:

Okeh 40279 *Tokio Blues*..............	7.00 -	10.00
40303 *Why Couldn't It Be Poor Little Me*....	7.00 -	10.00
40326 *Sob Sister Sadie*..............	7.00 -	10.00
40341 *All Aboard For Heaven*..............	5.00 -	8.00
40357 *If You Knew Susie*..............	5.00 -	8.00
40358 *Isn't She The Sweetest Thing?*........	5.00 -	8.00
40369 *Let Me Linger Longer In Your Arms*..	8.00 -	12.00
40387 *Steppin' In Society*..............	5.00 -	8.00
40412 *Ukelele Lady*..............	4.00 -	7.00
40438 *Indian Nights*..............	4.00 -	6.00
40451 *Marquerite*..............	5.00 -	8.00
40472 *Brown Eyes, Why Are You Blue?*.....	5.00 -	8.00
40484 *Mighty Blue*..............	15.00 -	20.00
40529 *Tomorrow Morning*..............	5.00 -	8.00
40550 *Pretty Little Baby*..............	5.00 -	8.00
40560 *Behind The Clouds*..............	4.00 -	7.00
40580 *So Does Your Ole Mandarin*........	5.00 -	8.00
40590 *Let's Talk About My Sweetie*........	8.00 -	12.00
40603 *The Blue Room*..............	5.00 -	8.00
40632 *Roses Remind Me Of You*..........	4.00 -	7.00
Okeh 40649 *Baby Face*..............	7.00 -	10.00
40651 *Barcelona*..............	4.00 -	6.00

JAMES MELTON:

Brunswick 20115 (12-inch)..............	5.00 -	8.00
Columbia 2065-D, 2084-D..............	5.00 -	8.00

MEMPHIS BELL-HOPS:

Challenge 134 *Li'l Farina*..............	30.00 -	40.00
135 *Animal Crackers*..............	30.00 -	40.00

MEMPHIS DADDY & HIS BOYS:

Silvertone 5023 *Georgia Bo Bo*..............	50.00 -	75.00

MEMPHIS FIVE (See ORGINAL MEMPHIS FIVE)

MEMPHIS HOT SHOTS:

I'm So In Love With You; issued contemporaneously on Clarion 5391-C, Harmony 1377-H, Velvet Tone 2455-V..............	15.00 -	20.00
Shout, Sister, Shout; issued contemporaneously on Clarion 5381-C, Harmony 1368-H, Velvet Tone 2445-V..............	8.00 -	12.00

MEMPHIS JAZZERS:

Miss Golden Brown; In Harlem's Araby; issued contemporaneously on Gray Gull, Radiex, Supreme	10.00 -	15.00

MEMPHIS JUG BAND:

Bluebird 5040 *Oh Ambulance Man*..............	20.00 -	30.00
5430 *Kansas City Blues*..............	15.00 -	20.00
5675 *Stonewall Blues*..............	50.00 -	75.00
Okeh 8955 *Jazzbo Stomp*..............	40.00 -	60.00
8956 *Boodle Bum Bum*..............	40.00 -	60.00

8958 *Gator Wobble*	40.00 -	60.00
8960 *Mary Anna Cut Off*	40.00 -	60.00
8963 *My Love Is Cold*	40.00 -	60.00
8966 *Jug Band Quartette*	40.00 -	60.00
Victor 20552 *Sun Brimmers*	50.00 -	75.00
20576 *Newport News*	50.00 -	75.00
20781 *Sunshine Blues*	50.00 -	75.00
20809 *Memphis Boy*	50.00 -	75.00
21066 *Beale Street Mess Around*	50.00 -	75.00
21185 *State of Tennessee Blues*	50.00 -	75.00
21278 *Coal Oil Blues*	50.00 -	75.00
21412 *Bob Lee Junior Blues*	50.00 -	75.00
21524 *Snitchin' Gambler Blues*	50.00 -	75.00
21657 *Evergreen Money Blues*	50.00 -	75.00
21740 *Sugar Pudding*	50.00 -	75.00
23251 *Fourth Street Mess Around*	80.00 -	110.00
23347 *Taking Your Place*	80.00 -	110.00
23421 *Meningitis Blues*	90.00 -	120.00
38015 *On The Road Again*	50.00 -	75.00
38540 *Whitewash Station Blues*	50.00 -	75.00
38537 *Jug Band Waltz*	50.00 -	75.00
38551 *I Can't Stand It*	50.00 -	75.00
38558 *K. C. Moan*	50.00 -	75.00
38578 *Feed You Friend With a Long-Handled Spoon*	50.00 -	75.00
38586 *Tired Of Your Driving Me*	50.00 -	75.00
38599 *Bumble Bee Blues*	50.00 -	75.00
38605 *Cave Man Blues*	50.00 -	75.00
38620 *Cocaine Habit Blues*	50.00 -	75.00
Vocalion 03175 *Take Your Fingers Off It*	30.00 -	40.00
03050 *Little Green Slippers*	15.00 -	25.00
03081 *My Love Is Cold*	15.00 -	25.00
03182 *Boodle Bum Bum*	15.00 -	25.00

MEMPHIS MELODY BOYS:

Buddy 8005 *Washboard Blues*	25.00 -	35.00

MEMPHIS MELODY MEN:

Superior 2723 *Minnie The Moocher*	15.00 -	20.00
2734 *New Moten Stomp*	15.00 -	20.00

MEMPHIS NIGHT HAWKS:

Vocalion 1736 *Sweet Feet*	40.00 -	50.00
1744 *Biscuit Roller*	40.00 -	50.00
2593 *Shanghai Honeymoon*	40.00 -	50.00

MEMPHIS SHEIKS:

Victor 23256 *He's In The Jailhouse Now*	90.00 -	120.00

MEMPHIS STOMPERS:

Electradisk 1930 *Somebody Stole My Gal*	15.00 -	20.00
Victor 21270 *Kansas City Blues*	8.00 -	12.00
21541 *Memphis Stomp*	8.00 -	12.00
21709 *Yea Alabama*	8.00 -	12.00
23371 *Stompin' Away*	12.00 -	15.00

THE MEMPHIS STRUTTERS:

Champion 15415 *Canned Heat Blues*	75.00 -	100.00

MENDELLO'S DANCE ORCHESTRA:

Banner 6205 *Baby's Coming Back*	7.00 -	10.00
6206 *Cool Papa*	7.00 -	10.00
6213 *High Hattin' Hattie*	7.00 -	10.00
6214 *Dixie Drag*	7.00 -	10.00
7246 *Easy*	7.00 -	10.00
7248 *Sunday Afternoon*	7.00 -	10.00

JOHNNY MERCER:

Decca 142 *The Bathtub Ran Over Again*	5.00 -	8.00

BENNY MEROFF ANDD HIS ORCHESTRA:

Brunswick 4709 *The Talk Of The Town*	5.00 -	8.00
Columbia 3065-D *Yankee In Havana*	8.00 -	12.00
Okeh 40847, 40967, 41079	5.00 -	8.00
40912 *Just An Hour Of Love*	15.00 -	25.00
41171 *Smiling Skies*	15.00 -	25.00

ROY MERRITT & HIS ORCHESTRA:

Champion 15637 *Me and the Man in the Moon*	8.00 -	12.00

CYRIL MERRIVALE & HIS ORCHESTRA; CYRIL MERRIVALE'S ORCHESTRA:

Parlophone PNY-34016 *I'm Following You*	8.00 -	15.00
34020 *I'm Following You*	8.00 -	15.00
34024 *Cryin' For The Carolines*	8.00 -	15.00
34025 *Have A Little Faith In Me*	8.00 -	15.00
34045 *Montana Call*	8.00 -	15.00
34046 *The Moon Is Low*	8.00 -	15.00
34047 *Montana Call*	8.00 -	15.00
34048 *The Moon Is Low*	8.00 -	15.00
34049 *Leven-Thirty Saturday Night*	8.00 -	15.00
34053 *It Must Be You*	8.00 -	15.00
34056 *It Must Be You*	8.00 -	15.00
34086 *Sharing*	8.00 -	15.00
34087 *Sharing*	8.00 -	15.00
34088 *The Song Without a Name*	8.00 -	15.00
34089 *The Song Without a Name*	8.00 -	15.00
34092 *Lo Lo*	8.00 -	15.00

*Note: Duplication of titles is due to the issuance of vocal and non-vocal takes.

METOMKIN INN ORCHESTRA:

Champion 15458 *So Long*	7.00 -	10.00

METROPOLITAN DANCE PLAYERS:

Harlem's Araby; issued contemporaneously on Globe, Grey Gull, Nadsco, Radiex	8.00 -	12.00

METZGER'S CAMPUS/NIGHT OWLS:

Superior 2629 *When Dreams Come True*	10.00 -	15.00
2646 *It's That Rhythm*	10.00 -	15.00

KEN MEYERS:

Regal 8183 *Stampede*	5.00 -	8.00

VIC MEYERS AND HIS ORCHESTRA; VIC MEYERS' MUSIC:

Brunswick 2501, 2630, 2664, 2733, 2800	4.00 -	7.00
Columbia 1456-D, 1530-D, 1516-D, 2026-D	4.00 -	7.00
Vocalion 15056 *Three O'Clock Blues*	7.00 -	10.00

MEZZ MEZZROW AND HIS ORCHESTRA/SWING BAND; MEZZROW-LADNIER QUINTET:

Bluebird 6319 *The Panic Is On*	8.00 -	12.00
6320 *Lost*	8.00 -	12.00
6321 *I'se a-Muggin'*	8.00 -	12.00
10085, 10087, 10090	4.00 -	7.00
Brunswick 6778 *Swingin' With Mezz*	8.00 -	12.00
7551 *Dissonance*	8.00 -	12.00
Victor 25019 *Sendin' The Vipers*	6.00 -	9.00
25202 *Old Fashioned Love*	6.00 -	9.00
25612 *Hot Club Stomp*	6.00 -	9.00
25636 *Blues In Disguise*	6.00 -	9.00

MIAMI LUCKY SEVEN:

Challenge 757 *So Tired*	---	
Gennett 3165 *Fallin' Down*	8.00 -	12.00
3174 *Slippery Elm*	8.00 -	12.00
5473 *Red Hot Mama*	7.00 -	10.00
5585 *Boll Weevil Blues*	7.00 -	10.00

ERNEST MICHALL (CLARINET BAND); ERNEST MICHALL & HIS NEW ORLEANS BOYS:

Black Patti 8046 *Sidewalk Blues*	60.00 -	80.00
Challenge 372 *Embarrassment Blues*	30.00 -	40.00
Champion 15455 *Lazybones Blues*	30.00 -	40.00

MICHIGAN MELODY MAKERS:

Pennington 1453, 1455	5.00 -	8.00

MICKEY MOUSE & THE TURTLES (See WILLIAMS' WASHBOARD BAND)

THE MIDNIGHT AIREDALES:
Columbia 1981-D *Swanee Shuffle*............. 8.00 - 12.00
THE MIDNIGHT ROUNDERS:
Vocalion 1218 *Shake Your Shimmy*........... 75.00 - 100.00
1237 *Bull Fiddle Rag*..................... 50.00 - 75.00
THE MIDNIGHT SERENADERS:
Broadway 1216 *Tin Roof Blues*........... 8.00 - 12.00
Paramount 20657 *Tin Roof Blues*........... 8.00 - 12.00
THE MIDWAY DANCE ORCHESTRA:
Columbia 33-D *The Black Sheep Blues*...... 8.00 - 12.00
51-D *Cotton Pickers' Ball*............. 10.00 - 15.00
MIDWAY GARDEN ORCHESTRA:
Claxtonola 40272 *Black Sheep Blues*........ 30.00 - 50.00
40273 *Lots O' Mama*............. 15.00 - 20.00
Harmograph 863 *Black Sheep Blues*........ 30.00 - 50.00
864 *Sobbin' Blues*............. 15.00 - 20.00
Paramount 20272 *Black Sheep Blues*........ 30.00 - 50.00
20273 *Sobbin' Blues*......... 15.00 - 20.00
Puritan 11273 *Lots O' Mama*............. 15.00 - 20.00
Triangle 11311 *Sobbin' Blues*............. 15.00 - 20.00
EDDIE MILES & HIS FLORENTINE CLUB ORCHESTRA:
Gennett 6200 *One O'Clock Baby*............ 7.00 - 10.00
6247 *Is It Possible?*................. 7.00 - 10.00
BUBBER MILEY & HIS MILEAGE MAKERS:
Victor 23010 *The Penalty Of Love*........... 15.00 - 25.00
38138 *I Lost My Gal From Memphis*....... 15.00 - 25.00
38146 *Black Maria*.................. 15.00 - 25.00
EMMETT MILLER (Acc. by HIS GEORGIA CRACKERS):
Bluebird 6550, 6577..................... 4.00 - 7.00
Okeh 40239, 40465, 40545............... 4.00 - 8.00
Okeh 41062 *I Ain't Got Nobody*........... 7.00 - 10.00
41095 *Anytime*................... 5.00 - 8.00
41135 *Take Your Tomorrow*........... 7.00 - 10.00
41182 *You're The Cream In My Coffee*...... 7.00 - 10.00
41205 *The Lion Tamers*............. 6.00 - 10.00
41280 *Right Or Wrong*............. 6.00 - 10.00
41305 *Lovin' Sam*............... 7.00 - 10.00
41342 *Sweet Mama*............. 8.00 - 12.00
41377 *The Pickaninnies' Paradise*...... 8.00 - 12.00
41438 *God's River Blues*............. 7.00 - 10.00
GLENN MILLER AND HIS ORCHESTRA:
Bluebird, most issues................. 3.00 - 5.00
Brunswick, 7915 *I Got Rhythm*........... 7.00 - 12.00
7923 *Sleepy Time Gal*........... 7.00 - 12.00
8034 *My Fine Feathered Friend*...... 7.00 - 12.00
8041 *Sweet Stranger*............. 7.00 - 12.00
8062 *Doin' The Jive*........... 7.00 - 12.00
8152 *Don't Wake Up My Heart*....... 7.00 - 12.00
8173 *Dippermouth Blues*........... 7.00 - 12.00
Columbia 3052-D *A Blues Serenade*........ 30.00 - 40.00
3058-D *Solo Hop*............. 30.00 - 40.00
Decca 1239 *How Am I To Know*........ 8.00 - 12.00
1284 *Wistful And Blue*............. 8.00 - 12.00
1342 *I'm Sitting On Top Of The World*...... 7.00 - 10.00
Decca, most other issues............. 2.00 - 4.00
Victor, most issues................. 2.00 - 4.00
JOHNNIE MILLER'S NEW ORLEANS FROLICKERS:
Columbia 1546-D *Dipper Mouth Blues*........ 20.00 - 30.00
RAY MILLER & HIS ORCHERSTRA:
Brunswick 2546, 2606, 2613, 2632, 2681, 2724, 2753,
2778, 2830, 2855, 2989................. 4.00 - 7.00
Brunswick 3132 *Stomp Your Stuff*........... 5.00 - 8.00
3133 *Oh! Oh! Oh! What A Night*........ 5.00 - 8.00
3328 *Mercy Percy*............. 5.00 - 8.00
3676 *Blue Baby*............. 5.00 - 8.00
3677 *Weary Blues*............. 5.00 - 8.00
3716 *I Ain't Got Nobody*........... 5.00 - 8.00
3749 *My Honey's Lovin' Arms*........ 7.00 - 10.00
3828 *Sorry*................. 7.00 - 10.00

3829 *Is She My Girl Friend?*............. 5.00 - 8.00
3920 *Who Wouldn't Be Jealous Of You?*..... 7.00 - 10.00
3947 *Angry*.................. 7.00 - 10.00
4131 *Rose Of Mandalay*............. 5.00 - 8.00
4194 *Mississippi, Here I am*........... 7.00 - 10.00
4224 *That's A Plenty*............. 7.00 - 10.00
4687 *Hoosier Hop*............. 5.00 - 8.00
4692 *Harlem Madness*............. 5.00 - 8.00
LUCKY MILLINDER WITH MILLS BLUE RHYTHM BAND; MILLS BLUE RHYTHM BAND:
Bluebird 5688 *The Growl*................. 8.00 - 12.00
Brunswick 6156 *Moanin'*.............. 15.00 - 25.00
6199 *Snake Hips*............. 10.00 - 15.00
6229 *Savage Rhythm*............. 10.00 - 15.00
Columbia 2963-D *Let's Have a Jubilee*...... 10.00 - 15.00
2994 *Keep the Rhythm Going*........ 10.00 - 15.00
3020-D *Back Beats*............. 10.00 - 15.00
3038-D *African Lullaby*............. 10.00 - 15.00
3071-D *Harlem Heat*............. 10.00 - 15.00
3078-D *Truckin'*............. 10.00 - 15.00
3083-D *Dinah Lou*............. 10.00 - 15.00
3087-D *Congo Caravan*............. 8.00 - 12.00
3111-D *Yes! Yes!*............. 10.00 - 15.00
3134-D *Everything Is Still Okay*........ 10.00 - 15.00
3135-D *Red Rhythm*............. 10.00 - 15.00
3147-D *Merry-Go-Round*........... 10.00 - 15.00
3148-D *In a Sentimental Mood*....... 10.00 - 15.00
3156-D *Balloonacy*............. 10.00 - 15.00
3157-D *Showboat Shuffle*........... 10.00 - 15.00
3158-D *Algiers Stomp*............. 10.00 - 15.00
3162-D *Big John's Special*........... 10.00 - 15.00
Variety 503 *Jungle Madness*............. 8.00 - 12.00
546 *Rhythm Jam*............. 8.00 - 12.00
604 *The Lucky Swing*............. 8.00 - 12.00
624 *Camp Meeting Jamboree*........ 8.00 - 12.00
634 *Jammin' For The Jack-Pot*........ 8.00 - 12.00
Victor 22763 *Heebie Jeebies*............. 10.00 - 15.00
22800 *Moanin'*............. 7.00 - 10.00
24442 *Harlem After Midnight*............ 10.00 - 15.00
24482 *Break It Down*............. 10.00 - 15.00
Vocalion 3808 *Ble Rhythm Fantasy*........... 8.00 - 12.00
3817 *Rhythm Jam*............. 8.00 - 12.00
THE MILLS BROTHERS
Brunswick 6197, 6225, 6240, 6269, 6276, 6278, 6305,
6330, 6357, 6430, 6785, 6913............. 5.00 - 10.00
6517 *Doin' The New Low-Down*............ 10.00 - 15.00
6519 *Diga Diga Doo*............. 10.00 - 15.00
6225 *Smoke Rings*............. 7.00 - 10.00
6894 *Swing It, Sister*............. 7.00 - 10.00
Decca 165, 166, 167, 228, 380, 402, 497, 1148.. 3.00 - 6.00
Note: In the February, 1979 issue of GOLDMINE'S
RECORD SWAPPER, an advertiser offers "up
to $950.00 for a Mills Brothers 78 on the Gennett
label cut in 1928. Titles unknown." The author
has not verified the existence of any Gennett
issues by The Mills Brothers.
MILLS CAVALCADE ORCHESTRA:
Columbia 3066-D *Lovely Liza Lee*............ 5.00 - 8.00
MILLS' MERRY MAKERS:
Titles, issued contemporaneously on Cameo, Lincoln
and Romeo: *In a Great Big Way; The Junior-
Senior Prom; Milwaukee Walk*............. 8.00 - 12.00
Harmony 1099-H *When You're Smiling*........ 10.00 - 15.00
1104-H *St. James' Infirmary*............. 10.00 - 15.00
Pathe-Actuelle 37027 *Moanin' Low*............. 7.00 - 10.00
Perfect 15208 *Moanin' Low*............. 7.00 - 10.00
Velvet Tone 7121-V *Farewell Blues*............. 10.00 - 15.00
MILLS MUSICAL CLOWNS:
Pathe-Actuelle 36930 *Railraod Man*............ 8.00 - 12.00
36944 *Futuristic Rhythm*............. 8.00 - 12.00
36974 *Wipin' The Pan*............. 5.00 - 8.00

Perfect 15111 *Railroad Man*	8.00 -	12.00
15125 *Futuristic Rhythm*	8.00 -	12.00
15155 *Wipin' The Pan*	5.00 -	8.00

MILLS SWINGPHONIC ORCHESTRA:

Master 119, 126	5.00 -	8.00

MILLS' TEN BLACK BERRIES:

Titles, issued contemporaneously on Clarion, Diva, Velvet Tone: *Black and Tan Fantasy; Double Check Stomp; East St. Louis Toodle-oo; Hot and Bothered; The Mooche; Sweet Mama* ... 15.00 - 20.00

FLOYD MILLS & HIS MARYLANDERS:

Gennett 6909 *Hard Luck*	25.00 -	35.00

IRVING MILLS & HIS HOTSY TOTSY GANG/MODERNISTS/ORCHESTRA:

Brunswick 4482 *Sweet Savannah Sue*	10.00 -	15.00
4498 *Some Fun*	10.00 -	15.00
4559 *Harvey*	10.00 -	15.00
4587 *Star Dust*	10.00 -	15.00
4641 *Manhattan Rag*	10.00 -	15.00
4674 *My Little Honey and Me*	10.00 -	15.00
4838 *Railroad Man*	10.00 -	15.00
4920 *Barbaric*	12.00 -	18.00
4983 *Deep Harlem*	20.00 -	30.00
4998 *What A Night!*	12.00 -	18.00
Victor 38105 *At The Prom*	20.00 -	30.00

WARREN MILLS & HIS BLUES SERENADERS:

Victor 35962 (12-inch) *St. Louis Blues*	8.00 -	12.00

MISSISSIPPI MAULERS:

Columbia 1545-D *My Angeline*	8.00 -	12.00

MISSISSIPPI TRIO:

Supertone 9528 *Doin' That Thing*	40.00 -	60.00
Van Dyke 77039 *Coal Black Blues*	15.00 -	20.00

THE MISSOURIANS:

Victor 38067 *Market Street Stomp*	20.00 -	30.00
38071 *Ozark Mountain Blues*	20.00 -	30.00
38084 *Scotty Blues*	25.00 -	35.00
38103 *Vine Street Drag*	25.00 -	35.00
38120 *Stoppin' The Traffic*	25.00 -	35.00
38145 *Two Hundred Squabble*	30.00 -	40.00

MISSOURI DANCE ORCHESTRA; MISSOURI JAZZ BAND:

Banner 1621 *Stomp Off, Let's Go*	7.00 -	10.00
6202 *I Could Stand A Lot of Loving*	5.00 -	8.00
7106 *Know Nothin' Blues*	5.00 -	8.00
7140 *Straight Back Home*	5.00 -	8.00
7157 *Puttin' On The Dog*	5.00 -	8.00
7160 *If I Can Ba-Ba-Baby You*	5.00 -	8.00
7193 *Raggedy Maggie*	5.00 -	8.00
Challenge 900 *If I Can Ba-Bab-Baby You*	5.00 -	8.00
Conqueror 7110 *Ready For The River*	7.00 -	10.00
7487 *The Man From The South*	7.00 -	10.00
Domino 3592 *Stomp Off, Let's Go*	7.00 -	10.00
3594 *Sweet Man*	8.00 -	12.00
4010 *Tiger Rag*	7.00 -	10.00
4184 *Ready For The River*	7.00 -	10.00
4497 *Nobody's Sweetheart*	7.00 -	10.00
Oriole 528 *Then I'll Be Happy*	7.00 -	10.00
536 *Sleepy Time Gal*	7.00 -	10.00
Perfect 15273 *Nobody's Sweetheart*	7.00 -	10.00
Regal 8361 *Bye-Bye Pretty Baby*	5.00 -	8.00
8942 *Nobody's Sweetheart*	7.00 -	10.00
8959 *Sing You Sinners*	7.00 -	10.00
9925 *Stomp Off, Let's Go*	7.00 -	10.00
9970 *My Charleston Dancing Man*	5.00 -	8.00

EDDIE MITCHELL & HIS ORCHESTRA:

Gennett 5612 *Pleasure Mad*	10.00 -	15.00

THE MODERNISTS:

Titles, issued contemporaneously on Banner, Conqueror, Melotone, Oriole, Perfect, Romeo: *Solitude; I'm Getting Sentimental Over You* .. 7.00 - 12.00

MIFF MOLE'S (LITTLE) MOLERS; MIFF MOLE:

Brunswick 7842 *How Could You?*	8.00 -	12.00
Okeh 40758 *Alexander's Ragtime Band*	15.00 -	20.00
40784 *The Darktown Strutters' Ball*	15.00 -	20.00
40848 *Hurricane*	15.00 -	20.00
40890 *Imagination*	15.00 -	20.00
40932 *My Gal Sal*	15.00 -	20.00
40984 *The New Twister*	15.00 -	20.00
41098 *Crazy Rhythm*	15.00 -	20.00
41153 *Wild Oat Joe*	15.00 -	20.00
41232 *That's A Plenty*	15.00 -	20.00
41273 *Birmingham Bertha*	15.00 -	20.00
41371 *Navy Blues*	15.00 -	20.00
41445 *After You've Gone*	15.00 -	20.00
Parlophone (English) R-647 *You Made Me Love You*	20.00 -	30.00
Premium 852, 853	5.00 -	8.00
Vocalion 3468 *Love and Learn*	7.00 -	10.00

TOOTS MONDELLO & HIS ORCHESTRA:

Brunswick 8031, 8061, 8094, 8105	4.00 -	6.00

J. NEAL MONTGOMERY & HIS ORCHESTRA:

Okeh 8682 *Atlanta Low Down*	40.00 -	60.00

ART MOONEY & HIS ORCHESTRA:

Vogue R-711 *Seems Like Old Times*	10.00 -	15.00
R-713 *I've Been Working on the Railroad*	10.00 -	15.00
R-730 *Piper's Junction*	10.00 -	15.00
R-732 *In The Moonmist*	10.00 -	15.00

THE MOONLIGHT REVELERS:

Grey Gull 1767 *Baby Knows How*	20.00 -	30.00
1775 *Alabama Shuffle*	20.00 -	30.00
1786 *Memphis Stomp*	20.00 -	30.00

MOONLIGHT SERENADERS:

Bell 383 *Hot Stuff Blues*	4.00 -	6.00

GRANT MOORE & HIS NEW ORLEANS BLACK DEVILS:

Vocalion 1622 *Original Dixieland One-Step*	35.00 -	50.00

WEBSTER MOORE & HIS HIGH HATTERS:

Harmony 1197-H *I Wonder How It Feels*	7.00 -	10.00
Velvet Tone 2197-V *I Wonder How It Feels*	7.00 -	10.00

FATE MORABLE'S SOCIETY SYNCOPATORS:

Okeh 40113 *Frankie and Johnny*	60.00 -	90.00

MORAN AND MACK:

Columbia 935-D, 1094-D, 1198-D	3.00 -	5.00
Columbia 1350-D *Two Black Crows, Part 7/8*	4.00 -	6.00
1560-D *Two Black Crows in Jail*	5.00 -	8.00
1652-D *Two Black Crows in Hades*	5.00 -	8.00
1929-D *Foolishments*	7.00 -	10.00
Columbia Personal 170330 *Two Black Crows in the AEF*	15.00 -	20.00

(Note: Above is a one-sided record made for Bobbs-Merrill Co.)

CHAUNCEY MOREHOUSE & HIS SWING SIX/ORCHESTRA:

Brunswick 8122 *Plastered In Paris*	7.00 -	10.00
8142 *Oriental Nocturne*	7.00 -	10.00
Variety 608 *Blues In B Flat*	7.00 -	10.00
638 *My Gal Sal*	7.00 -	10.00

RUSS MORGAN AND HIS ORCHESTRA; MUSIC IN THE RUSS MORGAN MANNER:

Brunswick, most issues	3.00 -	5.00
Columbia 3050-D *Tidal Wave*	8.00 -	12.00
3067-D *Sliphorn Sam*	8.00 -	12.00
Columbia 3063-D, 3064-D	4.00 -	7.00
Decca, most issues	2.00 -	4.00
Odeon ONY-36094 *Washin' the Blues from My Soul (instrumental)*	7.00 -	10.00
ONY-36097, ONY-36140	7.00 -	10.00

SAM MORGAN'S JAZZ BAND:

Columbia 14213-D *Sing On*	60.00 -	80.00

14258-D *Steppin' On The Gas*	60.00 -	80.00
14267-D *Down By The Riverside*	60.00 -	80.00
14351-D *Short Dress Gal*	75.00 -	100.00
14539-D *Over In The Glory Land*	75.00 -	100.00

THOMAS MORRIS & HIS ORCHESTRA/SEVEN HOT BABIES; THOMAS MORRIS PAST JAZZ MASTERS:

Okeh 4867 *Lonesome Journey Blues*	15.00 -	20.00
4940 *Those Blues*	15.00 -	20.00
8055 *Original Charleston Strut*	15.00 -	20.00
8075 *Just Blues, That's All*	15.00 -	20.00
Victor 20179 *Ham Gravy*	15.00 -	20.00
20180 *Georgia Grind*	15.00 -	20.00
20316 *Who's Dis Heah Stranger?*	15.00 -	20.00
20331 *P.D.Q Blues*	15.00 -	20.00
20364 *The Mess*	15.00 -	20.00
20493 *The Chinch*	15.00 -	20.00

LEE MORSE:

Columbia 1922-D, 2136-D, 2165-D, 2333-D, 2348-D	5.00 -	8.00
2417-D *Walkin' My Baby Back Home*	8.00 -	12.00
2497-D *It's The Girl!*	8.00 -	12.00

LEE MORSE'S BLUE GRASS BOYS:

Pathe-Actuelle 36541, 36545, 36546, 36556	4.00 -	7.00
Perfect 14722, 14726, 14727, 14737	4.00 -	7.00

BENNY MORTON & HIS ORCHESTRA:

Columbia 2902-D *Get Goin'*	15.00 -	25.00
2924-D *Taylor Made*	15.00 -	25.00

FERD (JELLY ROLL) MORTON: FRED (JELLY ROLL) MORTON; JELLY ROLL MORTON'S INCOMPARABLES/JAZZ BAND/JAZZ KIDS/KINGS OF JAZZ/STEAMBOAT FOUR/STOMPS KINGS/TRIO; JELLY ROLL MORTON & HIS ORCHESTRA/RED HOT PEPPERS:

Autograph 606 *Fish Tail Blues*	150.00 -	300.00
607 *Weary Blues*	150.00 -	300.00
623 *Wolverine Blues*	150.00 -	300.00
Broadway 11397 *Mr. Jelly Lord*	75.00 -	100.00
Buddy 8015 *Bucktown Blues*	50.00 -	75.00
Carnival 11397 *Mr. Jelly Lord*	75.00 -	100.00
Champion 15105 *Mr. Jelly Lord*	75.00 -	100.00
Gennett 3043 *Tia Juana*	35.00 -	50.00
3259 *Mr. Jelly Lord*	75.00 -	100.00
5218 *Grandpa's Spells*	50.00 -	80.00
5289 *Wolverine Blues*	50.00 -	80.00
5323 *The Pearls*	50.00 -	80.00
5486 *New Orleans (Blues) Joys*	50.00 -	80.00
5515 *Tom Cat Blues*	50.00 -	80.00
5552 *Big Foot Ham*	50.00 -	80.00
5590 *Stratford Hunch*	50.00 -	80.00
5632 *Tia Juana*	50.00 -	80.00
Mitchell 11397 *Mr. Jelly Lord*	75.00 -	100.00
Okeh 8105 *London Blues*	75.00 -	100.00
Oriole 1007 *The Pearls*	35.00 -	50.00
Paramount 12216 *Mamanita*	100.00 -	150.00
14032 *Froggie Moore*	7.00 -	10.00

20332 *Mr. Jelly Lord*	75.00 -	100.00
Puritan 11332 *Mr. Jelly Lord*	75.00 -	100.00
11397 *Mr. Jelly Lord*	75.00 -	100.00
12216 *Mamanita*	100.00 -	150.00
Rialto (unnumbered) *London Blues*	250.00 -	500.00
Silvertone 4028 *Mamanita*	50.00 -	80.00
4036 *Stratford Hunch*	50.00 -	80.00
4040 *Tom Cat Blues*	50.00 -	80.00
4041 *Perfect Rag*	50.00 -	80.00
4048 *Tia Juana*	50.00 -	80.00
Triangle 11397 *Mr. Jelly Lord*	75.00 -	100.00
Victor 20221 *Black Bottom Stomp*	15.00 -	20.00
20252 *Sidewalk Blues*	15.00 -	20.00
20296 *Steamboat Stomp*	20.00 -	30.00
20405 *Someday Sweetheart*	20.00 -	30.00
20415 *Doctor Jazz*	15.00 -	20.00
20431 *Cannon Ball Blues*	20.00 -	30.00
20772 *Hyena Stomp*	20.00 -	30.00
20948 *Beale Street Blues*	15.00 -	25.00
21064 *Wolverine Blues*	15.00 -	20.00
21345 *Jungle Blues*	20.00 -	30.00
21658 *Shoe Shiner's Drag*	15.00 -	20.00
22681 *Blue Blood Blues*	20.00 -	30.00
Victor 23004 *Mushmouth Shuffle*	30.00 -	40.00
23019 *Fickle Fay Creep*	30.00 -	50.00
23307 *Gambling Jack*	75.00 -	100.00
23321 *Oil Well*	80.00 -	120.00
23334 *Low Gravy*	75.00 -	100.00
23351 *Strokin' Away*	75.00 -	100.00
23424 *Primrose Stomp*	100.00 -	130.00
23429 *Load Of Coal*	100.00 -	130.00
38010 *Kansas City Stomps*	15.00 -	25.00
38024 *Georgia Swing*	15.00 -	25.00
38055 *Deep Creek*	15.00 -	25.00
38075 *Burnin' The Iceberg*	20.00 -	30.00
38078 *New Orleans Bump*	20.00 -	30.00
38093 *Courthouse Bump*	20.00 -	30.00
38108 *Turtle Twist*	20.00 -	30.00
38113 *Down My Way*	25.00 -	40.00
38125 *Ponchatrain*	25.00 -	40.00
38135 *Little Lawrence*	25.00 -	40.00
38527 *Freakish*	35.00 -	50.00
38601 *My Little Dixie Home*	25.00 -	35.00
38627 *Pep*	40.00 -	60.00
Vocalion 1019 *Fat Meat and Greens*	40.00 -	60.00
1020 *The Pearls*	40.00 -	60.00

TOM MORTON'S ORCHESTRA; TOMMY MORTON'S GRANGERS:

Harmony 930-H *Birmingham Bertha*	5.00 -	8.00
937-H *Broadway Baby Dolls*	5.00 -	8.00

(Note: Above titles also issued on Diva and Velvet Tone.)

Pathe-Actuelle 36544 *How Could Red Riding Hood?*	5.00 -	8.00
36548 *Baby Mine*	5.00 -	8.00
36549 *When I Kissed You I Kissed The Blues Goodbye*	5.00 -	8.00
Perfect 14725 *How Could Red Riding Hood?*	5.00 -	8.00

14729 *Baby Mine*...................... 5.00 - 8.00
14730 *When I Kissed You I Kissed The Blues*
    Goodbye........................ 5.00 - 8.00

**CURTIS MOSBY & HIS DIXIELAND BLUE
  BLOWERS:**
Columbia 1191-D *Weary Stomp*............. 15.00 - 25.00
1192-D *Tiger Stomp*...................... 15.00 - 20.00
1442-D *Blue Blowers Blues*............... 15.00 - 20.00
40001-D *Between You And Me*............. 20.00 - 25.00

MIKE MOSIELLO'S RADIO STARS:
Van Dyke 901 *Wow Wow Blues*............. 8.00 - 12.00
909 *Meanest Kind of Blues*............... 8.00 - 12.00
914 *Two Red Lips*....................... 8.00 - 12.00

SID MOSLEY'S BLUE BOYS:
Supertone 9686 *Asphalt Walk*............. 50.00 - 75.00

**SNUB MOSELY AND HIS
  BAND/ORCHESTRA:**
Decca 7728, 7768, 8586, 8614, 8626, 8636..... 4.00 - 7.00
Sonora .... 4.00 - 7.00

**BENNIE MOTEN'S KANSAS CITY OR-
  CHESTRA; BUSTER MOTEN-BENNIE
  MOTEN:**
Bluebird 5078 *The Only Girl I Ever Loved*..... 7.00 - 10.00
5585 *Milenberg Joys*................... 7.00 - 10.00
6032 *Moten Swing*.................... 7.00 - 10.00
6204 *Moten Stomp*.................... 5.00 - 8.00
6218 *New Orleans*.................... 7.00 - 10.00
6304 *Terrific Stomp*.................. 7.00 - 10.00
6431 *It's Hard To Laugh Or Smile*........ 8.00 - 12.00
6638 *Mary Lee*...................... 7.00 - 10.00
6709 *New Moten Stomp*............... 7.00 - 10.00
6710 *New Vine Street Blues*............ 8.00 - 12.00
6711 *Now That I Need You*............. 15.00 - 20.00
6719 *The Count*..................... 10.00 - 15.00
6851 *Sweetheart Of Yesterday*.......... 7.00 - 10.00
7938 *Moten's Blues*.................. 7.00 - 10.00
Okeh 8100 *Elephant's Wobble*............ 30.00 - 50.00
8184 *Goofy Dust*.................... 35.00 - 50.00
8194 *South*........................ 35.00 - 50.00
8213 *Baby Dear*..................... 40.00 - 60.00
8242 *18th Street Strut*................ 35.00 - 50.00
8255 *South Street Blues*.............. 40.00 - 60.00
8277 *Kater Street Rag*................ 40.00 - 60.00
Victor 20406 *Thick Lip Stomp*........... 15.00 - 20.00
20422 *Missouri Wobble*............... 15.00 - 20.00
20485 *Kansas City Shuffle*............. 8.00 - 12.00
20811 *White Lightnin' Blues*........... 15.00 - 20.00
20855 *Dear Heart*.................... 15.00 - 20.00
20946 *12th Street Rag*................ 15.00 - 20.00
20955 *Moten Stomp*.................. 8.00 - 12.00
21199 *Ding Dong Blues*............... 15.00 - 20.00
21584 *The New Tulsa Blues*............ 15.00 - 20.00
21693 *Kansas City Breakdown*.......... 15.00 - 20.00
21739 *Justrite*..................... 15.00 - 20.00
22660 *As Long As I Love You*.......... 20.00 - 30.00
22680 *Ya Got Love*.................. 20.00 - 30.00
22734 *When I'm Alone*............... 20.00 - 30.00
22793 *That Too, Do*................. 20.00 - 30.00
22958 *Oh! Eddie*.................... 25.00 - 35.00
23007 *New Vine Street Blues*........... 25.00 - 35.00
23023 *Liza Lee*..................... 25.00 - 35.00
23028 *Somebody Stole My Gal*.......... 15.00 - 20.00
23030 *Bouncin' Round*............... 25.00 - 35.00
23037 *Rumba Negro*................. 25.00 - 35.00
23342 *Small Black*................... 60.00 - 80.00
23357 *The Jones Law Blues*............ 60.00 - 80.00
23378 *The Only Girl I Ever Loved*....... 60.00 - 80.00
23384 *Moten Swing*................. 60.00 - 80.00
23391 *The Count*.................... 60.00 - 80.00
23393 *Prince Of Wails*............... 60.00 - 80.00
23429 *Professor Hot Stuff*............. 100.00 - 130.00

24216 *Lafayette*...................... 30.00 - 40.00
24381 *Milenberg Joys*................ 30.00 - 40.00
24893 *South*........................ 4.00 - 7.00
38012 *Slow Motion*.................. 15.00 - 20.00
38021 *South*........................ 10.00 - 15.00
38037 *Tough Breaks*................. 15.00 - 20.00
38048 *Sad Man Blues*................ 20.00 - 30.00
38072 *Moten's Blues*................ 15.00 - 20.00
38081 *Terrific Stomp*................ 15.00 - 20.00
38091 *Kansas City Squabble*........... 15.00 - 20.00
38104 *Rite Tite*..................... 15.00 - 20.00
38114 *Mary Lee*..................... 15.00 - 20.00
38123 *It Won't Be Long*.............. 20.00 - 30.00
38132 *When Life Seems So Blue*........ 20.00 - 30.00
38144 *Boot It*...................... 20.00 - 30.00

MOUNT CITY BLUE BLOWERS:
Bluebird 6270, 6456.................... 5.00 - 8.00
Brunswick 2581, 2602, 2648, 2804, 2849, 2908.. 4.00 - 7.00
Champion 40059 *Thanks A Millon*........ 6.00 - 10.00
40060 *Red Sails In The Sunset*......... 6.00 - 10.00
40073 *Eeeney Meeney Miney Mo*........ 6.00 - 10.00
40076 *I'm Shootin' High*.............. 6.00 - 10.00
40081 *The Broken Record*............. 8.00 - 12.00
40082 *Rhythm In My Nursery Rhymes*.... 8.00 - 12.00
40091 *Mama Don't Allow It*........... 8.00 - 12.00
40098 *You Hit The Spot*.............. 8.00 - 12.00
40090 *Wah-Hoo!*................... 8.00 - 12.00
40103 *High Society*.................. 8.00 - 12.00
Columbia 1946-D *Indiana*.............. 7.00 - 10.00
Okeh 41515 *Georgia On My Mind*........ 20.00 - 30.00
41526 *You Rascal, You*.............. 20.00 - 30.00
Victor 38087 *Tailspin Blues*............ 15.00 - 20.00
38100 *Hello, Lola*................... 15.00 - 20.00
Vocalion 2957 *What's The Reason*........ 9.00 - 12.00
2973 *Indiana*...................... 9.00 - 12.00

**KEN "GOOF" MOYER; KEN MOYER'S
  NOVELTY TRIO:**
Banner 1872, 1891..................... 5.00 - 8.00
Domino 3841, 3861.................... 5.00 - 8.00
Pathe-Actuelle 36511, 36528............. 5.00 - 8.00
Perfect 14692, 14709................... 5.00 - 8.00
Regal 8203 .... 5.00 - 8.00

**JIMMY MUNDY AND HIS OR-
  CHESTRA/SWING CLUB SEVEN:**
Variety 598 *Ain't Misbehavin'*........... 10.00 - 15.00
Varsity 8136 *A Lover Is Blue*........... 5.00 - 8.00
8148 *Sunday Special*................ 5.00 - 8.00

**LYLE "SPUD" MURPHY AND HIS
  ORCHESTRA:**
Bluebird 10151, 10157, 10539, 10875........ 4.00 - 7.00
Decca 1853, 2040, 2109................. 4.00 - 7.00

**BILLY MURRAY (& HIS MERRY MELODY
  MEN/& THE SEVEN BLUE BABIES):**
Edison 52448 *Doin' The Raccoon*......... 10.00 - 15.00
52454 *Don't Do That To The Poor Puss Cat*. 7.00 - 10.00
52518 *Ever Since The Movies Learned To Talk* 10.00 - 15.00

GLADYS MURRAY:

Banner 1464 *Big Bad Bill Is Sweet William Now.*	12.00 -	20.00
1479 *Nobody Knows What A Red Head Mama*		
Can Do	12.00 -	20.00
Regal 9760 *Everybody Loves My Baby*	12.00 -	20.00
9782 *I'm Done Done Done With You*	12.00 -	20.00

THE MUSICAL COMRADES:

Tremont 0515, 0526, 0537, 0544	5.00 -	8.00

THE MUSICAL MANIACS:

Vocalion 3655, 3691	4.00 -	7.00

MUSICAL STEVEDORES:

Columbia 14406-D *Happy Rhythm*	20.00 -	40.00

MUSICAL TRIO:

Madison 1920 *Beale Street Blues*	5.00 -	8.00

THE MUSICAL VOYAGERS:

Parlophone PNY-34152 *Can This Be Love?*	8.00 -	15.00
PNY-34153 *Fine and Dandy*	8.00 -	15.00

MUSTANG BAND OF SOUTHERN METHODIST UNIVERSTIY:

Decca 705 *Peruna*	5.00 -	8.00
706 *Limehouse Blues*	5.00 -	8.00

VICK MYERS' ATLANTA MELODY ARTISTS:

Okeh 40281 *Blue-Eyed Sally*	8.00 -	12.00
40364 *Flag That Train*	10.00 -	15.00
40386 *Sweet Man Blues*	10.00 -	15.00
40434 *Nantucket Nan*	10.00 -	15.00
40614 *I'd Rather Be Alone*	8.00 -	12.00

PHIL NAPOLEAN & HIS EMPERORS OF RHYTHM/ORCHERSTRA/WHISPERING RHYTHM; NAPOLEON'S EMPERORS:

Edison 51908 *Tiger Rag*	15.00 -	20.00
51960 *It Made You Happy When You Made Me*		
Cry	10.00 -	15.00
51962 *The Cat*	10.00 -	15.00
51996 *Underneath The Weeping Willow*	7.00 -	10.00
51997 *La Lo La*	7.00 -	10.00
52021 *Clarinet Marmalade*	15.00 -	20.00
52147 *Five Pennies*	15.00 -	20.00
Variety 656, 669	4.00 -	6.00
Victor 20605, 20647	5.00 -	8.00
38057 *Mean To Me*	12.00 -	16.00
38069 *You Can't Cheat a Cheater*	12.00 -	16.00
Vocalion 3792, 3860	4.00 -	6.00

WILLIAM NAPPI & HIS ORCHESTRA:

Columbia 1042-D *I'll Dream Of You*	8.00 -	12.00
1262-D *If You Just Knew*	8.00 -	12.00

SAM NASH & HIS ORCHESTRA:

Parlophone PNY-34098 *Can I Help It?*	8.00 -	12.00
PNY-34099 *I Love You So Much*	8.00 -	12.00
PNY-34187 *I've Found What I Wanted In You*	10.00 -	15.00
PNY-34197 *I'm Crazy 'Bout My Baby*	10.00 -	15.00

NASHVILLE JAZZERS:

St. Louis Blues, issued contemporaneously on Madison, Van Dyke	10.00 -	15.00

NATIONAL MUSIC LOVERS DANCE ORCHESTRA:

National Music Lovers 1097, 1152, 1156, 1186..	5.00 -	10.00

NAYLOR'S SEVEN ACES:

Gennett 5375 *Hugo (I Go Where You Go)*	15.00 -	20.00
5376 *Whe Wouldn't Do (What I Asked Her To)*	15.00 -	20.00
5386 *So I Took The Fifty Thousand Dollars* ..	15.00 -	20.00
5392 *31st Street Blues*	20.00 -	30.00
5393 *Ringleberg Blues*	20.00 -	30.00
5432 *Twilight Rose*	15.00 -	20.00
5470 *Say, Say, Sadie*	15.00 -	20.00
5638 *Susquehanna Home*	15.00 -	20.00
5643 *Bye Bye Baby*	15.00 -	20.00
Victor 19688 *Sweet Georgia Brown*	5.00 -	8.00

NOBBY NEALE & AL LYONS:

Paramount 12775 *Go To It*	15.00 -	20.00

ARNETT NELSON & HIS HOT FOUR:

Oh! Red; issued contemporaneously on Banner, Conqueror, Melotone, Oriole, Perfect, Romeo	8.00 -	12.00

CHUCK NELSON & HIS BOYS:

Champion 40016 *West End Blues*	10.00 -	15.00

DAVE NELSON & THE KING'S MEN:

Victor 22639 *I Ain't Got Nobody*	20.00 -	30.00
23039 *Some Of These Days*	20.00 -	30.00

JEWELL NELSON:

Columbia 14390-D *Beating Me Blues*	12.00 -	16.00

OZZIE NELSON & HIS ORCHESTRA:

Bluebird 6875, 6965, 6974, 7256, 7502, 7517, 7726, 7814	4.00 -	7.00
Bluebird, most other issues	3.00 -	5.00
Brunswick 4897, 4922, 4979, 6018	4.00 -	7.00
Brunswick 6060 *Dream A Little Dream Of Me*..	8.00 -	12.00
Brunswick 6131, 6155, 6186, 6228, 6313, 6347, 6372, 6373, 6410, 6413, 6443, 6447, 6547, 6551...	4.00 -	7.00
Brunswick 6861 *Dr. Heckle and Mr. Jibe*	5.00 -	8.00
7523 *Tiger Rag*	5.00 -	8.00
7651 *Streamline Strut*	5.00 -	8.00
7659 *Stompin' at the Savoy*	5.00 -	8.00
Brunswick, most other issues	3.00 -	6.00
Vocalion 2547, 2558, 2559, 2581, 2582, 2600, 2601, 2625, 2636, 2642	4.00 -	8.00

(D.C.) NELSON'S PARAMOUNT SERENADERS:

Paramount 12494 *Phillips Street Stomp*	40.00 -	60.00
12543 *New Orleans Breakdown*	40.00 -	60.00

RUBY NEWMAN AND HIS ORCHESTRA:

Brunswick 7632, 7633	4.00 -	7.00
Decca, most issues	2.00 -	4.00
Victor 22931, 22934	4.00 -	7.00
Victor 24042, 24043, 24048, 24072, 24073, 24074	3.00 -	5.00
Victor 24894, 25005, 25327, 25328, 25337, 25344	3.00 -	5.00
Victor 25401 *Make-Believe Ballroom*	4.00 -	7.00
Victor 25402, 25405, 25468, 26470, 25543, 25546	3.00 -	5.00

NEW ORLEANS BLACK BIRDS:

Victor 38027 *Playing The Blues*	10.00 -	15.00

NEW ORLEANS BLUE FIVE:

Victor 20316 *The King of the Zulus*	15.00 -	20.00
20364 *My Baby Doesn't Squawk*	15.00 -	20.00
20653 *South Rampart Street Blues*	25.00 -	35.00

NEW ORLEANS BLUES BAND:

Varsity 6029 *Big Blues*	10.00 -	15.00

NEW ORLEANS BOOTBLACKS:

Columbia 14337-D *Flat Foot*	30.00 -	40.00
14465-D *Mixed Salad*	40.00 -	50.00

NEW ORLEANS FEETWARMERS:

Victor 23358 *Lay You Racket*	75.00 -	100.00
23360 *Maple Leaf Rag*	50.00 -	75.00
24150 *I've Found a New Baby*	40.00 -	60.00

NEW ORLEANS FIVE:

Oriole 371 *Memphis Blues*	7.00 -	10.00

NEW ORLEANS JAZZ BAND:

Banner 1318 *Tin Roof Blues*	10.00 -	15.00
1445 *Copenhagen*	10.00 -	15.00
1544 *Some Of These Days*	10.00 -	15.00
1556 *My Sweet Louise*	10.00 -	15.00
1618 *The Camel Walk*	8.00 -	12.00
1624 *Melancholy Lou*	8.00 -	12.00
6049 *Tiger Rag*	7.00 -	10.00
Domino 335 *It Had To Be You*	10.00 -	15.00
338 *Limehouse Blues*	10.00 -	15.00
387 *How Could You Leave Me Now?*	10.00 -	15.00
389 *I'm Gonna Get Acquainted in a Quaint Old Fashioned Town*	10.00 -	15.00
403 *Alabamy Stay At Home*	10.00 -	15.00
3439 *Hot Sax*	15.00 -	20.00
3509 *Some Of These Days*	10.00 -	15.00
3524 *My Sweet Louise*	10.00 -	15.00
3590 *The Camel Walk*	8.00 -	12.00
3594 *Melancholy Lou*	8.00 -	12.00
Regal 9615 *Tin Roof Blues*	10.00 -	15.00
9739 *Copenhagen*	10.00 -	15.00

9839 *Some Of These Days*.	10.00 -	15.00
9852 *My Sweet Louise*.	10.00 -	15.00
9920 *Melancholy Lou*.	8.00 -	12.00
9923 *The Camel Walk*.	8.00 -	12.00

NEW ORLEANS LUCKY SEVEN:

Okeh 8544 *Goose Pimples*.	25.00 -	40.00

NEW ORLEANS OWLS:

Columbia 489-D *Stomp Off, Let's Go*.	15.00 -	20.00
605-D *The Owls' Hoot*.	15.00 -	20.00
688-D *West End Romp*.	15.00 -	20.00
823-D *Blowin' Off Steam*.	15.00 -	20.00
862-D *White Ghost Shivers*.	20.00 -	30.00
943-D *Eccentric*.	15.00 -	20.00
1045-D *Dynamite*.	15.00 -	20.00
1158-D *Meat On The Table*.	15.00 -	20.00
1261-D *Goose Pimples*.	15.00 -	20.00
1547-D *That's A Plenty*.	15.00 -	20.00

NEW ORLEANS PEPSTERS:

Van Dyke 77038 *Close Fit Blues*.	15.00 -	20.00
81836 *The Harlem Stomp Down*.	15.00 -	20.00
81843 *The Rackett*.	15.00 -	20.00

NEW ORLEANS RAMBLERS:

Melotone 12133 *No Wonder I'm Blue*.	15.00 -	25.00
12230 *That's The Kind Of Man For Me*. . . .	15.00 -	25.00

NEW ORLEANS RHYTHM KINGS (FORMERLY FRIARS SOCIETY ORCHESTRA):

Bluebird 10956 *She's Cryin' For Me*.	7.00 -	10.00
Buddy 8001 *Tin Roof Blues*.	50.00 -	75.00
8002 *Angry*.	90.00 -	130.00
8003 *Weary Blues*.	90.00 -	130.00
8004 *Clarinet Marmalade*.	90.00 -	130.00
Decca 161 *San Antonio Shout*.	7.00 -	10.00
162 *Panama*.	7.00 -	10.00
229 *Original Dixieland One-Step*.	7.00 -	10.00
388 *Dust Off That Old Piano*.	7.00 -	10.00
401 *Baby Brown*.	7.00 -	10.00
464 *Sensation*.	7.00 -	10.00
Gennett 3076 *Milenburg Joys*.	80.00 -	100.00
Gennett 5102 *Wolverine Blues*.	35.00 -	50.00
5104 *Maple Leaf Rag*.	35.00 -	50.00
5105 *That's A Plenty*.	30.00 -	40.00
5106 *Da Da Strain*.	35.00 -	50.00
5217 *Milenberg Joys*.	80.00 -	100.00
5219 *Sobbin' Blues*.	90.00 -	120.00
5220 *Mr. Jelly Lord*.	80.00 -	100.00
5221 *London Blues*.	90.00 -	130.00
Victor 19645 *She's Cryin' For Me*.	15.00 -	20.00

NEW ORLEANS STRUTTERS:

Champion 15398 *Fourth Avenue Stomp*.	75.00 -	100.00

NEW ORLEANS WANDERERS:

Columbia 698-D *Perdido Street Blues*.	30.00 -	50.00
735-D *Papa Dip*.	30.00 -	50.00

NEW ORLEANS WILD CATS WITH TAP DANCING JOE:

14662-D *Baby Mine*.	25.00 -	35.00
14668-D *Wild Cat Stomp*.	25.00 -	35.00

NEWPORT SYNCOPATORS:

Van Dyke 81850 *Ring Around The Moon*.	15.00 -	25.00
81851 *Because I'm Lonesome*.	15.00 -	25.00
81854 *Desert Blues*.	15.00 -	25.00
81879 *The Terror*.	15.00 -	25.00

FRANK NEWTON & HIS (CAFE SOCIETY ORCHESTRA/UPTOWN SERENADERS: FRANK NEWTON QUINTET:

Bluebird 10176 *The World Is Waiting For The Sunrise*.	7.00 -	10.00
10186 *Minor Jive*.	7.00 -	10.00
10216 *Who?*.	7.00 -	10.00
Blue Note 14 *After Hour Blues*.	7.00 -	10.00
501 *Daybreak Blues*.	7.00 -	10.00

Variety 518 *You Showed Me The Way*.	10.00 -	15.00
550 *'Cause My Baby Says It's So*.	10.00 -	15.00
571 *I Found A New Baby*.	10.00 -	15.00
616 *Where Or When*.	10.00 -	15.00
647 *Who's Sorry Now?*.	10.00 -	15.00
Vocalion 3777 *Easy Living*.	8.00 -	12.00
3811 *You Showed Me The Way*.	8.00 -	12.00
3839 *The Onyx Hop*.	8.00 -	12.00
4821 *Tab's Blues*.	5.00 -	8.00
4851 *Jam Fever*.	5.00 -	8.00
5410 *Parallel Fifths*.	7.00 -	10.00

THE NEWTOWN PIPPINS:

Gennett 6413 *Isabella (Tell Your Fella)*.	10.00 -	20.00
6741 *Caroline*.	10.00 -	20.00

THE NEW YORKERS:

Brunswick 6164 *Parkin' In The Moonlight*.	8.00 -	12.00
QRS 1027 *Kickin' a Hole in the Sky*.	15.00 -	20.00
1053 *Let Me Sing And I'm Happy*.	15.00 -	20.00

NEW YORK SYNCOPATORS:

Odeon ONY-36148 *It's a Great Life*.	10.00 -	15.00
ONY-36149 *When Kentucky Bids The World "Good Morning"*.	10.00 -	15.00
ONY-36152 *Satan's Holiday*.	10.00 -	15.00
ONY-36157 *I'll Be Blue, Just Thinking Of You*	10.00 -	15.00
ONY-36158 *I Got Rhythm*.	10.00 -	15.00
ONY-36159 *Ukelele Moon*.	10.00 -	15.00
ONY-36165 *Cheerful Little Earful*.	10.00 -	15.00
ONY-36189 *I'm So In Love With You*. . . .	15.00 -	20.00
ONY-36190 *I Can't Realize You Love Me*. . . .	15.00 -	20.00
ONY-36194 *The King's Horses*.	10.00 -	15.00
ONY-36206 *Dream A Little Dream Of Me*. . .	10.00 -	15.00
ONY-36208 *Just A Crazy Song*.	10.00 -	15.00
Okeh 40757 *There Ain't No Maybe In My Baby's Eyes*.	6.00 -	10.00
40860 *Bless Her Little Heart*.	6.00 -	10.00
40965 *Mary*.	6.00 -	10.00
41003 *I've Been Looking For a Girl Like You*.	6.00 -	10.00
41202 *Dream Train*.	6.00 -	10.00
41264 *The One That I Love Loves Me*.	6.00 -	10.00
Parlophone PNY-34155 *I'm Tickled Pink With a Blue-Eyed Baby*.	10.00 -	15.00

NICK NICHOLS & HIS ORCHESTRA:

Grey Gull 1820 *Breakin' A Leg*.	8.00 -	12.00

RAY NICHOLS & HIS FOUR TOWERS ORCHESTRA:

Bluebird 5902 *Who's Sorry Now?*.	7.00 -	10.00
5904 *Restless*.	5.00 -	8.00
6013 *Black Coffee*.	5.00 -	8.00
Bluebird, other issues.	3.00 -	6.00

RED NICHOLS & HIS FIVE PENNIES/ ORCHESTRA/CAPTIVATORS; RED NICHOLS' STOMPERS; LORING NICHOLS & HIS ORCHESTRA; RED NICHOLS & HIS WORLD-FAMOUS PENNIES:

Bluebird 5547 *Rockin' In Rhythm*.	5.00 -	8.00
5548 *Rollin' Home*.	5.00 -	8.00
5549 *The Prize Waltz*.	5.00 -	8.00
5552 *Straight From The Shoulder*.	5.00 -	8.00
5553 *Runnin' Wild*.	5.00 -	8.00
5583 *Old White's Whiskers*.	5.00 -	8.00
Bluebird 10179, 10190, 10200, 10328, 10332, 10360, 10408, 10451, 10522, 10593, 10683.	4.00 -	7.00
Brunswick 3407 *Washboard Blues*.	8.00 -	12.00
3477 *Buddy's Habits*.	8.00 -	12.00
3490 *Back Beats*.	8.00 -	12.00
3550 *Alabama Stomp*.	8.00 -	12.00
3597 *Mean Dog Blues*.	8.00 -	12.00
3626 *Feelin' No Pain*.	8.00 -	12.00
3627 *Riverboat Shuffle*.	8.00 -	12.00
3850 *Whispering*.	8.00 -	12.00

3854 *Avalon*	8.00 -	12.00
3855 *Five Pennies*	8.00 -	12.00
3931 *I Never Knew*	8.00 -	12.00
3955 *There'll Come a Time*	8.00 -	12.00
3961 *Panama*	8.00 -	12.00
3989 *Original Dixieland One-Step*	8.00 -	12.00
3991 *I'm Marching Home To You*	8.00 -	12.00
4243 *Who's Sorry Now?*	8.00 -	12.00
4286 *Roses Of Picardy*	8.00 -	12.00
4363 *Chinatown, My Chinatown*	8.00 -	12.00
4373 *Indiana*	8.00 -	12.00
4701 *Sometimes I'm Happy*	8.00 -	12.00
4724 *I Want To Be Happy*	8.00 -	12.00
4778 *Rose Of Washington Square*	8.00 -	12.00
4790 *Smiles*	10.00 -	15.00
4839 *After You've Gone*	10.00 -	15.00
4844 (Canadian issue) *Five Pennies* (plays *My Gal Sal,* which was not issued on U.S. Brunswick)	30.00 -	50.00
4877 *China Boy*	10.00 -	15.00
4885 *The Sheik Of Araby*	10.00 -	15.00
4925 *Carolina In The Morning*	10.00 -	15.00
4944 *Sweet Georgia Brown*	10.00 -	15.00
4957 *I Got Rhythm*	10.00 -	15.00
4982 *Yours And Mine*	10.00 -	15.00
6014 *Building A Nest For Many*	5.00 -	8.00
6012 *My Honey's Lovin' Arms*	10.00 -	15.00
6014 *Blue Again*	10.00 -	15.00
6026 *On Revival Day*	10.00 -	15.00
6029 *Sweet and Hot*	10.00 -	15.00
6035 *The Peanut Vendor*	8.00 -	12.00
6058 *Bugaboo*	7.00 -	10.00
6068 *Keep a Song In Your Soul*	10.00 -	15.00
6070 *Were You Sincere?*	8.00 -	12.00
6118 *Love Is Like That*	8.00 -	12.00
6133 *You Rascal, You*	8.00 -	12.00
6138 *Little Girl*	8.00 -	12.00
6149 *Moan, You Moaners*	8.00 -	12.00
6160 *Fan It*	8.00 -	12.00
6164 *How The Time Can Fly*	8.00 -	12.00
6191 *Singin' The Blues*	8.00 -	12.00
6198 *Honolulu Blues*	8.00 -	12.00
6219 *Junk Man Blues*	8.00 -	12.00
6234 *Haunting Blues*	8.00 -	12.00
6241 *Twenty-One Years*	8.00 -	12.00
6266 *Clarinet Marmalade*	8.00 -	12.00
6312 *Goofus*	8.00 -	12.00
6348 *Our Home Town Mountain Band*	10.00 -	15.00
6451 *Love, Nuts and Noodles*	10.00 -	15.00
6461 *Everybody Loves My Baby*	10.00 -	15.00
6534 *Dinah Lou*	10.00 -	15.00
6767 *Slow and Easy*	10.00 -	15.00
Brunswick 6681, 6711, 6718, 6753, 6814, 6815, 6816, 6817, 6818, 6819, 6820, 6821, 6822, 6823, 6827, 6828, 6830, 6831, 6832, 6833, 6834, 6835, 6836, 6839, 6841, 6842, 6843, 6844, 6845	5.00 -	10.00
6824, 6825, 6826, 6829, 6834, 6837, 6838, 6840, 7358, 7460	6.00 -	10.00
20062 (12-inch) *Poor Butterfly*	8.00 -	12.00
20070 (12-inch) *Dear Old Southland*	8.00 -	12.00
20091 (12-inch) *Some Of These Days*	8.00 -	12.00
20092 (12-inch) *It Had To Be You*	8.00 -	12.00
20107 (12-inch) *California Medley*	10.00 -	15.00
20110 (12-inch) *New Orleans Medley*	10.00 -	15.00
Okeh 5648, 5676	4.00 -	7.00
University 507 *Perfidia*	4.00 -	7.00
Variety 502 *They All Laughed*	5.00 -	8.00
524 *Wake Up and Live*	5.00 -	8.00
545 *Troublesome Trumpet*	5.00 -	8.00
595 *Humoresque*	5.00 -	8.00
655 *Twilight In Turkey*	5.00 -	8.00
Victor 21056 *Sugar*	8.00 -	12.00
21560 *Five Pennies*	8.00 -	12.00

Vocalion 3816 *Love's Old Sweet Song*	5.00 -	8.00
3827 *Humoresque*	5.00 -	8.00
3833 *Cream Puff*	5.00 -	8.00
Vocalion 15498 *Washboard Blues*	15.00 -	20.00
15566 *Alabama Stomp*	15.00 -	20.00
15536 *Back Beats*	10.00 -	15.00

NICK NICHOLSON & HIS BAND:

Champion 15699 *True Blue*	10.00 -	15.00

THE NIGHT OWLS:

Silvertone 3549 *Pump Tillie*	30.00 -	50.00

TOM NILES & HIS ORCHESTRA:

Parlophone PNY-34032 *The Perfect Song*	10.00 -	15.00
PNY-34033 *Amos 'n' Andy*	10.00 -	15.00

RAY NOBLE & HIS ORCHESTRA:

Brunswick 8098 *Crazy Rhythm*	5.00 -	8.00
8180 *Alexander's Ragtime Band*	5.00 -	8.00
Brunswick, most other issues	3.00 -	5.00
Columbia, most issues	2.00 -	5.00
Victor 24879 *Down By The River*	7.00 -	10.00
25070 *Let's Swing It*	5.00 -	8.00
Victor 24865, 24891, 25040, 25082, 25094, 25104, 25105, 25187, 25190, 25200, 25209, 25223, 25240, 25241, 25277, 25282, 25336, 25346, 25422, 25428, 25448, 25459, 25504, 25507	3.00 -	6.00

JIMMIE NOONE'S APEX CLUB ORCHESTRA: JIMMIE NOONE & HIS ORCHESTRA: JIMMIE NOONE TRIO:

Bluebird 8609 *They God My Number Now*	8.00 -	12.00
8649 *Then You're Drunk*	8.00 -	12.00
Brunswick 6174 *I Need Lovin'*	25.00 -	35.00
6192 *River, Stay 'Way From My Door*	25.00 -	35.00
Decca 1584 *I Know That You Know*	7.00 -	10.00
1621 *Four Or Five Times*	7.00 -	10.00
1730 *I'm Walkin' This Town*	8.00 -	12.00
7553 *Sweet Lorraine*	8.00 -	12.00
Vocalion 1184 *I Know That You Know*	25.00 -	40.00
Vocalion 1185 *Four Or Five Times*	25.00 -	40.00
1188 *Ready For The River*	35.00 -	50.00
1207 *Apex Blues*	35.00 -	50.00
1215 *Oh, Sister! Ain't That Hot?*	35.00 -	50.00
1229 *A Monday Date*	35.00 -	50.00
1238 *It's Tight Like That*	25.00 -	35.00
1240 *She's Funny That Way*	35.00 -	50.00
1267 *Chicago Rhythm*	35.00 -	50.00
1272 *Love Me Or Leave Me*	30.00 -	50.00
1296 *Birmingham Bertha*	30.00 -	50.00
1415 *True Blue Lou*	30.00 -	50.00
1416 *Satisfied*	30.00 -	50.00
1439 *He's A Good Man To Have Around*	40.00 -	60.00
1466 *Cryin' For The Carolines*	30.00 -	50.00
1471 *Should I?*	30.00 -	-50.00
1490 *Deep Trouble*	40.00 -	60.00
1497 *When You're Smiling*	30.00 -	50.00
1506 *On Revival Day*	30.00 -	50.00
1518 *Virginia Lee*	30.00 -	50.00
1531 *Little White Lies*	30.00 -	50.00
1554 *Three Little Words*	30.00 -	50.00
1580 *Trav'lin' All Alone*	30.00 -	50.00
1584 *You Rascal, You*	30.00 -	50.00
2619 *Inka Dinka Doo*	20.00 -	30.00
2620 *Delta Blues*	20.00 -	30.00
2779 *Apex Blues*	20.00 -	30.00
2862 *Liza*	20.00 -	30.00
2888 *Shine*	20.00 -	30.00
2907 *It's Easy To Remember*	20.00 -	30.00
2908 *Lullaby Of Broadway*	20.00 -	30.00
15819 *Ain't Misbehavin'*	40.00 -	60.00
15823 *Anything You Want*	40.00 -	60.00

NORTH-WEST MELODY BOYS:

Champion 15362 *After I've Called You Sweetheart*	15.00 -	20.00
15363 *Sugar Foot Strut*	15.00 -	20.00
15365 *Rain*	15.00 -	20.00
Gennett 6278 *Sugar Foot Strut*	15.00 -	20.00

RED NORVO; RED NORVO & HIS SWING SEXTETTE/SEPTET/OCTET/ORCHESTRA:

Brunswick 6562 *Hole In The Wall*............	8.00 -	12.00
6906 *In A Mist*......................	8.00 -	12.00
7732, 7744, 7761, 7767, 7813, 7815, 7868, 7928, 7932, 7970, 7975, 8068, 8069, 8085, 8088, 8089, 8103, 8135, 8145, 8171, 8182, 8194, 8202, 8227, 8230, 8240, 8288.................	5.00 -	8.00
Columbia 2927-D *Tomboy*..................	10.00 -	15.00
3026-D *The Night Is Blue*..............	10.00 -	15.00
3059-D *Old Fashioned Love*.............	10.00 -	15.00
3079-D *Bughouse*......................	10.00 -	15.00
Decca 670, 691, 779...................	4.00 -	7.00
Vocalion 4083, 4109, 4282, 4345, 4432, 4548, 4632, 4648, 4698, 4738, 4785, 4818, 4833, 4953, 5009	3.00 -	6.00

SAM NOWLIN:

Champion 16828 *So What*.................	10.00 -	15.00

JACK OAKIE:

Titles, issued contemporaneously on Banner, Melotone, Oriole, Perfect, Romeo: *Miss Brown To You; Why Dream*..................	8.00 -	12.00
Melotone 13236 *College Rhythm*..........	10.00 -	15.00

(JIMMIE/JIMMY O'BRYANT'S (FAMOUS ORIGINAL) WASHBOARD BAND:

Paramount 12246 *Red Hot Mama*...........	30.00 -	50.00
12260 *Shoodlum Blues*.................	30.00 -	50.00
12265 *Brand New Charleston*...........	30.00 -	50.00
12277 *Georgia Breakdown*..............	30.00 -	50.00
12287 *Clarinet Getaway*...............	30.00 -	50.00
12288 *Blue Eyed Sally*................	30.00 -	50.00
12294 *Steppin' On The Gas*............	30.00 -	50.00
12297 *The Joys*......................	30.00 -	50.00
12308 *Down To The Bricks*.............	30.00 -	50.00
12312 *Charleston Fever*...............	30.00 -	50.00
12321 *Milenberg Joys*.................	30.00 -	50.00
12329 *Thirty-Eight And Two*...........	30.00 -	50.00
12339 *Chicago Skiffle*................	30.00 -	50.00
12346 *Shake That Thing*...............	30.00 -	50.00
20400 *Alabamy Bound*..................	30.00 -	50.00

HUSK O'HARE'S SUPER ORCHESTRA OF CHICAGO; HUSK O'HARE'S WOLVERINES:

Gennett 4850 *Tiger Rag*...............	10.00 -	15.00
5009 *San*............................	10.00 -	15.00
Vocalion 15646 *Milenberg Joys*.........	50.00 -	75.00

OKEH MELODIANS:

Okeh 40941, 40960......................	5.00 -	8.00

OKEH MELODY STARS:

Okeh 8282 *Look Out, Mr. Jazz*..........	15.00 -	20.00

OLD SOUTHERN JUG BAND:

Silvertone 3061 *Hatchet Head Blues*...........	25.00 -	40.00
Vocalion 14958 *Hatchet Head Blues*...........	25.00 -	40.00

ANNA OLIVER & YOUNG'S CREOLE JAZZ BAND:

Paramount 12060 *What's The Use Of Lovin'*...	60.00 -	80.00

EARL OLIVER'S JAZZ BABIES:

Edion 51698, 51724, 51745, 51760, 51776, 51877, 51900, 51929......................	5.00 -	10.00
51762 *Lulu-Lou*.......................	10.00 -	15.00

JOE "KING" OLIVER; KING OLIVER'S (CREOLE) JAZZ BAND; KING OLIVER & HIS DIXIE SYNCOPATORS:

Autograph 617 *King Porter*.............	350.00 -	600.00
Bluebird 5466 *St. James Infirmary*............	5.00 -	8.00
6546 *Call Of The Freaks*..............	8.00 -	12.00
6778 *Boogie Woogie*...................	8.00 -	12.00
7242 *What You Want Me To Do?*.........	8.00 -	12.00
10707 *Shake It And Break It*..............	7.00 -	10.00
Brunswick 3398 *Showboat Shuffle*............	15.00 -	20.00
3741 *Farewell Blues*..................	15.00 -	20.00
4028 *Four Or Five Times*..............	20.00 -	30.00

4469 *I'm Watching The Clock*..............	20.00 -	30.00
6053 *Papa De Da Da*..............	25.00 -	35.00
6065 *I'm Crazy 'Bout My Baby*.............	25.00 -	35.00
Claxtonola 40292 *Riverside Blues*........	90.00 -	125.00
Columbia 13003-D *Chattanooga Stomp*........	30.00 -	40.00
14003-D *Camp Meeting Blues*........	30.00 -	40.00
Gennett 5132 *Weather Bird Rag*..........	125.00 -	200.00
5133 *Canal Street Blues*.............	125.00 -	200.00
5134 *Mandy Lee Blues*...............	125.00 -	200.00
5135 *Froggie Moore*.................	125.00 -	200.00
5184 *Snake Rag*.....................	125.00 -	200.00
5274 *Krooked Blues*.................	175.00 -	300.00
5275 *Zulus Ball*....................	*Extremely Rare*	
Harmograph 890 *Mabel's Dream*............	90.00 -	125.00
Okeh 4906 *Sobbin' Blues*............	75.00 -	100.00
4918 *Dipper Mouth Blues*.............	75.00 -	100.00
4933 *Snake Rag*.....................	75.00 -	100.00
4975 *Jazzin' Babies' Blues*..........	75.00 -	100.00
8148 *Room Rent Blues*...............	75.00 -	100.00
8235 *Mabel's Dream*.................	75.00 -	100.00
40000 *Buddy's Habits*...............	75.00 -	100.00
40034 *Riverside Blues*..............	75.00 -	100.00
Paramount 12088 *The Southern Stomps*........	125.00 -	175.00
20292 *Mabel's Dream*................	90.00 -	125.00
Puritan 11292 *Mabel's Dream*............	90.00 -	125.00
Victor 22298 *When You're Smiling*............	8.00 -	12.00
22681 *Olga*.........................	20.00 -	30.00
23001 *Struggle Buggy*...............	30.00 -	40.00
23009 *Shake It and Break It*............	30.00 -	40.00
23011 *You Were Only Passing Time With Me*	30.00 -	40.00
23029 *I Can't Stop Loving You*............	35.00 -	50.00
23388 *New Orleans Shout*................	75.00 -	100.00
38034 *West End Blues*................	20.00 -	30.00
38039 *Call Of The Freaks*..............	30.00 -	40.00
38049 *My Good Man Sam*................	30.00 -	40.00
38090 *Too Late*.....................	30.00 -	40.00
38101 *Sweet Like This*................	30.00 -	40.00
38109 *Frankie and Johnny*..............	30.00 -	40.00
38124 *I Must Have It*................	30.00 -	40.00
38134 *Boogie Woogie*.................	30.00 -	40.00
38137 *Edna*.........................	30.00 -	40.00
38521 *Freakish Light Blues*..............	30.00 -	40.00
Vocalion 1007 *Too Bad*.................	35.00 -	50.00
1014 *Jackass Blues*..................	35.00 -	50.00

1033 Sugar Foot Stomp	35.00 -	50.00
1049 Tack Annie	50.00 -	75.00
1059 Dead Man Blues	20.00 -	30.00
1112 Willie The Weeper	50.00 -	75.00
1113 Doctor Jazz	100.00 -	150.00
1114 Showboat Shuffle	50.00 -	75.00
1152 Farewell Blues	35.00 -	50.00
1189 West End Blues	50.00 -	75.00
1190 Sweet Emmaline	50.00 -	75.00
1225 Speakeasy Blues	50.00 -	75.00
15394 Deep Henderson	25.00 -	35.00
15493 Dead Man Blues	25.00 -	35.00
15503 Snag It	25.00 -	35.00

GEORGE OLSEN & HIS MUSIC:

Columbia 2790-D Let's Make Up	5.00 -	8.00
2791-D The Last Round-Up	5.00 -	8.00
2803-D Bless Your Heart	5.00 -	8.00
2810-D Savage Serenade	7.00 -	10.00
2811-D It's Only a Paper Moon	7.00 -	10.00
2837-D There's a Home in Wyomin'	5.00 -	8.00
2842-D Everything I Have Is Yours	5.00 -	8.00
2843-D Sing a Low-Down Tune	5.00 -	8.00
2848-D Roll Out of Bed with a Smile	5.00 -	8.00
2857-D Surprise	5.00 -	8.00
2860-D The Colonel From Kentucky	5.00 -	8.00
2872-D I'm Weaving Rainbows	5.00 -	8.00
2878-D This Little Piggie Went to Market	5.00 -	8.00
2881-D Wagon Wheels	5.00 -	8.00
2891-D Old Man Jingle	5.00 -	8.00
Decca 1785, 1786, 1824	3.00 -	5.00
Victor 19374, 19375, 19405, 19419, 19457, 19573, 19580, 19610, 19633, 19710, 19715	4.00 -	7.00
Victor 19761 Hot Aire	5.00 -	8.00
Victor 19834, 19852, 20024, 20029	4.00 -	7.00
Victor 20101, 20105, 20112, 20116	3.00 -	6.00
Victor 20322 I'm Tellin' The Birds-Tellin' The Bees	15.00 -	25.00
Victor 20327, 20337, 20352, 20359, 20367	3.00 -	6.00
Victor 20394 Thinking of You	5.00 -	8.00
20425 Sam, The Old Accordion Man	7.00 -	10.00
Victor 22279, 22430, 22935, 22937, 22947, 22967, 22968, 22994, 22998, 24002, 24069, 24070, 24090, 24124, 24125, 24138	3.00 -	6.00
Victor 24139 It's Gonna Be You	7.00 -	10.00
Victor 24165, 24166, 24220, 24221, 24229	4.00 -	7.00

OLE OLSEN AND HIS ORCHESTRA:

Pathe-Actuelle 36488 Sadie Green	8.00 -	12.00
36510 Take Your Time	8.00 -	12.00
Perfect 14669 Snag It	8.00 -	12.00
14691 Take Your Time	8.00 -	12.00

D. ONIVAS & HIS ORCHESTRA:

Pathe-Actuelle 036196 Louisville Blues	15.00 -	20.00

ORESTE & HIS QUEENSLAND ORCHESTRA:

Edison 51857 Ev'rything's Peaches	8.00 -	12.00
51885 Thinking Of You	8.00 -	12.00
51886 Hello! Swanee-Hello	8.00 -	12.00
51920 Yankee Rose	8.00 -	12.00
51983 I'm Looking Over a Four-Leaf Clover	8.00 -	12.00
51988 Coronado Nights	8.00 -	12.00
52017 High Hat Harry	10.00 -	15.00
52057 Rosa Lee	7.00 -	10.00
52058 She's Got It	7.00 -	10.00
52167 I'm Walkin' On Air	10.00 -	15.00
52169 When the Morning Glories Wake Up	10.00 -	15.00
52214 Danger! (Look Out For that Gal)	10.00 -	15.00
52272 Borneo	15.00 -	20.00
52273 Lila	15.00 -	20.00
52383 Ten Little Miles From Town	10.00 -	15.00
52466 Cross Roads	10.00 -	15.00
52560 Where The Shy Little Violets Grow	10.00 -	15.00
52592 Me and The Clock (Tick-I-Ty Tock and You)	15.00 -	20.00

ORIGINAL ATLANTA FOOTWARMERS:

Bell 585 Hot Licks	15.00 -	20.00

ORIGINAL CRESCENT CITY JAZZERS:

Okeh 40101 Sensation Rag	35.00 -	50.00

ORIGINAL DIXIELAND FIVE:

Victor 25502 Original Dixieland One-Step	7.00 -	10.00
25524 Tiger Rag	7.00 -	10.00
25525 Clarinet Marmalade	7.00 -	10.00

ORIGINAL DIXIELAND JAZZ BAND:

Aeolian Vocalion 1205 Barnyard Blues	20.00 -	30.00
1206 Ostrich Walk	20.00 -	30.00
1242 Reisenweber Rag	20.00 -	30.00
12097 Oriental Jazz	20.00 -	30.00
Bluebird 7442 Please Be Kind	5.00 -	8.00
7444 In My Little Red Book	5.00 -	8.00
7454 Drop a Nickel In The Slot	5.00 -	8.00
Columbia A-2297 Indiana	8.00 -	12.00
Okeh 4738 Toddlin' Blues	15.00 -	25.00
4841 Tiger Rag	15.00 -	25.00
Victor 18255 Livery Stable Blues	7.00 -	10.00
18457 At The Jazz Band Ball	7.00 -	10.00
18472 Skeleton Jangle	7.00 -	10.00
18483 Sensation Rag	7.00 -	10.00
18513 Clarinet Marmalade Blues	7.00 -	10.00
18564 Lazy Daddy	7.00 -	10.00
18717 Palesteena	4.00 -	7.00
18722 Broadway Rose	5.00 -	8.00
18729 Home Again Blues	7.00 -	10.0
18772 Jazz Me Blues	7.00 -	10.00
18798 Royal Garden Blues	7.00 -	10.00
18850 Bow Wow Blues	7.00 -	10.00
Vocalion 3084 I Live For Love	7.00 -	10.00
3099 You Stayed Away Too Long	7.00 -	10.00

ORIGINAL DIXIE RAG PICKERS:

My Own Blues, issued contemporaneously on Grey Gull, Mitchell, Radiex	10.00 -	15.00

ORIGINAL INDIANA FIVE:

Banner 1931 Indiana Shuffle	7.00 -	10.00
6006 Some Of These Days	7.00 -	10.00
6008 Sugar	8.00 -	12.00
6023 Struttin' Jerry	7.00 -	10.00
6028 The Lighthouse Blues	8.00 -	12.00
6031 Rarin' To Go	7.00 -	10.00
6032 My Melancholy Baby	7.00 -	10.00
7027 My Melancholy Baby	7.00 -	10.00
7057 Where Will I Be?	8.00 -	12.00
7084 Moten Stomp	7.00 -	10.00
7137 Somebody's Making a Fuss Over Somebody	8.00 -	12.00
Bell 463 Brown Sugar	10.00 -	15.00
490 St. Louis Blues	10.00 -	15.00
547 Low-Down Sawed-Off Blues	10.00 -	15.00
Cameo 924 Pensacola	8.00 -	12.00
1138 Memphis Blues	8.00 -	12.00
8154 Nobody's Sweetheart	10.00 -	15.00
Conqueror 7143 Moten Stomp	7.00 -	10.00
Domino 3901 Indiana Shuffle	7.00 -	10.00
3971 Some Of These Days	7.00 -	10.00
3995 My Melancholy Baby	7.00 -	10.00
3997 Struttin' Jerry	7.00 -	10.00
3998 The Lighthouse Blues	8.00 -	12.00
4165 Moten Stomp	7.00 -	10.00
Emerson 3069 Can You Picture That?	15.00 -	20.00
3070 Gettin' The Blues	15.00 -	20.00
3079 My Baby Knows How	15.00 -	20.00
3088 There Ain't No Maybe In My Baby's Eyes	15.00 -	20.00
3119 St. Louis Blues	15.00 -	20.00
3131 Memphis Blues	15.00 -	20.00
Gennett 3059 Sweet Georgia Brown	10.00 -	15.00
3060 Everything Is Hotsy Totsy Now	10.00 -	15.00
3083 Say, Arabella	10.00 -	15.00
3093 Two Tired Eyes	10.00 -	15.00
3106 Croonin' At Tune	10.00 -	15.00

3112 *Red Hot Henry Brown*	10.00 -	15.00
3121 *Oh! Boy, What A Girl*	10.00 -	15.00
3148 *I'm Goin' Out If Lizzie Comes In*	10.00 -	15.00
3150 *Siberia*	10.00 -	15.00
3153 *Pretty Puppy*	10.00 -	15.00
3165 *Melancholy Lou*	10.00 -	15.00
3166 *I'm Gonna Hang Around My Sugar*	10.00 -	15.00
3181 *Everybody Stomp*	10.00 -	15.00
3182 *Everybody's Doin' The Charleston Now*	10.00 -	15.00
3183 *No Man's Mama*	10.00 -	15.00
3218 *Pensacola*	10.00 -	15.00
3230 *Fallen Arches*	10.00 -	15.00
Harmony 47-H *Everybody Stomp*	8.00 -	12.00
58-H *Everybody's Doin' The Charleston Now*	8.00 -	12.00
106-H *I'd Rather Be Alone*	8.00 -	12.00
134-H *Running After You*	8.00 -	12.00
179-H *So Is Your Old Lady*	8.00 -	12.00
217-H *Spanish Mamma*	8.00 -	12.00
245-H *I'd Leave Ten Men Like Yours To Love One Man Like Mine*	8.00 -	12.00
267-H *Florida Low-Down*	8.00 -	12.00
327-H *Delilah*	7.00 -	10.00
387-H *Stockholm Stomp*	8.00 -	12.00
432-H *Play It, Red*	8.00 -	12.00
459-H *Struttin' Jerry*	8.00 -	12.00
501-H *Someday, Sweetheart*	7.00 -	10.00
510-H *Clementine*	7.00 -	10.00
632-H *Junk Man's Dream*	8.00 -	12.00
Lincoln 2499 *Hard-To-Get Gertie*	8.00 -	12.00
2808 *Nobody's Sweetheart*	10.00 -	15.00
National Music Lovers 1191 *Cow Bell Blues*	10.00 -	15.00
Okeh 4056 *Indiana Stomp*	15.00 -	20.00
40599 *Hard-To-Get Gertie*	15.00 -	20.00
Olympic 1443 *Two-Time Dan*	10.00 -	15.00
1444 *Bebe*	10.00 -	15.00
Pathe-Actuelle 021070 *Stavin' Change*	7.00 -	10.00
036019 *Tin Roof Blues*	7.00 -	10.00
036044 *Jubilee Blues*	8.00 -	12.00
36377 *I'd Rather Be Alone*	8.00 -	12.00
36379 *Lo-Nah*	8.00 -	12.00
36420 *Sittin' Around*	8.00 -	12.00
36428 *Hard-To-Get Gertie*	7.00 -	10.00
Perfect 14173 *Mean, Mean Mama*	7.00 -	10.00
14200 *St. Louis Gal*	7.00 -	10.00
14225 *Back O'Town Blues*	8.00 -	12.00
14558 *I'd Rather Be Alone*	8.00 -	12.00
14560 *Lo-Nah*	8.00 -	12.00
14601 *Too Bad*	8.00 -	12.00
14609 *Hard-To-Get Gertie*	7.00 -	10.00
Regal 8248 *Coffee Pot Blues*	7.00 -	10.00
8337 *Some Of These Days*	7.00 -	10.00
8354 *Struttin' Jerry*	7.00 -	10.00
8356 *My Melancholy Baby*	7.00 -	10.00
8368 *The Lighthouse Blues*	8.00 -	12.00
8592 *Moten Stomp*	7.00 -	10.00
Velvet Tone 1501-V *I'm Coming, Virginia*	7.00 -	10.00
1510-V *Clementine*	7.00 -	10.00

ORIGINAL INDIANA SYNCOPATORS:

Olympic 1439 *Louisville Lou*	10.00 -	15.00

ORIGINAL JAZZ HOUNDS:

Columbia 14086-D *Fo-Day Blues*	20.00 -	30.00
14094-D *Slow Down*	20.00 -	30.00
14124-D *Cannon Ball Blues*	20.00 -	30.00
14207-D *Lucy Long*	25.00 -	35.00

ORIGINAL LOUISIANA FIVE:

Titles, issued contemporaneously on Puritan, Triangle: *The Hoodoo Man; Louisiana Toddle; San; Too Tired* .... 10.00 - 15.00

ORIGINAL MEMPHIS FIVE:

This band recorded a large number of records for the following labels: Arto, Banner, Bell, Broadway, Brunswick, Claxtonola, Columbia, Edison, Emerson, Famous, Globe, Grey Gull, Harmograph, Nordskog, Oriole, Paramount, Pathe-Actuelle, Perfect, Puritan, Radiex, Regal, Triangle, Victor, Vocalion, and possibly others. Often, a given title will be found issued contemporaneously on several labels. The records, with some notable exceptions listed below, are of minimal value...

	4.00 -	8.00
Arto 9149 *Cuddle Up Blues*	8.00 -	12.00
9153 *Pacific Coast Blues*	8.00 -	12.00
9168 *Chicago*	7.00 -	10.00
9177 *Indigo Blues*	8.00 -	12.00
9185 *The Wicked Dirty Fives*	8.00 -	12.00
9192 *Railroad Man*	8.00 -	12.00
9199 *Hot 'N' Cold*	8.00 -	12.00
9204 *Papa Blues*	8.00 -	12.00
Banner 1336 *31st Street Blues*	7.00 -	10.00
1346 *Forgetful Blues*	7.00 -	10.00
1360 *Big Boy*	7.00 -	10.00
1373 *Sioux City Sue*	7.00 -	10.00
1375 *A Man Never Knows When A Woman's Gonna Change Her Mind*	7.00 -	10.00
Bell P-149 *Lonesome Mamma Blues*	8.00 -	12.00
P-153 *Pacific Coast Blues*	8.00 -	12.00
P-168 *Got To Cool My Doggies Now*	7.00 -	10.00
P-177 *That Da Da Strain*	8.00 -	12.00
P-185 *Stop Your Kiddin'*	8.00 -	12.00
P-192 *Great White Way Blues*	8.00 -	12.00
P-199 *Hot 'N' Cold*	8.00 -	12.00
P-204 *Sweet Mama, Please Come Back To Me*	8.00 -	12.00
P-210 *Farewell Blues*	8.00 -	12.00
P-216 *Laughin' Cryin' Blues*	8.00 -	12.00
P-224 *You've Got To See Mama Ev'ry Night*	8.00 -	12.00
P-262 *Steppin' Out*	7.00 -	10.00
Brunswick 3039 *Chinese Blues*	8.00 -	12.00
3630 *Lovely Lee*	8.00 -	12.00
Chautauqua 11138 *Deedle-Deedle-Dum*	30.00 -	40.00
Claxtonola 40139 *Buzz Mirandy*	8.00 -	12.00
40192 *Four O'Clock Blues*	8.00 -	12.00
40281 *St. Louis Gal*	8.00 -	12.00
Columbia 308-D *Doo Wacka Doo*	7.00 -	10.00
480-D *Indiana Stomp*	8.00 -	12.00
502-D *'Tain't Cold*	8.00 -	12.00
2577-D *St. Louis Gal*	15.00 -	20.00
2588-D *Anything*	15.00 -	20.00
Edison 51204 *Shufflin' Mose*	8.00 -	12.00
51246 *The Jelly-Roll Blues*	10.00 -	15.00
Emerson 10723 *I've Got A Cross-Eyed Papa*	8.00 -	12.00
10725 *Lots O'Mama*	8.00 -	12.00
10740 *Sioux City Sue*	8.00 -	12.00
10741 *31st Street Blues*	15.00 -	20.00
10782 *Red Hot Mama*	8.00 -	12.00
10783 *You Know Me, Alabam'*	8.00 -	12.00
10815 *The Meanest Blues*	8.00 -	12.00
10820 *Take Me*	8.00 -	12.00
Famous 3125 *Lonesome Mama Blues*	8.00 -	12.00
3132 *Buzz Mirandy*	8.00 -	12.00
3136 *I'm Going Away To Wear You Off My Mind*	8.00 -	12.00
3186 *Haunting Blues*	8.00 -	12.00
Harmograph 951 *Superstitious Blues*	8.00 -	12.00
975 *The Meanest Blues*	8.00 -	12.00
992 *Mama's Boy*	8.00 -	12.00
Nordskog 3013 *Pacific Coast Blues*	15.00 -	20.00
Pathe-Actuelle 11471 *Nothin'*	15.00 -	20.00
036117 *Africa*	7.00 -	10.00
036134 *I'm Going Back To Those Who Won't Go Back On Me*	7.00 -	10.00
036141 *Somebody Stole My Gal*	7.00 -	10.00
036151 *Choo Choo*	8.00 -	12.00
036168 *Mama's Boy*	8.00 -	12.00
36358 *Jacksonville Gal*	10.00 -	15.00

36384 *Throw Down Blues*	10.00 -	15.00
36413 *Military Mike*	10.00 -	15.00
36422 *Indiana Stomp*	10.00 -	15.00
36565 *Go, Joe, Go*	10.00 -	15.00
36623 *Wistful And Blue*	10.00 -	15.00
Perfect 14298 *Africa*	7.00 -	10.00
14315 *I'm Going Back To Those Who Won't Go Back On Me*	7.00 -	10.00
14322 *Somebody Stole My Gal*	7.00 -	10.00
14349 *Mama's Boy*	8.00 -	12.00
14539 *Nobody's Rose*	10.00 -	15.00
14565 *Thrown Down Blues*	10.00 -	15.00
14594 *Bass Ale Blues*	10.00 -	15.00
14603 *Indiana Stomp*	10.00 -	15.00
14741 *One Sweet Letter From You*	10.00 -	15.00
14757 *Go, Joe, Go*	10.00 -	15.00
14804 *What Do I Care What Somebody Said*	10.00 -	15.00
Victor 19480 *Meanest Blues*	5.00 -	8.00
19594 *Throw Down Blues*	5.00 -	8.00
19805 *Military Mike*	5.00 -	8.00
20039 *Static Strut*	5.00 -	8.00
Vocalion 15623 *Lovey Lee*	10.00 -	15.00
15712 *My Angeline*	15.00 -	20.00
15761 *Fireworks*	15.00 -	20.00
15805 *Memphis Blues*	20.00 -	30.00
15810 *Kansas City Kitty*	30.00 -	40.00

ORIGINAL MEMPHIS MELODY BOYS:

Gennett 3097 *Made a Monkey Out Of Me*	15.00 -	25.00
5123 *Wonderful Dream*	20.00 -	30.00
5157 *Blue Grass Blues*	20.00 -	30.00

ORIGINAL MIDNIGHT RAMBLERS ORCHESTRA:

Autograph (unnumbered) *Owl Strut*	20.00 -	30.00

ORIGINAL NEW ORLEANS RHYTHM KINGS:

Okeh 40327 *Golden Leaf Strut*	30.00 -	50.00
40422 *Baby*	30.00 -	50.00

ORIGINAL ST. LOUIS CRACKERJACKS:

Decca 7235 *Swing Jackson*	7.00 -	10.00
7236 *Crackerjack Stomp*	7.00 -	10.00
7248 *Echo In The Dark*	7.00 -	10.00
7265 *Chasing The Blues Away*	7.00 -	10.00

ORIGINAL TAMPA FIVE:

Dandy 5154 *My Own Blues*	12.00 -	18.00
5248 *Heebie Jeebies*	12.00 -	18.00

ORIGINAL TUXEDO JAZZ ORCHESTRA:

Okeh 8198 *Black Rag*	75.00 -	100.00
8215 *Original Tuxedo Rag*	75.00 -	100.00

THE ORIGINAL WOLVERINES:

Brunswick 3707 *Shim-Me-Sha-Wabble*	10.00 -	15.00
4000 *Royal Garden Blues*	10.00 -	15.00
Vocalion 15635 *Royal Garden Blues*	15.00 -	20.00
15708 *Limehouse Blues*	15.00 -	20.00
15732 *There's a Rainbow Round My Shoulder*	10.00 -	15.00
15751 *Sweethearts On Parade*	10.00 -	15.00
15768 *I'll Never Ask For More*	10.00 -	15.00
15784 *He, She and Me*	25.00 -	35.00
15795 *Some Sweet Day*	10.00 -	15.00

ORIGINAL YELLOW JACKETS:

Vocalion 03504 *Business After Midnight*	15.00 -	20.00
03549 *Swingin' At The Chat 'n' Chew*	15.00 -	20.00
03591 *Cross Street Swing*	15.00 -	20.00

HAROLD ORTLI & HIS OHIO STATE COLLEGIANS:

Okeh 40332 *My Daddy Rocks Me*	20.00 -	30.00

ORY'S SUNSHINE ORCHESTRA:

Sunshine 3003 *Ory's Creole Trombone*	150.00 -	200.00

GEORGE OSBORN & HIS ORCHESTRA:

Gennett 6215 *Brainstorm*	20.00 -	30.00

WILL OSBORNE & HIS ORCHESTRA:

Banner, most issues	3.00 -	6.00

Columbia 3080-D *That's What You Think*	7.00 -	10.00
3081-D *I Wish I Were Aladdin*	5.00 -	8.00
Columbia, most other issues	2.00 -	5.00
Conqueror, most issues	3.00 -	6.00
Melotone 12099 *Hello! Beautiful*	7.00 -	10.00
12189 *Star Dust*	5.00 -	8.00
Melotone, most other issues	3.00 -	6.00
Oriole, most issues	3.00 -	6.00
Perfect, most issues	3.00 -	6.00
Romeo, most issues	3.00 -	6.00

OSCAR'S CHICAGO SWINGERS:

Decca 7186 *I Wonder Who's Boogiein' My Woogie*	7.00 -	10.00
7201 *Try Some Of That*	7.00 -	10.00

GLEN OSWALD'S SERENADERS:

Victor 19733 *Bucktown Blues*	5.00 -	8.00

RED OWENS & HIS GANG:

Champion 15759 *Chicago Rhythm*	25.00 -	35.00
16423 *Hard Luck*	25.00 -	35.00

THE OXFORD RHYTHM MAKERS:

Parlophone PNY-34045 *Puttin' On The Ritz*	10.00 -	15.00
PNY-34046 *With You*	10.00 -	15.00

HAROLD OXLEY AND HIS POST LODGE ORCHESTRA:

Okeh 40134 *Step, Henrietta*	7.00 -	10.00
40180 *I Don't Know Why*	8.00 -	12.00

PACIFIC COAST PLAYERS:

Radiex 1326 *Jazzing Around*	8.00 -	12.00

HOT LIPS PAGE & HIS BAND; HOT LIPS PAGE TRIO:

Bluebird 7567, 6568, 7583, 7680, 7682, 7684, 8634, 8660, 8981	4.00 -	7.00
Decca 7433, 7451, 7699, 7714, 7757	4.00 -	7.00

WALTER PAGE'S BLUE DEVILS:

Vocalion 1463 *Blue Devil Blues*	50.00 -	75.00

PALLEDO ORCHESTRA OF ST. LOUIS:

Okeh 40521 *What-Cha-Call-'Em Blues*	20.00 -	30.00

CHARLIE PALLOY & HIS ORCHESTRA:

Crown 3389 *You're Telling Me*	5.00 -	8.00
3392 *Brother, Can You Spare A Dime?*	7.00 -	10.00
3410 *What A Perfect Combination*	7.00 -	10.00
3512 *Pettin' In The Park*	7.00 -	10.00

GLADYS PALMER:

Decca 7106 *I'm Livin' In A Great Big Way*	7.00 -	10.00
7017 *Get Behind Me, Satan*	7.00 -	10.00

PALMER HOUSE VICTORIANS (See JULES HERBUVEAUX):

PALMETTO NIGHT CLUB ORCHESTRA:

Champion 15308 *Darktown Shuffle*	15.00 -	20.00

PALOOKA WASHBOARD BAND:

Decca 7378 *We Gonna Move*	10.00 -	15.00
7398 *You Done Tore Your Pants With Me*	10.00 -	15.00

LOUIS PANICO & HIS ORCHESTRA:

Brunswick 4736 *Wabash Blues*	6.00 -	10.00

PAPALIA & HIS ORCHESTRA:

Okeh 40347 *Cross-Word Mama, You're Puzzling Me*	25.00 -	40.00

THE PARAMOUNTEERS:

Publix 2008-P *I Have To Have You*	10.00 -	15.00

PARAMOUNT PICKERS:

Paramount 12779 *Salty Dog*	75.00 -	100.00

TONY PARENTI; ANTHONY PARENTI & HIS FAMOUS MELODY BOYS; (TONY) PARENTI'S LIBERTY SYNCOPATORS/ NEW ORLEANIANS:

Old Man Rhythm, issued contemporaneously on Banner, Cameo, Jewel, Oriole, Romeo	15.00 -	20.00
Brunswick 4148 *Gumbo*	15.00 -	20.00
Columbia 545-D *Midnight Papa*	20.00 -	30.00
836-D *Up Jumped The Devil*	20.00 -	30.00
1264-D *African Echoes*	20.00 -	30.00
1548-D *In The Dungeon*	20.00 -	30.00
Okeh 40308 *That's A Plenty*	15.00 -	20.00

Victor 19647 *Creole Blues*............ 15.00 - 20.00
19697 *Dizzy Lizzy*............ 15.00 - 20.00
19698 *Be Yourself*............ 15.00 - 20.00

PARHAM'S BLACK PATTI BAND:
Black Patti 8038 *Um-Te-Da-Da-Da*........... 125.00 - 200.00

TINY PARHAM & HIS "FORTY" FIVE; TINY PARHAM & HIS MUSICIANS:
Bluebird 5146 *Black Cat Moan*............ 8.00 - 12.00
6031 *Subway Sobs*............ 8.00 - 12.00
6570 *Washboard Wiggles*............ 8.00 - 12.00
7005 *Blue Island Blues*............ 10.00 - 15.00
8130 *Stuttering Blues*............ 8.00 - 12.00
Paramount 12586 *Jim Jackson's Kansas City Blues* 100.00 - 150.00
Victor 21553 *Cuckoo Blues*............ 25.00 - 35.00
21659 *Snake Eyes*............ 25.00 - 35.00
22778 *Sud Buster's Dream*............ 25.00 - 35.00
22842 *Rock Bottom*............ 20.00 - 30.00
23027 *Blue Moon Blues*............ 30.00 - 40.00
23386 *Nervous Tension*............ 75.00 - 100.00
23410 *Steel String Blues*............ 75.00 - 100.00
23426 *Golden Lily*............ 75.00 - 100.00
23432 *My Dreams*............ 75.00 - 100.00
38009 *Jogo Rhythm*............ 20.00 - 30.00
38041 *Subway Sobs*............ 20.00 - 30.00
38047 *Blue Melody Blues*............ 20.00 - 30.00
38054 *Voodoo*............ 25.00 - 35.00
38060 *Stompin' On Down*............ 25.00 - 35.00
38076 *Echo Blues*............ 25.00 - 35.00
38082 *Jungle Crawl*............ 25.00 - 35.00
38111 *Dixieland Doin's*............ 25.00 - 35.00
38126 *Fat Man Blues*............ 30.00 - 40.00

CHARLIE PARKER QUINTET (& OTHER COMBINATIONS):
Dial 1002, 1006, 1007, 1012, 1013, 1015, 1058.. 5.00 - 8.00

ED PARKER & HIS ORCHESTRA:
Okeh 41537 *Potatoes Are Cheaper, Tomatoes Are Cheaper*............ 8.00 - 12.00

PARK LANE ORCHESTRA:
Brunswick 3513 *You Can't Cry Over My Shoulder* 7.00 - 10.00

ART PAYNE AND HIS ORCHESTRA:
Gennett 5063 *Some Winter Night*............ 5.00 - 8.00
5064 *Jingle Bells*............ 5.00 - 8.00
5631 *Oh Maud*............ 8.00 - 12.00
6644 *Igloo Stomp*............ 10.00 - 20.00
6694 *Jo-Anne*............ 10.00 - 20.00

RAY PEARL AND HIS ORCHESTRA:
Vocalion 3408, 3420, 3522, 3536............ 4.00 - 8.00

PAUL PENDARVIS AND HIS ORCHESTRA:
Columbia 2973-D, 2974-D, 3025-D, 3032-D, 3082-D, 3091-D............ 4.00 - 7.00

ANDY PENDLETON:
Okeh 8625 *Sweet Emmaline*............ 7.00 - 10.00
Victor 23389 *Thinking Of You*............ 10.00 - 15.00

TWIN-SIX GUITAR JACK PENEWELL:
Autograph 608 *Penewell Blues*............ 20.00 - 30.00

THE PENNSYLVANIA SYNCOPATORS:
Emerson 10773 *I Can't Get The One I Want*... 8.00 - 12.00
10868 *My Sweet Louise*............ 10.00 - 15.00

ALBERT PERKINS:
Ajax 17125 *Levee Man*............ 20.00 - 30.00
Harmograph 983 *Sweet Mandy*............ 20.00 - 30.00

GERTRUDE PERKINS:
Columbia 14313-D *Gold Daddy Blues*......... 15.00 - 20.00

RED PERKINS & HIS DIXIE RAMBLERS:
Champion 16288 *Hard Times Stomp*......... 20.00 - 30.00
16439 *Old Man Blues*............ 20.00 - 30.00
16661 *My Baby Knows How*............ 20.00 - 30.00

PERRY & HIS STOMP BAND:
Black Patti 8037 *Ash Can Stomp*............ 50.00 - 75.00

PERRY'S HOT DOGS:
Banner 1615 *There Ain't No Flies On Auntie*... 5.00 - 8.00

1641 *Has Been Blues*............ 5.00 - 8.00
1714 *Say Mister Have You Met Rosie's Sister*. 5.00 - 8.00

PERRY'S ORCHESTRA:
Paramount 20431 *Headin' For Louisville*....... 8.00 - 12.00
Puritan 11431 *That Certain Party*............ 8.00 - 12.00

SAM PERRY'S RUBE BAND:
Supertone 9039 *Bass Blues*............ 25.00 - 35.00

TEDDY PETERS:
Vocalion 1006 *Georgia Man*............ 50.00 - 75.00

JACK PETTIS AND HIS BAND/PETS:
Banner 1907 *Stockholm Stomp*............ 5.00 - 8.00
1908 *St. Louis Shuffle*............ 5.00 - 8.00
Banner 1911, 1927, 1929............ 4.00 - 7.00
Banner 1940 *I'm Back In Love Again*............ 5.00 - 8.00
1942 *Ain't She Sweet?*............ 5.00 - 8.00
Domino 3883 *Stockholm Stomp*............ 5.00 - 8.00
3884 *St. Louis Shuffle*............ 5.00 - 8.00
Domino 3895, 3897............ 4.00 - 7.00
Domino 3914 *That's My Hap-Hap-Happiness*... 5.00 - 8.00
3916 *I'm Back In Love Again*............ 5.00 - 8.00
4080 *Candied Sweets*............ 5.00 - 8.00
4094 *Once Over Lightly*............ 5.00 - 8.00
Okeh 41410 *Bag O'Blues*............ 20.00 - 25.00
41411 *Freshman Hop*............ 20.00 - 30.00
Regal 8221 *St. Louis Shuffle*............ 5.00 - 8.00
8229 *Stockholm Stomp*............ 5.00 - 8.00
Regal 8225, 8243, 8244............ 4.00 - 7.00
Regal 8263 *That's My Hap-Hap-Happiness*..... 5.00 - 8.00
8267 *Ain't She Sweet?*............ 5.00 - 8.00
Regal 8463 *Candied Sweets*............ 5.00 - 8.00
8483 *Steppin' It Off*............ 5.00 - 8.00
Victor 21559 *Doin' The New Low Down*....... 7.00 - 10.00
21793 *Freshman Hop*............ 7.00 - 10.00
38105 *Bugle Call Blues*............ 20.00 - 30.00
Vocalion 15703 *Hot Heels*............ 20.00 - 30.00
15761 *Broadway Stomp*............ 20.00 - 30.00

PHILLIPS' LOUISVILLE JUG BAND:
Brunswick 7187 *Smackin' The Sax*............ 35.00 - 50.00
7194 *Tiger Rag*............ 35.00 - 50.00
7207 *Soldier Boy Blues*............ 35.00 - 50.00

SIDNEY PHILLIPS & HIS ORCHESTRA:
Brunswick 8133, 8187, 8332............ 4.00 - 6.00
Variety 654............ 4.00 - 6.00
Vocalion 3934............ 4.00 - 6.00

THE PICCADILLY PLAYERSS (& SINGERS/&THE RADIO GIRL):
Edison (thin) 14023 *Susianna*............ 12.00 - 16.00
14032 *The One In The World*............ 12.00 - 16.00
14034 *Hittin' The Ceiling*............ 12.00 - 16.00
14035 *Someday Soon*............ 12.00 - 16.00
14036 *Maybe—Who Knows?*............ 12.00 - 16.00
14038 *You Ought To See My New Baby*..... 12.00 - 16.00
14056 *Tip Toe Thru The Tulips With Me*.... 15.00 - 20.00
Edison (thick) 52167 *Someday, Sweetheart*...... 10.00 - 15.00
52169 *She Don't Wanna*............ 10.00 - 15.00
52198 *What'll You Do?*............ 10.00 - 15.00
52215 *Rose Room*............ 10.00 - 15.00
52232 *Feelin' Good*............ 10.00 - 15.00
52273 *That's What I Call Keen*............ 15.00 - 20.00
52280 *My One And Only*............ 10.00 - 15.00
52327 *You're Just A Great Big Baby Doll*.... 10.00 - 15.00
52363 *Old Man Sunshine*............ 10.00 - 15.00
52391 *Take Your Tomorrow*............ 10.00 - 15.00
52442 *I'm Sorry, Sally*............ 10.00 - 15.00
52478 *Easy Goin'*............ 10.00 - 15.00
52527 *Susianna*............ 10.00 - 15.00
52545 *You Were Meant For Me*............ 10.00 - 15.00
52562 *My Lucky Star*............ 10.00 - 15.00
52565 *I'm Thirsty For Kisses, Hungry For Love* 10.00 - 15.00
52574 *On With The Dance!*............ 10.00 - 15.00
52590 *I've Made a Habit Of You*............ 10.00 - 15.00

52613 *Walking With Susie*	10.00 -	15.00
52635 *You Ought To See My New Baby*	10.00 -	15.00

WALTER PICHON:

Victor 38544, *Yo Yo*	30.00 -	40.00

THE PICKENS SISTERS:

Victor 22929, 22965, 22975, 24025, 24180, 24190,		
24335, 24468, 24471, 24625, 24630, 24751,		
24753, 24815	3.00 -	6.00

PICKETT-PARHAM APOLLO SYNCOPATORS:

Paramount 12441 *Mojo Strut*	75.00 -	100.00

CHARLES PIERCE & HIS ORCHESTRA:

Paramount 12619 *China Boy*	60.00 -	90.00
12640 *Jazz Me Blues*	60.00 -	90.00
20616 *Nobody's Sweetheart*	60.00 -	90.00

PIERROT SYNCOPATORS:

Crown (Canadian) 81008 *Somebody's Making A Fuss*		
Over Somebody	8.00 -	12.00
81020 *Dixie Drag*	7.00 -	10.00
81109 *The Rainbow Man*	5.00 -	10.00
81161 *Piccolo Pete*	7.00 -	10.00

PINKIE'S BIRMINGHAM FIVE:

Gennett 3208 *Carolina Stomp*	10.00 -	15.00

PIRON'S NEW ORLEANS ORCHESTRA:

Columbia 99-D *Ghost Of The Blues*	8.00 -	12.00
14007-D *Sud Bustin' Blues*	10.00 -	15.00
Okeh 40021 *Bouncing Around*	20.00 -	30.00
40189 *Lou'siana Swing*	20.00 -	30.00
Victor 19233 *New Orleans Wiggle*	7.00 -	10.00
19255 *West Indies Blues*	7.00 -	10.00
19646 *Red Man Blues*	10.00 -	15.00

THE PLANTATION SERENADERS:

Champion 15386 *Missouri Squabble*	25.00 -	40.00
15402 *I Call You Sugar*	25.00 -	40.00
Silvertone 5138 *Jackass Blues*	35.00 -	50.00
5502 *I Call You Sugar*	25.00 -	40.00

PLETCHER'S ELI PROM TROTTERS:

QRS Q-1055 *That's Where You're Wrong*	20.00 -	30.00

STEW PLETCHER & HIS ORCHESTRA:

Bluebird 6343 *You Never Looked So Beautiful*	7.00 -	10.00
6344 *I Don't Want To Make History*	7.00 -	10.00
6345 *I Hope Gabriel Likes My Music*	7.00 -	10.00

THE PODS OF PEPPER:

Columbia 14590-D *You've Had Your Way*	25.00 -	40.00
14664-D *I Was A Good Loser Until I Lost You*	25.00 -	40.00

BEN POLLACK & HIS CALIFORNIANS/(PARK CENTRAL) ORCHESTRA/PICK-A-RIB BOYS; BEN POLLACK'S ORCHESTRA:

Titles, issued contemporaneously on Banner, Cameo, Conqueror, Domino, Jewel, Oriole, Perfect, Regal, Romeo: *Fall In Love With Me; If I Could Be With You (One Hour Tonight); I'm A Ding Dong Daddy; I've Got Five Dollars; Rollin' Down The River; Sing-Song Girl; Sweet and Hot; There's A Wah Wah Girl In Agua Caliente; You Didn't Have To Tell Me*	8.00 -	15.00
Brunswick 7747, 7751, 7764	6.00 -	10.00
Columbia 2870-D *Got The Jitters*	12.00 -	16.00
2879-D *Deep Jungle*	12.00 -	16.00
2886-D *Goin' To Heaven On A Mule*	7.00 -	12.00
2901-D *Dancing In The Moonlight*	7.00 -	12.00
2905-D *Here Goes*	7.00 -	12.00
2906-D *The Voodoo*	7.00 -	12.00
2910-D *Alone On The Range*	7.00 -	12.00
2929-D *Sleepy Head*	7.00 -	12.00
2931-D *Freckly Face, You're Beautiful*	7.00 -	12.00
Decca 1424, 1435, 1458, 1465, 1476, 1488, 1517, 1546	4.00 -	7.00
Hit-of-the-Week 1026, 1027	4.00 -	7.00
Variety 504 *Deep Elm*	7.00 -	10.00
556 *Peckin'*	7.00 -	10.00

Victor 20394 *When I First Met Mary*	5.00 -	8.00
20408 *'Deed I Do*	8.00 -	12.00
20425 *He's The Last Word*	7.00 -	10.00
20461 *You're The One For Me*	25.00 -	35.00
21184 *Memphis Blues*	8.00 -	12.00
21437 *Singapore Sorrows*	8.00 -	12.00
21743 *Buy, Buy For Baby*	7.00 -	10.00
21827 *Sentimental Baby*	8.00 -	12.00
21858 *Futuristic Rhythm*	8.00 -	12.00
21941 *Louise*	7.00 -	10.00
21944 *On With The Dance!*	8.00 -	12.00
22071 *In The Hush of the Night*	7.00 -	10.00
22074 *Bashful Baby*	10.00 -	15.00
22089 *True Blue Lou*	7.00 -	10.00
22101 *Sweetheart, We Need Each Other*	8.00 -	12.00
22106 *Where The Sweet Forget-Me-Nots Remember*	8.00 -	12.00
22147 *Song of the Blues*	8.00 -	12.00
22158 *You've Made Me Happy Today*	8.00 -	12.00
22252 *I'd Like To Be A Gypsy*	5.00 -	8.00
22267 *Keep Your Undershirt On*	8.00 -	12.00
24284 *Two Tickets To Georgia*	10.00 -	15.00
Vocalion 3769 *The Moon Is Grinning At Me*	7.00 -	10.00
3819 *In a Sentimental Mood*	7.00 -	10.00

HARRY POLLOCK'S BLUE DIAMONDS/CLUB MAURICE DIAMONDS:

Gennett 3377 *Alabama Stomp*	10.00 -	15.00
6026 *There Ain't No Maybe In My Baby's Eyes*	7.00 -	10.00
6067 *You Can't Cry Over My Shoulder*	7.00 -	10.00
6069 *Underneath The Weeping Willow*	7.00 -	10.00
6083 *What Do I Care What Somebody Said?*	7.00 -	10.00
6383 *There Ain't No Sweet Man That's Worth The Salt of My Tears*	7.00 -	10.00

BOB POPE AND HIS (HOTEL CHARLOTTE) ORCHESTRA:

Titles, issued contemporaneously on Banner, Melotone, Oriole, Perfect, Romeo; *Always; Blue Skies; Nero; Rockin' Chair; Whoa Babe!*	7.00 -	10.00
Bluebird 6283 *Early Bird*	7.00 -	10.00
6284 *Moon Rose*	7.00 -	10.00
6285 *Breakin' In a Pair of Shoes*	7.00 -	10.00
6286 *Shoe-Shine Boy*	7.00 -	10.00
6299 *That Never-To-Be Forgotten Night*	7.00 -	10.00
6300 *Stop That Dog*	7.00 -	10.00
6452 *Big Chief De Sota*	7.00 -	10.00
6453 *On Your Toes*	7.00 -	10.00
6454 *Let's Sing Again*	7.00 -	10.00
6471 *Swamp Fire*	7.00 -	10.00
6502 *On Teh Alamo*	7.00 -	10.00
6508 *Madhouse*	7.00 -	10.00

PORTER'S BLUE DEVILS:

Gennett 5210 *Original Charleston Strut*	10.00 -	15.00
5249 *Steamboat Sal*	10.00 -	15.00
5251 *Somebody's Wrong*	8.00 -	12.00
5252 *Walk, Jenny, Walk*	8.00 -	12.00
5282 *Hot Dawg!*	8.00 -	12.00
5305 *When It's Night Time In Italy*	8.00 -	12.00

COLE PORTER:

Victor 24766, 24825, 24843, 24859	5.00 -	10.00

DICK PORTER & HIS ORCHESTRA:

Vocalion 3355 *Sweet Thing*	8.00 -	12.00
3469 *There's No Two Ways About It*	8.00 -	12.00
3478 *Poor Robinson Crusoe*	8.00 -	12.00

KING PORTER & HIS ORCHESTRA:

Champion 15305 *Oh Miss Hannah!*	10.00 -	15.00

PORT OF HARLEM JASSMEN/SEVEN:

Blue Note 3 *Rocking The Blues*	7.00 -	10.00
6 *Pounding Heart Blues*	7.00 -	10.00
7 *Blues For Tommy*	7.00 -	10.00
14 *Port Of Harlem Blues*	7.00 -	10.00

POWELL'S JAZZ MONARCHS:
Okeh 8333 *Laughing Blues* .... 35.00 - 50.00
DICK POWELL:
Brunswick 4884, 7469 .... 5.00 - 8.00
Conqueror 8183, 8184 .... 5.00 - 8.00
Perfect 12919, 12920 .... 5.00 - 8.00
Romeo 2084 .... 5.00 - 8.00
Vocalion 15647, 15648, 15674, 15675, 15686, 15699,
15700 .... 7.00 - 12.00
MEL POWELL & HIS ORCHESTRA:
Commodore 543, 544 .... 5.00 - 10.00
TEDDY POWELL AND HIS ORCHESTRA:
Bluebird, most issues .... 2.00 - 5.00
Decca .... 3.00 - 5.00
**TOMMY POWELL AND HIS HI-DE-HO
BOYS:**
Decca 7231 *That Cat Is High* .... 7.00 - 10.00
WALTER POWELL & HIS ORCHESTRA:
Vocalion 4612 *Devil's Holiday* ...... 5.00 - 10.00
**OLLIE POWERS' HARMONY
SYNCOPATORS/ORCHESTRA:**
Claxtonola 40263 *Play That Thing* .. 80.00 - 120.00
Harmograph 851 *Play That Thing* ... 80.00 - 120.00
Paramount 12059 *Jazzbo Jenkins* .... 80.00 - 120.00
Puritan 11263 *Play That Thing* ..... 80.00 - 120.00
**ANDY PREER & THE COTTON CLUB
ORCHESTRA:**
Gennett 6056 *I've Found A New Baby* .... 50.00 - 75.00
EVELYN PREER:
Banner 1895 *Sunday* .... 8.00 - 12.00
Domino 3864 *Cock-a-Doodle, I'm Off My Noodle* 8.00 - 12.00
Victor 20306 *Make Me Know It* ...... 15.00 - 20.00
**SAMMY PRICE AND HIS FOUR
QUARTERS/TEXAS BLUSICIANS:**
Brunswick 7136 *Blue Rhythm Stomp* .... 30.00 - 50.00
Decca 7732, 7781, 7811, 7820, 7836, 7850, 8505,
8515, 8547, 8557, 8566, 8575, 8601, 8624, 8649 4.00 - 8.00
VIC PRICE AND HIS ORCHESTRA:
Gennett 6411 *When* .... 10.00 - 15.00
6440 *I'm More Than Satisfied* .... 10.00 - 15.00
6443 *Speedy Boy* .... 10.00 - 15.00
6475 *Back In Your Own Back Yard* .... 10.00 - 15.00
6612 *Here's That Party Now In Person* ... 10.00 - 15.00
Herwin 8046 *Everywhere You Go* ..... 10.00 - 15.00
8049 *Back In Your Own Back Yard* .... 10.00 - 15.00
8052 *Mary Ann* .... 10.00 - 15.00
Supertone 9003 *Back In Your Own Back Yard* .. 10.00 - 15.00
9006 *Speedy Boy* .... 10.00 - 15.00
9043 *Here's That Party Now In Person* ..... 10.00 - 15.00
**LOUIS PRIMA & HIS NEW ORLEANS
GANG:**
Brunswick 7320 *I Still Want You* .... 7.00 - 10.00
7335 *Star Dust* .... 7.00 - 10.00
7376 *House Rent Party Day* .... 7.00 - 10.00
7394 *Sing It 'Way Down Low* .... 7.00 - 10.00
7419 *I'm Livin' In A Great Big Way* ... 7.00 - 10.00
7431 *Swing Me With Rhythm* .... 7.00 - 10.00
7448 *The Lady In Red* .... 7.00 - 10.00
7456 *Basin Street Blues* .... 7.00 - 10.00
7471 *It's The Rhythm In Me* .... 7.00 - 10.00
7479 *Let's Swing It* .... 7.00 - 10.00
7499 *Plain Old Me* .... 7.00 - 10.00
7524 *Jamaica Shout* .... 7.00 - 10.00
7531 *Solitude* .... 7.00 - 10.00
7586 *I've Got My Fingers Crossed* .... 7.00 - 10.00
7596 *Sweet Sue* .... 7.00 - 10.00
7628 *Sing, Sing, Sing* .... 7.00 - 10.00
7657 *Alice Blue Gown* .... 7.00 - 10.00
7666 *Lazy River* .... 7.00 - 10.00
7680 *Swing Me A Lullaby* .... 7.00 - 10.00
7709 *Confessin'* .... 7.00 - 10.00

7740 *Let's Get Together And Swing* .... 7.00 - 10.00
Decca 1618, 1674, 1871, 1953, 2242, 2279, 2660,
2749 .... 3.00 - 6.00
Hit, most issues .... 2.00 - 3.00
Majestic, most issues .... 2.00 - 3.00
Varsity 8245, 8247 .... 3.00 - 5.00
Vocalion 3376 *Pennies From Heaven* .. 7.00 - 10.00
3388 *The Goose Hangs High* .... 7.00 - 10.00
3509 *Fifty-Second Street* .... 7.00 - 10.00
3628 *Danger, Love At Work* .... 7.00 - 10.00
3657 *Tin Roof Blues* .... 7.00 - 10.00
3921 *Rhythm On The Radio* .... 7.00 - 10.00
ALBERTA PRIME:
Blu-Disc T-1007 *Parlor Social De Luxe* .... 100.00 - 200.00
**PRINCETON TRIANGLE CLUB DANCE
ORCHESTRA:**
Columbia Personal (170615/170614) *Make Time.* 15.00 - 20.00
Note: The vocalist "J.M. Stewart" on the flip side is
actor Jimmy Stewart.)
PRINCETON TRIANGLE CLUB JAZZ BAND:
Personal Record 30-P *Join The Navy* .... 12.00 - 18.00
31-P *Pirate Gold* .... 12.00 - 18.00
59-P *I'll Build An Igloo For You* ..... 12.00 - 18.00
63-P *Broke Again* .... 12.00 - 18.00
84-P *Twilight* .... 12.00 - 18.00
85-P *Pretty Please* .... 12.00 - 18.00
100-P *Rhythmic Refrain* .... 12.00 - 18.00
114-P *You Know Who* .... 12.00 - 18.00
**JACK PURVIS; JACK PURVIS & HIS
ORCHESTRA:**
Odeon ONY-36093 *When You're Feelin' Blue* ... 25.00 - 35.00
Okeh 8782 *Down Georgia Way* .... 20.00 - 30.00
8808 *Dismal Dan* .... 20.00 - 30.00
41404 *Copyin' Louis* .... 20.00 - 30.00
**FRANKIE QUARTELL & HIS LITTLE CLUB
ORCHESTRA/MELODY BOYS:**
Brunswick 4183 *Sweet Baby* .... 10.00 - 15.00
Okeh 40257 *Heart Broken Strain* ..... 15.00 - 20.00
40258 *Prince Of Wails* .... 15.00 - 25.00
QUEEN CITY BLOWERS:
Champion 15030 *Stomp Off, Let's Go* .... 20.00 - 30.00
MAE QUESTAL:
Decca 346, 447, 540, 653, 680, 769, 832, 876 ... 3.00 - 5.00
Victor 24261 *Sweet Betty* .... 8.00 - 12.00
QUINTONES:
Vocalion 4928 *Chew-Chew-Chew (Your Bubble
Gum)* .... 10.00 - 15.00
5172 *When My Sugar Walks Down The Street* 10.00 - 15.00
5409 *Midnight Jamboree* .... 10.00 - 15.00
5509 *Sly Mongoose* .... 10.00 - 15.00
5596 *Harmony In Harlem* .... 10.00 - 15.00
Q.R.S. BOYS:
QRS 7062 *Wiggle Yo' Toes* .... 20.00 - 30.00
7067 *Black Boy Blues* .... 20.00 - 30.00
**LOU RADERMAN & HIS PELHAM HEATH
INN ORCHESTRA:**
Harmony 607-H *Ol' Man River* .... 8.00 - 15.00
611-H *Oh Gee! Oh Joy!* .... 8.00 - 15.00
THE RADIOLITES:
Columbia 1432-D *Sweet Lorraine* ..... 5.00 - 8.00
Columbia 2540-D *I Don't Know Why* ... 7.00 - 10.00
IKE RAGON & HIS ORCHESTRA:
Vocalion 03513 *Maple Leaf Rag* ...... 10.00 - 15.00
03547 *Truckin' On The Old Camp Ground* ... 10.00 - 15.00
RAG PICKERS:
Autograph (unnumbered) *Suite 16* .... 25.00 - 40.00
MA RAINEY (AND HER GEORGIA BAND):
Paramount 12080 *Last Minute Blues* .... 20.00 - 30.00
12081 *Bad Luck Blues* .... 20.00 - 30.00
12082 *Walking Blues* .... 20.00 - 30.00
12083 *Southern Blues* .... 20.00 - 30.00

12098 *Dream Blues*	15.00 -	25.00
12200 *Ma Rainey's Mystery Record*	25.00 -	35.00
12215 *Lucky Rock Blues*	25.00 -	35.00
12222 *Farewell Daddy Blues*	20.00 -	30.00
12227 *South Bound Blues*	30.00 -	40.00
12238 *Jelly Bean Blues*	75.00 -	100.00
12242 *Toad Frog Blues*	25.00 -	35.00
12252 *See See Rider Blues*	75.00 -	100.00
12257 *Cell Bound Blues*	25.00 -	35.00
12284 *Explaining The Blues*	25.00 -	35.00
12290 *Louisiana Hoo Doo Blues*	25.00 -	35.00
12295 *Stormy Sea Blues*	25.00 -	35.00
12303 *Night Time Blues*	25.00 -	35.00
12311 *Rought and Tumble Blues*	25.00 -	35.00
12332 *Slave To The Blues*	25.00 -	40.00
12338 *Chain Gang Blues*	25.00 -	40.00
12352 *Seeking Blues*	25.00 -	40.00
12357 *Stack O'Lee Blues*	25.00 -	40.00
12364 *Broken Hearted Blues*	25.00 -	40.00
12374 *Titanic Man Blues*	25.00 -	35.00
12384 *Sissy Blues*	25.00 -	40.00
12395 *Down In The Basement*	25.00 -	40.00
12419 *Grievin' Hearted Blues*	20.00 -	30.00
12438 *Don't Fish In My Sea*	20.00 -	30.00
12455 *Morning Hour Blues*	20.00 -	30.00
12508 *Misery Blues*	50.00 -	75.00
12526 *Gone Daddy Blues*	50.00 -	75.00
12548 *Big Boy Blues*	50.00 -	75.00
12566 *Oh Papa Blues*	50.00 -	75.00
12590 *Georgia Cake Walk*	40.00 -	60.00
12603 *Moonshine Blues*	40.00 -	60.00
12612 *Ice Bag Papa*	40.00 -	60.00
12647 *Blues The World Forgot*	40.00 -	60.00
12668 *Prove It On Me Blues*	40.00 -	60.00
12687 *Victim Of The Blues*	40.00 -	60.00
12706 *Traveling Blues*	40.00 -	60.00
12718 *Big Feeling Blues*	50.00 -	75.00
12735 *Tough Luck Blues*	35.00 -	50.00
12760 *Sleep Talking Blues*	35.00 -	50.00
12804 *Log Camp Blues*	50.00 -	75.00
12902 *Runaway Blues*	50.00 -	75.00
12926 *Sweet Rough Man*	50.00 -	75.00
12963 *Daddy Goodbye Blues*	50.00 -	75.00

RAMONA AND HER GANG/GRAND PIANO:

Victor 24260 *A Penny For Your Thoughts*	7.00 -	10.00
24268 *What Have We Got To Lose?*	7.00 -	10.00
24303 *I've Got To Sing A Torch Song*	7.00 -	10.00
24310 *Was My Face Red?*	7.00 -	10.00
24316 *Raisin' The Rent*	7.00 -	10.00
24389 *You Excite Me!*	7.00 -	10.00
24408 *Ah! The Moon Is Here*	7.00 -	10.00
24440 *I'm No Angel*	7.00 -	10.00
24445 *Not For All the Rice In China*	7.00 -	10.00
25138 *Every Now And Then*	7.00 -	10.00
25156 *Barrel-House Music*	7.00 -	10.00

RAMPART STREET WASHBOARD BAND:

Titles, issued contemporaneously on Banner, Conqueror, Oriole, Perfect, Romeo: *Forty and Tight; Piggly Wiggle* ... 50.00 - 75.00

CLARK RANDALL & HIS ORCHESTRA:

Brunswick 7415 *Troublesome Trumpet*	8.00 -	12.00
7436 *Drifting Tide*	8.00 -	12.00
7466 *Jitter Bug*	8.00 -	12.00

DUKE RANDALL & HIS BOYS:

Champion 15491 *Squeeze Me*	75.00 -	100.00

SLATZ RANDALL & HIS ORCHESTRA:

Brunswick 4331, 4779, 6304	4.00 -	8.00

AMANDA RANDOLPH & HER ORCHESTRA:

Bluebird 6615, 6616, 6617, 6619	4.00 -	7.00

TED RAPH & HIS ORCHESTRA:

Columbia 2440-D, 2450-D	5.00 -	10.00

JIMMY RASCHEL & HIS ORCHESTRA:

Champion 16534 *It Don't Mean A Thing*	15.00 -	20.00

REB'S LEGION CLUB FORTY FIVES:

Hollywood (unnumbered) *My Mammy's Blues*	50.00 -	100.00

RED & HIS BIG TEN:

Victor 23026 *That's Where The South Begins*	10.00 -	15.00
23033 *At Last I'm Happy*	10.00 -	15.00

RED AND MIFF'S STOMPERS:

Edison 51854 *Alabama Stomp*	30.00 -	40.00
51878 *Black Bottom Stomp*	30.00 -	40.00
Victor 20778 *Delirium*	10.00 -	15.00
21183 *Feelin' No Pain*	10.00 -	15.00
21397 *Slippin' Around*	10.00 -	15.00

THE RED CAPS:

Victor 23382 *Niagara Falls*	20.00 -	30.00

THE RED DEVILS:

Ballin The Jack, issued contemporaneously on Banner, Oriole, Romeo ... 20.00 - 30.00

Columbia 14586-D *Tiger Rag*	20.00 -	30.00

THE RED HEADS:

Melotone 12443 *Feelin' No Pain*	5.00 -	8.00)
12495 *Bugaboo*	4.00 -	7.00
Oriole 2555 *Nobody's Sweetheart*	5.00 -	8.00
2574 *Bugaboo*	4.00 -	7.00
Pathe-Actuelle 11347 *Get A Load Of This*	15.00 -	20.00
36347 *Nervous Charlie*	10.00 -	15.00
36384 *Fallen Arches*	10.00 -	15.00
36387 *Poor Papa*	10.00 -	15.00
36419 *'Tain't Cold*	10.00 -	15.00
36458 *Dynamite*	10.00 -	15.00
36492 *Wild And Foolish*	10.00 -	15.00
36527 *Alabama Stomp*	10.00 -	15.00
36536 *The Hurricane*	10.00 -	15.00
36557 *Heebie Jeebies*	10.00 -	15.00
36576 *That's No Bargain*	10.00 -	15.00
Pathe-Actuelle 36583 *Tell Me Tonight*	10.00 -	15.00
36593 *You Should See My Tootsie*	10.00 -	15.00
36701 *A Good Man Is Hard To Find*	10.00 -	15.00
36707 *Nothin' Does-Does Like It Used To Do-Do-Do*	10.00 -	15.00
Perfect 14528 *Headin' For Louisville*	10.00 -	15.00
14565 *Fallen Arches*	10.00 -	15.00
14568 *Poor Papa*	10.00 -	15.00
14600 *Hangover*	10.00 -	15.00
14639 *Hi-Diddle-Diddle*	10.00 -	15.00
14673 *Wild And Foolish*	10.00 -	15.00
14708 *Brown Sugar*	10.00 -	15.00
14717 *The Hurricane*	10.00 -	15.00
14738 *Black Bottom Stomp*	10.00 -	15.00
14757 *That's No Bargin*	10.00 -	15.00
14764 *Here Or There*	10.00 -	15.00
14774 *You Should See My Tootsie*	10.00 -	15.00
14882 *Baltimore*	10.00 -	15.00
14888 *Nothin' Does-Does Like It Used To Do-Do-Do*	10.00 -	15.00

RED HOT SYNCOPATORS:

Bell 445 *Jackass Blues*	15.00 -	20.00
456 *Heebie Jeebies*	15.00 -	20.00

THE RED HOTTERS:

Silverton 3526 *St. Louis Blues*	10.00 -	15.00
3527 *Gin Houn' Blues*	10.00 -	15.00
3560 *Third Alley Breakdown*	80.00 -	100.00

DON REDMAN & HIS ORCHESTRA:

Titles, issued contemporaneously on Banner, Conqueror, Melotone, Oriole, Perfect, Romeo; *A Little Bit Later On; Bugle Call Rag; I Gotcha; Lazy Weather; Moonrise On The Lowlands; Too Bad; We Don't Know From Nothin'; Who Wants To Sing My Love Song?* ... 10.00 - 15.00

Bluebird 10061 *Down Home Rag*	5.00 -	8.00
10071 *Milenberg Joys*	5.00 -	8.00

10081 *'Deed I Do*...........	5.00 -	8.00
10095 *Auld Lang Syne*...........	5.00 -	8.00
10615 *You Ain't Nowhere*...........	5.00 -	8.00
10765 *Shim-Me-Sha-Wabble*...........	5.00 -	8.00
Brunswick 6211 *Chant of the Weed*...........	10.00 -	15.00
6233 *I Heard*...........	10.00 -	15.00
6273 *How'm I Doin'?*...........	10.00 -	15.00
6344 *It's A Great World After All*...........	10.00 -	15.00
6354 *Tea For Two*...........	10.00 -	15.00
6368 *Hot And Anxious*...........	10.00 -	15.00
6401 *Ain't I The Lucky One?*...........	10.00 -	15.00
6412 *Two-Time Man*...........	10.00 -	15.00
6429 *Nagasaki*...........	10.00 -	15.00
6517 *Doin' The New Low-Down*...........	10.00 -	15.00
6520 *Doin' The New Low-Down*...........	7.00 -	10.00
6523 *How Ya Feelin?*...........	10.00 -	15.00
6560 *Sophisticated Lady*...........	10.00 -	15.00
6585 *I Won't Tell*...........	10.00 -	15.00
6622 *Lazy Bones*...........	10.00 -	15.00
6684 *I Found A New Way To Go*...........	10.00 -	15.00
6745 *Got The Jitters*...........	10.00 -	15.00
6935 *Lonely Cabin*...........	10.00 -	15.00
Variety 580 *On The Sunny Side Of The Street*..	10.00 -	15.00
605 *Stormy Weather*...........	10.00 -	15.00
635 *The Man On The Flying Trapeze*.......	10.00 -	15.00
Victor 26206 *Jump Session*...........	5.00 -	8.00
26258 *Igloo*...........	5.00 -	8.00
26266 *Ain't I Good To You?*...........	5.00 -	8.00
Vocalion 3354 *Bugle Call Rag*...........	10.00 -	15.00
3359 *We Don't Know From Nothin'*...........	10.00 -	15.00
3823 *Exactly Like You*...........	10.00 -	15.00
3829 *Sweet Sue*...........	10.00 -	15.00
3836 *The Man On The Flying Trapeze*......	10.00 -	15.00

RED ONION JAZZ BABIES:

Gennett 5607 *Terrible Blues*...........	100.00 -	150.00
5627 *Cake Walking Babies*...........	100.00 -	150.00
Silvertone 4029 *Cake Walking Babies*...........	100.00 -	150.00
4032 *Santa Claus Blues*...........	100.00 -	150.00
5024 *Brotherly Love*...........	10.00 -	15.00

REUBEN "RIVER" REEVES & HIS RIVER BOYS/TRIBUTARIES:

Vocalion 1292 *River Blues*...........	50.00 -	70.00
1297 *Bugle Call Blues*...........	60.00 -	80.00
1407 *Moanin' Low*...........	60.00 -	80.00
1411 *Texas Special Blues*...........	60.00 -	80.00
2638 *Screws, Nuts and Bolts*...........	30.00 -	40.00
2723 *Zuddan*...........	30.00 -	40.00
15836 *Head Low*...........	50.00 -	75.00
15839 *Shoo Shoo Boogie Boo*...........	50.00 -	75.00

REILLY-FARLEY AND THEIR ONYX CLUB BOYS (See Riley-Farley);

LEO REISMAN AND HIS ORCHESTRA:

Columbia 701-D, 776-D, 973-D, 1467-D, 1561-D.	4.00 -	7.00
Victor L-16005 *Music From The Cat and The Fiddle*	7.00 -	10.00
Victor L-16026, L-16028...........	7.00 -	10.00
(Above are Long-Playing "Program Transcriptions.")		
Victor 22306 *Puttin' On The Ritz*...........	5.00 -	8.00
22398 *Happy Feet*...........	5.00 -	8.00
22433 *Rollin' Down The River*...........	5.00 -	8.00
Victor 22459, 22537, 22538, 22546, 22605, 22606, 22647, 22668, 22670, 22696...........	4.00 -	7.00
Victor 22746 *Without That Gal!*...........	5.00 -	8.00
22755 *New Sun In The Sky*...........	5.00 -	8.00
22757 *Without That Gal!*...........	5.00 -	8.00
Victor 22794, 22798...........	4.00 -	7.00
Victor 22836 *White Heat*...........	7.00 -	10.00
Victor 22839, 22849...........	4.00 -	7.00
Victor 22851 *Bend Down, Sister*...........	8.00 -	12.00
Victor 22869, 22870, 22904, 22912, 22913, 22914, 22915, 22927, 22954, 22961...........	4.00 -	7.00
Victor 24011 *If It Ain't Love*...........	5.00 -	8.00

Victor 24029, 24044, 24047...........	4.00 -	7.00
Victor 24048 *Got The South In My Soul*.......	5.00 -	8.00
Victor 24126, 24131, 24132, 24156...........	4.00 -	7.00
Victor 24157 *A Rainy Day*...........	5.00 -	8.00
24193 *I've Got You On My Mind*...........	7.00 -	10.00
Victor 24192, 24259, 24262, 24269...........	4.00 -	7.00
Victor 24312 *My Temptation*...........	5.00 -	8.00
24315 *Happy Is The Day Is Long*...........	7.00 -	10.00
Victor 24358 *Smoke Rings*...........	6.00 -	10.00
Victor 24398, 24399, 24407...........	4.00 -	7.00
Victor 24418 *Easter Parade*...........	5.00 -	8.00
24419 *Savage Serenade*...........	5.00 -	8.00
24428 *Not For All the Rice In China*........	5.00 -	8.00
Victor 24429, 24448...........	4.00 -	7.00

HENRY "KID" RENA'S JAZZ BAND:

Delta 800, 801, 802, 803, 804, 805, 806, 807....	7.00 -	10.00

JACQUES RENARD AND HIS ORCHESTRA:

Brunswick 4918 *Lucky Seven*...........	5.00 -	8.00
4919 *Can This Be Love?*...........	5.00 -	8.00
4939 *Three Little Words*...........	5.00 -	8.00
4940 *Readin', 'Ritin', Rhythm*...........	5.00 -	8.00
Brunswick, most other issues...........	3.00 -	5.00
Columbia 3086-D, 3090-D...........	4.00 -	7.00
Victor 20728 *Just Call On Me*...........	5.00 -	8.00

DUNK RENDLEMAN & THE ALABAMIANS; RENDLEMAN'S DANCE ORCHESTRA:

Gennett 6233 *Hot Heels*...........	15.00 -	20.00
6322 *Mean Dog Blues*...........	15.00 -	20.00
Silvertone 5052 *Hot Heels*...........	15.00 -	20.00

HARRY RESER'S ROUNDERS/ SYNCOPATORS; HARRY RESER AND HIS ORCHESTRA:

Columbia 1109-D *Shaking The Blues Away*.....	5.00 -	8.00
Columbia 1087-D, 1378-D, 1696-D, 1761-D, 1806-D, 1835-D, 1884-D, 1973-D...........	3.00 -	5.00
Columbia 2818-D, 2833-D...........	4.00 -	6.00
Columbia 2840-D *My Galveston Gal*...........	5.00 -	8.00
Edison 14032 *I'm Still Caring*...........	10.00 -	15.00
Edison 52184 *Highways Are Happy Ways*......	5.00 -	8.00
52282 *Hey! Hey! Hazel*...........	5.00 -	8.00
52525 *That's The Good Old Sunny South*....	7.00 -	10.00

FRANKIE REYNOLDS AND HIS ORCHESTRA:

Bluebird 7137 *Chicken On The Apple*........	5.00 -	8.00
7241 *Lady, Be Good*...........	7.00 -	10.00

LEW REYNOLDS FLEXO RECORDING ORCHESTRA:

Flexo 123 *At Last I'm Happy*...........	10.00 -	20.00
124 *You're Driving Me Crazy*...........	10.00 -	20.00
125 *To Whom It May Concern*...........	10.00 -	20.00
128 *What A Fool I've Been*...........	10.00 -	20.00
133 *Casey Jones*...........	10.00 -	20.00
134 *I Surrender Dear*...........	10.00 -	20.00
138 *Ho Hum!*...........	10.00 -	20.00

LYST REYNOLDS' LOGOLA ORCHESTRA:

Gennett 6235 *What Do We Do On a Dew-Dew Dewy Day*...........	10.00 -	15.00
6263 *Barbara*...........	10.00 -	15.00

ROSS REYNOLDS & HIS PALAIS GARDENS ORCHESTRA:

Gennett 5611 *Creole*...........	15.00 -	20.00

THE RHYTHM ACES:

Brunswick 4244 *Jazz Battle*...........	40.00 -	60.00
7120 *I Got The Stinger*...........	40.00 -	60.00

THE RHYTHMAKERS:

Titles, issued contemporaneously on Banner, Melotone, Oriole; *I Would Do Anything For You; Mean Old Bed Bug Blues; Yellow Dog Blues; Yes, Suh!*...........	15.00 -	25.00

THE RHYTHM KINGS:

Victor 23279 *You Rascal, You*...........	20.00 -	30.00
23283 *Please Tell Me*...........	20.00 -	30.00

THE RHYTHM MAKERS:
Vocalion 15763 *Wabash Blues*.............. 35.00 - 50.00
THE RHYTHM WRECKERS:
Vocalion 3341 *Sugar Blues*................ 5.00 - 8.00
    3390 *Wabash Blues*................... 5.00 - 8.00
    3523 *Twelfth Street Rag*............ 5.00 - 8.00
    3566 *St. Louis Blues*............... 5.00 - 8.00
    3608 *September In The Rain*......... 5.00 - 8.00
    3642 *Desert Blues*.................. 5.00 - 8.00
    3670 *Blue Yodel No. 3*............. 5.00 - 8.00
RIALTO DANCE ORCHESTRA:
Domino 356 *I Can't Get The One I Want*...... 7.00 - 10.00
    416 *Copenhagen*.................. 10.00 - 15.00
FRED/FREDDIE RICH AND HIS (LA PALINA/RADIO/TIMES SQUARE) ORCHESTRA:
Banner 0508 *Sweetheart, We Need Each Other*.. 5.00 - 8.00
    0835 *Sing Something Simple*............ 5.00 - 8.00
    6360 *I Get The Blues When It Rains*....... 8.00 - 15.00
    6477 *Sweetness*..................... 5.00 - 8.00
    6503 *Little By little*................. 5.00 - 8.00
    6508 *Piccolo Pete*.................. 5.00 - 8.00
Cameo 0108 *Sweetheart, We Need Each Other*.. 5.00 - 8.00
    0435 *Sing Something Simple*......... 5.00 - 8.00
    872 *Shake That Thing*............. 5.00 - 8.00
    9183 *To Be In Love*............... 5.00 - 8.00
    9229 *Sweetness*................... 5.00 - 8.00
    9233 *Piccolo Pete*................. 5.00 - 8.00
    9265 *Little By Little*.............. 5.00 - 8.00
    9300 *Singin' In The Rain*............ 5.00 - 8.00
Columbia 1838-D *Singin' In The Rain*........ 5.00 - 8.00
    1893-D *Don't Hang Your Dreams on a Rainbow* 5.00 - 8.00
    1924-D *Wishing And Waiting For Love*...... 5.00 - 8.00
    1965-D *Revolutionary Rhythm*.......... 8.00 - 12.00
    1979-D *I Don't Want Your Kisses*....... 5.00 - 8.00
    2043-D *Dixie Jamboree*............... 8.00 - 12.00
    2132-D *Strike Up The Band!*........... 8.00 - 12.00
    2299-D *Sing Something Simple*.......... 8.00 - 12.00
    2328-D *I Got Rhythm*............... 8.00 - 12.00
    2387-D *Tie A Little String Around Your Finger* 8.00 - 12.00
    2484-D *Pardon Me Pretty Baby*......... 8.00 - 12.00
    2536-D *As Time Goes By*............. 7.00 - 10.00
Columbia 2534-D, 2751-D, 2752-D, 2868-D, 2872-D 5.00 - 10.00
Columbia 3613-X *Don't Hang Your Dreams on a Rainbow*.................... 10.00 - 20.00
(Note: No. 3613-X is part of a Spanish series having green labels and utilizing instrumental versions of songs which, for U.S. market, have vocal choruses. See Columbia 1893-D.)
Gennett 6001 *Don't Take That Black Bottom Away* 10.00 - 15.00
    6015 *I Love To Baby You*............. 7.00 - 10.00
    6016 *Sweeter Than You*............. 7.00 - 10.00
    6133 *I'm On My Merry Way*.......... 7.00 - 10.00
    6151 *Ask Me Another*............... 7.00 - 10.00
    6159 *I Adore You*................ 7.00 - 10.00
Harmony 64-H *I'm Sitting On Top Of The World* 7.00 - 10.00
    119-H *Bell Hoppin' Blues*........... 7.00 - 10.00
Hit-of-the-Week J-4 *Little Girl*........... 5.00 - 8.00
    K-1 *It's The Girl*................. 5.00 - 8.00
Okeh 41489 *When I Take My Sugar To Tea*.... 8.00 - 12.00
Pathe-Actuelle 36389, 36394, 36401......... 4.00 - 7.00
    36452 *Up And At 'Em*.............. 7.00 - 10.00
Perfect 14570, 14575, 14582............. 4.00 - 7.00
    14633 *Up And At 'Em*.............. 7.00 - 10.00
Regal 8761 *I Get The Blues When It Rains*..... 5.00 - 8.00
Vocalion 5420 *How High The Moon*......... 7.00 - 10.00
    5507 *I'm Forever Blowing Bubbles*..... 7.00 - 10.00
CHUCK RICHARDS:
Vocalion 2877 *Blue Interlude*.............. 10.00 - 15.00
PETE RICHARDS & HIS ORCHESTRA:
Champion 15402 *Bugs*............... 25.00 - 40.00
    15455 *Michigan Stomp*.............. 25.00 - 40.00

DICK RICHARDSON & HIS BAND/ORCHESTRA:
Parlophone PNY-34091 *Dancing With Tears In My Eyes*.................. 8.00 - 15.00
    PNY-34092 *Promises*.............. 8.00 - 15.00
    PNY-34129 *Out Of Breath*.......... 8.00 - 15.00
    PNY-34130 *I Am Only Human After All*.... 8.00 - 15.00
INEZ RICHARDSON:
Black Swan 2023 *My June Love*.............. 10.00 - 15.00
BUD RICHIE & HIS BOYS:
Champion 16109 *Slappin' The Bass*......... 25.00 - 40.00
Champion 40010 *Rockin' Chair*.......... 10.00 - 15.00
HARRY RICHMAN:
Brunswick 4677 *Puttin On The Ritz*.......... 5.00 - 8.00
Champion 2701-D, 2965-D, 2995-D, 3017-D.... 4.00 - 8.00
Decca 700, 701.................... 4.00 - 8.00
Vocalion 15412, 15457, 15511, 15540, 15560, 15725 6.00 - 10.00
BOB RICKETTS' BAND:
Gennett 5156 *Mean Mean Mama*............ 5.00 - 8.00
THE RIFFERS:
Columbia 14677-D *Rhapsody In Love*........ 8.00 - 12.00
MIKE RILEY, EDDIE FARLEY & THEIR ONYX CLUB BOYS:
Decca 578 *The Music Goes 'Round and 'Round*. 5.00 - 8.00
    619 *I Never Knew*............... 6.00 - 10.00
    641 *Blue Clarinet Stomp*.......... 6.00 - 10.00
    683 *I'm Gonna Clap My Hands*........ 6.00 - 10.00
    684 *I Wish I Were Aladdin*.......... 6.00 - 10.00
    994 *Trouble Don't Like Music*........ 6.00 - 10.00
    1031 *Jingle Bells*................ 6.00 - 10.00
    1041 *With Thee I Swing*............ 6.00 - 10.00
    1263 *I'm Hatin' This Waitin' Around*..... 6.00 - 10.00
    1271 *That's Southern Hospitality*....... 6.00 - 10.00
    655, 1662.................... 4.00 - 7.00
JUSTIN RING & HIS OKEH ORCHESTRA:
Okeh 40869, 40904, 40972............ 4.00 - 7.00
    41295 *True Blue Lou*............. 7.00 - 10.00
JOHNNY RINGER'S ROSEMONT ORCHESTRA:
Gennett 6183 *Buffalo Rhythm*............ 15.00 - 20.00
    6199 *Swamp Blues*.............. 15.00 - 20.00
    6264 *Moonlit Waters*............. 15.00 - 20.00
    6280 *The Varsity Drag*............ 15.00 - 20.00
VINCENT RIZZO AND HIS HOTEL SYLVANIA ORCHESTRA OF PHILA.:
Okeh 40130, 40135.................. 4.00 - 6.00
Okeh 40725 *Clap Yo' Hands*............ 7.00 - 10.00
ROANE'S PENNSYLVANIANS:
Victor 22919 *Chinatown, My Chinatown*....... 7.00 - 10.00
    22922 *Between The Devil and The Deep Blue Sea* 7.00 - 10.00
    24036 *Goodbye Blues*............. 7.00 - 10.00
EVERETT ROBBINS & HIS SYNCOPATING ROBBINS:
Autograph (unnumbered) *You Didn't Want Me*.. 20.00 - 30.00
JOESPH ROBECHAUX & HIS NEW ORLEANS RHYTHM BOYS:
Vocalion 2539 *King Kong Stomp*............ 15.00 - 25.00
    2540 *Lazy Bones*................ 15.00 - 25.00
    2545 *Jig Music*................. 15.00 - 25.00
    2575 *Ring Dem Bells*............. 15.00 - 25.00
    2592 *Shake It And Break It*.......... 15.00 - 25.00
    2610 *Why Should I Cry For You?*....... 15.00 - 25.00
    2646 *Zola*.................... 15.00 - 25.0
    2796 *Foot Scuffle*............... 15.00 - 25.00
    2827 *Every Tub*................ 15.00 - 25.00
    2881 *Just Like A Falling Star*......... 15.00 - 25.00
ORLANDO ROBERSON:
Variety 513 *Just a Quiet Evening*.......... 8.00 - 12.00
CLIFF ROBERTS' DANCE ORCHESTRA:
Regal 10117 *Rough House Rosie*............ 7.00 - 10.00
DICK ROBERTSON (& HIS ORCHESTRA):
Brunswick 4367 *Some Sweet Day*........... 6.00 - 10.00

Champion 40077 *Moon Over Miami*........... 7.00 - 10.00
  40078 *With All My Heart*................. 7.00 - 10.00
  40087 *Lights Out*...................... 7.00 - 10.00
  40088 *Alone*........................ 7.00 - 10.00
  40092 *But Where Are You?*............ 7.00 - 10.00
  40093 *I'd Rather Lead A Band*............ 7.00 - 10.00
  40104 *Welcome Stranger*............... 7.00 - 10.00
  40105 *Is It True What They Say About Dixie?* 7.00 - 10.00
  40106 *The Touch Of Your Lips*........... 7.00 - 10.00
  40111 *Robins and Roses*.............. 7.00 - 10.00
  40116 *The Glory Of Love*............. 7.00 - 10.00
  40117 *She Shall Have Music*.......... 7.00 - 10.00
  40118 *On The Beach At Bali Bali*...... 7.00 - 10.00
Crown 3306 *Minnie The Moocher*........... 7.00 - 10.00
Crown 3427, 3428, 3438, 3440, 3491......... 4.00 - 8.00
Decca 1125, 1131, 1169, 1181, 1209, 1215, 1260,
  1283, 1334, 1335, 1367, 1374, 1407, 1415, 1436,
  1487, 1498, 1511, 1512, 1536, 1585, 1599, 1601,
  1619, 1620.................... 4.00 - 8.00
Decca, most other issues (blue label).......... 3.00 - 5.00
Edison 52194, 52379, 52473, 52551......... 5.00 - 10.00
Melotone 12082 *Would You like To Take A Walk?* 5.00 - 8.00
  12162 *Moonlight Saving Time*............. 5.00 - 8.00
  12163 *I Wanna Sing About You*.......... 5.00 - 8.00
  12408 *Holding My Honey's Hand*.......... 5.00 - 8.00
  12417 *West Bound Freight*............... 10.00 - 15.00
  12418 *Bull Fiddle Blues*............... 10.00 - 15.00

ROBINSON'S KNIGHTS OF REST:
Champion 16607 *Mean Baby Blues*........... 35.00 - 50.00

BILL ROBINSON:
Brunswick 4535, 6134, 6520.............. 5.00 - 10.00

BOB ROBINSON & HIS BOB CATS; BOB ROBINSON TRIO:
Bluebird 6929, 7898...................... 7.00 - 10.00
Crying For Love, issued contemporaneously on
  Banner, Melotone, Oriole, Perfect, Romeo,
  Vocalion...................... 7.00 - 10.00

ELZADIE ROBINSON:
Paramount 12417 *Barrel House Man*......... 40.00 - 60.00
  12420 *Houston Bound*.................... 40.00 - 60.00
  12469 *Baltimore Blues*.................. 40.00 - 60.00
  12509 *Whiskey Blues*.................. 40.00 - 60.00
  12544 *Tick Tock Blues*................. 40.00 - 60.00
  12573 *St. Louis Cyclone Blues*............ 30.00 - 50.00
  12627 *Love Crazy Blues*................ 30.00 - 50.00
  12635 *Elzadie's Policy Blues*............ 50.00 - 75.00
  12676 *Mad Blues*...................... 40.00 - 60.00
  12689 *Wicked Daddy*.................. 40.00 - 60.00
  12701 *Arkansas Mill Blues*.............. 40.00 - 60.00
  12724 *Rowdy Man Blues*............... 40.00 - 60.00
  12745 *Unsatisfied Blues*............... 40.00 - 60.00
  12768 *Cheatin' Daddy*................. 40.00 - 60.00
  12795 *My Pullman Porter Man*........... 40.00 - 60.00
  12900 *Driving Me South*................ 40.00 - 60.00

("BANJO")IKEY ROBINSON & HIS (BULL FIDDLE) BAND/WINDY CITY FIVE:
Brunswick 4963 *Got Butter On It*............ 40.00 - 60.00
  4964 *Rock Me Mama*.................. 30.00 - 40.00
  7052 *Rock Pile Blues*................. 30.00 - 40.00
  7057 *Got Butter On It*................. 40.00 - 60.00
  7059 *Rock Me Mama*.................. 30.00 - 40.00
  7068 *Without A Dime*.................. 30.00 - 40.00
Champion 40011 *Swing It*............. 10.00 - 15.00
  50073 *Sunshine*.................... 10.00 - 15.00
Decca 7430 *Scrunch-Lo*............... 8.00 - 12.00
  7650 *Sunshine*.................. 8.00 - 12.00

ROB ROBINSON (AND MEADE LUX LEWIS):
Paramount 13028 *I Got Some Of That*......... 40.00 - 75.00
  13030 *Don't Put That Thing*............. 40.00 - 75.00
  13064 *I Don't Want It Now*............. 40.00 - 75.00

CARSON ROBINSON'S KANSAS CITY JACK-RABBITS/MADCAPS; THE CARSON ROBISON ORCHESTRA:
Edison (thin) 14085 *Nonsense*............... 10.00 - 15.00
Okeh 41389 *Nothin'*................. 7.00 - 10.00
Victor 38074 *Nonsense*................. 15.00 - 25.00

WILLARD ROBISON & HIS ORCHESTRA; WILLARD ROBISON'S DEEP RIVER FOUR:
Autograph 600 *The Rhythm Rag*............. 20.00 - 30.00
Pathe-Actuelle 36723, 36744, 36757, 36766, 36783,
  36785, 36796.................... 5.00 - 8.00
  36724 *I'm More Than Satisfied*........... 40.00 - 60.00

Perfect 14904, 14925, 14938, 14942, 14963, 14966,
  14977 .... 5.00 - 8.00
  14905 *I'm More Than Satisfied*............ 40.00 - 60.00

TOM ROCK & HIS ORCHESTRA:
Odeon ONY-36157 *I'll Be Blue, Just Thinking Of You*. 8.00 - 15.00
  ONY-36158 *A Peach Of A Pair*......... 8.00 - 15.00
  ONY-36159 *My Love For You*......... 8.00 - 15.00
  ONY-36164 *The Little Things In Life*........ 8.00 - 15.00
  ONY-36179 *Would You Like To Take A Walk?* 8.00 - 15.00

ROCKY MOUNTAIN TRIO:
Gennett 3184 *Grand Opera Blues*............. 8.00 - 12.00
  3288 *Blowin' Off Steam*............. 8.00 - 12.00

IKE RODGERS (& HIS BIDDLE STREET BOYS):
Broadway 5081 *It Hurts So Good*............ 80.00 - 100.00
  7086 *Malt Can Blues*................. 60.00 - 80.00
Paramount 12816 *It Hurts So Good*.......... 80.00 - 100.00

GIL RODIN & HIS ORCHESTRA; GIL RODIN'S BOYS:
Titles, issued contemporaneously on Banner, Con-
  queror, Melotone, Oriole, Perfect, Romeo; *Love's*
  Serenade; Restless; Right About Face; What's The
  Reason .... 6.00 - 10.00
It's So Good, on Banner, Conqueror, Domino, Regal 8.00 - 12.00
Crown 3016 *If I Could Be With You One Hour*
  Tonight .... 15.00 - 25.00
  3017 *Beale Street Blues*................. 15.00 - 25.00
  3045 *Ninety-Nine Out Of a Hundred Wanna Be*
  Loved .... 15.00 - 20.00
  3046 *Hello, Beautiful*................ 15.00 - 25.00

BUDDY ROGERS (AND HIS CALIFORNIA CAVLIERS); CHARLES "BUDDY" ROGERS:
Columbia 2143-D *Sweepin' The Clouds Away*... 7.00 - 10.00
  2183-D *My Future Just Passed*......... 7.00 - 10.00
Victor 24001, 24015, 24031, 24049........... 5.00 - 8.00

GINGER ROGERS:
Bluebird 7981 *I Used To Be Color Blind*....... 7.00 - 10.00
Decca 638 *Eeny, Meeny, Miney Mo*.......... 7.00 - 10.00
**MACK ROGERS & HIS GUNTER HOTEL
ORCHESTRA:**
Bluebird 5603 *Casa Loma Stomp*............ 8.00 - 12.00
5835 *Baby, Won't You Please Come Home?*.. 8.00 - 12.00
RODNEY ROGERS RED PEPPERS:
Brunswich 3744 *Milenberg Joys*............. 4.00 - 7.00
WILL ROGERS:
Victor 45347, 45369, 45374................. 5.00 - 8.00
**B.A. ROLFE & HIS LUCKY STRIKE
DANCE/PALAIS D'OR ORCHESTRA:**
Edison (thin) 14003, 14033, 14048, 14049, 14050,
14059, 14068................. 10.00 - 15.00
Edison (thick) 51799, 51814, 51829, 51848, 51888,
51890, 52037, 52057, 52059, 52105, 52223,
52244, 52261, 52295, 52300, 52319, 52321,
52326, 52342, 52343, 52353, 52366, 52445,
52480................. 8.00 - 20.00*
(*Records of greatest collector interest are those hav-
ing a different orchestra on the flip side; reference
to such other orchestra may be made herein).
THE ROLLICKERS:
Edison 52600 *Lonely Little Cinderella*........ 7.00 - 12.00
ADRIAN ROLLINI & HIS ORCHESTRA:
Titles, issued contemporaneously on Banner, Con-
queror, Melotone, Oriole, perfect, Romeo; *Ah!
But Is It Love?; And So, Goodbye; Beloved; By
A Waterfall; Coffee In The Morning and Kisses
In The Night; Dream On; Got The Jitters; Have
You Ever Been Lonely?; Hustlin' And Bustlin'
For Baby; If I Had Somebody To Love; I Gotta
Get Up and Go To Work; I'll Be Faithful; I Raised
My Hat; Ol' Pappy; On The Wrong Side Of The
Fence; Savage Serenade; Sittin' On A Backyard
Fence; Sittin' On A Log; Song of Surrender; Sweet
Madness; Who Walks In When I Walk Out?; You
Must Believe Me; You've Got Everything; You've
Got Me Cryin' Again*................... 6.00 - 12.00
Decca 265 *Sugar*..................... 8.00 - 12.00
359 *Davenport Blues*................. 8.00 - 12.00
Master 114 *Slap That Bass*.............. 7.00 - 10.00
Vocalion 2672 *Butterfingers*............. 8.00 - 12.00
2673 *Waitin' At The Gate For Katy*...... 8.00 - 12.00
2675 *A Hundred Years From Today*........ 8.00 - 12.00
TODD ROLLINS AND HIS ORCHESTRA:
Titles, issued contemporaneously on Banner,
Melotone, Oriole, Perfect, Romeo; *The Boogie
Man; Christmas Night In Harlem; Fare Thee Well
To Harlem; Get Goin'; Jimmy Had A Nickel;
Jungle Fever; Junk Man; Moon Country; Take
A Lesson From The Lark*................. 5.00 - 8.00
Romeo 2222 *Let's Go Places and Do Things*.... 5.00 - 8.00
PHIL ROMANO AND HIS ORCHESTRA:
Victor 19803 *I'm Goin' Out If Lizzie Comes In*. 5.00 - 8.00
THEODORE ROOSEVELT:
Victor 35250 (12-inch) *The Farmer and the Business
Man*..................... 5.00 - 8.00
DAVID ROSE & HIS ORCHESTRA:
Bluebird 5708 *Jig-Saw Rhythm*............. 7.00 - 10.00
VINCENT ROSE & HIS ORCHESTRA:
Titles, issued contemporaneously on Banner, Con-
queror, Melotone, Oriole, Perfect, Romeo; *Lear-
ning; Stars Fell On Alabama*................. 9.00 - 12.00
Additional titles: *My Dog Loves Your Dog; Nasty
Man' Without That Gal*................. 5.00 - 8.00
ROSELAND DANCE ORCHESTRA:
Ajax 17119 *Where's My Sweetie Hiding?*....... 8.00 - 12.00
Banner 6129 *There's A Rickety Rackety Shack*.. 7.00 - 12.00
6154 *Sorry*..................... 7.00 - 12.00

Domino 3441 *Araby*..................... 7.00 - 12.00
3445 *I'll See You In My Dreams*........... 7.00 - 12.00
**TIMME ROSENKRANTZ & HIS BARREL-
HOUSE BARONS:**
Victor 25876, 25883................. 4.00 - 8.00
HARRY ROSENTHAL & HIS ORCHESTRA:
Columbia 2982-D *Say When*............. 10.00 - 15.00
2986-D *You're The Top*............. 10.00 - 15.00
3016-D *The Hunkadola*............. 7.00 - 10.00
3019-D *My Heart Is An Open Book*........ 7.00 - 10.00
ROSE ROOM ORCHESTRA:
Banner 6202 *How About Me?*............. 5.00 - 8.00
6268 *Glad Rag Doll*................. 5.00 - 8.00
Domino 4386 *Waiting at the End of the Road*.. 5.00 - 8.00
Regal 8831 *Waiting at the End of the Road*.... 5.00 - 8.00
ARTHUR ROSS AND HIS WESTERNERS:
Harmony 723-H *Take Your Tomorrow*........ 7.00 - 10.00
748-H *Where The Shy Little Violets Grow*... 7.00 - 10.00
793-H *A Room With a View*............. 5.00 - 8.00
892-H *She's My Girl*................. 5.00 - 8.00
(Note: Above titles also issued on Diva and Velvet
Tone.)
ROSS DE LUXE SYNCOPATORS:
Victor 20952 *Mary Bell*............. 30.00 - 40.00
20961 *Skad-O-Lee*................. 30.00 - 40.00
21077 *Monia*..................... 30.00 - 40.00
21537 *Believe Me, Dear*................. 30.00 - 40.00
THE ROUNDERS:
Domino 4386 *Lovable and Sweet*............ 5.00 - 8.00
Regal 8688 *Where The Shy Little Violets Grow*. 5.00 - 8.00
8781 *When My Dreams Come True*........ 5.00 - 8.00
8831 *Lovable and Sweet*................. 5.00 - 8.00
RUSSELL'S ROVING REVELERS:
Champion 15701 *Alfalfa*................. 15.00 - 20.00
**LUIS RUSSELL & HIS BURNING EIGHT/
ORCHESTRA; (LUIS) RUSSELL'S HEEBIE
JEEBIE STOMPERS/HOT SIX:**
Titles, issued contemporaneously on Banner,
Melotone, Oriole, Perfect, Romeo: *At The
Darktown Strutters' Ball; Ghost Of The Freaks;
Hokus Pocus; My Blue Heaven; Ol' Man River;
Primitive*..................... 15.00 - 25.00
Melotone 12000 *I Got Rhythm*............. 15.00 - 25.00
Okeh 8424 *Plantation Joys*............. 90.00 - 130.00
8454 *Sweet Mumtaz*............. 80.00 - 100.00
8656 *The Call Of The Freaks*............. 20.00 - 30.00
8734 *Jersey Lightnin'*................. 20.00 - 30.00
8760 *Savoy Shout*................. 20.00 - 30.00
8766 *Feelin' The Spirit*................. 20.00 - 30.00
8780 *Saratoga Shout*................. 20.00 - 30.00
8811 *Louisiana Swing*................. 20.00 - 30.00
8830 *Muggin' Lightly*................. 20.00 - 30.00
8849 *High Tension*................. 20.00 - 30.00
Vocalion 1010 *29th and Dearborn*........... 50.00 - 75.00
1579 *Saratoga Drag*................. 50.00 - 75.00
Victor 22789 *Goin' To Town*............. 15.00 - 25.00
22793 *You Rascal, You*................. 15.00 - 25.00
22815 *Freakish Blues*................. 15.00 - 25.00
PEE WEE RUSSELL'S RHYTHMAKERS:
Hot Rhythm Society 17, 1000, 1001.......... 4.00 - 6.00
RED RUSSELL'S RHYTHM:
Superior 2719 *Mood Indigo*................. 15.00 - 20.00
TED RUSSELL & HIS ORCHESTRA:
Champion 40040 *I Wished On The Moon*...... 5.00 - 8.00
40041 *In The Middle Of a Kiss*............. 5.00 - 8.00
40042 *Rhythm Is Our Business*............. 5.00 - 8.00
40056 *Santa Claus Is Comin' To Town*...... 5.00 - 8.00
40057 *You Are My Lucky Star*............. 5.00 - 8.00
40066 *Here's To Romance*............. 5.00 - 8.00
40071 *I Found A Dream*............. 5.00 - 8.00
40072 *You Took My Breath Away*............. 5.00 - 8.00

40079 *I Fell Like A Feather In My Breeze*...	5.00 -	8.00
40089 *Dinner For One, Please James*.......	5.00 -	8.00
40109 *Melody From The Sky*.............	5.00 -	8.00
40110 *Knick-Knacks on The Mantel*........	5.00 -	8.00

DAN RUSSO & HIS ORIOLE ORCHESTRA;
DAN RUSSO & HIS ORIOLES:

Brunswick 4490, 4672, 4708............	4.00 -	7.00
Columbia 2641-D *I'm a Ding Dong Daddy*.....	8.00 -	12.00
2642-D *Noah's Ark*...................	8.00 -	12.00

ST. LOUIS LEVEE BAND:

Okeh 8404 *Soap Suds*.................	90.00 -	120.00

ST. LOUIS RHYTHM KINGS:

Columbia 349-D *Papa De Da Da*.............	7.00 -	10.00

ST. LOUIS SYNCOPATORS:

Majestic 1431 *Way Down Yonder In New Orleans*	8.00 -	15.00
Olympic 1436 *Long Lost Mama*.............	8.00 -	15.00
1437 *The Snakes' Hips*..............	8.00 -	15.00

SAM 'N' HENRY (See CORRELL and
GOSDEN):

EDGAR SAMPSON & HIS ORCHESTRA:

Vocalion 4942 *Pick Your Own Lick*...........	8.00 -	12.00

JOE SANDERS (AND HIS ORCHESTRA):

Decca 658, 659, 676, 692, 843, 850, 952, 955, 956	4.00 -	7.00
Victor 24033 *Intangibility*.................	7.00 -	10.00

RED SANDERS AND HIS ORCHESTRA:

Gennett 3147 *What Could Be Sweeter Than You?*	7.00 -	10.00
3148 *On The Bam Bam Bamy Shore*.......	10.00 -	15.00
3166 *When You See That Aunt Of Mine*....	10.00 -	15.00
3178 *Show Me The Way To Go Home*......	7.00 -	10.00

JIMMY SAUTER'S NIGHT OWLS:

Gennett 6755 *Avalon Town*.................	7.00 -	10.00
6769 *Glad Rag Doll*...................	7.00 -	10.00

HELEN SAVAGE:

Brunswick 4536 *It's Bad For Your Soul*........	30.00 -	40.00

SAVANNAH NIGHT HAWKS:

Champion 15641 *Nightmare*.................	60.00 -	80.00

SAVANNAH SIX:

Harmony 56-H *Hot Aire*.............	8.00 -	12.00
58-H *Jacksonville Gal*.................	8.00 -	12.00

THE SAVANNAH SYNCOPATORS:

Brunswick 3245 *Deep Henderson*.............	15.00 -	20.00
3281 *Jackass Blues*..................	15.00 -	20.00
3361 *Sugar Foot Stomp*..............	15.00 -	20.00
3373 *Wa Wa Wa*..................	15.00 -	20.00
6046 *Who's Blue?*..................	35.00 -	50.00
6176 *Radio Rhythm*.................	25.00 -	40.00
7124 *My Melancholy Baby*..............	40.00 -	60.00

JAN SAVITT & HIS TOP HATTERS:

Bluebird 7281, 7283, 7295, 7490, 7493, 7504, 7593, 7595, 7607, 7666, 7670, 7679, 7733, 7737, 7748, 7783, 7786, 7797, 10005, 10013, 10018.....	4.00 -	7.00
Decca, blue label, most issues..............	3.00 -	5.00
Variety 506 *How Could You?*.................	7.00 -	10.00
542 *Supposing*....................	7.00 -	10.00
585 *Cross Country Hop*..............	7.00 -	10.00
Victor, most issues...................	3.00 -	5.00

SAVOY BEARCATS:

Victor 20182 *Senegalese Stomp*.............	20.00 -	30.00
20307 *Bearcat Stomp*..................	20.00 -	30.00
20406 *Stampede*..................	20.00 -	30.00

THE SCARE CROW:

Gennett 7209 *Traveling Blues*.................	60.00 -	90.00
7229 *Easy Creeping Mama*..............	60.00 -	90.00
7275 *The Scare Crow Ball*..............	60.00 -	90.00

REX SCHEPP:

Autograph 630 *Russian Rag*.............	8.00 -	12.00

ELMER SCHOEBEL & HIS FRIARS SOCIETY
ORCHESTRA:

Brunswick 4652 *Copenhagen*..............	20.00 -	30.00

ADRIAN SCHUBERT AND HIS
(DANCE/SALON) ORCHESTRA:

Crown 3004, 3007, 3011, 3034, 3036, 3052, 3062, 3066, 3087, 3088, 3110..................	3.00 -	6.00
Crown 3129 *Moonlight Saving Time*...........	5.00 -	8.00
Crown 3151, 3164, 3178..............	3.00 -	6.00
Crown 3181 *This Is The Missus*..............	5.00 -	8.00
Crown 3191, 3206, 3207, 3225, 3226, 3245, 3257, 3258, 3269, 3274, 3282, 3303, 3316, 3318, 3335, 3348, 3350, 3359, 3364, 3388, 3408, 3411, 3439, 3483..........................	3.00 -	6.00
Crown 3484 *I've Got To Sing a Torch Song*....	5.00 -	8.00
Crown 3493, 3496, 3508..............	4.00 -	7.00
Domino 4606 *When Love Comes in the Moonlight*	5.00 -	8.00
4609 *Living a Life of Dreams*..............	7.00 -	10.00

BERNIE SCHULTZ & HIS CRESCENT
ORCHESTRA:

Gennett 6216 *Sweet Violets*.................	10.00 -	20.00
6234 *Hold Everything*.................	10.00 -	20.00
6235 *Show Me That Kind of a Girl*........	10.00 -	20.00

ARTHUR SCHUTT (AND HIS ORCHESTRA):

Okeh 41243, 41345, 41346, 41391..........	5.00 -	8.00
41359 *Cryin' For The Carolines*.........	7.00 -	10.00
41360 *I'm Following You*.................	7.00 -	10.00
41392 *It Must Be You*.............	7.00 -	10.00
41400 *'Leven-Thirty Saturday Night*........	8.00 -	12.00

CECIL SCOTT & HIS BRIGHT
BOYS/ORCHESTRA:

Victor 38098 *In A Corner*.................	35.00 -	50.00
38117 *Bright Boy Blues*.................	35.00 -	50.00

LEONARD SCOTT/BLUE SCOTT & HIS BLUE
BOYS:

Bluebird 6520 *Rubbin', Rubbin'*..............	10.00 -	15.00
6557 *At The Bottom*.................	10.00 -	15.00
Vocalion 03311 *She's Got Something Good*.....	10.00 -	15.00

LLOYD SCOTT & HIS ORCHESTRA:

Victor 20495 *Happy Hour Blues*..............	30.00 -	40.00
21491 *Harlem Shuffle*..............	30.00 -	40.00

THE SCRANTON SIRENS ORCHESTRA:

Okeh 40297 *Why Should I Believe In You?*.....	25.00 -	35.00
40329 *Common Street Blues*..............	25.00 -	40.00

SEARCY TRIO:

Okeh 8360 *Kansas Avenue Blues*.............	20.00 -	30.00

SEATTLE HARMONY KINGS:
Victor 19772, 20133, 20142.................	4.00 -	8.00

GENE SEDRIC & HIS HONEY BEARS:
Vocalion 4552, 4576......................	5.00 -	8.00

RAY SEELEY & HIS ORCHESTRA:
Odeon ONY-36106 *I Love You So Much*......	10.00 -	15.00
ONY-36107 *Can I Help It?*...............	10.00 -	15.00
ONY-36192 *I Found What I Wanted In You*.	10.00 -	15.00
ONY-36203 *I'm Crazy 'Bout My Baby*.......	10.00 -	15.00

EMIL SEIDEL & HIS ORCHESTRA:
Gennett 6295 *The Best Things In Life Are Free*.	20.00 -	30.00
6309 *Down South*.............	15.00 -	25.00
6324 *Together, We Two*...........	15.00 -	25.00
6327 *For My Baby*...............	10.00 -	15.00
6340 *One More Night*...........	8.00 -	12.00
6355 *Counting The Days*........	8.00 -	12.00
6367 *Beautiful*..................	8.00 -	12.00

BEN SELVIN & HIS ORCHESTRA:
Columbia 2150-D *Let Me Sing And I'm Happy*..	5.00 -	8.00
2255-D *It's Easy To Fall In Love*...........	5.00 -	8.00
2287-D *Dixiana*..................	5.00 -	8.00
2323-D *My Man From Caroline*........	5.00 -	8.00
2356-D *Cheerful Little Earful*.......	7.00 -	10.00
2366-D *Yours And Mine*...........	7.00 -	10.00
2381-D *Would You Like To Take A Walk?*...	7.00 -	10.00
2400-D *99 Out Of A Hundred Wanna Be Loved*	7.00 -	10.00
2421-D *Smile, Darn Ya, Smile*.........	7.00 -	10.00
2426-D *Lean To Croon*.................	7.00 -	10.00
2463-D *Now You're In My Arms*...........	7.00 -	10.00
2487-D *Let's Drink A Drink To The Future*..	7.00 -	10.00
2491-D *Sing Another Chorus, Please*........	7.00 -	10.00
2499-D *Hikin' Down The Highway*.........	7.00 -	10.00
2501-D *My Sweet Tooth Says "I Wanna"*....	7.00 -	10.00
2515-D *This Is The Missus*................	7.00 -	10.00
2554-D *Little Mary Brown*............	7.00 -	10.00
2661-D *Crazy People*.................	7.00 -	10.00
2669-D *Cabin In The Cotton*............	7.00 -	10.00
2731-D *Young And Healthy*.............	7.00 -	10.00
2789-D *Morning, Noon and Night*.........	7.00 -	10.00
Columbia 18000-D *"Hot Cha" medley*......	8.00 -	12.00
(Note: Above is a "longer playing" record.)		
Vocalion 14851 *San*...................	5.00 -	8.00
14853 *Red Hot Mama*...................	5.00 -	8.00
14871 *Susquehanna Home*...............	5.00 -	8.00
15038 *Charleston*...................	5.00 -	8.00
15083 *Let's Wander Away*...............	5.00 -	8.00
15110 *Brown Eyes, Why Are You Blue?*.....	5.00 -	8.00
15154 *Sleepy Time Gal*.................	5.00 -	8.00

SEMINOLE SYNCOPATORS:
Okeh 40228 *Blue Grass Blues*...............	35.00 -	50.00

BOYD SENTER (& HIS SENTERPEDES/ZO-BO-KA-ZOOS):
Titles, on Autograph (unnumbered): *Bucktown Blues; Gertie; Laugh; Mobile Blues; Omaha Blues; Powder Rag*..................	20.00 -	30.00
Autograph (unnumbered) *Mr. Jelly Lord*......	30.00 -	50.00
Banner 0620, 0621, 0622, 1633.............	5.00 -	8.00
Clarion 5054-C, 5112-C, 5181-C, 5194-C....	5.00 -	8.00
Diva 6034-G, 6044-G.....................	5.00 -	8.00
Domino 3604 *Fat Mama Blues*..............	5.00 -	8.00
Okeh 40755, 40777, 40819, 40836, 40861, 40888, 40949, 41018......................	5.00 -	8.00
41059, 41115, 41163..................	7.00 -	10.00
Pathe-Actuelle 36256, 36270, 36285, 36320, 36336, 36351, 36359, 36397, 36424, 36483, 36493, 36528..................	5.00 -	8.00
Perfect 14437, 14451, 14466, 14501, 14517, 14532, 14540, 14578, 14605, 14664, 14674, 14709..	5.00 -	8.00
Regal 9937 *Fat Mama Blues*.............	5.00 -	8.00
Velvet Tone 7070-V, 7118-V, 7120-V, 7121-V...	5.00 -	8.00
Victor 21864, 21912, 22010.............	5.00 -	8.00
22303 *Copenhagen*..................	10.00 -	15.00
22464 *No One*...................	7.00 -	10.00
22812 *Waterloo*.................	7.00 -	10.00
23032 *Smiles*.................	10.00 -	15.00

THE SEPIA SERENADERS:
Bluebird 5770 *Ridiculous Blues*..............	15.00 -	20.00
5782 *Breakin' The Ice*.............	15.00 -	20.00
5803 *Alligator Crawl*.............	15.00 -	20.00

THE SEVEN ACES (See WARNER'S SEVEN ACES)

THE 7 BLUE BABIES:
Edison 52495 *That's Her Now!*..............	15.00 -	20.00
52602 *Heigh Ho! Ev'robody, Heigh Ho!*......	10.00 -	15.00

SEVEN BROWN BABIES:
Ajax 17011 *Do Doodle Oom*................	20.00 -	30.00
17011 *Dicty Blues*.................	20.00 -	30.00

THE SEVEN GALLON JUG BAND:
Columbia 2087-D *Wipe 'Em Off*..............	20.00 -	30.00

THE SEVEN HOT AIR MEN:
Columbia 2092-D *Harlem Madness*...........	8.00 -	12.00
2175-D *Red Hot Chicago*.................	8.00 -	12.00

SEVEN LITTLE CLOUDS OF JOY:
Brunswick 7180 *You Rascal, You*..............	25.00 -	40.00

SEVEN LITTLE POLAR BEARS:
Cameo 1060 *Don't Take That Black Bottom Away*	5.00 -	8.00

SEVEN MISSING LINKS:
Perfect 14480 *Angry*......................	5.00 -	8.00

SEVEN WILD MEN:
Harmony 191-H, 193-H.................	4.00 -	7.00

HATCH SEWARD:
Broadway 5063 *Honky Train Blues*...........	75.00 -	100.00

TERRY SHAND AND HIS ORCHESTRA:
Decca, blue label, most issues.................	3.00 -	5.00
Vocalion 4113, 4131......................	4.00 -	8.00

SHARKEY'S NEW ORLEANS BOYS/SHARKS OF RHYTHM:
Decca 1014 *Everybody Loves My Baby*........	6.00 -	10.00
Vocalion 3353 *Mudhole Blues*..............	7.00 -	12.00
3380 *High Society*.................	7.00 -	12.00
3400 *When You're Smiling*.............	7.00 -	12.00
3410 *Blowin' Off Steam*.................	7.00 -	12.00
3450 *Big Boy Blue*.................	7.00 -	12.00
3470 *Swing Like A Rusty Gate*.............	7.00 -	12.00

FRED SHARP'S DIXIE PLAYERS:
Champion 15216 *I'm Looking Over a Four-Leaf Clover*..................	15.00 -	20.00

CHARLIE SHAVERS QUINTET:
Vogue 754 *She's Funny That Way*..............	15.00 -	20.00

SHAW

755 *Serenade To A Pair Of Nylons*..........	15.00 -	20.00
756 *If I Had You*........................	15.00 -	20.00

ART(IE) SHAW & HIS NEW MUSIC/OR-CHESTRA/STRINGS:

Bluebird 7746, 7759, 7772, 7875, 7889, 7952, 10001, 10054, 10055, 10075, 10079, 10091, 10125, 10126, 10127, 10128, 10134, 10141, 10148, 10178, 10188, 10195, 10202, 10215, 10307, 10319, 10320, 10324, 10334, 10345, 10347, 10385, 10406, 10412, 10430, 10446, 10468, 10482, 10492	3.00 -	5.00
Brunswick 7688, 7698, 7721, 7735, 7741, 7750, 7771, 7778, 7787, 7794, 7806, 7827, 7835, 7841, 7852, 7895, 7899, 7907, 7914, 7934, 7936, 7942, 7947, 7952, 7965, 7971, 7976, 7986, 8010, 8019, 8050, 8054	5.00 -	10.00
Musicraft, most issues....................	2.00 -	4.00
Victor, most issues.....................	2.00 -	5.00

JOEL SHAW & HIS ORCHESTRA:

Crown 3244, 3271, 3273, 3302, 3304, 3306, 3311, 3312, 3319, 3332, 3333, 3349, 3352, 3362, 3381, 3382, 3383, 3413, 3414, 3423, 3442, 3444, 3451, 3453	5.00 -	10.00

MILT SHAW & HIS DETROITERS:

Okeh 41158, 41196....................	4.00 -	7.00
Vocalion 15665, 15666, 15697..........	6.00 -	10.00

TED SHAWNE & HIS ORCHESTRA:

Parlophone PNY-34126 *I Ain't Got Nobody*....	10.00 -	15.00
PNY-34027 *Rockin' Chair*................	10.00 -	15.00
PNY-34032 *Song Of The Islands*...........	10.00 -	15.00
PNY-34033 *Blue, Turning Grey Over You*...	10.00 -	15.00
PNY-34129 *I'm In The Market For You*.....	10.00 -	15.00
PNY-34131 *I'm A Ding Dong Daddy*........	10.00 -	15.00
PNY-34172 *The Peanut Vendor*...........	10.00 -	15.00
PNY-34173 *Sweethearts On Parade*........	10.00 -	15.00
Odeon ONY-41276 *Ain't Misbehavin'*..........	10.00 -	15.00

HARRY "FREDDIE" SHAYNE:

Champion 50061 *Lonesome Man Blues*........	10.00 -	15.00

BERT SHEFTER & HIS ORCHESTRA/RHYTHM OCTET:

Decca 2525, 2584, 2653..................	4.00 -	6.00
Victor 25614, 25622, 25632..................	4.00 -	7.00

OLLIE SHEPARD:

Decca, Okeh.........................	5.00 -	8.00

SHERIDAN ENTERTAINERS:

Banner 6025 *Sing Me A Baby Song*........	5.00 -	8.00

SISSLE

6026 *Dew Dew Dewy Day*.................	5.00 -	8.00
Challenge 658 *Dew Dew Dewy Day*...........	5.00 -	8.00

SHERMAN CLUB ORCHESTRA:

Challenge 715 *Muddy Water*.............	80.00 -	100.00

SHERMAN'S GLOBE TROTTERS:

Bell 615 *Louisiana*......................	15.00 -	20.00

SHERMAN SUNDODGERS:

Herwin 8059 *Happy Go Lucky Lane*..........	15.00 -	20.00

NAT SHILKRET & THE VICTOR ORCHESTRA:

Victor 20469 *I Love You But I Don't Know Why*	15.00 -	20.00
20471 *What Does It Matter?*..............	5.00 -	8.00
20508 *Ain't She Sweet?*..............	5.00 -	8.00
20634 *Fifty Million Frenchmen Can't Be Wrong*	5.00 -	8.00
20675 *Me and My Shadow*..............	5.00 -	8.00
20882 *Baby's Blue*..................	5.00 -	8.00
20926 *Zulu Wail*..................	5.00 -	8.00
21080 *Nothin'*..................	5.00 -	8.00
21515 *When Sweet Susie Goes Steppin' By*...	5.00 -	8.00
21603 *Moonlight Madness*..............	5.00 -	8.00
21996 *Susianna*..................	5.00 -	8.00
22258 *When I'm Looking At You*..........	5.00 -	8.00
22306 *Singing A Vagabond Song*..........	5.00 -	8.00
22472 *Dixiana*..................	5.00 -	8.00

SHREVEPORT SIZZLERS:

Okeh 8918 *Zonky*......................	20.00 -	30.00
41561 *You've Got To Be Modernistic*.......	20.00 -	30.00

AL SIEGEL & HIS ORCHESTRA:

Blue Grass Blues; So Long To You And The Blues; issued contemporaneously on Claxtonola, Paramount, Puritan.......................	15.00 -	20.00

SIGLER'S BIRMINGHAM MERRYMAKERS:

Okeh 40280 *Mama's Gone Goodbye*..........	20.00 -	30.00
40310 *I Love Her*..................	20.00 -	30.00

FRANK SIGNORELLI AND HIS ORCHESTRA:

Pathe-Actuelle 36518 *She's Still My Baby*......	10.00 -	15.00
36523 *Don't Be Angry With Me*...........	10.00 -	15.00
36535 *St. Louis Hop*................	10.00 -	15.00
Perfect 14699 *She's Still My Baby*..........	10.00 -	15.00
14704 *Don't Be Angry With Me*...........	10.00 -	15.00
14716 *A Blues Serenade*..............	10.00 -	15.00

SILVER SLIPPER ORCHESTRA:

Challenge 806 *There'll Come A Day*...........	75.00 -	100.00

JOHNNY SILVESTER AND HIS ORCHESTRA (See JOHNNY SYLVESTER):

OMER SIMEON:

Brunswick 7109 *Beau-Koo Jack*..............	40.00 -	60.00

LESTER SIMMONS & HIS ORCHESTRA:

Champion 15475 *I've Got Somebody Now*.....	10.00 -	15.00

HOWARD SIMMS:

Harmograph 841 *Pensacola Joe*..............	20.00 -	30.00

JOSEPH SIMPKINS & HIS RUBE BAND:

Champion 15581 *Bass Blues*..............	25.00 -	40.00

ARTHUR SIMS & HIS CREOLOE ROOF ORCHESTRA:

Okeh 8373 *Soapstick Blues*..................	40.00 -	60.00
40675 *As Long As I Have You*.............	40.00 -	60.00

THE SINGING BOYS & THEIR NOVELTY ORCHESTRA:

Harmony 928-H, 1087-H..................	4.00 -	7.00

SIOUX CITY SIX:

Gennett 5569 *Flock O'Blues*.................	60.00 -	90.00

NOBLE SISSLE; (NOBLE) SISSEL/SISSLE & (EUBIE) BLAKE; NOBLE SISSLE & HIS (INTERNATIONAL) OR-CHESTRA/SIZZLIN' SYNCOPATORS SWINGSTERS:

Brunswick 6073 *Got The Bench, Got The Park*.	15.00 -	25.00
6111 *Roll On, Mississippi, Roll On*..........	15.00 -	25.00
6129 *Basement Blues*..................	15.00 -	25.00
Decca 153 *Under The Creole Moon*..........	8.00 -	12.00

154 *Loveless Love*	8.00 -	12.00
766 *I Wonder Who Made Rhythm*	7.00 -	10.00
778 *That's What Love Did To Me*	7.00 -	10.00
847 *I Take To You*	7.00 -	10.00
2129 *Blackstick*	5.00 -	8.00
7429 *Viper Mad*	5.00 -	8.00
Edison 50754 *Crazy Blues*	7.00 -	10.00
51572 *Broken Busted Blues*	7.00 -	10.00
Emerson 10296 *Broadway Blues*	5.00 -	8.00
10326 *Crazy Blues*	5.00 -	8.00
10357 *Boll Weevil Blues*	5.00 -	8.00
10365 *Low Down Blues*	5.00 -	8.00
10367 *Royal Garden Blues*	5.00 -	8.00
Emerson 10385 *Baltimore Buzz*	5.00 -	8.00
10396 *Oriental Blues*	5.00 -	8.00
10443 *Arkansas Blues*	5.00 -	8.00
10484 *I'm A Doggone Struttin' Fool*	5.00 -	8.00
Okeh 40776 *'Deed I Do*	7.00 -	10.00
40824 *Slow River*	7.00 -	10.00
40859 *Sometimes I'm Happy*	5.00 -	8.00
40877 *Broken Hearted*	5.00 -	8.00
40882 *Give Me A Night In June*	5.00 -	8.00
40917 *Pickaninny Shoes*	7.00 -	10.00
Paramount 12002 *Bandana Days*	10.00 -	15.00
12007 *Crazy Blues*	12.00 -	18.00
Variety 552 *I'm Just Wild About Harry*	7.00 -	10.00
648 *Characteristic Blues*	7.00 -	10.00
Victor 19086, 19253, 19494	4.00 -	7.00
Vocalion 3840 *Characteristic Blues*	7.00 -	10.00

SIX BLACK DIAMONDS:

Issued contemporaneously on Banner, Domino, Regal: *Those Panama Mamas*	10.00 -	15.00
Banner 1318, 1322, 1346. 1348, 1349, 1385	4.00 -	8.00
Banner 6383 *Where Has Mammy Gone?*	5.00 -	8.00
Domino 3510 *Sweet Georgia Brown*	5.00 -	8.00
Oriole 497 *Melancholy Lou*	8.00 -	12.00
Regal 8022 *Say Mister Have You Met Rosie's Sister*	5.00 -	8.00
9725 *Dixie Flyer Sam*	12.00 -	16.00
Regal 9612, 9628, 9643, 9646	4.00 -	8.00

THE SIX HOTTENTOTS:

Titles, issued contemporaneously on Banner, Domino, Regal: *Hurricane; I'm In Love Again; Melancholy Charlie; The Memphis Blues; Rosy Cheeks, Sometimes I'm Happy*	8.00 -	12.00

SIX JOLLY JESTERS:

Vocalion 1449 *Oklahoma Stomp*	20.00 -	25.00
15843 *Six Or Seven Times*	35.00 -	50.00

SIX JUMPING JACKS:

Brunswick 3064 *Charleston Ball*	5.00 -	8.00
3095 *Masculine Women! Feminine Men!*	5.00 -	8.00

SIX MEN AND A GIRL:

Varsity 8190, 8193	4.00 -	7.00

THE SIZZLERS:

Edison 52463 *Diga Diga Doo*	7.00 -	10.00

CHARLEY SKEETE'S ORCHESTRA:

Edison 51775 *Deep Henderson*	35.00 -	50.00

DUDE SKILES & HIS VINE STREET BOYS:

Variety 516, 584	4.00 -	7.00

SKILLET DICK & HIS FRYING PANS:

Champion 15883 *Asphalt Walk*	50.00 -	75.00
15996 *Rock and Gravel*	50.00 -	75.00

SLIM & HIS HOT BOYS:

Victor 38044 *That's A Plenty*	20.00 -	30.00

SLIM AND SLAM:

Vocalion 3981, 4021, 4110, 4163, 4225, 4346, 4461, 4521, 4594	4.00 -	8.00

FATS SMITH & HIS RHYTHM KINGS:

Vocalion 03528 *If I Had You In My Arms*	10.00 -	15.00

FRED SMITH & HIS SOCIETY ORCHESTRA:

Black Swan 2052, 2114, 2119	6.00 -	10.00

HARL SMITH AND HIS ORCHESTRA:

Pathe-Actuelle 036158 *Rose Marie*	7.00 -	10.00
Perfect 14339 *Bring Back Those Rock-A-Bye Baby Days*	7.00 -	10.00

JABBO SMITH & HIS RHYTHM ACES: (see also THE RHYTHM ACES):

Brunswick 7058 *Little Willie Blues*	40.00 -	60.00
7061 *Take You Time*	40.00 -	60.00
7065 *Let's Get Together*	40.00 -	60.00
7069 *Michigander Blues*	40.00 -	60.00
7071 *Ace Of Rhythm*	40.00 -	60.00
7078 *Decatur Street Tutti*	40.00 -	60.00
7087 *Lina Blues*	40.00 -	60.00
7101 *Tanguay Blues*	40.00 -	60.00
7111 *Band Box Stomp*	40.00 -	60.00
Decca 1712, 1980	4.00 -	7.00

JOE SMITH'S MARTHA LEE CLUB ORCHESTRA:

Okeh 40322 *Don't Bother Me*	8.00 -	12.00

KATE SMITH:

Columbia 911-D *One Sweet Letter From You*	8.00 -	12.00

LEROY SMITH & HIS ORCHESTRA:

Blu-Disc 1001 *Stop And Listen*	35.00 -	50.00
Everybody's 1020 *Harlem's Araby*	30.00 -	40.00
1027 *Dixie Dreams*	30.00 -	40.00
Victor 21328 *St. Louis Blues*	7.00 -	10.00
21472 *St. Louis Blues*	4.00 -	6.00

LLOYD SMITH'S GUT-BUCKETEERS:

Vocalion 1560 *Wake Up, Sinners*	75.00 -	100.00
1573 *That's My Stuff*	75.00 -	100.00

SAMMY SMITH'S STOMPERS:

Clarion 5417-C *Blues In My Heart*	10.00 -	15.00
Velvet Tone 2477-V *Blues In My Heart*	10.00 -	15.00

STUFF SMITH & HIS ORCHESTRA/ONYX CLUB BOYS

Decca 1279 *Onyx Club Spree*	8.00 -	12.00
1287 *Where Is The Sun?*	8.00 -	12.00
Varsity 8063 *Sam The Vegetable Man*	7.00 -	10.00
8081 *My Blue Heaven*	7.00 -	10.00
8242 *I've Got You Under My Skin*	7.00 -	10.00
8251 *It's Up To You*	7.00 -	10.00
Vocalion 3169 *I'se A Muggin'*	7.00 -	10.00
3170 *I Hope Gabriel Likes My Music*	7.00 -	10.00
3200 *'Tain't No Use*	7.00 -	10.00
3201 *After You've Gone*	7.00 -	10.00
3234 *I've Got A Heavy Date*	7.00 -	10.00
3270 *It Ain't Right*	7.00 -	10.00
3300 *Knock Knock, Who's There*	7.00 -	10.00
3316 *Here Comes The Man With The Jive*	7.00 -	10.00

TED SMITH'S RHYTHM ACES:

Champion 16321 *Minnie The Moocher*	25.00 -	30.00
16332 *Boogie Woogie*	25.00 -	30.00
16420 *New Moten Stomp*	25.00 -	30.00
40006 *Jig Time*	10.00 -	15.00

WILLIE "THE LION" SMITH (& HIS ORCHESTRA): WILLIE SMITH (THE LION) & HIS CLUBS:

Commodore 518, 519, 521, 522, 523, 524, 525	4.00 -	7.00
Decca 1291 *The Swampland Is Calling Me*	7.00 -	10.00
1308 *More Than That*	7.00 -	10.00
1366 *Knock Wood*	7.00 -	10.00
1380 *Get Acquainted With Yourself*	7.00 -	10.00
1503 *Achin' Hearted Blues*	7.00 -	10.00
1957 *I've Got To Think It Over*	5.00 -	8.00
7073 *There's Gonna Be The Devil To Pay*	7.00 -	10.00
7074 *Streamline Gal*	7.00 -	10.00
7086 *Sittin' At The Table*	7.00 -	10.00
7090 *Swing, Brother, Swing*	7.00 -	10.00
General 1712 *Peace On You*	7.00 -	10.00
1713 *Rushin'*	7.00 -	10.00

MARVIN SMOLEV & HIS SYNCOPATORS:

Titles, issued contemporaneously on Grey Gull,

Radiex: *Apart From You; Because I'm Lonesome; Desert Blues; No-One But Betty Brown; Ring Around The Moon; She's Just The Baby For Me; Soubrette; The Terror; We'll Be Married In June*   15.00 - 30.00

JACK SNEED AND HIS SNEEZERS:
Decca 7522 *Big Joe Louis* . . . . 7.00 - 10.00

SNOOKS & HIS MEMPHIS RAMBLERS/STOMPERS; SNOOKS & HIS PARAMOUNT THEATRE ORCHESTRA:
Melotone 12203 *That's My Desire* . . . . 7.00 - 10.00
12210 *Just One More Chance* . . . . 7.00 - 10.00
12245 *Goodnight, Sweetheart* . . . . 7.00 - 10.00
12259 *When It's Sleepy Time Down South* . . . 7.00 - 10.00
Victor 22629 *I'm Happy When You're Happy* . . 5.00 - 8.00
22662 *Smile, Darn Ya, Smile* . . . . 5.00 - 8.00
22684 *Bon Soir* . . . . 5.00 - 8.00
22704 *You Don't Need Glasses* . . . . 5.00 - 8.00
22720 *Dip Your Brush In The Sunshine* . . . . . 5.00 - 8.00
22779 *Sweet Georgia Brown* . . . . 5.00 - 8.00
22813 *Kissable Baby* . . . . 5.00 - 8.00
22815 *Japanese Sandman* . . . . 15.00 - 25.00
22895 *Nothin' To Do But Love* . . . . 5.00 - 8.00
22988 *'Neath The Silvery Moon* . . . . 5.00 - 8.00
23038 *Hello, Beautiful!* . . . . 7.00 - 10.00

BOB SNYDER & HIS ORCHESTRA:
Vocalion 2660 *My Dog Loves Your Dog* . . . . . . 7.00 - 10.00
2661 *Nasty Man* . . . . 7.00 - 10.00
2707 *Love Thy Neighbor* . . . . 7.00 - 10.00

JOE SODJA'S SWINGTETTE:
Variety 609 *Limehouse Blues* . . . . 5.00 - 8.00

JACKIE SOUDERS AND HIS ORCHESTRA:
Columbia 837-D *Every Little Thing* . . . . 5.00 - 8.00

EDDIE SOUTH & HIS ALABAMIANS/ ORCHESTRA:
Victor 21151 *By The Waters Of Minnetonka* . . . 5.00 - 8.00
21155 *The Voice Of The Southland* . . . . 5.00 - 8.00
21605 *That's What I Call Keen* . . . . 7.00 - 10.00
24324 *Old Man Harlem* . . . . 8.00 - 12.00
24343 *Gotta Go!* . . . . 8.00 - 12.00
24383 *Nagasaki* . . . . 8.00 - 12.00

SOUTHAMPTON SOCIETY ORCHESTRA:
Pathe-Actuelle 36643 *I'm In Love Again* . . . . . . 8.00 - 12.00
Perfect 14395 *Poplar Street Blues* . . . . 10.00 - 15.00
14824 *I'm In Love Again* . . . . 8.00 - 12.00

THE SOUTHERNERS:
Gennett 3061 *Craving* . . . . 8.00 - 12.00
3198 *Clap Hands! Here Comes Charley* . . . . . 8.00 - 12.00
3199 *Rhythm Of The Day* . . . . 8.00 - 12.00
3204 *That Certain Party* . . . . 8.00 - 12.00
3212 *Someone's Stolen My Sweet Sweet Baby* . 8.00 - 12.00
3265 *My Bundle Of Love* . . . . 8.00 - 12.00
3266 *But I Do - You Know I Do* . . . . 8.00 - 12.00

THE SOUTHERN FIVE:
LaBelle 1410 *I Wish I Could Shimmy Like My Sister Kate* . . . . 8.00 - 12.00
Melody 1410 *I Wish I Could Shimmy Like My Sister Kate* . . . . 8.00 - 12.00

SOUTHERN MELODY ARTISTS:
Okeh 41216 *When The World Is At Rest* . . . . . . 7.00 - 10.00

SOUTHERN MELODY SYNCOPATORS:
Marathon 229 *I'm on the Crest of a Wave* . . . .
232 *Sonny Boy* . . . .
234 *High Up on a Hill Top* . . . .
235 *Roses of Yesterday* . . . .
(Note: Above are 7-inch records.)

SOUTHERN ORCHESTRA:
Victor 707 *West Indies Rhythm* . . . . 5.00 - 8.00

SOUTHERN RHYTHM MASTERS:
Van Dyke 81891 *Sweetheart It's You* . . . . 10.00 - 15.00

THE SOUTHERN SERENADERS:
Harmony 4-H *I Miss My Swiss* . . . . 15.00 - 20.00

5-H *Alone At Last* . . . . 15.00 - 20.00
Silvertone 2770 *I've Found a New Baby* . . . . . . 10.00 - 15.00

SOUTHLAND SYNCOPATORS:
Vocalion 15544 *Brown Sugar* . . . . 7.00 - 10.00

SOUTH SHORE MELODY BOYS:
Champion 15036, 15037 . . . . 8.00 - 12.00
15638 *Jo-Anne* . . . . 10.00 - 20.00
15639 *Blue Night* . . . . 10.00 - 20.00

SOUTH STREET RAMBLERS:
Q.R.S. 7019 *Endurance Stomp* . . . . 60.00 - 90.00

SOUTH STREET TRIO:
Victor 20402 *Need More Blues* . . . . 20.00 - 30.00
21135 *Dallas Blues* . . . . 20.00 - 30.00
21249 *Suitcase Breakdown* . . . . 20.00 - 30.00
38509 *South Street Stomp* . . . . 20.00 - 30.00

BUD SPAIGHT'S HARMONY KINGS:
Broadway 1389 *Don't Lose It* . . . . 10.00 - 15.00

MUGGSY SPANIER & HIS RAGTIME BAND:
Bluebird 10384, 10417, 10506, 10518, 10532, 10682, 10719, 10766 . . . . 3.00 - 5.00

PAUL SPECHT & HIS ORCHESTRA:
Columbia 627-D *Static Strut* . . . . 7.00 - 10.00
1186-D *Roll Up The Carpets* . . . . 7.00 - 10.00
1307-D *St. Louis Shuffle* . . . . 7.00 - 10.00
1836-D *Hittin' The Ceiling* . . . . 5.00 - 8.00
2106-D *Keepin' Myself For You* . . . . 7.00 - 10.00
2472-D *Falling In Love* . . . . 7.00 - 10.00
2482-D *I Found a Million Dollar Baby* . . . . . . 5.00 - 8.00
Harmony 1423-H *Keepin' Out of Mischief Now* . 7.00 - 10.00

MIKE SPECIALE & HIS (CARLTON TERRACE) ORCHESTRA:
Edison 51612 *When The Dear Old Summer Goes* 7.00 - 10.00
52498 *My Inspiration Is You* . . . . 7.00 - 10.00
Perfect 14375 *There'll Be Some Changes Made* . 5.00 - 8.00
14405 *Breakin' The Leg* . . . . 7.00 - 10.00
14456 *Row, Row, Rosie* . . . . 5.00 - 8.00
14494 *Walking The Rails* . . . . 7.00 - 10.00
14526 *Mammy Chasing Blues* . . . . 7.00 - 10.00
14536 *I Love My Baby (My Baby Loves Me)* . 7.00 - 10.00
14568 *Tentin' Down in Tennessee* . . . . 10.00 - 15.00
14569 *Dinah* . . . . 7.00 - 10.00

SPENCER TRIO:
Decca 1873 *John Henry* . . . . 7.00 - 10.00
1941 *Baby, Won't You Please Come Home* . . . 7.00 - 10.00

HERBERT SPENCER AND HIS ORCHESTRA:
Banner 7055 *She's a Great, Great Girl* . . . . 7.00 - 10.00
7057 *Lila* . . . . 7.00 - 10.00
Regal 8516 *Lila* . . . . 7.00 - 10.00

WALLY SPENCER'S GEORGIANS:
Champion 15304 *Buffalo Rhythm* . . . . 15.00 - 25.00
15307 *Rubber Heels* . . . . 15.00 - 20.00
15308 *Swamp Blues* . . . . 15.00 - 20.00
15362 *Who's That Knockin' At My Door?* . . . 15.00 - 20.00
15363 *The Varsity Drag* . . . . 15.00 - 20.00
15366 *Gold Digger* . . . . 40.00 - 60.00

SPIKE'S SEVEN PODS OF PEPPER ORCHESTRA:
Nordskog 3009 *Ory's Creole Trombone* . . . . . . 125.00 - 175.00

REB SPIKES MAJORS AND MINORS:
Columbia 1193-D *My Mammy's Blues* . . . . 20.00 - 30.00

PHILIP SPITALNY & HIS ORCHESTRA:
Brunswick 4917 *Maybe It's Love* . . . . 5.00 - 8.00
Edison (thin) 14035 *I Want To Meander in the Meadow* . . . . 10.00 - 15.00
14050 *Same Old Moon* . . . . 10.00 - 15.00
14058 *Waiting at the End of the Road* . . . . . . 10.00 - 15.00
14062 *Just You, Just Me* . . . . 10.00 - 15.00
14069 *I May Be Wrong* . . . . 10.00 - 15.00
14076 *Bottoms Up* . . . . 12.00 - 18.00
14086 *If I Can't Have You* . . . . 12.00 - 18.00
Edison 52568 *An Eyeful Of You* . . . . 10.00 - 15.00

52577 *To Be In Love*.....................	7.00 -	10.00
52589 *Here We Are*.....................	7.00 -	10.00
52605 *When My Dreams Come True*.......	7.00 -	10.00
52622 *I Want To Meander in the Meadow*...	10.00 -	15.00
52637 *So Sentimental*....................	7.00 -	10.00
Victor 20115 *Hello Baby*.................	5.00 -	8.00
20108 *Jackass Blues*.................	7.00 -	10.00
20475 *Rippin' It Off*..................	7.00 -	10.00

(See Also: THE HOUR OF CHARM ALL GIRL
 ORCHESTRA)

DICK STABILE AND HIS ORCHESTRA:

Bluebird 7388 *In the Shade of the Old Apple Tree*	5.00 -	8.00
Decca 716 *Just Because*..................	5.00 -	8.00
977 *Ja Da*......................	5.00 -	8.00
Vocalion 3368 *Riffin' at the Ritz*............	5.00 -	8.00

JESS STACY (& HIS ORCHESTRA):

Commodore 506, 507, 529, 1503.............	3.00 -	5.00
Varsity 8064, 8076, 8121, 8132, 8140.........	5.00 -	8.00

BILL STAFFON & HIS ORCHESTRA:

Bluebird 6048, 6049, 6082, 6115, 6175........	4.00 -	8.00

**JESSE STAFFORD & HIS (PALACE HOTEL)
 ORCHESTRA:**

Brunswick 4048 *Cinderella Blues*............	5.00 -	8.00
4129 *Doin' The Raccoon*..............	5.00 -	8.00
4548 *I Don't Want Your Kisses*...........	5.00 -	8.00
4630 *I'm Following You!*..............	5.00 -	8.00
Brunswick 4629, 4822, 4823, 4824, 6126.......	4.00 -	7.00

MARY STAFFORD:

Columbia A-3365, A-3390, A-3418, A-3426, A-3493, A-3511..............................	4.00 -	7.00
Pathe-Actuelle 7502 *Take Your Finger Off It*...	10.00 -	15.00
Perfect 102 *Take Your Finger Off It*.........	10.00 -	15.00

HENRY STARR:

Flexo 148 *Mr. Froggie*....................	20.00 -	30.00

STATE STREET RAMBLERS:

Champion 16247 *Tiger Moan*...............	50.00 -	75.00
16279 *Georgia Grind*.................	50.00 -	75.00
16320 *Kentucky Blues*...............	50.00 -	75.00
16350 *Richmond Stomp*...............	50.00 -	75.00
16464 *Careless Love*.................	50.00 -	75.00
40007 *Barrel House Stomp*.............	10.00 -	15.00
40009 *Georgia Grind*.................	10.00 -	15.00
40070 *Sic 'Em Tige*..................	10.00 -	15.00
40086 *Careless Love*.................	10.00 -	15.00
Gennett 6232 *Cootie Stomp*...............	75.00 -	100.00
6249 *There'll Come A Day*.............	75.00 -	100.00
6454 *My Baby*...................	75.00 -	100.00
6485 *Shanghai Honeymoon*.............	75.00 -	100.00
6552 *Endurance Stomp*...............	75.00 -	100.00
6569 *Brown-Skin Mama*...............	50.00 -	75.00
6589 *Tuxedo Stomp*.................	50.00 -	75.00
6641 *Yearning And Blue*.............	50.00 -	75.00
6692 *Oriental Man*.................	50.00 -	75.00

STATE STREET SWINGERS:

Vocalion 03284 *Chicago Rhythm*...........	10.00 -	15.00
03319 *Whippin' That Jelly*...........	10.00 -	15.00
03347 *You Waited Too Long*..........	10.00 -	15.00
03364 *Swing Cat Swing*.............	10.00 -	15.00
03395 *Rattlesnakin' Daddy*...........	10.00 -	15.00
03572 *You Can't Do That To Me*...........	10.00 -	15.00

**STEAMBOAT JOE & HIS LAFFIN'
 CLARINET:**

Black Patti 8020 *Texas Shuffle*.............	20.00 -	30.00
Gennett 6103 *Texas Shuffle*................	20.00 -	30.00

BLUE STEELE & HIS ORCHESTRA:

Victor 20971, 21400, 21530, 22436, V-40140...	3.00 -	7.00
21183 *Betty Jean*..................	10.00 -	15.00
21262 *Washington and Lee Swing*.........	8.00 -	12.00
21355 *Be My Baby*.................	8.00 -	12.00
23014 *Shooin' Flies*.................	15.00 -	20.00

JOE STEELE & HIS ORCHESTRA:

Victor 38066 *Coal-Yard Shuffle*..............	40.00 -	60.00

BILLY STENNETT'S CAROLINA STOMPERS:

Broadway 1193 *Down Where The Sun Goes Down*	15.00 -	20.00
1194 *Buffalo Rhythm*.....................	15.00 -	20.00

**LEITH STEVENS AND HIS SATURDAY
 NIGHT SWING CLUB ORCHESTRA:**

Vocalion 4210 *Memphis Blues*...............	5.00 -	8.00
4350 *Twelfth Street Rag*..............	5.00 -	8.00

**CARLYLE STEVENSON'S BON TON/EL
 PATIO ORCHESTRA:**

Hollywood 1024 *Eccentric*................	40.00 -	60.00
Sunset 1114 *Charleston*.................	15.00 -	20.00
1117 *Milenburg Joys*..............	15.00 -	20.00
1119 *Cecilia*..................	10.00 -	15.00
1120 *Collegiate*.................	10.00 -	15.00
1134 *Remember*.................	10.00 -	15.00

**REX STEWART & HIS FIFTY-SECOND
 STREET STOMPERS/ORCHESTRA; REX
 STEWART'S BIG SEVEN:**

Bluebird 10946 *Without A Song*............	7.00 -	10.00
11057 *Linger Awhile*...............	7.00 -	10.00
11258 *Some Saturday*...............	7.00 -	10.00
Hot Record Society 2004 *Diga Diga Doo*......	7.00 -	10.00
2005 *Bugle Call Rag*...............	7.00 -	10.00
Okeh 3831, 3844, 5448, 5510...............	4.00 -	8.00
Variety 517 *Rexatious*..................	7.00 -	10.00
618 *Back Room Romp*...............	7.00 -	10.00
664 *Sugar Hill Shim-Sham*.............	7.00 -	10.00
Vocalion 2880 *Stingaree*..................	10.00 -	15.00
3831 *Tea And Trumpets*.............	7.00 -	10.00
3844 *Sugar Hill Shim-Sham*.............	7.00 -	10.00
5448 *Fat Stuff Serenade*.............	5.00 -	8.00
5510 *San Juan Hill*................	7.00 -	10.00

**SAMMY STEWART & HIS ORCHESTRA;
 SAMMY STEWART'S TEN KNIGHTS OF
 SYNCOPATION:**

Paramount 20340 *My Man Rocks Me*........	30.00 -	40.00
20359 *Copenhagen*.................	30.00 -	40.00
Puritan 11340 *My Man Rocks Me*...........	30.00 -	40.00
11359 *Copenhagen*...............	30.00 -	40.00
Vocalion 15724 *'Cause I Feel Low Down*......	35.00 -	50.00
15734 *Crazy Rhythm*...............	35.00 -	50.00

**JACK STILLMAN'S ORIOLES; JACK
 STILLMAN'S ORIOLE ORCHESTRA;
 STILLMAN'S ORIOLES:**

Bell 368, 382.............................	4.00 -	7.00
Bell 457 *Gone Again Gal*.................	7.00 -	10.00
Emerson 3082 *Gone Again Gal*.............	7.00 -	10.00
3103 *High, High, High Up In The Hills*......	7.00 -	10.00
3106 *My Little Bunch of Happiness*........	7.00 -	10.00
Gennett 3183 *Cooler Hot*...............	10.00 -	15.00
3226 *Go Away and Don't Come Back*.......	7.00 -	10.00
3233 *Where Were You Then?*.............	7.00 -	10.00
3237 *Charleston of the Evening*.............	7.00 -	10.00
3244 *Lantern of Love*...............	7.00 -	10.00
3407 *Faustine*..................	7.00 -	10.00
Paramount 20423 *I Wonder Where My Baby Is Tonight*............................	8.00 -	12.00
20427 *Clap Hands, Here Comes Charley*.....	8.00 -	12.00
20455 *Blue Bonnet (You Make Me Feel Blue)*.	8.00 -	12.00
Pathe-Actuelle 36304 *My. Cooler Hot*........	5.00 -	8.00
36305 *Charleston of the Evening*........	5.00 -	8.00
36441 *Blue Bonnet*................	5.00 -	8.00
36443 *Tonight's My Night with Baby*........	5.00 -	8.00
36465 *Come On and Do Your Red Hot Business*	8.00 -	12.00
Perfect 14485 *Mr. Cooler Hot*.............	5.00 -	8.00
14486 *Charleston of the Evening*........	5.00 -	8.00
14622 *Blue Bonnet*...............	5.00 -	8.00
14624 *Tonight's My Night With Baby*.......	5.00 -	8.00
14646 *Come On and Do Your Red Hot Business*	8.00 -	112.00

BERT STOCK & HIS ORCHESTRA:

Gennett 7059 *Honeysuckle Rose*.............. 12.00 - 16.00
7075 *'Tain't No Sin*.............. 12.00 - 16.00

THE STOMPIN' SIX:
Sunset 1098 *Jimtown Blues*.............. 100.00 - 150.00
1099 *Down And Out Blues*.............. 100.00 - 150.00

THE STOMP SIX:
Autograph 626 *Everybody Loves My Baby*..... 100.00 - 150.00

EDDIE STONE & HIS ORCHESTRA:
Vocalion 3555, 3576, 3585, 3703, 3750, 3984, 3996,
4101 .... 3.00 - 6.00

JESSE STONE & HIS BLUES SERENADERS/ORCHESTRA:
Okeh 8471 *Boot To Boot*.............. 60.00 - 80.00
Variety 521 *Wind Storm*.............. 10.00 - 15.00

CHARLEY STRAIGHT & HIS ORCHESTRA:
Brunswick 3136 *What A Man!*.............. 5.00 - 8.00
3224 *Hobo's Prayer*.............. 7.00 - 10.00
3324 *Tell Me Tonight*.............. 5.00 - 8.00
3899 *That's What I Call Keen*.............. 5.00 - 8.00
3900 *Sentimental Baby*.............. 5.00 - 8.00
3945 *Too Busy*.............. 5.00 - 8.00
Harmograph 862 *Easy Melody*.............. 10.00 - 15.00
Paramount 20244 *Buddy's Habits*.............. 15.00 - 20.00
Paramount 20264 *Arkansas Mule*.............. 7.00 - 10.00
20266 *That Old Gang Of Mine*.............. 7.00 - 10.00
20270 *Tweet Tweet*.............. 7.00 - 10.00
20271 *Sweet Henry*.............. 7.00 - 10.00

STRAND ROOF ORCHESTRA:
Domino 3456 *Prince of Wails*.............. 15.00 - 20.00

ELLIS STRATAKOS & HIS HOTEL JUNG ORCHESTRA:
Vocalion 15792 *Weary River*.............. 25.00 - 40.00

STRAUN'S PULLMAN PORTERS:
Gennett 3005 *Casey Jones*.............. 6.00 - 10.00

HAL STUART & HIS GANG:
Bell 602 *Hot Coffee*.............. 15.00 - 20.00
Champion 15680 *Avalon Town*.............. 5.00 - 8.00

JOE SULLIVAN:
Columbia 2876-D *Gin Mill Blues*.............. 15.00 - 20.00
2925-D *Onyx Bringdown*.............. 15.00 - 20.00
Commodore 538, 540.............. 3.00 - 5.00
Decca 600 *Little Rock Getaway*.............. 7.00 - 10.00
Okeh 5496, 5531, 5647.............. 4.00 - 7.00
Vocalion 5496, 5531, 5556.............. 4.00 - 7.00

MAXINE SULLIVAN:
Victor 25802, 25810, 25894, 25895, 26124, 26132 .... 3.00 - 6.00
Vocalion 3654, 3679, 3848, 3885, 3993, 4015, 4068 .... 4.00 - 7.00

SUNNY AND THE D'C'NS:
Blu-Disc 1003 *Oh- How I Love My Darling!*.... 150.00 - 250.00

SUNSET DANCE ORCHESTRA:
Champion 15038 *High Society*.............. 20.00 - 30.00

THE SUNSHINE BOYS:
Columbia 1834-D, 2303-D.............. 4.00 - 7.00

SUPER SYNCOPATORS:
Autograph (unnumbered) *Jimtown Blues*....... 30.00 - 50.00
625 *South Bound*.............. 30.00 - 50.00

SUPERIOR DANCE KINGS:
Superior 2801 *Sweet Georgia Brown*.......... . . .

WILBUR (C.) SWEATMAN'S ORIGINAL JAZZ BAND/ORCHESTRA; WILBUR SWEATMAN'S BROWNIES; WILBUR SWEATMAN (& HIS ACME SYNCOPATORS/JAZZ BAND/ORCHESTRA):
Columbia A-2611, A-2645, A-2663, A-2682, A-2707, A-2721, A-2752, A-2768, A-2775, A-2818, A-2994 .... 3.00 - 6.00
Edison 51438 *Battleship Kate*.............. 10.00 - 15.00
Emerson 5163, 7161, (6 and 7 inch records)..... 6.00 - 10.00
Gennett 5584 *Battleship Kate*.............. 15.00 - 20.00
Pathe 20145, 20147, 20167.............. 7.00 - 10.00
Victor 23254 *Got 'Em Blues*.............. 15.00 - 20.00

38597 *Sweat Blues*.............. 15.00 - 20.00
Vocalion 2945 *Battleship Kate*.............. 7.00 - 10.00
2983 *The Hooking Cow Blues*.............. 9.00 - 12.00

SAMMY SWIFT'S JAZZ BAND:
Black Swan 2042 *Blue Danube Blues*.......... 10.00 - 15.00
2082 *The Carolina Shout*.............. 10.00 - 15.00
2113 *That Red-Head Gal*.............. 10.00 - 15.00
2117 *Way Down Yonder In New Orleans*.... 10.00 - 15.00
10078 *The Carolina Shout*.............. 10.00 - 15.00

JOHN(NY) SYLVESTER & HIS ORCHESTRA/ PLAYMATES;
Gennett 3384 *No-One But You*.............. 15.00 - 25.00
6026 *A Blues Serenade*.............. 15.00 - 20.00
6027 *Song Of The Wanderer*.............. 10.00 - 15.00
6056 *Indiana Butterfly*.............. 10.00 - 15.00
6061 *No-One But You*.............. 15.00 - 20.00
6095 *Mine*.............. 10.00 - 15.00
6099 *St. Louis Blues*.............. 15.00 - 20.00
Herschel Gold Seal 2010 *No-One But You*..... 15.00 - 25.00
Pathe-Actuelle 036086 *Sweet Man Joe*.......... 10.00 - 15.00
036154 *I Wanna Jazz Some More*.............. 10.00 - 15.00
036211 *King Porter Stomp*.............. 10.00 - 15.00
36331 *I'm Goin' Out If Lizzie Comes In*..... 8.00 - 12.00
36354 *I Would Rather Be Alone in the South*. 8.00 - 12.00
36502 *Looking at the World Thru' Rose-Colored Glasses* .... 7.00 - 10.00
36555 *Idolizing*.............. 5.00 - 8.00
36556 *I've Got The Girl*.............. 5.00 - 8.00
36599 *What's The Use?*.............. 7.00 - 10.00
Perfect 14267 *Clearing House Blues*.......... 10.00 - 15.00
14335 *Temperamental Papa*.............. 10.00 - 15.00
14512 *I'm Goin' Out If Lizzie Comes In*..... 8.00 - 12.00
14535 *I Would Rather Be Alone in the South*. 8.00 - 12.00
14683 *Looking at the World Thru' Rose-Colored Glasses* .... 7.00 - 10.00
14736 *Idolizing*.............. 5.00 - 8.00
14737 *I've Got The Girl*.............. 5.00 - 8.00
14780 *Rosie O'Ryan*.............. 7.00 - 10.00

SYNCO JAZZ BAND:
Pathe 22099, 22107, 22122, 22207.............. 6.00 - 10.00
Pathe-Actuelle 020461, 020499, 020558, 020665, 020699, 020770, 020778.............. 3.00 - 5.00

THE SYNCOPATING FIVE:
Gennett (unnumbered) *Lips*.............. 10.00 - 20.00

THE SYNCOPATING SEVEN:
Gennett (unnumbered) *Toot-Toot Tootsie*.... 100.00 - 150.00
(unnumbered) *Strutting At The Strutters' Ball*. 100.00 - 150.00

WILLIAM HOWARD TAFT:
Victor (12-inch) 35256 *Labor and Capital*..... 5.00 - 8.00

TAMPA BLUE JAZZ BAND:
Okeh 4357, 4405, 4453, 4461, 4544, 4573, 4595, 4671, 4773, 4777, 4791, 4803, 4816, 4826... 4.00 - 8.00

FRANK TANNER'S RHYTHM KINGS:
Bluebird 6667 *You Don't Love Me*.............. 7.00 - 10.00
6686 *Wrappin' It Up*.............. 7.00 - 10.00
6690 *Sailor Man Rhythm*.............. 7.00 - 10.00
6719 *Death In B Flat*.............. 10.00 - 15.00
6750 *Texas Teaser*.............. 7.00 - 10.00

CARROLL C. TATE:
Victor 21061 *You Live On In Memory*........ 10.00 - 15.00

ERSKINE TATE'S VENDOME ORCHESTRA:
Okeh 4907 *Chinaman Blues*.............. 50.00 - 80.00
Vocalion 1027 *Static Strut*.............. 75.00 - 100.00
15372 *Static Strut*.............. 75.00 - 100.00

ART TATUM (& HIS BAND/SWINGSTERS):
Brunswick 6543 *St. Louis Blues*.............. 8.00 - 12.00
6553 *Tea For Two*.............. 8.00 - 12.00
Decca 155 *Moon Glow*.............. 7.00 - 10.00
156 *Cocktails For Two*.............. 7.00 - 10.00
306 *Star Dust*.............. 7.00 - 10.00
468 *The Shout*.............. 7.00 - 10.00

741 *When A Woman Loves A Man*........	7.00 -	10.00
1197 *Body And Soul*..................	7.00 -	10.00
1198 *With Plenty Of Money And You*......	7.00 -	10.00
1373 *(I Would Do) Anything For You*......	7.00 -	10.00
1603 *Stormy Weather*................	7.00 -	10.00
2052 *The Skeik Of Araby*.............	5.00 -	8.00
2456 *Tea For Two*..................	4.00 -	7.00
8526 *Battery Bounce*................	7.00 -	10.00
8536 *Stompin' At The Savoy*..........	7.00 -	10.00
8563 *Corrine Corrina*...............	7.00 -	10.00
8577 *Rock Me, Mama*...............	7.00 -	10.00

JASPER TAYLOR & HIS ORIGINAL WASHBOARD BAND/STATE STREET BOYS:

Paramount 12409 *Stomp Time Blues*..........	90.00 -	125.00
Vocalion 1196 *Jasper Taylor Blues*...........	80.00 -	100.00

RAY/ROY TAYLOR & HIS (SINGING) ORCHESTRA:

Champion 15342 *Somebody And Me*.........	10.00 -	15.00
15343 *Show Me That Kind Of A Girl*......	10.00 -	15.00
Superior 356 *Sweet Violets*.............	15.00 -	20.00
359 *Show Me That Kind Of A Girl*........	15.00 -	20.00

TAYLOR'S DIXIE ORCHESTRA:

Victor 23277 *Everybody Loves My Baby*.......	35.00 -	50.00

JACK TEAGARDEN (& HIS CHICAGOANS/ORCHESTRA):

Brunswick 6716 *A Hundred Years From Today*.	8.00 -	12.00
6741 *Blue River*....................	8.00 -	12.00
6780 *Ol' Pappy*....................	8.00 -	12.00
6993 *Stars Fell On Alabama*...........	8.00 -	12.00
7652 *Junk Man*....................	8.00 -	12.00
Columbia 2588-D *You Rascal, You*..........	15.00 -	20.00
2803-D *Shake Your Hips*.............	15.00 -	20.00
2913-D *Plantation Moods*.............	15.00 -	20.00
35206, 35215, 35224, 35233, 35245, 35252, 35297, 35323	4.00 -	7.00
Crown 3051 *Rockin' Chair*..............	20.00 -	30.00
Domino 4646 *Just A Little Dance, Mam'selle*...	7.00 -	10.00
4651 *Son Of The Sun*...............	7.00 -	10.00
Hot Record Society 2006, 2007............	4.00 -	7.00
Perfect 15361 *You're Simply Delish*..........	9.00 -	12.00
15363 *Son Of The Sun*.............	7.00 -	10.00

THE TEMPO KINGS:

Pathe-Actuelle 36385 *Rhythm Of The Day*.....	7.00 -	10.00
Perfect 14566 *Rhythm Of The Day*...........	7.00 -	10.00

TEN BLACK BERRIES:

Titles, issued contemporaneously on Banner, Cameo, Challenge, Conqueror, Domino, Jewel, Oriole, Perfect, Regal, Romeo: *Jungle Blues; Rent Party Blues; St. James Infirmary; When You're Smiling*	10.00 -	15.00
Banner 0839 *Tiger Rag*..............	8.00 -	12.00
Jewel 6089 *Tiger Rag*..............	8.00 -	12.00
Oriole 2089 *St. Louis Blues*...........	8.00 -	12.00
Regal 10145 *St. Louis Blues*...........	8.00 -	12.00
Romeo 976 *Sorority Stomp*............	10.00 -	15.00
1453 *Tiger Rag*.................	8.00 -	12.00

TEN BLACK DIAMONDS:

Freshman Hop, issued contemporaneously on Banner, Cameo, Romeo	10.00 -	15.00

TEN FRESHMEN:

Pathe-Actuelle 37054 *Bag O' Blues*...........	10.00 -	15.00
Perfect 15235 *Bag O' Blues*............	10.00 -	15.00

TENNESSEE CHOCOLATE DROPS:

Vocalion 1517 *Vine Street Drag*..............	20.00 -	30.00

TENNESSEE MUSIC MEN:

Clarion 5389-C *Georgia On My Mind*........	15.00 -	20.00
5392-C *You Rascal You*.............	15.00 -	20.00
5446-C *Loveless Love*..............	15.00 -	20.00
5461-C *Bugle Call Rag*.............	15.00 -	20.00
5467-C *Choo Choo*................	15.00 -	20.00

5469-C *Baby Won't You Pleasee Come Home*.	15.00 -	20.00
5474-C *Shim-Me-Sha-Wabble*..............	12.00 -	16.00
Harmony 1375-H *Georgia On My Mind*.......	15.00 -	20.00
1378-H *You Rascal You*.............	15.00 -	20.00
1406-H *Loveless Love*..............	15.00 -	20.00
1415-H *Bugle Call Rag*.............	15.00 -	20.00
1420-H *Choo Choo*................	15.00 -	20.00
1422-H *Baby, Won't You Please Come Home*.	15.00 -	20.00
1427-H *Shim-Me-Sha-Wabble*...........	12.00 -	16.00
Velvet Tone 2453-V *Georgia On My Mind*.....	15.00 -	20.00
2456-V *You Rascal You*.............	15.00 -	20.00
2506-V *Loveless Love*..............	15.00 -	20.00
2521-V *Bugle Call Rag*.............	15.00 -	20.00
2527-V *Choo Choo*................	15.00 -	20.00
2529-V *Baby, Won't You Please Come Home*.	15.00 -	20.00
2534-V *Shim-Me-Sha-Wabble*...........	12.00 -	16.00

THE TENNESSEE TOOTERS:

Vocalion 14952 *Prince Of Wails*..............	10.00 -	15.00
14967 *Hot-Hot-Hottentot*..............	10.00 -	15.00
14985 *Everybody Loves My Baby*..........	10.00 -	15.00
15004 *Red Hot Henry Brown*...........	8.00 -	12.00
15022 *Jimtown Blues*...............	8.00 -	12.00
15068 *Milenberg Joys*..............	8.00 -	12.00
15086 *Charleston*................	8.00 -	12.00
15109 *Deep Elm*.................	8.00 -	12.00
15135 *I Ain't Got Nobody*...........	8.00 -	12.00
15169 *Hot Aire*.................	8.00 -	12.00
15201 *Fallin' Down*...............	8.00 -	12.00
15388 *Hobo's Prayer*..............	10.00 -	15.00
15487 *Crazy Quilt*...............	8.00 -	12.00
15488 *You're Burnin' Me Up*.........	8.00 -	12.00

BOB TERRY & HIS ORCHESTRA:

Champion 40093 *My Heart And I*...........	8.00 -	12.00
40094 *It's Been So Long*...........	8.00 -	12.00

THELMA TERRY & HER PLAY BOYS:

Columbia 1390-D *Voice of the Southland*......	8.00 -	12.00
1532-D *Starlight and Tulips*...........	4.00 -	7.00
1588-D *Dusky Stevedore*............	8.00 -	12.00
1706-D *Mama's Gone, Goodbye*..........	8.00 -	12.00

TEXAS BLUES DESTROYERS:

Ajax 17065 *Lenox Avenue Shuffle*...........	15.00 -	20.00
Pathe-Actuelle 036160 *Lenox Avenue Shuffle*...	15.00 -	20.00
Perfect 14314 *Lenox Avenue Shuffle*........	15.00 -	20.00
Vocalion 14913 *Lenox Avenue Shuffle*........	15.00 -	20.00

TEXAS TEN:

Banner 1540 *Sweet Georgia Brown*...........	5.00 -	8.00
Regal 9835 *Charleston*................	5.00 -	8.00

TEXAS TODDLERS:

Varsity 5081 *Keepin' Out Of Mischief Now*....	5.00 -	8.00

THEM BIRMINGHAM NIGHT OWLS:

Champion 15338 *Sugar*.................	80.00 -	120.00

HENRY THIES AND HIS (CASTLE FARM/HOTEL SINTON) ORCHESTRA:

Gennett 3118 *Angry*.............	10.00 -	15.00
Victor 21890 *Sweet Liza*.............	5.00 -	8.00
22476 *Here Comes Emily Brown*..........	7.00 -	10.00

THOMAS' DEVILS:
Brunswick 7064 *Boot It, Boy*.............. 35.00 - 50.00
THOMAS' MUSCLE SHOALS DEVILS:
Okeh 8225 *Wash Woman Blues*............. 30.00 - 50.00
EDDIE THOMAS' COLLEGIANS:
Columbia 1154-D *Sugar*................. 5.00 - 8.00
GEORGE THOMAS & HIS BOYS:
Champion 15434 *Blue Hawaii*............. 35.00 - 50.00
HERSAL THOMAS:
Okeh 8227 *Suitcase Blues*................ 15.00 - 25.00
HOCIEL THOMAS:
Buddy 8020 *I Must Have It*.............. 15.00 - 25.00
  8021 *Worried Down With The Blues*........ 15.00 - 25.00
Gennett 3004 *I Can't Feel Frisky Without My Liquor* 15.00 - 25.00
  3006 *I Must Have It*.................. 15.00 - 25.00
Okeh 8222 *Fish Tail Dance*............... 15.00 - 25.00
  8258 *Adam And Eve Got The Blues*........ 35.00 - 50.00
  8289 *Gambler's Dream*................. 35.00 - 50.00
  8297 *Deep Water Blues*............... 35.00 - 50.00
  8326 *Sunshine Baby*................. 35.00 - 50.00
  8346 *Listen To Ma*................. 35.00 - 50.00
HOWARD THOMAS & HIS ORCHESTRA:
Champion 16380 *Business In F*........... 30.00 - 40.00
  16387 *In The Shade Of The Old Apple Tree*.. 15.00 - 20.00
  16656 *Rose Of Washington Square*......... 15.00 - 20.00
  40080 *Business In F*................. 15.00 - 20.00
MILLARD G. THOMAS (& HIS CHICAGO
NOVELTY ORCHESTRA):
Ajax 17045 *Lazy Drag*................ 15.00 - 20.00
  17052 *More*................. 15.00 - 20.00
  17053 *Hard Luck Blues*.............. 15.00 - 20.00
  17056 *Worryin' Blues*.............. 15.00 - 20.00
  17074 *Blue Ivories*................. 15.00 - 20.00
JOHNNY THOMPSON:
Columbia 14285-D *Back In Your Own Backyard* 8.00 - 12.00
KAY THOMPSON AND THE BOYS/HER
ORCHESTRA:
Brunswick 7560 *You Hit The Spot*........ 8.00 - 12.00
  7564 *Out Of Sight, Out Of Mind*.......... 8.00 - 12.00
Victor 25564 *There's A Lull In My Life*....... 5.00 - 8.00
  25582 *It Had To Be You*................ 5.00 - 8.00
CLAUDE THORNHILL AND HIS
ORCHESTRA:
Brunswick 7951, 7957................. 4.00 - 7.00
Columbia, most issues................. 2.00 - 4.00
Harmony 1038 *Lullaby of the Rain*........ 4.00 - 7.00
Okeh 6124, 6168, 6178, 6202, 6234....... 3.00 - 5.00
V-Disc (12-inch) 612 *Stealin' Apples*....... 5.00 - 8.00
Vocalion 3595 *Gone With The Wind*........ 5.00 - 8.00
  3616 *Stop! You're Breaking My Heart*....... 5.00 - 8.00
THE THREE BARBERS:
Pathe-Actuelle 36414 *Down Town Rag*....... 10.00 - 15.00
Perfect 14565 *Down Town Rag*........ 10.00 - 15.00
THREE BLACK DIAMONDS:
Lincoln 2331 *Freakish Blues*............. 7.00 - 10.00
THREE BLUES CHASERS:
Okeh 8595 *Nothin' But Blues*............. 7.00 - 10.00
THE THREE BOSWELL SISTERS:
Okeh 41444 *Heebie Jeebies*............. 10.00 - 15.00
  41470 *Gee, But I'd Like To Make You Happy* 10.00 - 15.00
THE THREE DEUCES:
Commodore 537, 539.................. 3.00 - 5.00
THREE HAPPY DANDIES:
Silvertone 3057 *Freakish Blues*............ 8.00 - 12.00
THREE HOT ESKIMOS:
Pathe-Actuelle 036298 *Black Cat Blues*........ 7.00 - 10.00
Perfect 14479 *Black Cat Blues*......... 7.00 - 10.00
THE THREE JACKS:
Okeh 41102 *Chile Blues*............. 5.00 - 8.00
THREE JOLLY MINERS:
Vocalion 1003 *Pig Alley Stomp*........... 10.00 - 15.00

  1004 *Chicago Back Step*............. 10.00 - 15.00
  15009 *Freakish Blues*............. 10.00 - 15.00
  15051 *Black Cat Blues*............. 10.00 - 15.00
  15087 *Lake George Blues*............. 10.00 - 15.00
  15111 *Plain Old Blues*............. 10.00 - 15.00
  15141 *Texas Shuffle*............. 10.00 - 15.00
  15164 *House Party Stomp*............. 10.00 - 15.00
  15269 *Pig Alley Stomp*............. 10.00 - 15.00
  15271 *Chicago Back Step*............. 10.00 - 15.00
THE THREE KEYS:
Brunswick 6388 *Jig Time*............. 7.00 - 10.00
  6411 *Nagasaki*............. 7.00 - 10.00
  6423 *Wah-Dee-Dah*............. 5.00 - 8.00
  6522 *That Doggone Dog of Mine*............. 5.00 - 8.00
  6567 *Rasputin*............. 5.00 - 8.00
Columbia 2706-D *Mood Indigo*............. 7.00 - 10.00
Vocalion 2523 *Heebie Jeebies*............. 7.00 - 10.00
  2569 *I Found A New Baby*............. 7.00 - 10.00
Vocalion 2730 *Someone Stole Gabriel's Horn*... 7.00 - 10.00
  2732 *Fit as a Fiddle*............. 7.00 - 10.00
  2744 *Basin Street Blues*............. 5.00 - 8.00
  2755 *(I Would Do) Anything For You*....... 5.00 - 8.00
  2765 *Oh! By Jingo*............. 5.00 - 8.00
THREE MONKEY CHASERS:
Harmony 23-H *Corn Bread Wiggle*............. 5.00 - 8.00
  50-H *Uncle Remus Stomp*............. 5.00 - 8.00
THE THREE PEPPERS:
Decca 2239, 2557, 2609, 2751, 3342, 8508... 4.00 - 7.00
Variety 523 *Alexander's Ragtime Band*........ 5.00 - 8.00
  590 *The Duck's Yas Yas*............. 5.00 - 8.00
  630 *Serenade in the Night*............. 5.00 - 8.00
  650 *Swingin' at the Cotton Club*............. 5.00 - 8.00
Vocalion 3803 *Swing Out, Uncle Wilson*....... 5.00 - 8.00
  3805 *The Midnight Ride of Paul Revere*..... 5.00 - 8.00
THREE'S A CROWD:
Bluebird 10014, 10051, 10160............. 4.00 - 7.00
THE THREE T'S:
Victor 25273 *I'se A Muggin'*................ 5.00 - 8.00
THREE-FIFTEEN & HIS SQUARES:
Vocalion 03515 *Three Fifteen Blues*.......... 15.00 - 20.00
  03560 *Mollie Mae Blues*............. 15.00 - 20.00
BUD THURSTON:
Champion 15489 *My Senorita*.............. 12.00 - 15.00
LE ROY TIBBS & HIS CONNIE'S INN
ORCHESTRA:
Columbia 14309-D *One O'Clock Blues*......... 20.00 - 30.00
TIM TIMOTHY & HIS FRIVOLITY CLUB
ORCHESTRA:
Edison 52311 *My Pet*...................... 7.00 - 10.00
KLIEN TINDULL'S PARAMOUNT
SERENADERS:
Paramount 12377 *Down On The Amazon*...... 20.00 - 30.00
THE TIN PAN PARADERS:
Gennett 6456 *My Pet*.................... 7.00 - 10.00
  6488 *Mama's Grown Young, Papa's Grown Old* 7.00 - 10.00
  6504 *Who Wouldn't Be Blue*............. 7.00 - 10.00
  6520 *When Sweet Susie Goes Steppin' By*.... 7.00 - 10.00
  6849 *She Only Laughs At Me*............. 7.00 - 10.00
  6921 *Believe It Or Not*............. 7.00 - 10.00
  6965 *If I Were You I'd Fall In Love With Me* 7.00 - 10.00
  6967 *I'm Finding The Long Way Home*...... 7.00 - 10.00
  7012 *Clowning*............. 7.00 - 10.00
  7072 *Wake Up Your Feet*............. 7.00 - 10.00
  7132 *Harmonica Harry*............. 10.00 - 15.00
  7146 *You've Got That Thing*............. 10.00 - 15.00
  7148 *Puttin' On The Ritz*............. 10.00 - 15.00
  7174 *Chinnin' and Chattin' with May*............. 10.00 - 15.00
Supertone 9333 *My Scandinavian Gal*........ 5.00 - 8.00
  9416 *She Only Laughs At Me*............. 5.00 - 8.00
  9464 *Now I'm In Love*............. 5.00 - 8.00
  9477 *I Lift Up My Finger and I Say "Tweet Tweet"* 5.00 - 8.00

9544 *I Gotta Have You*................... 5.00 - 8.00
9616 *The Man From The South*........... 8.00 - 12.00
9620 *Just Can't Be Bothered With Me*...... 8.00 - 12.00
9634 *The Free And Easy*.............. 8.00 - 12.00
TINSLEY'S WASHBOARD BAND:
Victor 24405 *Shoutin' In The Amen Corner*.... 12.00 - 16.00
BEN TOBIER & HIS CALIFORNIA CYCLONES:
Champion 16425 *Hot And Heavy*............. 20.00 - 30.00
Superior 2571 *Hot And Heavy*.............. 20.00 - 30.00
TOBIN'S MIDNIGHT SERENADERS:
Okeh 40297 *I'm Afraid To Care For You*...... 25.00 - 35.00
SKEETS TOLBERT AND HIS GENTLEMEN OF SWING:
Decca 7570, 7591, 7630, 7653, 7669, 7717, 7722, 7751, 7791, 8506, 8516, 8528, 8534, 8565, 8579, 8589, 8608, 8617, 8631, 8641 .... 4.00 - 8.00
TOM AND JERRY:
Champion 15507 *Dustin' The Keys*.......... 20.00 - 30.00
PINKY TOMLIN:
Brunswick 7377, 7378, 7502, 7525, 7594, 7653, 7731, 7811, 7849, 7897 .... 4.00 - 7.00
TOMMY "RED" TOMPKINS & HIS ORCHESTRA:
Variety 543 *Monopoly Swing*............ 7.00 - 10.00
610 *I Never Had a Dream*........... 7.00 - 10.00
Vocalion 3271 *What The Heart Believes*...... 7.00 - 10.00
3293 *Viper's Dream*.............. 7.00 - 10.00
TRAM, BIX & EDDIE:
Okeh 40871 *For No Reason At All In C*....... 20.00 - 30.00
TRAM, BIX & LANG:
Okeh 40916 *Wringin' And Twistin'*........... 20.00 - 30.00
THE TRAVELERS:
Melotone 12113 *Sweet And Hot*............ 8.00 - 12.00
12148 *I've Got A Sweet Somebody*........ 8.00 - 12.00
12227 *I Apologize*................ 6.00 - 10.00
12230 *I Can't Get Mississippi Off My Mind*.. 15.00 - 25.00
Okeh 41259 *Am I Blue*............. 7.00 - 12.00
41260 *Breakaway*................ 7.00 - 12.00
41471 *Fine And Dandy*............. 7.00 - 12.00
VINCENT TRAVERS AND HIS ORCHESTRA:
Titles, issued contemporaneously on Banner, Melotone, Oriole, Perfect, Romeo, Vocalion: *Love Is Good For Anything That Ails You; Was It Rain?* .... 5.00 - 8.00
TRAVIS-CARLTON ORCHESTRA:
Gennett 3099 *Headin' For Home*............ 8.00 - 12.00
3216 *Somebody's Eyes*.......... 8.00 - 12.00
THE TRAYMORE ORCHESTRA:
Vocalion 15556 *Black And Tan Fantasy*....... 15.00 - 20.00
PAUL TRAMAINE AND HIS ARISTOCRATS/ORCHESTRA:
Columbia 2130-D, 2200-D, 2229-D............ 4.00 - 8.00
Columbia 2302-D *Gospel Train*.......... 5.00 - 8.00
2462-D *I Wanna Sing About You*......... 7.00 - 10.00
2510-D *I Can't Get Mississippi Off My Mind*. 7.00 - 10.00
Victor V-40176 *Four-Four Rhythm*.......... 15.00 - 20.00
V-40230 *Sarah Lee*.............. 10.00 - 15.00
GEORGE H. TREMER:
Gennett 6242 *Spirit Of '49 Rag*......... 40.00 - 60.00
ALPHONSE TRENT & HIS ORCHESTRA:
Champion 15956 *St. James Infirmary*......... 60.00 - 80.00
16587 *I've Found A New Baby*......... 60.00 - 80.00
Gennett 6664 *Louder and Funnier*........... 60.00 - 80.00
6710 *Nightmare*.............. 60.00 - 80.00
JO TRENT AND THE D'C'NS:
Blu-Disc 1003 *Deacon Jazz*.......... 125.00 - 250.00
TRIANGLE HARMONY BOYS:
Gennett 6275 *Sweet Patootie*................. 75.00 - 100.00
6322 *Canned Heat Blues*.............. 75.00 - 100.00
TROMBONE RED AND HIS BLUE SIX:

Columbia 14612-D *Greasy Plate Stomp*........ 40.00 - 60.00
CHARLIE TROUTT'S MELODY ARTISTS:
Columbia 1030-D *Transportation Blues*......... 5.00 - 8.00
1265-D *Transportation Blues, Parts 3/4*...... 5.00 - 8.00
Okeh 40589 *Mountain City Blues*............. 15.00 - 20.00
40627 *Sweet Child (I'm Wild About You)*.... 25.00 - 40.00
THE TROY HARMONISTS:
Pathe-Actuelle 7508 *Great Scott*.............. 15.00 - 20.00
Perfect 108 *Great Scott*.............. 15.00 - 20.00
FRANKIE TRUMBAUER & HIS ORCHESTRA; FRANKIE TRUMBAUER'S AUGMENTED ORCHESTRA:
Brunswick 6146 *Crazy Quilt*................. 8.00 - 12.00
6159 *Honeysuckle Rose*................. 8.00 - 12.00
6763 *Juba Dance*................. 7.00 - 10.00
6788 *Emaline*.................. 7.00 - 10.00
6912 *China Boy*................ 7.00 - 10.00
6997 *In A Mist*................. 7.00 - 10.00
7613 *Breakin' In A Pair Of Shoes*... 7.00 - 10.00
7629 *Announcer's Blues*.......... 7.00 - 10.00
7663 *'S Wonderful*............. 7.00 - 10.00
7665 *Ain't Misbehavin'*.......... 7.00 - 10.00
7687 *Diga Diga Doo*........... 7.00 - 10.00
Columbia 2710-D *Business In Q*........ 10.00 - 15.00
2729-D *The Newest St. Louis Blues*.... 10.00 - 15.00
2879-D *Bass Drum Dan*.......... 10.00 - 15.00
18002-D *Sizzling One-Step Medley*.... 8.00 - 12.00
Okeh 40772 *Singin' The Blues*............ 15.00 - 20.00
40822 *Ostrich Walk*............ 20.00 - 30.00
40843 *I'm Coming, Virginia*......... 20.00 - 30.00
40871 *Trumbology*............. 20.00 - 30.00
40879 *Blue River*............. 20.00 - 30.00
40903 *Three Blind Mice*......... 20.00 - 30.00
40926 *Humpty Dumpty*........... 20.00 - 30.00
40966 *A Good Man Is Hard To Find*..... 20.00 - 30.00
40979 *There'll Come A Time*...... 20.00 - 30.00
41019 *Lila*............. 20.00 - 30.00
Okeh 41039 *My Pet*............. 20.00 - 30.00
41044 *Jubilee*............ 20.00 - 30.00
41100 *Dusky Stevedore*......... 20.00 - 30.00
41128 *High Up On A Hill Top*..... 20.00 - 30.00
41145 *Take Your Tomorrow*........ 20.00 - 30.00
41209 *Futuristic Rhythm*........ 20.00 - 30.00
41231 *Louise*............. 20.00 - 30.00
41252 *Nobody But You*......... 15.00 - 20.00
41268 *Shivery Stomp*......... 15.00 - 20.00
41286 *Baby, Won't You Please Come Home?*. 20.00 - 30.00
41301 *How Am I To Know?*...... 10.00 - 15.00
41313 *Turn On The Heat*....... 10.00 - 15.00
41326 *My Sweeter Than Sweet*......... 10.00 - 15.00
41330 *What Wouldn't I Do For That Man?*.. 10.00 - 15.00
41421 *Happy Feet*......... 15.00 - 20.00
41431 *Deep Harlem*......... 15.00 - 20.00
41432 *What's The Use?*........ 15.00 - 20.00
41450 *Choo Choo*........ 15.00 - 20.00
Victor 24812 *Blue Moon*................. 8.00 - 12.00
24834 *Troubled*............. 8.00 - 12.00
TRUMP'S AMBASSADOR BELL HOPS ORCHESTRA:
Okeh 1 *What A Man*..................... . . .
GEORGE TUCKER & HIS NOVELTY BAND:
Champion 15638 *Doin' The New Low Down*... 25.00 - 40.00
15639 *Spiked Beer*............. 25.00 - 40.00
ORRIN TUCKER AND HIS ORCHESTRA:
Columbia, most issues............. 2.00 - 5.00
Vocalion, most issues............. 3.00 - 6.00
SOPHIE TUCKER:
Columbia 826-D *Some Of These Days*........ 4.00 - 8.00
Okeh 4565, 4590, 4617, 4817, 4818, 4837, 4839, 40054, 40895, 40921, 41010, 41058, 41249.... 4.00 - 8.00
Okeh 40068 *I've Got a Cross-Eyed Papa*....... 8.00 - 12.00

40129 *Hula Lou*	8.00 -	12.00
40813 *One Sweet Letter From You*	8.00 -	12.00
40837 *After You've Gone*	8.00 -	12.00
Victor 21993, 21994, 21995, 22049	4.00 -	8.00

AL TURK'S (PRINCESS) ORCHESTRA:

Okeh 8362 *Snag It*	30.00 -	50.00
8377 *Mean Man*	30.00 -	50.00
40648 *I'm Just Wild About Animal Crackers*	20.00 -	30.00
40653 *Snag It*	20.00 -	30.00
40660 *Shanghai Honeymoon*	20.00 -	30.00
Olympic 1461 *Copenhagen*	25.00 -	40.00
1463 *King Porter Stomp*	25.00 -	40.00

JOE TURNER AND HIS MEMPHIS MEN:

Columbia 1813-D *Freeze And Melt*	15.00 -	20.00

LLOYD TURNER AND HIS VILLA VENICE ORCHESTRA:

Okeh 40674 *My Mama's In Town*	7.00 -	10.00

TUXEDO SYNCOPATORS:

Titles, issued contemporaneously on Globe, Madison:

Horse Feathers; Torrid Rhythm; Zoolithique.	15.00 -	25.00

TWIN CITIES DANCE ORCHESTRA:

Challenge 257 *I'm Looking Over A Four-Leaf Clover*	15.00 -	20.00

TWIN CITY BELL HOPS:

Champion 15174 *No-One But You*	15.00 -	25.00

TWO BLACK CROWS (See MORAN & MACK):

SUGAR UNDERWOOD:

Victor 21538 *Dew Drop Alley Stomp*	15.00 -	20.00

UNIVERSAL DANCE ORCHESTRA:

Madison 1620 *Pepper Blues*	8.00 -	12.00

UNIVERSAL SEXTETTE:

Lincoln 2417 *Milenberg Joys*	6.00 -	10.00

UNIVERSITY EIGHT:

Lincoln 2543 *Ya Gotta Know How To Love*	5.00 -	8.00
2566 *She Knows Her Onions*	5.00 -	8.00
2606 *Crazy Words-Crazy Tune*	5.00 -	8.00
2626 *Ain't She Sweet?*	5.00 -	8.00
2674 *Arkansas Blues*	7.00 -	10.00

UNIVERSITY ORCHESTRA:

Gennett 6815 *Button Up Your Overcoat*	8.00 -	12.00
6862 *I've Got A Feeling I'm Falling*	8.00 -	12.00
6892 *Singin' in the Rain*	8.00 -	12.00
6920 *I'm In Seventh Heaven*	8.00 -	12.00
6980 *Hang On To Me*	8.00 -	12.00
7011 *Miss Wonderful*	8.00 -	12.00
7042 *Lady Luck*	8.00 -	12.00
7117 *Happy Days Are Here Again*	8.00 -	12.00
7234 *Swingin' in a Hammock*	8.00 -	12.00
7257 *Hullabaloo*	15.00 -	20.00

UNIVERSITY SEXTETTE:

Lincoln 2093, 2105, 2116, 2127, 2130, 2142, 2154, 2166, 2167, 2176, 2216, 2219, 2229, 2231, 2241, 2242	4.00 -	7.00
Lincoln 2168 *Mean Blues*	5.00 -	8.00
2208 *Doodle Doo Doo*	5.00 -	8.00
2238 *Hard Hearted Hannah*	5.00 -	8.00
2245 *She Loves Me*	5.00 -	8.00
2256 *A New Kind Of Man*	5.00 -	8.00
2264 *Talkin' To Myself*	4.00 -	8.00
2268 *Copenhagen*	7.00 -	10.00
2270 *Them Ramblin' Blues*	5.00 -	8.00
2276 *Dear One*	5.00 -	8.00
2279 *I'm Satisfied Beside That Sweetie O'Mine*	5.00 -	8.00
Lincoln 2288 *Doo Wacka Doo*	5.00 -	8.00
2290 *Oh! Mabel*	5.00 -	8.00
2302 *Happy*	5.00 -	8.00
2306 *I Ain't Got Nobody To Love*	5.00 -	8.00
2307 *Ain't My Baby Grand*	5.00 -	8.00
2311 *I Like You Best Of All*	5.00 -	8.00
2315 *No One*	5.00 -	8.00
2328 *Nobody Knows What A Red Head Mama Can Do*	5.00 -	8.00

2330 *Don't Bring Lulu*	5.00 -	8.00
2337 *Cheatin' On Me*	5.00 -	8.00
2339 *Lady of the Nile*	4.00 -	7.00
2340 *Sweet Georgia Brown*	6.00 -	10.00
2343 *Ah Ha!*	5.00 -	8.00
2352 *If You Knew Susie*	5.00 -	8.00
2355 *Charleston*	5.00 -	8.00
2371 *Yes, Sir! That's My Baby*	5.00 -	8.00
2380 *Oh, Say! Can I See You Tonight?*	5.00 -	8.00
2382 *I Want To See A Little More Of What I Saw In Arkansas*	5.00 -	8.00
2387 *Tryin' To Keep Away From You*	5.00 -	8.00
2403 *Sweet Man*	7.00 -	10.00
2435 *Show Me The Way To Go Home*	5.00 -	8.00
2441 *Freshie*	5.00 -	8.00
2463 *In My Gondola*	5.00 -	8.00
2517 *What a Man!*	5.00 -	8.00
2557 *Static Strut*	7.00 -	10.00
2578 *Lay Me Down To Sleep In Carolina*	5.00 -	8.00
2598 *Lonely Eyes*	5.00 -	8.00
2697 *Vo-Do-Do-De-O Blues*	8.00 -	12.00
2745 *Is She My Girl Friend?*	7.00 -	10.00
2795 *Farewell Blues*	8.00 -	12.00
2809 *Steamboat Bill*	8.00 -	12.00
2864 *On The Vagabond Trail*	4.00 -	6.00
2865 *Mother*	4.00 -	6.00
3260 *What Do We Get From Boston?*	5.00 -	8.00

UNIVERSITY SIX:

Harmony 36-H *The Camel Walk*	7.00 -	10.00
37-H *Desdemona*	7.00 -	10.00
71-H *Smile a Little Bit*	7.00 -	10.00
73-H *In Your Green Hat*	7.00 -	10.00
106-H *Fallin' Down*	8.00 -	12.00
134-H *Dustin' The Donkey*	8.00 -	12.00
155-H *Georgianna*	7.00 -	10.00
160-H *Sittin' Around*	7.00 -	10.00
209-H *Ace In The Hole*	10.00 -	15.00
224-H *Tiger Rag*	10.00 -	15.00
230-H *I Ain't Got Nobody*	8.00 -	12.00
245-H *St. Louis Hop*	8.00 -	12.00
262-H *That's A Good Girl*	7.00 -	10.00
296-H *My Baby Knows How*	7.00 -	10.00
316-H *It Takes A Good Woman*	7.00 -	10.00
Harmony 367-H *The Cat*	8.00 -	12.00
382-H *It's OK Katy With Me*	7.00 -	10.00
399-H *Rosy Cheeks*	5.00 -	8.00
414-H *Beale Street Blues*	10.00 -	15.00
425-H *Yes She Do . No She Don't*	7.00 -	10.00
433-H *Lazy Weather*	5.00 -	8.00
444-H *Bless Her Little Heart*	5.00 -	8.00
466-H *Swanee Shore*	5.00 -	8.00
474-H *Pastafazoola*	5.00 -	8.00
489-H *Oh, Doris! Where Do You Live?*	5.00 -	8.00
510-H *Zulu Wail*	7.00 -	10.00
529-H *Manhattan Mary*	5.00 -	8.00
534-H *Is She My Girl Friend?*	5.00 -	8.00
551-H *Changes*	5.00 -	8.00
557-H *Tell Me, Little Daisy*	5.00 -	8.00
565-H *Mine - All Mine*	5.00 -	8.00
570-H *Under The Clover Moon*	5.00 -	8.00
581-H *Let A Smile Be Your Umbrella*	5.00 -	8.00
591-H *What Do You Say?*	5.00 -	8.00
617-H *Stay Out Of The South*	5.00 -	8.00
619-H *Speedy Boy*	5.00 -	8.00
652-H *Chilly-Pom-Pom-Pee*	4.00 -	7.00
653-H *C-O-N-S-T-A-N-T-I-N-O-P-L-E*	4.00 -	7.00

(Note: Above titles, issued also on Diva and Velvet Tone, are of equal value and interest.)

THE VAGABONDS:

Gennett 3099 *I'm Gonna Charleston Back To Charleston*	8.00 -	12.00
3100 *Ukelele Lady*	8.00 -	12.00

3128 *Normandy*	7.00 -	10.00
3137 *Sweet Man*	8.00 -	12.00
3282 *Could I? I Certainly Could*	8.00 -	12.00
3283 *I'd Climb The Highest Mountain*	8.00 -	12.00
3361 *The Birth of the Blues*	10.00 -	15.00
3362 *Looking at the World Thru' Rose-Colored Glasses*	8.00 -	12.00
5288 *Rememb'ring*	5.00 -	8.00
5291 *Sittin' In A Corner*	5.00 -	8.00
5362 *California, Here I Come*	5.00 -	8.00
5447 *Shine*	7.00 -	10.00
5448 *Don't Mind The Rain*	7.00 -	10.00
5485 *Where The Dreamy Wabash Flows*	7.00 -	10.00
5501 *Nobody's Child*	7.00 -	10.00
5502 *Knock at the Door*	7.00 -	10.00
5504 *You Know Me, Alabam!*	7.00 -	10.00
5529 *Sing a Little Song*	7.00 -	10.00
5539 *I Want To Be Happy*	7.00 -	10.00
5540 *Rose Marie*	7.00 -	10.00
5568 *Nancy*	7.00 -	10.00
5602 *Back Where The Daffodils Grow*	7.00 -	10.00
5630 *Somebody Like You*	7.00 -	10.00
Gennett 6398 *You Gotta Be Good To Me*	10.00 -	15.00

SYD VALENTINE & HIS PATENT LEATHER KIDS:

Gennett 7026 *Patent Leather Stomp*	50.00 -	75.00
7071 *Asphalt Walk*	50.00 -	75.00

RUDOLPH VALENTINO:

Special Record (unnumbered) *Kashmiri Song*	30.00 -	40.00

RUDY VALLEE AND HIS CONNECTICUT YANKEES:

Titles, issued contemporaneously on Banner, Conqueror, Melotone, Oriole, Perfect, Romeo: *All's Fair In Love And War; Bojangles of Harlem' Call of the Prairie; The Coronation Waltz; Dream Time; Empty Saddles; A Fine Romance; The Glory of Love; I'm on a Wild Goose Chase; I Was Saying to the Moon; Rhythm on the Range; Seventh Heaven; She Shall Have Music; Speaking of the Weather; That's Southern Hospitality; These Foolish Things; Turn Off the Moon; Us on a Bus; The Waltz In Swing Time; The Way You Look Tonight; The Whiffenpoof Song; Who Loves You? Would You?* .... 4.00 - 8.00

Bluebird 5097, 5098, 5114, 5115, 5118, 5132, 5171, 5172, 5175, 5177, 5182, 7067, 7069, 7078, 7120, 7135, 7140, 7226, 7238, 7331, 7342, 7368, 7543, 7645, 7649, 7667	4.00 -	8.00
Columbia 2700-D *Maori*	7.00 -	10.00
2702-D *Strange Interlude*	7.00 -	10.00
2714-D *Say It Isn't So*	7.00 -	10.00
2715-D *Me Minus You*	7.00 -	10.00
2724-D *Please*	7.00 -	10.00
2725-D *Brother, Can You Spare A Dime?*	8.00 -	12.00
2730-D *Till Tomorrow*	7.00 -	10.00
2733-D *The Language Of Love*	7.00 -	10.00
2737-D *I'm Playing With Fire*	7.00 -	10.00
2738-D *A Jug Of Wine, A Loaf Of Bread*	7.00 -	10.00
2744-D *Hey! Young Fella*	7.00 -	10.00
2746-D *Pretending You Care*	7.00 -	10.00
2756-D *Meet Me In the Gloaming*	7.00 -	10.00
2764-D *Old Man Harlem*	7.00 -	10.00
2771-D *I Lay Me Down To Sleep*	7.00 -	10.00
2773-D *I've Got To Sing A Torch Song*	7.00 -	10.00

(Note: Above Columbia records are pressed of "royal blue" shellac.)

Diva 2759-G *Doin' The Raccoon*	5.00 -	8.00
Harmony 724-H *Right Out Of Heaven*	7.00 -	10.00
834-H *Caressing You*	7.00 -	10.00
Hit-of-the-Week A-3-4, B-1-2, C-1-2, C-3-4, M-4-5, MM-4-5	4.00 -	8.00

Velvet Tone 1759-V *Bye And Bye Sweetheart*	5.00 -	8.00
Victor 21868, 21869, 21880, 21924, 21963, 21967, 21983, 21998, 22029, 22034, 22062, 22084, 22090, 22118, 22136, 22193, 22196, 22227, 22261, 22284, 22321, 22361, 22412, 22419, 22435, 22445, 22473, 22489, 22506, 22545, 22560, 22572, 22574, 22585, 22595, 22611, 22615, 22672, 22679, 22742, 22751, 22752	4.00 -	8.00
Victor 22773, 22774, 22783	4.00 -	8.00
Victor 22783 *This Is The Missus*	7.00 -	10.00
Victor 24458 *My Dancing Lady*	5.00 -	8.00
24459 *Flying Down To Rio*	5.00 -	8.00
24475 *Puddin' Head Jones*	5.00 -	8.00
24476 *What Is There To Say?*	5.00 -	8.00
24554 *Goin' To Heaven on a Mule*	5.00 -	8.00
24558 *Carolina*	5.00 -	8.00
24580 *You Oughta Be In Pictures*	7.00 -	10.00
24581 *Nasty Man*	7.00 -	10.00
24642 *The Sweetest Music This Side of Heaven*	7.00 -	10.00
24646 *So Help Me*	7.00 -	10.00
24697 *Panama*	7.00 -	10.00
24702 *Somewhere in Your Heart*	7.00 -	10.00
24721 *The Drunkard Song*	7.00 -	10.00
24722 *Out in the Cold Again*	7.00 -	10.00
24723 *P.S. — I Love You*	7.00 -	10.00
24739 *The Tattooed Lady*	5.00 -	8.00

(Copies of Victor 24739 having white labels with simulated handwriting in red are not particularly scarce.

24827 *Sweet Music*	7.00 -	10.00
24833 *Fare Thee Well, Annabelle*	7.00 -	10.00
24838 *On the Good Ship Lollipop*	7.00 -	10.00
24895 *You Opened My Eyes*	5.00 -	8.00
24899 *Seein' Is Believen'*	5.00 -	8.00
25089 *His Majesty The Baby*	5.00 -	8.00
25092 *The Gentleman Obviously Doesn't Believe*	5.00 -	8.00
25109 *Plain Old Me*	5.00 -	8.00
Victor 25231, 25233, 25234, 25260, 25267, 25313, 25835, 25836	3.00 -	7.00
Victor 27823, 27841, 27842, 27843, 27844	2.00 -	4.00

VAN'S COLLEGIANS/VAN & HIS HALF MOON HOTEL ORCHESTRA:

Gennett 6472 *Louisiana*	10.00 -	15.00
6629 *My Blue Ridge Mountain Home*	10.00 -	15.00
Pathe-Actuelle 36422 *Jig Walk*	8.00 -	12.00
36432 *Whose Who Are You*	8.00 -	12.00
Perfect 14603 *Jig Walk*	8.00 -	12.00
14613 *Whose Who Are You*	8.00 -	12.00

FRED VAN EPS; VAN EPS TRIO; VAN-EPS-BANTA DANCE ORCHESTRA; VAN EPS BANJO ORCHESTRA:

Columbia A-1417, A-1593, A-1594, A-2034, A-5618	5.00 -	7.00
Edison 51324, 51514	5.00 -	7.00
Pathe 20087, 20094, 29030, 29081, 29082, 29083	7.00 -	10.00
Perfect 11160 *Grace and Beauty*	7.00 -	10.00
Victor 16667, 16845, 16934, 17033, 17168, 17308, 17575, 17601, 18376	4.00 -	7.00

PAUL VAN LOAN AND HIS ORCHESTRA:

Cameo 820 *Deep Elm*	5.00 -	8.00
848 *Pretty Little Baby*	5.00 -	8.00
853 *Cross My Heart Mother*	5.00 -	8.00

VARSITY EIGHT:

Titles, issued contemporaneously on Banner, Lincoln, Romeo: *Sorority Stomp; Dance Your Blues Away*	10.00 -	15.00

Titles, issued contemporaneously on Banner, Conqueror, Domino, Jewel, Oriole, Perfect, Regal, Romeo: *Fraternity Blues; Never Swat A Fly; One Pair Of Pants At A Time; Sweetheart Of My Student Days; Toodle-Oo; When Kentucky Bids The World 'Good Morning!'; Who's Calling You*

Sweetheart Tonight?....................	5.00 -	8.00
Cameo 400, 420, 426, 444, 445, 454, 456, 480, 505,		
507, 516, 571, 574, 580, 593, 617, 633, 640, 753	4.00 -	8.00
Cameo 498 *Mean Blues*....................	5.00 -	8.00
556 *San*..............................	5.00 -	8.00
559 *Doodle Doo Doo*...................	5.00 -	8.00
567 *You Know Me, Alabam'*.............	5.00 -	8.00
577 *Charleston Cabin*.................	5.00 -	8.00
588 *Hard Hearted Hannah*.............	5.00 -	8.00
602 *A New Kind Of Man*...............	5.00 -	8.00
605 *Them Ramblin' Blues*.............	5.00 -	8.00
606 *No-One Knows What It's All About*.....	5.00 -	8.00
620 *Taklin' To Myself*...............	5.00 -	8.00
632 *Copenhagen*.....................	7.00 -	10.00
635 *Those Panama Mamas*.............	5.00 -	8.00
641 *Doo Wacka Doo*...................	5.00 -	8.00
646 *Oh! Mabel*......................	5.00 -	8.00
680 *Ain't My Baby Grand?*.............	5.00 -	8.00
694 *No One*.........................	5.00 -	8.00
695 *I Like You Best Of All*.............	5.00 -	8.00
711 *He's The Kind Of Man You Like*......	5.00 -	8.00
714 *Don't Bring Lulu*.................	5.00 -	8.00
724 *If You Knew Susie*.................	5.00 -	8.00
725 *Cheatin' On Me*..................	5.00 -	8.00
730 *Sweet Georgia Brown*.............	6.00 -	10.00
732 *Ah Ha!*.........................	5.00 -	8.00
741 *Charleston*......................	5.00 -	8.00
750 *Yes, Sir! That's My Baby*.........	5.00 -	8.00
772 *Oh, Say! Can Is See You Tonight?*......	5.00 -	8.00
774 *Row, Row, Rosie!*.................	5.00 -	8.00
780 *Tryin' To Keep Away From You*.......	5.00 -	8.00
782 *Fallin' Down*....................	7.00 -	10.00
797 *Sweet Man*......................	7.00 -	10.00
817 *Milenberg Joys*..................	7.00 -	10.00
824 *I'm Gonna Hang Around My Sugar*.....	7.00 -	10.00
832 *Show Me The Way To Go Home*.......	5.00 -	8.00
835 *Freshie*........................	5.00 -	8.00
837 *She Doesn't*....................	5.00 -	8.00
870 *T. N. T.*.......................	7.00 -	10.00
925 *What A Man!*....................	5.00 -	8.00
975 *Static Strut*...................	7.00 -	10.00
986 *I'd Give A Lot Of Love*.............	5.00 -	8.00
1016 *Lay Me Down To Sleep in Carolina*....	5.00 -	8.00
1017 *Precious*......................	5.00 -	8.00
1020 *She Knows Her Onions*...........	5.00 -	8.00
1040 *Susie's Feller*.................	7.00 -	10.00
1049 *My Baby Knows How*.............	7.00 -	10.00
1077 *Lonely Eyes*...................	5.00 -	8.00
1110 *Crazy Words . Crazy Tune*......	7.00 -	10.00
1114 *Ain't She Sweet?*...............	7.00 -	10.00
1209 *Arkansas Blues*.................	8.00 -	12.00
1232 *Vo-Do-De-O Blues*.............	8.00 -	12.00
1245 *Clementine*....................	8.00 -	12.00
1266 *Steamboat Bill*.................	8.00 -	12.00
1280 *Is She My Girl Friend?*..........	7.00 -	10.00
8141 *Farewell Blues*.................	8.00 -	12.00
9233 *What Do We Get From Boston?*.......	5.00 -	8.00
Perfect 15473 *Popeye (The Sailor Man)*.....	5.00 -	8.00
Romeo 1035 *What Do We Get From Boston?*..	5.00 -	8.00
1068 *Send Love Through The Breeze*........	5.00 -	8.00

VARSITY SEVEN:

Varsity 8135 *Scratch My Back*...........	8.00 -	12.00
8147 *It's Tight Like That*.............	8.00 -	12.00
8173 *How Long, How Long Blues*......	8.00 -	12.00
8179 *Shake It And Break It*.............	8.00 -	12.00

**JOE VENUTI (& HIS NEW YORKERS/
ORCHESTRA); JOE VENUTI'S BLUE
FOUR; JOE VENUTI & HIS BLUE FIVE;
JOE VENUTI-EDDIE LANG BLUE FIVE;
JOE VENUTI-EDDIE LANG & THEIR ALL-
STAR ORCHESTRA; JOE VENUTI & RUSS
MORGAN:**

Titles, issued contemporaneously on Banner, Con-		
queror, Melotone, Oriole, Perfect, Romeo: *Alice*		
In Wonderland; Build A Little House; Cheese		
And Crackers; Cinderella's Fella; Doin' The Up-		
town Lowdown; Easter Parade; Everything I		
Have Is Yours; Heat Wave; I Want To Ring Bells;		
Moon Glow; My Dancing Lady; No More Love;		
One Minute To One; You Must Have Taken My		
Heart; You're My Past, Present and Future..	5.00 -	8.00
Bluebird 5293 *Fiddlesticks*...........	7.00 -	10.00
5520 *Everybody Shuffle*...........	7.00 -	10.00
10280 *Doin' Things*.................	5.00 -	8.00
Columbia 914-D *Stringint The Blues*...........	8.00 -	12.00
2535-D *There's No Other Girl*...........	8.00 -	12.00
2589-D *The Wolf Wobble*...........	8.00 -	12.00
2765-D *Raggin' The Scale*...........	8.00 -	12.00
2782-D *Vibraphonia*...............	8.00 -	12.00
2783-D *Isn't It Heavenly?*...........	8.00 -	12.00
2834-D *Doin' The Uptown Lowdown*.....	8.00 -	12.00
3103-D *Eeny Meeny Miney Mo*...........	7.00 -	10.00
3104-D *Stop, Look and Listen*...........	7.00 -	10.00
3105-D *Red Velvet*.................	7.00 -	10.00
Decca 624 *Nothing But Notes*...........	7.00 -	10.00
625 *Tap Room Blues*...........	7.00 -	10.00
669 *Vibraphonia No. 2*...........	7.00 -	10.00
Melotone 12277 *Farewell Blues*...........	20.00 -	30.00
12294 *Beale Street Blues*...........	20.00 -	30.00
Okeh 40762 *Wild Cat*...........	8.00 -	12.00
40825 *Doin' Things*...........	8.00 -	12.00
40853 *Kickin' The Cat*...........	10.00 -	15.00
40897 *A Mug Of Ale*...........	10.00 -	15.00
40947 *Penn Beach Blues*...........	10.00 -	15.00
41025 *The Wild Dog*...........	10.00 -	15.00
41051 *Tain't So, Honey, Tain't So*...........	10.00 -	15.00
41056 *Because My Baby Don't Mean "Maybe"*		
Now...........	10.00 -	15.00
41076 *The Man From The South*...........	10.00 -	15.00
41087 *Pickin' Cotton*...........	10.00 -	15.00
41133 *I Must Have That Man*...........	10.00 -	15.00
41144 *The Blue Room*...........	10.00 -	15.00
41192 *Weary River*...........	10.00 -	15.00
41251 *My Honey's Lovin' Arms*...........	10.00 -	15.00
41263 *I'm In Seventh Heaven*...........	10.00 -	15.00
41320 *Chant Of The Jungle*...........	10.00 -	15.00
41361 *Apple Blossoms*...........	10.00 -	15.00
41427 *Promises*...........	10.00 -	15.00
41432 *Raggin' The Scale*...........	10.00 -	15.00
41451 *Out Of Breath*...........	10.00 -	15.00
41469 *I've Found A New Baby*...........	10.00 -	15.00
41506 *Pardon Me, Pretty Baby*...........	10.00 -	15.00
41586 *Fiddlesticks*...........	10.00 -	15.00
Victor 21561 *Doin' Things*...........	8.00 -	12.00
23015 *My Man From Caroline*...........	15.00 -	20.00
23018 *Wasting My Love On You*...........	15.00 -	20.00
23021 *The Wild Dog*...........	10.00 -	15.00
23039 *Gettin' Hot*...........	20.00 -	30.00
24946 *Phantom Rhapsody*...........	8.00 -	12.00
Vocalion 15858 *Farewell Blues*...........	20.00 -	30.00
15864 *Beale Street Blues*...........	20.00 -	30.00

VICKSBURG BLOWERS:

Gennett 6089 *Monte Carlo Joys*.............	30.00 -	40.00

VICKSBURG TEN:

Champion 15477 *Clarinet Marmalade*.........	15.00 -	20.00

**DON VOORHEES & HIS (EARL CARROLL
VANITIES) ORCHESTRA:**

Cameo 1134 *Pardon The Glove*.............	7.00 -	10.00
Columbia 765-D, 835-D, 881-D, 954-D, 990-D,		
1078-D, 1123-D, 1124-D, 1126-D, 1129-D,		
1180-D, 1284-D....................	4.00 -	8.00
Edison 51855 *Just One More Kiss*.............	7.00 -	10.00
51888 *Somebody's Eyes*.............	7.00 -	10.00

51890	*Sunday*	7.00 -	10.00				
51919	*Blue Skies*	7.00 -	10.00				
51927	*Muddy Water*	7.00 -	10.00				

WABASH **129** **WASHBOARD**

51890 *Sunday*	7.00 -	10.00
51919 *Blue Skies*	7.00 -	10.00
51927 *Muddy Water*	7.00 -	10.00
51962 *Pardon The Glove*	10.00 -	15.00
51963 *Never Without You*	7.00 -	10.00
51997 *I'll Always Remember You*	10.00 -	15.00
51999 *Dancing The Devil Away*	10.00 -	15.00
52024 *Room For Two*	6.00 -	10.00
52070 *Show Me That Kind Of A Girl*	8.00 -	12.00
52072 *Oh! Doris, Where Do You Live?*	8.00 -	12.00
Pathe-Actuelle 36567, 36594	4.00 -	7.00
Perfect 14748, 14775	4.00 -	7.00

WABASH TRIO:

Titles, issued contemporaneously on Grey Gull, Radiex; *Coal Black Blues; Hoppin' Round; Lone Western Blues* .... 8.00 - 12.00

(JIMMY) WADE'S CLUB ALABAM MOULIN ROUGE MOULIN ROUGH ORCHESTRA; JIMMY WADE & HIS DIXIELANDERS:

Black Patti 8019 *Original Black Bottom Dance*	80.00 -	120.00
Gennett 6105 *Original Black Bottom Dance*	60.00 -	90.00
Harmograph 893 *Mobile Blues*	50.00 -	75.00
Paramount 20295 *Someday Sweetheart*	40.00 -	60.00
Puritan 11295 *Someday Sweetheart*	40.00 -	60.00
11363 *You've Got Ways I'm Crazy About*	40.00 -	60.00
Vocalion 1236 *Mississippi Wobble*	50.00 -	75.00

SOL S. WAGNER & HIS ORCHESTRA:

Gennett 5311 *My Sweet Girl*	8.00 -	12.00
5313 *Oklahoma Indian Jazz*	8.00 -	12.00
5323 *Dream Daddy*	35.00 -	50.00
Okeh 40827 *South Wind*	8.00 -	12.00
40838 *You Don't Like It-Not-Much*	8.00 -	12.00
40923 *Countin' The Days*	8.00 -	12.00

HERMAN WALDMAN AND HIS ORCHESTRA:

Bluebird 5437 *Cocktails For Two*	5.00 -	8.00
5439 *Out For No Good*	5.00 -	8.00
5478 *Home on the Range*	5.00 -	8.00
Brunswick 4649 *Marbles*	8.00 -	12.00
6181 *Lazy River*	8.00 -	12.00

EDDIE WALKER & HIS ORCHESTRA:

Columbia 2380-D *Personally, I Love You*	5.00 -	8.00
2404-D *Walkin' My Baby Back Home*	10.00 -	20.00

TED WALLACE & HIS ORCHESTRA/SWING MUSIC:

Bluebird 6251, 6252, 6253, 6254	4.00 -	7.00
Okeh 40749 *When I First Met Mary*	7.00 -	10.00
40751 *Usen't You Used To Be My Sweetie?*	7.00 -	10.00
40760 *Ain't She Sweet?*	7.00 -	10.00
40778 *The Cat*	7.00 -	10.00
40850 *Love and Kisses*	7.00 -	10.00
40915 *Zulu Wail*	8.00 -	12.00
40961 *Changes*	8.00 -	12.00
41014 *Buffalo Rhythm*	15.00 -	20.00

TRIXIE WALLACE:

Claxtonola 40393 *Copenhagen*	20.00 -	30.00

THOMAS ("FATS") WALLER (WITH MORRIS'S HOT BABIES); FATS WALLER & HIS BUDDIES/ RHYTHM:

Bluebird	3.00 -	5.00
Columbia 14593-D *I'm Crazy 'Bout My Baby*	25.00 -	35.00
Okeh 4757 *Birmingham Blues*	20.00 -	30.00
Victor 20357 *St. Louis Blues*	7.00 -	10.00
20470 *Soothin' Syrup Stomp*	20.00 -	30.00
20492 *Rusty Pail*	20.00 -	30.00
20655 *Stompin' The Bug*	20.00 -	30.00
20776 *Savannah Blues*	20.00 -	30.00
20890 *Beale Street Blues*	15.00 -	20.00
21127 *I Ain't Got Nobody*	15.00 -	20.00
21202 *He's Gone Away*	15.00 -	20.00

21358 *The Digah's Stomp*	20.00 -	30.00
21525 *Hog Maw Stomp*	20.00 -	30.00
22092 *Ain't Misbehavin'*	7.00 -	10.00
22108 *Sweet Savannah Sue*	10.00 -	15.00
22371 *St. Louis Blues*	5.00 -	10.00
23260 *That's All*	20.00 -	30.00
23331 *Sugar*	15.00 -	20.00
Victor 24641, 24648, 24708, 24714, 24737, 24738, 24742, 24801, 24808, 24826, 24830, 24846, 24853, 24863, 24867, 24888, 24889, 24892, 24898, 25015, 25026, 25037, 25039, 25044, 25063	4.00 -	8.00
25075 through 26002	3.00 -	6.00
38050 *Harlem Fuss*	20.00 -	30.00
38086 *Lookin' Good But Feelin' Bad*	20.00 -	30.00
38110 *When I'm Alone*	20.00 -	30.00
38119 *Ridin' But Walkin'*	20.00 -	30.00
38508 *Numb Fumblin'*	15.00 -	20.00
38554 *Valentine Stomp*	20.00 -	30.00
38568 *Turn On The Heat*	15.00 -	20.00
38613 *Smashing Thirds*	20.00 -	25.00

EDDIE WALTERS:

Columbia 2137-D, 2290-D	5.00 -	8.00
2232-D *It Must Be Love*	8.00 -	12.00

THE WANDERERS:

Bluebird 5834 *A Good Man Is Hard To Find*	7.00 -	10.00
5869 *I Ain't Got Nobody*	7.00 -	10.00
5887 *Tiger Rag*	7.00 -	10.00
5994 *Footwarmer*	7.00 -	10.00

BILLY WARD: .... 15.00 - 25.00

Oriole 4472 *Squeeze Me*	15.00 -	25.00

JOE WARD'S SWANEE CLUB ORCHESTRA:

Cameo 9026 *Traffic Jam*	7.00 -	10.00

WARING'S PENNSYLVANIANS:

Victor L-16016, L-16018 (Program Transcriptions - Long Playing)	7.00 -	10.00
21508 *Stack O'Lee Blues*	5.00 -	8.00
Victor 21836, 22266	4.00 -	7.00
22325 *Red-Hot Chicago*	7.00 -	10.00
22978 *How Am I Doin'?*	8.00 -	12.00
24030 *I Heard*	7.00 -	10.00
Victor 24051 *Holding My Honey's Hand*	5.00 -	8.00
24062 *Old Yazoo*	5.00 -	8.00
Victor 24168, 24169, 24179, 24181, 24186, 24214	4.00 -	8.00

BUD WARNER & HIS RED CAPS:

Bell 1174 *Down Home Special*	75.00 -	100.00

WARNER'S SEVEN ACES:

Columbia 305-D *Cheatin' On Me*	5.00 -	8.00
336-D *The Blues Have Got Me*	5.00 -	8.00
Columbia 491-D *Go Get'Em, Caroline*	5.00 -	8.00
605-D *Breakin' The Leg*	15.00 -	20.00
656-D *So Is Your Old Lady*	5.00 -	8.00
816-D *Don't Take That Black Bottom Away*	5.00 -	8.00
863-D *Who'll Be The One?*	5.00 -	8.00
1001-D *There's Everything Nice About You*	5.00 -	8.00
1046-D *That's My Hap-Hap-Happiness*	5.00 -	8.00
Okeh 4888 *In a Tent*	7.00 -	10.00
4911 *Dream Girl of P.K.A.*	7.00 -	10.00
4924 *Mean Eyes*	8.00 -	12.00
40080 *Ace of Spades*	8.00 -	12.00
40198 *Bessie Couldn't Help It*	8.00 -	12.00
40201 *Love Time*	7.00 -	10.00

WASHBOARD RHYTHM BAND:

Columbia 14680-D *Going, Going, Gone*	35.00 -	50.00

WASHBOARD RHYTHM BOYS/KINGS:

Titles, issued contemporaneously on Banner, Melotone, Oriole, Perfect, Romeo: *Dog and Cat; I Cover The Waterfront; Lazybones; Learn To Croon; Mississippi Basin; Old Man Blues; St. Louis Blues; Some Of These Days* ...... 15.00 - 20.00

Bluebird 6157 *Arlena*	7.00 -	12.00
6186 *Street Walkin' Blues*	7.00 -	12.00

6278 Hot Nuts..........................	7.00 -	12.00
Victor 22719 *A Porter's Love Song To A*		
Chambermaid.	15.00 -	20.00
22814 *Shoot 'Em.*	15.00 -	20.00
22958 *Pepper Steak.*	25.00 -	35.00
23301 *Georgia On My Mind.*	20.00 -	30.00
23303 *Boola Boo.*	20.00 -	30.00
23323 *If You Don't Love Me.*	20.00 -	30.00
23337 *All This World Is Made Of Glass.*	20.00 -	30.00
23348 *My Silent Love.*	20.00 -	30.00
23357 *Depression Stomp.*	20.00 -	30.00
23364 *Say It Isn't So.*	20.00 -	30.00
23367 *Ash Man Crawl.*	20.00 -	30.00
23368 *The Boy In The Boat.*	20.00 -	30.00
23373 *How Deep Is The Ocean?.*	20.00 -	30.00
23375 *A Nickel For a Pickel.*	20.00 -	30.00
23380 *Sloppy Drunk Blues.*	20.00 -	30.00
23403 *Nobody's Sweetheart.*	20.00 -	30.00
23405 *Sophisticated Lady.*	20.00 -	30.00
23408 *Bug-A-Boo.*	20.00 -	30.00
23413 *Move Turtle.*	20.00 -	30.00
23415 *Hard Corn.*	20.00 -	30.00
Vocalion 1724 *Sentimental Gentleman From Georgia*	15.00 -	20.00
1725 *The Scat Song.*	15.00 -	20.00
1729 *Syncopate Your Sins Away.*	15.00 -	20.00
1730 *Oh! You Sweet Thing.*	15.00 -	20.00
1731 *Angeline.*	15.00 -	20.00
1732 *Blue Drag.*	15.00 -	20.00
1733 *Old Yazoo.*	15.00 -	20.00
1734 *Spider Crawl.*	15.00 -	20.00

WASHBOARD SERENADERS:

Victor 38127 *Kazoo Moan.*	20.00 -	30.00
38610 *Teddy's Blues.*	25.00 -	35.00

WASHBOARD TRIO:

Paramount 12682 *Washboard Rag.*	35.00 -	50.00
Radiex 1485 *Yellow Dog Blues.*	———	

WASHBOARD WONDERS:

Silvertone 3548 *Shake That Thing.*	30.00 -	40.00
3549 *Skoodlum Blues.*	30.00 -	40.00

BENNIE WASHINGTON'S SIX ACES:

Okeh 8269 *Compton Ave. Blues.*	———	

BUCK WASHINGTON:

Columbia 2925-D *Old Fashioned Love.*	12.00 -	16.00

STEVE WASHINGTON & HIS ORCHESTRA:

Vocalion 2598 *Sing A Little Low-Down Tune...*	15.00 -	20.00
2607 *Blue River.*	12.00 -	15.00

THE WASHINGTONIANS:

Titles issued contemporaneously on Cameo, Lincoln, Romeo: *East St. Louis, Toodle-Oo; Hot And Bothered; Jubilee Stomp; The Mooche; Move Over, Saratoga Swing; Take It Easy; Who Said "It's Tight Like That"?*	15.00 -	20.00
Additional titles, issued contemporaneously on Cameo, Lincoln, Romeo: *It's Tight Like That; Mississippi, Here I Am.*	5.00 -	8.00
Blu-Disc 1002 *Choo Choo.*	150.00 -	300.00
Brunswick 3526 *Black And Tan Fantasy.*	10.00 -	15.00
4009 *Black Beauty.*	10.00 -	15.00
4044 *Jubilee Stomp.*	10.00 -	15.00
Diva 2577-G *Bugle Call Rag.*	12.00 -	16.00
2601-G *Stack O'Lee Blues.*	12.00 -	16.00
Harmony 577-H *Bugle Call Rag.*	12.00 -	16.00
601-H *Stack O'Lee Blues.*	12.00 -	16.00
Pathe-Actuelle 36333 *Trombone Blues.*	40.00 -	60.00
Perfect 14514 *Trombone Blues.*	40.00 -	60.00
Puritan 11437 *Rainy Nights.*	75.00 -	100.00
Triangle 11437 *Rainy Nights.*	75.00 -	100.00
Velvet Tone 1577-V *Bugle Call Rag.*	12.00 -	16.00
1601-V *Stack O'Lee Blues.*	12.00 -	16.00
Vocalion 15704 *Take It Easy.*	15.00 -	20.00
15710 *Jubilee Stomp.*	20.00 -	30.00

ETHEL WATERS: ETHEL WATERS' JAZZ MASTERS:

Black Swan 2010 *Down Home Blues.*	15.00 -	20.00
2021 *There'll Be Some Changes Made.*	15.00 -	20.00
2035 *Royal Garden Blues.*	15.00 -	20.00
2037 *Bugle Blues.*	15.00 -	20.00
2038 *Dyin' With The Blues.*	15.00 -	20.00
2074 *Struggle.*	15.00 -	20.00
2077 *Tiger Rag.*	15.00 -	20.00
10077 *Struggle.*	15.00 -	20.00
10073 *Tiger Rag.*	15.00 -	20.00
14117 *Jazzin' Babies Blues.*	15.00 -	20.00
14120 *Georgia Blues.*	15.00 -	20.00
14128 *At The New Jump Steady Ball.* ...	15.00 -	20.00
14145 *Brown Baby.*	15.00 -	20.00
14146 *Memphis Man.*	15.00 -	20.00
14148 *Long-Lost Mama.*	15.00 -	20.00
14151 *Lost Out Blues.*	15.00 -	20.00
14154 *Ethel Sings 'Em.*	15.00 -	20.00
14155 *All The Time.*	15.00 -	20.00
Brunswick 6517 *I Can't Give You Anything But Love*	8.00 -	12.00
6521 *St. Louis Blues.*	10.00 -	15.00
6564 *Stormy Weather.*	8.00 -	12.00
6617 *Shadows On The Swanee.*	10.00 -	15.00
6885 *You've Seen Harlem At Its Best.*	10.00 -	15.00
Cardinal 2036 *The New York Glide.*	15.00 -	20.00
Columbia 379-D *Sweet Georgia Brown.* ...	8.00 -	12.00
433-D *Sympathetic Dan.*	7.00 -	10.00
472-D *Pickaninny Blues.*	7.00 -	10.00
487-D *Sweet Man.*	8.00 -	12.00
561-D *I've Found A New Baby.*	10.00 -	15.00
1837-D *Birmingham Bertha.*	8.00 -	12.00
1871-D *True Blue Lou.*	8.00 -	12.00
1905-D *Shoo Shoo Boogie Boo.*	8.00 -	12.00
1933-D *Trav'lin All Alone.*	7.00 -	10.00
2184-D *Porgy.*	7.00 -	10.00
2222-D *My Kind Of Man.*	15.00 -	20.00
2288-D *You're Lucky To Me.*	7.00 -	10.00
2346-D *I Got Rhythm.*	8.00 -	12.00
2409-D *When You Lover Has Gone.*	12.00 -	16.00
2481-D *Without That Gal.*	12.00 -	16.00
2511-D *River, Stay 'Way From My Door.*	12.00 -	16.00
2826-D *Harlem On My Mind.*	12.00 -	16.00
2853-D *A Hundred Years From Today.*	12.00 -	16.00
14093-D *Down Home Blues.*	7.00 -	10.00
14112-D *Maybe Not At All.*	10.00 -	15.00
14116-D *No Man's Mama.*	7.00 -	10.00
14125-D *Bring Your Greenbacks.* ...	10.00 -	15.00
14132-D *Throw Dirt In Your Face.* ...	8.00 -	12.00
14134-D *I Wonder What's Bacome Of Joe?.* ...	8.00 -	12.00
14146-D *You'll Want Me Back.*	7.00 -	10.00
14153-D Heebie Jeebies.	8.00 -	12.00
14162-D *Take What You Want.*	8.00 -	12.00
14170-D *I'm Coming, Virginia.*	8.00 -	12.00
Columbia 14182-D *Jersey Walk.*	8.00 -	12.00
14199-D *Satisfyin' Papa.*	8.00 -	12.00
14214-D *Take You Black Bottom Outside.*	10.00 -	15.00
14229-D *Smile!.*	8.00 -	12.00
14264-D *Someday, Sweetheart.*	8.00 -	12.00
14297-D *I'm Saving It All For You.* ...	8.00 -	12.00
14353-D *My Handy Man.*	10.00 -	15.00
14365-D *West End Blues.*	10.00 -	15.00
14380-D *Do What Yo Did Last Night.*	10.00 -	15.00
14411-D *Lonesome Swallow.*	10.00 -	15.00
14458-D *Long Lean Lanky Mama.*	10.00 -	15.00
14565-D *Georgia Blues.*	10.00 -	15.00
Decca 140 *Moon Glow.*	5.00 -	8.00
141 *I Ain't Gonna Sin No More.*	8.00 -	12.00
234 *When It's Sleepy Time Down South.*	5.00 -	8.00
Liberty Music Shop 188 *Thief In The Night.*	7.00 -	10.00

310 *Taking A Chance On Love*	7.00 -	10.00
311 *Cabin In the Sky*	7.00 -	10.00
Paramount 12169 *Down Home Blues*	15.00 -	20.00
12170 *There'll Be Some Changes Made*	15.00 -	20.00
12171 *Royal Garden Blues*	15.00 -	20.00
12173 *Bugle Blues*	15.00 -	20.00
12174 *Dying With The Blues*	15.00 -	20.00
12175 *Jazzin' Babies Blues*	15.00 -	20.00
12176 *At The New Jump Steady Ball*	15.00 -	20.00
12177 *Georgia Blues*	15.00 -	20.00
12178 *Brown Baby*	15.00 -	20.00
12179 *Memphis Man*	15.00 -	20.00
12180 *Long-Last Mama*	15.00 -	20.00
12181 *Lost Out Blues*	15.00 -	20.00
12182 *Ethel Sings 'Em*	15.00 -	20.00
12189 *Tell 'Em 'Bout Me*	20.00 -	30.00
12230 *Black Spatch Blues*	30.00 -	40.00
12313 *Craving Blues*	75.00 -	100.00
Vocalion 14680 *Pleasure Mad*	6.00 -	10.00

WATSON'S PULLMAN PORTERS:

Gennett 6353 *Barbecue Blues*	40.00 -	60.00
6378 *Down Home Special*	40.00 -	60.00

EL WATSON:

Victor 20951 *Narrow Gauge Blues*	15.00 -	25.00
21440 *El Watson's Fox Chase*	12.00 -	16.00
21585 *Bay Rum Blues*	15.00 -	25.00

LU WATTERS' YERBA BUENA JAZZ BAND:

Jazz Man 1, 2, 3, 4, 5, 6, 7, 13, 14, 15, 17	7.00 -	10.00
Mercury 11026, 11065, 11090	3.00 -	5.00
West Coast 101, 103, 104, 111, 152	5.00 -	8.00

CHICK WEBB & HIS LITTLE CHICKS/ ORCHESTRA; CHICK WEBB'S SAVOY ORCHESTRA:

Brunswick 6156 *Blues In My Heart*	15.00 -	25.00
Columbia 2875-D *On The Sunny Side Of The Street*	12.00 -	16.00
2883-D *Let's Get Together*	12.00 -	16.00
2920-D *Imagination*	12.00 -	16.00
2926-D *Stompin' At The Savoy*	12.00 -	16.00
Decca 172 *Blue Minor*	7.00 -	10.00
173 *That Rhythm Man*	7.00 -	10.00
483 *Don't Be That Way*	7.00 -	10.00
494 *Love And Kisses*	7.00 -	10.00
588 *Rhythm And Romance*	7.00 -	10.00
640 *I'll Chase The Blues Away*	7.00 -	10.00
785, 830, 831, 995, 1032, 1065, 1087, 1114, 1115, 1123, 1213, 1220, 1273, 1513, 1521, 1586, 1681, 1716, 1759	4.00 -	8.00
Okeh 41571 *If It Ain't Love*	15.00 -	20.00
41572 *Blue Minor*	15.00 -	20.00
Vocalion 1607 *Heebie Jeebies*	30.00 -	40.00
3100 *If It Ain't Love*	10.00 -	15.00
3101 *True*	10.00 -	15.00
3246 *Stompin' At The Savoy*	7.00 -	12.00

MALCOLM WEBB & HIS GANG:

Champion 15420 *Friday Night*	15.00 -	25.00

CARL WEBSTER'S YALE COLLEGIANS:

Okeh 41393 *Puttin' On The Ritz*	10.00 -	15.00
Personal Record 139-P *If I'm Without You*	15.00 -	20.00

JULIAN WEBSTER AND HIS BAY STATE ACES:

Edison 52061 *Just Once Again*	5.00 -	8.00

ANSON WEEKS AND HIS (HOTEL MARK HOPKINS) ORCHESTRA:

Brunswick 6524, 6526, 6569, 6575, 6604, 6619, 6639, 6661, 6665, 6727, 6730, 6772, 6795, 6944, 6946, 6965, 6969, 6983, 6989, 6990, 6997, 7349, 7350	4.00 -	7.00
Brunswick 7477, 7510, 7515, 7518	4.00 -	7.00
Brunswick 20120 *"Strike Me Pink" medley*	8.00 -	12.00
(Note: Brunswick 20120 is a 12-inch record)		
Columbia 2211-D *Ro-Ro-Rolin' Along*	5.00 -	8.00
40004-D *Susianna*	7.00 -	10.00

Decca 1134, 1139, 1140	4.00 -	8.00

TED WEEMS & HIS ORCHESTRA:

Bluebird 5130, 5131, 5148, 5235, 5236, 5239, 5289, 5290	4.00 -	8.00
Columbia 2956-D, 2957-D, 2975-D, 2976-D	5.00 -	8.00
Decca 820, 822, 895, 921, 958, 959, 969	4.00 -	7.00
Decca (blue label), most other issues	3.00 -	5.00
Victor L-16025 (Long-Playing "Program Transcription")	8.00 -	12.00
19722, 20475, 21364, 21729, 22032, 22037, 22038, 22138, 22238, 22304, 22406, 22411, 22426, 22499, 22515, 22564, 22637, 22644, 22646, 22648, 22829, 22838, 22881, 24053, 24227, 24265, 24266, 24302, 24308	4.00 -	8.00

LEW WEINER'S GOLD AND BLACK ACES:

Gennett 6540 *Louisiana Bo Bo*	20.00 -	30.00

LAWRENCE WELK & HIS ORCHESTRA:

Gennett 6697 *Doin' The New Low Down*	25.00 -	40.00
6712 *Spiked Beer*	25.00 -	40.00
20341 *Shanghai Honeymoon*	25.00 -	40.00

DICKEY WELLS' SHIM SHAMMERS; DICKIE WELLS' ORCHESTRA:

Columbia 2829-D *Baby, Are You Satisfied?*	15.00 -	20.00
Signature	4.00 -	8.00

PETE WENDLING:

Okeh 4868, 4984	5.00 -	8.00

MAE WEST:

Brunswick 6495 *Easy Rider*	7.00 -	12.00
6675 *I'm No Angel*	7.00 -	12.00
6676 *They Call My Sister Honkey-Tonk*	7.00 -	12.00

THEADOR WEST:

Ajax 17118 *Hot Jelly Blues*	15.00 -	20.00
17129 *Blues, Just Blues*	15.00 -	20.00

FRANK WESTPHAL & HIS ORCHESTRA:

Columbia 32-D, A-3693, A-3743, A-3872, A-3911, A-3929	4.00 -	8.00

WE THREE:

Pathe-Actuelle 36464 *Trumpet Sobs*	15.00 -	20.00
36492 *Plenty Off Center*	15.00 -	20.00
Perfect 14645 *Trumpet Sobs*	15.00 -	20.00
14673 *Plenty Off Center*	15.00 -	20.00

WHISTLER & HIS JUG BAND:

Gennett 5554 *Chicago Flip*	30.00 -	50.00
5614 *Jail House Blues*	30.00 -	50.00
Okeh 8469 *Low Down Blues*	30.00 -	50.00
8816 *Pig Meat Blues*	25.00 -	40.00
Victor 23305 *Hold That Tiger*	35.00 -	50.00

BOB WHITE'S DIXIE TRIO:

Puritan 11400 *Alabamy Bound*	30.00 -	50.00

STEVE WHITE'S DANCELAND ORCHESTRA:

Sunset 1132 *Slippery Elm*	15.00 -	25.00

TED WHITE'S COLLEGIANS:

Oriole 931 *Hurricane*	8.00 -	12.00
960 *12th Street Rag*	5.00 -	8.00
1359 *Makin' Whoopee!*	5.00 -	8.00
1392 *Doin' The Raccoon*	5.00 -	8.00
1398 *Come on, Baby*	5.00 -	8.00
1503 *Wedding Bells*	5.00 -	8.00
1544 *Shirt Tail Stomp*	8.00 -	12.00
1664 *Sweetness*	5.00 -	8.00
1694 *Little By Little*	5.00 -	8.00

PAUL WHITEMAN & HIS (CONCERT) ORCHESTRA:

Columbia 1401-D, 1402-D, 1448-D, 1465-D, 1701-D, 1736-D, 1755-D, 1771-D, 1845-D, 1862-D, 2010-D, 2163-D, 2171-D	4.00 -	7.00
1441-D *Because My Baby Don't Mean "Maybe" Now*	7.00 -	10.00
1444-D *That's My Weakness Now*	7.00 -	10.00
1464-D *Pickin' Cotton*	5.00 -	8.00
1478-D *Felix The Cat*	10.00 -	15.00

1491-D Georgie Porgie	8.00 -	12.00	
1496-D I'd Rather Cry Over You	7.00 -	10.00	
1505-D Out O' Town Gal	8.00 -	12.00	
1683-D Makin' Woopee	5.00 -	8.00	
1723-D How About Me?	5.00 -	8.00	
1822-D When My Dreams Come True	8.00 -	12.00	
1877-D I'm In Seventh Heaven	8.00 -	12.00	
1945-D China Boy	8.00 -	12.00	
1974-D Waiting At The End Of The Road	8.00 -	12.00	
1993-D When You're Counting The Stars Alone	8.00 -	12.00	
2023-D Great Day	5.00 -	8.00	
2047-D Should I?	5.00 -	8.00	
2098-D After You've Gone	7.00 -	10.00	
2164-D A Bench In The Park	7.00 -	10.00	
2170-D I Like To Do Things For You	7.00 -	10.00	
2277-D The New Tiger Rag	7.00 -	10.00	
2491-D Choo Choo	7.00 -	10.00	
Columbia (12-inch) 50068 My Melancholy Baby	8.00 -	12.00	
(12-inch) 50103-D Sweet Sue	8.00 -	12.00	
Victor L-16001 George White's Scandals Medley	10.00 -	15.00	
L-16002 I'm Sorry, Dear plus 2 more tunes	10.00 -	15.00	
L-16017 Willow, Weep For Me plus 2 more tunes	10.00 -	15.00	
(above are long-playing "Program Transciptions")			
Victor 20092 Bell Hoppin' Blues	5.00 -	8.00	
20177 When The Red, Red, Robin Comes Bob, Bob, Bobbin' Along	5.00 -	8.00	
20418 Wistful and Blue	4.00 -	7.00	
20627 Side By Side	7.00 -	10.00	
20679 Magnolia	7.00 -	10.00	
20751 I'm Coming, Virginia	7.00 -	10.00	
20883 It Won't Be Long Now	4.00 -	7.00	
21103 Changes	5.00 -	8.00	
21119 Whiteman Stomp	7.00 -	10.00	
21214 Lonely Melody	5.00 -	8.00	
21218 Ol' Man River	5.00 -	8.00	
21228 Smile	5.00 -	8.00	
21240 Back In Your Own Backyard	7.00 -	10.00	
21274 From Monday On	7.00 -	10.00	
21301 Coquette	5.00 -	8.00	
21338 When	7.00 -	10.00	
21365 When You're With Somebody Else	5.00 -	8.00	
21388 My Angel	4.00 -	7.00	
21389 My Pet	7.00 -	10.00	
Victor 21398 You Took Advantage of Me	7.00 -	10.00	
21438 Louisiana	8.00 -	12.00	
21453 It Was The Dawn of Love	7.00 -	10.00	
21464 Sugar	8.00 -	12.00	
22883 'Leven Pounds of Heaven	5.00 -	8.00	
22984 Lawd, You Made the Night Too Long	5.00 -	8.00	
24078 San	10.00 -	15.00	
24105 Love Nest	10.00 -	15.00	
24140 You're Telling Me	7.00 -	10.00	
24400 It's Only a Paper Moon	8.00 -	12.00	
24403 Shanghai Lil	8.00 -	12.00	
24571 Fare-Thee-Well To Harlem	8.00 -	12.00	
24615 Christmas Night In Harlem	8.00 -	12.00	
24668 G Blues	8.00 -	12.00	
24704 Pardon My Southern Accent	5.00 -	8.00	
Victor 25806 Dodging a Divorcee	5.00 -	8.00	
25088 And Then Some	5.00 -	8.00	
25091 I'm in the Mood for Love	5.00 -	8.00	
25113 The Duke Insists	5.00 -	8.00	
25150 Sugar Plum	5.00 -	8.00	
Victor 25192, 25238, 25319, 25404, 25675, 26415	4.00 -	7.00	
25366 Mississippi Mud	8.00 -	12.00	
25367 San	8.00 -	12.00	
25368 From Monday On	8.00 -	12.00	
25369 Louisiana	8.00 -	12.00	
25370 Changes	8.00 -	12.00	
(*25366 through 25370 were issued as a set)			
27685 Loveable	5.00 -	8.00	

27686 Forget-Me-Not	5.00 -	8.00	
27687 Dancing Shadows	3.00 -	6.00	
27688 From Monday On	5.00 -	8.00	
27689 Back In Your Own Back Yard	5.00 -	8.00	
(*27685 through 27689 were issued as a set)			
Victor L-35001 Grand Canyon Suite	10.00 -	15.00	
L-35002 Grand Canyon Suite	10.00 -	15.00	
35822, 35877, 35912, 35933, 35934	4.00 -	7.00	
*39000 A Night With Paul Whiteman At The Biltmore	15.00 -	20.00	
*39003 Let 'Em Eat Cake — Program	15.00 -	20.00	
(*12-inch picture records, in the style of the more familar Vogue issues)			
55225 Rhapsody In Blue (12-inch) record)	5.00 -	8.00	
*67-2000 A Night With Paul Whiteman At The Biltmore	15.00 -	20.00	

PAUL WHITEMAN'S RHYTHM BOYS:

Columbia 1455-D Wa Da Da	8.00 -	12.00	
1629-D Rhythm King	8.00 -	12.00	
1819-D Louise	8.00 -	12.00	
2223-D A Bench In The Park	8.00 -	12.00	
Victor 20783 Mississippi Mud, etc	8.00 -	12.00	
21302 From Monday On	8.00 -	12.00	
24095 Bahama Mamas	5.00 -	8.00	
24190 Jig Time	5.00 -	8.00	
24240 Mississippi Mud, etc	5.00 -	8.00	
24349 From Monday On	8.00 -	12.00	

WHITE WAY PLAYERS:

Van Dyke 71816 Ev'rybody Dance	10.00 -	15.00	

JACK WHITNEY AND HIS ORCHESTRA:

Clarion 5270-C Please Don't Talk About Me When I'm Gone	7.00 -	10.00	
5344-C You Forgot Your Gloves	5.00 -	8.00	
5366-C So Sure of You	5.00 -	8.00	
Harmony 1335-H You Forgot Your Gloves	5.00 -	8.00	
1354-H So Sure Of You	5.00 -	8.00	
Parlophone PNY-34194 If You Should Ever Need Me	10.00 -	15.00	
Velvet Tone 2408-V You Forgot Your Gloves	5.00 -	8.00	
2430-V So Sure Of You	5.00 -	8.00	

THE WHOOPEE MAKERS:

Titles, issued contemporaneously on Banner, Jewel, Oriole, Regal, Romeo: Rockin' Chair; Them There Eyes	10.00 -	15.00	
Banner 6548 Saturday Night Function	10.00 -	15.00	
Cameo 9036 Hottentot	10.00 -	15.00	
9037 Misty Mornin'	10.00 -	15.00	
9306 Saturday Night Function	10.00 -	15.00	
Columbia 14367-D Sister Kate	7.00 -	10.00	
Conquerror 7428 Flaming Youth	10.00 -	15.00	
Domino 4428 Flaming Youth	10.00 -	15.00	
Lincoln 3065 Hottentot	10.00 -	15.00	
3066 Misty Mornin'	10.00 -	15.00	
3330 Saturday Night Function	10.00 -	15.00	
Pathe-Actuelle 36781 Jubilee Stomp	12.00 -	16.00	
36787 Take It Easy	12.00 -	16.00	
36899 The Mooche	12.00 -	16.00	
36915 Hot and Bothered	12.00 -	16.00	
36923 Misty Mornin'	12.00 -	16.00	
36945 Bugle Call Rag	12.00 -	16.00	
37013 Tiger Rag	9.00 -	12.00	
37036 Twelfth Street Rag	9.00 -	12.00	
37042 Dirty Dog	9.00 -	12.00	
37059 Doin' The Voom Voom	12.00 -	16.00	
Perfect 14962 East St. Louis Toodle-Oo	12.00 -	16.00	
14968 Take It Easy	12.00 -	16.00	
15080 Move Over	12.00 -	16.00	
15096 Hot And Bothered	12.00 -	16.00	
15104 Misty Mornin'	12.00 -	16.00	
15126 Bugle Call Rag	12.00 -	16.00	
15194 Tiger Rag	9.00 -	12.00	

15217 *Twelfth Street Rag*..................	9.00 -	12.00
15223 *The Sorority Stomp*................	9.00 -	12.00
15240 *Doin' The Voom Voom*..........	12.00 -	16.00
15376 *Happy Feet*.....................	7.00 -	10.00
15418 *Them There Eyes*...............	10.00 -	15.00
Romeo 840 *Misty Mornin'*............	10.00 -	15.00
Vocalion 15763 *Dardanella*...........	25.00 -	40.00
15768 *I've Never Been Loved*.........	25.00 -	40.00
15769 *Freshman Hop*.................	25.00 -	40.00

HAL WHITE'S SYNCOPATORS:

Domino 3444 *Everybody Loves My Baby*		
(instrumental)........................	10.00 -	15.00
3444 *Everybody Loves My Baby* (vocal chorus)	30.00 -	50.00

ZACH WHYTE'S CHOCOLATE BEAU BRUMMELS:

Gennett 6781 *Mandy*..................	90.00 -	130.00
6798 *It's Tight Like That*.............	75.00 -	100.00
7086 *Good Feelin' Blues*.............	80.00 -	120.00

LEE WILEY:

Gala 1 *Baby's Awake Now*............	7.00 -	10.00
2 *I've Got Five Dollars*..............	7.00 -	10.00
3 *You Took Advantage Of Me*........	7.00 -	10.00
4 *As Though You Were There*........	7.00 -	10.00
Liberty Music Shop 281 *My One And Only*....	7.00 -	10.00
282 *I've Got A Crush On You*........	7.00 -	10.00
283 *Sam And Delilah*................	7.00 -	10.00
284 *Sweet And Low Down*............	7.00 -	10.00
294 *You Do Something To Me*........	5.00 -	8.00
295 *Easy To Love*...................	5.00 -	8.00
296 *Find Me A Primitive Man*........	7.00 -	10.00
297 *Let's Do It*.....................	7.00 -	10.00

WILLIAM'S COTTON CLUB ORCHESTRA:

Victor 24083 *Red Blues*..............	7.00 -	10.00

WILLIAMS' PURPLE KNIGHTS:

Victor 22625 *Dinah*..................	7.00 -	10.00

WILLIAMS' WASHBOARD BAND:

Bluebird 5183 *I Want To Ring Bells*....	7.00 -	10.00
5202 *Mickey Mouse And The Turtle*........	7.00 -	10.00
5204 *Hard Corn*.....................	7.00 -	10.00
5230 *Move Turtle*...................	7.00 -	10.00

WILLIAMS & MOORE:

QRS 7016 *Block And Tackle Blues*..........	50.00 -	70.00

BILL WILLIAMS & HIS GANG:

Champion 15215 *Make Me Know It*.........	50.00 -	75.00
15216 *Georgia Bo Bo*................	50.00 -	75.00
15226 *She Looks Like Helen Brown*........	10.00 -	15.00

CLARENCE WILLIAMS (& HIS WASHBOARD BAND/ORCHESTRA); CLARENCE WILLIAMS' BLUE FIVE/JAZZ KINGS/JUG BAND/NOVELTY BAND/ ORCHESTRA/STOMPERS/TRIO/ WASHBOARD FOUR/WASHBOARD FIVE:

Banner 32021 *Papa De-Da-Da*.........	15.00 -	20.00
32063 *Shout, Sister, Shout*..............	15.00 -	20.00
Bluebird 6918, 6919, 6932.............	5.00 -	8.00
Brunswick 3580 *Slow River*..........	12.00 -	18.00
3664 *Baltimore*.....................	12.00 -	18.00
3667 *Slow River*....................	12.00 -	18.00
3703 *Baltimore*.....................	12.00 -	18.00
7000 *Cushion Foot Stomp*............	12.00 -	18.00
7017 *Baltimore*.....................	12.00 -	18.00
Columbia 1735-D *Have You Ever Felt That Way?*	15.00 -	20.00
2806-D *High Society*................	15.00 -	20.00
2829-D *Chizzlin' Sam*...............	15.00 -	20.00
2863-D *Organ Grinder Blues*.........	15.00 -	20.00
14193-D *Candy Lips*................	10.00 -	15.00
14241-D *I'm Goin' Back To Bottomland*......	15.00 -	20.00
14244-D *Shootin' The Pistol*.........	15.00 -	20.00
14287-D *Dreaming The Hours Away*......	15.00 -	20.00
14314-D *Any Time*..................	15.00 -	20.00
14326-D *Red River Blues*............	35.00 -	50.00

14341-D *Farm Hand Papa*............	20.00 -	30.00
14348-D *Walk That Broad*............	25.00 -	35.00
14422-D *Mountain City Blues*.........	15.00 -	20.00
14434-D *In Our Cottage Of Love*.....	15.00 -	20.00
14447-D *Whoop It Up*...............	15.00 -	20.00
14460-D *Freeze Out*................	15.00 -	20.00
14468-D *Railroad Rhythm*............	15.00 -	20.00
14488-D *Zonky*....................	15.00 -	20.00
14502-D *I've Found A New Baby*......	15.00 -	20.00
14555-D *High Society Blues*..........	15.00 -	20.00
14666-D *Baby, Won't You Please Come Home?*	15.00 -	25.00
Domino 4687 *Baby, Won't You Please Come Home?*	15.00 -	20.00
Jewel 6164 *Hot Lovin'*..............	15.00 -	20.00
Okeh 4893 *Mixing The Blues*.........	15.00 -	20.00
4925 *Wild Cat Blues*................	20.00 -	30.00
4966 *Achin' Hearted Blues*...........	20.00 -	30.00
4975 *New Orleans Hop Scop Blues*.....	75.00 -	100.00
4993 *Old Fashioned Love*............	20.00 -	30.00
8020 *Pullman Porter Blues*...........	6.00 -	10.00
8021 *Roumania*....................	6.00 -	10.00
8027 *Brown Skin (Who You For)*.....	6.00 -	10.00
8029 *The Dance They Call The Georgia Hunch*	6.00 -	10.00
8171 *Texas Moaner Blues*............	35.00 -	50.00
8181 *Everybody Loves My Baby*.......	35.00 -	50.00
8204 *Temptation Blues*..............	10.00 -	15.00
8215 *Papa De-Da-Da*...............	50.00 -	75.00
8245 *Coal Cart Blues*...............	35.00 -	50.00
8254 *Santa Claus Blues*.............	35.00 -	50.00
8267 *Get It Fixed*..................	15.00 -	20.00
8272 *Livin' High Sometimes*.........	35.00 -	50.00
8286 *I've Found A New Baby*.........	25.00 -	35.00
8440 *Candy Lips*...................	15.00 -	20.00
8443 *Senegalese Stomp*..............	15.00 -	20.00
8462 *Cushion Foot Stomp*............	15.00 -	20.00
8465 *Black Snake Blues*.............	15.00 -	20.00
8510 *Close Fit Blues*................	15.00 -	20.00
8525 *Yama Yama Blues*..............	15.00 -	20.00
8572 *Log Cabin Blues*...............	15.00 -	20.00
8584 *Red River Blues*...............	30.00 -	50.00
8592 *Lazy Mama*...................	30.00 -	50.00
Okeh 8604 *Wildflower Rag*...........	15.00 -	20.00
8617 *Organ Grinder Blues*...........	15.00 -	20.00
8629 *Walk That Broad*...............	15.00 -	20.00
8645 *In The Bottle Blues*............	35.00 -	50.00
8663 *Freeze Out*....................	15.00 -	20.00
8672 *Steamboat Days*...............	15.00 -	20.00
8706 *High Society*..................	20.00 -	30.00
8738 *I've Got What It Takes*.........	20.00 -	30.00
8752 *You Don't Understand*..........	20.00 -	30.00
8763 *I've Found A New Baby*.........	20.00 -	30.00
8790 *Worn Out Blues*...............	20.00 -	30.00
8798 *He Wouldn't Stop Doin' It*......	20.00 -	30.00
8806 *You Rascal, You*...............	15.00 -	20.00
8821 *Shout, Sister, Shout!*...........	20.00 -	30.00
8826 *Kansas City Man Blues*.........	20.00 -	30.00
8842 *Papa De-Da-Da*...............	20.00 -	30.00
40006 *Shreveport*..................	20.00 -	30.00
40172 *My Own Blues*...............	6.00 -	10.00
40260 *Mandy, Make Up Your Mind*......	35.00 -	50.00
40321 *Cake-Walking Babies From Home*......	35.00 -	50.00
40541 *Dinah*......................	15.00 -	20.00
40598 *What's The Matter Now?*.......	15.00 -	20.00
41561 *Mister, Will You Serenade?*.....	15.00 -	25.00
Oriole 2141 *Papa De-Da-Da*..........	10.00 -	15.00
2164 *Hot Lovin'*...................	15.00 -	20.00
Paramount 12435 *Shut Your Mouth*....	35.00 -	50.00
12517 *Bottomland*..................	25.00 -	35.00
12839 *Midnight Stomp*..............	75.00 -	125.00
12870 *Pane In The Glass*............	75.00 -	125.00
12884 *Speakeasy*...................	75.00 -	125.00
12885 *Squeeze Me*..................	75.00 -	125.00

Perfect 15387 *Baby, Won't You Please Come Home?*	15.00 -	20.00
15403 *Hot Lovin'*	15.00 -	20.00
QRS 7004 *Speakeasy*	75.00 -	125.00
7005 *Squeeze Me*	75.00 -	125.00
7039 *Midnight Stomp*	75.00 -	125.00
7034 *Bozo*	75.00 -	125.00
7040 *I'm Through*	75.00 -	125.00
7044 *Sister Kate*	75.00 -	125.00
Romeo 1529 *Hot Lovin'*	15.00 -	20.00
Victor 38063 *Lazy Mama*	20.00 -	30.00
38524 *Too Low*	15.00 -	20.00
38630 *I'm Not Worryin'*	15.00 -	25.00
Vocalion 1088 *Cushion Foot Stomp*	20.00 -	30.00
1130 *Baltimore*	20.00 -	30.00
Vocalion 2541 *Breeze*	5.00 -	8.00
2563 *The Right Key But The Wrong Keyhole*	10.00 -	15.00
2584 *Chocolate Avenue*	10.00 -	15.00
2602 *Harlem Rhythm Dance*	10.00 -	15.00
2616 *Swaller-Tail Coat*	10.00 -	15.00
2629 *Jimmy Had A Nickel*	10.00 -	15.00
2630 *How Can I Get It?*	10.00 -	15.00
2654 *New Orleans Hop Scop Blues*	10.00 -	15.00
2674 *As Long As I Live*	10.00 -	15.00
2676 *St. Louis Blues*	10.00 -	15.00
2689 *I Can't Dance, I Got Ants In My Pants.*	10.00 -	15.00
2718 *Pretty Baby, Is It Yes Or No?*	10.00 -	15.00
2736 *After Tonight*	10.00 -	15.00
2759 *Let's Have A Showdown*	10.00 -	15.00
2778 *Bimbo*	10.00 -	15.00
2788 *Trouble*	10.00 -	15.00
2805 *Ain't Gonna Give You None Of My Jelly Roll*	10.00 -	15.00
2838 *Big Fat Mama*	10.00 -	15.00
2854 *Chizzlin' Sam*	10.00 -	15.00
2871 *Organ Grinder Blues*	10.00 -	15.00
2889 *Tell The Truth*	10.00 -	15.00
2899 *I Saw Stars.*	10.00 -	15.00
2909 *Jungle Crawl*	10.00 -	15.00
2927 *Milk Cow Blues*	10.00 -	15.00
2938 *Black Gal*	10.00 -	15.00
2958 *I Can See You All Over The Place*	10.00 -	15.00
2991 *Yama Yama Blues*	10.00 -	15.00
3195 *This Is My Sunday Off*	10.00 -	15.00
03350 *Mississippi Basin*	15.00 -	20.00
25009 *Black-Eyed Susan Brown*	10.00 -	15.00
25010 *High Society*	10.00 -	15.00

COOTIE WILLIAMS & HIS ORCHESTRA/RUG CUTTERS:

Okeh 5618 *Black Butterfly*	5.00 -	8.00
5690 *Give It Up*	5.00 -	8.00
6224 *Ain't Misbehavin'*	5.00 -	8.00
6336 *Top And Bottom*	5.00 -	8.00
6370 *West End Blues*	5.00 -	8.00
Variety 527 *Downtown Uproar*	7.00 -	10.00
555 *Diga Diga Doo*	7.00 -	10.00
Vocalion 3814 *Blue Reverie*	7.00 -	10.00
3818 *Diga Diga Doo*	7.00 -	10.00
3890 *I Can't Give You Anything But Love...*	8.00 -	12.00
3922 *Pigeons And Peppers*	8.00 -	12.00
3960 *Echoes Of Harlem*	7.00 -	10.00
4061 *Carnival In Caroline*	7.00 -	10.00
4086 *Ol' Man River*	7.00 -	10.00
4324 *Blue Is The Evening*	7.00 -	10.00
4425 *Swing Pan Alley*	7.00 -	10.00
4574 *The Boys From Harlem*	7.00 -	10.00
4646 *Mobile Blues*	7.00 -	10.00
4726 *Boudoir Benny*	7.00 -	10.00
4958 *Black Beauty*	5.00 -	8.00
5411 *Beautiful Romance*	5.00 -	8.00
5618 *Blues A-Poppin'*	5.00 -	8.00
5690 *Give It Up*	5.00 -	8.00

DOUGLAS WILLIAMS (FOUR) (& HIS ORCHESTRA):

Victor 21269 *Roadhouse Stomp*	10.00 -	15.00
21413 *Far Away Texas Blues*	20.00 -	30.00
21695 *Kind Daddy*	20.00 -	30.00
23264 *Darktown Jubilee*	40.00 -	60.00
23303 *Thrill Me*	40.00 -	60.00
23337 *Clarinet Jiggles*	40.00 -	60.00
23362 *Memphis Gal*	40.00 -	60.00
23387 *Leaving Blues*	40.00 -	60.00
38031 *Riverside Stomp*	15.00 -	20.00
38518 *Neal's Blues*	35.00 -	50.00
38850 *P-Wee Strut*	35.00 -	50.00
38623 *Louisiana Hop*	35.00 -	50.00

FESS WILLIAMS & HIS JOY BOYS:

Vocalion 15690 *Dixie Stomp*	75.00 -	100.00

FESS WILLIAMS & HIS ROYAL FLUSH (SAVOY) ORCHESTRA:

Brunswick 3532 *Variety Stomp*	15.00 -	20.00
3589 *Alligator Crawl*	15.00 -	20.00
3596 *Razor Edge*	10.00 -	15.00
Champion 15118 *Ya Gotta Know How To Love*	15.00 -	20.00
15120 *It's Breaking My Heart*	15.00 -	20.00
Diva 2189-G *My Mama's In Town*	10.00 -	15.00
Gennett 3182 *Green River Blues*	15.00 -	20.00
3210 *Caroline*	15.00 -	20.00
3259 *Wimmin—Aah!*	75.00 -	100.00
3336 *Ya Gotta Know How To Love*	15.00 -	20.00
Harmony 189-H *My Mama's In Town*	10.00 -	15.00
Okeh 8322 *Make Me Know It*	30.00 -	40.00
Velvet Tone 1189-V *My Mama's In Town*	10.00 -	15.00
Victor 22864 *Hot Mama*	15.00 -	20.00
23003 *Everything's O.K. With Me*	15.00 -	20.00
23005 *Dinah*	15.00 -	20.00
23025 *She's Still Dizzy*	15.00 -	20.00
24153 *Playing My Saxophone*	15.00 -	20.00
38506 *Here 'Tis*	15.00 -	20.00
38062 *Betsy Brown*	15.00 -	20.00
38604 *Do Shuffle*	15.00 -	20.00
38065 *Sweet Savannah Sue*	15.00 -	20.00
38077 *Hot Town*	15.00 -	20.00
38095 *Buttons*	15.00 -	20.00
38106 *Slide, Mr. Jelly*	15.00 -	20.00
38128 *Big Shot*	15.00 -	20.00
38131 *I'm Feelin' Devilish*	15.00 -	20.00
Vocalion 1054 *Heebie Jeebies*	10.00 -	15.00
1058 *High Fever*	20.00 -	30.00
1085 *White Ghost Shivers*	20.00 -	30.00
1087 *Gambler's Blues*	20.00 -	30.00
1117 *Ozark Blues*	15.00 -	20.00
15492 *High Fever*	15.00 -	20.00
15550 *Variety Stomp*	12.00 -	18.00

HOD WILLIAMS AND HIS ORCHESTRA:

Bluebird 7104, 7119, 7141	4.00 -	7.00

JOHN WILLIAMS & HIS MEMPHIS STOMPERS:

Black Patti 8009 *Pee Wee Blues*	75.00 -	100.00
Vocalion 1453 *Lotta Sax Appeal*	40.00 -	60.00

JOHN WILLIAMS' SYNCO JAZZERS:

Herwin 92018 *Goose Grease*	75.00 -	100.00
Paramount 12457 *Goose Grease*	75.00 -	100.00

(DRUMMER MAN) JOHNNY WILLIAMS & HIS BOYS/SWING SEXTETTE:

Variety 594 *Where's My Sweetie Hiding?*	7.00 -	10.00
638 *I'll Build A Stairway To Paradise*	7.00 -	10.00
Vocalion 3826 *Little Old Lady*	7.00 -	10.00
3827 *I'll Build A Stairway To Paradise*	7.00 -	10.00
5077 *Milenberg Joys*	5.00 -	8.00
5213 *Clarinet Marmalade*	5.00 -	8.00

LEONA WILLIAMS & HER DIXIE BAND:

Columbia A-3565 *Cruel Daddy Blues*	5.00 -	8.00

A-3599 *Achin' Hearted Blues*.............	5.00 -	8.00
A-3642 *Got To Cool My Doggies Now*......	5.00 -	8.00
A-3696 *Sugar Blues*..............	5.00 -	8.00
A-3713 *I Wish I Could Shimmy Like My Sister*		
Kate.............	5.00 -	8.00
A-3736 *Mexican Blues*...............	5.00 -	8.00
A-3815 *Bring It With You When You Come*..	5.00 -	8.00
A-3835 *If Your Man Is Like My Man*.......	5.00 -	8.00

MARY LOU WILLIAMS:

Brunswick 7178 *Night Life*.............	30.00 -	40.00
Decca 781 *Mary's Special*.............	7.00 -	10.00
1021 *Isabelle*..............	7.00 -	10.00
1155 *Clean Pickin'*.............	7.00 -	10.00
2796, 2797, 18122.............	3.00 -	6.00

MIDGE WILLIAMS & HER JAZZ JESTERS:

Variety 519 *Walkin' The Dog*.............	5.00 -	8.00
566 *Let's Begin Again*.............	5.00 -	8.00
620 *That Old Feeling*..............	7.00 -	10.00
670 *The One Rose (That's Left In My Heart)*.	8.00 -	12.00
Vocalion 3779 *I Know Now*.............	7.00 -	10.00
3801 *An Old Flame Never Dies*.............	8.00 -	12.00
3812 *Walkin' The Dog*.............	5.00 -	8.00
3821 *I'm Getting Sentimental Over You*......	5.00 -	8.00
3838 *I Was Born To Swing*..............	7.00 -	10.00
3865 *Fortune Tellin' Man*.............	8.00 -	12.00
3900 *Singin' The Blues*.............	7.00 -	10.00
3961 *Goodnight, Angel*.............	7.00 -	10.00
04026 *Love Is Like Whiskey*.............	7.00 -	10.00
4177 *In Any Language*.............	7.00 -	10.00
4192 *Don't Wake Up My Heart*.............	7.00 -	10.00

SAMMY WILLIAMS (& HIS THREE NATURALS):

Autograph (unnumbered) *House Of David Blues*.	35.00 -	50.00
Mandy, Make Up Your Mind.............	35.00 -	50.00
Vocalion 4197 *All Alone*.............	5.00 -	8.00
4229 *Some Sweet Day*.............	5.00 -	8.00
4243 *My Walking Stick*.............	5.00 -	8.00
4259 *Ain't She Sweet?*.............	5.00 -	8.00

SPEED WILLIAMS' ORCHESTRA:

Superior 2818 *Tin Roof Blues*.............	60.00 -	100.00

TE ROY WILLIAMS & HIS ORCHESTRA:

Titles, issued contemporaneously on Diva, Harmony, Velvet-Tone; *Lindberg Hop; On Malinda*....	20.00 -	30.00

WILLIMASON'S BEALE STREET FROLIC ORCHESTRA:

Victor 20555 *Memphis Scrontch*.............	20.00 -	30.00
21410 *Scandinavian Stomp*.............	20.00 -	30.00

VIRGINIA WILLRICH & HER TEXAS RANGERS:

Okeh 41328 *Same Old Moon*.............	20.00 -	30.00

WILSHIRE DANCE ORCHESTRA:

Sunset 1059 *My Best Girl*.............	8.00 -	12.00
1088 *Charleston Charley*.............	8.00 -	12.00

WILSON'S T.O.B.A. BAND:

Paramount 12408 *Steady Roll*.............	60.00 -	80.00

CHICKEN WILSON AND SKEETER HINTON:

QRS 7051 *Myrtle Avenue Stomp*.............	40.00 -	60.00
7052 *House Snake Blues*.............	40.00 -	60.00

DUKE WILSON & HIS TEN BLACK BERRIES:

Banner 32607 *Mary's Idea*.............	15.00 -	20.00
Banner 32643 *Beale Street Blues*.............	10.00 -	15.00
32733 *House Of David Blues*.............	15.00 -	20.00
Domino 0127 *House Of David Blues*.........	15.00 -	20.00
Melotone 12662 *House Of David Blues*........	15.00 -	20.00
Oriole 2466 *How'm I Doin' (Hey Hey)*.........	15.00 -	20.00
2488 *Beale Street Blues*.............	10.00 -	15.00
2677 *House Of David Blues*.............	15.00 -	20.00
Perfect 15603 *How'm I Doin' (Hey Hey)*.......	15.00 -	20.00
15617 *Beale Street Blues*.............	10.00 -	15.00
15632 *Bull Fiddle Blues*.............	7.00 -	10.00

15697 *Once Or Twice*.............	15.00 -	20.00
15738 *Goodbye Blues*.............	15.00 -	20.00
15753 *House Of David Blues*.............	15.00 -	20.00
Romeo 1858 *Beale Street Blues*.............	10.00 -	15.00

EDITH WILSON (& HER/JOHNNY DUNN'S JAZZ BAND/HOUNDS):

Brunswick 4685 *Black And Blue*.............	10.00 -	15.00
Columbia A-3479 *Vampin' Liza Jane*.............	7.00 -	10.00
A-3506 *Old Time Blues*.............	7.00 -	10.00
A-3537 *The West Texas Blues*.............	7.00 -	10.00
A-3558 *Birmingham Blues*.............	7.00 -	10.00
A-3634 *Mammy, I'm Thinking Of You*......	7.00 -	10.00
A-3653 *He May Be Your Man (But He Comes To See Me Sometimes)*.............	7.00 -	10.00
A-3674 *Lonesome Mama Blues*.............	7.00 -	10.00
A-3746 *Evil Blues*.............	7.00 -	10.00
A-3787 *He Used To Be Your Man But He's My Man Now*.............	7.00 -	10.00
14008-D *Daddy, Change Your Mind*........	15.00 -	20.00
14027-D *Muscle Shoals Blues*.............	7.00 -	10.00
14054-D *Double Crossin' Papa*.............	10.00 -	15.00
14066-D *There'll Be Some Changes Made*....	7.00 -	10.00
Diva 6025-G *I Don't Know And I Don't Care Blues*	15.00 -	20.00
Velvet Tone 7051-V *Daddy, Change Your Mind*.	15.00 -	20.00
Victor 38624 *I'll Get Even With You*.........	15.00 -	20.00

GARLAND WILSON:

Okeh 41556 *Rockin' Chair*.............	8.00 -	12.00

GEORGE WILSON AND JIMMY HINTON:

Paramount 12843 *Chicken Wilson Blues*.......	50.00 -	70.00
QRS 7060 *Frog Eye Stomp*.............	50.00 -	70.00

LENA WILSON:

Ajax 17014 *Down South Blues*.............	15.00 -	20.00
17025 *He Wasn't Born In Araby*.............	15.00 -	20.00
Black Swan 14129 *The Wicked Fives' Blues*....	15.00 -	20.00
Brunswick 2464, 2590.............	5.00 -	8.00
Clarion 5036-C *Chiropractor Blues*.............	8.00 -	12.00
Columbia 14618-D *My Man O'War*.............	15.00 -	25.00
Diva 6038-G *Baby, It Upsets Me So*.............	10.00 -	15.00
6045-G *Chiropractor Blues*.............	10.00 -	15.00
Emerson 10745 *I Don't Love Nobody*........	7.00 -	10.00
Harmograph 2543 *Deceitful Blues*.............	15.00 -	20.00
Paramount 12029 *Deceitful Blues*.............	15.00 -	20.00
12042 *Memphis, Tennessee*.............	15.00 -	20.00
Pathe-Actuelle 020910, 032015.............	5.00 -	7.00
Perfect 12044, 12094.............	5.00 -	7.00
Silvertone 3010 *Afternoon Blues*.............	10.00 -	15.00
Victor 19085 *Triflin' Blues*.............	4.00 -	7.00
Vocalion 14631 *Your Time Now*.............	4.00 -	7.00
14651 *Afternoon Blues*.............	10.00 -	15.00

ROY WILSON & HIS GEORGIA CRACKERS:

Melotone 12026 *Swamp Blues*.............	20.00 -	30.00

TEDDY WILSON (& HIS ORCHESTRA) TEDDY WILSON QUARTET:

Brunswick 7498 *What A Little Moonlight Can Do*	7.00 -	10.00
7501 *Miss Brown To You*.............	7.00 -	10.00
7511, 7520, 7543, 7550, 7554, 7563, 7522, 7572, 7577, 7581, 7599, 7612, 7640, 7663, 7684, 7699, 7702, 7729, 7736, 7762, 7768, 7781, 7789, 7797, 7816, 7824, 7840, 7844, 7859, 7867, 7877, 7884, 7893, 7903, 7911, 7917, 7926, 7940, 7943, 7954, 7960, 7964, 7973, 8008, 8015, 8025, 8053, 8070, 8112, 8116, 8141, 8153, 8199, 8207, 8259, 8265, 8270, 8281, 8283, 8314, 8319, 8438, 8455...	5.00 -	10.00
Columbia 35207, 35220, 35232, 35298, 35354, 35372, 35711, 35737.............	3.00 -	5.00

WOODROW WILSON:

Victor (12-inch) 35252 *Democratic Principles*....	5.00 -	8.00
35253 *The Tariff*.............	5.00 -	8.00

DALE WIMBROW (THE DEL-MAR-VA SONGSTER) & HIS RUBEVILLE TUNERS:

Edison 51894 *So Long North (I'm Headin' South)*	7.00 -	10.00
52292 *Oshkosh*.............	10.00 -	15.00

WINDY RHYTHM KINGS:

Broadway 1294 *Piggly Wiggly Blues*.........	60.00 -	100.00
Paramount 12770 *Piggly Wiggly Blues*........	60.00 -	100.00

WINEGAR'S PENN. BOYS:

Edison 52097 *Shaking The Blues Away*.......	8.00 -	15.00
52099 *Ooh! Maybe It's You*..............	8.00 -	15.00
52221 *Since My Best Gal Turned Me Down**.	15.00 -	20.00
52224 *Stay Out Of The South*............	7.00 -	10.00
52241 *Since My Best Gal Turned Me Down*..	10.00 -	15.00
52255 *Say So!*.....................	5.00 -	10.00
52305 *My Gal Sal*....................	10.00 -	15.00
52321 *Ida! Sweet As Apple Cider*.......	10.00 -	15.00
52381 *Imagination*...................	8.00 -	12.00
52596 *Dream Mother*..................	5.00 -	10.00

(*The only copy seen of 52221 plays same song both
sides, although flip side is labelled *A Good Man
Is Hard To Find*)

JACK WINN'S/WYNN'S DALLAS DANDIES:

Melotone 12008 *Lovey Lee*.............	8.00 -	12.00
12027 *Wild Man Blues*..................	10.00 -	15.00
12051 *Loved One*......................	35.00 -	50.00
12064 *Melancholy*.....................	10.00 -	15.00
Vocalion 15860 *Loved One*..............	35.00 -	50.00

CHIC WINTERS' (HOTEL GRAMATIN) ORCHESTRA:

Gennett 3294, 3314, 3320, 3340	5.00 -	10.00
Pennington 1437 *Rainy Nights*..........	90.00 -	130.00

JULIE WINTZ AND HIS (HOFBRAU/ MAYFLOWER) ORCHESTRA; JULIE WINTZ AND GEORGE ZIMMER'S JERSEY COLLEGIANS:

Harmony 436-H *Vo-Do-Do-Deo Blues*........	5.00 -	8.00
438-H *Magnolia*....................	5.00 -	8.00
1092-H *The Man from the South*..........	7.00 -	10.00
1104-H *Harmonica Harry*..............	7.00 -	10.00
1169-H *After You've Gone*.............	7.00 -	10.00
Pathe-Actuelle 36451 *Deep Henderson*.......	7.00 -	10.00
36460 *Spanish Mamma*.................	7.00 -	10.00
Perfect 14632 *Deep Henderson*..........	7.00 -	10.00
14641 *Spanish Mamma*..............	7.00 -	10.00
Velvet Tone 2092-V *The Man from the South*..	7.00 -	10.00
2104-V *Harmonica Harry*.............	7.00 -	10.00

BILL WIRGES & HIS ORCHESTRA:

Pathe-Actuelle 036262, 036352	4.00 -	7.00
Perfect 14443, 14533	4.00 -	7.00

WISCONSIN ROOF ORCHESTRA:

Broadway 1177 *Wob-A-Ly Walk*..............	10.00 -	15.00
1178 *Whispering*..................	10.00 -	15.00
1180 *When You're Smiling*..............	10.00 -	15.00
Paramount 20561 *Who's That Knockin' At My Door?*	10.00 -	15.00
20619 *Wob-A-Ly Walk*..............	10.00 -	15.00
20621 *Whispering*.................	10.00 -	15.00
20622 *When You're Smiling*............	10.00 -	15.00

WISCONSIN U SKYROCKETS:

Parmount 12641 *Slow Beef*.............	75.00 -	100.00
12642 *Postage Stomp*...............	75.00 -	100.00

WOLVERINE ORCHESTRA; THE WOLVERINES:

Brunswick 3332 *Crazy Quilt*..............	8.00 -	12.00
Gennett 5408 *Jazz Me Blues*.............	60.00 -	80.00
5453 *Copenhagen*..................	60.00 -	80.00
5454 *Riverboat Shuffle*.............	60.00 -	80.00
5542 *Lazy Daddy*..................	60.00 -	80.00
5565 *Tia Juana*...................	60.00 -	80.00
5620 *Prince Of Wails*..............	20.00 -	30.00

WOODING'S GRAND CENTRAL RED CAPS:

Victor 22718 *I Can't Get Enough Of You*......	10.00 -	20.00

BABE WOODS & HIS PALS:

Champion 15468 *Let's Misbehave*...........	10.00 -	15.00

ALLISTER WYLIE & HIS CORONADO HOTEL ORCHESTRA:

Brunswick 4143 *Come On, Baby!*...........	10.00 -	15.00

(ALBERT) WYNN'S (AND HIS) GUT BUCKET FIVE/CREOLE JAZZ BAND:

Okeh 8350 *When*....................	50.00 -	75.00
Vocalion 1218 *Crying My Blues Away*........	60.00 -	80.00
1220 *Parkway Stomp*.................	75.00 -	100.00
1252 *She's Crying For Me*.............	75.00 -	100.00

JACK WYNN'S DALLAS DANDIES; See JACK WINN'S DALLAS DANDIES

BILLY WYNNE & HIS GREENWICH VILLAGE INN ORCHESTRA:

Edison 51549 *When My Sugar Walks Down The Street*	7.00 -	12.00
51566 *Pango Pango Maid*.................	7.00 -	12.00
51573 *Say, Arabella*.................	7.00 -	12.00
51580 *Steppin' In Society*.............	7.00 -	12.00
51603 *Cecilia*....................	7.00 -	12.00
51606 *Charleston Baby O'Mine*........	7.00 -	12.00
51715 *Everything's Gonna Be All Right*..	7.00 -	12.00
Harmony 33-H, 34-H, 54-H, 57-H.......	4.00 -	7.00

THE YACHT CLUB BOYS:

Columbia 2887-D *We Own A Salon*.......	7.00 -	10.00
2908-D *The Great American Tourist*........	7.00 -	10.00

YALE COLLEGIANS:

Edison 52108 *You'll Do It Someday*...........	8.00 -	12.00
Okeh 41474 *Blue Again*.................	8.00 -	12.00

JIMMY YANCEY:

Bluebird 8630	4.00 -	8.00
Session 10001, 10003, 10005.........	5.00 -	8.00
Vocalion 05464, 05490...............	4.00 -	8.00

THE YANKEE SIX:

Okeh 40335 *Oh! Those Eyes*............	15.00 -	25.00
40348 *Jimtown Blues*..............	20.00 -	30.00

THE YANKEE TEN (DANCE) ORCHESTRA:

Oriole 684 *Baby Face*....................	5.00 -	8.00
846 *Ain't She Sweet?*.............	5.00 -	8.00
933 *Sometimes I'm Happy*............	8.00 -	12.00
1455 *Makin' Whoopee*...............	5.00 -	8.00
1726 *Look What You've Done To Me*....	12.00 -	16.00

DUKE YELLMAN AND HIS ORCHESTRA:

Edison 52225 *Missouri Squabble*..........	10.00 -	15.00
52227 *I'm More Than Satisfied*.........	10.00 -	15.00
52328 *Fireworks*.................	10.00 -	15.00
52353 *Louisiana*.................	10.00 -	15.00
52470 *If You Want The Rainbow*.......	10.00 -	15.00

YOUNG'S CREOLE JAZZ BAND:

Claxtonola 40272 *Tin Roof Blues*.............	90.00 -	120.00
Harmograph 863 *Tin Roof Blues*.........	90.00 -	120.00
Paramount 12060 *Every Saturday Night*.......	90.00 -	120.00
12088 *Dearborn Street Blues*........	100.00 -	150.00
20272 *Tin Roof Blues*.............	90.00 -	120.00
Puritan 11272 *Tin Roof Blues*.........	90.00 -	120.00

CLARENCE YOUNG'S HARMONY SYNCOPATORS:

Harmograph 874 *Jazzbo Jenkins*............	60.00 -	80.00

PATSY YOUNG:

Diva, Harmony, Velvet Tone	4.00 -	8.00

VICTOR YOUNG & HIS ORCHESTRA:

Brunswick 6128 *Sing A Little Jingle*..........	7.00 -	10.00
6554 *Two Tickets To Georgia*.........	7.00 -	10.00
6747 *This Little Piggie Went To Market*.....	7.00 -	10.00
20106 (12-inch) *Face The Music*......	10.00 -	15.00
Decca 279 *Mr. And Mrs. Is The Name*.....	5.00 -	8.00

BARNEY ZEEMAN'S KENTUCKY CARDINALS:

Gennett 3299 *I'd Rather Be Alone*...........	8.00 -	12.00
3360 *Horses*...................	8.00 -	12.00

BOB ZURKE & HIS DELTA RHYTHM BAND:

Victor	3.00 -	5.00

ZUTTY & HIS BAND:

Decca 431 *Look Over Yonder*............	5.00 -	8.00
432 *Clarinet Marmalade*..............	5.00 -	8.00
465 *Royal Garden Blues*..............	5.00 -	8.00

BLUES; RHYTHM & BLUES
1920s to early 1950s

All records in this section are 78 RPM unless otherwise stated. An asterisk (*) after price indicates that the record is known or likely to exist in 45 rpm form, with the same label and catalog number. The price of such 45 rpm records usually is substantially higher than the 78 rpm counterpart. Some issues are listed in this section (78 rpm) and in the 45 rpm section.

(PEG LEG) BEN ABNEY:

Bluebird 6496 *Dirty Double Crosser*	10.00 -	15.00
6628 *I'm Rattlesnakin' Daddy*	10.00 -	15.00
8121 *'Way Down In Town*	10.00 -	15.00

KATHERINE ADKINS:

Okeh 8363 *Individual Blues*	10.00 -	15.00

GARFIELD AKERS:

Vocalion 1442 *Cottonfield Blues*	150.00 -	200.00
1481 *Dough Roller Blues*	150.00 -	200.00

ALABAMA FOUR:

Victor 21136 *Queen Street Rag*	10.00 -	20.00

ALABAMA JIM (AND GEORGE):

Gennett 6905 *Crossin' Beale Street*	40.00 -	60.00
6918 *All Over You*	40.00 -	60.00
6949 *Deep Blue Sea*	40.00 -	60.00

ALABAMA SAM:

Titles, issued contemporaneously on Banner, Conqueror, Melotone, Oriole, Perfect, Romeo; *Red Cross Blues; You Gonna Need Me*	20.00 -	30.00

ALABAMA SHIEKS:

Victor 23261 *Sittin' On Top Of The World*	50.00 -	70.00
23265 *Travelin' Railroad Man Blues*	50.00 -	70.00

ALABAMA SLIM:

Savoy 5553 *Boar Hog Blues*	7.00 -	10.00

MOZELLE ANDERSON (AND BLIND JAMES BECK):

Black Patti 8003 *Mozelle Blues*	75.00 -	100.00
8004 *Room Rent Blues*	75.00 -	100.00
8029 *Tall Man Blues*	75.00 -	100.00
Brunswick 7159 *Tight In Chicago*	20.00 -	30.00

ALEXANDER BROTHERS:

Champion 16493 *Limehouse Blues*	10.00 -	20.00
16497 *Tiger Rag*	10.00 -	20.00
16499 *St. Louis Blues*	10.00 -	20.00

LITTLE DAVID ALEXANDER:

Ebony 1005 *Dupree Blues*	20.00 -	30.00

HILDA ALEXANDER:

Brunswick 7069 *He's Tight Like This*	75.00 -	100.00

ORA ALEXANDER:

Columbia 14626-D *Sweetest Daddy In Town*	20.00 -	30.00
14646-D *Ugle Man Blues*	20.00 -	30.00
14651-D *Rider Needs A Fast Horse*	20.00 -	30.00

TEXAS ALEXANDER:

Freedom 1538 *Crossroads*	25.00 -	40.00
Okeh 8498 *Section Gang Blues*	15.00 -	25.00
8511 *Corn-Bread Blues*	15.00 -	25.00
8526 *Farm Hand Blues*	15.00 -	25.00
8542 *Sabine River Blues*	15.00 -	25.00
8563 *Bell Cow Blues*	15.00 -	25.00
8578 *Death Bed Blues*	15.00 -	25.00
8591 *Deep Blue Sea Blues*	15.00 -	25.00
8603 *West Texas Blues*	15.00 -	25.00
8624 *Sittin' On A Log*	15.00 -	25.00
8640 *Blue Devil Blues*	15.00 -	25.00
8658 *'Frisco Train Blues*	40.00 -	60.00
8673 *Tell Me Woman Blues*	40.00 -	60.00
8688 *St. Louis Fair Blues*	15.00 -	25.00
8705 *Gold Tooth Blues*	25.00 -	40.00
8731 *Awful Moaning Blues*	25.00 -	40.00
8745 *Double Crossing Blues*	25.00 -	40.00
8751 *Peaceful Blues*	25.00 -	40.00
8764 *Broken Yo Yo*	25.00 -	40.00

8771 *Texas Special*	25.00 -	40.00
8785 *Thirty Day Blues*	25.00 -	40.00
8801 *Yellow Girl Blues*	25.00 -	50.00
8813 *She's So Far*	25.00 -	50.00
8823 *Last Stage Blues*	25.00 -	50.00
8835 *Days Is Lonesome*	25.00 -	50.00
8890 *Seen Better Days*	25.00 -	50.00
Vocalion 02743 *Blues In My Mind*	25.00 -	35.00
02764 *Prairie Dog Hole Blues*	25.00 -	35.00
02772 *Worried Blues*	25.00 -	35.00
02856 *Justice Blues*	30.00 -	40.00
02876 *Lonesome Valley Blues*	30.00 -	40.00
02894 *Katy Crossing Blues*	30.00 -	40.00
02912 *Deceitful Blues*	30.00 -	40.00

MAY ALIX (& HER HARMOGRAPH JAZZ BOYS):

Famous 3193 *Come On Home*	15.00 -	25.00
3237 *Loveless Love*	15.00 -	25.00
Harmograph 791 *Aggravatin' Papa*	25.00 -	40.00
816 *You Shall Reap Just What You Sow*	15.00 -	25.00
873 *Experience Blues*	35.00 -	50.00
Paramount 20243 *Loveless Love*	20.00 -	30.00
Puritan 11199 *Come On Home*	20.00 -	30.00
11243 *Loveless Love*	20.00 -	30.00

GEORGE ALLISON & WILLIE WHITE:

Paramount 12960 *How I Feel My Love*	40.00 -	60.00

TESSIE AMES:

Silvertone 3565 *Rider Blues*	15.00 -	20.00
3576 *High Yellow Blues*	20.00 -	30.00
3577 *Ada Jane's Blues*	20.00 -	30.00

AMOS:

Bluebird 5780 *Mean Mistreatin' Woman*	15.00 -	20.00
5862 *Muddy Water Blues*	15.00 -	20.00

IRA AMOS:

Modern 817 *Blue And Disgusted*	8.00 -	15.00
Octave 23-20 *I'm Lonesome*	8.00 -	15.00

BLIND JOE AMOS:

Vocalion 1116 *C & O Blues*	80.00 -	100.00

CURTIS AMY:

Gold Star 618 *Sleepin Blues*	15.00 -	25.00

"TALKING" BILLY ANDERSON:

Columbia 14216-D *Adam And Eve*	15.00 -	25.00
14274-D *Cow Cow Blues*	20.00 -	30.00

JELLY ROLL ANDERSON:

Gennett 6135 *Free Woman Blues*	60.00 -	80.00
6181 *Good Time Blues*	120.00 -	150.00
6226 *Salt Tear Blues*	150.00 -	200.00
Herwin 92014 *Salt Tear Blues*	50.00 -	75.00
92020 *Free Women Blues*	60.00 -	80.00

JIMMIE ANDERSON:

Broadway 5111 *Ko Ko Mo Blues*	150.00 -	200.00

LOUISE ANDERSON:

Gennett 6424 *Papa, You're Too Slow*	30.00 -	40.00

MAYBELLE ANDERSON:

Supertone 9429 *Moanful Wailin' Blues*	60.00 -	80.00

MISSOURI ANDERSON:

Vocalion 1041 *Somebody Else's Blues*	30.00 -	40.00

PINK ANDERSON & SIMMIE DOOLEY:

Columbia 14336-D *Gonna Tip Out Tonight*	15.00 -	25.00
14400-D *C.C. & O. Blues*	15.00 -	25.00

ED ANDREWS:

Okeh 8137 *Barrel House Blues*	15.00 -	20.00

MOSE ANDREWS:
Decca 7338 *Ten Pound Hammer* .... 15.00 - 25.00
ANDY BOY:
Bluebird 6858 *House Raid Blues* .... 15.00 - 20.00
  6893 *Jive Blues* .... 15.00 - 20.00
  6940 *Yellow Gal Blues* .... 15.00 - 20.00
  7075 *Evil Blues* .... 15.00 - 20.00
ROOSEVELT ANTRIM:
Bluebird 7149 *Complaint To Make* .... 20.00 - 30.00
  7475 *Station Boy Blues* .... 20.00 - 30.00
ARCHIBALD:
Colony 105 *Crescent City Bounce* .... 7.00 - 10.00
Imperial 5068, 5082, 5089, 5101, 5212 .... 5.00 - 10.00
ARKANSAS SHORTY:
Bluebird 6545 *Greyhound Bus* .... 15.00 - 20.00
  6571 *Double Crossing Buddy* .... 15.00 - 20.00
  6983 *Blue as a Fool Can Be* .... 15.00 - 20.00
MAY ARMSTRONG:
Brunswick 7010 *Joe Boy Blues* .... 25.00 - 35.00
Vocalion 1129 *Joe Boy Blues* .... 25.00 - 35.00
RICHARD ARMSTRONG:
Randy's 104 *Gene Nobel's Boggie* .... ———
SHELLEY ARMSTRONG:
Champion 50008 *How Long How Long Blues* ... 15.00 - 20.00
  50024 *Chain Gang Bound* .... 20.00 - 30.00
  50028 *B & O Blues* .... 15.00 - 20.00
  50029 *D.B.A. Blues* .... 15.00 - 20.00
Decca 7127 *My Old Pal Blues* .... 12.00 - 16.00
  7350 *B & O Blues* .... 8.00 - 12.00
KOKOMO ARNOLD:
Decca 7026 *Milk Cow Blues* .... 15.00 - 20.00
  7044 *Back To The Woods* .... 15.00 - 20.00
  7050 *Sissy Man Blues* .... 15.00 - 20.00
  7059 *Milk Cow Blues—No. 2* .... 15.00 - 20.00
  7069 *Chain Gang Blues* .... 15.00 - 20.00
  7070 *How Long, How Long Blues* .... 15.00 - 20.00
  7083 *Feels So Good* .... 15.00 - 20.00
  7092 *Slop Jar Blues* .... 15.00 - 20.00
  7103 *Tonic Head Blues* .... 15.00 - 20.00
  7116 *Milk Cow Blues—No. 3* .... 15.00 - 20.00
  7133 *Monday Morning Blues* .... 15.00 - 20.00
  7139 *Southern Railroad Blues* .... 15.00 - 20.00
  7147 *Policy Wheel Blues* .... 15.00 - 20.00
  7156 *Back Door Blues* .... 15.00 - 20.00
  7163 *Milk Cow Blues—No. 4* .... 15.00 - 20.00
  7165 *Desert Blues* .... 15.00 - 20.00
  7172 *Sundown Blues* .... 15.00 - 20.00
  7181 *Stop Look and Listen* .... 15.00 - 20.00
  7198 *Model 'T' Woman Blues* .... 15.00 - 20.00
  7212 *Bull Headed Woman Blues* .... 15.00 - 20.00
  7242 *Coffin Blues* .... 15.00 - 20.00
  7261 *Lonesome Road Blues* .... 15.00 - 20.00
  7267 *Salty Dog* .... 15.00 - 20.00
  7275 *Fool Man Blues* .... 15.00 - 20.00
  7285 *Laugh And Grin Blues* .... 15.00 - 20.00
  7306 *Long And Tall* .... 15.00 - 20.00
  7319 *Black Mattie* .... 15.00 - 20.00
  7347 *Red Beans And Rice* .... 15.00 - 20.00
  7361 *Big Ship Blues* .... 15.00 - 20.00
  7390 *Back On The Job* .... 15.00 - 20.00
  7417 *Head Cuttin' Blues* .... 15.00 - 20.00
  7431 *Neck Bone Blues* .... 15.00 - 20.00
  7449 *Rocky Road Blues* .... 15.00 - 20.00
  7464 *Kid Man Blues* .... 15.00 - 20.00
  7485 *Something's Hot* .... 15.00 - 20.00
  7510 *Midnight Blues* .... 15.00 - 20.00
  7540 *Bad Luck Blues* .... 15.00 - 20.00
Decca 48000 *Milk Cow Blues* .... 4.00 - 7.00
MILDRED AUSTIN:
Champion 15530 *Sing That Song With Feeling* .. 20.00 - 30.00
BABY BONNIE:
Buddy 8021 *I Got Your Water On* .... 25.00 - 35.00

  8023 *Home, Sweet Home Blues* .... 25.00 - 35.00
Gennett 3041 *Longing Blues* .... 20.00 - 35.00
  5593 *I Got Your Water On* .... 20.00 - 35.00
  5616 *Backbiting Moan* .... 20.00 - 35.00
  5644 *Longing Blues* .... 20.00 - 35.00
Silvertone 4031 *Backbiting Moan* .... 20.00 - 35.00
  4034 *I Got Your Water On* .... 20.00 - 35.00
BABY BOY:
Sampson 633 *Taxi Driver* .... 30.00 - 50.00
BABY DOO:
Decca 7763 *The Death Of Walter Barnes* .... 10.00 - 15.00
  7773 *I'm Gonna Walk Your Log* .... 10.00 - 15.00
(VOCALIST) BABY FACE (LEROY) (TRIO):
Chess 1447 *Take A Little Walk With Me* ...... 10.00 - 20.00
J.O.B. 100 *Take A Little Walk With Me* ...... 50.00 - 75.00
Parkway 104 *Boll Weevil* .... 80.00 - 100.00
  501 *Rollin' And Tumblin'* .... 80.00 - 100.00
Savoy 1122 *Red Headed Woman* .... 10.00 - 20.00
THE BACK PORCH BOYS:
Apollo 392 *Big Hip Mama* .... 10.00 - 15.00
  406 *Sweet Woman Blues* .... 10.00 - 15.00
DE FORD BAILEY:
Bluebird 5147 *Ice Water Blues* .... 8.00 - 12.00
Brunswick 146 *Pan-American Blues* .... 15.00 - 20.00
  147 *Muscle Shoals Blues* .... 15.00 - 20.00
  148 *Alcoholic Blues* .... 15.00 - 20.00
  149 *Fox Chase* .... 15.00 - 20.00
  434 *Up Country Blues* .... 10.00 - 15.00
Victor 23336 *John Henry* .... 30.00 - 40.00
  23831 *John Henry* .... 30.00 - 40.00
  38014 *Ice Water Blues* .... 20.00 - 30.00
KID BAILEY:
Brunswick 7114 *Rowdy Blues* .... 150.00 - 300.00
RED MIKE BAILEY:
Paramount 13077 *Neck Bone Blues* .... 75.00 - 100.00
HOUSTON BAINES:
Blues & Rhythm 7001 *Going Home* .... 10.00 - 15.00
BLIND BOBBY BAKER:
Pathe-Actuelle 7533 *Macon Georgia Cut-Out* ... 20.00 - 30.00
Perfect 133 *Macon Georgia Cut-Out* .... 20.00 - 30.00
C.B. BAKER:
Sittin' In With 625 *Skin To Skin* .... 15.00 - 25.00
DOROTHY BAKER:
Decca 7080 *Steady Grinding Blues* .... 20.00 - 30.00
KATHERINE BAKER:
Gennett 6125 *I Helped You, Sick Man* .... 30.00 - 50.00
  6157 *Chicago Fire Blues* .... 30.00 - 50.00
  6194 *Wild Woman Blues* .... 30.00 - 50.00
  6228 *Money Woman Blues* .... 30.00 - 50.00
  6321 *Mistreated Blues* .... 30.00 - 50.00
Herwin 92017 *My Man Left Me Blues* .... 40.00 - 60.00
  92022 *Chicago Fire Blues* .... 40.00 - 60.00
  90237 *Daddy Sunshine Blues* .... 40.00 - 60.00
  92038 *Wild Woman Blues* .... 40.00 - 60.00
  92039 *Mistreated Blues* .... 40.00 - 60.00
VIOLA BAKER:
Okeh 8141 *Sweet Man Blues* .... 10.00 - 15.00
WILLIE BAKER:
Gennett 6751 *Weak-Minded Blues* .... 80.00 - 100.00
  6766 *No No Blues* .... 80.00 - 100.00
  6812 *Bad Luck Moan* .... 80.00 - 100.00
  6846 *Crooked Woman Blues* .... 80.00 - 100.00
BANJO JOE:
Paramount 12571 *Poor Boy, Long Ways From Home* ... 40.00 - 60.00
  12588 *Jonestown Blues* .... 40.00 - 60.00
  12604 *Jazz Gypsy Blues* .... 40.00 - 60.00
BARBECUE BOB:
Columbia 14205-D *Barbecue Blues* .... 15.00 - 25.00
  14222-D *Mississippi Heavy Water Blues* ...... 15.00 - 25.00
  14246-D *Honey You Don't Know My Mind* .. 15.00 - 25.00
  14257-D *Brown-Skin Gal* .... 15.00 - 25.00

14268-D	*It Won't Be Long Now*	15.00 -	25.00
14280-D	*Crooked Woman Blues*	15.00 -	25.00
14299-D	*Thinkin' Funny Blues*	15.00 -	25.00
14316-D	*Goin' Up The Country*	20.00 -	30.00
14331-D	*Waycross Georgia Blues*	20.00 -	30.00
14350-D	*My Mistake Blues*	20.00 -	30.00
14372-D	*Blind Pig Blues*	20.00 -	30.00
14383-D	*Cold Wave Blues*	20.00 -	30.00
14412-D	*Dollar Down Blues*	20.00 -	30.00
14424-D	*It's Just Too Bad*	20.00 -	30.00
14436-D	*It's a Funny Little Thing*	25.00 -	35.00
14449-D	*Good Time Rounder*	25.00 -	35.00
14461-D	*Bad Time Blues*	25.00 -	35.00
14479-D	*Yo Yo Blues*	30.00 -	40.00
14507-D	*Me And My Whiskey*	30.00 -	40.00
14523-D	*Yo You Blues No. 2*	30.00 -	40.00
14546-D	*Telling It To You*	30.00 -	40.00
14588-D	*The Spider And The Fly*	30.00 -	40.00
14573-D	*California Blues*	30.00 -	40.00
14581-D	*Jambooger Blues*	30.00 -	40.00
14591-D	*Atlanta Moan*	30.00 -	40.00
14614-D	*It Just Won't Quit*	30.00 -	40.00

JOHN HENRY BARBEE:
Vocalion 04417 *Six Weeks Old Blues* ... 10.00 - 20.00

BAREFOOT BILL:

Columbia 14481-D	*Big Rock Jail*	60.00 -	90.00
14510-D	*My Crime Blues*	60.00 -	90.00
14526-D	*Squabblin' Blues*	60.00 -	90.00
14561-D	*One More Time*	60.00 -	90.00

WILEY BARNER:
Gennett 6261 *My Gal Treats Me Mean* ... 35.00 - 50.00

FAE BARNES:

Black Swan 12153	*I Just Want A Daddy*	12.00 -	16.00
Paramount 12099	*Good-Bye Blues*	10.00 -	15.00
12136	*I Just Want A Daddy*	10.00 -	15.00

WILLIE BARNES:

Champion 15378	*My Gal Treats Me Mean*	30.00 -	40.00
Silverton 5121	*My Gal Treats Me Mean*	60.00 -	80.00

MARTHA BARR:
Broadway 5017 *Memphis Earthquake* ... 40.00 - 60.00

BARRELL HOUSE ANNIE:
Vocalion 03542 *Must Get Mine In Front* ... 10.00 - 15.00

BARREL HOUSE BUCK:

Decca 7013	*Lamp Post Blues*	15.00 -	20.00
7030	*Mercy Mercy Blues*	15.00 -	20.00

BARRELHOUSE FRANKIE:
Paramount 13019 *Smother Me Blues* ... 40.00 - 60.00

BARRELHOUSE SAMMY (THE COUNTRY BOY):
Atlantic 891 *Kill It Kid* ... 15.00 - 25.00

VIOLA BARTLETTE:

Paramount 12322	*Tennessee Blues*	30.00 -	40.00
12345	*Quit Knocking On My Door*	30.00 -	40.00
12351	*Anna Mina Forty And St. Louis Shorty*	50.00 -	/75.00
12363	*Out Bound Train Blues*	50.00 -	75.00
12369	*Sunday Morning Blues*	50.00 -	75.00

SLIM BARON (& EDDIE MAPP) (& JAMES MOORE):

Paramount 13114	*Fourth Avenue Blues*	75.00 -	100.00
QRS 7081	*It's Tight Like That*	75.00 -	100.00
7088	*I'm Hot Like That*	75.00 -	100.00
7089	*Fouth Avenue Blues*	75.00 -	100.00

TIPPY BARTON:
Vocalion 1742 *High Brown Cheater* ... 15.00 - 20.00

BAT THE HUMMING BIRD:
Varsity 6068 *Humming Blues* ... 10.00 - 15.00

DEACON L. J. BATES:
Paramount 12585 *He Arose From The Dead* ... 25.00 - 40.00

WILL BATTS:

Vocalion 02531	*Country Woman*	50.00 -	75.00
02542	*Cadillac Baby*	50.00 -	75.00

A. & J./ANDREW AND JIM BAXTER:

Victor 20962	*K.C. Railroad Blues*	50.00 -	75.00
21475	*The Moore Girl*	90.00 -	130.00
23394	*Done Wrong Blues*	80.00 -	100.00
23404	*Operator Blues*	80.00 -	100.00
38002	*Georgia Stomp*	50.00 -	75.00
38603	*It Tickles Me*	75.00 -	100.00

HELEN BAXTER:

Banner 1920	*I Wants A Real Man*	15.00 -	20.00
1958	*Scrubbin' Blues*	15.00 -	20.00

BEALE STREET ROUNDERS:
Vocalion 1555 *I'm Sittin' On Top Of The World* 50.00 - 75.00

BEALE STREET SHEIKS:

Paramount 12518	*It's A Good Thing*	60.00 -	100.00
12531	*Half Cup Of Tea*	60.00 -	100.00
12552	*Blues In 'D'*	60.00 -	100.00
12576	*Beale Town Bound*	60.00 -	100.00
12591	*Jazzin' The Blues*	60.00 -	100.00
12758	*Rockin' On The Hill Blues*	80.00 -	110.00
12774	*Hunting Blues*	80.00 -	110.00
12894	*Fillin' In Blues*	80.00 -	110.00

LOTTIE BEAMAN:

Brunswick 7147	*Going Away Blues*	30.00 -	50.00
Paramount 12201	*Honey Blues*	15.00 -	25.00
12235	*Regular Man Blues*	20.00 -	30.00
12254	*Sugar Daddy Blues*	20.00 -	30.00

HELEN BEASLEY:
Brunswick 7077 *Tia Juana Blues* ... 20.00 - 30.00

WALTER BEASLEY:

Okeh 8540	*Georgia Skin*	15.00 -	20.00
8564	*Sore Feet Blues*	15.00 -	20.00

CHARLES/ELDER CHARLIE BECK:

Bluebird 8244	*Changes*	7.00 -	10.00
8271	*You Can't Hurry God*	7.00 -	10.00
8317	*Dry Bones*	7.00 -	10.00
8337	*Talk On Talkers*	7.00 -	10.00
Decca 7320	*If I Have To Run*	10.00 -	15.00
Decca 7344	*I'm A Stranger*	7.00 -	10.00
7372	*Love, Oh Love Divine*	7.00 -	10.00
7418	*That's The Way I Do*	7.00 -	10.00
Okeh 8907	*When The World's On Fire*	20.00 -	30.00

JOHNNY BECK (THE BLIND BOY):
Sittin' In With 531 *Locked In Jail Blues* ... 15.00 - 20.00

SON BECKY:

Vocalion 03942	*Sunrise Blues*	20.00 -	30.00
03967	*Sweet Woman Blues*	20.00 -	30.00
04081	*Cryin' Shame Blues*	20.00 -	30.00

WILLIE BEE:
Vocalion 03907 *Ramblin' Mind Blues* ... 8.00 - 12.00

BROTHER BELL:
Blues & Rhythm 7002 *If You Feel Froggish* ... 7.00 - 12.00

ED BELL:

Columbia 14595-D	*She's A Fool Gal*	50.00 -	75.00
Paramount 12524	*Ham Bone Blues*	75.00 -	100.00
12546	*Mean Conductor Blues*	75.00 -	100.00

BABY BENBOW:
Okeh 8098 *Down Home Gal* ... 5.00 - 8.00

ELOISE BENNETT:

Black Patti 8006	*Sting Me, Mr. Strange Man*	40.00 -	60.00
Gennett 6147	*I Can't Be Satisfied With One*	20.00 -	30.00
Paramount 12412	*Effervescent Daddy*	20.00 -	30.00

WILL BENNETT:
Vocalion 1464 *Railroad Bill* ... 75.00 - 100.00

GLADYS BENTLEY:

Okeh 8610	*Ground Hog Blues*	10.00 -	15.00
8612	*Moanful Wailin' Blues*	10.00 -	15.00
8634	*Wild Geese Blues*	15.00 -	20.00
8707	*Big Gorilla Man*	15.00 -	25.00

GLORY BERNARD:

Grey Gull 7035	*South Bound Blues*	15.00 -	20.00
7036	*Cockroach Blues*	15.00 -	20.00

BESSEMER MELODY BOYS:

Victor 23252, 38606	7.00 -	10.00

BIDDLEVILLE QUINTETTE:

QRS 7070 *Wasn't That a Mighty Day?*	15.00 -	20.00
7071 *Holy Is Thy Name*	15.00 -	20.00
7072 *Got The Heaven In My View*	15.00 -	20.00
7073 *Didn't It Rain?*	15.00 -	20.00
7075 *Jesus Is The Rock*	15.00 -	20.00
7076 *The Lord Giveth*	15.00 -	20.00

BIG BILL (& HIS JUG BUSTERS/MEMPHIS FIVE/ORCHESTRA) BIG BILL & THOMPS:

Titles, issued contemporaneously on Banner, Melotone, Oriole, Perfect, Romeo: *Ash Hauler; Barrel House When It Rains; Big Bill Blues; Big Bill's Milk Cow No.2; Black Mare Blues; Black Widow Spider; Border Blues; Bricks In My Pillow; Bull Cow Blues No. 3; C and A Blues; C.C. Rider; Cherry Hill; Come Home Early; Detroit Special; Dirty No-Gooder; Dying Day Blues; Evil Hearted Me; Falling Rain; Get Away; Good Boy; Hard Headed Woman; Hattie Blues; Hobo Blues; Horny Frog; I'm A Southern Man; It's Too Late Now; I Wanta See My Baby Cry; I Want My Hands On It; I Want You By My Side; Let Her Go—She Don't Know; Let Me Be Your Winder; Let's Reel and Rock; Little Bug; Louise, Louise, Blues; Low Down Woman Blues; Low Land BLues; Made A Date With An Angel; Married Life's A Pain; Match Box Blues; Mean Old World; My Big Money; My Gal Is Gone; My Old Lizzie; My Woman -Mistreated Me; Of Babe; Play Your Hand; Pneumonia Blues; Prowlin' Ground Hog; Rising Sun Shine On; Serve It To me Right; Seven-Eleven; Somebody's Got To Go; Something Good; Southern Flood Blues; Tell We Wat You Been Doing; Terrible Flood Blues; These Ants Keep Biting Me; W.P.A. Blues; You Do Me Any Old Way; You Know I Gotta Reason; You Know I Need Lovin'; You May Need My Help Someday* — 10.00 - 15.00

Titles issued contemporaneously on Banner, Melotone, Oriole, Perfect, Romeo: *Bull Cow Blues; How You Want It Done?, Long Tall Mama; M and O Blues; Mistreatin' Mama Blues; Rukus Juice Blues; Shelby County Blues; Too-Too Train Blues; Worrying You Off My Mind* — 15.00 - 25.00

Bluebird 5476 *Bull Cow Blues*	10.00 -	15.00
5535 *Friendless Blues*	10.00 -	15.00
5571 *At The Break Of Day*	10.00 -	15.00
5474 *Serve It To Me Right*	10.00 -	15.00
5706 *Hungry Man Blues*	10.00 -	15.00
5998 *The Southern Blues*	10.00 -	15.00
6060 *Mountain Blues*	10.00 -	15.00
6111 *I'm Just A Bum*	10.00 -	15.00
6230 *Down The Line Blues*	10.00 -	15.00
Columbia 30002, 30009, 30016, 30135	3.00 -	7.00
Conqueror	4.00 -	8.00
Paramount 12656 *House Rent Stomp*	75.00 -	100.00
12707 *Down In The Basement Blues*	75.00 -	100.00
Vocalion	4.00 -	8.00

BIG BLOKE:

Varsity 6051 *Everybody Likes That Thing*	10.00 -	15.00

BIG CHIEF (& HIS) TRIO:

Sittin' In With 523 *Big Chief's Blues*	7.00 -	10.00
530 *Poor Man's Blues*	7.00 -	10.00

ESTHER BIGEOU:

Okeh 8025 *Stingaree Blues*	8.00 -	12.00
8026 *The Memphis Blues*	8.00 -	12.00
8029 *Nervous Blues*	8.00 -	12.00
8053 *Aggravatin' Papa*	7.00 -	10.00
8054 *Four O'Clock Blues*	7.00 -	10.00
8056 *The Gulf Coast Blues*	7.00 -	10.00
8057 *Beale Street Mama*	7.00 -	10.00
8058 *Beale Street Blues*	7.00 -	10.00
8065 *The Hesitating Blues*	7.00 -	10.00
Okeh 8118 *West Indies Blues*	15.00 -	20.00
8125 *Panama Limited Blues*	7.00 -	10.00

BIG JOE (AND HIS RHYTHM/WASHBOARD BAND):

Bluebird 7022 *Brother James*	25.00 -	35.00
7065 *Rootin' Ground Hog*	25.00 -	35.00
8814 *We Can't Agree*	7.00 -	10.00
8864 *What Will I Do?*	7.00 -	10.00
8956 *Got To Go Blues*	7.00 -	10.00
8986 *It Ain't No Lie*	7.00 -	10.00
9013 *Sleeping By Myself*	5.00 -	8.00
Okeh 06141 *I Love You Baby*	7.00 -	10.00
06175 *When You Said Goodbye*	7.00 -	10.00

BIG JOHN:

Acorn 304 *Too Late Blues*	———	

BIG MACEO:

Bluebird 8772, 8798, 8827, 8939, 8973, 9012	5.00 -	8.00
34-0703, 34-0735, 34-0743	3.00 -	6.00
Fortune 137, 805	7.00 -	10.00
Specialty 320, 346	5.00 -	10.00
RCA Victor 20-1870, 20-2028, 20-2173, 20-2353, 20-2505, 20-2687	3.00 -	6.00

BIG OSCAR:

Decca 7067 *Mistreatment Blues*	10.00 -	15.00

BIG MEMPHIS MA RAINEY:

Sun 184 *Baby, No, No*	40.00 -	60.00

BIG RICHARD:

Varsity 6063 *Pig Meat Mama*	8.00 -	12.00

BIG SISTER:

Varsity 6063 *Pig Meat Mama*	8.00 -	12.00

BIG THREE TRIO:

Columbia 30019, 30055, 30103, 30108, 30110, 30125	3.00 -	6.00
Okeh	3.00 -	6.00

BIG WILLIE:

Apollo 450 *Bogey Man*	8.00 -	12.00

D.H. BILBRO:

Victor 23831 *Chester Blues*	30.00 -	40.00

BILL AND SLIM:

Champion 16015 *Papa's Gettin' Hot*	35.00 -	50.00

BILLY & JESSE:

Brunswick 7099 *Put Your Mind On It*	15.00 -	20.00

BILLY BIRD:

Columbia 14381-D *Mill Man Blues*	15.00 -	25.00
14418-D *Alabama Blues*	15.00 -	25.00

BIRMINGHAM QUARTET:

Columbia 14154-D, 14190-D, 14224-D, 14263-D, 14311-D, 14567-D	7.00 -	12.00

BIRMINGHAM SAM:

Savoy 5558 *Landing Blues*	7.00 -	10.00

BLACK ACE:

Decca 7281 *Trifling Woman*	20.00 -	30.00
7340 *Whiskey And Woman*	20.00 -	30.00
7387 *Christmas Time Blues*	20.00 -	30.00

BLACK BOY SHINE:

Vocalion 03417 *Sugarland Blues*	15.00 -	20.00
03454 *Crazy Woman Blues*	15.00 -	20.00
03484 *Back Home Blues*	15.00 -	20.00
03551 *Wrong Doing Woman Blues*	15.00 -	20.00
03613 *Grey With Worry Blues*	15.00 -	20.00
03624 *Bed And Breakfast Blues*	15.00 -	20.00
03687 *Business Woman Blues*	15.00 -	20.00
03757 *Coal Woman Blues*	15.00 -	20.00
04003 *Hobo Blues*	15.00 -	20.00
(Note: First four titles issued contemporaneously on Banner, Melotone, Oriole, Perfect, Romeo:	15.00 -	20.00

BLACK DIAMOND:

Jaxyson 50 *Lonesome Blues*	10.00 -	20.00

BLACK IVORY KING:

Decca 7307 *The Flying Crow*	15.00 -	20.00
7355 *Match Box Blues*	15.00 -	20.00

BLACK SPIDER DUMPLIN':
Bluebird 6972 *John D. Blues*............ 15.00 - 20.00
  6995 *Sold It To The Devil*............ 10.00 - 15.00
  7001 *Death Of The Gambler*............ 10.00 - 15.00
FRANKIE BLACK:
Champion 50000 *Wayback Blues*......... 20.00 - 30.00
  50036 *Bad Liquor Blues*............ 20.00 - 30.00
  50049 *Alley Sally Blues*............ 20.00 - 30.00
LEWIS BLACK:
Columbia 14291-D *Gravel Camp Blues*......... 20.00 - 30.00
  14429-D *Rock Island Blues*............ 20.00 - 30.00
MAMIE BLACKBURN:
Herwin 92015 *Bird Nest Blues*............ 50.00 - 75.00
FRANCIS/SCRAPPER BLACKWELL:
Bluebird 5914 *A Blues*............ 10.00 - 15.00
  5973 *Springtime Blues*............ 40.00 - 60.00
Champion 16361 *Back Door Blues*............ 35.00 - 50.00
  16370 *Rambling Blues*............ 35.00 - 50.00
  16452 *Down South Blues*............ 35.00 - 50.00
Gennett 7158 *Springtime Blues*............ 40.00 - 60.00
Vocalion 1192 *Kokomo Blues*............ 35.00 - 50.00
  1213 *Trouble Blues*............ 35.00 - 50.00
  1276 *Non-Skid Tread*............ 35.00 - 50.00
  1417 *Mr. Scrapper's Blues*............ 35.00 - 50.00
  02752 *Morning Mail Blues*............ 35.00 - 50.00
WILLIE "61" BLACKWELL:
Bluebird 8810, 8845, 8876, 8921............ 10.00 - 15.00
SUNNY BLAIR:
Meteor 5006 *Please Send My Baby Back*....... 10.00 - 20.00*
RPM 354 *Five Foot Three Blues*........... 15.00 - 20.00*
BLIND ARTHUR
Paramount 12892 *Blind Arthur's Breakdown*.... 75.00 - 100.00
BLIND BLAKE:
Paramount 12387 *Early Morning Blues*........ 25.00 - 40.00
  12413 *Skeedle Loo Doo Blues*............ 25.00 - 40.00
  12431 *Too Tight*............ 25.00 - 40.00
  12442 *Tampa Bound*............ 25.00 - 40.00
  12464 *Buck-Town Blues*............ 25.00 - 40.00
  12479 *One Time Blues*............ 25.00 - 40.00
  12497 *Bad Feeling Blues*............ 25.00 - 40.00
  12565 *Southern Rag*............ 25.00 - 40.00
  12583 *Hard Road Blues*............ 25.00 - 40.00
  12597 *Wabash Rag*............ 25.00 - 40.00
  12606 *Brownskin Mama Blues*............ 25.00 - 40.00
  12634 *C.C. Pill Blues*............ 50.00 - 75.00
  12643 *Tootie Blues*............ 30.00 - 40.00
  12657 *Detroit Bound Blues*............ 30.00 - 40.00
  12673 *Hot Potatoes*............ 50.00 - 75.00
  12681 *South Bound Rag*............ 50.00 - 75.00
  12695 *Low Down Loving Gal*............ 30.00 - 40.00
  12710 *Back Door Slam Blues*............ 30.00 - 40.00
  12723 *No Dough Blues*............ 30.00 - 40.00
  12737 *Search Warrant Blues*............ 30.00 - 40.00
  12754 *Notoriety Woman Blues*............ 30.00 - 40.00
  12767 *Ramblin' Mama Blues*............ 30.00 - 40.00
  12794 *Hookworm Blues*............ 30.00 - 40.00
  12810 *Poker Woman Blues*............ 30.00 - 40.00
  12824 *Georgia Bound*............ 30.00 - 40.00
  12863 *Fightin' The Jug*............ 50.00 - 80.00
  12867 *Third Degree Blues*............ 40.00 - 60.00
  12888 *Police Dog Blues*............ 40.00 - 60.00
  12904 *Ice Man Blues*............ 40.00 - 60.00
  12918 *Cold Love Blues*............ 50.00 - 75.00
  12964 *Keep It Home*............ 50.00 - 75.00
  12994 *Hard Pushing Papa*............ 50.00 - 75.00
  13016 *Ain't Gonna Do That No More*....... 50.00 - 75.00
  13035 *Playing Policy Blues*............ 50.00 - 75.00
  13103 *Rope Stretchin' Blues*............ 60.00 - 90.00
  13115 *Dissatisfied Blues*............ 60.00 - 90.00
  13123 *Night And Day Blues*............ 60.00 - 90.00
  13137 *Depression's Gone From Me Blues*.... 60.00 - 90.00

BLIND GARY:
Titles, issued contemporaneously on Banner,
Melotone, Oriole, Perfect, Romeo: *Cross And Evil
Woman Blues; I'm Throwin' Up My Hand*... 15.00 - 20.00
BLIND MACK:
Vocalion 03167 *Rootin' Ground Hog Blues*..... 30.00 - 40.00
BLIND NORRIS:
Decca 7290 *Sundown Blues*............ 15.00 - 25.00
BLIND PERCY & HIS BLIND BAND:
Paramount 12584 *Coal River Blues*........... 40.00 - 60.00
BLIND SAMMIE:
Columbia 14484-D *Travelin' Blues*............ 90.00 - 120.00
  14551-D *Razor Ball*............ 90.00 - 120.00
  14632-D *Broke Down Engine Blues*............ 90.00 - 120.00
  14657-D *Atlanta Strut*............ 90.00 - 120.00
BLIND WILLIE (& PARTNER):
Regal 3260 *How About You*............ 20.00 - 30.00
Vocalion 02568 *Weary Hearted Blues*......... 60.00 - 90.00
  02577 *Death Cell Blues*............ 60.00 - 90.00
  02595 *Warm It Up To Me*............ 60.00 - 90.00
  02622 *It's A Good Little Thing*............ 60.00 - 90.00
  02623 *Lord Have Mercy If You Please*...... 60.00 - 90.00
  02668 *My Baby's Gone*............ 60.00 - 90.00
BLUE BELLE:
Okeh 9483 *High Water Blues*............ 15.00 - 25.00
  8538 *Sneakin' Lizard Blues*............ 15.00 - 25.00
  8553 *Dead Sea Blues*............ 15.00 - 25.00
  8588 *Ghost Creepin' Blues*............ 15.00 - 25.00
  8659 *Good Feelin' Blues*............ 15.00 - 25.00
  8704 *Death Valley Moan*............ 15.00 - 25.00
BLUE BILL:
Bluebird 6795 *More Blues*............ 15.00 - 25.00
BLUE BOY:
Varsity 6052 *Back-Biter Blues*............ 10.00 - 15.00
  6059 *Electric Chair*............ 10.00 - 15.00
THE BLUE BOYS:
Okeh 45314 *Memphis Stomp*............ 15.00 - 20.00
BLUE HARMONY BOYS:
Paramount 12889 *Take It Out Too Deep*....... 30.00 - 40.00
  12901 *Sweet Miss Stella Blues*............ 30.00 - 40.00
  12976 *Ragged But Right*............ 30.00 - 40.00
THE BLUEJACKS:
Dot 1000 *Late Hour Blues*............ 7.00 - 10.00
BLUES BIRDHEAD:
Okeh 8824 *Harmonica Blues*............ 20.00 - 30.00
BLUE SMITTY & HIS STRING MEN:
Chess 1522 *Sad Story*............ 8.00 - 12.00
THE BLUES KING:
Solo 10-0003 *Me And My Baby*............. 8.00 - 12.00
THE BLUES MAN:
Specialty 501 *My Baby's Blues*............ ...
THE BLUES ROCKERS:
Aristocrat 407 *Trouble In My Home*....... 15.00 - 25.00
  413 *Blues Rockers' Bop*............ 15.00 - 25.00
Chess 1483 *My Mama's Baby Child*........... 7.00 - 10.00
LOUIS BLUIE AND TED BOGAN:
Bluebird 5490 *I'm Through With You*......... 20.00 - 30.00
  5593 *Ted's Stomp*............ 20.00 - 30.00
CALVIN BOAZ WITH MARVIN JOHNSON & HIS ORCHESTRA:
G & G 1029 *Saffronia Bee*............ 8.00 - 12.00
LUCILLE BOGAN:
Brunswick 7051 *New Way Blues*............ 25.00 - 40.00
  7083 *Coffee Grindin' Blues*............ 25.00 - 40.00
  7145 *My Georgia Blues*............ 25.00 - 40.00
  7163 *Dirty Treatin' Blues*............ 25.00 - 40.00
  7168 *Black Angel Blues*............ 25.00 - 40.00
  7193 *Crawlin' Lizard Blues*............ 25.00 - 40.00
  7210 *Alley Boogie*............ 25.00 - 40.00
Okeh 8071, 8074............ 8.00 - 12.00
  8079 *Pawn Shop Blues*............ 10.00 - 15.00

Paramount 12459 *Sweet Patunia*.............	30.00 -	50.00
12504 *Kind Stella Blues*.................	30.00 -	50.00
12514 *Doggone Wicked Blues*........	30.00 -	50.00
12560 *War Time Man Blues*.........	30.00 -	50.00
12577 *Cravin' Whiskey Blues*........	30.00 -	50.00

HOUSTON BOINES:

RPM 364 *Monkey Motion*..................	15.00 -	25.00

LELA BOLDEN:

Okeh 8139 *Southern Woman Blues*........	20.00 -	30.00

ZU ZU BOLLIN:

Torch 6910 *Headlight Blues*.............	7.00 -	10.00*
6912 *Stavin' Chain*.................	10.00 -	15.00*

PILLIE BOLLIN (AND BAREFOOT BILL):

Columbia 14544-D *I Don't Like That*....	15.00 -	20.00
14654-D *Brown Skin Woman*.............	15.00 -	20.00

HATTIE BOLTEN:

Vocalion 04470 *Down Home Shake*.........	7.00 -	12.00

BROTHER SON BONDS; BROWNSVILLE SON BONDS; SON BONDS:

Bluebird 8927 *80 Highway Blues*.............	15.00 -	20.00
8950 *Come Back Home, Little Girl*.........	15.00 -	20.00
Champion 50064 *Weary Worried Blues*.......	20.00 -	30.00
Decca 7022 *All Night Long*.............	20.00 -	30.00
7024 *In My Father's House*.........	20.00 -	30.00
7039 *Ain't That News?*.............	20.00 -	30.00

THE BOOGIE MAN:

Acorn 308 *Do The Boogie*.................	5.00 -	8.00*

CHARLEY BOOKER:

Blues & Rhythm 7003 *Rabbit Blues*.......	15.00 -	25.00
Modern 878 *Moonrise Blues*.............	10.00 -	15.00*

CONNIE MAC/MACK BOOKER:

Freedom 1520 *Come Back Baby*........	5.00 -	8.00

JOHN LEE BOOKER:

Chance 1108 *Miss Lorraine*.................	8.00 -	12.00*
1110 *Graveyard Blues*.................	8.00 -	12.00*
1122 *609 Boogie*.................	8.00 -	12.00*
De Luxe 6004 *Lovin' Guitar Man*........	4.00 -	7.00*
6032 *Stuttering Blues*.............	4.00 -	7.00*
6046 *Real Real Gone*.............	4.00 -	7.00*
Rockin' 525 *Pouring Down Rain*.......	5.00 -	8.00*

ALONZO BOONE:

Supertone 9428 *Kansas City Blues*...........	150.00 -	250.00

CALVIN BOSTICK & HIS TRIO:

Chess 1444 *All Of My Life*.............	6.00 -	10.00
1451 *Fleetwood Blues*.................	6.00 -	10.00
1530, 1571..............	4.00 -	7.00*

EDDIE BOYD (& HIS CHESS MEN); LITTLE EDDIE BOYD (& HIS BOOGIE BAND):

Chess 1523 *Cool Kind Treatment*.............	5.00 -	8.00
1533, 1541, 1552, 1561.................	3.00 -	5.00*
J.O.B. 1005 *I'm Pleading*.............	5.00 -	10.00*
1007 *Five Long Years*.............	3.00 -	6.00*
RCA Victor..................	3.00 -	5.00

ERNIE BOYD:

Regal 3305 *I Gotta Find My Baby*...........	8.00 -	15.00

GEORGE BOYD:

Bluebird 5573 *I'm Sorry Blues*.............	30.00 -	40.00

RAYMOND BOYD:

Okeh 8528 *Unkind Mama*.................	25.00 -	35.00

ROBERT BOYD:

Wasco 201 *East St. Louis Baby*.............	10.00 -	15.00

CALVIN BOZE:

Aladdin 3055 *Safronia B.*.............	3.00 -	6.00*
3072 *Stinkin; From Drinkin'*.........	3.00 -	6.00*
3110 *Fish Tail*.................	3.00 -	6.00*
3122 *Hey Lawdy, Miss Claudie*.........	3.00 -	6.00*

ISHMAN BRACEY/BRACY (& HIS NEW ORLEANS NEHI BOYS):

Paramount 12941 *Jake Liquor Blues*.........	175.00 -	250.00
12970 *Suitcase Full Of Blues*.........	175.00 -	250.00
13038 *Pay Me No Mind*.........	175.00 -	250.00

Victor 21349 *Saturday Blues*.................	100.00 -	150.00
21691 *Trouble-Hearted Blues*.........	100.00 -	150.00
38560 *The Four Day Blues*.........	100.00 -	150.00

MISSISSIPPI BRACY:

Okeh 8867 *Cherry Ball*.............	150.00 -	200.00
8904 *I'll Overcome Someday*.............	150.00 -	200.00

AUNTIE MARY BRADFORD:

Paramount 12617 *Loafing Blues*.............	30.00 -	40.00

MARY H. BRADFORD:

Okeh 8102 *Chattanooga Blues*.............	20.00 -	30.00
8123 *Waco Texas Blues*.................	20.00 -	30.00

WALTER BRADFORD:

Sun 176 *Dreary Nights*.....................	100.00* -	UP

(The issuance of the above record has not been verified.)

BIG CHARLEY BRADIX:

Aristocrat 418 *Wee Wee Hours*.............	80.00 -	120.00
Blues Bonnet 153 *Dollar Diggin' Woman*......	25.00 -	40.00
Colonial 108 *Boogie Like You Wanna*........	15.00 -	20.00

MARIE BRADLEY:

Paramount 12456 *Down Home Moan*........	20.00 -	35.00
12466 *Stormy Hailing Blues*.............	35.00 -	50.00

TOMMIE BRADLEY (& JAMES COLE):

Champion 16149 *Adam And Eve*........	80.00 -	100.00
16308 *When You're Down And Out*.......	80.00 -	100.00
16339 *Four Day Blues*.............	80.00 -	100.00
16696 *Window Pane Blues*.........	80.00 -	100.00
16782 *Where Have You Been So Long?*........	80.00 -	100.00
50050 *Adam And Eve*.................	20.00 -	30.00

VELMA BRADLEY:

Broadway 5075 *'Fore Day Creep*.............	20.00 -	30.00

JEAN BRADY:

Okeh 06254 *My Mellow Man*.................	5.00 -	8.00

DOBBY BRAGG (AND CHARLIE MCFADDEN):

Paramount 12827 *Fire Detective Blues*.........	125.00 -	175.00
13004 *We Can Sell That Thing*.............	125.00 -	175.00
13044 *Little Snow Blues*.............	125.00 -	175.00
13083 *Don't Look Strange At Me*.........	125.00 -	175.00
13093 *You Got That Thing*.................	50.00 -	75.00

FRANK BRASSWELL:

Titles issued contemporaneously on Banner, Oriole, Perfect, Romeo: *Mountain Girl Blues; Western Blues*............. 10.00 - 15.00

JACKIE BRENSTON:

Chess 1458 *Rocket '88*.............	7.00 -	10.00*
1469 *My Real Gone Rocket*.............	5.00 -	10.00*
1472 *Juiced*.............	5.00 -	10.00*
1496 *Leo The Louse*.............	5.00 -	10.00*
1532 *Starvation*.............	5.00 -	10.00*

EVELYN BRICKEY:

Okeh 8256 *Down In The Valley Blues*........	8.00 -	12.00

GRACE BRIM:

J.O.B. 117 *Hospitality Blues*.............	10.00 -	15.00*

JOHN BRIM (& HIS COMBO/GARY KINGS/STOMPERS); JOHN BRIM TRIO:

Checker 769 *Rattlesnake*.............	7.00 -	10.00*
Chess 1588, 1624.................	4.00 -	7.00*
Fortune 801 *Strange Man*.............	10.00 -	15.00*
J.O.B. 110 *Trouble In The Morning*.........	10.00 -	15.00*
Parrot 799 *Gary Stomp*.............	7.00 -	10.00*
Random 201 *Dark Clouds*.............	15.00 -	20.00*

MRS. JOHN BRIM:

Random 202 *Going Down The Line*...........	7.00 -	12.00

FLORENCE BRISTOL:

Up-To-Date 2019 *How Come You Do Me Like You Do?*.............	75.00 -	125.00

DUSTY BROOKS:

Sun 182 *Heaven On Fire*.............	35.00 -	50.00*

EMORY BROOKS:

Champion 15416 *The Worried Man Blues*......	100.00 -	150.00

JUNIOR BROOKS:
RPM 343 *Lone Town Blues*............... 10.00 - 15.00*
BIG BILL BROOMSLEY:
Paramount 13084 *Station Blues*........ 75.00 - 100.00
BIG BILL BROONZY (& HIS FAT FOUR):
Mercury 8122, 8126, 8139, 8160, 8261, 8271, 8284 4.00 - 7.00
BROTHER BELL; (See BELL):
**BROTHER BLUES & THE BACK ROOM
   BOYS:**
Abbey 3015 *Day Break*................. 5.00 - 8.00
**BROTHER GEORGE & HIS SANCTIFIED
   SINGERS:**
Conqueror 9361....................... 4.00 - 7.00
Okeh 5671, 5729, 05893, 06019......... 4.00 - 7.00
Vocalion 05261, 5465.................. 4.00 - 7.00
ADA BROWN:
Okeh 8101 *Evil Mama Blues*............ 30.00 - 40.00
  8123 *Ill-Natured Blues*................ 30.00 - 40.00
  8694 *Down Home Dance*................ 8.00 - 12.00
Vocalion 1009 *Panama Limited Blues*... 40.00 - 60.00
ALBERTA BROWN:
Columbia 14321-D *Lonely Blues*........ 20.00 - 30.00
BESSIE BROWN:
Banner 1833 *What's The Matter Now?*....... 8.00 - 12.00
Brunswick 4346 *The Blues Singer From Alabam'* 15.00 - 20.00
  4409 *He Just Don't Appeal To Me*........ 15.00 - 20.00
Dominao 3781 *How Could I Be Blue?*...... 8.00 - 12.00
Regal 8143 *What's The Matter Now?*...... 8.00 - 12.00
Vocalion 1182 *Arkansas Blues*........ 10.00 - 15.00
  15688 *The Man I Love*................. 10.00 - 15.00
BILL BROWN:
Varsity 6064 *Goin' Away And Leavin; My Baby* 10.00 - 15.00
CHOCOLATE BROWN:
Paramount 12944 *Itching Heel*............... 40.00 - 60.00
  1298 *Cherry Hill Blues*................ 40.00 - 60.00
DANIEL BROWN:
Paramount 12663 *Now Is The Needy Time*..... 30.00 - 50.00
DUDLEY BROWN:
Supertone 9524 *Western Traveler Blues*........ 40.00 - 60.00
ELIZA BROWN:
Columbia 14466-D *Get On Out Of Here*....... 10.00 - 15.00
  14471-D *Peddlin' Man*.................... 10.00 - 15.00
  14478-D *Take A Little Bit*............... 10.00 - 15.00
FLOSSIE (AND DUKE) BROWN:
Champion 15814 *Shake It Daddy*......... 40.00 - 60.00
  15858 *Pig Meat Mama*.................. 40.00 - 60.00
FREDDIE BROWN:
Paramount 12910 *Whip It To A Jelly*........ 35.00 - 50.00
GABRIEL BROWN:
Beacon 5021 .... 4.00 - 8.00
Joe Davis 5003, 5004, 5006, 5008, 5015, 5016, 5017,
  5020, 5021, 5025, 5026, 5027, 5028....... 4.00 - 8.00
Gennett 5003, 5004................... 4.00 - 8.00
GATEMOUTH BROWN:
Aladdin 198, 199..................... 4.00 - 7.00
Peacock 1500, 1504, 1505, 1508, 1561, 1568.... 4.00 - 7.00
Peacock (higher numbers)................ 3.00 - 5.00*
"HI" HENRY BROWN:
Vocalion 1692 *Skin Man Blues*.......... 200.00 - 250.00
  1715 *Hospital Blues*................. 200.00 - 250.00
  1728 *Titanic Blues*.................. 200.00 - 250.00
ELDER J. C. BROWN:
Herwin 93004 *Where Shall I Be?*......... 50.00 - 75.00
**JAMES "WIDEMOUTH" BROWN—HIS
   GUITAR & ORCHESTRA:**
Jax 306 *Boogie Woogie Night Hawk*......... 8.00 - 12.00*
JOE BROWN:
Okeh 8491 *Cotton Patch Blues*......... 15.00 - 20.00
TEXAS JOHNNY BROWN:
Atlantic 876 *There Go The Blues*....... 10.00 - 15.00
JUDSON BROWN:
Brunswick 7220 *You Don't Know My Mind Blues* 75.00 - 100.00

KITTY BROWN:
Banner 1436, 1437, 1452................. 7.00 - 12.00
Paramount 12223 *Keep On Going*.......... 12.00 - 16.00
LEE BROWN:
Chicago 104 *Bobby Town Boogie*.......... 8.00 - 15.00)
Decca 7386 *Pitchin' Boogie*............ 15.00 - 20.00
  7504 *Carpenter Man Blues*............. 15.00 - 20.00
Decca 7575, 7587..................... 5.00 - 8.00
Decca 7615 *Forsaken Blues*............. 7.00 - 10.00
  7626 *Low Down Fellin'*................ 7.00 - 10.00
  7654 *Lock And Key Blues*.............. 10.00 - 15.00
  7686 *My Driving Wheel*................ 10.00 - 15.00
Decca 7697, 7710, 7726, 7744, 7775, 7790.... 5.00 - 8.00
King 4157 *New Little Girl*............. 7.00 - 10.00
Queen 4157 *Brownie's Boogie*........... 7.00 - 10.00
LIL BROWN:
Black Patti 8007 *Moanful Mama*.......... 40.00 - 60.00
  8008 *Three Card Monte Blues*.......... 40.00 - 60.00
LOTTIE BROWN:
Supertone 9286 *Wayward Girl Blues*...... 50.00 - 75.00
  9289 *Don't Speak To Me*............... 50.00 - 75.00
  9367 *Goin' Away Blues*................ 50.00 - 75.00
  9429 *Blue World Blues*................ 50.00 - 75.00
LUCILLE BROWN:
Superior 2552 *Pay With Money*.......... 35.00 - 50.00
  2633 *Can't Get Enough*................ 35.00 - 50.00
ORA BROWN:
Paramount 12481 *Jinx Blues*............ 30.00 - 40.00
  12500 *Jailhouse Moan*................. 30.00 - 40.00
RICHARD "RABBIT" BROWN:
Victor 20578 *James Alley Blues*......... 90.00 - 130.00
  21475 *Never Let The Same Bee Sting You Twice* 90.00 - 130.00
  35840 (12-inch) *Sinking Of The Titanic*....... 90.00 - 130.00
ROY BROWN:
De Luxe 1098, 1128, 1166, 3154, 3189, 3198, 3212,
  3226, 3300, 3301, 3302, 3304, 3308, 3312, 3319 3.00 - 6.00
Gold Star 636 *Deep Sea Diver*.......... 7.00 - 10.00
King .... 3.00 - 5.00*
Miltone 3198.......................... 3.00 - 6.00
SAMMY BROWN:
Gennett 6337 *Barrel House Blues*............. 125.00 - 175.00
SKEET BROWN:
Vocalion 1205 *Skeet Skat Blues*......... 15.00 - 20.00
WILLIE BROWN:
Champion 50023 *M And O Blues*.......... 50.00 - 75.00
Paramount 13090 *M And O Blues*......... 200.00 - 300.00
  13099 *Kicking In My Sleep Blues*....... 200.00 - 300.00
YODELING KID BROWN:
Vocalion 1205 *Policy Blues*............ 15.00 - 20.00
ALTA BROWNE:
Gennett 3308 *Couldn't Hear Nobody Pray*..... 15.00 - 20.00
  3318 *Nobody Knows Da Trouble I See*...... 15.00 - 20.00
BRYANT'S JUBILEE QUARTET/QUINTETTE:
Gennett 6608 *Who Stole The Lock Off The Hen
   House Door?*...................... 10.00 - 20.00
QRS 7018 *When The World's On Fire*..... 15.00 - 25.00
  7020 *Do You Call That Religion?*........ 15.00 - 25.00
GLADYS BRYANT:
Harmograph 818 *Beale Street Mama*.......... 25.00 - 40.00
  2539 *Triflin' Blues*................. 15.00 - 20.00
  2540 *Laughin' Cryin' Blues*........... 15.00 - 20.00
Paramount 12026 *Laughin' Cryin' Blues*....... 15.00 - 20.00
  12027 *Triflin' Blues*................. 15.00 - 20.00
  12031 *Beale Street Mama*.............. 25.00 - 40.00
**ELDER RICHARD BRYANT ('S SANCTIFIED
   SINGERS):**
Okeh 8559 *Come Over Here*............. 15.00 - 25.00
  8579 *How Much I Owe For Love Divine*.... 15.00 - 25.00
Victor 21357 *The Master Come And Called To Me* 12.00 - 16.00
  21694 *A Wild Man In Town*............. 15.00 - 25.00
  38507 *Everybody Was There*............ 15.00 - 25.00

JOHN BULLARD (QUARTET):

De Luxe 6019 *Spoiled Hambone Blues*	7.00 -	10.00*
6035 *Mary Lou*	7.00 -	10.00*
Index 300 *Callin' The Blues*	10.00 -	15.00

BULL CITY RED:

Titles, issued contemporaneously on Banner, Melotone, Oriole, Perfect, Romeo: *Black Woman And Poison Blues; I Won't Be Dogged Around; Now I'm Taking To You; Mississippi River; Pick And Shovel Blues; Richmond Blues* .... 15.00 - 25.00

BUMBLE BEE SLIM (& HIS THREE SHARKS):

Titles, issued contemporaneously on Banner, Melotone, Oriole, Perfect, Romeo, *Big Six; Bumble Bee's New Muddy Water; Goodbye; I'm Having So Much Trouble; I'm Needing Someone; My Big Moments; Rising River Blues; Rough Treatment; She Never; 12 O'clock Midnight; 12 O'clock Southern Train; Woman For Every Man* ..... 7.00 - 10.00

Bluebird 5563, 6521, 6559, 6586, 6612, 6635, 6649, 6834	5.00 -	8.00
Decca 7021 *Cruel Hearted Woman Blues*	5.00 -	8.00
7031 *Ain't It A Crying Shame?*	7.00 -	12.00
7045 *The Longest Day You Live*	7.00 -	12.00
7053 *Bleeding Heart Blues*	7.00 -	12.00
7054 *Let's Pitch A Boogie Woogie*	7.00 -	12.00
7071 *My Black Gal Blues*	7.00 -	12.00
7079 *Mean Bloody Murder Blues*	7.00 -	12.00
7089 *Good Evening Blues*	7.00 -	12.00
7098 *The Death Of Leroy Carr*	7.00 -	12.00
7101 *Sail On Sail On Blues*	7.00 -	12.00
7121 *I'll Take You Back*	7.00 -	12.00
7126 *Smoky Mountain Blues*	7.00 -	12.00
7138 *Happy Life Blues*	7.00 -	12.00
7145 *Some Old Rainy Days*	7.00 -	12.00
7162 *Deep Bass Blues*	7.00 -	12.00
7170 *No Good Woman*	7.00 -	12.00
Decca (others)	7.00 -	12.00
Fidelity 3004 *Ida Red*	5.00 -	8.00*
Paramount 13102 *Yo Yo String Blues*	50.00 -	75.00
13109 *Chain Gang Bound*	50.00 -	75.00
13132 *Honey Bee Blues*	50.00 -	75.00
Vocalion 1691 *Piney Woods Working Man*	25.00 -	35.00
1719 *Greasy Greens*	25.00 -	35.00
1720 *B And O Blues*	25.00 -	35.00
02713 *Busy Devil*	15.00 -	20.00
02728 *Baby So Long*	15.00 -	20.00
02742 *East St. Louis Blues*	15.00 -	20.00
02773 *Wrecked Life Blues*	15.00 -	20.00
02809 *Helping Hand Blues*	15.00 -	20.00
02829 *Rough Road Blues*	15.00 -	20.00
02865 *Cold-Blooded Murder*	15.00 -	20.00
02885 *Burned Down Mill*	15.00 -	20.00
02903 *Running Bad Luck Blues*	15.00 -	20.00
02930 *Blues Before Daylight*	15.00 -	20.00
02970 *Way Down In Georgia*	15.00 -	20.00
03005 *Lemon Squeezing Blues*	15.00 -	20.00
03037 *I Keep On Drinking*	15.00 -	20.00
03054 *When The Sun Goes Down*	15.00 -	20.00
03090 *Big 80 Blues*	10.00 -	15.00
03130 *Sometimes Blues*	10.00 -	15.00
03165 *Cold Blooded Murder No.2*	10.00 -	15.00
03197 *When Somebody Loses*	10.00 -	15.00
03209 *Can't You Trust Me No More?*	10.00 -	15.00
03221 *Dumb Tricks Blues*	10.00 -	15.00
03242 *Back In Jail Again*	10.00 -	15.00
03267 *Wet Clothes Blues*	10.00 -	15.00
03298 *Any Time At Night*	10.00 -	15.00
03328 *Hard Rocks In My Bed*	10.00 -	15.00
03384 *Meet Me At The Landing*	10.00 -	15.00
03418 *Slave Man Blues*	10.00 -	15.00

03446 *Fast Life Blues*	10.00 -	15.00
Vocalion 03473 *12 O'clock Midnight*	10.00 -	15.00
03506 *She Never*	10.00 -	15.00
03550 *Big Six*	10.00 -	15.00
03582 *Woman For Every Man*	10.00 -	15.00
03611 *Good Bye*	10.00 -	15.00
03637 *Rough Treatment*	10.00 -	15.00
03698 *Just Yesterday*	10.00 -	15.00
03767 *The Old Life I'm Living*	10.00 -	15.00
03870 *When Your Deal Goes Down*	10.00 -	15.00
03929 *Rock Hearted Woman*	10.00 -	15.00
04042 *If I Make It Over*	10.00 -	15.00
04661 *Where Was You Last Night?*	10.00 -	15.00

ALLEN BUNN:

Aollo 436 *She'll Be Sorry*	5.00 -	8.00*
439 *I Got You Covered*	5.00 -	8.00*
442, 447	3.00 -	5.00*

TEDDY BUNN & SPENCER WILLIAMS:

Victor 23253 *Tampa Twirl*	35.00 -	50.00
38592 *Pattin' Dat Cat*	35.00 -	50.00
38602 *Goose And Gander*	35.00 -	50.00
38617 *Blow It Up*	35.00 -	50.00

PINETOP BURKS:

Titles, issued contemporaneously on Banner, Melotone, Oriole, Perfect, Romeo, Vocalion: *Mountain Jack Blues; Shake The Shack* ..... 15.00 - 20.00

Vocalion 03979 *Jack Of All Trades Blues*	15.00 -	20.00
04107 *Fannie Mae Blues*	15.00 -	20.00

HATTIE BURLESON:

Brunswick 7042 *Superstitious Blues*	35.00 -	50.00
7054 *Bye Bye Baby*	35.00 -	50.00
Paramount 13050 *Clearin' House Blues*	40.00 -	60.00
13138 *Dead Lover Blues*	50.00 -	75.00

DAN BURLEY:

Circle 1020 *South Side Shake*	10.00 -	20.00
1021 *Big Cat, Little Cat*	10.00 -	20.00
1022 *Shotgun House Rag*	10.00 -	20.00

EDDIE BURNS:

Deluxe 6024 *Dealing With The Devil*	5.00 -	10.00*

(CHARLIE) BURSE (& HIS MEMPHIS MUD-CATS); CHARLIE CURSE WITH THE MEMPHIS JUG BAND; BURSE & SHADE; BURSE & STEPHEN:

Champion 16481 *I Got Good Taters*	100.00 -	150.00
16599 *Fishing In The Dark*	100.00 -	150.00
16654 *Tappin' That Thing*	100.00 -	150.00
Okeh 8959 *Bottle It Up And Go*	50.00 -	75.00
Vocalion 03080 *Bottle It Up And Go*	40.00 -	60.00
05017, 05070, 05123, 05192, 05299, 05393, 05551	5.00 -	8.00

CLARA BURSTON:

Champion 16125 *Try That Man O'Mine*	30.00 -	50.00
16216 *Pay With Money*	30.00 -	50.00
16756 *Good And Hot*	30.00 -	50.00
Gennett 7319 *Pay With Money*	30.00 -	50.00
Paramount 12881 *Georgia Man Blues*	40.00 -	60.00
13003 *C.P. Blues*	40.00 -	60.00
13045 *Ginger Snappin'*	40.00 -	60.00

BUDDIE (BUDDY) BURTON:

Gennett 6453 *Silvery Moon*	20.00 -	35.00
6471 *It's No-One But You*	20.00 -	35.00
Paramount 12625 *Ham-Fatchet Blues*	30.00 -	40.00

W. H. BURTON-MARCUS MOMAN-(CLIFF) MOORE:

Paramount 12787 *St. Louis Blues*	40.00 -	60.00
12789 *Roll That Jelly*	40.00 -	60.00

FRANK BUSBY:

Decca 7295 *Prisoner Bound*	7.00 -	10.00

MARY BUTLER:

Brunswick 7046 *Bungalow Blues*	30.00 -	50.00
7049 *Mad Dog Blues*	30.00 -	50.00

SAM BUTLER:

BUTLER

Vocalion 1056 *Heaven Is My View*........... 35.00 - 50.00
1057 *Poor Boy Blues*.................... 35.00 - 50.00
TRIXIE BUTLER:
Bluebird 6392 *Take It Easy Greasy*........... 8.00 - 12.00
6429 *You Got The Right Key*............. 10.00 - 15.00
BUTTERBEANS AND SUSIE:
Okeh 8147, 8180.................. 5.00 - 8.00
8163 *Construction Gang*.................... 30.00 - 40.00
8182 *Kiss Me Sweet*.................... 30.00 - 40.00
8192, 8199, 8202, 8209, 8219, 8224, 8233, 8241,
8303, 8307, 8319, 8323, 8335............ 6.00 - 10.00
8355 *He Likes Is Slow*.................... 25.00 - 35.00
8392, 8399, 8432, 8520............ 7.00 - 10.00
8502 *I Wannt Hot Dog For My Roll*....... 10.00 - 15.00
8556 *Gonna Make You Sorry*............. 10.00 - 15.00
8598, 8614, 8670, 8687, 8701............ 8.00 - 12.00
8769 *Ain't Gonna Do That No More*....... 15.00 - 20.00
8833 *Times Is Hard*.................... 12.00 - 16.00
8893 *Broke Down Mama*............. 15.00 - 20.00
8911 *Radio Papa*.................... 15.00 - 20.00
8950 *Papa Ain't No Santa Claus*............ 15.00 - 20.00
JOHN BYRD:
Paramount 12997 *Billy Goat Blues*........... 100.00 - 150.00
JOSEPHINE BYRD:
Columbia 14349-D *Mosquito Blues*........... 15.00 - 20.00
ROLAND BYRD:
Atlantic 947 *Hey Little Girl*................. 8.00 - 12.00*
ROY ("BALD HEAD") BYRD; ROY BYRD & HIS BLUES JUMPERS:
Atlantic 897 *She Walks Right In*.............. 8.00 - 12.00
Federal 12061 *K.C. Blues*.................... 6.00 - 10.00*
12073 *Rockin' With Fes*.................... 6.00 - 10.00*
Mercury 8175 *Bald Head*.................... 6.00 - 10.00
8184 *Oh Well*.................... 6.00 - 10.00
BOBBY (BOBBIE) CADILLAC:
Columbia 14413-D *Carbolic Acid Blues*........ 15.00 - 20.00
14505-D *Easin' In*.................... 15.00 - 20.00
14604-D *I Can't Stand That*.............. 15.00 - 20.00
ROBERT CAFFREY:
Chess 1470 *Ida Bee*.................... 10.00 - 15.00*
PERRY CAIN:
Gold Star 632 *All The Way From Texas*....... 10.00 - 15.00
JOE CALICOTT:
Brunswick 7166 *Fare Thee Well Blues*.......... 90.00 - 120.00
BOB CALL:
Brunswick 7137 *31 Blues*.................... 50.00 - 75.00
Coral 65009 *Talkin' Baby Blues*.............. 5.00 - 10.00
BOB CAMP (& HIS BUDDIES/THE NIGHTHAWKS):
Decca 48112, 48118.................. 5.00 - 8.00
Essex 714 *Pitch A Boogie*.................. 8.00 - 12.00*
Southern 121, 130.................. 7.00 - 10.00
BOB CAMPBELL:
Vocalion 02798 *Starvation Farm Blues*....... 75.00 - 100.00
02830 *Shotgun Blues*.................... 75.00 - 100.00
CARL CAMPBELL (WITH HENRY HAYES 4 KINGS):
Freedom 1521 *Ooh Wee Baby*.................. 5.00 - 8.00
Peacock 1538 *Early Morning Blues*............ 5.00 - 8.00
CHARLIE CAMPBELL:
Vocalion 03571 *Pepper Sauce Mama*......... 30.00 - 40.00
GENE CAMPBELL:
Brunswick 7139 *Bended Knee Blues*.......... 40.00 - 60.00
7154 *Western Plain Blues*.................... 40.00 - 60.00
7161 *Freight Train Yodeling Blues*........... 40.00 - 60.00
7170 *Wandering Blues*.................... 40.00 - 60.00
7177 *Wash And Iron Woman Blues*........ 40.00 - 60.00
7184 *Lazy Woman Blues*.................... 40.00 - 60.00
7197 *Wedding Day Blues*.................... 40.00 - 60.00
7206 *Face To Face Blues*.................... 40.00 - 60.00
7214 *Doggone Mean Blues*.................... 40.00 - 60.00

CARR

7225 *Crooked Woman Blues*.............. 40.00 - 60.00
7226 *Turned Out Blues*.............. 40.00 - 60.00
7227 *Married Life Blues*.............. 40.00 - 60.00
CANNON & WOODS:
Brunswick 7138 *Fourth And Beale*............. 40.00 - 60.00
CAROLINA PEANUT BOYS:
Victor 23267 *Got A Letter From My Baby*..... 80.00 - 110.00
23274 *You Got Me Rollin'*.............. 80.00 - 110.00
23319 *Spider's Nest Blues*.............. 80.00 - 110.00
CAROLINA SLIM:
Acorn 319 *Pleading Blues*.............. 7.00 - 10.00
323 *Worry You Off My Mind*............. 7.00 - 10.00
324 *Rag Mama*.............. 7.00 - 10.00
3015 *Mama's Boogie*.............. 7.00 - 10.00
CAROLINA WASHBOARD TRIO:
Varsity 6036 *That Thing Blues*.............. 10.00 - 15.00
DORA CARR: DORA CARR-CHAS. DAVENPORT:
Okeh 8130 *You Might Pizen Me*............. 8.00 - 15.00
8244 *Good Woman's Blues*.............. 8.00 - 15.00
8250 *Cow Cow Blues*.............. 8.00 - 15.00
8284 *Fifth Street Blues*.............. 8.00 - 15.00
GUNTER LEE CARR:
Decca 48167, 48170.................. 3.00 - 6.00
LEROY CARR; (AND/WITH SCRAPPER BLACKWELL):
Bluebird 5877 *Ain't It A Shame*.............. 15.00 - 20.00
5915 *Big Four Blues*.............. 15.00 - 20.00
5946 *Just A Rag*.............. 15.00 - 20.00
5963 *Going Back Home*.............. 15.00 - 20.00
Vocalion 1191 *My Own Lonesome Blues*....... 15.00 - 20.00
1200 *Tennessee Blues*.............. 15.00 - 20.00
1214 *Low Down Dirty Blues*.............. 15.00 - 20.00
1232 *Prison Bound Blues*.............. 20.00 - 30.00
1259 *How About Me?*.............. 20.00 - 30.00
1261 *Tired Of Your Low Down Ways*....... 20.00 - 30.00
1279 *You Don't Mean Me No Good*........ 20.00 - 30.00
1290 *Straight Alky Blues*.............. 20.00 - 30.00
1400 *Naptown Blues*.............. 20.00 - 30.00
1405 *Wrong Man Blues*.............. 20.00 - 30.00
1412 *Gambler's Blues*.............. 20.00 - 30.00
1423 *Gettin' All Wet*.............. 20.00 - 30.00
1432 *Prison Cell Blues*.............. 20.00 - 30.00
1435 *Love Hides All Faults*.............. 20.00 - 30.00
1454 *The Dirty Dozen*.............. 20.00 - 30.00
1460 *I'm Going Back To Tennessee*........ 20.00 - 30.00
1473 *Rainy Day Blues*.............. 20.00 - 30.00
1483 *That's Tellin' 'Em*.............. 20.00 - 30.00
1499 *Blue With The Blues*.............. 20.00 - 30.00
1519 *I Know That I'll Be Blue*.............. 20.00 - 30.00
1527 *Memphis Town*.............. 20.00 - 30.00
1541 *Papa Wants A Cookie*.............. 20.00 - 30.00
1574 *Jail Cell Blues*.............. 20.00 - 30.00
1585 *Big House Blues*.............. 20.00 - 30.00
1593 *Papa's On The House Top*.............. 20.00 - 30.00
1605 *Low Down Dog Blues*.............. 20.00 - 30.00
1624 *Let's Disagree*.............. 20.00 - 30.00
1636 *Papa's Got Your Water On*.............. 20.00 - 30.0
1651 *What More Can I Do?*.............. 20.00 - 30.0
1693 *The Depression Blues*.............. 20.00 - 30.00
1703 *Midnight Hour Blues*.............. 20.00 - 30.00
1709 *I Keep The Blues*.............. 20.00 - 30.00
1716 *Quittin' Papa*.............. 20.00 - 30.00
02657 *Blues Before Sunrise*.............. 20.00 - 30.00
02681 *Blues She Gave Me*.............. 20.00 - 30.00
02791 *Barrel House Woman*.............. 20.00 - 30.00
02820 *I Believe I'll Make A Change*.............. 20.00 - 30.00
02875 *Longing For My Sugar*.............. 20.00 - 30.00
02893 *Cruel Woman Blues*.............. 20.00 - 30.00
02922 *Stormy Weather Blues*.............. 20.00 - 30.00
02950 *My Woman's Gone Wrong*.............. 20.00 - 30.00

02969 *Bo Bo Stomp*	20.00 -	30.00
02986 *George Street Blues*	20.00 -	30.00
03034 *Tight Time Blues*	20.00 -	30.00
03067 *Black Wagon Blues*	20.00 -	30.00
03107 *Muddy Water*	20.00 -	30.00
03157 *My Good For Nothin' Gal*	20.00 -	30.00
03233 *Blue Night Blues*	20.00 -	30.00
03296 *Good Woman Blues*	20.00 -	30.00
03349 *Big Four Blues*	20.00 -	30.00

ALICE CARTER:

Okeh 8070, 8076	5.00 -	8.00

ALICE LESLIE CARTER:

Titles, issued contemporaneously on Arto, Bell, Globe: *The Also-Ran Blues; Aunt Hagar's Blues, Cry Baby Blues; Dangerouse Blues; Decatur Street Blues; Down Home Blues; Got To Have My Daddy Blues; I Want Some Lovin' Blues; You'll Think Of Me Blues* .... 10.00 - 15.00

BO CARTER (& WALTER JACOBS):

Bluebird 5489 *Bo Carter Special*	15.00 -	20.00
5536 *Howlin' Tome Cat Blues*	15.00 -	20.00
5594 *Pin In You Cushion*	15.00 -	20.00
5629 *Beans*	15.00 -	20.00
5704 *Nobody's Business*	15.00 -	20.00
5825 *Backache Blues*	15.00 -	20.00
5861 *Old Shoe Blues*	15.00 -	20.00
5912 *Mashing That Thing*	15.00 -	20.00
5997 *Skin Ball Blues*	15.00 -	20.00
6024 *Blue Runner Blues*	15.00 -	20.00
6058 *Please Warm My Weiner*	15.00 -	20.00
6124 *When You Left*	15.00 -	20.00
6295 *Cigarette Blues*	15.00 -	20.00
6315 *Ride My Mule*	15.00 -	20.00
6363 *Rolling Blues*	15.00 -	20.00
6407 *It's Too Wet*	15.00 -	20.00
6444 *Fat Mouth Blues*	15.00 -	20.00
6529 *T Baby Blues*	15.00 -	20.00
6589 *I Get The Blues*	30.00 -	40.00
6659 *Doubled Up In a Knot*	15.00 -	20.00
6695 *Sue Cow*	10.00 -	15.00
6735 *Worried G Blues*	15.00 -	20.00
7073 *Got To Work Somewhere*	15.00 -	20.00
7213 *The Ins And Outs Of My Girl*	15.00 -	20.00
7927 *Shake 'Em On Down*	15.00 -	20.00
7952 *Lucille, Lucille*	15.00 -	20.00
7968 *Shoo That Chicken*	15.00 -	20.00
8045 *Let's Get Drunk Again*	12.00 -	18.00
8078 *World In A Jug*	8.00 -	12.00
8093 *Old Devil*	12.00 -	18.00
8122 *Whiskey Blues*	12.00 -	18.00
8147 *Santa Claus*	12.00 -	18.00
8159 *Trouble In Blues*	12.00 -	18.00
8397 *The County Farm Blues*	12.00 -	18.00
8423 *Lock The Lock*	12.00 -	18.00
8459 *Baby Ruth*	12.00 -	18.00
8495 *Policy Blues*	12.00 -	18.00
8514 *My Little Mind*	12.00 -	18.00
8555 *Honey*	12.00 -	18.00
Columbia 14661-D *Pussy Cat Blues*	35.00 -	50.00
14671-D *New Auto Blues*	35.00 -	50.00
Okeh 8852 *I'm An Old Bumble Bee*	35.00 -	50.00
8858 *Times Is Tight Like That*	35.00 -	50.00
8870 *Mean Feeling Blues*	35.00 -	50.00
8887 *Pin In Your Cushion*	35.00 -	50.00
8888 *Loveless Love*	35.00 -	50.00
8889 *Howling Tom Cat Blues*	35.00 -	50.00
8897 *Ants In My Pants*	35.00 -	50.00
8906 *Blue Runner Blues*	35.00 -	50.00
8923 *What Kind Of Scent Is This?*	35.00 -	50.00
8930 *Last Go Round*	35.00 -	50.00
8935 *I Want You To Know*	35.00 -	50.00

8952 *Baby, How Can It Be?*	35.00 -	50.00
Vocalion 03091 *Pussy Cat Blues*	10.00 -	15.00
03259 *Ants In My Pants*	8.00 -	12.00

BUNNY CARTER:

Conqueror 7266 *Midnight Special Blues*	60.00 -	90.00

CHARLIE CARTER:

Broadway 5076 *Long Gone Lost John*	20.00 -	30.00

GEORGE CARTER:

Paramount 12750 *Hot Jelly Roll Blues*	80.00 -	100.00
12769 *Weeping Willow Woman*	80.00 -	100.00

GOREY/GORY CARTER (AND/WITH HIS GUITAR & ROCKIN' RHYTHM ORCHESTRA/HEPCATS):

Coral 65058, 65064	4.00 -	7.00
Freedom 1502, 1506, 1511, 1518, 1522, 1525, 1536	4.00 -	8.00
Modern 819 *Seven Days*	5.00 -	8.00
Sittin' In With 556, 572	5.00 -	8.00

HARRY CARTER:

Bluebird 6009 *Letter From Texas*	20.00 -	30.00
6095 *Hoo Doo Blues*	20.00 -	30.00
6210 *Deep Blues Ocean Blues*	20.00 -	30.00

JOSEPHINE CARTER:

Okeh 8002, 8015	5.00 -	8.00

LEROY CARTER:

Vocalion 03120 *Black Widow Spider*	20.00 -	30.00

NELSON CARTER & HIS GUITAR:

Sittin' In With 557 *My Baby Left Me*	10.00 -	15.00

"SPIDER" CARTER:

Brunswick 7181 *Dry Spell Blues*	90.00 -	120.00
7188 *Don't Leave Me Blues*	90.00 -	120.00

CARVER BOYS:

Paramount 3182 *No One To Welcome Me Home*	30.00 -	40.00
3198 *Darling Nellie Gray*	30.00 -	40.00
3233 *I'll Be With You When The Roses Bloom Again*	30.00 -	40.00
12822 *Sisco Harmonica Blues*	30.00 -	40.00

CASEY BILL (AND THE BROWN BOMBERS OF SWING):

Bluebird 6212 *Long-Eared Mule*	10.00 -	15.00
6243 *My Stove Won't Work*	10.00 -	15.00
6262 *Howlin' Dog Blues*	10.00 -	15.00
6356 *Somebody's Got To Go*	10.00 -	15.00
6390 *Let Me Be Your Butcher*	10.00 -	15.00
6465 *I'm A Stranger In Your Town*	10.00 -	15.00
6519 *Casey Blues*	10.00 -	15.00
8004 *You Gotta Do Your Duty*	8.00 -	12.00
8060 *Midnight Blues*	8.00 -	12.00
Vocalion 03186 *W.P.A. Blues*	10.00 -	15.00
03220 *Flood Water Blues*	10.00 -	15.00
03250 *Keyhole Blues*	10.00 -	15.00
03274 *Big Bill Blues*	10.00 -	15.00
03330 *Back Door Blues*	10.00 -	15.00
03373 *Gonna Take My Time*	10.00 -	15.00
03407 *Talkin' To Myself*	10.00 -	15.00
03437 *Streamline Woman*	10.00 -	15.00
03464 *Big Katy Adam*	10.00 -	15.00
03496 *Jinx Blues*	10.00 -	15.00
03529 *Round And Round*	7.00 -	10.00
03561 *I've Been Tricked*	7.00 -	10.00
03592 *No Good Woman*	7.00 -	10.00
03859 *Sales Lady*	10.00 -	15.00
03860 *New Round And Round*	8.00 -	12.00
03930 *Rooster Blues*	10.00 -	15.00
04001 *Go Ahead, Buddy*	10.00 -	15.00
04066 *Red Hot Blues*	10.00 -	15.00
04138 *Spider Blues*	10.00 -	15.00

CEDAR CREEK SHEIK:

Bluebird 6467 *Don't Use That Stuff*	15.00 -	25.00
6528 *She's Totin' Something Good*	15.00 -	25.00
6587 *What A Pity*	15.00 -	25.00
6634 *Don't Credit My Stuff*	15.00 -	25.00
6939 *Ford V-8*	15.00 -	25.00

CHARLIE CHAPMAN:
Broadway 5079 *Moanin' The Blues*............ 50.00 - 75.00
   5091 *Back To The Wood Blues*.......... 50.00 - 75.00
   5108 *She's Got Good Stuff*............ 50.00 - 75.00
HENRY CHARLES:
Broadway 5094 *Henry Charles Blues*....... 75.00 - 100.00
THE CHARLESTON BLUES TRIO:
Champion 15734 *Lighthouse Blues*.......... 25.00 - 40.00
   15755 *Runnin' Wild*................. 25.00 - 40.00
CHATMAN BROTHERS:
Bluebird 6657 *Stir In Now*............... 20.00 - 30.00
   6682 *Hold It At The Bottom*.......... 20.00 - 30.00
   6717 *Wake Me Just Before Day*........ 20.00 - 30.00
   7167 *Radio Blues*................... 20.00 - 30.00
   8139 *Jumping Out Blues*............. 20.00 - 30.00
ANDY CHATMAN:
Brunswick 7185 *Shakin' The Jelly*........ 40.00 - 60.00
BO CHATMAN:
Brunswick 7048 *Good Old Turnip Greens*...... 40.00 - 60.00
PETER CHATMAN:
Okeh 05799 *Last Pair Of Shoes Blues*..... 7.00 - 10.00
   05845 *Miss Ora Lee Blues*............ 7.00 - 10.00
   05908 *The Jive Blues*............... 7.00 - 10.00
HARRY CHATMON:
Vocalion 03143 *Black Ants Blues*......... 20.00 - 30.00
CHICAGO FIVE:
Bluebird 6543 *I'm A Gamblin' Man*........ 8.00 - 12.00
THE CHICAGO SHEIKS:
Superior 2798 *Beedle Um Bum*............ 40.00 - 60.00
CHICAGO SUNNY BOY:
Meteor 5004 *Western Union Man*.......... 10.00 - 15.00*
VIRGIL CHILDERS:
Bluebird 7441 *Somebody Stole My Jane*....... 15.00 - 25.00
   7464 *Red River Blues*............... 15.00 - 25.00
   7487 *Travelin' Man*................. 15.00 - 25.00
BUDDY CHILES:
Gold Star 660 *Jet Black Woman*........... 10.00 - 15.00
ANNA LEE CHISHOLM:
Paramount 12213 *Georgia Sam Blues*....... 20.00 - 30.00
BUDDY CHRISTIAN'S FOUR CRY-BABIES:
Okeh 8332 *Nina Lee*..................... 7.00 - 10.00
BLIND CLYDE CHURCH:
Victor 23271 *Number Nine Blues*.......... 35.00 - 50.00
DOT CLARK:
Supertone 9288 *Papa, You're Too Slow*....... ———
ETHEL CLARK:
Silvertone 3521 *Black Man Blues*......... 25.00 - 35.00
   3523 *Jelly Roll Blues*.............. 40.00 - 60.00
LONNIE CLARK:
Paramount 12871 *Broke Down Engine*........ 80.00 - 100.00
GEORGE CLARKE:
Bluebird 7485 *Prisoner Blues*............ 20.00 - 30.00
JIM CLARKE:
Vocalion 1536 *Fat Fanny Stomp*........... 75.00 - 100.00
DOCTOR CLAYTON:
Bluebird 8901, 8938, 9003, 9021, 34-0702.. 4.00 - 7.00
RCA Victor 20-1995, 20-2153, 20-2323..... 3.00 - 5.00
JESSE CLAYTON:
Vocalion 1598 *Neckbone Blues*............ 15.00 - 20.00
PETER J. CLAYTON:
Bluebird 6071 *Peter's Blues*............. 15.00 - 25.00
   6096 *Yo Yo Jive*.................. 15.00 - 20.00
PETER CLEIGHTON:
Conqueror 9447 *Roaming Gambler*.......... 5.00 - 8.00
   9948 *Back Door Man Blues*........... 8.00 - 12.00
Okeh 06375 *Love Is Gone*............... 7.00 - 10.00
   06398 *Slick Man Blues*.............. 7.00 - 10.00
   06464 *Streamline Love*............. 7.00 - 10.00
   06514 *Something Going On Wrong*....... 7.00 - 10.00
ALBERT CLEMENS:
Bluebird 5930 *Policy Blues*............. 30.00 - 40.00

BIG BOY CLEVELAND:
Gennett 6108 *Quill Blues*............... 90.00 - 120.00
KAISER CLIFTON:
Victor 23278 *Cash Money Blues*........... 50.00 - 80.00
   38600 *Teach Me Right From Wrong*.... 50.00 - 80.00
JAMES COLE; JAMES COLE'S WASHBOARD
    BAND/FOUR:
Champion 16150 *Sweet Lizzie*............. 75.00 - 100.00
   16308 *I Love My Mary*............... 75.00 - 100.00
   16718 *Mistreated The Only Friend You Had*.. 75.00 - 100.00
   40047 *Runnin' Wild*................. 15.00 - 25.00
KID COLE:
Vocalion 1186 *Sixth Street Moan*......... 30.00 - 40.00
   1187 *Hard Hearted Mama Blues*........ 30.00 - 40.00
LUCY COLE:
Champion 15549 *Empty Bed Blues*.......... 20.00 - 30.00
Supertone 9285 *Empty Bed Blues*.......... 20.00 - 30.00
WALTER COLE:
Champion 16104 *Everybody Got Somebody*.... 20.00 - 30.00
Gennett 7318 *Everybody Got Somebody*....... 20.00 - 30.00
BOB COLEMAN:
Paramount 12731 *Cincinnati Underworld Moan*. 50.00 - 75.00
   12791 *Sing Song Blues*............. 50.00 - 75.00
ELLEN COLEMAN:
Edison 51200 *Cruel Back Bitin' Blues*....... 15.00 - 20.00
   51242 *She Walked Right Up And Took*..... 12.00 - 16.00
JAYBIRD COLEMAN:
Black Patti 8055 *Boll Weevil*............ 150.00 - 250.00
Columbia 14534-D *Man Trouble Blues*......... 75.00 - 100.00
Gennett 6245 *Man Trouble Blues*.......... 150.00 - 200.00
   6276 *No More Good Water*........... 150.00 - 200.00
LONNIE COLEMAN:
Columbia 14440-D *Old Rock Island Blues*....... 20.00 - 30.00
WALTER COLEMAN:
Decca 7157 *Smack That Thing*............ 20.00 - 30.00
   7168 *I'm Going To Cincinnati*......... 20.00 - 30.00
CHASEY COLLINS:
Bluebird 6187 *Atlanta Town*............. 35.00 - 50.00
   6261 *Walking Blues*............... 35.00 - 50.00
SAM COLLINS:
Black Patti 8025 *The Jail House Blues*........ 100.00 - 150.00
   8026 *Yellow Dog Blues*............. 100.00 - 150.00
Gennett 6146 *Yellow Dog Blues*.......... 90.00 - 120.00
   6167 *The Jail House Blues*.......... 90.00 - 120.00
   6181 *Devil In The Lion's Den*........ 90.00 - 120.00
   6260 *Dark Cloudy Blues*........... 90.00 - 120.00
   6291 *Lead Me All The Way*.......... 90.00 - 120.00
   6307 *Midnight Special Blues*........ 90.00 - 120.00
   6379 *Hesitation Blues*............ 90.00 - 120.00
Herwin 92043 *Riverside Blues*........... 100.00 - 150.00
Superior 330 *Midnight Special Blues*........ 90.00 - 120.00
   350 *Hesitation Blues*............ 90.00 - 120.00
   369 *Dark Cloudy Blues*........... 90.00 - 120.00
BIG TOM COLLINS:
King 4483 *Heartache Blues*.............. 5.00 - 8.00
   4568 *Watchin' My Stuff*............ 5.00 - 8.00
VIE COLLINS:
Silvertone 3518 *Nobody Knows*............ ———
   3519 *Who'll Drive My Blues Away*....... ———
   3538 *Confessin' Blues*............. 20.00 - 30.00
   3539 *Reckless Don't Care Mama Blues*.... 20.00 - 30.00
   3540 *Midnight Special*............ 20.00 - 30.00
CONNIE'S/CONNEY'S COMBO (WITH L.C.
    WILLIAMS):
Freedom 1508 *Ugly Mae*................. 4.00 - 7.00
   1510 *That's Alright*.............. 4.00 - 7.00
BEN CONWAY:
Herwin 93014 *Sing Song Blues*........... 60.00 - 80.00
ANN COOK:
Victor 20579 *Mama Cookie*.............. 35.00 - 50.00
DONALD COOKS (& HIS BAND):
Jade 202 *Dolphin Street Stomp*.......... 5.00 - 8.00

SILVER COOKS WITH THE GONDOLIERS:
Peacock 1510 *Mr. Ticket Agent*............ 15.00 - 25.00
RATTLESNAKE COOPER:
Talent 804 *Rattlesnake Blues*............ 30.00 - 50.00
MARTHA COPELAND:
Columbia 14161-D, 14189-D, 14196-D........ 7.00 - 10.00
14208-D, 14227-D, 14237-D, 14248-D, 14262-D,
14281-D, 14310-D, 14327-D............ 8.00 - 12.00
14352-D *Desert Blues*.................. 10.00 - 15.00
14377-D *Mama's Well Has Done Gone Dry*.. 10.00 - 15.00
Okeh 8091, 8112........................ 7.00 - 10.00
Victor 20548 *Hard-Headed Mama*......... 10.00 - 15.00
20769 *Stole My Man Blues*............. 10.00 - 15.00
COTTON TOP MOUNTAIN SACTIFIED
  SINGER:
Brunswick 7100 *Give Me That Old Time Religion* 50.00 - 75.00
7119 *She's Coming Round The Mountain*.... 50.00 - 75.00
JAMES COTTON:
Sun 199 *Straighten Up Baby*.............. 10.00 - 15.00*
206 *Cotton Crop Blues*.................. 10.00 - 15.00*
SYLVESTER COTTON:
Modern 655 *Ugly Woman Blues*............ 6.00 - 10.00
Sensation 7000 *Ugly Woman Blues*........... 8.00 - 15.00
LITTLE WILLIE COTTON:
Swing Time 319 *Gonna Shake It Up And Go*... 10.00 - 15.00
DIPPER BOY COUNCIL:
Titles, issued contemporaneously on Banner, Conqueror, Melotone, Oriole, Perfect, Romeo: *I'm Grievin' and I;m Worryin'; Poor And Ain't Got A Dime; Runaway Man Blues; Working Man Blues* . . . . 15..00 - 20.00
COUNTRY JIM:
Imperial 5062 *Rainy Morning Blues*........... 7.00 - 10.00
5073 *Old River Blues*..................... 7.00 - 10.00
5091 *Good Looking Mama*............... 5.00 - 8.00
5095 *Phillipine Blues*................. 5.00 - 8.00
COUNTRY PAUL:
King 4517 *Your Picture Done Faded*........ 7.00 - 12.00*
4532 *One More Time*.................. 7.00 - 12.00*
4560 *Black Cat Trail*.................. 7.00 - 12.00*
4573 *Side Walk Boogie*................. 7.00 - 12.00*
(MISS) COUNTRY SLIM:
Hollywood 1005 *What Wrong Have I Done*.... 10.00 - 15.00
COUSIN JOE:
Savoy 5527 *Weddin' Day Blues*........... 5.00 - 8.00
Signature 1013 *Come Down Baby*............ 5.00 - 8.00
BLIND/BOGUS BEN COVINGTON:
Brunswick 7121 *Boodle-De-Bum Bum*......... 35.00 - 50.00
Paramount 12693 *Adam And Eve In The Garden* 75.00 - 100.00
CRAMER BROTHERS:
Broadway 8058 *Love Always Has Its Way*..... 15.00 - 20.00
8059 *Sara Jane*...................... 15.00 - 20.00
Broadway 8060 *In The Good Old Summertime*.. 15.00 - 20.00
8071 *On Top Of Old Smoky*............. 15.00 - 20.00
8180 *Simpson County*.................. 15.00 - 20.00
BOB CRANE:
Herwin 93018 *Ghost Woman Blues*.......... 90.00 - 120.00
JAMES CRAWFORD:
Gennett 6536 *Flood And Thunder*............ 30.00 - 40.00
ROSETTA CRAWFORD:
Decca 7567, 7584....................... 7.00 - 10.00
Okeh 8096 *Down On The Levee Blues*........ 25.00 - 35.00
Pathe-Actuelle 7505 *Misery*............. 15.00 - 25.00
Perfect 105 *Misery*.................... 15.00 - 25.00
PEE WEE CRAYTON:
Aladdin 3112 *Day Break*................. 4.00 - 6.00*
Modern 624, 643, 658, 675, 707, 719, 732, 742, 763,
774, 796, 816, 892.................... 4.00 - 7.00*
KATIE CRIPPEN:
Black Swan 2003 *Blind Man's Blues*.......... 15.00 - 20.00
2018 *That's My Cup Blues*.............. 15.00 - 20.00
Same titles on Claxtonola, Paramount, Puritan.. 15.00 - 20.00

DAVID CROSS:
Brunswick 7079 *Then My Gal's In Town*...... 25.00 - 40.00
(ARTHUR) "BIG BOY" CRUDUP:
Bluebird 8858 *Death Valley Blues*............ 8.00 - 12.00
8896 *Black Pony Blues*................ 8.00 - 12.00
9019 *Raised To My Hand*............... 8.00 - 12.00
Bluebird 34-0704 *Mean Old Frisco Blues*...... 5.00 - 8.00
34-0717 *My Mamma Don't Allow Me*....... 5.00 - 8.00
34-0725 *Rock Me Mama*................ 5.00 - 8.00
34-0738 *Cool Disposition*................. 5.00 - 8.00
34-0746 *She's Gone*................... 5.00 - 8.00
RCA Victor 20-1949 *Ethel Mae*......... 5.00 - 8.00
20-2105 *I Want My Lovin'*.............. 5.00 - 8.00
20-2205 *That's All Right*.............. 5.00 - 8.00
20-2387 *That's Your Red Wagon*......... 5.00 - 8.00
20-2565 *Train Fore Blues*............. 5.00 - 8.00
20-2757 *Dirty Road Blues*............. 5.00 - 8.00
20-2989 *Boy Friend Blues*............. 5.00 - 8.00
20-3140 *Just Like A Spider*............ 5.00 - 8.00
20-3261 *Chicago Blues*............... 5.00 - 8.00*
20-4367 *Love Me Mama*................ 5.00 - 8.00*
20-4572 *Goin' Back To Georgia*......... 5.00 - 8.00*
20-4753 *Late In The Evening*........... 5.00 - 8.00*
20-4933 *Second Man Blues*............. 5.00 - 8.00*
20-5070 *Lookin' For My Baby*........... 5.00 - 8.00*
20-5167 *Nelvina*.................... 5.00 - 8.00*
20-5563 *The War Is Over*............. 5.00 - 8.00*
22-0007 *Gonna Be Some Changes Made*..... 5.00 - 8.00*
22-0029 *Crudup's Vicksburg Blues*........ 5.00 - 8.00*
22-0048 *Hoodoo Lady Blues*............ 5.00 - 8.00*
22-0061 *Come Back Baby*.............. 5.00 - 8.00*
22-0074 *Dust My Broom*.............. 5.00 - 8.00*
22-0092 *Mean Old Santa-Fe*............ 5.00 - 8.00*
22-0100 *Lonesome World To Me*........ 5.00 - 8.00*
22-0105 *She's Just Like Caldonia*........ 5.00 - 8.00*
22-0117 *Nobody Wants Me*............ 5.00 - 8.00*
22-0126 *Roberta Blues*.............. 5.00 - 8.00*
22-0141 *Too Much Competition*.......... 5.00 - 8.00*
(* 45 rpm issues have catalog number prefixes 47 - or 50-instead of 20 - or 22 -' catalog numbers may also be different in some cases. See 45 rpm section.)
PERCY LEE CRUDUP:
Checker 754 *Tears In My Eyes*.............. 5.00 - 8.00*
DENNIS CRUMPTON & ROBERT SUMMERS:
Titles, issued contemporaneously on Banner, Melotone, Oriole, Perfect, Romeo: *Everybody Ought To Pray Sometime; Go I'll Send Thee.* 20.00 - 30.00
BEN CURRY:
Champion 50019 *You Rascal You*............ 20.00 - 30.00
Paramount 13118 *Fat Mouth Blues*.......... 100.00 - 150.00
13122 *Hot Dog*..................... 100.00 - 150.00
13140 *The New Dirty Dozen*............ 100.00 - 150.00
ELDER CURRY:
Okeh 8857 *Memphis Flu*................. 15.00 - 20.00
8879 *Hard Times*.................... 15.00 - 20.00
8892 *None Good But One*............. 15.00 - 20.00
8910 *Prove All Things*............... 15.00 - 20.00
DADDY STOVEPIPE (AND MISSISSIPPI
  SARAH):
Bluebird 5913 *The Spasm*.............. 35.00 - 50.00
6023 *35 Depression*.................. 35.00 - 50.00
Claxtonola 40335 *Sundown Blues*.......... 25.00 - 40.00
Gennett 5459 *Stove Pipe Blues*............ 25.00 - 40.00
DUSKY DAILEY:
Titles, issued contemporaneously on Banner, Melotone, Oriole, Perfect, Romeo, Vocalion: *Flying Crow Blues; I Want You, I Need You; I Would Do Anything For You; Screamin' And Hollerin' Blues.* 10.00 - 15.00
Vocalion 04963 *Miss Georgia Blues*.......... 8.00 - 12.00

04977 *Can Cutter Blues*.................	8.00 -	12.00
05044 *Lost Lovin' Blues*.................	8.00 -	12.00
05110 *Misunderstandin' Man*.............	8.00 -	12.00

DALLAS RED:
Selective 112 *Cold Blooded Blues*...........	5.00 -	8.00

DALLAS STRING BAND (WITH COLEY JONES):
Columbia 14290-D *Dallas Rag*...........	40.00 -	60.00
14389-D *Hokum Blues*...............	40.00 -	60.00
14410-D *Chasin' Rainbows*..............	40.00 -	60.00
14574-D *Sugar Blues*....................	40.00 -	60.00

LEROY DALLAS:
Sittin' In With 522 *Jump Little Children*.......	8.00 -	15.00
526 *Good Morning Blues*.................	8.00 -	15.00
537 *Your Sweet Man's Blues*.............	8.00 -	15.00

(JULIUS DANIELS (AND TORRENCE):
Victor 20499 *I'm Gonna Tell God How You Doin'*	50.00 -	75.00
20658 *Ninety Nine Year Blues*.............	50.00 -	75.00
21065 *Richmond Blues*.................	50.00 -	75.00
21359 *Can't Put The Bridle On That Mule*...	50.00 -	75.00

BLIND (BLUES) DARBY:
Decca 7328 *Heart Trouble Blues*.............	15.00 -	20.00
7816 *Spike Driver*......................	15.00 -	20.00
Vocalion 02953 *I'm Gonna Wreck Your Vee Eight*	25.00 -	35.00
02988 *Pokino Blues*..................	25.00 -	35.00
03177 *Sweet Memories Blues*.............	25.00 -	35.00

TEDDY DARBY:
Paramount 12828 *My Laona Blues*...........	100.00 -	150.00
12907 *What Am I To Do?*.............	100.00 -	150.00
Victor 23311 *Deceiving Blues*..............	150.00 -	200.00

GENEVIEVE DAVIS:
Victor 20648 *I've Got Something*...........	30.00 -	40.00

GEORGE DAVIS:
Decca 7756, 7799....................	5.00 -	10.00

BLIND JOHN(NY) DAVIS (TRIO):
MGM 10574 *No Mail Today*...............	5.00 -	8.00
10738 *My Love*.......................	5.00 -	8.00
10919 *Telegram To My Baby*...........	5.00 -	8.00
10976 *The Day Will Come*.............	5.00 -	8.00
Vocalion 04079 *Jersey Cow Blues*...........	7.00 -	12.00
01489 *Alley Woman Blues*.............	7.00 -	12.00
04580 *Anna Lou Breakdown*.............	7.00 -	12.00

HENRYETTE DAVIS:
Okeh 8371 *Another Sweet Daddy*.............	15.00 -	20.00
8395 *Mail Box Blues*..................	15.00 -	20.00

SONNY BOY DAVIS:
Talent 802 *I Don't Live Here No More*........	20.00 -	30.00

WALTER DAVIS:
Bluebird 5031 *M. & O. Blues*.............	15.00 -	20.00
5038 *Blue Sea Blues*.................	15.00 -	20.00
5077 *Howling Wind Blues*.............	15.00 -	20.00
5094 *Hijack Blues*..................	15.00 -	20.00
5129 *Worried Man Blues*.............	15.00 -	20.00
5143 *Red Cross Blues*...............	15.00 -	20.00
5192 *Moonlight Blues*...............	15.00 -	20.00
5228 *Evil Woman*..................	15.00 -	20.00
5305 *Red Cross Blues—No. 2*.............	15.00 -	20.00
5324 *You Don't Smell Right*.............	15.00 -	20.00
5361 *What's The Use Of Worryinn'?*........	15.00 -	20.00
5390 *Oil Field Blues*.................	15.00 -	20.00
5411 *Story Weather Blues—No. 2*.............	20.00 -	30.00
5879 *Sloppy Drunk Again*.............	15.00 -	25.00
5931 *Sweet Sixteen*....................	20.00 -	30.00
5965 *Minute Man Blues*.............	15.00 -	25.00
5982 *Sad And Lonesome Blues*.............	15.00 -	25.00
6040 *Dentist Blues*..................	15.00 -	20.00
6059 *I Can Tell By The Way You Smell*.....	10.00 -	15.00
6074 *Pearly May*..................	10.00 -	15.00
6125 *Santa Claus*..................	20.00 -	30.00
6167 *Moonlight Is My Spread*.............	10.00 -	15.00
6201 *Katy Blues*..................	10.00 -	15.00

6228 *Blues At Midnight*..................	10.00 -	15.00
6354 *Carpenter Man*..................	10.00 -	15.00
6410 *Fallin' Rain*..................	8.00 -	12.00
6468 *Jacksonville*..................	8.00 -	12.00
6498 *Think You Need A Shot*..........	8.00 -	12.00
6971 *Nightmare Blues*..................	8.00 -	12.00
6996 *Good Gal*....................	8.00 -	12.00
7021 *Fifth Avenue Blues*.............	8.00 -	12.00
7064 *Angel Child*..................	8.00 -	12.00
7292 *Guiding Rod*..................	8.00 -	12.00
7329 *Holiday Blues*..................	8.00 -	12.00
7375 *Big Jack Engine Blues*..........	8.00 -	12.00
7512 *Walking The Avenue*..........	8.00 -	12.00
7551 *Easy Goin' Mama*..........	8.00 -	12.00
7589 *Million-Dollar*..................	8.00 -	12.00
7643 *Candy Man*..................	8.00 -	12.00
7663 *Friendless Blues*..................	8.00 -	12.00
7693 *13 Highway*..................	8.00 -	12.00
7745 *Call Me Anytime*..................	8.00 -	12.00
7792 *Love Will Kill You*..........	8.00 -	12.00
7836 *Homesick*..................	8.00 -	12.00
7978 *Cuttin' Off My Days*..........	8.00 -	12.00
8002 *Early This Mornin'*..........	8.00 -	12.00
8026 *Smoky Mountain*..........	8.00 -	12.00
8058 *Mercy Blues*..................	8.00 -	12.00
8107 *Troubled And Weary*..........	8.00 -	12.00
8227 *Corinne*..................	8.00 -	12.00
8261 *Big Four Blues*..................	8.00 -	12.00
8282 *Green And Lucky*..........	8.00 -	12.00
8312 *Bachelor Blues*..................	8.00 -	12.00
8343 *Froggy Bottom*..................	8.00 -	12.00
8367 *Doctor Blues*..................	8.00 -	12.00
8393 *Sundown Blues*..................	8.00 -	12.00
8434 *Jungle Blues*..................	8.00 -	12.00
8470 *Western Land*..................	8.00 -	12.00
8510 *Come Back Baby*..................	8.00 -	12.00
8534 *The Way I Love You*..........	8.00 -	12.00
8574 *Four Foot Eleven*..........	8.00 -	12.00
8600 *Can't See Your Face*..........	8.00 -	12.00
8664 *Just Thinking*..................	8.00 -	12.00
8694 *Soon Forgotten*..................	8.00 -	12.00
8737 *Friends Must Part*..........	8.00 -	12.00
8773 *The Only Woman*..................	8.00 -	12.00
8802 *All My Money Gone*..........	8.00 -	12.00
8833 *I'll Be Back After A While*..........	8.00 -	12.00
8860 *You Keep On Crying*..........	8.00 -	12.00
8926 *Teasin' Brown Skin*..........	8.00 -	12.00
8961 *Frisco Blues*..................	8.00 -	12.00
8998 *Hello Baby*..................	5.00 -	8.00
9027 *Goodbye*..................	5.00 -	8.00
Bullet 305 *Move Back To The Woods*.........	5.00 -	10.00
311 *I Would Hate To Hate You*............	5.00 -	10.00
321 *Santa Claus Blues*............	5.00 -	10.00
326 *Stop That Train In Harlem*........	5.00 -	10.00
341 *I Just Can't Help It*..........	5.00 -	10.00
Montgomery Ward (many titles same as Bluebird, above).....................	5.00 -	10.00
Victor 23250 *Blue Sea Blues*..........	50.00 -	80.00
23282 *What Made Me Love You So?*.....	50.00 -	80.00
23291 *Railroad Man Blues*............	50.00 -	80.00
23302 *Mr. Davis Blues—No. 2*..........	50.00 -	80.00
23308 *Howling Wind Blues*..........	50.00 -	80.00
23315 *Strange Land Blues*..........	50.00 -	80.00
23325 *Lonesome Hill Blues*..........	50.00 -	80.00
23333 *Worried Man Blues*..........	30.00 -	50.00
23343 *Hijack Blues*..................	30.00 -	50.00
23355 *South-West Missouri Blues*.....	30.00 -	50.00
23414 *Night Creepin'*..................	30.00 -	50.00
23418 *L & N Blues*..................	30.00 -	50.00
23423 *Red Cross Blues*..........	30.00 -	50.00
38618 *Mr. Davis' Blues*..........	40.00 -	60.00

BLIND WILLIE DAVIS:

Paramount 12658 *When The Saints Go Marching In*	50.00 -	75.00
12726 *You Enemy Cannot Harm You*......	75.00 -	100.00
12979 *I Believe I'll Go Back Home*.........	90.00 -	120.00

RUTH DAY:

Columbia 14642-D *Painful Blues*............	20.00 -	30.00

TEXAS BILL DAY (& BILLIKEN JOHNSON):

Columbia 14494-D *Goin' Back To My Baby*....	20.00 -	30.00
14514-D *Elm Street Blues*................	20.00 -	30.00
14587-D *Good Mornin' Blues*.............	20.00 -	30.00

WILL DAY:

Columbia 14318-D *Sunrise Blues*............	30.00 -	40.00

JOE DEAN:

Vocalion 1544 *Mexico Bound Blues*..........	50.00 -	75.00

JAMES/JIMMY DE BERRY (& HIS MEMPHIS PLAYBOYS):

Okeh 05800 *Spider Bite Blues*............	7.00 -	10.00
Sun 185 *Take A Little Chance*............	25.00 -	40.00*
Vocalion 05084 *You Can Go*............	7.00 -	10.00
05247 *Insane Jealous Blues*............	7.00 -	10.00
05349 *You Played A Trick On Me*....	7.00 -	10.00

MERCY DEE:

Bayou 003 *Please Understand*............	10.00 -	15.00
013 *Happy Bachelor*................	7.00 -	10.00
Colony 102 *Straight And Narrow*......	5.00 -	15.00
107 *Old Fashioned Ways*..........	5.00 -	8.00
111 *Birdbrain Baby*..............	5.00 -	8.00
Imperial 5104 *Empty Life*............	5.00 -	8.00
5110 *Big Foot Country*............	5.00 -	8.00
5118 *Bought Love*................	5.00 -	8.00
5127 *Pay Off*....................	5.00 -	8.00
Spire 11-001 *Lonesome Cabin Blues*......	7.00 -	10.00
11-002 *Travelin' Alone Blues*........	7.00 -	10.00

MATTIE DELANEY:

Vocalion 1480 *Tallahatchie River Blues*.......	20.00 -	30.00

TOME DELANEY:

Columbia 14082-D *Georgia Stockade Blues*.....	7.00 -	12.00
14122-D *Bow Legged Mama*..............	7.00 -	12.00

THE DELLS:

Vee Jay 134 *Tell The World*................	20.00 -	40.00*

DELTA BOYS:

Bluebird 8852 *Black Gal Swing*............	15.00 -	25.00
8891 *When The Saints Go Marching In*......	15.00 -	25.00
8915 *Get Up And Go*................	15.00 -	25.00

DELTA JOE:

Chance 1115 *4 O'clock Blues*................	15.00 -	25.00*

DELTA JOHN:

Regent 1001 *Goin' Mad Blues*..............	7.00 -	10.00

DELTA RHYTHM BOYS:

Atlantic 889, 899, 900, 905, 1023.....	3.00 -	5.00
Decca 8514, 8522, 8530, 8542......	3.00 -	5.00

DESCRIPTIVE NOVELTY (See BLIND LEMON JEFFERSON)

DETROIT COUNT:

JVB 75830 *Hastings Street Opera*............	15.00 -	20.00
75831 *Hastings St. Woogie Man*...........	15.00 -	20.00
King 4264 *Hastings Street Opera*...........	8.00 -	12.00
4265 *I'm Crazy About You*..........	10.00 -	15.00
4279 *Little Tillie Willie*.............	10.00 -	15.00

THE DEVIL'S DADDY-IN-LAW:

Conqueror 9204 *Lookin' For My Baby*........	10.00 -	15.00
Vocalion 04643 *Lookin' For My Baby*......	10.00 -	15.00

PEARL DICKSON:

Columbia 14286-D *Little Rock Blues*.......	20.00 -	30.00

PERE DICKSON:

Victor 23335 *Red Hot Papa*..............	40.00 -	60.00

TOM DICKSON:

Okeh 8570 *Worry Blues*............	80.00 -	100.00
8590 *Death Cell Blues*............	80.00 -	100.00

DIRTY RED:

Aladdin 194 *Home Last Night*............	10.00 -	15.00
207 *Hotel Boogie*................	10.00 -	15.00

FLOYD DIXON (TRIO) (WITH JOHNNY MOOR'S THREE BLAZERS):

Aladdin 3069, 3073, 3074, 3075, 3078, 3082, 3083, 3084, 3101, 3111, 3135, 3144, 3151, 3166, 3196, 3230............	3.00 -	5.00*
Modern 653, 664, 700, 724, 725, 744, 761, 776, 797	3.00 -	7.00
Supreme 1528, 1535, 1546, 1547.............	5.00 -	8.00
Swing Time 261, 287..............	5.00 -	8.00

MARY DIXON:

Columbia 14415-D *Daddy You Got Ev'rything*..	15.00 -	20.00
14442-D *All Around Mama*................	15.00 -	20.00
14459-D *Black Dog Blues*................	15.00 -	20.00
14532-D *Unhappy Blues*...............	15.00 -	20.00
Vocalion 1199 *Dusky Stevedore*.............	20.00 -	30.00

PERRY DIXON:

Columbia 14522-D *Back To Georgia Blues*......	30.00 -	40.00

DOCTOR CLAYTON'S BUDDY:

RCA Vitor 20-2733, 20-2954, 20-3085, 20-3255.	3.00 -	6.00

DR. HEPCAT (See L. DURST):

FATS DOMINO:

Imperial 5058 *The Fat Man*................	15.00 -	20.00
5065 *Boogie Woogie Baby*................	15.00 -	20.00
5077 *Hide Away Blues*...............	15.00 -	20.00
5085 *Brand New Baby*...............	10.00 -	15.00
5099 *Every Night About This Time*........	10.00 -	15.00
5114 *What's The Matter Baby*.........	15.00 -	20.00
5123 *Don't You Lie To Me*..........	15.00 -	20.00
5138 *No, No Baby*...............	10.00 -	15.00
5145 *Rockin' Chair*...............	8.00 -	12.00
5167 *I'll Be Gone*...............	10.00 -	15.00

BLIND JOE DONNELL:

Broadway 5089 *There's A Hand Writing On The Wall*........	30.00 -	40.00

MATTIE DORSEY:

Paramount 12521 *Mattie Blues*.............	30.00 -	40.00
12554 *Stingaree Blues*...................	30.00 -	40.00

BIG BILL DOTSON & HIS GUITAR:

Blues & Rhythm 7004 *Dark Old World*........	8.00 -	12.00

DAISY DOUGLAS:

Columbia 14175-D *Down-Hearted Blues*......	8.00 -	12.00

K.C. DOUGLAS:

Down Town 2004 *Mercury Boogie*...........	10.00 -	15.00

DOWN HOME BOYS:

Bluebird 6331 *You Do It*...............	15.00 -	20.00
Victor 38567 *It's All Gone Now*.............	40.00 -	60.00

DOWN HOME TRIO:

Down Town 2017 *Down Town Shuffle*........	20.00 -	30.00

DOWN SOUTH BOYS:

Varsity 6009 *The New Stop And Listen Blues*...	10.00 -	15.00
6010 *Down On My Bended Knees*..........	15.00 -	20.00

LITTLE BUDDY DOLE:

Vocalion 05111 *Grief Will Kill You*............	15.00 -	20.00
05246 *Sweet Man Blues*.................	15.00 -	20.00
05771 *Renewed Love Blues*...............	15.00 -	20.00

ARIZONA DRANES:

Okeh 8352 *John Said He Saw A Number*......	15.00 -	20.00
8353 *It's All Right Now*............	15.00 -	20.00
8380 *In That Day*...............	15.00 -	20.00
8419 *I'm Going Home on the Morning Train*.	15.00 -	20.00
8438 *I'm Glad My Lord Saved Me*.........	15.00 -	20.00
8600 *I Shall Wear a Crown*.............	15.00 -	20.00
8646 *Don't You Want To Go?*.............	15.00 -	20.00

DRIFTIN' SLIM/SMITH:

Modern 849 *My Little Machine*.............	8.00 -	15.00*
RPM 370 *Good Morning Baby*.............	10.00 -	15.00*

SLIM DUCKETT & PIG NORWOOD:

Okey 8871 *You Gotta Stand Judgment For Yourself*	20.00 -	30.00
8899 *When The Saints Go Marching In*......	20.00 -	30.00

SIDEWHEEL SALLIE/SALLY DUFFIE:

Paramount 12519 *King Papa Blues*..........	25.00 -	40.00
12545 *Bunker Hill Blues*.............	25.00 -	40.00
12581 *Kid Man Blues*.............	25.00 -	40.00

BERNICE DUKE:

Broadway 5038 *Back Door Blues*	30.00 -	40.00
5088 *Gold Mansion Blues*	30.00 -	40.00

DUKE BAYOU & HIS MYSTIC 6:

Apollo 440 *Rub A Little Boogie*	7.00 -	10.00

WILLIE DUKES:

Champion 16126 *Snake Hip Twirl*	15.00 -	20.00
16745 *Sweet Poplar Bluff Blues*	40.00 -	60.00
50055 *Snake Hip Twirl*	7.00 -	10.00

ANDREW DUNHAM:

Sensation 23 *Hattie Mae*	10.00 -	15.00

FRED DUNN & HIS BARRELHOUSE RHYTHM:

Signature 1026, 1027, 32010	5.00 -	8.00

CHAMPION JACK DUPREE; JACK DUPREE & HIS BAND:

Alert 421 *Highway 51*	7.00 -	10.00
Apollo 407, 413, 421	5.00 -	8.00
Continental 6064, 6065, 6066	5.00 -	8.00
Joe Davis 5100, 5101, 5102, 5103, 5104, 5105, 5106, 5107, 5108	4.00 -	7.00
Okeh 05656, 05713, 05769, 05823, 06068, 06104, 06152, 06197, 06597, 06642	5.00 -	10.00

L. DURST (DR. HEPCAT):

Peacock 1509 *Hattie Green*	30.00 -	50.00
Uptown 201 *Hattie Green*	50.00 -	80.00

JIMMY EAGER & HIS TRIO:

Sabre 100 *Please Mr. Doctor*	7.00 -	10.00*

AMOS EASTON (& HIS ORCHESTRA):

Specialty 410 *Strange Angel*	5.00 -	8.00
Vocalion 1694 *M and O Blues*	20.00 -	30.00

EBONY THREE:

Decca 7503, 7527	5.00 -	8.00

EDDIE AND OSCAR:

Victor 23324 *Flying Crow Blues*	75.00 -	100.00

EDDY TEDDY:

Brunswick 7223 *Alcohol Mama*	25.00 -	35.00

BERNICE EDWARDS (BLACK BOY SHINE & HOWLING SMITH):

Paramount 12620 *Southbound Blues*	40.00 -	60.00
12633 *Long Tall Mama*	40.00 -	60.00
12653 *Sunshine Blues*	40.00 -	60.00
12713 *Jack Of All Trades*	40.00 -	60.00
12741 *Born To Die Blues*	40.00 -	60.00
12766 *Hard Hustlin' Blues*	40.00 -	60.00
Vocalion 03036 *Bantam Rooster Blues*	35.00 -	50.00
03168 *Hot Mattress Stomp*	35.00 -	50.00

BIG BOY EDWARDS:

Titles, issued contemporaneously on Banner, Melotone, Oriole, Perfect, Romeo, Vocalion: *It Was No Dream; Louise*	15.00 -	20.00
Vocalion 02866 *Who Did You Give My Barbecue To?*	15.00 -	20.00
02932 *Hoodoo Blues*	15.00 -	20.00
03079 *Dancing The Blues Away*	15.00 -	20.00

CARRIE EDWARDS:

Columbia 14652-D *Dirty Mistreater*	15.00 -	20.00
Okeh 8938 *Hard Time Blues*	15.00 -	20.00

FRANK EDWARDS:

Okeh 06393 *Terraplane Blues*	10.00 -	15.00
06493 *Sweet Man Blues*	10.00 -	15.00

HONEYBOY EDWARDS:

Artist 102 *Build A Cave*	8.00 -	15.00

J.D. EDWARDS:

Imperial 5245 *Hobo*	5.00 -	8.00*

PIANO KID EDWARDS:

Paramount 13051 *Piano Kid Special*	80.00 -	110.00
13086 *Hard Luck Gamblin' Man*	80.00 -	100.00

(BIG BOY) TEDDY EDWARDS; BIG TEDDY BOY EDWARDS:

Bluebird 5628 *Who Did You Give My Barbecue To?*	15.00 -	20.00

5813 *Love Will Provide For Me*	15.00 -	20.00
5826 *Louise*	15.00 -	20.00
Decca 7184 *Louisiana*	15.00 -	20.00
Melotone 12037 *Them Things*	15.00 -	25.00
12097 *Lovin' Blues*	15.00 -	25.00
Vocalion 02698 *Lovin' Blues*	15.00 -	25.00

TENDERFOOT EDWARDS:

Paramount 12873 *Seven Sister Blues*	150.00 -	200.00
12952 *Up On The Hill Blues*	150.00 -	200.00

W.C. ELKINS & HIS DEXTRA SINGERS:

QRS 7045 *Climbing Up The Mountain*	15.00 -	25.00
7046 *Oh, Mother, Don't You Weep*	15.00 -	25.00
7047 *Roll, Roll, Chariot*	15.00 -	25.00
7063 *Eloi*	15.00 -	25.0
7066 *Ride On, Moses*	15.00 -	25.00
7068 *A Wheel In A Wheel*	15.00 -	25.00

BIG BOY ELLIS & HIS RHYTHM:

Lenox 521 *Dices Dices*	7.00 -	10.00

BILLY (THE KID) EMERSON:

Sun 195 *No Teasin' Around*	15.00 -	20.00*
214 *Move Baby Move*	5.00 -	8.00*
219 *Red Hot*	5.00 -	8.00*
233 *Something For Nothing*	5.00 -	8.00*

JACK ERBY:

Columbia 14570-D *Hot Peter*	15.00 -	20.00

JOHN ERBY:

Columbia 14151-D *Lonesome Jimmy Blues*	15.00 -	20.00

LEROY ERVIN:

Gold Star 628 *Rock Island Blues*	15.00 -	20.00
Swing 415 *Rock Island Blues*	15.00 -	20.00

(SLEEPY) JOHN ESTES; JOHN ESTES-JAMES RACHEL:

Bluebird 7677 *Diving Duck Blues*	20.00 -	30.00
7849 *The Girl I Love, She Got Long Curly Hair*	20.00 -	30.00
Bluebird 8871 *Little Laura Blues*	15.00 -	20.00
8950 *Working Man Blues*	15.00 -	20.00
Champion 50001 *Stop That Thing*	20.00 -	30.00
50048 *Drop Down Mama*	20.00 -	30.00
50068 *Someday Baby Blues*	20.00 -	30.00
Decca 7279 *Someday Baby Blues*	15.00 -	20.00
7289 *Married Woman Blues*	15.00 -	20.00
7325 *Down South Blues*	15.00 -	20.00
7342 *Vernita Blues*	15.00 -	20.00
7354 *Hobo Jungle Blues*	15.00 -	20.00
7365 *Need More Blues*	15.00 -	20.00
7414 *Government Money*	15.00 -	20.00
7442 *Floating Bridge*	12.00 -	16.00
7473 *Brownsville Blues*	15.00 -	20.00
7491 *Liquor Store Blues*	15.00 -	20.00
7516 *Easin' Back To Tennessee*	15.00 -	20.00
7561 *Everybody Oughta Make A Change*	15.00 -	2.00
7766 *Drop Down*	15.00 -	20.00
7789 *Mailman Blues*	15.00 -	20.00
7814 *Jailhouse Blues*	15.00 -	20.00
Victor 23318 *Expressman Blues*	150.00 -	200.00
23397 *Stack O'Dollars*	150.00 -	200.00
38549 *Diving Duck Blues*	100.00 -	150.00
38582 *Black Mattie Blues*	100.00 -	150.00
38595 *T-Bone Steak Blues*	100.00 -	150.00
38614 *Milk Cow Blues*	100.00 -	150.00
38628 *Poor John Blues*	100.00 -	150.00

JOE EVANS:

Titles, issued contemporaneously on Oriole, Perfect, Romeo: *Boogity Woogity; Down In Black Bottom; Early Some Morning Blues; Georgia Rose; Mill Man Blues; New Huntsville Jail; Oh You Son Of A Gun; Shook It This Morning Blues*	30.00 -	40.00
Gennett 6259 *Little Son Of A Gun*	50.00 -	80.00

EVANS AND McCLAIN:

Titles, issued contemporaneously on Banner, Oriole, Perfect, Romeo: *So Sorry Dear; Sourwood Mountain*	30.00 -	40.00

DOROTHY EVERETTS:

Columbia 14444-D *Macon Blues*. . . . . 20.00 - 30.00

LOTTIE EVERSON (& HER BUDDY):

Champion 15591 *Lost Lover Blues*. . . . . 40.00 - 60.00

15636 *Blue World Blues*. . . . . 40.00 - 60.00

15755 *Wayward Girl Blues*. . . . . 40.00 - 60.00

EXCELSIOR (NORFOLK) QUARTETTE:

Black Swan 2060 *Jelly Roll Blues*. . . . . 10.00 - 15.00

Gennett 4881 *Kitchen Mechanic Blues*. . . . . 7.00 - 10.00

Okeh 4481 *Kitchen Mechanic Blues*. . . . . 7.00 - 10.00

8033 *Roll Them Bones*. . . . . 7.00 - 10.00

8035 *Down By The Old Mill Stream*. . . . . 7.00 - 10.00

8038 *Goodbye, My Coney Island Baby*. . . . . . 7.00 - 10.00

FAMOUS HOKUM BOYS:

Titles, issued contemporaneously on Banner, Oriole,
Perfect, Romeo: *Ain't Going There No More;
Black Cat Rag; Come On In; Come On Mama;
Do That Thing; Eagle Riding Papa; Guitar Rag;
It's All Used Up; Nancy Jane; Papa's Getting Hot;
Pat That Bread; Pie-Eating Strut; Pig Mean Strut;
Rollin' Mill; Saturday Night Rub; Somebody's
Been Using That Thing; That Stuff I Got; That's
The Way She Likes It; You Can't Get Enough
Of That Stuff; You Do It*. . . . . 25.00 - 40.00

THE FAT MAN:

J.O.B. 103 *You've Got To Stop This Mess*. . . . . 20.00 - 30.00

FEATHERS AND FROGS:

Paramount 12812 *How You Get That Way*. . . . 25.00 - 40.00

BEN FERGUSON:

Victor 23297 *Please Don't Holler, Mama*. . . . . . 25.00 - 40.00

TROY FERGUSON:

Columbia 14483-D *College Blues*. . . . . 15.00 - 20.00

14644-D *You Better Keep It At Home*. . . . . . 15.00 - 20.00

ALFRED FIELDS:

Okeh 06020, 06129. 7.00 - 10.00

Vocalion 05018, 05727. . . . . 7.00 - 10.00

FINE ART(S) TRIO (SIPPIN AT THE PIANO):

Fine Art 203 *Caught In The Web Of Sin*. . . . . . 10.00 - 15.00

204 *Here I Go Wher The Morning Glories Grow* 10.00 - 15.00

THE FIVE BREEZES:

Bluebird 8590 *Sweet Louise*. . . . . 10.00 - 15.00

8614 *My Buddy Blues*. . . . . 10.00 - 15.00

8679 *Swingin' The Blues*. . . . . 10.00 - 15.00

8710 *Just A Jitterbug*. . . . . 10.00 - 15.00

FIVE JINKS:

Bluebird 6857 *I'm Moaning All Day For You*. . . 7.00 - 10.00

6905 *Cushion Foot*. . . . . 7.00 - 10.00

6951 *There Goes My Headache*. . . . . 7.00 - 10.00

THE FIVE SHARPS:

Jubilee 5104 *Stormy Weather/Sleepy Cowboy*
(Almost legendary among Rhythm & Blues collectors, this record was reportedly sold at auction
for over $3,800.00. Only two or three copies are
known, despite the seemingly inordinate publici-
ty given this record over the years). . . . . Rare

THE FLAMINGOS:

Parrot 811 *I Really Don't Want To Know*. . . . . . 20.00 - 30.00*

NAPOLEON FLETCHER:

Bluebird 5383 *She Showed It All*. . . . . 25.00 - 35.00

NELLIE FLORENCE:

Columbia 14342-D *Jacksonville Blues*. . . . . 25.00 - 35.00

THE FLORIDA KID:

Bluebird 8589, 8625, 8680, 8743. . . . . 10.00 - 15.00

ELL-ZEE FLOYD:

Brunswick 7181 *Snow Bound And Blues*. . . . . . 80.00 - 120.00

FLYIN' LINDBURG:

Decca 7066 *No Good Woman Blues*. . . . . 15.00 - 25.00

A.C. FOREHAND:

Victor 20547 *Mother's Prayer*. . . . . 10.00 - 15.00

BLIND MAMIE FOREHAND:

Victor 20574 *Honey In The Rock*. . . . . 10.00 - 15.00

FOREST CITY JOE:

Aristocrat 3101 *Memory of Sonny Boy*. . . . . . . 40.00 - 60.00

DESSA FOSTER & HOWLING SMITH:

Melotone 12117 *Tell It To The Judge*. . . . . 20.00 - 30.00

EVELYN FOSTER:

Champion 15569 *Park No More Mama Blues*. . . 25.00 - 40.00

15590 *Beating Blues*. . . . . 25.00 - 40.00

JIM FOSTER:

Champion 15301 *Riverside Blues*. . . . . 100.00 - 150.00

15320 *The Jail House Blues*. . . . . 100.00 - 150.00

15359 *Pork Chop Blues*. . . . . 100.00 - 150.00

15397 *Dark Cloudy Blues*. . . . . 100.00 - 150.00

15453 *It Won't Be Long*. . . . . 100.00 - 150.00

15472 *Hesitation Blues*. . . . . 100.00 - 150.00

Silvertone 5127 *Yellow Dog Blues*. . . . . 100.00 - 150.00

5131 *Do That Thing*. . . . . 100.00 - 150.00

5172 *I Want To Be Like Jesus In My Heart*. . 100.00 - 150.00

LEROY FOSTER & MUDDY WATERS:

Aristocrat 1234 *Locked Out Boogie*. . . . . 25.00 - 40.00

RUDY FOSTER:

Paramount 12981 *Corn Trimmer Blues*. . . . . . . 125.00 - 175.00

FOUR BLACKAMOORS:

Decca 7850 *Break It Up Charlie*. . . . . 7.00 - 10.00

8512 *Romance in the Dark*. . . . . 7.00 - 10.00

THE FOUR BLUEJACKETS:

Mercury 8017 *Baby Baby Please Come Home*. . 5.00 - 8.00

THE FOUR BLUES:

DeLuxe 1002 *The Things You Want Most Of All* 5.00 - 8.00

1004 *Blues Can Jump*. . . . . 5.00 - 8.00

4 DEEP TONES:

Coral 65061 *Just In Case You Change Your Mind* 5.00 - 8.00

65062 *The Night You Said Goodbye*. . . . . . . 5.00 - 8.00

THE FOUR DOTS:

Dot 1043 *My Dear*. 7.00 - 10.00

FOUR PODS OF PEPPER:

Brunswick 7103 *Ain't Got No Mama Now*. . . . . 15.00 - 20.00

THE FOUR ROCKETS:

Aladdin 3007 *Travelin' Light*. . . . . 8.00 - 12.00

THE FOUR SOUTHERNERS:

Decca 7291 *Dan The Back Door Man*. . . . . 5.00 - 8.00

FOUR SOUTHERN SINGERS:

Bluebird 8392 *Old Man Harlem*. . . . . 8.00 - 12.00

Victor 24262 *Mammy Lou*. . . . . 8.00 - 12.00

24328 *Hamebone Am Sweet*. . . . . 8.00 - 12.00

JOHN D. FOX:

Gennett 6352 *The Worried Man Blues*. . . . . 100.00 - 150.00

Superior 389 *The Worried Man Blues*. . . . . 80.00 - 100.00

ELI FRAMER:

Victor 23409 *Framer's Blues*. . . . . 80.00 - 120.00

FRANKIE AND CLARA:

Paramount 13010 *Frankie and Clara*. . . . . 50.00 - 75.00

BUCK FRANKLIN:

Victor 23310 *Crooked World Blues*. . . . . 75.00 - 100.00

EMERY FRANKLIN:

Cava-Tone 251 *Lonesome Day*. . . . . 7.00 - 10.00

TINY FRANKLIN:

Gennett 5345 *Shorty George Blues*. . . . . 20.00 - 30.00

5346 *Up The Country Blues*. . . . . 20.00 - 30.00

Silvertone 4049 *Houston Blues*. . . . . 20.00 - 30.00

4050 *Shorty George Blues*. . . . . 20.00 - 30.00

FREEZONE:

Paramount 12803 *Indian Squaw Blues*. . . . . . . 40.00 - 60.00

JOE (PAPOOSE) FRITZ:

Modern 750 *Wrong Doing Woman*. . . . . 7.00 - 10.00

Peacock 1606 *Real Fine Girl*. . . . . 7.00 - 10.00

Sittin' In With 559 *Please Get Off My Mind*. . . . 7.00 - 10.00

574 *I'm So Sorry*. 7.00 - 10.00

584 *Cool Cool Baby Blues*. . . . . 7.00 - 10.00

591 *Lady Bear Boogie*. . . . . 7.00 - 10.00

602 *Please, My Darling*. . . . . 7.00 - 10.00

BLIND BOY FULLER:

Titles, issued contemporaneously on Banner, Conqueror, Melotone, Oriole, Perfect, Romeo, Vocalion: *Ain't It A Crying Shame?; Babe, You Got To Do Better; Baby, I Don't Have To Worry; Baby You Gotta Change Your Mind; Big Red Blues; Black And Tan; Boots And Shoes; Careless Love; Cat Man Blues; Death Valley; Evil Hearted Woman; Homesick And Lonesome Blues; Hungry Calf Blues; If You Don't Give Me What I Want; I'm A Rattlesnakin' Daddy; I'm Climbin' On Top Of The Hill; I'm Going To Move; Let Me Squeeze Your Lemon; Log Cabin Blues; Looking For My Woman; Mama Let Me Lay It On You; Mamie; Mistreater, You're Going To Be Sorry; Mojo Hidin' Woman; My Baby Don't Mean Me No Good; My Best Gal Gonna Leave Me; My Brownskin Sugar Plum; New Louise, Louise Blues; New Oh Red; Rag, Mama Rag; Shaggy Like A Bear; She's Funny That Way; Somebody's Been Playing With That Thing; Snake Woman Blues; Stealing Bo-Hog; Sweet Honey Hole; Throw You Yas Yas Back In Jail; Tom Cat Blues; Truckin' My Blues Away; Trucklin' My Blues Away-No. 2; Untrue Blues; Walking My Troubles Away; When You Gal Picks Up And Leaves; Wires All Down; Worried And Evil Man Blues* .... 8.00 - 12.00

Conqueror 9038, 9075, 9076, 9157, 9158, 9171, 9202, 9280, 9281, 9310, 9311, 9344, 9373, 9374, 9376, 9377, 9580, 9757, 9758 .... 5.00 - 8.00

Decca 7330, 7878, 7892, 7899, 7903 .... 5.00 - 8.00

Okeh 05657, 05712, 05756, 05685, 05933, 06231 4.00 - 7.00

Vocalion 04054, 04106, 04137, 04175, 04237, 04343, 04391, 04456, 04519, 04557, 04603, 04675 .. 7.00 - 10.00

04732, 04782, 04843, 04897, 05030, 05083, 05150, 05218, 05273, 05324, 05476, 05527, 05540 .. 5.00 - 8.00

ROCKY FULLER:

Checker 753 *Soon One Morning* .... 10.00 - 15.00*

LOWELL FULSON/FULSOM (WITH GUITAR/ORCHESTRA):

Aladdin 3088, 3104 .... 4.00 - 8.00

Big Town 1068, 1070, 1071, 1072, 1074, 1077 .. 4.00 - 7.00

Down Beat 116, 119, 120, 121 .... 4.00 - 7.00

Down Town 2002, 2021 .... 7.00 - 10.00

Gilt Edge 5041, 5043 .... 5.00 - 10.00

RPM 305 .... 5.00 - 10.00

Scotty's 101 *Scotty's Blues* .... 6.00 - 10.00

Swing Time 110, 111, 112, 113, 114, 115, 116, 117, 119, 120, 121, 122, 123, 133, 134, 167, 196, 197, 201, 202, 203, 219, 220, 226, 227, 230, 231, 237, 243, 272, 295, 301, 308, 315, 320, 325, 330, 335, 338 .... 4.00 - 8.00*

Trilon 185, 186, 192, 193 .... 5.00 - 10.00

BOB GADDY & HIS ALLEY CATS:

Jackson 2303 *Bicycle Boogie* .... 5.00 - 8.00*

Jax 308 *Little Girl's Boogie* .... 5.00 - 8.00*

(LITTLE) BILL GAITHER (LEROY'S BUDDY):

Decca 7141 *Georgia Woman Stomp* .... 8.00 - 12.00

7625 *I Got Your Water On* .... 5.00 - 8.00

Okeh 05655, 05714, 05770, 05824, 06044, 06092, 06128, 06164, 06208, 06561, 06659 .... 5.00 - 8.00

(PVT.) CECIL GANT (& HIS TRIO):

Bullet 250, 255, 256, 257, 264, 265, 272, 280, 289, 299, 300, 313, 320 .... 3.00 - 6.00

Decca 48171, 48185, 48190, 48200, 48212, 48231, 48249 .... 3.00 - 6.00

4-Star 1176, 1284, 1339, 1377, 1452, 1526, 1561, 1584, 1606 .... 3.00 - 6.00

Gilt-Edge 501, 502, 503, 504, 505, 506, 508, 509, 510, 511, 512, 513, 514, 515, 516, 517, 518, 519, 525, 534 .... 4.00 - 8.00

HATTIE GARLAND:

Black Patti 8005 *Strange Woman's Dream* ..... 40.00 - 60.00

CLARENCE ("BON TON") GARLOW (& HIS GUITAR/ORCHESTRA):

Aladdin 3179 *New Bon Ton Roula* .... 4.00 - 8.00*

3225 *I'm Hurt* .... 4.00 - 8.00*

Feature 1000 *New Bon Ton Roula* .... 10.00 - 15.00

Lyric 100 *Louisiana Blues* .... 10.00 - 15.00

101 *Wrong Doing Woman* .... 10.00 - 15.00

Marcy's 5001 *She's So Fine* .... 10.00 - 15.00

5002 *Bon Ton Roula* .... 10.00 - 15.00

CORA GARNER:

Columbia 14659-D *Wouldn't Stop Doing It* ..... 10.00 - 20.00

BOB GEDDINS (& HIS CAVALIERS):

Cavatone 5, 103 .... 6.00 - 12.00

Trilon 1058 *Irma Jean* .... 6.00 - 12.00

GEORGIA BILL:

Okeh 8924 *Georgia Rag* .... 100.00 - 150.00

8936 *Stomp Down Rider* .... 100.00 - 150.00

THE GEORGIA BROWNS:

Titles, issued contemporaneously on Banner, Melotone, Oriole, Perfect, Romeo: *Decatur Street 81; It Must Have Been Her; Tampa Strut; Who Stole De Lock?* .... 30.00 - 50.00

GEORGIA COTTON PICKERS:

Columbia 14577-D *Diddle-Da-Diddle* .... 50.00 - 75.00

14594-D *She Looks So Good* .... 50.00 - 75.00

GEORGIA PINE BOY:

Champion 50009 *One In A Hundred* .... 15.00 - 25.00

50041 *Look Who's Coming Down The Road* .. 15.00 - 25.00

50057 *What's The Matter With You* .... 15.00 - 20.00

Decca 7822 *Please Baby* .... 15.00 - 20.00

GEORGIA SLIM:

Titles, issued contemporaneously on Banner, Melotone, Oriole, Perfect, Romeo: *Evil Hearted Woman; I've Been Mistreated; New Root Man Blues; Ocean Wide Blues; Separatin' Blues; Sweet Woman Blues* .... 25.00 - 35.00

GEORGIA TOM:

Titles, issued contemporaneously on Banner, Jewel, Melotone, Oriole, Perfect, Romeo: *Don't Leave Me Here; Don't Mean To Mistreat You; The Duck's Yas Yas Yas; Mama's Leaving Town; My Texas Blues; Pig Meat Strut; Six Shooter Blues; You Got Me In This Mess* .... 10.00 - 15.00

Champion 16237 *Been Mistreated Blues* .... 35.00 - 50.00

16360 *Don't Leave Me Blues* .... 35.00 - 50.00

Decca 7362 *Levee Bound Blues* .... 5.00 - 8.00

Gennett 6919 *My Texas Blues* .... 35.00 - 50.00

6933 *Suicide Blues* .... 35.00 - 50.00

7008 *Pig Meat Blues* .... 35.00 - 50.00

7041 *Rollin' Mill Stomp* .... 35.00 - 50.00

7130 *Six Shooter Blues* .... 35.00 - 50.00

7190 *Dark Hour Blues* .... 35.00 - 50.00

Supertone 9506 *My Texas Blues* .... 35.00 - 50.00

9507 *Pig Meat Blues* .... 35.00 - 50.00

9508 *Eagle Ridin' Papa* .... 35.00 - 50.00

9512 *Rollin' Mill Stomp* .... 35.00 - 50.00

9647 *Second-Hand Woman Blues* .... 35.00 - 50.00

Vocalion 1216 *Grievin' Me Blues* .... 12.00 - 20.00

1246 *Lonesome Man Blues* .... 12.00 - 20.00

1282 *If You Want Me To Love You* .... 12.00 - 20.00

1685 *Don't Leave Me Here* .... 10.00 - 15.00

GEORGIA TOM & JANE LUCAS:

Champion 16171 *Terrible Operation Blues* ...... 35.00 - 50.00

16215 *What's That I Smell* .... 35.00 - 50.00

16289 *Double Trouble Blues* .... 35.00 - 50.00

50015 *Terrible Operation Blues* .... 10.00 - 15.00

Decca 7259 *Terrible Operation Blues* .... 7.00 - 10.00

GEORGIA TOM & HANNAH MAY:

Titles, issued contemporaneously on Oriole (8033,

8034, 8041), Perfect (169, 170, 171), Romeo
(5033, 5034, 5041): *Come On Mama; It's Been
So Long; Rent Man Blues; Terrible Operation
Blues; What's That I Smell* .... 15.00 - 20.00
Same Titles on Banner, Melotone; and on Oriole,
Perfect, Romeo (different numbers than above): 15.00 - 20.00

**GEORGIA TOM & TAMPA RED (AND
FRANKIE JAXON) (THE BLACK HILL
BILLIES):**
Vocalion 1246 *Long Ago Blues* .... 15.00 - 20.00
1286 *Pat That Bread* .... 75.00 - 100.00
1450 *Kunjine Baby* .... 25.00 - 40.00

CLIFFORD GIBSON:
Bluebird 5110 *Jive Me Blues* .... 20.00 - 30.00
Paramount 12866 *Tired Of Being Mistreated* .... 80.00 - 120.00
12923 *Stop Your Rambling* .... 80.00 - 120.00
QRS 7079 *Tired Of Being Mistreated* .... 80.00 - 120.00
7082 *No No Blues* .... 80.00 - 120.00
7083 *Stop Your Rambling* .... 80.00 - 120.00
7087 *Whiskey Moan Blues* .... 80.00 - 120.00
7090 *Morgan Street Blues* .... 80.00 - 120.00
Victor 23255 *Old Timer Rider* .... 90.00 - 120.00
23290 *Railroad Man Blues* .... 90.00 - 120.00
38562 *Ice And Snow Blues* .... 75.00 - 100.00
38572 *Don't Put That Thing On Me* .... 75.00 - 100.00
38577 *Levee Camp Moan* .... 75.00 - 100.00
38590 *Bad Luck Dice* .... 75.00 - 100.00
38612 *Society Blues* .... 75.00 - 100.00

BILL/JAZZ GILLUM (& HIS JAZZ BOYS):
Bluebird 5565 *Early In The Morning* .... 10.00 - 15.00
6409 *Jockey Blues* .... 8.00 - 12.00
6445 *Sarah Jane* .... 8.00 - 12.00
7253, 7341, 7524, 7563, 7615, 7718, 7769, 7821
7986, 8027, 8106, 8189, 8221, 8257, 8287, 8505,
8529, 8739, 8778, 8816, 8846, 8872, ... 6.00 - 10.00
8943, 8975, 9004, 9034, 9042, 34-0707, 34-0709,
34-0730, 34-0741, 34-0747. .... 5.00 - 8.00
RCA Victor .... 4.00 - 6.00
                                          3.00 - 5.00

BOYD GILMORE:
Modern 860 *Ramblin' On My Mind* .... 7.00 - 12.00
872 *Take A Little Walk With Me* .... 7.00 - 12.00

GENE GILMORE:
Decca 7661 *Brown Skin Woman* .... 5.00 - 8.00
7763 *The Natchez Fire* .... 10.00 - 15.00
7773 *She Got Something There* .... 10.00 - 15.00

THE GIRL FRIEND:
Varsity 6045 *Good And Hot* .... 10.00 - 15.00

GITFIDDLE JIM:
Victor 23268 *Paddlin' Blues* .... 100.00 - 150.00

RUBY GLAZE & HOT SHOT WILLIE:
Bluebird 5362 *Rollin' Mama Blues* .... 50.00 - 75.00
5391 *Lonesome Day Blues* .... 50.00 - 75.00
6007 *Rollin' Mama Blues* .... 10.00 - 15.00
Victor 23328 *Rollin' Mama Blues* .... 75.00 - 100.00
23353 *Lonesome Day Blues* .... 75.00 - 100.00

EMERY GLEN:
Columbia 14283-D *Two Ways To Texas* ...... 30.00 - 40.00
14472-D *Back Door Blues* .... 30.00 - 40.00

LILLIAN GLINN:
Columbia 14275-D *Doggin' Me Blues* .... 15.00 - 25.00
14300-D *Come Home Daddy* .... 15.00 - 25.00
14315-D *Shake It Down* .... 15.00 - 25.00
14330-D *Best Friend Blues* .... 15.00 - 25.00
14360-D *Lost Letter Blues* .... 15.00 - 25.00
14421-D *Atlanta Blues* .... 20.00 - 30.00
14433-D *Black Man Blues* .... 20.00 - 30.00
14493-D *Don't Leave Me Daddy* .... 20.00 - 30.00
14519-D *Shreveport Blues* .... 20.00 - 30.00
14559-D *I Love That Thing* .... 20.00 - 30.00
14617-D *Cannon Ball Blues* .... 20.00 - 30.00

MAE GLOVER (AND JAMES PARKER):

Champion 15814 *Shake It Daddy* .... 40.00 - 60.00
15858 *Gas Man Blues* .... 40.00 - 60.00
16238 *My Man Blues* .... 40.00 - 60.00
16244 *Two Timin' Mama* .... 40.00 - 60.00
16268 *Hoboken Prison Blues* .... 40.00 - 60.00
16351 *Grasshopper Papa* .... 40.00 - 60.00
16408 *North Wind Blues* .... 50.00 - 75.00
Gennett 6948 *Pig Meat Mama* .... 50.00 - 75.00
6964 *Shake It Daddy* .... 50.00 - 75.00
7040 *Gas Man Blues* .... 50.00 - 75.00

GOLDEN LEAF QUARTET/QUARTETTE:
Brunswick 7032 *Alabama Camp Meetin'* ...... 8.00 - 15.00
7050 *I Wouldn't Mind Dying* .... 8.00 - 15.00
7150 *Central Georgia Blues* .... 8.00 - 15.00
7169 *Let Me Ride* .... 8.00 - 15.00
7176 *Shake My Righteous Hand* .... 8.00 - 15.00
7221 *I Sing Because I'm Happy* .... 8.00 - 15.00
7228 *Let God Use You* .... 8.00 - 15.00

GOLDRUSH:
Jaxyson 6 *All My Money Is Gone* .... 10.00 - 15.00

FANNIE MAE GOOSBY:
Brunswick 7029 *Dirty Moaner Blues* .... 15.00 - 20.00
7030 *Fortune Teller Blues* .... 15.00 - 20.00
Okeh 8079 *Grievous Blues* .... 10.00 - 15.00
8095, 8121, 8128 .... 6.00 - 10.00

JAMES/JIMMIE GORDON:
Bluebird 5661 *Neck Bone Blues* .... 20.00 - 30.00
Champion 50075 *Graveyard Blues* .... 10.00 - 15.00
Decca 7007 *Bed Springs Blues* .... 10.00 - 15.00
7020 *Yo Yo Mama Blues* .... 8.00 - 12.00
7099 *Bed Springs Blues-No. 2* .... 8.00 - 12.00
Decca 7230, 7250, 7264, 7268, 7282. ...... 5.00 - 8.00
Decca (higher numbers). .... 3.00 - 6.00

ROSCOE GORDON:
Chess 1487 *Booted* .... 5.00 - 8.00*
Duke 109 *Too Many Women* .... 5.00 - 8.00*
Flip 227 *Weeping Blues* .... 10.00 - 15.00*
RPM 322 *Roscoe's Boogie* .... 5.00 - 10.00*
324 *Ouch, Pretty Baby* .... 5.00 - 10.00*
336 *Dime A Dozen* .... 5.00 - 10.00*
350 *No More Doggin'* .... 5.00 - 10.00*
365 *Two Kinds Of Women* .... 5.00 - 10.00*
Sun 227 *Weeping Blues* .... 15.00 - 20.00*

SLIM GORDON:
Vocalion 1743 *Leg Iron Blues* .... 20.00 - 30.00

GEORGIA GORHAM:
Black Swan 2017 *Broadway Blues* .... 8.00 - 12.00

GOSPEL CAMP MEETING SINGERS:
Vocalion 1283 *Come And Go To That Land* ... 10.00 - 15.00

GOSPEL MINNIE:
Decca 7063 *Let Me Ride* .... 10.00 - 15.00

EMMA GOVER:
Pathe-Actuelle 021006, 021060, 021061 .... 7.00 - 10.00
Perfect 12065, 12073, 12074 .... 7.00 - 10.00

JACK GOWDLOCK:
Victor 23419 *Rollin' Dough Blues* .... 75.00 - 100.00

RUBY GOWDY:
Champion 15635 *Breath And Britches Blues* .... 35.00 - 50.00
Gennett 6570 *Moanful Wailin' Blues* .... 40.00 - 60.00
6708 *Florida Flood Blues* .... 40.00 - 60.00

GRAND CENTRAL RED CAP QUARTET:
Columbia 14621-D *My Little Dixie Home* ...... 8.00 - 12.00

**(COOT) GRANT AND (KID
WESLEY)/(SOCKS/SOX) WILSON:**
Titles, issued contemporaneously on Banner,
Melotone, Oriole, Perfect, Romeo: *Do It Again;
Water Trough Blues* .... 8.00 - 15.00
Cameo 9015 *Ducks* .... 20.00 - 30.00
Columbia 14637-D *You Can't Do That To Me* .. 15.00 - 20.00
14649-D *Deceiving Man Blues* .... 15.00 - 20.00
Decca 7500 *Uncle Joe* .... 5.00 - 8.00

Okeh 8944 *Do Your Duty*.................. 15.00 - 20.00
Paramount 12272 *Rock, Aunt Dinah, Rock*..... 15.00 - 20.00
  12317 *Come On Coot Do That Thing*....... 35.00 - 50.00
  12324 *You Dirty Mistreater*............. 35.00 - 50.00
  12337 *Find Me At The Greasy Spoon*....... 35.00 - 50.00
  12379 *Scoop It*...................... 20.00 - 30.00
  12831 *Big Trunk Blues*................. 20.00 - 30.00
  12833 *Uncle Joe*..................... 20.00 - 30.00
Pathe-Actuelle 7540 *Mama Didn't Do It*..... 15.00 - 20.00
Perfect 140 *Mama Didn't Do It*............. 15.00 - 20.00
QRS 7065 *Uncle Joe*........................ 25.00 - 35.00
  7085 *Big Trunk Blues*................. 25.00 - 35.00
  7092 *Take It Right Back*.............. 25.00 - 35.00
Romeo 819 *Ducks*........................... 20.00 - 30.00
Vocalion 02613, 02799, 03121.............. 8.00 - 12.00

LEE GRAVES:
Mercury 8214, 8222........................ 5.00 - 8.00

(BLIND) ROOSEVELT GRAVES AND (HIS)
  BROTHER:
Paramount 12820 *Guitar Boogie*............. 75.00 - 100.00
  12859 *Bustin' The Jug*................. 75.00 - 100.00
  12891 *Staggerin' Blues*................ 75.00 - 100.00
  12913 *Happy Sunshine*................. 75.00 - 100.00
  12961 *St. Louis Rambler Blues*......... 75.00 - 100.00
  12974 *When I Lay My Burdens Down*....... 75.00 - 100.00

BETTY GRAY:
Titles, issued contemporaneously on Cameo, Lincoln,
  Romeo: *Loud And Wrong; Mean Old Bed Bug
  Blues*.................................. 10.00 - 15.00

GENEVA GRAY:
Okeh 8449 *Fortune Teller Blues*............ 20.00 - 30.00

CHRISTINA GRAY:
Okeh 8757 *The Reverend Is My Man*........ 15.00 - 25.00

BOY GREEN:
Regis 120 *A and B Blues*................... 10.00 - 15.00

L.M./LEE/LEOTHUS GREEN:
Bluebird 7353 *My Best Friend*.............. 15.00 - 25.00
Decca 7016 *Memphis Fives*.................. 20.00 - 30.00
  7032 *Doctorin' Fool Blues*............ 20.00 - 30.00
  7062 *Round The World Blues*........... 20.00 - 30.00
  7346 *The Way I Feel*................. 15.00 - 25.00
  7368 *Sealskin Black Woman*............ 15.00 - 20.00
  7437 *Country Gal Blues*.............. 15.00 - 20.00
Gennett 6934 *Pork Chop Stomp*.............. 60.00 - 80.00
Paramount 12865 *Five Minute Blues*......... 60.00 - 80.00
Vocalion 1401 *Railroad Blues*.............. 50.00 - 75.00
  1422 *The Way I Feel Blues*........... 50.00 - 75.00
  1441 *Little Eddie Jones*............. 50.00 - 75.00
  1467 *Dud-Low Joe*................... 50.00 - 75.00
  1485 *Death Bell Blues*.............. 50.00 - 75.00
  1501 *Bootleggin' My Jelly*........... 50.00 - 75.00
  1510 *Wash Day And No Soap*.......... 50.00 - 75.00
  1533 *Gambling Man Blues*............ 50.00 - 75.00
  1562 *Pork Chop Blues*............... 50.00 - 75.00
  1566 *Train Number 14*............... 50.00 - 75.00
  1648 *Five Minute Blues*............. 50.00 - 75.00

L.C. GREEN:
Dot 1103 *When The Sun Is Shining*.......... 7.00 - 10.00*
  1128 *Little School Girl*............. 7.00 - 10.00*
  1147 *Little Machine*................. 7.00 - 10.00*
Von 42 *Going Down To The River Blues*...... 20.00 - 30.00

LIL GREEN:
Bluebird.................................. 3.00 - 6.00

PORK CHOP GREEN:
Gennett 7116 *She Walks Like A Maltee Cat*.... 60.00 - 80.00

R. GREEN & TURNER:
J & M Fullbright 123 *Central Avenue Blues*.... 10.00 - 15.00

RUTH GREEN:
Okeh 8140 *Sad And Lonely Blues*............ 15.00 - 25.00

SLIM GREEN:
Murray 501 *Tricky Woman Blues*............. 15.00 - 20.00

FLOYD GRIFFIN:
Supertone 9521 *Ocean Wave Blues*........... 50.00 - 70.00
  9522 *You Broke My Heart Baby*......... 50.00 - 70.00
  9523 *Back-Biter Blues*............... 50.00 - 70.00
  9525 *Easy Papa*..................... 50.00 - 70.00

MARIE GRIFFIN:
Paramount 13015 *Blue And Disgusted*........ 30.00 - 40.00

TOMMY GRIFFIN:
Bluebird 6696 *I'm Gonna Try That Meat*...... 25.00 - 35.00
  6734 *Young Heifer Blues*.............. 25.00 - 35.00
  6756 *Dream Book Blues*............... 25.00 - 35.00
  6793 *On My Way Blues*................ 25.00 - 35.00
  6834 *Dying Sinner Blues—Part 2*....... 25.00 - 35.00
  6872 *Mistreatin' Papa*............... 25.00 - 35.00
Bluebird 7179 *Hey Hey Blues*............... 10.00 - 15.00
  7194 *Young Heifer Blues*............. 10.00 - 15.00
Vocalion 1479 *Bell Tolling Blues*.......... 40.00 - 60.00
  1507 *Mistreatment Blues*............. 40.00 - 60.00

MARIE GRINTER:
Buddy 8023 *Morning Dove Blues*............. 25.00 - 35.00
Gennett 3004 *Morning Dove Blues*........... 25.00 - 35.00
Gennett 6551 *Road House Blues*............. 35.00 - 50.00
  6738 *St. Louis Man*................. 35.00 - 50.00
Okeh 8384 *East And West Blues*............. 15.00 - 20.00
Supertone 9304 *Road House Blues*........... 35.00 - 50.00
  9530 *Charleston Blues*............... 30.00 - 40.00

BLIND ARTHUR GROOM & BRO.:
Paramount 12874 *Telephone To Glory*........ 25.00 - 40.00

THE GROOVY FIVE:
Groovy 103 *Wrong Love Blues*............... 7.00 - 10.00

THE GROOVY TRIO:
Groovy 101 *Too Late Baby*.................. 7.00 - 10.00

HELEN GROSS:
Ajax 17036 *Haunted House Blues*............ 25.00 - 40.00
  17037 *Hard Luck Blues*................ 25.00 - 40.00
  17042 *I Wanna Jazz Some More*.......... 25.00 - 40.00
  17046 *Rockin' Chair Blues*............ 25.00 - 40.00
  17049 *What'll I Do?*.................. 25.00 - 40.00
  17050 *Strange Man*................... 25.00 - 40.00
  17051 *My Man Ain't Yo' Man*........... 25.00 - 40.00
  17060 *Ticket Agent, Ease Your Window Down* 25.00 - 40.00
  17062 *Chicago Monkey Man Blues*........ 25.00 - 40.00
  17071 *Neglected Blues*................ 25.00 - 40.00
  17077 *If You Can't Ride Slow And Easy*.... 25.00 - 40.00
  17082 *Conjure Man Blues*.............. 25.00 - 40.00
  17086 *Bitter Feelin' Blues*........... 25.00 - 40.00
  17090 *Last Journey Blues*............. 25.00 - 40.00
  17133 *Workin' Woman's Blues*.......... 25.00 - 40.00

CREOLE GEORGE GUESNON:
Bluebird 6706 *Goodbye Good Luck To You*.... 15.00 - 20.00
Decca 7740, 7792......................... 5.00 - 8.00

GUITAR SLIM:
Titles, issued contemporaneously on Banner,
  Melotone, Oriole, Perfect, Romeo: *Ain't It A
  Shame?, Katie May-Katie May*............. 30.00 - 50.00
Imperial 5278, 5310....................... 3.00 - 6.00*
Specialty 482, 490, 527, 536, 542, 551, 557, 569. 3.00 - 5.00*

GULF COAST QUARTET:
Columbia 14012-D *Alabama Blues*.......... 8.00 - 12.00

ELDER J.J. HADLEY:
Paramount 12799 *Prayer Of Death*........... 80.00 - 110.00

JAMES HALL:
Vocalion 04231 *My Jivin' Woman*............ 7.00 - 10.00
  04316 *Street Walkin' Woman*........... 7.00 - 10.00

HALLELUJAH JOE (& CONGREGATION):
Decca 7047 *If I Be Lifted Up*.............. 8.00 - 12.00
  7118 *The Great Love*................ 7.00 - 10.00
  7302 *Twenty Minutes In Hell*.......... 7.00 - 10.00
  7802 *Highway 61*................... 7.00 - 10.00

HAM GRAVY:
Vocalion 03275 *Mama Don't Allow—No. 1*.... 8.00 - 12.00
  03375 *Mama Don't Allow—No. 2*......... 8.00 - 12.00

"BEANS" HAMBONE & EL MORROW:
Victor 23280 *Beans*.......................... 50.00 - 75.00
GEORGE HAMILTON:
Champion 15726 *Atlanta Rag*.............. 40.00 - 60.00
  15756 *Givin' It Away*................... 40.00 - 60.00
HAMMIE AND SON:
Decca 7040 *Tennessee Worried Blues*......... 15.00 - 25.00
STICK HORSE HAMMOND:
Gotham 504 *Truck'em On Down*............ 20.00 - 30.00
J.O.B. 100 *Gambling Man*................... 75.00 - 100.00
  105 *Highway 51*...................... 50.00 - 75.00
Royalty 906 *Too Late Baby*............... 50.00 - 75.00
R.T. HANEN:
Victor 23288 *Happy Days Blues*........... 90.00 - 130.00
GEORGE HANNAH:
Paramount 12786 *The Snitches Blues*.......... 40.00 - 60.00
  12788 *Gutter Man Blues*................ 40.00 - 60.00
  13024 *Freakish Man Blues*............. 75.00 - 100.00
  13048 *Alley Rat Blues*................. 75.00 - 100.00
Vocalion 1047 *Hurry Home Blues*........ 15.00 - 25.00
LANE HARDIN:
Bluebird 6242 *Hard Time Blues*........... 50.00 - 75.00
LUCIUS HARDY:
Paramount 12598 *Jelly Bean Man*............. 25.00 - 35.00
MATTIE HARDY:
Conqueror 9203 *Striped Ape Bleus*........... 10.00 - 15.00
Vocalion 04660 *Striped Ape Blues*......... 10.00 - 15.00
TRILBY HARGENS:
Herwin 92012 *Goofer Dust Blues*........ 75.00 - 100.00
HARLEM STARS:
E & W 100 *All Right Baby*............. 10.00 - 15.00
HARMONICA FRANK:
Chess 1475 *Swamp Root*................ 10.00 - 15.00*
  1494 *Howlin' Tomcat*............. 10.00 - 15.00*
Sun 205 *The Great Medical Menagerist*....... 30.00 - 40.00*
HARMONY HOUNDS:
Columbia 14119-D *Done Got De Blues*.... 6.00 - 10.00
JOSIE HARLEY:
Paramount 12025 *2 A.M. Blues*............. 10.00 - 15.00
HARRIS & HARRIS:
Victor 21285 *That Same Cat*............ 20.00 - 30.00
  3859 *Teasing Brown*............... 50.00 - 80.00
ALFONCY HARRIS:
Vocalion 02902 *All Alone Blues*.......... 20.00 - 30.00
  02971 *No Good Guy*................ 20.00 - 30.00
  02996 *Absent Freight Train Blues*..... 20.00 - 30.00
BOB HARRIS; LITTLE BOBBY HARRIS:
Derby 770, 773.................... 5.00 - 8.00
Jackson 2301 *Friendly Advice*........... 5.00 - 8.00
Par 1304 *Heavyweight Mama*............... 7.00 - 10.00
CLARENCE HARRIS:
Bluebird 8138 *Try My Whiskey Blues*....... 10.00 - 15.00
JAMES HARRIS:
Broadway 5061 *Forty-Four Blues*............ 75.00 - 100.00
JOHN HARRIS:
Victor 23284 *Prowling Wolf Blues*........ 80.00 - 120.00
LILLINA HARRIS:
Banner 1173, 1212, 1224.............. 7.00 - 10.00
Regal 9445, 9497, 9510............... 7.00 - 10.00
MAGNOLIA HARRIS AND HOWLING SMITH:
Melotone 12077 *Mama's Quittin' and Leavin'*... 35.00 - 50.00
Vocalion 1602 *Mama's Quittin' and Leavin'*..... 35.00 - 50.00
MARY HARRIS:
Champion 50045 *Happy New Year Blues*...... 10.00 - 15.00
MAXINE HARRIS:
Champion 15490 *Satisfied Blues*.......... 20.00 - 30.00
OTIS HARRIS:
Columbia 14428-D *Waking Blues*.......... 25.00 - 35.00
PEPPERMINT HARRIS:
Modern 936 *Black Cat Bone*............ 5.00 - 8.00

Sittin' In With 543, 554, 568, 576, 578, 587, 597, 612,
  623, 638, 650.......................... 4.00 - 7.00
WILLIAM HARRIS:
Gennett 6306 *I'm Leavin' Town*............ 150.00 - 250.00
  6661 *Bull Frog Blues*............... 150.00 - 250.00
  6677 *Kitchen Range Blues*............ 150.00 - 250.00
  6693 *Leavin' Here Blues*............. 150.00 - 250.00
  6707 *Kansas City Blues*.............. 150.00 - 250.00
  6737 *I'm A Roamin' Gambler*........... 150.00 - 250.00
  6752 *Electric Chair Blues*........... 150.00 - 250.00
  6904 *Nothin' Right Blues*............ 150.00 - 250.00
WILLIE HARRIS:
Brunswick 7092 *West Side Blues*.......... 90.00 - 120.00
  7149 *Lonesome Midnight Dream*........... 90.00 - 120.00
SMOKEY/SMOKY HARRISON:
Paramount 12920 *Hop Head Blues*......... 80.00 - 100.00
  12936 *St. Peter's Blues*............. 80.00 - 100.00
  12984 *Mail Coach Blues*............. 80.00 - 100.00
HATTIE HART:
Victor 23273 *You Wouldn't, Would You, Papa?*. 50.00 - 75.00
Vocalion 02821 *Coldest Stuff In Town*........ 50.00 - 75.00
  02855 *I'm Missing That Thing*............ 50.00 - 75.00
HARUM SCARUMS:
Broadway 5097 *I'm The Lonesome One*........ 20.00 - 35.00
Crown 3324 *I'm The Lonesome One*.......... 20.00 - 35.00
  3358 *Where Did You Stay Last Night?*..... 20.00 - 35.00
Paramount 13054 *Alabama Scratch*........ 30.00 - 50.00
  13104 *Come On In*.................. 30.00 - 50.00
CLEO HARVES WITH LIGHTNING GUITAR:
Okla Tornado 105 *Skinny Woman Boogie*..... 8.00 - 12.00
WILLIE HATCHER:
Bluebird 8003 *They're Mean To Me*........ 8.00 - 12.00
BERT (SNAKE-ROOT) HATTON:
Vocalion 1101 *Down In Black Bottom*......... 35.00 - 50.00
BUDDY BOY HAWKINS:
Paramount 12475 *Number Three Blues*...... 50.00 - 75.00
  12489 *Jailhouse Fire Blues*.......... 50.00 - 75.00
  12539 *Awful Fix Blues*.............. 50.00 - 75.00
  12558 *Yellow Woman Blues*........... 50.00 - 75.00
ROY HAWKINS:
Down Town 2018, 2020, 2024, 2025, 2026..... 5.00 - 8.00
Modern........................... 3.00 - 5.00
WALTER HAWKINS:
Paramount 12802 *Voice Throwin' Blues*........ 50.00 - 75.00
  12814 *A Rag Blues*................. 50.00 - 75.00
BILL HAYES & HIS BAND/ORCHESTRA:
Jade 211 *I'm Just Another Fool*............. 4.00 - 7.00
Sittin' In With 551, 560................. 4.00 - 7.00
DADDY MOON HAYES & HIS BOYS:
Gennett 6122 *Gang Of Brown Skin Women*.... 150.00 - 200.00
Champion 15283 *Two Little Tommie Blues*..... 150.00 - 200.00
NAP HAYES AND MATHEW PRATER:
Okeh 45231 *Nothin' Doin*................... 15.00 - 20.00
BLIND ROGER HAYS:
Brunswick 7047 *On My Way To Heaven*....... 25.00 - 35.00
EDDIE HEAD:
Columbia 14548-D *Down On Me*............ 15.00 - 20.00
  14589-D *Within My Mind*.............. 15.00 - 20.00
JOHNNIE HEAD:
Paramount 12628 *Fare Thee Blues*............ 30.00 - 40.00
(BIG) BERTHA HENDERSON:
Chance 1143 *Rock, Daddy, Rock*............. 7.00 - 10.00*
Paramount 12645 *So Sorry Blues*........... 40.00 - 60.00
  12655 *Lead Hearted Blues*.............. 40.00 - 60.00
  12697 *Leavin' Gal Blues*.............. 40.00 - 60.00
KATHERINE HENDERSON:
Broadway 5034 *West End Blues*............ 40.00 - 60.00
Paramount 12840 *If You Like Me*.......... 75.00 - 100.00
QRS 7024 *West End Blues*............... 40.00 - 60.00
  7032 *Lonesome Lovesick Blues*.......... 75.00 - 100.00
  7041 *If You Like Me*................. 75.00 - 100.00
  7054 *What Can You Do Without Me?*....... 75.00 - 100.00

LEROY HENDERSON:

Vocalion 02979 *Good Scuffler Blues*	10.00 -	15.00
03020 *Deep Sea Diver*	10.00 -	15.00

ROSA HENDERSON:

Ajax 17021 *When You Walked Out*	15.00 -	25.00
17049 *I Can't Get The One I Want*	25.00 -	40.00
17055 *Strut Yo' Puddy*	20.00 -	30.00
17060 *Hard-Hearted Hannah*	25.00 -	40.00
17069 *Memphis Bound*	20.00 -	30.00
17081 *Twelfth Street Blues*	20.00 -	30.00
17116 *It Takes a Two-Time Papa*	25.00 -	40.00
Brunswick 2589 *I'm A Good Gal*	10.00 -	15.00
2612 *Clearing House Blues*	10.00 -	15.00
Columbia A-3958 *I Need You*	5.00 -	8.00
Columbia 14130-D *Let's Talk About My Sweetie*	10.00 -	15.00
14627-D *Doggone Blues*	20.00 -	30.00
Edison 51476 *Undertaker's Blues*	40.00 -	50.00
51478 *Don't Advertise Your Man*	40.00 -	50.00
Emerson 10747 *West Indies Blues*	8.00 -	12.00
10763 *Four-Flushin' Papa*	15.00 -	20.00
Pathe-Actuelle 7519 *Git Goin'*	8.00 -	12.00
7522 *Slow Up Papa*	8.00 -	12.00
7529 *Black Snake Moan*	15.00 -	20.00
7534 *I'm Saving It All For You*	15.00 -	20.00
7535 *Dyin' Crap Shooter's Blues*	10.00 -	15.00
7538 *Police Blues*	10.00 -	15.00
032021 *Every Day Blues*	10.00 -	15.00
Perfect 119 *Some Day You'll Come Back To Me*	8.00 -	12.00
122 *Hock Shop Blues*	8.00 -	12.00
129 *Fortune Teller Blues*	15.00 -	20.00
134 *Gay Catin' Daddy*	15.00 -	20.00
135 *Dyin' Crap Shooter's Blues*	10.00 -	15.00
138 *Police Blues*	10.00 -	15.00
Victor 19084, 19157	4.00 -	7.00
Victor 19124 *Midnight Blues*	7.00 -	10.00
Vocalion 1011 *Fulton Street Blues*	50.00 -	75.00
1021 *Chicago Policeman Blues*	20.00 -	30.00
1025 *Daddy, Come Back*	20.00 -	30.00
1038 *Rough House Blues*	20.00 -	30.00
1177 *Get It Fixed*	30.00 -	40.00
14635 *Down South Blues*	8.00 -	12.00
14652 *So Long To You And The Blues*	8.00 -	12.00
14682 *Every Woman's Blues*	8.00 -	12.00
14708 *I Want My Sweet Daddy Now*	8.00 -	12.00
14770 *Do Right Blues*	10.00 -	15.00
14795 *My Papa Doesn't Two-Time No Time*	8.00 -	12.00
14825 *Barbadoes Blues*	10.00 -	15.00
14831 *Barrel House Blues*	8.00 -	12.00
14832 *Chicago Monkey Man Blues*	8.00 -	12.00
14995 *Penitentiary Bound Blues*	10.00 -	15.00
15011 *Low Down Daddy*	15.00 -	20.00
15044 *Get It Fixed*	15.00 -	20.00
15215 *And I Don't Mean If*	15.00 -	20.00

CURTIS HENRY:

Bluebird 6845 *G-Man Blues*	15.00 -	20.00
6888 *The Worried Blues*	15.00 -	20.00

HOUND HEAD HENRY:

Vocalion 1208 *Freight Train Special*	40.00 -	60.00
1209 *Hound Head Blues*	40.00 -	60.00
1210 *Laughin' Blues*	40.00 -	60.00
1288 *My Silver Dollar Mama*	40.00 -	60.00

LENA HENRY:

Vocalion 14873, 14910	7.00 -	10.00
14902 *Sinful Blues*	15.00 -	20.00

ROBERT HENRY:

King 4624 *Miss Anna B.*	10.00 -	15.00
4646 *Old Battle Ax*	10.00 -	15.00

"SLOPPY" HENRY:

Okeh 8178 *Tom Cat Rag*	15.00 -	25.00
8305 *Traveling Blues*	15.00 -	25.00
8334 *Goose-Pecked Man*	15.00 -	25.00
8368 *Foggy Morning Blues*	15.00 -	25.00
8630 *Canned Heat Blues*	35.00 -	50.00
8683 *Hobo Blues*	35.00 -	50.00
8805 *Say I Do It*	35.00 -	50.00
8845 *Royal Palm Special Blues*	35.00 -	50.00

LAURA HENTON:

Brunswick 7129 *I Can Tell The World About This*	40.00 -	60.00
7144 *Plenty Good Room In My Father's Kingdom*	40.00 -	60.00
Columbia 14388-D *He's Coming Soon*	30.00 -	40.00

CLARA HERRING:

Gennett 6591 *Beating Blues*	30.00 -	40.00

EDNA HICKS:

Ajax 17006 *Just Thinkin'*	25.00 -	40.00
17008 *Mistreatin' Daddy*	15.00 -	20.00
17012 *Kind Lovin' Blues*	15.00 -	20.00
Brunswick 2463 *Gulf Coast Blues*	5.00 -	8.0
Columbia 14001-D *No Name Blues*	7.00 -	10.00
Gennett 5195 *Bleeding Hearted Blues*	7.00 -	10.00
5234 *Tin Roof Blues*	8.00 -	12.00
Paramount 12023 *Hard Luck Blues*	15.00 -	20.00
Paramount 12024 *Mistreatin' Daddy*	15.00 -	20.00
12069 *Uncle Sam Blues*	15.00 -	20.00
12089 *Cemetery Blues*	15.00 -	20.00
12090 *Where Can That Somebody Be?*	20.00 -	30.00
12204 *Down On The Levee Blues*	35.00 -	50.00
Vocalion 14650 *You've Got Everything*	15.00 -	20.00
14659 *Wicked Dirty Fives*	10.00 -	15.00

MINNIE HICKS:

Broadway 5099 *Sweet Rider*	50.00 -	75.00
Melotone 12549 *Jim Jam Blues*	50.00 -	75.00

ROBERT HICKS:

Columbia 14231-D *When The Saints Go Marching In*	20.00 -	30.00

ROBERT AND CHARLIE HICKS:

Columbia 14531-D *Darktown Gamblin'*	30.00 -	40.00

BILLY HIGGINS:

Ajax 17125 *Levee Blues*	15.00 -	25.00
17135 *Ain't Trustin' Nobody No More*	15.00 -	25.00

BERTHA "CHIPPIE" HILL:

Okeh 8273 *Low Land Blues*	25.00 -	35.00
8312 *Trouble In Mind*	25.00 -	35.00
8339 *Lonesome, All Alone And Blue*	25.00 -	35.00
8367 *Panama Limited Blues*	25.00 -	35.00
8420 *Pratt City Blues*	25.00 -	35.00
8437 *Mess, Katie, Mess*	25.00 -	35.00
8453 *Lovesick Blues*	25.00 -	35.00
8473 *Do Dirty Blues*	25.00 -	35.00
Vocalion 1224 *Weary Money Blues*	20.00 -	30.00
1248 *Hangman Blues*	25.00 -	35.00
1264 *Hard Time Blues*	20.00 -	30.00
1406 *Pratt City Blues*	25.00 -	35.00

CHARLIE HILL:

Gennett 6904 *Papa Charlie Hill Blues*	150.00 -	250.00

CHIPPIE HILL (See BERTHA "CHIPPIE" HILL):

HENRY HILL:

Federal 12030, 12037, 12044, 12083	4.00 -	7.00*

KING SOLOMON HILL:

Champion 50022 *Tell Me Baby*	50.00 -	75.00
Crown 3325 *Whoopee Blues*	50.00 -	75.00
Paramount 13116 *Whoopee Blues*	200.00 -	250.00
13125 *My Buddy Blind Papa Lemon*	200.00 -	250.00
13129 *The Gone Dead Train*	200.00 -	250.00

ROBERT HILL:

Bluebird 6680 *It Is So Good*	15.00 -	25.00
6706 *Pal, How I Miss You Tonight*	15.00 -	25.00
6716 *Just Smilin'*	15.00 -	25.00
6741 *Tell Me What's Wrong With You*	15.00 -	25.00
6776 *Lumber-Yard Blues*	15.00 -	25.00
6795 *G Blues*	15.00 -	25.00
6963 *You Gonna Look Like A Monkey*	15.00 -	25.00

RAYMOND HILL:

Sun 204 *Bourbon Street Jump*	20.00 -	30.00*

SAM HILL FROM LOUISVILLE:

Brunswick 7195 *Near The End*..............	40.00 -	60.00
7216 *Things 'Bout Coming My Way*........	40.00 -	60.00

SAMMY HILL:

Victor 38588 *Needin' My Woman Blues*......	75.00 -	100.00

OTIS HINTON:

Timely 1003 *Walkin' Down Hill*............	7.00 -	12.00*

MATTIE HITE:

Columbia 14503-D *Texas Twist*..............	20.00 -	30.00

CHA CHA HOGAN:

Talent 810 *My Walking Baby*................	10.00 -	15.00

WALTER HOGAN:

Herwin 93011 *The Duck's Yas Yas*..........	50.00 -	75.00

ANDREW HOGG:

Crown 122 *Dark Clouds*....................	7.00 -	10.00*
Decca 7303 *Family Trouble Blues*............	15.00 -	20.00
Exclusive 89 *He Knows How Much We Can Bear*	5.00 -	8.00

JOHN HOGG:

Mercury 8230 *Got A Mean Woman*........	7.00 -	10.00
Octive 705, 706..........................	10.00 -	15.00

SMOKEY/SMOKY HOGG:

Bullett 285 *Hard Times*................	7.00 -	10.00
Colony 103 *In This World Alone*..........	7.00 -	10.00
Fidelity 3007 *Crawdad*...................	4.00 -	7.00
Imperial 5106, 5111......................	4.00 -	7.00
Independent 300 *Misery Blues*...........	7.00 -	10.00
Jade 210, 212...........................	5.00 -	8.00
Macy's 5003 *You Gotta Go*...............	7.00 -	12.00
5008 *Change Your Ways*...............	7.00 -	12.00
Mercury 8228, 8235.....................	4.00 -	6.00
Ray's 33 *Penitentiary Blues*..............	7.00 -	10.00
35 *I Used To Be Rich*................	7.00 -	10.00
Sittin' In With...........................	4.00 -	7.00
Specialty................................	4.00 -	7.00
Top Hat 1023 *Baby Shake Your Leg*........	7.00 -	10.00

THE HOKUM BOYS (WITH PIANO & GUITAR); THE HOKUM BOYS AND JANE LUCAS:

Broadway 5060 *It's All Worn Out*............	25.00 -	35.00
5078 *Cut That Out*...................	25.00 -	35.00
Brunswick 7070 *You Ain't Livin' Right*........	15.00 -	20.00
Champion 16081 *Pig Meat Strut*.........	40.00 -	60.00
16237 *Hip Shakin' Strut*.............	40.00 -	60.00
16360 *Hokum Stomp*................	40.00 -	60.00
Okeh 8747 *Gin Mill Blues*.............	20.00 -	30.00
8788 *That's My Business*...............	20.00 -	30.00
Paramount 12714 *Selling That Stuff*..........	20.00 -	30.00
12746 *Pat-A-Foot Blues*..............	25.00 -	40.00
12777 *Better Cut That Out*...........	25.00 -	40.00
12778 *Selling That Stuff*.............	25.00 -	40.00
12796 *It's All Worn Out*.............	25.00 -	40.00
12811 *Hokum Blues*................	25.00 -	40.00
12821 *Ain't Goin' That Way*.........	25.00 -	40.00
12858 *Went To His Head*...........	25.00 -	40.00
12882 *I Was Afraid Of That*.........	25.00 -	40.00
12897 *Let Me Have It*..............	25.00 -	40.00
12919 *Gambler's Blues-No. 2*.........	25.00 -	40.00
12935 *The Folks Down Stairs*.........	25.00 -	40.00
Vocalion 03156, 03232, 03265, 03386, 03406, 03463, 03516, 03572.................	7.00 -	12.00

ROSA HOLLEY:

Vocalion 1179 *Lookin' For The Blues*........	40.00 -	60.00

TONY HOLLINS:

Okeh 06351, 06523, 06605..............	5.00 -	8.00

THE HOLLYWOOD FOUR FLAMES:

Recorded In Hollywood 164 *I'll Always Be A Fool*	8.00 -	12.00*
165 *Young Girl*....................	8.00 -	12.00*

HAPPY HOLMES:

Victor 21075 *Solid Ground*.................	15.00 -	20.00

SONNY BOY HOLMES:

Recorded in Hollywood 223 *Walking And Crying Blues*.............................	10.00 -	15.00

225 *I Got Them Blues*.................	10.00 -	15.00

SPEEDY HOLMES:

Supertone 9364 *Mister Mary Blues*...........	15.00 -	25.00

WINSTON HOLMES AND CHARLIE TURNER:

Paramount 12798 *Rounders Lament*...........	30.00 -	50.00
12815 *Skinner*..........................	30.00 -	50.00

WRIGHT HOLMES:

Gotham 508 *Drove Home Blues*............	15.00 -	20.00
511 *Quinsella*......................	15.00 -	20.00
Milton 5221 *Alley Special*...............	15.00 -	20.00

THE HOME WRECKERS:

Bluebird 5341 *Home Wreckin' Blues*..........	30.00 -	40.00

THE HONEY DRIPPER (ROOSEVELT SYKES):

Decca 7160, 7164, 7173, 7188, 7197, 7252.....	7.00 -	10.00
7324 and higher numbers.................	5.00 -	8.00

EARL HOOKER:

King 4600 *Race Track*.....................	7.00 -	10.00*
Rockin' 519 *On The Hook*................	7.00 -	10.00*

JOHN LEE HOOKER:

Chart 609, 614..........................	4.00 -	7.00*
Chess 1467, 1482, 1505, 1513..............	5.00 -	8.00*
JVB 30 *Boogie Rambler*.................	10.00 -	15.00
Modern 627, 663, 688, 714, 730, 746, 767, 790, 814, 829, 835, 847, 867, 876, 886, 897, 901, 908, 916, 923, 931, 935, 942, 948, 958, 966, 978......	3.00 -	6.00*
Regal 3295 *Boogie Chillen*..............	5.00 -	8.00
3304 *Notoriety Woman*..............	7.00 -	12.00
Sensation 21, 26, 30, 33, 34.................	5.00 -	8.00

LIGHTNIN' HOPKINS:

Aladdin 165, 167, 168, 204, 209, 3005, 3015, 3028, 3035, 3052, 3063, 3077, 3096, 3117, 3262...	3.00 -	6.00*
Gold Star 613, 616, 634, 637, 640, 641, 646, 652, 656, 662, 664, 665, 666, 669, 673, 3131.....	6.00 -	12.00
671 *Henny Penny Blues*..............	25.00 -	40.00
Jax 315, 321, 635, 642, 660..............	4.00 -	7.00
Mercury 8276, 8293, 70081, 70191..........	3.00 -	5.00*
Modern 529, 543, 552, 568, 594, 621, 673..	3.00 -	6.00
RPM 337, 346, 351, 359, 378, 388, 398.......	3.00 -	6.00
Sittin' In With 599, 611, 621, 635, 642, 647, 649, 752, 658, 660, 661...........................	4.00 -	7.00
TNT 8002 *Lightning Jump*.............	8.00 -	12.00
8008 *Moanin' Blues*.................	8.00 -	12.00

J.D. HORTON:

Bullet 350 *Cadillac Blues*.................	15.00 -	20.00

SHAKEY/WALTER HORTON:

Chess 1529 *Walter's Boogie*	7.00 -	10.00*
Cobra 5002 *Need My Baby*..............	7.00 -	10.00*

SON HOUSE:

Paramount 12990 *Dry Spell Blues*	150.00 -	250.00
13013 *Preachin' The Blues*.................	150.00 -	250.00
13042 *My Black Mama*	150.00 -	250.00
13096 *Clarksdale Moan*...................	150.00 -	250.00
13111 *What Am I To Do Blues*...............	200.00 -	250.00

EMERSON HOUSTON:

Bluebird 5791 *Hard Luck Blues*..............	30.00 -	40.00

LAWYER HOUSTON:

Atlantic 916 *Dallas Be Bop Blues*............	10.00 -	15.00

SOLDIER BOY HOUSTON:

Atlantic 971 *Western Rider Blues*............	10.00 -	15.00*

JOHN HENRY HOWARD:

Gennett 3117 *I've Started For The Kingdom*....	25.00 -	40.00
3124 *Black Snake*.................	25.00 -	40.00

JOHNNY HOWARD:

DeLuxe 6044 *Hastings Street Jump*...........	20.00 -	30.00*

ROSETTA HOWARD:

Decca 7370, 7392, 7410, 7447, 7459, 7515, 7531, 7551, 7618, 7627, 7640, 7658, 7687, 7801...	5.00 -	8.00

WHISTLING BOB HOWE & FRANKIE GRIGGS:

Decca 7085 *The Hottest Stuff In Town*........	7.00 -	10.00

PEG LEG HOWELL (& HIS GANG): PEG LEG HOWELL & EDDIE ANTHONY/JIM HILL:

Columbia 14177-D *New Prison Blues*	25.00 -	40.00
14194-D *Coal Man Blues*	25.00 -	40.00
14210-D *New Jelly Roll Blues*	25.00 -	40.00
14238-D *Sadie Lee Blues*	25.00 -	40.00
14270-D *Hobo Blues*	25.00 -	40.00
14298-D *Peg Leg Stomp*	25.00 -	40.00
14320-D *Rock And Gravel Blues*	25.00 -	40.00
14356-D *Fairy Blues*	25.00 -	40.00
14382-D *Turkey Buzzard Blues*	25.00 -	40.00
14426-D *Monkey Man Blues*	25.00 -	40.00
14438-D *Rolling Mill Blues*	25.00 -	40.00
14456-D *Turtle Dove Blues*	25.00 -	40.00
14473-D *Skin Game Blues*	25.00 -	40.00
14535-D *Ball And Chain Blues*	25.00 -	40.00

HOWLIN' WOLF:

Chess 1479, 1497, 1510, 1515, 1528, 1557, 1566	5.00 -	8.00*
RPM 333, 340, 347	4.00 -	8.00

ED "FATS" HUDSON:

Champion 16414 *Fats' Hard Luck Blues*	40.00 -	60.00

HATTIE HUDSON:

Columbia 14279-D *Black Hand Blues*	20.00 -	30.00

LUTHER HUFF:

Trumpet 132, 141	7.00 -	10.00*

WILLIE B. HUFF:

Big Town 105 *Operator 209*	8.00 -	12.00*

PEE WEE HUGHES & THE DELTA DUO:

Deluxe 3228 *Santa Fe Blues*	10.00 -	15.00

15.00

PAPA HARVEY HULL & THE DOWN HOME BOYS & LONG "CLEVE" REED:

Black Patti 8001 *France Blues*	150.00 -	200.00
8002 *Don't You Leave My Here*	150.00 -	200.00

HELEN HUMES:

Okeh 8467 *A Worried Woman's Blues*	15.00 -	20.00
8529 *Alligator Blues*	15.00 -	20.00
8545 *If Papa Has Outside Lovin'*	15.00 -	20.00
8674 *Garlic Blues*	15.00 -	20.00
8825 *Race Horse Blues*	15.00 -	20.00

D.A. HUNT:

Sun 183 *Lonesome Ol' Jail*	40.00 -	60.00*

HUNTER BROTHERS:

Superior 2836 *Stove Pipe Stomp*	40.00 -	60.00

ALBERTA HUNTER:

Black Swan 2008 *Bring Back The Joys*	20.00 -	25.00
2019 *Someday Sweetheart*	20.00 -	25.00
Bluebird 8485, 8539	5.00 -	8.00
Columbia 14450-D *My Particular Man*	20.00 -	30.00
Decca 7633, 7644, 7727	4.00 -	6.00
Okeh 8268 *Your Jelly Roll Is Good*	20.00 -	30.00
8278 *Everybody Does It Now*	20.00 -	30.00
8294 *I'm Hard To Satisfy*	20.00 -	30.00
8315 *Empty Cellar Blues*	20.00 -	30.00
8365 *You For Me, Me For You*	15.00 -	20.00
8383 *Everybody Mess Around*	20.00 -	30.00
8393 *Wasn't It Nice?*	20.00 -	30.00
8409 *Don't Forget To Mess Around*	20.00 -	30.00
Paramount 12001 *Daddy Blues*	15.00 -	20.00
12005 *Down Hearted Blues*	15.00 -	20.00
12006 *Jazzin' Baby Blues*	15.00 -	25.00
12007 *Lonesome Monday Morning Blues*	15.00 -	25.00
12008 *You Can't Have It All*	15.00 -	25.00
12010 *After All These Years*	15.00 -	25.00
12012 *Someday Sweetheart*	15.00 -	25.00
12014 *Bring Back The Joys*	15.00 -	25.00
12016 *'Tain't Nobody's Bizness*	15.00 -	25.00
12017 *Chirping The Blues*	15.00 -	25.00
12018 *Bring It With You When You Come*	20.00 -	30.00
12019 *Loveless Love*	20.00 -	30.00
12020 *Vamping Brown*	20.00 -	30.00
12021 *Bleeding Hearted Blues*	20.00 -	30.00
12036 *Michigan Water Blues*	25.00 -	40.00
12043 *Mistreated Blues*	20.00 -	30.00
12049 *Stingaree Blues*	25.00 -	40.00
12065 *Experience Blues*	25.00 -	40.00
12066 *Miss Anna Brown*	20.00 -	30.00
12093 *Old-Fashioned Love*	15.00 -	20.00
Victor 20497 *I'll Forgive You 'Cause I Love You*	10.00 -	15.00
20651 *My Old Daddy's Got A Brand New...*	10.00 -	15.00
20771 *Sugar*	20.00 -	30.00
21539 *I'm Going To See My Ma*	20.00 -	30.00

IVORY JOE HUNTER:

Pacific	5.00 -	8.00

LOST JOHN HUNTER & THE BLIND BATS:

4 Star 1492 *Cool Down Mama*	8.00 -	12.00
1511 *Boogie For Me Baby*	8.00 -	12.00

LEE HUNTER:

Gold Star 651 *Lee's Boogie*	12.00 -	16.00

SLIM HUNTER:

Superior 2808 *Mistreatin' Mama*	40.00 -	60.00
2837 *Big Bill Blues*	40.00 -	60.00

MISSISSIPPI JOHN HURT:

Okeh 8560 *Nobody's Dirty Business*	100.00 -	150.00
8654 *Stack O'Lee Blues*	100.00 -	150.00
8666 *Blessed Be The Name*	100.00 -	150.00
8692 *Spike Driver Blues*	100.00 -	150.00
8724 *Louis Collins*	100.00 -	150.00
8759 *Avalon Blues*	100.00 -	150.00

J.B. HUTTO:

Chance 1165 *Dim Lights*	10.00 -	15.00*

HATTIE HYDE:

Victor 23374 *Special Question Blues*	40.00 -	60.00

J.B. & HIS BAYOU BOYS:

J.O.B. 1008 *The Mountain*	6.00 -	10.00*

J.B. & HIS HAWKS:

Chance 1155 *Combination Boogie*	15.00 -	20.00*

JACKIE BOY & LITTLE WALTER:

Sun 174 *Sellin' My Whiskey* (possibly unissued)	—	

JACK O'DIAMONDS:

Paramount 12786 *The Ducks Yas Yas*	60.00 -	80.00
12791 *Smiling Blues*	60.00 -	80.00

JACKSON BLUE BOYS:

Columbia 14397-D *Sweet Alberta*	20.00 -	30.00

BESSIE JACKSON:

Titles, issued contemporaneously on Banner, Melotone, Oriole, Perfect, Romeo: *Alley Boogie, B.D. Woman Blues; Baking Powder Blues; Barbecue Bess; Black Angel Blues; Boogan Ways Blues; Changed Way Blues; Down In Boogie Alley; Drinking Blues; Forty-Two Hundred Blues; Groceries On The Shelf; House Top Blues; I Hate That Train Called The M. & O.; Jump Steady Daddy; Lonesome Midnight Blues; Man Stealer Blues; Mean Twister; My Baby Came Back; My Man Is Boogan Me; New Muscle Shoals Blues; Pig Iron Sally; Reckless Woman; Red Cross Man; Roll And Rattler; Seabord Blues; Shave 'Em Dry; Skin Game Blues; Sloppy Drunk Blues; Stew Meat Blues; Superstitious Blues; That's What My Baby Likes; Tired As I Can Be; Tricks Ain't Walkin' No more; Troubled Mind; Walkin' Blues; You Got To Die Someday*	20.00 -	30.00

BO WEAVIL JACKSON:

Paramount 12389 *Pistol Blues*	60.00 -	80.00
12390 *When The Saints Come Marching Home*	60.00 -	80.00
12423 *Who Do You Moan?*	60.00 -	80.00

(PAPA) CHARLIE JACKSON (AND BLIND BLAKE):

Okeh 8954 *Skoodle-Um-Skoo*	15.00 -	25.00
8957 *If I Got What You Want*	15.00 -	25.00
Paramount 12219 *Papa's Lawdy Lawdy Blues*	15.00 -	20.00

12236	*Salty Dog Blues*	15.00 -	20.00
12259	*The Cat's Got The Measles*	15.00 -	20.00
12264	*Coffee Pot Blues*	15.00 -	20.00
12281	*Shake That Thing*	15.00 -	20.00
12289	*Drop That Sack*	15.00 -	20.00
12296	*Take Me Back Blues*	15.00 -	20.00
12305	*Mama, Don't You Think I Know?*	15.00 -	20.00
12320	*Maxwell Street Blues*	15.00 -	20.00
12335	*Texas Blues*	15.00 -	20.00
12348	*Jackson's Blues*	15.00 -	20.00
12358	*Butter And Egg Man Blues*	15.00 -	20.00
12366	*The Judge Cliff Davis Blues*	15.00 -	20.00
12375	*Up The Way Bound*	15.00 -	20.00
12383	*Bad Luck Woman Blues*	15.00 -	20.00
12422	*Fat Mouth Blues*	15.00 -	25.00
12461	*Coal Man Blues*	15.00 -	25.00
12501	*Skoodle Um Skoo*	15.00 -	25.00
12553	*Baby Don't You Be So Mean*	15.00 -	25.00
12574	*Bright Eyes*	15.00 -	25.00
12602	*Long Gone Lost John*	15.00 -	25.00
12660	*Ash Tray Blues*	20.00 -	30.00
12675	*I Like To Love My Baby*	20.00 -	30.00
12700	*Lexington Kentucky Blues*	20.00 -	30.00
12721	*Corn Liquor Blues*	20.00 -	30.00
12736	*Don't Break Down On Me*	20.00 -	30.00
12765	*We Can't Buy It No More*	20.00 -	30.00
12797	*Tailor Made Lover*	20.00 -	30.00
12853	*Forgotten Blues*	20.00 -	30.00
12905	*I'll Be Gone Babe*	30.00 -	40.00
12911	*Papa Charlie And Blind Blake Talk About It*	30.00 -	40.00
12956	*Self Experience*	30.00 -	40.00

DEACON JACKSON:

Herwin 93031	*All I Want Is That Pure Religion.*	35.00 -	50.00

FRANKIE JACKSON:

Okeh 8359	*Hannah Fell In Love With My Piano*	10.00 -	20.00

GEORGE JACKSON & BESSIE JONES:

Superior 2555	*I'm Long Gone*	35.00 -	50.00

HANDY JACKSON:

Sun 177	*Got My Application Baby*	40.00 -	60.00

JIM JACKSON:

Victor 21236	*My Monday Woman Blues*	15.00 -	25.00
21268	*Bootlegging Blues*	15.00 -	25.00
21387	*Old Dog Blue*	15.00 -	25.00
21671	*I'm Gonna Move To Louisiana*	15.00 -	25.00
38003	*This Mornin' She Was Gone*	15.00 -	25.00
38505	*What A Time*	15.00 -	25.00
38517	*Traveling Man*	15.00 -	25.00
38525	*Going 'Round The Mountain*	15.00 -	25.00
Vocalion 1144	*Jim Jackson's Kansas City Blues — Part 1/2*	10.00 -	15.00
1145	*Mobile Central Blues*	15.00 -	20.00
1146	*He's In The Jailhouse Now*	20.00 -	30.00
1155	*Jim Jackson's Kansas City Blues — Part 3/4*	12.00 -	15.00
1164	*I'm A Bad Bad Man*	20.00 -	30.00
1284	*Hey Mama, It's Nice Like That*	20.00 -	30.00
1295	*Foot Achin' Blues*	20.00 -	30.00
1413	*Ain't You Sorry Mama?*	20.00 -	30.00
1428	*Jim Jackson's Jamboree*	20.00 -	30.00
1477	*Hesitation Blues*	20.00 -	30.00

LILLIAN JACKSON:

Supertone 9281	*I'm All Broke Out With The Blues*	30.00 -	40.00
9287	*Sing That Song With Feeling*	30.00 -	40.00
9294	*Cow Cow Blues*	30.00 -	40.00

LIL'/LITTLE SON JACKSON:

Gold Star 638	*Roberta Blues*	8.00 -	15.00
642	*Ground Hog Blues*	8.00 -	15.00
653	*No Money, No Love*	8.00 -	15.00
663	*Cairo Blues*	8.00 -	15.00
668	*Gambling Blues*	8.00 -	15.00
Imperial 5100	*Ticket Agent Blues*	5.00 -	8.00*
5108	*Tough Luck Blues*	5.00 -	8.00*
5113	*Rockin' And Rollin'*	5.00 -	8.00*

5119	*Rocky Road*	5.00 -	8.00*
5125	*Young Woman Blues*	5.00 -	8.00*
5131	*Time Changes Things*	5.00 -	8.00*
5137	*Restless Blues*	5.00 -	8.00*
5144	*Red Light*	5.00 -	8.00*
5156, 5165, 5175, 5192, 5204, 5218, 5229, 5237, 5248, 5259, 5268, 5276, 5286, 5300, 5312, 5319, 5339		3.00 -	5.00*
Modern 840	*Talkin' Boogie*	7.00 -	10.00
Sittin' In With 643	*Gambling Blues*	7.00 -	10.00

LULU JACKSON:

Vocalion 1193	*Careless Love Blues*	12.00 -	18.00
1206	*After You've Had Your Way*	15.00 -	25.00
1242	*Lost Lover Blues*	15.00 -	25.00
1276	*Little Rosewood Casket*	15.00 -	25.00

MONROE "MOE" JACKSON:

Mercury 8127	*Move It On Over*	7.00 -	10.00

ODIS JACKSON:

Fechi 90	*Pretty Baby*	7.00 -	10.00

PORKCHOP JACKSON:

Supertone 9510	*Lonesome Man Blues*	50.00 -	75.00

SADIE JACKSON:

Columbia 14181-D	*Original Black Bottom Dance*	8.00 -	12.00

VIOLET JACKSON:

Gennett 6090	*Blue And All By Myself*	20.00 -	30.00
6147	*I Can't Be Satisfied With One*	20.00 -	30.00

(BLIND/NEW ORLEANS) WILLIE JACKSON (& BROTHER):

Broadway 5050	*Telephone To Glory*	25.00 -	40.00
Columbia 14136-D	*Willie Jackson's Blues*	15.00 -	20.00
14156-D	*Bad, Bad Mama*	15.00 -	20.00
14165-D	*Who'll Chop Your Suey When I'm Gone*	15.00 -	20.00
14184-D	*Numbers on the Brain*	15.00 -	20.00
14218-D	*Railroad Man Blues*	15.00 -	20.00
14284-D	*Kansas City Blues*	15.00 -	20.00
14432-D	*Corn And Bunion Blues*	20.00 -	30.00
Crown 3326	*Telephone To Glory*	20.00 -	30.00
Herwin 92035	*Telephone To Glory*	25.00 -	40.00
93005	*Rock Of Ages*	35.00 -	50.00

WALTER JACOBS (& THE CARTER BROTHERS):

Bluebird 6673	*Rats Been On My Cheese*	20.00 -	30.00
Montgomery Ward 7064	*How Did It Happen*	20.00 -	30.00
Okeh 45468	*Sheiks Special*	25.00 -	40.00
45482	*Mississippi Low Down*	25.00 -	40.00

ELMER JAMES:

Trumpet 186	*Gonna Find My Baby*	7.00 -	10.00*

ELMO/ELMORE JAMES (& HIS BROOMDUSTERS):

Meteor 5000, 5003		5.00 -	8.00*
Trumpet 146	*Dust My Broom*	5.00 -	8.00*

FRANK JAMES:

Champion 16798	*Mistreated Blues*	50.00 -	75.00
16809	*Frank's Lonesome Blues*	50.00 -	75.00
50017	*Forsaken Blues*	25.00 -	35.00
50018	*Snake Hip Blues*	25.00 -	35.00

JESSE JAMES:

Decca 7213	*Southern Casey Jones*	15.00 -	20.00
Sittin' In With 569	*Forgive Me Blues*	8.00 -	12.00

PAULINE JAMES:

Gennett 6147	*You Used To Be Sugar Blues*	20.00 -	30.00

SADIE JAMES:

Victor 20575	*Mama, Fold Your Hands*	20.00 -	30.00

SKIP JAMES:

Paramount 13065	*Cherry Ball Blues*	150.00 -	200.00
13066	*22-20 Blues*	150.00 -	200.00
13072	*How Long "Buck"*	150.00 -	200.00
13088	*Devil Got My Woman*	150.00 -	200.00
13098	*Special Rider Blues*	150.00 -	200.00
13106	*Hard Luck Child*	150.00 -	200.00
13108	*Be Ready When He Comes*	150.00 -	200.00
13111	*Drunken Spree*	175.00 -	250.00

SPRINGBACK JAMES:

Titles, issued contemporaneously on Banner, Melotone, Oriole, Perfect, Romeo, Vocalion:

Hard Driving Mama; Hellish Ways	20.00 -	30.00
Bluebird 6777 See For Yourself	20.00 -	30.00
6824 New Red Cross Blues	20.00 -	30.00
7116 Poor Coal Passer	20.00 -	30.00
Champion 50076 Lonesome Love Blues	25.00 -	35.00
Decca 7091 Rusty Can Blues	20.00 -	30.00
7119 Stingaree Mama Blues	20.00 -	30.00

SUNNY JAMES:

Down Town 2010 Excuse Me Baby	15.00 -	20.00

ULYSSES JAMES:

Cava-Tone 250 Poor Boy	5.00 -	8.00

W. LAWRENCE JAMES:

Paramount 12450 Oh Cap'n	20.00 -	30.00

JAMMIN' JIM:

Savoy 1106 Shake Boogie	7.00 -	10.00

JAZZBO TOMMY & HIS LOWLANDERS:

Titles, issued contemporaneously on Banner, Melotone, Oriole, Perfect, Romeo; Blaze Face Cow; You Don't Mean Me No Good .... 40.00 - 60.00

GEORGE JEFFERSON:

Bluebird 7926 Honey Bee	7.00 -	10.00
Champion 15452 Why Should I Grieve After You've Gone	50.00 -	75.00
15472 When A Man Is Treated Like A Dog	90.00 -	130.00
Gennett 6378 Bearcat Blues	50.00 -	75.00

BLIND LEMON JEFFERSON:

Okeh 8455 Black Snake Moon	35.00 -	50.00
Paramount 12347 Booster Blues	30.00 -	50.00
12354 Got The Blues	30.00 -	50.00
12367 Black Horse Blues	30.00 -	50.00
12373 Jack O'Diamond Blues	30.00 -	50.00
12394 Beggin' Back	30.00 -	50.00
12407 Stocking Feet Blues	30.00 -	50.00
12425 Wartime Blues	30.00 -	50.00
12443 Bad Luck Blues	30.00 -	50.00
12454 Rabbit Foot Blues	30.00 -	50.00
12474 Match Box Blues	30.00 -	50.00
12487 Teddy Bear Blues	30.00 -	50.00
12493 Weary Dog Blues	30.00 -	50.00
12510 Right Of Way Blues	30.00 -	50.00
12541 Rambler Blues	30.00 -	50.00
12551 Chinch Bug Blues	30.00 -	50.00
12578 Gone Dead On You Blues	30.00 -	50.00
12585 He Arose From The Dead	30.00 -	50.00
12593 Lonesome House Blues	40.00 -	60.00
12608 'Lectric Chair Blues	40.00 -	60.00
12622 'Prison Cell Blues	40.00 -	60.00
12631 Mean Jumper Blues	40.00 -	60.00
12639 Lemon's Cannon Ball Moan	40.00 -	60.00
*12650 Piney Woods Mama Blues	40.00 -	60.00
12666 Blind Lemon's Penitentiary Blues	40.00 -	60.00
12679 Lock Step Blues	40.00 -	60.00
12685 How Long How Long	40.00	-60.00
12692 Happy New Year Blues	40.00 -	60.00
12712 Maltese Cat Blues	40.00 -	60.00
12728 Competition Bed Blues	40.00 -	60.00
12739 Eagle Eyed Mama	40.00 -	60.00
12756 Tin Cup Blues	40.00 -	60.00
12771 Oil Well Blues	40.00 -	60.00
12801 Peach Orchard Mama	50.00 -	80.00
12852 Long Distance Moan	50.00 -	80.00
12872 Bed Springs Blues	50.00 -	80.00
12880 Pneumonia Blues	50.00 -	80.00
**12886 Hometown Skiffle	50.00 -	80.00
12899 Mosquito Moan	50.00 -	80.00
12921 Cat Man Blues	50.00 -	80.00
12933 The Cheaters Spell	50.00 -	80.00
12946 Empty House Blues	50.00 -	80.00

(*Note: Paramount 12650 is designated "Blind Lemon Jefferson's Birthday Record," and bears a portrait of the artist.)

(**Note: Paramount 12886 is designated "Descriptive Novelty," performed by several artists. Since Blind Lemon Jefferson's name appears first, it is included in his output.)

JELLY BELLY & SLIM SEWARD:

Apollo 412 Sorry Woman Blues	7.00 -	10.00

JEKINS AND JENKINS:

Columbia 14040-D Hen Pecked Man	10.00 -	15.00
14100-D Sister, It's Too Bad	10.00 -	15.00
Gennett 3335 Miserable Blues	10.00 -	15.00

HAZEKIAH JENKINS:

Columbia 14585-D The Panic Is On	15.00 -	20.00

ROBERT JENKINS:

Parkway 103 Steelin' Boogie	10.00 -	15.00

JIM JAM:

Varsity 6044 Diamond Ring Blues	15.00 -	20.00
6054 Window Pane Blues	15.00 -	20.00

JOE JOE:

Varsity 6032 Humming Blues	7.00 -	10.00

JIMMY & WALTER:

Sun 180 Before Long	35.00 -	50.00*

JOHNSON AND JACKSON:

Champion 15835 Everybody Likes That Thing	25.00 -	40.00

JOHNSON AND SMITH:

Champion 16411 Brown Skin Shuffle	40.00 -	60.00

JOHNSON BOYS:

Okeh 8708 Violin Blues	15.00 -	20.00

JOHNSON-NELSON-PORKCHOP:

Okeh 8577 In The Mornin'	10.00 -	15.00

ALEC JOHNSON (& HIS BAND):

Columbia 14378-D Mysterious Coon	35.00 -	50.00
14416-D Next Week Sometime	35.00 -	50.00
14446-D Sundown Blues	35.00 -	50.00

BABE JOHNSON:

Silvertone 3562 Worried 'Bout Him Blues	30.00 -	40.00

BESSIE JOHNSON; BESSIE JOHNSON'S SANCTIFIED SINGERS:

Okeh 8725 No Room At The Hotel	15.00 -	20.00
8765 The Whole World In His Hand	15.00 -	20.00

BIG BILL JOHNSON:

Champion 16081 Saturday Night Rub	40.00 -	60.00
16172 That Won't Do	40.00 -	60.00
16327 The Baker's Blues	40.00 -	60.00
16396 Big Bill Blues	40.00 -	60.00
16426 Mr. Conductor Man	40.00 -	60.00
50060 Big Bill Blues	15.00 -	20.00
50069 Too Too Train Blues	15.00 -	20.00
Gennett 7210 Skoodle Do Do	40.00 -	60.00
7230 I Can't Be Satisfied	40.00 -	60.00

BILLIKEN/BILLIKIN JOHNSON & FRED ADAMS/WITH NEAL ROBERTS:

Columbia 14293-D Sun Beam Blues	30.00 -	40.00
14405-D Wild Jack Blues	30.00 -	40.00

BUD JOHNSON:

Champion 15614 Kitchen Range Blues	150.00 -	250.00
15675 Hot Time Blues	150.00 -	250.00

BUSTER JOHNSON:

Champion 16718 Undertaker Blues	80.00 -	100.00

CONRAD JOHNSON:

Gold Star 622 Howling On Dowling	7.00 -	10.00

EASY PAPA JOHNSON:

Melotone 12048 Drinkin' Woman Blues	25.00 -	35.00
12086 Cotton Seed Blues	25.00 -	35.00
Vocalion 02669 No Good Woman Blues	25.00 -	35.00
02697 Papa Sweetback Blues	25.00 -	35.00

EDDIE JOHNSON & HIS ORCHESTRA:

Colony 101 Juice Head	5.00 -	8.00
Imperial 5120 Corn Licker Blues	5.00 -	8.00

EDITY (NORTH) JOHNSON:

Okeh 8748 *Heart Aching Blues*	40.00 -	60.00
Paramount 12823 *Honey Dripper Blues*	50.00 -	75.00
12864 *Can't Make Another Day*	50.00 -	75.00
12915 *Honey Dripper Blues No. 2*	40.00 -	60.00
12939 *Eight Hour Woman*	40.00 -	60.00
13032 *Whispering To My Man*	40.00 -	60.00
QRS 7048 *You Ain't No Good Blues*	35.00 -	45.00
Vocalion 1433 *Honey Dripper Blues*	30.00 -	40.00

EDNA JOHNSON:

Gennet 5367 *I'm Drifting From You Blues*	10.00 -	15.00

ELIZABETH JOHNSON:

Okeh 8593 *Empty Bed Blues*	35.00 -	50.00
8789 *Be My Kid Blues*	20.00 -	30.00

ELNORA JOHNSON:

Black Patti 8033 *Freakish Papa*	30.00 -	40.00
8039 *Red Cap Porter Blues*	30.00 -	40.00

ELVIRA JOHNSON:

Gennett 3337 *Numbers on the Brain*	20.00 -	30.00
Champion 15126 *Numbers on the Brain*	20.00 -	30.00
15127 *How Could I Be Blue?*	20.00 -	30.00

FANNIE JOHNSON:

Cameo 1144 *Slow Up Papa*	10.00 -	15.00
1158 *Black Snake Blues*	10.00 -	15.00
Romeo 416 *Back Water Blues*	8.00 -	12.00
453 *Dyin' Crap-Shooter's Blues*	8.00 -	12.00

FRANK JOHNSON:

Herwin 92038 *Trouble 'Bout My Soul*	75.00 -	100.00

GLADYS JOHNSON:

Variety 5033 *I'm Savin' It All For You*	10.00 -	15.00
5048 *Slow Up Papa*	10.00 -	15.00
5085 *Black Snake Blues*	10.00 -	15.00

HARRY "SLICK" JOHNSON:

Peacock 1560 *My Baby's Coming Home*	7.00 -	10.00

JAMES "STEADY ROLL" JOHNSON:

Okeh 8287 *Newport Blues*	10.00 -	15.00

JAMES (STUMP) JOHNSON & HIS PIANO:

QRS 7049 *The Snitchers Blues*	40.00 -	60.00
7050 *My Babe Blues*	40.00 -	60.00

JELLY ROLL JOHNSON:

Champion 15281 *Free Woman Blues*	40.00 -	60.00
Silvertone 5121 *Free Woman Blues*	50.00 -	75.00

JESSE JOHNSON:

Paramount 12829 *I Wish I Had Died In Egyptland*	35.00 -	50.00

JULIA JOHNSON:

Gennett 6519 *Hard Headed Daddy*	15.00 -	25.00

KI KI JOHNSON:

QRS 7001 *Lone Grave*	35.00 -	50.00
7003 *Lady, Your Clock Ain't Right*	35.00 -	50.00

LEROY "COUNTRY" JOHNSON:

Freedom 1509 *Loghouse On The Hill*	10.00 -	15.00

LIL JOHNSON:

Bluebird 6112 *Keep On Knocking*	7.00 -	10.00
Champion 50002 *Get 'Em From The Peanut Man*	10.00 -	15.00
50052 *Snake Man Blues*	10.00 -	15.00
Vocalion 1299 *Never Let Your Left Hand Know*	15.00 -	25.00
1410 *House Rend Scuffle*	15.00 -	25.00
03199 *Press My Button*	10.00 -	15.00
03241 *Get 'Em From The Peanut Man* (The New Hot Nuts)	10.00 -	15.00
03251 *My Stove's In Good Condition*	10.00 -	15.00
03266 *Two Timin' Man*	7.00 -	10.00
03299 *Murder In The First Degree*	10.00 -	15.00
03312 *Hottest Gal In Town*	10.00 -	15.00
03331 *Ramblin' Man Blues*	10.00 -	15.00
03374 *Black And Evil Blues*	10.00 -	15.00
03397 *Crazy About My Rider*	10.00 -	15.00
03428 *New Shave 'Em Dry*	10.00 -	15.00
03455 *River Hip Papa*	10.00 -	15.00
03483 *You Can't Bet On Love*	10.00 -	15.00
03530 *I'm A Sales Lady*	10.00 -	15.00
03562 *Meat Balls*	10.00 -	15.00
03600 *Goofer Dust Swing*	10.00 -	15.00
03604 *Joe Louis Fight*	10.00 -	15.00
03604 *Winner Joe (The Knock-Out King)*	10.00 -	15.00
03666 *Mellow Stuff*	10.00 -	15.00
03710 *Broken-Hearted Blues*	10.00 -	15.00
03941 *When Your Troubles Are Like Mine*	10.00 -	15.00
03978 *Ain't That A Shame?*	10.00 -	15.00
04067 *Snake In The Grass*	10.00 -	15.00

Titles, issued contemporaneously on Banner, Melotone, Oriole, Perfect, Romeo: *Get 'Em From The Peanut Man; If You Can Dish It; I;m Bettin' On You; Press My Button; Take It Easy, Greasy; That Bonus Done Gone Through* ... 8.00 - 15.00

LONNIE JOHNSON (& BLIND WILLIE DUNN/& CLARENCE WILLIAMS/& SPENCER WILLIAMS):

Aladdin 197, 3029, 3047	4.00 -	7.00
Bluebird 8322, 8338, 8363, 8387, 8530, 8564... 8684, 8748, 8779, 8804, 8980, 9006, 9022, 34-0708, 34-0714, 34-0732, 34-0742	6.00 - 4.00 -	10.00 7.00
Columbia 14667-D *Home Wreckers Blues*	20.00 -	30.00
14676-D *Unselfish Love*	20.00 -	30.00
Decca 7388, 7397, 7427, 7445, 7461, 7487, 7509, 7537	7.00 -	10.00
Disc 5060, 5061, 5062, 5063, 5064, 5065	5.00 -	8.00
King	3.00 -	5.00
Okeh 8523 *Mr. Johnson's Blues*	12.00 -	16.00
8282 *Love Story Blues*	12.00 -	16.00
8291 *Bed Of Sand*	12.00 -	16.00
8309 *Lonesome Jail Blues*	12.00 -	16.00
8340 *A Good Happy Home*	12.00 -	16.00
8358 *Good Old Wagon*	12.00 -	16.00
8376 *Baby Please Tell Me*	12.00 -	16.00
8391 *Oh! Doctor, The Blues*	12.00 -	16.00
8411 *Lonnie's Got The Blues*	12.00 -	16.00
8417 *Johnson Trio Stomp*	12.00 -	16.00
8435 *Ball And Chain Blues*	12.00 -	16.00
8451 *You Drove A Good Man Away*	12.00 -	16.00
8466 *South Bound Water*	12.00 -	16.00
8484 *Treat 'Em Right*	12.00 -	16.00
8497 *Roaming Rambler Blues*	12.00 -	16.00
8505 *Fickle Mamma Blues*	12.00 -	16.00
8512 *St. Louis Cyclone Blues*	12.00 -	16.00
8524 *Tin Can Alley Blues*	12.00 -	16.00
8537 *Kansas City Blues*	12.00 -	16.00
8557 *Life Saver Blues*	12.00 -	16.00
8558 *Playing With The Strings*	12.00 -	16.00
8574 *Crowing Rooster Blues*	12.00 -	16.00
8575 *Blues In G*	12.00 -	16.00
8586 *Bed Bug Blues No. 2*	12.00 -	16.00
8601 *Wrong Woman Blues*	12.00 -	16.00
8618 *Broken Levee Blues*	12.00 -	16.00
8635 *Careless Love*	12.00 -	16.00
8637 *Two Tone Stomp*	12.00 -	16.00
8664 *It Feels So Good—Part 1/2*	7.00 -	10.00
8691 *Death Is On Your Track*	12.00 -	16.00
Okeh 8695 *Bull Frog Moan*	12.00 -	16.00
8697 *It Feels So Good—Part 3/4*	7.00 -	10.00
8709 *Mr. Johnson's Blues—No. 2*	12.00 -	16.00
8722 *From Now On Make Your Whoopee At Home*	12.00 -	16.00
8754 *Sundown Blues*	12.00 -	16.00
8762 *Wipe It Off*	20.00 -	30.00
8768 *She's Making Whoopee In Hell Tonight*	12.00 -	16.00
8775 *The Dirty Dozen*	12.00 -	16.00
8786 *Headed For Southland*	12.00 -	16.00
8796 *Don't Drive Me From Your Door*	12.00 -	16.00
8802 *The Bull Frog And The Toad*	15.00 -	20.00
8812 *Keep It To Yourself*	15.00 -	20.00
8822 *Deep Sea Blues*	15.00 -	20.00
8831 *No More Troubles Now*	15.00 -	20.00

8846 *Let All Married Women Alone*	15.00 -	20.00
8875 *Just A Roaming Man*	15.00 -	25.00
8886 *I Just Can't Stand These Blues*	15.00 -	25.00
8898 *Beautiful But Dumb*	15.00 -	25.00
8909 *I Have To Do My Time*	15.00 -	25.00
8916 *The Best Jockey In Town*	15.00 -	25.00
8926 *Sleepy Water Blues*	15.00 -	25.00
8937 *Sam, You're Just A Rat*	15.00 -	25.00
8946 *Racketeers Blues*	15.00 -	25.00
40695 *Nile Of Genago*	15.00 -	25.00
Paradise 110 *Tomorrow Night*	8.00 -	12.00
123 *Lonesome Day Blues*	8.00 -	12.00

LOUISE JOHNSON:

Paramount 12992 *All Night Long Blues*	90.00 -	120.00
13008 *On The Wall*	90.00 -	120.00

MARGARET JOHNSON:

Okeh 8107 *E Flat Blues*	15.00 -	20.00
8162 *Absent Minded Blues*	15.00 -	20.00
8185 *Changeable Daddy Of Mine*	30.00 -	40.00
8193 *Who'll Chop Your Suey When I'm Gone?*	15.00 -	20.00
8220 *Nobody's Blues But Mine*	15.00 -	20.00
8230 *I'm A Good-Hearted Mama*	15.00 -	20.00
8405 *Mama, Papa Don't Wanna Come Back Home*	15.00 -	20.00
8418 *Heavy Burden Blues*	15.00 -	20.00
8506 *Stinging Bee Blues*	15.00 -	20.00
Victor 20178 *My Man's Done Done Me Dirty*	15.00 -	20.00
20333 *Graysom Street Blues*	15.00 -	25.00
20652 *Good Woman Blues*	15.00 -	25.00
20982 *Dead Drunk Blues*	15.00 -	25.00

MARTHA JOHNSON:

Superior 2753 *Goin' Away Blues*	40.00 -	60.00

MARY JOHNSON:

Brunswick 7081 *Western Union Blues*	50.00 -	75.00
7093 *Muddy Creek Blues*	50.00 -	75.00
7153 *Dawn Of Day Blues*	20.00 -	30.00
7160 *Death Cell Blues*	20.00 -	30.00
7175 *Morning Sun Blues*	20.00 -	30.00
Champion 16570 *Mary Johnson Blues*	35.00 -	50.00
50062 *Mary Johnson Blues*	10.00 -	15.00
Decca 7012 *Those Black Man Blues*	15.00 -	20.00
7014 *Black Gal Blues*	15.00 -	20.00
7305 *Delmar Avenue*	10.00 -	15.00
Paramount 12931 *Dream Daddy Blues*	50.00 -	75.00
12996 *Barrel House Flat Blues*	60.00 -	90.00

MERLINE JOHNSON:

Bluebird 6985 *He Roars Like A Lion*	20.00 -	30.00
7032 *My Baby Left Me*	20.00 -	30.00
7166 *Pallet On The Floor*	20.00 -	30.00

PORKCHOP JOHNSON:

Champion 15796 *Pork Chop Stomp*	50.00 -	70.00
Supertone 9516 *Pork Chop Stomp*	50.00 -	70.00

RAY JOHNSON:

Mercury 70203, 70231	5.00 -	8.00*

RED JOHNSON:

Mercury 70141, 70194	5.00 -	8.00*

ROBERT JOHNSON:

Titles, issued contemporaneously on Banner, Melotone, Oriole, Perfect, Romeo, Vocalion: *Come On In My Kitchen; Cross Road Blues; Dead Shrimp Blues; From Four Until Late; Hell Hound On My Trail; I Believe I'll Dust My Broom; I'm A Steady Rollin' Man; Kind Hearted Woman Blues; Last Fair Deal Gone Down; Malted Milk; Milkcow's Calf Blues; Ramblin' On My Mind; Stones In My Passway; Terraplane Blues; They're Red Hot; 32-20 Blues* ... 75.00 - 100.00

Vocalion 03601 *Sweet Home Chicago*	75.00 -	100.00
04002 *Honeymoon Blues*	75.00 -	100.00
04108 *Me And The Devil Blues*	75.00 -	100.00
04630 *Love In Vain*	75.00 -	100.00

ROCKHEART JOHNSON:

Victor 20-4967, 20-5136	6.00 -	10.00*

RUTH JOHNSON:

Paramount 13060 *Rockin' Chair*	20.00 -	30.00

SAM (SUITCASE) JOHNSON:

Sittin' In With 608 *Sam's Boogie*	10.00 -	15.00

SARA JOHNSON:

Banner 1882 *Papa If You Can't Do Better*	10.00 -	15.00
Domino 3852 *Papa If You Can't Do Better*	10.00 -	15.00
Regal 8196 *Papa If You Can't Do Better*	10.00 -	15.00

SHERMAN JOHNSON (& HIS CLOUDS OF JOY):

Nashboro 507 *Back Alley Boogie*	8.00 -	12.00
Trumpet, 198, 190	4.00 -	7.00*

SONNY BOY JOHNSON & HIS BLUE BLAZERS:

Murray 505 *Come And Go With Me*	10.00 -	15.00
507 *Swimming Pool Blues*	10.00 -	15.00

STOVEPIPE JOHNSON:

Vocalion 1203 *Devilish Blues*	20.00 -	30.00
1211 *I Ain't Got Nobody*	30.00 -	40.00

STUMP JOHNSON: (See also JAMES "STUMP" JOHNSON)

Bluebird 5159 *Don't Give My Lord Away*	40.00 -	60.00
5247 *Money Johnson*	40.00 -	60.00
Paramount 12862 *Kind Babe Blues*	60.00 -	90.00
12906 *Soaking Wet Blues*	60.00 -	90.00
12938 *You Buzzard You*	60.00 -	90.00
Victor 23327 *Barrel Of Whiskey Blues*	50.00 -	75.00

T.C. JOHNSON & "BLUE COAT" TOM NELSON:

Okeh 8838 *J. C. Johnson's Blues*	30.00 -	45.00

TILLIE JOHNSON:

Gennett 6438 *Chicago Man Blues*	30.00 -	40.00
6471 *My Baby*	30.00 -	40.00

TOMMY JOHNSON:

Paramunt 12950 *Alcohol And Jake Blues*	175.00 -	250.00
12975 *Slidin' Delta*	175.00 -	250.00
13000 *Black Mare Blues*	175.00 -	250.00
Victor 21279 *Big Road Blues*	150.00 -	200.00
21409 *Bye-Bye Blues*	150.00 -	200.00
38535 *Canned Heat Blues*	150.00 -	200.00

BLIND WILLIE JOHNSON:

Columbia 14276-D *Jesus Make Up My Dying Bed*	20.00 -	30.00
14303-D *Nobody's Fault But Mine*	20.00 -	30.00
14343-D *Mother's Children Have A Hard Time*	20.00 -	30.00
14391-D *Jesus Is Coming Soon*	20.00 -	30.00
14425-D *Keep Your Lamp Trimmed And Burning*	20.00 -	30.00
14490-D *Let Your Light Shine On*	20.00 -	30.00
14504-D *You'll Need Somebody On Your Bond*	20.00 -	30.00
14520-D *God Moves On The Water*	20.00 -	30.00
14530-D *John The Revelator*	30.00 -	50.00
14537-D *The Rain Don't Fall On Me*	25.00 -	40.00
14545-D *When The War Was On*	25.00 -	40.00
14556-D *Can't Nobody Hide From God*	25.00 -	40.00
14582-D *The Soul Of A Man*	25.00 -	40.00
14597-D *Go With Me To That Land*	25.00 -	40.00
14624-D *Take Your Stand*	25.00 -	40.00

JOLLY JIVERS:

Vocalion 02532 *Whatcha Gonna Do?*	40.00 -	60.00
25015 *Hungry Man's Scuffle*	40.00 -	60.00

JOLLY JUG BAND:

Varsity 6037 *Tappin' That Thing*	15.00 -	20.00

JOLLY TWO:

Vocalion 25014 *Frisco Blues*	35.00 -	50.00
25018 *Guitar Stomp*	35.00 -	50.00

ALBERTA JONES (TRIO) (AND HER RED PEPPERS):

Buddy 8024 *Sud Bustin' Blues*	30.00 -	40.00
8025 *Home Alone Blues*	30.00 -	40.00
8033 *It Must Be Hard*	30.00 -	40.00

8034 *Take Your Fingers Off It*............	30.00 -	40.00
Gennett 3144 *Home Alone Blues*............	15.00 -	20.00
3306 *Take Your Finger Off It*............	15.00 -	20.00
3403 *Lucky Number Blues*............	25.00 -	30.00
6424 *Dying Blues*..................	25.00 -	35.00
6439 *Shake A Little Bit*...............	25.00 -	35.00
6535 *My Slow and Easy Man*...........	25.00 -	35.00
6642 *Wild Geese Blues*...............	25.00 -	35.00
7252 *On Revival Day*..............	25.00 -	35.00
7274 *I Lost My Man*...............	25.00 -	35.00
Herwin 92001 *Lucky Number Blues*......	25.00 -	35.00
Silvertone 4052 *Home Alone Blues*.......	15.00 -	20.00
5025 *Lucky Number Blues*............	20.00 -	30.00
Supertone 9284 *Dying Blues*..........	25.00 -	30.00
9290 *Shake A Little Bit*.............	25.00 -	30.00

ANNA JONES:

Harmograph 859 *Trixie Blues*............	20.00 -	25.00
Paramount 12043 *You Can't Do What My Last Man Did*............	20.00 -	25.00
12052 *Trixie Blues*.................	20.00 -	25.00

BESSIE JONES:

Superior 2633 *Stop Bitin' Other Women In The Back*	35.00 -	50.00
Supertone 9474 *I Ain't Givin' Nobody None*....	25.00 -	40.00
9509 *Pig Meat Mama*.................	25.00 -	40.00

"BO" JONES:

Vocalion 1452 *Leavenworth Prison Blues*.......	50.00 -	70.00

CLINT JONES:

Columbia 14322-D *Right Or Wrong*..........	7.00 -	10.00
Okeh 8587 *Blue Valley Blues*..............	7.00 -	10.00

COLEY JONES:

Columbia 14288-D *Traveling Man*............	20.00 -	30.00
14489-D *Drunkard's Special*...............	20.00 -	30.00

CURTIS JONES:

Bluebird 7387 *Good Old Easy Street*..........	8.00 -	12.00
7452 *Schoolmate Blues*.................	8.00 -	12.00
8412, 8455..............	7.00 -	10.00
Conqueror 9030, 9031, 9032, 9077, 9161, 9196, 9273, 9279, 9358..............	7.00 -	10.00
9768, 9944, 9945, 9946.................	5.00 -	8.00
Okeh 05744, 05834, 05907, 05947, 05996, 06069, 06105, 06140, 06186, 06428, 06594, 06615..	5.00 -	8.00
Parrot 782 *Cool Playing Blues*............	7.00 -	10.00*
Vocalion 03756, 03953, 03990, 04027, 04080, 04120, 04162, 04249, 04330, 04392..........	7.00 -	10.00

EDDIE (GUITAR SLIM) JONES (& HIS PLAYBOYS):

Imperial 5134 *Bad Luck Is On Me*............	5.00 -	8.00*
Jim Bullet 603 *Feelin' Sad*..............	5.00 -	8.00*

ELIJAH JONES:

Bluebird 7526 *E. Stuff Stomp*............	20.00 -	30.00
7565 *Big Boat*..................	20.00 -	30.00
7616 *Katy Fly*..................	20.00 -	30.00
7655 *Lonesome Man*.................	20.00 -	30.00

ELSIE JONES WITH SMILIN' JOE:

Flip 1003 *Old Man's Sweetheart*.............	————

FLOYD JONES (& HIS TRIO) (WITH SNOOKY & MOODY):

Chess 1498 *Dark Road*..................	10.00 -	15.00*
1527 *Early Morning*.................	10.00 -	15.00*
J.O.B. 1001 *Big World*..............	20.00 -	30.00*
1013 *On The Road Again*.............	20.00 -	30.00
Old Swingmaster 22 *Stockyard Blues*..........	15.00 -	25.00

FRANKIE JONES:

Vocalion 04206 *My Lincoln*............	8.00 -	12.00
04266 *Jockey Blues*.................	8.00 -	12.00

REV. (GEORGE) JONES (& CONGREGATION):

Champion 15816 *The Heavenly Airplane*......	15.00 -	25.00
Gennett 6979 *The Heavenly Airplane*........	15.00 -	25.00
Supertone 9518 *The Heavenly Airplane*........	15.00 -	25.00

JAKE JONES:

Brunswick 7130 *Monkeyin' Around*...........	30.00 -	40.00

JOSEPHINE JONES:

Ajax *Just One Word Of Conclusion*...........	10.00 -	15.00

JULIA JONES:

Champion 15265 *Save My Jelly*............	15.00 -	25.00
Gennett 5177 *That Thing Called Love*........	8.00 -	12.00
5233 *Deceitful Blues*..................	8.00 -	12.00
Starr 9407 *That Thing Called Love*............	8.00 -	12.00

LITTLE HAT JONES:

Okeh 8712 *Two String Blues*............	50.00 -	70.00
8735 *Corpus Blues*.................	50.00 -	70.00
8794 *Little Hat Blues*.................	50.00 -	70.00
8815 *Kentucky Blues*.................	50.00 -	70.00
8829 *Cherry Street Blues*...............	50.00 -	70.00

MAGGIE JONES:

Black Swan 14153 *I Just Want A Daddy*.......	10.00 -	15.00
Columbia 14044-D, 14047-D, 14070-D, 14081-D, 14092-D	8.00 -	12.00
14050-D *Poor House Blues*.............	15.00 -	20.00
14055-D *Screamin' The Blues*............	15.00 -	20.00
14059-D *If I Lose, Let Me Lose*...........	15.00 -	20.00
14063-D *Anybody Here Want To Try My Cabbage?*......................	15.00 -	20.00
14074-D *Cheatin' On Me*...............	12.00 -	18.00
14102-D, 14167-D....................	12.00 -	18.00
14114-D *South Street Blues*.............	12.00 -	18.00
14127-D *I'm A Back-Bitin' Mama*...........	12.00 -	18.00
14139-D *I'm Leaving You*..............	12.00 -	18.00
14243-D *The Man I Love Is Oh So Good*....	15.00 -	20.00
Pathe-Actuelle 021062, Perfect 12075.........	5.00 -	10.00
Paramount 12099 *Goodbye Blues*...........	10.00 -	15.00
12136 *I Just Want A Daddy*.............	10.00 -	15.00

MARY JONES:

Gennett 6860 *You Lied About That Woman*...	15.00 -	20.00

ELDER OTIS JONES:

Bluebird 6466 *Repentance*.................	10.00 -	15.00
6626 *I Am The Vine*.................	10.00 -	15.00
7720 *O Lord, I'm Your Child*.............	10.00 -	15.00

SONNY JONES:

Vocalion 05056 *Dough Roller*...............	12.00 -	18.00
05124 *I'm Pretty Good At It*.............	12.00 -	18.00

WILLIE (DOC) JONES:

Peacock 1540 *Do You Want To Roll*..........	5.00 -	10.00
Vocalion 1194 *Willie's Weary Blues*...........	20.00 -	30.00

CHARLIE/CHARLEY JORDAN/JORDON:

Victor 23304 *Working Man Blues*.............	80.00 -	120.00
23372 *Greyhound Blues*...............	80.00 -	120.00
Vocalion 1511 *Big Four Blues*.............	50.00 -	75.00
1528 *Raidin' Squad Blues*.............	50.00 -	75.00
1543 *Just A Spoonful*.............	50.00 -	75.00
1551 *Running Mad Blues*.............	50.00 -	75.00
1557 *Dollar Bill Blues*.............	50.00 -	75.00
1568 *Tough Times Blues*.............	50.00 -	75.00
1611 *You Run And Tell Your Daddy*....	50.00 -	75.00
1627 *Starvation Blues*.............	50.00 -	75.00
1645 *Tight Haired Mama Blues*....	50.00 -	75.00
1657 *Hungry Blues*.............	50.00 -	75.00
1666 *Silver Dollar Blues*.............	50.00 -	75.00
1696 *Stir It Up*..................	50.00 -	75.00
1707 *Cherry Wine Woman*.............	50.00 -	75.00
1717 *Honey Sucker Blues*.............	50.00 -	75.00
02763 *Bottle Passing Blues*.............	50.00 -	75.00

JENNIE JORDAN:

Champion 15267 *Blue And All By Myself*......	20.00 -	30.00

JIMMY JORDAN:

Columbia 14622-D *Jelly Killed Old Sam*........	20.00 -	30.00
14647-D *She's Dangerous With That Thing*...	20.00 -	30.00
14655-D *There Is No Justice*.............	20.00 -	30.00

LUKE JORDAN:

Victor 20957 *Traveling Coon*.............	60.00 -	80.00

21076 *Cocaine Blues*	60.00 -	80.00
23400 *If I Call You Mama*	75.00 -	100.00
38564 *My Gal's Done Quit Me*	60.00 -	80.00

CHARLEY JORDON: (See also CHARLIE/CHARLEY JORDAN):

Decca 7015 *Rolling Moon Blues*	15.00 -	20.00
7065 *Tight Time Blues*	15.00 -	20.00
7130 *Christmas Christmas Blues*	15.00 -	20.00

JUBILEE GOSPEL TEAM:

Paramount 12835 *Dry Bones In The Valley*	10.00 -	15.00
12836 *Station Will Be Changed*	10.00 -	15.00
12837 *I Know The Lord Has Laid His Hands On Me*	10.00 -	15.00
12838 *I Have Crossed The Separating Line*	10.00 -	15.00
13113 *Jesus Is Mine*	10.00 -	15.00
QRS 7013 *Dry Bones In The Valley*	15.00 -	20.00
7014 *Station Will Be Changed*	15.00 -	20.00.
7015 *Oh Lord, Remember Me*	15.00 -	20.00
7026 *I Know The Lord Has Laid His Hands On Me*	15.00 -	20.00
7027 *I Have Crossed The Separating Line*	15.00 -	20.00
7053 *I'm 'Termined To Pray Right On*	15.00 -	20.00
7058 *When The Train Comes Along*	15.00 -	20.00

JUNIOR BLUES:

RPM 320 *Whiskey Head Woman*	10.00 -	15.00

KANSAS CITY BLUES STRUMMERS:

Vocalion 1048 *String Band Blues*	30.00 -	40.00

KANSAS CITY KITTY:

Bluebird 5726, 5756	5.00 -	8.00
Vocalion 1508 *You Got That Stuff*	15.00 -	20.00
1534 *Room Rent Blues*	15.00 -	20.00
1545 *Fish House Blues*	15.00 -	20.00
1565 *Killing Floor Blues*	15.00 -	20.00
1575 *Who's Been Here Since I Been Gone?*	15.00 -	20.00
1600 *Root Man Blues*	15.00 -	20.00
1612 *Knife Man Blues*	15.00 -	20.00
1632 *Scronchin'.*	15.00 -	20.00
1642 *That Thing's A Mess*	15.00 -	20.00

KANSAS JOE (& MEMPHIS MINNIE):

Bluebird 6260 *Something Gonna Happen To You*	15.00 -	25.00
Columbia 14439-D *When The Levee Breaks*	50.00 -	75.00
14542-D *I Want That*	50.00 -	75.00
Vocalion 1500 *What Fault You Find Of Me?*	50.00 -	75.00
1523 *Can I Do It For You?*	50.00 -	75.00
1535 *Cherry Ball Blues*	50.00 -	75.00
1550 *North Memphis Blues*	50.00 -	75.00
1570 *Botherin' That Thing*	50.00 -	75.00
1576 *She Wouldn't Give Me None*	50.00 -	75.00
1612 *Pile Drivin' Blues*	50.00 -	75.00
1631 *I Called You This Morning*	50.00 -	75.00
1643 *Preachers Blues*	50.00 -	75.00
1660 *Pickin' The Blues*	50.00 -	75.00
1668 *My Wash Women's Gone*	50.00 -	75.00
1677 *I'm Fixed For You*	50.00 -	75.00
1686 *Joliet Bound*	50.00 -	75.00
1688 *You Stole My Cake*	50.00 -	75.00
1705 *Dresser Drawer Blues*	50.00 -	75.00

KANSAS KATIE:

Bluebird 8944 *Deep Sea Diver*	8.00 -	12.00
8999 *He's My Man*	8.00 -	12.00

KEGHOUSE:

Okeh 8583 *Keghouse Blues*	30.00 -	40.00
Vocalion 1239 *Canned Heat Blues*	30.00 -	40.00

JACK KELLY (& HIS SOUTH MEMPHIS JUG BAND):

Titles, issued contemporaneously on Banner, Conqueror, Melotone, Oriole, Perfect, Romeo: *Believe I'll Go Back Home; Cold Iron Bed; Highway No. 61 Blues; Highway No. 61 Blues No. 2; Ko-Ko-Mo Blues; President Blues; Red Ripe Tomatoes; R.F.C. Blues.*

	60.00 -	80.00

Vocalion 05031 *Diamond Buyer Blues*	15.00 -	25.00
05193 *Neck Bone Blues*	15.00 -	25.00
05312 *Men Fooler Blues*	15.00 -	25.00

WILLIE KELLY:

Victor 23259 *Kelly's Special*	60.00 -	80.00
23263 *Side Door Blues*	60.00 -	80.00
23270 *Big Time Woman*	60.00 -	80.00
23286 *Don't Squeeze Me Too Tight*	60.00 -	80.00
23299 *Nasty But It's Clean*	60.00 -	80.00
23320 *Hard Luck Man Blues*	60.00 -	80.00
23416 *Sad And Lonely Day*	60.00 -	80.00
38608 *Kelly's 44 Blues*	50.00 -	75.00
38619 *32-20 Blues*	50.00 -	75.00

SAM KELLY & HIS HARMONICA:

Von 43 *Ramblin' Around Blues*	20.00 -	30.00

ROBERT KELTON & HIS TRIO:

Aladdin 3054, 3187	5.00 -	8.00

TINY KENNEDY:

Trumpet 187 *Strange Kind Of Feeling*	4.00 -	7.00*
188 *Blues Disease*	4.00 -	7.00*

KID AND COOT:

Columbia 14363-D *Keyhole Blues*	15.00 -	20.00

KID COLEY:

Bluebird 5248 *Clair And Pearley Blues*	20.00 -	30.00
Victor 23293 *Tricks Ain't Walkin' No More*	50.00 -	80.00
23369 *Freight Train Blues*	50.00 -	80.00

KID STORMY WEATHER:

Vocalion 03145 *Short Hair Blues*	30.00 -	40.00

LENA (AND SYLVESTER) KIMBROUGH:

Meritt 2201 *Cabbage Head Blues*	75.00 -	100.00

LOTTIE KIMBROUGH (AND WINSTON HOLMES):

Gennett 6607 *Wayward Girl Blues*	60.00 -	80.00
6624 *Rolling Log Blues*	60.00 -	80.00
6660 *Blue World Blues*	60.00 -	80.00

SYLVESTER KIMBROUGH:

Brunswick 7135 *Garbage Can Blues*	35.00 -	50.00

KING TUT:

Sittin' In With 542, 550	5.00 -	8.00

B.B. ("BLUES BOY")KING:

Bullett 309 *Miss Martha King*	8.00 -	12.00
315 *Got The Blues*	8.00 -	12.00
RPM 304, 311, 318, 323, 330, 339, 348, 355, 360, 363, 374, 380, 386, 391, 395, 403, 408, 411, 412, 416, 421, 425, 430	3.00 -	6.00*

JULIUS KING:

Tennessee 123 *I Want A Slice Of Your Pudding*	7.00 -	10.00

RICHARD KING & HIS ORCHESTRA:

Khoury's 800 *Ride, Daddy, Ride*	5.00 -	8.00

WEE WILLIE KIRK:

Bullet 340 *Your Love Was So Nice And Warm.*	10.00 -	15.00

(LITTLE) EDDIE KIRKLAND:

King 4659, 4680	5.00 -	8.00*
RPM 367 *That's All Right*	8.00 -	12.00*

LILLIE MAE KIRKMAN:

Vocalion 04951 *Hop Head Blues*	8.00 -	12.00
04991 *When You Leave Me Honey*	8.00 -	12.00

JESSIE KNIGHT:

Checker 797 *Nothing But Money*	4.00 -	7.00*

BIG BOY KNOX:

Bluebird 6904 *Texas Blues*	20.00 -	30.00
6952 *Blue Man Blues*	20.00 -	30.00

CHARLIE KYLE:

Victor 21707 *Kyle's Worried Blues*	50.00 -	75.00
38625 *Walking Blues*	50.00 -	75.00

RUBE LACY:

Paramount 12629 *Mississippi Jail House Groan*	80.00 -	120.00

RUTH LADSON & THREE SHADOWS:

Okeh 06667 *Kicking My Man Around*	7.00 -	10.00

JUSTINE LAMAR:

Decca 7238 *Always Mine*	5.00 -	8.00

ERNEST LANE:
Blues & Rhythm 700 *What's Wrong Baby* ..... 8.00 - 12.00
WILLIE LANE:
Talent 805 *Prowlin' Ground Hog* .... 30.00 - 40.00
  806 *Black Cat Rag* .... 30.00 - 40.00
SOPHISTICATED JIMMY LA RUE:
Champion 50070 *Money Truckin' Blues* .... 8.00 - 12.00
  50071 *Two Old Maids In A Folding Bed Blues* 10.00 - 15.00
LOUIS LASKY:
Vocalion 02955 *Teasin' Brown Blues* .... 20.00 - 30.00
LAUGHING CHARLEY:
Columbia 14272-D *Chain Gang Trouble* .... 25.00 - 35.00
LAZY BILL & HIS BLUE RHYTHMS:
Chance 1148 *I Had A Dream* .... 10.00 - 15.00*
LAZY SLIM JIM:
Savoy 868 *Sugaree* .... 5.00 - 8.00
(HUDDIE) LEADBELLY:
Titles, issued contemporaneously on Banner, Melotone, Oriole, Perfect, Romeo: *Becky Deem, She Was A Gamblin' Gal; Four Day Worry Blues; Honey, I'm All Out And Down; New Black Snake Moan; Packin' Trunk Blues; Pig Meat Papa* .. 25.00 - 40.00
Bluebird 8550 *Sail On, Little Girl, Sail On* ...... 8.00 - 12.00
  8559 *T.B. Blues* .... 8.00 - 12.00
  8570 *Easy Rider* .... 8.00 - 12.00
  8709 *Roberta* .... 8.00 - 12.00
  8750 *New York City* .... 8.00 - 12.00
  8791 *Leaving Blues* .... 8.00 - 12.00
HUDDIE LEDBETTER WITH THE GOLDEN GATE QUARTET:
Victor 27266, 27267, 27268 .... 3.00 - 6.00
BERTHA LEE:
Vocalion 02650 *Mind Reader Blues* .... 75.00 - 100.00
BESSIE LEE:
Silvertone 3525 *He Likes It Slow* .... 20.00 - 30.00
  3534 *Sorrowful Blues* .... 20.00 - 30.00
CAROLINE LEE:
Oriole 353 *Thunderstorm Blues* .... 10.00 - 15.00
ELIZA CHRISTMAS LEE:
Gennett 4801 *Arkansas Blues* .... 7.00 - 10.00
EMMA DELL LEE & TRIO:
Khoury's 900 *No Good Daddy* .... 5.00 - 8.00
JERRY LEE:
Herwin 93011 *The Snitches Blues* .... 35.00 - 50.00
  93014 *Smiling Blues* .... 50.00 - 75.00
JOHN LEE:
Federal 12054 *Down At The Depot* .... 7.00 - 10.00*
  12089 *Blind's Blues* .... 7.00 - 10.00*
Gotham 515 *Mean Old Train* .... 7.00 - 10.00
J.O.B. 114 *Rhythm Rockin' Boogie* .... 15.00 - 20.00
JOHNNY LEE:
DeLuxe 6009 *I Came To See You Baby* .... 5.00 - 8.00
MAE BELLE LEE & GEORGE RAMSEY:
Paramount 13069 *Bumble Bee No. 2* .... 30.00 - 40.00
RUSSELL LEE & DAISY WRIGHT:
Okeh 8263 *Vampire Brown* .... 5.00 - 8.00
TOMMY LEE:
Delta 403 *Highway 80 Blues* .... 7.00 - 10.00*
VERDI LEE (& CHARLEY JORDAN):
Decca 7130 *Christmas Tree Blues* .... 15.00 - 20.00
  7142 *Get It If You Can* .... 15.00 - 20.00
J.B. LENOIR/LENORE (& HIS BAYOU BOYS/COMBO):
Chess 1449 *My Baby Told Me* .... 8.00 - 12.00*
  1463 *Deep In Debt Blues* .... 8.00 - 12.00*
J.O.B. 112 *Let's Roll* .... 10.00 - 15.00*
  1008 *The Mountain* .... 5.00 - 10.00*
  1012 *The Mojo* .... 5.00 - 10.00*
  1016 *I'll Die Trying* .... 5.00 - 10.00
  1102 *Play A Little While* .... 5.00 - 10.00*
Parrot 802 *Eisenhower Blues/I'm In Korea* ..... 7.00 - 15.00*

  802 *Tax Paying Blues/I'm In Korea* .... 7.00 - 10.00*
  809 *Mama Talk To Your Daughter* .... 4.00 - 7.00*
  814 *What Have I Done* .... 4.00 - 7.00*
  821 *I Lost My Baby* .... 4.00 - 7.00*
LEROY'S BUDDY:
Decca 7179, 7180, 7194, 7202, 7223, 7233, 7246, 7258, 7271, 7298, 7308, 7335, 7356, 7374, 7394 6.00 - 10.00
Decca (higher numbers) .... 5.00 - 8.00
LEVEE JOE:
Conqueror 8658 *Flood Water Blues* .... 8.00 - 12.00
LEWIS BRONZEVILLE FIVE:
Bluebird 8433 *Cotton Blossom Blues* .... 10.00 - 15.00
  8445 *Natchez Mississippi Blues* .... 10.00 - 15.00
  8460 *Low Dow Gal Blues* .... 10.00 - 15.00
  8480 *It Can Happen To You* .... 10.00 - 15.00
Montgomery Ward 8898 *Laughing At Life* ..... 10.00 - 15.00
  8899 *Linda Brown* .... 10.00 - 15.00
  8900 *Mississippi Fire Blues* .... 10.00 - 15.00
  8901 *Oh! Mabel Oh!* .... 10.00 - 15.00
ARCHIE LEWIS:
Champion 16677 *Miss Handy Hanks* .... 30.00 - 40.00
BUDDY LEWIS:
Swing Time 312 *You've Got Good Business* .... 10.00 - 15.00*
ERNEST LEWIS:
Parrot 791 *West Coast Blues* .... 7.00 - 10.00*
FURRY LEWIS:
Victor 21664 *Kassie Jones* .... 75.00 - 100.00
  23345 *Cannon Ball Blues* .... 80.00 - 120.00
  38506 *Judge Harsh Blues* .... 60.00 - 80.00
  38519 *Mistreatin' Mama* .... 60.00 - 80.00
Vocalion 1111 *Rock Island Blues* .... 75.00 - 100.00
  1115 *Mr. Furry's Blues* .... 75.00 - 100.00
  1116 *Sweet Papa Moan* .... 75.00 - 100.00
  1132 *Good Looking Girl Blues* .... 75.00 - 100.00
  1133 *Big Chief Blues* .... 75.00 - 100.00
  1134 *Mean Old Bedbug Blues* .... 75.00 - 100.00
  1474 *John Henry* .... 75.00 - 100.00
  1547 *Creeper's Blues* .... 75.00 - 100.00
IDA LEWIS:
Silvertone 3556 *Tennessee Blues* .... 35.00 - 50.00
JOHNNY LEWIS ORCHESTRA:
Rockin' 517 *She's Taking All My Money* .... 20.00 - 30.00*
KATE LEWIS:
Broadway 5016 *Mercy Blues* .... 30.00 - 40.00
PETE (GUITAR) LEWIS:
Federal 12066, 12076, 12103, 12112 .... 4.00 - 7.00*
RAY LEWIS:
Imperial .... 3.00 - 5.00*
SAMMY LEWIS:
Sun 218 *I Feel So Worried* .... 15.00 - 20.00*
PAPA LIGHTFOOT:
Aladdin 3171 *P.L. Blues* .... 7.00 - 10.00*
  3304 *Jumpin' With Jarvis* .... 7.00 - 10.00*
Imperial 5289 *Mean Old Train* .... 10.00 - 15.00*
PRESTON LILLARD:
Champion 15416 *Barrel House Blues* .... 100.00 - 150.00
  15436 *The Jockey Blues* .... 60.00 - 80.00
LILLIE MAE:
Columbia 14600-D *Buggy Jail House Blues* ..... 20.00 - 30.00
Okeh 8920 *Mama Don't Want It* .... 20.00 - 30.00
CHARLEY/CHARLIE LINCOLN:
Columbia 14305-D *Jealous Hearted Blues* ...... 25.00 - 35.00
  14332-D *Ugly Papa* .... 25.00 - 35.00
  14420-D *Gamblin' Charley* .... 25.00 - 35.00
  14475-D *Country Breakdown* .... 25.00 - 35.00
  14550-D *Mama Don't Rush Me* .... 25.00 - 35.00
JOE LINTHECOME:
Gennett 7131 *Humming Blues* .... 20.00 - 30.00
VIRGINIA LISTON:
Okeh 8092 *Bed Time Blues* .... 8.00 - 12.00
  8115 *Sally Long Blues* .... 8.00 - 12.00

8122 *Shreveport Blues*	8.00 -	12.00
8126 *You Can Have It*	8.00 -	12.00
8134 *House Rent Stomp*	8.00 -	12.00
8138 *I Don't Love Nobody*	15.00 -	20.00
8151 *Don't Agitate Me Blues*	8.00 -	12.00
8160 *Mississippi Blues*	8.00 -	12.00
8173 *You've Got The Right Key, But The Wrong Keyhole*	30.00 -	40.00
8175 *Weeping Willow Blues*	10.00 -	15.00
8187 *Early In The Morning*	30.00 -	40.00
8196 *Night Latch Key Blues*	10.00 -	15.00
8218 *You Can Dip Your Bread In My Gravy, But You Can't Have None Of My Chops*	10.00 -	15.00
8223 *Black Sheep Blues*	10.00 -	15.00
8234 *I'm Sick Of Fattening Frogs For Snakes*	10.00 -	15.00
8247 *Make Me A Pallet*	20.00 -	30.00
Vocalion 1031 *Titanic Blues*	25.00 -	35.00
1032 *Rolls-Royce Papa*	25.00 -	35.00

LITTLE BILL:

Bluebird 6972 *You Can't Love Me And Someone Else Too*	10.00 -	15.00

LITTLE BROTHER:

Bluebird 6658 *Chinese Man Blues*	20.00 -	30.00
6697 *Louisiana Blues — Part 2*	20.00 -	30.00
6733 *Crescent City Blues*	20.00 -	30.00
6766 *Tantalizing Blues*	20.00 -	30.00
6811 *Santa Fe Blues*	20.00 -	30.00
6825 *Never Go Wrong Blues*	20.00 -	30.00
6894 *Farish Street Jive*	20.00 -	30.00
6916 *Out West Blues*	20.00 -	30.00
7178 *West Texas Blues*	20.00 -	30.00
7277 *Sorrowful Blues*	20.0 -	30.00
7806 *Misled Blues*	20.00 -	30.00
10177 *Farish Street Jive*	10.00 -	15.00
10953 *Crescent City Blues*	10.00 -	15.00
Montgomery Ward 7111 *Louisiana Blues*	15.00 -	20.00
7112 *Tantalizing Blues*	15.00 -	20.00

LITTLE DAVID:

Decca 7211 *Standing By A Lamp Post*	15.00 -	25.00
7270 *Ramblin' Mind Blues*	15.00 -	25.00
Regal 3271 *Shackles 'Round My Body*	15.00 -	20.00
RPM 371 *Crying Blues*	5.00 -	8.00*

LITTLE HUDSON & HIS RED DEVIL TRIO:

J.O.B. 1015 *Rough Treatment*	20.00 -	30.00*

LITTLE JIMMY:

Acorn 301 *Rock That Boogie*	———	

LITTLE JOHNNY:

Aristocrat 405 *Shelby County Blues*	75.00 -	100.00

LITTLE JUNIOR'S BLUE FLAMES:

Sun 187, 192	6.00 -	10.00*

LITTLE MILTON:

Delta 403 *Little Milton's Boogie*	10.00 -	15.00
Sun 194 *Beggin' My Baby*	5.00 -	8.00*
209 *Alone And Blue*	10.00 -	15.00*
220 *Looking For My Baby*	8.00 -	12.00*

LITTLE MR. MIDNIGHT:

Regal 3287 *Four O'Clock Blues*	———	

LITTLE PAPA JOE:

Blue Lake 116 *Looking For My Baby*	15.00 -	20.00*

LITTLE SISTER:

Varsity 6050 *My Back To The Wall*	10.00 -	15.00

LITTLE SON JOE:

Okeh 06707 *Black Rat Swing*	4.00 -	7.00
Vocalion 04707 *Diggin' My Potatoes*	10.00 -	15.00
04776 *A.B.C. Blues*	10.00 -	15.00
04978 *My Black Buffalo*	10.00 -	15.00
05004 *Key To The World*	10.00 -	15.00

LITTLE T-BONE:

Miltone 5223 *Christmas Blues*	8.00 -	12.00

LITTLE WALTER (TRIO) (& HIS JUKES/NIGHT CAPS):

Chance 1116 *I Just Keep Loving Her*	10.00 -	15.00
Checker 758 *Juke*	7.00 -	10.00*
764 *Mean Old World*	7.00 -	10.00*
767 *Tonight With A Fool*	5.00 -	8.00*
770 *Off The Wall*	5.00 -	8.00*
Checker 780, 786, 793, 799, 805, 811, 817, 825.	4.00 -	7.00*
833, 838, 845, 852, 859, 867, 890	3.00 -	5.00
Ora Nelle 711 *Ora Nelle Blues*	30.00 -	50.00
Regal 3296 *Muskadine Blues*	50.00 -	75.00

LITTLE WILLIE LITTLEFIELD:

Eddie's 1202 *Little Willie's Boogie*	7.00 -	10.00
1205 *Chicago Bound*	7.00 -	10.00
1212 *Boogie Woogie Playgirl*	7.00 -	10.00
Freedom 1502 *Littlefield Boogie*	5.00 -	8.00
Modern	3.00 -	5.00*

JESSE LOCKETT & HIS ORCHESTRA:

Gulf 3000 *Blacker The Berry*	10.00 -	15.00

JAMES (BLAZER BOY) LOCKS:

Regal 3231 *Blazer Boy Blues*	10.00 -	15.00

ROBERT LOCKWOOD:

Bluebird 8820 *Take A Little Walk With Me*	15.00 -	25.00
8877 *Black Spider Blues*	15.00 -	25.00

ROBERT LOCKWOOD, JR./ROBERT JR. LOCKWOOD:

J.O.B. 1107 *Sweet Woman From Maine*	15.00 -	25.00*
Mercury 8260 *Dust My Broom*	7.00 -	10.00

CRIPPLE CLARENCE LOFTON:

Titles, issued contemporaneously on Banner, Conqueror, Melotone, Oriole, Perfect: *Brown Skin Girls; You Done Tore Your Playhouse Down*	20.00 -	35.00
Solo Art 12003 *Streamline Train*	15.00 -	25.00
12009 *Pine Top's Boogie Woogie*	15.00 -	25.00
Vocalion 02951 *Monkey Man Blues*	25.00 -	35.00

POOR BOY LOFTON:

Decca 7010 *Poor Boy Blues*	50.00 -	75.00
7049 *Rainy Day Blues*	50.00 -	75.00
7076 *Jake Leg Blues*	50.00 -	75.00

WILLIE LOFTON TRIO:

Bluebird 6229 *Beer Garden Blues*	40.00 -	60.00

RAY LOGAN:

Paramount 12310 *Lost John Blues*	50.00 -	75.00

CLARENCE LONDON:

Fidelity 3009 *One Rainy Morning*	7.00 -	10.00

JOHNNY LONDON:

Sun 175 *Flat Tire*	75.00 -	100.00*

LOTTIE AND WINSTON:

Superior 2717 *Wayward Girl Blues*	40.00 -	60.00

JOE HILL LOUIS:

Checker 763 *Dorothy May*	10.00 -	15.00*
Columbia 30182, 30221	7.00 -	10.00
Modern 795, 813, 822, 828, 839, 856	6.00 -	10.00
Sun 178 *We All Gotta Go Sometime*	60.00 -	90.00*

LESLIE LOUIS:

Rockin' 509 *Ridin' Home*	25.00 -	35.00*

LOUISIANA JOHNNY:

Vocalion 02980 *Policy Blues*	15.00 -	20.00
03497 *Whiskey Head Woman*	15.00 -	20.00

HOT SHOT LOVE:

Sun 196 *Wolf Call Boogie*	25.00 -	40.00*

WILLIE LOVE & HIS THREE ACES; WILLIE LOVE'S THREE ACES:

Trumpet 137 *Take It Easy Baby*	5.00 -	8.00
147 *My Own Boogie*	5.00 -	8.00
172, 173, 174, 175, 209	3.00 -	6.00*

LOVIN' SAM (FROM DOWN IN 'BAM); LOVIN' SAM & BURNS CAMPBELL ORCHESTRA/HIS SWING RASCALS:

Bluebird 7514, 7629, 7916	5.00 -	8.00
Brunswick 7073 *She's Givin' It Away*	15.00 -	20.00
7075 *What You Gonna Do?*	15.00 -	20.00
7090 *Get Your Mind On It*	15.00 -	20.00

7094 *I Ain't No Ice Man*...............	15.00 -	20.00
7098 *You Rascal You*.................	15.00 -	20.00
7117 *Huggin' And Kissin' Gwine On*.......	15.00 -	20.00
7131 *Get It In Front*................	15.00 -	20.00
7167 *You Rascal You—No. 2*............	15.00 -	20.00
7183 *Ugly Child*..................	15.00 -	20.00
7198 *Three Sixes*.................	15.00 -	20.00
7218 *That New Kinda Stuff*............	15.00 -	20.00
Vocalion 03686 *Spo-Dee-O-Dee*...........	7.00 -	10.00

FLORENCE LOWERY:

Vocalion 1106 *Poor Girl Blues*..........	20.00 -	30.00
1107 *Thirty Day Blues*.............	20.00 -	30.00

JANE LUCAS (& GEORGIA TOM):

Champion 16215 *Fix It*..............	30.00 -	50.00
Vocalion 03314 *I Can't Last Long*.........	15.00 -	20.00
03346 *Mr. Freddie Blues*...........	15.00 -	20.00

LONNIE LYONS (COMBO); LONNIE LYONS, HIS PIANO & ORCHESTRA:

Freedom 1504, 1507, 1512, 1519, 1523.....	5.00 -	8.00
Sittin' In With 566 *I Need Romance*.........	5.00 -	8.00

SMILING SMOKEY LYNN:

Peacock 1555, 1579.......................	5.00 -	8.00

ALURA MACK:

Gennett 6767 *Old Fashioned Blues*..........	25.00 -	40.00
6797 *My Kitchen Man*...............	25.00 -	40.00
6813 *West End Blues*..............	25.00 -	40.00
6876 *Loose Like That*..............	25.00 -	40.00
6890 *Beef Blood Blues*.............	25.00 -	40.00
6964 *The Long Lost Blues*...........	25.00 -	40.00
7273 *Monkey Blues*................	25.00 -	40.00
7295 *Everybody's Man Is Mine*..........	25.00 -	40.00

BILLY AND MARY MACK:

Okeh 8195 *My Heart-Breakin' Gal*..........	15.00 -	20.00
8274 *Fetch It When You Come*...........	10.00 -	15.00
8296 *You Don't Want Much*............	10.00 -	15.00
8339 *Oh! Me Oh! My Blues*...........	25.00 -	40.00

IDA MAY MACK:

Victor 21690 *Mr. Moore Blues*............	30.00 -	40.00
38030 *Elm Street Blues*.............	30.00 -	40.00
38532 *Wrong Doin' Daddy*.............	30.00 -	40.00

MARY MACK:

Vocalion 03462 *You Drink Too Much*........	7.00 -	10.00

RED MACK:

Atlas 117 *Black Man's Blues*..............	———	

MACON ED (AND TAMPA JOE):

Okeh 8676 *Worrying Blues*..............	25.00 -	40.00
8855 *Try That Thing*...............	25.00 -	40.00
8877 *Tickle Britches*..............	25.00 -	40.00
8896 *Mean Florida Blues*............	25.00 -	40.00

SIDNEY MAIDEN:

Imperial 5189 *Honey Bee Blues*............	7.00 -	10.00

HELENA MANLEY:

Okeh 8111 *Loving Blues*................	7.00 -	10.00

LEOLA MANNING:

Vocalion 1446 *He Fans Me*..............	20.00 -	30.00
1492 *The Arcade Building Moan*.........	20.00 -	30.00
1529 *Laying In The Graveyard*............	20.00 -	30.00

MARTIN AND ROBERT:

Brunswick 7007 *Dollar Blues*............	20.00 -	30.00
Vocalion 1127 *South Street Blues*..........	20.00 -	30.00

ARETHA MARTIN:

Champion 15340 *Lost Man Blues*..........	40.00 -	60.00
15360 *Tea-Rollin' Blues*............	40.00 -	60.0
Silvertone 5129 *Lost Man Blues*..........	40.00 -	60.00

CARL MARTIN:

Bluebird 5745 *Kid Man Blues*............	30.00 -	40.00
6139 *Old Time Blues*..............	30.00 -	40.00
Champion 50074 *High Water Flood Blues*......	15.00 -	25.00
Decca 7114 *Let's Have A New Deal*.........	15.00 -	25.00
Okeh 8961 *Badly Mistreated Man*.........	40.00 -	60.00
Vocalion 03003 *Badly Mistreated Man*.......	20.00 -	30.00

03047 *Good Morning, Judge*..............	20.00 -	30.00
03496 *That New Kind Of Stuff*...........	15.00 -	20.00

DAISY MARTIN:

Banner 1262 *Feelin' Blue*..............	5.00 -	8.00
Gennett 4712 *Spread Yo' Stuff*.............	7.00 -	10.00
Okeh 8001 *I Won't Be Back 'Til You Change Your Ways*...................	5.00 -	8.00
8008 *Everybody's Man Is My Man*..........	5.00 -	8.00
8009 *I Didn't Start In To Love You*........	5.00 -	8.00
8010 *Sweet Daddy*.............	5.00 -	8.00
8013 *Nightmare Blues*.............	5.00 -	8.00
8027 *If You Don't Want Me Please Don't Dog Me 'Round*......................	5.00 -	8.00
Regal 9548 *Feelin' Blue*..............	5.00 -	8.00

DOLLY MARTIN:

Decca 7080 *All Men Blues*..............	20.00 -	30.00

BLIND GEORGE MARTIN:

Broadway 5040 *Worried Blues*............	25.00 -	40.00
5053 *Southern Rag*.................	25.00 -	40.00
5080 *Hookworm Blues*.............	35.00 -	50.00
5084 *Goodbye Mama Moan*...........	50.00 -	75.00

OLLIS MARTIN:

Gennett 6306 *Police And High Sheriff Come Ridin' Down*.....................	150.00 -	250.00

SARA MARTIN:

Okeh 4904, 8041, 8058, 8060, 8062, 8063, 8065, 8078, 8083, 8084, 8085, 8086, 8087, 8088, 8093, 8097, 8104, 8117, 8136, 8146, 8161, 8172, 8191, 8214, 8226, 8237, 8249, 8303, 8354........	5.00 -	10.00
8043 *'Tain't Nobody's Biz-ness If I Do*......	10.00 -	15.00
8045 *Last Go Round Blues*...........	10.00 -	15.00
8061 *Come Home Papa Blues*..........	10.00 -	15.00
8064 *Laughin' Cryin' Blues*..........	10.00 -	15.00
8067 *Yodeling Blues*.............	10.00 -	15.00
8082 *Hesitation Blues*.............	10.00 -	15.00
8090 *Blind Man Blues*.............	10.00 -	15.00
8099 *Graveyard Dream Blues*..........	15.00 -	25.00
8108 *Squabbling Blues*.............	10.00 -	15.00
8154 *He's Never Gonna Throw Me Down*....	10.00 -	15.00
8166 *Jug Band Blues*..............	20.00 -	30.00
8176 *I Got The Crying Blues*..........	20.00 -	30.00
8211 *I Ain't Got No Man*............	20.00 -	30.00
8203 *Things Done Got Too Much*.........	15.00 -	20.00
8262 *Alabamy Bound*.............	15.00 -	20.00
8270 *I'm Gonna Hoodoo You*..........	15.00 -	20.00
8283 *Down At The Razor Ball*..........	15.00 -	20.00
8292 *Forget Me Not Blues*...........	15.00 -	20.00
8304 *Give Me Just a Little Of Your Time*....	10.00 -	15.00
8325 *Careless Man Blues*............	15.00 -	20.00
8336 *What's The Matter Now?*...........	15.00 -	20.00
8374 *Some Sweet Day*.............	15.00 -	20.00
8394 *Look Out, Mr. Jazz*...........	10.00 -	15.00
8412 *Shipwrecked Blues*............	10.00 -	15.00
8427 *Georgia Stockade Blues*..........	15.00 -	20.00
8442 *The Prisoner's Blues*...........	15.00 -	20.00
8461 *Cushion Foot Stomp*...........	15.00 -	20.00
8513 *Orn'ry Blues*.............	10.00 -	15.00
Paramount 12841 *Death Sting Me Blues*......	75.00 -	100.00
QRS 7035 *Hole In The Wall*.............	75.00 -	100.00
7042 *Death Sting Me Blues*...........	75.00 -	100.00
7043 *Kitchen Man Blues*............	75.00 -	100.00

MARY AND MACK:

Bluebird 6894 *You Gotta Quit Your Low Down Ways*.........................	20.00 -	30.00
7908 *Black*.................	30.00 -	40.00

THE MASKED MARVEL:

Paramount 12805 *Mississippi Bo Weavil Blues*...	100.00 -	150.00

MINNIE MATHES:

Vocalion 04431 *Ball Game Blues*............	5.00 -	8.00

EMMETT MATHEWS:

Paramount 13087 *Upside Down*............	30.00 -	40.00

LENA MATLOCK:

Champion 16170 *Stop Bitin' Other Women In The Back* .... 30.00 - 40.00

MAE MATTHEWS:

Gennett 6438 *Dirty Woman Blues* .... 30.00 - 40.00
6439 *Satisfied Blues* .... 30.00 - 40.00

CLAUDE MAXWELL:

Sterling 3006 *Bad Woman Blues* .... 7.00 - 10.00

HANNAH MAY (& THE STATE STREET FOUR):

Titles, issued contemporaneously on Banner, Oriole, Perfect, Romeo: *Pussy Cat Blues; What You Call That?* .... 12.00 - 15.00
Vocalion 03313 *Kansas City Hill* .... 8.00 - 12.00

TINY MAYBERRY:

Decca 7496 *Oh That Nasty Man* .... 6.00 - 10.00
7520 *Mayberry Blues* .... 6.00 - 10.00
7593 *Mailman Blues* .... 6.00 - 10.00

ETHEL MAYES:

Harmograph 781 *Sugar Blues* .... 12.00 - 15.00
842 *Goin' Down To The Levee* .... 15.00 - 25.00
2544 *Gulf Coast Blues* .... 15.00 - 20.00

BERT (M.) MAYS:

Paramount 12614 *Mama's Man Blues* .... 50.00 - 70.00
12632 *Midnight Rambler's Blues* .... 50.00 - 70.00
Vocalion 1223 *Michigan River Blues* ...... 30.00 - 40.00

PALMER McABEE:

Victor 21352 *McAbee's Railroad Piece* ..... 15.00 - 20.00

CONNIE McBOOKER:

Eddie's 1928 *Short Baby Boogie* .... 10.00 - 15.00

ARTHUR McCLAIN (AND JOE EVANS):

Titles, issued contemporaneously on Banner, Oriole, Perfect, Romeo: *Cream And Sugar Blues; Old Hen Cackle* .... 25.00 - 40.00

ERNEST McCLAY & HIS TRIO:

Murray 506 *Big Timing Woman* .... 15.00 - 20.00

TOMMY McCLENNAN:

Bluebird 8347 *You Can Mistreat Me Here* ..... 10.00 - 15.00
8373 *Bottle It Up And Go* .... 7.00 - 10.00
8408 *Cotton Patch Blues* .... 10.00 - 15.00
8444 *Brown Skin Girl* .... 10.00 - 15.00
8499 *New Highway No. 51* .... 10.00 - 15.00
8545 *My Baby's Doggin' Me* .... 10.00 - 15.00
8605 *My Little Girl* .... 10.00 - 15.00
8669 *My Baby's Gone* .... 10.00 - 15.00
8689 *Katy Mae Blues* .... 10.00 - 15.00
8704, 8725, 8853, 8897, 8957, 9005, 9015, 9037, 34-0706, 34-0716 .... 7.00 - 12.00

LILI McCLINTOCK:

Columbia 14575-D *Furniture Man* .... 20.00 - 30.00
14602-D *Sow Good Seeds* .... 20.00 - 30.00

MATTHEW McCLURE:

Champion 16514 *True Love Blues* .... 30.00 - 40.00

McCOY AND JOHNSON:

Bluebird 5385 *I Never Told A Lie* .... 30.00 - 40.00
Victor 23313 *I Never Told A Lie* .... 60.00 - 80.00
23352 *Georgia Skin* .... 60.00 - 80.00

("PAPA") CHARLES/CHARLIE McCOY (AND BO CARTER/WITH CHATMAN'S MISSISSIPPI HOT FOOTERS):

Brunswick 7118 *It Ain't No Good* .... 20.00 - 30.00
7141 *Last Time Blues* .... 40.00 - 60.00
7156 *Your Valves Need Grinding* .... 40.00 - 60.00
7165 *Glad Hand Blues* .... 40.00 - 60.00
Okeh 8853 *Mississippi I'm Longing For You* ... 75.00 - 100.00
8863 *It Is So Good—Part 1* .... 75.00 - 100.00
8873 *You Gonna Need Me* .... 75.00 - 100.00
8881 *It Is So Good—Part 2* .... 75.00 - 100.00
Vocalion 1683 *Boogie Woogie* .... 60.00 - 80.00
1712 *Too Long* .... 60.00 - 80.00
1726 *Bottle It Up* .... 60.00 - 80.00

ROBERT/LEE McCOY:

Bluebird 6995 *Prowling Night Hawk* .... 15.00 - 25.00
7045 *Lonesome World* .... 15.00 - 25.00
7090 *G-Man* .... 15.00 - 25.00
7115 *Tough Luck* .... 15.00 - 25.00
7303 *Mean Black Cat* .... 15.00 - 25.00
7386 *Take It Easy, Baby* .... 15.00 - 25.00
7416 *My Friend Has Forsaken Me* .... 15.00 - 25.00
7440 *C N A* .... 15.00 - 25.00

VIOLA/VOLET McCOY:

Ajax 17010 *Lonesome Daddy Blues* .... 15.00 - 20.00
17069 *Keep On Going* .... 15.00 - 20.00
Banner 1357, 1371, 1394 .... 6.00 - 10.00
Brunswick 2591 *If Your Good Man Quits You* .. 6.00 - 10.00
Cameo 1066, 1097, 1144, 1189, 1225 .... 6.00 - 10.00
Columbia 14395-D *I Want A Good Man* .... 10.00 - 15.00
Edison 51478 *Memphis Bound* .... 40.00 - 50.00
Gennett 5108, 5128, 5162, 5175 .... 7.00 - 10.00
5151 *Gulf Coast Blues* .... 10.00 - 15.00
Regal 9653, 9667, 9690 .... 6.00 - 10.00
Vocalion 1002 *South Street Blues* .... 10.00 - 15.00
14632, 14633, 14653, 14689, 14801, 14818 ... 6.00 - 10.00
14912 *Keep On Going* .... 10.00 - 15.00
15245 *Stomp Your Blues Away* .... 20.00 - 30.00
15268 *South Street Blues* .... 10.00 - 15.00

WILLIAM McCOY:

Columbia 14302-D *Mama Blues* .... 12.00 - 18.00
14393-D *How Long Baby* .... 20.00 - 30.00
14453-D *Central Tracks Blues* .... 20.00 - 30.00
15269-D *Mama Blues* .... 12.00 - 18.00

JIMMY McCRACKLIN (& HIS BLUES BLASTERS/ORCHESTRA):

Aladdin 3089 *Bad Luck And Trouble* .... 5.00 - 8.00
Cava-Tone 251 *Jimmy's Blues* .... 7.00 - 10.00
Courtney 123 *You Had Your Chance* .... 7.00 - 10.00
Down Town 2023 *Bad Condition Blues* .... 8.00 - 12.00
2027 *Low Down Mood* .... 8.00 - 12.00
Excelsior 182 *You Deceived Me* .... 7.00 - 10.00
Globe 102 *Miss Mattie Left Me* .... 5.00 - 8.00
104 *Highway 101* .... 5.00 - 8.00
109 *Street Loafin' Woman* .... 5.00 - 8.00
J & M Fullbright 123 *Special For You* ..... 8.00 - 12.00
124 *Rock And Rye* .... 8.00 - 12.00
Modern 722, 728, 741, 762, 806 .... 4.00 - 7.00
Old Swingmaster 24, 25 .... 5.00 - 8.00
Peacock 1605, 1615, 1639 .... 4.00 - 7.00 *
RPM 317 *Your Heart Ain't Right* .... 5.00 - 8.00
Swing Time 260, 264, 270, 285, 286, 291 ... 4.00 - 7.00
Trilon 197 *Rock And Rye* .... 6.00 - 10.00
231 *Big Foot Mama* .... 6.00 - 10.00
244, 245 .... 4.00 - 7.00

JAMES McCRAVY:

Columbia 14641-D *Shove It Up It There* .... 12.00 - 15.00

ROBERT McCULLUM:

Aristocrat 413 *Jackson Town Woman* .... 15.00 - 20.00

HATTIE McDANIEL(S):

Merritt 2202 *Brown-Skin Baby Doll* .... 75.00 - 100.00
Okeh 8434 *Boo Hoo Blues* .... 60.00 - 90.00
8569 *I Thought I'd Do It* .... 15.00 - 20.00
Paramount 12751 *Dentist Chair Blues* ...... 30.00 - 40.00
12790 *That New Love Maker Of Mine* .... 30.00 - 40.00

WILLARD McDANIEL:

Specialty 415, 424 .... 4.00 - 7.00

KATHERINE McDAVID:

Okeh 8295 *Underground Blues* .... 10.00 - 15.00

HELEN McDONALD:

Gennett 5193 *Squawkin' My Blues* .... 10.00 - 15.00

TEE McDONALD:

Decca 7018 *Beef Man Blues* .... 15.00 - 20.00

TECUMSEH McDOWELL:

Bluebird 5286 *My Man Blues* .... 40.00 - 60.00
Sunrise 3367 *So-Called Friend* .... 40.00 - 60.00

BLACK PATCH McFADDEN:

Paramount 13021 *Whiskey Head Man*........ 80.00 - 100.00

CHARLES/CHARLIE McFADDEN; "SPECKS"
CHARLIE McFADDEN:

Bluebird 5160 *Piggly Wiggly Blues*......... 30.00 - 40.00
  5203 *Times Are So Tight*................. 30.00 - 40.00
  5325 *Last Journey Blues*................. 30.00 - 40.00
  5384 *Lonesome Ghost Blues*............. 30.00 - 40.00
Decca 7317 *People, People*.............. 8.00 - 12.00
Okeh 8894 *Don't Bite That Thing*......... 35.00 - 50.00
Paramount 12928 *Groceries On The Shelf*...... 75.00 - 100.00
  13076 *Groceries On The Shelf No. 2*.. 75.00 - 100.00
Sunrise 3241 *People, People*........... 30.00 - 40.00
  3284 *Friendless Man*................ 30.00 - 40.00
  3406 *Low Down Rounders Blues*..... 30.00 - 40.00
Victor 23420 *Lonesome Ghost Blues*.... 50.00 - 75.00

BUCK MacFARLAND:

Paramount 12982 *St. Louis Fire Blues*..... 50.00 - 75.00

BROWNIE McGHEE (& SONNY TERRY/&
HIS JOOK BLOCK BUSTERS):

Alert 400, 401, 402, 403, 404, 405, 406, 407, 408,
  409, 410, 411, 412, 413, 420............. 5.00 - 10.00
Conqueror 9563, 9564, 9566, 9765, 9766, 9937, 9938,
  9939, 9940.......................... 4.00 - 8.00
Derby 776, 783........................... 5.00 - 8.00
Disc 6057, 6058, 6059, 6088............. 4.00 - 6.00*
Harlem 2323, 2329....................... 4.00 - 7.00*
Jax 304, 307, 310, 312, 322............... 4.00 - 7.00*
Savoy 704, 714, 747, 760, 778, 872, 899, 5533, 5534,
  5538, 5541, 5548, 5550, 5551, 5557, 5559, 5561,
  5565 .... 4.00 - 7.00
Sittin' In With 302, 517................. 7.00 - 10.00
Okeh 05875, 05812, 05881, 05933, 06007, 06056,
  06265, 06329, 06419, 06437, 06472, 06524,
  06579, 06698......................... 5.00 - 10.00

STICKS McGHEE (& HIS BUDDIES):

Atlantic 873 *Drinkin' Wine Spo-Dee-O-Dee*..... 7.00 - 10.00
  881 *Lonesome Road Blues*........... 7.00 - 10.00
  898, 909, 912, 926, 937, 955, 991...... 4.00 - 7.00*
Decca 48104 *Drinkin' Wine Spo-Dee-O-Dee*..... 5.00 - 8.00*
Essex 709 *My Little Rose*.............. 5.00 - 10.00
Harlem 1018 *Drinkin' Wine Spo-Dee-O-Dee*.... 15.00 - 20.00
  King 4610, 4628, 4672, 4700, 4783, 4800.... 3.00 - 5.00*

ELDERS McINTORSH & EDWARD; LONNIE
McINTORSH:

Okeh 8647 *The 1927 Flood*.......... 15.00 - 20.00
  8671 *Take A Stand*................. 15.00 - 20.00
  8698 *Since I Laid My Burden Down*........ 15.00 - 20.00
Victor 21271 *The Lion And The Tribes Of Judah* 20.00 - 30.00
  21411 *Arise And Shine*.............. 20.00 - 30.00

ARTHUR/ART McKAY:

Decca 7068 *Central Limited Blues*..... 15.00 - 20.00
  7364 *She Squeezed My Lemon*........ 15.00 - 20.00

McKENZIE AND CRUMP:

Paramount 12857 *That's A Married Man's Weakness* 20.00 - 30.00

BILLIE McKENZIE:

Vocalion 03385 *Romeo And Juliet*........... 7.00 - 10.00

WILLIE MAE McKENZIE:

Vocalion 03507 *Oh, Babe*............. 7.00 - 10.00
  03552 *I'm Getting Even With You*......... 7.00 - 10.00
  03562 *Little Red Wagon*............. 7.00 - 10.00

BILL McKINLEY:

Titles, issued contemporaneously on Banner,
  Melotone, Oriole, Perfect, Romeo: *I Went To The*
  Gypsy; She Keeps On Kickin'............ 8.00 - 12.00

(DAVID) PETE McKINLEY:

Fidelity 3008 *Black Snake Blues*........... 10.00 - 15.00
Gotham 505 *Shreveport Blues*......... 15.00 - 25.00

SADIE McKINNEY:

Victor 20565 *Rock Away*.............. 15.00 - 20.00

JIMMY McLAIN:

Vocalion 04444 *Tailor Made Blues*...... 8.00 - 12.00

CAB McMILLAN & HIS FADEAWAYS:

Macy's 5011 *I'm Young And Able*.......... 5.00 - 8.00

DENNIS McMILLON:

Regal 3232 *Poor Little Angel*................. 10.00 - 20.00
  3257 *I Woke Up One Morning*............ 10.00 - 20.00

FRED McMULLEN (AND RUTH WILLIS):

Titles, issued contemporaneously on Banner,
  Melotone, Oriole, Perfect, Romeo: *De Kalb Chain*
  Blues; Just Can't Stand It; Poor Stranger Blues;
  Rolling Mama; Wait And Listen.......... 30.00 - 40.00

BLACK BOTTOM McPHAIL:

Vocalion 1690 *Mix That Thing*.............. 40.00 - 60.00
  1721 *Down In Black Bottom*......... 40.00 - 60.00
  04220 *New Whiskey Man*........... 15.00 - 20.00
  04317 *Don't Go Down In Black Bottom*..... 15.00 - 20.00

OZIE (DAYBREAK) McPHERSON:

Paramount 12327 *You Gotta Know How*...... 30.00 - 40.00
  12350 *Standing on the Corner Blues*........ 40.00 - 50.00
  12355 *Nobody Rolls Their Jelly Roll Like Mine* 40.00 - 50.00
  12362 *I Want My Loving*................. 40.00 - 50.00

BLIND WILLIE McTELL; BLIND WILLIE &
KATE McTELL:

Decca 7078 *Ticket Agent Blues*............. 35.00 - 50.00
  7093 *Dying Gambler*..................... 35.00 - 50.00
  7117 *Hillbilly Willie's Blues*.............. 35.00 - 50.00
  7140 *We Got To Meet Death One Day*...... 35.00 - 50.00
  7810 *Cold Winter Day*................. 30.00 - 40.00
Regal 3272 *It's My Desire*.............. 80.00 - 120.00
Victor 21124 *Mr. McTell Got The Blues*...... 80.00 - 120.00
  21474 *Writin' Paper Blues*.............. 80.00 - 120.00
  38001 *Three Women Blues*............. 80.00 - 120.00
  38032 *Dark Night Blues*.............. 80.00 - 120.00
  38580 *Drive Away Blues*............. 80.00 - 120.00

MEMPHIS EDDIE:

RPM 301, 308, 310, 315.............. 5.00 - 10.00

MEMPHIS JIMMY:

RCA Victor 20-1887, 20-2278............. 4.00 - 8.00

MEMPHIS JOE:

Vocalion 1277 *Plenty Gals Blues*.............. 35.00 - 50.00

MEMPHIS MINNIE & KANSAS JOE (& HER
JUG BAND/& HER COMBO/WITH LITTLE
JOE & HIS BAND):

Titles, issued contemporaneously on Banner,
  Melotone, Oriole, Perfect, Romeo: *Bumble Bee;*
  Bumble Bee No. 2; Fishin' Blues; I'm Talkin' 'Bout
  You; Kind Treatment Blues; Outdoor Blues;
  Where Is My Good Man................. 30.00 - 40.00
Bluebird 6187 *When The Sun Goes Down*...... 25.00 - 35.00
  6199 *Doctor, Doctor Blues*............. 15.00 - 20.00
  6202 *Hustlin' Woman Blues*.......... 20.00 - 30.00
Checker 771 *Me And My Chauffeur*.......... 5.00 - 8.00*
Columbia .... 3.00 - 5.00
Conqueror 9025, 9026, 9162, 9198, 9275, 9282, 9372,
  9763, 9764, 9934, 9935, 9936........... 8.00 - 12.00
Decca 7019 *Chickasaw Train Blues*...... 15.00 - 20.00
  7023 *Hole In The Wall*................ 15.00 - 20.00
  7037 *Keep It To Yourself*.............. 15.00 - 20.00
  7038 *You Got To Move*............. 15.00 - 20.00
  7048 *You Can't Give It Away*......... 15.00 - 20.00
  7084 *Sylvester And His Mule Blues*...... 15.00 - 20.00
  7102 *Down In New Orleans*......... 15.00 - 20.00
  7125 *Jockey Man Blues*............. 15.00 - 20.00
  7146 *Squat It*.................... 15.00 - 20.00
J.O.B. 1101 *Kissing In The Dark*............. 8.00 - 12.00*
Okeh 05670, 05728, 05811, 06288, 06410, 06505,
  06224, 06707......................... 8.00 - 12.00
  8948 *My Butcher Man*............. 35.00 - 50.00
Regal 3259 *Kidman Blues*............. 10.00 - 15.00
Vocalion 1476 *Bumble Bee*.............. 35.00 - 50.00
  1512 *I'm Gonna Bake My Biscuits*...... 35.00 - 50.00
  1556 *Bumble Bee—No. 2*.......... 35.00 - 50.00

1588 *Frankie Jean*	35.00 -	50.00
1601 *Garage Fire Blues*	35.00 -	50.00
1603 *Good Girl Blues*	35.00 -	50.00
1618 *New Dirty Dozen*	35.00 -	50.00
1631 *Plymouth Rock Blues*	35.00 -	50.00
1638 *Dirt Dauber Blues*	35.00 -	50.00
1653 *Tricks Ain't Walkin' No More*	35.00 -	50.00
1658 *Soo Cow Soo*	35.00 -	50.00
1673 *Don't Bother It*	35.00 -	50.00
1682 *Minnie Minnie Bumble Bee*	35.00 -	50.00
1688 *Socket Blues*	35.00 -	50.00
1698 *Outdoor Blues*	35.00 -	50.00
1711 *Fishin' Blues*	35.00 -	50.00
1718 *Jailhouse Trouble Blues*	35.00 -	50.00
02711 *Stinging Snake Blues*	35.00 -	50.00
Vocalion 03046 *Joe Louis Strut*	10.00 -	15.00
03144 *Biting Bug Blues*	10.00 -	15.00
03187 *Ain't Nobody Home But Me*	10.00 -	15.00
03222 *Ice Man (Come On Up)*	10.00 -	15.00
03258 *I'm A Gamblin' Woman*	10.00 -	15.00
03285 *If You See My Rooster (Please Run Him Home)*	10.00 -	15.00
03398 *Dragging My Heart Around*	10.00 -	15.00
03436 *I Don't Want You No More*	10.00 -	15.00
03474 *It's Hard To Be Mistreated*	10.00 -	15.00
03541 *Ball And Chain Blues*	10.00 -	15.00
03581 *Black Cat Blues*	10.00 -	15.00
03612 *Down In The Alley*	8.00 -	12.00
03651 *Keep On Sailing*	8.00 -	12.00
03697 *No Need You Doggin' Me*	8.00 -	12.00
03768 *Living The Best I Can*	8.00 -	12.00
03894 *My Baby Don't Want Me No More*	8.00 -	12.00
03966 *Walking And Crying Blues*	8.00 -	12.00
04250 *I've Been Treated Wrong*	8.00 -	12.00
04295 *Good Biscuits*	8.00 -	12.00
04356 *Keep On Walking*	8.00 -	12.00
04506 *I'd Rather See Him Dead*	8.00 -	12.00
04694 *Good Soppin'*	8.00 -	12.00
04797 *Bad Outside Friends*	8.00 -	12.00
04858 *Call The Fire Wagon*	8.00 -	12.00
04898 *Don't Lead My Baby Wrong*	8.00 -	12.00
05004 *Poor And Wandering Woman Blues*	8.00 -	12.00

MEMPHIS MOSE:

Brunswick 7102 *Pig Meat Papa*	35.00 -	50.00
7134 *Blue Moanin' Blues*	35.00 -	50.00
7143 *Billie The Grinder*	35.00 -	50.00

MEMPHIS SAM AND JOHN:

Gennett 6987 *It's Just All Right*	30.00 -	50.00

MEMPHIS SLIM (& HIS/THE HOUSE ROCKERS; & HIS SOLID BAND):

Bluebird 8584 *Beer Drinking Woman*	8.00 -	12.00
8615 *Empty Room Blues*	8.00 -	12.00
8645 *Shelby Country Blues*	8.00 -	12.00
8749 *Two Of A Kind*	7.00 -	10.00
8784 *Me, Myself, And I*	7.00 -	10.00
8834 *Whiskey Store Blues*	7.00 -	10.00
8903 *Old Taylor*	7.00 -	10.00
8945 *Whiskey And Gin Blues*	7.00 -	10.00
8974 *Caught The Old Coon At Last*	7.00 -	10.00
9028 *Lend Me Your Love*	7.00 -	10.00
Chess 1491 *Walking Alone*	5.00 -	8.00*
Federal 12007, 12015, 12021, 12033	5.00 -	8.00
Hy-Tone 10, 17, 19	5.00 -	8.00
King 4284, 4312, 4324, 4327	3.00 -	6.00
Master 1010, 1020, 1030	5.00 -	8.00
Mercury 8251, 8266, 8281, 70063	3.00 -	5.00
Miracle 102, 103, 110, 111, 125, 132, 145, 153	5.00 -	8.00
Old Swingmaster 1010	5.00 -	10.00
Peacock 1517, 1602	5.00 -	8.00
Premium 850, 860, 867, 873, 878, 903	5.00 -	8.00

SARA MESSON:

Oriole 325 *Nobody Knows The Way I Feel*	10.00 -	15.00

ANNA MEYERS:

Pathe-Actuelle 020870 *That Da Da Strain*	7.00 -	10.00
020877 *Evil Minded Blues*	7.00 -	10.00
Perfect 12031 *That Da Da Strain*	7.00 -	10.00
12038 *Last Go Round Blues*	7.00 -	10.00

HAZEL MEYERS:

Ajax 17007 *Love Ain't Blind No More*	15.00 -	20.00
17019 *Mississippi Blues*	15.00 -	20.00
17026 *Heart Breakin' Joe*	15.00 -	20.00
17039 *Papa Don't Ask Mama Where She Was*	20.00 -	30.00
17040 *I'm Every Man's Mama*	20.00 -	30.00
17047 *War Horse Mama*	20.00 -	30.00
17048 *Hateful Blues*	20.00 -	30.00
17054 *Lonesome for That Man Of Mine*	20.00 -	30.00
17077 *Lost My Sweetie Blues*	25.00 -	35.00
17082 *He Used To Be Mine*	25.00 -	35.00
Banner 1358 *Plug Ugly*	7.00 -	10.00
Bell P-255 *Down Hearted Blues*	10.00 -	15.00
Emerson 10748 *Don't Know and Don't Care Blues*	15.00 -	20.00
Harmograph 925 *'Tain't A Doggone Thing But The Blues*	15.00 -	20.00
967 *Pipe Dream Blues*	15.00 -	20.00
Okeh 8364 *Blackville After Dark*	35.00 -	50.00
Pathe-Actuelle 032053 *Pipe Dream Blues*	10.00 -	15.00
Perfect 12132 *Pipe Dream Blues*	10.00 -	15.00
Regal 9654 *Plug Ugly*	7.00 -	10.00
Silvertone 3011 *Graveyard Dream Blues*	7.00 -	10.00
3012 *Maybe Someday*	15.00 -	20.00
Vocalion 14688 *Graveyard Dream Blues*	8.00 -	12.00
14709 *Awful Moanin' Blues*	15.00 -	20.00
14725 *Mason-Dixon Blues*	15.00 -	20.00
14861 *Maybe Someday*	15.00 -	20.00

MIDNIGHT RAMBLERS:

Vocalion 03395 *Out With The Wrong Woman*	10.00 -	15.00
03517 *Down In The Alley*	10.00 -	15.00

AMOS MILBURN:

Aladdin 159, 160, 161, 173, 174	5.00 -	9.00
Aladdin (higher numbers)	3.00 -	5.00*

JOSIE MILES:

Ajax 17057 *Lovin' Henry Blues*	25.00 -	35.00
17066 *Believe Me, Hot Mama*	25.00 -	35.00
17070 *South Bound Blues*	25.00 -	35.00
17076 *Sweet Man Joe*	25.00 -	35.00
17080 *A to Z Blues*	25.00 -	35.00
17083 *Picnic Time*	15.00 -	20.00
17087 *Cross Word Papa*	15.00 -	20.00
17090 *I'm A Cabaret Nightingale*	15.00 -	20.00
17092 *It Ain't Gonna Rain No Mo*	15.00 -	20.00
17127 *At The Cake Walk Steppers Ball*	25.00 -	35.00
17134 *Give Me Just A Little Bit Of Love*	25.00 -	35.00
Banner 1498 *Bitter Feelin' Blues*	8.00 -	12.00
1499 *Let's Agree To Disagree*	10.00 -	15.00
1516 *Ghost Walkin' Blues*	10.00 -	15.00
1534 *Low Down Daddy Blues*	7.00 -	10.00
Black Swan 14121 *When You're Crazy Over Daddy*	15.00 -	20.00
14130 *If You Want To Keep Your Daddy Home*	20.00 -	30.00
14133 *When I Dream Of Old Tennessee Blues*	15.00 -	20.00
14136 *Four O'Clock Blues*	15.00 -	20.00
14139 *Low Down 'Bama Blues*	15.00 -	20.00
Domino 3468 *Bitter Feelin' Blues*	10.00 -	15.00
3469 *Let's Agree To Disagree*	10.00 -	15.00
3485 *Ghost Walkin' Blues*	10.00 -	15.00
3504 *Low Down Daddy Blues*	8.00 -	12.00
Edison 51476 *Sweet Man Joe*	40.00 -	50.00
51477 *Temper'mental Papa*	40.00 -	50.00
Gennett 5261 *Kansas City Man Blues*	8.00 -	12.00
5292 *Graveyard Dream Blues*	8.00 -	12.00
5307 *I Want My Sweet Daddy Now*	8.00 -	12.00
5339 *Awful Moanin' Blues*	8.00 -	12.00
5359 *War Horse Mamma*	12.00 -	16.00
5391 *31st. Street Blues*	8.00 -	12.00
Paramount 12156 *When You're Crazy Over Daddy*	15.00 -	20.00

12157 *If You Want To Keep Your Daddy Home*	20.00 -	30.00
12158 *When I Dream Of Old Tennessee Blues*	15.00 -	20.00
12159 *Four O'Clock Blues*	15.00 -	20.00
12160 *Low Down 'Bama Blues*	15.00 -	20.00
Regal 9796 *Let's Agree To Disagree*	10.00 -	15.00
9797 *Bitter Feelin' Blues*	10.00 -	15.00
9831 *Low Down Daddy Blues*	8.00 -	12.00
Silvertone 4043, 4048, 4051	8.00 -	12.00

LIZZIE MILES; LIZZIE MILES & THE MELROSE STOMPERS:

Titles, issued contemporaneously on Banner, Conqueror, Domino, Regal: *Banjo Papa; If You Can't Control Your Man; Lonesome Ghost Blues; Mean Old Bed Bug Blues; Police Blues; Second Hand Daddy; Shake It Down; Shootin' Star Blues; When You Get Tired Of Your New Sweetie.*

	7.00 -	12.00
Bluebird 5064 *Electrician Bleus*	10.00 -	15.00
Brunswick 2462 *My Pillow and Me*	7.00 -	10.00
Columbia A-3897, A-3920	5.00 -	7.00
14335-D *My Diff-rent Kind O'Man*	25.00 -	40.00
Emerson 10586 *Aggravatin' Papa*	10.00 -	15.00
10603 *Tell Me Gypsy*	10.00 -	15.00
10613 *Your Time Now*	10.00 -	15.00
Okeh 8031 *Muscle Shoals Blues*	8.00 -	12.00
8032 *State Street Blues*	8.00 -	12.00
8037 *Wicked Blues*	7.00 -	10.00
8039 *Lonesome Monday Morning Blues*	7.00 -	10.00
8040 *Hot Lips*	7.00 -	10.00
8048 *Sweet Smellin' Mama*	8.00 -	12.00
8050 *The Black Bottom Blues*	8.00 -	12.00
8052 *The Yellow Dog Blues*	8.00 -	12.00
Okeh 8456 *Slow Up Papa*	20.00 -	30.00
Victor 19083, 19124, 19158	5.00 -	8.00
23281 *My Man O'War*	25.00 -	35.00
23298 *Electrician Blues*	25.00 -	35.00
23306 *Good Time Papa*	25.00 -	35.00
38607 *Good Time Papa*	25.00 -	35.00
38571 *I Hate A Man Like You*	40.00 -	60.00
Vocalion 05165 *That's All Right Daddy*	5.00 -	8.00
05260 *Mellow Rhythm*	5.00 -	8.00
05325 *He's Red Hot To Me*	5.00 -	8.00
05392 *Twenty Grand Blues*	5.00 -	8.00

MILLER AND RODGERS:

Gennett 6782 *Everybody's Been Using That Thing*	30.00 -	40.00
Paramount 12778 *I Would If I Could*	30.00 -	40.00

AL MILLER (& HIS MARKET STREET BOYS/SWING STOMPERS); AL MILLER'S STRING BAND:

Black Patti 8047 *Someday Sweetheart*	40.00 -	60.00
8049 *Saturday Night Hymn*	40.00 -	60.00
Brunswick 7063 *I Would If I Could*	20.00 -	30.00
7084 *It Ain't Killed Nobody Yet*	20.00 -	30.00
7097 *It Must Be Good*	20.00 -	30.00
7105 *Thirty First And State*	20.00 -	30.00
7140 *That Stuff You Sell*	20.00 -	30.00
7143 *Gimme A Li'l Taste*	20.00 -	30.00
7212 *That Stuff Ain't No Good*	20.00 -	30.00
Champion 50067 *Truckin' Old Fool*	10.00 -	15.00
50072 *Ain't That A Mess?*	10.00 -	15.00
Gennett 6875 *Mister Mary Blues*	30.00 -	40.00

EDDIE MILLER:

Titles, issued contemporaneously on Banner, Melotone, Oriole, Perfect, Romeo: *I'd Rather Drink Muddy Water; Whoopie.*

	40.00 -	60.00
Brunswick 7133 *Freight Train Blues*	50.00 -	75.00
7213 *School Day Blues*	50.00 -	75.00

JIM MILLER:

Vocalion 1737 *Joker Man Blues*	15.00 -	25.00

LILLIAN MILLER:

Gennett 6486 *Butcher Shop Blues*	50.00 -	75.00
6518 *Dead Drunk Blues*	50.00 -	75.00
Okeh 8381 *Kitchen Blues*	30.00 -	40.00

LUELLA MILLER (& HER DAGO HILL STRUTTERS:

Vocalion 1044 *Dago Hill Blues*	20.00 -	30.00
1080 *Down in the Alley*	20.00 -	30.00
1081 *Rattle Snake Groan*	20.00 -	30.00
1102 *Carrier Pigeon Blues*	20.00 -	30.00
1103 *Jackson's Blues*	30.00 -	40.00
1104 *Smiling Rose Blues*	30.00 -	40.00
1105 *North Wind Blues*	20.00 -	30.00
1147 *Tornado Groan*	20.00 -	30.00
1151 *Tombstone Blues*	20.00 -	30.00
1202 *'Frisco Blues*	20.00 -	30.00
1234 *Chicago Blues*	20.00 -	30.00

MAE BELLE MILLER:

Paramount 12985 *Long Tall Man Blues*	60.00 -	80.0

SODARISA/SODARISSA MILLER:

Paramount 12231 *Hot Springs Water Blues*	20.00 -	30.00
12243 *Don't Dog Me 'Round*	20.00 -	30.00
12261 *Broadway Daddy Blues*	20.00 -	30.00
12276 *Be Yourself*	20.00 -	30.00
12293 *Nobody Knows*	20.00 -	30.00
12306 *Midnight Special*	20.00 -	30.00
Victor 20404 *Lonesome Room Blues*	20.00 -	30.00

JOSIE MILLS:

Emerson 10874 *Low Down Daddy Blues*	7.00 -	10.00

MAUDE MILLS:

Titles, issued contemporaneously on Banner, Domino, Regal: *Anything That Happens Just Pleases Me; Black Snake Blues; Golden Brown Blues; Hard Headed Mama.*

	8.00 -	15.00
Emerson 10624 *Triflin' Blues*	8.00 -	12.00
Pathe-Actuelle 7526 *Somebody's Been Loving My Baby*	8.00 -	12.00
Perfect 126 *Somebody's Been Loving My Baby*	8.00 -	12.00

VIOLET MILLS:

Domino 437 *Worried Blues*	10.00 -	15.00
438 *Mad Mama's Blues*	10.00 -	15.00

IRENE MIMS:

Vocalion 1183 *Dirty Blues*	15.00 -	20.00

MISS FRANKIE:

Titles, issued contemporaneously on Banner, Domino, Regal: *Kissin' Mule Blues; Peepin' Jim Blues.*

	8.00 -	12.00

MISSISSIPPI BLACKSNAKES:

Brunswick 7196 *It's So Nice And Warm*	50.00 -	75.00
7202 *Five Pound Ax Blues*	50.00 -	75.00
7215 *Easy Going Woman Blues*	50.00 -	75.00
7222 *Bye Bye Baby Blues*	50.00 -	75.00

MISSISSIPPI BAND:

Titles, issued contemporaneously on Banner, Melotone, Oriole, Perfect, Romeo: *Barbecue Bust; Dangerous Woman; Hittin' The Bottle Stomp; Skippy Whippy.*

	30.00 -	50.00

MISSISSIPPI MATILDA:

Bluebird 6812 *Hard Working Woman*	30.00 -	40.00
7908 *A. & V. Blues*	30.00 -	40.00

THE MISSISSIPPI MOANER:

Vocalion 03166 *Mississippi Moan*	50.00 -	75.00

MISSISSIPPI MUD MASHERS:

Bluebird 5845 *Bring In On Home To Grandma*	10.00 -	15.00
5988 *Take My Seat And Sit Down*	10.00 -	15.00
7316 *Tiger Rag*	10.00 -	15.00

MISSISSIPPI MUD STEPPERS:

Okeh 45504 *Jackson Stomp*	40.00 -	60.00
45519 *Vicksburg Stomp*	40.00 -	60.00
45532 *Farewell Waltz*	40.00 -	60.00

MISSISSIPPI MUDDER:

Decca 7008 *I Got To Have A Little More*	20.00 -	30.00
7009 *Meat Cutter Blues*	20.00 -	30.00
7036 *Candy Man Blues*	20.00 -	30.00
7046 *Charity Blues*	20.00 -	30.00
7087 *Motherless And Fatherless Blues*	20.00 -	30.00

MISSISSIPPI SARA (& DADDY STOVEPIPE):

Vocalion 1662 *Greenville Strut*	25.00 -	40.00
1667 *Do You Love Him?*	25.00 -	40.00
1670 *Jail Cell Blues*	25.00 -	40.00
1676 *Jake Leg Blues*	25.00 -	40.00

MISSISSIPPI SHEIKS (WITH BO CARTER):

Bluebird 5452 *Pop Skull Blues*	15.00 -	25.00
5453 *Sales Tax*	15.00 -	25.00
5474 *Hitting The Numbers*	15.00 -	25.00
5516 *I Am The Devil*	15.00 -	25.00
5564 *Blues On My Mind*	15.00 -	25.00
5618 *She's Got Something Crazy*	15.00 -	25.00
5659 *Somebody's Got To Help Me*	15.00 -	25.0
5847 *Do Right Blues*	15.00 -	25.00
5881 *I Can't Go Wrong*	15.00 -	25.00
5949 *Lean To One Woman*	15.00 -	25.00
6006 *Dead Wagon Blues*	15.00 -	25.00
Champion 50003 *Tell Me To Do Right*	15.00 -	20.00
50004 *Please Baby*	15.00 -	20.00
50007 *Don't Wake It Up*	15.00 -	20.00
50013 *New Shake That Thing*	15.00 -	20.00
50021 *The New Stop And Listen Blues*	15.00 -	20.00
50030 *Shooting High Dice*	15.00 -	20.00
Columbia 14660-D *The World Is Going Wrong*	40.00 -	60.00
14672-D *Kind Treatment*	40.00 -	60.00
Okeh 8773 *Wintertime Blues*	25.00 -	35.00
8784 *Sitting On Top Of The World*	20.00 -	30.00
8807 *Driving That Thing*	40.00 -	60.00
8810 *Back To Mississippi*	40.00 -	60.00
8820 *Bootleggers' Blues*	40.00 -	60.00
8834 *Jail Bird Love Song*	40.00 -	60.00
8843 *River Bottom Blues*	40.00 -	60.00
8854 *Sitting On Top Of The World—No. 2*	40.00 -	60.00
8859 *Unhappy Blues*	40.00 -	60.00
8876 *Church Bell Blues*	40.00 -	60.00
8885 *She Ain't No Good*	40.00 -	60.00
8905 *Ram Rod Blues*	40.00 -	60.00
8922 *Please Baby*	40.00 -	60.00
8927 *Bed Spring Poker*	40.00 -	60.00
8933 *She's A Bad Girl*	40.00 -	60.00
8939 *Jake Leg Blues*	40.00 -	60.00
8947 *Kitty Cat Blues*	40.00 -	60.00
8951 *Shake Hands And Tell Me Goodbye*	40.00 -	60.00
8953 *Too Long*	40.00 -	60.00
Paramount 13134 *The New Stop And Listen Blues*	70.00 -	100.00
13142 *Shooting High Dice*	70.00 -	100.00
13143 *New Shake That Thing*	70.00 -	100.00
13152 *Don't Wake It Up*	70.00 -	100.00
13152 *Please Baby*	70.00 -	100.00
13156 *Tell Me To Do Right*	70.00 -	100.00

WALTER MITCHELL:

JVB 75827 *Pet Milk Blues*	35.00 -	50.00

MONARCH JAZZ QUARTET:

Okeh 8736 *Four Or Five Times*	10.00 -	15.00
8761 *I Ain't Got Nobody*	10.00 -	15.00
8931 *Pleading Blues*	10.00 -	15.00

MONKEY JOE (& HIS MUSIC GRINDERS):

Bluebird 6061 *Sweet Petunia Stomp*	10.00 -	15.0
6114 *Monkey Joe Got The Blues*	10.00 -	15.00
Okeh 05685, 06153	5.00 -	8.00
Vocalion 04161 *O.K. With Me Baby*	8.00 -	12.00
04219 *Hair Parted In The Middle*	8.00 -	12.00
04294 *Some Sweet Day*	8.00 -	12.00
04416 *Preach, Pray And Moan*	8.00 -	12.00
04471 *Rabbit Foot Blues*	7.00 -	10.00
04618 *New York Central*	7.00 -	10.00
04814 *Tailor Made Woman*	7.00 -	10.00
04871 *Good Business No. 2*	7.00 -	10.00
04926 *Wise To The Jive*	7.00 -	10.00
04978 *Mobile And K.C. Line*	7.00 -	10.00
05166 *Carry My Business On*	7.00 -	10.00
05274 *That Same Cat*	7.00 -	10.00
05348 *Mountain Baby Blues*	7.00 -	10.00

ALEX MONROE:

Bell 1190 *The Worried Man Blues*	100.00 -	150.00

"E" MONTGOMERY:

Melotone 12548 *Louisiana Blues*	60.00 -	80.00
Vocalion 02706 *Louisiana Blues*	60.00 -	80.00

LITTLE BROTHER MONTGOMERY:

Bluebird 6072 *Vicksburg Blues No. 2*	20.00 -	30.00
6140 *Pleading Blues*	20.00 -	30.00
Century 4009, 4010	5.00 -	10.00
Paramount 13006 *Vicksburg Blues*	80.00 -	120.00

SAM MONTGOMERY ("KINGS OF SPADES"):

Titles, issued contemporaneously on Banner, Melotone, Oriole, Perfect, Romeo: *Baby Please Don't Go; Blue Devil Blues; Honey Dripper; I'm Through With You; Kind of Knave; King of Knave No. 2; Low In Mind Blues; Mercy Mercy Blues*	15.00 -	25.00

JULIA MOODY:

Titles, issued contemporaneously on Banner, Regal: *Don't Forget, You'll Regret; Mad Mama's Blues; Worried Blues*	8.00 -	15.00
Black Swan 14132 *The Cootie Crawl*	15.00 -	20.00
14140 *Starvin' For Love*	15.00 -	20.00
14144 *Good Man Sam*	15.00 -	20.00
Columbia 14087-D *Strivin' Blues*	10.00 -	15.00
14103-D *Midnight Dan*	10.00 -	15.00
14121-D *That Chicago Wiggle*	10.00 -	15.00
Paramount 12153 *That Cootie Crawl*	15.00 -	20.00
12154 *Starvin' For Love*	15.00 -	20.00
12155 *Good Man Sam*	15.00 -	20.00

HENRY MOON AND GEORGE THOMAS:

Herwin 92025 *Neck Bones And Beans*	60.00 -	80.00

ETTA MOONEY:

Black Swan 14118 *Early Every Morn*	15.00 -	20.00
14134 *Cootie For Your Tootie*	15.00 -	20.00
Paramount 12151 *Early Every Morn*	15.00 -	20.00
12152 *Cootie For Your Tootie*	15.00 -	20.00

(WHISTLIN') ALEX (ANDER) MOORE:

Columbia 14496-D *West Texas Woman*	20.00 -	30.00
14518-D *Ice Pick Blues*	30.00 -	40.00
14596-D *Blue Bloomer Blues*	30.00 -	40.00
Decca 7288 *Blue Bloomer Blues*	15.00 -	20.00
7552 *Hard Hearted Woman*	15.00 -	20.00
RPM 326 *Neglected Woman*	8.00 -	12.00

ALICE MOORE:

Decca 7028 *Riverside Blues*	20.00 -	30.00
7056 *Lonesome Woman Blues*	20.00 -	30.00
7109 *Just Sitting Here Wondering*	10.00 -	15.00
7132 *Blue Black And Evil Blues*	10.00 -	15.00
7153 *Daddy Calling Mama*	10.00 -	15.00
7190 *Grass Cutter Blues*	10.00 -	15.00
7227 *Money Tree Man*	10.00 -	15.00
7253 *I'm Going Fishing Too*	10.00 -	15.00
7293 *New Blue Black And Evil Blues*	10.00 -	15.00
7327 *Midnight Creepers*	10.00 -	15.00
7369 *Don't Deny Me Baby*	10.00 -	15.00
7380 *Doggin' Man Blues*	10.00 -	15.00
7393 *Push Cart Pusher*	10.00 -	15.00
Paramount 12819 *Black And Evil Blues*	60.00 -	80.00
12868 *My Man Blues*	60.00 -	80.00
12947 *Serving Time Blues*	70.00 -	90.00
12973 *Have Mercy Blues*	70.00 -	90.00
13107 *Lonesome Dream Blues*	70.00 -	90.00

ARAH "BABY" MOORE:

Victor 20553 *Drop Down Blues*	20.00 -	30.00

BILL MOORE:

Paramount 12613 *Barbershop Rag*	75.00 -	100.00
12636 *Ragtime Millionaire*	75.00 -	100.00
12648 *One Way Gal*	75.00 -	100.00

(KID) PRINCE MOORE:

Titles, issued contemporaneously on Banner, Melotone, Oriole, Perfect, Romeo: *Bug Juice Blues; Church Bells; Honey Dripping Papa; Sign Of Judgment* .... 15.00 - 20.00

Decca 7475 *Single Man Blues* .... 8.00 - 12.00

7514 *Ford V-8 Blues* .... 8.00 - 12.00

7539 *That's Lovin' Me* .... 8.00 - 12.00

MONETTE MOORE:

Ajax 17124 *Memphis Blues* .... 15.00 - 25.00

Columbia 14105-D *Get It Fixed* .... 15.00 - 20.00

Decca 7161 *Rhythm Shop Swing* .... 6.00 - 10.00

Harmograph 781 *Sugar Blues* .... 10.00 - 15.00

Paramount 12015 *Sugar Blues* .... 10.00 - 15.00

12028 *I Just Want A Daddy* .... 10.00 - 15.00

12030 *Gulf Coast Blues* .... 10.00 - 15.00

12046 *I'll Go To My Grave With The Blues* .. 20.00 - 30.00

12067 *Muddy Water Blues* .... 15.00 - 20.00

12210 *Friendless Blues* .... 15.00 - 20.00

Victor 20356 *If You Don't Like Potatoes* .... 20.00 - 30.00

20484 *Moaning Sinner Blues* .... 20.00 - 30.00

Vocalion 14903 *I Wanna Jazz Some More* ...... 15.00 - 20.00

14911 *Death Letter Blues* .... 15.00 - 20.00

ROSIE MAE MOORE:

Victor 21280 *Staggering Blues* .... 30.00 - 40.00

21408 *School Girl Blues* .... 30.00 - 40.00

WILLIAM MOORE:

Paramount 12761 *Raggin' The Blues* .... 90.00 - 120.00

EDDIE MORGAN:

Bluebird 5757 *Rock House Blues* .... 30.00 - 40.00

CLARA MORRIS:

Bluebird 8700 *I Stagger In My Sleep* .... 5.00 - 8.00

8767 *Poker Playing Daddy* .... 5.00 - 8.00

MOSBY AND SYKES:

Champion 16513 *Mosby Stomp* .... 40.00 - 60.00

BUDDY MOSS:

Titles, issued contemporaneously on Banner, Conqueror, Melotone, Oriole, Perfect, Romeo: *Bachelors' Blues; Back To My Used-To-Be; Best Gal; B & O Blues No. 2; Broke Down Engine; Bye Bye Mama; Can't Use You No More; Cold Country Blues; Daddy Don't Care; Dough Rolling Papa; Evil Hearted Papa; Going To Your Funeral In A Vee-Eight Ford; Gravy Server; Hard Road Blues; Hard Times Blues; Insane Blues; Jealous Hearted Man; Jinx Man Blues; Love Me Baby; Love Me; Married Man's Blues; Misery Man Blues; Mistreated Boy; My Baby Wont's Pay Me No Mind; New Lovin' Blues; Oh Lordy Mama; Oh Lordy Mama No. 2; Prowlin' Gambler Blues; Prowling Woman; Red River Blues; Restless Night Blues; See What You Done Done; Shake It All Night Long; Sleepless Night; Somebody Keeps Calling Me; Someday Baby; Some Lonesome Day; Stinging Bull Nettle; Stop Hanging Around; T.B.'s Killing Me; Too Doggone Jealous; Travelin' Blues; Tricks Ain't Walking No More; Undertaker Blues; Unkind Woman; When I'm Dead And Gone; When The Hearse Rolls Me From My Door; Worrysome Woman; You Got To Give Me Some Of It; Your Hard Head Will Bring You Sorrow Some Day* .... 15.00 - 20.00

Okeh 06473, 06515, 06679 .... 7.00 - 10.00

TEDDY MOSS:

Gennett 6993 *Texas Dream Blues* .... 50.00 - 70.00

7010 *You Broke My Hear Baby* .... 50.00 - 70.00

7055 *Ocean Wave Blues* .... 50.00 - 70.00

7084 *Back-Biter Blues* .... 50.00 - 70.00

7158 *Rocky Luck Blues* .... 60.00 - 90.00

MR. FREDDIE:

Bluebird 5995 *4A Highway* .... 35.00 - 50.00

6025 *Your Good Man Is Gone* .... 35.00 - 50.00

6261 *Let's Go Riding* .... 35.00 - 50.00

MUDDY WATERS:

Aristocrat 406 *Screamin' And Cryin'* .... 75.00 - 100.00

412 *Rollin' And Tumblin'* .... 15.00 - 25.00

1302 *Little Anna Mae* .... 20.00 - 30.00

1304 *She Ain't Nowhere* .... 20.00 - 30.00

1305 *I Feel Like Going Home* .... 12.00 - 18.00

1306 *Train Fare Home* .... 15.00 - 20.00

1307 *Mean Red Spider* .... 15.00 - 25.00

1310 *Muddy Jumps One* .... 15.00 - 20.00

1311 *Little Geneva* .... 25.00 - 35.00

Chess 1426 *Rollin' Stone* .... 8.00 - 12.00

1434 *You're Gonna Need My Help I Said* .... 8.00 - 12.00

1441 *Louisiana Blues* .... 8.00 - 12.00*

1452 *Long Distance Call* .... 8.00 - 12.00*

1468 *Honey Bee* .... 8.00 - 12.00*

1480 *My Fault* .... 8.00 - 12.00*

1490 *Early Morning Blues* .... 8.00 - 12.00*

1509 *All Night Long* .... 5.00 - 8.00*

1514 *Please Have Mercy* .... 5.00 - 8.00*

1526 *Gone To Main Street* .... 5.00 - 8.00*

1537 *Sad, Sad Day* .... 5.00 - 8.00*

MUMBLES:

Modern 809 *Little Boy Blue* .... 10.00 - 15.00

RPM 338 *Black Gal* .... 10.00 - 15.00

MABEL NANCE:

Silvertone 3547 *The Stomps* .... 35.00 - 50.00

(CHARLIE) DAD NELSON (& HIS GUITAR):

Paramount 12401 *Red River Blues* .... 30.00 - 45.00

12430 *Mississippi Strut* .... 30.00 - 45.00

12467 *Traveling Daddy* .... 30.00 - 45.00

12492 *Cleveland Stomp* .... 30.00 - 45.00

PEPPERMINT NELSON:

Gold Star 626 *Peppermint Boogie* .... 10.00 - 20.00

RED NELSON:

Bluebird 7265 *Relief Blues* .... 10.00 - 15.00

7918 *Black Gal Stomp* .... 10.00 - 15.00

7960 *Working Man Blues* .... 10.00 - 15.00

Decca 7136 *Grand Trunk Blues* .... 20.00 - 30.00

7154 *Detroit Special* .... 20.00 - 30.00

7155 *Sweetest Thing Born* .... 15.00 - 20.00

7171 *Streamline Train* .... 15.00 - 20.00

7185 *Empty Bed Blues* .... 10.00 - 15.00

7256 *Gambling Man* .... 10.00 - 15.00

7263 *Gravel In My Bed* .... 10.00 - 15.00

Vocalion 03001 *Six Cold Feet In The Ground* .. 35.00 - 50.00

ROMEO NELSON:

Vocalion 1447 *Head Rag Hop* .... 75.00 - 100.00

1494 *Dyin' Rider Blues* .... 75.00 - 100.00

SONNY BOY NELSON:

Bluebird 6672 *Street Walkin'* .... 25.00 - 35.00

6718 *Lovin' Blues* .... 25.00 - 35.00

7091 *Low Down* .... 25.0 - 35.00

7849 *Long Tall Woman* .... 20.00 - 30.00

"BLUE COAT" TOM NELSON:

Okeh 8838 *Blue Coat Blues* .... 35.00 - 50.00

BLIND (GUSSIE) NESBIT/NESBITT:

Columbia 14576-D *Pure Religion* .... 15.00 - 25.00

Decca 7113 *He's The Joy Of My Salvation* ..... 7.00 - 10.00

7131 *Motherless Children* .... 7.00 - 10.00

SCOTTIE NESBITT:

Bluebird 7125 *Sundown Blues* .... 10.00 - 15.00

7155 *Troubled And Blue* .... 10.00 - 15.00

HAMBONE WILLIE NEWBERN:

Okeh 8679 *Roll And Tumble Blues* .... 150.00 - 200.00

8693 *Way Down In Arkansas* .... 150.00 - 200.00

8740 *She Could Toddle-Oo* .... 150.00 - 200.00

JACK NEWMAN:

Vocalion 04265 *Blackberry Wine* .... 8.00 - 12.00

04344 *New Prison Blues* .... 8.00 - 12.00

MANNY NICHOLS:

FCB 125 *Walkin Talkin Blues*	30.00 -	50.00
Imperial 5162 *No One To Love Me*	12.00 -	16.00*
5173 *Worried Life Blues*	12.00 -	16.00*

NICK NICHOLS:

Columbia 2071-D *Frankie And Johnny*	15.00 -	20.00
14512-D *Riverside Blues*	15.00 -	25.00

FREDDIE "REDD" NICHOLSON:

Brunswick 7152 *Dirty No Gooder*	40.00 -	60.00
7204 *Freddie's Got The Blues*	50.00 -	75.00
7220 *Tee Roller's Rub*	75.00 -	100.00

"BOZO" NICKERSON:

Vocalion 1487 *What's The Matter Now? Part 1/2*	40.00 -	60.00
1525 *Bozo's Blues*	40.00 -	60.00
1604 *What's The Matter Now? Part 3/4*	40.00 -	60.00

THE NIGHTHAWKS:

Aristocrat 413 *Jackson Town Gal*	25.00 -	35.00
2301 *Black Angel Blues*	20.00 -	30.00

ROBERT NIGHTHAWK (& HIS NIGHTHAWKS BAND):

Chess 1484 *Return Mail Blues*	10.00 -	15.00*
States 131 *Maggie Campbell*	7.00 -	10.00*
United 102 *Kansas City Blues*	10.00 -	15.00*
105 *Take It Easy Baby*	10.00 -	15.00*

WILLIE NIX (& HIS COMBO):

Chance 1163 *Nervous Wreck*	10.00 -	15.00*
Checker 756 *Truckin' Little Woman*	5.00 -	8.00*
RPM 327 *Lonesome Bedroom Blues*	8.00 -	12.00
Sabre 104 *All By Myself*	10.00 -	15.00*
Sun 179 *Baker Shop Boogie*	50.00 -	75.00*

ELMORE NIXON:

Mercury 70061 *Playboy Blues*	4.00 -	7.00*
Peacock 1537, 1572	5.00 -	8.00
Savoy 878, 889, 1105	4.00 -	7.00
Sittin' In With 546, 580, 601	6.00 -	10.00

GEORGE NOBLE:

Titles, issued contemporaneously on Banner, Melotone, Oriole, Perfect, Romeo: *If You Lose Your Good Gal, Don't Mess With Mine; The Seminole Blues*	80.00 -	120.00
Vocalion 02905 *New Milk Cow Blues*	80.00 -	120.00
02923 *Bed Spring Blues*	80.00 -	120.00
02954 *On My Death Bed*	80.00 -	120.00

DIXIE NOLAN—JOHNNY HARDGE:

Victor 38556 *Worried Love*	20.00 -	30.00

NORA AND DELLE:

Decca 7852 *Army Camp Blues*	5.00 -	8.00
7858 *Keep A Knockin'*	5.00 -	8.00

NORFOLK JAZZ QUARTET:

Decca 7333, 7349, 7383, 7443	5.00 -	10.00
Okeh 4318, 4345, 4366, 4380, 4391, 8007, 8019, 8022, 8028, 8034	7.00 -	15.00
Paramount 12032 *Ain't It A Shame?*	8.00 -	15.00
12054 *Sad Blues*	8.00 -	15.00
12055 *Dixie Blues*	8.00 -	15.00
12218 *Jelly Roll's First Cousin*	8.00 -	15.00
12453 *Louisiana Bo Bo*	8.00 -	15.00
12844 *Please Give Me Some Of That*	8.00 -	15.00

BEN NORSINGLE:

Brunswick 7041 *Rover's Blues*	40.00 -	60.00
7043 *Black Cat Blues*	40.00 -	60.00

HATTIE NORTH:

Vocalion 1433 *Honey Dripper Blues*	30.00 -	40.00

NUGRAPE TWINS:

Columbia 14187-D, 14251-D	6.00 -	10.00

OAK CLIFF T-BONE:

Columbia 14506-D *Trinity River Blues*	50.00 -	75.00

JIMMIE/JIMMY ODEN:

Bluebird 5260 *My Dream Blues*	20.00 -	30.00
Champion 16540 *I Have Made Up My Mind*	40.00 -	60.00
16613 *Patrol Wagon Blues*	40.00 -	60.00

50044 *Patrol Wagon Blues*	15.00 -	25.00
Sunrise 3343 *Warning Spirit Blues*	20.00 -	30.00

OLD MAN ODEN:

Decca 7017 *Six Feet In The Ground*	20.00 -	30.00
7412 *Silk Worm Blues*	15.00 -	20.00
7545 *Thick And Thin*	15.00 -	20.00

OLD CED ODOM:

Decca 7241 *Hotter Than Fire*	7.00 -	10.00
7247 *Break 'Er Down*	7.00 -	10.00
7276 *Fore Day In The Morning*	7.00 -	10.00

OLD PAL SMOKE SHOP FOUR:

Vocalion 1046 *Black Cat Blues*	35.00 -	50.00

OLD SOUTH QUARTETTE:

Broadway 5031 *Pussy Cat Rag*	15.00 -	20.00
QRS 7006 *Pussy Cat Rag*	15.00 -	20.00
7025 *No Hiding Place Down Here*	15.00 -	20.00
7029 *Watermelon Party*	15.00 -	20.00

ONE ARM SLIM:

Bluebird 7806 *Howling Man Blues*	20.00 -	30.00
Vocalion 04676 *Crap Shootin' Blues*	10.00 -	15.00

ONE STRING SAM:

J.V.B. 40 *I Need A Hundred Dollars*	25.00 -	40.00

THE ORIOLES:

Jubilee 5000 *Barbra Lee*	8.00 -	12.00
5001 *Dare To Dream*	10.00 -	15.00
5002 *It Seems So Long Ago*	10.00 -	15.00
5005 *Tell Me So*	7.00 -	10.00*
5008 *I Challenge Your Kiss*	7.00 -	10.00*
Natural 5000 *Barbra Lee*	8.00 -	12.00

JOHN OSCAR:

Brunswick 7080 *In The Gutter*	30.00 -	40.00
7104 *Mama Don't Allow No Easy Riders Here*	20.00 -	30.00
7203 *Whoopee Mama Blues*	50.00 -	75.00
Decca 7029 *Got To Be Worried Now*	10.00 -	15.00

DUKE OWENS & BUD WILSON:

Gennett 6366 *When A Man Is Treated Like A Dog*	40.00 -	60.00

"BIG BOY" GEORGE OWENS:

Gennett 6006 *Kentucky Blues*	60.00 -	80.00

MARSHALL OWENS:

Paramount 13117 *Texas Blues*	150.00 -	200.00
13131 *Texas Blues—Part 2*	150.00 -	200.00

WILLIE "SCARE CROW" OWENS:

Brunswick 7213 *Cut It Out*	50.00 -	75.00

ROBERT N. PAGE:

Victor 21067 *Ride End Shine On The Dummy Line*	10.00 -	15.00

STAR PAGE:

Paramount 12684 *Georgia Blues*	20.00 -	30.00

DUKE PAIGE:

Juke Box 520 *Two Faced Woman Blues*	7.00 -	10.00

SYLVESTER PALMER:

Columbia 14492-D *Lonesome Man Blues*	30.00 -	40.00
14524-D *Broke Man Blues*	30.00 -	40.00

FRANK PALMES:

Paramount 12893 *Troubled 'Bout My Soul*	75.00 -	100.00

PALMETTO JAZZ QUARTET:

Okeh 8011 *My Jazz Gal*	10.00 -	15.00
8016 *Sweet Mamma (Papa's Getting Mad)*	10.00 -	15.00
8023 *Baseball Blues*	10.00 -	15.00
8028 *"U" Need Some Loving*	10.00 -	15.00
8034 *Norfolk Religion*	10.00 -	15.00

PAPA CHARLIE'S BOYS:

Bluebird 6408 *Let My Peaches Be*	10.00 -	15.00
6602 *Gypsy Woman Blues*	10.00 -	15.00

PAPA EGG SHELL:

Brunswick 7082 *I'm Goin' Up In The Country*	60.00 -	80.00
7095 *Whole Soul Blues*	60.00 -	80.00

PAPA FREDDIE:

Okeh 8422 *Way Back Down Home*	60.00 -	80.00

PAPA TOO SWEET:

Okeh 8651 *Big Fat Mama*	30.00 -	40.00

EVA PARKER:

PARKER		
Victor 20414 *You Got Yourself Another Woman*	15.00 -	20.00
38020 *Careless Love*	15.00 -	20.00

LITTLE JUNIOR PARKER & HIS BLUE FLAMES:

Modern 864 *You're My Angel*	7.00 -	10.00

MEL PARKER:

Victor 23387 *Don't Treat Me Like A Dog*	35.00 -	50.00

MONISTER PARKER:

Nucraft 100 *Black Snake Blues*	20.00 -	30.00

SHORTY BOB PARKER:

Decca 7470 *Death Of Slim Green*	10.00 -	15.00
7488 *Tired Of Being Drug Around*	10.00 -	15.00
7526 *Rain And Snow*	10.00 -	15.00

TURNER PARRISH:

Champion 16509 *Four Day Blues*	40.00 -	60.00
16629 *Graveyard Blues*	40.00 -	60.00
16645 *Trenches*	50.00 -	80.00
50027 *Graveyard Blues*	10.00 -	15.00
50046 *Fives*	10.00 -	15.00

LILA PATTERSON:

Broadway 5005 *Grievin' Hearted Blues*	30.00 -	45.00
5010 *Don't Fish In My Sea*	30.00 -	45.00
5018 *Dead Drunk Blues*	30.00 -	45.00

PATTON AND LEE:

Vocalion 02904 *Troubled 'Bout My Mother*	90.00 -	120.00

CHARLEY PATTON:

Paramount 12792 *Banty Rooster Blues*	100.00 -	150.00
12854 *It Won't Be Long*	100.00 -	150.00
12869 *A Spoonful Blues*	100.00 -	150.00
12877 *Pea Vine Blues*	100.00 -	150.00
12883 *Lord I'm Discouraged*	100.00 -	150.00
12909 *High Water Everywhere*	100.00 -	150.00
12924 *Rattlesnake Blues*	100.00 -	150.00
12943 *Magnolia Blues*	100.00 -	150.00
12953 *Mean Black Moan*	100.00 -	150.00
12972 *Green River Blues*	100.00 -	150.00
12986 *I Shall Not Be Moved*	125.00 -	175.00
12998 *Hammer Blues*	125.00 -	175.00
13014 *Moon Going Down*	125.00 -	175.00
13031 *Some Happy Day*	125.00 -	175.00
13040 *Devil Sent The Rain*	125.00 -	175.00
13070 *Dry Well Blues*	125.00 -	175.00
13080 *Some Summer Day*	125.00 -	175.00
13110 *Frankie And Albert*	125.00 -	175.00
13133 *Joe Kirby*	125.00 -	175.00
Vocalion 02651 *Poor Me*	100.00 -	120.00
02680 *High Sheriff Blues*	100.00 -	120.00
02782 *Love My Stuff*	100.00 -	120.00
02931 *Revenue Man Blues*	100.00 -	120.00

RUBY PAUL:

Paramount 12592 *Red Letter Blues*	60.00 -	80.00

GUILFORD (PEACHTREE) PAYNE:

Okeh 8103 *Peachtree Man Blues*	7.00 -	10.00

PEANUT THE KIDNAPPER:

Titles, issued contemporaneously on Banner, Conqueror, Melotone, Oriole, Perfect, Romeo: *Eighth avenue Blues; Silver Spade Blues; Suicide Blues; Swagger Woman Blues*	40.00 -	60.00

ALICE PEARSON:

Paramount 12507 *Memphis Earthquake*	40.00 -	60.00
12523 *Greyhound Blues*	40.00 -	60.00
12547 *Black Sow Blues*	40.00 -	60.00

BILL PEARSON:

Brunswick 7053 *Detroit Blues*	30.00 -	40.00

DAVID PEARSON:

Okeh 8847 *Friendless Blues*	40.00 -	60.00

MEMPHIS EDDIE PEE:

Globe 103, 108	5.00 -	10.00

ROBERT PEEPLES:

Paramount 12995 *Fat Greasy Baby*	100.00 -	150.00
13033 *Mama's Boy*	100.00 -	150.00

PEETIE'S BOY:

Decca 7767 *Gonna Keep It For My Daddy*	8.00 -	12.00
7819 *Friar's Point Blues*	8.00 -	12.00

PEETIE WHEATSTRAW'S BUDDY:

Hy-Tone 38 *Miss Irene*	10.00 -	15.00

MORRIS PEJOE:

Checker 766 *Gonna Buy Me A Telephone*	5.00 -	8.00*

CORA PERKINS:

Okeh 8348 *Today Blues*	10.00 -	15.00

DOLLY PERKINS:

Emerson 10761 *My Doggone Lazy Man*	10.00 -	15.00

CHARLES "SPECK" PERTUM:

Brunswick 7128 *Broken Down Blues*	50.00 -	75.00
7146 *Gambler's Blues*	50.00 -	75.00

PETE AND REPEAT:

Brunswick 7055 *Hymn-Singing Bill*	15.00 -	25.00
7104 *Toodle-Oodle-Oo*	20.00 -	30.00

CHARLEY PETERS:

Herwin 92036 *Lord I'm Discouraged*	90.00 -	130.00

ARTHUR PETTIES/PETTIS:

Brunswick 7182 *Good Boy Blues*	60.00 -	80.00
7209 *Quarrellin' Mama Blues*	60.00 -	80.00
Victor 21282 *Two Time Blues*	40.00 -	60.00

ROBERT PETWAY:

Bluebird 8726 *Rockin' Chair Blues*	10.00 -	15.00
8756 *Sleepy Woman Blues*	10.00 -	15.00
8786 *My Little Girl*	10.00 -	15.00
8838 *Catfish Blues*	10.00 -	15.00
8987 *Boogie Woogie Woman*	7.00 -	10.00
9008 *My Baby Left Me*	10.00 -	15.00

WASHINGTON PHILLIPS:

Columbia 14277-D *Lift Him Up That's All*	15.00 -	20.00
14333-D *Denomination Blues*	15.00 -	20.0
14369-D *Paul And Silas In Jail*	15.00 -	20.00
14404-D *Jesus Is My Friend*	15.00 -	20.00
14448-D *Train Your Child*	15.00 -	20.00
14511-D *I've Got The Key To The Kingdom*	15.00 -	20.00
14566-D *The Church Needs Good Deacons*	15.00 -	20.00

PIANO RED:

RCA Victor	3.00 -	6.00

PICANINNY/PICKANINNY JUG BAND:

Champion 15995 *Diamond Ring Blues*	35.00 -	50.00
16615 *Bottle It Up And Go*	75.00 -	100.00

WALTER/FATS PICHON:

DeLuxe 3069 *Pinetop's Boogie*	7.00 -	10.00
3072 *Cherry*	7.00 -	10.00
Raynac 1101 *Fat And Greasy*	7.00 -	10.00

CHARLIE PICKETT:

Decca 7707 *Down The Highway*	15.00 -	20.00
7762 *Trembling Blues*	15.00 -	20.00

DAN PICKETT:

Gotham 201 *Laughing Rag*	10.00 -	20.00
510 *Early One Morning*	10.00 -	20.00
512 *Chicago Blues*	10.00 -	20.00
516 *Lemon Man*	10.00 -	20.00
542 *Baby How Long*	10.00 -	20.00

PIG 'N' WHISTLE BAND:

Regal 3277 *Talking To You Mama*	25.00 -	35.00

PIGMEAT PETE (AND CATJUICE CHARLIE):

Columbia 14452-D *Can You Do That To Me?*	15.00 -	20.00
14463-D *Do It Right*	15.00 -	20.00
14485-D *My Friend John*	15.00 -	20.00
14513-D *Our Family Doctor*	15.00 -	20.00
14563-D *In Kentucky*	15.00 -	20.00
14588-D *Hard Times*	20.00 -	30.00
14598-D *Honey You Done Gone Too Far*	20.00 -	30.00
14640-D *Rockin' Chair Mary*	20.00 -	30.00

PIGMEAT TERRY:

Champion 50043 *Black Sheep Blues*	15.00 -	20.00
Decca 7829 *Moaning The Blues*	15.00 -	20.00

PINETOP:

Bluebird 6041 *Workhouse Blues*.............	20.00 -	30.00
6125 *Every Day I Have The Blues*.........	20.00 -	30.00
6202 *Got The Blues About My Baby*.......	20.00 -	30.00

PINETOP AND LINDBERG:

Victor 23330 *East Chicago Blues*............	100.00 -	150.00
23359 *Louisiana Bound*..................	100.00 -	150.00

PINETOP SLIM:

Colonial 106 *Applejack Boogie*...........	15.00 -	20.00

PINEWOOD TOM (& HIS BLUES HOUNDS):

Titles, issued contemporaneously on Banner, Conqueror, Melotone, Oriole, Perfect, Romeo: *Badly Mistreated Man; Bed Springs Blues; Black Gal; Black Man; Broad Players Blues; Cherry Picker; D.B.A. Blues; Did You Read That Letter?; Evil Man Blues; Friendless City Blues; Gone Dry Blues; Gone Mother Blues; Good Gal; Greenville Sheik; Homeless and Hungry Blues; Mean Mistreater Mama; Milk Cow Blues; New D.B.A. Blues; New Mean Mistreater Blues; New Milk Cow Blues; No More Ball And Chain; Pigmeat And Whiskey Blues; Prodigal Son; She's Alright With Me; Silicosis Is Killin' Me; Sissy Man; Stormy Weather No. 1; Talking About My Time; Tweet Tweet Mama Blues; Welfare Blues; When The Sun Goes Down*....................

	15.00 -	20.00

JAMES PLATT:

Champion 15860 *Sympathizin' Blues*...........	40.00 -	60.00
15880 *Easy Papa*....................	40.00 -	60.00
15927 *Back-Biter Blues*..............	40.00 -	60.00
16059 *Texas Dream Blues*............	40.00 -	60.00

FRANK PLUITT:

Bluebird 5383 *Found A Note On My Door*.....	25.00 -	35.00
Sunrise 3464 *Found A Note On My Door*......	25.00 -	35.00
Victor 23428 *Meningitis Blues*.............	60.00 -	90.00

POOR BILL:

Varsity 6020 *A Hundred Women*............	10.00 -	15.00

POOR CHARLIE:

Vocalion 03652 *My Little Machine*............	10.00 -	15.00

POOR JAB:

Champion 16483 *Poor Jab Blues*..............	100.00 -	150.00
16630 *Get It From Behind*................	100.00 -	150.00
16654 *Come Along Little Children*..........	100.00 -	150.00

POOR JIM (WITH DAN JACKSON):

Titles, issued contemporaneously on Banner, Conqueror, Melotone, Oriole, Perfect, Romeo: *Blue And Worried Woman; Squeaky Work Bench Blues; Stack O'Dollars Blues; Sugar Farm Blues*

	75.00 -	100.00

JENNY POPE:

Vocalion 1438 *Whiskey Drinkin' Blues*........	30.00 -	40.00
1489 *Mr. Postman Blues*.................	40.00 -	60.00
1522 *Bull Frog Blues*..................	50.00 -	75.00

FLOSSIE PORTER:

Champion 15101 *Ain't Got Nobody to Grind My Coffee*..................................	25.00 -	35.00
15102 *Mama's Losin' A Mighty Good Chance*	25.00 -	35.00

SONNY PORTER:

Columbia 14366-D *Deck Hand Blues*.........	10.00 -	15.00

NETTIE POTTER:

Banner 1483 *A Good Man Is Hard To Find*....	10.00 -	15.00
1484 *Blind Man Blues*..................	10.00 -	15.00
Pathe-Actuelle 032122 *Nobody Knows The Way I Fell*..................................	10.00 -	15.00
032124 *Meat Man Blues*.................	10.00 -	15.00
Regal 9764 *Who Calls You Sweet Mama Now?*.	10.00 -	15.00
9781 *Blind Man Blues*.................	10.00 -	15.00
9782 *A Good Man Is Hard To Find*........	10.00 -	15.00

LOUIS POWELL:

Vocalion 04040 *Mushmouth Blues*..........	8.00 -	12.00

JULIA/JULIUS POWERS:

Harmograph 827 *Weary Way Blues*..........	25.00 -	35.00
829 *Bama Bound Blues*.................	15.00 -	25.00

847 *Any Woman's Blues*.................	15.00 -	25.00
858 *Chicago Bound Blues*..............	15.00 -	25.00
872 *Chattanooga Blues*................	25.00 -	35.00
883 *Moanin' Groanin' Blues*...........	50.00 -	75.00
897 *Mama Doo Shee Blues*.............	30.00 -	40.00

BUD PRESTON'S STRING BAND:

Champion 15509 *Those Next Mornin' Blues*....	75.00 -	100.00

L.C. PRIGETT:

Victor 20953 *Sure As You Take A Woman From*	12.00 -	18.00
21359 *Frogtown Blues*..................	50.00 -	75.00

WES PRINCE & HIS RHYTHM PRINCES:

Excelsior 167, 170...................	6.00 -	10.00

HELEN PROCTOR:

Decca 7666 *Cheatin' On Me*................	6.00 -	10.00
7703 *Let's Call It A Day*.............	6.00 -	10.00

SNOOKY PRYOR:

J.O.B. 101 *Boogy Fool*...................	30.00 -	40.00
115 *Going Back On The Road*..........	10.00 -	15.00
Parrot 807 *Crosstown Blues*..............	7.00 -	10.00*

PULLMAN PORTERS QUARTETTE:

Paramount 12607 *Pullman Passenger Train*.....	10.00 -	15.00

JOE PULLEM/PULLUM (& HIS ORCHESTRA/ROBERT COOPER):

Bluebird 5459 *Black Gal What Makes Your Head So Hard?*...........................	15.00 -	20.00
5534 *Cows, See That Train Comin'*..........	15.00 -	25.00
5592 *Black Gal What Makes Your Head So Hard No. 2*..............................	20.00 -	30.00
5661 *McKinney Street Stomp*............	20.00 -	30.00
5844 *Mississippi Flood Blues*...........	20.00 -	30.00
5859 *Careful Drivin' Mama*.............	20.00 -	30.00
5898 *Rack It Back And Tell It Right*.....	20.00 -	30.00
5947 *Black Gal No. 4*.................	15.00 -	25.00
6071 *Joe Louis Is The Man*.............	15.00 -	25.00
6093 *Bad Break Blues*.................	15.00 -	25.00
6123 *I Can't Control Myself*...........	15.00 -	25.00
6185 *Ice Man Blues*..................	15.00 -	25.00
6276 *Hard Working Man Blues*..........	15.00 -	25.00
6298 *Telephone Blues*.................	15.00 -	25.00
Bluebird 6314 *Swing Them Blues*............	8.00 -	12.00
6372 *Woman Trouble Blues*............	8.00 -	12.00
6426 *Hattie Green*...................	8.00 -	12.00
Montgomery Ward 4833 *I Believe In You*.....	15.00 -	20.00
4986 *Traveling Blues*.................	15.00 -	20.00
Swing Time 267 *My Woman*...............	8.00 -	12.00

DOUG QUATTLEBAUM:

Gotham 519 *Lizzie Lou*....................	15.00 -	20.00*

SIS QUANDER:

Pathe-Actuelle 7528 *Mama Is Waiting For You*.	8.00 -	12.00
7530 *Black Snake Blues*...............	8.00 -	12.00
Perfect 128 *Mama Is Waiting For You*......	8.00 -	12.00
130 *Black Snake Blues*..............	8.00 -	12.00

RUFUS AND BEN QUILLIAN (WITH JAMES McCRAVY):

Columbia 14560-D *Keep It Clean*.............	12.00 -	16.00
14584-D *Working It Slow*...............	12.00 -	16.00
14616-D *It's Dirty But Good*...........	12.00 -	16.00
14639-D *Workin' It Fast*..............	12.00 -	16.00

YANK RACHELL (AND DAN SMITH):

Bluebird 7525 *Rachel Blues*...............	15.00 -	20.00
7602 *Lake Michigan Blues*.............	15.00 -	20.00
7694 *It's All Over*...................	15.00 -	20.00
7731 *Texas Tommy*..................	15.00 -	20.0
Bluebird 8732 *38 Pistol Blues*............	8.00 -	12.00
8768 *Biscuit Baking Woman*...........	8.00 -	12.00
8796 *Insurance Man Blues*............	8.00 -	12.00
8840 *Army Man Blues*...............	8.00 -	12.00
8951 *Yellow Yam Blues*..............	8.00 -	12.00
8993 *Rainy Day Blues*...............	8.00 -	12.00
9033 *Peach Tree Blues*...............	8.00 -	12.00
34-0715 *Katy Lee Blues*..............	8.00 -	12.00

RCA Victor 20-2955 *38 Pistol Blues*.......... 5.00 - 8.00
Vocalion 02649 *Gravel Road Woman*......... 75.00 - 100.00
CARL RAFFERTY:
Bluebird 5429 *Mr. Carl's Blues*.............. 20.00 - 30.00
RAILROAD BILL:
Melotone 12373 *M And O Blues*.............. 15.00 - 20.00
RAINEY, BIG MEMPHIS MA:
Sun 184 *Baby No No*...................... 40.00 - 60.00*
RAMBLIN' BOB:
Bluebird 7987 *Big Apple Blues*............. 15.00 - 25.00
8020 *Ol' Mose*......................... 15.00 - 25.00
8059 *Good Gamblin'*..................... 15.00 - 25.00
8067 *Freight Train Blues*............... 15.00 - 25.00
GEORGE RAMSEY (AND MAE BELLE LEE):
Paramount 13067 *Times Done Get Hard*...... 30.00 - 40.00
13068 *Bumble Bee No. 1*................ 30.00 - 40.00
13071 *Perfect Mess Blues*.............. 30.00 - 40.00
JACK RANGER:
Okeh 8795 *Thieving Blues*................. 40.00 - 60.00
8847 *Lonesome Grave Blues*............ 40.00 - 60.00
RUBY RANKIN (and GEORGE HAMILTON):
Champion 15736 *Shadow Blues*............. 35.00 - 50.00
15756 *Mistreated Mama Blues*.......... 35.00 - 50.00
15857 *Got Jelly On My Mind*........... 35.00 - 50.00
15902 *Southern High Water Blues*...... 35.00 - 50.00
16057 *Southern High Water Blues*...... 35.00 - 50.00
HERMAN RAY:
Decca 48105, 48107..................... 3.00 - 6.00
RED AND HIS WASHBOARD BAND:
Vocalion 03965 *Prowling Groundhog No. 2*.... 10.00 - 15.00
THE RED DEVIL:
Vocalion 03954 *Huntsman Blues*............ 8.00 - 12.00
RED HOT OLD MAN MOSE:
Paramount 12605 *Shrimp Man*.............. 30.00 - 40.00
RED ONION JOE AND HIS UKE THUMPERS:
Champion 15928 *Humming Blues*........... 20.00 - 30.00
JIMMY REED:
Chance 1142 *High And Lonesome*........... 8.00 - 12.00*
Vee Jay 100 *High And Lonesome*......... 5.00 - 8.00*
105 *Jimmy's Boogie*................. 5.00 - 8.00*
Vee Jay 119, 132, 153, 168, 186, 203, 226, 237. 3.00 - 5.00*
LONG CLEVE REED & THE DOWN-HOME BOYS:
Black Patti 8030 *Mama You Don't Know How.* 150.00 - 200.00
SADIE REED:
Champion 15435 *Fall Or Summer Blues*....... 30.00 - 40.00
WILLIE REED:
Columbia 14407-D *Dreaming Blues*.......... 30.00 - 40.00
Vocalion 03093 *All Worn Out And Dry Blues*.. 20.00 - 30.00
SLIM REESE:
Sittin' In With 581 *Got The World In A Jug*... 5.00 - 8.00
BLIND JOE REYNOLDS:
Broadway 5106 *Outside Woman Blues*........ 150.00 - 200.00
Paramount 12927 *Nehi Blues*.............. 150.00 - 200.00
12983 *Cold Woman Blues*............... 150.00 - 200.00
TEDDY REYNOLDS:
Sittin' In With 558, 571, 586, 594, 613........ 5.00 - 8.00
BLIND WILLIE REYNOLDS:
Victor 23258 *Third Street Woman Blues*....... 90.00 - 120.00
MACK RHINEHART & BROWNIE STUBBLEFIELD:
Titles, issued contemporaneously on Banner, Melotone, Oriole, Perfect, Romeo: *Blues After Sundown; Broke And Hungary; Clay County Blues; Dirty No Gooder; I Can't Take It Any More; If I Leave Here Running; Lonesome House Blues; Lost Woman Blues; Open Back Door Blues; T.P.N. Moaner; Up-town Blues; You Don't Know My Mind*.................... 30.00 - 50.00
WALTER RHODES:
Columbia 14289-D *The Crowing Rooster*...... 30.00 - 40.00

RHYTHM WILLIE (& HIS GANG):
Okeh 05856 *Bedroom Stomp*.............. 7.00 - 12.00
05960 *Boarding House Blues*........... 7.00 - 12.00
Premium 866 *Wailin' Willie*............. 7.00 - 10.00
RICHARD BROTHERS:
Strate-8 1500 *Stolen Property*............ 35.00 - 50.00*
ROBERT RICHARD:
JVB 75828 *Cadillac Woman*.............. 35.00 - 50.00
King 4274 *Wigwam Woman*.............. 10.00 - 15.00
SETH RICHARD:
Columbia 14325-D *Lonely Seth Blues*....... 25.00 - 35.00
UNCLE CHARLIE RICHARDS:
Pathe-Actuelle 7521 *Levee Blues*.......... 10.00 - 15.00
7527 *Sore Bunion Blues*............... 10.00 - 15.00
Perfect 121 *Levee Blues*............... 10.00 - 15.00
127 *Sore Bunion Blues*............. 10.00 - 15.00
"MOOCH" RICHARDSON:
Okeh 8554 *T And T Blues*............... 25.00 - 35.00
8576 *Big Kate Adams Blues*........... 25.00 - 35.00
8611 *Helena Blues*.................. 25.00 - 35.00
RICHMOND STARLIGHT (JAZZ) QUARTET:
QRS 7028 *Gone Jazz Crazy*............. 15.00 - 20.00
7056 *Oh, You Better Mind*............ 15.00 - 20.00
EHTEL RIDLEY:
Ajax 17126 *Get It Fixed*............... 15.00 - 25.00
17131 *He Was A Good Man*............ 15.00 - 25.00
Columbia A-3941, A-3965................ 5.00 - 8.00
Victor 19111 *Memphis, Tennessee*......... 8.00 - 12.00
WILLIE (BOODLE IT) RIGHT:
Okeh 05959 *Down South Blues*........... 7.00 - 10.00
06008 *Sunny Land Blues*............. 7.00 - 10.00
06057 *West Texas Blues*............. 7.00 - 10.00
ISSIE RINGGOLD:
Columbia 1450]9-D *He's A Good Meat Cutter*.. 20.00 - 30.00
HUBERT ROBERTSON & HIS ORCHESTRA:
Eddies 1211 *Lonely Traveler*............ 5.00 - 8.00
GIP ROBERTS:
JVB 29 *Sandman*..................... 10.00 - 15.00
HELEN ROBERTS:
Silvertone 3570 *Lonely Blues*............ 30.00 - 40.00
SISTER MINNIE PEARL ROBERTS:
Brunswick 7179 *You Make Your Troubles So Hard* 15.00 - 20.00
SALLY ROBERTS:
Okeh 8485 *Gonna Ramble Blues*.......... 15.00 - 25.00
8500 *Black Hearse Blues*............. 15.00 - 25.00
SNITCHER ROBERTS:
Okeh 8750 *Low Moaning Blues*.......... 40.00 - 60.00
8781 *Snitcher's Blues*.............. 40.00 - 60.00
ROBINSON BROTHERS:
Black & White 107, 108................. 7.00 - 10.00
ROBINSON & MACK:
Okeh 8259 *I Beg To Be Excused*.......... 10.00 - 15.00
8298 *It's All The Same To Me*......... 10.00 - 15.00
8321 *Booze*...................... 10.00 - 15.00
ALEXANDER ROBINSON:
Paramount 12649 *My Baby*.............. 35.00 - 50.00
HUBERT ROBINSON (& HIS YARDBIRDS):
Jade 206 *Hard Lovin' Daddy*............ 5.00 - 8.00
Macy's 5005, 5007, 5010, 5015............ 5.00 - 8.00
JAMES "BAT" ROBINSON:
Champion 16236 *Bat's Own Blues*......... 40.00 - 60.00
16745 *Humming Blues*............... 40.00 - 60.00
MABEL ROBINSON:
Decca 8568, 8580, 8601................. 4.00 - 7.00
MUSHMOUTH ROBINSON:
Black & White 105 *Boogie Boo Blues*........ 5.00 - 8.00
NETTIE ROBINSON:
Pathe-Actuelle 7523 *I've Got The Right Man Now* 10.00 - 15.00
Perfect 123 *I've Got The Right Man Now*...... 10.00 - 15.00
JIMMY ROGERS (& HIS TRIO/ROCKING FOUR):
Chess 1435 *That's All Right*............. 8.00 - 15.00*

1442 *Going Away Baby*................	8.00 -	15.00*
1453, 1476.................	7.00 -	10.00*
1506, 1519, 1543, 1574, 1616, 1643.......	3.00 -	6.00*
1659, 1687, 1721................	3.00 -	5.00

MAE ROGERS:
Champion 16530 *My Time Blues*.......... 35.00 - 50.00

MAY ROGERS:
Champion 15590 *Road House Blues*......... 35.00 - 50.00

WALTER ROLAND:
Titles, issued contemporaneously on Banner, Conqueror, Melotone, Oriole, Perfect, Romeo: *Back Door Blues; Bad Dream Blues; Big Mama; Club Meeting Blues; Cold Blooded Murder; Collector Man Blues; C.W.A. Blues; Dices' Blues; Early This Morning; Early In The Morning No. 2; Every Morning Blues; 45 Pistol BLues; House Lady Blues; Last Year Blues; Man, Man, Man; Money Taker Woman; O.B.O. Blues; Overall Blues; Penniless Blues; Red Cross Blues No. 2; Sail On Little Girl No. 2; Schoolboy Blues; Screw Worm; Slavin' Blues; S.O.L. Blues; Talkin' Low Blues; T Model Blues; Worn Out Man Blues; You Gonna Want Me*.............. 30.00 - 40.00

MAMIE ROMER:
Oriole 325 *A Good Man Is Hard To Find*...... 10.00 - 15.00

BAYLESS ROSE:
Champion 16037 *Black Dog Blues*............ 35.00 - 50.00
16772 *Frisco Blues*.............. 35.00 - 50.00
Gennett 7250 *Black Dog Blues*........... 35.00 - 50.00

LUCY ROSE:
Champion 15471 *Papa, You're Too Slow*...... 30.00 - 40.00

BERTHA ROSS:
Gennett 6227 *My Jelly Blues*............... 40.00 - 60.00
6243 *Lost Man Blues*............. 40.00 - 60.00
Superior 331 *Tea Rollin' Blues*.......... 40.00 - 60.00

DOCTOR/DR. ROSS (& HIS JUMP & JIVE BOYS):
Chess 1504 *Dr. Ross Boogie*............. 10.00 - 15.00*
Sun 193 *Chicago Breakdown*............... 20.00 - 30.00*
212 *The Boogie Disease*.................. 20.00 - 30.00*

DOLLY ROSS:
Brunswick 7005 *Hootin' Owl Blues*......... 12.00 - 16.00
Vocalion 1166 *Hootin' Owl Blues*........... 12.00 - 16.00

LOUISE ROSS:
Columbia 14118-D *No Home Blues*........ 15.00 - 20.00

LUCY ROSS:
Champion 15715 *West End Blues*......... 25.00 - 40.00
15754 *Loose Like That*............... 25.00 - 40.00
15775 *Cotton Belt Blues*.............. 25.00 - 40.00

OLLIE ROSS:
Brunswick 7045 *Ox Meat Blues*........... 35.00 - 50.00

TED ROSS:
Champion 15859 *Mother-In-Law Blues*........ 40.00 - 60.00
15882 *Clickety-Clack Blues*.............. 40.00 - 60.00

WILL ROWLAND & HIS BAND (Vocal, JESSE LOCKETT):
Gold Star 657 *Don't Lose Your Mind*........ 7.00 - 10.00

LAURA RUCKER:
Paramount 13030 *I'm The Lonesome One*...... 40.00 - 60.00
13075 *Little Joe*.................. 40.00 - 60.00
13138 *Fancy Tricks*............... 50.00 - 75.00

OLLIE RUPERT:
Victor 20577 *Ain't Goin' To Be Your Low Down Dog*.............. 50.00 - 75.00

LILLIAN RUSH:
Champion 15510 *Do What You Did Last Night*. 30.00 - 40.00
15529 *There's Been Some Changes Made*..... 30.00 - 40.00

BLIND TIM RUSSELL:
Herwin 93008 *I've Crossed The Separation Line*. 40.00 - 60.00

GEORGE "HAMBONE" RUTHERS:
Champion 15795 *Street Walkin' Blues*........ 25.00 - 35.00

ST. LOUIS BESSIE:
Vocalion 1559 *Sugar Man Blues*............. 30.00 - 40.00
1615 *Meat Cutter Blues*................. 30.00 - 40.00

ST. LOUIS JIMMY:
Apollo 420 *Chicago Woman Blues*........... 7.00 - 10.00
Aristocrat 7001 *Florida Hurricane*......... 15.00 - 25.00
Bluebird 8889 *Going Down Slow*............ 8.00 - 12.00
8933 *Lost Ball Blues*............... 8.00 - 12.00
9016, 9040, 34-0718, 34-0727...... 5.00 - 10.00
Bullet 270 *Going Down Slow*........... 8.00 - 12.00
278 *Sittin' And Thinkin'*............. 8.00 - 12.00
291 *Mr. Brown Boogie*............. 8.00 - 12.00
Herald 407 *Hard Luck Boogie*........... 5.00 - 8.00*
J.O.B. 101 *Mother's Day*............. 50.00 - 75.00
Mercury 8137 *Shame On You Baby*........... 5.00 - 8.00
Miracle 134 *Biscuit Roller*................. 5.00 - 8.00
RCA Victor 20-2650 *Dog House Blues*....... 3.00 - 6.00

ST. LOUIS JOHNNY:
Champion 50071 *Sister Kelly Blues*........... 15.00 - 20.00

ST. LOUIS RED MIKE:
Bluebird 7744 *Red Mike Blues*.............. 10.00 - 15.00
7781 *Wash My Hands Nice And Clean*...... 10.00 - 15.00
7896 *Gamblin' Man Blues*............ 10.00 - 15.00

SALLY SAD:
Varsity 6033 *Don't Say Goodbye*............ 10.00 - 15.00
6040 *Gin House Blues*............ 10.00 - 15.00
6058 *Mistreated Mamma Blues*....... 10.00 - 15.00
6066 *Gypsy Woman Blues*............ 10.00 - 15.00

SALTY DOG SAM:
Titles, issued contemporaneously on Banner, Melotone, Oriole, Perfect, Romeo: *Graveyard Digger's Blues; I'm Still Sitting On Top Of The World; Lonesome Road Blues; New Salty Dog; Signifying Blues; Slow Mama Slow*......... 100.00 - 150.00

SAM AND OSCAR:
Brunswick 7208 *You Can't Get That Stuff No More* 15.00 - 20.00
7212 *I Done Caught That Rascal Now*...... 15.00 - 20.00

SAMMY SAMPSON:
Titles, issued contemporaneously on Banner, Oriole, Perfect, Romeo: *I Got The Blues For My Baby; Meanest Kind Of Blues; Police Station Blues; State Street Woman; Tadpole Blues; They Can't Do That*......... 25.00 - 40.00

CLARENCE SAMUELS:
Aristocrat 1001 *Boogie Woogie Blues*......... 10.00 - 15.00
DeLuxe 3219 *Stompin' At The Jubilee*......... 4.00 - 8.00
Freedom 1533, 1541, 1544................. 4.00 - 8.00
Swing Time 131, 149................. 4.00 - 8.00

BESSIE SANDERS (& HER DIXIE DUDES):
Champion 15101 *It Must Be Hard*........... 15.00 - 20.00
15102 *Take Your Fingers Off It*........... 15.00 - 20.00
15106 *Home Alone Blues*.............. 25.00 - 35.00
15180 *Lucky Number Blues*............. 25.00 - 35.00
15471 *Shake A Little Bit*............. 25.00 - 35.00
15490 *Dying Blues*................. 25.00 - 35.00
15550 *Where Have All The Black Men Gone?* 25.00 - 35.00
15613 *Wild Geese Blues*............. 25.00 - 35.00
15635 *Red Beans And Rice*........... 25.00 - 35.00
16058 *I Lost My Man*................. 25.00 - 35.00
16216 *Bring It Back Daddy*............. 25.00 - 35.00

GERTRUDE SAUNDERS:
Vocalion 1131 *Don't Let Your Love Come Down* 10.00 - 15.00

THE SCARE CROW:
Champion 16014 *Easy Creeping Mama*........ 60.00 - 90.00
16036 *Traveling Blues*.............. 60.00 - 90.00
16103 *Ornery Blues*............. 60.00 - 90.00
16194 *That Black Bottom Dance*........... 60.00 - 90.00

BEVERLY SCOTT & HIS TRIO:
Murray 503 *Shaking The Boogie*......... 10.00 - 20.00

ELLIE SCOTT:
Vocalion 1461 *Sunshine Special*............. 30.00 - 40.00

LANNIE SCOTT TRIO:
Savoy 614 *Lannie's Boogie Woogie*............. 5.00 - 8.00

LULU SCOTT:
Bluebird 7706 *Baby Can I Holler*............. 7.00 - 10.00

MAE SCOTT:
Paramount 12048 *Squawkin' The Blues*........ 15.00 - 20.00

ROOSEVELT SCOTT:
Vocalion 05137 *Do You Call That Right?*...... 10.00 - 15.00
  05206 *Browskin Woman Swing*............. 10.00 - 15.00
  05371 *Tender Foot Blues*................. 10.00 - 15.00
  05415 *Look Up And Down*................. 10.00 - 15.00
  05502 *Doctor Bill Blues*................. 10.00 - 15.00
  05550 *Down In The Gutter*............... 10.00 - 15.00

SONNY SCOTT:
Vocalion 02533 *No Good Biddie*............. 50.00 - 75.00
  02586 *Black Horse Blues*................ 50.00 - 75.00
  02614 *Fire Wood Man*.................... 50.00 - 75.00
  25012 *Noal Mountain Blues*............. 50.00 - 75.00
  25013 *Working Man's Moan*............. 50.00 - 75.00
  25016 *Naked Man Blues*................. 50.00 - 75.00
  25017 *Red Rooster Blues*................ 50.00 - 75.00

IRENE SCRUGGS:
Champion 16102 *Borrowed Love*............. 30.00 - 50.00
  16148 *My Back To The Wall*............. 30.00 - 50.00
  16756 *The Voice of the Blues*............. 30.00 - 50.00
Gennett 7296 *You've Got What I Want*...... 35.00 - 50.00
Okeh 8142 *Why He Left Me I Don't Know*.... 15.00 - 20.00
  8156 *My Daddy's Calling Me*............. 15.00 - 20.00
  8476 *Lonesome Valley Blues*............. 15.00 - 20.00
Paramount 13023 *Good Meat Grinder*........ 75.00 - 100.00
  13046 *Back To The Wall*............... 75.00 - 100.00
Vocalion 1017 *Home Town Blues*............. 75.00 - 100.00

CHARLIE SEGAR:
Decca 7027 *Southern Hospitality*............. 15.00 - 20.00
  7075 *Cow Cow Blues*................... 15.00 - 20.00
Vocalion 05441 *Key To The Highway*......... 7.00 - 10.00
  05539 *Lonesome Graveyard Blues*........... 7.00 - 10.00

HOWARD SERRATT:
Sun 198 *Troublesome Waters*............. 25.00 - 40.00*

TOMMY SETTLERS & HIS BLUES MOANER:
Paramount 13049 *Low Down Blues Moan*...... 80.00 - 100.00
  13056 *Big Bed Bug*..................... 80.00 - 100.00
  13120 *Blowing The Bugle Blues*............. 80.00 - 100.00

TOMMY SETTLES WITH EZIEKIEL LOWE & LEE BUNKLEY:
Titles, issued contemporaneously on Banner, Melotone, Oriole, Perfect, Romeo: *Don't Want You No More; Pearlie Mae Blues*............. 40.00 - 60.00

SLIM SEWARD & FAT BOY HAYES:
MGM 10306, 10770...................... 7.00 - 10.00

GEORGE SEYMOUR:
Herwin 93016 *Southland Blues*............. 30.00 - 40.00

WILL SHADE:
Champion 16599 *She Done Sold It Out*........ 100.00 - 150.00
  16630 *Get It From The Front*............. 100.00 - 150.00
Victor 21725 *Better Leave That Stuff Alone*.... 75.00 - 100.00

ALLEN SHAW:
Vocalion 02844 *Moanin' The Blues*........... 90.00 - 120.00

THE SHA-WEEZ:
Aladdin 3170 *No One To Love Me*............. 15.00 - 20.00*

JOHNNY SHINES:
J.O.B. 116 *Cool Driver*.................... 30.00 - 50.00*
  1010 *Brutal Hearted Woman*............. 30.00 - 50.00*

SHOE SHINE JOHNNY:
Chess 1443 *Joliet Blues*.................. 15.00 - 25.00

JAYDEE SHORT:
Paramount 13040 *Drafted Mama*............. 100.00 - 150.00
  13043 *Telephone Arguin' Blues*........... 100.00 - 150.00
  13091 *Flaggin' It To Georgia*............. 100.00 - 150.00

JELLY JAW SHORT:
Vocalion 1704 *Snake Doctor Blues*........... 75.00 - 100.00
  1708 *Let Me Mash That Thing*........... 75.00 - 100.00

SHORTY GEORGE:
Brunswick 7106 *Jones Law Blues*............. 35.00 - 50.00

SHREVEPORT HOME WRECKERS:
Victor 23275 *Home Wreckin' Blues*.......... 60.00 - 80.00

SHUFFLIN' SAM & HIS RHYTHM:
Vocalion 03329 *Good Liquor*............. 10.00 - 15.00

BILL SIMPSON:
Lin 100 *Jelly Roll Man*................. 7.00 - 10.00

COLETHA SIMPSON:
Brunswick 7089 *Riverside Blues*............. 40.00 - 60.00
  7112 *Black Man Blues*.................. 40.00 - 60.00

FRANKIE LEE SIMS:
Blue Bonnet 147 *Home Again Blues*......... 25.00 - 40.00
  148 *Single Man Blues*.................. 25.00 - 40.00

HENRY SIMS:
Paramount 12912 *Farrell Blues*............. 150.00 - 200.00
  12940 *Be True Be True Blues*............. 150.00 - 200.00

JOE SIMS AND CLARENCE WILLIAMS:
Paramount 12435 *Shut Your Mouth*.......... 50.00 - 75.00

SKOODLE DUM DOO AND SHEFFIELD:
Manor 1056 *West Kinney Street Blues*........ 10.00 - 15.00
Regis 107 *Gas Ration Blues*.............. 10.00 - 15.00

SLEEPY JOE & HIS WASHBOARD BAND:
Savoy 753 *Amen Blues*................. 7.00 - 10.00

SLOKE & IKE:
Decca 7315 *Chocolate Candy Bars*........... 10.00 - 15.00
  7375 *Slocum Blues*.................... 10.00 - 15.00

SLUEFOOT JOE:
QRS 7080 *House Top Blues*............. 90.00 - 120.00
  7084 *Grab It And Run*................. 90.00 - 120.00
  7086 *Shouting Baby Blues*............. 90.00 - 120.00
  7091 *Rocky Road Moan*................. 90.00 - 120.00

SMITH AND HARPER:
Titles, issued contemporaneously on Banner, Melotone, Oriole, Perfect, Romeo: *Insurance Policy Blues; Poor Girl*................. 35.00 - 50.00

ANNIE SMITH:
Harmograph 896 *Moonshine Blues*........... 35.00 - 45.00

BESSIE SMITH:
Columbia A-3844 *Down Hearted Blues*........ 8.00 - 12.00
  A-3877 *Beale Street Mamma*............. 8.00 - 12.00
  A-3888 *Oh Daddy Blues*............... 7.00 - 10.00
  A-3898 *'Tain't Nobody's Business If I Do*..... 8.00 - 12.00
  A-3900 *Mama's Got The Blues*............. 8.00 - 12.00
  A-3936 *Bleeding Hearted Blues*............. 8.00 - 12.00
  A-3939 *Lady Luck Blues*................. 8.00 - 12.00
  A-3942 *Nobody In Town Can Bake A Sweet Jelly Roll Like Mine*.................. 8.00 - 12.00
  A-4001 *Graveyard Dream Blues*............. 8.00 - 12.00
  13000-D *My Sweetie Went Away*............. 8.00 - 12.00
  13001-D *Any Woman's Blues*............. 10.00 - 15.00
  13005-D *Sam Jones Blues*............. 8.00 - 12.00
  13007-D *Far Away Blues*............. 8.00 - 12.00
  14000-D *Chicago Bound Blues*............. 10.00 - 15.00
  14005-D *Frosty Mornin' Blues*............. 8.00 - 12.00
  14010-D *Eavesdropper's Blues*............. 10.00 - 15.00
  14018-D *Ticket Agent Ease Your Window Down*............. 8.00 - 12.00
  14020-D *Sorrowful Blues*............. 8.00 - 12.00
  14023-D *Hateful Blues*............. 8.00 - 12.00
  14025-D *Pinchbacks-Take 'Em Away*............. 8.00 - 12.00
  14031-D *Mountain Top Blues*............. 10.00 - 15.00
  14032-D *House Rent Blues*............. 10.00 - 15.00
  14037-D *Rainy Weather Blues*............. 10.00 - 15.00
  14042-D *Weeping Willow Blues*............. 10.00 - 15.00
  14051-D *Dying Gambler's Blues*............. 10.00 - 15.00
  14052-D *Sinful Blues*............. 8.00 - 12.00
  14056-D *Sobbin' Hearted Blues*............. 20.00 - 30.00
  14064-D *Cold In Hand Blues*............. 20.00 - 30.00
  14075-D *Soft Pedal Blues*............. 10.00 - 15.00
  14079-D *You've Been A Good Old Wagon*... 20.00 - 30.00
  14083-D *Careless Love*............. 20.00 - 30.00
  14090-D *Nashville Woman's Blues*............. 20.00 - 30.00

14095-D	*J.C. Holmes Blues*	20.00 -	30.00
14098-D	*Nobody's Blues But Mine*	10.00 -	15.00
14109-D	*New Gulf Coast Blues*	10.00 -	15.00
14115-D	*Red Mountain Blues*	10.00 -	15.00
14123-D	*Lonesome Desert Blues*	10.00 -	15.00
14129-D	*What's The Matter Now?*	10.00 -	15.00
14133-D	*Jazzbo Brown From Memphis Town*	10.00 -	15.00
14137-D	*Hard Driving Papa*	10.00 -	15.00
14147-D	*Baby Doll*	10.00 -	15.00
14158-D	*Lost Your Head Blues*	10.00 -	15.00
14172-D	*One And Two Blue*	15.00 -	20.00
14179-D	*Young Woman's Blues*	15.00 -	20.00
14195-D	*Back Water Blues*	15.00 -	20.00
14197-D	*After You've Gone*	15.00 -	20.00
14209-D	*Them's Graveyard Words*	15.00 -	20.00
14219-D	*Alexander's Ragtime Band*	15.00 -	20.00
14232-D	*Trombone Cholly*	15.00 -	20.00
14250-D	*Mean Old Bed Bug Blues*	15.00 -	20.00
14260-D	*Sweet Mistreater*	12.00 -	18.00
14273-D	*Foolish Man Blues*	15.00 -	20.00
14292-D	*Thinking Blues*	12.00 -	18.00
14304-D	*Pickpocket Blues*	15.00 -	20.00
14312-D	*Empty Bed Blues*	10.00 -	15.00
14324-D	*Spider Man Blues*	15.00 -	20.00
14338-D	*Standin' In The Rain Blues*	15.00 -	20.00
14354-D	*Devil's Gonna Git You*	15.00 -	20.00
14375-D	*Washwoman's Blues*	15.00 -	20.00
14384-D	*Slow And Easy Man*	15.00 -	20.00
14399-D	*You Ought To Be Ashamed*	15.00 -	20.00
14427-D	*I'm Wild About That Thing*	12.00 -	16.00
14435-D	*I've Got What It Takes*	15.00 -	20.00
14451-D	*Take It Right Back*	15.00 -	20.00
14464-D	*He's Got Me Goin'*	15.00 -	25.00
14476-D	*Wasted Life Blues*	15.00 -	25.00
14487-D	*You Don't Understand*	15.00 -	25.00
14516-D	*Keep It To Yourself*	15.00 -	25.00
14527-D	*Blue Spirit Blues*	15.00 -	25.00
14538-D	*Moan, You Moaners*	15.00 -	25.00
14554-D	*Hustlin' Dan*	15.00 -	25.00
14569-D	*Hot Springs Blues*	15.00 -	20.00
14611-D	*In The House Blues*	25.00 -	35.00
14634-D	*Safety Mama*	25.00 -	35.00
14663-D	*Shipwreck Blues*	25.00 -	35.00
Okeh 8945	*Do Your Duty*	20.00 -	30.00
8949	*Gimme a Pigfoot*	20.00 -	30.00

BESSIE MAE SMITH:

Paramount 12922	*St. Louis Daddy*	60.00 -	80.00

CLARA SMITH:

Black Patti 8034	*Sand Raisin' Blues*	50.00 -	75.00
8035	*Clara Blues*	50.00 -	75.00
Columbia 12-D	*Kansas City Man Blues*	7.00 -	10.00
A-3943	*Every Woman's Blues*	7.00 -	10.00
A-3961	*Kind Lovin' Blues*	7.00 -	10.00
A-3966	*All Night Blues*	7.00 -	10.00
A-3991	*Irresistible Blues*	8.00 -	12.00
A-4000	*Awful Moanin' Blues*	7.00 -	10.00
13002-D	*Don't Never Tell Nobody*	7.00 -	10.00
13007-D	*Far Away Blues*	8.00 -	12.00
14006-D	*It Won't Be Long Now*	8.00 -	12.00
14009-D	*31st. Street Blues*	10.00 -	15.00
14013-D	*I'm Gonna Tear Your Playhouse Down*	8.00 -	12.00
14016-D	*My Doggone Lazy Man*	8.00 -	12.00
14019-D	*The Clearing House Blues*	8.00 -	12.00
14021-D	*Cold Weather Papa*	10.00 -	15.00
14022-D	*Mean Papa, Turn In Your Key*	10.00 -	15.00
14026-D	*Don't Advertise Your Man*	8.00 -	12.00
14034-D	*Deep Blues Sea Blues*	10.00 -	15.00
14039-D	*Basement Blues*	8.00 -	12.00
14041-D	*Freight Train Blues*	10.00 -	15.00
14045-D	*Death Letter Blues*	10.00 -	15.00
14049-D	*San Francisco Blues*	8.00 -	12.00
14053-D	*Steel Drivin' Sam*	8.00 -	12.00

14058-D	*Nobody Knows The Way I Feel Dis Mornin'.*	20.00 -	30.00
14062-D	*Broken Busted Blues*	20.00 -	30.00
14069-D	*When I Steps Out*	8.00 -	12.00
14073-D	*Courthouse Blues*	20.00 -	30.00
14077-D	*Shipwrecked Blues*	20.00 -	30.00
14085-D	*Different Way Blues*	8.00 -	12.00
14097-D	*Kitchen Mechanic Blues*	8.00 -	12.00
14098-D	*My Man Blue*	8.00 -	12.00
14104-D	*Alley Rat Blues*	8.00 -	12.00
14108-D	*The Market Street Blues*	8.00 -	12.00
14117-D	*I'm Tired Of Bein' Good*	10.00 -	15.00
14126-D	*Disappointed Blues*	8.00 -	12.00
14138-D	*Rock, Church, Rock*	8.00 -	12.00
14143-D	*Salty Dog*	10.00 -	15.00
14150-D	*Whip It To A Jelly*	8.00 -	12.00
14160-D	*Separation Blues*	8.00 -	12.00
14183-D	*Get On Board*	8.00 -	12.00
14192-D	*Cheatin' Daddy*	10.00 -	15.00
14202-D	*Percolatin' Blues*	8.00 -	12.00
14223-D	*Black Woman's Blues*	8.00 -	12.00
14240-D	*Black Cat Moan*	8.00 -	12.00
14256-D	*Troublesome Blues*	8.00 -	12.00
14294-D	*Race Track Blues*	10.00 -	15.00
14319-D	*It's All Coming Home To You*	10.00 -	15.00
14344-D	*Steamboat Man Blues*	15.00 -	20.00
14368-D	*Ain't Got Nobody To Grind My Coffee*	15.00 -	20.00
14398-D	*It's Tight Like That*	15.00 -	20.00
14409-D	*Empty House Blues*	15.00 -	20.00
14419-D	*Got My Mind On That Thing*	20.00 -	30.00
14462-D	*Papa I Don't Need You Now*	20.00 -	30.00
14536-D	*Where Is My Man?*	20.00 -	30.00
14553-D	*Don't Fool Around On Me*	15.00 -	25.00
14568-D	*You're Getting Old On Your Job*	15.00 -	25.00
14580-D	*Woman To Woman*	12.00 -	16.00
14592-D	*Good Times*	15.00 -	20.00
14619-D	*Ol' Sam Tages*	15.00 -	25.00
14633-D	*You Dirty Dog*	20.00 -	30.00
14645-D	*Street Department Papa*	20.00 -	30.00
14653-D	*So Long Jim*	20.00 -	30.00

CLEMENTINE SMITH:

Banner 1483	*I'm Done Done Done With You*	10.00 -	15.00
1484	*Nobody Knows The Way I Feel This Morning*	7.00 -	12.00
Pathe-Actuelle 032067	*Hard Luck Blues*	8.00 -	12.00
Perfect 12146	*Hard Luck Blues*	8.00 -	12.00
Regal 9779	*Nobody Knows What A Red Head Mama Can Do*	10.00 -	15.00
9781	*Nobody Knows The Way I Feel This Morning*	7.00 -	12.00

ELIZABETH SMITH:

Victor 20297	*No Sooner Blues*	15.00 -	20.00
20334	*When My Wants Run Out*	20.00 -	30.00
21539	*Police Done Tore My Playhouse Down*	15.00 -	20.00

ETHEL SMITH:

Champion 16613	*Jelly Roll Mill*	40.00 -	60.00

FLOSSIE SMITH & THE RED HOTS TWINS:

Superior 2603	*Hokum Stomp*	40.00 -	60.00
2699	*That's The Way She Likes It*	40.00 -	60.00

"FUNNY PAPER" SMITH:

Vocalion 1558	*Howling Wife Blues—No. 1/2*	75.00 -	100.00
1590	*Good Coffee Blues*	75.00 -	100.00
1614	*Howling Wolf Blues—No. 3/4*	75.00 -	100.00
1633	*Corn Whiskey Blues*	75.00 -	100.00
1641	*Seven Sisters Blues—Part 1/2*	75.00 -	100.00
1655	*Hungry Wolf*	75.00 -	100.00
1664	*Forty-Five Blues*	75.00 -	100.00
1674	*Fool's Blues*	75.00 -	100.00
1679	*County Jail Blues*	75.00 -	100.00

GRACE SMITH:

National 9051	*What's on the Rail for the Lizard*	5.00 -	8.00

GUY SMITH:
Paramount 12806 *Southland Blues*............ 30.00 - 40.00

HAZEL SMITH:
Okeh 8620 *West End Blues*................. 30.00 - 50.00

HENRY SMITH:
Dot 1220 *Good Rocking Mama*............ 7.00 - 10.00*
Fortune 802 *Dog Me Blues*................ 7.00 - 10.00*

HORACE SMITH:
Gennett 7025 *Mother-n-Law Blues*........ 60.00 - 80.00
7056 *Clickety-Clack Blues*................ 60.00 - 80.00

IKE SMITH'S CHICAGO BOYS:
Champion 50040 *Fighting Joe Louis*...... 10.00 - 15.00

IVA/IVY SMITH (AND CHARLIE DAVEN-PORT/AND HER BUDDIES):
Champion 16080 *Milkman Blues*............. 35.00 - 50.00
Gennett 6829 *Shadow Blues*............... 35.00 - 50.00
6861 *Gin House Blues*.................... 35.00 - 50.00
6875 *Mistreated Mama Blues*............. 35.00 - 50.00
7024 *Wringin' And Twistin' Papa*........ 35.00 - 50.00
7040 *Doin' That Thing*.................. 35.00 - 50.00
7101 *Cheating Only Blues*............... 35.00 - 50.00
7231 *That's The Kind Of Girl I'm Looking For* 35.00 - 50.00
7251 *Milkman Blues*..................... 35.00 - 50.00
Paramount 12436 *Rising Sun Blues*....... 35.00 - 50.00
12447 *Sad And Blue*..................... 35.00 - 50.00
12472 *Barrel House Mojo*................ 35.00 - 50.00
12496 *Ninety-Nine Years Blues*.......... 35.00 - 50.00
Supertone 9509 *Shadow Blues*............ 35.00 - 50.00
9515 *No Good Man Blues*................. 35.00 - 50.00
9527 *Wringing And Twistin' Papa*........ 35.00 - 50.00
9528 *Somebody's Got To Knock A Jug*...... 35.00 - 50.00
9531 *Mistreated Mama Blues*............. 35.00 - 50.00
9533 *Southern High Waters Blues*........ 35.00 - 50.00

JANE SMITH:
Silvertone 3563 *Kentucky Blues*.......... 15.00 - 20.00

JULIA SMITH:
Oriole 771 *Crap Shootin' Papa, Mama Done Caught Your Dice*.......................... 8.00 - 12.00
772 *I Needs Plenty Of Grease In My Frying Pan* 8.00 - 12.00
816 *Harlem Blues*....................... 8.00 - 12.00

LAURA SMITH:
Don't You Leave Me Here, issued contemporaneously on Banner, Domino, Regal............. 10.00 - 15.00
Okeh 8157 *Texas Moaner Blues*........... 20.00 - 30.00
8169 *Two-Faced Woman Blues*............ 20.00 - 30.00
8179 *Gravier Street Blues*.............. 20.00 - 30.00
8186 *I'm Gonna Get Myself A Real Man*.... 20.00 - 30.00
8246 *Disgusted Blues*................... 20.00 - 30.00
8252 *Face To Face*..................... 20.00 - 30.00
8316 *I'll Get Even With You*............ 20.00 - 30.00
8331 *Them Has Been Blues*.............. 20.00 - 30.00
8366 *Cool Can Blues*................... 20.00 - 30.00
8445 *Hateful Blues*.................... 20.00 - 30.00
Pathe-Actuelle 7520 *When A Gator Hollers*.... 15.00 - 20.00
7525 *I'm Gonna Kill Myself*............. 15.00 - 20.00
Perfect 120 *When A Gator Hollers*....... 15.00 - 20.00
125 *I'm Gonna Kill Myself*............. 15.00 - 20.00
Victor 20775 *Lonesome Refugee*.......... 15.00 - 20.00
20945 *Red River Blues*................. 15.00 - 20.00

MAMIE SMITH (& HER JAZZ BAND/HOUNDS); MAMIE SMITH'S JAZZ HOUNDS:
Ajax 17058 *Good Time Ball*.............. 15.00 - 20.00
17063 *Remorseful Blues*................ 15.00 - 20.00
Okeh 4113 *That Thing Called Love*....... 7.00 - 10.00
4169 *Crazy Blues*..................... 7.00 - 10.00
4194 *Fare Thee Honey Blues*........... 7.00 - 10.00
4228 *If You Don't Want Me Blues*....... 7.00 - 10.00
4253 *Don't Care Blues*................ 7.00 - 10.00
4254 *Royal Garden Blues*.............. 10.00 - 15.00
4295 *Jazzbo Ball*..................... 8.00 - 12.00

4296 *That Thing Called Love*.......... 10.00 - 15.00
4305 *You Can't Keep A Good Man Down*... 8.00 - 12.00
4351 *Dangerous Blues*................. 8.00 - 12.00
4416 *Sax-O-Phoney Blues*.............. 8.00 - 12.00
4427 *Mamma Whip! Mamma Spank!*....... 8.00 - 12.00
4445 *The Wang Wang Blues*............ 8.00 - 12.00
4446 *Down Home Blues*................ 8.00 - 12.00
4471 *Weepin'*......................... 8.00 - 12.00
4511 *Sweet Man O'Mine*............... 8.00 - 12.00
4542 *Oh, Joe (Please Don't Go)*........ 8.00 - 12.00
4578 *Doo-Dah Blues*.................. 8.00 - 12.00
4600 *A-Wearin' Away The Blues*........ 8.00 - 12.00
4623 *I Want A Jazzy Kiss*............. 8.00 - 12.00
4630 *Lonesome Mama Blues*............ 10.00 - 15.00
4631 *Mean Daddy Blues*............... 10.00 - 15.00
4658 *Alabama Blues*.................. 8.00 - 12.00
4670 *Got To Cool My Doggies Now*..... 8.00 - 12.00
4689 *That Da Da Strain*.............. 8.00 - 12.00
4752 *I Ain't Gonna Give Nobody None O' This Jelly Roll*........................... 8.00 - 12.00
4767 *The Darktown Flappers Ball*...... 8.00 - 12.00
4781 *I'm Gonna Get You*.............. 10.00 - 15.00
4856 *Mean Man*....................... 10.00 - 15.00
4926 *Kansas City Man Blues*.......... 10.00 - 15.00
4935 *Good Looking Papa*.............. 8.00 - 12.00
4960 *Mistreatin' Daddy Blues*........ 8.00 - 12.00
8024 *Rambling Blues*................. 8.00 - 12.00
8030 *Carolina Blues*................. 10.00 - 15.00
8036 *Strut Yout Material*............ 10.00 - 15.00
8072 *Those Longing For you Blues*..... 10.00 - 15.00
8864 *Don't Advertise Your Man*........ 25.00 - 35.00
8915 *Golfing Papa*................... 25.00 - 35.00
Victor 20210 *Goin' Crazy With The Blues*... 15.00 - 20.00
20233 *Sweet Virginia Blues*.......... 15.00 - 20.00

MANDY SMITH:
Jewel 5138, 5188, 5207, 5230, 5254, 5309..... 7.00 - 10.00
Oriole 1059, 1118, 1147, 1170, 1197, 1249..... 7.00 - 10.00

PINE TOP SMITH:
Vocalion 1245 *Pine Top's Boogie Woogie*...... 50.00 - 75.00
1256 *Big Boy They Can't Do That*....... 50.00 - 75.00
1266 *I'm Sober Now*.................. 50.00 - 75.00
1298 *Jump Steady Blues*.............. 50.00 - 75.00

ROBERT SMITH:
Independent 301 *Freeway Boogie*........... 6.00 - 10.00

RUBY SMITH:
Bluebird 7654 *Dream Man Blues*.......... 7.00 - 10.00
7794 *Flyin' Mosquito Blues*........... 7.00 - 10.00
7864 *Hard Up Blues*................. 7.00 - 10.00
Vocalion 04903 *Back Water Blues*........ 10.00 - 15.00

SIX CYLINDER SMITH:
Paramount 12968 *Pennsylvania Woman Blues*... 90.00 - 120.00

SPARK PLUG SMITH:
Titles, issued contemporaneously on Banner, Melotone, Oriole, Perfect, Romeo: *Deserted Man Blues; In A Shanty In Old Shanty Town; Make It Tight; Mama's Doughnut; Motherless Boy; New Blues Heaven; Stopped Clock Blues; Sweet Evening Breeze; Vampire Woman; You Put That Thing On Me*................. 15.00 - 20.00

SUSIE SMITH:
Ajax 17064 *House Rent Blues*............ 15.00 - 25.00
17073 *Salt Water Blues*.............. 15.00 - 25.00
17075 *Bullet Wound Blues*............ 15.00 - 25.00
17079 *The Bye Bye Blues*............. 15.00 - 25.00
17081 *Meat Man Pete*................. 15.00 - 25.00
17086 *Nobody Knows The Way I Feel Dis Mornin'*........................... 15.00 - 25.00
17089 *Sore Bunion Blues*............. 15.00 - 25.00
17093 *Scandal Blues*................. 15.00 - 25.00
17095 *How Can I Miss You*............ 15.00 - 25.00
17127 *Texas Special Blues*........... 15.00 - 25.00

17132 *Undertaker's Blues*		15.00 -	25.00
17134 *Crepe Hanger Blues*		15.00 -	25.00

THUNDER SMITH (AND ROCKIE):

Aladdin 166 *Little Mama Boogie*		10.00 -	15.00
Down Town 2011 *Thunder's Unfinished Boogie*		15.00 -	25.00
2012 *New Worried Life Blues*		15.00 -	25.00
2013 *Low Down Dirty Ways*		15.00 -	25.00
Gold Star 615 *Cruel Hearted Woman*		15.00 -	25.00
644 *Santa Fe Blues*		15.00 -	25.00

TRIXIE SMITH:

Black Swan 2039 *Trixie's Blues*		15.00 -	20.00
2044 *Long Lost Weary Blues*		15.00 -	20.00
14114 *Pensacola Blues*		15.00 -	20.00
14127 *My Man Rocks Me*		15.00 -	20.00
14132 *I'm Through With You*		15.00 -	20.00
14138 *I'm Gonna Get You*		15.00 -	20.00
14142 *Log Cabin Blues*		15.00 -	20.00
14149 *Triflin' Blues*		15.00 -	20.00
Decca 7469 *Trixie Blues*		7.00 -	10.00
7489 *My Unusual Man*		7.00 -	10.00
7528 *Jack, I'm Mellow*		7.00 -	10.00
7617 *No Good Man*		7.00 -	10.00
Paramount 12161 *Trixie's Blues*		12.00 -	18.00
12162 *Long Lost Weary Blues*		12.00 -	18.00
12163 *Pensacola Blues*		12.00 -	18.00
12164 *My Man Rocks Me*		12.00 -	18.00
12165 *I'm Through With You*		12.00 -	18.00
12166 *I'm Gonna Get You*		12.00 -	18.00
12167 *Log Cabin Blues*		12.00 -	18.00
12168 *Triflin' Blues*		12.00 -	18.00
12208 *Sorrowful Blues*		20.00 -	30.00
12211 *Freight Train Blues*		20.00 -	30.00
12232 *Praying Blues*		20.00 -	30.00
12245 *Choo Choo Blues*		20.00 -	30.00
12256 *Mining Camp Blues*		50.00 -	75.00
12262 *Railroad Blues*		50.00 -	75.00
12330 *Love Me Like You Used To Do*		25.00 -	40.00
12336 *Black Bottom Hop*		25.00 -	40.00

EILLIAM & VERSEY SMITH:

Paramount 12505 *When That Great Ship Went Down*		20.00 -	30.00
12516 *I Believe I'll Go Back Home*		20.00 -	30.00

SMOKEHOUSE CHARLEY:

Champion 15794 *My Texas Blues*		35.00 -	50.00
15815 *Pig Meat Blues*		35.00 -	50.00
15834 *Broke Man's Blues*		35.00 -	50.00
15903 *Rollin' Mill Stomp*		35.00 -	50.00

SMOKEY JOE:

Flip 502 *Split Personality*		25.00 -	35.00*
Sun 228 *Split Personality*		15.00 -	20.00*

SNOOKY AND MOODY:

Old Swing-Master 18 *Calling Up My Baby Blues*		15.00 -	25.00

EDDIE SNOW:

Sun 226 *Ain't That Right*		15.00 -	25.00*

HATTIE SNOW:

Gennett 7039 *Don't Say Goodbye*		40.00 -	60.00
7070 *Make That Gravel Fly*		40.00 -	60.00
7115 *Two Train Blues*		40.00 -	60.00

Q. ROSCOE SNOWDEN:

Okeh 8119 *Misery Blues*		8.00 -	12.00

SONNY BOY & LONNIE:

Continental 6050, 6052, 6053, 6054		7.00 -	10.00

SONNY BOY & SAM:

Continental 6055 *Mama Blues*		7.00 -	10.00

SOUTH CAROLINA QUARTETTE:

QRS 7012 *Paul And Silas*		12.00 -	20.00
7061 *I'm A Pilgrim*		12.00 -	20.00

SOUTHERN BLUES SINGERS:

Gennett 6828 *Lighthouse Blues*		20.00 -	30.00
6845 *Runnin' Wild*		20.00 -	30.00

SOUTHERN JUBILEE QUARTET:

Black Patti 8036 *Listen To The Lambs*		20.00 -	30.00

SOUTH MEMPHIS JUG BAND:

Vocalion 02585 *Doctor Medicine*		50.00 -	75.00

SOUTHERN (NEGRO) QUARTETTE:

Columbia A-3444 *I'm Wild About Moonshine*		7.00 -	10.00
A-3450 *I Ain't Givin' Nothin' Away*		7.00 -	10.00
A-3489 *He Took It Away From Me*		7.00 -	10.00
14038-D *Hampton Road Blues*		7.00 -	10.00
14043-D *Moanin' Groanin' Blues*		7.00 -	10.00
14048-D *My Man Rocks Me (With One Steady Roll)*		7.00 -	10.00

SOUTHERN SANCTIFIED SINGERS:

Brunswick 7074 *Soon We'll Gather At The River*		20.00 -	30.00

SOUTHERN UNIVERSITY QUARTET:

Bluebird 5846 *All Over The World*		7.00 -	10.00
5932 *I'm Tired Of Living In The Country*		7.00 -	10.00
6142 *I'm Troubled In Mind*		7.00 -	10.00

CHARLIE SPAND:

Okeh 05699 *Rock And Rye*		15.00 -	20.00
05757 *Gold Tooth Mama*		15.00 -	20.00
05894 *Big Alley Rat Blues*		15.00 -	20.00
05946 *Gone Mother Blues*		15.00 -	20.00
Paramount 12790 *Soon This Morning*		60.00 -	90.00
12817 *Back To The Woods Blues*		60.00 -	90.00
12856 *Moanin' The Blues*		60.00 -	90.00
12887 *In The Barrel Blues*		60.00 -	90.00
12917 *Mississippi Blues*		60.00 -	90.00
12930 *Room Rent Blues*		60.00 -	90.00
13005 *She's Got Good Stuff*		75.00 -	100.00
13022 *Mistreatment Blues*		75.00 -	100.00
13047 *Thirsty Woman Blues*		50.00 -	100.00
13101 *Georgia Mule Blues*		90.00 -	120.00
13112 *Hard Times Blues*		90.00 -	120.00

THE SPANIELS:

Chance 1141 *Baby, It's You*		10.00 -	15.00*

SPARKLING FOUR QUARTETTE:

QRS 7011 *Keep On To Galilee*		15.00 -	20.00

SPARKS BROTHERS:

Bluebird 5193 *61 Highway*		40.00 -	60.00
5247 *Chicago's Too Much For Me*		40.00 -	60.00
Sunrise 3273 *Down on the Levee*		40.00 -	60.00
3330 *Chicago's Too Much For Me*		40.00 -	60.00

MILTON SPARKS:

Bluebird 6096 *Grinder Blues*		20.00 -	30.00
6126 *I Wake Up In The Morning*		20.00 -	30.00
6521 *Ina Blues*		20.00 -	30.00
6529 *Erie Train Blues*		20.00 -	30.00

HENRY SPAULDING:

Brunswick 7085 *Cairo Blues*		50.00 -	75.00

BLOSSOM SPEARS:

Champion 15267 *Indian Brown Blues*		20.00 -	30.00

SPECKLED RED:

Bluebird 7985 *St. Louis Stomp*		8.00 -	12.00
8012 *Try Me One More Time*		8.00 -	12.00
8036 *You Got To Fix It*		8.00 -	12.00
8069 *Welfare Blues*		8.00 -	12.00
8113 *Down On The Levee*		8.00 -	12.00
Brunswick 7116 *The Dirty Dozen*		40.00 -	60.00
7137 *House Dance Blues*		40.00 -	60.00
7151 *The Dirty Dozen—Part No. 2*		40.00 -	60.00
7164 *Speckled Red's Blues*		40.00 -	60.00
7200 *We Got To Get That Thing Fixed*		40.00 -	60.00

MAMIE SPENCER:

Oriole 795 *Scrubbin' Blues*		12.00 -	16.00

BIG BOY SPIRES & HIS TRIO:

Chance 1137 *About To Lose My Mind*		10.00 -	15.00*
Checker 752 *One Of These Days*		7.00 -	10.00*

SWEET PEASE SPIVEY & HER/DOT SCOTT'S RHYTHM DUKES:

Decca 7204 *Grievin' Me*		7.00 -	10.00
7237 *410 Blues*		7.00 -	10.00

(ORIGINAL) VICTORIA SPIVEY (AND CHICAGO FOUR/DOT SCOTT'S RHYTHM DUKES/HER HALLELUJAH BOYS:

Decca 7203 *Black Snake Swing*	8.00 -	12.00
7222 *T.B.'s Got Me Blues*	8.00 -	12.00
Okeh 8338 *No More Jelly Bean Blues*	10.00 -	15.00
8351 *Dirty Woman's Blues*	10.00 -	15.00
8370 *Hoodoo Man Blues*	10.00 -	15.00
8389 *Humored And Petted Blues*	10.00 -	15.00
8401 *Big Houston Blues*	10.00 -	15.00
8410 *Santa Fe Blues*	10.00 -	15.00
8464 *Idle Hour Blues*	10.00 -	15.00
8481 *The Alligator Pond Went Dry*	10.00 -	15.00
8494 *T.B. Blues*	10.00 -	15.00
8517 *Garter Snake Blues*	10.00 -	15.00
8531 *Blood Thirst Blues*	10.00 -	15.00
8550 *Red Lantern Blues*	10.00 -	15.00
8565 *Your Worries Ain't Like Mine*	10.00 -	15.00
8581 *Murder In The First Degree*	10.00 -	15.00
8615 *Organ Grinder Blues*	35.00 -	50.00
8626 *New Black Snake Blues, Part 1/2*	8.00 -	12.00
8634 *Mosquito, Fly And Flea*	15.00 -	20.00
8652 *Furniture Man Blues—Part 1/2*	10.00 -	15.00
8713 *How Do You Do It That Way?*	30.00 -	40.00
8733 *You Done Lost Your Good Thing Now— Part 1/2*	15.00 -	20.00
8744 *Toothache Blues—Part No. 1/2*	15.00 -	20.00
Victor 23349 *Baulin Water Blues*	20.00 -	30.00
38546 *Telephoning The Blues*	30.00 -	40.00
38584 *New York Blues*	20.00 -	30.00
38589 *Haunted By The Blues*	20.00 -	30.00
38609 *You've Gotta Have What It Takes*	15.00 -	-25.00
Vocalion 1606 *Nebraska Blues*	20.00 -	30.00
1640 *Low Down Man Blues*	20.00 -	30.00
03243 *Toothache Blues—Part 1/2*	8.00 -	12.00
03260 *Furniture Man Blues—Part 1/2*	8.00 -	12.00
03366 *I Ain't Gonna Let You See My Santa Claus*	10.00 -	15.00
03405 *Detroit Moan*	10.00 -	15.00
03505 *One Hour Mama*	10.00 -	15.00
03639 *Good Cabbage*	10.00 -	15.00

"MR. FREDDIE" SPRUELL:

Paramount 12665 *Tom Cat Blues*	75.00 -	100.00

STABLE BOY SAM:

Vocalion 1739 *Mama's Doughnut*	15.00 -	20.00

STATE STREET BOYS:

Okeh 8962 *Don't Tear My Clothes*	20.00 -	30.00
8964 *Crazy About You*	20.00 -	30.00
8965 *Sweet To Mama*	20.00 -	30.00
Vocalion 03302 *She Caught The Train*	20.00 -	30.00
03004 *Crazy About You*	20.00 -	30.00
03049 *Sweet To Mama*	20.00 -	30.00
03131 *Mobile And Western Line*	20.00 -	30.00

STEAMBOAT BILL & HIS GUITAR:

Champion 15674 *No No Blues*	75.00 -	100.00
15694 *Weak-Minded Blues*	75.00 -	100.00
15716 *Bad Luck Moan*	75.00 -	100.00
15735 *Rag Baby*	75.00 -	100.00

STEELE AND JOHNSON:

Champion 16395 *Selling That Stuff*	40.00 -	60.00

VOL STEVENS:

Victor 21356 *Vol Stevens Blues*	60.00 -	80.00

DAN STEWART:

Vocalion 1536 *New Orleans Blues*	80.00 -	100.00

MAE STEWART:

Silvertone 3518 *I Was Born A Brownskin*	20.00 -	30.00
3520 *You Ain't Foolin' Me*	20.00 -	30.00
3541 *Going To The Nation*	20.00 -	30.00

PRISCILLA STEWART:

Paramount 12205 *True Blues*	20.00 -	30.00
12224 *Mecca Flat Blues*	20.00 -	30.00
12240 *Delta Bottom Blues*	20.00 -	30.00

12253 *The Woman Ain't Born*	20.00 -	30.00
12286 *Priscilla Blues*	20.00 -	30.00
12299 *Going To The Nation*	20.00 -	30.00
12360 *It Must Be Hard*	25.00 -	40.00
12402 *Biscuit Roller*	25.00 -	40.00
12463 *Lonesome Hour Blues*	25.00 -	40.00
12465 *P.D.Q. Blues*	25.00 -	40.00
12740 *A Little Bit Closer*	25.00 -	35.00

ARBEE STIDHAM:

Abco 100, 107	4.00 -	6.00*
Checker 751, 758	4.00 -	7.00*
RCA Victor	3.00 -	5.00
Sittin' In With 596, 606, 617	5.00 -	8.00

FRANK STOKES:

Victor 21272 *Downtown Blues*	80.00 -	100.00
21672 *Mistreatin' Blues*	80.00 -	100.00
21738 *Stomp That Thing*	80.00 -	100.00
23341 *I'm Going Away Blues*	100.00 -	150.00
23411 *Frank Stoke' Dream*	100.00 -	150.00
38500 *Tain't Nobody's Business If I Do*	80.00 -	100.00
38512 *I Got Mine*	80.00 -	100.00
38531 *Take Me Back*	80.00 -	100.00
38548 *South Memphis Blues*	90.00 -	120.00
38589 *Right Now Blues*	90.00 -	120.00

JOE STONE:

Bluebird 5169 *Back Door Blues*	35.00 -	50.00
Sunrise 3250 *It's Hard Time*	35.00 -	50.00

LUTHER STONEHAM:

Mercury 8275 *Sittin' And Wonderin'*	8.00 -	12.00*

STOVEPIPE No. 1 (AND DAVID CROCKETT):

Columbia 201-D *Turkey In The Straw*	7.00 -	10.00
15011-D *Lonesome John*	7.00 -	10.00
Okeh 8514 *Court Street Blues*	20.00 -	30.00
8543 *Bed Slats*	20.00 -	30.00

FREEMAN STOWERS:

Gennett 6814 *Railroad Blues*	25.00 -	40.00
Gennett 6830 *Texas Wildcat Chase*	25.00 -	40.00
Supertone 9396 *Sunrise on the Farm*	25.00 -	35.00

MARY STRAINE:

Black Swan 14115 *Ain't Got Nothing Blues*	15.00 -	20.00
14123 *Last Go Round Blues*	15.00 -	20.00
14150 *Chirpin' The Blues*	15.00 -	20.00
Paramount 12132 *Ain't Got Nothing Blues*	12.00 -	16.00
12149 *Last Go Round Blues*	12.00 -	16.00
12150 *Chirpin' The Blues*	12.00 -	16.00

JIMMY STRANGE:

Victor 23317 *No Limit Blues*	75.00 -	100.00

JOHNNIE STRAUSS:

Decca 7035 *Old Market Street Blues*	15.00 -	25.00
7081 *Hard Working Woman*	15.00 -	25.00

STREAMLINE MAE:

Okeh 06045 *Romance In The Dark*	7.00 -	10.00
06093 *School Boy Blues*	7.00 -	10.00

SUGAR CANE JOHNNY:

Bluebird 5948 *Who Pumped The Wind In The Doughnuts?*	30.00 -	40.00

THE SUGARMAN:

Sittin' In With 609 *Which Woman Do I Love*	10.00 -	15.00

ANNIE SUMMERFORD:

Okeh 8174 *'Fo Day Blues*	40.00 -	60.00

SUNNY BOY & HIS PALS:

Champion 15283 *Don't You Leave ME Here*	150.00 -	200.00
Gennett 6106 *France Blues*	150.00 -	200.00

SUNNY JIM AND WHISTLIN' JOE:

Champion 15361 *Black Snake Blues*	40.00 -	60.00

SUNNYLAND SLIM & HIS SUNNY (LAND) BOYS/TRIO; SUNNYLAND SLIM & MUDDY WATERS (COMBO); SUNNYLAND TRIO:

Apollo 416 *Bad Times*	8.00 -	12.00
Aristocrat 1301 *Fly Right, Little Girl*	15.00 -	25.00

1304 *She Ain't Nowhere*	15.00 -	25.00
Blue Lake 105 *Going Back To Memphis*	8.00 -	12.00*
107 *Shake It Baby*	8.00 -	12.00*
Ebony 1009 *Shake It Baby*	———	
Hytone 32 *Jivin' Boogie*	8.00 -	12.00
33 *My Heavy Load*	8.00 -	12.00
33 *Miss Bessie Mae*	8.00 -	12.00
37 *I've Done You Wrong*	8.00 -	12.00
J.O.B. 102 *Down Home Child*	35.00 -	50.00
1002 *Pet Rabbit*	20.00 -	30.00
1003 *Mary Lee*	20.00 -	30.00
1105 *Shake It Baby*	10.00 -	15.00*
1108 *Four Day Bounce*	10.00 -	15.00*
Mercury 8132, 8264, 8277	7.00 -	10.00*
Regal 3327 *Orphan Boy Blues*	15.00 -	20.00
Sunny 101 *Back To Korea Blues*	30.00 -	50.00
Tempo Tone 1001 *Hard Times*	20.00 -	30.00
1002 *Blue Baby*	20.00 -	30.00

THE SWALLOWS:

King 4458, 4466, 4501, 4515, 4521, 4612, 4632.	7.00 -	10.00*

SWAN AND LEE:

Okeh 8732 *Fishy Little Thing*	10.00 -	15.00

SWEET PAPA STOVEPIPE:

Paramount 12404 *Mama's Angel Child*	20.00 -	30.00

SWEET PAPA TADPOLE:

Vocalion 1592 *Have You Ever Been Worried In Mind*	20.00 -	30.00
1680 *Black Spider Blues*	20.00 -	30.00
1687 *Your Baby Can't Get Enough*	20.00 -	30.00

SWEET PEA(S):

Bluebird 7224, 8114, 8146	5.00 -	8.00
Victor 23361 *Day Breakin' Blues*	35.00 -	50.00
38565 *Heart-Breakin' Blues*	35.00 -	50.00

SYKES AND JOHNSON:

Champion 16558 *Steady Grinding*	40.00 -	60.00

ISABEL SYKES:

Bluebird 5170 *Don't Rush Yourself*	15.00 -	25.00

ROOSEVELT SYKES:

Black & White 100 *This Tavern Boogie*	8.00 -	12.00
Bluebird 5323 *New 44 Blues*	15.00 -	25.00
5342 *Working Dollar Blues*	15.00 -	25.00
34-0721, 34-0729	4.00 -	7.00
Bullet 319 *Candy Man Blues*	10.00 -	15.00
Champion 16586 *Highway 61 Blues*	50.00 -	75.00
50012 *Highway 61 Blues*	15.00 -	20.00
Decca 7011 *Ethel Mae Blues*	15.00 -	20.00
7280 *Mister Sykes Blues*	8.00 -	12.00
7586 *Have You Seen Ida B.*	8.00 -	12.00
7597 *Love Will Wear You Down*	8.00 -	12.00
Okeh 06219, 06387, 06455, 06542, 06709	5.00 -	10.00
8702 *Boot That Thing*	35.00 -	50.00
8727 *The Way I Feel Blues*	35.00 -	50.00
8742 *Henry Ford Blues*	35.00 -	50.00
8749 *Skeet And Garret*	35.00 -	50.00
8776 *Roosevelt's Blues*	35.00 -	50.00
8787 *Poor Boy Blues*	35.00 -	50.00
8819 *Bury That Thing*	35.00 -	50.00
RCA Victor	5.00 -	8.00
Regal 3269 *Rock It*	8.00 -	12.00
3286 *Drivin' Wheel*	8.00 -	12.00
3306 *Mailbox Blues*	8.00 -	12.00
3324 *Green Onion Top*	8.00 -	12.00
Sunrise 3404 *New 44 Blues*	15.00 -	25.00
3423 *Devil's Island Gin Blues*	15.00 -	25.00
United 101, 120, 129, 139, 152	4.00 -	7.00*

HANNAH SYLVESTER:

Emerson 10625 *Midnight Blues*	15.00 -	20.00
Famous 3237 *Farewell Blues*	15.00 -	20.00
Paramount 12033 *Midnight Blues*	15.00 -	20.00
12034 *The Wicked Fives*	15.00 -	20.00
20243 *Farewell Blues*	15.00 -	20.00
Puritan 11243 *Farewell Blues*	15.00 -	20.00

BLIND JOE/JOEL TAGGART (& BERTHA/EMMA/JAMES TAGGART):

Decca 7033 *I Wonder Will My Mother Be On That Train?*	15.00 -	20.00
7034 *I Ain't No Sinner Now*	15.00 -	20.00
Paramount 12611 *Been Listening All The Day*	20.00 -	30.00
12717 *I've Crossed The Separation Line*	30.00 -	50.00
12744 *Mother's Love*	30.00 -	50.00
12780 *Scandulous And A Shame*	30.00 -	50.00
13020 *Wonder Will My Troubles Then Be Over*	30.00 -	50.00
13059 *Pressin' Up That Shiny Way*	30.00 -	50.00
13081 *Satan Your Kingdom Must Come Down*	30.00 -	50.00
13094 *I Ain't No Sinner Now*	30.00 -	50.00
Vocalion 1061 *Take Your Burden To The Lord*	20.00 -	30.00
1062 *I Will Not Be Removed*	20.00 -	30.00
1063 *I'll Be Satisfied*	20.00 -	30.00
1070 *Keep On The Firing Line*	20.00 -	30.00
1123 *The Storm Is Passing Over*	20.00 -	30.00

TALLAHASSEE TIGHT:

Titles, issued contemporaneously on Banner, Conqueror, Domino, Melotone, Oriole, Perfect, Romeo: *Black Gal; Black Snake Blues; Coast Line Blues; Homesick Blues; Jealous Man; Lonesome And Worried Blues; Quincey Wimmems; Ramblin' Mind Blues; Screaming Woman; Tallahassee Women*	20.00 -	30.00

TAMPA KID:

Decca 7278 *Keep On Trying*	8.00 -	12.00

TAMPA RED, "THE GUITAR WIZARD", TAMPA RED'S HOKUM JUG BAND; TAMPA RED & THE CHICAGO FIVE/HOKUM JUG BAND:

Titles, issued contemporaneously on Banner, Melotone, Oriole, Perfect, Romeo: *Dead Cats On The Line; Georgia Hound Blues; How Long How Long Blues; Mama Don't Allow No Easy Riders Here; New Strangers Blues; Reckless Man Blues*	15.00 -	20.00
Bluebird 5450 *I'll Find My Way*	12.00 -	16.00
5515 *I'll Kill Your Soul*	12.00 -	16.00
5546 *Mean Mistreater Blues*	15.00 -	20.00
5572 *Somebody's Been Using That Thing*	15.00 -	20.00
5617 *Kingfish Blues*	15.00 -	20.00
5673 *I'm Just Crazy Bout You*	15.00 -	20.00
5723 *Witchin' Hour Blues*	12.00 -	16.00
5744 *Worried Devil Blues*	12.00 -	16.00
5779 *Happy Jack*	12.00 -	16.00
5812 *Stockyard Fire*	12.00 -	16.00
5878 *Shake It Up A Little*	12.00 -	16.00
5929 *Don't Dog Your Woman*	12.00 -	16.00
5981 *Worthy Of You*	12.00 -	16.00
6037 *My Baby Said Yes*	12.00 -	16.00
6059 *Keep On Dealin'*	10.00 -	15.00
6126 *Rowdy Woman Blues*	20.00 -	30.00
6166 *You Missed A Good Man*	7.00 -	10.00
6211 *Drinkin' My Blues Away*	12.00 -	16.00
6241 *Waiting Blues*	12.00 -	16.00
6353 *Let's Get Drunk And Truck*	7.00 -	10.00
6388 *She Don't Know My Mind*	10.00 -	15.00
6425 *Nutty And Buggy Blues*	12.00 -	16.00
6443 *When You Were A Gal Of Seven*	7.00 -	10.00
6498 *She Don't Know My Mind—Part 2*	8.00 -	12.00
6532 *All Night Long*	7.00 -	10.00
6578 *That's The Way I Do*	7.00 -	10.00
6620 *You Stole My Heart*	7.00 -	10.00
6681 *Blue And Evil Blues*	10.00 -	15.00
6755 *Stop Truckin' And Suzi-Q*	7.00 -	10.00
6787 *If It Wasn't For You*	7.00 -	10.00
6825 *Someday I'm Bound To Win*	20.00 -	30.00
6832 *Cheatin' On Me*	7.00 -	10.00
6968 *You Got To Learn To Do It*	6.00 -	10.00
6990 *I See You Can't Take It*	5.00 -	8.00
7010 *My Gal Is Gone*	10.00 -	15.00

7058 *I Give My Love To You*	5.00 -	10.00
7091 *When Love Comes In*	15.00 -	20.00
7115 *Taking It And Make My Get Away*	10.00 -	15.00
7225 *Harlem Swing*	5.00 -	8.00
7236 *I'm Gonna Get High*	6.00 -	10.00
7269 *Oh Babe, Oh Baby*	7.00 -	10.00
7276 *Wrong Idea*	8.00 -	12.00
7315 *Deceitful Friend Blues*	8.00 -	12.00
7364 *Whoopee Mama*	8.00 -	12.00
7499 *The Most Of Us Do*	5.00 -	8.00
7538 *We Gonna Get High Together*	5.00 -	8.00
7591 *A Lie In My Heart*	5.00 -	8.00
7642 *Grouchy Hearted Woman*	8.00 -	12.00
7675 *Got To Leave My Woman*	8.00 -	12.00
7743 *Rock It In Rhythm*	5.00 -	8.00
7793 *Sweetest Gal In Town*	5.00 -	8.00
7822 *When I Had A Good Woman*	8.00 -	12.00
7879 *Crazy With The Blues*	8.00 -	12.00
7976 *Checkin' Up On You*	5.00 -	8.00
8011 *Mr. Rhythm Man*	5.00 -	8.00
8046 *Blues For My Baby*	5.00 -	8.00
8086 *Hellish Old Feeling*	5.00 -	8.00
8179 *Please Don't Throw Me Down*	5.00 -	8.00
8205 *Poor Old Gal Blues*	5.00 -	8.00
8238 *No Good Woman Blues*	5.00 -	8.00
8266 *Booze Head Woman*	5.00 -	8.00
8291 *Sad Letter Blues*	5.00 -	8.00
8327 *Sweet Mellow Woman Blues*	5.00 -	8.00
8353 *Ready For Rhythm*	5.00 -	8.00
8368 *I Got A Big Surprise For You*	5.00 -	8.00
8407 *Dangerous Woman Blues*	5.00 -	8.00
8454 *I Don't Care No More*	5.00 -	8.00
8475 *You Say We're Through*	5.00 -	8.00
8575 *Baby Take A Chance With Me*	5.00 -	8.00
8635 *It Hurts Me Too*	5.00 -	8.00
8654 *Anna Lou Blues*	5.00 -	8.00
8715 *I Want To Swing*	7.00 -	10.00
8744 *This Ain't No Place For Me*	7.00 -	10.00
8780 *Hard Road Blues*	7.00 -	10.00
8821 *Noonday Hour Blues*	7.00 -	10.00
8890, 8919, 8962, 8991, 9009, 9024, 34-0700, 34-0711, 34-0724, 34-0731, 34-0740	4.00 -	7.00
Paramount 12685 *Through Train Blues*	35.00 -	50.00
Vocalion 1216 *It's Tight Like That*	15.00 -	20.00
1228 *It's Tight Like That*	25.00 -	35.00
1237 *You Can't Come In*	25.00 -	35.00
1244 *It's Tight Like That—No. 2*	15.00 -	25.00
1251 *Jelly Whippin' Blues*	15.00 -	25.00
1254 *Down In The Alley*	30.00 -	40.00
1258 *It's Tight Like That*	20.00 -	30.00
1268 *Juicy Lemon Blues*	15.00 -	25.00
1274 *Boot It Boy*	30.00 -	40.00
1277 *The Duck Yas-Yas-Yas*	35.00 -	50.00
1281 *Mess, Katie, Mess*	30.00 -	40.00
1286 *Pat That Bread*	15.00 -	25.00
1294 *It's So Nice*	15.0 -	25.00
1404 *Prison Bound Blues*	20.00 -	30.00
1409 *Givin' It Away*	15.00 -	25.00
1418 *Strange Woman Blues*	15.00 -	25.00
1420 *Come On, Mama, Do That Dance*	25.00 -	35.00
1426 *You Better Tighten Up On It*	15.0 -	25.00
1429 *Strewin' You Mess*	15.00 -	25.00
1430 *Saturday Night Scrontch*	25.00 -	35.00
1450 *Corrine, Corrina*	15.00 -	25.00
1456 *That Stuff You Sell*	15.00 -	25.00
1469 *Mrs. Baker's Blues*	15.00 -	25.00
1484 *Moanin' Heart Blues*	15.00 -	25.00
1491 *Dying Mercy Blues*	15.00 -	25.00
1496 *Corrine Corrina—No. 2*	15.00 -	25.00
1521 *You Rascal You*	30.00 -	40.00
1538 *The Dirty Dozen—No. 2*	15.00 -	20.00

1540 *You Rascal You*	20.00 -	30.00
1571 *Poor Old Bachelor Blues*	15.00 -	25.00
1572 *Dying Mercy Blues*	20.00 -	30.00
1577 *It's My Time Blues*	15.00 -	25.00
1596 *Jinx Doctor Blues*	20.00 -	30.00
1608 *Bear Cat's Kittens*	20.00 -	30.00
1619 *Boogie Woogie Dance*	20.00 -	30.00
1623 *Cryin' Shame Blues*	20.00 -	30.00
1628 *They Call It Boogie Woogie*	20.00 -	30.00
1637 *Cotton Seed Blues*	20.00 -	30.00
1654 *Georgia Hound Blues*	20.00 -	30.00
1656 *Depression Blues*	20.00 -	30.00
1661 *Stop And Listen Blues*	20.00 -	30.00
1671 *Please Mister Blues*	25.00 -	35.00
1685 *Dead Cats On The Line*	20.00 -	30.00
1699 *No Matter How She Done It*	20.00 -	30.00
1700 *Turpentine Blues*	20.00 -	30.00
1706 *Reckless Man Blues*	20.00 -	30.00
02720 *That Stuff Is Here*	20.00 -	30.00
02753 *Black Angel Blues*	20.00 -	30.00
02774 *Denver Blues*	20.00 -	30.00

FRANK TANNEHILL:
Titles, issued contemporaneously on Banner, Melotone, Oriole, Perfect, Romeo, Vocalion:

I.G.N. Blues; Steel Mill Blues	12.00 -	18.00
Bluebird 7945 *Warehouse Blues*	10.00 -	15.00
8028 *Door Bell Blues*	10.00 -	15.00
8762 *Lillie Mae*	10.00 -	15.00
8803 *Sweet Jelly Roll*	10.00 -	15.00

SAM TARPLEY:

Champion 16327 *Try Some Of That*	40.00 -	60.00
16782 *That Stuff*	40.00 -	60.00
Superior 2584 *Try Some Of That*	35.00 -	50.00

SLIM TARPLEY:

Paramount 13062 *Alabama Hustler*	50.00 -	75.00

TARTER AND GAY:

Victor 38017 *Brownie Blues*	40.00 -	60.00

TASKIANA FOUR:

Victor 20183, 20184	5.00 -	7.00
20852 *Dixie Bo-Bo*	10.00 -	15.00

HATTIE TATE:

Supertone 9288 *There's Been Some Changes Made*	———	

ROSE TATE:

Champion 15302 *My Man Left Me Blues*	30.00 -	50.00
15319 *Wild Woman Blues*	30.00 -	50.00
15417 *Money Woman Blues*	30.00 -	50.00
Silvertone 5133 *My Man Left Me Blues*	30.00 -	50.00
5168 *Mistreated Blues*	30.00 -	50.00

TAYLOR'S WEATHERBIRDS:

Victor 23309 *Coal Camp Blues*	75.00 -	100.00

TAYLOR AND ANDERSON:

Champaion 15951 *Corrine Corrina*	40.00 -	60.00
50016 *You Rascal, You*	10.00 -	15.00
Supertone 9646 *You Rascal, You*	40.00 -	60.00

CHARLES/CHARLEY TAYLOR:

Paramount 12949 *Where My Shoes At?*	75.00 -	100.00
12967 *Heavy Suitcase Blues*	75.00 -	100.00
13121 *C.P. Railroad Blues*	75.00 -	100.00

EDNA TAYLOR:

Paramount 12057 *Good Man Blues*	25.00 -	35.00

EVA TAYLOR (& HER BOY FRIENDS):
Titles, issued contemporaneously on Banner, Melotone, Oriole, Perfect, Romeo: *Crazy Blues;*

The Stuff Is Here And It's Mellow	8.00 -	12.00
Black Swan 2103 *New Moon*	10.00 -	15.00
Edison 14046 *West End Blues*	20.00 -	30.00
52646 *West End Blues*	20.00 -	30.00
Okeh 3055 (12-inch) *Farewell Blues*	20.00 -	30.00
4740 *Baby, Won't You Please Come Home*	8.00 -	12.00
4805 *Down Hearted Blues*	8.00 -	12.00
4927 *Oh! Daddy Blues*	15.00 -	20.00

8047 *You Missed A Good Woman When You Picked All Over Me*.................	8.00 -	12.00
8049 *12th Street Rag*.................	12.00 -	15.00
8050 *You Can Have My Man*...........	12.00 -	15.00
8051 *My Pillow And Me*.................	12.00 -	15.00
8067 *Yodeling Blues*.................	12.00 -	15.00
8068 *You'll Never Have No Luck By Quittin' Me*	12.00 -	15.00
8069 *Church Street Sobbin' Blues*......	12.00 -	15.00
8073 *Barefoot Blues*.................	15.00 -	20.00
8082 *Hesitation Blues*.................	8.00 -	12.00
8089 *Original Charleston Strut*.............	10.00 -	15.00
8114 *Old Fashioned Love*.............	15.00 -	20.00
8129 *Jazzin' Babies Blues*.............	15.00 -	20.00
8145 *Ghost Of The Blues*.............	15.00 -	20.00
8183 *Terrible Blues*.................	15.00 -	20.00
8286 *I've Found A New Baby*.............	25.00 -	35.00
8342 *You Can't Shush Katie (The Gabbiest Gal In Town)*.................	60.00 -	90.00
8407 *Morocco Blues*.............	20.00 -	30.00
8414 *Scatter Your Smiles*.............	20.00 -	30.00
8444 *I Wish You Would*.............	30.00 -	40.00
8463 *Red Hot Flo*.............	20.00 -	30.00
8518 *May We Meet Again*.............	15.00 -	20.00
8585 *Chloe*.............	10.00 -	15.00
8665 *Happy Days And Lonely Nights*......	15.00 -	25.00
40330 *Pickin' On Your Baby*.............	35.00 -	50.00
40655 *Senorita Mine*.............	10.00 -	15.00
40671 *When The Red, Red Robin Comes Bob, Bob*	15.00 -	20.00
40715 *Candy Lips*.............	20.00 -	30.00
Victor 38575 *Don't You Understand*.........	25.00 -	40.00

BLIND JEREMIAH TAYLOR:

Herwin 93027 *Mother's Love*.............	40.00 -	60.00

MONTANA TAYLOR (& THE JAZOO BOYS):

Circle 1008 *In The Bottom*.................	5.00 -	8.00
1009 *Low Down Boogie*.................	5.00 -	8.00
1010 *Sweet Sue*.................	5.00 -	8.00
1015 *Montana's Blues*.................	5.00 -	8.00
Vocalion 1275 *Whoop And Holler Stomp*......	75.00 -	100.00
1419 *Detroit Rocks*.................	75.00 -	100.00

SALLIE TAYLOR:

Supertone 9365 *Seven Men Blues*.............	25.00 -	40.00
9392 *West End Blues*.................	25.00 -	40.00
9426 *Old Fashioned Blues*.................	25.00 -	40.00
9440 *Loose Like That*.................	25.00 -	40.00
9530 *The Long Lost Blues*.................	25.00 -	40.00

WALTER TAYLOR:

Champion 15972 *Yo-Yo Blues*.............	40.00 -	60.00
16059 *Broadcasting Blues*.............	40.00 -	60.00
Gennett 7144 *Corrine Corrina*.............	40.00 -	60.00
7157 *Broadcasting Blues*.............	40.00 -	60.00
7171 *Deal Rag*.............	40.00 -	60.00
7189 *It Ain't No Good*.............	40.00 -	60.00
Suptertone 9681 *Yo-Yo Blues*.............	40.00 -	60.00
9682 *Thirty-Eight And Plus*.............	40.00 -	60.00

"BIG ROAD" WEBSTER TAYLOR:

Vocalion 1271 *Sunny Southern Blues*...........	40.00 -	60.00

T.C.I SECTION CREW:

Paramount 12478 *Section Gang Song*..........	15.00 -	20.00

TEARDROPS:

Sampson 634 *Come Back To Me*.............	10.00 -	20.00

JOHNNIE/JOHNNY TEMPLE:

Bluebird 8913 *Sundown Blues*.............	7.00 -	10.00
8968 *Big Woman Blues*.............	7.00 -	10.00
Decca 7244 *Louise Louise Blues*.............	8.00 -	12.00
7316 *Peepin' Through The Keyhole*........	8.00 -	12.00
7337 *So Lonely And Blue*.............	7.00 -	10.00
7385 *Hoodoo Women*.............	5.00 -	8.00
7416 *Snapping Cat*.............	7.00 -	10.00
7444 *Mean Baby Blues*.............	5.00 -	8.00
7456 *County Jail Blues*.............	5.00 -	8.00
7495 *Fare You Well*.............	5.00 -	8.00

7532 *Stavin' Chain*.............	5.00 -	8.00
7547 *Big Leg Woman*.............	5.00 -	8.00
7564 *Mississippi Woman's Blues*.............	5.00 -	8.00
7573 *What A Fool I've Been*.............	5.00 -	8.00
7583 *Grinding Mill*.............	5.00 -	8.00
7599 *If I Could Holler*.............	5.00 -	8.00
7632 *The Sun Goes Down In Blood*........	5.00 -	8.00
7643 *Down In Mississippi*.............	5.00 -	8.00
7660 *Streamline Blues*.............	5.00 -	8.00
7678 *Cherry Ball*.............	5.00 -	8.00
7735 *Good Woman Blues*.............	5.00 -	8.00
7750 *Skin And Bones Woman*.............	5.00 -	8.00
7772 *Lovin' Woman Blues*.............	5.00 -	8.00
7782 *Rommin' House Blues*.............	5.00 -	8.00
7800 *Fix It Up And Go*.............	7.00 -	10.00
7817 *Bow Leg Woman*.............	7.00 -	10.00
7825 *Corrine Corrina*.............	7.00 -	10.00
Vocalion 02987 *Jacksonville Blues*.............	15.00 -	20.00
03068 *Big Boat Whistle*.............	15.00 -	20.00

TENNESSEE SHAKERS:

Brunswick 7199 *Grind So Fine*.............	50.00 -	75.00

TENNESSEE TRIO:

Vocalion 5472 *Knox County Stomp*...........	20.00 -	35.00

NAT TERRY:

Imperial 5150 *Take It Easy*.................	10.00 -	15.00

SONNY ("HOOTIN") TERRY (& HIS BUCKSHOT FIVE/NIGHT OWLS):

Capitol 931, 15237, 40003, 40043, 40061, 40097, 40121.............	4.00 -	6.00
Gotham 517, 518.............	6.00 -	10.00
Gramercy 1004/1005 *Hootin' Blues*.............	5.00 -	8.00
Harlem 2327 *Dangerous Woman*.............	5.00 -	8.00*
Jackson 2327 *Harmonica Train*.............	5.00 -	8.00*
Jax 305 *I Don't Worry*.............	5.00 -	8.00*
Okeh 05453 *Harmonica Blues*.............	7.00 -	12.00
05538 *Harmonica Stomp*.............	7.00 -	12.00
05684 *Blowing The Blues*.............	7.00 -	12.00
Red Robin 110 *Harmonica Hop*.............	5.00 -	8.00*

TEXAS RED & JIMMY:

Viceroy 3333 *Black Snake Blues*.............	15.00 -	20.00*

TEXAS SLIM:

King 4283, 4315, 4323, 4329, 4334, 4366, 4377.	5.00 -	8.00

TEXAS TOMMY:

Brunswick 7044 *Jail Break Blues*.............	30.00 -	40.00
Varsity 6035 *Ridin' Papa*.............	10.00 -	15.00
6039 *Broke and Hungry*.............	10.00 -	15.00

SAM THEARD ("LOVIN' SAM FROM DOWN IN 'BAM):

Decca 7025 *That Rhythm Gal*.............	7.00 -	12.00
7146 *Till I Die*.............	12.00 -	18.00

(See also LOVIN' SAM)

AL "FATS" THOMAS:

Checker 759 *Dog Days*.............	70.00 -	10.00*

ANDREW THOMAS:

Swing With The Stars 1038 *Chicago Blues*......	10.00 -	20.00

ANDY THOMAS:

Gold Star 645 *My Baby Quit Me Blues*........	10.00 -	20.00
659 *In Love Blues*.............	10.00 -	20.00

BESSIE THOMAS:

Supertone 9282 *Harbor Blues*.............	35.00 -	50.00

BUD THOMAS:

Supertone 9511 *Street Walkin' Blues*.............	25.00 -	35.00

EARL THOMAS:

Decca 7195 *Sugar Girl Blues*.............	15.00 -	20.00
7221 *Rent Day Blues*.............	15.00 -	20.00

ELVIE THOMAS:

Paramount 12977 *Motherless Child Blues*......	90.00 -	120.00

F.T. THOMAS:

Gennett 6963 *Street Walkin' Blues*.............	25.00 -	40.00

GEORGE THOMAS:

Paramount 12826 *Fast Stuff Blues*.............	40.00 -	60.00

HENRY THOMAS:

Bluebird 5343 *My Sweet Candy*	20.00 -	30.00
5411 *Sick With The Blues*	20.00 -	30.00
Sunrise 3424 *She's Got What I Want*	20.00 -	30.00
Vocalion 1094 *John Henry*	75.00 -	100.00
1137 *Red River Blues*	75.00 -	100.00
1138 *The Little Red Caboose*	75.00 -	100.00
1139 *Woodhouse Blues*	75.00 -	100.00
1140 *Jonah In The Wilderness*	75.00 -	100.00
1141 *Run, Mollie, Run*	75.00 -	100.00
1197 *Texas Easy Street Blues*	75.00 -	100.00
1230 *Bull Doze Blues*	75.00 -	100.00
1249 *Texas Worried Blues*	75.00 -	100.00
1286 *Arkansas*	75.00 -	100.00
1443 *Don't Leave Me Here*	75.00 -	100.00
1468 *Lovin' Babe*	75.00 -	100.00

JESSE THOMAS; JESSE (BABYFACE) THOMAS:

Club (unnumbered) *You Are My Dreams*	15.00 -	20.00
(unnumbered) *I Wonder Why*	7.00 -	10.00
Freedom 1513 *Guess I'll Walk Alone*	7.00 -	10.00
Hollywood 1072 *Cool Kind Lover*	3.00 -	6.00*
Miltone 232 *Same Old Stuff*	20.00 -	30.00
233 *Mountain Key Blues*	20.00 -	30.00
Modern 710 *Texas Blues*	7.00 -	10.00
Specialty 419 *When You Say I Love You*	4.00 -	7.00*
Swing Time 240 *I Can't Stay Here*	8.00 -	12.00
241 *Now's The Time*	8.00 -	12.00
Victor 23381 *Down In Texas Blues*	80.00 -	100.00
38555 *Blue Goose Blues*	60.00 -	80.00

JOSEPHINE THOMAS:

Pathe-Actuelle 032122 *Memphis Bound*	8.00 -	12.00
Perfect 12201 *Memphis Bound*	8.00 -	12.00

L.J. THOMAS:

Chess 1493 *Sam's Drag*	5.00 -	8.00*

RAMBLIN' THOMAS:

Paramount 12609 *Back Gnawing Blues*	60.00 -	80.00
12616 *Sawmill Moan*	60.00 -	80.00
12637 *Lock And Key Blues*	60.00 -	80.00
12670 *No Baby Blues*	60.00 -	80.00
12708 *Ramblin' Man*	60.00 -	80.00
12752 *Good Time Blues*	60.00 -	80.00

RAMBLING THOMAS:

Victor 23332 *Ground Hog Blues*	60.00 -	80.00
23365 *Ground Hog Blues No. 2*	60.00 -	80.00

RUFUS THOMAS:

Chess 1466 *Night Walkin' Blues*	5.00 -	10.00*
1492 *No More Doggin' Around*	50.00 -	10.00*
1517 *Juanita*	5.00 -	10.00*
Sun 181 *Walkin' In The Rain*	8.00 -	12.00*
188 *Tiger Man*	8.00 -	12.00*
Talent 807 *I'm So Worried*	15.00 -	20.00

SIPPIE THOMAS:

Victor 38502 *I'm A Mighty Tight Woman*	40.00 -	60.00

WASHINGTON THOMAS:

Champion 15489 *Time Enough*	12.00 -	15.00
15511 *Silvery Moon*	12.00 -	15.00

JIM THOMPKINS:

Brunswick 7200 *Bedside Blues*	50.00 -	75.00

EDWARD THOMPSON:

Paramount 13018 *West Virginia Blues*	150.00 -	200.00

EVELYN THOMPSON:

Vocalion 1075 *Someday, Sweetheart*	10.00 -	15.00
1083 *After You've Gone*	10.00 -	15.00
1084 *One More Kiss*	10.00 -	15.00
15529 *One More Kiss*	10.00 -	15.00
15548 *One Sweet Letter From You*	15.00 -	20.00

MARGARET THORNTON:

Black Patti 8041 *Jockey Blues*	75.00 -	100.00

WILLIE MAE (BIG MAMA) THORNTON:

Peacock	3.00 -	5.00*

THE THRILLERS:

Big Town 109 *The Drunkard*	7.00 -	10.00*

ANDY TIBBS:

Aristocrat 1104 *Going Down Fast*	4.00 -	7.00

SLIM TINSLEY:

Globe 117 *606 Blues*	6.00 -	10.00
118 *Big Shot Mama*	6.00 -	10.00

JAMES TISDOM:

Universal-Fox 100 *Last Affair Blues*	15.00 -	25.00
101 *Throw This Dog A Bone*	15.00 -	25.00
102 *Overhaul Blues*	15.00 -	25.00

KINGFISH BILL TOMLIN:

Paramount 13034 *Hot Box*	100.00 -	150.00
13057 *Dupree Blues*	100.00 -	150.00

TOMMY AND JIMMY:

Superior 2555 *Where You Been So Long?*	35.00 -	50.00

THE TOO BAD BOYS:

Paramount 12861 *Ballin' The Jack*	20.00 -	30.00

TOO TIGHT HENRY:

Brunswick 7189 *Squinch Owl Moan*	20.00 -	30.00
Columbia 14374-D *Charleston Contest*	15.00 -	20.00

GEORGE TOREY:

Titles, issued contemporaneously on Banner, Melotone, Oriole, Perfect, Romeo: *Lonesome Man Blues; Married Woman Blues*	50.00 -	75.00

JIM TOWEL:

Brunswick 7060 *Buckwheat Cakes*	25.00 -	35.00

HENRY TOWNSEND:

Bluebird 5966 *She's Got A Mean Disposition*	30.00 -	40.00
6589 *She's Got A Mean Disposition*	30.00 -	40.00
7453 *Lose Your Man*	15.00 -	25.00
7474 *A Ramblin' Mind*	15.00 -	25.00
Columbia 14491-D *Mistreated Blues*	60.00 -	80.00
14529-D *Henry's Worry Blues*	60.00 -	80.00
Paramount 13097 *Doctor, Oh Doctor*	100.00 -	150.00

JESSE TOWNSEND:

Victor 23322 *No Home Blues*	40.00 -	60.00

SAM TOWNSEND:

Brunswick 7116 *Curbstone Blues*	40.00 -	60.00
Columbia 14571-D *I'm Missing That*	30.00 -	40.00

TRIANGLE QUARTETTE:

Broadway 5071 *She Done Quit Me Blues*	15.00 -	20.00
Paramount 12781 *She Done Quit Me Blues*	15.00 -	20.00

RICH TRICE:

Decca 7701 *Come On Baby*	15.00 -	25.00

WELLY TRICE:

Decca 7358 *Come On In Here Mama*	15.00 -	25.00

DORETHEA TROWBRIDGE:

Bluebird 5431 *Bad Luck Blues*	40.00 -	60.00

TUB JUG WASHBOARD BAND:

Paramount 12671 *Tub-Jug Rag*	35.00 -	50.00

BESSIE TUCKER:

Bluebird 5128 *Bogy Man Blues*	20.00 -	30.00
Sunrise 3208 *Bogy Man Blues*	20.00 -	30.00
Victor 21692 *Black Name Moan*	25.00 -	35.00
21708 *The Dummy*	25.00 -	35.00
23385 *Bogey Man Blues*	30.00 -	40.00
23392 *T.B. Moan*	30.00 -	40.00
38018 *Fryin' Pan Skillet Blues*	25.00 -	35.00
38526 *Bessie's Moan*	30.00 -	40.00
38538 *Old Black Mary*	30.00 -	40.00
38542 *Katy Blues*	30.00 -	40.00

ANNIE TURNER:

Bluebird 6707 *Black Pony Blues*	15.00 -	25.00
6788 *Workhouse Blues*	15.00 -	25.00

BABY FACE TURNER:

Modern 882 *Gonna Let You Go*	10.00 -	15.00*

BEE TURNER:

Paramount 13017 *Rough Treatin' Daddy*	50.00 -	75.00

CHARLIE TURNER AND WINSTON HOLMES:

Paramount 12793 *The Death Of Holmes' Mule*..	35.00 -	50.00

IKE TURNER:

Chess 1459 *I'm Lonesome Baby*	5.00 -	8.00*

(BIG) JOE TURNER (& THE ALL STARS):

Bayou 015 *Blues Jump The Rabbit*	7.00 -	10.00
Coral 65004 *Blues On Central Avenue*........	5.00 -	8.00
Decca 4093 *Rocks In My Bed*	5.00 -	8.00
7824 *Doggin' The Dog*...........	7.00 -	10.00
7827 *Jumpin' Down Blues*........	7.00 -	10.00
7856 *Somebody's Got To Go*......	5.00 -	8.00
7868 *Nobody In Mind*.............	5.00 -	8.00
7885 *Blues In The Night*..........	5.00 -	8.00
7889 *Sun Risin' Blues*............	5.00 -	8.00
Excelsior.....................	3.00 -	5.00
Freedom 1531 *Still In The Dark*.............	7.00 -	10.00
National 9011 *Watch That Jive*	5.00 -	8.00
Vocalion 4607 *Goin' Away Blues*............	10.00 -	15.00

LAVINIA TURNER:

Pathe-Actuelle 020544, 020572, 020627, 020705, 020878	5.00 -	8.00
Perfect 12005, 12032, 12033, 12034, 12039.....	5.00 -	8.00

SMILEY TURNER:

Mercury 8161 *Lonely Boy Blues*	5.00 -	8.00

BLIND SQUIRE TURNER:

Bluebird 5307 *She Thinks She's Slick*	35.00 -	50.00
5412 *Low Mellow*.....................	35.00 -	50.00
5491 *Pitty Pat Blues*....................	35.00 -	50.00

JOHN D. TWITTY:

Titles, issued contemporaneously on Banner, Melotone, Oriole, Perfect, Romeo, Vocalion: *A Gang Of Trouble; Walking Blues*..........	8.00 -	12.00

TWO BOYS FROM SAVANNAH:

Supertone 9485 *It's Just All Right*.............	30.00 -	50.00
9529 *Messed Up Blues*.................	30.00 -	50.00

THE TWO CHARLIES:

Titles, issued contemporaneously on Banner, Melotone; Oriole; Perfect; Romeo: *Don't Put Your Dirty Hands On Me; Got Your Water On; I Couldn't Stay Here; Pork Chops Blues*.....	30.00 -	40.00

THE TWO OF SPADES:

Columbia 14072-D *Meddlin' With The Blues*....	15.00 -	20.00

TWO POOR BOYS:

Titles, issued contemporaneously on Banner, Oriole, Perfect, Romeo: *John Henry Blues; Sitting On Top Of The World; Take A Look At That Baby; Two White Horses In A Line*..............	30.00 -	40.00

TYUS & TYUS:

Columbia 14638-D *Dad's Ole Mule*............	15.00 -	20.00

CHARLES (& EFFIE) TYUS:

Okeh 8133 *Omaha Blues*.................	8.00 -	12.00
8149 *I Want To Go Back To The Farm*.....	8.00 -	12.00
8200 *Cuddle Up Closer, It's Winter Time*.....	10.00 -	15.00
8330 *Good Old Bygone Days*..........	8.00 -	12.00
8459 *Alibi-ing Papa*..................	10.00 -	15.00

UMBRIAN GLEE CLUB:

Vocalion 1012 *Swing Along*.................	8.00 -	12.00
1013 *Rain Song*.....................	8.00 -	12.00

UNCLE SKIPPER:

Decca 7353 *Cutting My A B C's*.............	15.00 -	20.00
7455 *Look What Shape I'm In*..........	15.00 -	20.00

LOUISE VANT:

Okeh 8264 *Show Me The Way To Go Home*...	20.00 -	30.00
8275 *I'm Tired Of Everything But You*......	20.00 -	30.00
8281 *Just A Little But Bad*...........	20.00 -	30.00
8293 *Do Right Blues*.................	20.00 -	30.00
8310 *Pensacola Blues*................	15.00 -	20.00
8341 *Daddy, Don't You Try To Pull That Two-Time Thing On Me*................	8.00 -	12.00

CALLIE VASSAR:

Gennett 5172 *All Night Blues*...............	15.00 -	25.00
5173 *Original Stomps*...................	15.00 -	25.00

EDITH VAUGHAN:

Oriole 298 *Mad Mama's Blues*...............	10.00 -	15.00
311 *Broken Busted Can't Be Trusted Blues*...	10.00 -	15.00

THE VELVETONES:

Columbia 30224 *I'm Disillusioned*............	———	

JOHN P. VIGAL:

Black Swan 14115 *Fowler Twist*...............	15.00 -	20.00
Paramount 12132 *Fowler Twist*...............	15.00 -	20.00

WALTER VINCENT:

Brunswick 7126 *Your Friends Gonna Use It Too*	40.00 -	60.00
7141 *Overtime Blues*.....................	40.00 -	60.00
7190 *Mississippi Yodelin' Blues*..........	40.00 -	60.00
Decca 7169 *Losin' Blues*................	15.00 -	20.00
7178 *The Wrong Man*...............	15.00 -	20.00

WALTER VINCSON:

Bluebird 8828 *Every Dog Must Have His Day*..	10.00 -	15.00
8908 *Gulf Coast Boy*.................	10.00 -	15.00
8963 *Rosa Lee Blues*..................	10.00 -	15.00

OTTO VIRGIAL:

Bluebird 6213 *Bad Notion Blues*.............	15.00 -	25.00
6279 *Seven Year Itch*.................	15.00 -	25.00

THE VIRGINIA FOUR:

Decca 7662 *Dig My Jelly Roll*...............	8.00 -	12.00
7808 *Queen Street Rag*................	8.00 -	12.00

THE VOCALEERS:

Red Robin 130 *Shim Sham Shimmy*...........	———	
(The existence of this record has not been verified. It Is known that labels for such issue were printed. Offers of hundreds of dollars have been made. Note that the title was issued on Red Robin 130 by CHAMPION JACK DUPREE, and a simple printing error may be all that's involved.)		

VON BATTLE, JOSEPH:

JVB 75828 *Looking For My Woman*.........	15.00 -	20.00

UNCLE BUD WALKER:

Okeh 8828 *Stand Up Suitcase Blues*...........	50.00 -	75.00

JAMES WALKER:

Silvertone 3553 *Lost John Blues*.............	60.00 -	80.00

MONROE WALKER:

Columbia 14549-D *High Powered Mama*.......	30.00 -	40.00

PRETTY BOY WALKER:

Vocalion 1713 *The Break I'm Gettin'*.........	20.00 -	30.00

T-BONE WALKER:

Black & White 110, 111, 115, 121, 122, 123, 125, 126, 127...........................	4.00 -	7.00
Capitol 10033 *Mean Old World*	5.00 -	8.00
Capitol (others).......................	3.00 -	5.00
Comet 50, 51, 52, 53..................	4.00 -	6.00
Imperial 5071, 5081, 5086, 5094, 5103, 5116, 5147, 5153, 5161, 5171, 5181, 5193............	4.00 -	7.00*
Imperial (5202 through 5330).............	3.00 -	5.00*
Mercury 8016 *My Baby Left Me*.............	5.00 -	8.00
Old Swing-Master 11 *She Is Going To Ruin Me*.	7.00 -	10.00
Rhumboogie 4000, 4002, 4003..............	5.00 -	10.00

WILLIAM WALKER:

Gennett 7100 *I'll Remember You*.............	15.00 -	20.00

WILLIE WALKER:

Columbia 14578-D *South Carolina Rag*.......	30.00 -	40.00

FRANCES WALLACE:

Brunswick 7076 *Low Down Man Blues*........	20.00 -	30.00

INEZ WALLACE:

Black Swan 14137 *Radio Blues*...............	12.00 -	16.00
14144 *Come Back Dear*...............	12.00 -	16.00
14147 *Kissin' Daddy*.................	12.00 -	16.00
Paramount 12145 *Radio Blues*...............	10.00 -	15.00
12146 *Kissin' Daddy*.................	10.00 -	15.00
12155 *Come Back Dear*...............	10.00 -	15.00

MINNIE WALLACE:

Bluebird 5144 *Dirty Butter*.................	20.00 -	30.00
Victor 38547 *Dirty Butter*.................	40.00 -	60.00
Vocalion 03106 *Field Mouse Stomp*...........	30.00 -	40.00
03154 *Let's All Do That Thing*...........	30.00 -	40.00

SIPPIE WALLACE:

Okeh 8106 *Up The Country Blues*	15.00 -	20.00
8144 *Underworld Blues*	10.00 -	15.00
8159 *Stranger's Blues*	10.00 -	15.00
8168 *Mama's Gone, Goodbye*	10.00 -	15.00
8177 *Sud Bustin' Blues*	15.00 -	20.00
8190 *Let My Man Alone Blues*	10.00 -	15.00
8197 *Off And On Blues*	15.00 -	20.00
8205 *Every Dog Has His Day*	40.00 -	60.00
8206 *Devil Dance Blues*	40.00 -	60.00
8212 *Trouble Everywhere I Roam*	30.00 -	40.00
8232 *Section Hand Blues*	15.00 -	20.00
8243 *Murder's Gonna Be My Crime*	20.00 -	30.00
8251 *The Man I Love*	20.00 -	30.00
8276 *Advice Blues*	20.00 -	30.00
8288 *I'm Leaving You*	10.00 -	15.00
8301 *A Jealous Woman Like Me*	30.00 -	40.00
8328 *Jack O'Diamonds Blues*	35.00 -	50.00
8345 *The Mail Train Blues*	30.00 -	50.00
8381 *I Must Have It*	20.00 -	30.00
8439 *Bedroom Blues*	20.00 -	30.00
8470 *Lazy Man Blues*	35.00 -	50.00
8499 *Dead Drunk Blues*	35.00 -	50.00

WESLEY WALLACE:

Paramount 12958 *Fanny Lee Blues*	100.00 -	150.00

PEGGY WALLER AND GEORGE RAMSEY:

Paramount 13037 *Blacksnake Wiggle*	35.00 -	50.00

CHARLOTTE WALSH:

Silvertone 3567 *Cool Daddy Blues*	30.00 -	40.00

WALTER & BYRD:

Paramount 12945 *Wasn't It Sad About Lemon*	35.00 -	50.00

LORRAINE WALTON:

Bluebird 7577 *Whiskey Blues*	8.00 -	12.00
7630 *Freight Train Blues*	8.00 -	12.00
Vocalion 03989 *If You're A Viper*	8.00 -	12.00

SQUARE WALTON:

RCA Victor 20-5493 *Pepper Head Woman*	7.00 -	10.00*
20-5584 *Bad Hangover*	7.00 -	10.00*

AMY WARD:

Silvertone 3566 *Uptown Daddy*	20.00 -	30.00
3568 *Riverside Blues*	20.00 -	30.00
3573 *Nobody Knows*	20.00 -	30.00

EDDIE WARE & HIS BAND:

Chess 1461, 1507	5.00 -	8.00*
States 130 *That's The Stuff I Like*	7.00 -	10.00*

REV. I.B. WARE:

Vocalion 1235 *You Better Quit Drinking Shine*	15.00 -	20.00

OZIE WARE:

Titles, issued contemporaneously on Cameo, Lincoln, Pathe-Actuelle, Perfect, Romeo: *He Just Don't Appeal To Me; Hit Me In The Nose Blues* .. 15.00 - 20.00

Victor 21777 *I Done Caught You Blues*	20.00 -	30.00

PETER WARFIELD:

Miltone 5249 *Morning Train Blues*	15.00 -	20.00

BABY BOY WARREN (& HIS BUDDY):

Blue Lake 106 *Mattie Mae*	5.00 -	8.00*
Drummond 3002 *Baby Boy Blues*	8.00 -	15.00*
3003 *Stop Breakin' Down*	7.00 -	10.00*
Federal 12008 *Forgive Me Darling*	5.00 -	8.00*
Gotham 507 *My Special Friend Blues*	10.00 -	15.00
JVB 26 *Hello Stranger*	20.00 -	30.00
Staff 706 *My Special Friend Blues*	20.00 -	30.00
707 *Lonesome Cabin Blues*	20.00 -	30.00
709 *Forgive Me Darling*	20.00 -	30.00

WASHBOARD PETE:

Savoy 5556 *Christmas Blues*	7.00 -	12.00

WASHBOARD SAM (& HIS WASHBOARD BAND); WASHBOARD SAM'S BAND:

Bluebird 5983 *Ocean Blues*	12.00 -	18.00
6355 *You Done Tore Your Playhouse Down*	10.00 -	15.00
6518 *Give Me Lovin'*	10.00 -	15.00

6556 *Cherry Hill Blues*	10.00 -	15.00
6765 *Razor Cuttin' Man*	8.00 -	12.00
6794 *Out With The Wrong Woman*	8.00 -	12.00
6870 *Big Woman*	8.00 -	12.00
6970 *Easy Ridin' Mama*	7.00 -	10.00
7001 *We Gonna Move*	7.00 -	10.00
7048 *I Drink Good Whiskey*	7.00 -	10.00
7096 *Lowland Blues*	7.00 -	10.00
7148 *Out With The Wrong Woman*	10.00 -	15.00
7179 *I Love All My Women*	10.00 -	15.00
7194 *You Done Tore Your Playhouse Down*	10.00 -	15.00
7291 *Washboard's Barrel House Song*	7.00 -	10.00
7328 *Beer Garden Blues*	7.00 -	10.00
7365 *Gonna Be Some Walkin' Done*	7.00 -	10.00
7403 *Second Story Man*	7.00 -	10.00
7440 *Want To Woogie Some More*	15.00 -	25.00
7501 *Don't Leave Me Here*	7.00 -	10.00
7526 *Down At The Old Village Store*	20.00 -	30.00
7552 *My Woman's A Sender*	7.00 -	10.00
7601 *Phantom Black Snake*	7.00 -	10.00
7655 *The Gal I Love*	20.00 -	30.00
7664 *Yellow, Black And Brown*	7.00 -	10.00
7732 *Serve It Right*	7.00 -	10.00
7780 *Sophisticated Mama*	7.00 -	10.00
7834 *Policy Writer's Blues*	7.00 -	10.00
7866 *Jumpin' Rooster*	7.00 -	10.00
7906 *Bucket's Got A Hole In It*	7.00 -	10.00
7977 *Walkin' In My Sleep*	7.00 -	10.00
7993 *Warehouse Blues*	7.00 -	10.00
8018 *Gonna Kill My Baby*	5.00 -	8.00
8044 *Rack 'Em Back*	5.00 -	8.00
8076 *Suspicious Blues*	7.00 -	10.00
8184 *That Will Get It*	7.00 -	10.00
8211 *Diggin' My Potatoes*	5.00 -	8.00
8243 *Good Old Easy Street*	5.00 -	8.00
8270 *This Time Is My Time*	5.00 -	8.00
8323 *Has My Gal Been By Here?*	5.00 -	8.00
8342 *Jersey Cow Blues*	5.00 -	8.00
8358 *So Early In The Morning*	5.00 -	8.00
8377, 8424, 8450, 8469, 8500, 8525, 8540, 8554, 8569, 8599, 8644, 8675, 8699, 8727, 8761, 8792, 8815, 8844, 8878, 8909, 8937, 8967, 8997, 9007, 9018, 9039, 34-0705, 34-0710	4.00 -	8.00
Chess 1545 *Diggin' My Potatoes*	5.00 -	8.00*
Montgomery Ward 7050 *Don't 'Low*	7.00 -	10.00
7062 *Razor Cuttin' Man*	7.00 -	10.00
7497 *Towboat Blues*	7.00 -	10.00
7498 *Barbecue*	7.00 -	10.00
7499 *Want To Woogie Some More*	7.00 -	10.00
7500 *Down At The Old Village Store*	10.00 -	15.00
7588, 7590, 7759, 7760, 7761, 8801, 8804	4.00 -	8.00
RCA Victor	3.00 -	5.00
Vocalion 02937 *Don't Tear My Clothes*	7.00 -	10.00
03365 *Mixed Up Blues*	10.00 -	15.00

Titles, issued contemporaneously on Banner, Conqueror, Melotone, Oriole, Perfect, Romeo: *Don't Tear My Clothes; I'm A Prowlin' Groundhog.* 7.00 - 10.00

WASHBOARD WALTER (& HIS BAND):

Paramount 12954 *Narrow Face Blues*	60.00 -	80.00
12991 *Disconnected Mama*	60.00 -	80.00
13100 *Wuffin' Blues*	60.00 -	80.00

WASHBOARD WILLIE & HIS SUPER SUDS OF RHYTHM:

JVB 59 *Cherry Red Blues*	15.00 -	20.00
70 *Washboard Blues*	15.00 -	20.00*

ALBERTA WASHBURN:

Superior 2668 *Skeeter Blues*	40.00 -	60.00
2739 *Pig Meat Mama*	40.00 -	-60.00
2783 *Forty-Four Blues*	40.00 -	60.00
2826 *Hoboken Prison Blues*	40.00 -	60.00

BOOKER T. WASHINGTON:

Bluebird 8352 *Just Want To Think*	15.00 -	20.00

8378 *Cotton Club Blues*...............	15.00 -	20.00
8413 *Cozy Corner Blues*...............	15.00 -	20.00
8449 *Wrapped Up In Bad Luck*...........	15.00 -	20.00

D.C. WASHINGTON:

Gold Star 661 *Happy Home Blues*...........	15.00 -	25.00

ELIZABETH WASHINGTON:

Bluebird 5229 *Riot Call Blues*.............	40.00 -	50.00
Sunrise 3312 *You Put That Thing On Me*.....	40.00 -	50.00
Victor 23425 *Mistreated Blues*.............	60.00 -	80.00

ISABELLE WASHINGTON:

Black Swan 14141 *I Want To*.............	15.00 -	20.00
Paramount 12135 *I Want To*.............	12.00 -	16.00

LIZZIE WASHINGTON:

Black Patti 8054 *Mexico Blues*...........	40.00 -	60.00
Champion 15282 *Skeleton Key Blues*........	40.00 -	60.00
15303 *East Coast Blues*...............	30.00 -	40.00
15319 *Sport Model Mamma Blues*.......	30.00 -	40.00
Gennett 6126 *Working Man Blues*.........	30.00 -	50.00
6134 *Skeleton Key Blues*...........	30.00 -	50.00
6195 *Fall Or Summer Blues*..........	30.00 -	50.00
6321 *Brick Flat Blues*.............	30.00 -	50.00
6408 *Lord Have Mercy Blues*........	30.00 -	50.00
Herwin 92013 *East Coast Blues*........	35.00 -	50.00
92021 *My Low Down Brown*.......	35.00 -	50.00
92039 *Lord Have Mercy Blues*.....	35.00 -	50.00
92040 *Mexico Blues*............	35.00 -	50.00
92041 *Brick Flat Blues*..........	35.00 -	50.00
92042 *Ease Away Blues*..........	35.00 -	50.00
Vocalion 1459 *Whiskey Head Blues*.....	30.00 -	40.00

LOUIS WASHINGTON:

Vocalion 02634 *Run, Sinner, Run*...........	20.00 -	30.00
02658 *Standin' On A Rock*.............	20.00 -	30.00

WALTER (COWBOY) WASHINGTON:

Bluebird 6917 *Ice Pick Mama*.............	15.00 -	25.00
7314 *I Need You Blues*.............	15.00 -	25.00

CROWN PRINCE WATERFORD:

Aladdin 534, 535.......................	4.00 -	6.00
Capitol 40074, 40103, 40132, 40137......	4.00 -	6.00
King 4310, 4374, 4393................	4.00 -	6.00
Torch 6911 *Eatin' Watermelon*...........	6.00 -	10.00

KITTY WATERS:

Pathe-Actuelle 7531 *Back Water Blues*........	7.00 -	10.00
7537 *Loud And Wrong*.................	7.00 -	10.00
Perfect 131 *Back Water Blues*............	7.00 -	10.00
137 *Loud And Wrong*................	7.00 -	10.00

KATIE WATKINS:

Viceroy 3333 *Trying To Get You Off My Mind.*	15.00 -	20.00*

VIOLA WATKINS:

Jubilee 5007 *Jelly And Bread*.............	5.00 -	8.00

DEEK WATSON & THE BROWN DOTS:

Manor	3.00 -	6.00

YOUNG JOHN WATSON:

Federal 12120 *Highway 60*.............	5.00 -	8.0*
12131 *Motor Head Baby*.............	5.00 -	8.00*
12143 *Walkin' To My Baby*.........	5.00 -	8.00*
12157 *What's Going On*.............	5.00 -	8.00*
12175 *Space Guitar*.................	5.00 -	8.00*

MOJO WATSON:

Atlas 1080 *All Alone*.................	7.00 -	10.00

JAMES WAYNE/WAYNES:

Imperial 5151, 5160, 5166, 5258.......	5.00 -	8.00*
Sittin' In With 573, 588, 607, 622, 639...	6.00 -	10.00

WEAVER AND BEASLEY:

Okeh 8530 *Bottleneck Blues*.............	20.00 -	30.00

CURLEY WEAVER (& HIS GUITAR/& EDDIE MAPP/& CLARENCE MOORE/& RUTH WILLIS):

Titles, issued contemporaneously on Banner, Melotone, Oriole, Perfect, Romeo: *Birmingham Gambler, Black Woman; City Cell Blues; Early Morning Blues; Leg Iron Blues; No No Blues; Some Cold Rainy Day; Tippin' Tom*........ 35.00 - 50.00

Champion 50065 *Two Faced Woman*..........	20.00 -	30.00
50077 *Fried Pie Blues*.............	20.00 -	30.00
Columbia 14386-D *No No Blues*...........	30.00 -	40.00
Decca 7077 *Early Morning Blues*...........	12.00 -	15.00
7664, 7906.......................	5.00 -	8.00
Okeh 8928 *Baby Boogie Woogie*...........	40.00 -	60.00
QRS 7077 *Dirty Deal Blues*.............	60.00 -	80.00
Sittin' In With 547 *My Baby's Gone*........	15.00 -	20.00
646 *Some Rainy Day*................	8.00 -	12.00

SYLVESTER WEAVER:

Okeh 8109 *Guitar Rag*.................	15.00 -	25.00
8152 *Smoketown Strut*.............	15.00 -	25.00
8207 *Weaver's Blues*.............	15.00 -	25.00
8460 *True Love Blues*.............	20.00 -	30.00
8480 *Guitar Rag*.................	20.00 -	30.00
8504 *Penitentiary Bound Blues*.....	15.00 -	25.00
8522 *What Makes A Man Blue?*......	15.00 -	25.00
8534 *Black Spider Blues*............	15.00 -	25.00
8549 *Rock Pile Blues*.............	15.00 -	25.00
8608 *Polecat Blues*.............	15.00 -	25.00

BOOGIE BILL WEBB:

Imperial 5257 *Bad Dog*.................	8.00 -	12.00*

TINY WEBB TRIO:

Globe 108 *G.I. Blues*.................	4.00 -	7.00

MARGARET WEBSTER:

Diva 6040-G *How Can I Get It*...........	10.00 -	15.00
Velvet Tone 7066-V *How Can I Get It*.......	10.00 -	15.00
7076-V *Wipe 'Em Off*.................	10.00 -	15.00

BARREL HOUSE WELCH:

Paramount 12759 *Dying Pickpocket Blues*......	30.00 -	40.00

KANSAS CITY BILL WELDON:

Vocalion 03078 *Race Horse Filly Blues*.......	8.00 -	15.00
03198 *Doctor's Blues*................	8.00 -	15.00

WILL WELDON:

Victor 21134 *Turpentine Blues*.............	60.00 -	80.00

TUDIE WELLS:

Pathe-Actuelle 032006 *Uncle Sam Blues*.......	7.00 -	10.00
Perfect 12085 *Uncle Sam Blues*............	7.00 -	10.00

NOLAN WELSH:

Okeh 8372 *St. Peter Blues*.............	40.00 -	60.00
8425 *Bouncing Blues*................	15.00 -	20.00

CHARLEY WEST:

Bluebird 7033 *Poor Boy Blues*.............	10.00 -	15.00
8085 *Rollin' Stone Blues*.............	10.00 -	15.00

WESTERN KID:

Gennett 7210 *Mountain Girl Blues*............	40.00 -	60.00
7230 *Western Blues*................	40.00 -	60.00

PERRY WESTON:

Vocalion 03699 *Border Blues*.............	15.00 -	20.00

LITTLE DAVID WHEATON:

Capitol 40009, 40034, 40139.............	12.00 -	18.00

PEETIE WHEATSTRAW:

Titles, issued contemporaneously on Banner, Conqueror, Melotone, Oriole, Perfect, Romeo; Vocalion: *Froggie Blues; Good Whiskey Blues; Kidnappers Blues; The Last Dime; Letter Writing Blues; Long Lonesome Drive; Mistreated Love Blues; Remember And Forget Blues*........ 10.00 - 15.00

Bluebird 5451 *Devil's Son-In-Law*............	10.00 -	15.00
Conqueror 8858, 8925, 9027, 9028............	6.00 -	10.00
Decca 7007 *Doin' The Best I Can*.............	10.00 -	15.00
7018 *Throw Me In The Alley*.............	15.00 -	20.00
7061 *Good Home Blues*................	10.00 -	15.00
7082 *Numbers Blues*................	10.00 -	15.00
7111 *Whiskey Head Blues*.............	10.00 -	15.00
7123 *Good Hustler Blues*.............	10.00 -	15.00
7129 *Santa Claus Blues*.............	10.00 -	15.00
7144 *King Spider Blues*.............	10.00 -	15.00
7159 *Coon Can Shorty*.............	10.00 -	15.00
7167 *Deep Sea Love*.............	10.00 -	15.00
7177 *Poor Millionaire Blues*.............	10.00 -	15.00

WHIDBY192WHITE

7187	Meat Cutter Blues	10.00 -	15.00
7200	Low Down Rascal	10.00 -	15.00
7228	Country Fool Blues	10.00 -	15.00
7243	False Hearted Woman	8.00 -	12.00
7257	I Don't Want No Pretty-Faced Woman	8.00 -	12.00
7272	Beggar Man Blues	8.00 -	12.00
7292	Crapshooter's Blues	8.00 -	12.00
7311	Working On The Project	8.00 -	12.00
7348	Crazy With The Blues	8.00 -	12.00
7379	New Working On The Project	8.00 -	12.00
7391	Give Me Black Or Brown	8.00 -	12.00
7403	Sick Bed Blues	8.00 -	12.00
7422	Devilment Blues	8.00 -	12.00

7441, 7453, 7465, 7479, 7498, 7529, 7544, 7568, 7578, 7589, 7605, 7641, 7657, 7676, 7692, 7738, 7753, 7778, 7788, 7798, 7815, 7823, 7837, 7844, 7857, 7879, 7886, 7894, 7901 .... 5.00 - 8.00

7904	Southern Girl Blues	15.00 -	20.00
Vocalion 1552	Tennessee Peaches Blues	20.00 -	30.00
1569	School Days	20.00 -	30.00
1597	Strange Man Blues	20.00 -	30.00
1620	Mama's Advice	20.00 -	30.00
1649	Ain't It A Pity And A Shame	20.00 -	30.00
1672	C And A Blues	20.00 -	30.00
1722	Police Station Blues	20.00 -	30.00
1727	Can't See Blues	20.00 -	30.00
02783	Back Door Blues	12.00 -	16.00
02810	C And A Train Blues	12.00 -	16.00
02843	Keyhole Blues	12.00 -	16.00
02942	Blues At My Door	8.00 -	12.00
02978	Good Whiskey Blues	8.00 -	12.00
03035	Up The Road Blues	8.00 -	12.00
03066	King Of Spades	8.00 -	12.00
03119	Sorrow Hearted Blues	8.00 -	12.00
03155	Johnnie Blues	8.00 -	12.00
03185	True Blue Woman	8.00 -	12.00
03231	Jungle Man Blues	8.00 -	12.00
03249	Froggie Blues	8.00 -	12.00
03273	Mistreated Love Blues	8.00 -	12.00
03348	Block And Tackle	8.00 -	12.00
03396	Sweet Home Blues	8.00 -	12.00
03444	Cut Out Blues	8.00 -	12.00

LULU WHIDBY:
Black Swan 2005 Home Again Blues .... 10.00 - 15.00
Home Again Blues also issued contemporaneously on Claxtonola, Paramount, Puritan .... 8.00 - 12.00

WHISTLIN' PETE AND DADDY STOVEPIPE:
Gennett 6212 Black Snake Blues .... 40.00 - 60.00

WHISTLIN' RUFUS:
Bluebird 5306 Sweet Jelly Rollin' .... 5.00 - 8.00
5360 Sweet Thing .... 5.00 - 8.00

BOB WHITE:
Bluebird 8595 I'm The Woogie Man .... 10.00 - 15.00

BUKKA WHITE:
Conqueror 9072 Shake 'Em On Down .... 60.00 - 80.00
Okeh 05625 Good Gin Blues .... 60.00 - 80.00
05683 District Attorney Blues .... 60.00 - 80.00
05743 Sleepy Man Blues .... 60.00 - 80.00
Vocalion 03711 Shake 'Em On Down .... 60.00 - 80.00
05489 High Fever Blues .... 60.00 - 80.00
05526 Strange Place Blues .... 60.00 - 80.00
05588 Black Train Blues .... 60.00 - 80.00

CLARA WHITE (Accompanied by SAM HILL/HARRY SIMS):
Oriole 263 Clearing House Blues .... 7.00 - 10.00
264 Buzzin' Around .... 7.00 - 10.00
265 You Don't Know My Mind .... 7.00 - 10.00

FLORENCE WHITE:
Victor 20584 Cold Rocks Was My Pillow ...... 15.00 - 20.00

GEORGIA WHITE:
Decca 7072 Your Worries Ain't Like Mine ..... 7.00 - 10.00

7100	Dupree Blues	7.00 -	10.00
7122	Honey Dripper Blues	7.00 -	10.00
7135	Easy Rider Blues	7.00 -	10.00
7143	Your Worries Ain't Like Mine No. 2	7.00 -	10.00
7149	If You Can't Get Five, Take Two	7.00 -	10.00
7152	Tell Me Baby	7.00 -	10.00
7166	Can't Read, Can't Write	7.00 -	10.00
7174	Rattlesnakin' Daddy	7.00 -	10.00
7183	New Hot Nuts (Get 'Em From The Peanut Man)	7.00 -	10.00
7192	Trouble In Mind	7.00 -	10.00
7199	I Just Want Your Stingaree	7.00 -	10.00
7209	Pigmeat Blues	7.00 -	10.00
7216	No Second Hand Woman	7.00 -	10.00
7254	Your Hellish Ways	5.00 -	8.00
7269	Sinking Sun Blues	5.00 -	8.00
7277	You Don't Know My Mind	5.00 -	8.00
7287	Little Red Wagon	5.00 -	8.00
7309	Toothache Blues	5.00 -	8.00
7323	When My Love Comes Down	5.00 -	8.00
7332	New Trouble In Mind	5.00 -	8.00
7357	Biscuit Roller	5.00 -	8.00
7377	Georgia Man	5.00 -	8.00
7389	Red Cap Porter	5.00 -	8.00
7405	All Night Blues	5.00 -	8.00
7419	Strewin' Your Mess	5.00 -	8.00
7436	The Stuff Is Here	5.00 -	8.00
7450	Almost Afraid To Love	5.00 -	8.00
7477	Too Much Trouble	5.00 -	8.00
7521	Trouble In Mind Swing	5.00 -	8.00
7534	Dead Man's Blues	5.00 -	8.00
7562	My Worried Mind Blues	5.00 -	8.00
7596	Married Woman Blues	5.00 -	8.00
7608	Fire In The Mountain	5.00 -	8.00
7620	Beggin' My Daddy	5.00 -	8.00
7631	Hydrant Love	5.00 -	8.00
7652	Do It Again	5.00 -	8.00
7672	I'm Doing What My Heart Says Do	5.00 -	8.00
7689	Furniture Man	5.00 -	8.00
7741	Jazzin' Babies Blues	5.00 -	8.00
7754	Sensation Blues	5.00 -	8.00
7783	Papa Pleaser	5.00 -	8.00
7807	Worried Head Blues	5.00 -	8.00
7841	Come Around To My House	5.00 -	8.00
7853	Territory Blues	5.00 -	8.00
7866	Mail Plane Blues	5.00 -	8.00

GLADYS WHITE:
Oriole 746 I'm Saving It All For You .... 10.00 - 15.00
772 Papa, If You Can't Do Better .... 10.00 - 15.00

GRACE WHITE:
Silvertone 3542 Friendless Blues .... 15.00 - 20.00

JOSH/JOSHUA WHITE:
Titles, issued contemporaneously on Banner, Conqueror, Melotone, Oriole, Perfect, Romeo: Baby, Won't You Doodle-Doo-Doo; Bad Depression Blues; Big House Blues; Black And Evil Blues; Blood Red River; Can't Help But Crying Sometimes; Crying Blues; Death's Coming Back After You; Double Crossing Women; Downhearted Man Blues; Down On Me; Four And Twenty Elders; Got A Key To The Kingdom; High Brown Cheater; How About You?; Howlin' Wolf Blues; I Don't Intend To Die In Egyptland; I Got A Home In That Rock; Jesus Gonna Make Up My Dying Bed; Lay Some Flowers On My Grave; Lazy Black Snake Blues; Little Brother Blues; Lord, I Want To Die Easy; Motherless Children; My Father Is A Husband-man; My Soul Is Gonna Live With God; On My Way; Paul And Silas Bound In Jail; Pickin' Low Cotton; Pure Religion Hallilu; So Sweet, So Sweet;

That Suits Me; There's A Man Going Round Taking Names; Things About Coming My Way; This Heart Of Mine; While The Blood Runs Warm In Your Veins; You Sinner You . . . . 20.00 - 30.00

WASHINGTON WHITE:
Victor 23295 *The Panama Limited* . . . . 90.00 - 120.00
   38615 *Promise True And Grand* . . . . 90.00 - 120.00

ELSIE WHITMAN:
Paramount 12172 *Sweet Daddy It's You I Love.* 12.00 - 16.00

ESSIE WHITMAM:
Black Swan 2036 *If You Don't Believe I Love You* 12.00 - 16.00

MARGARET WHITMIRE:
Brunswick 7024 *Tain't A Cow In Texas* . . . . 15.00 - 20.00
Vocalion 1173 *Tain't A Cow In Texas* . . . . 15.00 - 20.00

(JAMES) "BOODLE IT" WIGGINS:
Paramount 12662 *Evil Woman Blues* . . . . 80.00 - 100.00
   12860 *Forty-Four Blues* . . . . 80.00 - 100.00
   12878 *Weary Heart Blues* . . . . 80.00 - 100.00
   12916 *Gotta Shave 'Em Dry* . . . . 80.00 - 100.00

BILL WILBER:
Champion 50053 *Greyhound Blues* . . . . 30.00 - 40.00

WILEY AND WILEY:
Brunswick 7022 *The Dixie Drug Store Down On* 15.00 - 20.00
Columbia 14610-D *Irene's Bakershop Blues* . . . . . 15.00 - 20.00
   14630-D *Jumpin' Judy Blues* . . . . 15.00 - 20.00
Okeh 8385 *Dear Old Campanion* . . . . 15.00 - 20.00
Vocalion 1171 *The Dixie Drug Store Down On.* 15.00 - 20.00

ARNOLD WILEY:
Apollo 391 *Wiley's Boogie* . . . . 7.00 - 10.00
Brunswick 7113 *Windy City* . . . . 25.00 - 40.00
Paramount 12955 *Jumping Blues* . . . . 30.00 - 40.00

DOC WILEY:
Bullet 323 *Play Your Hand* . . . . 7.00 - 10.00

GEESHIE WILEY:
Paramount 12951 *Skinny Leg Blues* . . . . 80.00 - 100.00
   13074 *Pick Poor Robin Clean* . . . . 80.00 - 100.00

ROBERT WILKINS:
Brunswick 7125 *Falling Down Blues* . . . . 90.00 - 120.00
   7158 *Get Away Blues* . . . . 90.00 - 120.00
   7168 *Police Sergeant Blues* . . . . 90.00 - 120.00
   7205 *Long Train Blues* . . . . 90.00 - 120.00
Victor 21741 *Rolling Stone* . . . . 80.00 - 100.00
   23379 *Jail House Blues* . . . . 90.00 - 130.00

TIM WILKINS:
Vocalion 03176 *Black Rat Blues* . . . . 60.00 - 80.00
   03223 *Dirty Deal Blues* . . . . 60.00 - 80.00

B. WILLIAMS:
Top Tunes 101 *Mortgaged Love* . . . . 8.00 - 12.00

BESSIE WILLIAMS:
Domino 361, 362, 363, 364 . . . . 8.00 - 12.00
   412 *I Wanna Jazz Some More* . . . . 10.00 - 15.00
   413 *Family Skeleton Blues* . . . . 10.00 - 15.00
   424 *Deep River Blues* . . . . 8.00 - 12.00

BILL WILLIAMS (& SAMMY SAMPSON):
Titles, issued contemporaneously on Banner, Oriole, Perfect, Romeo: *Mr. Conductor Man; No Good Buddy* . . . . 25.00 - 40.00

BILYE WILLIAMS:
Acorn 310 *Disgusted Blues* . . . . 7.00 - 10.00

BLIND BOY WILLIAMS:
Sittin' In With 538 *Just Drifting* . . . . 8.00 - 12.00

EDDIE WILLIAMS & THE BROWN BUDDIES:
Selective 121 *Unfaithful Woman* . . . . 5.00 - 8.00
Supreme 1528, 1535, 1542, 1546, 1547, 1548 . . . 4.00 - 6.00

BOODLE IT WILLIAMS:
Broadway 5086 *Evil Woman Blues* . . . . 80.00 - 100.00

BROTHER WILLIAMS' MEMPHIS SANC-TIFIED SINGERS:
Vocalin 1482 *He's Got The Whole World In His Hands* . . . . 20.00 - 30.00

ELLIS WILLIAMS:
Columbia 14482-D *Smokey Blues* . . . . 25.00 - 35.00

ELSIE WILLIAMS:
Decca 7399 *Bind It Back* . . . . 5.00 - 8.00

GEORGE ("BULLET") WILLIAMS:
Broadway 5085 *Frisco Leaving Birmingham* . . . . . 50.00 - 75.00
Paramount 12651 *The Escaped Convict* . . . . 50.00 - 75.00
   12680 *Touch Me Light Mama* . . . . 50.00 - 75.00

GEORGE WILLIAMS (AND BESSIE BROWN):
Columbia A-3974, 13006-D, 14002-D, 14011-D,
14015-D, 14017-D, 14030-D, 14065-D, 14078-D,
14135-D, 14148-D, 14201-D . . . . 4.00 - 8.00
14033-D, 14046-D, 14049-D, 14071-D, 14543-D 5.00 - 108.00
Diva 6027-G Velvet Tone 7053-V . . . . 5.00 - 8.00

GUSSIE WILLIAMS:
Okeh 8934 *It's Too Slippery* . . . . 25.00 - 35.00

HENRY WILLIAMS AND EDDIE ANTHONY:
Columbia 14328-D *Georgia Crawl.* . . . . 15.00 - 25.00

"JABO" WILLIAMS:
Paramount 13127 *Ko Ko Mo Blues* . . . . 150.00 - 200.00
   13130 *Fat Mama Blues* . . . . 150.00 - 200.00
   13136 *House Lady Blues* . . . . 150.00 - 200.00
   13141 *Pratt City Blues* . . . . 150.00 - 200.00

(BIG) JOE WILLIAMS (& HIS 9-STRING GUITAR); JOE WILLIAMS' WASHBOARD BLUES SINGERS:
Bluebird 5900 *Little Leg Woman* . . . . 30.00 - 40.00
   5930 *Providence Help The Poor People* . . . . . 30.00 - 40.00
   5948 *My Grey Pony* . . . . 30.00 - 40.00
   5996 *49 Highway Blues* . . . . 30.00 - 40.00
   6200 *Wild Cow Blues* . . . . 30.00 - 40.00
   6231 *Worried Man Blues* . . . . 30.00 - 40.00
   7719 *Get Your Head Trimmed Down* . . . . 25.00 - 35.00
   7770 *Peach Orchard Mama* . . . . 25.00 - 35.00
   8738 *Crawlin' King Snake* . . . . 10.00 - 15.00
   8774 *I'm Getting Wild About Her* . . . . 10.00 - 15.00
   8969 *Please Don't Go* . . . . 10.00 - 15.00
   9025 *Highway 49* . . . . 8.00 - 12.00
   34-0739 *Vitamin A* . . . . 5.00 - 8.00
Bullet 337 *Jivin' Woman* . . . . 8.00 - 12.00
Columbia 30099, 30107, 30119, 30129, 30191,
37945, 38055, 38190 . . . . 4.00 - 7.00
Trumpet 151 *Delta Blues* . . . . 7.00 - 10.00*
   169 *Overhauling Blues* . . . . 7.00 - 10.00*
   171 *She Left Me A Mule* . . . . 7.00 - 10.00*
Vocalion 1457 *Mr. Devil Blues* . . . . 40.00 - 60.00

JOHNNY WILLIAMS:
Gotham 506 *Wandering Blues* . . . . 6.00 - 10.00
Staff 704 *Highway Blues* . . . . 8.00 - 15.00
   710 *Wandering Blues* . . . . 8.00 - 15.00
   717 *I Got Lucky* . . . . 15.00 - 20.00
   718 *Prison Bound* . . . . 8.00 - 12.00
Swing Time 225 *I Got Lucky* . . . . 5.00 - 8.00
   266 *Prison Bound* . . . . 5.00 - 8.00

L.C. WILLIAMS (with J.C. CONNEY'S COM-BO); L.C. (LIGHTNIN' JR.) WILLIAMS:
Bayou 008 *All Through My Dreams* . . . . 10.00 - 15.00
Dot 1052 *You Never Miss The Water.* . . . . 5.00 - 8.00
Freedom 1501, 1517, 1524 . . . . 5.00 - 8.00
   1529 *All Through My Dreams* . . . . 6.00 - 10.00
Gold Star 614 *Trying, Trying* . . . . 7.00 - 10.00
   623 *Hole In The Wall* . . . . 8.00 - 12.00
   648 *I Won't Be Here Long* . . . . 8.00 - 12.00
Imperial 5195 *Mean And Evil Blues* . . . . 5.00 - 8.00*
Jax 640 *Baby Child* . . . . 8.00 - 12.00
   648 *Fannie Mae* . . . . 8.00 - 12.00
Mercury 8276 *Don't Want No Woman* . . . . 5.00 - 8.00
Sittin' In With 640 *So Sorry* . . . . 8.00 - 12.00
   648 *Fannie Mae* . . . . 8.00 - 12.00

LESTER WILLIAMS:
Macy's 5000, 5004, 5006, 5009, 5016 . . . . 6.00 - 10.00
Specialty 422, 431, 437, 450 . . . . 4.00 - 6.00*

LIGHTNIN' JR. WILLIAMS (see L.C. WILLIAMS); (PAPA) LONNIE WILLIAMS; PAPA LONNIE WILLIAMS & GEORGE HOLMES:

Champion 15695 *Somebody's Been Using That Thing*	15.00 -	20.00
Sittin' In With 567 *New Road Blues*	8.00 -	15.00
593 *Wavin' Sea Blues*	8.00 -	15.00

LULU WILLIAMS:

Titles, issued contemporaneously on Banner, Oriole, Perfect, Romeo: *Careless Love Blues; You're Going To Leave The Old Home, Jim*	15.00 -	25.00

MAMIE WILLIAMS:

Silvertone 5134 *Ease Away Blues*	30.00 -	40.00

RABBITS FOOT WILLIAMS:

Black Patti 8052 *Mistreatin' Mama*	175.00 -	250.00
Champion 15339 *Mill Log Blues*	150.00 -	200.00
15379 *Man Trouble Blues*	150.00 -	200.00
Silvertone 5172 *I'm Gonna Cross The River*	100.00 -	150.00

SONNY BOY WILLIAMS:

Decca 7888, 7898, 8513, 8532, 8643, 8651	3.00 -	5.00

SUNNY WILLIAMS TRIO:

Super Disc 1030, 1058	5.00 -	8.00

SUSAN WILLIAMS:

Lincoln 2612 *Someday You'll Come Back To Me*	8.00 -	12.00
2651 *Black Water Blues*	8.00 -	12.00
2690 *Gay-Cattin' Daddy*	8.00 -	12.00

JAMES WILLIAMSON & HIS TRIO:

Chance 1121 *Lonesome Ole Train*	20.00 -	30.00*
1131 *Homesick*	20.00 -	30.00

SONNY BOY WILLIAMSON:

Ace 511 *Boppin' With Sonny*	4.00 -	6.00*
Bluebird 7012 *Skinny Woman*	20.00 -	30.00
7059 *Sugar Mama Blues*	20.00 -	30.00
7098 *Blue Bird Blues*	20.00 -	30.00
7302 *Early In The Morning*	15.00 -	20.00
7352 *Suzanna Blues*	15.00 -	20.00
7404 *Frigidaire Blues*	15.00 -	20.00
7428 *Collector Man Blues*	15.00 -	20.00
7500 *Sunny Land*	15.00 -	20.00
7536 *You Can Lead Me*	15.00 -	20.00
7576 *Miss Louisa Blues*	15.00 -	20.00
7603 *Beauty Palor*	15.00 -	20.00
7665 *Decoration Blues*	15.00 -	20.00
7707 *Honey Bee Blues*	15.00 -	20.00
7756 *You Give An Account*	15.00 -	20.00
7805 *Deep Down In The Ground*	15.00 -	20.00
7847 *Shannon Street Blues*	15.00 -	20.00
7979, 7995	7.00 -	10.00
8010 *Number Five Blues*	8.00 -	15.00
8034, 8094	7.00 -	10.00
8237 *Good For Nothing Blues*	8.00 -	15.00
8265 *Bad Luck Blues*	8.00 -	15.00
8307 *Doggin' My Love Around*	8.00 -	15.00
8333 *T.B. Blues*	8.00 -	15.00
8357 *Good Gal Blues*	8.00 -	15.00
8383 *New Jail House Blues*	8.00 -	15.00
8403 *Joe Louis And John Henry Blues*	8.00 -	15.00
8439 *Miss Ida Lee*	8.00 -	15.00
8474 *Honey Bee Blues*	8.00 -	15.00
8580 *War Time Blues*	7.00 -	10.00
8610 *Welfare Store Blues*	7.00 -	10.00
8674 *My Little Machine*	7.00 -	10.00
8731 *Western Union Man*	7.00 -	10.00
8766 *Big Apple Blues*	7.00 -	10.00
8797 *Mattie Mae Blues*	7.00 -	10.00
8822 *Sloppy Drunk Blues*	7.00 -	10.00
8866 *Million Years Blues*	7.00 -	10.00
8914 *She Was A Dreamer*	7.00 -	10.00
8955 *Drink On, Little Girl*	7.00 -	10.00
8992 *My Black Name Blues*	5.00 -	8.00
9031 *Ground Hog Blues*	5.00 -	8.00

34-0701 *She Don't Love Me That Way*	5.00 -	8.00
34-0713, 34-0722, 34-0736, 34-0744	4.00 -	7.00
Checker 824, 834, 847, 864, 883	3.00 -	6.00*
RCA Victor	3.00 -	6.00
Trumpet 129 *Eyesight To The Blind*	5.00 -	10.00*
139 *Do It If You Wanna*	5.00 -	10.00*
140 *Stop Crying*	5.00 -	10.00*
144 *West Memphis Blues*	5.00 -	10.00*
145 *Pontiac Blues*	5.00 -	10.00*
166, 168, 212, 215, 228	4.00 -	7.00*

WILLIE MAE:

Vocalion 03404 *I'd Rather Drink Muddy Water*	15.00 -	25.00

LITTLE SON WILLIS:

Swing Time 304 *Bad Luck And Trouble*	10.00 -	15.00*
305 *Harlem Blues*	10.00 -	15.00*
306 *Nothing But The Blues*	10.00 -	15.00*
341 *Roll Me Over Slow*	10.00 -	15.00*

MAC WILLIS:

Elko 254 *Pretty Woman*	10.00 -	20.00

MARY WILLIS:

Okeh 8921 *Rough Alley Blues*	30.00 -	40.00
8932 *Merciful Blues*	30.00 -	40.00

MILTON WILLIS COMBO:

Lucky 7 5001 *Little Joe's Boogie*	5.00 -	8.00

RALPH ('BAMA) WILLIS (& HIS ALABAMA TRIO); RALPH WILLIS' COUNTRY BOYS:

Abbey 3002 *Cool That Thing*	15.00 -	20.00
Jubilee 5034, 5044, 5078	6.00 -	10.00*
King 4611, 5631	7.00 -	10.00*
Prestige 919, 923	5.00 -	8.00
Regis 118 *Worried Blues*	10.00 -	15.00
Signature 32012, 32016	7.00 -	10.00
20th Century 20-09, 20-11, 20-12	7.00 -	10.00

RUTH WILLIS:

Titles, issued contemporaneously on Banner, Melotone, Oriole, Perfect, Romeo: *I'm Still Sloppy Drunk; Man Of My Own*	15.00 -	20.00

TURNER WILLIS:

Trilon 1058 *Re-Enlistment Blues*	6.00 -	12.00

WILSON AND REED:

Champion 15264 *France Blues*	100.00 -	150.00

JIMMY WILSON (& HIS ALL STARS):

Aladdin 3087, 3140, 3169, 3241	3.00 -	6.00*
Cavatone 252 *Mistake In Life*	4.00 -	7.00

LEOLA WILSON WITH WESLEY WILSON AND COOT GRANT:

Columbia 14669-D *I Can't Get Enough*	25.00 -	35.00
14775-D *Dirty Spoon Blues*	25.00 -	35.00

LEOLA B. WILSON:

Paramount 12392 *Ashley St. Blues*	35.00 -	50.00
12403 *Dishrag Blues*	35.00 -	50.00
12426 *Wilson Dam*	35.00 -	50.00
12444 *Down The Country*	35.00 -	50.00

EDNA WINSTON:

Victor 20407 *Peepin' Jim*	15.00 -	20.00
20424 *Pail In My Hand*	15.00 -	20.00
20654 *Joogie Blues*	15.00 -	20.00
20857 *Rent Man Blues*	15.00 -	20.00

KATIE WINTERS:

Gennett 6107 *Indian Brown Blues*	20.00 -	30.00

BIG BOY WOODS:

Bell 1173 *The Jail House Blues*	80.00 -	100.00
1180 *Do That Thing*	80.00 -	100.00
1181 *Dark Cloudy Blues*	80.00 -	100.00

BUDDY WOODS:

Vocalion 03906 *Muscat Hill Blues*	12.00 -	16.00
04604 *Jam Session Blues*	10.00 -	15.00
04745 *Low Life Blues*	10.00 -	15.00

EVA WOODS:

Silvertone 3522 *You Gotta Know How*	20.00 -	30.00
3557 *He's My Man*	20.00 -	30.00

OSCAR WOODS:

Decca 7219 *Lone Wolf Blues*.................. 15.00 - 20.00
   7904 *Evil Hearted Woman Blues*........... 15.00 - 20.00

EMMA WRIGHT:

Columbia 14413-D *Lonesome Trail Blues*....... 15.00 - 25.00

THE YAS YAS GIRL:

Titles, issued contemporaneously on Banner, Con-
queror, Melotone, Oriole, Perfect, Romeo,
Vocalion: *Blues Everywhere; Crime Don't Pay;
Got A Man In The 'Bama Mines; Grandma And
Grandpa; I'd Rather Drink Muddy Water—No.
2; I Drink Good Whiskey; Jackass For Sale; New
Drinking My Blues Away; Patrol Wagon Blues;
Sold It To The Devil; Working On The Project;
You Got To Pay*........................ 8.00 - 12.00

Conqueror 9079 *Don't You Leave Me Here*.... 7.00 - 10.00
   9147 *Don't You Make Me High*........... 7.00 - 10.00
   9205 *Breakin' 'Em Down Tonight*.......... 7.00 - 10.00
   9375 *Want To Woogie Some More*......... 5.00 - 8.00
   9449 *You're A Pain In The Neck To Me*.... 5.00 - 8.00
   9451 *I'll Try To Forget*................. 5.00 - 8.00
   9601 *I Won't Sell My Love*............... 5.00 - 8.00
   9949 *Good Old Easy Street*............. 5.00 - 8.00
   9950 *Milk Man Blues*................... 5.00 - 8.00

Okeh 05870 *Worried Heart Blues*............ 5.00 - 8.00
   05932 *You Know It Ain't Right*........... 5.00 - 8.00
   05984 *Got The Blues For My Baby*........ 5.00 - 8.00
   06032 *Evil Old Nightmare*............... 5.00 - 8.00
   06340 *Blues Before Daybreak*............ 5.00 - 8.00
   06446 *Good Old Easy Street*............. 5.00 - 8.00
   06570 *Froggy Bottom*................... 5.00 - 8.00

Vocalion 04013 *He May Be Your Man*........ 8.00 - 12.00
   04094 *Love Shows Weakness*............. 8.00 - 12.00
   04150 *About My Time To Check*........... 8.00 - 12.00
   04188 *Jelly Bean Blues*................... 7.00 - 10.00
   04331 *You Can't Shoot Your Pistol*........ 7.00 - 10.00
   04455 *Don't You Make Me High*........... 7.00 - 10.00
   04545 *Whiskey Fool*..................... 7.00 - 10.00
   04719 *Reckless Life Blues*............... 7.00 - 10.00
   04775 *Grieving Heart Blues*.............. 7.00 - 10.00
   04830 *Easy Towing Mama*............... 7.00 - 10.00
   04885 *Got A Mind To Ramble*............ 7.00 - 10.00
   05105 *Fine And Mellow*................. 7.00 - 10.00
   05180 *I'd Rather Be Drunk*.............. 5.00 - 8.00
   05219 *I Need You By My Side*............ 7.00 - 10.00
   05286 *I Got To Have It Daddy*........... 5.00 - 8.00
   05337 *I'll Try To Forget*................. 5.00 - 8.00
   05382 *Mama's Bad Luck Child*........... 7.00 - 10.00
   05501 *You Don't Know My Mind*........ 5.00 - 8.00
   05576 *Stop And Listen*.................. 5.00 - 8.00
   05614 *Black Gypsy Blues*............... 5.00 - 8.00

BLIND RICHARD YATES:

Black Patti 8021 *Sore Bunion Blues*........... 40.00 - 60.00
Champion 15264 *I'm Gonna Moan My Blues Away* 100.00 - 150.00
   15281 *Sore Bunion Blues*................. 40.00 - 60.00
Gennett 6104 *Sore Bunion Blues*............. 40.00 - 60.00

BILLE YOUNG:

Victor 23339 *You Done Played Out Blues*...... 40.00 - 60.00

JOHNNY YOUNG:

Ora Nelle 712 *Worried Man Blues*........... 15.00 - 20.00

MAN YOUNG:

Old Swing-Master 19 *Let Me Ride Your Mule*.. 15.00 - 20.00

THE ZA ZU GIRL:

Titles, issued contemporaneously on Banner,
Melotone, Oriole, Perfect, Romeo, Vocalion: *He
Left Me; My Righteous Man*.............. 7.00 - 10.00

COUNTRY/WESTERN; OLD TIME SINGING; STRING BANDS; ETC.
1920s to early 1950s—78 RPM
(All Records in this section are 78 RPM)
(Note: * after listing means that the record may exist also in 45 RPM form).

ROY ACUFF & HIS CRAZY TENNES-SEANS/SMOKY MOUNTAIN BOYS:
Titles, issued contemporaneously on Banner, Conqueror, Melotone, Oriole, Perfect, Romeo: *All Night Long; Charmin' Betsy' Gonna Have A Big Time Tonight; Gonna Raise A Ruckus Tonight; Great Speckle Bird; Great Speckle Bird No. 2; My Gal Sal; My Mountain Home Sweet Home; New Greenback Dollar; Sailing Along; Red Lips; Sailing Along; She No Longer Belongs To Me; Steamboat Whistle Blues; Steel Guitar Blues; Steel Guitar Chimes; Tell Mother I'll Be There; Trouble Trouble; Yes Sir, That's My Baby; You're The Only Star (In My Blue Heave); You've Gotta See Mama Every Night* .... 5.00 - 8.00
Conqueror 9123, 9170, 9255, 9257, 9324, 9404, 9432 .... 4.00 - 7.00
Vocalion 03255, 04252, 04374, 04376, 04466, 04505, 04531, 04590, 04657, 04730, 04795, 04867, 04909, 04915, 05041 .... 4.00 - 8.00

CHARLIE ADAMS & THE LONE STAR PLAYBOYS:
Decca 28397, 46335, 46358, 46373, 46391 ...... 4.00 - 7.00*
Imperial 8100, 8113 .... 4.00 - 7.00

CLARENCE ADAMS:
Challenge 229, 232 .... 5.00 - 8.00

AIKEN COUNTRY STRING BAND:
Okeh 45143 *Carolina Stompdown* .... 10.00 - 15.00
45219 *Charleston Rag* .... 10.00 - 15.00
45294 *Harrisburg Itch* .... 10.00 - 15.00

AKINS BIRMINGHAM BOYS:
Columbia 15348-D *I Walked And Walked* ...... 5.00 - 8.00

ALABAMA FOUR:
Broadway 8209 *Looking This Way* .... 5.00 - 8.00

ALEXANDER & MILLER:
Supertone 9398 *Medley* .... 5.00 - 8.00

WELDON ALLARD:
Imperial 8117 *Too Late You Say* .... 3.00 - 6.00

ALLEGHENY HIGHLANDERS:
Brunswick 324, 325 .... 7.00 - 10.00

ALLEN BROTHERS:
Bluebird 5001 *Fruit Jar Blues* .... 5.00 - 8.00
5104 *Triple Blues* .... 10.00 - 15.00
5165 *Shake It, Ida, Shake It* .... 10.00 - 15.00
5224 *Reckless Night Blues* .... 10.00 - 15.00
5317 *Slide, Daddy, Slide* .... 10.00 - 15.00
5380 *New Chattanooga Blues* .... 10.00 - 15.00
5403 *Brown's Ferry Blues* .... 5.00 - 8.00
5448 *No Low Down Hanging Around* .... 7.00 - 10.00
5470 *Chattanooga Mama* .... 10.00 - 15.00
5533 *It Can't Be Done* .... 10.00 - 15.00
5668 *Shanghai Rooster Blues* .... 10.00 - 15.00
5700 *Roll Down The Line* .... 10.00 - 15.00
5701 *Glorious Night Blues* .... 10.00 - 15.00
5702 *When You Leave, You'll Leave Me Sad.* .... 10.00 - 15.00
5772 *Skipping And Flying* .... 10.00 - 15.00
Bluebird 6148, 6149, 6195 .... 4.00 - 8.00
Columbia 15175-D *Salty Dog Blues* .... 20.00 - 30.00
15270-D *Ain't That Skippin'?* .... 20.00 - 30.00
Victor 23507 *Price Of Cotton Blues* .... 30.00 - 40.00
23514 *New Salty Dog* .... 15.00 - 25.00
23536 *No Low Down Hanging Around* ...... 15.00 - 25.00
23551 *Roll Down The Line* .... 30.00 - 50.00
23567 *Chattanooga Mama* .... 30.00 - 50.00
23578 *Pile Drivin' Papa* .... 30.00 - 50.00
23590 *Slide, Daddy, Slide* .... 30.00 - 50.00
23607 *Mother-In-Law Blues* .... 30.00 - 50.00

23623 *Unlucky Man* .... 30.00 - 50.00
23631 *Moonshine Bill* .... 30.00 - 50.00
23662 *It Can't Be Done* .... 30.00 - 50.00
23678 *Maybe Next Week Some Time No. 2* .. 30.00 - 50.00
23692 *Window Shade Blues* .... 60.00 - 80.00
23707 *Glorious Night Blues* .... 40.00 - 70.00
23756 *Rough Neck Blues* .... 30.00 - 50.00
23773 *Slipping Clutch Blues* .... 30.00 - 50.00
23786 *Red Hot Rambling Dan* .... 30.00 - 50.00
23805 *Warm Knees Blues* .... 30.00 - 50.00
23817 *Midnight Mama* .... 30.00 - 50.00
40003 *Frisco Blues* .... 15.00 - 20.00
40210 *Prisoner's Dream* .... 15.00 - 20.00
40266 *Skipping And Flying* .... 20.00 - 30.00
40276 *Enforcement Blues* .... 20.00 - 30.00
40303 *Jake Walk Blues* .... 10.00 - 15.00
40326 *Shanghai Rooster Blues* .... 20.00 - 30.00
Vocalion 02817 *Red Pajama Sal* .... 15.00 - 20.00
02818 *Salty Dog Blues* .... 15.00 - 20.00
02841 *Midnight Mama* .... 15.00 - 20.00
02853 *Daddy Park Your Car* .... 15.00 - 20.00
02874 *The Prisoner's Dream* .... 15.00 - 20.00
02890 *New Deal Blues* .... 15.00 - 20.00
02891 *Tiple Blues* .... 15.00 - 20.00
02939 *Allen Brothers' Rag* .... 15.00 - 20.00

CLAY ALLEN:
Decca 46324, 46360 .... 3.00 - 6.00*

ALLEN, LEE & AUSTIN:
Columbia 14266-D *Chattanooga Blues* .... 20.00 - 30.00

ALLEN, JULES (THE SINGING COWBOY):
Victor 21470 *Jack O'Diamonds* .... 5.00 - 8.00
21627 *Home On The Range* .... 5.00 - 8.00
23598 *Sweetie Dear* .... 15.00 - 20.00
23757 *The Cow Trail To Mexico* .... 15.00 - 20.00
23834 *The Dying Cowboy* .... 15.00 - 20.00
40022 *Zebra Dun* .... 5.00 - 10.00
40068 *The Texas Cowboy* .... 5.00 - 10.00
40118 *Two Fragments* .... 5.00 - 10.00
40167 *Chisholm Trail* .... 7.00 - 10.00
40178 *The Cowboy's Dream* .... 7.00 - 10.00
40263 *Punchin' The Dough* .... 10.00 - 15.00

ALLEY, SHELLEY LEE & HIS ALLEY CATS:
Globe 112 *Low Down Blues* .... 4.00 - 7.00
Vocalion 03891, 03939, 03975, 04145, 04201, 04276, 04371, 04451, 04600, 04670, 04728, 04793, 04879, 04986, 05053 .... 3.00 - 5.00

ALLISON'S SACRED HARP SINGERS:
Gennett 6499 *Sweet Canaan* .... 8.00 - 12.00
Gennett 6583 *Weeping Pilgrim* .... 8.00 - 12.00

ANDERSON, LEROY (THE RED HEADED BRIER HOPPER):
Champion 45024 *The Pine Tree On The Hill* ... 5.00 - 8.00
45045 *The Fatal Derby Day* .... 5.00 - 8.00
45055 *A Mother's Wayward Son* .... 5.00 - 8.00
45059 *Gambling On The Sabbath* .... 5.00 - 8.00

LES "CARROT TOP" ANDERSON:
Cormac 1107 *Queen of the Saddle* .... 7.00 - 10.00
1108 *He's Just A Hobo* .... 7.00 - 10.00
Decca 46250, 26259, 46303, 46326, 46352 ...... 3.00 - 5.00

ANGLIN BROTHERS/TWINS:
Vocalion 02963, 04078, 04579, 04692, 04774, 04896 .... 4.00 - 8.00

ANN, JUDY AND ZEKE WITH PETE:
Okeh 45576 *Me And My Still* .... 5.00 - 8.00
45578 *Mississippi Waters* .... 5.00 - 8.00

APPALACHIAN VAGABOND:
Vocalion 5450 *The Peddler And His Wife* ...... 15.00 - 20.00

APPLEBLOSSOM, CAPTAIN:

Okeh 45373 *Time Table Blues*.............	5.00 -	8.00
45416 *The Book Of Etiquette*.............	5.00 -	8.00

ARKANSAS BAREFOOT BOYS:

Okeh 45217 *Eighth Of January*.............	20.00 -	30.00

ARKANSAS CHARLIE:

Vocalion 5270 *Goodbye Old Paint*...........	7.00 -	10.00
5292 *The Texas Trail*................	7.00 -	10.00
5298 *He Was A Travelin' Man*..........	7.00 -	10.00
5355 *The Poor Fish*..................	7.00 -	10.00
5367 *We All Grow In Time*.............	7.00 -	10.00
5384 *Old Zip Coon*..................	7.00 -	10.00
5401 *The Sheriff And The Robber*........	7.00 -	10.00

ARKANSAS WOODCHOPPER:

Champion 45058 *Frankie And Johnny*........	7.00 -	10.00
45192 *Old And Only In The Way*........	7.00 -	10.00
Columbia 15463-D *The Dying Cowboy*......	8.00 -	12.00
Gennett 7036 *In The Jailhouse Now*........	15.00 -	20.00
7065 *Home On The Range*.............	15.00 -	20.00
7095 *Zeb Tuney's Gal*................	15.00 -	20.00
7126 *Take Me Back To Colorado*........	15.00 -	20.00
7154 *Old And Only In The Way*........	15.00 -	20.00
7184 *A Hard Luck Guy*...............	15.00 -	20.00
7264 *The Little Green Valley*...........	15.00 -	20.00
Supertone 9569 *Barney McCoy*..........	10.00 -	15.00
9570 *In The Jailhouse Now*...........	10.00 -	15.00
9571 *The Cowboy's Dream*............	10.00 -	15.00
9628 *If Brother Jack Were Here*........	10.00 -	15.00
9639 *Prisoner At The Bar*............	10.00 -	15.00
9643 *The Little Green Valley*..........	10.00 -	15.00
9664 *A Hard Luck Guy*..............	10.00 -	15.00
9665 *Write Me A Song About Father*......	10.00 -	15.00

ARMSTRONG'S PLAYERS: (see also NICHOLSON'S PLAYERS):

Supertone 9644 *Medley*..............	5.00 -	8.00
9661 *Sweet Bunch Of Daisies*..........	5.00 -	8.00
9733 *Muskakatuck Waltz*.............	7.00 -	10.00

ARMSTRONG & ASHLEY:

Paramount 3291 *No More Dying*...........	7.00 -	10.00

ARMSTRONG & JACOBS:

Supertone 9661 *Let Me Call You Sweetheart*...	5.00 -	10.00

ARNOLD, GENE:

Victor 23785, 23777, 23780, 23803, 23818, 23827, 23839.............	4.00 -	7.00

ARTHUR & REXROAT:

Vocalion 5323 *I Tickled Her Under The Chin*...	15.00 -	20.00
5335 *The White Rose*................	15.00 -	20.00

CHARLINE ARTHUR:

Bullet 707 *I've Got The Boogie Blues*..........	3.00 -	5.00

EMRY ARTHUR (& HENRY ARTHUR/ & THE CUMBERLAND SINGERS/ & DELLA HATFIELD):

Paramount 3221 *The Broken Wedding*........	15.00 -	20.00
3222 *The Bluefield Murder*.............	15.00 -	20.00
3237 *She Lied To Me*...............	15.00 -	20.00
3243 *Blood Stained Dress*.............	15.00 -	20.00
3249 *Jennie My Own True Love*..........	15.00 -	20.00
3251 *Sunshine And Shadows*...........	15.00 -	20.00
3289 *The Married Man*...............	15.00 -	20.00
3290 *Short Life Of Trouble*...........	15.00 -	20.00
3295 *She Lied To Me*...............	15.00 -	20.00
3298 *Careless Love*.................	15.00 -	20.00
3301 *I Tickled Her Under The Chin*.......	15.00 -	20.00
Vocalion 5225 *In The Heart Of The City That Has No Heart*.............	10.00 -	15.00
5228 *Where Gates Swing Outward Never*....	10.00 -	15.00
5229 *Let That Liar Alone*...........	15.00 -	20.00
5230 *Nobody's Business*.............	15.00 -	20.00
5234 *Wandering Gypsy Girl*...........	15.00 -	20.00
5249 *The Rich Man And Joseph Smith*......	15.00 -	20.00
5264 *Train Whistle Blues*............	15.00 -	20.00

5288 *My Girl-She's A Lulu*...........	15.00 -	20.00
5340 *Frankie Baker*................	15.00 -	20.00
5351 *Prison Bound Blues*............	15.00 -	20.00
5354 *My Mother-In-Law*.............	15.00 -	20.00
5358 *The Blind Boy*................	15.00 -	20.00
5385 *The Bootleggers Song*............	15.00 -	20.00
5396 *Remember The Old Folks Back Home*..	15.00 -	20.00

ASHFORD QUARTET:

Brunswick 393, 402, 456..................	3.00 -	6.00

ASHLEY'S MELODY MAKERS/MEN:

Victor 23661 *I Never Felt So Blue*...........	15.00 -	20.00
23767 *Come Back Lottie*................	20.00 -	30.00
40158 *Bath House Blues*...............	15.00 -	20.00
40199 *Sweetest Flower Waltz*...........	15.00 -	20.00
40300 *Somewhere In Arkansas*...........	15.00 -	20.00

ASHLEY & FOSTER:

Vocalion 02554 *Greenback Dollar*.........	5.00 -	8.00
02611 *Sideline Blues*................	10.00 -	15.00
02647 *Frankie Silvers*..............	10.00 -	15.00
02666 *Faded Roses*................	10.00 -	15.00
02750 *One Dark And Stormy Night*........	10.00 -	15.00
02780 *Baby, All Night Long*...........	10.00 -	15.00
02789 *Ain't No Use To High Hat Me*......	10.00 -	15.00
02900 *My North Carolina Home*...........	10.00 -	15.00

CLARENCE ASHLEY:

Columbia 15489-D *Dark Holler Blues*.......	15.00 -	25.00
15522-D *Little Sadie*...............	15.00 -	25.00
15654-D *Old John Hardy*.............	20.00 -	30.00

CLYDE ASHLEY:

Superior 2558 *Down In Arkansas*...........	15.00 -	25.00
2605 *The Ramblin' Railroad Boy*........	15.00 -	25.00
2636 *The Hand Car Yodel*.............	15.00 -	25.00
2676 *High Silk Hat And Gold Top Walking Cane*	15.00 -	25.00
2711 *The Bootlegger's Plea*...........	15.00 -	25.00
2723 *Leaving Town Blues*............	15.00 -	25.00
Superior 2751 *My Alabama Home*...........	15.00 -	25.00
2778 *Alimony Woman*...............	15.00 -	25.00
2833 *In 1992*..................	15.00 -	25.00

THOMAS C./TOM ASHLEY:

Conqueror 8103 *The Fiddlers Contest*.........	5.00 -	8.00
Gennett 6404 *Four Night's Experience*.........	15.00 -	20.00
Romeo 5113 *Haunted Road Blues*...........	5.00 -	8.00

ASPARAGUS JOE:

Champion 15688 *Hand Me Down My Walking Cane*	6.00 -	10.00
15709 *Asleep At The Switch*............	6.00 -	10.00
15752 *Boston Burglar*...............	6.00 -	10.00
15970 *Waiting For The Railroad Train*......	6.00 -	10.00
16012 *Nutty Song*..................	6.00 -	10.00
16071 *The Lightning Express*............	10.00 -	15.00
16118 *The Roving Gambler*............	10.00 -	15.00

BOB ATCHER & BONNIE BLUE EYES:

Vocalion 04882, 04898, 05001, 05069.........	3.00 -	5.00

AUGUSTA TRIO:

Champion 15729 *Down Yonder*.............	7.00 -	10.00
15768 *Back Up And Push*.............	7.00 -	10.00
45159 *Whistlin' Rufus*..............	3.00 -	6.00

AUSTIN AND LEE ALLEN (See ALLEN)

GENE AUTRY (& JIMMY LONG); GENE AUTRY TRIO:

Titles, issued contemporaneously on Banner, Conqueror, Melotone, Oriole, Perfect, Romeo: *Always Dreaming Of You; Atlanta Bound; Bear Cat Papa Blues; Birmingham Daddy; Blue Days; Cowboy's Yodel; The Crime I Didn't Do; Dallas County Jail Blues; The Death Of Jimmie Rodgers; Don't Take Me Back To The Chain Gang; Do Right Daddy Blues; Eleven Months In Leavenworth; A Gangster's Warning; He's In The Jail House Now No. 2; High Steppin' Mama Blues; I'll Always Be A Rambler; Jailhouse Blues; Methodist Pie; Missouri I'm Calling; My Alabama Home; My*

Cross-Eyed Girl; Night Time; Pistol Packin' Papa; Rheumatism Blues; T.B. Blues; That's How I Got My Start; True Blue Bill; Uncle Noah's Ark; Wild Cat Mama Blues; The Yodeling Hobo....... 7.00 - 12.00

Additional titles, issued contemporaneously on Banner, Conqueror, Melotone, Oriole, Perfect, Romeo: After 21 Years; Alone With My Sorrows; Angel Baby; The Answer To Nobody's Darling; The Answer To Red River Valley; The Answer To 21 Years; At The Old Barn Dance; Back To Old Smokey Mountain; Beautiful Texas; The Convict's Dream; Cowboy's Heaven; Don't Waste Your Tears On Me; Dust Pan Blues; The End Of The Trail; Good Luck Old Pal; Gosh! I Miss You All The Time; Guns And Guitars; Have You Found Someone Else; A Hill Billy Wedding In June; Hold On Little Dogies; If I Could Bring Back My Buddy; I Hate To Say Goodbye To The Prairie; I'll Be Thinking Of You Little Girl; I'll Be True While You're Gone; I'll Go Riding down That Texas Trail; I'm Always Dreaming Of You; It's Roundup Time In Reno; The Last Round Up; Little Farm Home; Little Ranch House On The Circle B; Louisana Moon; Memories Of That Silver Haired Daddy Of Mine; Mexicali Rose; Mississippi Valley Blues; Moonlight And Skies; My Carolina Mountain Rose; My Old Pal Of Yesterday; My Old Saddle Pal; Nobody's Darling But Mine; Old Buckaroo Goodbye; The Old Covered Wagon; The Old Folks Back Home; Old Missouri Moon; Ole Faithful; The One Rose; Rhythm Of The Range; Ridin; The Range; Sail Along Silv'ry Moon; Seven More Days; Silver Haired Daddy Of Mine; Some Day In Wyomin'; The Stump Of The Old Pine Tree; Texas Plains; That Old Feather Bed On The Farm; That Ramshackled Shack; That's Why I'm Nobody Darling; There's A Gold Mine In The Sky; There's A Little Old Lady In Waiting; There's An Empty Cot In the Bunkhouse Tonight; Tumbling Tumbleweeds; Watching The Clouds Roll By; 'Way Out West In Texas; When The Golden Leaves Are Falling; When It's Springtime In The Rockies; When Jimmie Rodgers Said Goodbye; When The Tumbleweeds Come Tumbling Down Again; Why Don't You Come Back To Me; With A Song In My Heart; The Yellow Rose Of Texas; You're The Only Star.................. 4.00 - 8.00

Titles, issued contemporaneously on Clarion, Diva, Velvet Tone: Blue Yodel No. 5; Dust Pan Blues; Hobo Yodel; Left My Gal In The Mountains 15.00 - 20.00

California Blues; Cowboy Yodel; Daddy And Home; Frankie And Johnny; A Gangster's Warning; I'll Be Thinking Of You Little Girl; Lullaby Yodel; My Alabama Home; My Rough And Rowdy Ways; No One To Call Me Darling; Pictures Of My Mother; Slue Foot Lue; Stay Away From My Chicken House; That's How I Got My Start; That's Why I Left The Mountains; True Blue Bill; Waiting For A Train; Why Don't You Come Back To Me......................... 15.00 - 25.00

Champion 16030 I'll Be Thinking Of You Little Girl 25.00 - 40.00
16050 In The Shadow Of The Pine.......... 25.00 - 40.00
16073 Hobo Bill's Last Ride.............. 25.00 - 40.00
16096 Hobo Yodel.................. 25.00 - 40.00
16119 Dust Pan Blues.............. 25.00 - 40.00
16166 High Powered Mama........... 25.00 - 40.00
16210 Mean Mama Blues............ 25.00 - 40.00
16230 Any Old Time.............. 25.00 - 40.00
16245 Blue Days................. 25.00 - 40.00
16275 T. B. Blues............... 25.00 - 40.00
16328 True Blue Bill............. 35.00 - 50.00

16372 Dad In The Hills.............. 35.00 - 50.00
16485 That's How I Got My Start......... 35.00 - 50.00
Champion 45025 Pistol Packin' Papa...... 10.00 - 15.00
45027 Bear Cat Papa Blues............ 10.00 - 15.00
45060 Dad In The Hills.............. 10.00 - 15.00
45071 In The Shadow Of The Pine...... 10.00 - 15.00
45073 T.B. Blues............... 10.00 - 15.00
45156 Money Ain't No Use Anyway....... 5.00 - 8.00
45172 Yodeling Hobo.............. 7.00 - 10.00
45183 I'll Always Be A Rambler...... 10.00 - 15.00
Columbia (red label), most issues....... 2.00 - 3.00
Decca 5426, 5464, 5488, 5501, 5517, 5527..... 3.00 - 6.00
Gennett 7243 Cowboy Yodel.............. 50.00 - 80.00
7265 In The Shadow Of The Pine...... 50.00 - 80.00
7290 Hobo Bill's Last Ride.......... 50.00 - 80.00
7310 Train Whistle Blues.......... 50.00 - 80.00
Q.R.S. 1044 Living In The Mountains........ 75.00 - 100.00
Superior 2561 The Girl I Left Behind..... 90.00 - 130.00
2596 Dad In The Hills.............. 40.00 - 60.00
2637 Pistol Packin' Papa........... 40.00 - 60.00
2660 Mean Mama Blues.............. 40.00 - 60.00
2681 That's How I Got My Start....... 40.00 - 60.00
2710 Blue Days................. 40.00 - 60.00
2732 Money Ain't No Use Anyway....... 40.00 - 60.00
2769 Hobo Bill's Last Ride.......... 40.00 - 60.00
Supertone 9702 Hobo Bill's Last Ride...... 25.00 - 35.00
9704 They Cut Down The Old Pine Tree.... 25.00 - 35.00
9705 Whisper Your Mother's Name...... 25.00 - 35.00
9706 Train Whistle Blues.......... 25.00 - 35.00
Victor 23530 Bear Cat Papa.............. 50.00 - 75.00
23548 Do Right Daddy.............. 50.00 - 75.00
23561 There's A Good Gal In The Mountains 50.00 - 75.00
23589 High Steppin' Mama........... 50.00 - 75.00
23617 She's A Low Down Mamma........ 50.00 - 75.00
23630 Rheumatism Blues............ 50.00 - 75.00
23642 Wild Cat Mama.............. 50.00 - 75.00
23673 I'm Always Dreaming Of You...... 50.00 - 75.00
23707 Black Bottom Blues........... 60.00 - 80.00
23720 Kentucky Lullaby............ 60.00 - 80.00
23725 The Gangster's Warning........ 60.00 - 80.00
23726 Back To Old Smoky Mountain...... 60.00 - 80.00
23783 Cowboy's Heaven............. 60.00 - 80.00
23792 Louisiana Moon............. 60.00 - 80.00
23810 Your Voice Is Calling........ 60.00 - 80.00
40200 My Alabama Home............. 50.00 - 75.00
Vocalion 02991, 03007, 03070, 03097, 03101, 03138, 03229, 03262, 03291, 03317, 03358, 03448.. 5.00 - 10.00
04091, 04146, 04172, 04246, 04262, 04267, 04274, 04340, 04375, 04415..................... 3.00 - 6.00

HARVEY AYERS (See GROVER RANN)
GREEN BAILEY:
Gennett 6702 The Santa Barbara Earthquake... 15.00 - 25.00
6732 If I Die A Railroad Man.............. 15.00 - 25.00
MR. & MRS. BAKER:
Victor 20863 The Newmarket Wreck.......... 5.00 - 10.00
BUDDY BAKER:
Victor 21549 Box Car Blues................. 10.00 - 15.00
V-40017 Matrimonial Intentions............. 10.00 - 15.00
CHARLES BAKER (THE WYOMING COWBOY):
Champion 16614 Just Plain Folks............. 8.00 - 12.00
45044, 45052.......................... 4.00 - 6.00
ELDON BAKER'S BROWN COUNTY REVELERS:
Vocalion 04217 Lost John.................. 7.00 - 10.00
04279 I Will Meet You................ 7.00 - 10.00
04355 Happy Cowboy................. 5.00 - 8.00
04441 Dear Old Dixieland.............. 5.00 - 8.00
LUKE BALDWIN:
Champion 15792 Hungry Hash House Blues.... 10.00 - 15.00
15811 Daddy And Home............... 10.00 - 15.00
15853 California Blues............. 10.00 - 15.00

15877 *Alabama Blues*	10.00 -	15.00
15945 *I Love The Jailer's Daughter*	10.00 -	15.00
16009 *The Yodeling Cowboy*	15.00 -	20.00
16075 *The Handcar Yodel*	15.00 -	20.00
16142 *It Won't Happen Again*	15.00 -	20.00
16162 *Don't Ever Marry A Widow*	15.00 -	20.00
16186 *The Bootlegger's Plea*	15.00 -	20.00
16232 *The Ramblin' Railroad Boy*	15.00 -	20.00
16254 *When The Roses Bloom In Dixie*	15.00 -	20.00
16313 *Leaving Town Blues*	15.00 -	25.00
16317 *Alimony Woman*	15.00 -	25.00
16343 *Travelin' Blues*	15.00 -	25.00
16443 *In 1992*	15.00 -	25.00

BENTLEY BALL:
Columbia A-3084 *The Gallows Tree* ———

WOLFE BALLARD (& CLAUDE SAMUELS):

Broadway; Paramount	3.00 -	6.00
Herwin 75545 *I Want A Pardon For Daddy*	8.00 -	12.00

JOHN BALTZELL ("CHAMPION OLD TIME FIDDLER"):

Banner 2151 *Turkey in the Straw*	5.00 -	8.00
2159 *Sailor's Hornpipe*	5.00 -	8.00
Conqueror 7741 *The Girl I Left Behind*	5.00 -	8.00
Edison 51236, 51354, 51548, 51995, 52022	5.00 -	8.00
52281 *Emmett Quadrille*	7.00 -	10.00
52294 *Arkansas Traveler*	7.00 -	10.00
52313 *Flowers Of Edinburgh Hornpipe*	7.00 -	10.00
52370 *Soldier's Joy Hornpipe*	7.00 -	10.00
52395 *My Highland Fling*	7.00 -	10.00
52425 *Starlight Waltz*	7.00 -	10.00
52450 *S.J. Rafferty Reel*	7.00 -	10.00
Paramount 3015 *Turkey In The Straw*	5.00 -	8.00
3017 *Sailor's Hornpipe*	5.00 -	8.00

BANG BOYS:
Vocalion 03372 *When Lulu's Gone*   15.00 - 20.00

BANJO JOE:
Columbia 15238-D *Engineer Joe*   10.00 - 15.00
(See also: WILLARD HODGIN)

EMMETT BANKSTON & RED HENDERSON:
Okeh 45292 *Six Nights Drunk*   10.00 - 15.00

GLEN BARBER:

Hallmark 1110 *Styles And Ways Of The World*	5.00 -	8.00*
Stampede 104 *Ring Around The Moon*	5.00 -	8.00*

JOHNNY BARFIELD (& HOYT BRYANT, ACC. BY BERT LAYNE & HIS GEORGIA SERENADERS):

Bluebird	3.00 -	5.00
Bullet 620 *Doin' The Boogie Woogie*	5.00 -	8.00
Champion 16406 *Back To My Georgia Home*	20.00 -	30.00
16415 *Highway Hobo*	20.00 -	30.00

JERRY BARLOW:

Lyric 703 *Just Thinking Of You*	4.00 -	6.00
O.T. 103 *Louisiana Baby*	4.00 -	7.00

(YODELING) FRANKIE BARNES:

Champion 16366 *Hokey Pokey*	7.00 -	10.00
Superior 2746 *Nervy Bum*	7.00 -	10.00

H.M. BARNES & HIS BLUE RIDGE RAMBLERS:

Brunswick 310 *Who Broke The Lock On The Hen House Door?*	7.00 -	10.00
313 *Old Joe Clark*	7.00 -	10.00
327 *Goin' Down The Road Feelin' Bad*	8.00 -	12.00
361 *Our Director March*	5.00 -	10.00
397 *Mandolin Rag*	5.00 -	10.00
463 *Honolulu Rag*	8.00 -	12.00

THE BARNSTORMERS:
Silverton 5401 *Party Quadrille*   5.00 - 8.00

BARNYARD STEVE:
Okeh 45366 *Out On The Farm*   7.00 - 10.00

BARTLETT'S BOOSTERS:
Paramount 3245 *The Bumble Bee*   7.00 - 10.00

JOHN BARTON:
Broadway 8051, 8052   5.00 - 8.00

KENNETH BARTON: (See BORTON)

DR. HUMPHREY BATES & HIS POSSUM HUNTERS:

Brunswick 232 *Goin' Up Town*	15.00 -	25.00
239 *Billy In The Low Ground*	15.00 -	25.00
243 *Bill Pickle Rag*	15.00 -	25.00
271 *Old Joe*	15.00 -	25.00
275 *Greenback Dollar Bill*	15.00 -	25.00
Vocalion 5238 *Ham Beats All Meat*	15.00 -	25.00

RAY BATTS:
Bullet 754 *Bear Cat Daddy*   7.00 - 10.00*

BAXTER FAMILY TRIO:
Superior 2557 *I Am Coming Home*   10.00 - 15.00

JOHNNY BAXTER:
Superior 2811 *I Want My Rib*   20.00 - 30.00

MUMFORD BEAN & HIS ITAWAMBIANS:
Okeh 45303 *Flow Rain Waltz*   15.00 - 25.00

JOHNNIE BEE:
Talent 744 *Hang-Over Blues*   5.00 - 8.00

JERRY BEHRENS:

Okeh 45535 *Drifting Along*	10.00 -	15.00
45564 *Nobody's Business*	10.00 -	15.00

DICK BELL:
Challenge 425 *Shut Up In Coal Creek Mine*   5.00 - 8.00

BENTLEY BOYS:
Columbia 15565-D *Henhouse Blues*   20.00 - 30.00

BEVERLY HILL BILLIES: (See also GLEN RICE)

Brunswick 421 *Red River Valley*	5.00 -	8.00
441 *My Pretty Quadroon*	5.00 -	8.00
455 *Mellow Mountain Moon*	5.00 -	8.00
462 *Peek A Boo*	5.00 -	8.00
506 *Wonder Valley*	5.00 -	8.00
514 *Strawberry Roan*	5.00 -	8.00
519 *Prairie Skies*	5.00 -	8.00

BIG JEFF & THE RADIO PLAYBOYS:

Dot 1004 *Juke Box Boogie*	5.00 -	8.00
1058 *Step It Up And Go*	5.00 -	8.00
1064 *Fast Women, Slow Horses And Wine*	5.00 -	8.00*
1088 *Move On Baby*	5.00 -	8.00*
World Records 1520 *Poppin' Bubble Gum*	5.00 -	8.00*

BUD & JOE BILLINGS; BUD BILLINGS TRIO:

Victor 23500, 23534, 23539, 23556, 23706, 23709, 23715	5.00 -	10.00
23725 *I Wonder If He's Singing*	60.00 -	80.00
23732, 23735, 23740, 23744, 23784	5.00 -	10.00
40082, 40267, 40299	3.00 -	6.00

DOUG BINE & HIS DIXIE RAMBLERS:
Bluebird 6677, 6705, 6789, 6847, 8133   3.00 - 6.00

BINKLEY BROTHERS' DIXIE CLODHOPPERS:

Victor 21758 *All Go Hungry Hash House*	10.00 -	15.00
40048 *Give Me Back My Fifteen Cents*	10.00 -	15.00
40129 *When I Had But Fifty Cents*	10.00 -	15.00

BIRD'S KENTUCKY CORN CRACKERS:
Victor 23608 *Ship That's Sailing High*   15.00 - 20.00

CONNIE BIRD:
Gennett 6929 *Little Mamie*   15.00 - 20.00

ELMER BIRD'S HAPPY FOUR/STRING BAND:

Champion 16421 *Kentucky Stomp*	30.00 -	50.00
45168 *Kentucky Stomp*	15.00 -	20.00
Gennett 7064 *Kentucky Stomp*	30.00 -	50.00
7182 *Muscle Shoals Blues*	40.00 -	70.00
Superior 2598 *Sleepy Creek*	30.00 -	50.00

LOUIS BIRD:
Vocalion 5428 *It's Funny What Whiskey Will Do*   7.00 - 10.00

NAT BIRD & TOM COLLINS:
Brunswick 376 *Hornpipe Medley*   5.00 - 8.00

L.O. BIRKHEAD & R.M. LANE:
Columbia 15757-D *Robinson County* .... 20.00 - 30.00
JASPER BISBEE:
Edison 51381, 51382 .... 5.00 - 8.00
BILLY BISHOP:
Champion 15331 *Medley Of Old Favorites* ..... 4.00 - 7.00
Gennett 6203 *Medley Of Old Favorites* .... 8.00 - 12.00
Supertone 9171 *Medley Of Old Favorites* ...... 4.00 - 7.00
LESTER PETE BIVINS:
Bluebird 6886, 6950 .... 5.00 - 8.00
BLACK BROTHERS:
Okeh 45244, 45253, 45270, 45296, 45312, 45336,
45345, 45374, 445487, 45493, 45572 .... 4.00 - 7.00
JIMMY BLACK:
Okeh 45275, 45298 .... 4.00 - 7.00
DAD BLACKARD'S MOONSHINERS:
Victor 21130 *Sandy River Belle* .... 10.00 - 15.00
CHARLEY BLAKE:
Supertone 9476 *Daddy And Home* .... 8.00 - 12.00
9489 *Back Home In Tennessee* .... 8.00 - 12.00
9534 *California Blues* .... 8.00 - 12.00
9540 *Go 'Long Mule No. 2* .... 8.00 - 12.00
9556 *She'll Be Coming 'Round The Mountain.* 8.00 - 12.00
9559 *Jackson County* .... 8.00 - 12.00
9600 *Alabama Blues* .... 8.00 - 12.00
9641 *I Love The Jailer's Daughter* .... 8.00 - 12.00
9714 *My Old Log Cabin Home* .... 8.00 - 12.00
9722 *The Yodeling Cowboy* .... 8.00 - 12.00
9724 *My Rough And Rowdy Ways* .... 8.00 - 12.00
CURLEY BLAKE (See CHARLEY BLAKE):
GUY BLAKEMAN & HIS BLUE GRASS
SERENADERS:
Chess 1525 *I Ain't Gonna Give Nobody None Of
My Jelly Roll.* .... 4.00 - 7.00
BLALOCK & YATES:
Columbia 15576-D *Pride Of The Ball* .... 10.00 - 15.00
DAN BLANCHARD:
Champion 15526 *The West Plains Explosion* .... 7.00 - 10.00
15578 *Just A Little West Of West Virginia* ... 7.00 - 10.00
BLANKENSHIP FAMILY:
Victor 23583 *Jack And Mae* .... 20.00 - 30.00
FRANK BLEVINS' TAR HEEL RATTLERS:
Columbia 15210-D *Old Aunt Betsy* .... 20.00 - 30.00
15280-D *Nine Pound Hammer* .... 20.00 - 30.00
15765-D *I've Got No Honey Babe Now* ...... 75.00 - 100.00
Velvet Tone 7101-V *Old Aunt Betsy* .... 15.00 - 20.00
7103-V *Fly Around My Pretty Little Miss* .... 15.00 - 20.00
RUBYE BLEVINS:
Bluebird 5404, 5973 .... 3.00 - 6.00
BLIND ANDY: (See also ANDREW JENKINS)
Okeh 40393 *Floyd Collins In The Sand Cave* ... 5.00 - 8.00
45007 *The Little Newsboy* .... 5.00 - 8.00
45043 *Charming Billy* .... 5.00 - 8.00
45197 *Little Marian Parker* .... 5.00 - 8.00
45319 *The Alabama Flood* .... 6.00 - 10.00
45343 *Tragedy On Daytona Beach* .... 6.00 - 10.00
45347 *Ramblin' Yodel Sam* .... 6.00 - 10.00
45454 *Stop And Look For The Train* .... 6.00 - 10.00
BLUE BOYS:
Okeh 45314 *Memphis Stomp* .... 20.00 - 30.00
BLUE MOON MELODY BOYS:
Champion 15542 *My Blue Ridge Mountain Home* 7.00 - 10.00
BLUE RIDGE CORNSHUCKERS:
Victor 20835 *Old Time Corn Shuckin'* .... 8.00 - 12.00
BLUE RIDGE DUO (GENE AUSTIN &
GEORGE RENEAU):
Edison 51422 *Little Brown Jug* .... 7.00 - 10.00
51498 *Life's Railway To Heaven* .... 7.00 - 10.00
51502 *Turkey In The Straw* .... 7.00 - 10.00
51515 *Blue Ridge Blues* .... 7.00 - 10.00

BLUE RIDGE HIGHBALLERS (Led by Charley
La Prade, Fiddler):
Columbia 15070-D *Under The Double Eagle* .... 8.00 - 12.00
15081-D *Fourteen Days In Georgia* .... 8.00 - 12.00
15089-D *Round Town Girls* .... 8.00 - 12.00
15096-D *Going Down To Lynchburg Town* ... 8.00 - 12.00
15132-D *Darned* .... 8.00 - 12.00
15168-D *Soldier's Joy* .... 8.00 - 12.00
Paramount 3077 *I'm Tired Of Living Here Alone* 10.00 - 15.00
3083 *Red Wing* .... 10.00 - 15.00
BLUE RIDGE HILLBILLIES:
Bluebird 6541, 6609, 6786, 7070 .... 4.00 - 7.00
BLUE RIDGE MOUNTAINEER:
Edison 51832 *The Sinking Of The Titanic* ..... 10.00 - 15.00
BLUE RIDGE MOUNTAINEERS:
Gennett 6870 *Old Flannigan* .... 15.00 - 20.00
BLUE RIDGE MOUNTAIN ENTERTAINERS:
Conqueror 7942 *Goodnight Waltz* .... 5.00 - 8.00
BLUE RIDGE MOUNTAIN GIRLS:
Champion 16701 *The First Whippoorwill Song*.. 10.00 - 15.00
16715 *Woman's Answer To 21 Years* .... 10.00 - 15.00
16743 *She Came Rolling Down The Mountain* 10.00 - 15.00
16752 *New Answer To 21 Years* .... 10.00 - 15.00
16763 *My Heart Is Where The Mohawk Flows* 10.00 - 15.00
16778 *When It's Prayer Meetin' Time In The
Hollow* .... 10.00 - 15.00
16795 *Memories of That Silver Haired Daddy*. 10.00 - 15.00
Champion 45077, 45083, 45090, 45100, 45198.. 4.00 - 7.00
BLUE RIDGE MOUNTAIN SINGERS:
Columbai 15550-D *Lorena* .... 8.00 - 12.00
15580-D *Give My Love To Nell* .... 8.00 - 12.00
15647-D *The Engineer's Last Run* .... 10.00 - 20.00
15678-D *Mansion Of Aching Hearts* .... 10.00 - 20.00
BLUE RIDGE PLAYBOYS:
Vocalion 03425, 03526, 03558, 03765 .... 4.00 - 8.00
BLUE SKY BOYS TRIO:
Bluebird 6480, 6538, 6567, 6621, 6669, 6714, 6764,
6808, 6854, 6901, 7113, 7132, 7173, 7311, 7348,
7411, 7472, 7550, 7661, 7755, 7803, 7878, 7933,
7984 .... 4.00 - 6.00
Bluebird (higher numbers) .... 3.00 - 5.00
Montgomery Ward .... 3.00 - 5.00
BUD BLUE:
Okeh 45254 *A Blind Mother's Prayer* .... 5.00 - 8.00
BOA'S PINE CABIN BOYS:
Vocalion 02594 *Hurry, Johnny, Hurry* .... ———
BOB & MONTE:
Vocalion 5279 *The Utah Trail* .... 4.00 - 6.00
5343 *Old Virginia Lullaby* .... 5.00 - 8.00
5373 *Back To Hawaii And You.* .... 5.00 - 8.00
5387 *From The Heart Of The West* .... 5.00 - 8.00
(LOY) BODINE (& HOWARD KEESEE):
Champion 16305 *I Still Got Ninety-Nine* .... 20.00 - 30.00
16391 *Where The Old Red River Flows* ..... 20.00 - 30.00
Superior 2608 *Wabash Cannon Ball* .... 20.00 - 30.00
2809 *A Gangster's Warning* .... 20.00 - 30.00
"DOCK" BOGGS:
Brunswick 118 *Down South Blues* .... 15.00 - 20.00
131 *Country Blues* .... 15.00 - 20.00
132 *Danville Girl* .... 15.00 - 20.00
133 *Hard Luck Blues* .... 15.00 - 20.00
Vocalion 5144 *Hard Luck Blues* .... 15.00 - 20.00
CAP. M.J. BONNER (THE TEXAS FIDDLER):
Victor 19699 *Medley—Yearling's In The Canebreak
etc.* .... 15.00 - 20.00
BOONE COUNTY ENTERTAINERS:
Supertone 9163 *Arkansas Traveler* .... 5.00 - 8.00
9177 *Fiddlin' Bootleggers* .... 10.00 - 15.00
9181 *The Blind Man And His Child* .... 7.00 - 10.00
9182 *Something Wrong With My Gal.* ...... 7.00 - 10.00
9492 *Virginia Bootleggers* .... 7.00 - 10.00

CLAUDE BOONE (& WALTER HURDT):
Bluebird 7817 *The Poor Widow*		5.00 -	8.00
7008 *The Hobo Blues*		5.00 -	8.00

REV. EDWARD (& MRS.) BOONE (& MISS OLIVE BOONE):
Gennett 6903 *Will David Play His Harp*		8.00 -	12.00
7208 *Springing Up Within My Soul*		10.00 -	15.00
7225 *Flowers On The Open Grave*		10.00 -	15.00
7248 *Salvatin Is For All*		10.00 -	15.00
7321 *A Mansion There For Me*		10.00 -	15.00

JIMMY BOONE:
Superior 2638 *The Brakeman's Reply*		20.00 -	30.00
2661 *Crazy Blues*		20.00 -	30.00
2698 *Box Car Blues*		20.00 -	30.00
2742 *The Fatal Run*		20.00 -	30.00
2775 *Hobo Jack's Last Ride*		20.00 -	30.00
2831 *The Cowboy Song*		20.00 -	30.00

BOOTS & HIS BUDDIES:
Talent 709 *Poor Little Joe*		4.00 -	7.00

BENNY BORG (THE SINGING SOLDIER):
Columbia 15148-D *I Want A Pardon For Daddy*		5.00 -	8.00
15183-D *Pictures From Life's Other Side*		5.00 -	8.00

GODFREY BORTON:
Bell 1186 *Don't Forget Me, Little Darling*		5.00 -	8.00
1187 *Two Little Orphans*		5.00 -	8.00

KENNETH BORTON:
Challenge 331 *That's What The Old Bachelor's Made Of*		5.00 -	8.00

LEO BOSWELL (& DEWEY BOSWELL):
Columbia 15290-D *The Fatal Rose Of Red*		7.00 -	10.00
15469-D *Memory That Time Cannot Erase*		8.00 -	12.00

(MR. & MRS.) CHRIS BOUCHILLON:
Columbia 15120-D *Talking Blues*		5.00 -	8.00
15151-D *Born In Hard Luck*		5.00 -	8.00
15178-D *Let It Alone*		7.00 -	10.00
15213-D *Christ Visits The Barber Shop*		7.00 -	10.00
15244-D *You Look Awful Good To Me*		7.00 -	10.00
15262-D *New Talking Blues*		7.00 -	10.00
15289-D *I've Been Married Three Times*		7.00 -	10.00
15317-D *Oyster Stew*		7.00 -	10.00
15345-D *Adam And Eve*		7.00 -	10.00
15373-D *Speed Maniac*		7.00 -	10.00
15508-D *Girls Of Today*		8.00 -	12.00

BOWERS & LEWIS:
Superior 2659 *Put On Your Old Gray Bonnet*		10.00 -	15.00

EARL BOWERS:
Superior 2526 *I Tickled Her Under The Chin*		10.00 -	15.00
2607 *The Contented Hobo*		10.00 -	15.00

BOWMAN SISTERS:
Columbia 15473-D *My Old Kentucky Home*		5.00 -	8.00
15621-D *Old Lonesome Blues*		10.00 -	15.00

CHARLIE BOWMAN & HIS BROTHERS:
Columbia 15357-D *Gonna Raise The Ruckus Tonight*		15.00 -	20.00
15387-D *The Moonshiner And His Money*		15.00 -	20.00
Vocalion 5118 *Hickman Rag*		15.00 -	20.00
15377 *Hickman Rag*		15.00 -	20.00

DONNIE BOWSHIER:
King 1219 *We'll Never Part*		———*	

AARON BOYD:
Champion 15652 *The Santa Barbara Earthquake*		12.00 -	18.00

BILL BOYD & HIS COWBOY RAMBLERS:
Bluebird 5608, 5667, 5740, 5788, 5945, 6109, 6119, 6161, 6177, 6235, 6308, 6323, 6328, 6346, 6351, 6384, 6420, 6486, 6492, 6523, 6599, 6670, 6694, 6715, 6731, 6772, 6807, 6889, 6959, 7004, 7006, 7053, 7088, 7128, 7189, 7260, 7299, 7345, 7437, 7507, 7521, 7531, 7573, 7624, 7662, 7691, 7739, 7754, 7788, 7880, 7867, 7910, 7921, 7940, 7971, 7989		4.00 -	7.00

JOHN BOYD AND HIS SOUTHERNERS:
Vocalion 03661 *Doin' The Raccoon*		4.00 -	7.00

BOYS FROM WILDCAT HOLLOW:
Champion 15633 *The Fiddlin' Bootleggers*		10.00 -	15.00
45010 *The Fiddlin' Bootleggers*		5.00 -	8.00

VIRGEL BOZMAN & CIRCLE C BOYS:
O.T. 112 *Troubles, Troubles*		4.00 -	7.00

BRANCH & COLEMAN:
Okeh 45556 *My Free Wheelin' Baby*		10.00 -	15.00
45561 *Telegraph Shack*		10.00 -	15.00
45568 *Since My Darling Went Away*		10.00 -	15.00

ERNEST BRANCH:
Champion 16286 *Lulu Love*		10.00 -	15.00

HOMER BRIARHOPPER:
Bluebird 6903 *If You Ever Had The Blues*		10.00 -	15.00

BRIER HOPPER (BROTHERS); (See also RED HEADED BRIER HOPPER):
Champion 16648 *Answer To Ninety-Nine Years*		15.00 -	20.00
16692 *Bring Back My Blue-Eyed Boy*		15.00 -	20.00
16708 *Lorena*		15.00 -	20.00
Champion 45032, 45066		4.00 -	7.00

BILLY BRIGGS:
Imperial 8102, 8104, 8111		3.00 -	6.00

BRITT BROTHERS; BRITT & FORD; ELTON BRITT:
Titles, issued contemporaneously on Banner, Melotone, Oriole, Perfect, Romeo: *Alpine Milkman Yodel; Answer To 99 Years; Chime Bells, Dear Old Daddy; Good Night, Little Girl Of My Dreams; In The Hills Of Pennsylvania; I Was Born In The Mountains; My Mother's Tears; Old Fashioned Dipper; There's A Home In Wyomin'; When It's Harvest Time In Old New England; When You Played The Old Church Organ; The Wrong Man And The Wrong Woman*		4.00 -	7.00

MAYNARD BRITTON:
Champion 16543 *The Drunkard's Hell*		15.00 -	20.00
45051 *The Drunkard's Hell*		8.00 -	12.00
Superior 2563 *I Don't Want No Woman*		20.00 -	35.00
2524 *Always Blue, Lonesome Too*		20.00 -	35.00

BROCK SISTERS:
Paramount 3163 *Bring Me Back My Darling*		——	

BROCK & DUDLEY:
Columbia 15645-D *I'll Remember You Love*		8.00 -	12.00

BILLY BROOKS:
Columbia 15614-D *Freight Train Blues*		10.00 -	15.00

BOB BROOKS:
Columbia 15676-D *Wandering Lamb*		5.00 -	8.00
15689-D *Red River Valley*		5.00 -	8.00

CHARLIE (C.S.) BROOKS (& CHARLIE TURNER):
Columbia 15733-D *My Mammy's Cabin*		5.00 -	8.00
15756-D *Will You Love Me When I'm Old*		5.00 -	8.00

(RICHARD) BROOKS & REUBEN PUCKETT):
Brunswick 273 *Long Gone*		10.00 -	15.00
281 *She's More To Be Pitied Than Censured*		10.00 -	15.00
301 *The Longest Way Home*		10.00 -	15.00
317 *All In, Down And Out*		10.00 -	15.00
Victor 20541 *Something's Going To Happen*		10.00 -	15.00
20542 *Hello Central, Give Me Heaven*		10.00 -	15.00

BROWN'S MUSICAL BROWNIES (See MILTON BROWN)

BROWN'S HAPPY FOUR:
Champion 16549 *Bootlegger's Dream*		15.00 -	20.00

BROWN & BUNCH:
Supertone 9375 *Let Her Go, I'll Meet Her*		8.0 -	12.00
9443 *My Carolina Home*		8.00 -	12.00

BROWN, GRAY & DILLY:
Vocalion 5432 *A Fiddlers Tryout In Georgia*		20.00 -	30.00

HERSAL/HERSHAL/HERSCHEL BROWN & HIS BOYS/HAPPY FIVE/WASHBOARD BAND; HERSCHEL BROWN & L.K. SENTELL:

Okeh 45247 *New Talking Blues*............	15.00 -	20.00
45250 *Home Brew Party*..................	20.00 -	30.00
45286 *I Wish That Gal Was Mine*........	20.00 -	30.00
45337 *New Talking Blues No. 2*........	20.00 -	30.00
45354 *Alabama Breakdown*.............	20.00 -	30.00
45484 *Spanish Rag*....................	20.00 -	30.00
45494 *County Fair*...................	20.00 -	30.00
Victor 21403 *Down Yonder*............	10.00 -	15.00
40070 *Shanghai Rag*....................	15.00 -	25.00

JIMMY BROWN:

Champion 16812 *Keep A Light In Your Window Tonight*....................	10.00 -	15.00
45074 *Keep A Light In Your Window Tonight*	4.00 -	7.00

(MILTON) BROWN'S (MUSICAL) BROWNIES:

Bluebird 5444 *Oh You Pretty Woman*........	7.00 -	10.00
(Note: Some copies issued as by FORT WORTH BOYS)		
Bluebird 5484, 5558, 5610, 5654, 5690, 5715, 5775, 5808........	5.00 -	8.00

OSCAR BROWN:

Champion 15523 *You're A Little Too Small*....	10.00 -	15.00

THOMAS BROWN:

Brunswick 593 *On The Plains Of Texas*.......	5.00 -	8.00

BILL BRUNER:

Okeh 45400 *My Pal Of Yesterday*...........	10.00 -	15.00
45438 *He's In The Jailhouse Now*........	15.00 -	20.00
45463 *A Gal Like You*..................	15.00 -	20.00
45497 *My Old Home Town Girl*...........	15.00 -	20.00

(HOYT) "SLIM" BRYANT (& HIS RIVERSIDERS):

Champion 16407 *Peach Picking Time In Georgia*	20.00 -	30.00
Crown 3384 *Wreck Of The Old 97*............	10.00 -	15.00
Superior 2812 *The Rabbit Hunt*..............	20.00 -	30.00

BUCKEYE BOYS:

Champion 16168 *Duck Foot Sue*.............	5.00 -	8.00
45160, 45200...............................	3.00 -	6.00
Superior 2616 *That Old Fashioned Phonograph*.	10.00 -	15.00

BUCK MOUNTAIN BAND:

Okeh 45428 *Don't Let The Blues Get You Down*	15.00 -	25.00

ALVIN BUNCH:

Supertone 9180 *Only A Miner Killed In The Ground*	8.00 -	12.00

CARL BUNCH:

Bell 1186 *True And Trembling Brakeman*......	8.00 -	12.00

SAM BUNCH:

Supertone 9372 *My Sarah Jane*...............	7.00 -	10.00

JACK & JIM BURBANK:

Superior 2741 *Try Not To Forget*............	10.00 -	15.00
2761 *On The Banks Of The Brandywine*.....	10.00 -	15.00
2825 *Oh Mary Don't You Weep*..........	10.00 -	15.00

JACK BURDETTE & BERT MOSS:

Superior 2696 *That Old Tiger Rag*........	20.00 -	30.00

BURKE BROTHERS:

Victor 40294 *Lonesome And Lonely*..........	8.00 -	12.00

(FIDDLIN') JIM BURKE (& JESSE COAT):

Champion 15396 *Cripple Creek*.............	5.00 -	8.00
15449 *Waynesburgh*...................	7.00 -	10.00
15500 *Billy In The Low Ground*.......	7.00 -	10.00
15564 *Smoky Row*....................	8.00 -	12.00
15603 *Brick Yard Joe*.................	8.00 -	12.00
15668 *Shoot That Turkey Buzzard*......	8.00 -	12.00
15690 *Knoxville Rag*...................	10.00 -	15.00
15749 *Jack's Creek Waltz*.............	8.00 -	12.00
15788 *The Devil In Georgia*...........	7.00 -	10.00
15783 *Johnny Inchin' Along*..........	7.00 -	10.00
15921 *Sally Gooden*..................	7.00 -	10.00
16027 *Rye Straw*.....................	10.00 -	15.00
16208 *The Drunken Man's Dream*........	10.00 -	15.00

Silvertone 8179 *And The Cat Came Back*......	6.00 -	10.00
8185 *Arkansas Traveler*.................	6.00 -	10.00
Supertone 9164 *Buck Creek Gal*............	6.00 -	10.00
9165 *And The Cat Came Back*.............	6.00 -	10.00
9168 *Cripple Creek*.....................	6.00 -	10.00
9169 *Dance With The Girl With The Hole*...	6.00 -	10.00
9172 *Arkansas Traveler*.................	6.00 -	10.00
9173 *Brick Yard Joe*....................	6.00 -	10.00
9176 *Billy In The Low Ground*...........	6.00 -	10.00
9260 *Knoxville Girl*....................	8.00 -	12.00
9311 *Run Smoke Run*....................	7.00 -	10.00
9355 *New Money*........................	7.00 -	10.00
9390 *The Devil In Georgia*..............	7.00 -	10.00
9650 *Chicken Reel*.....................	7.00 -	10.00

PETE BURKE TRIO:

Humming Bird 1007 *Super Boogie Woogie*......	—*	

ABNER BURKHARDT:

Champion 15261, 15279, 15356, 15669.........	5.00 -	8.00

BURNETT BROTHERS:

Victor 23727 *Old Shoes A-Draggin'*...........	7.00 -	10.00
23730 *Countin' Cross Ties*.................	7.00 -	10.00
23745 *Rockin' Chair*......................	7.00 -	10.00

BURNETTE & MILLER:

Superior 2764 *Twenty-One Years*............	10.00 -	15.00

BURNETT & RUTHERFORD:

Columbia 15113-D *Pearl Bryan*..............	5.00 -	8.00
15122-D *Lost John*.......................	5.00 -	8.00
15133-D *A Short Life Of Trouble*............	5.00 -	8.00
15187-D *My Sweetheart In Tennessee*........	5.00 -	8.00
15209-D *Ladies On A Steamboat*............	7.00 -	10.00
15204-D *Curley Headed Woman*............	7.00 -	10.00
15314-D *All Night Long Blues*............	10.00 -	15.00

BURNETTE & RUTTLEDGE:

Columbia 15567-D *Blackberry Blossoms*........	10.00 -	15.00

SMILIE BURNETTE:

Titles issued contemporaneously on Banner, Melotone, Oriole, Perfect, Romeo, include: *He Was A Traveling Man; Mama Don't Like Music; Matilda Higgins; Peg Leg Jack*.............	8.00 -	12.00

DAPHNE BURNS:

Paramount 3032 *Weeping Willow Tree*.......	7.00 -	10.00

RUBEN BURNS:

Champion 15376 *The Burglar Man*...........	8.00 -	12.00
Gennett 6222 *The Burglar Man*............	8.00 -	12.00

(JOHN) BURTON (& BODINE):

Superior 2522 *I Don't Want You Mama*......	30.00 -	40.00
2573 *Memphis Special Blues*............	30.00 -	40.00
2618 *Little Old Home Down In New Orleans*.	30.00 -	40.00
2672 *Treasure Untold*...................	30.00 -	40.00
2810 *Pal Of My Sunny Days*............	35.00 -	50.00
2823 *The Longest Train I Ever Saw*........	35.00 -	50.00

RUSSELL & LOUIS BURTON:

Champion 16454 *Down In Tennessee*..........	15.00 -	25.00
Superior 2703 *The Old Corn Mill*...........	15.00 -	25.00

BUSTER & JACK:

Montgomery Ward 4084 *Guitar Duet Blues*.....	15.00 -	20.00
Victor 23257 *Guitar Duet Blues*...........	30.00 -	40.00

DWIGHT BUTCHER:

Champion 45187 *Broken Hearted Cowboy*......	5.00 -	8.00
Victor 23772 *Lonesome Cowboy*............	20.00 -	30.00
23794 *By A Little Bayou*................	20.00 -	30.00
23802 *Alarm Clock Blues*...............	25.00 -	40.00
23810 *Your Voice Is Calling*............	40.00 -	60.00
23819 *Pistol Pete*......................	25.00 -	35.00
23826 *My Rambling Days Are Over*........	25.00 -	35.00

ALBERT CAIN:

Okeh 45557 *Pickin' On The Old Guitar*......	15.00 -	20.00
45567 *Runnin' Wild*....................	15.00 -	20.00

CALDWELL BROTHERS:

Supertone 9343 *Somebody's Waiting For Me*....	7.00 -	10.00

CALDWELL & BUNCH:

Superior 2791 *My Bones Is Gonna Rise Again*..	15.00 -	20.00

BOB CALEN:

Okeh 45372 *Carolina Rolling Stone*......... 10.00 - 15.00

HANK CALDWELL & THE SADDLE KINGS:

D'Oro 103 *Alibi*...................... ——

SAM CALDWELL:

Supertone 9185 *The Prisoner's Lament*........ 7.00 - 10.00

CALLAHAN BROTHERS; HOMER CALLAHAN; WALTER CALLAHAN:

Titles, issued contemporaneously on Banner, Conqueror, Melotone, Oriole, Perfect, Romeo; include: *Asheville Blues; Brown's Ferry Blues; Cowboy Jack; Days Are Blue; Don't You Remember The Time; Going To Heaven On My Own Expense; Gonna Quit Drinkin' When I Die; Gonna Quit My Rowdy Ways; Green Back Dollar; I Don't Want To Hear Your Name; Katie Dear; Little Poplar Log House On The Hill; Lonesome And Wear Blues; Maple On The Hill; Mean Mama; New Birmingham Jail No. 3; North Carolina Moon; Once I Had A Darling Mother Rattle Snake Daddy; Rounder's Luck; St. Louis Blues; She's Killing Me; She's My Curley Headed Baby No. 2; T.B. Blues No. 2; True Lover...* 5.00 - 10.00

Vocalion 02973 *Take The News To Mother*.... 5.00 - 10.00

03108 *Just One Year*.................... 5.00 - 10.00

03171 *Freight Train Blues*................ 5.00 - 10.00

03335 *She's My Curley Headed Baby No. 3*.. 5.00 - 10.00

04358, 04359, 04360, 04361, 04362, 04363... 3.00 - 6.00

CALOWAY'S WEST VIRGINIA MOUNTAINEERS:

Gennett 6546 *The Corn Shuckers' Frolic*....... 15.00 - 25.00

AARON CAMPBELL'S MOUNTAINEERS:

Champion 16689 *The Flying Trapeze*.......... 10.00 - 15.00

16740 *Mother's Knee*.................. 10.00 - 15.00

16751 *Daisies Won't Tell*.............. 15.00 - 20.00

45008, 45038, 45086.................... 4.00 - 6.00

ORAN CAMPBELL:

Champion 15429, 15502.................. 5.00 - 8.00

HARMON CANADA:

Gennett 6961 *My Little Home In Tennessee*.... 8.00 - 12.00

6972 *Born In Hard Luck*.............. 8.00 - 12.00

WARREN CAPLINGER & CUMBERLAND MOUNTAIN ENTERTAINERS/THE DIXIE HARMONIZERS:

Brunswick 224 *Nobody's Business*........... 15.00 - 20.00

241 *Big Ball In Town*.............. 15.00 - 20.00

Gennett 6915 *The Music Man*............. 20.00 - 30.00

Vocalion 5222 *Chicken Reel*................ 15.00 - 20.00

5237 *When The Redeemed Are Gathered In*.. 10.00 - 15.00

5240 *Jerusalem Mourn*.............. 10.00 - 15.00

KEN CARD:

Champion 45148 *The Last Flight Of Wiley Post*. 5.00 - 8.00

CARLISLE BROTHERS:

Titles, issued contemporaneously on Banner, Melotone, Oriole, Perfect, Romeo, include: *The Little Dobie Shack; Looking For Tomorrow; Ramshackled Shack On The Hill; Sunshine And Daisies* .... 4.00 - 7.00

Bluebird .... 3.00 - 6.00

(SMILING) BILL CARLISLE:

Bluebird 6478, 6568, 6600, 6608, 6775, 6938, 7019, 7087, 7153, 7414, 7613.................. 4.00 - 6.00

Melotone 7-02-64 *House Cat Mama*.......... 5.00 - 8.00

(Note: Also issued on Banner, Oriole, Perfect, Romeo)

Vocalion 02520 *Rattle Snake Daddy*.......... 7.00 - 10.00

02946 *I'm Gonna Kill Myself*............. 7.00 - 10.00

CLIFF/CLIFFORD CARLISLE:

Titles, issued contemporaneously on Banner, Conqueror, Melotone, Oriole, Perfect, Romeo, include: *Birmingham Jail No. 2; Blue Eyes; Chicken Roost Blues; Desert Blues; Don't Marry The*

Wrong Woman; Fussin' Mama; Gamblin' Dan; Going Back To Alabama; Hen Pecked Man; I Don't Mind; I'm Glad I'm A Hobo; Just A Lonely Hobo; Louisiana Blues; My Two Time Mama; On The Banks Of The Rio Grande; Shanghai Rooster Yodel; Wreck Of No. 52; Written Letter.... 5.00 - 10.00

Additional titles: *The Bunch Of Cactus On The Wall; Casey County Jail; Childhood Dreams; Dang My Rowdy Soul; Dream A Little Dream Of Me; Georgia Moon; Goodbye Old Pal; Lonely Valley; Lonesome For Caroline; Longing For You; Memories That Haunt Me; Memories That Make Me Cry; On The Prairie; Seven Years With The Wrong Woman; When It's Roundup Time In Texas; Where Romance Calls; Won't Somebody Pal With Me*........................ 4.00 - 7.00

Bluebird 6350 *Rambling Yodeler*............. 5.00 - 10.00

6405 *A Stretch Of 28 Years*................ 5.00 - 10.00

6439 *Cowboy Johnny's Last Ride*.......... 5.00 - 10.00

6458 *You'll Miss Me When I'm Gone*....... 5.00 - 10.00

6493 *When I Feel Froggie, I'm Gonna Hop*... 5.00 - 10.00

6524 *Wigglin' Mama*.................. 5.00 - 10.00

6540, 6631, 6647..................... 5.00 - 8.00

6754, 6791, 6830, 6855, 6980, 7031, 7094, 7147, 7290, 7702, 7717, 7740, 7790, 7817, 8199, 8228 4.00 - 7.00

Champion 15969 *Memphis Yodel*............. 15.00 - 20.00

15992 *Desert Blues*.................. 15.00 - 20.00

16028 *Virginia Blues*................ 15.00 - 20.00

Champion - *I'm Lonely And Blue*........... 15.00 - 20.00

16140 *Crazy Blues*.................. 15.00 - 20.00

16165 *No Daddy Blues*................ 15.00 - 20.00

16212 *Box Car Blues*................ 20.00 - 30.00

16239 *High Steppin' Mama*............. 20.00 - 30.00

16270 *Hobo Jack's Last Ride*.......... 20.00 - 30.00

16329 *Nobody Wants Me*.............. 20.00 - 30.00

16419 *Memories That Haunt Me*......... 20.00 - 30.00

16434 *She's Waiting For Me*............. 20.00 - 30.00

16447 *The Fatal Run*................. 20.00 - 30.00

45029, 45042, 45132, 45134, 45139, 45140, 45147, 45155, 45162, 45179, 45186.............. 5.00 - 8.00

Gennett 7153 *Down In The Jailhouse On My Knees* 15.00 - 20.00

7187 *Desert Blues*.................. 15.00 - 20.00

7206 *Memphis Yodel*................ 15.00 - 20.00

7244 *Virginia Blues*................. 15.00 - 20.00

7288 *I'm Lonely And Blue*.............. 15.00 - 25.00

CAROLINA BUDDIES:

Columbia 15537-D *The Murder Of The Lawson Family* .... 8.00 - 12.00

15641-D *The Story That The Crow Told Me*.. 10.00 - 15.00

15652-D *Otto Wood The Bandit*............ 10.00 - 15.00

15663-D *Work Don't Bother Me*........... 10.00 - 15.00

15770-D *Mistreated Blues*................ 10.00 - 15.00

CAROLINA MANDOLINE BAND:

Okeh 45191 *Georgia Camp Meeting*.......... 10.00 - 15.00

CAROLINA NIGHT HAWKS:

Columbia 15256-D *Governor Al Smith For President* 5.00 - 8.00

CAROLINA RAMBLERS STRING BAND:

Melotone 13047 *Chinese Breakdown*.......... 7.00 - 10.00

CAROLINA TAR HEELS:

Victor 20544 *I'm Going To Georgia*......... 8.00 - 12.00

20545 *Bring Me A Leaf From The Sea*...... 8.00 - 12.00

20931 *I Love My Mountain Home*........ 8.00 - 12.00

20941 *Bulldog Down In Sunny Tennessee*... 8.00 - 12.00

21193 *My Mamma Scolds Me*............. 10.00 - 15.00

23516 *Farm Girl Blues*............... 15.00 - 20.00

23546 *The Hen House Door Is Locked*...... 15.00 - 20.00

23611 *Got The Farm Land Blues*......... 20.00 - 30.00

23671 *Nobody Cares If I'm Blue*.......... 20.00 - 30.00

23682 *Times Ain't Like They Used To Be*.... 20.00 - 30.00

40007 *Peg And Awl*................. 10.00 - 15.00

40024 *Roll On, Boys*................. 10.00 - 15.00

40053 *I Don't Like The Blues No More*	10.00 -	15.00
40077 *Rude And Rambling Man*	10.00 -	15.00
40100 *My Home's Across The Blue Ridge Mountains*	10.00 -	15.00
40128 *Somebody's Tall And Handsome*	10.00 -	15.00
40177 *The Old Gray Goose*	10.00 -	15.00
40219 *I'll Be Washed*	10.00 -	15.00

CAROLINA TWINS:

Victor 21363 *Off To War I'm Going*	5.00 -	8.00
21575 *One Dark And Rainy Night*	5.00 -	8.00
23502 *Since My Baby's Gone Away*	15.00 -	20.00
40044 *When You Go A-Courtin'*	5.00 -	10.00
40098 *Mr. Brown, Here I Come*	5.00 -	10.00
40123 *New Orleans Is The Town I Like Best*	5.00 -	10.00
40243 *Change In Business All Around*	7.00 -	10.00
40310 *Southern Jack*	7.00 -	10.00

BOYDEN CARPENTER:

Champion 16519 *The Hobos Convention*	10.00 -	15.00

JOHN CARPENTER:

Bell 1178 *Sourwood Mountain*	5.00 -	8.00

CARROLL COUNTY RAMBLERS:

Vocalion 5433 *Georgia Wobble Blues*	25.00 -	35.00

CARSON BROTHERS & SMITH/SPRINKLE:

Okeh 45013, 45023	5.00 -	8.00
45398 *The Highway Man*	7.00 -	10.00

BERT CARSON:

Superior 2520 *My Red Haired Lady*	15.00 -	20.00

FIDDLIN' JOHN CARSON (& HIS VIRGINIA REELERS/with MOONSHINE KATE):

Bluebird 5401 *New Comin' Round The Mountain*	10.00 -	15.00
5447 *Stockade Blues*	10.00 -	15.00
5483 *The Storm That Struck Miami*	10.00 -	15.00
5560, 5652, 5742, 5787, 5959, 6022, 6247	5.00 -	10.00
Montgomery Ward 4848, 4849, 4851, 4852	4.00 -	7.00
Okeh 4890 *The Little Old Log Cabin In The Lane*	10.00 -	15.00

(Note: The existence of an unnumbered issue of the above record, of which 500 copies were supposedly pressed, has not been confirmed.)

Okeh 4994 *Papa's Billy Goat*	10.00 -	15.00
7003 (12-inch) *Sugar In The Gourd*	40.00 -	60.00
7004 (12-inch) *John Henry Blues*	40.00 -	60.00
7006 (12-inch) *The Baggage Coach Ahead*	40.00 -	60.00
7008 (12-inch) *The Lightning Express*	40.00 -	60.00
40020 *Billy In The Low Ground*	8.00 -	15.00
40038 *Casey Jones*	8.00 -	15.00
40050 *Tom Watson Special*	8.00 -	15.00
40071 *The Kickin' Mule*	8.00 -	15.00
40095 *Dixie Boll Weevil*	8.00 -	15.00
40108 *Arkansas Traveler*	8.00 -	15.00
40181 *Old And In The Way*	10.00 -	15.00
40196 *I'm Nine Hundred Miles From Home*	10.00 -	15.00
40204 *Alabama Gal*	10.00 -	15.00
40230 *Turkey In The Straw*	10.00 -	15.00
40238 *Nancy Rowland*	10.00 -	15.00
40263 *Old Dan Tucker*	10.00 -	15.00
40306 *Steamboat Bill*	10.00 -	15.00
40343 *My North Georgia Home*	10.00 -	15.00
40363 *Charming Betsy*	10.00 -	15.00
40411 *The Honest Farmer*	10.00 -	15.00
40419 *The Boston Burglar*	10.00 -	15.00
40444 *Bully Of The Town*	10.00 -	15.00
40446 *Little Mary Phagan*	10.00 -	15.00
45001 *Run Along Home With Lindy*	10.00 -	15.00
45011 *Soldier's Joy*	10.00 -	15.00
45018 *Hell Broke Loose In Georgia*	10.00 -	15.00
45028 *The Grave Of Little Mary Phagan*	10.00 -	15.00
45032 *The Drunkard's Hiccoughs*	10.00 -	15.00
45035 *Liberty*	10.00 -	15.00
45040 *Georgia Wagner*	10.00 -	15.00
45045 *Everybody Works But Father*	10.00 -	15.00
45049 *Good-Bye Liza Jane*	10.00 -	15.00

45056 *The Batchelor's Hall*	10.00 -	15.00
45068 *Fire In The Mountain*	10.00 -	15.00
45077 *Long Way To Tipperary*	10.00 -	15.00
45096 *Don't Let Your Deal Go Down*	10.00 -	15.00
45122 *Cotton-Eyed Joe*	10.00 -	15.00
45139 *Swanee River*	10.00 -	15.00
45159 *Hell Bound For Alabama*	10.00 -	15.00
45167 *Turkey In The Hay*	10.00 -	15.00
45176 *Engineer On The Mogull*	10.00 -	15.00
45186 *Quit That Ticklin' Me*	10.00 -	15.00
45198 *Old Joe Clark*	10.00 -	15.00
45214 *Going Down To Cripple Creek*	15.00 -	20.00
45259 *Ain't No Bugs On Me*	15.00 -	20.00
45273 *Old And In The Way*	15.00 -	20.00
45290 *John Makes Good Licker*	15.00 -	20.00
45301 *Be Kind To A Man When He's Down*	15.00 -	20.00
45321 *Going To The County Fair*	15.00 -	20.00
45338 *Hawk And Buzzard*	15.00 -	20.00
45353 *My Ford Sedan*	15.00 -	20.00
45369 *John Makes Good Licker, Part 3/4*	15.00 -	20.00
45384 *You'll Never Miss Your Mother, No. 2*	20.00 -	30.00
45402 *Times Are Not Like They Used To Be*	20.00 -	30.00
45415 *Corn Licker And Barbecue, Part 1/2*	20.00 -	30.00
45434 *Sunny Tennessee*	20.00 -	30.00
45440 *Kate's Snuff Box*	20.00 -	30.00
45445 *The Raccoon And The Possum*	20.00 -	30.00
45448 *Who's The Best Fiddler?*	20.00 -	30.00
45458 *John In The Army*	20.00 -	30.00
45471 *The Last Old Dollar Is Gone*	20.00 -	30.00
45488 *On The Banks Of Old Tennessee*	20.00 -	30.00
45498 *The Dominicker Duck*	20.00 -	30.00
45513 *My Home In Dixie-Land*	20.00 -	30.00
45542 *Take The Train To Charlotte*	20.00 -	30.00
45555 *I Intend To Make Heaven My Home*	25.00 -	40.00
45569 *Didn't He Ramble*	25.00 -	40.00

ROSA LEE CARSON:

Okeh 45005 *The Drinker's Child*	8.00 -	12.00

CARTER BROTHERS (& SON):

Okeh 45202 *Saddle Up The Grey*	15.00 -	25.00
45289 *Give The Fiddler A Dream*	15.00 -	25.00
Vocalion 5295 *Give Me A Chaw Tobacco*	20.00 -	30.00
5297 *Jenny On The Railroad*	20.00 -	30.00

CARTER FAMILY:

Titles, issued contemporaneously on Banner, Conqueror, Melotone, Oriole, Perfect, Romeo: *Broken Hearted Lover; By The Touch Of Her Hand; Cannon Ball Blues; Can The Circle Be Unbroken; East Virginia Blues No. 2; The Fate Of Dewey Lee; Gathering Flowers on the Hillside; Glory To The Lamb; God Gave Noah The Rainbow Sign; He Took A White Rose From Her Hair; I'm Thinking Tonight Of My Blue Eyes; Keep On The Sunny Side; Kissing Is A Crime; Let's Be Lovers Again; Little Darling Pal Of Mine; On The Rocks Where Moses Stood; River Of Jordan; Worried Man Blues*

	8.00 -	12.00
Bluebird 5006 *Keep On The Sunny Side*	5.00 -	8.00

5058 Where We'll Never Grow Old.........	5.00 -	8.0
5096 Meet Me By The Moonlight Alone.....	5.00 -	8.00
5122 When The Springtime Comes Again....	5.00 -	8.00
5161 Will The Roses Bloom In Heaven?.....	5.00 -	8.00
5185 Amber Tresses..................	5.00 -	8.00
5243 Mid The Green Fields Of Virginia......	5.00 -	8.00
5272 God Gave Noah The Rainbow Sign....	5.00 -	8.00
5301 My Clinch Mountain Home.........	5.00 -	8.00
5356 Wildwood Flower.................	5.00 -	8.00
5406 Anchored In Love................	5.00 -	8.00
5468 Sow 'Em On The Mountain.........	5.00 -	8.00
5529 I'll Be All Smiles Tonight...........	5.00 -	8.00
5543 A Distant Land To Roam...........	5.00 -	8.00
5586 Darling Daisies..................	5.00 -	8.00
5650 The East Virginia Blues...........	5.00 -	8.00
5716 I'm Working On A Building.........	5.00 -	8.00
5771 One Little Word.................	5.00 -	8.00
5817 I'll Aggravate Your Soul...........	5.00 -	8.00
5856 Longing For Old Virginia..........	5.00 -	8.00
5908 My Heart's Tonight In Texas.........	5.00 -	8.00
5911 I'll Be Home Some Day...........	5.00 -	8.00
5924 Little Moses...................	5.00 -	8.00
5927 Lulu Wall....................	5.00 -	8.00
5956 The Mountains Of Tennessee.........	5.0 -	8.00
5961 On a Hill Lone And Gray..........	5.00 -	8.00
5974 Sailor Boy....................	5.00 -	8.00
5990 Kitty Waltz...................	5.00 -	8.00
5993 The Church In The Wildwood........	5.00 -	8.00
6000 Lonesome For You...............	5.00 -	8.00
6020 Worried Man Blues...............	5.00 -	8.00
6033 Diamonds In The Rough...........	5.00 -	8.00
6036 Carter's Blues.................	5.00 -	8.00
6053 When I'm Gone.................	5.00 -	8.00
6055 Where Shall I Be?...............	5.00 -	8.00
6106 Two Sweethearts................	5.00 -	8.00
6117 Lonesome Valley................	5.00 -	8.00
6176 Fond Affection.................	5.00 -	8.00
6223 Engine One-Forty-Three...........	5.00 -	8.00
6257 I Never Loved But One...........	5.00 -	8.00
6271 Little Log Cabin By The Sea........	5.00 -	8.00
6762 The Carter Family & Jimmie Rodgers In Texas..........................	8.00 -	12.00
8350 Wabash Cannon Ball.............	5.00 -	8.00
8868 Dark And Stormy Weather.........	5.00 -	8.00
Decca 5240 My Dixie Darling...........	7.00 -	10.00
5241 My Native Home...............	7.00 -	10.00
5242 No Depression.................	7.00 -	10.00
5254 Just Another Broken Heart.........	7.00 -	10.00
5263 My Honey Lou.................	7.00 -	10.00
5283 You've Been A Friend To Me........	7.00 -	10.00
5304 Bonnie Blue Eyes...............	7.00 -	10.00
5318 Sweet Heaven In My View.........	7.00 -	10.00
5359 In The Shadow Of The Pines........	7.00 -	10.00
5386 The Last Move For Me...........	7.00 -	10.00
5411 The Only Girl.................	7.00 -	10.00
5430 Lover's Lane..................	7.00 -	10.00
5447 He Never Came Back.............	7.00 -	10.00
5452 Honey In The Rock.............	7.00 -	10.00
5467 Jim Blake's Message.............	7.00 -	10.00
5479 Hello Stranger.................	7.00 -	10.00
5494 Lord I'm In Your Care...........	7.00 -	10.00
5518 Broken Down Tramp.............	7.00 -	10.00
5532 Goodbye To The Plains...........	7.00 -	10.00
5565 Stern Old Bachelor..............	7.00 -	10.00
5579 Happy In The Prison.............	7.00 -	10.00
5596 Coal Miner's Blues..............	7.00 -	10.00
5612 Who's That Knockin' On My Window..	7.00 -	10.00
5632 Little Joe....................	7.00 -	10.00
5649 Bring Back My Boy..............	7.00 -	10.00
5662 Cuban Soldiers.................	7.00 -	10.00
5677 Farewell Nellie................	7.00 -	10.00

5692 You Are My Flower..............	7.00 -	10.00
5702 Charlie And Nellie..............	7.00 -	10.00
5722 Reckless Motorman..............	7.00 -	10.00
Montgomery Ward (Many titles, same as on Bluebird and Victor, valued approximately the same as Bluebird issues)................	5.00 -	10.00
Victor 20877 The Poor Orphan Child.........	8.00 -	12.00
20937 Storms Are On The Ocean........	8.00 -	12.00
21074 Little Log Cabin By The Sea.......	8.00 -	12.00
21434 Keep On The Sunny Side.........	8.00 -	12.00
21517 Chewing Gum................	8.00 -	12.00
21638 Will You Miss Me When I'm Gone?...	8.00 -	12.00
23513 On The Rock................	20.00 -	30.00
23523 Where Shall I Be?.............	20.00 -	30.00
23541 Lonesome Valley..............	20.00 -	30.00
23554 There's Someone A Waiting For Me...	20.00 -	30.00
23569 Can't Feel At Home............	20.00 -	30.00
23574 Jimmie Rodgers Visits The Carter Family	20.00 -	30.00
23585 Sow 'Em On The Mountain........	20.00 -	30.00
23599 My Old Cottage Home..........	20.00 -	30.00
23618 Let The Church Roll On..........	20.00 -	30.00
23626 Weary Prodigal Son............	20.00 -	30.00
23641 Dying Soldier................	20.00 -	30.00
23656 I Have Never Loved But One........	25.00 -	40.00
23672 Where We'll Never Grow Old.......	25.00 -	40.00
23686 'Mid The Green Fields Of Virginia....	25.00 -	40.00
23701 Amber Tresses...............	25.00 -	40.00
23716 Carter's Blues...............	25.00 -	40.00
23731 Wabash Cannon Ball...........	25.00 -	40.00
23748 Will The Roses Bloom In Heaven?....	25.00 -	40.00
23761 Sweet As The Flowers In May Time...	25.00 -	40.00
23776 The Church In The Wildwood.......	25.00 -	40.00
23791 Two Sweet Hearts.............	40.00 -	60.00
23807 I Wouldn't Mind Dying..........	40.00 -	60.00
23821 Gold Watch And Chain..........	40.00 -	60.00
23835 I Loved You Better Than I Know.....	50.00 -	75.00
23845 On The Sea Of Galilee..........	50.00 -	75.00
40000 Wildwood Flower.............	8.00 -	12.00
40036 I Have No One..............	8.00 -	12.00
40058 Foggy Mountain Top...........	8.00 -	12.00
40089 Engine One-Forty-Three..........	8.00 -	12.00
40110 Little Moses................	8.00 -	12.00
40126 Sweet Fern.................	8.00 -	12.00
40150 Diamonds In The Rough.........	8.00 -	12.00
40190 Bring Back My Blue-Eyed Boy......	8.00 -	12.00
40207 The Homestead On The Farm.......	10.00 -	15.00
40229 When The Roses Bloom In Dixieland..	15.00 -	20.00
40255 Western Hobo...............	15.00 -	20.00
40277 Lover's Farewell..............	15.00 -	20.00
40293 When The World's On Fire........	15.00 -	20.00
40317 Worried Man Blues............	20.00 -	30.00
40328 Don't Forget This Song..........	20.00 -	30.00
Vocalion 02990 Broken Hearted Lover......	15.00 -	20.00
03027 Can The Circle Be Unbroken......	10.00 -	15.00
03112 Lonesome Valley.............	10.00 -	15.00
03160 The Storms Are On The Ocean......	10.00 -	15.00
04390 Don't Forget Me Little Darling......	10.00 -	15.00

(BUSTER) CARTER & (PRESTON) YOUNG:

Columbia 15690-D *I'll Roll In My Sweet Baby's Arms*	30.00 -	50.00
15702-D *It Won't Hurt No More*..........	30.00 -	50.00
15758-D *Bill Morgan And His Gal*.........	30.00 -	50.00

FLOYD CARTER:

Oriole 8847 *Flemington Kidnap Trial*.........	5.00 -	8.00

WILF CARTER:

Bluebird 5536, 5545, 5871, 6009, 6107, 6208, 6380,		
6814, 6826, 6827.................	5.00 -	8.00
Bluebird (lower numbers/Canadian issues)......	5.00 -	10.00
Bluebird (higher numbers)................	3.00 -	6.00

CARTWRIGHT BROTHERS:

Columbia 15220-D *Kelly Waltz*...........	4.00 -	7.00
15346-D *On The Old Chisholm Trail*.......	8.00 -	12.00
15410-D *Utah Carroll*..................	8.00 -	12.00
15677-D *Over The Waves*...............	10.00 -	15.00
Victor 40147 *San Antonio*..............	8.00 -	12.00
40198 *The Dying Ranger*.............	8.00 -	12.00
40247 *The Wandering Cowboy*...........	8.00 -	12.00

CARVER BOYS:

Paramount 3182 *No One To Welcome Me Home*	15.00 -	20.00
3198 *The Brave Engineer*.................	15.00 -	20.00
3199 *Tim Brook*..................	15.00 -	20.00
3233 *Simpson County*...............	15.00 -	20.00

CASEY'S OLD TIME FIDDLERS:

Victor 23560 *Casey's Old Time Waltz*.........	15.00 -	20.00

CLAUDE CASEY (& THE PINE STATE PLAYBOYS):

Bluebird 7863, 7883..................	4.00 -	7.00

ELRY CASH:

Columbia 15399-D *My Old New Hampshire Home*	8.00 -	12.00
15457-D *Then My Love Began To Wane*.....	8.00 -	12.00

CASS COUNTY BOYS:

Bluebird 8006, 8824..................	4.00 -	7.00

THOMPSON CATES:

Paramount 3103 *Curse Of An Aching Heart*....	7.00 -	10.00

CAULEY FAMILY:

Melotone 13113 *New River Train*..............	5.00 -	8.00
13114 *Duplin County Blues*................	5.00 -	8.00
(Note: Probably also issued on Banner, Oriole, Perfect, Romeo)		

(JACK) CAWLEY'S (OKLAHOMA) RIDGE RUNNERS:

Victor 23521 *White River Stomp*...........	20.00 -	30.00
23540 *Cross Tie Blues*.................	20.00 -	30.00
23570 *The Vine-Covered Cottage*...........	20.00 -	30.00
40175 *Ft. Worth Rag*.................	20.00 -	30.00
40254 *Oklahoma Waltz*...............	20.00 -	30.00

CEDAR CREST SINGERS: (See also WILLIAM REXROAT):

Vocalion 5294 *Dying For Someone To Love Me*	15.00 -	20.00

LEON CHAPPELEAR (THE LONE STAR COWBOY):

Champion 16497 *Little Joe The Wrangler*......	15.00 -	20.00
40568 *Little Joe The Wrangler*...........	4.00 -	6.00
45167 *Trifling Mama Blues*...............	7.00 -	10.00

CHARLESTON ENTERTAINERS:

Supertone 9718 *Wait Till The Sun Shines Nellie*.	5.00 -	8.00

CHEZZ CHASE:

Paramount 3178 *Log Cabin Blues*............	5.00 -	8.00

CHENOWETH'S CORNFIELD SYMPHONY ORCHESTRA:

Okeh 45025 *Arkansaw Wampus Cat*.........	15.00 -	20.00

CHEROKEE RAMBLERS:

Decca 5402 *Back Up And Push*.........	5.00 -	8.00

TED CHESNUT:

Gennett 6480 *The Letter From Home*........	15.00 -	20.00
6513 *The Death Of J.B. Marcum*........	15.00 -	20.00
6603 *Bring Back My Boy*.............	15.00 -	20.00
6638 *The Drunkard's Doom*.............	15.00 -	20.00
6673 *Only A Tramp*.............	15.00 -	20.00

CHIEF SHUNATONA, DOUG MaTAGUE, AND SNOOKUM:

Columbia 15781-D *Cowboy Tom's Roundup*....	50.00 -	75.00

CHILDERS & WHITE:

Okeh 45208 *Red River Valley*..............	7.00 -	10.00
45213 *Don't Grieve Your Mother*..........	7.00 -	10.00

BILL CHILDERS:

Okeh 45203 *Bury Me Not On The Lone Prairie*.	7.00 -	10.00

(MR. & MRS.) W.C. CHILDERS:

Champion 16467 *Strawberry Roan*............	15.00 -	20.00
45103, 45166.............	4.00 -	7.00
Gennett 6931 *The Grand Roundup*...........	15.00 -	20.00
6943 *Over The Hills To The Poor House*........	15.00 -	20.00
6973 *Your Mother's Always Waiting*........	15.00 -	20.00
7021 *Workin' Habits*..............	15.00 -	20.00
7066 *Crepe On The Little Cabin Door*.....	15.00 -	20.00
7113 *I'll Smoke My Long Stemmed Pipe*.....	20.00 -	30.00
7223 *Two Little Girls In Blue*........	20.00 -	30.00
7292 *The Prison Warden's Secret*..........	20.00 -	30.00
Paramount 3181 *Amber Tresses Tied In Blue*...	15.00 -	20.00

LEW CHILDRE:

Champion 16011 *Moonshine Blues*............	20.00 -	30.00
Gennett 7183 *Moonshine Blues*.............	20.00 -	30.00
7312 *The Old Grey Mare*...............	20.00 -	30.00

BILL CHITWOOD (& GEORGIA MOUNTAIN-EERS/BUD LANDRESS):

Brunswick 2884 *Furniture Man*..............	5.00 -	8.00
Okeh 45100 *Fourth Of July At The County Fair*	6.00 -	10.00
45110 *Smiling Watermelon*.................	6.00 -	10.00
45131 *Preacher Blues*.................	6.00 -	10.00
45162 *Kitty Hill*.................	6.00 -	10.00
45236 *Bill Wishes He Was Single Again*......	6.00 -	10.00
Silvertone 3048 *Howdy Bill*...............	7.00 -	10.00
3049 *Over The Sea*.................	7.00 -	10.00
3050 *Hen Cackle*.................	7.00 -	10.00

HARRY CHOATES:

Allied 103, 104....................	5.00 -	10.00
Cajun Classics 1007/1010 *Hackberry Hop*......	5.00 -	8.00
Gold Star 1314, 1319, 1326, 1330, 1333, 1335, 1336,		
1343, 1380, 1385, 1388.................	4.00 -	7.00
Macy's 124, 134, 141, 147, 158..............	4.00 -	7.00

BEN CHRISTIAN & HIS TEXAS COWBOYS:

Four Star 1270 *Moonlight Island*............	4.00 -	7.00
Melody 501 *You Played The Game And Lost*...	4.00 -	7.00
502 *Moonlight Island*.................	5.00 -	7.00

HOMER CHRISTOPHER (& RANEY VAN WINK/& WIFE):

Okeh 45041 *Southern Railroad*...............	5.00 -	8.00
45097 *Red Wing*.................	5.00 -	8.00
45117 *Going Slow*.................	5.00 -	8.00
45138 *Hilo March*.................	5.00 -	8.00
45147 *Home Town Rag*.................	5.00 -	8.00
45195 *Old Fashioned Waltz*.................	5.00 -	8.00
45277 *March In "D"*.................	5.00 -	8.00
Victor 20656 *Lost Mamma Blues*.............	7.00 -	10.00
Victor 21128 *Going Slow*..............	5.00 -	8.00

CHUCK WAGON GANG:

Banner, Canqueror, Melotone, Oriole, Perfect, Romeo (various titles).............	3.00 -	5.00
Vocalion 02938, 03028, 03224, 03434, 03472, 04105, 04342.................	3.00 -	6.00

CHUMBLER'S BREAKDOWN GANG:

Q.R.S. 9016 *May I Sleep In Your Barn Tonight?*	35.00 -	50.00

CHUMBLER FAMILY:

Columbia 15481-D *Jacobs Ladder*............	8.00 -	12.00
15513-D *I'm Going Home To My Wife*......	8.00 -	12.00

GENE CLARDY & STAN CLEMENTS:

Vocalion 5418 *Black Mustache*.............	8.00 -	12.00
5462 *Sleeping Time Waltz*..............	8.00 -	12.00

CLARK BROTHERS (See JOHN CLARK):
DUKE CLARK:
Champion 16470 *Make A Change In Business*..	15.00 -	25.00
16565 *Thirty Minutes Behind The Time*......	15.00 -	25.00
16624 *11:29 Blues*......................	20.00 -	30.00
Superior 2687 *The Wreck Of The F.F. & V*.....	20.00 -	30.00

FRANK CLARK:
Champion 15946 *Sad And Lonely Blues*.......	15.00 -	25.00

JOHN CLARK:
Champion 15565 *The Prisoner's Lament*......	8.00 -	12.00
15586 *Falling By The Wayside*............	8.00 -	12.00

LUTHER B. CLARK (Acc. by BLUE RIDGE HIGHBALLERS):
Columbia 15069-D *Bright Sherman Valley*......	7.00 -	10.00
15096-D *Wish To Lord I Had Never Been Born*	7.00 -	10.00

THEO. & GUS CLARK:
Okeh 45339 *Wimbush Rag*.................	20.00 -	30.00

CLARKE & HOWELL:
Supertone 9500 *Flop Eared Mule*...........	10.00 -	15.00
9536 *Birmingham Jail*.................	10.00 -	15.00

AL CLAUSER & HIS OKLAHOMANS:
Gulf 105 *Soldier's Return*.................	5.00 -	8.00

CLAYTON & HIS MELODY MOUNTAINEERS:
Vocalion 5434 *Lookout Valley Waltz*.......	10.00 -	15.00

CLEM & HARRY:
Champion 16667 *In The Old Town Hall*......	8.00 -	12.00

HARMON CLEM & PRINCE ALBERT HUNT:
Okeh 45360 *Oklahoma Rag*.................	30.00 -	40.00

STANLEY CLEMENTS:
Okeh 45562 *The Habit I Never Have Had*.....	8.00 -	12.00

CLIFF & RAY:
Vocalion 03721, 04204, 04293, 04743........	4.00 -	8.00

BOB CLIFFORD:
Vocalion 5488 *My Two Time Mama*.........	7.00 -	10.00
5492 *Shanghai Rooster Yodel No. 2*........	7.00 -	10.00
5499 *Hobo Jack's Last Ride*...........	7.00 -	10.00

CLINCH VALLEY BOYS:
Champion 15297 *Little Red Caboose Behind The Train*....................	7.00 -	10.00
15316 *Just As The Sun Went Down*........	7.00 -	10.00
Supertone 9248 *Just As The Sun Went Down*...	7.00 -	10.00

FRANK CLOUTIER & HIS VICTORIA CAFE ORCHESTRA:
Gennett 6305 *Moonshiner's Dance*..........	8.00 -	12.00

JESSE COAT (& JOHN BISHOP):
Champion 15585 *East Bound Train*...........	10.00 -	15.00
15611 *The Dying Girl's Message*.........	10.00 -	15.00
15712 *She Ain't Built That Way*..........	10.00 -	15.00
15854 *The Virginia Moonshiner*..........	10.00 -	15.00
15922 *The Fellow That Looks Like Me*.....	10.00 -	15.00

COBB & PROW:
Champion 16167 *My Pretty Snow Dear*.......	10.00 -	15.00

COBB & UNDERWOOD:
Champion 16144 *Black Sheep Blues*..........	15.00 -	20.00
45146 *Black Sheep Blues*.............	5.00 -	8.00
Gennett 7311 *Black Sheep Blues*..........	15.00 -	20.00

OSCAR L. COFFEY:
Gennett 6481 *My Dear Old Mountain Home*...	15.00 -	20.00
6496 *Six Feet Of Earth*................	15.00 -	20.00

TINY COLBERT & HIS ENTERTAINERS:
Blue Bonnet 133 *Bumble Bee Baby*.........	7.00 -	10.00
150 *Our Own Sweet Baby Boy*.........	3.00 -	5.00

JAMES COLE STRING BAND:
Vocalion 5226 *I Got A Gal*...............	15.00 -	20.00

JIM COLE'S (TENNESSEE) MOUNTAINEERS:
Crown 3102 *I'm Pining For The Pines And Caroline*	8.00 -	12.00
3122 *Rocky Mountain Sal*.............	8.00 -	12.00
3142 *Down In The Valley*............	8.00 -	12.00
3158 *Old Folks' Dance Medley*........	8.00 -	12.00
Paramount 3279 *Rocky Mountain Sal*........	20.00 -	30.00

REX COLE'S MOUNTAINEERS:
Melotone 12055 *Wilderness*.................	5.00 -	8.00

BERNICE COLEMAN acc. by WEST VIRGINIA RAMBLERS:
Champion 16456 *The Ring My Mother Wore*...	10.00 -	15.00

DUTCH COLEMAN:
Vocalion 5391 *New Ground Blues*............	20.00 -	30.00
5408 *The Clayton Case*..............	20.00 -	30.00
5467 *Gonna Raise Some Bacon At Home*....	20.00 -	30.00

BIFF COLLIE:
Macy's 126 *I Want A Gal (To Cook For Me)*...	7.00 -	10.00

BILL COLLINS:
Victor 20673 *When The Moon Shines*........	7.00 -	10.00

POP COLLINS & HIS BOYS:
Edison 52426 *The Train That Never Arrived*...	7.00 -	10.00
52507 *Pappy's Buried On The Hill*.........	7.00 -	10.00

UNCLE TOM COLLINS:
Okeh 45119 *Four Sons Of A Gun*...........	8.00 -	12.00
45132 *Little Brown Jug*...............	8.00 -	12.00
45140 *Chicken You Can't Roost Too High For Me*	8.00 -	12.00

COLT BROTHERS:
Melotone 12106 *Eleven More Months & Ten More Days*........................	5.00 -	8.00
12314 *Eleven More Months...part ¾*........	5.00 -	8.00
12333 *That Goes On For Days And Days*....	5.00 -	8.00
12348 *Hang It On The Hen House*.......	5.00 -	8.00
12449 *In 1992*.......................	5.00 -	8.00
12458 *Our Home Town Mountain Band*.....	5.00 -	8.00
12483 *Somethin' I Et*................	5.00 -	8.00
12506 *After The Old Barn Dance*........	5.00 -	8.00
12601 *The Last Words I Said*...........	5.00 -	8.00
(Note: Above probably issued contemporaneon Banner, Oriole, Perfect, Romeo.)		

FIDDLIN' COLVIN:
Victor 40271 *Old Lady Blues*..............	20.00 -	30.00

HITER COLVIN:
Victor 23815 *Indian War Woop*..............	30.00 -	40.00
40239 *Rabbit Up The Gum Stump*..........	20.00 -	30.00

PETER J. CONLON:
Okeh 45030 *Barn Dance*.................	5.00 -	8.00

CARL CONNER:
Columbia 15076-D *The Story Of Gerald Chapman*	8.00 -	12.00

HERB COOK:
Columbia 15729-D *Arkansas Sweetheart*.......	10.00 -	15.00
15778-D *Just A Little Happiness*............	10.00 -	15.00

JAMES COOK'S OLD TIME FIDDLERS:
Vocalion 5265 *Medley Of Old Fiddler's Favorites*	15.00 -	20.00

JOE COOK:
Bluebird 5135 *Got That Old Fashioned Love*...	5.00 -	8.00
6884 *Sweet Little Girl In Blue*..........	5.00 -	8.00
7362 *Nobody Knows My Name*..........	5.00 -	8.00

COON CREEK GIRLS:
Vocalion 04278, 04413, 04504, 04659........	4.00 -	8.00

COON HOLLOW BOYS:
Champion 15748 *Coon Hollow Boys At The Still*	10.00 -	15.00

WALTER COON (& HIS JOY BOYS):
Gennett 7002 *Huskin' Bee*.................	10.00 -	15.00
7005 *The Boys Best Friend*.............	15.00 -	20.00
7079 *Polly Wolly Doodle*.............	15.00 -	20.00
7097 *Fly Away Birdie To Heaven*........	15.00 -	25.00

CORN COB CRUSHERS:
Champion 16373 *Dill Pickle Rag*............	15.00 -	20.00
16449 *Lonesome Road Blues*..........	15.00 -	20.00
45178 *Lonesome Road Blues*..........	10.00 -	15.00

ARTHUR CORNWALL & JOHN GIBSON:
Champion 16429 *Walking The Highway*.......	15.00 -	20.00

COUCH & WILKS RAMBLERS:
Bluebird 7552 *Fourteen Days In Georgia*......	7.00 -	10.00

COURVILLE & McGEE:
Vocalion 5315 *Courville & McGee Waltz*......	20.00 -	30.00

COX & HENSON:
Champion 16694 *National Blues*............	20.00 -	30.00

(BILL) COX & (CLIFF) HOBBS:

Titles, issued contemporaneously on Banner, Conqueror, Melotone, Oriole, Perfect, Romeo, include: *Alimony Woman; Barefoot Boy With Boots On; Best Friend I Ever Had; Blue Eyed Sally; Blue Ridge Mountain Blues; Bring Back The Sunshine And Roses; Brown Eyes; Brown's Ferry Blues; The Clouds Gwine Roll Away; The Democratic Donkey; Down In Dixie Land; East Cairo Street Blues; The Fate Of Will Rogers And Wiley Post; Fiddling Soldier; The Ganster's Yodel; Hard Luck Blues; I Get Those Drunken Blues; I Long For Your Love Each Day; Lay My Head Beneath The Rose; Long Chain Charlie Blues; Married Life Blues; Midnight Special; My Gamblin' Days; New Mama; N.R.A. Blues; Ramblin' Hobo; Sally Let Your Bangs Hang Down; Sweethearts And Kisses; Sweet Kentucky Lou; The Trial Of Bruno Hauptmann; When The Women Get In Power; Where The Red Roses Grow; Will And Wiley's Last Flight* ....

....	5.00 -	10.00
Champion 45007, 45021, 45092, 45106, 45141, 45157	7.00 -	10.00
Gennett 6928 *California Blues*	25.00 -	35.00
6946 *Daddy And Home*	25.00 -	35.00
6974 *Hungry Hash House Blues*	25.00 -	35.00
7004 *When We Meet On That Beautiful Shore*	25.00 -	35.00
7037 *Back Home In Tennessee*	25.00 -	35.00
7052 *When We Sing Of Home*	25.00 -	35.00
7080 *Alabama Blues*	25.00 -	35.00
7155 *I Love The Jailer's Daughter*	25.00 -	35.00
7226 *My Rough And Rowdy Ways*	25.00 -	35.00
7266 *The Hand Car Yodel*	25.00 -	35.00
Vocalion 03043, 03161, 03253, 03380	5.00 -	8.00
04077, 04148, 04235, 04341, 04454, 04641, 04811, 04869, 05055	3.00 -	6.00

RICHARD COX (& HIS NATIONAL FIDDLERS):

Champion 16475 *Sleeping Lulu*	20.00 -	30.00
16563 *East Tennessee Blues*	20.00 -	30.00
16693 *Chewing Chawin' Gum*	20.00 -	30.00
Champion 45040 *It Ain't No Good*	10.00 -	15.00

GENE CRABB:

Richtone 353 *Truck Stop Lucy*	———	

RILEY CRABTREE:

(Star) Talent 719, 724, 756, 761	4.00 -	8.00

EDWARD L. CRAIN (THE TEXAS COWBOY):

Columbia 15710-D *Bandit Cole Younger*	15.00 -	25.00
Crown 3238 *Twenty-One Years*	10.00 -	15.00
3239 *Little Joe The Wrangler*	10.00 -	15.00
3250 *Cowboy's Home Sweet Home*	10.00 -	15.00
3275 *The Old Chisholm Trail*	10.00 -	15.00

CRAMER BROTHERS

(BOB) CRANFORD & (ERNEST) THOMPSON (with THE RED FOX CHASERS):

Champion 16243 *That Sweetie Of Mine*	20.00 -	30.00
16261 *Otto Wood*	20.00 -	30.00
16490 *Sweet Fern*	20.00 -	30.00
16676 *Katy Cline*	20.00 -	30.00
16768 *Two Babes In The Woods*	20.00 -	30.00
45061, 45097	5.00 -	8.00
Gennett 6636 *Stolen Love*	20.00 -	30.00
6672 *Something Wrong With My Gal*	20.00 -	30.00
6901 *Little Sweetheart Pal Of Mine*	20.00 -	30.00
6945 *Devilish Mary*	20.00 -	30.00
6959 *How I Love My Mabel*	20.00 -	30.00

AL CRAVER (& CHARLIE WELLS):

Columbia 15031-D, 15034-D, 15044-D, 15046-D, 15049-D, 15053-D, 15056-D, 15060-D, 15065-D, 15086-D, 15098-D, 15109-D, 15121-D, 15126-D, 15135-D, 15146-D, 15169-D, 15192-D, 15218-D, 15223-D, 15251-D, 15256-D	3.00 -	5.00

15449-D, 15512-D, 15530-D, 15546-D, 15561-D, 15585-D	5.00 -	8.00

ALVIN CRAWFORD:

Superior 2528 *I Sit Broken Hearted*	20.00 -	30.00

CRAZY HILL BILLIES BAND:

Okeh 45575 *Danced All Night With A Bottle In My Hand*	10.00 -	15.00
45579 *Going Down The Road Feeling Bad*	10.00 -	15.00

CROCKER & CANNON:

Challenge 423 *Two Faithful Lovers*	5.00 -	8.00

CROCKETT FAMILY MOUNTAINEERS; CROCKETT'S KENTUCKY MOUNTAINEERS:

Brunswick 290 *Hard Cider Song*	10.00 -	15.00
291 *Medley*	10.00 -	15.00
353 *Bonaparte's Retreat*	10.00 -	15.00
394 *After The Ball*	10.00 -	15.00
Crown 3074 *Lightnin' Express*	10.00 -	15.00
3075 *Buffalo Gals Medley*	10.00 -	15.00
3121 *Sweet Betsy From Pike*	10.00 -	15.00
3172 *Cripple Creek*	10.00 -	15.00
3188 *Skip To My Lou*	10.00 -	15.00
Paramount 3277 *Granny's Old Arm Chair*	15.00 -	25.00
3302 *Roving Gambler*	15.00 -	25.00
3303 *Take Me Back To Old Kentucky*	15.00 -	25.00

JOHNNY (& ALBERT) CROCKETT (& CROCKETT'S KENTUCKY MOUNTAINEERS):

Brunswick 372 *Fresno Blues*	10.00 -	15.00
Crown 3101 *I Was Born About 10,000 Years Ago*	10.00 -	15.00
Paramount 3278 *The Blind Man's Lament*	20.00 -	30.00
Specialty 702 *Just A Minute*	4.00 -	7.00

BALLARD CROSS:

Vocalion 5359 *My Poodle Dog*	7.00 -	10.00
5377 *The Wabash Cannon Ball*	7.00 -	10.00
5402 *Down Where The Swanee River Flows*	7.00 -	10.00

BOB CROSS & HIS TROUBADOURS:

Personality 321/322 *Black Mountain Rag*	5.00 -	8.00
323/324 *Combination Rag*	5.00 -	8.00

(HUGH) CROSS (& McCARTT/BOB NICHOLS/RILEY PUCKETT):

Columbia 15143-D *Sweet Rosie O'Grady*	5.00 -	8.00
15182-D *I'm Going Away From The Cotton Fields*	5.00 -	8.00
15206-D *Red River Valley*	5.00 -	8.00
15231-D *The Mansion Of Aching Hearts*	5.00 -	8.00
15266-D *Where The Morning Glories Grow*	5.00 -	8.00
15337-D *Clover Blossoms*	8.00 -	12.00
15365-D *Never No More Blues*	8.00 -	12.00
15421-D *Go Feather Your Nest*	8.00 -	12.00
15439-D *Wabash Cannon Ball*	8.00 -	12.00
15455-D *Gonna Raise A Ruckus Tonight*	10.00 -	15.00
15458-D *Pretty Little Blue-Eyed Sally*	5.00 -	8.00
15478-D *Smiles*	7.00 -	10.00
15480-D *I Left My Gal In The Mountains*	7.00 -	10.00
15482-D *Kickapoo Medicine Show*	15.00 -	20.00
15613-D *My Little Home In Tennessee*	10.00 -	15.00

CROWDER BROTHERS:

Titles, issued contemporaneously on Banner, Conqueror, Melotone, Oriole, Perfect, Romeo, include: *Blonde Headed Baby; Depot Blues; Dying In Ashville Jail; Got No Use For Women; Lonesome Lost Gal Blues; New Maple On The Hill; The Sailing Ship* ......

......	7.00 -	10.00
Vocalion 03030 *Got No Use For Women*	7.00 -	10.00

(PAUL) CRUTCHFIELD (& CLOTWORTHY):

Okeh 45261 *Death's River*	5.00 -	8.00
45266 *Uncle Hiram's Trip To The City*	5.00 -	8.00

CRUTHERS BROTHERS:

Okeh 45307 *Carolina Moon*	7.00 -	10.00

CRYSEL BOYS with ALLEN BULLARD:

Titles, issued contemporaneously on Banner,

Melotone, Oriole, Perfect, Romeo: *Crazy Blues; My Gal Kate* .... 10.00 - 15.00

CRYSTAL SPRING RAMBLERS:
Vocalion 03856 *Down In Arkansas* .... 5.00 - 8.00

CUMBERLAND RIDGE RUNNERS:
Conqueror 8310 *I'm Here To Get My Baby Out Of Jail* .... 5.00 - 8.00
Melotone 12981 *Roundin' Up The Yearlings* .... 5.00 - 8.00
Perfect 12993 *Roundin' Up The Yearlings* ...... 5.00 - 8.00

CUMBERLAND STRING BAND:
Superior 2536 *Wink The Other Eye* .... 20.00 - 30.00

DAVE CUTRELL:
Okeh 45057 *Pistol Pete's Midnight Special* ..... 10.00 - 15.00

DA COSTA WOLTZ'S SOUTHERN BROAD-CASTERS (featuring FRANK JENKINS/PRICE GOODSON):
Gennett 6187 *Lost Train Blues* .... 20.00 - 30.00
6220 *John Brown's Dream* .... 20.00 - 30.00
6223 *Roving Cowboy* .... 20.00 - 30.00
6240 *Evening Star Waltz* .... 20.00 - 30.00

VERNON DALHART:
This artist recorded for almost every label during the 1920's. Most of his records command minimal premiums. The selective listing following represents only a tiny fraction of his recorded output.
Black Patti 8027 *The Mississippi Flood* .... 10.00 - 20.00
8028 *Barbara Allen* .... 10.00 - 20.00
Buddy 8037 *The Great Titanic* .... 10.00 - 20.00
Edison (thin) 11002 *The West Plains Explosion* .. 10.00 - 15.00
20001 *Eleven Cent Cotton* .... 10.00 - 15.00
20003 *Big Rock Candy Mountain* .... 10.00 - 15.00
20010 *Dixie Way* .... 10.00 - 15.00
Edison (thick) 51459, 51541, 51557, 51584, 51597, 51605, 51607, 51608, 51609, 51610, 51611, 51620, 51621, 51637, 51643, 51649, 51669, 51670, 51693, 51741, 51718, 51729, 51735, 51749, 51807, 51827, 51856, 51883, 51901, 51949, 51974, 52020, 52029, 52088, 52095, 52118, 52134, 52144, 52174, 52229, 52248, 52307, 52335, 52423, 52434, 52457, 52472, 52487, 52533, 52558, 52566, 52599, 52628 .. 5.00 - 10.00
52077 *My Horses Ain't Hungry* .... 10.00 - 15.00
Herschel Gold Seal 2005 *The Miami Storm* ..... 10.00 - 15.00
2018 *Just A Melody* .... 10.00 - 15.00
Herwin 75501 *Blue Ridge Mountain Blues* ...... 10.00 - 20.00
75505 *The Prisoner's Song* .... 10.00 - 20.00
Herwin 75506 *The New River Train* .... 10.00 - 20.00
75507 *Jesse James* .... 10.00 - 20.00
75517 *The Life Of Tom Watson* .... 10.00 - 20.00
75531 *Papa's Billy Goat* .... 10.00 - 20.00
75540 *The Wreck Of The Royal Palm* ...... 10.00 - 20.00
75546 *The Mississippi Flood* .... 10.00 - 20.00

(TOMMY) DANDURAND & THE BARN DANCE FIDDLERS/HIS BARN DANCE GANG OF WLS/HIS GANG;
Gennett 6273 *Buffalo Gal* .... 12.00 - 18.00
6351 *McLeod's Reel* .... 12.00 - 18.00
Supertone 9156 *Big Town Fling* .... 6.00 - 10.00
9157 *Buffalo Girl* .... 6.00 - 10.00
9158 *Haste To The Wedding* .... 6.00 - 10.00
9159 *McLeod's Reel* .... 6.00 - 10.00
9160 *The Irish Washerwoman* .... 6.00 - 10.00
9162 *Devil's Dream* .... 6.00 - 10.00

(TOM) DARBY & (JIMMIE) TARLTON:
Columbia 15197-D *Birmingham Town* .... 8.00 - 12.00
15212-D *Birmingham Jail* .... 8.00 - 12.00
15254-D *After The Ball* .... 15.00 - 20.00
15293-D *The Irish Police* .... 15.00 - 20.00
15219-D *Mexican Rag* .... 15.00 - 20.00
15330-D *Heavy Hearted Blues* .... 15.00 - 20.00

15360-D *The Rainbow Division* .... 15.00 - 20.00
15375-D *Birmingham Jail No. 2* .... 15.00 - 20.00
15388-D *If You Ever Learn To Love Me* ..... 15.00 - 20.00
15403-D *Down In The Old Cherry Orchard* ... 20.00 - 30.00
15419-D *Slow Wicked Blues* .... 20.00 - 30.00
15436-D *Sweet Sarah Blues* .... 20.00 - 30.00
15452-D *Black Jack Moonshine* .... 20.00 - 30.00
15477-D *All Bound Down In Texas* .... 20.00 - 30.00
15492-D *Little Bessie* .... 20.00 - 30.00
15511-D *Freight Train Ramble* .... 20.00 - 30.00
15528-D *Jack And May* .... 20.00 - 30.00
15552-D *Faithless Husband* .... 20.00 - 30.00
15572-D *My Little Blue Heaven* .... 20.00 - 30.00
15591-D *The Maple On The Hill* .... 20.00 - 30.00
15611-D *Hard Time Blues* .... 35.00 - 50.00
15624-D *Beggar Joe* .... 35.00 - 50.00
15674-D *The Black Sheep* .... 35.00 - 50.00
15684-D *Gamblin' Jim* .... 35.00 - 50.00
15701-D *Rising Sun Blues* .... 40.00 - 60.00
15715-D *Going Back To My Texas Home* .... 40.00 - 60.00

MOUNTAIN DEW DARE:
Okeh 45170 *Don't Love A Smiling Sweetheart* .. 5.00 - 8.00

CHUCK DARLING:
Bluebird 5285 *Harmonica Rag* .... 5.00 - 8.00
Victor 40330 *Blowin' The Blues* .... 20.00 - 30.00

DAVE AND HOWARD:
Victor 23566 *Bay Rum Blues* .... 30.00 - 40.00
23577 *Serves 'Em Fine* .... 30.00 - 40.00

CARL DAVENPORT & HIS GANG:
Vocalion 5371 *Broken Hearted Lover* .... 8.00 - 12.00
5394 *Double Eagle March* .... 8.00 - 12.00

EMMETT DAVENPORT:
Supertone 9178 *The Dingy Miner's Cabin* ..... 8.00 - 12.00
9179 *The Dying Girl's Message* .... 8.00 - 12.00
9388 *She Ain't Built That Way* .... 8.00 - 12.00
9539 *The Virginia Moonshiner* .... 8.00 - 12.00
9642 *Johnny The Drunkard* .... 8.00 - 12.00
9774 *An Old Fashioned Picture Of Mother* ... 8.00 - 12.00

HOMER DAVENPORT & THE YOUNG BROTHERS:
Silvertone 4089 *Down In Tennessee Blues* ..... 10.00 - 15.00

DAVIS & NELSON:
Paramount 3186 *I Shall Not Be Moved* .... 15.00 - 20.00
3187 *I Don't Bother Work* .... 15.00 - 20.00
3188 *I Don't Want Your Greenback Dollar* ... 15.00 - 20.00
3227 *Charming Betsy* .... 15.00 - 20.00
Q.R.S. 9014 *I Don't Want Your Greenback Dollar* 15.00 - 20.00
9018 *I Don't Bother Work* .... 15.00 - 20.00

DAVIS, STOKES & LAYNE:
Gennett 6548 *Way Down In Alabam'* .... 20.00 - 30.00

DAVIS TRIO:
Paramount 3238 *Sleepy Hollow* .... 15.00 - 20.00

C.W./CHARLIE DAVIS:
Gennett 6637 *Sweet Bunch Of Daisies* .... 10.00 - 15.00
Timely Tunes 1559 *Down In A Southern Town*. 10.00 - 15.00

CLAUDE DAVIS (TRIO) (& BOB NICHOLS):
Brunswick 503 *Over In The Hills Of California* .. 5.00 - 8.00
Columbia 15397-D *We Were Pals Together* ..... 5.00 - 8.00
15466-D *Underneath The Southern Moon* .... 5.00 - 8.00
15740-D *Standing By The Highway* .... 8.00 - 12.00

EVA DAVIS:
Columbia 129-D *Wild Bill Jones* .... 5.00 - 8.00

JEWELL DAVIS:
Okeh 45152 *Thinking Of The Days I've Done Wrong* 5.00 - 8.00

JIMMIE DAVIS:
Bluebird 5005 *She's A Hum-Dum Dinger* .... 15.00 - 20.00
5156 *The Keyhole In The Door* .... 20.00 - 30.00
5187 *I Wonder If She's Blue* .... 20.00 - 30.00
5359 *I Want Her Tailor-Made* .... 20.00 - 30.00
5394 *Beautiful Texas* .... 7.00 - 10.00
5425 *Alimony Blues* .... 20.00 - 30.00

5496	Arabella Blues	15.00 -	20.00
5570	Easy Rider Blues	20.00 -	30.00
5635	Triflin' Mama Blues	20.00 -	30.00
5697	I'll Get Mine Bye And Bye	20.00 -	30.00
5699	Red Nightgown Blues	20.00 -	30.00
5751	Sewing Machine Blues	20.00 -	30.00
5806	I'll Be Happy Today	20.00 -	30.00
5965	Minute Man, Part 1/2	20.00 -	30.00
6040	Dentist Blues	20.00 -	30.00
6167	Moonlight	15.00 -	20.00
6236	Sweet Sixteen	15.00 -	20.00
6249	The Davis Limited	15.00 -	20.00
6272	Organ Grinder Blues	15.00 -	20.00
6437	Yo Yo Mama	15.00 -	20.00
7071	My Dixie Sweetheart	15.00 -	20.00
Victor 23517	Arabella Blues	30.00 -	50.00
23525	In Arkansas	30.00 -	50.00
23544	Penitentiary Blues	30.00 -	50.00
23559	Before You Say Farewell	30.00 -	50.00
23573	Pea Pickin' Papa	30.00 -	50.00
23587	She's A Hum-Dinger	30.00 -	50.00
23601	The Davis Limited	30.00 -	50.00
23620	Market House Blues	30.00 -	50.00
23628	Wild And Reckless John	30.00 -	50.00
23648	Lonely Hobo	30.00 -	50.00
23659	Red Nightgown Blues	40.00 -	60.00
23674	Davis' Salty Dog	40.00 -	60.00
23688	1982 Blues	40.00 -	60.00
23703	High Behind Blues	40.00 -	60.00
23718	Cowboy's Home Sweet Home	40.00 -	60.00
23746	Shotgun Wedding	40.00 -	60.00
23749	Bury Me In Old Kentucky	40.00 -	60.00
23752	Hold 'Er Newt	40.00 -	60.00
23763	Organ Grinder Blues	50.00 -	75.00
23778	The Gambler's Return	50.00 -	75.00
23793	Yo Yo Mama	50.00 -	80.00
40154	The Barroom Message	20.00 -	30.00
40215	Out Of Town Blues	30.00 -	40.00
40286	Doggone That Train	30.00 -	40.00
40302	My Louisiana Girl	30.00 -	40.00
40332	Settling Down For Life	20.00 -	30.00

STAN DAVIS:
Okeh 45401 The Body In The Bag ... 10.00 - 15.00
DAVE DAWSON'S STRING BAND:
Superior 2517 Over The Waves ... 10.00 - 15.00
2575 Grey Eagle ... 10.00 - 15.00
DECKERS:
Paramount 3281 When It's Night Time In Nevada ... 10.00 - 20.00
3323 That Little Boy Of Mine ... 10.00 - 20.00
ROSCOE & SAM DELLINGER:
Bluebird 6852 The Ohio River Floods ... 5.00 - 10.00
6868 Tellin' The Stars ... 5.00 - 10.00
DELMORE BROTHERS:

Bluebird 5299	Lonesome Yodel Blues	10.00 -	15.00
5338	The Frozen Girl	10.00 -	15.00
5258	I'm Leaving You	10.00 -	15.00
5403	Browns Ferry Blues	5.00 -	8.00
5467	Ramblin' Minded Blues	8.00 -	12.00
5531	Blue Railroad Train	8.00 -	12.00
5589	Smoky Mountain Bill	8.00 -	12.00
5653	I'm Mississippi Bound	8.00 -	12.00
5741	Lonesome Jailhouse Blues	8.00 -	12.00
5857	Hey! Hey! I'm Memphis Bound	8.00 -	12.00
5893	Brown's Ferry Blues, Part 2	8.00 -	12.00
5925	Lorena, The Slave	7.00 -	10.00
5957	I Long To See My Mother	7.00 -	10.00
6002	I Got The Knasas City Blues	7.00 -	10.00
6019	The Fugitive's Lament	7.00 -	10.00
6034	Alabama Lullaby	7.00 -	10.00
6312	The Nashville Blues	7.00 -	10.00
6349	I'm Worried Now	7.00 -	10.00

6386	Lonesome Yodel Blues No. 2	7.00 -	10.00
6401	Carry Me Back To Alabama	7.00 -	10.00
6522	The Lover's Warning	7.00 -	10.00
6841	Southern Moon	7.00 -	10.00
6915	No Drunkard Can Enter There	7.00 -	10.00
6949	False Hearted Girl	7.00 -	10.00
6998	No One	7.00 -	10.00
7029	Don't Forget Me, Darling	7.00 -	10.00
7129	Singing My Troubles Away	7.00 -	10.00
7192	They Say It Is Sinful To Flirt	7.00 -	10.00
7262	The Budded Rose	7.00 -	10.00
7300	Weary Lonesome Blues	7.00 -	10.00
7337	Lead Me	7.00 -	10.00
7383	The Farmers Girl	7.00 -	10.00
7436	Goodbye Booze	7.00 -	10.00
7496	'Cause I Don't Mean To Cry	5.00 -	10.00
7560	Big Ball In Texas	5.00 -	10.00
7672	Wonderful There	5.00 -	10.00
7741	Brother, Take Warning	5.00 -	10.00
7778	Alcatraz Island Blues	5.00 -	10.00
7913	Leavin' On That Train	5.00 -	10.00
7957	Where Is My Sailor Boy?	5.00 -	10.00
7991	The Cannon Ball	5.00 -	10.00
8031	Fifteen Miles From Birmingham	5.00 -	10.00
8052	Home On The River	5.00 -	10.00
8177	Baby, You're Throwing Me Down	5.00 -	10.00
8204	Wabash Blues	5.00 -	10.00
8215	I Loved You Better Than You Knew	5.00 -	10.00
8230	Gambler's Yodel	5.00 -	10.00
8247	Nothing But The Blues	5.00 -	10.00
8264	I'm Alabama Bound	5.00 -	10.00
8290	A Better Range Is Home	5.00 -	10.00
8404	Scatterbrain Mama	5.00 -	10.00
8418	Back To Birmingham	5.00 -	10.00
8451	Over The Hills	5.00 -	10.00
8488	The Eastern Gate	5.00 -	10.00
8557	Rainin' On The Mountain	5.00 -	10.00
8613	Storms Are On The Ocean	5.00 -	10.00
8637	Heart Of Sorrow	5.00 -	10.00
8687	That Yodelin' Gal, Miss Julie	5.00 -	10.00

(Note: Some of above titles were also issued on Mont-
gomery Ward label.)
Columbia 15724-D Got The Kansas City Blues .. 50.00 - 80.00
Decca 5878, 5890, 5897, 5907, 5925, 5970, 6000,
6051, 6080 ... 3.00 - 6.00
King 509, 514, 518, 525, 527, 533 ... 3.00 - 5.00
MORGAN DENMON:
Okeh 45075 Naomi Wise ... 7.00 - 10.00
45105 I've Still Got Ninety-Nine ... 7.00 - 10.00
45306 The Two Drummers ... 8.00 - 12.00
45327 The Drunkard's Dream ... 8.00 - 12.00
DICK DEVALL:
Timely Tunes 1563 Out On The Lone Star Cow Trail 8.00 - 12.00
**CHARLES M. (BUDDY) DE WITTE (THE
SINGING MOONSHINER/
MOUNTAINEER; THE VAGABOND
YODELER):**
Champion 16371 Vagabond Yodel ... 20.00 - 30.00
16444 Vagabond Yodel No. 2 ... 20.00 - 30.00
16658 My Kentucky Cabin ... 20.00 - 30.00
16680 Rose Of Mother's Day ... 20.00 - 30.00
16759 The Girl I Met In Bluefield ... 20.00 - 30.00
16825 The Sad, Sad Story ... 20.00 - 30.00
AL DEXTER & HIS TROOPERS:
Vocalion 03435 New Jellyroll Blues ... 7.00 - 10.00
03569, 03719, 03927, 03988 ... 5.00 - 8.00
04174, 04277, 04327, 04405, 04988, 05042 ... 4.00 - 7.00
DEZURIK SISTERS:
Vocalion 04616, 04704, 04781 ... 4.00 - 7.00
DICKSON & CARROLL:
Superior 2523 Advice To Husband Seekers ... 15.00 - 20.00

BOB DICKSON:
Victor 23633, 23679 . . . . 5.00 - 8.00

M.S. DILLEHAY:
Victor 40155 *Mother-In-Law* . . . . 10.00 - 15.00

JOHN DILLESHAW & THE STRING MARVEL:
Okeh 45328 *Cotton Patch Rag* . . . . 20.00 - 30.00

(SEVEN FOOT) DILLEY (see DILLY)

JOHN DILLINGSHAW:
Vocalion 5459 *Farmer's Blues* . . . . 30.00 - 40.00

DILLY, LINDSEY, LINDSEY,, GRAY & BROWN; DILLY, TUCKER, LEE, STOKES & MELVIN; (SEVEN FOOT) DILLY & HIS DILL PICKLES:
Brunswick 489 *A Bootlegger's Joine In Atlanta* . . 20.00 - 30.00
575 *Kenesaw Mountain Rag* . . . . 20.00 - 30.00
Vocalion 5419 *Square Dance Fight On Bald Top Mountain* . . . . 30.00 - 40.00
5421 *Bust Down Stomp* . . . . 30.00 - 40.00
5436 *Georgia Bust Down* . . . . 30.00 - 40.00
5446 *Lye Soap* . . . . 30.00 - 40.00
5454 *A Georgia Barbecue At Stone Mountain* . 30.00 - 40.00

DIX & WILSON:
Bluebird 5397, 5472 . . . . 4.00 - 7.00

DIXIE CRACKERS:
Paramount 3151 *The Old Bell Cow* . . . . 10.00 - 15.00

DIXIE HARMONIZERS:
Gennett 6872 *Gonna Raise A Ruckus Tonight* . . 25.00 - 40.00

DIXIE MOUNTAINEERS:
Edison 52057 *Hop Light Ladies* . . . . 10.00 - 15.00

DIXIE STRING BAND:
Paramount 3164 *Atlanta Special* . . . . 10.00 - 15.00
3166 *Show Me The Way To Go Home* . . . . . . 10.00 - 15.00

DIXIELAND SWINGSTERS:
Bluebird 7857, 7882, 7899, 7948 . . . . 4.00 - 6.00

DIXIE RAMBLERS: (see also DOUG BINE)
Bluebird 6118, 6179, 6248, 6352, 6442 . . . . 4.00 - 8.00

DIXIE REELERS:
Bluebird 6461, 6713, 6738, 6831 . . . . 4.00 - 8.00

DIXIE STRING BAND:
Columbia 15273-D *Dixie Waltz* . . . . 7.00 - 10.00
Silvertone 3516 *Soldier's Joy* . . . . 7.00 - 10.00

DIXON'S CLOD HOPPERS:
Melotone 12007 *Steamboat Bill* . . . . 5.00 - 8.00
12052 *Wreck On The Southern Old 97* . . . . . . 5.00 - 8.00

DIXON BROTHERS:
Bluebird 6327 *Intoxicated Rat* . . . . 5.00 - 10.00
6441 *Weave Room Blues* . . . . 5.00 - 10.00
6462 *Answer To Maple On The Hill* . . . . 5.00 - 10.00
6582 *My Girl In Sunny Tennessee* . . . . 5.00 - 10.00
6630, 6691, 6809, 6867, 6979, 7020, 7263, 7449, 7674, 7767, 7801 . . . . 4.00 - 8.00

DIXON TRIO:
Victor 23790 *Carolina Lullaby* . . . . 10.00 - 20.00

BOB DIXON:
Victor 23752 *There Ain't No Man In The Moon* 30.00 - 50.00
23764 *Old Bill Smith* . . . . 10.00 - 15.00
23787 *What Are We Gonna Use For Money* . 10.00 - 15.00

JOHNNY DODDS:
Okeh 45417 *The Railroad Boomer* . . . . 50.00 - 80.00
45462 *No One To Call Me Darling* . . . . 50.00 - 80.00
45472 *Slu Foot Lue* . . . . 50.00 - 80.00
45560 *Cowboy Yodel* . . . . 50.00 - 80.00

DONALDSON QUARTET:
Victor 23788 *Hannah From Panama* . . . . 7.00 - 10.00

DONALDSON TRIO:
Bluebird 5003, 5035, 5060, 5134, 5166, 5221 . . . 3.00 - 6.00

LOUIE DONALDSON & HOKE RICE:
Gennett 6885 *The Gang's All Here* . . . . 15.00 - 20.00

BUSTER DOSS & HIS ARKANSAS PLAYBOYS:
Talent 734 *Playboy Boogie* . . . . 4.00 - 7.00

EVAN DOUGLAS & NATE SMITH:
Champion 15651 *If I Could Only Blot Out The Past* 10.00 - 15.00
15711 *If I Only Had A Home* . . . . 10.00 - 15.00

THE DOWN HOMERS: (see also WOWO DOWN HOMERS)
Voque 736 *Out Where The West Winds Blow* . . 12.00 - 16.00

DOYLE BROS:
TNT 113 *T.N.T. Baby* . . . . ———

FRANK DUDGEON:
Champion 16532 *Atlanta Bound* . . . . 20.00 - 30.00
16575 *Sweet Betsy From Pike* . . . . 20.00 - 30.00
16580 *The Crime I Didn't Do* . . . . 20.00 - 30.00
16602 *Birmingham Jail No. 2* . . . . 20.00 - 30.00

FRANK DUNBAR:
Superior 2538 *Nobody's Darling On Earth* . . . . 15.00 - 20.00

DUNCAN BOYS:
Supertone 9676 *Kentucky Stomp* . . . . 10.00 - 15.00

DUNCAN SISTERS:
Columbia 15745-D *Dusty Roads* . . . . 5.00 - 8.00

UNCLE ECK DUNFORD:
Victor 20880 *The Whip-Poor-Will Song* . . . . . . 10.00 - 15.00
20938 *Barney McCoy* . . . . 10.00 - 15.00
21131 *My First Bicycle Ride* . . . . 10.00 - 15.00
21244 *The Taffy-Pulling Party* . . . . 10.00 - 15.00
21578 *Sweat Summer Has Gone Away* . . . . . . 10.00 - 15.00
40060 *Old Shoes And Leggin's* . . . . 10.00 - 15.00

BARNEY DUNROE:
Champion 15523 *Six Feet Of Earth* . . . . 10.00 - 15.00

DUPREE'S ROME BOYS:
Okeh 45320 *Wedding Bells Waltz* . . . . 15.00 - 20.00
45356 *Cat Rag-Breakdown* . . . . 15.00 - 20.00

DYE'S SACRED HARP SINGERS:
Gennett 6889 *Amazing Grace* . . . . 15.00 - 20.00

DYKES' MAGIC CITY TRIO:
Brunswick 120 *Cotton-Eyed Joe* . . . . 15.00 - 20.00
125 *Ida Red* . . . . 15.00 - 20.00
127 *Poor Ellen Smith* . . . . 15.00 - 20.00
128 *Hook And Line* . . . . 15.00 - 20.00
129 *Huckleberry Blues* . . . . 15.00 - 20.00
130 *Far Beyond The Blue Sky* . . . . 15.00 - 20.00
Vocalion 5143 *Frankie* . . . . 15.00 - 20.00
5181 *Callahan's Reel* . . . . 15.00 - 20.00

DICK DYSON (& HIS MUSICAL TEXANS):
Blue Bonnet 126 *Waited Too Long Blues* . . . . . 4.00 - 7.00
Tri-State 113 *Hell's Fire* . . . . ———

EARL & BILL:
Vocalion 15014 *On The Oregon Trail* . . . . 5.00 - 8.00

EAST TEXAS SERENADERS:
Brunswick 282 *Acorn Stomp* . . . . 7.00 - 10.00
298 *Deacon Jones* . . . . 7.00 - 10.00
379 *Three-In-One Two Step* . . . . 7.00 - 10.00
429 *McKinney Waltz* . . . . 7.00 - 10.00
453 *Babe* . . . . 7.00 - 10.00
538 *Ozark Rag* . . . . 7.00 - 10.00
562 *Mineola Rag* . . . . 7.00 - 10.00
Columbia 15229-D *Combination Rag* . . . . 5.00 - 8.00

GARNER ECKLER & ROLAND GAINES (YODELING TWINS):
Champion 45043 *Moonlight And Skies* . . . . 5.00 - 8.00
45087 *Mountain Rangers Lullaby* . . . . 5.00 - 8.00

GEORGE EDGIN'S CORN DODGERS:
Columbia 15754-D *My Ozark Mountain Home* . 30.00 - 50.00

DAVE EDWARDS & HIS ALABAMA BOYS:
Decca 5470, 5478, 5493, 5507, 5522, 5536, 5564 4.00 - 7.00

HAROLD EDWARDS:
Champion 15702 *Who Cares What You Have Been* 7.00 - 10.00

ELK CREEK TRIO:
Champion 15584 *Silvery Bell* . . . . 5.00 - 8.00

ELKINS' STRINGED STEPPERS:
Okeh 45079 *Speed* . . . . 15.00 - 20.00

RAY ELKINS:
Champion 15831 *The Boy's Best Friend* . . . . . . 8.00 - 12.00

ELLIOTT (& MITCHELL):

Victor 23646 *When It's Springtime In The Blue Ridge*
Mountains . . . . 8.00 - 12.00
   23652 *When The Oriole Sings Again* . . . . 8.00 - 12.00

ELM CITY QUARTET:

Champion 16827 *The Tree Song* . . . . 7.00 - 10.00

ELMER & JUD:

Broadway 8052 *Turkey In The Straw* . . . . 5.00 - 8.00
Conqueror 7332 *Turkey In The Straw* . . . . . . 5.00 - 8.00
Oriole 1414 *Turkey In The Straw* . . . . 5.00 - 8.00

EVANS' OLD TIMERS:

Champion 16512 *Honeysuckle Time* . . . . 35.00 - 50.00
   16531 *The Old Elm Tree* . . . . 35.00 - 50.00
   16709 *No Low Down Hanging Around* . . . . . . 50.00 - 80.00

CLYDE EVANS BAND:

Columbia 15597-D *How I Got My Gal* . . . . 10.00 - 15.00

JOHN B. EVANS:

Brunswick 237 *Three Night's Experience* . . . . 8.00 - 12.00
   276 *The Last Mile Of The Way* . . . . 8.00 - 12.00
Supertone 2051 *Mother's Grave* . . . . 7.00 - 10.00

CLAY EVERHEART & THE NORTH CAROLINA COOPER BOYS:

Columbia 15737-D *Standing By A Window* . . . . . 40.00 - 60.00

BOB FAGAN:

Challenge 839 *She Was A Moonshiner's Daughter* 7.00 - 10.00

JIMMIE FAIR:

Kentucky 532 *I'll Walk Alone* . . . . 4.00 - 7.00
   533 *Just A Little Lovin'* . . . . 4.00 - 7.00
   538 *Anytime* . . . . 4.00 - 7.00

J.D. FARLEY:

Victor 40269 *Bill Was A Texas Lad* . . . . 10.00 - 15.00

FARM HANDS:

Paramount 3294 *The Old Hayloft Waltz* . . . . . . 10.00 - 15.00

HARVEY FARR:

Supertone 9320 *The Santa Barbara Earthquake* . . 8.00 - 12.00
   9372 *The Fate Of Ellen Smith* . . . . 8.00 - 12.00

FAY & THE JAYWALKERS:

Paramount 3100 *My Baby Don't Love Me* . . . . . 12.00 - 18.00
   3156 *Longing For Home* . . . . 12.00 - 18.00

BOB FERGUSON (& HS SCALAWAGGERS):

Columbia 15297-D, 15433-D, 15476-D, 15529-D,
   15553-D, 15616-D, 15664-D . . . . 4.00 - 8.00
   15677-D *The Strawberry Roan* . . . . 8.00 - 12.00
   15704-D, 15727-D, 15732-D, 15739-D, 15759-D,
   15782-D . . . . 4.00 - 8.00
Victor 23697, 23704, 23715 . . . . 8.00 - 12.00

JOHN FERGUSON:

Challenge 158 *Wild Bill Jones* . . . . 10.00 - 15.00
   159 *Railroad Daddy* . . . . 10.00 - 15.00
   324 *Wild Bill Jones* . . . . 10.00 - 15.00
   325 *Frankie's Gamblin' Man* . . . . 8.00 - 12.00
Supertone 9259 *Down Where The Swanee River*
Flows . . . . 6.00 - 10.00

FIDDLER JOE & HIS BOYS:

Okeh 45042 *Turkey In The Straw* . . . . 7.00 - 10.00

FLANNERY SISTERS:

Decca 5000, 5256, 5284 . . . . 4.00 - 7.00

ALAN FLATT & HIS BAND:

Jamboree 508 *It's All Over Now* . . . . 5.00 - 8.00
   511 *I'm Movin' On* . . . . 5.00 - 8.00

FLEMING & TOWNSEND:

Bluebird 5002, 5106, 5186, 5256, 5378, 5426, 5470,
   5497, 5566, 5634, 5694, 5695, 5696, 5821, 5874 4.00 - 8.00
Decca 5419, 5427, 5445, 5463, 5487, 5516 . . . . 4.00 - 8.00
Melotone 13231 *She's Just That Kind* . . . . 8.00 - 12.00
(Note: Probably issued also on Banner, Oriole, Perfect,
   Romeo.)
Victor 23509 *She's Always On My Mind* . . . . . . 20.00 - 30.00
   23520 *I'll Tell You About Women* . . . . 20.00 - 30.00
   23543 *Gonna Quit Drinkin'* . . . . 20.00 - 30.00
   23557 *Ramblin' Boy* . . . . 20.00 - 30.00

   23563 *I'm Leavin' This Town* . . . . 20.00 - 30.00
   23575 *Sweet Daddy From Tennessee* . . . . 20.00 - 30.00
   23594 *How Can You Be Mean To Me* . . . . . . 20.00 - 30.00
   23604 *Come And Drift With Me* . . . . 20.00 - 30.00
   23625 *I Feel So Blue* . . . . 20.00 - 30.00
   23635 *Blowin' The Blues* . . . . 25.00 - 35.00
   23666 *First Time In Jail* . . . . 25.00 - 35.00
   23676 *Yes, I Got Mine* . . . . 25.00 - 35.00
   23694 *Bad Reputations* . . . . 30.00 - 50.00
   23710 *That Lonesome Train* . . . . 30.00 - 50.00
   23758 *Blues Have Gone* . . . . 30.00 - 50.00
   23771 *When It's Hottest Down South* . . . . . . 30.00 - 50.00
   23789 *Picture On My Dresser* . . . . 30.00 - 50.00
   23793 *Do-Do-Daddling Thing* . . . . 30.00 - 50.00
   23814 *Right Always Wins* . . . . 30.00 - 50.00
   23829 *Gambler's Advice* . . . . 30.00 - 50.00
   40297 *She's Just That Kind* . . . . 15.00 - 25.00
   40321 *I'm Blue And Lonesome* . . . . 15.00 - 25.00

FLETCHER & FOSTER:

Champion 16121 *Travelin' North* . . . . 20.00 - 30.00
Victor 40232 *Charlotte Hot Step* . . . . 20.00 - 30.00

OTTO & JIM FLETCHER:

Superior 2669 *True And Trembling Brakeman* . . . 35.00 - 50.00
   2726 *When The Cactus Is In Bloom* . . . . 35.00 - 50.00
   2749 *Columbus Stockade Blues* . . . . 35.00 - 50.00
   2777 *The Chicken Roost Blues* . . . . 35.00 - 50.00

TEX FLETCHER (& JOE ROGERS); TEX FLETCHER'S LONELY COWBOYS:

Decca 5300, 5302, 5320, 5332, 5391, 5403, 5441,
   5460, 5489, 5500, 5520 . . . . 3.00 - 6.00

TIM FLORA & RUFUS LINGO:

Okeh 45311 *Stuttering Billy* . . . . 8.00 - 12.00

FLOYD COUNTY RAMBLERS:

Victor 23759 *Barn Dance* . . . . 20.00 - 30.00
   40307 *Sunny Tennessee* . . . . 20.00 - 30.00
   40331 *Aunt Dinah's Quilting Party* . . . . 20.00 - 30.00

ELZIE FLOYD & LEO BOSWELL:

Columbia 15150-D *Nellie Dare* . . . . 7.00 - 10.00
   15167-D *The Two Orphans* . . . . 7.00 - 10.00

DAVID FOLEY:

Challenge 393 *I'll Never Be Yours* . . . . 8.00 - 12.00
   394 *Poor Little Joe* . . . . 8.00 - 12.00
   397 *Train No. 45* . . . . 8.00 - 12.00

(RAMBLING) RED FOLEY (Acc. by THE CUMBERLAND RIDGE RUNNERS):

Titles, issued contemporaneously on Banner,
   Melotone, Oriole, Perfect, Romeo: *Blonde Headed*
   Girl; The Dying Rustler; Echoes of My Planta-
   tion Home; I Got The Freight Train Blues; Just
   One Little Kiss; The Lone Cowboy; Seven Long
   Years; Single Life Is Good Enough For Me . . 7.00 - 10.00

FORD & GRACE:

Okeh 45157 *Kiss Me Cindy* . . . . 7.00 - 10.00
   45237 *Hide Away* . . . . 7.00 - 10.00

JACK FORD:

Chess 4858 *That's All You Gotta Do* . . . . 4.00 - 7.00

OSCAR FORD:

Columbia 15437-D *Henry Ford's Model A* . . . . . 8.00 - 12.00

15554-D *Me And My Gal*................	8.00 -	12.00
15599-D *The Farmer's Dream*............	10.00 -	15.00
15634-D *Georgia Is My Home*............	10.00 -	15.00
15673-D *Little Nan*...................	10.00 -	15.00

FORT WORTH BOYS (see MILTON BROWN)
FORT WORTH DOUGHBOYS:

Bluebird 5257 *Nancy Jane*..............	40.00 -	60.00
Montgomery Ward 4416 *Nancy Jane*.......	40.00 -	60.00
Victor 23653 *Nancy Jane*...............	80.00 -	120.00

JOE FOSS & HIS HUNGRY SANDLAPPERS:

Columbia 15268-D *Oh! How She Lied*.......	7.00 -	10.00

(J.D.) FOSTER (& J.D. JAMES); FOSTER & (T.S.) YOUNG; JOHN FOSTER:

Champion 16733 *My Boyhood Happy Days*....	15.00 -	20.00
16753 *Some Day I'll Wander Back Again*.....	15.00 -	20.00
45037, 45102......................	5.00 -	8.00
Gennett 6434 *When I Was Single My Pockets Would Jingle*.	15.00 -	20.00
6791 *My Sarah Jane*..................	15.00 -	20.00

OWEN FOSTER:

Victor 20934 *Wilkes County Blues*.......	10.00 -	15.00

SALLY FOSTER & THE TRAVELERS:

Decca 5229, 5308, 5333, 5352, 5387......	3.00 -	5.00

FOUR BUZZ SAWS:

Vocalion 5471 *The Tree Song*...........	5.00 -	8.00

FOUR PICKLED PEPPERS:

Bluebird	3.00 -	5.00

FOUR VIRGINIANS:

Okeh 45163 *Two Little Lads*...........	10.00 -	15.00
45181 *Swing Your Partner*.............	10.00 -	15.00

FOX CHASERS:

Okeh 45477 *Red Wing*.................	15.00 -	25.00
45496 *Forked Deer*..................	15.00 -	25.00

FOX & DAVIS:

Supertone 9406 *Monroe County Quickstep*.....	10.00 -	15.00

CODY FOX & HIS YELLOW JACKETS:

Vocalion 03493 *I Only Want A Buddy*.......	5.00 -	8.00

CURLEY FOX:

Decca 5169 *Tennessee Roll*.............	5.00 -	8.00
5185 *Yum Yum Blues*.................	5.00 -	8.00
5213 *Listen To The Mockingbird*..........	5.00 -	8.00

GLEN FOX & JOE WILSON:

Vocalion 5490 *My Dixie Home*...........	5.00 -	8.00
5495 *The Old Covered Bridge*...........	5.00 -	8.00
5496 *The Roundup In The Spring*..........	5.00 -	8.00

OSCAR FOX:

Supertone 9325 *My Dear Old Mountain Home*..	7.00 -	10.00

DUEL FRADY:

Victor 20930 *Leavenworth*...............	7.00 -	10.00

LEE FRAZIER:

Champion 16626 *The Ice Man Blues*..........	20.00 -	30.00

FREDERICK & MASON:

Victor 20965 *Missouri Waltz*.............	5.00 -	10.00

FREED & MOORE:

Vocalion 14865 *Harmonica Blues*...........	7.00 -	10.00
14917 *Banjo Blues*...................	7.00 -	10.00
15116 *Plantation Medley*...............	7.00 -	10.00

FREEMAN & ASHCRAFT:

Columbia 15442-D *Alabama Rag*............	20.00 -	30.00

FREENY'S BARN DANCE BAND:

Okeh 45508 *Don't You Remember The Time*...	20.00 -	30.00
45524 *The Leake County Two Step*........	20.00 -	30.00
45533 *Mississippi Square Dance*..........	20.00 -	30.00

THE FRONTIERSMEN:

Bullet 708 *Honky Tonk Hop*.............	4.00 -	7.00

FRUIT JAR GUZZLERS:

Paramount 3095 *Sourwood Mountain*.......	20.00 -	30.00
3099 *Black Sheep Of The Family*.........	20.00 -	30.00
3106 *Yes, I'm Free*..................	20.00 -	30.00
3113 *Kentucky Bootlegger*..............	20.00 -	30.00
3116 *Cripple Creek*..................	20.00 -	30.00

3121 *Steel Driving Man*.................	20.00 -	30.00
3148 *Old Joe Clark*...................	20.00 -	30.00

JEP FULLER:

Vocalion 5074, 15125...................	4.00 -	7.00

CLARENCE (& CLAUDE) GANUS:

Vocalion 5272 *Memories Of Floyd Collins*.....	8.00 -	12.00
5284 *Down In Indiana*................	8.00 -	12.00
5312 *Just The Thought Of Mother*.........	8.00 -	12.00
5385 *I Love Nobody But You*............	10.00 -	15.00
5386 *Sleeping At The Foot Of The Bed*......	8.00 -	12.00
5396 *The Dying Soldier*...............	8.00 -	12.00
5409 *Take A Tater And Wait*............	8.00 -	12.00
5417 *I'm Going Away*.................	8.00 -	12.00
5452 *Won't The Angels Let Mama Come*....	8.00 -	12.00

GARDNER & DAVID:

Diva 6010-G *John Hardy*................	5.00 -	8.00

BLIND UNCLE GASPARD:

Vocalion 5320 *Markeville Blues*...........	15.00 -	20.00
5333 *Natchitocheo*..................	15.00 -	20.00

AUBREY GASS:

Capitol 1427 *K.C. Boogie*...............	5.00 -	8.00
Gold Star 1318 *Delivery Man Blues*..........	5.00 -	8.00

JOHNNIE GATES:

Columbia 15573-D *Saw Mill Blues No. 1*.......	10.00 -	15.00
15661-D *Saw Mill Blues No. 2*..........	10.00 -	15.00

GATWOOD SQUARE DANCE BAND:

Columbia 15363-D *Third Party*............	8.00 -	12.00

RED GAY & JACK WELLMAN:

Brunswick 523 *Flat Wheel Train Blues*........	10.00 -	15.00

WHIT GAYDON:

Victor 40315 *Tennessee Coon Hunt*..........	10.00 -	15.00

NORMAN GAYLE:

Champion 15447 *Train No. 45*............	10.00 -	15.00
15465 *She's Mine All Mine*.............	10.00 -	15.00
15501 *Sally Gooden*.................	10.00 -	15.00

GEORGE'S HOT SHOTS:

Victor 23729 *We Do It Just The Same*.......	10.00 -	15.00

GEORGIA CRACKERS:

Okeh 40598 *Diamond Joe*..............	10.00 -	15.00
45111 *Georgia Black Bottom*............	10.00 -	15.00
45192 *Stockade Blues*................	10.00 -	15.00

GEORGIA MELODY BOYS:

Broadway 8119 *Cabin Home*.............	7.00 -	10.00

GEORGIA ORGAN GRINDERS:

Columbia 15394-D *Back Up And Push*.......	20.00 -	30.00
15415-D *Charming Betsy*..............	20.00 -	30.00
15445-D *Georgia Man*................	20.00 -	30.00

GEORGIA POT LICKERS:

Brunswick 595 *Up Jumped The Rabbit*.......	8.00 -	12.00

GEORGIA SERENADERS:

Supertone 9473 *Gonna Raise a Ruckus Tonight*.	10.00 -	15.00

GEORGIA WILDCATS:

Victor 23640 *She's Waiting For Me*..........	20.00 -	30.00

GEORGIA YELLOW HAMMERS:

Victor 20549 *Fourth Of July*..............	5.00 -	8.00
20550 *Pass Around The Bottle*...........	5.00 -	8.00
20928 *Mary, Don't You Weep*...........	8.00 -	12.00
20943 *My Carolina Girl*...............	10.00 -	15.00
20173 *Tennessee Coon*...............	10.00 -	15.00
21195 *G Rag*......................	10.00 -	15.00
21362 *The Song Of The Doodle Bug*.......	10.00 -	15.00
21486 *The Old Rock Jail*...............	10.00 -	15.00
21626 *Moonshine Hollow Band*..........	10.00 -	15.00
23542 *No One To Welcome Me*...........	15.00 -	25.00
23547 *Child Hood Days*...............	15.00 -	25.00
23683 *Peaches Down In Georgia*..........	20.00 -	30.00
40004 *Warhorse Game*................	10.00 -	15.00
40069 *The Sale Of Simon Slick*..........	10.00 -	15.00
40091 *Kiss Me Quick*.................	10.00 -	15.00
40138 *Big Ball In Memphis*.............	15.00 -	20.00

FRANK GERARD-HOWARD DIXON-MUTT EVANS:
Bluebird 7895 *Honey, Baby Mine*............ 7.00 - 10.00

GIBBS BROTHERS & CLYDE DAVIS:
Vocalion 5447 *I Love My Toodlum-Doo*...... 15.00 - 20.00
5464 *Strolling Home With Jenny*............ 15.00 - 20.00

HUGH GIBBS STRING BAND:
Paramount 3001 *I'm Goin' Crazy*............ 15.00 - 25.00
3002 *Almost Persuaded*.................... 15.00 - 25.00
3003 *Chicken Feed*....................... 15.00 - 25.00
3004 *In The Good Old Summertime*......... 15.00 - 25.00

GRINNELL GIGGERS: (see GRINNELL)

CECIL GILL (YODELING COUNTRY BOY):
Silver Star 100, 101...................... 4.00 - 7.00

GIRLS OF THE GOLDEN WEST:
Bluebird 5155, 5167, 5189, 5226, 5288, 5318, 5382, 5394, 5427, 5718, 5719, 5737, 5732, 6004, 6054, 6163, 6164, 6178, 6255 .... 4.00 - 7.00
Victor 23857 *The Cowgirl's Dream*.......... 15.00 - 20.00
Vocalion 04022, 04053, 04103, 04147, 04234, 04292, 04373 .... 4.00 - 7.00

SHORTY GODWIN:
Columbia 15411-D *Turnip Greens*........... 8.00 - 12.00

GOLDEN MELODY BOYS:
Paramount 3068 *The Cross Eyed Butcher*...... 5.00 - 8.00
3074 *Would You Ever Think Of Me*......... 5.00 - 8.00
3081 *Cabin Home*......................... 5.00 - 8.00
3087 *Way Down In Arkansas*.............. 5.00 - 8.00
3107 *Freak Melody*....................... 5.00 - 8.00
3124 *Jack And May*...................... 5.00 - 8.00
3137 *When The Lilac Blooms*............. 5.00 - 8.00
3153 *Uncle Ebner & Ebner At The Rehersal*.. 5.00 - 8.00
3169 *Guitar Rag*......................... 5.00 - 8.00

DAN GOLDEN:
Champion 15525 *Good Old Turnip Greens*..... 10.00 - 15.00

GOOD'S BOX WHITTLERS:
Vocalion 5352 *Election Day In Kentucky*...... 10.00 - 15.00

HERALD GOODMAN & HIS TENNESSEE VALLEY BOYS:
Bluebird 7868, 7935, 7999, 8033........... 3.00 - 6.00

PRICE GOODSON:
Gennett 6154 *Lonesome Road Blues*.......... 20.00 - 30.00

GOOSE CREEK GULLY JUMPERS:
Superior 2639 *Let Me Call You Sweetheart*..... 10.00 - 15.00
2738 *Medley*............................ 10.00 - 15.00

ALEX GORDON:
Conqueror 7269 *A Message From Home Sweet Home* .... 10.00 - 15.00
7270 *The Burial Of Wild Bill*............ 10.00 - 15.00

TOMMY GORDON & HIS CORN HUSKERS:
Superior 2614 *Halfway To Arkansas*......... 20.00 - 30.00
2712 *Wild Hog In The Woods*............ 20.00 - 30.00

TED GOSSETT'S BAND:
Champion 16116 *Fox Chase*............... 15.00 - 20.00
16310 *Bow Legged Irishman*............. 15.00 - 20.00
Gennett 7308 *Fox Chase*.................. 15.00 - 25.00

GRADY FAMILY:
Columbia 15633-D *Carolina's Best*........... 10.00 - 15.00

GRAHAM BROTHERS:
Victor 23654 *Ninety-Nine Years*........... 8.00 - 12.00
23664 *Gene, The Fighting Marine*......... 8.00 - 12.00
23668 *Spring's Tornado*................. 8.00 - 12.00
23670 *Don't Hang Me*................... 8.00 - 12.00
23690 *Bobby Boy*........................ 8.00 - 12.00

HENRY GRAHAM:
Bell 1167 *The Marion Parker Murder*....... 7.00 - 10.00
1177 *The Sinking Of The Submarine S-4*.... 7.00 - 10.00

GRANT BROTHERS & THEIR MUSIC:
Columbia 15322-D *Tell It To Me*.......... 10.00 - 15.00
15460-D *Goodbye My Honey, I'm Gone*..... 15.00 - 20.00

GRANT TRIO:

Victor 23667 *Under The Old Umbrella*......... 8.00 - 12.00
23743 *Say A Prayer For Baby*............ 8.00 - 12.00

GRAPEVINE COON HUNTERS:
Brunswick 584 *The Broan Waltz*............ 7.00 - 10.00

GRAVES & TANNER:
Vocalion 5342 *The Bum's Rush*............ 8.00 - 12.00

GRAY & NELSON:
Supertone 9309 *Mandolin Rag*............. 8.00 - 12.00
9377 *Farewell Waltz*.................... 8.00 - 12.00
9397 *Martha Campbell*.................. 8.00 - 12.00
9670 *Waltz The Hall*................... 8.00 - 12.00

A.A. GRAY & SEVEN FOOT DILLY:
Vocalion 5430 *Streak O'Lean-Streak O'Fat*..... 20.00 - 30.00
5458 *The Old Ark's A'Moving*............ 20.00 - 30.00

"MOMMIE" GRAY/OWEN GRAY/OTTO GRAY'S (OKLAHOMA) COWBOY BAND:
Champion 16027 *It Can't Be Done*.......... 10.00 - 15.00
Gennett 6376 *It Can't Be Done*........... 15.00 - 25.00
6387 *In The Baggage Coach Ahead*....... 15.00 - 25.00
Gennett 6405 *The Drunkard's Lone Child*.... 15.00 - 25.00
7222 *Down Where The Swanee River Flows*.. 20.00 - 30.00
Superior 2550 *I Can't Be Done*........... 15.00 - 25.00
Vocalion 5250 *It Can't Be Done*.......... 15.00 - 20.00
5267 *Tom Cat Blues*.................... 15.00 - 20.00
5301 *Be Home Early Tonight, My Dear*.... 15.00 - 20.00
5327 *The Terrible Marriage*............. 15.00 - 20.00
5337 *Midnight Special*................. 15.00 - 20.00
5479 *Who Stole The Lock*............... 15.00 - 20.00

(G.B.) GRAYSON & (HENRY) WHITTER (See also WHITTER & GRAYSON):
Bluebird 5498, 7072..................... 4.00 - 7.00
Gennett 6304 *Nobody's Darling*........... 20.00 - 30.00
Victor 21139 *Don't Go Out Tonight My Darling* 10.00 - 15.00
21189 *Train Forty-Five*................. 10.00 - 15.00
21625 *Rose Conley*..................... 10.00 - 15.00
23565 *Going Down The Lee Highway*...... 20.00 - 30.00
40038 *Joking Henry*.................... 7.00 - 10.00
40063 *Red And Green Signal Lights*...... 10.00 - 15.00
40268 *I Have Lost You Darling*.......... 15.00 - 20.00
40324 *I've Always Been A Rambler*....... 15.00 - 20.00

GREAT GAP ENTERTAINERS:
Broadway 8137 *Barn Dance On The Mountain*.. 10.00 - 15.00
8140 *Pussy Cat Rag*.................... 10.00 - 15.00
8200 *O Wasn't I Getting Away*.......... 10.00 - 15.00

GREEN'S STRING BAND:
Champion 16115 *Zenda Waltz*............. 10.00 - 15.00
16249 *Gray Eagle*..................... 10.00 - 15.00
16489 *Rickett's Hornpipe*.............. 10.00 - 15.00
Gennett 7307 *Glide Waltz*............... 10.00 - 15.00

GREEN & RUSSELL:
Supertone 9377 *Goodnight Waltz*.......... 8.00 - 12.00

UNCLE GEORGE GREEN & HIS BOYS:
Champion 15828 *Louisiana Hop*........... 8.00 - 12.00
15896 *Polly Wolly Doodle*.............. 8.00 - 12.00

JERRY GREEN:
Specialty 712 *Naggin' Women And Braggin' Men* 5.00 - 8.00*
714 *Are You Goin' My Way?*............. ———

AMOS GREENE:
Supertone 9651 *Down In The Jailhouse On My Knees* .... 12.00 - 18.00
9671 *Memphis Yodel*................... 12.00 - 18.00
9707 *I'm Lonely And Blue*............. 12.00 - 18.00
9708 *Yodeling Them Blues Away*........ 12.00 - 18.00
9709 *Just A Lonely Hobo*.............. 12.00 - 18.00

CLARENCE GREENE (& THE WISE BROTHERS):
Columbia 15311-D *Fond Affection*......... 15.00 - 20.00
15461-D *Johnson City Blues*............ 15.00 - 20.00
15580-D *Pride Of The Ball*............. 15.00 - 20.00
Victor 40141 *Little Bunch Of Roses*....... 15.00 - 20.00

LEM GREEN:
Okeh 45418 *Eleven More Months & Ten More Days* 8.00 - 12.00

PROFESSOR & MRS. GREER:
Paramount 3195 *Black Jack Davy* .... 10.00 - 15.0
  3236 *Sweet William And Fair Ellen* .... 10.00 - 15.00
BOBBY GREGORY:
Okeh 45350 *The Runaway Boys* .... 10.00 - 15.00
  45473 *Hoopee Scoopee* .... 10.00 - 15.00
  45500 *Little Pal Of Mine* .... 10.00 - 15.00
WALLACE GREY:
Champion 15832 *Little Mamie* .... 8.00 - 12.00
REX GRIFFIN:
Decca 5088, 5089, 5118, 5147, 5202, 5227, 5250,
  5269, 5294, 5383, 5395 .... 4.00 - 7.00
TAYLOR GRIGGS MELODY MAKERS (See TAYLOR'S MELODY MAKERS):
GRINNELL GIGGERS:
Victor 23511 *Duck Shoes Rag* .... 15.00 - 20.00
  23632 *Cotton Picker's Rag* .... 15.00 - 20.00
  23675 *Plow Boy Hop* .... 15.00 - 20.00
  40275 *Giggers Waltz* .... 10.00 - 15.00
BILL GRUBBS & HIS OKLAHOMA RAMBLERS:
Blue Bonnet 101 *My Gal Alice* .... 4.00 - 7.00
  105 *I'm Gonna Wake Up In Waco* .... 4.00 - 7.00
GUNBOAT BILLY & THE SPARROW:
Crown 3077 *Eleven More Months And Ten More Days* .... 7.00 - 10.00
Paramount 3273 *Eleven More Months And Ten More Days* .... 7.00 - 10.00
Victor 23698 *I'm Glad I'm A Bum* .... 5.00 - 8.00
  23714 *Four Stone Walls* .... 5.00 - 8.00
  24024 *Oh For The Life Of A Hobo* .... 5.00 - 8.00
HARDROCK GRUNTER & THE PEBBLES:
Bama 104 *Birmingham Bounce* .... 5.00 - 8.00
  202 *Lonesome Blues* .... 5.00 - 8.00
(E.E) HACK'S STRING BAND:
Champion 16292 *Kentucky Plow Boy's March* .. 15.00 - 20.00
  45149 *Wink The Other Eye* .... 5.00 - 8.00
Columbia 15418-D *Too Tight Rag* .... 10.00 - 15.00
  15466-D *Black Lake Waltz* .... 8.00 - 12.00
HACKBERRY RAMBLERS:
Bluebird 2002 *Bring It Down To The Jailhouse, Honey* .... 8.00 - 12.00
  2003 *Jolie Blonde* .... 8.00 - 12.00
  2005 *Vinton High Society* .... 8.00 - 12.00
  2010 *Rambling* .... 8.00 - 12.00
  2013 *Cajun Crawl* .... 8.00 - 12.00
  2017 *Rice City Stomp* .... 8.00 - 12.00
  2019 *Dobie Shack* .... 8.00 - 12.00
  2021, 2066, 6069, 6110, 6120, 6136, 6181, 6289, 6368 .... 8.00 - 12.00
RED HADLEY'S WRANGLERS:
Meteor 5017 *Brother, That's All* .... 5.00 - 8.00*
EWEN HAIL:
Brunswick 141 *Cowboy's Lament* .... 5.00 - 8.00
  433 *Cowboy's Lament* .... 5.00 - 8.00
Vocalion 5146 *Cowboy's Lament* .... 5.00 - 8.00
THERON HALE & DAUGHTERS:
Victor 40019 *Turkey Gobbler* .... 8.00 - 12.00
  40046 *Jolly Blacksmith* .... 8.00 - 12.00
TRAVIS B. HALE (& E.J. DERRY, JR.):
Victor 20796 *Oh Bury Me Out On The Prairie* .. 5.00 - 8.00
  20866 *Long Gone* .... 7.00 - 10.00
AMBROSE HALEY'S OZARK RAMBLERS:
Vocalion 03590 *It Looks Like Rain In Cherry Blossom Lane* .... 5.00 - 8.00
  03648 *How's Your Folks & My Folks* .... 5.00 - 8.00
  03709 *I Can't Lose That Longing For You* ... 5.00 - 8.00
HALL BROTHERS:
Bluebird 6843 *Little Mohee* .... 5.00 - 8.00
  6925 *Whistle, Honey, Whistle* .... 7.00 - 10.00
  7103 *Little Girl, You've Done Me Wrong* .... 7.00 - 10.00
  7363 *Spartanburg Jail* .... 7.00 - 10.00

  7462 *Alcatraz Prisoner* .... 7.00 - 10.00
  7728 *The Wrong Road* .... 7.00 - 10.00
  7801 *Hitch-Hike Blues* .... 7.00 - 10.00
Clarion 5183-C *That Goes On For Days And Days* 5.00 - 8.00
HALL TRIO:
Victor 23782 *The Answer To 21 Years* .... 10.00 - 15.00
  23797 *It Makes No Difference* .... 10.00 - 15.00
  23799 *I'm Twisting Loops In Pretzels* .... 10.00 - 15.00
  23836 *Absolutely Free* .... 10.00 - 15.00
  23838 *Shepherd Of The Air* .... 10.00 - 15.00
ROY HALL (& HIS BLUE RIDGE ENTERTAINERS):
Bluebird 8561 *New San Antonio Rose* .... 5.00 - 8.00
  8656 *Don't Let Your Sweet Love Die* .... 5.00 - 8.00
  8863 *Polecat Blues* .... 5.00 - 8.00
  8959 *I Wonder Where You Are Tonight* ..... 5.00 - 8.00
Bullet 704 *Mule Boogie* .... 5.00 - 8.00
  712 *Ain't You Afraid* .... 5.00 - 8.00
Vocalion 04627 *Good For Nothing Gal* .... 5.00 - 10.00
  04717 *Lonesome Dove* .... 5.00 - 10.00
  04771 *Where The Roses Never Fade* .... 5.00 - 10.00
  04842 *Come Back Little Pal* .... 5.00 - 10.00
HALTON BROTHERS:
Champion 16628 *Hook And Line* .... 15.00 - 20.00
STUART HAMBLEN (COWBOY JOE) (& HIS COVERED WAGON JUBILEE):
Bluebird 5242 *Boy In Blue* .... 5.00 - 8.00
Decca 5001, 5077, 5109, 5145 .... 4.00 - 7.00
Victor 23685 *My Brown-Eyed Texas Rose* ...... 10.00 - 15.00
  40109 *Boy In Blue* .... 8.00 - 12.00
  40242 *Wrong Keyhole* .... 8.00 - 12.00
  40306 *Standin' On The Pier In The Rain* ..... 10.00 - 15.00
Victor 40311 *Sailor's Farewell* .... 10.00 - 15.00
  40319 .... 10.00 - 15.00
PAUL HAMBLIN:
Victor 40260 *Strawberry Roan* .... 10.00 - 15.00
  40280 *Prairie Maiden* .... 10.00 - 15.00
WYZEE HAMILTON (Acc. by HAMILTON HARMONIANS):
Gennett 6272 *Old Sefus Brown* .... 15.00 - 25.00
HAMLIN QUARTETTE:
Herwin 75572 *Darling Nellie Gray* .... 10.00 - 15.00
JOHN HAMMOND:
Champion 15356 *Drunken Hiccoughs* .... 8.00 - 12.00
Gennett 6256 *Little Birdie* .... 15.00 - 20.00
Supertone 9249 *Little Birdie* .... 7.00 - 10.00
SID HAMPTON (THE YODELIN' MAN FROM DIXIE LAND):
Columbia 15555-D *Kicking Mule* .... 8.00 - 12.00
  15583-D *The Hills Of Tennessee* .... 8.00 - 12.00
WILLIAM HANSON:
Okeh 45506 *Stop And Listen Blues* .... 15.00 - 25.00
  45523 *Gambling On The Sabbath* .... 15.00 - 25.00
HAPPY HOLLOW HOODLUMS:
Decca 5098 *Down Home Rag* .... 5.00 - 8.00
HAPPY HAYSEEDS:
Victor 23722 *Ladies' Quadrille* .... 15.00 - 25.00
  23774 *Cottonwood Reel* .... 15.00 - 25.00
HAPPY JACK:
Columbia 15720-D *I'm Only Suggesting This* .... 7.00 - 10.00
HAPPY VALLEY FAMILY:
Vocalion 04251 *Lily Of The Valley* .... 5.00 - 8.00
  04296 *My Clinch Mountain Home* .... 5.00 - 8.00
  04484 *Going Down To The Valley* .... 5.00 - 8.00
(Note: Above titles and others were also issued on Banner, Melotone, Oriole, Perfect, and Romeo.)
TEX HARDIN:
Champion 16552 *The Trail To California* .... 10.00 - 15.00
BILLY HARDISON (See TENNESSEE DRIFTERS):
HARKINS & MORAN:
Broadway 8055 *Hand Me Down My Walking Cane* 8.00 - 12.00

8056 *Bully Of The Town*................	8.00 -	12.00
8064 *Lazy Tennessee*................	8.00 -	12.00
8081 *Land Where We'll Never Grow Old*...	8.00 -	12.00
8114 *John Henry*................	8.00 -	12.00
8115 *The Gambler's Dying Words*.........	8.00 -	12.00
8117 *In The Sweet Bye And Bye*.........	8.00 -	12.00
8157 *Kitty Wells*................	8.00 -	12.00

HARKINS & OWENS:

Broadway 8214 *A Mother's Plea*............	8.00 -	12.00

HARKINS & PERRY:

Broadway 8129 *Life's Railway To Heaven*......	8.00 -	12.00

(SID) HARKREADER & (GRADY) MOORE;
HARKREADER & (BLYTHE) POTEET:

Paramount 3022 *Bully Of The Town*........	25.00 -	40.00
3023 *John Henry*................	25.00 -	40.00
3024 *There's A Little Rosewood Casket*.....	25.00 -	40.00
3025 *The Gambler's Dying Words*........	25.00 -	40.00
3033 *Mockingbird Breakdown*............	25.00 -	40.00
3035 *Only As Far As The Gate*........	25.00 -	40.00
3043 *Kitty Wells*................	25.00 -	40.00
3044 *Bits Of Blues*................	25.00 -	40.00
3052 *Land Where We'll Never Grow Old*....	25.00 -	40.00
3054 *It Looks To Me Like A Big Night Tonight*	25.00 -	40.00
3061 *The Old Rugged Cross*........	25.00 -	40.00
3063 *Lazy Tennessee*................	25.00 -	40.00
3094 *Life's Railway To Heaven*.........	25.00 -	40.00
3104 *Take Me Back To Carolina Home*......	25.00 -	40.00
3112 *Sweet Bird*................	25.00 -	40.00
3118 *Wang Wang Blues*................	25.00 -	40.00
3141 *Red River Valley*................	25.00 -	40.00
3183 *On The Bowery*................	25.00 -	40.00
3296 *Land Where We'll Never Grow Old*....	25.00 -	40.00
Vocalion 5063 *Never River Train*........	15.00 -	20.00
5066 *Oh, Where Is My Boy Tonight*........	15.00 -	20.00
5082 *Struttin' Round*................	15.00 -	20.00
5114 *Dark Eyes*................	15.00 -	20.00
14887 *Soldier's Joy*................	15.00 -	20.00
15035 *New River Train*................	15.00 -	20.00
15075 *The Dying Girl's Messge*........	15.00 -	20.00
15193 *Struttin' Round*................	15.00 -	20.00
15366 *Dark Eyes*................	15..00 -	20.00

HARMONICA BILL:

Champion 16393 *The Prisoner's Radio*........	15.00 -	20.00
16399 *Answer To The Gypsy's Warning*.....	15.00 -	20.00
16425 *Georgia The Dear Old State I Love*....	15.00 -	20.00

HOMONICA JIM:

Superior 2789 *The Prisoner's Radio*...........	15.00 -	20.00
2806 *Great Grandad And Grandma*........	15.00 -	20.00

RICHARD HAROLD:

Columbia 15426-D *Sweet Bird*...............	8.00 -	12.00
15586-D *The Battleship Maine*...........	8.00 -	12.00

HARPER BROTHERS:

Brunswick 469 *Dreamy Rock Mountain Moon*..	5.00 -	8.00
505 *Blue Pacific Moonlight*...............	5.00 -	8.00

HARPER FAMILY TRIO:

Supertone 9645, 9649, 9656, 9729...........	4.00 -	7.00

HARPER & HALL:

Superior 2678 *Down The Lane To Home Sweet Home*...............	15.00 -	20.00
2799 *Life's Railway To Heaven*............	15.00 -	20.00

HARPER & PAGE:

Supertone 9314 *Sweet William*.............	7.00 -	10.00

HARPER & TURNER:

Supertone 9262, 9266, 9316, 9353, 9391, 9658..	4.00 -	8.00
9640 *Sweet Adeline At The Still*............	5.00 -	10.00
9656 *There's A Vacant Chair At Home Sweet Home*...............	5.00 -	10.00
9678 *No Never Alone*................	5.00 -	10.00
9725 *I Surrender All*................	5.00 -	10.00
9726 *Beautiful Garden Of Prayer*..........	5.00 -	10.00

DIXIE HARPER & HER BLUEBONNET

BRATS:

Royalty P-31 *Sweeter Than The Flowers*.......	5.00 -	8.00
P-38/39 *Lovesick Blues*................	5.00 -	8.00

AUNT IDY HARPER & THE COON CREEK GIRLS:

Vocalion 04203, 04354.....................	4.00 -	8.00

JACK HARPER:

Vocalion 5494 *The Tramp's Last Ride*.........	7.00 -	10.00

OSCAR HARPER'S TEXAS STRING BAND:

Okeh 45227 *Bouquet Waltz*................	20.00 -	30.00
Vocalion 5403 *Sally Johnson*................	20.00 -	30.00

OSCAR & DOC HARPER:

Okeh 45397 *Beaumont Rag*................	20.00 -	30.00
45420 *Terrell Texas Blues*................	20.00 -	30.00
45485 *Bitter Creek*................	20.00 -	30.00

ROY HARPER & EARL SHIRKEY: (See also SHIRKEY & HARPER):

Columbia 15429-D *Bootlegger's Dream*........	15.00 -	20.00
Columbia 15467-D *Cowboy's Lullaby*.........	15.00 -	20.00

KELLY HARRELL (& HENRY NORTON):

Okeh 40486 *Wild Bill Jones*................	8.00 -	12.00
Victor 19596 *New River Train*................	5.00 -	8.00
20103 *My Horses Ain't Hungry*........	5.00 -	8.00
20171 *Rovin' Gambler*................	5.00 -	8.00
20242 *Butcher's Boy*................	5.00 -	8.00
20527 *Bright Sherman Valley*........	5.00 -	8.00
20535 *Bye And Bye You Will Forget*........	5.00 !	8.00
20657 *I'm Nobody's Darling On Earth*........	5.00 -	8.00
20797 *Charles Giteau*................	6.00 -	10.00
20867 *I Love My Sweetheart The Best*........	6.00 -	10.00
20935 *Row Us Over The Tide*........	6.00 -	10.00
21069 *For Seven Long Years*........	8.00 -	12.00
21520 *My Wife, She Has Gone*........	8.00 -	12.00
23741 *I Heard Somebody Call*........	15.00 -	20.00
40047 *Oh, My Pretty Monkey*........	8.00 -	12.00
40095 *She Just Kept Kissing On*...........	8.00 -	12.00

EARL HARRIS:

Okeh 45566 *Gene, The Fighting Marine*.......	5.00 -	8.00

GEORGE HARRIS:

Columbia 15543-D *That's The Blue Heaven For Me*	10.00 -	15.00

J.D. HARRIS:

Okeh 45024 *Cackling Hen*................	10.00 -	15.00

SIM HARRIS:

Oriole 916 *Pass Around The Bottle*........	7.00 -	10.00
946 *The Fatal Wedding*................	7.00 -	10.00
947 *Bully Of The Town*................	7.00 -	10.00

HAPPY BUD HARRISON:

Vocalion 5344 *Mail Man Blues*........	8.00 -	12.00
5350 *I'm Glad I'm Free*................	8.00 -	12.00
5370 *Ball And Chain Blues*........	8.00 -	12.00
5405 *Mama Don't Allow No Easy Riders*....	8.00 -	12.00

HART BROTHERS:

Paramount 3162 *The Miner's Prayer*.........	10.00 -	15.00
3176 *The Empty Cradle*................	10.00 -	15.00
3262 *Lamp Lighting Time In The Valley*.....	10.00 -	15.00
3265 *The Prodigal Son*................	10.00 -	15.00

HART & CATES:

Okeh 45499 *In The Valley Of Broken Hearts*...	7.00 -	10.00

HART & OGLE:

Paramount 3297 *They Cut Down The Old Pine Tree*	8.00 -	12.00

HARTMAN'S HEARTBREAKERS; DICK HARTMAN'S TENNESSEE RAMBLERS:

Bluebird 5796, 5797, 5837, 5875, 5876, 5891, 5909, 5962, 5992, 6003, 6089, 6105, 6122, 6135, 6162, 6180, 6207, 6226, 6227, 6274, 6481, 6494, 6516, 6542, 6566, 6622, 6656..................	3.00 -	6.00

BOB HARTSELL:

Bluebird 7439 *Rambling Freight Train Yodel*....	5.00 -	8.00
7473 *Rock Me To Sleep In My Rocky Mountain Home*................	5.00 -	8.00

(ROY) HARVEY (& COLEMAN/LEONARD

COPELAND/BOB HOKE/JESS JOHNSON/HIS NORTH CAROLINA RAMBLERS/POSEY RORER):
Brunswick 223 *There'll Come A Time* .... 10.00 - 15.00
234 *I'll Be There Mary Dear* .... 10.00 - 15.00
250 *The Bluefield Murder* .... 10.00 - 15.00
268 *Budded Roses* .... 10.00 - 15.00
Champion 16187 *No Room For A Tramp* ...... 15.00 - 25.00
16213 *When The Bees Are In The Hives* ..... 15.00 - 25.00
16255 *Railroad Blues* .... 20.00 - 30.00
16281 *Gambling Blues* .... 20.00 - 30.00
16312 *Called To The Foreign Fields* .... 20.00 - 30.00
16331 *You're Bound To Look Like A Monkey* 20.00 - 30.00
16662 *The Great Reaping Day* .... 20.00 - 30.00
16781 *Jefferson Street Rag* .... 30.00 - 40.00
45011, 45035, 45117 .... 5.00 - 8.00
Columbia 15155-D *Daisies Won't Tell* ...... 8.00 - 12.00
15514-D *Beckley Rag* .... 15.00 - 20.00
15582-D *Lonesome Weary Blues* .... 15.00 - 20.00
15637-D *Greasy Wagon* .... 20.00 - 30.00
15714-D *Dark Eyes* .... 30.00 - 50.00
Gennett 6303 *The Old Clay Pipe* .... 20.00 - 30.00
6350 *We Will Outshine The Sun* .... 20.00 - 30.00
Vocalion 5243 *Sweet Refrain* .... 15.00 - 20.00

OVERTONE HATFIELD:
Columbia 15687-D *A Gangster's Warning* ...... 50.00 - 75.00

HAUULEA ENTERTAINERS:
Okeh 45461 *Twelfth Street Rag* .... 10.0 - 15.00
45490 *Railroad Blues* .... 10.00 - 15.00

HAWAIIAN PALS:
Victor 23588 *It's Awful What Whiskey Will Do.* 8.00 - 12.00

BUDDY HAWK & HIS BUDDIES:
Atlantic 7074 *Painting The Big Town* .... ----

HAWKINS & PUCKETT:
Bluebird 5691 *Down In The Valley* .... 7.00 - 10.00

UNCLE BEN HAWKINS (& HIS BOYS):
Challenge 244 *The Poor Tramp Has To Live*... 7.00 - 10.00
Champion 15248 *Round Town Gals* .... 7.00 - 10.00
Silvertone 5001 *The Poor Tramp Has To Live.*. 7.00 - 10.00
5003 *Long Eared Mule* .... 7.00 - 10.00
Supertone 9255 *When The Roses Bloom Again.*. 7.00 - 10.00
9400 *The New River Train* .... 7.00 - 10.00

UNCLE BILLY HAWKINS:
Champion 15084 *Turkey In The Straw* .... 5.00 - 8.00

UNCLE JIM HAWKINS:
Challenge 101 *Hell Broke Loose In Georgia*..... 5.00 - 8.00
109 *Turkey In The Straw* .... 5.00 - 8.00
111 *Dixie* .... 5.00 - 8.00
112 *Billy In The Low Ground* .... 5.00 - 8.00
301 *Arkansas Traveler* .... 5.00 - 8.00
304 *Hell Broke Loose In Georgia* .... 5.00 - 8.00
Champion 15098 *Seneca Square Dance* .... 7.00 - 10.00

TED HAWKINS' MOUNTAINEERS:
Columbia 15752-D *Roamin' Jack* .... 20.00 - 30.00

HAYES & JENKINS:
Superior 2537 *I Played On My Spanish Guitar*.. 15.00 - 20.00

DEWEY HAYES (THE CAROLINA TROUBADOUR):
Columbia 15753-D *Bring Back The One I Love*.. 15.00 - 20.00

ED HAYES:
Okeh 45025 *Big White Rooster And The Little Brown Hen* .... 10.00 - 15.00

SELMA & DEWEY HAYES:
Victor 23629 *Broken Heart* .... 8.00 - 12.00

HAYWOOD COUNTY RAMBLERS:
Victor 23779 *Buncombe Chain Gang* .... 40.00 - 60.00

BILL HELMS & HIS UPSON COUNTY BAND:
Victor 21649 *Georgia Blues* .... 10.00 - 15.00
40079 *Alabama Jubilee* .... 8.00 - 12.00

BILL HELMS & RILEY PUCKETT:
Columbia 15774-D *Lost Love* .... 30.00 - 50.00

ERNEST HELTON:
Okeh 45010 *Royal Clog* .... 15.00 - 20.00

HENDERSON BROTHERS:
Vocalion 03128 *The Grave Beneath The Pines*.. 7.00 - 10.00

RED HENDERSON:
Okeh 45283 *Auto Ride Through Alabama* ...... 7.00 - 10.00

(FISHER) HENDLEY (& HIS ARISTOCRATIC PIGS/CAROLINA TAR HEELS/& SMALL)
Bluebird 6555 *Another Man's Wife* .... 7.00 - 10.00
Okeh 45012 *Let Your Shack Burn Down* .... 10.00 - 15.00
Victor 23528 *Shuffle, Feet, Shuffle* .... 15.00 - 20.00
Vocalion 02530 *Greasy Possum* .... 7.00 - 10.00
02543 *Answer To Big Rock Candy Mountain*. 7.00 - 10.00
02612 *Going Down Town* .... 7.00 - 10.00
02679 *Hook And Line* .... 7.00 - 10.00
04516, 04556, 04658, 04718, 04780, 04881, 04937, 05016 .... 4.00 - 7.00

(CHIEF) HENRY'S STRING BAND:
Victor 40195 *Cherokee Rag* .... 10.00 - 15.00
40225 *Choctow Waltz* .... 10.00 - 15.00
40281 *Indian Tom Tom* .... 10.00 - 15.00

HENSLEY, TAYLOR & WALKER:
Vocalion 02639 *It's Hard To Make Gertie* ...... 10.00 - 15.00
02640 *Scottdale Stomp* .... 10.00 - 15.00
02678 *Match Box Blues* .... 15.00 - 20.00

HERMAN BROTHERS:
Broadway 8165 *Turkey In The Straw* .... 5.00 - 8.00

HERNANDEZ BROTHERS:
Victor 40081 *When You And I Were Young, Maggie* 5.00 - 10.00

ZEB HERRELSON & M.B. PADGETT:
Okeh 45078 *Soldier's Joy* .... 5.00 - 8.00

BENNIE HESS (& HIS NATION'S PLAY BOYS):
Opera 102 *I'm Not Gonna Fool With You* ..... 5.00 - 10.00
104 *Drink Drink Drink* .... 5.00 - 10.00
1013 *Bennie Hess Boogie* .... 5.00 - 10.00
1015 *Novelty Yodel No. 1* .... 5.00 - 8.00
1018 *To Be Loved* .... 5.00 - 8.00
1019 *Texas Stars* .... 5.00 - 8.00

HICKORY NUTS:
Okeh 45169 *The Louisville Burglar* .... 10.00 - 15.00
45220 *There'll Be No Liars There* .... 10.00 - 15.00

HI-FLYERS:
Vocalion 03684, 03964, 04011, 04093, 04589, 04671, 04703, 05000, 05054 .... 4.00 - 7.00

LEN & JOE HIGGINS:
Columbia 15243-D *Kentucky Wedding Chimes*.. 7.00 - 10.00
15354-D *Slippery Elm Tree* .... 10.00 - 15.00

HIGHLANDERS:
Paramount 3171 *Flop-Eared Mule* .... 30.00 - 50.00
3184 *Richmond Square* .... 30.00 - 50.00
3200 *Tennessee Blues* .... 30.00 - 50.00

HIGH NEIGHBOR BOYS:
Vocalion 04555, 04691, 04773, 04895 .... 4.00 - 7.00

LUKE HIGHNIGHT & HIS OZARK STRUTTERS:
Vocalion 5325 *There's No Hell In Georgia* ..... 30.00 - 40.00
5339 *Fort Smith Breakdown* .... 30.00 - 40.00

HILL'S VIRGINIA MOUNTAINEERS:
Supertone 9170 *Forked Deer* .... 5.00 - 8.00

BOB HILL:
Victor 23718 *He Was A Good Man* .... 30.00 - 40.00

EZRA HILL & HENRY JOHNSON:
Champion 15750 *Birmingham Jail* .... 10.00 - 15.00

FRANK HILL:
Supertone 9319 *Lonely Village Churchyard* ..... 6.00 - 10.00
9612 *I'll Not Forget You Daddy* .... 6.00 - 10.00

JESS HILLARD (See HILLIARD)
HILLBILLIES:
Vocalion 5016 *East Tennessee Blues* .... 7.00 - 10.00
5017 *Blue Eyed Girl* .... 7.00 - 10.00
5018 *Kitty Wells* .... 7.00 - 10.00

5019 *Sally Ann*	7.00 -	10.00
5020 *Cluck, Old Hen*	7.00 -	10.00
5021 *Texas Gals*	7.00 -	10.00
5022 *Sourwood Mountains*	7.00 -	10.00
5023 *Buck-Eyed Rabbits*	7.00 -	10.00
5024 *Cumberland Gap*	7.00 -	10.00
5025 *Bristol Tennessee Blues*	7.00 -	10.00
5115 *Cripple Creek*	7.00 -	10.00
5116 *Mississippi Sawyer*	7.00 -	10.00
5117 *Old Joe Clark*	7.00 -	10.00
5173 *Hear Dem Bells*	7.00 -	10.00
5178 *Sweet Bunch Of Daisies*	7.00 -	10.00
5179 *Black-Eyed Susie*	7.00 -	10.00
5182 *Baby, Your Time Ain't Long*	7.00 -	10.00
5183 *Wasn't She A Dandy*	7.00 -	10.00
Vocalion 5186 *Darling Nellie Gray*	7.00 -	10.00
15367 *Cripple Creek*	7.00 -	10.00
15368 *Mississippi Sawyer*	7.00 -	10.00
15369 *Old Joe Clark*	7.00 -	10.00

HARRY HILLIARD:

Champion 16337 *Blue Yodel No. 9*	20.00 -	30.00
Superior 2663 *The Mystery Of No 5*	25.00 -	35.00

JESS HILLIARD (& HIS ACES/WEST VIRGINIA HILLIBILLIES):

Champion 16333 *Cackling Hen*	15.00 -	20.00
16347 *Pea Pickin' Papa*	20.00 -	30.00
16368 *Penitentiary Blues*	20.00 -	30.00
16398 *Ninety-Nine Years*	20.00 -	30.00
16525 *Red Night Gown Blues*	25.00 -	40.00
16564 *Mississippi Moon*	25.00 -	40.00
16571 *The Barnyard Stomp*	25.00 -	40.00
16617 *99 Years Blues*	25.00 -	40.00
16638 *Hell Up Flat Rock*	25.00 -	40.00
16640 *Tall Mamma Blues*	25.00 -	40.00
16651 *Austin Breakdown*	25.00 -	40.00
16670 *Dixie Rag*	25.00 -	40.00
Champion 45001, 45003, 45026, 45047, 45091, 45095	5.00 -	10.00
Superior 2695 *The Rambler's Blues*	30.00 -	40.00

HINSON, PITTS & COLEY:

Bluebird 7438 *Whoa, Mule, Whoa*	5.00 -	8.00

W.A. HINTON:

Victor 23555 *Leather Breeches*	30.00 -	40.00

HOBBS BROTHERS:

Conqueror 7332 *Patty On The Turnpike*	4.00 -	7.00
Paramount 3219 *Devil's Dream*	7.00 -	10.00
3220 *Patty On The Turnpike*	7.00 -	10.00
3224 *Hell Among The Yearlings*	7.00 -	10.00
Q.R.S. 9003 *Turkey In The Straw*	7.00 -	10.00

GEORGE HOBSON:

Silvertone 3045 *The Lighting Express*	5.00 -	8.00
3047 *The Baggage Coach Ahead*	5.00 -	8.00

WILLARD HODGIN (BANJO JOE):

Edison 52204 *Courtin' The Widow*	10.00 -	15.00
52243 *Girl That Lived On Polecat Creek*	10.00 -	15.00
52278 *Judge Done Me Wrong*	10.00 -	15.00
52332 *Ugle Gal's Got Something Hard To Beat*	10.00 -	15.00
Victor 21485 *Don't Get One Woman*	8.00 -	12.00

ADOLPH HOFNER:

Bluebird 7597, 7641, 7701, 7752, 7833, 7900, 7931, 7955, 7988	4.00 -	7.00

GEORGE HOLDEN:

Challenge 385 *The Marion Parker Murder*	7.00 -	10.00
392 *The Preacher And The Bear*	7.00 -	10.00

HOLMES & TAYLOR:

Superior 2713 *The Pretty Quadroon*	15.00 -	20.00

GEORGE HOLMES:

Superior 2525 *A Mother's Plea*	10.00 -	15.00

SALTY HOLMES:

Bluebird 5303 *I Want My Mama*	8.00 -	12.00

HOME TOWN BOYS:

Columbia 15736-D *Still Got Ninety-Nine*	15.00 -	25.00

15762-D *Home Town Rag*	15.00 -	25.00

HONEYBOY & SASSAFRAS:

Brunswick 417 *The Lighthouse Song*	5.00 -	8.00
509 *The Chicken Sermon*	5.00 -	8.00
585 *Some Family*	5.00 -	8.00

HONOLULU STROLLERS:

Okeh 45226 *Ole Oaken Bucket*	5.00 -	8.00
45239 *Mighty Lak' A Rose*	5.00 -	8.00
Victor 23600 *Don't Say No*	8.00 -	12.00

HOOSIER HOT SHOTS:

This largely corn-ball but popular group recorded many titles during the 1930's which were issued on Banner, Conqueror, Melotone, Oriole, Perfect, Romeo, Vocalion. Since the records are generally of minimal value, no detailed listing is presented.

AL HOPKINS & HIS BUCKLE BUSTERS:

Brunswick 103 *Round Town Girls*	7.00 -	10.00
104 *Bristol Tennessee Blues*	7.00 -	10.00
105 *Sally Ann*	7.00 -	10.00
106 *Governor Alf Taylor's Fox Chase*	7.00 -	10.00
174 *Sweet Bunch Of Daisies*	5.00 -	8.00
175 *Black Eyed Susie*	5.00 -	8.00
176 *Down The Meadow Lane*	5.00 -	8.00
177 *The Nine Pound Hammer*	5.00 -	8.00
179 *Johnson Boys*	5.00 -	8.00
180 *Echoes Of The Chimes*	5.00 -	8.00
181 *Hear Dem Bells*	5.00 -	8.00
182 *Bug In The Taters*	5.00 -	8.00
183 *Baby Your Time Ain't Long*	5.00 -	8.00
184 *Down To The Club*	5.00 -	8.00
185 *Sleep Baby Sleep*	5.00 -	8.00
186 *Ride That Mule*	5.00 -	8.00
187 *Wasn't She A Dandy?*	5.00 -	8.00
189 *Hear Dem Bells*	5.00 -	8.00
295 *Old Dan Tucker*	5.00 -	8.00
318 *Carolina Moonshiner*	5.00 -	8.00
321 *Polka Medley*	5.00 -	10.00
335 *Wild Hoss*	5.00 -	10.00

ANDY HOPKINS:

Supertone 9490 *Put Me Off At Buffalo*	8.00 -	12.00
9601 *Crepe On The Little Cabin Door*	8.00 -	12.00
9655 *I'll Smoke My Long Stemmed Pipe*	8.00 -	12.00
9713 *The Prison Warden's Secret*	8.00 -	12.00

DOC HOPKINS:

Broadway 8337 *Methodist Pie*	7.00 -	10.00

DAN HORNSBY (NOVELTY) ORCH./QUARTETTE/(LION'S DEN) TRIO:

Columbia 15276-D *On Mobile Bay*	5.00 -	8.00
15321-D *The Shelby Disaster*	7.00 -	10.00
15381-D *She Was Bred In Old Kentucky*	5.00 -	8.00
15444-D *Hinky Dinky Dee*	5.00 -	8.00
15578-D *I'm Sorry I Made You Cry*	5.00 -	8.00
15628-D *The Lunatic's Lullaby*	5.00 -	7.00
15769-D *Dear Old Girl*	7.00 -	10.00
15771-D *Three Blind Mice*	7.00 -	10.00

JOHNNY HORTON:

Abbott 100 *Candy Jones*	8.00 -	12.00*
101 *Happy Millionaire*	8.00 -	12.00*
102 *Plaid And Calico*	8.00 -	12.00*
103 *Birds And Butterflies*	8.00 -	12.00*
104 *In My Home In Shelby County*	8.00 -	12.00*
105 *Shadows On The Bayou*	8.00 -	12.00*
106 *Smokey Joe's Barbeque*	8.00 -	12.00*
107 *It's A Long Rocky Road*	8.00 -	12.00*
108 *Betty Lorraine*	8.00 -	12.00*
109 *Rhythm In My Baby's Walk*	8.00 -	12.00*
Cormac 1193 *Plaid And Calico*	15.00 -	25.00
Cormac 1197 *Birds And Butterflies*	15.00 -	25.00

WILLIAM B. HOUCHENS:

Gennett 5240 *Turkey In The Straw*	7.00 -	10.00

KENNETH HOUCHINS (& SLIM COX):

Champion 16473 *Fancy Nancy*	15.00 -	20.00

16484 *Do Right Daddy Blues*	15.00 -	20.00
16501 *Tennessee Blues*	15.00 -	20.00
16553 *The Wanderer's Warning*	15.00 -	20.00
16584 *The Yodeling Drifter*	15.00 -	20.00
16603 *Mean Old Ball And Chain Blues*	15.00 -	20.00
16619 *Bay Rum Blues*	15.00 -	20.00
16636 *I'm Just A Yodeling Rambler*	15.00 -	20.00
16637 *The Old Missouri Moon*	15.00 -	20.00
16650 *Back To Old Smoky Mountain*	15.00 -	20.00
16669 *Behind These Grey Walls*	15.00 -	20.00
16679 *Homesick For Heaven*	15.00 -	20.00
16695 *Our Old Family Album*	15.00 -	20.00
16755 *Louisiana Moon*	15.00 -	20.00
16775 *My Little Ozark Mountain Home*	15.00 -	20.00
16787 *Blue Ridge Lullaby*	20.00 -	30.00
16793 *When Jimmie Rodgers Said Goodbye*	20.00 -	30.00
16807 *The Gangster's Brother*	20.00 -	30.00
Champion 45028 *Cowboy's Meditation*	7.00 -	10.00
45030 *Blue Ridge Lullaby*	7.00 -	10.00
45049 *Louisiana Moon*	7.00 -	10.00
45054 *The End Of Memory Lane*	7.00 -	10.00
45062 *When Jimmie Rodgers Said Goodbye*	10.00 -	15.00
45078 *Back To Old Smoky Mountain*	7.00 -	10.00

LAKE HOWARD:
Titles, issued contemporaneously on Banner, Melotone, Oriole, Perfect, Romeo: *Chewing Chewing Gum; Don't Let Your Deal Go Down; Forsaken Love; Get Your Head In Here; I Have No One To Leave Me; It's None Of Your Business; Little Annie; Love Me Darling; Love Me; Lover's Farewell; New Chattanooga Mama; Streamlined Mama; Within My Father's House* .... 8.00 - 12.00

J.H. HOWELL'S CAROLINA HILLBILLIES:
Bluebird 7162 *Lost John*	8.00 -	12.00
7409 *The Burning Of Cleveland School*	8.00 -	12.00
8219 *Mollie Married a Travelin' Man*	8.00 -	12.00

UNCLE STEVE HUBBARD (& HIS BOYS):
Gennett 6088 *Big Town Fling*	10.00 -	15.00
6101 *Two Step Quadrille*	10.00 -	15.00
6121 *Devil's Dream*	10.00 -	15.00
6436 *Over The Ocean Waves*	10.00 -	15.00
Supertone 9161 *Soldier's Joy*	7.00 -	10.00

HUGH & SHUG'S RADIO PALS:
Decca 5406, 5407, 5428, 5431, 5451, 5466, 5506, 5534 .... 3.00 - 5.00

DAN HUGHEY:
Champion 15428 *The Fatal Wedding*	7.00 -	10.00
15466 *Froggie Went A-Courtin'*	7.00 -	10.00
15502 *Sweet Kitty Wells*	7.00 -	10.00
15631 *An Old Camp Meeting*	7.00 -	10.00
15687 *Four Thousand Years Ago*	7.00 -	10.00
15710 *The Red River Valley*	7.00 -	10.00
15731 *The Little Mohee*	7.00 -	10.00
15771 *Will The Angels Play Their Harps For Me*	8.00 -	12.00
15851 *Cindy*	8.00 -	12.00
15876 *After The Ball*	8.00 -	12.00
15923 *Old Number Three*	10.00 -	15.00
16029 *Charlie Brooks*	10.00 -	15.00

HUMPHRIES BROTHERS:
Okeh 45464 *Black And White Rag*	10.00 -	15.00
45478 *After The Ball*	10.00 -	15.00
45489 *Ragged Ann Rag*	10.00 -	15.00
45501 *What Made The Wild Cat Wild*	10.00 -	15.00

PRINCE ALBERT HUNT'S TEXAS RAMBLERS:
Okeh 45230 *Blues In A Bottle*	20.00 -	30.00
45375 *Wake Up Jacob*	20.00 -	30.00
45446 *Houston Slide*	20.00 -	30.00

DAVE HUNT:
Champion 15565 *Katy Lee*	10.00 -	15.00
15610 *Wake Up In The Morning*	10.00 -	15.00

WALTER HURDT & HIS BOYS/SINGING COWBOYS:
Bluebird 7915 *My Skinny Sarah Jane*	5.00 -	8.00
7959 *I've Always Loved My Old Guitar*	5.00 -	8.00

ZACK HURT:
Okeh 45212 *Gambler's Lament*	5.00 -	8.00

HUTCHENS BROTHERS:
Champion 15464 *Praise The Lord, It's So*	5.00 -	8.00
15485 *I'm On The Sunny Side*	5.00 -	8.00
15567 *Climbing Up The Golden Stairs*	5.00 -	8.00
15588 *I'm Free Again*	5.00 -	8.00
15632 *I Feel Like Traveling On*	6.00 -	10.00
15671 *I Wants My Lulu*	6.00 -	10.00
15693 *Why Not Tonight*	6.00 -	10.00
15753 *At The Battle Front*	6.00 -	10.00
15900 *No Never Alone*	8.00 -	12.00
15944 *Old Kentucky Dew*	8.00 -	12.00
15971 *Life's Railway To Heaven*	8.00 -	12.00
16101 *I Surrender All*	8.00 -	12.00
16122 *Down The Lane To Home Sweet Home*	10.00 -	15.00

JOHN HUTCHENS:
Champion 15414 *The Preacher And The Bear*	7.00 -	10.00
15427 *The Sinking Of The Submarine S-4*	7.00 -	10.00
15467 *The Wreck Of The Virginian Train*	7.00 -	10.00
15483 *The Volunteer Organist*	7.00 -	10.00
15503 *I Got Mine*	7.00 -	10.00
15549 *He Included Me*	7.00 -	10.00
15550 *The Vestris Disaster*	10.00 -	15.00
15751 *Hard Luck Jim*	10.00 -	15.00

FRANK HUTCHISON (& SHERMAN LAWSON):
Okeh 45064 *Worried Blues*	15.00 -	20.00
45083 *The West Virginia Rag*	15.00 -	20.00
45089 *The C & O Excursion Train*	15.00 -	20.00
45093 *The Wild Horse*	15.00 -	20.00
45106 *Stackalee*	15.00 -	20.00
45114 *Worried Blues*	15.00 -	20.00
45121 *Logan County Blues*	15.00 -	20.00
45144 *All Night Long*	15.00 -	20.00
45258 *The Miner's Blues*	15.00 -	20.00
45274 *Hutchison's Rag*	15.00 -	20.00
45313 *The Burglar Man*	15.00 -	20.00
45361 *Johnny And Jane*	15.00 -	20.00
45378 *Cannon Ball Blues*	15.00 -	20.00
45425 *Railroad Bill*	20.00 -	30.00
45452 *Hell Bound Train*	20.00 -	30.00
45570 *Cumberland Gap*	25.00 -	35.00
Velvet-Tone 7107-V *Worried Blues*	15.00 -	20.00

H.K. HUTCHISON:
Gennett 6464 *Good Old Turnip Greens*	15.00 -	20.00

JERRY IRBY (& THE TEXAS RANCHERS):
Cireco 101 *Almost Every Time*	4.00 -	7.00
Globe 113 *Nails In My Coffin*	5.00 -	8.00
114 *Steel Guitar Special*	5.00 -	8.00
115 *Don't You Weep*	5.00 -	8.00
120 *Super Boogie Woogie*	5.00 -	8.00
Gulf 103 *Nails In My Coffin*	5.00 -	8.00
Imperial 8014 *Hillbilly Boogie*	5.00 -	8.00

HARVEY IRWIN:
Okeh 45014 *The Blind Child*	5.00 -	8.00
45052 *Sunny Tennessee*	5.00 -	8.00

WALLIE & TEX ISABELL:
Eddie's 1219 *Sugar Cain Gal*	5.00 -	8.00

JACK & BILL:
Okeh 45368 *The Lonesome Road*	7.00 -	10.00

JACK HARMONICA PLAYERS:
Vocalion 5353 *Mouth Harp Blues*	15.00 -	20.00

JACK & TONY:
Okeh 45421 *Since I Gave My Heart To You*	10.00 -	15.00
45422 *The Burial Of The Miner's Child*	10.00 -	15.00

JACKSON COUNTY BARN OWLS:
Champion 16031 *Bake That Chicken Pie*	20.00 -	30.00

JACKSON COUNTY RAMBLERS:
Champion 16284 *Carolina Girl* . . . . 15.00 - 20.00

JACK JACKSON:
Columbia 15497-D *I'm Just A Black Sheep* . . . . . 8.00 - 12.00
     15662-D *Flat Tire Blues* . . . . 8.00 - 12.00

AUNT MOLLY JACKSON:
Columbia 15731-D *Kentucky Miner's Wife* . . . . . 10.00 - 15.00

JACOBY BROS.:
TNT 1002 *There's No Use To Go Wrong* . . . . . . 5.00 - 8.00
     1004 *Cannonball* . . . . 5.00 - 8.00
     1009 *Bicycle Wreck* . . . . 5.00 - 8.00*

BEN JARRELL (Acc. by DA COSTA WOLTZ'S SOUTHERN BROADCASTERS):
Gennett 6143 *Merry Girl* . . . . 15.0 - 20.00
     6164 *I Know My Name Is Written There* . . . . 10.00 - 15.00
     6176 *When You Ask A Girl To Leave Her Happy Home* . . . . 15.00 - 20.00

JARVIS & JUSTICE:
Brunswick 333 *Guian Valley Waltz* . . . . 8.00 - 12.00
     358 *Muskrat Rag* . . . . 10.00 - 15.00

(BLIND ANDREW) JENKINS (& FRANK HICKS/CARSON ROBINSON/ WHITWORTH):
Okeh 45232 *On The Banks Of The Old Omaha.* 5.00 - 8.00
     45234 *In The Baggage Coach Ahead* . . . . 5.00 - 8.00
     45246 *Silver Threads Among The Gold* . . . . . 5.00 - 8.00
     45264 *My Dixie Home* . . . . 5.00 - 8.00
     45331 *I'll Be All Smiles Tonight* . . . . 5.00 - 8.00
     45443 *Don't Stop Praying* . . . . 5.00 - 8.00
     45481 *The Little Flower Girl* . . . . 6.00 - 10.00

FRANK JENKINS (& HIS PILOT MOUNTAINEERS):
Gennett 6165 *Home Sweet Home* . . . . 15.00 - 20.00
     7034 *Sunny Home In Dixie* . . . . 15.00 - 20.00

"GOOBY" JENKINS:
Okeh 45069 *Fiddlin' Bill* . . . . 8.00 - 12.00
     45082 *The Prisoner's Dream* . . . . 8.00 - 12.00
     45088 *Georgia Girl* . . . . 8.00 - 12.00
     45115 *Hopeful Walter Booth* . . . . 8.00 - 12.00

OSCAR JENKINS' MOUNTAINEERS:
Broadway 8249 *Burial OF Wild Bill* . . . . 7.00 - 10.00
Paramount 3240 *The Railway Flagman's Sweetheart* 7.00 - 10.00

JENNINGS BROS.:
Champion 15148 *Cripple Creek* . . . . 5.00 - 8.00

HERB JENNINGS:
Champion 15198 *The Death Of John Henry* . . . . 7.00 - 10.00
     15209 *The Roving Gambler* . . . . 7.00 - 10.00

JESSE'S STRING FIVE:
Bluebird 6443 *River Blues* . . . . 7.00 - 10.00

JOHNNY & SLIM:
Superior 2752 *Back To My Georgia Home* . . . . . 20.00 - 30.00

WHITEY JOHNS:
Challenge 852 *The Farm Relief Song* . . . . 5.00 - 8.00
     895 *The Prisoner's Rosary* . . . . 5.00 - 8.00
Paramount 3190 *The Little Old Sod Shanty* . . . . . 7.00 - 10.00

JOHNSON BROTHERS:
Victor 20661 *Down In Happy Valley* . . . . 12.00 - 16.00
     20662 *Sweet Nellie Brown* . . . . 12.00 - 16.00
     20891 *The Soldier's Poor Little Boy* . . . . 12.,00 - 16.00
     20940 *Careless Love* . . . . 12.00 - 16.00
     21243 *Two Brothers Are We* . . . . 12.00 - 16.00
     21532 *Old Timer From Caroliner* . . . . 12.00 - 16.00
     21646 *The Crime Of The D'Autremount Brothers* 12.00 - 16.00

JOHNSON & HARVEY:
Champion 16449 *Birdie* . . . . 15.00 - 20.00

EARL JOHNSON (& HIS CLODHOPPERS/ DIXIE ENTERTAINERS):
Okeh 45092 *Ain't Nobody's Business* . . . . 8.00 - 12.00
     45101 *John Henry Blues* . . . . 8.00 - 12.00
     45112 *Shortenin' Bread* . . . . 8.00 - 12.00
     45123 *Johnson's Old Grey Mule* . . . . 8.00 - 12.00
     45129 *I'm Satisfied* . . . . 8.00 - 12.00

     45156 *Twinkle Little Star* . . . . 8.00 - 12.00
     45171 *Johnnie Get Your Gun* . . . . 8.00 - 12.00
     45183 *They Don't Roost Too High For Me* . . . 8.00 - 12.00
     45194 *In The Shadow Of The Pines* . . . . 8.00 - 12.00
     45209 *Red Hot Breakdown* . . . . 15.00 - 20.00
     45223 *Mississippi Jubilee* . . . . 15.00 - 20.00
     45269 *Wire Grass Drag* . . . . 15.00 - 20.00
     45300 *G Rag* . . . . 15.00 - 20.00
     45383 *All Night Long* . . . . 15.00 - 20.00
     45406 *Poor Little Joe* . . . . 15.00 - 20.00
     45412 *Bringing In The Sheaves* . . . . 15.00 - 20.00
     45528 *Take Me Back To My Old Mountain Home* 15.00 - 20.00
     45545 *There's No Place Like Home* . . . . 15.00 - 20.00
     45559 *Way Down In Georgia* . . . . 15.00 - 20.00
Victor 23638 *I Lost My Gal* . . . . 20.00 - 30.00
     40212 *Fiddlin' Rufus* . . . . 15.00 - 20.00
     40304 *Green Mountain Polka* . . . . 15.00 - 20.00

EDWARD JOHNSON:
Champion 15048 *Sand Cave* . . . . 4.00 - 7.00

GENE JOHNSON:
Timely Tunes 1550 *T.B. Blues* . . . . 15.00 - 25.00
     1551 *Jimmie The Kid* . . . . 15.00 - 25.00
     1552 *Do Right Daddy Blues* . . . . 15.00 - 25.00

HENRY JOHNSON:
Champion 15732 *When The Snowflakes Fall Again* 10.00 - 15.00

JAMES JOHNSON:
Columbia 15453-D *Papa Please Buy Me An Airship* 10.00 - 15.00

JESS JOHNSON (& ROY HARVEY):
Champion 16255 *The Dying Brakeman* . . . . 20.00 - 30.00
     16780 *By A Cottage In The Twilight* . . . . 20.00 - 30.00

JIMMIE/JIMMY JOHNSON'S STRING BAND:
Champion 16389 *Washington Quadrille* . . . . 15.00 - 20.00
     16430 *Ching Chow* . . . . 15.00 - 20.00
     16506 *Bury Me On The Prairie* . . . . 15.00 - 20.00
     16516 *Drink More Cider* . . . . 15.00 - 20.00
     16541 *Old Blind Dog* . . . . 15.00 - 20.00
     16559 *Jennie Baker* . . . . 15.00 - 20.00
Superior 2821 *Step Lively* . . . . 15.00 - 25.00

JULIAN JOHNSON & LEON HYATT:
Bluebird 7510 *T.B. Killed My Daddy* . . . . 10.00 - 15.00

PAUL (AND CHARLES) JOHNSON:
Gennett 7313 *Wild Cat Hollow* . . . . 25.00 - 40.00
Superior 2612 *Wild Cat Hollow* . . . . 25.00 - 40.00

SMILIN' TUBBY JOHNSON:
Champion 15247 *I'm A Stern Old Bachelor* . . . . . 5.00 - 8.00
     15260 *Whoa, Mule, Whoa* . . . . 5.00 - 8.00
     15278 *Oh, Suzanna* . . . . 5.00 - 8.00
     15298 *Little Brown Jug* . . . . 5.00 - 8.00
     15430 *Oh, Dem Golden Slippers* . . . . 5.00 - 8.00

JONES BROTHERS:
Melotone 12017 *The Memory That Time Cannot Erase* . . . . 5.00 - 8.00
     12179 *The Little Green Valley* . . . . 5.00 - 8.00

BUDDY JONES:
Decca 5345, 5372, 5414, 5476, 5490, 5521, 5538, 5539 . . . . 4.00 - 8.00

CARL JONES:
Okeh 45516 *The Wild Man Of Borneo* . . . . 10.00 - 15.00
     45540 *My Tennessee Girl* . . . . 10.00 - 15.00

COLON JONES & RILEY PUCKETT:
Columbia 15774-D *That Saxophone Waltz* . . . . . . 20.00 - 30.00

DEMPSEY JONES:
Champion 16356 *The Cross-Eyed Butcher* . . . . . . 8.00 - 12.00
     16416 *Jack And May* . . . . 8.00 - 12.00
     16697 *Cabin Home* . . . . 8.00 - 12.00

FLOYD JONES:
Paramount 3029 *My Dream Of The Big Parade.* 10.00 - 15.00
     3030 *Someone Is Waiting Your Light* . . . . 10.00 - 15.00

GENE JONES:
Gold Star 1382 *Stop, Look And Listen* . . . . 4.00 - 6.00

GRANDPA JONES:

King 502, 508, 513, 517, 524	3.00 -	5.00

HIRAM JONES:

Homestead 16492 *Sailor's Hornpipe*	10.00 -	15.00

ROY JONES:

Columbia 15428-D *Southern Yodel Blues*	20.00 -	30.00

JORDAN BROTHERS:

Bluebird 7123 *Answer To Birmingham Jail*	8.00 -	12.00
7235 *Goin' Back Home*	8.00 -	12.00

JORDAN & RUPERT:

Supertone 9494 *It Won't Be Long Till My Grave Is Made*	7.00 -	10.00

JERRY JORDAN:

Supertone 9407 *The Cat's Got The Measles And The Whooping Cough*	10.00 -	15.00
9454 *The Baldheaded End Of A Broom*	7.00 -	10.00

JUDY & JEN, ACCOMP. BY THE HILLTOPPERS:

Vogue 744 *Flat River, Missouri*	12.00 -	18.00

JUERLING & JUSTIS:

Supertone 9099 *Grasshopper Polka*	———	

DICK JUSTICE:

Brunswick 336 *Brown Skin Blues*	15.00 -	20.00
367 *Henry Lee*	15.00 -	20.00
395 *Cocaine*	15.00 -	20.00

BOB KACKLEY (& BEN WEAVER):

Okeh 45531 *The Strawberry Roan*	10.00 -	15.00

KARL (DAVIS) & HARTY (TAYLOR):

Banner, Conqueror, Melotone, Perfect, Oriole, Romeo	3.00 -	5.00

ALFRED G. KARNES:

Victor 20840 *Where We'll Never Grow Old*	5.00 -	8.00
20933 *To The Work*	5.00 -	8.00
40076 *Days Of My Childhood Plays*	7.00 -	10.00
40327 *Called To The Foreign Field*	10.00 -	15.00

KAY BROTHERS:

Victor 23508 *Got The Jake Let Too*	15.00 -	20.00

BUELL KAZEE (& SOOKIE HOBBS):

Brunswick 144 *John Hardy*	7.00 -	10.00
145 *Rock Island*	7.00 -	10.00
154 *East Virginia*	7.00 -	10.00
155 *The Ship That's Sailing High*	7.00 -	10.00
156 *The Little Mohee*	7.00 -	10.00
157 *The Old Maid*	7.00 -	10.00
206 *The Faded Coat Of Blue*	7.00 -	10.00
210 *Red Wing*	7.00 -	10.00
211 *The Orphan Girl*	7.00 -	10.00
212 *The Cowboy's Farewell*	7.00 -	10.00
213 *The Butcher's Boy*	7.00 -	10.00
215 *Little Bessie*	7.00 -	10.00
216 *In The Shadow Of The Pines*	7.00 -	10.00
217 *Poor Boys Long Ways From Home*	7.00 -	10.00
218 *Gambling Blues*	7.00 -	10.00
330 *The Hobo's Last Ride*	7.00 -	10.00
338 *A Mountain Boy Makes His First Record*	7.00 -	10.00
351 *The Blind Man*	7.00 -	10.00
436 *The Little Mohee*	7.00 -	10.00
437 *The Old Maid*	7.00 -	10.00
481 *The Cowboy Trail*	7.00 -	10.00
Vocalion 5221 *In The Shadow Of The Pines*	8.00 -	12.00
5231 *Little Bessie*	8.00 -	12.00

HANK KEENE (& HIS CONNECTICUT HILLBILLIES):

Bluebird 5241, 5254, 5339, 6035	4.00 -	7.00
Brunswick 516 *The Run Away Boy*	7.00 -	10.00

(HOWARD) KEESE/KEESEE (& LOY BODINE):

Champion 16097 *Indiana Pal Of Mine*	20.00 -	30.00
16260 *The Mystery Of Number 5*	20.00 -	30.00
16374 *The Longest Train I Ever Saw*	20.00 -	30.00
16446 *Pal Of My Sunny Days*	20.00 -	30.00
Gennett 7082 *Blue Yodel No. 5*	20.00 -	30.00
7113 *My Dear Old Sunny South By The Sea*	20.00 -	30.00

7166 *Memphis Special Blues*	20.00 -	30.00
7315 *A Sailor's Plea*	20.00 -	30.00

KELLY BROTHERS:

Decca 5027 *Precious One*	5.00 -	8.00
Victor 23822 *After You've Gone*	10.00 -	15.00
23828 *Floating Down A River*	10.00 -	15.00
23833 *Always Remember*	10.00 -	15.00
23853 *Stormy Hawaiian Weather*	10.00 -	15.00

R.D. KELLY & JULIUS DUNN:

Okeh 45510 *Moonlight On The Colorado*	10.00 -	15.00
45543 *Harem Scarem*	10.00 -	15.00

REX KELLY:

Paramount 3319 *Down By The Railroad Track*	15.00 -	20.00

KEN, CHUCK & JIM:

Champion 16579 *I Like Mountain Music*	10.00 -	15.00
16672 *Cattesburg*	10.00 -	15.00
45131 *Home On The Range*	4.00 -	7.00

KENTUCKY GIRLS:

Columbia 15364-D *Old And Only In The Way*	7.00 -	10.00

KENTUCKY MOUNTAIN BOYS:

Supertone 2026 *The Two Orphans*	5.00 -	8.00
2260 *Many Happy Returns Of The Day*	5.00 -	8.00

KENTUCKY RAMBLERS:

Paramount 3283 *With My Mother Dead And Gone*	25.00 -	35.00
3284 *The Prisoner's Sweetheart*	25.00 -	35.00
3285 *The Unfortunate Brakeman*	25.00 -	35.00
3300 *Some Mother's Boy*	25.00 -	35.00

KENTUCKY SERENADERS:

Champion 15770 *Gonna Raise A Ruckus Tonight*	10.00 -	15.00

KENTUCKY STRING TICKLERS:

Champion 16577 *Stove Pipe Blues*	20.00 -	30.00
16581 *Georgia Bust Down*	20.00 -	30.00
16681 *Leaving Here Blues*	20.00 -	30.00
45014 *Leaving Here Blues*	10.00 -	15.00

KENTUCKY THOROBREDS:

Paramount 3010 *I Love You Best Of All*	12.00 -	18.00
3011 *Mother's Advice*	12.00 -	18.00
3014 *This World Is Not My Home*	12.00 -	18.00
3036 *The Preacher And The Bear*	12.00 -	18.00
3059 *Till We Meet Again*	12.00 -	18.00
3071 *I've Waited Long For You*	12.00 -	18.00
3080 *I'll Not Marry At All*	12.00 -	18.00

KESSINGER BROTHERS:

Brunswick 220 *Wednesday Night Waltz*	7.00 -	10.00
235 *Turkey In The Straw*	7.00 -	10.00
238 *Garfield March*	7.00 -	10.00
247 *Arkansas Traveler*	7.00 -	10.00
256 *Devil's Dream*	7.00 -	10.00
267 *Sixteen Days In Georgia*	7.00 -	10.00
308 *Sourwood Mountain*	7.00 -	10.00
309 *Mississippi Sawyer*	7.00 -	10.00
315 *Dill Pickle*	8.00 -	12.00
323 *Old Jake Gillespie*	8.00 -	12.00
331 *Wild Goose Chase*	8.00 -	12.00
344 *Black Hawk Waltz*	8.00 -	12.00
352 *Midnight Serenade Waltz*	8.00 -	12.00
364 *Durang Hornpipe*	8.00 -	12.00
396 *Chinky Pin*	8.00 -	12.00
411 *Sopping The Gravy*	8.00 -	12.00
458 *Rat Cheese Under The Hill*	8.00 -	12.00
468 *Little Brown Jug*	8.00 -	12.00
480 *Chicken Reel*	8.00 -	12.00
484 *Mary Jane Waltz*	8.00 -	12.00
518 *Dixie*	8.00 -	12.00
521 *Liza Jane*	8.00 -	12.00
540 *Ragtime Annie*	8.00 -	12.00
554 *Shoo, Fly*	8.00 -	12.00
563 *Steamboat Bill*	8.00 -	12.00
567 *Mexican Waltz*	8.00 -	12.00
580 *Little Betty Brown*	8.00 -	12.00
592 *Regal March*	8.00 -	12.00
Vocalion 02565 *Brownstown Girl*	15.00 -	20.00

02566 *Kanawha County Rag*............	15.00 -	20.00
5248 *Patty On The Turnpike*............	15.00 -	20.00
5481 *Hot Foot*........................	15.00 -	20.00

KIDOODLERS:
Vocalion 03717, 03866, 03925, 03974, 04063, 04133, 04202, 04260, 04338, 04404, 04503, 04907, 04960 ....

	3.00 -	6.00

B.F. KINCAID (THE BRIER HOPPER OF WFIW):

Gennett 7309 *Lane County Bachelor*.....	15.00 -	20.00

BRADLEY KINCAID:
Titles, issued contemporaneously on Banner, Conqueror, Melotone, Oriole, Perfect, Romeo, Vocalion: *After The Ball; Bury Me Out On The Prairie; The Fatal Derby Day; The Fatal Wedding; For Sale, A Baby; Gooseberry Pie; The Innocent Prisoner; I Wish I Had Someone To Love Me; The Lightning Express; A Picture From Life's Other Side; Red River Valley; Somewhere, Somebody's Waiting For You; The True And Trembling Brakeman; Two Little Girls In Blue*

	5.00 -	8.00
Bluebird 5179 *Long Long Ago*..........	5.00 -	8.00
5201 *The Old Wooden Bucket*...........	5.00 -	8.00
5255 *House Carpenter*................	5.00 -	8.00
5321 *Sweet Betsy From Pike*...........	5.00 -	8.00
5377 *The Death Of Jimmie Rodgers*.....	8.00 -	12.00
5423 *Mrs. Jimmie Rodgers' Lament*.....	8.00 -	12.00
5486 *The Life Of Jimmie Rodgers*......	8.00 -	12.00
5569 *The Ship That Never Returned*....	5.00 -	8.00
5895 *The Letter Edged In Black*.......	5.00 -	8.00
5971 *In The Hills Of Kentucky*........	5.00 -	8.00
8410 *Zeb Turney's Gal*...............	5.00 -	8.00
8478 *Mammy's Precious Baby*..........	5.00 -	8.00
8501 *The Blind Girl*.................	5.00 -	8.00
Brunswick 403 *Give My Love To Neil*...	7.00 -	10.00
420 *Methodist Pie*...................	7.00 -	10.00
464 *Cindy*..........................	7.00 -	10.00
485 *Old Coon Dog*...................	7.00 -	10.00
Bullet 615 *Ain't We Crazy*...........	5.00 -	8.00
Champion 45039 *On Top Of Old Smoky*....	5.00 -	8.00
45057 *Four Thousand Years Ago*.......	5.00 -	8.00
45098 *Wreck On The C & O Road*.......	5.00 -	8.00
45130 *Angels In Heaven Know I Love You*..	5.00 -	8.00
Decca 5025 *Ain't We Crazy*...........	5.00 -	8.00
5026 *The Old Wooden Rocker*..........	5.00 -	8.00
5048 *The Cowboy's Dream*............	5.00 -	8.00
Gennett 6363 *The Fatal Wedding*......	10.00 -	15.00
6417 *Methodist Pie*.................	10.00 -	15.00
6462 *The Swapping Song*.............	10.00 -	15.00
6620 *The Cuckoo Is A Pretty Bird*....	10.00 -	15.00
6761 *Four Thousand Tears Ago*........	10.00 -	15.00
6823 *Pearl Bryan*...................	10.00 -	15.00
6856 *The Little Mohee*..............	10.00 -	15.00
6900 *Angels In Heaven Know I Love You*...	10.00 -	15.00
6944 *Let THat Mule Go Aunk! Aunk!*.....	10.00 -	15.00
6958 *Charlie Brooks*................	10.00 -	15.00
7020 *Old Number Three*..............	10.00 -	15.00
7053 *On Top Of Old Smoky*...........	10.00 -	15.00
7081 *After The Ball*................	10.00 -	15.00
7112 *Cindy*.........................	10.00 -	15.00
Superior 366 *Sourwood Mountain*......	10.00 -	15.00
2656 *Four Thousand Years Ago*.......	10.00 -	15.00
2770 *On Top Of Old Smoky*...........	10.00 -	15.00
2788 *Old Number Three*..............	10.00 -	15.00
Supertone 9208 *Bury Me On The Prairie*..	5.00 -	8.00
9209 *Froggie Went A-Courting*........	5.00 -	8.00
9210 *Methodist Pie*.................	5.00 -	8.00
9211 *The Fatal Wedding*.............	5.00 -	8.00
9212 *Two Sisters*...................	8.00 -	12.00
9350 *Give My Love To Neil*..........	5.00 -	8.00
9362 *Four Thousand Years Ago*.......	5.00 -	8.00
9402 *The Little Mohee*..............	5.00 -	8.00

9403 *The Red River Valley*..........	5.00 -	8.00
9404 *Pearl Bryan*...................	5.00 -	8.00
9452 *Angels In Heaven Know I Love You*...	5.00 -	8.00
9471 *Happy Days Long Ago*...........	5.00 -	8.00
9505 *Old Number Three*..............	5.00 -	8.00
9565 *The Blind Girl*................	5.00 -	8.00
9566 *On Top Of Old Smoky*...........	5.00 -	8.00
9648 *After The Ball*................	5.00 -	8.00
9666 *Pretty Little Pink*............	5.00 -	8.00

CHICKIE KING:

Speed 108 *Lov-ie Lov-ie*.............	———	

MARTIN KING:

Superior 2530 *We Parted By The Riverside*.....	15.00 -	20.00
2574 *Lane County Bachelor*..........	15.00 -	20.00

RANDY KING:

TNT 108 *Tied And Bound*.............	———	

KIRBY & PHILLIPS:

Bluebird 6367, 7056.................	4.00 -	6.00

FRED KIRBY:

Bluebird 6325 *In The Shade Of The Pine*......	5.00 -	8.00
6419 *I'm A Gold Diggin' Papa*........	5.00 -	8.00
6597 *My Heavenly Sweetheart*........	5.00 -	8.00
6763, 7009, 7164, 7190, 7261, 7310........	4.00 -	7.00

FRED KIRBY (& DON WHITE/CLIFF CARLISLE):

Bluebird 6540 *My Old Saddle Horse Is Missing*..	5.00 -	8.00

ROCKY KIRKLAND:

J-B 1503 *Candy Baby*................	———	

BERT KNOWLES:

Okeh 45427 *Blue Undertaker's Blues No. 2*.....	15.00 -	20.00

VANCE KNOWLES & RED LAY:

Bluebird 6585 *A Thousand Miles From Texas*...	5.00 -	8.00

DON KUTTER:

Challenge 326 *Two Little Orphans*..........	7.00 -	10.00
327 *That Bad Man Stackalee*.........	8.00 -	12.00

PIEREE LA DIEU:

Columbia 15278-D *The Shanty-Man's Life*......	10.00 -	15.00

SLIM LAKE:

Superior 2819 *Peach Picking Time In Georgia*...	25.00 -	35.00

BELLA LAM & HIS GREENE COUNTY SINGERS:
Okeh 45126, 45136, 45145, 45177, 45228, 45407, 45456 ....

	4.00 -	8.00

LAMBERT & HILLPOT:

Paramount 3013 *My Carolina Home*..........	4.00 -	7.00

G.E. LANCASTER:

Superior 2538 *Tennessee Yodel*.............	20.00 -	30.00

LEE LANDERS:

Champion 15727 *Blue Yodel No. 3*............	10.00 -	15.00
15767 *Lullaby Yodel*...............	10.00 -	15.00

UNCLE BUD LANDRESS:

Victor 21036 *Candy Pulling Time*...........	8.00 -	12.00
21354 *Coon Hunting In Moonshine Hollow*..	8.00 -	12.00
23606 *The Daddy Song*..............	10.00 -	15.00
40252 *Rubber Doll Rag*.............	10.00 -	15.00

DUKE LANE:

Supertone 9425 *Blue Yodel No. 4*...........	8.00 -	12.00
9496 *Waiting For A Train*...........	8.00 -	12.00

LAND & MILES:

Supertone 9314 *The Old New Hampshire Village*	7.00 -	10.00

(FIDDLIN') BOB LARKAN/LARKIN (& FAMILY/HIS MUSIC MAKERS):

Okeh 45205 *Kansas City Reel*...............	15.00 -	20.00
45229 *Beautiful Belle*.............	15.00 -	20.00
45349 *The Woman Wear No Clothes At All*..	15.00 -	25.00
Vocalion 5277 *Saturday Night Waltz*.........	15.00 -	25.00
5313 *McLeod's Reel*................	15.00 -	25.00
5329 *Arkansas Waltz*...............	15.00 -	25.00

CHARLIE LAWMAN:

Crown 3144 *There Must Be A Bright Tomorrow*	5.00 -	8.00
Paramount 3304 *There Must Be A Bright Tomorrow*	7.00 -	10.00

JIMMIE LAWSON:
Victor 20477 *Tennessee Blues*............... 10.00 - 15.00
ZORA LAYMAN:
Decca 5033, 5034......................... 4.00 - 7.00
BERT LAYNE (& HIS GEORGIA SERENADERS/MELODY BOYS):
Brunswick 502 *Nights Of Gladness*.......... 10.00 - 15.00
582 *I Ain't Got No Sweetheart*............ 10.00 - 15.00
Champion 16346 *The Rabbit Hunt*........... 20.00 - 30.00
BENNIE LEADERS:
Freedom 5012 *Boots Don't Leave Me*......... 5.00 - 8.00
5020 *I'll Be Jumped Up And Down*........ 5.00 - 8.00
5029 *Naggin' Woman*.................... 5.00 - 8.00
Nucraft 105 *Clean Town Blues*............ 5.00 - 8.00
Ok'ed 1050 *Hey Miss Fannie*............ 5.00 - 8.00
LEAKE COUNTY REVELERS:
Columbia 15149-D *Johnson Gal*............ 7.00 - 10.00
15189-D *Wednesday Night Waltz*........ 3.00 - 5.00
15205-D *The Old Hat*................... 5.00 - 8.00
15227-D *My Bonnie Lies Over The Ocean*.... 5.00 - 8.00
15264-D *Merry Widow Waltz*............ 5.00 - 8.00
15292-D *They Go Wild Over Me*.......... 7.00 - 10.00
15318-D *Crow Black Chicken*............ 8.00 - 12.00
15353-D *Rockin' Yodel*................ 8.00 - 12.00
15380-D *Bring Me A Bottle*............ 8.00 - 12.00
15409-D *Georgia Camp Meeting*.......... 8.00 - 12.00
15427-D *Memories Waltz*................ 5.00 - 8.00
15441-D *Dry Town Blues*................ 10.00 - 15.00
15470-D *Saturday Night Breakdown*........ 10.00 - 15.00
15501-D *Beautiful Bells*................ 7.00 - 10.00
15520-D *Leake County Blues*............ 8.00 - 12.00
15569-D *Mississippi Moon*............... 10.00 - 15.00
15625-D *Birds In The Brook*............ 10.00 - 15.00
15648-D *When It's Springtime In The Rockies* 10.00 - 15.00
15668-D *Mississippi Breakdown*.......... 15.00 - 20.00
15691-D *Texas Fair*.................... 15.00 - 20.00
15767-D *Lazy Kate*.................... 15.00 - 20.00
15776-D *Listen To The Mockingbird*....... 15.00 - 20.00
LEATHERMAN SISTERS:
Bluebird 6490, 6590..................... 3.00 - 6.00
STEVE LEDFORD & HIS MOUNTAINERS:
Bluebird 7626, 7742...................... 4.00 - 7.00
LEE BROTHERS TRIO:
Brunswick 501 *Cotton Mills Blues*............ 10.00 - 15.00
A. LEE, B. BROWN, P. MELVIN, H. RICE, P. LINDSEY & JUDGE LEE:
Brunswick 419 *A Bootlegger's Joint In Atlanta*.. 15.00 - 20.00
NANCY LEE & THE HILLTOPPERS:
Vogue 744 *Don't Tetch It*.............. 12.00 - 18.00
WOODY LEFTWICH & ROY LILLY:
Champion 16345 *Lonesome Road Blues*........ 15.00 - 20.00
MALCOLM LEGETTE:
Columbia 15424-D *Song Of The Tramp*........ 7.00 - 10.00
LEON'S LONE STAR COWBOYS:
Champion 45151 *Mistreated Blues*.......... 4.00 - 8.00
45152 *Sweet Sue*.................... 4.00 - 8.00
45165 *Weary Blues*.................... 4.00 - 8.00
45169 *Bugle Call Rag*.................... 4.00 - 8.00
45174 *Dinah*.................... 4.00 - 8.00
45185 *White River Stomp*.................... 4.00 - 8.00
45195 *Just Forget*.................... 4.00 - 8.00
45196 *Milenburg Joys*.................... 4.00 - 8.00
Decca 5280, 5288, 5289, 5301, 5323, 5328, 5340,
5361, 5377, 5388, 5396, 5511, 5530........ 3.00 - 6.00
JOE (& MARY) LESTER (& DICK MOSS);
Superior 2606 *My Old Cottage Home*........ 10.00 - 15.00
2632 *That Silver Haired Daddy Of Mine*..... 10.00 - 15.00
2654 *Missouri Is Calling*.................... 10.00 - 15.00
2675 *Yodel Your Troubles Away*.......... 15.00 - 20.00
2683 *Down And Out Blues*.................... 15.00 - 20.00
2702 *By The Ozark Trail*.................... 15.00 - 20.00

LEWIS BROTHERS:
Victor 40172 *Sally Johnson*.................. 15.00 - 20.00
40187 *When Summer Comes Again*........ 15.00 - 20.00
ARCHIE LEWIS:
Champion 16677 *Miss Handy Hanks*......... 15.00 - 20.00
TEXAS JIM LEWIS & LONE STAR COWBOYS:
Vocalion 03754, 03915, 03977............... 4.00 - 8.00
LIGHT CRUST DOUGHBOYS:
Okeh, most issues...................... 3.00 - 6.00
Vocalion 02992 *My Pretty Quadroon*......... 5.00 - 8.00
03017 *El Rancho Grande*............ 5.00 - 8.00
03065, 03141, 03239, 03610, 03660, 03867, 03926,
04158, 04216, 04261, 04326, 04403, 04468,
04559, 04560, 04638, 04701, 04702, 04770,
04825, 04921, 04965, 04973, 04974, 05039... 4.00 - 7.00
ADD LINDSAY:
Victor 21401 *Whoa Mule*.................. 7.00 - 10.00
RED LINDSEY:
Talent 711 *Penitentiary Blues*.................. 5.00 - 8.00
W.A. LINDSEY & ALVIN CONDER:
Okeh 45346 *Good Old Turnip Greens*......... 15.00 - 20.00
LITTLE JIMMIE (See ASHER SIZEMORE)
TOBE LITTLE:
Okeh 40460, 40479, 45090................... 4.00 - 8.00
DOCTOR LLOYD & HOWARD MAXEY:
Okeh 45150 *Western Union*............... 15.00 - 25.00
RUSTY LOCKE:
TNT 1012 *Milk Cow Blues*................ 5.00 - 8.00
HANK LOCKLIN:
Gold Star 1341 *Rio Grande Waltz*............ 8.00 - 12.00
Royalty 603 *Please Come Back And Stay*...... 8.00 - 12.00
604 *You've Been Talking In Your Sleep*...... 8.00 - 12.00
GEORGE E. LOGAN ("PETE THE HIRED MAN"):
Champion 45036 *By The Ozark Trail*......... 5.00 - 8.00
LOGAN COUNTY TRIO:
Challenge 302 *The Buckin' Mule*.............. 5.00 - 8.00
325 *Hand Me Down My Walking Cane*...... 5.00 - 8.00
LOG CABIN BOYS:
Banner 32903 *Ole Bill Jackson Brown*......... 5.00 - 8.00
Decca 5035, 5036, 5103, 5110............... 15.00 - 20.00
LONESOME COWBOY:
Champion 16767 *Memphis Gal*............ 15.00 - 20.00
45080 *Memphis Gal*................ 5.00 - 8.00
Perfect 12591 *I'm Just A Black Sheep*......... 4.00 - 7.00
Superior 2652 *The Yodeling Cowboy*.......... 20.00 - 30.00
LONESOME COWGIRL:
Champion 16767 *Lonesome Cowboy*.......... 15.00 - 20.00
Superior 2631 *Livin' In The Mountains*....... 15.00 - 20.00
2652 *My Mother Was A Lady*........... 15.00 - 20.00
LONESOME LUKE (& HIS FARMS BOYS):
Champion 16229 *Dogs In The Ash Can*....... 15.00 - 25.00
16269 *Beaver Valley Breakdown*............ 15.00 - 25.00
LONESOME PINE TWINS:
Banner 6041 *A Picture From Life's Other Side*.. 3.00 - 5.00
LONE STAR COWBOYS:
Bluebird 5283........................ 4.00 - 7.00
6001, 6052........................ 4.00 - 7.00
Champion 45046 *Dillinger's Warning*......... 5.00 - 8.00
Victor 23846 *Deep Elm Blues*........ 15.00 - 20.00
23850 *Wonderful Child*........... 10.00 - 15.00
LONE STAR RANGERS:
Broadway 8141 *The Prison Warden's Secret*.... 7.00 - 10.00
8142 *The Train That Never Arrived*........ 7.00 - 10.00
8144 *Farm Relief Song*........ 7.00 - 10.00
8150 *Eleven·More Months And Ten More Days* 7.00 - 10.00
3202 *The Train That Never Arrived*........ 7.00 - 10.00
3208 *Farm Relief Song*........ 7.00 - 10.00
3218 *Eleven More Months And Ten More Days* 7.00 - 10.00
Regal 8973 *Eleven More Months And Ten More Days*...................... 5.00 - 8.00

LONG BROTHERS:

Victor 23622 *Cross-Eyed Gal That Lived Upon The*
Hill .... 15.00 - 20.00
  23637 *Missouri Is Calling* .... 15.00 - 20.00

BEVERLY & JIM/JIMMIE/JIMMY LONG:

Bluebird 5139, 5188 .... 3.00 - 6.00
Champion 16659 *Two Little Orphans* ...... 12.00 - 16.00

CLAY LONG & HIS LONG HORNS:

Vocalion 04602, 04731, 04812 .... 4.00 - 7.00

JIMMIE/JIMMY LONG (& BEVERLY
  LONG/CLIFF KEISER):

Champion 16099 *Missouri I'm Calling You* .... 10.00 - 15.00
  16117 *That's Why I Left The Mountains* .... 10.00 - 15.00
  16164 *My Alabama Home* .... 15.00 - 20.00
  16190 *My Old Pal Of Yesterday* .... 10.00 - 15.00
  16214 *Listen To The Voice* .... 8.00 - 12.00
  16233 *Yodel Your Troubles Away* .... 10.00 - 15.00
  16280 *Have You Found Somebody Else To Love* 10.00 - 15.00
  16296 *Down And Out Blues* .... 15.00 - 20.00
  16311 *Let's Get Together* .... 15.00 - 20.00
  16632 *The Answer To 21 Years* .... 15.00 - 20.00
  16641 *Hang It In The Hen House* ...... 15.00 - 20.00
  16663 *The Old Folks Back Home* .... 10.00 - 15.00
  16671 *My California Mountain Rose* ..... 15.00 - 20.00
  45022, 45023, 45084, 45089 .... 4.00 - 6.00
Gennett 7287 *Blue Pining For You* .... 15.00 - 25.00
  7314 *Missouri Is Calling* .... 15.00 - 25.00
Victor 23705 *Doggone Blues* .... 15.00 - 25.00
  23724 *Down And Out* .... 15.00 - 25.00
  23824 *Alone With My Sorrows* .... 15.00 - 25.00

LOOKOUT MOUNTAIN BOYS:

Paramount 3164 *Down In Atlanta* .... 15.00 - 20.00
  3264 *Down In Atlanta* .... 15.00 - 20.00

LOOKOUT MOUNTAIN REVELERS:

Paramount 3105 *Barn Dance On The Mountain* . 15.0 - 20.00
  3111 *Pussy Cat Rag* .... 15.00 - 20.00
  3123 *Dreaming Of Mother* .... 10.00 - 15.00
  3143 *Bury Me Beneath The Willow* ..... 10.00 - 15.00

LOUISIANA LOU:

Bluebird 5424, 5484, 5636, 5749 ...... 3.00 - 6.00
Victor 23858 *Go 'Long Mule* .... 10.00 - 15.00

LOUISIANA ROUNDERS:

Decca 5483, 5495 .... 4.00 - 8.00

LOUISIANA STROLLERS:

Champion 45199 *Strollers Waltz* .... 4.00 - 6.00

(DADDY) JOHN LOVE:

Bluebird 6294 *My Little Red Ford* .... 10.00 - 15.00
  6491 *Cotton Mill Blues* .... 10.00 - 15.00
  6583 *Blue Days* .... 10.00 - 15.00
  6624 *Railroad Blues* .... 10.00 - 15.00
  6675 *Over The Hills In Carolina* ...... 10.00 - 15.00

RAMBLIN' RED LOWERY:

Vocalion 02665 *Ramblin' Red's Memphis Yodel.* ——

LUKE THE DRIFTER (See HANK WILLIAMS):

LULLABY LARKERS:

Champion 16257 *Shine On Harvest Moon* ...... 15.00 - 20.00
  16295 *The True And Trembling Breakman* ... 15.00 - 20.00
  16322 *When The Cactus Is In Bloom* ..... 15.00 - 20.00
  16364 *The Chicken Roost Blues* .... 15.00 - 20.00
  16417 *My Lonely Boyhood Days* .... 15.00 - 20.00
  45132, 45186 .... 5.00 - 8.00

LULU BELLE & SCOTTY:

Vocalion 04690, 04772, 04841, 04910, 04962 ... 4.00 - 7.00
Vogue 718 *Some Sunday Morning* .... 12.00 - 18.00
  719 *I Get A Kick Out Of Corn* .... 12.00 - 18.00
  720 *Time Will Tell* .... 12.00 - 18.00

BASCOM LAMAR LUNSFORD:

Brunswick 219 *Mountain Dew* .... 8.00 - 12.00
  227 *Lost John Dean* .... 8.00 - 12.00
  228 *Darby's Ram* .... 8.00 - 12.00
  229 *Lulu Wall* .... 8.00 - 12.00

  230 *Kidder Cole* .... 8.00 - 12.00
  231 *Dry Bones* .... 8.00 - 12.00
  314 *Dry Bones* .... 8.00 - 12.00
Columbia 15595-D *Speaking The Truth* ...... 15.00 - 20.00
Okeh 40155 *Jesse James* .... 15.00 - 20.00
  45008 *Fate Of Santa Barbara* .... 15.00 - 20.00
Vocalion 5246 *Lost John Dean* .... 10.00 - 15.00
  5252 *Little Turtle Dove* .... 10.00 - 15.00

TED LUNSFORD:

Champion 16287 *The Hobo's Return* .... 15.00 - 20.00

FRANK LUTHER:

This artist recorded for many labels in the 1920s and
  1930s. Most of his records are of minimal value
  or interest to the collector. Following are a few
  possible exceptions.

Broadway 8102 *Memphis Yodel* .... 5.00 - 8.00
Columbia 15588-D *Oklahoma Charley* .... 5.00 - 8.00
  15768-D *Carry Me Back To The Mountains* .. 5.00 - 8.00
Edison (thick) .... 4.00 - 8.00
Edison (thin) .... 8.00 - 12.00
Timely Tunes 1558 *Divorce Blues* .... 8.00 - 12.00
Victor 23737 *Sweetest Of All My Dreams* ..... 7.00 - 10.00
Vocalion 5227, 5278 .... 4.00 - 8.00

"MAC" (AND HIS HAYWIRE ORCHESTRA):
  (See also "RADIO MAC")

Victor 21343, 21420, 21421, 21487, 21704, 21761 3.00 - 6.00
Victor V-40016 *Trail To Mexico* .... 4.00 - 6.00

W.W. MacBETH:

Brunswick 373 *Southern Melodies* .... 5.00 - 8.00
  443 *Red Wing* .... 5.00 - 8.00
  571 *Darling Nellie Gray* .... 5.00 - 8.00

BOB MacGIMSEY:

Victor 23562 *Religion Ain't Nothin' To Play With* 7.00 - 10.00
  23584 *Bob's Medley* .... 7.00 - 10.00
  23612 *Southern Melodies* .... 7.00 - 10.00

MACK BROTHERS:

Decca 5073, 5086, 5125 .... 4.00 - 7.00

BILL MACK:

Imperial 8114 *Crazy Baby Boogie* .... 5.00 - 8.00
  8151 *Big Bad Daddy* .... 5.00 - 8.00*
  8174 *Play My Boogie* .... 5.00 - 8.00
  8192 *Forever I'll Wait For You* .... 4.00 - 6.00*

MACON QUARTETTE:

Columbia 15211-D *Uncle Joe* .... 5.00 - 8.00

UNCLE DAVE MACON; MACON & (SID)
  HARKREADER; UNCLE DAVE MACON &
  KIRK/SAM McGEE; UNCLE DAVE
  MACON & HIS FRUIT JAR DRINKERS:

Bluebird 5842 *One More River To Cross* ...... 15.00 - 25.00
  5873 *I'll Tickle Nancy* .... 15.00 - 25.00
  5926 *Just One Way To The Pearly Gates* .... 15.00 - 25.00
  7174 *From Jerusalem To Jericho* .... 15.00 - 20.00
  7234 *Travelin Down The Road* .... 15.00 - 20.00
  7350 *Bum Hotel* .... 15.00 - 20.00
  7385 *Fame Apart From God's Approval* .... 15.00 - 20.00
  7549 *She's Got The Money Too* .... 15.00 - 20.00
  7779 *Peek-A-Boo* .... 15.00 - 20.00
  7951 *Country Ham And Red Gravy* ...... 15.00 - 20.00

8279 *Working For My Lord*	15.00 -	20.00
8325 *Railroadin' And Gamblin'*	15.00 -	20.00
8341 *Beautiful Love*	15.00 -	20.00
8379 *Johnny Grey*	15.00 -	20.00
8422 *They're After Me*	15.00 -	20.00
Brunswick 112 *On The Dixie Bee Line*	15.00 -	20.00
114 *The Cross Eyed Butcher & The Cackling Hen*	15.00 -	20.00
263 *Governor Al Smith*	20.00 -	30.00
266 *Worthy Of Estimation*	20.00 -	30.00
292 *I'm The Child To Fight*	20.00 -	30.00
329 *From Earth To Heaven*	20.00 -	30.00
340 *Uncle Dave's Travels-Part 1*	20.00 -	30.00
349 *Uncle Dave's Travels-Part 2*	20.00 -	30.00
355 *Uncle Dave's Travels-Part 3*	20.00 -	30.00
362 *Uncle Dave's Travels-Part 4*	20.00 -	30.00
425 *Coming Round The Mountains*	20.00 -	30.00
Champion 16805 *When The Train Comes Along*	75.00 -	100.00
16822 *Don't Get Weary Children*	75.00 -	100.00
45048 *Don't Get Weary Children*	15.00 -	25.00
45105 *When The Train Comes Along*	15.00 -	25.00
Decca 5369 *Don't Get Weary Children*	10.00 -	15.00
5373 *Thank God For Everything*	10.00 -	15.00
Montgomery Ward 4819 *One More River To Cross*	10.00 -	15.00
7347 *The Bum Hotel*	10.00 -	15.00
7348 *Honest Confession Is Good For The Soul*	10.00 -	15.00
7349 *From Jerusalem To Jericho*	10.00 -	15.00
7350 *Two-In-One Chewing Gum*	10.00 -	15.00
7884 *She's Got The Money Too*	10.00 -	15.00
7885 *Johnny Grey*	10.00 -	15.00
8029 *Don't Get Weary Children*	10.00 -	15.00
Okeh 45507 *Tennessee Red Fox Chase*	50.00 -	80.00
45522 *Mysteries Of The World*	50.00 -	80.00
45552 *She's Got The Money Too*	50.00 -	80.00
Vocalion 5001 *Deliverance Will Come*	15.00 -	25.00
5002 *Arcade Blues*	15.00 -	25.00
5003 *The Old Man's Drunk Again*	15.00 -	25.00
5004 *Something's Always Sure To Tickle Me*	15.00 -	25.00
5005 *Sourwood Mountain Medley*	15.00 -	25.00
5006 *Sassy Sam*	15.00 -	25.00
5007 *My Girl's A High Born Lady*	15.00 -	25.00
5008 *Them Two Gals Of Mine*	15.00 -	25.00
5009 *I Ain't Got Long To Stay*	15.00 -	25.00
5010 *Sho' Fly, Don't Bother Me*	15.00 -	25.00
5011 *Uncle Ned*	15.00 -	25.00
5012 *Diamond In The Rough*	15.00 -	25.00
5013 *Tossing The Baby So High*	15.00 -	25.00
5014 *Never Make Love No More*	15.00 -	25.00
5040 *(She Was Always) Chewing Gum*	15.00 -	25.00
5041 *Papa's Billie Goat*	15.00 -	25.00
5042 *Down By The River*	15.00 -	25.00
5043 *The Fox Chase*	15.00 -	25.00
5046 *Jonah And The Whale*	15.00 -	25.00
5047 *Soldier's Joy*	15.00 -	25.00
5051 *All I've Got's Gone*	15.00 -	25.00
5060 *Run, Nigger, Run*	15.00 -	25.00
5061 *Old Dan Tucker*	15.00 -	25.00
5062 *The Girl I Left Behind Me*	15.00 -	25.00
5065 *Southern Whistling Coon*	15.00 -	25.00
Vocalion 5066 *Oh, Where Is My Boy Tonight*	15.00 -	25.00
5067 *All-Go-Hungry Hash House*	15.00 -	25.00
5070 *Save My Mother's Picture From The Sale*	15.00 -	25.00
5071 *Muskrat Medley*	15.00 -	25.00
5075 *Down By The Old Mill Stream*	15.00 -	25.00
5081 *Arkansas Travelers*	15.00 -	25.00
5082 *Struttin' Round*	15.00 -	25.00
5095 *I've Got The Mourning Blues*	15.00 -	25.00
5096 *On The Dixie Bee Line*	15.00 -	25.00
5097 *Way Down The Old Plank Road*	15.00 -	25.00
5098 *He Won The Heart Of My Sarah Jane*	15.00 -	25.00
5099 *Whoop 'Em Up Cindy*	15.00 -	25.00
5100 *Poor Sinners, Fare You Well*	15.00 -	25.00

5104 *Old Ties*	15.00 -	25.00
5109 *I Tickled Nancy*	15.00 -	25.00
5148 *Bake That Chicken Pie*	25.00 -	40.00
5149 *In The Shade Of The Old Apple Tree*	25.00 -	40.00
5151 *Carve That Possum*	25.00 -	40.00
5152 *Rockabout My Sara Jane*	25.00 -	40.00
5153 *Tell Her To Come Back Home*	25.00 -	40.00
5154 *Walk, Tom Wilson, Walk*	25.00 -	40.00
5155 *Sail Away, Ladies*	25.00 -	40.00
5156 *Sleepy Lou*	25.00 -	40.00
5157 *I's Gwine Back To Dixie*	25.00 -	40.00
5159 *Poor Old Dad*	25.00 -	40.00
5161 *The Mockingbird Song Medley*	25.00 -	40.00
5163 *When Ruebin Comes To Town*	25.00 -	40.00
5164 *Backwater Blues*	25.00 -	40.00
5165 *Go Along Mule*	25.00 -	40.00
5172 *More Like Your Dad Every Day*	25.00 -	40.00
5261 *The New Ford Car*	25.00 -	40.00
5316 *Jesus, Lover Of My Soul*	25.00 -	40.00
5341 *Farm Relief*	25.00 -	40.00
5356 *The Life And Death Of Jesse James*	25.00 -	40.00
5374 *We Need A Change In Business All Around*	25.00 -	40.00
5380 *Susie Lee*	25.00 -	40.00
5397 *Put Me In My Little Bed*	25.00 -	40.00
14847 *(She Was Always) Chewing Gum*	15.00 -	25.00
14848 *Keep My Skillet Good And Greasy*	15.00 -	25.00
14849 *Down By The River*	15.00 -	25.00
14850 *Old Maid's Last Hope (A Burglar Song)*	15.00 -	25.00
14864 *Jonah And The Whale*	15.00 -	25.00
14904 *All I've Got's Gone*	15.00 -	25.00
15032 *Run, Nigger, Run*	15.00 -	25.00
15033 *Old Dan Tucker*	15.00 -	25.00
15034 *Down In Arkansaw*	15.00 -	25.00
15063 *Watermelon Smilin' On The Vine*	15.00 -	25.00
15076 *All-Go-Hungry Hash House*	15.00 -	25.00
15100 *Save My Mother's Picture From The Sale*	15.00 -	25.00
15101 *Muskrat Medley*	15.00 -	25.00
15143 *Down By The Old Mill Stream*	15.00 -	25.00
15192 *Arkansas Travelers*	15.00 -	25.00
15319 *I've Got The Mourning Blues*	15.00 -	25.00
15320 *On The Dixie Bee Line*	15.00 -	25.00
15321 *Rise When The Rooster Crows*	15.00 -	25.00
15322 *He Won The Heart Of My Sarah Jane*	15.00 -	25.00
15323 *Whoop 'Em Up Cindy*	15.00 -	25.00
15324 *Poor Sinners, Fare You Well*	15.00 -	25.00
15325 *Old Ties*	15.00 -	25.00
15341 *I Tickled Nancy*	15.00 -	25.00
15439 *Uncle Dave's Beloved Solo*	15.00 -	25.00
15441 *In The Good Old Summer Time*	15.00 -	25.00
15442 *Something's Always Sure To Tickle Me*	15.00 -	25.00
15443 *Sourwood Mountain Medley*	15.00 -	25.00
15444 *Sassy Sam*	15.00 -	25.00
15445 *My Girl's A High Born Lady*	15.00 -	25.00
15446 *Them Two Girls Of Mine*	15.00 -	25.00
15447 *We Are Up Against It Now*	15.00 -	25.00
15448 *Sho' Fly Don't Bother Me*	15.00 -	25.00
15450 *Uncle Ned*	15.00 -	25.00
15451 *Hold On To The Sleigh*	15.00 -	25.00
15452 *Kissin' On The Sly*	15.00 -	25.00
15453 *Never Make Love No More*	15.00 -	25.00

MADDOX BROS. & ROSE:

4-Star 1184 *Midnight Train*	5.00 -	8.00
1185 *Milk Cow Blues*	5.00 -	8.00

MADDUX FAMILY:

Decca 5393 *Stone Rag*	4.00 -	7.00

MADISONVILLE STRING BAND:

Champion 16452 *B Flat Rag*	10.00 -	15.00
16503 *Next To Your Mother, Who Do You Love*	15.00 -	20.00
45005 *B Flat Rag*	7.00 -	10.00
Decca 5437 *B Flat Rag*	5.00 -	8.00
Superior 2756 *B Flat Rag*	10.00 -	15.00

MAGNOLIA

MAGNOLIA TRIO:

Okeh 45505 *My Carolina Sweetheart*	7.00 -	10.00
45521 *'Neath The Old Pine Tree At Twilight.*	7.00 -	10.00

JACK MAHONEY:

Columbia 15685-D *The Convict And The Bird* ..	10.00 -	15.00
15712-D *The Convict's Return*	10.00 -	15.00

**J.E. MAINER (& HIS MOUNTAINEERS);
WADE MAINER & SONS; WADE MAINER
& ZEKE MORRIS; WADE MARINER &
SON OF THE MOUNTAINEERS;
MAINERS MOUNTAINEERS; MAINER'S
SMILIN RANGERS:**

Bluebird 6065 *Maple On The Hill*	5.00 -	8.00
6088 *This World Is Not My Home*	7.00 -	10.00
6090 *Broken Hearted Blues*	7.00 -	10.00
6104 *Let Her Go, God Bless Her*	7.00 -	10.00
6160 *The City On The Hill*	7.00 -	10.00
6194 *Write A Letter To Mother*	7.00 -	10.00
6222 *Longest Train*	7.00 -	10.00
6290 *Fatal Wreck Of The Bus*	7.00 -	10.00
6293 *Maple On The Hill-Part 2*	7.00 -	10.00
6324 *Satisfied*	7.00 -	10.00
6347 *A Leaf From The Sea*	7.00 -	10.00
6383 *Just As The Sun Went Down*	7.00 -	10.00
6385 *When I Reach My Home Eternal*	7.00 -	10.00
6424 *New Lost Train Blues*	7.00 -	10.00
6440 *Behind The Parlor Door*	7.00 -	10.00
6460 *Nobody's Darling On Earth*	7.00 -	10.00
6479 *The Old And Faded Picture*	7.00 -	10.00
6489 *Cradle Days*	7.00 -	10.00
6539 *Got A Home In That Rock*	7.00 -	10.00
6551 *Come Back To Your Dobie Shack* ..	7.00 -	10.00
Bluebird 6584 *Watermelon On The Vine*	7.00 -	10.00
6596 *Shake Hands With Mother*	7.00 -	10.00
6624 *What Makes Him Do It?*	7.00 -	10.00
6629 *John Henry Was A Little Boy*	7.00 -	10.00
6653 *Cowboy's Pony In Heaven*	7.00 -	10.00
6675 *Budded Roses*	7.00 -	10.00
6704 *Been Foolin' Me Baby*	7.00 -	10.00
6738 *Won't Be Worried Long*	7.00 -	10.00
6752 *Hop Along Peter*	7.00 -	10.00
6784 *Just One Way To The Pearly Gates*	7.00 -	10.00
6792 *Seven And A Half*	7.00 -	10.00
6840 *Little Birdie*	7.00 -	10.00
6890 *Always Born A Gambler*	7.00 -	10.00
6936 *In The Land Beyond The Blue*	7.00 -	10.00
6993 *Little Rosebuds*	7.00 -	10.00
7114 *Answer To Two Little Rosebuds*	7.00 -	10.00
7151 *Answer To Greenback Dollar*	7.00 -	10.00
7165 *I'm Not Turning Backward*	7.00 -	10.00
7201 *Little Maggie*	7.00 -	10.00
7222 *In The Little Village Churchyard*	7.00 -	10.00
7249 *Wild Bill Jones*	7.00 -	10.00
7274 *Memory Lane*	5.00 -	10.00
7289 *Kiss Me Cindy*	5.00 -	10.00
7298 *Riding On Train 45*	5.00 -	10.00
7349 *Don't Go Out*	5.00 -	10.00
7384 *What Are You Goin' To Do, Brother?* ..	5.00 -	8.00
7412 *Lamp Lightin' Time In Heaven*	5.00 -	8.00
7424 *All My Friends*	5.00 -	8.00
7471 *If I Lose, Let Me Lose*	5.00 -	8.00
7483 *Don't Get To Deep In Love*	5.00 -	8.00
7523 *Floating Down The Stream Of Time*	5.00 -	8.00
7561 *I Won't Be Worried*	5.00 -	8.00
7586 *Your Best Friend Is Always Near*	5.00 -	8.00
7587 *Mountain Sweetheart*	5.00 -	8.00
7659 *I Once Loved A Young Man*	5.00 -	8.00
7730 *Just Over In Glory Land*	5.00 -	8.00
Bluebird 7753 *Where Romance Calls*	5.00 -	8.00
7845 *Mitchell Blues*	5.00 -	8.00
7965 *Great Reaping Day*	5.00 -	8.00

MARTIN

7965 *More Good Women Gone Wrong*	5.00 -	8.00
8042 *Sparkling Blue Eyes*	5.00 -	8.00
Bluebird (higher numbers)	4.00 -	7.00
King	3.00 -	5.00

JACK MAJOR:

Brunswick 252 *Tennessee Mountain Girl*	10.00 -	15.00
Columbia 15362-D *My Kentucky Mountain Sweetheart*	10.00 -	15.00

BLIND JOE MANGUM & FRED SHRIBER:

Okeh 40018 *Bacon And Cabbage*	8.00 -	12.00

MAPLE CITY FOUR:

Supertone 9193 *Roll Dem Bones*	5.00 -	8.00

MARKHAM BROS.:

Challenge 399 *I Am Resolved*	5.00 -	8.00
400 *Constantly Abiding*	5.00 -	8.00
401 *I'm On The Sunny Side*	7.00 -	10.00

ANDY MARLOW:

Champion 15875 *My Little Lady*	15.00 -	20.00
15879 *Blue Yodel No. 5*	15.00 -	20.00

MARLOW AND YOUNG:

Champion 15691 *Let Her Go I'll Meet Her*	7.00 -	10.00
15732 *My Carolina Home*	15.00 -	20.00
15750 *Six Months Ain't Long*	15.00 -	20.00

CHARLIE MARSHALL:

Vocalion 03045 *The Old Hitchin' Rail*	5.00 -	8.00

MARTIN BROTHERS:

Paramount 3194 *The Marion Massacre*	15.00 -	25.00
3217 *Whistling Rufus*	15.00 -	25.00
3248 *Don't Marry A Man If He Drinks*	15.00 -	25.00

MARTIN MELODY BOYS:

Columbia 15413-D *The Donald Rag*	15.00 -	20.00

**(ASA) MARTIN & (JAMES) ROBERTS;
MARTIN & ROSE; MARTIN & HOBBS:**

Titles, issued contemporaneously on Banner, Conqueror, Melotone, Oriole, Perfect, Romeo: *Aged Mother; Bronco Bill; Budded Roses; Bury Me Neath The Weeping Willow; Careless Love; The Contented Hobo; Crawdad Song; Darling Nellie Gray; Down On The Farm; The Dying Cowboy; The East Bound Train; Give My Love To Nellie, Jack; Good Bye Betty; Hang Down Your Head And Cry; Hot Corn; I Tickled Her Under The Chin; The Knoxville Girl; A Letter From Home Sweet Home; Lillie Dale; The Little Old Jail House; Little Shack Around The Corner; Low Down Hanging Around; Message Of A Broken Heart; My Blue Eyed Boy; My Dixie Home; My Lover On The Deep Blue Sea; My Old Homestead By The Sea; My Rocky Mountain Queen; Ninety-Nine Years; The Pine Tree On The Hill; Prisoner No. 999; The Roundup In The Spring; The Rovin' Moonshiner; Rycove Cyclone; Shadows And Dreams; She Ain't Built That Way; The Ship That Never Returned; Sunny Tennessee; Sweet Florine; There's A Little Box Of Pine On The 7:29; There's No Place Like Home; There's Someone Waiting For You; The Wandering Hobo; When It's Lamp Lighting Time In The Valley; When The Roses Bloom In Dixie; Where's My Sweetie Now...*

...	5.00 -	8.00
Champion 16049 *An Old Fashioned Picture Of Mother*	12.00 -	16.00
16272 *Mind Your Own Business*	12.00 -	16.00
16299 *The Contented Hobo*	12.00 -	16.00
16520 *Hot Corn*	15.00 -	25.00
16529 *Prisoner No. 949*	15.00 -	25.00
16536 *Wild Cat Rag*	15.00 -	25.00
16539 *The Little Old Jailhouse*	15.00 -	25.00
16557 *The Roving Moonshiner*	15.00 -	25.00
16568 *I Must See My Mother*	15.00 -	20.00
16589 *I'm On My Way Back Home*	15.00 -	20.00
16597 *Shadows And Dreams*	15.00 -	20.00

16610 *Wolf County Blues*	20.00 -	30.00
16611 *Gamblin' Cowboy*	20.00 -	30.00
16627 *Jakewalk Papa*	20.00 -	30.00
16769 *It's Funny When You Feel That Way*	20.00 -	30.00
Champion 45034 *Bronco Bill*	7.00 -	10.00
45065 *Hot Corn*	7.00 -	10.00
45067 *My Cabin Home Among The Hills*	5.00 -	8.00
45129 *She Ain't Built That Way*	5.00 -	8.00
45133 *Red River Valley Rose*	5.00 -	8.00
45142 *Take Those Lips Away*	5.00 -	8.00
Champion 45175 *The Dying Girl's Message*	5.00 -	8.00
45176 *Prisoner No. 949*	5.00 -	8.00
Decca 5444 *Take Those Lips Away*	4.00 -	7.00
Gennett 6531 *The Dingy Miner's Cabin*	15.00 -	20.00
6601 *The Old New Hampshire Valley*	15.00 -	20.00
6621 *The Dying Girl's Message*	15.00 -	20.00
6762 *Bad Campanions*	15.00 -	20.00
6808 *She Ain't Built That Way*	15.00 -	20.00
6975 *The Virginia Moonshiner*	15.00 -	20.00
7050 *Gwine Down To Town*	15.00 -	20.00
7068 *Down On The Farm*	15.00 -	20.00
7207 *Johnny The Drunkard*	15.00 -	20.00
7242 *Put On Your Old Gray Bonnet*	15.00 -	20.00
Vocalion 04529, 04569, 04673, 04759, 04827, 04894	4.00 -	8.00

CLYDE MARTIN & HIS HOOSIER RANGERS:
Champion 16409 *Shuber's Hoe Down*	10.00 -	15.0

DAN MARTIN:
Superior 2824 *The Cross-Eyed Butcher*	8.00 -	12.00

JOHN MARTIN:
Superior 2626 *Railroad Blues*	15.00 -	20.00
2658 *The Hobo's Pal*	15.00 -	20.00
2701 *The Wreck Of The C & O Sportsman*	15.00 -	20.00

JOHNNY MARTIN:
Supertone 9721 *Sweet Wimmin'*	15.00 -	20.00

MARVIN FAMILY:
Columbia 15474-D *Yodeling Them Blues Away*	10.00 -	15.00

MARVIN'S STRING BAND:
Supertone 9738 *Fox Chase*	7.00 -	10.00

FRANKIE MARVIN (& HIS GUITAR & JIM-MIE SMITH):

Following is a selective listing form the large number of records, mostly of minimal value, by the artist:
Crown 3125, 3204	5.00 -	8.00
Edison (thin) 11006 *Away Out On The Mountain*	10.00 -	15.00
20002 *Ben Dewberry's Final Run*	10.00 -	15.00
20011 *Oklahoma, Land Of The Sunny West*	———	

(Note: 20011 was not officially issued, but copies have been reported.)
Edison (thick) 52436, 52451, 52460, 52490, 52523, 52576, 52607	4.00 -	8.00
52650 *Blue Yodel No. 4*	8.00 -	12.00
Paramount 3275 *T.B. Blues*	7.00 -	10.00
3276 *The Gangster's Warning*	7.00 -	10.00
Timely Tunes 1553 *She's Just That Kind*	15.00 -	20.00
1554 *She's Always On My Mind*	10.00 -	15.00
1555 *I'm Blue And Lonesome*	10.00 -	15.00
Victor 23523 *Old Man Duff*	7.00 -	10.00
23561 *When It's Night-Time In Nevada*	30.00 -	40.00

JOHNNY MARVIN:

Most of the records by this artist are of little value or interest as country/western music.
Victor 23691 *I'm Gonna Yodel My Way To Heaven*	5.00 -	10.00
23708 *Seven Come Eleven*	5.00 -	10.00
23728 *Go Along Bum*	5.00 -	10.00

MASSEY FAMILY:
Vocalion 02993 *Sweet Mama Tree Top Tall*	5.00 -	8.00

JACK MATHIS:
Columbia 15344-D *Your Mother Still Prays For You*	5.00 -	-8.00
15450-D *Charming Bessie Lee*	5.00 -	8.00

JOHNNY MATHIS:
Talent 738 *Tell Me Why*	7.00 -	10.0

JIMMIE MATTOX:
Gennett 7227 *Good Bye Mama*	15.00 -	20.00

BILLIE MAXWELL (THE COWGIRL SINGER):
Victor 40148 *Billy Verero*	7.00 -	10.00
40188 *The Cowboy's Wife*	7.00 -	10.00
40241 *Haunted Hunted*	7.00 -	10.00

KEN MAYNARD:
Columbia 2310-D *The Cowboy's Lament*	25.00 -	40.00

DAVID McCARN:
Victor 23506 *Poor Man, Rich Man*	30.00 -	40.00
23532 *Hobo Life*	30.00 -	40.00
23555 *Gastonia Gallop*	30.00 -	40.00
40274 *Cotton Mill Colic*	20.00 -	30.00

McCARTT BROTHERS & PATTERSON:
Columbia 15454-D *Green Valley Waltz*	5.00 -	8.00

McCLAIN & HARPOLD:
Gennett 7224 *Bake That Chicken Pie*	10.00 -	15.00
Supertone 9716 *Bake That Chicken Pie*	10.00 -	15.00

McCLENDON BROTHERS:
Bluebird 6961 *My Little Mountain Lady*	5.00 -	8.00
7339 *Free As I Can Be*	8.00 -	12.00
7832 *Corns On My Feet*	5.00 -	8.00

HARRY McCLINTOCK (See "RADIO MAC" AND "MAC"

McCLUNG BROTHERS (& CLEVE CHAFFIN):
Brunswick 134 *Birdie*	10.00 -	15.00
135 *Chicken*	10.00 -	15.00
136 *It's A Long, Long Way To Tipperary*	10.00 -	15.00
Paramount 3161 *Alabama Jubilee*	20.00 -	30.00
3179 *Rock House Gamblers*	20.00 -	30.00

(SMILIN') ED McCONNELL:
Bluebird 5075, 5105, 5140, 5200, 5275	3.00 -	6.00
Champion 16209 *The Hell Bound Train*	10.00 -	15.00
16263 *Leave It There*	10.00 -	15.00
45137 *The Devil Song*	4.00 -	6.00
Victor 23808 *Tiny Toys*	8.00 -	12.00
23812 *The Royal Telephone*	8.00 -	12.00
23823 *Life's Railway To Heaven*	8.00 -	12.00
23825 *Where Is My Boy Tonight*	8.00 -	12.00
23844 *The Old Rugged Cross*	8.00 -	12.00
23848 *Leave It There*	8.00 -	12.00

EARL McCOY (& JESSIE BROCK/ALFRED MENG & CLEM GARNER):
Columbia 15499-D *Cotton Mill Girl*	15.00 -	20.00
15604-D *Off To War*	15.00 -	20.00
15622-D *Forty Per Cent*	15.00 -	20.00

FRANK & JAMES McCRAVY:
Brunswick 192, 193, 194, 424, 444, 452, 465, 467, 504, 515, 528, 535, 566, 572, 589	3.00 -	6.00
Columbia 15617-D *No More Dying*	5.00 -	8.00
15764-D *I Love You In The Same Old Way*	7.00 -	10.00
Okeh 45128, 45135, 45433, 45435, 45447, 45457, 45466	4.00 -	7.00
Vocalion 5193, 5194, 5195, 5255, 5293	4.00 -	7.00

LEWIS/LOUIS McDANIEL (& GID SMITH):
Timely Tunes 1560 *One More Kiss Before I Go*	8.00 -	12.00
Victor 23505 *I've Loved You So True*	8.00 -	12.00
40287 *We'll Talk About One Another*	7.00 -	10.00

McDONALD BROTHERS:
Vocalion 5406 *Poor Little Joe*	8.00 -	12.00

(LESTER) McFARLAND & (BOB) GARDNER:
Brunswick 107, 108, 109, 110, 111, 116, 160, 163, 164, 167, 168, 169, 170, 171, 190, 195, 199, 200, 201, 202, 203, 286, 293, 305, 307, 311, 316, 322, 326, 332, 334, 339, 350, 356, 366, 398, 409, 426, 432, 438, 439, 451, 454, 461, 466, 475, 479, 483, 492, 499, 520, 524, 525, 527, 537, 541, 548, 551, 553, 561, 568, 570, 578, 586, 588, 594, 596	4.00 -	7.00
Vocalion 5026, 5027, 5028, 5120, 5121, 5122, 5123, 5124, 5125, 5126, 5127, 5128, 5129, 5130, 5174,		

5177, 5184, 5187, 5191, 5192, 5259, 5285, 5307, 5322, 5364, 5369, 5381, 5392 . . . . 4.00 - 8.00

(Note: Other records by this duo usually command similar premiums.)

J.D. McFARLANE & DAUGHTER:
Okeh 45027 *Devil In The Wood Pile* . . . . 7.00 - 10.00

ALPHUS McFAYDEN:
Victor 21128 *Medley* . . . . 5.00 - 8.00

DENNIS McGEE:
Vocalion 5334 *Allen And Tassone* . . . . 15.00 - 25.00
5348 *Myself* . . . . 15.00 - 25.00

SAM (& KIRK) McGEE; KIRK & SAM McGEE; KIRK McGEE (& BLYTHE POTEET):
Champion 16804 *Brown's Ferry Blues* . . . . 40.00 - 60.00
45033 *Brown's Ferry Blues* . . . . 10.00 - 15.00
Decca 5348 *Brown's Ferry Blues* . . . . 10.00 - 15.00
Gennett 6704 *If I Only Had A Home* . . . . 25.00 - 40.00
6731 *If I Could Hear My Mother Pray Again* . 25.00 - 40.00
6778 *Only A Step To The Grave* . . . . 25.00 - 40.00
6960 *My Wife Left Me* . . . . 25.00 - 40.00
7022 *Kickin' Mule* . . . . 25.00 - 40.00
Vocalion 5094 *The Franklin Blues* . . . . 20.00 - 30.00
5101 *Knoxville Blues* . . . . 20.00 - 30.00
5150 *Salty Dog Blues* . . . . 20.00 - 30.00
5166 *Charming Bill* . . . . 20.00 - 30.00
5167 *Old Master's Runaway* . . . . 20.00 - 30.00
5169 *Salt Lake City Blues* . . . . 20.00 - 30.00
5254 *Easy Rider* . . . . 20.00 - 30.00
5310 *The Ship Without A Sail* . . . . 20.00 - 30.00
15318 *Buck Dancer's Choice* . . . . 20.00 - 30.00
15326 *Knoxville Blues* . . . . 20.00 - 30.00

McGHEE & COGER:
Gennett 6703 *The Vestris Disaster* . . . . 15.00 - 25.00
6795 *He Included Me* . . . . 10.00 - 15.00
6932 *Calling The Prodigal* . . . . 10.00 - 15.00

(JOHN) McGHEE & (FRANK) WELLING: (See also WELLING & McGHEE)
Brunswick 222 *He Abides* . . . . 7.00 - 10.00
251 *I Would Not Be Denied* . . . . 7.00 - 10.00
258 *Dwelling In Beulah Land* . . . . 7.00 - 10.00
272 *I Am Coming Home* . . . . 7.00 - 10.00
Champion 16479 *My Burdens Rolled Away* . . . . 7.00 - 10.00
16542 *He Abides* . . . . 7.00 - 10.00
Gennett 6334 *I've Been Redeemed* . . . . 7.00 - 10.00
6389 *Praise The Lord, It's So* . . . . 7.00 - 10.00
6435 *I Am Resolved* . . . . 7.00 - 10.00
6533 *I'm Free Again* . . . . 7.00 - 10.00
6657 *Get A Transfer* . . . . 10.00 - 15.00
6671 *I Wants My Lulu* . . . . 15.00 - 20.00
6690 *Why Not Tonight* . . . . 12.00 - 18.00
6749 *At The Battle Front* . . . . 12.00 - 18.00
6874 *I Have To Tell The Story* . . . . 12.00 - 18.00
7083 *Beautiful Garden Of Prayer* . . . . 12.00 - 18.00
7114 *No Never Alone* . . . . 15.00 - 20.00
7128 *Old Kentucky Dew* . . . . 15.00 - 20.00
7143 *He'll Understand* . . . . 15.00 - 20.00
7156 *Life's Railway To Heaven* . . . . 15.00 - 20.00
7185 *Where Is My Mamma* . . . . 15.00 - 20.00
7228 *Sweeping Through The Gates* . . . . . . 15.00 - 20.00
7247 *I'm Drifting Back To Dreamland* . . . . 15.00 - 20.00
7294 *I Surrender All* . . . . 15.00 - 20.00
7316 *I'm Forever Blowing Bubbles* . . . . . . 15.00 - 20.00
Paramount 3234 *The Prisoner's Child* . . . . 20.00 - 30.00
Superior 323 *He Keeps Me Singing* . . . . 20.00 - 30.00
345 *I Am Resolved* . . . . 15.00 - 25.00
Supertone 9626 *Down The Lane To Home Sweet Home* . . . . 7.00 - 10.00
Vocalion 5251 *The Lily Of The Valley* . . . . 8.00 - 12.00

JOHN McGHEE:
Gennett 6362 *The Sinking Of Submarine S-4* . . . 7.00 - 10.00
6103 *The Preacher And The Bear* . . . . 10.00 - 15.00

6149 *Aged Mother* . . . . 10.00 - 15.00
6450 *The Volunteer Organist* . . . . 10.00 - 15.00
6479 *Bill Bailey, Ain't That A Shame* . . . . . . 10.00 - 15.00
6546 *Hard Luck Jim* . . . . 10.00 - 15.00
6587 *The Hatfield-McCoy Feud* . . . . 15.00 - 25.00
6960 *Life Ain't Worth Living When You're Broke* 25.00 - 35.00
7096 *The Great Airplane Crash* . . . . 20.00 - 30.00
7168 *You're As Welcome As The Flowers In May* 20.00 - 30.00
Superior 325 *The Preacher And The Bear* . . . . . 10.00 - 15.00
344 *The Marian Parker Murder* . . . . 10.00 - 15.00
367 *The Sinking Of Submarine S-4* . . . . 7.00 - 10.00

KIRK McGHEE; SAM McGHEE (See McGEE)
MERLE McGINNIS:
Gennett 6990 *Highway Blues* . . . . 20.00 - 30.00

McGINTY'S OKLAHOMA COWBOY BAND:
Champion 15446 *It Can't Be Done* . . . . 8.00 - 12.00
15482 *Adam And Eve* . . . . 8.00 - 12.00
Okeh 45057 *The Cowboy's Dream* . . . . 10.00 - 15.00

LEON McGUIRE:
Vocalion 5393 *When The Blues Eyes Meet The Brown* . . . . 7.00 - 10.00

McKINNEY BROTHERS:
Champion 16830 *Old Uncle Joe* . . . . 10.00 - 15.00

McLAUGHLIN'S (OLD TIME) MELODY MAKERS:
Victor 21286 *Dill Pickles Rag* . . . . 8.00 - 12.00
40117 *Whistlin' Rufus* . . . . 8.00 - 12.00
Vocalion 5296 *Mississippi Shadows* . . . . 10.00 - 15.00
5330 *Hilarious Zeb* . . . . 10.00 - 15.00

McMANN & ROBERTS:
Supertone 9318 *If I Could Hear My Mother Pray Again* . . . . 7.00 - 10.00

(CLAYTON) McMICHEN'S MELODY MEN; McMICHEN-LAYNE STRING OR-CHESTRA; CLAYTON McMICHEN & DAN HORNSBY/RILEY PUCKETT; CLAYTON McMICHEN & HIS GEORGIA WILDCATS/HARMONY BOYS/HOME TOWN BAND:
Columbia 15111-D *Sweet Bunch Of Daisies* . . . . 5.00 - 8.00
15130-D *House Of David Blues* . . . . 5.00 - 8.00
*15140-D *A Fiddlers Convention In Georgia* . . 5.00 - 8.00
15190-D *St. Louis Blues* . . . . 5.00 - 8.00
*15201-D *A Corn Licker Still In Georgia* . . . . . 5.00 - 8.00
15202-D *The Missouri Waltz* . . . . 5.00 - 8.00
15224-D *Fifty Years Ago* . . . . 5.00 - 8.00
15247-D *Silver Threads Among The Gold* . . . . 5.00 - 8.00
15253-D *The Original Arkansas Traveler* . . . . . 7.00 - 10.00
*15258-D *A Corn Licker Still In Georgia* . . . . . 5.00 - 8.00
15288-D *Home Sweet Home* . . . . 5.00 - 8.00
15310-D *Ain't She Sweet* . . . . 8.00 - 12.00
15333-D *The Blind Child's Prayer* . . . . 8.00 - 12.00
15340-D *Lonesome Mama Blues* . . . . 8.00 - 12.00
15356-D *Down The Ozark Trail* . . . . 8.00 - 12.00
*15366-D *Corn Licker Still Part 5/6* . . . . 7.00 - 10.00
15391-D *When You're Far From The Ones Who Love You* . . . . 8.00 - 12.00
*15432-D *Corn Licker Still Part 7/8* . . . . 8.00 - 12.00
15464-D *The Dying Hobo* . . . . 10.00 - 15.00
*15503-D *A Night In A Blind Tiger* . . . . 10.00 - 15.00
15521-D *McMichen's Reel* . . . . 10.00 - 15.00
*15531-D *Corn Licker Still Part 9/10* . . . . 10.00 - 15.00
15540-D *Honolulu Moon* . . . . 15.00 - 20.00
*15549-D *Taking The Census* . . . . 15.00 - 20.00
*15598-D *Jeremiah Hopkins' Store At Sand Mountain* . . . . 15.00 - 20.00
*15618-D *Corn Licker Still Part 11/12* . . . . 15.00 - 20.00
*15632-D *Prohibition—Yes Or No* . . . . 15.00 - 20.00
*15667-D *Fiddler's Convention Part 3/4* . . . . . . 15.00 - 20.00
15686-D *The Arkansas Sheik* . . . . 20.00 - 30.00
*15700-D *A Bee Hunt On Hell For Sartin Creek* . 20.00 - 30.00

*15703-D *Corn Licker Still Part 13/14*......	20.00 -	30.00
15723-D *Yum Yum Blues*................	25.00 -	40.00
15775-D *Wild Cat Rag*..................	30.00 -	50.00

(*These "descriptive novelty" records credit several or more artists on the labels; since McMichen's name appears first, all are included in this listing.)

Crown 3384 *Singing An Old Hymn*.........	12.00 -	15.00
3385 *Georgia Wildcat Breakdown*......	12.00 -	15.00
3386 *Way Down In Caroline*.........	12.00 -	15.00
3397 *Arkansas Traveler*..............	12.00 -	15.00
3416 *Old Joe Clarke*...............	12.00 -	15.00
3419 *When The Bloom Is On The Sage*.....	12.00 -	15.00
3432 *Countin' Cross Ties*..........	12.00 -	15.00
Decca 5418, 5424, 5436, 5448, 5491.........	4.00 -	7.00
Okeh 45022 *Alabama Jubilee*..........	10.00 -	15.00
45034 *Bully Of The Town*..........	10.00 -	15.00
45330 *Ain't She Sweet?*...........	10.00 -	15.00

WHITEY McPHERSON:

Vocalion 03883 *Little Lady*............	4.00 -	7.00
03937 *Brakeman Blues*...........	4.00 -	7.00
04245 *Blue Ridge Mountain Blues*.....	4.00 -	7.00
04339 *Am I Blue*...............	4.00 -	7.00

ODDIE McWINDERS:

Crown 3398 *Down In Old Kentucky*.........	10.00 -	15.00

GRACE MEANS:

Supertone 9244 *Your Mother Still Prays For You*	5.00 -	8.00

"THE MEDICINE SHOW" (See EMMETT MILLER) **DAVID MEEK & HIS BOYS:**

Champion 15376 *Old Sefus Brown*..........	7.00 -	10.00

DICK MEEKS:

Supertone 9306 *Poor, But A Gentleman Still*....	8.00 -	12.00

MELTON & MINTER/WAGGONER:

Columbia 15423-D *In The Hills Of Old Kentucky*	7.00 -	10.00
Vocalion 5435 *Let Me Call You Sweetheart*....	7.00 -	10.00

MEMPHIS BOB:

Columbia 15735-D *Little Marion McLean*......	7.00 -	10.00

MERIDIAN HUSTLERS:

Paramount 3173 *Queen City Square Dance*.....	20.00 -	30.00

MERT'S HOMETOWN SERENADERS:

Vocalion 5338 *We Gotta Look Into This*.......	7.00 -	10.00

ARTHUR MILES:

Victor 40156 *The Lonely Cowboy*...........	8.00 -	12.00

PAUL MILES & THE RED FOX CHASERS:

Gennett 6461 *Under The Double Eagle*.......	15.00 -	20.00
6516 *The Arkansas Traveler*...............	15.00 -	20.00
6547 *Weeping Willow Tree*.............	15.00 -	20.00
6568 *Mississippi Sawyer*.............	15.00 -	20.00
6866 *The Red Fox...Makin' Licker, Part 1/2*.	20.00 -	30.00
6912 *The REd Fox...Makin' Licker, Part 3/4*	20.00 -	30.00
6930 *Virginia Bootleggers*.................	20.00 -	30.00

MILLER'S BULL FROG ENTERTAINERS:

Okeh 45348, 45358, 45386.................	5.00 -	8.00

MILLER & BURNETT:

Champion 15963 *Missouri Joe*............	5.00 -	8.00
15985 *Long White Robe*.............	5.00 -	8.00
Gennett 7164 *Missouri Joe*..............	10.00 -	15.00
7220 *Twenty-One Years*.............	10.00 -	15.00
Okeh 45442, 45541.....................	4.00 -	8.00

BOB MILLER (& HIS HINKY DINKERS/TRIO); CHARLOTTE MILLER & HINKY DINKERS:

Brunswick 404, 428, 4431.................	10.00 -	15.00
Champion 16008 *The Ohio Prison Fire*........	10.00 -	15.00
7239 *Five Cent Glass Of Beer*........	10.00 -	15.00
Okeh 45475 *Little Cotton Mill Girl*...........	10.00 -	15.00
45497 *Nebuchudneezer*.............	4.00 -	8.00
Victor 23693 *Twenty-One Years, Part 2*.......	4.00 -	8.00

DAVID MILLER:

Champion 15298 *Don't Forget Me, Little Darling*	8.00 -	12.00
15317 *The Lonesome Valley*.........	5.00 -	8.00
15334 *The Bad Man Stackalee*..............	5.00 -	8.00

Gennett 6175 *The Lonesome Valley*..........	8.00 -	12.00
6188 *The Bad Man Stacklee*.............	10.00 -	15.00
6333 *Sweet Floetta*..................	15.00 -	20.00
6349 *A Little Child Shall Lead Them*.......	10.00 -	15.00
6388 *Give My Love To Nellie, Jack*........	10.00 -	15.00
Superior 324 *Sweet Floetta*..............	12.00 -	18.00
368 *Give My Love To Nellie, Jack*........	12.00 -	18.00
384 *Two Little Orphans*..............	12.00 -	18.00
Supertone 9258 *Two Little Orphans*..........	12.00 -	18.00

EMMETT MILLER:

Okeh 45380 *The Medicine Show, Act 1/2*.....	7.00 -	10.00
45391 *The Medicine Show, Act 3/4*.....	7.00 -	10.00
45413 *The Medicine Show, Act 5/6*........	10.00 -	15.00

(Note: Although the labels of the above "descriptive novelty" records credit several artists, they are listed here, since Emmett Miller's name appears first.)

Okeh 45546 *Sam's New Job*..................	7.00 -	10.00

(Note: Other records by Emmett Miller are listed in the jazz and dance bands section.)

JOHN MILLER:

Superior 2839 *Highway Hobo*...............	10.00 -	15.00

STANLEY MILLER:

Champion 15297 *Be Kind To A Man When He Is Down*.............................	7.00 -	10.00
15315 *Lost Train Blues*....................	7.00 -	10.00

OWEN MILLS & FRANK WELLING (& McGHEE):

Paramount 3155 *A Mother's Plea*...........	7.00 -	12.00
3158 *Don't Forget Me Darling*.............	7.00 -	12.00
3159 *It's Hard To Be Shut Up In Prison*.....	7.00 -	12.00

MILNER & CURTIS WITH THE MAGNOLIA RAMBLERS:

Vocalion 5426 *Northeast Texas*...............	20.00 -	30.00

BILLY MILTON & ONE MAN BAND:

Gennett 6318 *Dill Pickles*..................	10.00 -	15.00

FLOYD MING'S PEP STEPPERS:

Victor 21294 *Indian War Whoop*............	20.00 -	30.00
21534 *Tupelo Blues*....................	20.00 -	30.00

MISSISSIPPI 'POSSUM HUNTERS:

Victor 23595 *Mississippi Breakdown*...........	20.00 -	30.00

MITCHELL FAMILY TRIO:

Superior 2641 *Picture On The Wall*...........	7.00 -	10.00
2657 *The Old Rugged Cross*................	7.00 -	10.00
2700 *Hide Me*........................	7.00 -	10.00
2776 *There Is Power In The Blood*........	7.00 -	10.00

MOATSVILLE STRING TICKLERS:

Columbia 15491-D *Moatsville Blues*...........	15.00 -	20.00

MODERN MOUNTAINEERS:

Bluebird 6911, 6976, 6997, 7047, 7247, 7323, 7423, 7470, 7671..........................	3.00 -	6.00

MONROE BROTHERS:

Bluebird 6309 *This World Is Not My Home*....	8.00 -	12.00
6363 *What Is Home Without Love?*.........	8.00 -	12.00
6422 *My Long Journey Home*..............	8.00 -	12.00
6477 *God Holds The Future In His Hands*...	8.00 -	12.00
6512 *Six Months Ain't Long*..............	8.00 -	12.00
6552 *Just A Song Of Old Kentucky*.........	8.00 -	12.00
6607 *On Some Foggy Mountain Top*........	8.00 -	12.00
6645 *New River Train*..................	8.00 -	12.00
6676 *The Old Crossroad*................	8.00 -	12.00
6729 *My Savior's Train*..................	8.00 -	12.00
6762 *Where Is My Sailor Boy?*........:....	10.00 -	15.00
6773 *Roll In My Sweet Baby's Arms*........	6.00 -	10.00
6820 *Will The Circle Be Unbroken*........	6.00 -	10.00
6829 *Forgotten Soldier Boy*..............	6.00 -	10.00
6866 *I Am Ready To Go*................	6.00 -	10.00
6912 *What Would The Profit Be?*.........	6.00 -	10.00
6960 *Katy Cline*.....................	6.00 -	10.00
7007 *I Am Going That Way*.............	6.00 -	10.00
7055 *Do You Call That Religion*..........	6.00 -	10.00

7093 *Weeping Willow Tree*	6.00 -	10.00
7122 *What Would You Give In Exchange?*	6.00 -	10.00
7145 *On My Way To Glory*	6.00 -	10.00
7191 *Let Us Be Lovers*	6.00 -	10.00
7273 *My Last Moving Day*	6.00 -	10.00
7326 *Sinner, You Better Get Ready*	6.00 -	10.00
7385 *On The Banks Of The Ohio*	8.00 -	12.00
7425 *I've Still Got Ninety-Nine*	5.00 -	8.00
7460 *On My Way Back Home*	5.00 -	8.00
7508 *Goodbye, Maggie*	5.00 -	8.00
7562 *A Beautiful Life*	5.00 -	8.00
7598 *Rollin' On*	5.00 -	8.00
Montgomery Ward (some titles as above.)	4.00 -	7.00

MONROE COUNTY BOTTLE TIPPERS:

Gennett 6585 *The Fiddlin' Bootleggers*	20.00 -	30.00

BILL MONROE & THE BLUE GRASS BOYS:

Bluebird 8568 *Mule Skinner Blues*	10.00 -	15.00
8611 *No Letter In The Mail*	10.00 -	15.00
8692 *Dog House Blues*	10.00 -	15.00
8813 *Tennessee Blues*	10.00 -	15.00
8861 *Blue Yodel No. 7*	10.00 -	15.0
Columbia (red label)	3.00 -	5.00

CHARLIE MONROE'S BOYS:

Bluebird 7862 *Great Speckled Bird*	5.00 -	8.00
7922 *Farther Along*	5.00 -	8.00
7949 *You're Gonna Miss Me*	5.00 -	8.00
7990 *When The World's On Fire*	5.00 -	8.00
8050 *Guided By Love*	5.00 -	8.00
8118 *Joy Bells In My Soul*	5.00 -	8.00

MONTANA SLIM:

Bluebird 6515 *Midnight, The Unconquered Outlaw*	5.00 -	8.00
6814 *Prairie Sunset*	5.00 -	8.00
6826 *Round-Up Time In Heaven*	5.00 -	8.00
6827 *Yodeling Cowgirl*	5.00 -	8.00
7618 *By The Grave Of Nobody's Darling*	5.00 -	8.00
8150, 8202, 8241, 8313, 8329, 8361, 8374, 8425, 8441, 8456, 8472, 8517, 8531, 8566, 8696, 8875, 8924, 8983	4.00 -	7.00

(Note: See also WILF CARTER:)

PATSY MONTANA (with THE PRAIRIE RAMBLERS):

Titles, issued contemporaneously on Banner, Conqueror, Melotone, Oriole, Perfect, Romeo, include: *Blazin' The Trail; A Cowboy Honeymoon; Give Me A Home In Montana; Gold Coast Express; I Wanna Be A Cowboy's Sweetheart; Lone Star; Pride Of The Prairie; Ridin' The Sunset Trail; Sweetheart Of The Saddle; Swingtime Cowgirl; With A Banjo On My Knee;*

	3.00 -	6.00
Vocalion 03010, 03135, 03268, 03292, 03377, 03422	4.00 -	7.00
04023, 04076, 04135, 04247, 04291, 04469, 04482, 04518, 04568, 04689, 04742, 05081	3.00 -	6.00
Vogue 721 *When I Gets To Where I'm Going*	10.00 -	15.00

PHIL MONTGOMERY:

Superior 2542 *That Old Covered Bridge*	15.00 -	20.00

TOMMY MOONEY (WITH BOBBY MOONEY) & HIS AUTOMOBILE BABIES:

Floto 78001 *Bingo Boogie*	———	
78003 *Rose Covered Garden*	———	

MOONSHINE DAVE:

Champion 15789 *Biscuit Jim*	10.00 -	15.00

MOONSHINE HARRY:

Supertone 9553 *Son Of A Gun*	10.00 -	15.00

MOONSHINE KATE (& HER PALS):

Okeh 45444 *Texas Blues*	15.00 -	20.00
45515 *Texas Bound*	15.00 -	20.00
45547 *The Poor Girl's Story*	20.00 -	30.00
45555 *My Man's A Jolly Railroad Man*	25.00 -	40.00

MOONSHINERS:

Victor 40223 *Fulton County*	10.00 -	15.00
40284 *Midnight Waltz*	10.00 -	15.00

MOORE, BURNETTE & RUTHERFORD:

Gennett 6706 *Cumberland Gap*	12.00 -	16.00

MOORE & FREED: (See also FREED & MOORE):

Vocalion 5131 *Harmonica Blues*	8.00 -	12.00
5132 *Plantation Medley*	8.00 -	12.00

MOORE & GREENE:

Champion 16357 *Cincinnati Rag*	25.00 -	35.00

MOORE & SMECK:

Vocalion 5133 *Dear Old Pal Of Mine*	7.00 -	10.00

BYRD MOORE (& HIS HOT SHOTS):

Champion 16498 *Oh Take Me Back*	20.00 -	30.00
Columbia 15496-D *Careless Love*	15.00 -	25.00
15536-D *Frankie Silvers*	15.00 -	25.00
Gennett 6549 *Hobo's Paradise*	35.00 -	50.00
6586 *Mama Toot Your Whistle*	40.00 -	60.00
6686 *Back Water Blues*	40.00 -	60.00
6763 *Snatch 'Em Back Blues*	40.00 -	60.00
6841 *When The Snowflakes Fall Again*	40.00 -	60.00
6991 *Mama Don't Allow No Low Down Hanging Round*	50.00 -	80.00

JOHN MOORE:

Broadway 8188 *Columbus Prison Fire*	8.00 -	12.00

LATTIE MOORE:

Speed 101 *Juke Joint Johnny*	7.00 -	10.00

O. MOORE:

Challenge 422 *The Drunkard's Doom*	7.00 -	-10.00

SAM MOORE & HARACE DAVIS:

Vocalion 14430 *Annie Laurie*	8.00 -	12.00

PEG MORELAND:

Victor 21548 *The Prisoner At The Bar*	7.00 -	10.00
21653 *Going Back To Dixie*	5.00 -	8.00
21724 *Maple In The Lane*	5.00 -	8.00
23510 *I Got Mine*	10.00 -	15.00
Victor 23539 *In Berry Picking Time*	10.00 -	15.00
23593 *Cowboy Jack*	10.00 -	15.00
40008 *Stay In The Wagon Yard*	5.00 -	8.00
4010 *He Never Came Back*	5.00 -	8.00
40137 *You're Gonna Miss Me*	5.00 -	8.00
40209 *When I Had But Fifty Cents*	7.00 -	10.00
40272 *Make Me A Cowboy Again*	7.00 -	10.00
40296 *In The Town Where I Was Born*	7.00 -	10.00

EVERETT MORGAN:

Champion 16616 *Texas Home*	15.00 -	20.00

MORRIS BROTHERS:

Bluebird 7903 *The Story Of Charlie Lawson*	8.00 -	12.00
7967 *Let Me Be Your Salty Dog*	8.00 -	12.00

FRANK MORRIS:

Paramount 3070 *Old Brown Pants*	7.00 -	10.00

WALTER MORRIS:

Columbia 15079-D *Crazy Coon*	7.00 -	10.00
15101-D *The Railroad Tramp*	7.00 -	10.00
15115-D *Sweet Marie*	7.00 -	10.00
15186-D *In The Time Of Long Ago*	7.00 -	10.00

ZEKE MORRIS:

Bluebird 7362 *Garden Of Prayer*	7.00 -	10.00

MORRISON BROTHERS BAND:

Victor 40323 *Dry And Dusty*	20.00 -	30.00

MORTON, BOND & WILLIAMS:

Champion 15653 *Cumberland Gap*	8.00 -	12.00

MORTON & CRANE:

Supertone 9497 *Budded Roses*	8.00 -	12.00
9535 *Put My Little Shoes Away*	8.00 -	12.00

JACK MOSER & HIS OKLAHOMA CAVALIERS:

Bluebird 6728, 6751	4.00 -	7.00

(BERT) MOSS & (JOE) LONG:

Superior 2539 *My Trouble Blues*	35.00 -	50.00
2559 *Jake Legs Blues*	35.00 -	50.00
2838 *Pig Ankle*	50.00 -	80.00

OTIS MOTE (& TOM):
Okeh 45389 *Tight Like That*	10.00 -	15.00
45429 *Home In The Rock*	7.00 -	10.00

BILL MOUNCE:
Bluebird	3.00 -	5.00

MURPHY BROTHERS:
Champion 16455 *When Katie Comes Down To The Gate*	10.00 -	15.00

CHARLES NABELL:
Okeh 40252 *The Great Round Up*	7.00 -	10.00
45021 *After The War It Over*	7.00 -	10.00
45031 *The Hills Of Old Kentucky*	7.00 -	10.00
45039 *The Scopes Trail*	7.00 -	10.00

NANCE FAMILY (& CLARENCE DOOLEY/with THE TRAPHILL TWINS:
Brunswick 542 *The Lawson Murder*	8.00 -	12.00
565 *Sweet Freedom*	8.00 -	12.00
Champion 16316 *A Mother's Advice*	10.00 -	15.00
16330 *I'm On My Way To Heaven*	10.00 -	15.00
16369 *Somebody's Knocking At Your Door*	10.00 -	15.00

NARMOUR & SMITH:
Bluebird 5615 *New Carroll County Blues No. 2.*	15.00 -	20.00
5616 *Sweet Milk And Peaches*	15.00 -	20.00
5637 *Someone I Love*	15.00 -	20.00
5669 *Gallop To Georgia*	15.00 -	20.00
5720 *New Carroll County Blues No. 2.*	15.00 -	20.00
5754 *Rose Waltz*	15.00 -	20.00
5810 *New Charleston No. 3.*	15.00 -	20.00
6234 *New Charleston No. 2.*	15.00 -	20.00
Okeh 45242 *The Sunny Waltz*	15.00 -	25.00
45263 *Whistling Coon*	15.00 -	25.00
45276 *Little Star*	15.00 -	25.00
45317 *Carroll County Blues*	20.00 -	30.00
45329 *Someone I Love*	20.00 -	30.00
45344 *Gallop To Georgia-Breakdown*	25.00 -	40.00
45377 *Charleston No. 2.*	25.00 -	40.00
45390 *Dry Gin Rag*	25.00 -	40.00
45414 *Avalon Blues*	25.00 -	40.00
45424 *Sweet Milk And Peaches-Breakdown*	25.00 -	40.00
45459 *Charleston No. 3.*	35.00 -	50.00
45469 *Jake Leg Rag*	35.00 -	50.00
45480 *Where The Southern Crosses The Dog.*	35.00 -	50.00
45492 *Texas Breakdown*	35.00 -	50.00
45536 *Tequila Hop Blues*	40.00 -	60.00
45548 *Limber Neck Blues*	40.00 -	60.00

LEN NASH (& HIS COUNTRY BOYS):
Brunswick 354 *On The Road To California*	8.00 -	12.00
387 *The Ozark Trail*	8.00 -	12.00
440 *Goin' Down To Town*	8.00 -	12.00
Supertone 2069 *The Trail To Mexico*	8.00 -	12.00

BUCK NATION (& RAY WHITLEY):
Decca 5065, 5066, 5075, 5081, 5105, 5114, 5124, 5172	4.00 -	8.00

NATIONAL BARN DANCE ORCHESTRA:
Bluebird 5212, 5213, 5214, 5215, 5216, 5217	3.00 -	6.00

AMOS NEAL:
Champion 15692 *She'll Be Coming 'Round The Mountain*	8.00 -	12.00

FIDDLIN' DAVE NEAL:
Challenge 102 *Seneca Square Dance*	5.00 -	8.00
103 *Sandy Land*	5.00 -	8.00
301 *Seneca Square Dance*	5.00 -	8.00

DAVID NEAL:
Supertone 9184 *Good Old Turnip Greens*	8.00 -	12.00

RUSH NEAL & WANDA NEAL:
Okeh 45124 *The Two Orphans*	7.00 -	10.00

FIDDLIN' FRANK NELSON:
Challenge 303 *Cripple Creek*	5.00 -	8.00

NELSTONE'S HAWAIIANS:
Victor 40273 *Mobile County Blues*	8.00 -	12.00

NETTLE BROS. STRING BAND:
Bluebird, most issues	3.00 -	5.00

BILL NETTLES (& HIS DIXIE BLUE BOYS):
Bullet 637 *High Falutin' Mama*	5.00 -	8.00
Vocalion 03634 *My Cross-Eyed Nancy Jane*	5.00 -	8.00
03662 *No Daddy Blues*	5.00 -	8.00
Vocalion 03694, 03903, 03952, 04012, 04075, 04615, 04655, 04757	4.00 -	7.00

JIM NEW:
Timely Tunes 1564 *Wreck Of The Six Wheeler*	10.00 -	15.00

NEW ARKANSAS TRAVELERS:
Victor 21288 *Handy Man*	7.00 -	10.00

NEW DIXIE DEMONS:
Decca 5140, 5141, 5148, 5163, 5171, 5253, 5257, 5259, 5264, 5271, 5277, 5292, 5314, 5343, 5362, 5363, 5392	3.00 -	6.00

THE NEWMAN BROTHERS (HANK & SLIM):
Vocalion 02807 *Mississippi River Blues*	———	
02808 *How Beautiful Heaven Must Be*	———	
02840 *Dear Old Mother*	———	
02852 *Good Old Country Town*	———	

CHARLIE NEWMAN (& BUD NEWMAN):
Okeh 45072 *Sweet Bunch Of Daisies*	5.00 -	8.00
45095 *Pretty Little Dear*	5.00 -	8.00
45116 *Susie Ann*	5.00 -	8.00
45184 *Blue Ridge Mountain Blues*	5.00 -	8.00
45200 *My Blues Ridge Mountain Queen*	5.00 -	8.00
45431 *The Old Traveling Man*	7.00 -	10.00

FRED NEWMAN:
Paramount 3177 *San Antonio*	10.00 -	15.00
3267 *San Antonio*	10.00 -	15.00

ROY NEWMAN & HIS BOYS:
Vocalion 03117 *I Can't Dance*	5.00 -	8.00
03598, 03752, 03878, 03938, 03963, 04025, 04578, 04639, 04740, 04792, 04866, 04959, 05014, 05066	4.00 -	7.00

NEWTON COUNTY HILLBILLIES:
Okeh 45520 *Happy Hour Breakdown*	20.00 -	30.00
45544 *Nine O'Clock Breakdown*	20.00 -	30.00
45549 *Going To The Wedding To Get Some Cake*	20.00 -	30.00

NICHOLS BROTHERS:
Victor 23582 *She's Killing Me*	20.0 -	30.00
23596 *Dear Old Tennessee*	20.00 -	30.00

BOB NICHOLS (& HUGH CROSS/RILEY PUCKETT):
Columbia 15114-D, 15136-D, 15161-D	4.00 -	7.00
15198-D *Let The Rest Of The World Go By*	5.00 -	-8.00
15216-D *In The Shade Of The Old Apple Tree*	5.00 -	8.00
15304-D *The Trail Of The Lonesome Pine*	5.00 -	8.00
15350-D *Dear Old Dixieland*	5.00 -	8.00
15480-D *Corrine Corrina*	10.00 -	15.00
15556-D *Smoky Mountain Home*	10.00 -	15.00
15590-D *The Killing Of Tom Slaughter*	15.00 -	20.00
15698-D *When It's Peach Pickin' Time In Georgia*	15.00 -	20.00

JOE & BOB NICHOLS:
Crown 3399 *Smoky Mountain Home*	7.00 -	10.00
3419 *Red Wing*	10.00 -	15.00
3447 *Blue Hills Of Virginia*	7.00 -	10.00

NICHOLSON'S PLAYERS:
Champion 15942 *Muskakatuck Waltz*	10.00 -	15.00
16007 *Sweet Bunch Of Daisies*	10.00 -	15.00
16137 *My Honey*	10.00 -	15.00
45193 *Let Me Call You Sweetheart*	4.00 -	7.00
Gennett 7125 *Muskakatuck Waltz*	10.00 -	15.00
7151 *Sweet Bunch Of Daisies*	10.00 -	15.00
7241 *Let Me Call You Sweetheart*	12.00 -	18.00

NITE OWLS:
Vocalion 03621, 03675, 03706, 03879, 03905, 03951, 03987, 04064, 04118, 04159, 04233, 04312, 04372, 04452, 04517, 04626, 04715, 04794, 04853, 04935	3.00 -	6.00

HOYLE/HOYAL NIX & HIS WEST TEXAS COWBOYS:
Talent 709 *A Big Ball's In Cowtown*	5.00 -	8.00

EDDIE NOACK:

Gold Star 1352 *Triflin' Mama Blues*............ 8.00 - 12.00

FLORA NOLES:

Okeh 45037 *Little Mohee*.................... 5.00 - 8.00

FATE NORRIS (& HIS PLAYBOYS/& THE TANNER BOYS):

Columbia 15124-D *New Dixie*.............. 5.00 - 8.00

15332-D *A Day At The County Fair*........ 5.00 - 8.00*

15435-D *Johnnie Get Your Gun*........... 10.00 - 15.00

(Note: The label of Columbia 15332-D credits several artists, but since Fate Norris' name appears first, the record is listed here.)

LAND NORRIS:

Okeh 40096 *Groundhog*................... 8.00 - 12.00

45006 *Ida Red*...................... 8.00 - 12.00

45017 *Pat That Butter Down*......... 8.00 - 12.00

45033 *Charming Betsy*.............. 8.00 - 12.00

45047 *The Old Grey Mare*............ 8.00 - 12.00

45058 *Getting Into Trouble*.......... 8.00 - 12.00

LYMON NORRIS:

Champion 16431 *In A Lonely Jail*........... 15.00 - 20.00

45070 *In A Lonely Jail*................... 5.00 - 8.00

NORTH CAROLINA COOPER BOYS:

Okeh 45174 *Red Rose Of Texas*............ 8.00 - 12.00

NORTH CAROLINA FOX CHASERS:

Supertone 9322 *Mountain Sweetheart*......... 10.00 - 15.00

NORTH CAROLINA HAWAIIANS:

Okeh 45248 *Soldier's Joy*.................. 4.00 - 7.00

45297 *Bully Of The Town*............... 5.00 - 8.00

45405 *Chinese Breakdown*.............. 8.00 - 12.00

NORTH CAROLINA RAMBLERS (& ROY HARVEY):

(See also ROY HARVEY)

Columbia 15106-D *Flyin' Clouds*........... 7.00 - 10.00

15127-D *Rag Time Annie*............... 7.00 - 10.00

15279-D *Mountain Reel*............... 7.00 - 10.00

Gennett 6288 *Poor Little Joe*........... 20.00 - 30.00

Paramount 3064 *Take Back The Ring*........ 20.00 - 30.00

3065 *Give My Love To Nell*............ 20.00 - 30.00

3072 *Blue Eyes*.................. 20.00 - 30.00

3079 *Bill Mason*................. 20.00 - 30.00

3136 *Sweet Sunny South*................ 20.00 - 30.00

NORTH CAROLINA RIDGE RUNNERS:

Columbia 15650-D *Nobody's Darling*......... 15.00 - 20.00

NORTH GEORGIA FOUR:

Paramount 3135 *I Can, I Do, I Will*........ 10.00 - 15.00

3149 *Amazing Grace*.................. 10.00 - 15.00

3174 *She Was A Lulu*............... 10.00 - 15.00

NORTHLANDERS:

Vocalion 5274 *Over The Waves*............ 6.00 - 10.00

FRANK NOVACK & HIS ROOTIN' TOOTIN' BOYS:

Vocalion 03525, 03557, 03588, 03658, 03877, 03913, 03936, 03962, 03998, 04052, 04117, 04171, 04232, 04290, 04370, 04467, 04567, 04744, 04777 .... 3.00 - 5.00

SLIM OAKDALE:

Crown 3433 *Lonesome Road Blues*............ 7.00 - 10.00

3461 *No Hard Times*................... 7.00 - 10.00

3476 *Roll Along Kentucky Moon*....... 7.00 - 10.00

3503 *Cowboy's Heaven*................ 7.00 - 10.00

3516 *When Jimmie Rodgers Said Goodbye*... 10.00 - 15.00

JESSE OAKLEY:

Supertone 9243 *Aged Mother*............ 8.00 - 12.00

9256 *I Got Mine*....................... 5.00 - 8.00

9257 *Sinking Of The Submarine S-4*....... 5.00 - 8.00

9674 *You're As Welcome As The Flowers In May* 5.00 - 8.00

OAK MOUNTAIN FOUR:

Champion 15874 *Medley*.............. 7.00 - 10.00

CHARLIE OAKS:

Vocalion 5068 *The John T. Scopes Trial*....... 5.00 - 8.00

5069 *Little Mary Phagan*............ 5.00 - 8.00

5072 *Poor Little Joe*...................... 5.00 - 8.00

5073 *The Kaiser And Uncle Sam*........ 5.00 - 8.00

5076 *The Fatal Wedding*............... 5.00 - 8.00

5105 *The Old Cottage Home*.......... 5.00 - 8.00

5110 *Darling Nellie Gray*............ 5.00 - 8.00

5111 *Ginger Blues*.................... 5.00 - 8.00

5112 *Home Of The Soul*............. 5.00 - 8.00

15094 *The John T. Scopes Trial*....... 7.00 - 10.00

15099 *Little Mary Phagan*........... 7.00 - 10.00

15103 *Poor Little Joe*............... 7.00 - 10.00

15104 *The Kaiser And Uncle Sam*........... 7.00 - 10.00

15144 *The Fatal Wedding*............ 7.00 - 10.00

15195 *Moonshine*................... 7.00 - 10.00

15342 *Boll Weevil*.................. 7.00 - 10.00

15343 *Darling Nellie Gray*........... 5.00 - 8.00

15344 *Ginger Blue*.................. 5.00 - 8.00

15345 *Home Of The Soul*............. 5.00 - 8.00

15346 *The Old Cottage Home*............ 5.00 - 8.00

W. LEE O'DANIEL & HILLBILLY BOYS/THE LIGHT CRUST DOUGHBOYS:

Vocalion 02842 *Saturday Night Rag*......... 7.00 - 10.00

03196 *Peach Pickin' Time In Georgia*........ 7.00 - 10.00

03412 *Everybody Kiss Your Partner*...... 5.00 - 8.00

03538 *Keep A Light In Your Window Tonight* 5.00 - 8.00

03568 *Back To Old Smoky Mountain*........ 5.00 - 8.00

03674 *When You Hear Me Call*........... 5.00 - 8.00

03753, 03902, 03950, 03986, 04049, 04102, 04185, 04244, 04311, 04353, 04388, 04440, 04542, 04588, 04656, 04727, 04778, 04852............ 4.00 - 7.00

CHESTER ODOM & HIS WESTERN RHYTHM BOYS:

Blue Bonnet 128 *You've Done Broke My Heart*. 4.00 - 7.00

144 *That's All*.................. 4.00 - 7.00

Royalty 301 *Don't Rob Another Man's Castle*.. 5.00 - 8.00

329 *Rag Time Annie*..................... 5.00 - 8.00

OKLAHOMA WRANGLERS (with THE WILLIS BROTHERS):

Sterling 202 *I Can't Go On This Way*........ 5.00 - 8.00

OLIVER & ALLEN:

Bluebird 7124, 7175, 7327, 7402............. 4.00 - 7.00

OWENS BROTHERS:

Columbia 15416-D *If You Don't Like My Ford Coupe, Don't You Cadillac Me*........ 10.00 - 15.00

Victor 40283 *Right Upon The Firing Line*...... 7.00 - 10.00

40309 *Harvest Field*.............. 7.00 - 10.00

E.B. OWENS:

Columbia 15414-D *Sweet Carlyle*............. 10.00 - 15.00

TEX OWENS:

Decca 5015, 5187............... 4.00 - 7.00

TOM OWENS' WLS BARN DANCE TRIO:

Challenge 104 *Ocean Waves*.............. 5.00 - 8.00

105 *Kings Head*...................... 5.00 - 8.00

106 *Hell On The Wabash*............... 5.00 - 8.00

107 *Buckwheat Batter*............... 5.00 - 8.00

306 *Ocean Waves*................... 5.00 - 8.00

Silvertone 3104 *Kings Head*............ 5.00 - 8.00

3105 *Buffalo Girls*.................. 5.00 - 8.00

3106 *Buckwheat Batter*............. 5.00 - 8.00

3107 *McLeod's Reel*................ 5.00 - 8.00

OZARKERS:

Okeh 45573 *There's More Pretty Girls Than One* 10.00 - 15.00

OZARK RAMBLER:

Paramount 3322 *The Wreck Of The 1262*..... 15.00 - 20.00

OZARK WARBLERS:

Paramount 3127 *Memories Of Floyd Collins*.... 15.00 - 20.00

JACK PADGETT:

Talent 729 *Boogie Woogie Gal*............. 7.00 - 10.00

BUTTERBALL PAIGE:

Bullet 695 *I'm Too Old To Boogie Anymore*.. 5.00 - 8.00

BILL PALMER (TRIO):

Bluebird 5009, 5010, 5012, 5013, 5034......... 4.00 - 7.00

Electradisk 1938 *Duck Foot Sue*........... 5.00 - 8.00

Victor 23723 *In The Hills Of Arkansas* .... 8.00 - 12.00

PAPPY, ZEKE, EZRA & ELTON:

Decca 5097, 5126, 5153 ...... 3.00 - 5.00

GEO. R. PARISEAU'S ORCHESTRA:

Champion 15987 *Moonshiner's Serenade* ...... 8.00 - 12.00

16802 *Falling Leaf* ...... 15.00 - 20.00

45009 *Falling Leaf* ...... 5.00 - 8.00

Gennett 6899 *Waggoner's Hornpipe* ...... 15.00 - 20.00

7033 *Fisher's Hornpipe* ...... 15.00 - 20.00

7203 *Moonshiner's Serenade* ...... 15.00 - 20.00

CHARLIE PARKER (& MACK WOOLBRIGHT):

Columbia 15154-D *Rabbit Chase* ...... 8.00 - 12.00

15236-D *Ticklish Reuben* ...... 8.00 - 12.00

15694-D *Will, The Weaver* ...... 12.00 - 16.00

CHUBBY PARKER (& HIS OLD TIME BANJO):

Champion 15393 *Uncle Ned* ...... 5.00 - 8.00

16143 *I'm A Stern Old Bachelor* ...... 8.00 - 12.00

16163 *The Old Wooden Rocker* ...... 8.00 - 12.00

16211 *Get Away Old Maids Get Away* ...... 8.00 - 12.00

Columbia 15296-D *Down On The Farm* ...... 7.00 - 10.00

Gennett 6077 *Nickety Nackety Now Now Now* . 8.00 - 12.00

6097 *I'm A Stern Old Bachelor* ...... 8.00 - 12.00

6120 *Little Brown Jug* ...... 8.00 - 12.00

6287 *Uncle Ned* ...... 8.00 - 12.00

6319 *My Little Old Sod Shanty* ...... 8.00 - 12.00

6374 *A Rovin' Little Darky* ...... 8.00 - 12.00

Melotone 12524 *Get Away, Old Maids* ...... 5.00 - 8.00

12525 *Walking The Last Mile* ...... 5.00 - 8.00

12526 *Many Times I've Wondered* ...... 5.00 - 8.00

12653 *Bringing In The Sheaves* ...... 5.00 - 8.00

Silvertone 5011 *Whoa Mule Whoa* ...... 5.00 - 8.00

5013 *Little Brown Jug* ...... 5.00 - 8.00

Supertone 9187 *Darling Nellie Gray* ...... 5.00 - 8.00

9188 *Whoa, Mule, Whoa* ...... 5.00 - 8.00

9190 *Oh, Dem Golden Slippers* ...... 5.00 - 8.00

9191 *Oh, Susanna* ...... 5.00 - 8.00

9192 *Uncle Ned* ...... 5.00 - 8.00

9723 *In Kansas* ...... 5.00 - 8.00

9731 *You'll Hear The Bell In The Morning* ... 5.00 - 8.00

9732 *Grandfather's Clock* ...... 5.00 - 8.00

DAN PARKER (& BILL PARKER):

Crown 3248 *They Cut Down The Old Pine Tree* 7.00 - 10.00

3265 *That Silver Haired Daddy Of Mine* ..... 7.00 - 10.00

3266 *Fifty Years Repentin'* ...... 7.00 - 10.00

3279 *Carry Me Back To The Mountains* ..... 7.00 - 10.00

3291 *Ninety-Nine Years* ...... 7.00 - 10.00

SILVIA PARKER-THE HAPPY BUCKEYE:

Champion 45094 *Old Bill Mosher's Ford* ...... 5.00 - 8.00

(DICK) PARMAN (OF KENTUCKY); PARMAN & SMITH:

Champion 16010 *I Love You Best Of All* ...... 10.00 - 15.00

16055 *The Trail Of The Lonesome Pine* ...... 10.00 - 15.00

16300 *In The Hills Of Old Kentucky* ...... 12.00 - 18.00

45189 *I Love You Best Of All* ...... 5.00 - 8.00

Gennett 6718 *She'll Be Coming Around The Mountain* ...... 15.00 - 20.00

6747 *Many Trouble Blues* ...... 15.00 - 20.00

6792 *Seven Long Years Of Trouble* ...... 15.00 - 20.00

7127 *Are You From Dixie* ...... 15.00 - 20.00

7204 *I Love You Best Of All* ...... 15.00 - 20.00

Paramount 3138 *We've Been Chums For Fifty Years* 15.00 - 20.00

V.D. PARMAN & SNYDER:

Okeh 45302 *Blue Bell* ...... 5.00 - 8.00

FIDDLIN' IKE PATE:

Champion 15085 *Medley* ...... 5.00 - 8.00

FIDDLIN' JIM PATE:

Victor 40170 *Texas Farewell* ...... 10.00 - 15.00

LUTHER PATRICK:

Gennett 6448 *Cornbread* ...... 10.00 - 15.00

COLONEL JOHN A. PATTEE:

Columbia 231-D *Old Money Must Quadrille* .... 8.00 - 12.00

PATTERSON'S PIEDMONT LOG ROLLERS:

Victor 20936 *I'll Never Get Drunk Anymore* ... 10.00 - 15.00

21132 *Sweet Sunny South* ...... 10.00 - 15.00

21187 *My Sweetheart Is Shy* ...... 10.00 - 15.00

35874 (12-inch) *Poor Little Joe* ...... 10.00 - 15.00

PATTERSON & CAPLINGER:

Gennett 7003 *The Black Sheep* ...... 15.00 - 20.00

PATT PATTERSON (& LOIS DEXTER):

Romeo 5022 *A Home On The Range* ...... 4.00 - 6.00

5031 *The Cowboy's Love Song* ...... 4.00 - 6.00

RED PATTERSON'S PIEDMONT LOG ROLLERS (See PATTERSON'S PIEDMONT LOG ROLLERS) SAM PATTERSON TRIO:

Edison 51644 *Old MacDonald Had A Farm* .... 7.00 - 10.00

52085 *Pictures From Life's Other Side* ...... 7.00 - 10.00

PAUL & JOHN:

Okeh 45280 *Band Rehersal For Old Settler's Union* 8.00 - 12.00

EZRA PAULETTE & THE BEVERLY HILLBILLIES:

Titles, issued contemporaneously on Banner, Melotone, Oriole, Perfect, Romeo: *The Old Arapahoe Trail; On The Texas Prairie; The Prisoner's Song' Rosalie; When The Wild Flowers Are In Bloom* ...... 5.00 - 8.00

Conqueror 8954, 8955, 8956, 9011 ...... 5.00 - 8.00

Vocalion 03164, 03263, 03882, 04104 ...... 5.00 - 8.00

PHIL PAVEY:

Okeh 45308 *Broncho Bustin' Blues* ...... 8.00 - 12.00

45355 *Utah Mormon Blues* ...... 8.00 - 12.00

LEON PAYNE:

Bullet 649, 670, 671, 679 ...... 3.00 - 6.00

PECK'S MALE QUARTET:

Q.R.S. 9029 *There Is Power In The Blood* ...... 8.00 - 12.00

9030 *The Home Over There* ...... 8.00 - 12.00

BERT PECK:

Brunswick 522 *Over The Hills To The Poor House* 7.00 - 10.00

FRED PENDLETON & HIS MELODY BOYS:

Champion 16457 *Come Take A Trip In My Airship* 15.00 - 20.00

JACK PENEWELL:

Paramount 3130 *When Irish Eyes Are Smiling* .. 5.00 - 8.00

3131 *Last Night I Was Dreaming* ...... 5.00 - 8.00

BESS PENNINGTON:

Vocalion 5423 *Jake And May* ...... 8.00 - 12.00

(OLD) HANK PENNY (& HIS RADIO COWBOYS):

Columbia 15766-D *My Blue Ridge Mountain Bride* 40.00 - 60.00

King 507, 512, 519, 521, 528, 534 ...... 3.00 - 5.00

Okeh, most issues ...... 3.00 - 5.00

Vocalion 04543, 04640, 04741, 04826, 04922, 05067 4.00 - 7.00

PERRY COUNTY MUSIC MAKERS:

Vocalion 5425 *Madaline* ...... 10.00 - 15.00

5443 *Got A Buddy I Must See* ...... 10.00 - 15.00

PETE THE HIRED MAN (GEORGE E. LOGAN):

Champion 45004 *Will The Roses Bloom In Heaven* 5.00 - 8.00

PETERSON'S HOBO ORCHESTRA:

Victor 20677 *Submarine Waltz* ...... 5.00 - 8.00

W.C./WALTER PETERSON:

Champion 45000, 45018 ...... 3.00 - 5.00

Gennett 6078 *Medley* ...... 8.00 - 12.00

6102 *Over The Waves* ...... 8.00 - 12.00

6221 *Medley* ...... 8.00 - 12.00

6274 *One-Two-Three-Four* ...... 8.00 - 12.00

6406 *Marching Through Georgia* ...... 8.00 - 12.00

6463 *Where The River Shannon Flows* ...... 8.00 - 12.00

6674 *Medley* ...... 8.00 - 12.00

Superior 349 *Over The Waves* ...... 5.00 - 8.00

9194 *Lazy Old Man* ...... 5.00 - 8.00

9195 *Bummelpetrus* ...... 5.00 - 8.00

9196 *Medley Of Old Timers* ...... 5.00 - 8.00

9197 *Medley*	5.00 -	8.00
9198 *Over The Waves*	5.00 -	8.00
9199 *One-Two-Three-Four*	5.00 -	8.00
9200 *Medley*	5.00 -	8.00
9201 *Marching Through Georgia*	5.00 -	8.00

NORMAN PHELPS' VIRGINIA ROUNDERS:

Decca 5191, 5192, 5193, 5204, 5212, 5224, 5225, 5237, 5245, 5252, 5268, 5307	4.00 -	8.00

WILLIE PHELPS:

Decca 5223 *The Terrible Tupelo Storm*	5.00 -	8.00

PHILYAW BROTHERS:

Vocalion 02974, 02997, 03011, 03111, 03379, 03419, 04065, 04119, 04186, 04218, 04314	3.00 -	6.00

PICKARD FAMILY:

Banner 6283 *Down In Arkansas*	5.00 -	8.00
Broadway 8179 *Thompson's Old Gray Mare*	5.00 -	8.00
Brunswick 348 *Down In Arkansas*	7.00 -	10.00
363 *Buffalo Gals*	7.00 -	10.00
385 *Get Me Out Of This Birmingham Jail*	7.00 -	10.00
Conqueror 7251 *Down In Arkansas*	5.00 -	8.00
Oriole 1502 *Rabbit In The Pea Patch*	5.00 -	8.00
Paramount 3213 *Rabbit In The Pea Patch*	5.00 -	8.00
3214 *Down In Arkansas*	5.00 -	8.00
3218 *On The Dummy Line*	7.00 -	10.00
3231 *Thompson's Old Gray Mare*	5.00 -	8.00
Q.R.S. 9022 *Down In Arkansas*	7.00 -	10.00
9006 *Thompson's Old Grey Mare*	7.00 -	10.00

OBED PICKARD:

Columbia 15141-D *Kitty Wells*	7.00 -	10.00
15246-D *The Old Gray Horse*	7.00 -	10.00

JACK PICKELL:

Columbia 15117-D *Don't You Love Your Daddy Too*	5.00 -	8.00

WILL PICKETT:

Bell 1169 *It Can't Be Done*	10.00 -	15.00

PIEDMONT MELODY BOYS:

Victor 23660 *Tell Him Now*	15.00 -	20.00

JOHNNY PIEMONTE:

Gennett 6348 *Over The Waves*	7.00 -	12.00

PIE PLANT PETE:

Champion 16770 *Medley Of Old Familiar Tunes*	12.00 -	16.00
45015, 45063, 45064, 45093	4.00 -	7.00
Decca 5014, 5030	4.00 -	7.00
Gennett 6748 *Boston Burglar*	10.00 -	15.00
6776 *Ben Tucker Reel*	10.00 -	15.00
6810 *Asleep At The Switch*	10.00 -	15.00
7167 *Waiting For The Railroad Train*	10.00 -	15.00
7205 *Nutty Song*	10.00 -	15.00
7289 *The Lightning Express*	10.00 -	15.00
Melotone 13277 *Stay On The Farm*	5.00 -	8.00
13278 *Do You Hear The Goldfish Sing?*	5.00 -	8.00
6-06-52 *Prairie Moon*	5.00 -	8.00
(Note: Above titles, and others, were also issued on Banner, Oriole, Perfect, Romeo.)		
Process 1014 *I'm Gonna Ride That Train*	————	
Supertone 9351 *Boston Burglar*	5.00 -	8.00
9363 *The Letter That Never Came*	6.00 -	10.00
9405 *Ben Tucker Reel*	6.00 -	10.00
9652 *Nutty Song*	6.00 -	10.00
9667 *Medley Of Old Familiar Tunes*	6.00 -	10.00
9668 *O Jailer Bring Back That Key*	6.00 -	10.00
9669 *Sand Will Do It*	6.00 -	10.00
9701 *The Lightning Express*	6.00 -	10.00
9712 *Good Old Turnip Greens*	6.00 -	10.00
9717 *Little Brown Jug*	6.00 -	10.00

PIERCE'S OKLAHOMA (COW) BOYS:

Bluebird 6610, 6632, 6646, 6785, 6822	4.00 -	7.00

WEBB PIERCE:

4 Star	3.00 -	5.00
Pacemaker 1015 *In The Jailhouse*	7.00 -	10.00

PINE KNOB SERENADERS:

Superior 2556 *Apple Cider*	12.00 -	18.00

PINE MOUNTAIN BOYS:

Victor 23582 *She Wouldn't Be Still*	20.00 -	30.00
23592 *Wild Woman Blues*	20.00 -	30.00
23605 *Apron String Blues*	20.00 -	30.00

PINE MOUNTAIN RAMBLERS:

Champion 15610 *Ramblin' Reckless Hobo*	10.00 -	15.00

PINE RIDGE BOYS:

Bluebird 8360 *The Convict And The Rose*	5.00 -	8.00
Bluebird 8671 *Railroad Boomer*	5.00 -	8.00
8940 *Lonesome For You*	5.00 -	8.00

PINE STATE PLAYBOYS: (See Also CLAUDE CASEY)

Bluebird 7451, 7535, 7704	4.00 -	7.00

PINSON, PITTS & COLEY:

Bluebird 76611 *In Old Wyoming*	10.00 -	15.00

PIPERS GAP RAMBLERS:

Okeh 45185 *I Ain't Nobody's Darling*	8.00 -	12.00

PLAINSMEN & RUFUS HALL:

Broadway 8183 *Bill Mason*	12.00 -	18.00

PLANTATION BOYS:

Bluebird 6678, 6981	4.00 -	7.00

PLEASANT FAMILY:

Broadway 8148 *Rabbit In The Pea Patch*	5.00 -	8.00
8149 *Down In Arkansas*	5.00 -	8.00
8150 *On The Dummy Line*	7.00 -	10.00

PLYMOUTH VERMONT OLD TIME BARN DANCE ORCHESTRA:

Okeh 45073 *Portland Fancy*	5.00 -	8.00

POHLMANN & HATHAWAY:

Supertone 9139 *Throw Out The Life Line*	————	

DOUG POINDEXTER:

Sun 202 *Now She Cares No More*	10.00 -	20.00*

TALMADGE POLLARD:

Bluebird 7176 *Mind Your Own Business*	5.00 -	8.00

CHARLIE POOLE (& ROY HARVEY/& THE NORTH CAROLINA RAMBLERS):

Columbia 15038-D *Don't Let Your Deal Go Down Blues*	6.00 -	10.00
15043-D *The Girl I Left In Sunny Tennessee*	6.00 -	10.00
15099-D *White House Blues*	6.00 -	10.00
15116-D *There'll Come A Time*	6.00 -	10.00
15138-D *Good Bye Booze*	6.00 -	10.00
15160-D *The Highwayman*	6.00 -	10.00
15179-D *Falling By The Wayside*	6.00 -	10.00
15193-D *You Ain't Talkin' To Me*	6.00 -	10.00
15215-D *If I Lose I Don't Care*	6.00 -	10.00
15286-D *Ramblin' Blues*	8.00 -	12.00
15307-D *I Cannot Call Her Mother*	8.00 -	12.00
15342-D *Jealous Mary*	8.00 -	12.00
15385-D *Hangman, Hangman, Slack The Rope*	10.00 -	15.00
15407-D *Bill Mason*	10.00 -	15.00
15425-D *Sweet Sunny South*	10.00 -	15.00
15456-D *The Wayward Boy*	10.00 -	15.00
15509-D *The Baltimore Fire*	15.00 -	20.00
15519-D *Sweet Sixteen*	15.00 -	20.00
15545-D *If The River Was Whiskey*	15.00 -	20.00
15584-D *A Young Boy Left His Home One Day*	15.00 -	20.00
Columbia 15601-D *Look Before You Leap*	20.00 -	30.00
15615-D *Southern Medley*	20.00 -	30.00
15636-D *Just Keep Waiting Till The Good Time Comes*	20.00 -	30.00
15672-D *Took My Gal A-Walkin'*	30.00 -	40.00
15688-D *Milwaukee Blues*	30.00 -	40.00
15711-D *Write A Letter To My Mother*	30.00 -	40.00

POPE'S ARKANSAS MOUNTAINEERS:

Victor 21295 *Hog Eye*	10.00 -	15.00
21469 *Cotton-Eyed Joe*	20.00 -	30.00
21577 *Jaw Bone*	20.00 -	30.00

POPLIN-WOODS TENNESSEE STRING BAND:

Victor 40080 *Are You From Dixie?*	10.00 -	15.00

ARCHIE PORTER & HIS HAPPY BUCKEYES:
Champion 16729 *Log Cabin Call*............ 15.00 - 20.00

POTTER & JAMES:
Supertone 9541 *Down On The Farm*......... 8.00 - 12.00

POWDER RIVER JACK & KITTY LEE:
Victor 23527 *Tying A Knot In The Devil's Tail.* 10.00 - 15.00

JACK & JOHNNIE POWELL:
Victor 23568 *By The Old Garden Gate*........ 5.00 - 8.00
40259 *You Ain't Talking To Me*............ 5.00 - 8.00

FIDDLIN' POWERS (& FAMILY):
Edison 51662 *Old Joe Clark*............ 8.00 - 12.00
51789 *Sourwood Mountains*................ 8.00 - 12.00
52083 *Cluck Old Hen*................ 10.00 - 15.00
Okeh 45154 *Old Virginia Reel*............ 7.00 - 10.00
45268 *Did You Ever See The Devil, Uncle Joe?* 7.00 - 10.00
Victor 19448 *Sour Wood Mountains*.......... 5.00 - 8.00
Victor 19449 *Cripple Creek*................ 5.00 - 8.00

PRAIRIE RAMBLERS:
Titles, issued contemporaneously on Banner, Conqueror, Melotone, Oriole, Perfect, Romeo, include: *Deep Elem Blues; Gonna Have a Feast Here Tonight; I'm Looking For The Bully Of The Town; Isle Of Capri; Jim's Windy Mule; Jug Rag; Just Come On In; The Lady In Red; Mistook In The Woman I Love; Nobody's Darling But Mine; On Treasure Island; The Oregon Trail; Put On An Old Pair Of Boots; Snowflakes; Swingin' Down The Old Orchard Lane; Truckin; Uncle Oph's Got The Coon; When I Grow Too Old To Dream; Woman's Answer To Nobody's Dream* 5.00 - 10.00
Bluebird 5302 *Blue River*.................... 6.00 - 10.00
5320 *Go Easy Blues*..................... 6.00 - 10.00
5322 *Gonna Have A Feast Here Tonight*..... 6.00 - 10.00
5395 *Next Year*...................... 6.00 - 10.00
Okeh 05851, 05878, 06053, 06102, 06230, 06243, and others...................... 3.00 - 5.00
Victor 23856 *Go Easy Blues*................. 25.00 - 35.00
23859 *Kentucky Blues*................... 25.00 - 35.00
Vocalion 03061 *Maple On The Hill, Part 2*..... 7.00 - 10.00
03085 *You Look Pretty In An Evening Gown* 5.00 - 8.00
03100 *This World Is Not My Home*........ 5.00 - 8.00
03115 *Jesus Hold My Hand*.............. 5.00 - 8.00
03332, 03422, 03469, 04039, 04092, 04134, 04427, 04601, 04672, 04796, 04868, 04899, 04936, 05002, 05081................ 4.00 - 7.00

PRAIRIE SERENADERS:
Champion 45164 *The Lonely Cowboy*......... 7.00 - 10.00
45190 *I'm The Last Of The Texas Rangers*... 7.00 - 10.00

CHARLIE PRESCOTT:
Challenge 335 *The Dixie Cowboy*............. 8.00 - 12.00

RAY PRICE:
Bullet 701 *Jealous Lies*..................... 20.00 - 30.00

WILLIAM PRICE:
Challenge 332 *Little Birdie*................. 5.00 - 8.00

B.L./SUNSHINE PRITCHARD:
Gennett 6902 *Son Of A Gun*................. 15.00 - 25.00
Paramount 3320 *Stone Mountain Wobble*...... 20.00 - 30.00

HOLLAND PUCKETT:
Gennett 6144 *Weeping Wilow Tree*........... 10.00 - 15.00
6163 *A Mother's Advice*................... 10.00 - 15.00
6189 *Drunken Hiccoughs*.................. 10.00 - 15.00
6206 *He Lives On High*.................... 10.00 - 15.00
6271 *The Dying Cowboy*.................... 10.00 - 15.00
6433 *Come And Kiss Me Baby Darling*...... 10.00 - 15.00
6532 *The Maple On The Hill*.............. 10.00 - 15.00
6720 *Little Bessie*...................... 10.00 - 15.00
Silvertone 25065 *The Dying Cowboy*.......... 10.00 - 15.00
Supertone 9324 *Little Bessie*............... 10.00 - 15.00

RILEY PUCKETT (& TED HAWKINS/RED JONES/CLAYTON McMICHEN):
Bluebird 5432 *The Old Spinning Wheel*........ 8.00 - 12.00

5471 *K.C. Railroad*.......... 8.00 - 12.00
5473 *Texas Hop*.......... 8.00 - 12.00
5514 *Kimball Blues*.......... 8.00 - 12.00
5532 *Careless Love*.......... 8.00 - 12.00
5587 *I'm Gettin' Ready To Go*.......... 8.00 - 12.00
5607 *Renfro Valley Home*.......... 8.00 - 12.00
5656 *Tokio Rag*.......... 8.00 - 12.00
5666 *Lost Love*.......... 8.00 - 12.00
5691 *Down In The Valley*.......... 8.00 - 12.00
5738 *Puckett Blues*.......... 8.00 - 12.00
5786 *Four Day Blues*.......... 8.00 - 12.00
5818 *Chain Gang Blues*.......... 8.00 - 12.00
6064 *Roll Back The Carpet*.......... 8.00 - 12.00
6067 *Don't Let Your Deal Go Down*.......... 7.00 - 10.00
6103 *Nobody's Business*.......... 7.00 - 10.00
6134 *Curly Headed Baby*.......... 7.00 - 10.00
6196 *Blue Ridge Mountain Blues*.......... 7.00 - 10.00
6291 *When I Grow Too Old To Dream*...... 7.00 - 10.00
6313 *Ole Faithful*.......... 7.00 - 10.00
6348 *Back To My Home In The Smoky Montains* 7.00 - 10.00
6404 *My Old Mule*.......... 7.00 - 10.00
7303 *Carolina Sunshine Girl*.......... 7.00 - 10.00
7717 *Old Maid's Brown Ferry*.......... 5.00 - 8.00
Columbia 107-D *Rock All Your Babies To Sleep*. 8.00 - 12.00
110-D *Hen Cackle*.......... 8.00 - 12.00
113-D *Casey Jones*.......... 8.00 - 12.00
119-D *Black-Eyed Alabama Gal*.......... 8.00 - 12.00
150-D *Johnson's Old Grey Mule*.......... 8.00 - 12.00
240-D *Just As The Sun Went Down*.......... 7.00 - 10.00
254-D *Blue Ridge Mountain Blues*.......... 7.00 - 10.00
405-D *Let Me Call You Sweetheart*.......... 8.00 - 12.00
15003-D *Swanee River*.......... 10.00 - 15.00
15015-D *Burglar Man*.......... 10.00 - 15.00
15033-D *Jesse James*.......... 10.00 - 15.00
15035-D *Just Break The News To Mother*.... 8.00 - 12.00
15036-D *I Wish I Was Single Again*........ 8.00 - 12.00
15045-D *Long Tongue Woman*.......... 8.00 - 12.00
15050-D *The Orphan Girl*.......... 8.00 - 12.00
15055-D *When I'm Gone You'll Soon Forget*. 8.00 - 12.00
15058-D *Down By The Old Mill Stream*...... 6.00 - 10.00
15063-D *You'd Be Surprised*.......... 6.00 - 10.00
15068-D *Hello Central Give Me Heaven*..... 6.00 - 10.00
15073-D *Wait Till The Sun Shines Nellie*.... 6.00 - 10.00
15074-D *Bully Of The Town*.......... 6.00 - 10.00
15078-D *Everybody Works But Father*...... 6.00 - 10.00
15088-D *Sauerkraut*.......... 6.00 - 10.00
15095-D *My Carolina Home*.......... 6.00 - 10.00
15102-D *Ida Red*.......... 6.00 - 10.00
15125-D *Put My Little Shoes Away*.......... 6.00 - 10.00
15139-D *Down In Arkansas*.......... 7.00 - 10.00
15163-D *Fuzzy Rag*.......... 8.00 - 12.00
15171-D *Little Log Cabin In The Lane*....... 7.00 - 10.00
15185-D *Alabama Gal*.......... 7.00 - 10.00
15196-D *My Poodle Dog*.......... 7.00 - 10.00
15198-D *That Old Irish Mother Of Mine*..... 5.00 - 8.00
15226-D *Red Wing*.......... 8.00 - 12.00
15232-D *Little Brown Jug*.......... 8.00 - 12.00
15250-D *All Bound 'Round With The Mason-Dixon Line*.................. 10.00 - 15.00
15261-D *Blue Yodel*.......... 10.00 - 15.00
15277-D *Little Maumee*.......... 10.00 - 15.00
15295-D *Slim Gal*.......... 10.00 - 15.00
15324-D *The Moonshiner's Dream*.......... 12.00 - 18.00
15358-D *Bill Johnson*.......... 12.00 - 18.00
15374-D *I'm Going To Georgia*.......... 12.00 - 18.00
15392-D *Don't Try It For It Can't Be Done*.. 12.00 - 18.00
15393-D *Carolina Moon*.......... 15.00 - 20.00
15408-D *Waiting For A Train*.......... 15.00 - 20.00
15448-D *McKinley*.......... 15.00 - 20.00
15505-D *Frankie And Johnny*.......... 15.00 - 20.00
15563-D *Dark Town Strutters Ball*.......... 15.00 - 20.00

15605-D *Waitin' For The Evenin' Mail*	20.00 -	30.00
15631-D *Somewhere In Old Wyoming*	20.00 -	30.00
15656-D *The Cat Came Back*	20.00 -	30.00
15708-D *There's A Hard Time Coming*	25.00 -	40.00
15719-D *All Bound Down In Prison*	25.00 -	40.00
15747-D *East Bound Train*	30.00 -	50.00
Decca 5438 *There's More Pretty Girls Than One*	7.00 -	10.00
5442 *Short Life Of Trouble*	7.00 -	10.00
5455 *Altoona Freight Wreck*	7.00 -	10.00
5472 *Gulf Coast Blues*	7.00 -	10.00
5523 *Somebody's Waiting For You*	5.00 -	8.00
5540 *Moonlight On The Colorado*	5.00 -	8.00

SI PUCKETT:

Supertone 9186 *The Maple On The Hill*	7.00 -	10.00
9254 *The Bright Sherman Valley*	7.00 -	10.00

PETE PYLE:

Bluebird 8581, 8711	3.00 -	6.00
Bullet 602 *Talking The Blues*	4.00 -	7.00

QUADRILLERS:

Paramount 3008 *Drunk Man Blues*	15.00 -	20.00
3009 *Cumberland Blues*	15.00 -	20.00

FRANK QUINN:

Okeh 45030 *Pop Goes The Weasel*	5.00 -	8.00

RADIO MAC:

Victor 23510 *Home Spun Gal*	10.00 -	15.00
23586 *He Sure Can Play*	10.00 -	15.00
24690 *Last Old Dollar*	10.00 -	15.00
23704 *Sweet Betsy From Pike*	8.00 -	12.00
23829 *Bald Top Mountain*	30.00 -	50.00
40101 *Ain't We Crazy*	5.00 -	8.00
40264 *Roamin'*	5.00 -	8.00

JAMES RAGAN & OLIVER BECK:

Challenge 390 *Please Papa Come Home*	8.00 -	12.00
401 *Walking On The Streets Of Glory*	7.00 -	10.00

RAGGEDY ANN'S MELODY MAKERS:

Okeh 45235 *Zenda Waltz*	5.00 -	8.00

RAILROAD BOYS:

Superior 2684 *By A Cottage In The Twilight*	15.00 -	20.00
2779 *You're Bound To Look Like A Monkey*	20.00 -	30.00

RAINEY OLD TIME BAND:

Columbia 15675-D *Engineer Frank Hawk*	15.00 -	20.00

RALEY BROTHERS:

Bluebird 7062 *Chicken Roost Blues*	7.00 -	10.00

RAMBLING DUET:

Bluebird 7131, 7233, 7450, 7484, 7534, 7574	4.00 -	7.00

RAMBLING KID & PROFESSOR:

Melotone 7-07-54 *Little Home In Tennessee*	8.00 -	12.00

RAMBLING RAMBLERS:

Vocalion 04628, 04758, 04949	4.00 -	7.00

RANCH BOYS:

Decca 5016, 5017, 5040, 5045, 5046, 5061, 5074, 5113, 5128, 5167, 5319, 5341, 5354	4.00 -	7.00

RAND & FOSTER:

Supertone 9326 *The Vestris Disaster*	8.00 -	12.00
9373 *Only A Step To The Grave*	8.00 -	12.00

GROVER RANN & HIS LOOKOUT MOUNTAINEERS:

Columbia 15638-D *Don't Stay After Ten*	20.00 -	30.00

RAY BROTHERS:

Bluebird 5789 *Winona Rag*	10.00 -	15.00
Victor 23552 *Mississippi Echoes*	15.00 -	20.00
23713 *Winona Rag*	15.00 -	20.00
40291 *Jake Leg Wobble*	15.00 -	20.00
40313 *Choctaw County Rag*	15.00 -	20.00

AULTON RAY/RAYL:

Champion 15332 *Maxwell Girl*	7.00 -	10.00
Gennett 6129 *True And Trembling Brakeman*	15.00 -	25.00
6177 *The Dixie Cowboy*	15.00 -	25.00
6205 *Maxwell Girl*	15.00 -	25.00
Herwin 75552 *True And Trembling Brakeman*	15.00 -	25.00
Silvertone 8150 *The Dixie Cowboy*	7.00 -	10.00

Superior 385 *The Dixie Cowboy*	15.00 -	20.00
Supertone 9250 *The Maxwell Girl*	7.00 -	10.00

REAVES' WHITE COUNTY RAMBLERS:

Vocalion 5218 *Ten Cent Piece*	20.00 -	30.00
5219 *Rattler Tree'd A Possum*	20.00 -	30.00
5224 *Down In Arkansas*	20.00 -	30.00
5247 *Drunkard's Hiccups*	20.00 -	30.00
5260 *Arkansas Pullet*	20.00 -	30.00

RECORD BOYS:

Vocalion 5136 *Harmonica Jim*	8.00 -	12.00

RECTOR TRIO:

Columbia 15658-D *Skyland Rag*	15.00 -	20.00

RED BRUSH ROWDIES/SINGERS:

Paramount 3122 *The Hatfield-McCoy Feud*	20.00 -	30.00
3140 *The Third Of July*	20.00 -	30.00
3143 *Beyond The Starry Plane*	20.00 -	30.00
3150 *Midnight Serenade*	20.00 -	30.00

RED HEADED BRIER HOPPER (LEROY ANDERSON):

Champion 16578 *Gooseberry Pie*	10.00 -	15.00
16668 *Three Wishes*	10.00 -	15.00
16678 *The Fatal Derby Day*	10.00 -	15.00
16708 *Is There No Chance For Me Tonight, Love*	10.00 -	15.00
16797 *The Wrong Man And The Wrong Woman*	15.00 -	20.00
16811 *A Mother's Wayward Son*	15.00 -	20.00
16820 *Gambling On The Sabbath*	20.00 -	30.00

RED HEADED FIDDLERS:

Brunswick 285 *Texas Quickstep*	20.00 -	30.00
388 *Rag Time Annie*	20.00 -	30.00
460 *The Fatal Wedding*	20.00 -	30.00
470 *Cheat 'Em*	20.00 -	30.00
526 *The Steeley Rag*	20.00 -	30.00

RED MOUNTAIN TRIO:

Columbia 15260-D *The Wang Wang Blues*	10.00 -	15.00
15369-D *Dixie*	10.00 -	15.00
15462-D *Carolina Sunshine*	15.00 -	20.00

RED RIVER COON HUNTERS:

Superior 2647 *The Wreck Of The West Bound Airliner*	20.00 -	30.00
2754 *By And By You Will Forgive Me*	20.00 -	30.00

RED & SON RAYMOND:

Champion 16797 *Mother's Beautiful Hands*	15.00 -	20.00

REED CHILDREN:

Columbia 15525-D *I'll Be All Smiles Tonight*	7.00 -	10.00

ALFRED & ORVILLE REED:

Victor 23550 *Beware*	10.00 -	15.00
23650 *Old Fashioned Cottage*	10.00 -	15.00

BLIND ALFRED REED:

Victor 20836 *The Wreck Of The Virginia*	10.00 -	15.00
20939 *You Must Unload*	7.00 -	10.00
21191 *Explosion In The Fairmount Mines*	10.00 -	15.00
21360 *Why Do You Bob Your Hair, Girls?*	10.00 -	15.00
21533 *The Fate Of Chris Lively And Wife*	10.00 -	15.00
40196 *Woman's Been After Man Ever Since*	10.00 -	15.00
40236 *Money Cravin' Folks*	10.00 -	15.00
40290 *Black And Blue Blues*	10.00 -	15.00

L.K. REEDER:

Okeh 45026 *Falling Leaf*	5.00 -	8.00

JACK REEDY & HIS WALKER MOUNTAIN STRING BAND:

Brunswick 221 *Chinese Breakdown*	15.00 -	25.00

JIMMY REESE:

Supertone 9613 *Blue Yodel No. 5*	10.00 -	15.00
9627 *You And My Old Guitar*	10.00 -	15.00

REEVES & MOODY:

Victor 20540 *Down Where The Watermelon Grows*	10.00 -	15.00
20929 *Rock All Our Babies To Sleep*	5.00 -	8.00
21188 *Sweet Evelina*	5.00 -	8.00

GOEBEL REEVES (THE TEXAS DRIFTER):

Titles, issued contemporaneously on Banner, Conqueror, Melotone, Oriole, Perfect, Romeo: *The*

Bar None Ranch; Big Rock Candy Mountain; The Cowboy's Dizzy Sweetheart; It's True I'm Just A Convict; Reckless Tex From Texas; The Wandering Boy; Where The Mississippi Washes ... 5.00 - 8.00

Brunswick 539 *Station H.O.B.O.*	7.00 -	10.00
Champion 539 *The Hobo's Grave*	10.00 -	15.00
16189 *Station H.O.B.O.*	10.00 -	15.00
16234 *The Drifter*	10.00 -	15.00
45181 *The Drifter's Buddy*	5.00 -	8.00
45194 *I Learned About Women From Her*	5.00 -	8.00
Conqueror 8442 *Cold And Hungry*	7.00 -	10.00
8443 *The Bar None Ranch*	7.00 -	10.00
Okeh 45365 *The Drifter*	8.00 -	12.00
45381 *The Tramp's Mother*	8.00 -	12.00
45408 *Blue Undertaker's Blues*	8.00 -	12.00
45449 *The Texas Drifter's Warning*	8.00 -	12.00
45491 *In The Land Of Never Was*	8.00 -	12.00

JIM REEVES:

Macy's 115 *Teardrops Of Regret*	35.00 -	50.00
132 *I've Never Been So Blue*	30.00 -	40.00

WALTER REGAN:

Superior 2524 *Just As Your Mother Was*	10.00 -	15.00
2585 *Moundsville Prisoner*	20.00 -	30.00

DICK REINHART:

Brunswick 386 *Rambling Lover*	8.00 -	12.00

GEORGE RENEAU ("THE BLIND MUSICIAN OF THE SMOKEY MOUNTAINS"):

Vocalion 5029 *Lonesome Road Blues*	6.00 -	10.00
5030 *Life's Railway To Heaven*	6.00 -	10.00
5031 *Little Brown Jug*	6.00 -	10.00
5032 *Arkansas Traveler*	6.00 -	10.00
5033 *Here, Rattler, Here*	6.00 -	10.00
5034 *Blue Ridge Blues*	6.00 -	10.00
5049 *Red Wing*	6.00 -	10.00
5050 *C & O Wreck*	6.00 -	10.00
5052 *The Baggage Coach Ahead*	6.00 -	10.00
5054 *The New Market Wreck*	6.00 -	10.00
5055 *I've Got The Railroad Blues*	6.00 -	10.00
5056 *The Prisoner's Song*	6.00 -	10.00
5057 *Little Rosewood Casket*	6.00 -	10.00
5058 *Wild Bill Jones*	6.00 -	10.00
5059 *Wild And Reckless Hobos*	6.00 -	10.00
5064 *My Redeemer*	6.00 -	10.00
5077 *Rovin' Gambler*	6.00 -	10.00
5078 *Gambling On The Sabbath Day*	6.00 -	10.00
5079 *Bad Companions*	6.00 -	10.00
5080 *The Hand Of Fate*	6.00 -	10.00
5083 *Railroad Lover*	6.00 -	10.00
5106 *Old Man On The Hill*	6.00 -	10.00
5107 *Old Rugged Cross*	6.00 -	10.00
5108 *Two Orphans*	6.00 -	10.00
14809 *Lonesome Road Blues*	8.00 -	12.00
14811 *Life's Railway To Heaven*	8.00 -	12.00
14812 *Little Brown Jug*	8.00 -	12.00
14813 *Arkansas Traveler*	8.00 -	12.00
14814 *Here, Rattler, Here*	8.00 -	12.00
14815 *Blue Ridge Blues*	8.00 -	12.00
14896 *Red Wing*	8.00 -	12.00
14897 *C & W Wreck*	8.00 -	12.00
14918 *The Baggage Coach Ahead*	8.00 -	12.00
14930 *The New Market Wreck*	8.00 -	12.00
14946 *I've Got The Railroad Blues*	8.00 -	12.00
14991 *The Prisoner's Song*	8.00 -	12.00
14997 *The Little Rosewood Casket*	8.00 -	12.00
14998 *Wild Bill Jones*	8.00 -	12.00
14999 *Wild And Reckless Hobos*	8.00 -	12.00
15046 *My Redeemer*	7.00 -	10.00
15148 *Rovin' Gambler*	7.00 -	10.00
15149 *Gambling On The Sabbath Day*	7.00 -	10.00
15150 *Bad Companions*	7.00 -	10.00
15182 *The Hand Of Fate*	7.00 -	10.00

15194 *Railroad Lover*	7.00 -	10.00
15347 *Old Man On The Hill*	7.00 -	10.00
15348 *The Old Rugged Cross*	7.00 -	10.00
15349 *Two Orphans*	7.00 -	10.00
15366 *On Top Of Old Smoky*	15.00 -	20.00

RENFRO VALLEY BOYS:

Paramount 3311 *Twenty-One Years*	15.00 -	20.00
3315 *My Renfro Valley Home*	15.00 -	20.00
3316 *The Yellow Rose Of Texas*	15.00 -	20.00
3321 *Loreena*	15.00 -	25.00

JIMMIE REVARD & THE OKLAHOMA PLAYBOYS:

Bluebird 6654, 6679, 6712, 6739, 6753, 6774, 6823, 6842, 6877, 6935, 6992, 7028, 7061, 7085, 7172, 7199, 7248, 7309, 7370, 7371, 7481, 7520, 7559, 7610, 7727, 7776, 7911, 7939, 7964	4.00 -	7.00
Bluebird (higher numbers)	4.00 -	5.00
Everstate 1011 *Holdin' The Sack*	4.00 -	7.00

WILLIAM REXROAT (& HIS CEDAR CREST SINGERS):

Vocalion 5290 *Fading Away*	10.00 -	15.00
5323 *Build Me A Bungalow*	10.00 -	15.00
5345 *We Shall Wear A Crown*	8.00 -	12.00

REYNOLDS & ROBINSON:

Superior 2653 *Rocky Mountain Rose*	————	

RALPH REYNOLDS & HIS DUDE RANCH WRANGLERS:

Globe 127, 128	3.00 -	6.00

RICE BROTHERS' GANG:

Decca, most issues	4.00 -	6.00

RICE, DAVIS & THOMAS:

Paramount 3309 *Circus Day Rag*	20.00 -	30.00
Q.R.S. 9019 *Circus Day Rag*	20.00 -	30.00

EDD RICE:

Vocalion 5220 *Cricket On The Hearth*	8.00 -	12.00

GLEN RICE & HIS BEVERLY HILLBILLIES:
(See also BEVERLY HILLBILLIES)

Brunswick 506 *My Old Iowa Home*	5.00 -	8.00
519 *Prairie Skies*	5.00 -	8.00
597 *Swiss Yodel*	5.00 -	8.00
598 *The Big Corral*	5.00 -	8.00
599 *Ridge Runnin' Roan*	5.00 -	8.00
600 *Cowboy Joe*	5.00 -	8.00

HOKE RICE & HIS HOKY POKY BOYS/SOUTHERN BAND/STRING BAND; HOKE RICE & HARRY STARK:

Brunswick 416 *Georgia Jubilee*	7.00 -	10.00
473 *Wabash Blues*	7.00 -	10.00
482 *Georgia Gal*	7.00 -	10.00
552 *Floating Down To Cotton Town*	7.00 -	10.00
Gennett 6839 *Waiting' For A Train*	15.00 -	20.00
6855 *Blue Yodel No. 4*	15.00 -	25.00
7067 *Unexplained Blues*	15.00 -	25.00
Paramount 3212 *I'm Lonely And Blue*	15.00 -	20.00
3229 *Chinese Breakdown*	15.00 -	25.00
3239 *Down In A Southern Town*	15.00 -	25.00
3308 *Macon Georgia Breakdown*	15.00 -	25.00
Q.R.S. 9012 *Waiting For A Train*	15.00 -	20.00
9015 *Down In A Southern Town*	15.00 -	25.00
9022 *Way Down South By The Sea*	15.00 -	25.00

RENUS RICH & CARL BRADSHAW:

Columbia 15341-D *Sleep Baby Sleep*	5.00 -	8.00

FRED RICHARDS:

Columbia 15483-D *Danville Blues*	10.00 -	15.00

RALPH RICHARDSON:

Okeh 45267 *Little Dog Yodel*	4.00 -	7.00

RIDGEL'S FOUNTAIN CITIANS:

Vocalion 5363 *Be Ready*	20.00 -	30.00
5389 *Little Bonnie*	20.00 -	30.00
5427 *Baby, Call Your Dog Off*	20.00 -	30.00
5455 *The Bald Headed End Of The Broom*	20.00 -	30.00

RILEY'S MOUNTAINEERS:
Supertone 9677 *Sunny Home In Dixie* .... 7.00 - 10.00
GEORGE RILEY:
Perfect 12653 *The Texas Drifter's Warning* ..... 5.00 - 8.00
(Probably also issued on Melotone, Oriole, Romeo.)
TEX RITTER:
Titles, issued contemporaneously on Banner, Conqueror, Melotone, Oriole, Perfect, Romeo, Vocalion: *A-Ridin' Old Paint; Every Day In The Saddle; Goodbye Old Paint; Rye Whiskey, Rye Whiskey* .... 8.00 - 12.00
Champion 45153 *Nobody's Darling But Mine* .... 8.00 - 10.00
45154 *The Oregon Trail* .... 7.00 - 10.00
45191 *Bill The Bar Fly* .... 7.00 - 10.00
45197 *Answer To Nobody's Darling But Mine* 7.00 - 10.00
45198 *The Hills Of Old Wyomin'.* .... 7.00 - 10.00
Decca 5076 *Lady Killin' Cowboy* .... 7.00 - 10.00
5112 *Thirty-Three Years In Prison* .... 7.00 - 10.00
5305 *Bill The Bar Fly* .... 5.00 - 8.00
5306 *Jailhouse Lament* .... 5.00 - 8.00
5315 *High, Wide And Handsome* .... 5.00 - 8.00
5389 *Down The Colorado Trail* .... 5.00 - 8.00
5405 *I'm Hittin' The Trail (For Home)* .... 5.00 - 8.00
5639, 5648, 5922 .... 4.00 - 7.00
Montgomery Ward 8020, 8032 .... 4.00 - 7.00
RIVERSIDE RAMBLERS:
Bluebird 6926, 7063, 7202, 7251, 7846, 7942, 7974 3.00 - 6.00
ROANE COUNTY RAMBLERS:
Columbia 15328-D *Home Town Blues* .... 15.00 - 20.00
15377-D *Tennessee Waltz* .... 10.00 - 15.00
15398-D *Roane County Rag* .... 15.00 - 20.00
15438-D *McCarroll's Breakdown* .... 15.00 - 20.00
15498-D *Johnson City Rag* .... 20.00 - 30.00
15570-D *Alabama Trot* .... 20.00 - 30.00
ROANOKE JUG BAND:
Okeh 45393 *Home Brew Rag* .... 25.00 - 40.00
45423 *Stone Mountain Rag* .... 25.00 - 40.00
GEORGE ROARK:
Columbia 15383-D *I Ain't A Bit Drunk* .... 7.00 - 10.00
SHORTBUCKLE ROARK & FAMILY:
Victor 40023 *My Mother's Hands* .... 7.00 - 10.00
FIDDLIN' DOC ROBERTS (TRIO):
Titles, issued contemporaneously on Banner, Conqueror, Melotone, Oriole, Perfect, Romeo: *Blue Grass Rag; Carroll County Blues; Charleston No. 1; Coal Tipple Blues; Cumberland Blues; Did You Ever See The Devil, Uncle Joe?; Down Yonder; Farewell Waltz; A Good Man Is Waiting For You; I Don't Love Nobody; In The Shadow Of The Pines; Ninety-Nine Years; Over The Waves; Pickin' And Playin'; Ragtime Chicken Joe; Sally Ann; Shortenin' Bread; Turkey In The Straw; The Waggoner; 'Way Down South; Wednesday Night Waltz* .... 5.00 - 8.00
Challenge 501 *All I've Got Is Done Gone* ..... 7.00 - 10.00
Champion 45099, 45135, 45136 .... 4.00 - 7.00
Gennett 3152 *Martha Campbell* .... 8.00 - 12.00
3162 *All I've Got Is Done Gone* .... 8.00 - 12.00
3235 *Billy In The Low Ground* .... 8.00 - 12.00
6025 *In The Shadow Of The Pine* .... 12.00 - 16.00
6257 *Waynesburgh* .... 12.00 - 16.00
6336 *Old Buzzard* .... 12.00 - 16.00
6390 *Billy In The Low Ground* .... 10.00 - 15.00
6495 *Old Zip Coon & Medley Of Reels* ...... 15.00 - 20.00
6588 *My Old Coon Dog* .... 15.00 - 20.00
6635 *Brickyard Joe* .... 15.00 - 20.00
6689 *Shippin' Sport* .... 15.00 - 20.00
6717 *Farewell Waltz* .... 15.00 - 20.00
6750 *Mandolin Rag* .... 15.00 - 20.00
6775 *Shoot That Turkey Buzzard* .... 15.00 - 20.00
6826 *Who's Been Here Since I Been Gone* .... 15.00 - 20.00

6942 *The Devil In Georgia* .... 15.00 - 20.00
7017 *Jack's Creek Waltz* .... 15.00 - 20.00
7049 *Johnny Inchin' Along* .... 15.00 - 20.00
7094 *My Baby Don't Love Me* .... 15.00 - 20.00
7110 *Hawk's Got A Chicken* .... 15.00 - 20.00
7221 *Rye Straw* .... 15.00 - 20.00
Superior 348 *And The Cat Came Back* .... 15.00 - 20.00
386 *Billy In The Low Ground* .... 15.00 - 20.00
2762 *Sally Gooden* .... 15.00 - 20.00
Supertone 9252 *In The Shadow Of The Pine* .... 7.00 - 10.00
9397 *Martha Campbell* .... 7.00 - 10.00
JAMES ROBERTS:
Titles, issued contemporaneously on Banner, Conqueror, Melotone, Oriole, Perfect, Romeo, include: *The Crepe On The Cabin Door; Down And Out Blues; Duval County Blues; May I Sleep In Your Barn Tonight, Mister?; String Bean Mama* 7.00 - 10.00
A.C. (ECK) ROBERTSON (& DR. J.B. CRANFILL/& FAMILY):
Victor 18956 *Arkansas Traveler* .... 5.00 - 8.00
19149 *Turkey In The Straw* .... 5.00 - 8.00
19372 *Sally Johnson* .... 5.00 - 8.00
40145 *Texas Wagoner* .... 10.00 - 15.00
40166 *The Island Unknown* .... 10.00 - 15.00
40205 *Great Big Taters* .... 10.00 - 15.00
40298 *Amarillo Waltz* .... 15.00 - 20.00
40334 *Brown Kelly Waltz* .... 15.00 - 20.00
TEXAS JIM ROBERTSON:
Bluebird 8186, 8606, 8706 .... 3.00 - 6.00
MELVIN ROBINETTE & BYRD MOORE:
Gennett 6841 *Birmingham Jail* .... 35.00 - 50.00
6884 *Flop Eared Mule* .... 35.00 - 50.00
6957 *That Old Tiger Rag* .... 35.00 - 50.00
7068 *Goodbye Sweetheart* .... 35.00 - 50.00
CARSON ROBINSON (& VERNON DALHART/FRANK LUTHER/THE PIONEERS):
This artist recorded seemingly countless records for many labels from the 1920s to the 1950s. Most of his records are of minimal value and interest to collectors of country music. A few selected exceptions are listed following (and also see the Jazz and the Rockabilly/Rock & Roll, etc., sections!)
Columbia 15548-D, 15627-D, 15644-D, 15768-D. 5.00 - 10.00
15773-D *Old Familiar Tunes* .... 8.00 - 12.00
15779-D *Missouri Valley* .... 8.00 - 12.00
Okeh 45537 *So I Joined The Navy* .... 5.00 - 8.00
Superior 2546 *When The Sun Goes Down Again* 8.00 - 12.00
2580 *Cross Eyed Sue* .... 8.00 - 12.00
ROCKY MOUNTAIN RANGERS:
Bluebird 6907, 6908 .... 4.00 - 7.00
HUGH RODEN (& ROY ROGERS/HIS TEXAS NIGHTHAWKS):
Okeh 45430 *Deep Sea Waltz* .... 10.00 - 15.00
45465 *Tulsa Waltz* .... 10.00 - 15.00
45540 *Hogs In The Potato Patch* .... 15.00 - 20.00
RODEO TRIO:
Victor 40136 *Arkansas Traveler* .... 5.00 - 8.00
40186 *Medley* .... 5.00 - 8.00
JESSIE RODGERS:
Bluebird 5443 *The Ramblers' Yodel* .... 7.00 - 10.00
5499 *Way Down In Mississippi* .... 7.00 - 10.00
5632 *Roughneck Blues* .... 7.00 - 10.00
5839 *Rattlesnake Daddy* .... 7.00 - 10.00
5853 *Headin' Home* .... 7.00 - 10.00
5910 *An Old Rugged Road* .... 7.00 - 10.00
5942 *Leave Me Alone* .... 15.00 - 20.00
5958 *Lonely Days In Texas* .... 7.00 - 10.00
6066 *Hummin' To My Honey* .... 7.00 - 10.00
6087 *Window Shopping Mama* .... 7.00 - 10.00
6116 *When I Was A Boy* .... 7.00 - 10.00

6143 *Jessie's Talking Blues*.................. 7.00 - 10.00
6196 *Give Your Love*..................... 7.00 - 10.00
6256 *When The Texas Moon Is Shining*...... 5.00 - 8.00
6311 *Little Prairie Town*.................. 5.00 - 8.00
6364 *San Antonio Blues*.................. 5.00 - 8.00
6402 *Tell You About A Gal Named Sal*...... 5.00 - 8.00
6924 *Troubled In Mind And Blues*.......... 5.00 - 8.00
7018 *Just One Little Kiss*................. 5.00 - 8.00
7042 *Back In Jail Again*.................. 5.00 - 8.00
7209 *I'm A Roaming Cowboy*............. 5.00 - 8.00

JIMMIE RODGERS:
Bluebird 5000 *Moonlight And Skies*.......... 7.00 - 10.00
5037 *Gambling Bar Room Blues*........... 10.00 - 15.00
5057 *Happy Till She Met You*............. 10.00 - 15.00
5061 *You've Got Me Crying Again*......... 10.00 - 15.00
5076 *Prairie Lullaby*................... 10.00 - 15.00
5080 *Mother, Queen Of My Heart*........ 10.00 - 15.00
5081 *Down The Old Road To Home*........ 10.00 - 15.00
5082 *Roll Along, Kentucky Moon*.......... 10.00 - 15.00
5083 *My Time Ain't Long*............... 10.00 - 15.00
5084 *What's It*....................... 10.00 - 15.00
5085 *Blue Yodel*...................... 7.00 - 10.00
5136 *Mississippi Moon*................. 8.00 - 12.00
5163 *Waiting For A Train*............... 7.00 - 10.00
5199 *When It's Harvest Time*............ 10.00 - 15.00
5223 *In The Jailhouse Now*.............. 6.00 - 10.00
5281 *Jimmie Rodgers' Last Blue Yodel*..... 20.00 - 30.00
5393 *My Blue-Eyed Jane*................ 6.00 - 10.00
5482 *Ben Dewberry's Final Run*........... 6.00 - 10.00
5556 *Yodeling Ranger*.................. 6.00 - 10.00
5609 *My Old Pal*...................... 6.00 - 10.00
5739 *I'm Lonesome Too*................. 8.00 - 12.00
5784 *In The Hills Of Tennessee*........... 8.00 - 12.00
5838 *Treasures Untold*................. 5.00 - 8.00
5892 *Why Did You Give Me Your Love*..... 10.00 - 15.00
5942 *My Good Gal's Gone*.............. 15.00 - 20.00
5991 *Daddy And Home*................. 5.00 - 8.00
6198 *Old Love Letters*................. 15.00 - 20.00
6225 *Sleep, Baby, Sleep*............... 5.00 - 8.00
6246 *The Sailor's Plea*................. 5.00 - 8.00
6275 *Mule Skinner Blues*............... 15.00 - 20.00
6698 *Why There's A Tear In My Eye*...... 15.00 - 25.00
6762 *The Carter Family & Jimmie Rodgers In Texas*........................ 10.00 - 15.00
6810 *I've Only Loved Three Women*........ 10.00 - 15.00
7280 *Yodeling My Way Back Home*........ 10.00 - 15.00
7600 *Take Me Back Again*.............. 10.00 - 15.00
Montgomery Ward (many titles as on Bluebird).. 7.00 - 10.00
4209 *Blue Yodel No. 9*................. 15.00 - 20.00
5014 *My Good Gal's Gone Blues*.......... 15.00 - 20.00
Victor 20864 *Soldier's Sweetheart*.......... 8.00 - 12.00
21142 *Away Out On The Mountain*........ 8.00 - 12.00
21245 *Ben Dewberry's Final Run*......... 8.00 - 12.00
21291 *Blue Yodel No. 2*................ 8.00 - 12.00
21433 *Treasures Untold*................. 8.00 - 12.00
21531 *Blue Yodel No. 3*................ 8.00 - 12.00
21574 *Dear Old Sunny South By The Sea*.... 8.00 - 12.00

21636 *Memphis Yodel*.................. 8.00 - 12.00
21757 *Daddy And Home*................ 8.00 - 12.00
22072 *Blue Yodel No. 5*................ 10.00 - 15.00
22143 *Frankie And Johnny*.............. 10.00 - 15.00
22220 *My Rough And Rowdy Ways*........ 10.00 - 15.00
22271 *Blue Yodel No. 6*................ 10.00 - 15.00
22319 *The Drunkard's Child*.............. 10.00 - 15.00
22379 *Train Whistle Blues*.............. 10.00 - 15.00
22421 *Hobo Bill's Last Ride*.............. 10.00 - 15.00
22488 *Any Old Time*.................... 10.00 - 15.00
22523 *High Powered Mama*.............. 10.00 - 15.00
22554 *Pistol Packin' Papa*............... 10.00 - 15.00
23503 *Blue Yodel No. 8*................ 20.00 - 30.00
23518 *Nobody Knows But Me*............. 20.00 - 30.00
23535 *T.B. Blues*..................... 20.00 - 30.00
23549 *Jimmie, The Kid*................. 20.00 - 30.00
23564 *I'm Lonesome, Too*............... 20.00 - 30.00
23574 *Moonlight And Skies*.............. 20.00 - 30.00
23580 *Blue Yodel No. 9*................ 40.00 - 60.00
23609 *What's It*...................... 35.00 - 50.00
23621 *Rodgers' Puzzle Record*............ 40.00 - 60.00
23636 *Gambling Polka Dot Blues*.......... 35.00 - 50.00
23651 *Roll Along Kentucky Moon*.......... 35.00 - 50.00
23669 *My Time Ain't Long*.............. 35.00 - 50.00
23681 *Home Call*...................... 35.00 - 50.00
23696 *Blue Yodel No. 10*................ 35.00 - 50.00
23711 *Hobo's Meditation*................ 35.00 - 50.00
23721 *Mother, The Queen Of My Heart*..... 35.00 - 50.00
23736 *Miss The Mississippi And You*....... 35.00 - 50.00
23751 *Whippin' That Old T.B.*............ 35.00 - 50.00
23766 *Gambling Bar Room Blues*.......... 50.00 - 75.00
23781 *Peach Pickin' Time In Georgia*....... 40.00 - 60.00
23796 *Blue Yodel No. 11*............... 50.00 - 75.00
23811 *The Southern Cannon Ball*.......... 60.00 - 80.00
23816 *Mississippi Delta Blues*............ 60.00 - 80.00
23830 *The Yodeling Ranger*.............. 75.00 - 100.00
23840 *Old Love Letters*................. 75.00 - 100.00
24456 *Blue Yodel No. 12*............... 60.00 - 80.00
40014 *Blue Yodel No. 4*................ 8.00 - 12.00
40054 *The Sailor's Plea*................ 8.00 - 12.00
40072 *My Little Lady*................... 8.00 - 12.00
40096 *My Carolina Sunshine Girl*.......... 8.00 - 12.00
18-6000 (picture record) *Blue Yodel No. 12*... 100.00 up

(Note: Valuations of several hundred dollars and up
have been placed on this sought-after disc;
however, only one actual transaction at such a
lofty figure has been verified.)

MRS. JIMMIE ROGERS:
Bluebird 6698 *We Miss Him When The Evening Shadows Fall*......................... 15.00 - 25.00
7339 *My Rainbow Trail*................. 10.00 - 15.00

ROE BROTHERS (& MORRELL):
Columbia 15156-D *The Ship That Never Returned* 8.00 - 12.00
15199-D *Goin' Down The Road Feelin' Bad*.. 8.00 - 12.00

ERNEST ROGERS:
Victor 20502 *Willie, The Chimney Sweeper*..... 5.00 - 8.00
20672 *The Flight of "Lucky" Lindberg*....... 10.00 - 15.00
20798 *Steamboat Bill*.................. 8.00 - 12.00
20870 *My Red-Haired Lady*.............. 8.00 - 12.00
21361 *Mythological Blues*................ 8.00 - 12.00

ROY ROGERS:
Vocalion 04050 *When A Cowboy Sings A Song*. 5.00 - 8.00
04051 *Listen To The Rhythm Of The Range*. 5.00 - 8.00
04091 *Hi-Yo Silver*..................... 5.00 - -8.00
04263 *I'm A Lonely Ranger*.............. 5.00 - 8.00
04389 *When The Sun Is Setting On The Prairie* 5.00 - 8.00
04453 *Colorado Sunset*.................. 5.00 - 8.00
Vocalion 04544 *Born To The Saddle*......... 5.00 - 8.00
04840 *Somebody's Smile*................ 5.00 - 8.00
04923 *Headin' For Texas And Home*........ 5.00 - 8.00
04961 *Let Me Build A Cabin*............. 5.00 - 8.00

ROLLING STONES:
Victor 40316 *Down By The Old Rio Grande*....   8.00 -   12.00
**POSEY RORER & THE NORTH CAROLINA
    RAMBLERS:**
Edison (thin) 11009 *A Wild And Reckless Hobo.*   ————
  20005 *As We Sat Beneath The Maple On The Hill*   ————
(Note: The above two discs were never officially
    released, but copies may have gotten out.)
Edison (thick) 52414 *As We Sat Beneath The Maple
    On The Hill*......................   35.00 -   50.00
ROSE FAMILY:
Bluebird 5004, 5036, 5074............   4.00 -   7.00
JACK ROSE:
Okeh 45370 *Jack And Babe Blues*............   10.00 -   15.00
ROSS' RHYTHM RASCALS:
Decca 5344, 5384, 5399, 5410, 5446, 5480, 5512,
  5528 ....   4.00 -   7.00
CARTER ROWLAND & SON:
Vocalion 5349 *Cotton-Eyed Joe*.............   10.00 -   15.00
GEORGE RUNNELS:
Champion 15394 *Write A Letter To My Mother*   10.00 -   15.00
FLOYD RUSSELL:
Supertone 9167 *Coal Creek March*...........   7.00 -   10.00
RUSTIC REVELERS:
Decca 5059 *Dixie Get Together*..............   5.00 -   8.00
  5062 *Chicken Reel*......................   5.00 -   8.00
  5063 *Fiddlin' Away*.....................   5.00 -   8.00
**RUTHERFORD &
    BURNETT/FOSTER/MOORE:**
Brunswick 490 *Six Months Ain't Long*........   10.00 -   15.00
  581 *My Boyhood Happy Days*..............   10.00 -   15.00
Gennett 6688 *Under The Pale Moonlight*......   15.00 -   20.00
  6746 *Let Her Go, I'll Meet Her*..........   15.00 -   20.00
  6760 *Good Night Waltz*.................   15.00 -   25.00
  6807 *Six Months Ain't Long*.............   15.00 -   25.00
  6873 *My Carolina Home*.................   15.00 -   25.00
  6913 *Taylor's Quickstep*................   15.00 -   25.00
  6976 *Richmond Blues*..................   15.00 -   25.00
Superior 2640 *My Carolina Home*...........   15.00 -   25.00
J.P./JOE RYAN:
Champion 16342 *It Just Suits Me*............   20.00 -   30.00
Gennett 7006 *Bed Bug Groan*...............   20.00 -   30.00
  7140 *Worried Daddy Blues*..............   20.00 -   30.00
Supertone 9542 *Sad And Lonely Blues*.......   10.00 -   15.00
SADDLE TRAMPS:
Vocalion 03609, 03649, 03940, 04037........   4.00 -   8.00
SALEM HIGHBALLERS:
Okeh 45455 *Going On To Town*.............   10.00 -   15.00
CURLEY SANDERS:
Talent 749 *Last On Your List*..............   5.00 -   8.00
DILLIARD SANDERS:
Supertone 9247 *I'll Never Be Yours*..........   8.00 -   12.00
**IRENE SANDERS (Acc. by AARON CAMP-
    BELL'S MOUNTAINEERS):**
Champion 16719 *Fond Affection*............   15.00 -   20.00
  45056 *Fond Affection*..................   5.00 -   8.00

LITTLE TOMMIE SANDS:
Freedom 5022 *Syrup Soppin' Blues*...........   7.00 -   10.00
SANDY CREEK WOOD CHOPPERS:
Supertone 9543 *Huskin' Bee*...............   7.00 -   10.00
  9680 *Polly Wolly Doodle*................   7.00 -   10.00
SANFORD & McCONNELL:
Victor 23765 *Over The Bar*................   7.00 -   10.00
SAXTON BROTHERS:
Superior 2537 *Going-A-Courtin'*.............   25.00 -   35.00
JIMMIE SCOTT:
Star Talent 781 *Rocky Road*...............   5.00 -   8.00
RAMBLIN' TOMMY SCOTT:
Macy's 130 *Smoky Mountain Sunset*.........   5.00 -   8.00
SCOTT COUNTY TRIO:
Supertone 9308 *Silvery Bell*...............   5.00 -   8.00
SCOTTSDALE STRING BAND:
Okeh 45074 *Aunt Hager's Blues*............   7.00 -   10.00
  45130 *Chinese Breakdown*...............   5.00 -   8.00
  45118 *Stone Mountain Wobble*...........   7.00 -   10.00
  45142 *Carolina Glide*.................   5.00 -   8.00
  45158 *Hiawatha Breakdown*.............   5.00 -   8.00
  45173 *Scottdale Stomp*................   8.00 -   12.00
  45188 *Down Yonder*...................   8.00 -   12.00
  45201 *Goin' Crazy Blues*................   8.00 -   12.00
  45256 *Share 'Em*.....................   7.00 -   10.00
  45279 *Silver Bell*....................   7.00 -   10.00
  45341 *Coughdrop Blues*...............   10.00 -   15.00
  45352 *The Moonshiner's Waltz*..........   10.00 -   15.00
  45379 *Honolulu Moon*.................   10.00 -   15.00
  45509 *Japanese Breakdown*.............   15.00 -   20.00
  45527 *Charleston Wobble*..............   15.00 -   20.00
SCOTTY THE DRIFTER:
Decca 5296 *Gooseberry Pie*................   5.00 -   8.00
LISTON SCROGGINS:
Brunswick 378 *Goodbye To Friends And Home.*   5.00 -   8.00
JOHN SEAGLE — LEONARD STOKES:
Victor 22060 *Life's Railway To Heaven*........   ————
  22289 *Will There Be Any Stars*............   ————
(UNCLE) JIM SEANY:
Challenge 324 *The Poor Tramp Has To Live*...   7.00 -   10.00
  398 *The Poor Tramp Has To Live*.........   7.00 -   10.00
Champion 15222 *Kenney Wagner's Surrender*...   8.00 -   12.00
  15233 *Sweet Bunch Of Violets*............   8.00 -   12.00
JILSON SETTERS:
Victor 21353 *The Wild Wagoner*............   7.00 -   10.00
  21407 *Forked Deer*...................   7.00 -   10.00
  21635 *Way Up On Clinch Mountain*.......   7.00 -   10.00
  40025 *Wild Horse Of Stoney Point*........   7.00 -   10.00
  40127 *Black Eyed Susie*................   7.00 -   10.00
BILL SHAFER:
Vocalion 5413 *Kicking Mule*...............   8.00 -   12.00
"TED" SHARP, HINMAN & SHARP:
Champion 16712 *Hell Among The Yearlings*....   15.00 -   25.00
  16739 *Where's My Other Foot*...........   15.00 -   25.00
  16766 *Goin' On Up To Town*...........   15.00 -   25.00
  45002, 45012, 45182.................   10.00 -   15.00
BERT/BURT SHAW:
Superior 2733 *Pea Pickin' Papa*............   20.00 -   30.00
  2760 *Doggone Them Blues*.............   20.00 -   30.00
  2805 *Ninety-Nine Years*...............   20.00 -   30.00
**MIKE SHAW & HIS ALABAMA
    ENTERTAINERS:**
Okeh 45518 *Tennessee River Bottom Blues*....   15.00 -   20.00
  45529 *Going Crazy*...................   15.00 -   20.00
SHELOR FAMILY:
Victor 20865 *Big Bend Gal*................   10.00 -   15.00
SHELTON BROTHERS (BOB & JOE):
Decca 5079, 5087, 5099, 5100, 5135, 5137, 5161,
  5170, 5173, 5177, 5180, 5184, 5187, 5190, 5198,
  5219, 5244, 5261, 5339, 5353, 5367, 5381, 5397,
  5409, 5422, 5440, 5456, 5468, 5471, 5475, 5484,
  5496, 5508, 5519, 5533.................   4.00 -   8.00

B.F. SHELTON:
Victor 40107 *Cold Penitentiary Blues* .... 25.00 - 35.00

BILL SHEPARD (Acc. by SHEPARD BROS. & ED WEBB):
Champion 16383 *Aunt Jane Blues* .... 15.00 - 25.00

ARKEY SHIBLEY:
Gilt-Edge 5021, 5030 .... 4.00 - 7.00

UNCLE JOE SHIPPEE:
Pathe 21164 *Old Time Fiddler* .... 7.00 - 10.00
Perfect 11237 *Old Time Fiddler* .... 7.00 - 10.00

EARL SHIRKEY & ROY HARPER:
15376-D *Poor Little Joe* .... 15.00 - 20.00
15490-D *My Yodeling Sweetheart* .... 20.00 - 30.00
15535-D *The Virginian Strike of '23* .... 20.00 - 30.00
15642-D *We Have Moonshine In The West Virginia Hills* .... 25.00 - 35.00

CHESLEY SHIRLEY (THE TEXAS RAMBLER):
Champion 16826 *The Last Great Roundup* ..... 10.00 - 15.00
45075 *Only Flirting* .... 5.00 - 8.00

SHORE'S SOUTHERN TRIO:
Gennett 6842 *Whistling Rufus* .... 15.00 - 20.00
6927 *Goin' Crazy* .... 15.00 - 20.00

BILL SHORES & MELVIN DUPREE:
Columbia 15506-D *West Texas Breakdown* ..... 15.00 - 20.00

SHORT BROTHERS:
Okeh 45206 *Whistling Coon* .... 8.00 - 12.00

SHORT CREEK TRIO:
Gennett 6272 *Hand Me Down My Walking Cane* 10.00 - 15.00
6364 *The Buckin' Mule* .... 10.00 - 15.00

CHIEF SHUNATONA, ET AL. (See CHIEF...)
CONNIE SIDES:
Columbia 15009-D *In The Shadow Of The Pine.* 7.00 - 10.00

BILL SIMMON (S' COWBOYS):
Victor 23533 *The Cowboy's Plea* .... 15.00 - 20.00
23603 *Rocky Mountain Blues* .... 15.00 - 20.00

MATT SIMMONS & FRANK MILLER:
Okeh 45148 *That Little Old Hut* .... 5.00 - 8.00

OLIVER SIMS:
Columbia 15103-D *Lost John* .... 7.00 - 10.00

ALLEN SISSON:
Edison 51522 *Farewell Ducktown-Reel* .... 7.00 - 10.00
51559 *Walking Water* .... 7.00 - 10.00
51690 *Katy Hill-Reel* .... 7.00 - 10.00
51720 *Gray Eagle-Reel* .... 7.00 - 10.00

ASHER SIZEMORE (& LITTLE JIMMY):
Bluebird 5445 *Goodbye To Jimmie Rodgers* ..... 25.00 - 40.00
5495 *Cowboy Jim* .... 25.00 - 40.00
Bluebird 5568 *Shake Hands With Mother* ...... 25.00 - 40.00
Bluebird 5717 *My West Virginia Home* .... 25.00 - 40.00
Bluebird 5774 *Memories Of Kentucky* .... 25.00 - 40.00
Bluebird 6021 *I Dreamed I Searched* .... 25.00 - 40.00

BILL SKIDMORE:
Columbia 15761-D *Behind The Big White House* 7.00 - 10.00

BOB SKILES (4 OLD TUNERS):
Okeh 45211 *Rye Waltz* .... 5.00 - 10.00
45225 *Casey Jones* .... 5.00 - 10.00
45243 *Wagner* .... 4.00 - 8.00

SKYLAND & SCOTTIE:
Bluebird 5357, 5906 .... 3.00 - 6.00

SLOAN & THREADGILL:
Brunswick 284 *Clover Blossoms* .... 8.00 - 12.00
299 *When The Harvest Is Shining* .... 8.00 - 12.00

LESTER SMALLWOOD:
Victor 40181 *Cotton Mill Girl* .... 20.00 - 30.00

(DR.) SMITH'S (CHAMPION) HOSS HAIR PULLERS:
Victor 21711 *Going Down The River* .... 20.00 - 30.00
40059 *Save My Mother's Picture From The Sale* 15.00 - 20.00
40124 *Just Give Me The Leavings* .... 15.00 - 20.00

SMITH'S GARAGE FIDDLE BAND:
Vocalion 5268 *Beaumont Rag* .... 10.00 - 15.00
5287 *Done Gone* .... 10.00 - 15.00
5306 *Dill Pickle Rag* .... 10.00 - 15.00
5336 *Miss Lola* .... 10.00 - 15.00
5375 *Tom & Jerry* .... 10.00 - 15.00

SMITH & WOODLIEFF:
Gennett 6809 *The Old Schoolhouse Playground.* 20.00 - 30.00
6840 *I Ain't Gonna Grieve My Lord Anymore* 20.00 - 30.00
6858 *I'd Rather Be With Rosy Nell* .... 20.00 - 30.00

ARTHUR SMITH (TRIO) (& HIS DIXIE LINERS):
Bluebird 5896 *Blackberry Blossom* .... 7.00 - 10.00
6322 *Chittlin' Cookin' Time* .... 7.00 - 10.00
6369 *Cheatham County Breakdown* .... 7.00 - 10.00
6442 *Fiddler's Blues* .... 7.00 - 10.00
6514 *Take Me Back To Tennessee* .... 7.00 - 10.00
6844 *Florida Blues* .... 7.00 - 10.00
6869 *Never Alone* .... 7.00 - 10.00
6913 *The Girl I Love Don't Pay Me No Mind* 7.00 - 10.00
6927 *Sugar Tree Stomp* .... 7.00 - 10.00
6994 *It's Hard To Please Your Mind* ...... 7.00 - 10.00
7043 *Walking In My Sleep* .... 7.00 - 10.00
7146 *Lonesome For You* .... 5.00 - 8.00
7203 *Beautiful Memories* .... 5.00 - 8.00
7221 *Across The Blue Ridge Mountains* ..... 5.00 - 8.00
7325 *Nellie's Blues Eyes* .... 5.00 - 8.00
7351 *Cheatham County Breakdown No. 2* .... 7.00 - 10.00
7437 *Answer To More Pretty Girls Than One.* 7.00 - 10.00
7498 *Henpecked Husband Blues* .... 7.00 - 10.00
7511 *Smith's Breakdown* .... 7.00 - 10.00
7547 *Her Little Brown Hand* .... 7.00 - 10.00
7651 *Lost Love* .... 7.00 - 10.00
7893 *The Gypsy's Warning* .... 7.00 - 10.00
7943 *Why Should I Wonder?* .... 7.00 - 10.00
7982 *Give Me Old Time Music* .... 5.00 - 8.00
Bluebird (higher numbers) .... 4.00 - 7.00

BLAINE & CAL SMITH:
Vocalion 04705, 04855, 04976 .... 3.00 - 6.00

CHARLES B. SMITH:
Columbia 15755-D *Walkin' Georgia Rose* .... 10.00 - 15.00

HANK SMITH:
Vocalion 5318 *Eleven Cent Cotton And Forty Cent Meat* .... 10.00 - 15.00

HARRY SMITH:
Okeh 45260 *The Death Of Floyd Collins* ...... 7.00 - 10.00

TRAVELIN' J. SMITH:
Columbia 15547-D *So I Joined The Navy* ...... 4.00 - 7.00

JIMMIE SMITH:
Timely Tunes 1556 *She's A Low Down Mama* .. 15.00 - 20.00
1557 *There's A Good Gal In The Mountains.* 15.00 - 20.00

JOE SMITH (THE COLORADO COWBOY):
Bluebird 5522 *John Dillinger* .... 5.00 - 8.00
5530 *Pining For The Pines In Caroline* ...... 5.00 - 8.00
5651 *That Silver-Haired Mother* .... 5.00 - 8.00
Champion 15808 *The Talkin' Blues* .... 8.00 - 12.00
45173 *Born In Hard Luck* .... 5.00 - 8.00

KID SMITH'S FAMILY:
Victor 23576 *Little Bessie* .... 15.00 - 20.00
Vocalion 03414 *I'm Not Angry With You Darling* 8.00 - 12.00

03415 *Mississippi Freight Train Blues*........	10.00 -	15.00
03443 *Ten Is Served And Ten To Serve*......	10.00 -	15.00

MARSHALL SMITH:

Columbia 15080-D *Jonah And The Whale*......	5.00 -	8.00

(MERRITT) SMITH & (KEITH) POOSER:

Okeh 45318 *Carolina Moon*...................	4.00 -	7.00
45326 *Softly And Tenderly*................	4.00 -	7.00
45362 *The Lonesome Road*.................	4.00 -	7.00
45474 *Death Is Only A Dream*...........	4.00 -	7.00

MERRITT SMITH & LEO BOSWELL:

Champion 16335 *On The Banks Of the Brandywine*	7.00 -	10.00
16344 *Oh Mary Don't You Weep*..........	7.00 -	10.00
16433 *Daisies Never Tell*.................	7.00 -	10.00
Columbia 15748-D *Try Not To Forget*........	8.00 -	12.00

R.B. SMITH & S.J. ALLGOOD:

Okeh 45010 *American And Spanish Fandango*..	8.00 -	12.00

SLIM SMITH:

Crown 3118 *Bread Line Blues*...............	8.00 -	12.00
Victor 23526 *Bread Line Blues*.............	10.00 -	15.00
Vocalion 05082 *Sad And Alone*.............	5.00 -	8.00

WALTER SMITH:

Gennett 6825 *The Cat's Got The Measles, The Dog's Got The Whoopin' Cough*.............	15.00 -	25.00

SMOKY MOUNTAIN BOYS:

Gennett 6871 *The Smoky Mountain Boys At The Still*...................	20.00 -	30.00

SMOKY MOUNTAIN FIDDLER TRIO:

Bluebird 6387 *Bonaparte's Retreat*.............	5.00 -	8.00

SMOKY MOUNTAIN RAMBLERS:

Vocalion 5422 *San Antonio*...............	20.00 -	30.00
5437 *Bear Mountain Rag*...............	20.00 -	30.00
5451 *Born In Tennessee*.................	20.00 -	30.00

SMYTH'S COUNTY RAMBLERS:

Victor 40144 *Way Down In Alabama*........	15.00 -	20.00

(LEO) SOILEAU & LAFLEUR/(MOISE) ROBIN:

Decca 5101, 5102, 5116, 5117, 5133, 5157, 5182, 5210, 5215, 5236, 5262, 5279, 5299, 5326...	3.00 -	6.00
Paramount 12808 *Easy Rider*...............	15.00 -	20.00
Victor 21769 *Basile*.....................	10.00 -	15.00
21770 *The Criminal*...................	10.00 -	15.00
22183 *Penitentiary Waltz*.............	10.00 -	15.00
22207 *Grosse Mama*.................	10.00 -	15.00

SOLOMON & HUGHES:

Victor 40244 *Ragtime Annie*...............	8.00 -	12.00

SONS OF THE PIONEERS:

Decca 5013 *Ridin' Home*...............	4.00 -	7.00
5047 *Moonlight On The Prairie*.............	5.00 -	8.00
5082, 5083, 5168, 5178, 5218, 5232, 5243, 5247, 5248, 5275, 5358.................	4.00 -	7.00
Vocalion 03399 *Power In The Blood*..........	5.00 -	8.00
03880 *Open Range Ahead*............	5.00 -	8.00
03881 *Smilin' Through*...............	5.00 -	8.00
03916 *I Love You, Nelly*.............	5.00 -	8.00
04136 *Billie The Kid*...............	5.00 -	8.00
04187 *Hear Dem Bells*.............	5.00 -	8.00
04264 *Cajon Stomp*.................	5.00 -	8.00
04328 *Send Him Home To Me*.........	5.00 -	8.00

SOUTHERN KENTUCKY MOUNTAINEERS:

Supertone 9310 *Cumberland Gap*...........	8.00 -	12.00

SOUTHERN MOONLIGHT ENTERTAINERS:

Vocalion 5372 *My Blue Ridge Mountain Queen*.	8.00 -	12.00
5388 *My Carolina Girl*.................	8.00 -	12.00
5407 *Buckin' Mule*.................	8.00 -	12.00
5440 *Then I'll Move To Town*.............	8.00 -	12.00
5460 *Lost John*.................	8.00 -	12.00

SOUTH GEORGIA HIGHBALLERS:

Okeh 45155 *Bibb County Grind*.............	15.00 -	20.00

SPANGLE & PEARSON:

Okeh 45287 *Patrick County Blues*.............	20.00 -	30.00

SPOONEY FIVE:

Columbia 15234-D *Chinese Rag*.............	8.00 -	12.00

CARL T. SPRAGUE:

Aurora 418 *Cowboy Love Song*.............	8.00 -	12.00
Bluebird 6258 *The Prisoner's Meditation*.......	7.00 -	10.00
Victor 19747 *Bad Companions*.............	5.00 -	8.00
20067 *Cowboy Love Song*.............	5.00 -	8.00
20122 *The Cowboy's Dream*.............	5.00 -	8.00
20534 *The Boston Burglar*.............	7.00 -	10.00
20932 *The Last Great Roundup*.............	7.00 -	10.00
21194 *Utah Carroll*.............	10.00 -	15.00
21402 *Cowman's Prayer*.............	10.00 -	15.00
40066 *Here's To The Texas Ranger*.............	10.00 -	15.00
40197 *The Last Longhorn*.............	10.00 -	15.00
40246 *The Wayward Daughter*.............	10.00 -	15.00

FRED STANLEY:

Columbia 15559-D *The Tie That Binds*......	8.00 -	12.00

JOHN STANLEY'S ORCHESTRA:

Superior 2691 *Moonshiner's Serenade*.........	15.00 -	25.00

ROBA STANLEY & WILLIAM PATTERSON:

Okeh 40213 *Devilish Mary*.............	7.00 -	10.00
45036 *Old Maid Blues*.............	10.00 -	15.00

STANTON'S JOY BOYS:

Superior 2671 *Huskin' Bee*.............	10.00 -	15.00

FRANK STANTON:

Superior 2521 *Creole Girl*.............	15.00 -	20.00
2544 *Poor Old Dad*.............	15.00 -	20.00

STAPLETON BROTHERS:

Columbia 15284-D *In A Cool Shady Nook*.....	5.00 -	8.00
Victor 23591 *Won't You Take Me Back Again*..	7.00 -	10.00

STEAMBOAT BILL & HIS GUITAR:

Champion 15674 *No, No, Blues*.............	10.00 -	15.00
15694 *Weak Minded Blues*.............	10.00 -	15.00
15752 *Boston Burglar*.............	10.00 -	15.00

JOE STEEN:

Bluebird 5567 *I'll Love Ya Till The Cows Come Home*.............	4.00 -	6.00
Champion 16258 *Railroad Jack*.............	10.00 -	15.00
Victor 23634 *Crazy Engineer*.............	10.00 -	15.00

UNCLE "BUNT" STEPHENS:

Columbia 15071-D *Louisburg Blues*.............	8.00 -	12.00
15085-D *Left In The Dark Blues*.............	8.00 -	12.00

STEVE'S HOT SHOTS:

Victor 23699 *Sour Apple Cider*.............	20.00 -	30.00
40308 *The Press*.............	20.00 -	30.00

OTIS STEWART:

Supertone 9242 *Adam And Eve*.............	8.00 -	12.00

CHARLES LEWIS STINE:

Columbia 15027-D *The Wreck On The C & O*..	7.00 -	10.00

OCIE STOCKARD:

Bluebird 7108, 7296, 7459, 7570, 7652, 7716, 8021	3.00 -	6.00

STOKES, MILLER, McKINNEY, MARTIN, WILLIAMS & BROWN:

Brunswick 422 *The Great Hatfield-McCoy Feud, Part 1/2*.............	12.00 -	16.00
423 *The Great Hatfield-McCoy Feud, Part 3/4*	12.00 -	16.00

LEONARD STOKES:

Bluebird 7349 *Will You Miss Me When I'm Gone*	7.00 -	10.00
7401 *There's A Green Hill Far Away*.......	5.00 -	8.00
Electradisk 1920 *He's Too Far Gone*..........	5.00 -	8.00

LOWE STOKES & HIS NORTH GEORGIANS/POT LUCKERS; LOWE STOKES & RILEY PUCKETT/MIKE WHITTEN:

Brunswick 491 *Prohibition Is A Failure*.......	12.00 -	18.00
549 *Four Cent Cotton*.................	12.00 -	18.00
Columbia 15241-D *Home Brew Rag*..........	10.00 -	15.00
15369-D *Wave That Frame*.............	10.00 -	15.00
15486-D *Take Me Back To Georgia*.............	15.00 -	20.00
15557-D *Left All Alone Again Blues*.............	15.00 -	25.00
15620-D *Everybody's Doing It*.............	15.00 -	25.00
15660-D *Bone Dry Blues*.............	20.00 -	30.00
15693-D *Sailing On The Robert E. Lee*.............	20.00 -	30.00

JIMMY STONE:

Imperial 8137 *Midnight Boogie*............... 5.00 - 8.00*

STONEMAN FAMILY:

Victor 40030 *Broken-Hearted Lover*.......... 10.00 - 15.00

40116 *Going Up The Mountain After Liquor.* 10.00 - 15.00

40206 *Too Late*........................ 10.00 - 15.00

(MR. & MRS.) ERNEST V. STONEMAN & HIS DIXIE MOUNTAINEERS/GRAYSON COUNTY BOYS; ERNEST V. STONEMAN (TRIO) (& FIDDLER JOE):

Banner 1993 *Hand Me Down My Walking Cane* 5.00 - 8.00

2157 *Pass Around The Bottle*.............. 5.00 - 8.00

2158 *It's Sinful To Flirt*................ 5.00 - 8.00

Broadway 8054 *Pass Around The Bottle*....... 5.00 - 8.00

8055 *Hand Me Down My Walking Cane*..... 5.00 - 8.00

Challenge 151 *Katy Cline*................. 5.00 - 8.00

152 *Barney McCoy*.................... 5.00 - 8.00

153 *Silver Bell*..................... 5.00 - 8.00

309 *Barney McCoy*.................... 5.00 - 8.00

312 *May I Sleep In Your Barn Tonight Mister* 5.00 - 8.00

665 *Pass Around The Bottle*.............. 5.00 - 8.00

Conqueror 7064 *Pass Around The Bottle*...... 5.00 - 8.00

7755 *Bully Of The Town*................ 5.00 - 8.00

Domino 0187 *The Old Hickory Cane*.......... 5.00 - 8.00

3964 *Hand Me Down My Walking Cane*..... 5.00 - 8.00

3984 *The Fatal Wedding*................. 5.00 - 8.00

3985 *Pass Around The Bottle*............. 5.00 - 8.00

Edison (thin) 20004 *He Is Coming After Me*.... ———

(There is some question as to whether the above disc was issued.)

Edison (thick) 51788 *Bad Companions*........ 12.00 - 16.00

51864 *Watermelon Hanging On The Vine*.... 12.00 - 16.00

51869 *Wild Bill Jones*................. 12.00 - 16.00

51909 *Bury Me Beneath The Weeping Willow Tree* 12.00 - 16.00

51935 *Once I Had A Fortune*............. 12.00 - 16.00

51938 *Hand Me Down My Walking Cane*.... 12.00 - 16.00

51951 *Bully Of The Town*................ 12.00 - 16.00

51994 *Kitty Wells*.................... 12.00 - 16.00

52026 *The Fate Of Talmadge Osborne*...... 12.00 - 16.00

52077 *The Orphan Girl*................ 10.00 - 15.00

52290 *When The Redeemed Are Gathered In.* 15.00 - 20.00

52299 *Unlucky Road To Washington*....... 15.00 - 20.00

52312 *Down On The Banks Of The Ohio*.... 15.00 - 20.00

52350 *All Go Hungry Hash House*......... 15.00 - 20.00

52369 *The Old Maid And The Burglar*...... 15.00 - 20.00

52386 *It's Sinful To Flirt*............... 15.00 - 20.00

52461 *The Prisoner's Lament*............. 15.00 - 20.00

52479 *He Is Coming After Me*........... 15.00 - 20.00

52489 *All I've Got's Gone*.............. 15.00 - 20.00

Gennett 3368 *May I Sleep In Your Barn Tonight Mister?*.......................... 7.00 - 10.00

3369 *Pretty Snow Deer*................ 7.00 - 10.00

3381 *Barney McCoy*.................. 7.00 - 10.00

6044 *Kenney Wagner's Surrender*.......... 10.00 - 15.00

6052 *Long Eared Mule*................ 10.00 - 15.00

6065 *Sweet Bunch Of Violets*............ 10.00 - 15.00

Herwin 75528 *Barney McCoy*............. 10.00 - 15.00

75529 *Silver Bell*.................... 10.00 - 15.00

75530 *Pretty Snow Deer*................ 10.00 - 15.00

75535 *The Poor Tramp Has To Live*........ 10.00 - 15.00

75541 *Sweet Bunch Of Violets*........... 10.00 - 15.00

Homestead 16490 *Pass Around The Bottle*..... 7.00 - 10.00

16498 *The Fatal Wedding*............... 7.00 - 10.00

16500 *Bully Of The Town*.............. 7.00 - 10.00

Okeh 7011 (12-inch) *John Hardy*.......... 20.00 - 30.00

40288 *The Titanic*................... 10.00 - 15.00

40312 *Freckled Face Mary Jane*.......... 10.00 - 15.00

40384 *Dying Girl's Farewell*............. 10.00 - 15.00

40405 *The Long Eared Mule*............ 10.00 - 15.00

40408 *The Lightning Express*............. 10.00 - 15.00

40430 *Uncle Sam And The Kaiser*......... 10.00 - 15.00

45009 *All I've Got's Gone*.............. 10.00 - 15.00

45015 *The Fancy Ball*................. 10.00 - 15.00

45036 *The Kicking Mule*............... 10.00 - 15.00

45044 *Asleep At The Switch*............. 10.00 - 15.00

45048 *In The Shadow Of The Pine*........ 10.00 - 15.00

45051 *The Religious Critic*.............. 10.00 - 15.00

45054 *The Texas Ranger*............... 10.00 - 15.00

45059 *The Old Hickory Cane*............ 10.00 - 15.00

45060 *My Pretty Snow Dear*............ 10.00 - 15.00

45062 *The All Go Hungry Hash House*...... 10.00 - 15.00

45065 *Katie Cline*.................... 10.00 - 15.00

45084 *The Fatal Wedding*.............. 10.00 - 15.00

45094 *Lonesome Road Blues*............ 10.00 - 15.00

45125 *The Mountaineer's Courtship*....... 10.00 - 15.00

Paramount 3021 *Pass Around The Bottle*..... 5.00 - 8.00

Pathe-Actuelle 32271 *The Old Hickory Cane*.... 5.00 - 8.00

32278 *The Fatal Wedding*.............. 5.00 - 8.00

32279 *Bully Of The Town*.............. 5.00 - 8.00

Perfect 12350 *Sinful To Flirt*.............. 5.00 - 8.00

12357 *Pass Around The Bottle*........... 5.00 - 8.00

12358 *Bully Of The Town*.............. 5.00 - 8.00

Regal 8324 *Hand Me Down My Walking Cane.* 5.00 - 8.00

8346 *Sinful To Flirt*................. 5.00 - 8.00

8347 *The Fatal Wedding*.............. 5.00 - 8.00

8369 *The Old Hickory Cane*............ 5.00 - 8.00

Romeo 597 *Bully Of The Town*........... 5.00 - 8.00

600 *Sinful To Flirt*................. 5.00 - 8.00

Silvertone 5004 *Sweet Bunch Of Violets*....... 7.00 - 10.00

Supertone 9255 *The Poor Tramp Has To Live..* 7.00 - 10.00

Victor 20223 *In The Golden Bye And Bye*..... 7.00 - 10.00

20224 *Hallelujah Side*................. 7.00 - 10.00

20235 *The Little Old Log Cabin In The Lane.* 7.00 - 10.00

20237 *All Go Hungry Hash House*......... 7.00 - 10.00

20294 *Sugar In The Gourd*............. 7.00 - 10.00

20302 *Old Joe Clark*................. 7.00 - 10.00

20531 *Going Down The Valley*.......... 10.00 - 15.00

20532 *The Great Reaping Day*.......... 10.00 - 15.00

20533 *I'll Be Satisfied*................. 10.00 - 15.00

20540 *Peekaboo*.................... 10.00 - 15.00

20671 *The Story Of The Mighty Mississippi..* 10.00 - 15.00

20672 *The Fate Of Talmadge Osborne*...... 10.00 - 15.00

20799 *The Old Hickory Cane*............ 10.00 - 15.00

20844 *Are You Washed In The Blood?*...... 10.00 - 15.00

20880 *The Mountaineer's Courtship*....... 10.00 - 15.00

21071 *I Am Resolved*................. 10.00 - 15.00

21129 *The Dying Girl's Farewell*.......... 10.00 - 15.00

21186 *I Know My Name Is There*........ 10.00 - 15.00

21264 *Possum Trot School Exhibition*....... 12.00 - 18.00

21518 *Serenade In The Mountains*.......... 12.00 - 18.00

21648 *The Raging Sea, How It Roars*....... 12.00 - 18.00

40078 *There's A Light Lit Up In Galilee*..... 10.00 - 15.00

Vocalion 02632 *Texas Ranger*............. 10.00 - 15.00

02655 *Nine Pound Hammer*............. 10.00 - 15.00

02901 *All I Got's Gone*............... 10.00 - 15.00

WILLIE STONEMAN:

Gennett 6565 *Katy Lee*................. 12.00 - 16.00

STONE MOUNTAIN BOYS:

Supertone 9456 *Makin' Licker In North Carolina* 10.00 - 15.00

STONE MOUNTAIN ENTERTAINERS:

Broadway 8159 *Red Wing*............... 6.00 - 10.00

STONE MOUNTAIN TRIO:

Brunswick 543 *Maple Leaf Waltz*........... 5.00 - 8.00

Vocalion 5457 *Stone Mountain Waltz*......... 8.00 - 12.00

SMOKEY STOVER:

Specialty 715 *What A Shame*............... ———*

DICK STRATTON & THE NITE OWLS:

Tennessee 795 *Pistol Boogie*.............. ———

HARLEY STRATTON:

Superior 2588 *The Red River Valley*......... 10.00 - 15.00

STRIPLING BROTHERS:

Decca 5018, 5019, 5041, 5049, 5069, 5207, 5246,

5267, 5291, 5313, 5417.................	4.00 -	8.00
Melotone 12173 *Moonlight Waltz*............	5.00 -	8.00
12181 *Big Footed Nigger In The Sandy Lot*..	5.00 -	8.00
Vocalion 02738 *June Rose Waltz*...........	8.00 -	12.00
02739 *Coal Mine Blues*..............	8.00 -	12.00
5321 *The Lost Child*...............	10.00 -	15.00
5365 *Railroad Bum*...............	10.00 -	15.00
5366 *Red River Waltz*............	10.00 -	15.00
5382 *New Born Blues*.............	10.00 -	15.00
5395 *Dance All Night With A Bottle In My Hand*	10.00 -	15.00
5412 *Wolves Howling*..................	10.00 -	15.00
5441 *Lost John*..................	10.00 -	15.00
5453 *Coal Mine Blues*..............	10.00 -	15.00
5468 *Midnight Waltz*...............	10.00 -	15.00

UNCLE "AM" STUART:

Vocalion 5035 *Cumberland Gap*...........	8.00 -	12.00
5036 *Sourwood Mountain*..............	8.00 -	12.00
5037 *Leather Breeches*.................	8.00 -	12.00
5038 *Billie In The Low Ground*.........	8.00 -	12.00
5039 *Forked Deer*................	8.00 -	12.00
5048 *Dixie*.................	8.00 -	12.00
5053 *George Boker*.............	8.00 -	12.00
14839 *Cumberland Gap*............	8.00 -	12.00
14840 *Sourwood Mountain*............	8.00 -	12.00
14841 *Leather Breeches*.............	8.00 -	12.00
14843 *Billie In The Low Ground*........	8.00 -	12.00
14846 *Forked Deer*...............	8.00 -	12.00
14888 *Dixie*..................	8.00 -	12.00
14919 *George Boker*..............	8.00 -	12.00

SUE & RAWHIDE (Acc. by THE CRAZY HILLBILLIES BAND):

Okeh 45577 *Falling Leaf*..................	10.00 -	15.00

SWAMP ROOTERS:

Brunswick 556 *Swamp Cat Rag*...........	15.00 -	20.00

SWEET BROTHERS:

Gennett 6620 *I Got A Bull Dog*............	15.00 -	20.00
6655 *Falling By The Wayside*...............	15.00 -	20.00

HERBERT SWEET:

Gennett 6567 *The Prisoner's Lament*.........	12.00 -	16.00

SWEET VIOLET BOYS:

Vocalion 03110, 03218, 03219, 03256, 03281, 03327, 03402, 03587, 03663, 03766, 04010, 04428, 04528, 04714, 04756..................	3.00 -	6.00

SWING BILLIES:

Bluebird 7121, 7143, 7161, 7338.............	4.00 -	7.00

CHARLES ROSS TAGGART:

Edison 51001 *A Country Fiddler At Home*.....	5.00 -	8.00
51048 *A Country Fiddler At The Telephone*..	5.00 -	8.00
51448 *Sister Sorrowful*..................	5.00 -	8.00
Victor 18036 *Old Country Fiddler At The Party*.	5.00 -	8.00

ARTHUR TANNER & HIS CORNSHUCKERS/& RILEY PUCKETT:

Columbia 15145-D *Knoxville Girl*.............	8.00 -	12.00
15180-D *Two Little Children*.............	8.00 -	12.00
15352-D *Sleep On Blue Eyes*.............	8.00 -	12.00
15479-D *Dr. Ginger Blue*.............	15.00 -	20.00
15577-D *Gather The Flowers*.............	15.00 -	20.00
Paramount 3159 *Devilish Mary*.............	8.00 -	12.00
3160 *The Lightening Express Train*...........	8.00 -	12.00
3161 *The Little Old Log Cabin In The Lane*..	8.00 -	12.00
3162 *The Knoxville Girl*................	8.00 -	12.00
3163 *When I Was Single My Pockets Would Jingle Jingle*...................	8.00 -	12.00
Silvertone 3514 *The Burglar Man*.............	8.00 -	12.00
3515 *The Knoxville Girl*..............	8.00 -	12.00

GID TANNER & HIS GEORGIA BOYS/SKILLET LICKERS; GID TANNER & FATE NORRIS/RILEY PUCKETT; TANNER, McMICHEN, PUCKETT, STOKES & NORRIS:

Bluebird 5433 *Mississippi Sawyer*.............	8.00 -	12.00

5434 *Cumberland Gap On A Buckin' Mule*...	8.00 -	12.00
5435 *Skillet Licker Breakdown*..............	8.00 -	12.00
5446 *Prosperity And Politics*...............	8.00 -	12.00
5488 *Ida Red*....................	5.00 -	8.00
5559 *Practice Night With The Skillet Lickers*..	8.00 -	12.00
5562 *Down Yonder*.................	5.00 -	8.00
5591 *Cotton Patch*.................	7.00 -	10.00
5633 *Hinkey-Dinkey-Dee*.............	7.00 -	10.00
5657 *Tanner's Rag*.................	7.00 -	10.00
5658 *Soldier's Joy*..................	5.00 -	8.00
5665 *On Tanner's Farm*.............	7.00 -	10.00
5748 *Three Nights Drunk*.............	7.00 -	10.00
5805 *I Ain't No Better Now*............	7.00 -	10.00
Columbia 119-D *Black Eyed Susie*.............	8.00 -	12.00
15010-D *Don't Grieve Your Mother*............	7.00 -	10.00
15017-D *Fox Chase*..................	7.00 -	10.00
15019-D *Georgia Railroad*..............	7.00 -	10.00
15059-D *Just Gimme The Leavings*...........	7.00 -	10.00
15084-D *Turkey In The Straw*.............	5.00 -	8.00
15091-D *Hand Me Down My Walking Cane*..	5.00 -	8.00
15104-D *Alabama Jubilee*..................	5.00 -	8.00
15105-D *Goodbye, Booze*.............	8.00 -	12.00
15108-D *Old Joe Clark*.............	7.00 -	10.00
15123-D *Shortening Bread*.............	7.00 -	10.00
15134-D *I Got Mine*.............	7.00 -	10.00
15142-D *John Henry*.............	7.00 -	10.00
15158-D *Dixie*.............	7.00 -	10.00
15165-D *Football Rag*.............	7.00 -	10.00
15170-D *The Old Gray Mare*.............	7.00 -	10.00
15188-D *The Darktown Strutters Ball*........	7.00 -	10.00
15200-D *She'll Be Coming 'Round The Mountain*	7.00 -	10.00
15204-D *Big Ball In Town*.................	7.00 -	10.00
15217-D *Please Do Not Get Offended*.......	7.00 -	10.00
15221-D *Uncle Bud*.................	7.00 -	10.00
15237-D *Casey Jones*.................	7.00 -	10.00
15249-D *Bile Them Cabbage Down*...........	7.00 -	10.00
15267-D *Slow Buck*.................	8.00 -	12.00
15283-D *Cotton-Eyed Joe*.................	8.00 -	12.00
*15298-D *Possum Hunt On Stump Mountain*.	10.00 -	15.00
15303-D *Cumberland Gap*.............	8.00 -	12.00
15315-D *Settin' In The Chimney Jamb*.........	8.00 -	12.00
15334-D *Liberty*.................	8.00 -	12.00
15382-D *Old Dan Tucker*.............	10.00 -	15.00
15404-D *Cotton Baggin'*.............	10.00 -	15.00
15420-D *Mississippi Sawyer*.............	10.00 -	15.00
15447-D *The Rovin' Gambler*.............	10.00 -	15.00
*15468-D *Hog Killing Day*.............	12.00 -	18.00
15472-D *Flatwoods*.............	10.00 -	15.00
15485-D *Cripple Creek*.............	10.00 -	15.00
15516-D *Hell's Broke Loose In Georgia*......	15.00 -	20.00
15562-D *Sal's Gone To The Cider Mill*.......	20.00 -	30.00
15589-D *Devilish Mary*.............	20.00 -	30.00
15612-D *Sugar In The Gourd*.............	20.00 -	30.00
15623-D *New Arkansas Traveler*.............	20.00 -	30.00
15640-D *Bully Of The Town No. 2*...........	20.00 -	30.00
15665-D *Don't You Cry My Honey*.........	20.00 -	30.00
15682-D *Ricketts Hornpipe*.................	20.00 -	30.00
15695-D *Giddup Napoleon*.................	20.00 -	30.00
15709-D *Fly Around My Pretty Little Miss*...	25.00 -	40.00
15716-D *You've Got To Stop Drinking 'Shine*.	25.00 -	40.00
15730-D *Miss McLeod's Reel*.............	25.00 -	40.00
15746-D *Four Cent Cotton*.............	35.00 -	50.00
15777-D *McMichen's Breakdown*...........	35.00 -	50.00

(*These "descriptive novelty" records credit several or more artists on the labels; since Tanner's name appears first, they are listed here.)

LUCY TANNER & THE SKILLET LICKERS:

Columbia 15538-D *Rock That Cradle, Lucy*....	15.00 -	20.00

JIMMIE TARLTON (& DARBY); LOUISE J. TARLTON:

Columbia 15629-D *New Birmingham Jail*.......	40.00 -	60.00

1565-D *Moonshine Blues*.................	40.00 -	60.00
15763-D *By The Old Oaken Bucket*.........	50.00 -	75.00
Montgomery Ward 4335 *Once I Had A Fortune*	10.00 -	15.00
Victor 23665 *Dixie Jail*..................	50.00 -	75.00
23680 *13 Years In Kilby Prison*.........	50.00 -	75.00
23700 *Ooze Up To Me*...................	50.00 -	75.00

TATE BROTHERS & (RHODA) HICKS:

Champion 15965 *Medley*...................	7.00 -	10.00
Gennett 7165 *Medley*.....................	10.00 -	15.00

TAYLOR'S KENTUCKY BOYS:

Gennett 6130 *Forked Deer*................	10.00 -	15.00

TAYLOR'S (LOUISIANA) MELODY MAKERS:

Victor 21768 *Big Ball Uptown*.............	10.00 -	15.00
23613 *'Mid The Shamrock Of Shannon*......	10.00 -	15.00
40261 *On The Bridge At Midnight*.........	10.00 -	15.00

TAYLOR & BUNCH:

Supertone 9352 *Six Months Ain't Long*.......	8.00 -	12.00

TAYLOR-GRIGGS LOUISIANA MELODY MAKERS:

Victor 40083 *Ione*......................	7.00 -	10.00
40184 *The Yodler's Serenade*..............	10.00 -	15.00

TAYLOR, MOORE & BURNETT:

Gennett 6760 *Knoxville Rag*..............	15.00 -	20.00

JIM TAYLOR & BILL SHELBY:

Champion 15730 *It's Sad To Leave You Sweetheart*	10.00 -	15.00
15772 *The Bald-headed End Of A Broom*....	10.00 -	15.00
15812 *I Ain't Gonna Grieve My Lord Anymore*	10.00 -	15.00
15855 *The Old Schoolhouse Playground*......	10.00 -	15.00
45072 *It's Sad To Leave You Sweetheart*.....	5.00 -	8.00

UNCLE FRANK TEMPLETON:

Bell 1172 *Over The Waves*.................	7.00 -	10.00

TENNESSEE DRIFTERS:

Dot 1001 *Boogie Beat Rag*................	7.00 -	10.00
1002 Mean Ole Boogie..................	7.00 -	10.00

TENNESSEE FIDDLERS:

Timely Tunes 1562 *Cottonwood Reel*.........	15.00 -	20.00

TENNESSEE MOUNTAINEERS:

Victor 20860 *Standing On The Promises*.......	10.00 -	15.00

TENNESSEE RAMBLERS:

Brunswick 255 *Arkansas Traveler*............	10.00 -	15.00
252 Medley Of Mountain Songs..........	10.00 -	15.00
257 *A Fiddlers Contest*.................	10.00 -	15.00
Vocalion 5362 *Give The Fiddler A Dram*.....	15.00 -	20.00
5398 *In My Dear Old Sunny South*........	15.00 -	20.00

TENNESSEE TRAVELERS:

Champion 15300 *Forked Deer*.............	7.00 -	10.00

TENNEVA RAMBLERS:

Victor 20861 *The Longest Train*............	10.00 -	15.00
21141 *Miss Liza, Poor Gal*..............	10.00 -	15.00
21289 *The Curtains Of Night*............	10.00 -	15.00
21406 *Seven Long Years In Prison*.........	10.00 -	15.00
21645 *I'm Goin' To Georgia*..............	10.00 -	15.00

JACK TETER:

Paramount 3235 *Silver Threads Among The Gold*	8.00 -	12.00

NORWOOD TEW:

Bluebird 6553 *Sailorman Blues*.............	7.00 -	10.00
6892 *My Old Crippled Daddy*.............	7.00 -	10.00
7288, 7618, 7791, 7950..................	5.00 -	8.00

TEXAS COWBOY BAND:

Supertone 9673 *New Harmony Waltz*..........	8.00 -	12.00

TEXAS DRIFTER:

Decca 5020 *The Yodeling Teacher*............	5.00 -	8.00
5021 *Cowboy's Lullaby*.................	5.00 -	8.00
Melotone 12016 *The Texas Drifter*........	5.00 -	8.00
12047 *The Oklahoma Kid*...............	5.00 -	8.00
12186 *Bright Sherman Valley*...........	5.00 -	8.00
12214 *Little Joe, The Wrangler*.........	5.00 -	8.00
12232 *Mother-In-Law Blues*.............	5.00 -	8.00
12242 *The Tramp's Mother*.............	5.00 -	8.00
12290 *John Law And The Hobo*.........	5.00 -	8.00
12302 *The Cowboy's Secret*.............	5.00 -	8.00
Vocalion 5484 *The Drifter*..............	7.00 -	10.00

TEXAS NIGHT HAWKS:

Okeh 453633 *Possum Rag*...............	10.00 -	15.00

TEXAS RANGER:

Superior 2774 *Eleven Cent Cotton-Forty Cent Meat*	10.00 -	15.00
2792 *All Aboard For Blanket Bay*..........	10.00 -	15.00
Supertone S-2055 *The Brakeman's Blues*.......	7.00 -	10.00

TEXAS RANGERS:

Decca 5022, 5107, 5139, 5183..............	4.00 -	7.00

TEXAS RHYTHM BOYS:

Royalty 600 *Benzedrine Blues*.............	5.00 -	8.00

GEORGE THOMAS & HIS BOYS/MUSIC:

Champion 15262 *Big Town Fling*...........	5.00 -	8.00
15280 *Larry O'Gaff*.................	5.00 -	8.00
15354 *Haste To The Wedding*............	5.00 -	8.00
15410 *Leather Breeches*...............	5.00 -	8.00
15434 *Blue Hawaii*....................	5.00 -	8.00

GRAYSON THOMAS & WILL LOTTY:

Champion 15395 *Nobody's Darling*...........	10.00 -	15.00

THOMPSON, CRANFORD & MILES:

Gennett 6602 *The Blind Man And His Child*...	15.00 -	20.00

THOMPSON & MILES WITH THE RED FOX CHASERS:

Gennett 6914 *Put My Little Shoes Away*.......	15.00 -	25.00
6930 *The Girl I Loved In Sunny Tennessee*...	20.00 -	30.00

BUD THOMPSON:

Crown 3418 *Five Cent Cotton*.............	8.00 -	12.00
½3430 *I'm A Fugitive From A Chain Gang*..	8.00 -	12.00
3489 *The Lie He Wrote Home*.............	8.00 -	12.00
3502 *When The White Azaleas Start Blooming*	8.00 -	12.00

ERNEST THOMPSON:

Columbia 130-D *Are You From Dixie*.........	8.00 -	12.00
145-D *Lightning Express*..................	8.00 -	12.00
147-D *Little Brown Jug*.................	8.00 -	12.00
153-D *Life's Railway To Heaven*............	8.00 -	12.00
189-D *Mississippi Sawyer*...............	8.00 -	12.00
190-D *Red Wing*.......................	8.00 -	12.00
216-D *In The Baggage Coach Ahead*.......	7.00 -	10.00
15001-D *Weeping Willow Tree*............	10.00 -	15.00
15002-D *Silly Bill*.....................	10.00 -	15.00
15006-D *Whistlin' Rufus*...............	10.00 -	15.00
15007-D *The Old Time Religion*............	10.00 -	15.00

ERNEST E. THOMPSON:

Gennett 7139 *Medley*..................	15.00 -	20.00

FLOYD THOMPSON & HIS HOMETOWNERS:

Vocalion 5233 *Sidewalks Of New York*.........	7.00 -	10.00
5236 *Little Brown Jug*..................	7.00 -	10.00
5242 *Oh My Darling Clementine*...........	7.00 -	10.00
5253 *The Trail Of The Lonesome Pine*.......	7.00 -	10.00
5258 *Billy Boy*.......................	7.00 -	10.00
5266 *I Wonder How She Did It*...........	7.00 -	10.00
5300 *When The Sunset Turns The Ocean Blue To Gold*..................................	7.00 -	10.00
5317 *Mountains Of Virginia*...............	7.00 -	10.00
5331 *Red Wing*....................	7.00 -	10.00

GEORGIA THOMPSON:

Columbia 15532-D *Cross Eyed Sue*...........	4.00 -	7.00

HANK THOMPSON (& HIS BRAZOS VALLEY BOYS):

Blue Bonnet 107 *My Starry-Eyed Texas Gal*....	8.00 -	12.00
123 *California Women*................	8.00 -	12.00
Globe 124 *Whoa Sailor!*................	7.00 -	12.00

HUGH THOMPSON:

Crystal 385 *Naggin' Wife*.................	———

UNCLE JIMMIE THOMPSON:

Columbia 15118-D *Billy Wilson*..............	10.00 -	15.00
Vocalion 5456 *Lynchburg*................	15.00 -	25.00

THREE 'BACCER TAGS:

Victor 23571 *Ain't Gonna Do It*..............	15.00 -	20.00

THREE GEORGIA CRACKERS:

Columbia 15630-D *I've Been Hoodooed*........	5.00 -	8.00
15653-D *Hannah-My Love*.................	5.00 -	8.00

THREE

THREE HOWARD BOYS:
Challenge 110 *Down In Tennessee Blues*....... 7.00 - 10.00
  304 *Down In Tennessee Blues*............. 7.00 - 10.00

THREE KENTUCKY SERENADERS:
Supertone 9246 *Pearl Bryant*............... 8.00 - 12.00
  9251 *Please, Papa, Come Home*............ 8.00 - 12.00
  9269 *We Will Outshine The Sun*........... 8.00 - 12.00

THREE MUSKETEERS:
Bluebird 8129 *Chattanooga Mama*........... 5.00 - 8.00

THREE OLD CRONIES:
Vocalion 5134 *Turkey In The Straw*.......... 7.00 - 10.00
  15305 *Turkey In The Straw*............... 7.00 - 10.00

THREE STRIPPED GEARS:
Okeh 45553 *Depression Blues*.............. 15.00 - 20.00
  45571 *Alabama Blues*.................... 15.00 - 20.00

THREE TOBACCO TAGS:
Bluebird 6668, 6730, 6853, 6902, 6948, 6999, 7044,
  7130, 7163, 7211, 7250, 7312, 7361, 7400, 7448,
  7482, 7533, 7692, 7715, 7777, 7877, 7912, 7973 4.00 - 7.00
Champion 16480 *The Teacher's Hair Was Red*.. 15.00 - 20.00
  16674 *Reno Blues*...................... 15.00 - 20.00

THREE TWEEDY BOYS/BROTHERS:
Champion 15486 *The Bully Of The Town*...... 7.00 - 10.00
  15548 *Sugar In The Gourd*............... 7.00 - 10.00
  15689 *Ida Red*......................... 7.00 - 10.00

THREE VIRGINIANS:
Okeh 45451 *June Tenth Blues*.............. 15.00 - 20.00

THREE WILLIAMSONS:
Bluebird 7819 *Fiddlers Blues*............. 7.00 - 10.00

TOBACCO TAGS:
Bluebird 8396, 8420...................... 4.00 - 7.00

TOM & CHUCK:
Victor 40305 *White River Road*............ 8.00 - 12.00

TOM & ROY:
Bluebird 5073, 5138, 5198, 5245............ 4.00 - 7.00
Victor 23800 *Grandfather's Clock*......... 7.00 - 10.00
  23804 *In My Old Cabin Home*............ 7.00 - 10.00
  23813 *Chant Of The Jungle*............. 7.00 - 10.00

TOMMIE & WILLIE:
Champion 16034 *By The Old Oak Tree*....... 8.00 - 12.00
  16231 *I'm The Last One Left On The Corner*. 10.00 - 15.00
  16240 *By My Side*...................... 10.00 - 15.00
  16259 *My Canary Has Circles Under His Eyes* 10.00 - 15.00
  16276 *Rocky Mountain Rose*.............. 10.00 - 15.00
  16301 *When It's Night Time In Nevada*..... 10.00 - 15.00
  16314 *If You Can't Sing, Whistle*........ 10.00 - 15.00
  16432 *There's A Little Box Of Pine On The 7:29* 10.00 - 15.00
  45006, 45180.......................... 4.00 - 7.00
Gennett 7246 *By The Old Oak Tree*......... 12.00 - 18.00

JED THOMPKINS:
Harmony 5096-H *Life's Railway To Heaven*.... 4.00 - 6.00
  5099-H *Mississippi Sawyer*............. 4.00 - 6.00
  5101-H *Coon Crap Game*................. 4.00 - 6.00
Velvet Tone 7034-V *Mississippi Sawyer*...... 4.00 - 6.00

JACK TOOMBS:
Excello 2033 *Two Cheaters In Love*......... 4.00 - 8.00*
  2041 *My Imagination*.................. 4.00 - 8.00*
Speed 111 *Pin Ball Fever*................. 8.00 - 12.00

WELBY TOOMEY:
Gennett 6005 *Roving Gambler*.............. 12.00 - 16.00
  6025 *Little Brown Jug*................. 12.00 - 16.00
Silvertone 8151 *Roving Gambler*........... 7.00 - 10.00
Supertone 9245 *Little Brown Jug*.......... 7.00 - 10.00
  9252 *Roving Gambler*.................. 7.00 - 10.00

GEORGE TOON & THE TENNESSEE DRIFTERS:
Dot 1008 *That There Gal O'Mine*........... 5.00 - 8.00
(Note: See also TENNESSEE DRIFTERS)

MITCHELL TOROK:
FBC 102 *Nacogdoches County Line*.......... 8.00 - 12.00
  115 *Piney Woods Boogie*............... 8.00 - 12.00

VAGABONDS

TRAVELERS:
Decca 5453, 5461....................... 3.00 - 6.00

CARL TRIMBLE:
Champion 16717 *Down On The Old Plantation*. 12.00 - 16.00
  45050 *In A Lonely Little Cottage*......... 5.00 - 8.00

ERNEST TUBB:
Bluebird 6693 *The Passing Of Jimmie Rodgers*.. 75.00 - 100.00
  7000 *Since That Black Cat Crossed My Path*.. 75.00 - 100.00
  8899 *Mean Old Bed Bug Blues*........... 50.00 - 75.00
  8966 *My Mother Is Lonely*............. 40.00 - 60.00
Decca 5825, 5846, 5900, 5910, 5920, 5938, 5958,
  5976, 5993, 6007, 6023, 6040............ 3.00 - 5.00

TUNE WRANGLERS:
Bluebird 6310, 6326, 6365, 6403, 6421, 6438, 6513,
  6554, 6655, 6692, 6703, 6828, 6856, 6900, 6947,
  6962, 6982, 7030, 7076, 7089, 7200, 7272, 7336,
  7413, 7571, 7612, 7673, 7703, 7766, 7830, 7867,
  7947, 7966, 7972, 7992, 8014............ 4.00 - 7.00

BUCK TURNER:
Title, issued contemporaneously on Banner,
  Melotone, Oriole, Perfect Romeo: *Sing Sing Blues* 8.00 - 12.00

CAL TURNER:
Champion 15524 *The Rowan County Feud*..... 12.00 - 18.00
  15544 *The Death Of J.B. Marcum*.......... 12.00 - 18.00
  15587 *Only A Tramp*................... 12.00 - 18.00
  15630 *By The Silvery Rio Grande*........ 12.00 - 18.00

DAVE TURNER:
Supertone 9318 *She'll Be Comin 'Round The Mountain*...................... 7.00 - 10.00
  9319 *That Old Covered Bridge*.......... 7.00 - 10.00
  9374 *Many Troubles Blues*............. 8.00 - 12.00
  9560 *We've Been Chums For Fifty Years*.... 8.00 - 12.00

HOBO JACK TURNER:
Various recordings issued on Diva, Harmony and
  Velvet Tone under this name are of little interest
  or value.

JACK TURNER:
Gennett 7305 *Honey Stay In Your Own Back Yard* 12.00 - 16.00

LEMUEL TURNER:
Victor 21292 *'Way Down Yonder Blues*........ 15.00 - 20.00
  40052 *Jake Bottle Blues*............... 15.00 - 20.00

BILL TUTTLE:
Columbia 15697-D *Gamblin' Bill Driv' On*..... 10.00 - 15.00

FRANK TUTTLE:
Velvet Tone 2148-V *The Prison Fire*.......... 4.00 - 7.00

TWEEDY BROTHERS: (See also THREE TWEEDY BOYS/BROTHERS)
Champion 16048 *Home Brew Rag*............ 15.00 - 20.00
Gennett 6447 *The Bully Of The Town*........ 8.00 - 12.00
  6483 *Sugar In The Gourd*............... 8.00 - 12.00
  6529 *Shortnin' Bread*................. 8.00 - 12.00
  6604 *Buckwheat Batter*................ 8.00 - 12.00
  6734 *Dixie*.......................... 8.00 - 12.00
  7240 *Home Brew Rag*................... 15.00 - 20.00
Superior 2784 *Home Brew Rag*............. 15.00 - 20.00
Supertone 9166 *Ida Red*................. 8.00 - 12.00
  9174 *Shortnin' Bread*................. 8.00 - 12.00

UNCLE BUD & HIS PLOWBOYS:
Oriole 8170 *Five Cent Cotton*.............. 5.00 - 8.00

CHAS. UNDERWOOD (Acc. by HACK'S STRING BAND):
Champion 16144 *Black Snake Moan*.......... 15.00 - 20.00
  16362 *I Want My Rib*................... 15.00 - 20.00

MARION UNDERWOOD (& SAM HARRIS):
Gennett 6155 *A Picture From Life's Other Side*. 10.00 - 15.00
  6177 *Just As The Sun Went Down*......... 10.00 - 15.00
  6240 *Coal Creek March*................. 15.00 - 20.00

VAGABONDS:
Bluebird 5072, 5103, 5124, 5137, 5197, 5282, 5297,
  5300, 5315, 5335, 5381, 5402, 5588, 6184... 4.00 - 8.00
Victor 23801 *In The Sleepy Hills Of Tennessee*.. 10.00 - 15.00
  23809 *The Old Rugged Cross*............ 10.00 - 15.00

23820 *Ninety-Nine Years*	15.00 -	20.00
23849 *My Pretty Quadroon*	15.00 -	20.00
23855 *In The Valley Of Yesterday*	15.00 -	20.00

VAGABOND YODELER:

Superior 2793 *No More To Ride The Rails*	15.00 -	25.00

VAL & PETE:

Okeh 45224 *Yodel Blues*	5.00 -	8.00

VANCE'S TENNESSEE BREAKDOWNERS:

Okeh 45151 *Tennessee Breakdown*	15.00 -	20.00

VASS FAMILY:

Decca 5425 *Jimmy Randall*	4.00 -	6.00
5432 *Deep Blue Sea*	4.00 -	6.00

BILLY VEST:

Titles, issued on Banner, Conqueror, Melotone, Oriole, Perfect, Romeo, include: *Big City Jail; Dear Old Texas*	6.00 -	10.00
Columbia 15669-D *She'll Never Find Another Daddy Like Me*	10.00 -	15.00
15692-D *Billy's Blue Yodel*	10.00 -	15.00

VIRGINIA DANDIES:

Crown 3145 *God's Getting Worried*	8.00 -	12.00
Paramount 3305 *Mid The Green Fields Of Virginia*	8.00 -	12.00

VIRGINIA MOUNTAIN BOOMERS:

Gennett 6567 *Ramblin' Reckless Hobo*	15.00 -	25.00
6687 *Cousin Sally Brown*	15.00 -	25.00
Supertone 9305 *Rambling Reckless Hobo*	15.00 -	20.00
9406 *East Tennessee Polka*	15.00 -	20.00

VIRGINIA POSSUM TAMERS:

Champion 15484 *The Wreck On The Mountain Road*	10.00 -	15.00
15522 *Turkey In The Straw*	10.00 -	15.00
15566 *Weeping Willow Tree*	10.00 -	15.00
15609 *The Blind Man And His Child*	10.00 -	15.00
15672 *Something Wrong With My Gal*	10.00 -	15.00
15769 *The Virginia Possum Tamers Makin' Licker*	12.00 -	18.00
15790 *Virginia Bootleggers*	12.00 -	18.00
15809 *The Virginia Possum Tamers Makin' Licker, Part 3/4*	12.00 -	18.00
15925 *Put My Little Shoes Away*	10.00 -	15.00
45079 *Virginia Bootleggers*	7.00 -	10.00

VIRGINIA RAMBLERS:

Timely Tunes 1561 *Rag Time Annie*	8.00 -	12.00

WILD BILL WADE:

Okeh 45550 *Weeping Daddy Blues*	10.00 -	15.00

GEORGE WADE & CAROLINIANS:

Bluebird 7904 *Long And Bony*	5.00 -	8.00
Columbia 15515-D *When We Go A-Courtin'*	8.00 -	12.00

GEORGE WALBURN'S FOOT-SCORCHERS; GEORGE WALBURN & EMMETT HETHCOX:

Columbia 15721-D *Dixie Flyer*	15.00 -	25.00
Okeh 45024 *Lee County Blues*	15.00 -	20.00
45066 *Home Brew*	15.00 -	20.00
45178 *Kansas City Railroad Blues*	15.00 -	20.00
45305 *Decatur Street Rag*	15.00 -	20.00

WALKER'S CORBIN RAMBLERS:

Vocalion 02468 *Nobody's Business*	10.00 -	15.00
02667 *Ned Went A-Fishin'*	10.00 -	15.00
02678 *The Dying Tramp*	12.00 -	18.00
02719 *I Had A Dream*	10.00 -	15.00
02771 *Dark Town Strutters Ball*	10.00 -	15.00
02790 *Stone Mountain Toddle*	10.00 -	15.00

DAVE WALKER:

Superior 2688 *Someone Owns A Cottage*	15.00 -	20.00

FRANCIS/FRANKIE WALLACE:

(Note: Most records issued under these names—pseudonyms for Frank Marvin—are of minimal value.)

Edison 52356 *Away Out On The Mountain*	5.00 -	8.00
52387 *Drowsy Moonlight*	5.00 -	8.00
Paramount 3180 *Yodeling Them Blues Away*	8.00 -	12.00

3190 *Mississippi Moonshine*	8.00 -	12.00
3203 *I'm Riding The Blinds On A Train Headed West*	10.00 -	15.00
3209 *I Don't Work For A Living*	5.00 -	8.00
3211 *Blue Yodel No. 5*	7.00 -	10.00
3272 *Jimmie Rodger's Blue Yodel*	5.00 -	8.00
Supertone 9082 *Blue Yodel No. 2*	5.00 -	8.00

JERRY WALLACE:

Superior 2577 *Waiting For The Railroad Train*	10.00 -	15.00
2643 *O Jailer Bring Back That Key*	10.00 -	15.00
2677 *Hand Me Down My Walking Cane*	10.00 -	15.00

"DOCK" WALSH:

Columbia 15047-D *The East Bound Train*	8.00 -	12.00
15057-D *The Educated Man*	8.00 -	12.00
15075-D *We Courted In The Rain*	8.00 -	12.00
15094-D *In The Pines*	8.00 -	12.00
15105-D *Traveling Man*	8.00 -	12.00
Victor 40237 *Bathe In The Beautiful Pool*	15.00 -	20.00
40325 *We're Just Plain Folks*	15.00 -	20.00

WALTER FAMILY:

Champion 16595 *Too Young To Get Married*	15.00 -	20.00
16622 *Flying Cloud Waltz*	15.00 -	20.00
16643 *Patty On The Turn Pike*	15.00 -	20.00
16653 *Shaker Ben*	15.00 -	20.00

WANNER & JENKINS/WHITE:

Champion 16306 *The Pretty Quadroon*	10.00 -	15.00
16348 *The Little Old Church In The Valley*	10.00 -	15.00
Columbia 15728-D *A Sweetheart's Promise*	10.00 -	15.00
Superior 2734 *That Little Boy Of Mine*	10.00 -	15.00

ENOS WANNER:

Champion 15791 *Over The Hills To The Poor House*	8.00 -	12.00
15810 *Don't Grieve Your Mother*	8.00 -	12.00
15830 *Put Me Off At Buffalo*	8.00 -	12.00
15898 *Crepe On The Little Cabin Door*	8.00 -	12.00
16052 *The Prison Warden's Secret*	10.00 -	15.00
16098 *Two Little Girls In Blue*	10.00 -	15.00
Superior 2722 *Strawberry Roan*	20.00 -	30.00

A.E. WARD & HIS PLOW BOYS:

Columbia 15734-D *Going To Leave Old Arkansas*	50.00 -	80.00

CROCKETT WARD & HIS BOYS:

Okeh 45179 *Deadheads And Suckers*	20.00 -	30.00
45304 *Ain't That Trouble In Mind?*	20.00 -	30.00

PRESTON WARD:

Kentucky 540, 541	3.00 -	6.00

TOMMY WARD:

Superior 2689 *Mississippi River Blues*	25.00 -	40.00

PAUL WARMACK & HIS GULLY JUMPERS:

Victor 40009 *Robertson County*	15.00 -	20.00
40067 *Little Red Caboose Behind The Train*	15.00 -	20.00

HANK WARNER:

Banner 5-11-61 *The Death Of Hughey P. Long*	7.00 -	10.00

(Note: Probably also issued on Melotone, Oriole, Perfect, and Romeo.)

YODELIN' JIMMY WARNER:

Champion 15562 *Blue Yodel No. 2*	5.00 -	8.00

WASHBOARD WONDERS:

Bluebird 6455 *You Gotta Eat Your Spinach, Baby*	6.00 -	10.00
6463 *All Quiet On The Old Front Porch*	6.00 -	10.00
6464 *It Ain't Right*	6.00 -	10.00
6495 *Feather Your Nest*	6.00 -	10.00
6526 *Meet Me At The Ice House*	6.00 -	10.00
6648 *Apple Tree*	6.00 -	10.00
6671 *Roll Your Own*	6.00 -	10.00
6737 *You're Everything Sweet*	6.00 -	10.00
6761 *Breeze*	4.00 -	6.00

W.L. "RUSTIC" WATERS:

Columbia 15705-D *Sweet Nora Shannon*	8.00 -	12.00

WATKINS BAND:

Victor 21405 *Gideon*	7.00 -	10.00

DR. CLAUDE WATSON & L.W. McCREIGHTON:

Okeh 45020 *Chicken Reel*	10.00 -	15.00
45034 *Ballin' The Jack And Nigger Blues*	10.00 -	15.00

GEORGE P. WATSON:

Edison 51530 *Love's A Magic Spell*..........	5.00 -	8.00
51691 *Medley Of J.K. Emmett's Yodel Songs.*	5.00 -	8.00
Victor 20190, 20247......................	3.00 -	5.00

HARVEY WATSON:

Challenge 328 *Drunken Hiccoughs*...........	8.00 -	12.00
329 *Bright Sherman Valley*.................	8.00 -	12.00
330 *Weeping Willow Tree*..................	8.00 -	12.00
Champion 15299 *A Mother's Advice*.........	7.00 -	10.00
15333 *He Lives On High*..................	7.00 -	10.00
15334 *Weeping Willow Tree*...............	8.00 -	12.00
15356 *Drunken Hiccoughs*................	8.00 -	12.00
15428 *The Dying Cowboy*.................	7.00 -	10.00
Supertone 9243 *Weeping Willow Tree*.......	8.00 -	12.00
9263 *He Lives On High*..................	7.00 -	10.00

LUIS WATSON:

Supertone 9167 *Home Sweet Home*.......	7.00 -	10.00
9175 *Wandering Boy*....................	7.00 -	10.00

TOM WATSON:

Silvertone 3262 *Georgia Railroad*.............	7.00 -	10.00

WATTS & WILSON:

Paramount 3006 *The Sporting Cowboy*.......	30.00 -	40.00
3007 *The Night Express*.................	30.00 -	40.00
3019 *The Chain Gang Special*............	30.00 -	40.00

OLD POP WATTS:

Phamous 701 *Kissin And Huggin'*.............	——

WILMER WATTS & THE LONELY EAGLES:

Broadway 8248 *Knockin' Down Casey Jones*....	30.00 -	50.00
Paramount 3210 *Knockin' Down Casey Jones*...	30.00 -	50.00
3232 *Charles Gitaw*.....................	30.00 -	50.00
3242 *Banjo Sam*.......................	30.00 -	50.00
3247 *She's A Hard Boiled Rose*...........	30.00 -	50.00
3254 *Cotton Mill Blues*.................	30.00 -	50.00
3271 *Banjo Sam*.......................	30.00 -	50.00
3282 *Sleepy Desert*....................	30.00 -	50.00
3299 *Bonnie Bess*.....................	30.00 -	50.00

WEAVER BROTHERS:

Columbia 15487-D *Prison Sorrows*...........	10.00 -	15.00

WEAVER & WIGGINS:

Broadway 8112 *The Sporting Cowboy*.........	20.00 -	30.00
8113 *The Night Express*.................	20.00 -	30.00
8114 *The Chain Gang Special*............	20.00 -	30.00

J.D. WEAVER:

Okeh 45016 *Arkansas Traveler*..............	8.00 -	12.00

WEBER & BROOKS:

Superior 2740 *The Utah Trail*...............	15.00 -	20.00

DAN WEBER:

Superior 2527 *Fair Florella*...............	20.00 -	30.00
2582 *Worried Daddy Blues*................	20.00 -	30.00

SAM WEBER:

Superior 2822 *My Ozark Mountain Home*......	25.00 -	35.00

WEEMS STRING BAND:

Columbia 15300-D *Greenback Dollar*.........	15.00 -	20.00

WELLING TRIO:

Champion 16035 *Will The Circle Be Unknown*..	10.00 -	15.00
16054 *Wait Till The Sun Shines Nellie*.......	10.00 -	15.00
16078 *Halleluiah All The Way*............	10.00 -	15.00
16120 *School Days*....................	10.00 -	15.00
Champion 45123, 45171....................	4.00 -	7.00
Gennett 7291 *Tie Me To Your Apron Strings Again*	15.00 -	25.00

WELLING & McGHEE: (See also McGHEE & WELLING)

Champion 16585 *The Hallelujah Side*..........	10.00 -	15.00
16598 *Nothing But The Blood*.............	10.00 -	15.00
16660 *Ring The Bells Of Heaven*..........	10.00 -	15.00
Gennett 6719 *Lonely Village Churchyard*......	10.00 -	15.00
7096 *Picture From Life's Other Side*.........	10.00 -	15.00
Melotone 5-12-59 *The Maple On The Hill*.....	7.00 -	10.00
Oriole 8056 *The Lonely Village Churchyard*....	7.00 -	10.00

(Note: The above titles on Melotone and Oriole, and those on Perfect, below, probably were issued contemporaneously on Banner, Conqueror, Melotone, Oriole, Perfect, Romeo.)

Paramount 3084 *In The Garden*.............	10.00 -	15.00
3093 *Haven Of Rest*....................	10.00 -	15.00
3102 *Are You Washed In The Blood*.......	10.00 -	15.00
3108 *My Mother's Bible*.................	10.00 -	15.00
3115 *At The Cross*.....................	10.00 -	15.00
3157 *Too Many Parties And Too Many Pals*.	15.00 -	20.00
3175 *I Love To Walk With Jesus*..........	10.00 -	15.00
3223 *Don't Sing Aloha When I Go*........	15.00 -	20.00
3286 *Where Is My Mama*.................	15.00 -	20.00
3310 *Almost Persuaded*..................	15.00 -	20.00
Perfect 12769 *The Crime At Quiet Dell*......	7.00 -	10.00
Perfect 12801 *Sweet Hour Of Prayer*.......	7.00 -	10.00
Vocalion 5241 *The Hallelujah Side*..........	8.00 -	12.00
5251 *The Lilly Of The Valley*.............	8.00 -	12.00
5263 *The Nearer, The Sweeter*...........	8.00 -	12.00
5299 *Go By The Way Of The Cross*.......	8.00 -	12.00

WELLING & SCHANNEN/SHANNON:

Paramount 3127 *S.O.S. Vestris*..........	7.00 -	12.00
3134 *I'm A Child Of The King*............	7.00 -	12.00
3142 *Are You A Christian?*..............	7.00 -	12.00

FRANK WELLING (& THE RED BRUSH ROWDIES):

Champion 16474 *My Little Mountain Home*....	15.00 -	20.00
16562 *I Can't Think Of Everything*........	15.00 -	20.00
16588 *The Old Man's Story*..............	15.00 -	20.00
16590 *Shake Hands With Mother Again*....	15.00 -	20.00
16594 *The Little Old Cross Road Store*....	15.00 -	20.00
16618 *Roll It Down Baby*................	15.00 -	20.00
16652 *Daddy's Lullaby*..................	15.00 -	20.00
16697 *Daddy And Son*..................	15.00 -	20.00
Gennett 6616 *Yodelin' Daddy Blues*.........	20.00 -	30.00
6671 *I Wants My Lulu*..................	15.00 -	20.00
7111 *Little Pal*........................	15.00 -	25.00
7142 *That's A Plenty*...................	15.00 -	25.00
Paramount 3119 *The Last Mile*............	15.00 -	25.00
3125 *She's My Mama, And I'm Her Daddy*...	15.00 -	25.00
3216 *A Plea To Young Wives*............	20.00 -	30.00
3287 *Busted Bank Blues*................	20.00 -	30.00
Supertone 9083 *Yodelin' Daddy Blues*........	10.00 -	15.00

WELLS BROTHERS STRING BAND:

Bluebird 7588 *Snow White Stone*............	5.00 -	8.00

WENATCHEE MOUNTAINEERS:

Titles, issued contemporaneously on Banner, Conqueror, Melotone, Oriole, Perfect, Romeo, include: *Bring Your Roses To Your Mother; Britt's Reel; By The Sleepy Rio Grande; Dear Old Southern Moon; I Like Mountain Music; The Little Rose Covered Shack; Texas Rag; When It's Harvest Time*...................... 5.00 - 8.00

JOE WERNER & THE RAMBLERS:

Bluebird 7539, 7575, 7639, 7690, 7923.........	4.00 -	7.00

C.A. WEST:

Gennett 7098 *A Mother's Advice*............	12.00 -	16.00
Supertone 9650 *Oh Willie Come Back*........	5.00 -	8.00

CAL WEST:

Vocalion 5361 *Cal West's Yodeling Blues*......	8.00 -	12.00

ED "JAKE" WEST:

Broadway 8109 *Waiting For The Train*........	4.00 -	7.00
Challenge 813 *Waiting For The Train*.........	5.00 -	8.00
Paramount 3154 *Waiting For The Train*.......	5.00 -	8.00

WALTON WEST:

Champion 45161 *'Leven Miles From Leavenworth*	5.00 -	8.00
45170 *In That Vine Covered Chapel*........	5.00 -	8.00

WESTERNERS:

Titles, issued contemporaneously on Banner, Conqueror, Melotone, Oriole, Perfect, Romeo, include: *Carry Me Back To The Lone Prairie; The Cowboy's Dream; Goin' Down To Santa Fe Town; Gol Darn Wheel; Good Old Turnip Greens; If Jesse James Rode Again; Is It True What They Say About Dixie?; My Gal On The Rio Grande; My Herdin' Song; Nobody To Love; Out On The Loco Range; Pretty Boy Floyd;*

Rancho Grande; Ridin' Down That Old Texas Trail; Roundup Time In Heaven; The Santa Fe Trail; Texas Star...................... 4.00 - 8.00

DON WESTON:

Champion 16748 *That Old Feather Bed On The Farm*...................... 15.00 - 20.00

   16764 *The Dying Cowgirl*.............. 15.00 - 20.00

   16779 *'Way Out West In Texas*......... 15.00 - 20.00

   16825 *That Mother And Daddy Of Mine*..... 20.00 - 30.00

   45053, 45101, 45107, 45110........... 4.00 - 7.00

WEST VIRGINIA COON HUNTERS:

Victor 20862 *Greasy String*............... 10.00 - 15.00

WEST VIRGINIA NIGHT OWLS:

Victor 21190 *Sweet Bird*.................. 10.00 - 15.00

   21533 *I'm Goin' To Walk On The Streets Of Glory* 10.00 - 15.00

WEST VIRGINIA RAIL SPLITTER:

Champion 15852 *In The Jail House Now*...... 10.00 - 15.00

   15897 *Barney McCoy*................ 10.00 - 15.00

   15943 *Old And Only In The Way*..... 10.00 - 15.00

   15990 *The Habit*.................. 10.00 - 15.00

   16053 *Zeb Turney's Gal*............ 10.00 - 15.00

   16095 *The Dying Ranger*........... 10.00 - 15.00

WEST VIRGINIA RAMBLERS:

Champion 16757 *O Dem Golden Slippers*...... 12.00 - 18.00

   45017 *O Dem Golden Slippers*...... 4.00 - 7.00

WEST VIRGINIA RIDGE RUNNERS:

Superior 2794 *Dill Pickle Rag*............ 15.00 - 20.00

WEST VIRGINIA SNAKE HUNTERS:

Brunswick 119 *Standin' In The Need Of Prayer*. 10.00 - 15.00

JIM WHALEN:

Champion 15545 *May I Sleep In Your Barn Tonight, Mister?*........................ 8.00 - 12.00

(FRANK) WHEELER & (MONROE) LAMB:

Victor 23537 *Jim Blake, The Engineer*........ 15.00 - 20.00

   23755 *Will You Sometimes Think Of Me*..... 15.00 - 20.00

   40169 *Jolly Group Of Cowboys*......... 10.00 - 15.00

   40248 *Since The Preacher Made Us One*..... 10.00 - 15.00

WEBB WHIPPLE:

Okeh 45574 *Don't Hang Me In The Morning*... 8.00 - 12.00

WHITE & DAWSON:

Superior 9541 *On The Banks Of The Silvery Stream* 8.00 - 12.00

FIDDLIN' BOB WHITE:

Bell 1171 *Cripple Creek*................. 5.00 - 8.00

   1188 *Billy In The Low Ground*........... 5.00 - 8.00

CLYDE WHITE:

Champion 16318 *Beside A Lonely River*....... 10.00 - 15.00

GEORGE WHITE:

Okeh 45241, 45257, 45287, 45335, 45351...... 4.00 - 7.00

   45382 *Dust Pan Blues*............... 5.00 - 8.00

   45432 *Livin' In The Mountains*........... 5.00 - 8.00

   45502 *I Am Just A Gambler*............ 5.00 - 8.00

JOHN WHITE:

Romeo 5066 *Strawberry Roan*............... 5.00 - 8.00

JOHNNIE/JOHNNY WHITE & HIS RHYTHM RIDERS:

Citation 102 *My Home In Tennessee*......... 4.00 - 6.00

Fortune 145 *Mean And Evil Blues*.......... 3.00 - 5.00

REUBEN WHITE:

Challenge 336 *Old Sefus Brown*............. 7.00 - 10.00

ZEB WHITE:

Vocalion 5189 *When You Were Sweet Sixteen*.. 8.00 - 12.00

RED WHITEHEAD & DUTCH COLEMAN:

Vocalion 5414 *Booneville Stomp*............. 20.00 - 30.00

WHITE MOUNTAIN ORCHESTRA:

Victor 23619 *Maxwell's Old Rye Waltz*....... 20.00 - 30.00

   40185 *Leather Britches*................. 15.00 - 20.00

RAY WHITELY (& ODIS ELDER); WHITLEY'S RANGE RAMBLERS:

Titles, issued contemporaneously on Banner, Conqueror, Melotone, Oriole, Perfect, Romeo: *Have You Written Your Mother Lately; The Morro*

Castle Disaster; Pretty Boy Floyd; Old Wishing Well; Singing A Song In Sing Sing; Sittin' On The Old Settee........................ 8.00 - 12.00

Decca 5078 *Big Bad Blues*................. 7.00 - 10.00

   5132 *Wiley Post*.................. 7.00 - 10.00

   5195 *Wah-Hoo*................... 7.00 - 10.00

   5205 *Blue Yodel Blues*............ 7.00 - 10.00

   5285 *Travelin'*.................. 5.00 - 8.00

   5293 *You Took My Candy*.......... 5.00 - 8.00

J.B. WHITMIRE & THE BLUE SKY TRIO:

Bluebird 7132, 7844...................... 3.00 - 6.00

(HENRY) WHITTER (& G.B. GRAYSON); WHITTER'S VIRGINIA BREAKDOWNERS; HENRY WHITTER & FIDDLER JOE: (See also GRAYSON & WHITTER)

Champion 15629 *Cluck Old Hen*............. 8.00 - 12.00

Gennett 6320 *Train Forty-Five*........... 15.00 - 20.00

   6373 *I'll Never Be Yours*........... 15.00 - 20.00

   6418 *Red Or Green*................ 15.00 - 20.00

   6436 *Old Jimmy Sutton*............ 15.00 - 20.00

   6656 *Cluck Old Hen*.............. 15.00 - 20.00

   6733 *Sally Goodin*............... 15.00 - 20.00

Herwin 75537 *Snow Storm*................. 15.00 - 20.00

Okeh 40015 *Lonesome Road Blues*............ 15.00 - 20.00

   40029 *Last Train Blues*............. 8.00 - 12.00

   40063 *Little Brown Jug*............ 8.00 - 12.00

   40064 *Tippy Two Step Blues*........ 7.00 - 10.00

   40077 *Western County*.............. 8.00 - 12.00

   40109 *Sydney Allen*................ 8.00 - 12.00

   40120 *Double Headed Train*......... 8.00 - 12.00

   40143 *New River Train*............. 8.00 - 12.00

   40169 *The Drunkard's Child*........ 8.00 - 12.00

   40187 *Rain Crow Bill Blues*........ 8.00 - 12.00

   40211 *Nellie Gray*................ 10.00 - 15.00

   40229 *Broken Engagement Blues*..... 10.00 - 15.00

   40237 *Ellen Smith*................ 10.00 - 15.00

   40269 *Rabbit Race*................ 10.00 - 15.00

   40296 *Keep My Skillet Good And Greasy*.... 10.00 - 15.00

   40320 *Round-Town Girl*............ 10.00 - 15.00

   40352 *The Long Tongued Woman*.......... 10.00 - 15.00

   40375 *Butcher Boy*................ 10.00 - 15.00

   40395 *My Darling's Black Mustache*........ 12.00 - 18.00

   40403 *Good-Bye, Old Booze*......... 12.00 - 18.00

   45003 *Liza Jane*.................. 10.00 - 15.00

   45045 *The Heart Of Old Galax*....... 10.00 - 15.00

   45046 *Put My Little Shoes Away*...... 10.00 - 15.00

   45053 *Many Times With You I've Wondered*. 10.00 - 15.00

   45061 *Hand Me Down My Walking Cane*.... 10.00 - 15.00

   45063 *The Burglar Man*............ 10.00 - 15.00

   45081 *George Collins*............. 10.00 - 15.00

Victor 20878 *Whitter's Fox Chase*.......... 5.00 - 8.00

   40061 *Poor Lost Boy*.............. 10.00 - 15.00

   40105 *Short Life Of Trouble*........ 10.00 - 15.00

   40135 *Little Maggie With A Dram Glass*.... 10.00 - 15.00

   40235 *Tom Dooley*................. 10.00 - 15.00

   40292 *Fox Chase No. 2*............ 15.00 - 20.00

PETE WIGGINS:

Okeh 45295 *The Gay Caballero*............. 5.00 - 8.00

   45412 *Everybody Does It In Hawaii*........ 5.00 - 8.00

MILLER WIKEL:

Gennett 6566 *Frail Wildwood Flower*.......... 15.00 - 20.00

Paramount 3205 *Young Charlotte*............. 15.00 - 25.00

RILEY WILCOX:

Bell 1179 *The Broken Engagement*.......... 7.00 - 10.00

WILEY, ZEKE & HOMER:

Bluebird 7426 *Greenback Dollar, Part 3*........ 5.00 - 8.00

   7452 *Someone To Love You When You're Old* 5.00 - 8.00

   7572 *I Will Never Turn Back*........ 5.00 - 8.00

   7628 *Under The Old Kentucky Moon*....... 5.00 - 8.00

WILKINS & SHARON:

Broadway 8204 *My Mother's Bible*........... 7.00 - 10.00

FRANK WILKINS:
Broadway 8205 *The Last Mile*............... 8.00 - 12.00
"DAD" WILLIAMS:
Brunswick 306 *Money Musk*................. 10.00 - 15.00
HANK WILLIAMS:
(Note: Some issues on MGM label are credited as by
  LUKE THE DRIFTER.)
MGM 10033, 10073, 10124, 10171, 10212, 10226,
  10271...................... 4.00 - 7.00
  10328, 10352, 10832.................... 3.00 - 5.00
  10401, 10434, 10461, 01506, 01560, 10609, 10645,
  10696, 10760, 10813, 10904, 10961, 11000,
  11054, 11100, 11160, 11202, 11283, 11318,
  11366, 11416.................... 4.00 - 7.00
  11479, 11533, 11574, 11628, 11707, 11768, 11861 4.00 - 8.00
  11975 *Message To My Mother*............. 5.00 - 8.00
  12029 *Alone And Forsaken*............... 6.00 - 10.00
  12077 *Someday You'll Call My Name*....... 7.00 - 10.00
  12127 *Thank God*...................... 7.00 - 10.00
  12185 *Thy Burdens Are Greater Than Mine*.. 7.00 - 10.00
  12244 *I Wish I Had A Nickel*............. 8.00 - 12.00
(Note: Early issues, to about –10401, designated
  "Metrolite," are later pressings; little difference in
  premium between the "original" and subsequent
  pressings exist.)
Sterling 201 *Never Again (Will I Knock On Your
  Door)*.................... 75.00 - 100.00
  204 *Wealth Won't Save Your Soul*......... 75.00 - 100.00
  208 *I Don't Care (If Tomorrow Never Comes)*. 75.00 - 100.00
  210 *Pan American*...................... 50.00 - 80.00
MARC WILLIAMS:
Brunswick 240 *Willie The Weeper*........... 8.00 - 12.00
  244 *The Cowboy's Dream*............... 8.00 - 12.00
  269 *Jesse James*...................... 8.00 - 12.00
  304 *Sam Bass*...................... 8.00 - 12.00
  377 *The Cowboy's Last Wish*............... 8.00 - 12.00
  430 *Cowboy Jack*...................... 8.00 - 12.00
  497 *The Dying Ranger*................... 8.00 - 12.00
  544 *Cole Younger*...................... 8.00 - 12.00
  564 *The Boys In Blue*.................. 8.00 - 12.00
Decca 5010 *Roy Bean*................... 7.00 - 10.00
  5011 *Sioux Indians*.................... 7.00 - 10.00
  5012 *Old Montana*................... 7.00 - 10.00
  5106 *Old Chism Trail*................. 5.00 - 8.00
  5196 *When They Changed My Name To A
  Number*.................... 5.00 - 8.00
  5216 *My Blue Heaven*.................... 5.00 - 8.00
  5327 *William And Mary*................. 5.00 - 8.00
Supertone 2051 *The Crepe Upon The Little Cabin
  Door*.................... 7.00 - 10.00
**MARVIN WILLIAMS (THE SUNSHINE
  YODELER):**
Okeh 45467 *Can't Sleep In Your Barn Tonight,
  Mister*.................... 7.00 - 10.00
  45483 *Back Where The Blue Bonnets Grow*.. 7.00 - 10.00
WILLIAMSON BROTHERS & CURRY:
Okeh 45108 *Cumberland Gap*............. 30.00 - 50.00
  45127 *Gonna Die With My Hammer In My Hand* 30.00 - 50.00
  45146 *Lonesome Road Blues*............... 30.00 - 50.00
BOB WILLS & SLEEPY JOHNSON:
Titles, issued on Banner, Melotone, Oriole, Perfect,
  Romeo (all numbered 6-11-58): *Harmony; Smith's
  Reel*.................... 15.00 - 20.00
BOB WILLS & HIS TEXAS PLAYBOYS:
The Antones 501 *Have I Stayed Away Too Long?* 10.00 - 15.00
(Note: Above is limited issue for Bob Wills Fan Club.
  There are others, of like value and interest.)
Columbia, most issues............... 3.00 - 5.00
MGM, most issues............... 3.00 - 5.00
Okeh, most issues............... 3.00 - 6.00
Vocalion 03076 *St. Louis Blues*............. 8.00 - 12.00
  03086 *Mexicali Rose*.................. 8.00 - 12.00
  03096 *Osage Stomp*.................... 8.00 - 12.00
  03139 *Black And Blue Rag*............... 8.00 - 12.00
  03173 *Wang Wang Blues*............... 8.00 - 12.00
  03206 *I Ain't Got Nobody*............... 8.00 - 12.00
  03230 *Blue River*.................... 8.00 - 12.00
  03264 *Never No More Blues*............... 8.00 - 12.00
  03295 *Oklahoma Rag*.................. 8.00 - 12.00
  03343 *Trouble In Mind*............... 7.00 - 10.00
  03344 *Basin Street Blues*............... 7.00 - 10.00
  03361 *Fan It*...................... 7.00 - 10.00
  03394 *Steel Guitar Rag*............... 7.00 - 10.00
  03424 *She's Killing Me*............... 7.00 - 10.00
  03451 *Right Or Wrong*............... 7.00 - 10.00
  03492 *Mean Mama Blues*............... 7.00 - 10.00
  03537 *Too Busy*...................... 7.00 - 10.00
  03578 *Swing Blues No. 2*............... 7.00 - 10.00
  03597 *Bleeding Hearted Blues*............. 7.00 - 10.00
  03614 *White Heat*.................... 7.00 - 10.00
  03659 *Rosetta*...................... 7.00 - 10.00
  03693 *The New St. Louis Blues*............. 7.00 - 10.00
  03924 *Maiden's Prayer*................. 6.00 - 10.00
  03977 *Sunbonnet Sue*............... 6.00 - 10.00
  04132 *Black Rider*.................. 6.00 - 10.00
  04184 *Empty Bed Blues*............... 6.00 - 10.00
  04275 *Gambling Polka Dot Blues*......... 6.00 - 10.00
  04325 *Tulsa Stomp*................. 5.00 - 8.00
  04387 *Loveless Love*.................. 5.00 - 8.00
  04439 *Moonlight And Roses*............. 5.00 - 8.00
  04515 *Oh, Lady Be Good*............... 5.00 - 8.00
  04566 *That's What I Like 'Bout The South*... 5.00 - 8.00
  04625 *Whoa, Babe*.................... 5.00 - 8.00
  04755, 04839, 04934, 04999, 05079, 05161, 05228,
  05282.................... 4.00 - 7.00
JOHNNIE LEE WILLIS:
Bullet 696, 700, 710, 711, 717, 721, 724, 726, 737,
  741, 743.................... 3.00 - 6.00
**FRANK WILSON & HIS BLUE RIDGE
  MOUNTAIN TRIO:**
Columbia 15372-D *Katy-Did Waltz*........... 7.00 - 10.00
**JIMMIE WILSON'S CATFISH STRING
  BAND; JIMMIE WILSON:**
Okeh 45019 *Let Me Call You Sweetheart*...... 7.00 - 10.00
  45029 *Over The Waves*................. 7.00 - 10.00
Victor 40163 *Catfish Whiskers*............. 7.00 - 10.00
  40216 *Catfish Medley March*............. 10.00 - 15.00
  40240 *Polecat Creek*............... 10.00 - 15.00
TOMMY WILSON:
Vocalion 5262 *The Sinking Of The Vestris*..... 8.00 - 12.00
JUSTIN WINFIELD:
Gennett 6619 *The New River Train*........... 15.00 - 20.00
  6733 *Say, Darling, Say*............... 20.00 - 30.00
WING'S ROCKY MOUNTAIN RAMBLERS:
Champion 16808 *Jackson County Rag*......... 15.00 - 25.00
  16819 *Whiskers*............... 15.00 - 25.00
  45019 *Ragged Ann*............... 10.00 - 15.00
F. WINGATE:
Supertone 9121 *Sleep, Baby, Sleep*........... 5.00 - 8.00
  9122 *Emmett's Cuckoo Song*............. 5.00 - 8.00
WISE STRING BAND:
Vocalion 5360 *Yellow Dog Blues*............. 10.00 - 15.00
HASKELL WOLFBERGER:
Vocalion 5390 *My Little Girl*................. 8.00 - 12.00
WONDER STATE HARMONISTS:
Vocalion 5275 *Turnip Greens*............... 8.00 - 12.00
  5291 *On The Wing*............... 8.00 - 12.00
  5346 *My Castle On The Nile*............. 8.00 - 12.00
SMOKY WOOD & HIS WOOD CHIPS:
Bluebird 7660, 7729.................... 3.00 - 6.00
JACK WOODCLIFF:
Paramount 3280 *I Wonder If She Cares To See Me
  Now*.................... 15.00 - 25.00

JAKE WOODFIELD:

Crown 3103 *There's A Mother Old And Gray Who Needs Me Know* .... 10.00 - 15.00

WOODIE BROTHERS:

Victor 23579 *Like Likker Better Than Me* ...... 15.00 - 20.00

EPHRIAM WOODIE & THE HENPECKED HUSBANDS:

Columbia 15564-D *Last Gold Dollar* .... 10.00 - 15.00

NORMAN WOODLIEFF:

Gennett 6824 *Brace Up And Be A Man* .... 15.00 - 25.00

FRANK WOODS:

Okeh—*Canadian Husking Bee/Money Musk* .... ———

LAWRENCE WOODS:

Champion 16517 *The Cyclone Of Rycove* ...... 15.00 - 20.00

SHEB WOOLEY (& THE CALUMET INDIANS):

Blue Bonnet 124 *Lazy Mazy* .... 7.00 - 10.00

125 *Peeping Through The Key Hole* .... 7.00 - 10.00

126 *Your Papa Ain't Steppin' Anymore* ...... 7.00 - 10.00

Bullet 603 *Oklahoma Honky-Tonk Gal* .... 7.00 - 10.00

KYLE WOOTEN:

Okeh 45511 *Lumber Camp Blues* .... 15.00 - 20.00

45526 *Choking Blues* .... 15.00 - 20.00

WORKMAN, RAMSEY & WOLFE:

Gennett 6659 *The South Salon Quadrille* .... 10.00 - 15.00

W O W O DOWN HOMERS: (See also THE DOWN HOMERS)

Vogue 786 *Boogie Woogie Yodel* .... 12.00 - 18.00

WRIGHT & McNEW (THE HOOSIER HAWAIIANS):

Champion 16336 *The Utah Trail* .... 15.00 - 20.00

EARL WRIGHT (Acc. by THE ARKANSAS CORN DODGERS):

Champion 16382 *My Ozark Mountain Home* ... 15.00 - 20.00

WYATT & BRANDON:

Columbia 15523-D *Evalina* .... 10.00 - 15.00

WYOMING COWBOY (CHARLES BAKER):

Champion 16724 *Utah Carroll* .... 12.00 - 18.00

16737 *Curly Joe* .... 12.00 - 18.00

45044, 45052 .... 4.00 - 7.00

IRA & EUGENE YATES:

Columbia 15581-D *Sarah Jane* .... 10.00 - 15.00

JIMMY YATES' BOLL WEEVILS:

Victor 21723 *Smiles* .... 10.00 - 15.00

40065 *Bloody War* .... 10.00 - 15.00

YELLOW JACKETS:

Champion 16070 *Heel And Toe Polka* .... 8.00 - 12.00

16161 *Medley* .... 8.00 - 12.00

Gennett 7262 *Medley* .... 10.00 - 15.00

YODELING TWINS (GARNER ECKLER & ROLAND GAINES):

Champion 16723 *Mountain Rangers Lullaby* .... 10.00 - 15.00

16747 *Moonlight And Skies* .... 10.00 - 15.00

YOUNG BROTHERS TENNESSEE BAND:

Columbia 15219-D *Are You From Dixie?* ...... 8.00 - 12.00

BUDDY YOUNG'S KENTUCKIANS:

Superior 2519 *Fire On The Mountain* .... 15.00 - 20.00

2655 *Eighth Of January* .... 15.00 - 20.00

2731 *Rocky Mountain Goat* .... 15.00 - 20.00

CLARENCE YOUNG:

Champion 15550 *The Lonely Village Churchyard* 10.00 - 15.00

15582 *Yodelin' Daddy Blues* .... 10.00 - 15.00

15924 *Little Pal* .... 10.00 - 15.00

15991 *That's A Plenty* .... 10.00 - 15.00

JACKSON YOUNG:

Champion 15318 *Take Me Back To The Sweet Sunny South* .... 8.00 - 12.00

15333 *I Know My Name Is There* .... 7.00 - 10.00

JESS YOUNG'S TENNESSEE BAND:

Columbia 15338-D *Fiddle Up* .... 10.00 - 15.00

15400-D *Sweet Bunch Of Daisies* .... 8.00 - 12.00

15431-D *Lovin' Henry* .... 10.00 - 15.00

15493-D *Old Weary Blues* .... 15.00 - 20.00

ZACK & GLENN:

Okeh 45212 *The Gambler's Lament* .... 4.00 - 7.00

45240 *Love's Old Sweet Song* .... 4.00 - 7.00

ZORA & THE HOMETOWNERS:

Decca 5459, 5460 .... 3.00 - 6.00

RHYTHM & BLUES; ROCK & ROLL; ROCKABILLY; BLUES; ETC.
1950s through Early 1960s

All records in this section are 45 rpm unless otherwise indicated. Albums and Extended-Play records are denoted by (LP) or (EP) between the name of the label and the record/catalog number. LPs and EPs must be in their original jackets; LPs and EPs lacking jackets or having damaged or defaced jackets are worth substantially less than the prices listed (and may, in fact, be virtually unsalable in many cases).

Collectors of 1950s records are particularly fussy about labels. The color, logo or style of type may distinguish first from subsequent pressings. An effort has been to designate, where repressings involving label variations are notorious, the label color (or other determinant) of the original or earliest pressing. In addition, the presence of writing, stickers, tears, or other damage to labels detracts from desirability and value moreso than with earlier 78 rpm records.

Although most of the records listed in this section are 45RPM, LPs and EPs, selected 78 RPM records are listed. These are the 78 RPM counterparts (having the same label and catalog/record number) of big-selling 45 RPM rock and roll hits of the late 1950s. Such records, common and of minimal value as 45s (and therefore not listed herein), are often quite scarce as 78s. By the late 1950s, the process of phasing out 78s in favor of 45s had nearly concluded. The major companies discontinued 78s in 1957-1958; some smaller labels continued to produce 78s as late as 1960. The market for these "late 78s" is in its formative stage, and prices are necessarily speculative. The greatly increased demand for these records parallels the rise in popularity of antique 78 rpm jukeboxes, whose owners often seek to fill them with 1950s oldies. But they are also the focus of increasing attention by record collectors. Perhaps the listing of "late 78s" will be greatly expanded as interested collectors discover additional (and even later!) 78s.

While the "late 78s" may be worth more than their 45 rpm counterparts, the opposite is generally true of records from the early to mid-50s. During this period, 45s, being relatively new, had not yet supplanted 78s, and often were issued in smaller quantities than 78s. This is particularly true of Rhythm and Blues, Blues, and Country records, whose pur-purchasers were among the last to discard their old 78s and record players in favor of the new format. Thus, for most of the records listed is this section, a 78 RPM copy would be worth less than its 45 RPM counterpart.

Readers will note the presence of a number of incomplete listings which lack label, catalog/record number, title, or price. These records are deemed worthy of inclusion notwithstanding missing information due to their having appeared in want lists or auction lists of knowledgeable collectors and dealers. It is expected that collectors will supply some of the missing information, or in some cases will advise the deletion of a record, in time for a fourth edition of this book.

THE ACADEMICS:
Ancho 101 *Too Good To Be True*	5.00 -	8.00
103 *Darla, My Darling*	5.00 -	8.00

THE ACCENTS:
Brunswick 55100 *Wiggle Wiggle*	3.00 -	5.00
55100 *Wiggle Wiggle* (78 RPM)	10.00 -	15.00
55123 *Ching A Ling*	3.00 -	5.00

JOHNNY ACE:
Duke (EP) *80 Memorial Album; (EP) 81*	8.00 -	12.00
(LP) *70 (10-inch)*	20.00 -	30.00
(LP) DLP 71 *Memorial Album*	10.00 -	15.00
102 *My Song*	10.00 -	15.00
107 *Cross My Heart*	7.00 -	10.00
112 *The Clock*	7.00 -	10.00
118 *Saving My Love For You*	7.00 -	10.00
128 *Please Forgive ME*	5.00 -	8.00
136 *Pledging My Love*	5.00 -	8.00
144 *Anymore*	4.00 -	7.00
148 *So Lonely*	4.00 -	7.00
Flair 1015 *Midnight Hours Journey*	8.00 -	12.00

SONNY ACE:
TNT 153 *If My Teardrops Could Talk*	4.00 -	8.00

ACORNS:
Unart 2006, 2015	3.00 -	5.00

ROY ACUFF:
Capitol (LP) T-617	8.00 -	12.00
Columbia (LP) 9004 (10") *Songs Of The Smoky Mountains*	10.00 -	15.00
(LP) 9010 (10") *Old Time Barn Dance*	10.00 -	15.00
Harmony (LP) 7082 *Great Speckled Bird*	7.00 -	10.00
MGM (LP) 3707 *Favorite Hymns*	5.00 -	8.00

ART ADAMS:
Cherry 1005 *Rock Crazy Baby*	20.00 -	30.00

FAYE ADAMS:
Herald 416, 444, 457, 512	4.00 -	7.00
Warwick (LP) 2031 *Shake A Hand*	10.00 -	15.00

BILLY ADAMS (& THE ROCK-A-TEERS):
Decca 30724 *Baby I'm Bugged*	7.00 -	10.00
Dot 15689 *You Heard Me Knocking*	8.00 -	12.00
Nau-Voo 805 *That's My Baby*	10.00 -	15.00

CHARLIE ADAMS:
Columbia 21239, 21355	5.00 -	8.00
21524 *Black Land Blues*	7.00 -	10.00
Decca 46335, 46358, 46373	6.00 -	10.00

WOODROW ADAMS (& THE BOOGIE BLUES BLASTERS/THE THREE B'S):
Checker 757 *Pretty Baby Blues*	15.00 -	25.00
Meteor 5018 *Wine Head Woman* (Red Label)	25.00 -	40.00

ADELPHIS:
Rim 2022 *Shine Again*	4.00 -	7.00

THE ADMIRALS:
King 4772 *Left With A Broken Heart*	20.00 -	30.00
4782 *Close Your Eyes*	20.00 -	30.00

ADMIRAL TONES:
Felsted 8563 *Rocksville, Pa.*	5.00 -	8.00

THE ADVENTURERS:
Columbia 42227 *Rock And Roll Uprising*	7.00 -	10.00

AGGIE DUKES:
Aladdin 3364 *Swing Low Sweet Cadillac*	———

JIM AKINS:
Marlo 1517 *Floating On A Cloud*	5.00 -	8.00

THE ALADDINS:
Aladdin 3275 *Cry Cry Baby*	15.00 -	20.00
3298 *I Had Dream Last Night*	20.00 -	30.00
3314 *All Of My Life*	20.00 -	30.00

STEVE ALAIMO & THE RED COATS:

Lifetime 6112 *The Girl Can't Help It* . . . .   7.00 -   10.00
Marlin 6064 *I Want You To Love Me* . . . .   5.00 -   8.00

DENNI ALAN:
Academy 434 *Turn-A-Bout Date* . . . .   15.00 -   20.00

MEL ALBERT:
Apollo 530 *Sugar Plum* . . . .   8.00 -   12.00

ANNIE ALFORD:
Groove 0172 *It's Heavenly* . . . .   15.00 -   20.00

THE ALGERS:
Nothern 3730 *Heavenly Father* . . . .   10.00 -   15.00

BILLY ALLEN & THE BACK BEATS:
Imperial 5500 *Please Give Me Something* . . . . . .   7.00 -   10.00

CHARLIE ALLEN:
Portrait 107 *Wheelin' And Dealin'* . . . .   7.00 -   10.00

CONNIE ALLEN:
King 4528 *Rocket 69* . . . .   8.00 -   12.00

DANNY ALLEN:
Valley 101 *Teenage Blues* . . . .   5.00 -   8.00

HAROLD ALLEN:
Mar Vel 1200 *Honky Tonkin Women* . . . .   10.00 -   15.00
1021 *If You Were Mine Again* . . . .   10.00 -   15.00

LEE ALLEN:
Ember (LP) ELP 200 *Walkin' With Mr. Lee* . . . . .   15.00 -   20.00

MILTON ALLEN:
RCA Victor 6994 *Just Look, Don't Touch* . . . . . .   7.00 -   10.00
7116 *Don't Bug Me Baby* . . . .   4.00 -   7.00
Robin 61824 *Anthing Goes* . . . .   5.00 -   8.00

RAY ALLEN:
Blast (LP) 6004 *Tribute To Six* . . . .   15.00 -   20.00

REX ALLEN:
Decca (LP) 8402 *Under Western Skies* . . . .   8.00 -   12.00
30674 *Knock Knock Rattle* . . . .   5.00 -   8.00

RONNIE ALLEN:
San 208 *Juvenile Delinquent* . . . .   7.00 -   10.00
209 *High School Love* . . . .   8.00 -   12.00
300 *Gonna Get My Baby* . . . .   5.00 -   8.00

TONY ALLEN (& THE
    CHAMPS/TWILIGHTERS):
(See also THE CHIMES)
Bethlehem 3002 *Just Like Before* . . . .   5.00 -   8.00
Crown (LP) CLP 5231 *Rock And Roll with* . . . . .   15.00 -   20.00
Dig 109 *I Found An Angel* . . . .   10.00 -   15.00
Kent 364 *Dreamin'* . . . .   ———
Ultra 104 *It Hurts Me So* . . . .   5.00 -   8.00

JOE ALLISON:
Dot 15714 *Baby Doll* . . . .   5.00 -   8.00

"ALL STAR ROCK & ROLL REVUE":
King (LP) 513 (various artists) . . . .   20.00 -   30.00

"ALL TIME COUNTRY & HILLBILLY
    FAVORITES":
Capitol (LP) 9103, 9107, (10") . . . .   8.00 -   12.00

"ALL TIME COUNTRY & WESTERN HITS":
King (LP) 537 . . . .   8.00 -   12.00

HERSCHEL ALMOND:
Ace 558 *Let's Get It On* . . . .   10.00 -   15.00

LUCKY JOE ALMOND:
Trumpet 199 *Rock Me* . . . .   9.00 -   12.00
221 *Gonna Roll And Rock* . . . .   9.00 -   12.00

HENRY ALSTON:
Skyline 551 *Once In A Beautiful Lifetime* . . . .   7.00 -   10.00

ALTON & THE FLAMES:
Dutchess 1568 *Nothing Sweeter* . . . .   8.00 -   12.00

ALVANS:
May 102 *What Can It Be?* . . . .   5.00 -   8.00

THE AMBASSADORS:
Bon 001 *Power Of Love* . . . .   8.00 -   12.00
Timely 1001 *Darling, I'm Sorry* . . . .   8.00 -   12.00

THE AMBERS:
Ebb 142 *Never Let You Go* . . . .   7.00 -   10.00

JOHNNY AMELIO:
Blue Moon 408 *Jo-Ann, Jo-Ann* . . . .   25.00 -   40.00

AMERICAN BEETLES:
Mammoth 102 *You're Getting To Me* . . . .   5.00 -   8.00

DOUG AMERSON:
IntraState 25 *Bop Man Bop* . . . .   25.00 -   35.00

ANDY ANDERSON (& THE
    DAWNBREAKERS/ROLLING STONES):
Apollo 535 *You Shake Me Up* . . . .   15.00 -   20.00
Century 601 *Gimme A Lock-A Yo' Hair* . . . .   15.00 -   20.00
602 *Gonna Sit Right Down And Cry* . . . .   15.00 -   20.00
Felsted 8508 *I-I-I- Love You* . . . .   5.00 -   8.00

BILL ANDERSON:
TNT 9015 *City Lights* . . . .   15.00 -   20.00

ELTON ANDERSON:
Trey 1002 *Wanta Come Back Home* . . . .   5.00 -   8.00
Vin 1001 *Roll On Train* . . . .   3.00 -   5.00*

GENE ANDERSON & THE KEYNOTES:
Top Ten 252 *I've Got It Bad* . . . .   3.00 -   5.00

JIMMY ANDERSON (& HIS JOY JUMPERS):
Excello 2220, 2227, 2257 . . . .   3.00 -   5.00
Zynn 1014 *I Wanna Boogie* . . . .   6.00 -   10.00

DEBBIE ANDREWS (with the MUSKETEERS):
United 144 *Don't Make Me Cry* . . . .   5.00 -   10.00

LEE ANDREWS & THE HEARTS:
Casino 110 *Baby Come Back* . . . .   15.00 -   20.00
Chess 1665 *Long Lonely Nights* . . . .   5.00 -   8.00
Gotham 318 *Bluebird Of Happiness* . . . .   12.00 -   16.00
320 *Lonely Room* . . . .   12.00 -   16.00
321 *Just Suppose* . . . .   12.00 -   16.00
Rainbow 250 *White Cliffs Of Dover* (red plastic) . .   75.00 -   100.00
252 *Maybe You'll Be There* (red plastic) . . . . . .   35.00 -   50.00
259 *The Fairest* . . . .   20.00 -   30.00
Rivera 965 *Maybe You'll Be There* . . . .   75.00 -   100.00
UnArt 151 *MMMaybe You'll Be There* . . . .   5.00 -   8.00

ANDY & THE LIVE WIRES:
Applause 1249 *Maggie* . . . .   7.00 -   10.00

JOHNNY ANGEL:
Excello 2077 *Baby I'm Confessin'* . . . .   10.00 -   15.00

THE ANGELOS:
Tollie 9003 *Bad Motorcycle* . . . .   5.00 -   8.00

THE ANGELS:
Caprice (LP) *And The Angels Sing* . . . .   15.00 -   20.00
Gee 1024 *The Glory Of Love* . . . .   10.00 -   15.00

PAUL ANKA:
ABC Paramount (LP) 240 *Paul Anka* . . . .   10.00 -   15.00
(LP) 296 *My Heart Sings* . . . .   10.00 -   15.00
(LP) 420 *Diana* . . . .   10.00 -   15.00
ABC Paramount (LP) 323, 360, 390, 409 . . . .   9.00 -   12.00
9831 *Diana* (78 RPM) . . . .   15.00 -   20.00
9880 *You Are My Destiny* (78 RPM) . . . .   12.00 -   16.00
RPM 499 *I Confess* . . . .   12.00 -   15.00

PATTI ANN:
Aladdin 3198 *Sorrowful Heart* . . . .   20.00 -   25.00
3280 *Shtiggy Boom* . . . .   8.00 -   12.00

ANNETTE & CECIL NULL:
Epic 9829 *Moment Of Silence* . . . .   ———

THE ANNUALS:
Marconn 1 *Once In A Lifetime* . . . .   15.00 -   20.00

THE ANSWERS:
United 214 *Have No Fear* . . . .   15.00 -   25.00

PAUL ANTHONY:
Roulette 4099 *Bop Bop Bop!* . . . .   4.00 -   7.00

VINCE ANTHONY:
Hilton 0007 *Too Hot To Handle* . . . .   7.00 -   10.00
Viking 1018 *Clarabel* . . . .   7.00 -   10.00

THE APOLLOS:
Harvard 803 *I Love You Darling* . . . .   35.00 -   50.00

DAVE APPELL:
President 1013 *Applejack* . . . .   7.00 -   10.00

THE AQUA-NITES:
Astra 1000, 2001 *Lover Don't You Weep* . . . . . .   8.00 -   12.00

THE AQUATONES:

Fargo 1001, 1005.........................	3.00 -	5.00
(LP) FLP 3001 *The Aquatones Sing*........	35.00 -	50.00

THE ARABIANS:

Carrie 1516 *My One Possession*...............	————	
JAM 3738 *Heaven Sent You*.............	15.00 -	20.00
Magnificent 102 *My Heart Beats Over*......	10.00 -	15.00
114 *Teardrops In The Night*..............	10.00 -	15.00
Teek 4824 *Condition Your Heart*...........	15.00 -	25.00
Twin Star 1018 *Heaven Sent You*..........	15.00 -	25.00

ARCHIBALD:

Imperial 5212 *Great Big Eyes*.............	15.00 -	20.00

ARIST-O-KATS:

Vita 168 *I Don't See Me In Your Eyes*....	10.00 -	15.00

SMOKEY ARMEN:

Peek-A-Boo 102 *Baby What Am I Gonna Do*...	15.00 -	20.00

BILLY BOY ARNOLD:

Cool 103 *Hello Stranger*................	10.00 -	20.00

EDDY ARNOLD:

Camden (LP) 471, 563...................	7.00 -	10.00
RCA Victor (LP) 1111 *Wanderin'*.........	15.00 -	20.00
1223 *All-Time Favorites*.................	10.00 -	15.00
1224 *Anytime*.......................	10.00 -	15.00
1225 *Chapel On The Hill*...............	15.00 -	20.00
1293 *A Dozen Hits*....................	8.00 -	12.00
1377 *A Little On The Lonely Side*.......	10.00 -	15.00
1484 *When They Were Young*..........	10.00 -	15.00
(LP) 3027 (10") *Country Classics*.......	20.00 -	30.00
3031 (10") *All-Time Hits*.............	15.00 -	20.00
3117 (10") *Eddy Arnold*.............	15.00 -	20.00
3230 (10") *An American Institution*......	15.00 -	20.00
3249 (10") *When It's Round-Up Time In Heaven*	15.00 -	20.00
Tops (LP) 1612 *Cowboy Songs Of The West*....	8.00 -	12.00

JACK ARNOLD & THE CHALECOS:

Wildcat W-00018 *Pistol Packing Mama*........	7.00 -	10.00

JAMES ARP:

Vellez 1515 *Let It Rock*....................	10.00 -	15.00

THE ARROGANTS:

Lute 6226 *Canadian Sunset*................	7.00 -	10.00

THE ARROWS:

Flash 132 *Annie Mae*...................	10.00 -	15.00
Hugo 11172 *No Other Arms*.............	10.00 -	15.00

RICHIE ARTHUR:

Platter—*Walkin' Down A Lonesome Road*.....	7.00 -	10.00

THE ARTISTICS:

S & G—*One Way*......................	8.00 -	12.00

LITTLE JOE ARTWOOD:

Kingsport 105 *Cue Ball Blues*..............	10.00 -	15.00

THE ASCOTS:

Ace 650 *Perfect Love*.....................	8.00 -	12.00
J & S 1628/1629 *What Love Can Do*......	10.00 -	15.00

JOHN ASHLEY:

Dot 15775 *Born To Rock*..................	8.00 -	12.00

BOB ATCHER:

Columbia (LP) 9006 (10") *Early American Folksongs*	10.00 -	15.00
(LP) 9013 (10") *Songs Of The Saddle*.........	10.00 -	15.00

CHUCK ATHA:

Fox 1169 *Just Me And My Baby*...........	15.00 -	20.00

CHET ATKINS:

RCA Victor (LP) 1090 *Session*...........	15.00 -	20.00
1197 *In Three Dimensions*...........	15.00 -	20.00
1236 *Stringin' Along*................	15.00 -	20.00
1383 *Finger—Style Guitar*...........	15.00 -	20.00
1544 *At Home*.....................	12.00 -	16.00
1577 *Hi-Fi In Focus*................	12.00 -	16.00
(LP) 3079 (10") *Galloping Guitar*.......	15.00 -	20.00
3163 (10") *Stringin' Along*............	12.00 -	16.00

DAVE ATKINS AND HIS OFFBEATS:

Back Beat 511 *Shake—Kum—Down*..........	5.00 -	8.00

THE ATLANTICS:

Linda 107 *Remember The Night*...........	4.00 -	7.00

AUDREY:

Plus 104 *Dear Elvis*..................	10.00 -	15.00

LITTLE AUGIE AUSTIN (& THE CHROMATICS):

Brunswick 55080 *My Heart Let Me Be Free*....	15.00 -	25.00
Pontiac 101 *I Thank My Lucky Star*.........	————	

BILLY AUSTIN & THE HEARTS:

Apollo 444 *Night Has Gone*.................	80.00 -	100.00

DON AUSTIN & THE SENSATIONAL DELLOS:

U-C 1031 *Why Did You Leave Me*...........	60.00 -	90.00
Mida 106 *So Shy*......................	10.00 -	15.00
109 *So Don't Go*....................	20.00 -	30.00

GENE AUTRY:

Columbia (LP) 9001 (10") *Western Classics*.....	8.00 -	12.00
(LP) 9002 (10") *Western Classics, Vol 2*......	8.00 -	12.00

FRANKIE AVALON:

Chancellor 1011 *De De Dinah* (78 RPM)......	15.00 -	20.00
(LP) 5001 *Frankie Avalaon*................	10.00 -	15.00
(LP) 5002 *Young Frankie Avalon*...........	10.00 -	15.00
(LP) 5004, 5009, 5011.................	8.00 -	12.00
(LP) 5022, 5027, 5031, 5032..........	8.00 -	12.00

THE AVALONS:

Casion 108 *You Do Something To Me*.....	15.00 -	20.00
Grove 0141 *Chains Around My Heart*........	25.00 -	35.00
0174 *It's Funny But It's True*..............	25.00 -	35.00
NPC 302 *Begin The Beguine*.........	5.00 -	8.00
UnArt 2007 *Heart's Desire*..............	8.00 -	12.00

THE AVONS:

Groove 0039 *Whatever Happened To Our Love*.	10.00 -	15.00
Hull 717 (black label) *Our Love Will Never End*.	15.00 -	20.00
717 (orange label) *Our Love Will Never End*..	8.00 -	12.00
722, 726, 728, 731, 754................	7.00 -	12.00
(LP) HLP *The Avons*..................	50.00 -	75.00

BABY DEE:

MGM 1179 *Hold The Light For Me*........	7.00 -	10.00

THE BACHELORS:

Earl 101 *Delores*......................	15.00 -	30.00
102 *Tell Me Now*..................	15.00 -	30.00

GAR BACON:

Baton 248 *There's Gonna Be Rocking Tonight*..	5.00 -	8.00

SHORTY BACON:

Ozark 1237 *Fire Of Love*..................	7.00 -	10.00

JACK BAILEY:

Ford 105 *Oh What Love Is*...............	7.00 -	10.00

LITTLE MARIE BAILEY:

Excello 2007 *Brownskin Woman Blues*........	10.00 -	15.00
2016 *My Baby's Blues*...............	10.00 -	15.00

MORRIS BAILEY:

Bailey 500 *Calendar Hanging On The Wall*.....	8.00 -	12.00

CHARLIE BAKER:

Mun Rab 106 *You Crack Me Up*............	10.00 -	15.00

DONNY BAKER:

Rainbow 219 *Drinking Wine Spo-Dee-O-Dee*....	15.00 -	20.00

LAVERNE BAKER:

Atlantic (EP) 566, 588................	10.00 -	15.00
1004, 1030, 1047...................	4.00 -	8.00
(LP) 1281 *Sings Bessie Smith*.............	15.00 -	20.00
(LP) 8007 *Lavern Baker*...............	15.00 -	20.00
(LP) 8030 *Blues Ballads*...............	15.00 -	20.00
(LP) 8036 *Precious Memories*...........	15.00 -	20.00
(LP) 8071 *See See Rider*...............	15.00 -	20.00
King 4556 *Trying*....................	8.00 -	12.00

RONNIE BAKER & THE DELTONES:

Laurie 3128 *My Story*..................	5.00 -	8.00

WILLIE BAKER:

DeLuxe 6023 *Before She Leaves Town*........	20.00 -	35.00
Rockin' 527 *Before She Leaves Town*........	20.00 -	35.00

EARL BALL:

Parthenon 101 *Party Of One*.............	7.00 -	10.00

THE BALLADS:

Franwil 5028 *Before You Fall In Love*........	10.00 -	15.00
Ron-Cris 1003 *Somehow*.................	8.00 -	12.00
Veltone 1738 *I Hope I Never Fall In Love*.....	10.00 -	15.00

HANK BALLARD (& THE MIDNIGHTERS):
(See THE MIDNIGHTERS)

Federal (EP) 333, 435, 451	7.00 -	10.00
King (LP) 541 *Their Greatest Juke Box Hits*	25.00 -	35.00
581 *Hank Ballard & The Midnighters*	25.00 -	35.00
(LP) 618, 674, 700, 748, 759, 781, 793	9.00 -	15.00

JERRY BALLARD:

Skippy 120 *Pinch Me*	5.00 -	8.00

THE BALTINEERS:

Teenage 1000 *Moments Like This*	20.00 -	30.00
1002 *Tears In My Eyes*	20.00 -	30.00

JAMES BANISTER & HIS COMBO:

States 141 *Gold Digger*	20.00 -	30.00

DICK BANKS:

Liberty 55145 *Dirty Dog*	10.00 -	15.00

OTIS BANKS:

Bow 304 *She's My Baby*	7.00 -	10.00

THE BANNERS:

MGM 12810 *My Own True Love*	8.00 -	12.00
12862 *Fortune Teller*	8.00 -	12.00

DON BARBER & THE DUKES:

Personality 3505 *Henrietta*	5.00 -	8.00

GLENN BARBER:

D 1098 *Go Home Letter*	5.00 -	8.00
Pic1 143 *I Created A Monster*	8.00 -	12.00
Starday 166 *Ice Water*	10.00 -	15.00
196 *Poor Man's Baby*	8.00 -	12.00
249 *Shadow My Baby*	8.00 -	12.00

PHIL BARCLAY & THE SLIDERS:

Doke 101 *Young Long John*	20.00 -	30.00
102 *I Love 'Em All*	20.00 -	30.00

BOBBY BARE:

Fraternity 861 *That's Where I Want To Be*	4.00 -	6.00

BARKER BROS:

Kent 302 *Hey Little Mama*	7.00 -	10.00

DELBERT BARKER:

King 4951 *No Good Robin Hood*	20.00 -	30.00

AL BARKLE:

M&M 4041 *Jumpin' From Six To Six*	15.00 -	20.00

DEAN BARLOW (featured with THE CRICKETS, which also see):

Jay-Dee 799, 803	4.00 -	7.00

DEAN BARLOW & THE MONTEREYS:

Onyx 513 *Dearest One*	10.00 -	15.00

JUKE BOY BARNER:

Irma 111 *Well Baby*	15.00 -	20.00

BENNY BARNES:

D 1052 *Happy Little Blue Bird*	5.00 -	8.00
Starday 401 *You Gotta Pay*	10.00 -	15.00

DAVID BARNES:

San 302 *Lovin' On My Mind*	10.00 -	15.00

JIMMY BARNES & THE GIBRALTARS:

Gibraltar 102 *Be Careful With My Love*	5.00 -	8.00

THE BARONS:

Decca (EP) ED-2400	10.00 -	15.00
29293 *Forget About Me*	15.00 -	20.00
48323 *A Year And A Day*	15.00 -	20.00
Imperial 5343 *Eternally*	10.00 -	15.00
5359, 5370, 5383, 5397	7.00 -	10.00
Spartan 400 *I've Been Hurt*	5.00 -	8.00

CHUCK BARR & THE ROCKABILLIES:

Elsan 100 *Susie Or Mary Lou*	8.00 -	12.00

THE BARRETT SINGERS:

Reserve 124 *Lonesome Road*	10.00 -	15.00

HUGH BARRETT:

Lucky Four 1015 *Devil's Love*	15.00 -	20.00

RICHARD BARRETT:

Seville 104 *Dream On*	7.00 -	10.00

BILLY BARRIX:

Chess 1662 *Cool Off Baby*	15.00 -	20.00

LONNIE BARRON:

Sage 230 *Teenage Queen*	8.00 -	12.00

DAVE BARRY & SARA BERNER:

RPM 469 *Out Of This World Wity Flying Saucers*	5.00 -	8.00

JAY BARRY:

ABC Paramount 10226 *Love Spell*	7.00 -	10.00

JEFF BARRY:

RCA Victor 7477 *It's Called Rock And Roll*	7.00 -	10.00
7797 *Lonely Lips*	7.00 -	10.00
7821 *All You Need Is A Quarter*	7.00 -	10.00

JOE BARRY:

Jin 144, 152	4.00 -	7.00

TEDDY BART:

Felsted 8514 *Headin' For A Weddin'*	———	

DAVE BARTHOLOMEW:

Bayou 005 *Country Gal*	10.00 -	15.00
Imperial 5322 *Another Mule*	7.00 -	10.00
(LP) 9162 *Fats Domino Presents*	10.00 -	15.00
(LP) 9217 *New Orleans House Party*	10.00 -	15.00

BART BARTON:

E & M 1651 *Ain't I'm A Mess*	10.00 -	15.00

BILLY (BOY) BARTON:

Gulf Reef 1001 *Monkey Business*	4.00 -	7.00
King 1478 *Do You Love Me*	4.00 -	7.00
Radio 117 *Doorway To Heaven*	4.00 -	6.00
Sims—*Even Steven*	5.00 -	8.00
Vidor 1007 *Crazy Lover*	7.00 -	10.00

DICK BARTON & THE REBELS:

Anthem 61712 *I Get The Blues*	15.00 -	20.00

OTTO BASH with THE RHYTHM ROCKERS:

Hidus 2008 *My Babe*	8.00 -	12.00

NORVEN BASKERVILLE & THE ADMIRATIONS:

X-tra 100 *Gonna Find My Pretty Baby*	10.00 -	15.00

TONY BASSETT:

Orchid 873 *Rocking Little Mama*	15.00 -	20.00

THE BATCHELORS:

Aladdin 3210 *Can't Help Lovin' You*	15.00 -	20.00

"BATTLE OF THE BLUES":

King (LP) 607, 627, 668	10.00 -	15.00

RAY BATTS:

Bullet—*Wild Man Boogie*	———	
Excello 2028 *Stealin' Sugar*	8.00 -	12.00

DAVE BAUCOM:

Giant 1101 *That'll Be The Day*	10.00 -	15.00

ALLEN BAUM:

Red Robin 124 *My Kinda Woman*	25.00 -	35.00

THE BAY BOPS:

Coral 61975 *Joanie*	7.00 -	10.00

BILL BEACH:

King 4940 *Peg Pants*	25.00 -	35.00

RUFUS BEACHAM:

Chart 617 *Don't Say You Love Me*	10.00 -	15.00
627 *I Can't Believe*	10.00 -	15.00

THE BEACH BOYS:

Candix 301 *Surfin'*	40.00 -	60.00
301 (same, but bears notation: "Dist. by ERA RECORD SALES, INC.)	20.00 -	35.00
331 *Surfin'*	20.00 -	35.00
Capitol (Custom) KFWB Promotional Souvenir *Spirit Of America*	40.00 -	60.00
SXA-1981 (7-inch, for juke boxes) *Surfer Girl* . . .	*15.00 -*	*25.00*
DU 2269 (7-inch, for juke boxes) *The Beach Boys Today*	20.00 -	30.00
PRO 2937 (Courtesy Of Downtown Salt Lake City Stores) *Salt Lake City*	75.00 -	100.00
(EP) PRO 2993 *Barbara Ann + 3*	20.00 -	30.00
4880 *Ten Little Indians*	5.00 -	8.00
(Note: Picture Sleeves for Cap. 4880 are scarce.)		
Capitol (EP) 5267 *4 by the Beach Boys*	15.00 -	20.00
"X" 301 *Surfin'*	75.00 -	100.00

DEAN BEARD (WITH THE CREW CATS/FOX FOUR SEVENS):

Atlantic 1137 *Rakin' And Scrapin'*	8.00 -	12.00

Atlantic 1137 *Rakin' And Scrapin' (78 RPM)*...	10.00 -	20.00
1162 *Party Party*.................	8.00 -	12.00
1182 *Hold Me Close*.................	8.00 -	12.00
Edmoral 1011 *Rakin' And Scrapin'*...........	15.00 -	25.00
Fox 405 *Red Rover*..................	15.00 -	20.00
408 *Sing Sing Sing*...............	15.00 -	20.00
Sangelo 1 *Party Party*..............	15.00 -	20.00

JIMMY BEASLEY:

Crown (LP) CLP 5014 *The Fabulous*.........	15.00 -	20.00

GOOD ROCKIN' (SAM) BEASLEY: (see also KID KING'S COMBO)

Excello 2011 *Happy Go Lucky*..............	10.00 -	15.00
2051 *Now Listen Baby*..................	5.00 -	8.00

THE BEATLES:

Atco (LP) 169 *Ain't She Sweet*...........	15.00 -	25.00
6302 *Sweet Georgia Brown*...............	5.00 -	8.00
6302 (DJ) *Sweet Georgia Brown*...........	15.00 -	20.00
6308 (DJ) *Ain't She Sweet*...............	15.00 -	20.00
(Note: Picture sleeve to Atco 6308 is very scarce; originals have sold for as much as $75.00.)		
Capitol SXA 2047 (7-inch, 33⅓ rpm) *Meet The Beatles*.......................	25.00 -	40.00
2056 (DJ) *Hello Goodbye*.................	15.00 -	20.00
SXA 2080 (7-inch, 33⅓ rpm) *Beatles Second Album*.......................	20.00 -	30.00
SXAS 2108 (7-inch, 33⅓ rpm) *Something New*	25.00 -	50.00
(EP) EAP 2121 *Four By The Beatles*.......	20.00 -	40.00
2138 (DJ) *Lady Madonna*.................	15.00 -	20.00
(LP) 2553 *Yesterday and Today* ("Butcher" cover: Beatles are sitting among doll parts and pieces of raw meat. Withdrawn shortly after issue and replaced with a more tasteful depiction of the Beatles gathered around a trunk.)...........	150.00 -	250.00
(LP) 2553 *Yesterday and Today* (with new cover pasted over "Butcher" cover, traces of which are visible).......................	75.00 -	100.00
2637 (DJ) *KFW Beatles*.................	75.00 -	100.00
5150 *Can't Buy Me Love* Picture Sleeve is quite scarce (the record is of negligible value.)		
(EP) EPR 5365 *4 by the Beatles*...........	8.00 -	12.00
5810 (DJ) *Penny Lane*.................	20.00 -	30.00
5964 (DJ) *All You Need Is Love*...........	15.00 -	20.00
Clarion (LP) 601 *The Amazing Beatles And Other Great English Group Sounds*...............	10.00 -	15.00
MGM 13213 (DJ) *My Bonnie*................	20.00 -	30.00
13227 (DJ) *Why*.................	20.00 -	30.00
(Note: Picture Sleeve for MGM 13227 is scarce)		
Radio Pulsebeat (LP) *The American Tour With Ed Rudy*.......................	20.00 -	30.00
#Swan 4152 (white label, red printing, without legend *Don't Drop Out*) *She Loves You*...........	25.00 -	40.00
Tollie 9008 (DJ) *Love Me Do*..............	20.00 -	30.00
Vee Jay 498 (DJ) *Love Me Do*..............	20.00 -	30.00
498 (DJ) *Please Please Me*...............	75.00 -	100.00
#498 *Please Please Me*...............	40.00 -	100.00
522 (DJ) *From Me To You*...............	15.00 -	20.00
581 (DJ) *Please Please Me*...............	15.00 -	25.00
(Note: Picture sleeve for Vee Jay 581 is scarce.)		
587 (DJ) *Do You Want To Know A Secret)*..	20.00 -	30.00
(Note: Picture sleeve for 587 is scarce.)		
(EP) 1-903 *Souvenir Of Their Visit To America*	20.00 -	30.00
#(LP) 1062 *Introducing The Beatles* Mono: reverse of jacket depicts "other fine albums of significant interest".......................	25.00 -	40.00
#(LP) 1062 same, but Stereophonic...........	50.00 -	75.00
#(LP) 1062 same, but reverse of jacket lists song titles in columns; Stereophonic.................	30.00 -	50.00
(LP) 1085 *The Beatles & Frank Ifield* (picture of Beatles on cover; not to be confused with nominally-valued version having a drawing of an old man on the cover) Mono.................	75.00 -	150.00

(LP) 1085 same as preceding, but stereo........	150.00 -	300.00

(Note: A sealed copy of this LP supposedly sold for $1000.00 or more.)

#Note: These records (and others) occur with seemingly minute variations in label and/or covers, which may affect prices drastically. One interesting variation of Vee Jay 498 has the group designated as "THE BEATTLES."

IMPORTANT: The generally applicable caveat concerning bootlegs and reissues deserves particular emphasis in the case of the BEATLES' records. Also note that in many instances picture sleeves are worth far more than the record. Mentioned above are some of the most sought-after sleeves, but there are others which, although of lesser scarcity and value, are desirable (even where the record, unlisted here, is of nominal value). Finally, where a record listed is a promotional copy ("DJ" after record number), it should not be inferred that the regular issue is of comparable value; the regular issue, unless it is also listed, is common and of little value.

THE BEATNICKS:

Key-Lock 913 *Blue Angel*..................	10.00 -	15.00

E.C. BEATTY:

Colonial 7009 *Little Blue Eyes*.............	5.00 -	8.00

THE BEAU-MARKS:

Shad 5021 *'Cause We're In Love*..............	5.00 -	8.00

THE BEAVERS:

Brunswick 65018 *If You See Tears In My Eyes*.	50.00 -	75.00
65026 *I'd Rather Be Wrong Than Blue*......	50.00 -	75.00

STAN BEAVERS:

Petal —*I Got A Rocket In My Pocket*.........	———	

THE BEES:

Imperial 5314 *Toy Bell*..................	25.00 -	35.00

THE BEL-AIRES/BELAIRES:

Flip 303 *This Paradise*..................	8.00 -	12.00
Raft 604 *Are You My Girl*..................	5.00 -	8.00

CARL BELEW:

Decca 30947 *Cool Gator Shoes*...............	7.00 -	10.00

BILL BELL & THE FOUR UNKNOWNS:

Mida 112 *Little Bitty Girl*...............	7.00 -	10.00

CARL BELL & THE NOVAIRS:

Laurie 3014 *Birth of The Beat*...............	5.00 -	8.00

DWAIN BELL:

Summit 110 *Rock & Roll On A Saturday Night*.	50.00 -	75.00

EDDIE/EDDY BELL:

Coed 512 *Countin' The Days*.................	5.00 -	8.00
Mercury 71677 *The Masked Man*.............	7.00 -	10.00

FREDDIE BELL & THE BELL BOYS:

Mercury (LP) 20289 *Rock and Roll*..........	15.00 -	20.00
Teen 101 *Hound Dog* (78 RPM).............	10.00 -	15.00

JOHNNY BELL:

Brunswick 55142 *Flip Flop And Fly*..........	7.00 -	10.00

TOMMY BELL:

ZII 9001 *Swamp Gal*.....................	35.00 -	50.00

THE BEL-LARKS:

Ransom—*A Million And One Dreams*........	15.00 -	20.00

THE BELLS:

Rama 166 *What Can I Tell Her Now*........	15.00 -	20.00

THE BELLTONES:

Grand (blue) 102 *Estelle* (red plastic)..........	100.00 -	200.00

TONY BELLUS:

NRC (LP) LPA 8 *Robbin The Cradle*.......	25.00 -	35.00

THE BELTONES:

Hull 721 *I Talk To My Echo*..............	10.00 -	15.00
Jell 188 *I Want To Be Loved*..............	10.00 -	15.00

THE BELVEDERES:

Baton 217 *Pepper Hot Baby*................	5.00 -	8.00
Lucky Four 1003 *Wage Assignment Blues*......	8.00 -	12.00
Trend 30-009 *Let's Get Married*..........	8.00 -	12.00

THE BELVIDEERS:

Buena Serra 1771 *Walking In The Garden*...... 35.00 - 50.00

JESSE BELVIN:

Cash 1056 *Beware*................. 8.00 - 12.00
J.R.M. 003/004 *Going Away Baby*.......... 7.00 - 10.00
Modern 1005 *Goodnight My Love*.......... 7.00 - 10.00
RCA Victor (LP) 2089................ 10.00 - 15.00
(LP) 2105 *Mr. Easy*.............. 10.00 - 15.00
Specialty 550 *Gone*.................. 5.00 - 8.00
559 *Where's My Girl*.......... 5.00 - 8.00

BOYD BENNETT (& HIS ROCKETS):

King (EP) *Rock And Roll*............ 12.00 - 15.00
(EP) 383 *Rock And Roll*........ 12.00 - 15.00
(LP) 532 *Boyd Bennett*.......... 75.00 - 100.00
(LP) 594 *Boyd Bennett*.......... 50.00 - 75.00
1413 *I've Had Enough*............ 7.00 - 10.00
1432 *You Upset Me Baby*......... 7.00 - 10.00
1275 *Tennessee Rock And Roll*........... 10.00 - 15.00
1494 *My Boy Flat Top*............ 4.00 - 7.00
4903 *Blue Suede Shoes*............ 7.00 - 10.00
4985 *Rockin' Up A Storm*........... 8.00 - 12.00
5094 *Put The Chain On The Door*........ 7.00 - 10.00
5115 *Move*.................. 10.00 - 15.00
Mercury 71479 *Boogie Bear*........... 5.00 - 8.00

JOE BENSON:

DeLuxe 6146 *Rock And Roll Jungle*......... 7.00 - 10.00

BROOK BENTON (& THE SANDMEN):

Camden (LP) 564................. 8.00 - 12.00
Epic (LP) LN-3573 *At His Best*........ 10.00 - 15.00
Mercury (LP) 20421 *It's Just A Matter Of Time*. 10.00 - 15.00
(LP) 20464 *Endlessly*............. 10.00 - 15.00
(LP) 20565 *So Many Ways*......... 8.00 - 12.00
Okeh 7058 *Ooh*................ 10.00 - 15.00
Vik 0311 *A Million Miles From Nowhere*...... 5.00 - 8.00

BUSTER BENTON:

Melloway 20668 *Hole In My Head*........... 7.00 - 10.00

MERV BENTON:

Marvel 401 *Twenty Flight Rock*......... 10.00 - 15.00

WALT BENTON (& THE SNAPPERS):

20th Fox 143 *Big Wheel*................ 15.00 - 20.00

SHIRLEY BERGERON:

Lanor 510 *French Rocking Boogie*........... 10.00 - 15.00

ROD BERNARD (& THE TWISTERS):

Argo 5327 *Pardon Mr. Gordon*......... 7.00 - 10.00
Argo 5327 *Pardon Mr. Gordon* (78 RPM)...... 10.00 - 15.00
5338 *My Life Is A Mystery*.......... 7.00 - 10.00
Jin 105 *Pardon Mr. Gordon*......... 12.00 - 16.00
(LP) 1007 *Rod Bernard*.............. 20.00 - 30.00

THE BERRY CUPS:

Khoury's 710 *Delores Darlin'*.......... 5.00 - 8.00

THE BERRY KIDS:

MGM 12379 *Go, Go, Go, Right Into Town*.... 7.00 - 10.00
MGM 12496 *You're My Teen Age Baby*..... 8.00 - 12.00

CHUCK BERRY:

Chess (LP) 1426 *After School Session*.......... 15.00 - 25.00
(LP) 1432 *One Dozen Berrys*........ 15.00 - 25.00
(LP) 1435 *Chuck Berry Is On Top*....... 15.00 - 25.00
(LP) 1448 *Rockin' At The Hops*......... 15.00 - 25.00
(Note: LPs must have black labels with silver printing.)
1604 *Maybelline* (silver top label)........... 7.00 - 10.00
1610 *Thirty Days* (silver top label)........... 7.00 - 10.00
1615, 1626, 1635, 1645, 1653, 1664 (silver top
label)....................... 5.00 - 8.00
1671, 1683, 1691, 1697, 1700, 1709, 1716, 1722,
1729, 1727, 1747.................. 3.00 - 6.00
1653 *School Day* (78 RPM)........... 7.00 - 10.00
1664 *Oh Baby Doll* (78 RPM)........... 7.00 - 10.00
1671 *Rock & Roll Music* (78 RPM)........ 8.00 - 12.00
1683 *Reeling And Rocking* (78 RPM)........ 8.00 - 12.00
1691 *Johnny B. Goode* (78 RPM)........ 8.00 - 12.00
1697 *Beautiful Belilah* (78 RPM)........ 7.00 - 10.00

1700 *Carol* (78 RPM)..................... 7.00 - 10.00
1709 *Sweet Little Rock And Roll* (78 RPM).. 10.00 - 15.00
1714 *Run, Rudolph, Run* (78 RPM)........ 7.00 - 10.00
1716 *Anthony Boy* (78 RPM)........ 8.00 - 12.00
1722 *Little Queenie* (78 RPM)........ 10.00 - 15.00
1729 *Back In The U.S.A.* (78 RPM)........ 15.00 - 20.00
1737 *Childhood Sweetheart* (78 RPM)........ 8.00 - 12.00
1747 *Let It Rock* (78 RPM)........ 15.00 - 20.00
(EP) 5118 *After School Session*........... 8.00 - 12.00
(EP) 5119 *Rock & Roll Music*........ 8.00 - 12.00
(EP) 5121 *Sweet Little Sixteen*........ 8.00 - 12.00
(EP) 5124 *Pickin' Berries*........ 8.00 - 12.00

LOU BERRY & THE BELL RAVES:

Dreem 1001 *What A Dolly*.......... 50.00 - 75.00
20th Fox 169 *What A Dolly*........ 30.00 - 50.00

MIKE BERRY & THE OUTLAWS:

Coral 62341 *Tribute To Buddy Holly*........ 8.00 - 12.00

RED BERRY & THE BELL RAVES: (See LOU BERRY, above)

RICHARD BERRY (& THE DREAMERS/PHARAOHS):

Crown (LP) 5371 *Richard Berry & The Dreamers* 15.00 - 20.00
Flair 1016, 1055, 1064, 1068............. 6.00 - 10.00
Flip 321 *Louie Louie*.......... 5.00 - 8.00
331, 336.................. 4.00 - 7.00
RPM 448 *Rockin' Man*......... 7.00 - 10.00
452 *I Am Bewildered*.......... 5.00 - 8.00

"THE BEST OF RHYTHM & BLUES":

Jubilee (LP) 1014.................. 15.00 - 20.00

BIG BOPPER:

D 1008 *Chantilly Lace*.......... 20.00 - 30.00
Mercury (LP) 20402 *Chantilly Lace*.......... 35.00 - 50.00
71343 *Chantilly Lace* (78 rpm)........ 25.00 - 40.00
71416, 71451, 71482.............. 5.00 - 8.00

BIG CONNIE:

Groove 0142 *Mumbles Blues*........... 7.00 - 10.00

BIG DADDY:

Gee (LP) 704 *Big Daddy's Blues*............ ———

BIG ED & HIS COMBO:

Checker 790 *Biscuit Baking Mama*........... 20.00 - 30.00

THE BIG FIVE:

Shad 5019 *Blue Eyes*.......... 7.00 - 10.00

BIG FOUR:

Moon 306 *Outa Tune*.......... 7.00 - 10.00

BIG MAC:

Tri-Mac 501 *Someday You're Gonna Sing The Blues* 10.00 - 15.00

BIG MACEO (with TAMPA RED):

Groove 5001 *Worried Life Blues*............. 8.00 - 11.00
RCA Victor 500-0002 (orange plastic) *If You Ever
Change Your Ways*.................. 15.00 - 20.00

BIG MAYBELLE:

Okeh 7060 *Whole Lotta Shakin' Goin' On*...... 10.00 - 15.00
Savoy (LP) 14011 *Blues, Candy And Big Maybelle* 15.00 - 20.00

BIG MEMPHIS MA RAINEY: (See MARAINEY)

BIG WALTER (& HIS COMBO/THE THUNDERBIRDS):

Global 409 *Watusie Freeze*................. 5.00 - 8.00
Goldband 1080 *Crazy Dream*................ 7.00 - 10.00
Myrl 406 *Feelin' A Little Worried*........... 5.00 - 8.00
Peacock 1661 *Gamblin' Woman*............. 7.00 - 10.00
States 145 *Hard Hearted Woman*............. 15.00 - 20.00
Teardrop 3130 *Get To Gitten'*............. 5.00 - 8.00
TNT 8005 *Calling Margie*............. 12.00 - 16.00
8006 *Oh No, No Blues*............. 15.00 - 20.00

DICK BILLS:

Crest 1089 *Rockin' And Rollin'*............. 10.00 - 15.00

BILLY & LILLIE:

Casino 105 *La Dee Dah*............. 5.00 - 8.00
Swan 4002 *La Dee Dah* (78 rpm)............. 15.00 - 20.00

BILLY BOY:

Vee Jay 146 *I Was Fooled*.............	8.00 -	12.00
171 *I Ain't Got You*.................	5.00 -	8.00
192 *Here's My Picture*..............	5.00 -	8.00
238, 260.............................	4.00 -	6.00

BILLY GUITAR & HIS NIGHTHAWKS:
Decca 30634 *Here Comes The Night*.........	10.00 -	15.00

BILLY THE KID:
Kapp 261 *Apron Strings*..............	10.00 -	15.00

LONG MAN BINDER:
United 194 *I'm A Lover*.................	8.00 -	12.00

BING BONGS:
Dragon 10205 *Ding-A-Ling-A-Ling-Ding-Dong*...	————	

BIP AND BOP:
Aladdin 3287 *Ding Dong Ding*.............	5.00 -	8.00

LARRY BIRDSONG:
Excello 2064, 2076.......................	5.00 -	8.00

OTIS BLACKWELL:
Davis (LP) 109 *Singin' The Blues*........	15.00 -	20.00
Jay-Dee 784, 787, 791...................	5.00 -	8.00

THE BLACKWELLS:
GB 125 *Here's The Question*..............	15.00 -	20.00

TOMMY BLAKE:
Buddy 107 *Cool It (Baby)*.............	20.00 -	30.00
RCA Victor 6925 *Freedom*...........	5.00 -	8.00
Sun 278 *Flat Foot Sam*.............	8.00 -	12.00
300 *I Dig You Baby*................	75.00 -	100.00

CLIFF BLAKELEY:
Starday 352 *High Steppin'*.............	15.00 -	20.00
369 *Get Off My Toe*.................	15.00 -	20.00

JIMMY BLAKELEY:
Starday 299 *Crazy Blues*.............	10.00 -	15.00

WELLINGTON BLAKELY:
Vee Jay 104 *Sailor Joe*...............	15.00 -	25.00

JACKIE BLANCHARD with THE ROCKING' IMPALAS:
Mida 111 *The King O'Hearts*.............	10.00 -	15.00

BILLY BLAND:
Old Town 1016 *The Fat Man*.............	7.00 -	10.00

BOBBY BLUE BLAND:
Crown (LP) 5258 *Two In Blues*.........	12.00 -	16.00
Duke (LP) 74 *Two Steps From The Blues*......	8.00 -	12.00
(LP) 77 *Call On Me*..................	8.00 -	12.00
(LP) 78 *Ain't Nothing You Can Do*.....	8.00 -	12.00
(Above LPs are MONO issues)		
Duke 141, 153, 170, 182, 185...........	4.00 -	7.00

GLENN BLAND:
Sarg 159 *Mean Gene*................	15.00 -	20.00
164 *When My Baby Passes By*........	15.00 -	20.00

BLANKENSHIP BROTHERS:
Skyline 106 *That's Why I'm Blue*..........	10.00 -	15.00

THE BLASERS:
United 191 *She Needs To Be Loved*..........	10.00 -	15.00

JULES BLATTNER:
Bobbin 105 *Rock And Roll Blues*............	15.00 -	20.00
K-Ark 609 *Lonesome*....................	10.00 -	15.00
Norman 509 *Slip 'N Slide*..............	5.00 -	8.00

BLAZER BOY (See also JAMES LOCKS):
Imperial 5199 *Mornin' Train*..............	20.00 -	30.00

STEVE BLEDSOE:
Witch 102 *Dumb Dumb Bunny*..............	8.00 -	12.00

THE BLENDAIRS:
Tin Pan Alley 252 *My Love Is Just For You*...	10.00 -	15.00

THE BLENDERS:
Class 236 *Little Rose*...................	8.00 -	12.00
Decca 31284 *Tell Me What's On Your Mind*...	8.00 -	12.00
48156 *Gone*........................	10.00 -	15.00
48244 *You Do The Dreamin'*.............	10.00 -	15.00
Paradise 111 *I Won't Tell The World*..........	10.00 -	15.00

THE BLENDS:
Casa Grande 5000 *A Thousand Miles Away*....	10.00 -	15.00
5037 *Someone To Care*.............	8.00 -	12.00

THE BLENDTONES:
MGM 12782 *Lilly*.....................	10.00 -	15.00

MARV BLIHOVE:
Lindy 113 *Cigarettes And Coffee Blues*........	10.00 -	15.00

THE BLOCKBUSTERS:
Aladdin 3319 *Why Baby Why*...............	5.00 -	8.00

THE BLUE ANGELS:
Edsel 781 *Deserie*.................	10.00 -	15.00

THE BLUE BELLES:
Atlantic 987 *The Story Of A Fool*..........	5.00 -	8.00

BLUE CHARLIE:
Nasco 6002 *I'm Gonna Kill That Hen*.......	15.00 -	25.00

THE BLUE CHIPS:
Groove 0006 *Promise*..............	5.00 -	8.00

THE BLUE DIAMONDS:
Savoy 1134 *No Money*...............	8.00 -	12.00

THE BLUE DOTS:
Ace 596 *Please Don't Tell 'Em*.............	7.00 -	10.00
De Luxe 6052 *You've Got To Live For Yourself*	20.00 -	30.00
6055 *Street Of Sorrow*.............	20.00 -	30.00
6061 *Save All Your Love For Me*......	20.00 -	30.00
6067 *Hold Me Tight*.............	20.00 -	30.00
NRC 504 *All You Gotta Do*............	5.00 -	8.00

BLUE FLAMES (See LITTLE JUNIOR)

THE BLUE JAYS:
Blue Jay 102 *Write Me A Letter*.............	35.00 -	50.00
Checker 782 *White Cliffs Of Dover*.........	100.00 -	150.00
Milestone 2008 *Lover's Island*.........	4.00 -	7.00
2010 *Let's Make Love*...............	5.00 -	8.00
Roulette 4169 *Barbara*.............	7.00 -	10.00

THE BLUE NOTES:
Josie 800 *If You Love Me*.............	15.00 -	20.00
823 *The Retribution Blues*.............	15.00 -	20.00
Lost—*She Is Mine*.................	15.00 -	20.00
TNT 150 *Darling Of Mine*.............	7.00 -	10.00
20th Century 1213 *Pucker Your Lips*..........	5.00 -	8.00
Value 213 *My Hero*....................	7.00 -	10.00

"THE BLUES":
Argo (LP) 4026........................	7.00 -	10.00

THE BLUES ROCKERS:
Excello 2062 *Calling All Cows*...............	8.00 -	12.00

BLUES SLIM:
Five-Four 5435 *Drivin' Me, Baby*.............	7.00 -	10.00

THE BLUES TOPPERS:
Duke 172 *Sleeping In An Ocean Of Tears*......	8.00 -	12.00

THE BLUE TONES:
King 5088 *Shake Shake*.............	10.00 -	15.00

TOOTER BOATMAN:
Twinkle 501 *More And More*.............	75.00 -	100.00

HARMON BOAZEMAN:
Sarg 145 *No Love In You*.............	20.00 -	30.00

BOB AND LUCILLE:
Ditto 121 *Eenie Meenie Miney Moe*.........	25.00 -	40.00
126 *What's The Password*.............	8.00 -	12.00
Imperial 5631 *Eenie Meenie Miney Moe*......	10.00 -	15.00

BOB AND RAY:
Nasco 6023 *Shorty Shorty*..............	8.00 -	12.00

BOB & THE ROCKABILLIES:
Blue Chip 011 *Your Kind Of Love*..........	8.00 -	12.00

BOB AND SHERI:
Safari 101 *The Surfer Moon*.................	100.00 up	

(DJ: white label; regular issue; blue label. Caution: Bootlegs exist of this early BEACH BOYS related disc.)

THE BOBBETTES:
Atlantic 1144 *Mr. Lee* (78 rmp).............	10.00 -	15.00

BOBBY & THE ORBITS:
Seeco 6067 *Felicia*.................	5.00 -	8.00

BILL BODAFORD & THE ROCKETS:
Back Beat 507 *Little Girl*.............	10.00 -	15.00

THE BON-AIRES:
Dootone 325 *It's Xmas Time*	10.00 -	15.00
King 4975 *Stop The World*	7.00 -	10.00

EDDIE BOND (& HIS STOMPERS):
Diplomat 8566 *The Monkey And The Baboon*	10.00 -	15.00
Ekko 1015 *Talkin' Off The Wall*	50.00 -	75.00
1016 *Love Makes A Fool*	20.00 -	30.00
Memphis 115 *Here Comes The Train*	8.00 -	12.00
Mercury 70826 *Rockin' Daddy*	15.00 -	20.00
70882 *Slip Slip Slippin' In*	15.00 -	20.00
70941 *Boppin' Bonnie*	15.00 -	25.00
71067 *You're Part Of Me*	5.00 -	8.00
71153 *Hershey Bar*	5.00 -	8.00
71237 *Backslidin'*	5.00 -	8.00
Stomper Time 1156 *You'll Never Be A Stranger*	10.00 -	15.00

LUTHER BOND & HIS EMERALDS:
Federal 12279 *He Loves You Baby*	10.00 -	15.00
12368 *Old Mother Nature*	10.00 -	15.00
Savoy 1124 *What If You*	10.00 -	15.00
1131 *Starlight, Starbright*	8.00 -	12.00
1159 *It's Written In The Stars*	8.00 -	12.00

GARY U.S. BONDS (See U.S. BONDS)

LEE BONDS:
Decca 29338 *I'm Lookin' For Some Lovin'*	5.00 -	8.00
Tennessee 826 *Wild Cattin' Woman*	7.00 -	10.00

U.S. BONDS:
Legrand (LP) 3001 *Dance Til Quarter To Three*	15.00 -	25.00
(LP) 3002 *Twist Up Calypso*	15.00 -	20.00

JOHNNY BONI:
Black-Crest 108 *Ruby Baby*	10.00 -	15.00

JUKE BOY BONNER:
Goldband 1102 *Call Me Juke Boy*	7.00 -	10.00

THE BONNEVILLES:
Munich 103 *Lorraine*	10.00 -	15.00

BOOGALOO:
Crest 1030 *Cops and Robbers* (red plastic)	10.00 -	15.00

BOOGIE JAKE:
Chess 1746 *Bad Luck And Trouble*	5.00 -	8.00
Instant 3314 *Early Morning Blues*	5.00 -	8.00

JOHN LEE BOOKER:
De Luxe 6004 *Blue Monday*	15.00 -	20.00
6032 *Pouring Down Rain*	10.00 -	15.00
6046 *Real Real Gone*	15.00 -	20.00
Rockin' 525 *Pouring Down Rain*	15.00 -	25.00

CONNIE BOOKS:
Citation 5001 *Black Magic And Witchcraft*	7.00 -	10.00

PAT BOONE:
Dot (LP) 3050, *Pat*	9.00 -	12.00
Republic 7049, 7062, 7084	5.00 -	8.00

THE BOP-CHORDS:
Holiday 2601 *Castle In The Sky*	15.00 -	20.00
2603 *When I Woke Up This Morning*	15.0 -	20.00
2608 *Baby*	12.00 -	16.00

"BOPPIN" (With THE ORIOLES, THE MARYLANDERS, etc al.)
Jubilee (LP) 1118	20.00 -	30.00

BILL BOWEN & THE ROCKETS:
Meteor 5033 *Have Myself A Ball*	25.00 -	35.00

JIMMY BOWEN:
Blue Moon 402 *I'm Stickin' With You*	50.00 -	75.00
Roulette 4001, 4010	4.00 -	7.00
Roulette 4001 *I'm Sticking' With You* (78rpm)	10.00 -	15.00
4010 *Warm Up To Me Baby* (78rpm)	10.00 -	15.00
4023 *It's Shameful*	4.00 -	7.00
4023 *It's Shameful* (78rpm)	10.00 -	15.00
(LP) 25004 *Jimmy Bowen*	20.00 -	30.00
Triple-D 797 *I'm Stickin' With You*	35.00 -	50.00

DOUG BOWLES:
Tune 206 *Cadillac Baby*	15.00 -	25.00

CECIL BOWMAN:
D 1048 *Man-A-Waitin'*	3.00 -	5.00
Saturday 336 *Blues Around My Door*	8.00 -	12.00

DONNIE BOWSER:
Era 3029 *Stone Heart*	5.00 -	8.00
Sage 265 *I Love You Baby*	8.00 -	12.00
276 *Got The Best Of Me*	10.00 -	15.00

LITTLE DONNIE BOWSHIER:
Dess 7002 *Rock And Roll Joys*	30.00 -	50.00

EDDIE BOYD:
Bea & Baby 101, 107, 108	4.00 -	7.00
Chess 1523 *Cool Kind Treatment*	8.00 -	12.00
1533 *The Tickler*	7.00 -	10.00
1541, 1552, 1561, 1573, 1576, 1582, 1595, 1606, 1621, 1634	5.00 -	8.00
1660, 1674	3.00 -	5.00
Herald 406 *I'm Goin' Downtown*	15.00 -	20.00
J.O.B. 1005 *I'm Pleading*	25.00 -	40.00
1007 *Five Long Years*	10.00 -	15.00
1009 *I'm Pleading*	20.00 -	30.00
1114 *I Love You*	25.00 -	35.00
Oriole 1316/1317 *Five Long Years*	4.00 -	7.00

JIMMY BOYD:
Columbia 21571 *Shakin' Down The Mississippi*	7.00 -	10.00

ROBERT BOYD:
Wasco 201 *Boyd's Bounce*	25.00 -	35.00

HELEN BOZEMAN:
Sandy 1011 *Sugar Baby*	10.00 -	15.00

TOMMY BRADEN:
United 177 *Do The Do*	5.00 -	8.00

ROCKIN' BRADLEY:
Fire 1007 *Look Out*	10.00 -	15.00

JACK BRADSHAW:
Mar-Vel 750 *Don't Tease Me*	8.00 -	12.00

JIMMY BRADSHAW:
McBrad 1000 *When School's Out*	7.00 -	10.00

TINY BRADSHAW:
King (LP) 501 *Selections*	15.00 -	20.00
4497 *Train Kept-A-Rollin'*	8.00 -	12.00

DOUG BRAGG:
D 1045 *Calling Me Back*	4.00 -	7.00
Dixie—*Pretty Little Thing*	10.00 -	15.00

JOHNNY BRAGG & THE MARIGOLDS:
Excello 2078 *Foolish Me*	8.00 -	12.00
2091 *Juke Box Rock 'n' Roll*	8.00 -	12.00

RONNIE BRANHAM:
Pep 117 *You Treat Me Like A Fool*	8.00 -	12.00

BOBBY BRANT:
White Rock 1114 *Piano Nellie*	20.00 -	30.00

NICKY BRAZZELL:
Sparr—*Betty Joe*	———	

JIMMY BREEDLOVE:
Atco 6094 *That's My Baby*	7.00 -	10.00
Diamond 144 *Jealous Fool*	7.00 -	10.00

JACKIE BRENSTON:
Federal 12283 *Gonna Wait For My Chance*	5.00 -	8.00
12291 *The Mistreater*	5.00 -	8.00

FRANKIE BRENT (& THE COUNTS):
Calvert 201 *No Rock 'n' Rollin' Here*	7.00 -	10.00
Strand 25014 *No Rock 'n' Rollin' Here*	5.00 -	8.00
Vik 0322 *Cold As Ice*	5.00 -	8.00

BRENTWOODS:
Dore 559 *Midnight Star*	4.00 -	7.00

ROBIN HOOD BRIANS:
Fraternity 803 *Dis a Itty Bit*	20.00 -	30.00

JAY BRINKLEY:
Kliff 101 *Guitar Smoke*	20.00 -	30.00

LARRY BRINKLEY:
Magic—*Right String But The Wrong Yo Yo*	———	
Westwood—*Jackson Dog*	———	

ELTON BRITT:
ABC Paramount (LP) 293 *Wandering Cowboy*	15.00 -	20.00
(LP) 322 *Beyond The Sunset*	15.00 -	20.00
RCA Vitor (LP) 1288 *Yodel Songs*	15.00 -	20.00

CHUCK BROOKS:
Dub 2844 *Spinning My Wheels*............. 10.00 - 15.00

LILLIAN BROOKS (& THE MOROCCOS):
King 4934 *For Only You*............. 7.00 - 10.00
4956 *Sweet Sweet William*............. 7.00 - 10.00

LOUIS BROOKS (& HIS HI-TOPPERS):
Excello 2042, 2056, 2063, 2100, 2119......... 4.00 - 8.00
2141, 2159............. 3.00 - 7.00

SONNY BROOKS:
Tip Top 1008 *I'm So Downhearted*............ 8.00 - 12.00

BIG BILLY BROONZY:
Columbia (LP) 111 *Big Bill's Blues*............. 15.00 - 20.00
EmArcy (LP) 20634 (10") *Folk Blues*.......... 20.00 - 30.00
Folkways (LP) 2326 *Sings Country Blues*...... 8.00 - 12.00
(LP) 3586 *Songs And Story*............. 7.00 - 10.00
Mercury (LP) 36137 *Blues*............. 15.00 - 25.00
Period (LP) 1114 (10") *Sings*............. 20.00 - 30.00

THE BROTHERS:
Argo 5318 *Deep Sleep*............. 7.00 - 10.00

BILLY BROWN:
Columbia 41029 *Did We Have A Party*....... 8.00 - 12.00
41100 *Meet Me In The Alley, Sally*....... 8.00 - 12.00
41297 *Flip Out*............. 5.00 - 8.00
41380 *Run 'Em Off*............. 3.00 - 5.00
Republic 2007 *Lost Weekend*............. 5.00 - 8.00

BOBBY BROWN & THE CURIOS:
Vaden 100 *Down At Big Mary's Place*........ 30.00 - 40.00

BUSTER BROWN:
Fire (LP) 102 *The New King Of The Blues*..... 35.00 - 50.00
1008 *Fannie Mae* (78rpm)............. 30.00 - 50.00
This is one of the last 78 rpm records to be issued,
   and as such, is much sought-after. Rumors of
   prices far in excess of those here quote remain
   unconfirmed.)

CHARLES BROWN:
Rose 101 *Mean, Mean Mama*................. 10.00 - 15.00
102 *Have You Heard The Gossip*.......... 10.00 - 15.00

CHARLIE BROWN:
Ace 561 *Educated Fool*................. 4.00 - 7.00
Aladdin (LP) 702 (10") *Mood Music*.......... 50.00 - 80.00
(LP) 809 *Mood Music*............. 50.00 - 80.00
3092 *Seven Long Days*............. 15.00 - 20.00
3116, 3176, 3209, 3220............. 7.00 - 10.00
3235, 3254, 3284, 3290, 3316, 3342, 3348.... 4.00 - 7.00
Imperial (LP) 9257 *Best Of The Blues*....... 15.00 - 25.00
Score (LP) 4011 *Drifting Blues*............. 50.00 - 75.00

DANNY BROWN:
Earth 702 *Standing On The Corner*.......... 7.00 - 10.00

DUSTY BROWN:
Bandera 2503 *Please Don't Go*............. 5.00 - 8.00
Parrot 820 *Yes She's Gone*............. 15.00 - 20.00

EARL "GOOD ROCKING" BROWN:
Kappa 207 *Turn Back The Time*............. 15.00 - 20.00

GATEMOUTH BROWN: (See also Blues 78 rpm
   section)
Cue 1050 *Leftover Blues*............. 4.00 - 7.00
Peacock 1616 *Boogie Uproar*............. 8.00 - 12.00
1619 *Please Tell Me Baby*............. 8.00 - 12.00
1637, 1653, 1662............. 4.00 - 7.00

GENE BROWN:
Dot 15709 *Big Door*............. 8.00 - 12.00

GUY BROWN with RED CAMPI & HIS BAND:
Echo 5002 *How Long Will It Be*............. 15.00 - 20.00

HYLO BROWN:
Capitol (LP) 1168............. 10.00 - 15.00

J.T. BROWN:
Meteor 5016 *Dumb Woman Blues*........... 10.00 - 15.00

JAMES BROWN (& THE FAMOUS FLAMES):
King (LP) 610 *Please, Please*............. 15.00 - 20.00
(LP) 743 *The Amazing James Brown*........ 10.00 - 15.00

JIM EDWARD & THE BROWNS:
RCA Victor (LP) 1438............. 10.00 - 15.00

(LP) 2144 *Sweet Sounds*.................. 10.00 - 15.00
(LP) 2174 *Town & Country*.............. 10.00 - 15.00

JIMMY BROWN:
Capitol 3255 *It's Over*.................... 8.00 - 12.00

MARCUS BROWN:
Khoury's 734 *Lover Lee*.................. 5.00 - 8.00

MILTON BROWN & HIS BROWNIES:
Decca (LP) 5561 (10") *Dance-O-Rama*......... 20.00 - 30.00

NAPPY BROWN:
Savoy (LP) 14002 *Sings*.................. 10.00 - 15.00
(LP) 14025 *The Right Time*.............. 10.00 - 15.00

ROY BROWN:
Home of the Blues 107 *Don't Break My Heart*.. 4.00 - 8.00
110 *Rocking All The Time*............. 7.00 - 10.00
115 *Sugar Baby*.................. 5.00 - 8.00
Imperial 5422, 5427, 5439.................. 3.00 - 6.00
5510 *Hip Shakin' Baby*............. 10.00 - 15.00
King (EP) 254 *Blues Boogie*............. 15.00 - 20.00
(LP) 607 *Roy Brown And Wynonie Harris*.... 40.00 - 60.00
4602 *Travelin' Man*.................. 8.00 - 12.00
4609 *Money Can't Buy Love*.......... 8.00 - 12.00
4627 *Gamblin' Man*.................. 8.00 - 12.00
4637 *Old Age Boogie*.................. 8.00 - 12.00
4669 *Caldonia's Wedding Day*.......... 8.00 - 12.00
4704, 4715, 4731, 4761, 4834.......... 7.00 - 10.00
King (higher numbers).................. 4.00 - 6.00

RUTH BROWN:
Atlantic 919 *Teardrops From My Eyes*....... 20.00 - 30.00
941 *I Know*.................. 10.00 - 15.00
973 *Have A Good Time*............. 8.00 - 12.00
978 *Three Letters*.................. 8.00 - 12.00
1005, 1023, 1027, 1036, 1044.......... 5.00 - 8.00
(LP) 1308 *Late Date With*............. 15.00 - 25.00
(LP) 8004 *Ruth Brown*............. 20.00 - 30.00
(LP) 8026 *Miss Rhythm*............. 15.00 - 25.00
(LP) 8080 *The Best Of Ruth Brown*........ 8.00 - 12.00
(Note: Above must be original MONO issues)

TOMMY BROWN:
Imperial 5476, 5533.................. 4.00 - 7.00

LITTLE WILLIE BROWN:
Chart 1485 *Things Ain't Like They Use To Be*.. 10.00 - 15.00
Do-Ra-Me 1404 *Cut It Out*............. 15.00 - 20.00
Suntan 1112 *Going Back To The Country*...... 15.00 - 20.00
Topic 223 *Do It Like That*............. 15.00 - 20.00

WINI BROWN & HER BOYFRIENDS:
Mercury 5870 *Here In My Heart*............. 20.00 - 30.00
8270 *Heaven Knows Why*............. 10.00 - 15.00

DORIS BROWNE:
Gotham 290 *Please Believe Me*............. 10.00 - 15.00
296 *Until The End Of Time*............. 10.00 - 15.00
298 *My Cherie*.................. 10.00 - 15.00
303 *When The Moon Is High*............. 10.00 - 15.00

EDWIN BRUCE:
Sun 276 *Rock Boppin' Baby*............. 4.00 - 7.00
292 *Sweet Woman*.................. 7.00 - 10.00

FRANK BRUNSON:
Groove 0173 *Charmaine*.................. 4.00 - 6.00

BILLY BRYAN:
Blaze 351 *Cradle Of Your Arms*............. 5.00 - 8.00
Festival 25002 *Please, Come Back Baby*...... 5.00 - 8.00

WES BRYAN:
Clock 1013 *Honey Baby*............. 7.00 - 10.00
United Artist 102, 122............. 5.00 - 8.00

THE BUCCANEERS:
Rama 21 *The Stars Will Remember*........... 100.00 - 150.00
24 *In The Mission Of St. Augustine*......... 75.00 - 125.00
Southern 101 *Fine Brown Frame*.......... 90.00 - 125.00

BUCHANAN & ANCELL:
Flying Saucer 501 *The Creature*............. 8.00 - 12.00

BUCHANAN & GOODMAN:
Luniverse 101, 102, 103, 105, 107, 108....... 4.00 - 8.00
(Note: 78 rpm issues of above are worth more)
Radioactive 101 *Flying Saucer*.............. 10.00 - 15.00
BUCHANAN & GREENFIELD:
Novel 711 *The Invasion*..................... 4.00 - 7.00
WES BUCHANAN:
Pep 114 *Give Some Love My Way*............ 25.00 - 40.00
GARY BUCK:
Petal 1011 *Savin' All My Love For You*....... 5.00 - 8.00
PETER BUCK:
Drew-Blan 1005 *That's Enough*.............. 5.00 - 8.00
THE BUCKEYES:
De Luxe 6110 *Since I Fell For You*........... 20.00 - 30.00
6126 *Dottie Baby*...................... 12.00 - 16.00
BUCKY & THE PREMIERES:
Nu-Phi 701 *Cruisin'*....................... 7.00 - 10.00
JOHN BULLARD:
De Luxe 6019 *Spoiled Hambone Blues*........ 25.00 - 40.00
NORMAN BULLOCK:
M & J 1-2 *Moanin' The Blues*............... 20.00 - 30.00
1108 *Lies, Lies, Lies*.................. 20.00 - 30.00
"BUNCH OF GOODIES":
Chess (LP) 1441............................ 10.00 - 15.00
BILLY BUNN & HIS BUDDIES:
RCA Victor 4483 *I Need A Shoulder To Cry On* 25.00 - 35.00
4657 *That's When Your Heartaches Begin*.... 20.00 - 30.00
RAY BURDEN:
Adonis 112 *A Hot Rodder's Dream*.......... 15.00 - 20.00
Cullman 6403 *That Kind Of Carrying On*...... 35.00 - 50.00
DAVE BURGESS:
Challenge 1018 *Maybelle*.................. 5.00 - 8.00
59027 *I Don't Want To Know*........... 5.00 - 8.00
59032 *Lovey Dovey Baby*.............. 5.00 - 8.00
Challenge 59037, 59045.................... 4.00 - 7.00
SONNY BURGESS:
Phillips 3551 *Sadie's Back In Town*.......... 8.00 - 12.00
Razorback 136 *Odessa*................... 8.00 - 12.00
Sun 247 *Red Headed Woman*.............. 7.00 - 10.00
263 *Ain't Got A Thing*................. 10.00 - 15.00
285 *My Bucket's Got A Hole In It*....... 5.00 - 8.00
304 *Thunderbird*..................... 15.00 - 20.00
JIM BURGETT:
Oro 1502 *Live It Up*...................... 15.00 - 20.00
BUDDY BURKE:
Bullseye 1002 *That Big Old Moon*........... 15.00 - 20.00
EDDIE BURKE:
D 1063 *Rock Mop*........................ 5.00 - 8.00
THE BURNETTE BROTHERS:
Imprial 5509 *Warm Love*.................. 10.00 - 15.00
DORSEY BURNETTE:
Abbott 190 *At A Distance*................. 5.00 - 8.00
Cee-Jam 16 *Bertha Lou*.................. 8.00 - 12.00
Imperial 5668 *Way In The Middle Of The Night* 10.00 - 15.00
5561, 5597........................... 4.00 - 7.00
JOHNNY BURNETTE (& THE ROCK 'N'
ROLL TRIO):
JOHNNY BURNETTE TRIO:
Coral (LP) 57080 *Johnny Burnette & The Rock 'N'*
Roll Trio.......................... 80.00 - 130.00
61651 *Tear It Up*..................... 15.00 - 25.00
61675 *Midnight Train*................. 12.00 - 20.00
61719 *The Train Kept A-Rollin'*.......... 12.00 - 20.00
61758 *Lonesome Train*................ 12.00 - 20.00
61869 *Butterfingers*.................. 12.00 - 20.00
61918 *Rock Billy Boogie*.............. 12.00 - 20.00
Freedom 44001 *I'm Restless*............. 5.00 - 8.00
44011 *Me And The Bear*.............. 5.00 - 8.00
44017 *Sweet Baby Doll*.............. 8.00 - 12.00
Liberty (LPs) 3179, 3183, 3190, 3206, 7183, 7190,
7197, 7206........................ 15.00 - 20.00

LINDA BURNETTE:
Perry 5 *Rattle Bones Rock*................. 12.00 - 18.00
MAC BURNEY & THE FOUR JACKS:
Aladdin 3274 *Tired Of Your Sexy Ways* (blue label) 15.00 - 25.00
EDDIE BURNS:
Chess 1672 *Treat Me Like I Treat You*....... 5.00 - 8.00
De Luxe 6024 *Dealing With The Devil*....... 15.00 - 20.00
Harvey 111, 115, 118.................... 3.00 - 6.00
JVB 82 *Treat Me Like I Treat You*.......... 20.00 - 30.00
JACKIE BURNS:
Del-Fi 4102 *Hey Then There Now*........... 4.00 - 7.00
SONNY BURNS:
Starday 209 *A Real Cool Cat*.............. 15.00 - 25.00
HAROLD BURRAGE:
Cobra 5004, 5012, 5018, 5022, 5026.......... 5.00 - 8.00
BOB BURTON:
Mar-Vel 953 *Tired Of Rocking*............. 15.00 - 20.00
WAYNE BUSBY:
Empire 506 *Goin' Back To Dixie*........... 20.00 - 30.00
EDDIE BUSH:
Jaxon 503 *Little Darling*................. 20.00 - 30.00
THE BUTANES:
Enrica 1007 *That's My Desire*.............. 5.00 - 8.00
SAM BUTERA & THE WITNESSES:
Capitol 4014 *Bim Bam*................... 10.00 - 15.00
CLIFF BUTLER & THE DOVES:
States 123 *When You Love*................ 30.00 - 40.00
JERRY BUTLER & THE IMPRESSIONS:
Abner 1013, 1017, 1023.................. 5.00 - 8.00
1013 *For Your Precious Love* (78rpm)....... 15.00 - 20.00
Falcon 1013 *For Your Precious Love*........ 10.00 - 15.00
Vee Jay 280 *For Your Precious Love* (Rare).... 100.00 up

BOBBY BYRD & THE BIRDS:
Cash 1031 *Let's Live Together As One*........ 15.00 - 20.00
ROBERT BYRD:
Jamie 1039 *Bippin' And Boppin'*.............. 7.00 - 10.00
ROY BYRD:
Federal 12061 *Curly Haired Baby*............ 25.00 - 40.00
12073 *Rockin' With Fes*................ 25.00 - 40.00
JERRY BYRNE:
Specialty 635 *Lights Out*.................. 7.00 - 10.00
EDD BYRNES:
Warner Bros. (LP) 1309 *Kookie*............. 10.00 - 15.00
JIMMIE BYRON:
Teen 113 *Sidewalk Rock*.................. 8.00 - 12.00
WILLIE C.:
Ruler 5000 *Slow Down Baby*............... 5.00 - 8.00
THE CABINEERS:
Prestige 904 *Each Time*.................. 80.00 - 120.00
917 *Baby Mine*...................... 80.00 - 120.00
THE CADETS:
Crown (LP) 5015 *Rockin' n' Rollin'*......... 20.00 - 30.00
(LP) 5370 *The Cadets*................ 15.00 - 20.00
(LP) CST 370 *The Cadets*............. 10.00 - 15.00
Modern 956 *I Cry*..................... 10.00 - 15.00
960, 969, 971, 985.................... 7.00 - 10.00
994, 1000, 1006, 1012, 1017, 1024.......... 4.00 - 7.00
THE CADILLACS:
Capitol 4825 *White Gardenia*.............. 6.00 - 10.00
Josie 759 *Carelessly*...................... ———
765 *Gloria*........................ 30.00 - 40.00
769 *Wishing Well*................... 40.00 - 60.00
773 *Sympathy*..................... 10.00 - 15.00
778 *Down The Road*................. 10.00 - 15.00
785 *Speedo*....................... 5.00 - 8.00
785 *Speedo* (78rpm)................. 8.00 - 12.00
792 *Zoom*........................ 5.00 - 8.00
792 *Zoom* (78rpm)................. 7.00 - 10.00
798, 805, 812, 820, 821, 846, 866.......... 4.00 - 7.00
*Jubilee (LP) 1045 *The Fabulous Cadillacs*...... 50.00 - 75.00
*(LP) 1089 *The Crazy Cadillacs*............. 40.00 - 60.00

*(LP) 1117 *The Cadillacs Meet The Orioles*... 25.00 - 40.00
(LP) 5009 *Twisting With The Cadillacs*...... 10.00 - 15.00
(*original issues have blue label)

AUBREY CAGLE:
Glee 100 *Be Bop Blues*........... 10.00 - 15.00
1958 *Come Along Little Girl*............ 7.00 - 10.00
10013 *Bop 'N' Stroll*............ 7.00 - 10.00
House Of Sound 104 *Real Cool*........ 7.00 - 10.00

ANDY CALDWELL:
Liberty 55142 *She's So Fine*......... 7.00 - 10.00

THE CALENDARS:
Swingin' 649 *One-Week Romance*........ 5.00 - 8.00

THE CALIFORNIANS:
Federal 12231 *My Angel*............ 15.00 - 20.00

BOB CALLAWAY:
Big Red—*Tick Tock*................ ———

DUDLEY CALLICUT & THE "GO" BOYS:
"DC" 0412 *Get Ready Baby*............ 10.00 - 15.00

BABY CALLOWAY:
Bay-Tone 106 *Midnight Blues*........ 5.00 - 8.00

THE CALVAES:
Checker 928 *So Bad*........... 5.00 - 8.00
Cobra 5003 *Fine Girl*........... 25.00 - 35.00
5014 *Lonely Lonely Village*........ 15.00 - 25.00

THE CALVANES:
Deck 579 *Dreamworld*........ 5.00 - 8.00
Dootone (EP) 205 .... 10.00 - 15.00
380 *Florabelle*............ 7.00 - 10.00

THE CALVEYS:
Comma 445 *The Wind*............ 5.00 - 8.00

THE CAMELOTS:
Aanko 1001, 1004............ 6.00 - 9.00
Ember 1108 *Searchin' For My Baby*.... 5.00 - 8.00

THE CAMEOS:
Dean 504 *Lost Lover*............ 15.00 - 20.00

THE CAMERONS:
Felsted 8638 *Guardian Angel*........ 5.00 - 8.00

DAVID CAMPANELLA & THE DELLCHORDS:
Kane 5593 *Over The Rainbow*........ 5.00 - 8.00

CECIL CAMPBELL:
MGM 12482 *Rock & Roll Fever*........ 20.00 - 30.00

DICK CAMPBELL:
Great 4703 *She's My Girl*............ 5.00 - 8.00

GLEN CAMPBELL:
Crest 1087, 1096............ 3.00 - 5.00

JO ANN CAMPBELL:
End (LP) 306 *I'm Nobody's Baby*....... 20.00 - 30.00
Gone 5014, 5021, 5037............ 4.00 - 7.00

LOUIS CAMPBELL:
Excello 2035 *The Natural Facts*........ 10.00 - 15.00

RAY CAMPI:
D 1047 *The Ballad Of Donna And Peggy Sue*... 10.00 - 15.00
Domino 700 *My Screamin' Mimie*....... 15.00 - 20.00
Dot 15617 *It Ain't Me*............ 20.00 - 30.00
TNT 145 *Catapillar*............ 50.00 - 75.00

CAMP MEETING CHOIR:
Mercury (LP) 25084 (10") *Negro Spirituals*...... 10.00 - 15.00

THE CAMPS:
Parkway 974 *The Ballad Of Batman*........ 5.00 - 8.00

FREDDY CANNON:
Swan (LP) 502 *The Explosive Freddy Cannon*... 25.00 - 35.00
(LP) 504 *Freddy Cannon Sings Happy Shades Of Blue*............ 20.00 - 30.00
(LP) 505 *Solid Gold Hits*............ 20.00 - 30.00
(LP) 506 *Twistin' All Night Long*........ 15.00 - 20.00
(LP) 507 *Palisades Park*............ 25.00 - 35.00
(LP) 511 *Freddy Cannon Steps Out*........ 25.00 - 40.00

THE CANUCKS with RAY PARK:
Diadon 60-116 *Rock Around The Barn*...... 8.00 - 12.00

JERRY CAPEHART:
Cash 1021 *Walking Stick Boogie*........ 12.00 - 16.00

THE CAPISTRANOS:
Duke 179 *Now Darling*................ 8.00 - 12.00

THE CAPITOLS:
Cindy 3002 *Rose-Marie*............ 20.00 - 30.00
Gateway 721 *Day By Day*............ 10.00 - 15.00
Pet 807 *Angel Of Love*............ 10.00 - 15.00

THE CAPRIS:
Gotham 7304 *God Only Knows*........ 10.00 - 15.00
7306 *It Was Moonglow*............ 15.00 - 20.00
7308 *It's A Miracle*............ 15.00 - 20.00
Lifetime 1001/1002 *Oh, My Darling*........ 15.00 - 20.00
Old Time 1103 *Tears In My Eyes*....... 5.00 - 8.00
Planet 1010 *There's A Moon Out Tonight*...... 25.00 - 35.00
20th Century 1201 *My Weakness*......... 10.00 - 15.00

THE CAPS:
White Star 102 *Daddy Dean*............ 5.00 - 8.00

CAPTAIN & TENILLE:
Butter-Castle 001 *The Way I Want To Teach You* ———

THE CAP-TANS:
Anna 1122 *I'm Afraid*............ 7.00 - 10.00
Dot 15114 *With All My Love*............ 25.00 - 40.00

BOBBY & TERRY CARAWAY:
Crest 1065 *Ballin' Keen*............ 15.00 - 20.00

LEONARD CARBO:
Vee Jay 291 *Pigtails And Blue Jeans*........ 7.00 - 10.00

THE CARDELLS:
Middle Tone 011 *Helen*............ 10.00 - 15.00

JACK CARDELL:
Rama 227 *Rock-A-Billy Yodler*........ 8.00 - 12.00

THE CARDINALS:
Atlantic 938 *Shouldn't I Know*............ 50.00 - 75.00
952 *I'll Always Love You*............ 25.00 - 40.00
958 *Wheel Of Fortune*............ 25.00 - 40.00
972 *She Rocks*............ 15.00 - 20.00
995 *You Are My Only Love*............ 10.00 - 15.00
1025 *Under A Blanket Of Blues*............ 12.00 - 18.00
1054, 1067, 1076, 1079............ 7.00 - 10.00
(Note: Above are yellow label)
1090, 1126............ 4.00 - 7.00
Rose 835 *Why Don't You Write Me?*........ ———

THE CARIBBEANS:
20th Fox 112 *Keep Her By My Side*........ 5.00 - 8.00

STEVE CARL:
Meteor 5046 *Curfew*............ 15.00 - 20.00

CARLISLE BROTHERS:
King (LP) 643 *Fresh From The Country*...... 8.00 - 12.00

"CARL, LEFTY AND MARTY"
Columbia (LP) 2544 (10").................. 25.00 - 35.00

CARLO:
Laurie 3151, 3157.................. 4.00 - 7.00

CARL CARLTON:
20th Fox——*She's A Bad Mama Jama*.... ———

THE CARNATIONS:
Lescay 3002 *Long Tall Girl*............ 7.00 - 10.00
Music City 736 *You Gave Peace Of Mind*...... 15.00 - 20.00
Savoy 1172 *The Angels Sent You To Me*...... 7.00 - 10.00

CAROLINA SLIM:
Sharp (LP) 2002 *Blues From The Cotton Fields*. 60.00 - 90.00

THE CAROLS:
Lamp 2001 *My Search Is Over*............ 15.00 - 20.00
Savoy 896 *Fifty Million Women*............ 12.00 - 16.00

THE CAROUSELS:
Jaguar 3029 *Rendezvous*............ 10.00 - 15.00

THE CARPETS:
Federal 12257 *Why Do I*............ 15.00 - 20.00
12269 *Lonely Me*............ 15.00 - 20.00

CATHY CARR:
Fraternity 734 *Ivory Tower* (78 rpm)........ 7.00 - 10.00
(LP) 1005 *Ivory Tower*............ 10.00 - 15.00

CARRIBIANS:
Brooks 2000 *Wonderland*............ ———

CURTIS CARRINGTON:
Fury 1018 *I'm Gonna Catch You*............ 5.00 - 8.00
THE CARROLL BROS.:
Cameo 140 *Red Hot*..................... 10.00 - 15.00
BILL CARROLL:
Dixie 2010 *I Feel So Good*............... 25.00 - 40.00
CHUCK CARROLL:
Happy Heart 133 *Mean Ole Blues*........... ————
EARL CARROLL & THE ORIGINAL CADILLACS:
Josie 829 *Buzz-Buzz-Buzz*............. 5.00 - 8.00
JIMMY CARROLL:
Fascination 2000 *Big Green Car*............. 10.00 - 15.00
JOHNNY CARROLL (& HIS HOT ROCK):
Decca 29940 *Rock 'N' Roll Ruby*............ 20.00 - 30.00
29941 *Wild Wild Women*.................. 20.00 - 30.00
30013 *Hot Rock*..................... 20.00 - 30.00
Phillips 3520 *That's The Way I Love*......... 15.00 - 20.00
WA 112 *Trudy*...................... 10.00 - 15.00
Warner Bros. 5042 *Bandstand Doll*....... 7.00 - 10.00
WAYNE CARROLL:
King 5123 *Chicken Out*................. 10.00 - 15.00
5134 *Rockin' Chair Mama*.......... 10.00 - 15.00
5146 *He Cheated*................. 5.00 - 8.00
THE CARTER KIDS:
Gambler 1638 *Gotta Rock*............... 7.00 - 10.00
THE CARTER RAYS:
Gone 5006 *My Secret Love*................ 15.00 - 20.00
Jubilee 5142 *Goodnight, Sweetheart, Goodnight*. 7.00 - 10.00
BILL CARTER:
Ozark 1234 *Cool Tom Cat*............. 10.00 - 15.00
Tally 111 *I Wanna Feel Good*.......... 8.00 - 12.00
BOB CARTER:
Den 11229 *The Fortunate Few*.............. 7.00 - 10.00
HARRY CARTER:
Mar-Vel 1300 *Jump Baby Jump*........ 10.00 - 15.00
1301 *You Made Me Love You Baby*....... 10.00 - 15.00
WILF CARTER:
Camden (LP) 527 *Montana Slim*........ 15.00 - 20.00
RIC CARTEY:
ABC Paramount 10415 *Something In My Eye*.. 4.00 - 6.00
NRC 503 *Scratchin' On My Screen*........ 20.00 - 30.00
RCA Victor 6751 *Ooh Eee*............. 8.00 - 12.00
6828 *Heart Throb*.......... 10.00 - 15.00
6920 *Let Me Tell You About Love*... 10.00 - 15.00
7011 *My Babe*............. 10.00 - 15.00
CASANOVA & THE CHANTS:
Sapphire 2254 *Geraldine*............. 8.00 - 12.00
CASANOVA, JR.:
Port 7001 *Sally Mae*................. 10.00 - 15.00
TONY CASANOVA:
American International 532 *Dairy Of A High School Bride*.............. 7.00 - 10.00
Crest 1053 *Yea! Yea! Come Another Day*...... 8.00 - 12.00
Dore 535 *Boogie Woogie Feeling*............. 8.00 - 12.00
THE CASANOVAS:
Apollo 471 *That's All*................. 15.00 - 20.00
474 *Hush-A-Mecca*............ 12.00 - 16.00
477 *Please Be My Love*........ 12.00 - 16.00
483 *My Baby's Love*........ 12.00 - 16.00
519 *Please Be Mine*........ 12.00 - 16.00
523 *You Are My Queen*....... 12.00 - 16.00
Planet 1027 *In My Land Of Dreams*....... 15.00 - 20.00
THE CASCADES:
Renee 105 *Pains In My Heart*............. 5.00 - 8.00
Valiant (LP) 405 *Rhythm Of The Rain*....... 20.00 - 30.00
AL CASEY:
Dot 15563 *Guitar Man*.................. 5.00 - 8.00
Highland 1002 *Teenage Blues*........... 7.00 - 10.00
Liberty 55117 *She Gotta Shake*........... 7.00 - 10.00
EDDIE CASH:
Peak 1001 *Doin' All Right*.............. 12.00 - 16.00

JOHNNY CASH:
Sun (EP) 111...*Sings Hank Williams*.......... 8.00 - 12.00
(EP) 112...*Country Boy*................. 8.00 - 12.00
221 *Hey Porter*................. 8.00 - 12.00
232 *Folsom Prisom Blues*........ 4.00 - 7.00
241 *I Walk The Line*........... 4.00 - 7.00
241 *I Walk The Line (78rpm)*.......... 10.00 - 15.00
258, 266, 279, 295, (78rpm)......... 7.00 - 10.00
283, 302, 309, 316, (78rpm)......... 10.00 - 15.00
(LP) 1240 *Greatest!*.............. 15.00 - 20.00
(LP) 1270 *All Aboard The Blue Train*...... 15.00 - 20.00
(LP) 1275 *The Original Sun Sound Of*.... 10.00 - 15.00
THE CASHMERES:
Herald 474 *Little Dream Girl*............. 8.00 - 12.00
Josie 894 *Where Have You Been*.......... 5.00 - 8.00
Mercury 70501 *My Sentimental Heart*........ 5.00 - 8.00
70617 *Don't Let It Happen Again*.......... 8.00 - 12.00
70679 *There's A Rumor*......... 8.00 - 12.00
THE CASINOS:
Fraternity (LP) 1019..................... 20.00 - 25.00
THE CASLONS:
Seeco 6078 *Anniversary Of Love*........... 8.00 - 12.00
TOMMY CASSELL:
Cassell 58 1/2 *Go Ahead On*................ 15.00 - 20.00
THE CASTALEERS:
Donna 1349 *That's Why I Cry*............. 7.00 - 10.00
Felsted 8504 *Come Back*............. 7.00 - 10.00
8512 *Lonely Boy*............. 7.00 - 10.00
8585 *You're My Dream*......... 7.00 - 10.00
(GEORGE CASTELLE &) THE CASTELLES:
Atco 6069 *Hey Baby, Baby*............. 8.00 - 12.00
Grand 101 *My Girl Awaits Me*........ 20.00 - 30.00
103 *This Silver Ring*........ 25.00 - 40.00
105 *Do You Remember*......... 25.00 - 40.00
109 *Over A Cup Of Coffee*...... 75.00 - 100.00
114 *Marcella*................ 30.00 - 40.00
118 *Over The Rainbow*........ 20.00 - 30.00
122 *Heavenly Father*........ 20.00 - 30.00
JOE CASTLE:
RCA Victor 7283 *That Ain't Nothin' But Right*. 7.00 - 10.00
THE CASTLE-TONES:
Rift 502 *Goodnight*.................... 8.00 - 12.00
504 *We Met At A Dance*.......... 8.00 - 12.00
JIMMY CASTOR & THE JUNIORS:
Wing 90078 *I Know The Meaning Of Love*.... 8.00 - 12.00
THE CASTROES:
Lasso—*Lucky Me*........................ ————
THE CASUALS (See "THE ORIGINAL CASUALS")
THE CASUALTEENS:
Felsted 8529 *Need You So*............. 5.00 - 8.00
THE CASUAL THREE:
Luniverse 109 *The Invisible Thing*....... 7.00 - 10.00
THE CATALINAS:
Back Beat 513 *Speechless*............. 12.00 - 15.00
Little 812 *Castle Of Love*............ 8.00 - 12.00
THE CATS:
Federal 12238 *After I Gave You My Heart*..... 10.00 - 15.00
12248 *You're So Nice*............. 10.00 - 15.00
THE CATS & THE FIDDLE:
RCA Victor 50-0077 *I Miss You So*.......... 10.00 - 15.00
JOHNNY CAVALIER:
Hi Class 105 *Knock Off The Rock*............ 10.00 - 15.00
JIM CAVALLO:
Sunnyside 3105 *Don't Move Me No More*...... 15.00 - 20.00
JIMMY CAVELLO:
Coral 61689, 61728, 61787.............. 5.00 - 8.00
JOHN W. CAVES:
Mem'ry Lane 102 *Rocket To The Moon*....... ————
THE CELLOS:
Apollo 510, 515......................... 5.00 - 8.00
516 *The Be-Bop Mouse*............. 7.00 - 10.00
524 *I Beg For Your Love*............. 8.00 - 12.00

THE CELTICS:
Al Jacks 2 *Can You Remember?* .... 50.00 - 80.00
War Conn 2216 *Darlene Darling* .... 30.00 - 50.00
THE CENTURIES:
Life 501 *In This Whole World* .... 8.00 - 12.00
THE CENTURY'S:
Fortune 533 *Take My Hand* .... 10.00 - 15.00
ERNIE CHAFFIN:
Hickory 1024 *I Can't Lose The Blues* .... 5.00 - 8.00
Sun 262, 275 .... 5.00 - 8.00
THE CHALETS:
Tru-Lite 101 *Who's Laughin'?* .... 8.00 - 12.00
THE CHALONS:
Dice 89 *Oh You* .... ———
THE CHAMBERLAIN BROS.:
Columbia 41227 *Baby Walked Out* .... 10.00 - 15.00
EDDIE CHAMBLEE:
United 160, 181 .... 5.00 - 8.00
JOHNNY CHAMPION:
Natural Sound 2004 *Beer Drinking Daddy* ...... 5.00 - 8.00
THE CHAMPIONS:
Ace 541 *I'm So Blue* .... 7.00 - 10.00
Chart 602 *Annie Met Henry* .... 7.00 - 10.00
611 *Mexico Bound* .... 7.00 - 10.00
620 *Pay Me Some Attention* .... 8.00 - 12.00
631 *Come On* .... 8.00 - 12.00
THE CHAMPS:
Challenge (LP) 601 *Go Champs Go* .... 15.00 - 20.00
1016 *Tequila* (78rpm) .... 10.00 - 15.00
59007 *El Rancho Rock* (78rpm) .... 8.00 - 12.00
THE CHANCELLORS:
XYZ 104 *I'm Coming Home* .... 7.00 - 10.00
THE CHANCETEERS:
Chess 1636 *Night Beat* .... 5.00 - 8.00
THE CHANDELIERS:
Angel Tone 521 *Blueberry Sweet* .... 10.00 - 15.00
Do-Well 102 *Once More* .... 7.00 - 10.00
ELAINE CHANDLER:
4 Star 1700 *Tiptoin' Thru The Teepee* .... ———
LEE CHANDLER:
Band Box 224 *Tree-Top* .... 8.00 - 12.00
250 *Sweet Dreams* .... 7.00 - 10.00
WAYLAND CHANDLER:
4 Star 1716 *Little Lover* .... 5.00 - 8.00
CLISTON CHANIER:
Post 2010 *Rockin' The Bop* .... 7.00 - 10.00
2016 *Rockin' Hop* .... 7.00 - 10.00
BRUCE CHANNEL:
Le Cam 953 *Hey! Baby* .... 15.00 - 20.00
Teen Ager 601 *Run, Romance, Run* .... 7.00 - 10.00
THE CHANNELS:
Fire 1001 *The Girl Next Door* .... 12.00 - 15.00
Fury 1021 *Bye Bye Baby* .... 4.00 - 7.00
Gone 5012 *That's My Desire* .... 5.00 - 8.00
5019 *Altar Of Love* .... 5.00 - 8.00
Whirlin Disc 100 *The Closer You Are* .... 10.00 - 15.00
102 *The Gleam In Your Eyes* .... 8.00 - 15.00
107 *I Really Love You* .... 8.00 - 15.00
109 *Flames In My Heart* .... 8.00 - 15.00
THE CHANTELS:
End (LP) 301 *We Are The Chantels* (group photo) .... 50.00 - 75.00
(LP) 301 *The Chantels* (juke box) .... 10.00 - 15.00
(LP) 312 *There's Our Song Again* .... 10.00 - 15.00
1001 *He's Gone* (black label) .... 7.00 - 10.00
1005 *Maybe* (black label) .... 7.00 - 10.00
1005 *Maybe* (78rpm) .... 15.00 - 20.00
1015 *Every Night* .... 5.00 - 8.00
1015 *Every Night* (78rpm) .... 10.00 - 15.00
1020 *I Love You So* .... 4.00 - 7.00
1020 *I Love You So* (78rpm) .... 10.00 - 15.00
Ludix 101 *Eternally* .... 3.00 - 5.00
Verve 10435 *It's Just Me* .... 5.00 - 8.00

THE CHANTERS:
Combo 78 *Why* .... 20.00 - 30.00
92 *I Love You* .... 20.00 - 30.00
De Luxe 6162, 6166, 6172, 6177, 6191, 6194, 6200 .... 5.00 - 10.00
Kem 2740 *Lonesome Me* .... 15.00 - 20.00
RPM 415 *Tell Me, Thrill Me* .... 20.00 - 30.00
THE CHANTICLEERS:
Lyric 103 *To Keep Your Love* .... 15.00 - 20.00
THE CHANTONES:
TNT 167 *Dear Diary* .... 7.00 - 10.00
THE CHANTS:
Nite Owl 40 *Heaven And Paradise* .... ———
JEAN CHAPEL:
RCA Victor 6892 *Oo-Ba La Baby* .... 7.00 - 10.00
Sun 244 *I Won't Be Rockin' Tonight* .... 8.00 - 12.00
THE CHAPERONES:
Josie 885 *Shining Star* .... 4.00 - 7.00
GENE CHAPMAN:
Westport 145 *Don't Come Cryin'* .... 5.00 - 8.00
BILL CHAPPELL:
Yucca 121 *Lovey Dove* .... 10.00 - 15.00
Yucca 156 *Down On the Farm Boogie* .... ———
THE CHARIOTEERS:
Columbia (LP) CL 6014 (10") *Sweet And Low* .. 50.00 - 80.00
Harmony (LP) 7089 .... 15.00 - 25.00
Josie 787 *Don't Play* .... 8.00 - 12.00
MGM 12569 *The Candles* .... 15.00 - 20.00
ANDY CHARLES & THE BLUES KINGS:
D 1061 *Baby Don't Go* .... 12.00 - 16.00
BOBBY CHARLES:
Chess 1609, 1617, 1628, 1638, 1658, 1670 ...... 4.00 - 8.00
RAY CHARLES:
Atlantic 976 *The Midnight Hour* (yellow label) .. 8.00 - 12.00
984 *The Sun's Gonna Shine Again* (yellow label) 8.00 - 12.00
999 *Mess Around* (yellow label) .... 7.00 - 10.00
1154 *Swanee River Rock* (78rpm) .... 7.00 - 10.00
(LP) 1289...*At Newport* .... 10.00 - 15.00
(LP) 1312...*Genius* .... 12.00 - 15.00
(LP) 1369 *The Genius After Hours* .... 10.00 - 15.00
2006 *Rockhouse* (78rpm) .... 10.00 - 15.00
2031 *What'd I Say* (78rpm) .... 15.00 - 25.00
2043 *I'm Movin' On* (78rpm) .... 15.00 - 20.00
(LP) 8006 *Ray Charles* (black label) .... 15.00 - 20.00
(LP) 8025 *Yes Indeed!* (black label) .... 10.00 - 15.00
(LP) 8029 *What'd I Say* .... 8.00 - 12.00
CHARLIE BOP TRIO:
Capitol 4100 *Mr. Big Feet* .... 7.00 - 10.00
THE CHARMERS:
Allison 921 *Magic Rose* .... 8.00 - 12.00
Central 1002 *The Beating Of My Heart* .... 20.00 - 30.00
Laurie 3142 *My Kind Of Love* .... 8.00 - 12.00
Timely 1011 *The Church On The Hill* .... ———
THE CHARMS: (See also OTIS WILLIAMS)
Chart 608 *Love's Our Inspiration* .... 7.00 - 10.00
613 *I Offer You* .... 7.00 - 10.00
623 *I'll Be True* .... 15.00 - 20.00
De Luxe (EP) 357, 364 .... 8.00 - 12.00
6000 *Heaven Only Knows* .... 30.00 - 50.00
6014 *Happy Are We* .... 20.00 - 30.00
6034 *Please Believe Me* .... 20.00 - 30.00
6050 *Quiet Please* .... 15.00 - 20.00
6056 *My Baby Dearest Darling* .... 15.00 - 20.00
6062, 6065, 6072, 6076, 6080, 6082, 6087 .... 5.00 - 10.00
Rockin' 516 *Heaven Only Knows* .... 35.00 - 50.00
THE CHARTERS:
Merry-Go-Round 103 *Lost In A Dream* .... 7.00 - 10.00
THE CHARTS:
Everlast 5001 *Deserie* .... 4.00 - 6.00
5002 *Why Do You Cry* .... 10.00 - 15.00
5006 *You're The Reason* .... 8.00 - 12.00
5008 *All Because Of Love* .... 8.00 - 12.00
5010 *My Diane* .... 7.00 - 10.00

5026 *Deserie*....................	4.00 -	7.00
Guyden 2021 *For The Birds*........	6.00 -	10.00

THE CHATEAUS:

Coral 62364 *Honest I Will*............	5.00 -	8.00
Warner Bros. 5043, 5071.............	5.00 -	8.00

EARL CHATMAN:

Fortune 844 *Take Two Steps Back*.......	5.00 -	8.00

THE CHAVELLES:

Vita 127 *Valley Of Love*...........	15.00 -	20.00

THE CHAVIS BROTHERS:

Ascot 2177 *Humpty Dumpty*............	5.00 -	8.00

BOOZOO CHAVIS:

Folk Star 1197 *Paper In My Shoe*......	15.00 -	20.00
1201 *Forty One Days*............	15.00 -	20.00
Goldband 1161 *Hamburgers And Popcorn*......	5.00	-8.00
Imperial 5374 *Boozoo Stomp*...............	12.00 -	16.00

CHUBBY CHECKER:

Parkway 804 *The Class* (78rpm)........	75.00 up	

(Note: the existence of this record in 78rpm form has not been confirmed.)

965 *You Just Don't Know*.............	8.00 -	12.00

THE CHECKER DOTS:

Peacock 1688 *Alpha Omega*.............	5.00 -	8.00

THE CHECKERS:

Federal 12375 *White Cliffs Of Dover*......	8.00 -	12.00
King 4558 *Flame In My Heart*.............	30.00 -	50.00
4581 *Night Curtains*..............	30.00 -	50.00
4626 *Ghost Of My Baby*...........	15.00 -	25.00
4673 *I Promise You*.............	15.00 -	25.00
4675 *White Cliffs Of Dover*.....	10.00 -	15.00
4710 *House With No Windows*.......	10.00 -	15.00
4719 *Over The Rainbow*..........	15.00 -	20.00
4751 *Mama's Daughter*.............	15.00 -	20.00
4764 *Trying To Hold My Gal*.......	15.00 -	20.00
5156 *Heaven Only Knows*........	10.00 -	15.00
Skyla 1120 *Blue Saturday*..........	4.00 -	7.00

BIG CHENIER & HIS NIGHT OWLS/THE R.B. ORCHESTRA:

Goldband 1051 *Let Me Hold Your Hand*......	7.00 -	10.00
1131 *The Dog And His Puppies*...........	5.00 -	8.00

CLIFTON CHENIER:

Argo 5262 *The Big Wheel*..........	4.00 -	6.00
Bayou 707 *Black Gal*.............	10.00 -	15.00
710 *Louisiana Rock*...........	10.00 -	15.00
Checker 939 *Bayou Drive*.........	3.00 -	5.00
Elko 920 *Louisiana Stomp*.........	20.00 -	30.00
Imperial 5352 *Louisiana Stomp*.......	10.00 -	15.00
Specialty 552, 556, 568.............	5.00 -	8.00
Zynn 506, 1004, 1011...............	5.00 -	8.00

THE CHEROKEES:

Grand 106 *Rainbow Of Love*...........	20.00 -	30.00
Peacock 1656 *Is She Real*............	15.00 -	20.00
United Artists 367 *My Heavenly Angel*.......	8.00 -	12.00

FRANKIE CHER-VALI:

Dot 15674 *My First Impression Of You*........	———	

THE CHESTERFIELDS:

Chess 1559 *I'm In Heaven*....................	———	

THE CHESTERS:

Apollo 521 *The Fires Burn No More*..........	10.00 -	15.00

THE CHESTNUTS:

Davis 447 *Love Is True*..........	10.00 -	15.00
452 *Forever I Vow*..................	10.00 -	15.00
Mercury 70489 *Don't Go*...........	10.00 -	15.00
Standard 100 *Who Knows Better Than I*.......	20.00 -	30.00

THE CHEVELLES:

Infinity 1007 *I'm Sorry*.............	4.00 -	7.00

THE CHEV-RONS:

Galt 100 *The Defense Rests*..........	8.00 -	12.00

CHICK & THE HOT RODS:

King 5537 *Jimmy Caught The Dickens*.......	4.00 -	7.00

THE CHIFFONS:

Laurie (LP) 2018 *He's So Fine*.........	15.00 -	20.00
(LP) 2036 *Sweet Talkin' Guy*.........	15.00 -	20.00

BUDDY CHILDRESS:

Dub 2838 *My Lovin' Arms*...............	8.00 -	12.00

THE CHIMES:

Flair 1051 *My Heart's Crying For You*........	15.00 -	20.00
House Of Beauty *3 Tears From An Angel's Eyes*	———	
Royal Roost 577 *Dearest Darling*............	10.00 -	15.00
Specialty 555 *Zindy Lou*............	8.00 -	12.00
570, 574.............	5.00 -	8.00

THE CHIPPENDALES:

Andie 5013 *What A Night*.............	5.00 -	8.00
Rust 5023 *The Day Will Come*........	5.00 -	8.00

THE CHIPS:

Josie 803 *Rubber Biscuit*...............	10.00 -	15.00

THE CHORALS:

Decca 29914 *In My Dream*............	10.00 -	15.00

THE CHORDCATS:

Cat 112 *A Girl To Love*....................	8.00 -	12.00

THE CHORDELLS:

Jaro 77005 *At Last*.............	10.00 -	15.00
Onyx 504 *Here's A Heart For You*..........	10.00 -	15.00

THE CHORDS:

Casino 451 *Tears In Your Eyes*........	7.00 -	10.00
Cat 104, 109.............	5.00 -	8.00
Metro 20015 *Elephant Walk*.........	5.00 -	8.00

"A CHRISTMAS GIFT FOR YOU":

Philles (LP) 4005 (various artists).............	20.00 -	30.00

JOHN CHRISTMON:

Excello 2031 *My Baby's Gone*.............	15.00 -	20.00

THE CHROMATICS: (See also LITTLE AUGIE AUSTIN)

Million 2010 *Here In The Darkness*..........	7.00 -	10.00

CHUCK & BILL:

Brunswick 55011 *Watch Your Step*...........	15.00 -	20.00

THE CHUCKLES:

West Side 1019 *On The Street Where You Live*.	4.00 -	7.00

CHUCK WAGON GANG:

Columbia (LP) 922 *Sacred Songs*.............	8.00 -	12.00
(LP) 9022 (10")........................	8.00 -	12.00

EUGENE CHURCH:

Class 235, 254.............	3.00 -	6.00
235 *Pretty Girls Everywhere* (78rpm)........	10.00 -	15.00
254 *Miami* (78rpm)...........	10.00 -	15.00

THE CINCINNATIANS:

Emerald 16116 *Magic Genie*.............	3.00 -	5.00

CINDY & SANDY:

Tailspin 102 *Make Believe Baby*.............	———	

THE CINERAMAS:

Rhapsody 71964 *Crying For You*............	7.00 -	10.00

PETE CIOLINO:

Recorte 401 *Daddy Joe*....................	10.00 -	15.00

CIRCLE C BAND:

Melco 105 *Ramshackled Shack*...............	———	

JIMMY CLANTON:

Ace 546 *Just A Dream* (78rpm)...............	10.00 -	15.00
668 *Heart Hotel*............	7.00 -	10.00
(LP) 1001 *Just A Dream*....................	15.00 -	20.00
(LP) 1007 *Jimmy's Happy*...........	10.00 -	15.00
(LP) 1008 *Jimmy's Blue*...........	10.00 -	15.00
(LP) 1011 *My Best To You*...........	10.00 -	15.00
(LP) 1014 *Teenage Millionaire*...........	10.00 -	15.00
(LP) 1026 *Venus In Blue Jeans*...........	10.00 -	15.00

THE CLAREMONTS:

Apollo 517 *Angel Of Romance*.............	7.00 -	10.00

CHARLES CLARK:

Artistic 1500 *Row Your Boat*.............	7.00 -	10.00

DEE CLARK:

Falcon 1002, 1005.............	5.00 -	8.00
1009 *Oh Little Girl*..................	15.00 -	20.00
Vee Jay (LP) 1037 *Hold On...It's Dee Clark*.....	15.00 -	20.00

FRED CLARK:

Federal 12136 *Ground Hog Snooper*	10.00 -	15.00

LEONARD CLARK & LAND OF SKY BOYS:

Klub 3108 *Come To Your Tommy Now*	8.00 -	12.00

SANFORD CLARK:

Dot 15534, 15556	3.00 -	5.00
Jamie 1107 *Sing 'Em Some Blues*	5.00 -	8.00
1120 *Bad Luck*	3.00 -	6.00
MCI 1003 *The Fool*	15.00 -	20.00
Project—*Tennessee Walk*	————	

THE CLASSICS:

Class 219 *If Only The Sky Was A Mirror*	8.00 -	12.00
Dart 1015 *Cinderella*	8.00 -	12.00
1]24 *Life Is But A Dream*	8.00 -	12.00
1032 *Angela Angela*	8.00 -	12.00
Musicnote 118, 1116	4.00 -	8.00
Promo 1010 *Blue Moon*	4.00 -	8.00

THE CLASSMATES:

Marquee 102 *Pretty Little Pet*	4.00 -	7.00

JOE CLAY:

Vik 0211 *Duck Tail*	10.00 -	15.00
0218 *Cracker Jack*	15.00 -	20.00

DOCTOR CLAYTON:

Groove 5006 *Honey Stealin' Blues*	10.00 -	15.00

DOUG CLAYTON:

Pure Gold—*Sally Ann*	————	

JOHNNY CLAYTON:

Dixie 838 *Never Again*	10.00 -	15.00

CLEAR WATERS:

Atomic H 203 *Boogie Woogie Baby*	15.00 -	20.00

EDDIE CLEARY:

Kawana 102 *Think It Over Baby*	8.00 -	12.00

THE CLEFS:

Chess 1521 *We Three*	50.00 -	80.00
Peacock 1643 *I'll Be Waiting*	12.00 -	16.00

THE CLEFTONES:

Gee (LP) 705 *Heart And Soul*	25.00 -	40.00
(LP) 707 *For Sentimental Reasons*	25.00 -	40.00
1000 *You Baby You*	5.00 -	8.00
1000 *You Baby You* (78rpm)	7.00 -	10.00
1011 *Little Girl Of Mine*	5.00 -	8.00
1016 *Neki-Hokey*	4.00 -	7.00
1016 *Neki-Hokey* (78rpm)	7.00 -	10.00
1064, 1067	3.00 -	5.00
Old Town—*The Masquerade Is Over*	40.00 -	60.00

HENRY CLEMENT:

Spot 1000 *Late Hour Blues*	5.00 -	8.00
Zynn 1006 *I'll Be Waiting*	5.00 -	8.00

JACK CLEMENT:

Sun 291 *Ten Years*	5.00 -	8.00

CLEO & THE CRYSTALIERS:

Cindy 3003 *Please Be My Guy*	20.00 -	30.00

THE CLICKS:

Josie 780 *Come Back To Me*	15.00 -	20.00

THE CLIMBERS:

J & S 1652 *My Darlin' Dear*	15.00 -	20.00

PATSY CLINE:

Decca 8611 *Patsy Cline*	10.00 -	15.00
Patsy Cline (EP) 16 *Try Again +3*	7.00 -	10.00

THE CLINTONIAN CUBS:

My Brothers 7 *She's Just My Style*	50.00 -	80.00

THE CLIPS:

Calvert—*Let Me Get Close To You Baby*	10.00 -	15.00

THE CLIQUES:

Modern 987, 995	5.00 -	8.00

THE CLOUDS:

Cobra 1005 *I Do*	75.00 -	100.00

THE CLOVERS:

Atlantic (EP) 504, 537, 590	8.00 -	12.00
934 *Don't You Know I Love You*	35.00 -	50.00
944 *Fool Fool Fool*	20.00 -	30.00

---

963 *One Mint Julep*	10.00 -	15.00
969 *Ting-A-Ling*	10.00 -	15.00
977 *I Played The Fool*	10.00 -	15.00
989 *Crawlin'*	10.00 -	15.00
1000 *Good Lovin'*	8.00 -	12.00
0101 *The Feeling Is So Good*	8.00 -	12.00
1022 *Lovey Dovey*	8.00 -	12.00
1035 *Your Cash Ain't Nothin' But Trash*	7.00 -	10.00
1046 *I Confess*	7.00 -	10.00
1052 *Blue Velvet*	5.00 -	8.00
1060 *Love Bug*	5.00 -	8.00
1073 *Nip Sip*	5.00 -	8.00
1083 *Devil Or Angel*	5.00 -	8.00
(Above are yellow label)		
Atlantic (higher number, red label)	3.00 -	6.00
(LP) 1248 *The Clovers* (black label)	30.00 -	40.00
(LP) 8009 *The Clovers* (black label)	25.00 -	40.00
(LP) 8034 *Clovers' Dance Party*	15.00 -	20.00
Popular (LP) 1001 *The Clovers In Clover*	15.00 -	20.00
United Artists (LP) 3033 *The Clovers In Clover*.	15.00 -	20.00
United Artists (LP) 3099 *Love Potion Number 9*.	25.00 -	35.00

THE CLUSTERS:

Tee Gee 102 *Pardon My Heart*	————	

THE COASTERS:

Atco (LP) 101 *The Coasters*	30.00 -	40.00
(LP) 111 *The Coasters' Greatest Hits*	20.00 -	30.00
(LP) 123 *One By One*	25.00 -	35.00
(LP) 135 *Coast Along With The Coasters*	15.00 -	20.00
6064 *Turtle Dovin'* (maroon label)	7.00 -	10.00
6073 *Brazil* (maroon label)	7.00 -	10.00
6087 *Searchin'* (maroon label)	7.00 -	10.00
Atco (higher numbers, yellow label)	3.00 -	6.00
6098 *My Baby Comes To Me*	7.00 -	10.00
6104 *What Is The Secret Of Your Success?* . . .	7.00 -	10.00
6111 *Gee, Golly* (78rpm)	8.00 -	12.00
6116 *Yakety Yak* (78rpm)	15.00 -	20.00
6126 *The Shadow Knows* (78rpm)	10.00 -	15.00
6132 *Charlie Brown* (78rpm)	20.00 -	30.00
6146 *Poison Ivy* (78 rpm)	25.00 -	35.00
(EP) 4501 Rock & Roll With	10.00 -	15.00
(EP) 4502 *Keep Rockin' With The Coasters* . . .	10.00 -	15.00
(EP) 4506 *The Coasters*	10.00 -	15.00
(EP) 4507 *The Coasters' Top Hits*	10.00 -	15.00

THE COBRAS:

Modern 964 *Sindy*	20.00 -	30.00

WILLIE COBBS:

C & F 300/301 *Five Long Years*	5.00 -	8.00
J.O.B. 1127 *Come On Home*	15.00 -	20.00

KIMBALL COBURN:

Hi 2010 *Please, Please*	7.00 -	10.00

THE COCHRAN BROTHERS:

Ekko 1003 *Two Blue Singing Stars*	35.00 -	50.00
1005 *Guilty Conscience*	50.00 -	75.00
3001 *Fool's Paradise*	50.00 -	75.00

EDDIE COCHRAN:

Crest 1026 *Skinny Jim*	20.00 -	30.00
Liberty (LP) 3061 *Singin' To My Baby*	60.00 -	80.00
(LP) 3172 *Eddie Cochran*	35.00 -	60.00
(LP) 3220 *Never To Be Forgotten*	35.00 -	60.00
Liberty 55056 *Sittin' In The Balcony* (78 rpm) . . .	10.00 -	15.00
55056, 55070, 55087	3.00 -	5.00
55112 *Cradle Baby*	6.00 -	10.00
55123 *Jeannie Jeannie Jeannie*	6.00 -	10.00
55138, 55144, 55166, 55177, 55203	3.00 -	5.00
55217, 55242, 55278	4.00 -	8.00

JACK(IE) (LEE) COCHRAN:

ABC Paramount 9930 *Buy A Car*	15.00 -	20.00
Decca 30206 *Mama Don't You Think I Know* . .	25.00 -	35.00
Jaguar 3031 *Georgia Lee Brown*	30.00 -	40.00
Sims 107 *Hip Shakin' Mama*	40.00 -	60.00
Spry 120 *Pity Me*	40.00 -	60.00
Viv 988 *Buy A Car*	20.00 -	30.00

WAYNE COCHRAN:

Gala 117 *Last Kiss*.............	3.00 -	5.00
Scottie 1303 *My Little Girl*.............	3.00 -	5.00

JIMMY COE (& HIS GAY CATS OF RHYTHM):

States 129 *Raid On The After Hour Joint*......	8.00 -	12.00
155 *The Jet*.........	8.00 -	12.00

THE CO-EDS:

Dwain 802 *With All My Heart*.............	7.00 -	10.00
Old Town 1027 *Love You Baby All The Time*..	8.00 -	12.00
1033 *I Love An Angel*.............	8.00 -	12.00

THE COINS:

Gee 10 *Can't Get No Place With You*........	150.00 -	200.00

COKE JINGLES (with THE SHIRELLES, THE FOUR SEASONS, JAN & DEAN, and ROY ORBISON):

....	10.00 -	20.00

AL COKER with THE COKER FAMILY:

Decca 30053 *Don't Go Baby*.............	10.00 -	20.00

ALVADEAN COKER:

Abbott 176 *We're Gonna Bop*.............	4.00 -	6.00

ANN COLE (& THE SUBURBANS):

Baton 232, 237, 240..............	5.00 -	8.00

DON COLE:

Kent 305 *Sweet Lovin' Honey*.............	15.00 -	25.00
RPM 502 *Snake-Eyed Mama*.............	15.00 -	25.00

LEE COLE:

Mist 1010 *Cool Baby*.............	15.00 -	25.00

LES COLE with THE ECHOES:

D 1010 *Rock-A-My Baby*.............	15.00 -	25.00

SONNY COLE:

Excell 124 *Robinson Crusoe Bop*.............	20.00 -	30.00

HONEY COLEMAN:

Combo 3 *Daddy Why Did You Leave Me*......	10.00 -	15.00

HOOKS COLEMAN:

Excello 2193 *Teen-Age Baby*.............	8.00 -	12.00

RAY COLEMAN:

Arcade 147 *Jukebox Rock & Roll*.............	20.00 -	30.00

COLLAY & THE SATELLITES:

Sho-Biz 102 *Little Girl Next Door*.............	10.00 -	15.00

THE COLLEGIANS:

Winley (LP) 6004 *Sing Along With The Collegians*	35.00 -	50.00
X-Tra 108 *Let's Go For A Ride*.............	15.00 -	20.00

GUS COLLETTI:

Tin Pan Alley—*Sample Kiss*.............	———	

BIFF COLLIE:

Starday 178, 251.............	5.00 -	10.00

THE COLLINS KIDS:

Columbia 21470 *Beetle Bug Bop*.............	7.00 -	10.00
21514 *The Rockaway Rock*.............	5.00 -	8.00
21543 *I'm In My Teens*.............	8.00 -	12.00
21560 *Rock And Roll Polka*.............	5.00 -	8.00
40824 *Move A Little Closer*.............	8.00 -	12.00
40921 *Hop, Skip And Jump*.............	8.00 -	12.00
41012 *Party*.............	10.00 -	15.00
41087 *Mama Worries*.............	8.00 -	12.00
41149 *Mercy*.............	10.00 -	15.00
41225 *Rock Boppin' Baby*.............	10.00 -	15.00
41329 *Sugar Plum*.............	8.00 -	12.00

AL COLLINS:

Ace 500 *I Got The Blues For You*.............	30.00 -	40.00

EDDIE COLLINS:

Fernwood 104 *Patience Baby*.............	———	

LORRIE & LARRY COLLINS (See THE COLLINS KIDS)

MARTY COLLINS:

Ammons 6083 *I'm Gonna Walk*.............	4.00 -	6.00
Renner 227 *She's Fine*.............	10.00 -	15.00

TOMMY COLLINS:

Capitol (LP) 776.............	10.00 -	15.00
(LP) 1196 *This Is*.............	10.00 -	15.00

THE COLONAIRS:

Ember 1017 *Can't Stand To Lose You*........	10.00 -	15.00

Tru-Lite 127 *Do-Pop-Si*.............	25.00 -	30.00

THE COLTS:

Vita 112 *Adorable*.............	8.00 -	12.00
121 *Sweet Sixteen*.............	10.00 -	15.00
130 *Never, No More*.............	10.00 -	15.00

CHUCK COMER:

Vaden—*Shall We Dance/Little More Lovin*—...	———	

THE COMIC BOOKS:

Dynamic Sound 2005 *The First Time In My Life*	8.00 -	12.00

THE COMMODORES:

Dot 15372 *Uranium*.............	10.00 -	15.00
RPM 488 *Hello Baby*.............	10.00 -	15.00

THE COMPANIONS:

Federal 12397 *Why Oh Why Baby*.............	8.00 -	12.00
Gina 722 *It's Too Late*.............	5.00 -	8.00

THE COMPOSERS:

Era 3118 *I Had A Dream*.............	7.00 -	10.00

BOBBY COMSTOCK & THE COUNTS:

Mohawk 124 *Everyday Blues*.............	4.00 -	7.00
Triumph 602 *Jealous Fool*.............	4.00 -	7.00

THE CONCORDS:

Ember 1007 *I'll Always Say Please*.............	10.00 -	15.00
Epic 9697 *Should I Cry*.............	7.00 -	10.00
Gramercy 304 *Cross My Heart*.............	7.00 -	10.00
Harlem 2328 *Monticello*.............	75.00 -	100.00
Herald 576 *Marlene*.............	5.00 -	8.00
578 *Cold And Frosty Morning*.............	5.00 -	8.00

TONY CONN:

Decca 30813 *Like Wow*.............	30.00 -	40.00
30865 *You Pretty Thing*.............	30.00 -	40.00

CONNY & THE BELLHOPS:

R 505 *Shot Road*.............	10.00 -	15.00
R 511 *Fafine/Are You Ashamed*.............	10.00 -	15.00

THE CONSTELLATIONS:

Groove 0140 *Come Sit By Me*.............	8.00 -	12.00

THE CONTINENTALS:

Hunter 3502 *It Doesn't Matter*.............	20.00 -	30.00
Whirlin' Disc 101 *Dear Lord*.............	15.00 -	20.00
105 *Picture Of Love*.............	15.00 -	20.00

THE CONTOURS:

Motown 1012 *Funny*.............	10.00 -	15.00

DALE COOK:

Specialty 596 *Forever*.............	5.00 -	8.00

L.C. COOKE:

Checker 903, 925.............	4.00 -	7.00

SAM COOKE:

Keen (LP) 2001, 2003, 2004.............	8.00 -	12.00
4-4002 *Desire Me* (78rpm).............	8.00 -	12.00
4-4009 *Lonely Island* (78rpm).............	8.00 -	12.00
44013 *You Send Me* (78rpm).............	10.00 -	15.00
Specialty 619 *Forever*.............	4.00 -	7.00
627 *I Don't Want To Cry*.............	5.00 -	8.00

COOKIE & THE CUPCAKES:

Khoury's 703 *Mathilda*.............	7.00 -	10.00
Lyric 1008 *All My Lovin' Baby*.............	5.00 -	8.00

THE COOKIES:

Josie 822 *King Of Hearts*.............	4.00 -	7.00

COOL BREEZE (See LITTLE COOL BREEZES)

THE COOLBREEZERS:

ABC Paramount 9865 *You Know I Go For You*	10.00 -	15.00
Bale 100 *The Greatest Love Of All*.............	8.00 -	12.00
102 *Christmas Ring*.............	12.00 -	16.00

EDDIE COOLEY & THE DIMPLES:

Roost 621 *Priscilla* (78rpm).............	8.00 -	12.00

SPADE COOLEY:

Columbia (LP) 9007 (10") *Sagebrush Swing*.....	15.00 -	20.00

DOLLY COOPER:

Dot 15495 *Big Rock Inn*.............	7.00 -	10.00

LITTLE COOPER & THE DRIFTERS:

Stevens 105 *Evening Train*.............	7.00 -	10.00

COWBOY COPAS:

Starday 501, 528, 542, 641.............	4.00 -	6.00

JOHNNY COPELAND:
Mercury 71280 *Rock 'n Roll Lilly*. . . . . ————

KEN COPELAND:
Lin 5017 *Fanny Brown*. 15.00 - 20.00

THE COPESETICS:
Premium 409 *Collegian*. . . . . 10.00 - 15.00

PAT CORDEL & THE CRESCENTS:
Club 1011 *Darling Come Back*. . . . . 15.00 - 20.00
Victory 1001 *Darling Come Back* (red plastic). . . 10.00 - 15.00

THE CORDELLS:
Bullseye 1017 *Believe In Me*. . . . . 10.00 - 15.00

THE CORDIALS:
Reveille 106 *Eternal Love*. . . . . 7.00 - 10.00
Seven Arts 707 *Dawn Is Almost Here*. . . . . 8.00 - 12.00
Whip 276 *My Heart's Desire*. . . . . 7.00 - 10.00

THE CORONETS:
Chess 1549 *Nadine*. 15.00 - 25.00
1549 *Nadine* (red plastic). . . . . 100.00 up
1553 *It Would Be Heavenly*. . . . . 25.00 - 40.00
1553 *It Would Be Heavenly* (red plastic). . . 100.00 up
Groove 014 *I Love You More*. . . . . 20.00 - 30.00
0116 *Hush*. . . . . 20.00 - 30.00

THE CORSAIRS:
Hytone 110 *Goodbye Darling*. . . . . 75.00 - 125.00

THE CORVAIRS:
Comet 2145 *True True Love*. . . . . 5.00 - 8.00

THE CORVELLS:
ABC Paramount 10324 *Take My Love*. . . . . 7.00 - 10.00
Lido 509 *We Made A Vow*. . . . . 10.00 - 15.00

THE CORVETS:
ABC Paramount 9891 *String Band Hop*. . . . . . . ————

THE COSMIC RAYS:
Saturn 222 *Bye Bye*. ————

NED COSTNER:
Hamilton 50030 *Jeopardy*. . . . . 7.00 - 10.00

ERNEST COTTON:
J.O.B. 1120 *Going Back To Memphis*. . . . . 15.00 - 20.00

JAMES COTTON:
Loma 2042 *Laying In The Weeds*. . . . . 5.00 - 8.00
Sun 199 *Straighten Up Baby*. . . . . 40.00 - 60.00
206 *Cotton Crop Blues*. . . . . 40.00 - 60.00

JERRY COULSTON & THE JADES:
Christy 131 *Bon-Bon Baby*. . . . . 7.00 - 10.00

THE COUNTRY DUDES (with CLAY ALLAN):
Azalea 121 *Have A Ball*. . . . . 10.00 - 15.00

THE COUNTRY G-J's:
Valley—*Go, Girl, Go*. . . . . ————

FRED COUPLAND (See BLUE TONES)

THE COUNTS:
Dot 1188 *Darling Dear*. . . . . 10.00 - 15.00
1199 *Baby Don't You Know*. . . . . 10.00 - 15.00
1210 *She Won't Say Yes*. . . . . 10.00 - 15.00
1226 *Baby I Want You*. . . . . 8.00 - 12.00
1235 *Let Me Go Lover*. . . . . 8.00 - 12.00
1243 *Love And Understanding*. . . . . 8.00 - 12.00
1265 *I Need You Tonight*. . . . . 8.00 - 12.00
1275 *To Our Love*. . . . . 8.00 - 12.00

KEITH COURDALE:
—*Steelwork Blues*. . . . . ————

COUSIN LEROY:
Ember 1016 *Highway 41*. . . . . 10.00 - 15.00
1023 *Up The River*. . . . . 8.00 - 12.00
Groove 0123 *Catfish*. . . . . 8.00 - 12.00
Herald 546 *Waitin' At The Station*. . . . . 8.00 - 12.00

BUDDY COVELLE:
Coral 62181 *Lorraine*. . . . . 20.00 - 30.00

C-QUINS:
Chess 1815 *My Only Love*. . . . . 5.00 - 8.00

RILEY CRABTREE:
Ekko 1019 *Meet Me At Joe's*. . . . . 5.00 - 8.00

BILL(Y) ("CRASH") CRADDOCK:
Colonial 721 *Birddoggin'*. . . . . 7.00 - 10.00

Columbia 41316, 41367, 41536. . . . . 3.00 - 5.00

JIMMY CRAIG:
Imperial 5592 *Oh! Little Girl!*. . . . . 10.00 - 15.00
Prism 1002 *Rocka Socka Hop*. . . . . 10.00 - 15.00

PEE WEE CRAIG:
Choice 1000 *Rambling Man*. . . . . 10.00 - 15.00

JIMMY CRAIN:
Spangle 2009 *Shig-A-Shag*. . . . . 10.00 - 15.00
Vincent 5047/5048 *Why Worry*. . . . . 7.00 - 10.00

BLACKIE CRAWFORD:
Coral 64118, 64128, 64161. . . . . 5.00 - 8.00

FRED CRAWFORD:
Starday 170 *You Gotta Wait*. . . . . 10.00 - 15.00
243 *Rock Candy Rock*. . . . . 10.00 - 15.00

SUGAR BOY CRAWFORD:
Imperial 5424, 5468. . . . . 3.00 - 6.00

PEE WEE CRAYTON:
Crown (LP) 5175 *Pee Wee Crayton*. . . . . 15.00 - 20.00
Fox 102 *Look Up And Live*. . . . . 10.00 - 15.00
Imperial 5288 *Every Dog Has His Day*. . . . . . . 10.00 - 15.00
5297 *Hurry Hurry*. . . . . 10.00 - 15.00
5321 *I Need Your Love*. . . . . 6.00 - 10.00
5338 *I Got News For You*. . . . . 6.00 - 10.00
5345 *Eyes Full Of Tears*. . . . . 6.00 - 10.00
5353 *Be Faithful*. . . . . 6.00 - 10.00
Post 2007 *Don't Go*. . . . . 7.00 - 10.00
Recorded in Hollywood 408 *Pappy's Blues*. . . . . 15.00 - 20.00
426 *I'm Your Prisoner*. . . . . 15.00 - 20.00
Vee Jay 214 *The Telephone Is Ringing*. . . . . . . 5.00 - 8.00
252 *I Don't Care*. . . . . 5.00 - 8.00
266 *Fiddle De Dee*. . . . . 4.00 - 6.00

THE CREATIONS:
Jamie 1197 *The Bells*. . . . . 4.00 - 7.00
Meridian 6283, 7552 *The Wedding*. . . . . 10.00 - 15.00
Penny 9022 *We're In Love*. . . . . 5.00 - 8.00
Tip Top 400 *Mommy and Daddy*. . . . . 15.00 - 20.00

THE CREATORS:
Dootone 463 *I've Had You*. . . . . 4.00 - 7.00
Dore 653 *Too Far To Turn Around*. . . . . 6.00 - 10.00
Hi-Q 5021 *Wear My Ring*. . . . . 6.00 - 10.00

THE CRESCENDOS:
Music City 831 *My Heart's Desire*. . . . . 8.00 - 12.00
Nasco 6005 *Oh Julie*(78rpm). . . . . 15.00 - 20.00
Scarlet 4007 *Strange Love*. . . . . 4.00 - 7.00
Tap 7027 *Oh Julie*. 10.00 - 15.00

THE CRESCENTS:
Hamilton 50033 *Hey There*. . . . . 5.00 - 8.00
Joyce 102 *Everybody Knew But Me*. . . . . 15.00 - 20.00

THE CRESTS:
Coed 501 *Pretty Little Angel*. . . . . 7.00 - 10.00
(LP) 901 *The Crests Sing All Biggies*. . . . . 30.00 - 40.00
(LP) 904 *16 Fabulous Hits*. . . . . 20.00 - 30.00
Coral 64203 *You Blew Out The Candles*. . . . . . . 5.00 - 8.00
Joyce 103 *Sweetest One*. . . . . 15.00 - 20.00
105 *No One To Love*. . . . . 15.00 - 20.00
(Note: 78 RPM pressings may exist of THE CRESTS'
Coed records; these would be of value. Canadian
78 RPM pressings have been seen.)

THE CREW CUTS:
Mercury (LP) 20144 *Rock And Roll Bash*. . . . . . 15.00 - 20.00

THE CRICKETS (featuring DEAN BARLOW):
Beacon 104 *Be Faithful*. . . . . 7.00 - 10.00
Davis (EP) 211 *The Crickets*. . . . . 10.00 - 15.00
459 *I'm Going To Live My Life Alone*. . . . . . 7.00 - 10.00
Jay Dee 777 *Dreams And Wishes*. . . . . 10.00 - 15.00
781 *Fine As Wine*. . . . . 10.00 - 15.00
785 *Your Love*. . . . . 10.00 - 15.00
786 *Just You*. . . . . 8.00 - 12.00
789 *Are You Looking For A Sweetheart?*. . . . 8.00 - 12.00
795 *I'm Going To Live My Life Alone*. . . . . . 8.00 - 12.00
Junior 396 *I Sold My Heart To The Junkman*. . . 10.00 - 15.00
MGM 11428 *You're Mine*. . . . . 15.00 - 25.00

11507 *For You I Have Eyes*............	15.00 -	25.00

THE CRICKETS (with BUDDY HOLLY):

Brunswick (LP) 54038 *The Chirping Crickets*....	60.00 -	90.00
55009 *That'll Be The Day* (78 rpm)........	25.00 -	35.00
55035 *Not Fade Away* (78 rpm)........	25.00 -	35.00
55053 *Maybe Baby* (78 rpm)........	25.00 -	35.00
55072 *Think It Over* (78 rpm)........	25.00 -	35.00
55094 *It's So Easy* (78 rpm)........	25.00 -	35.00
(EP) 71036 *Chirping Crickets*........	20.00 -	30.00
(EP) 71038 *Sound Of The Crickets*........	20.00 -	30.00
Coral (LP) 57320 *In Style With The Crickets*....	40.00 -	60.00
(EP) 81192 *The Crickets*........	20.00 -	30.00

G. DAVY CROCKETT:

Checker 1121 *Look Out Mabel*........	7.00 -	10.00
Chief 7010 *Look Out Mabel*........	15.00 -	20.00
U.S.A. 816 *Look Out Mabel*........	8.00 -	12.00

GEORGE CROMWELL:

Brunswick 55131 *Washed Up*........	8.00 -	12.00

JERRY CRONIN:

Flame 113 *A-Rock-A Me Baby*........	7.00 -	10.00

DILLAR CROOM & THE CROOM BROTHERS:

Vee Jay 283 *It's You Love*........	25.00 -	35.00

HAROLD CROSBY & THE PINE TREE BOYS:

Lorida 3/4 *The Bastille Blues*........	5.00 -	8.00

BOBBY CROWN & THE KAPERS:

Felco 102 *One Way Ticket*........	15.00 -	20.00

THE CROWNS: (See also ARTHUR LEE MAYE & THE CROWNS)

R n B 6901 *I'll Forget About You*........	15.00 -	20.00

THE CROWS:

Gee 1 *Perfidia*........	40.00 -	60.00
Rama 3 *Seven Lonely Days*........	80.00 -	120.00
5 Gee (red plastic)........	20.00 -	30.00
5 Gee (black plastic)........	10.00 -	15.00
10 *Heartbreaker*........	40.00 -	60.00
29 *Untrue*........	30.00 -	40.00
30 *Miss You*........	40.00 -	60.00
50 *Sweet Sue*........	40.00 -	60.00
Tico 1082 *Mambo Shevitz*........	35.00 -	50.00

(ARTHUR) "BIG BOY" CRUDUP:

Ace 503 *My Baby Boogies All The Time*.......	20.00 -	30.00
Fire (LP) 103 *Mean Old Frisco*........	40.00 -	60.00
1502, 1503........	4.00 -	6.00
Groove 0011 *I Love My Baby*........	15.00 -	20.00
0026 *She's Got No Hair*........	15.00 -	20.00
5005 *Rock Me Mama*........	10.00 -	15.00
RCA Victor 5070 *Pearly Lee*........	15.00 -	20.00
5167 *Keep On Drinkin'*........	15.00 -	20.00
5563 *My Wife And Women*........	15.00 -	20.00
50-0000 *That's All Right*........	25.00 -	40.00
50-0001 *Katie May*........	15.00 -	20.00
50-0013 *Crudup's Vicksburg Blues*........	15.00 -	20.00
50-0032 *Hoodoo Lady Blues*........	15.00 -	20.00
50-0046 *Mercy Blues*........	15.00 -	20.00

(Note: RCA Vic. 50-0000—50-0046, inclusive, are made of vivid orange plastic.)

RCA Victor 50-0074 *Dust My Broom*........	12.00 -	16.00
50-0092 *Mean Old Santa Fe*........	12.00 -	16.00
50-0100 *Lonesome World To Me*........	12.00 -	16.00
50-0101 *She's Just Like Caldonia*........	12.00 -	16.00
50-0117 *Nobody Wants Me*........	12.00 -	16.00
50-0126 *Roberta Blues*........	12.00 -	16.00
50-0141 *Too Much Competition*........	12.00 -	16.00

THE CRUISERS:

Finch 353 *The Moon Is Yours*........	10.00 -	15.00
Zebra 119 *Foolish Me*........	10.00 -	15.00

AL CRUM:

Glenn 3800 *Turn 'Em Up*........	5.00 -	8.00

SIMON CRUM:

Capitol (LP) 1880 *The Unpredictable Simon Crum*	10.00 -	15.00
3460 *Bop Cat Bop*........	7.00 -	10.00

MANNY CRUSE & THE SOUNDS QUARTETTE:

Dart 127 *Any Time Any Place*........	5.00 -	8.00

THE CRYSTALIERS:

Johnson 103 *Don't Cry*........	20.00 -	30.00

THE CRYSTALS:

Aladdin 3355 *I Do Believe*........	15.00 -	20.00
De Luxe 6013 *My Dear*........	30.00 -	50.00
6037 *Have Faith In Me*........	30.00 -	50.00
6077 *God Only Knows*........	30.00 -	50.00
Felsted 8566 *Blind Date*........	4.00 -	6.00
Luna 5001 *Come To Me Darling*........	30.00 -	50.00
Philles 100 *Oh Yeah, Maybe Baby*........	7.00 -	10.00
103 *Uptown*........	7.00 -	10.00
Rockin' 518 *Don't You Go*........	30.00 -	50.00

THE C TONES:

Everlast 5005 *On Your Mark*........	5.00 -	8.00

THE CUBANS:

Flash 133 *Tell Me*........	8.00 -	12.00

THE CUBS:

Savoy 1502 *Why Did You Make Me Cry*......	7.00 -	10.00

THE CUES:

Capitol 3310 *You're On My Mind*........	7.00 -	10.00

THE CUFF LINKS:

Dootone 413 *How You Lied*........	10.00 -	15.00
422 *It's Too Late Now*........	8.00 -	12.00
409 *Guided Missiles*........	8.00 -	12.00
Gait 543 *Only One Love*........	15.00 -	20.00

THE CUFFLINX:

Dootone 433 *So Tough*........	8.00 -	12.00
435 *A Fool's Fortune*........	8.00 -	12.00
438 *Lawful Wedding*........	8.00 -	12.00

BRUCE CULVER:

M.M.I. 1235 *Square Record*........	7.00 -	10.00

THE CUPIDS:

Aladdin 3404 *Lillie Mae*........	8.00 -	12.00
Decca 30279 *The Answer To Your Prayer*.....	8.00 -	12.00

PAT CUPP:

Crown (LP) 5364 *Pat Cupp and Ray Smith*....	15.00 -	20.00
RPM 461 *Do Me Now Wrong*........	20.00 -	30.00
473 *Long Gone Daddy*........	20.00 -	30.00
—*That's My Girl*........	———	

CURLEY JIM (MORRISON):

Mida 100 *Rock 'N' Roll Itch*........	7.00 -	10.00
108 *Sloppy Sloppy Suzie*........	7.00 -	10.00

EARL CURRY:

Post 2001 *Somebody Stole My Girl*........	8.00 -	12.00
2011 *Hobo*........	8.00 -	12.00
R & B 1313 *Try And Get Me*........	10.00 -	15.00
RPM 402 *One Whole Year Baby*........	15.00 -	20.00

JAMES CURRY:

Flash 110 *My Promise*........	8.00 -	12.00

DON CURTIS:

Kliff 104 *Rough Tough Man*........	20.00 -	30.00

EDDIE CURTIS:

Dot 15505 *You're Much Too Pretty For Me*....	5.00 -	8.00

EDDIE "TEX" CURTIS:

Gee 9 *Shake, Pretty Baby, Shake*........	75.00 -	100.00

MAC CURTIS:

King 4927 *If I Had Me A Woman*........	20.00 -	30.00
4949 *Grandaddy's Rockin'*........	25.00 -	35.00
4965 *You Ain't Treatin' Me Right*........	20.00 -	30.00
4995 *That Ain't Nothin' But Right*........	20.00 -	30.00
5059 *Say So*........	15.00 -	20.00
5107 *What You Want*........	15.00 -	20.00
5121 *Little Miss Linda*........	10.00 -	15.00
Shalimar 103 *Come On Back*........	5.00 -	8.00

C.C. CURTIS:

Audicon 109 *Aunt Minnie*........	5.00 -	8.00

THE CYCLONES: (See also BILL TAYLOR & THE CYCLONES)

Flip 324 *My Dear*........	4.00 -	7.00
Trophy 503 *Aftermath*........	5.00 -	8.00

CYMBAL

JOHNNY CYMBAL:

Kapp (LP) 3324 *Mr. Bass Man*	12.00 -	18.00

THE CYMBALS:

Amazon 709 *One Step Too Far*	5.00 -	8.00

BUDDY CYPRESS:

Flash 118 *I'm In Love With You*	7.00 -	10.00

CZARS OF RHYTHM:

De'Voice 782 *Please Don't Leave Me*	10.00 -	15.00

DADDY CLEANHEAD:

Specialty 541 *Back Home*	5.00 -	8.00

DICK D'AGOSTIN:

Accent 1046 *I'm You Daddy-O*	8.00 -	12.00
Dot 15773 *Nancy Lynne*	10.00 -	15.00
15867 *Night Walk*	4.00 -	7.00
Liberty 55218 *It's You*	3.00 -	5.00

DICK DALE & THE DEL-TONES:

Deltone (LP) 1001 *Surfer's Choice*	20.00 -	30.00
5014 *Jessie Pearl*	5.00 -	8.00
5019 *Eight Till Midnight*	5.00 -	8.00
5020 *Surf Beat*	5.00 -	8.00

JIMMIE DALE:

Drew-Blan 1003 *Emma Lee*	5.00 -	10.00

KENNY DALE:

Picture 310 *Cincy Lee*	7.00 -	10.00

LARRY DALE (& THE KING NOTES):

Atlantic 2133 *Drinkin' Wine Spo-Dee-O-Dee*	5.00 -	8.00
Elbridge 12763 *Crying Over You*	10.00 -	15.00

THE DALES:

Onyx 509 *If You Are Meant To Be*	10.00 -	15.00

JIMMY DALEY & THE DING-A-LINGS:

Decca (EP) 2431, 2432, 2480	5.00 -	8.00
(LP) 8429 *Ro*	12.00 -	16.00

CHUCK DALLAS:

K-C 102 *Come On Let's Go*	8.00 -	12.00

CHUCK DALLIS:

Glenn 2201 *Come On Let's Go*	10.00 -	15.00
2203 *Good Show, But No Go*	10.00 -	15.00
Mar-Vel 2204 *Joni Kaye*	10.00 -	15.00

BIG LLOYD DALTON:

Yucca 135 *Jenny*	7.00 -	10.00

DURWOOD DALY:

Caprock 108 *That's The Way It Goes*	7.00 -	10.00

TERRY DALY:

Mark 122 *You Don't Bug Me*	10.00 -	15.00

JOE D'AMBRA & THE EMBERS:

Mercury 71725 *Please Come Home*	5.00 -	8.00

DONNA DAMERON:

Dart 113 *Bopper 486609*	10.00 -	20.00

"DANCE THE ROCK & ROLL":

Atlantic (LP) 8013 (various artists)	10.00 -	15.00

"DANCE TUNES FROM THE VAULT":

Chess (LP) 1476 (various artists)	10.00 -	15.00

THE DANDELIERS:

B & F 1344 *Chop Chop Boom*	7.00 -	10.00
States 147 *My Autumn Love*	15.00 -	20.00
150 *My Loving Partner*	15.00 -	20.00
152 *May God Be With You*	20.00 -	30.00
160 *My Love*	20.00 -	30.00

THE DANDIES:

Peach 121 *Red Light*	7.00 -	10.00

EDDIE DANIELS:

Ebb 108 *Whoa-Whoa Baby*	10.00 -	15.00

JEFF DANIELS:

Astro 108 *Foxy Dan*	15.00 -	20.00
Big B 555 *Uh Uh Uh*	15.00 -	20.00
Big Howdy 777 *Switch Blade Sam*	15.00 -	20.00
Caravan—*Go Daddyo* (?)	———	
Meladee 117 *Daddy-O Rock*	30.00 -	50.00

THE DANLEERS:

Amp-3 2115 *One Summer Night*	10.00 -	15.00
Everest 19412 *Foolish*	5.00 -	8.00

DAVIS

Mercury 71356, 71401	4.00 -	6.00

DANNY & THE JUNIORS:

ABC Paramount 9871 *At The Hop* (78 rpm)	20.00 -	30.00
Singular 711 *At The Hop*	30.00 -	40.00

DANNY & THE MEMORIES:

Valiant 705 *Can't Help Lovin That Girl Of Mine*	5.00 -	8.00

DANNY BOY (& HIS BLUE GUITAR):

Dot 16140 *Send Me Some Lovin'*	7.00 -	10.00
Kent 300 *Don't Go Pretty Baby*	7.00 -	10.00
Tifco 824 *Wild Women*	7.00 -	10.00

CHARLES BUD DANT:

Decca (LP) 8430 *Holiday In The Golden West*	15.00 -	20.00

DANTE & THE EVERGREENS:

Madison (LP) 1002 *Dante & The Evergreens*	30.00 -	40.00

THE DAPPERS:

Epic 9423 *My Love Is Real*	10.00 -	15.00
Groove 0156 *Unwanted Love*	25.00 -	40.00
Peacock 1651 *Come Back To Me*	15.00 -	25.00
Rainbow 373 *Bop Bop Bu*	8.00 -	12.00

THE DAPS:

Marterry 5249 *Down And Out*	4.00 -	6.00

BOBBY DARIN (& THE JAYBIRDS):

Atco (LP) 102 *Bobby Darin*	15.00 -	20.00
(LP) 104 *That's All*	15.00 -	20.00
(LP) 115 *This Is Bobby Darin*	12.00 -	16.00
6117 *Splish Splash* (78rpm)	15.00 -	25.00
6127 *Queen Of The Hop* (78 rpm)	15.00 -	20.00
6133 *Plain Jane* (78 rpm)	15.00 -	20.00
Decca 29983 *Rock Island Line*	8.00 -	12.00
29922 *Sully Willie*	8.00 -	12.00
30031 *Hear Them Bells*	8.00 -	12.00
30225 *Dealer In Dreams*	8.00 -	12.00

DENVER DARLING:

Audio Lab (LP) 107	10.00 -	15.00

JOHNNY DARLING:

De Luxe 6167 *Baseball Baby*	———	

DARNELL & THE DREAMS:

West Side 1030 *I Had A Love*	5.00 -	8.00

DON DARNELL:

Brunswick 55144 *In My Own Little Way*	8.00 -	12.00

DARREL & THE OXFORDS:

Roulette 4174 *Picture In My Wallet*	5.00 -	8.00

JAMES DARREN:

Colpix (LP) 406 *Album No. 1*	15.00 -	20.00
(LP) 418 *Sings The Movies*	15.00 -	20.00
(LP) 424 *Sings For All Sizes*	15.00 -	20.00
(LP 428 *Love Among The Young*	15.00 -	20.00

THE DARTS:

Apt 25023 *On My Mind*	7.00 -	10.00

CHUCK DARTY:

Chart 642 *My Steady Girl*	15.00 -	20.00
Rama 229 *My Steady Girl*	8.00 -	12.00

FRANKIE DASH:

Cool 106 *Rock Rhythm Roll*	10.00 -	15.00

DAVE & THE STEREOS:

Pennant 1001 *Roamin' Romeo*	8.00 -	12.00

DAVEY & THE DOO RAYS:

Guyden 2002 *It's The Beat*	7.00 -	10.00

BOB DAVIES & THE RHYTHM JESTERS:

Rama 224 *Never Anymore*	7.00 -	10.00

AL DAVIS:

Manco——*Go Baby Go*	———	

BO DAVIS:

Crest 1027 *Let's Coast Awhile*	———	

BOB DAVIS:

Bandera 2505 *I Was Wrong*	5.00 -	8.00

DALE DAVIS & THE TOMCATS:

Stardale 100/101 *Gotta Rock*	15.00 -	25.00
104/105 *Why'd You Leave Me Blues*	15.00 -	25.00
701/702 *Bearcat Mama*	15.00 -	25.00

EDDIE DAVIS:

Fable—*Tick Tock Rock*	———	

EMMETT DAVIS:
M and B 101 *How About It Baby* . . . . 5.00 - 8.00

EUNICE DAVIS:
De Luxe 6068 *24 Hours A Day* . . . . 15.00 - 20.00
Grand 130 *Let's Have A Party* . . . . 8.00 - 12.00

GENE DAVIS:
Challenge 59091 *The Facts Of Life* . . . . 4.00 - 6.00
King 5076 *Who'll Dry My Tears* . . . . 5.00 - 8.00
R-Dell 107 *Curfew* . . . . 15.00 - 20.00

HARLEY DAVIS:
Cindy 3011 *Calling All Cats* . . . . 15.00 - 20.00

"HAPPY JACK" DAVIS with PIANO SLIM & THE STEREO-TONES:
Lluvia 5052 *Ten Cents Stew* . . . . 5.00 - 8.00

JIMMIE DAVIS:
Decca (LP) 5500 (10") . . . . 15.00 - 20.00
(LP) 8896 *You Are My Sunshine* . . . . 10.00 - 15.00

JUDGE DAVIS:
Flash 120 *Sawmill Section* . . . . 7.00 - 10.00

KEN DAVIS:
Star-Light 1006 *Shook Shake* . . . . 20.00 - 30.00

KING DAVIS:
Hollywood 422 *Waggin' Your Tail* . . . . 10.00 - 15.00

LARRY DAVIS:
Duke 192, 313, 328 . . . . 3.00 - 5.00

LARRY & DIXIE DAVIS:
Kangaroo 13 *Gonna Live It Up* . . . . 30.00 - 40.00

LENNY DAVIS:
Do-Ra-Me 1413 *Santan's Got You* . . . . 7.00 - 10.00

LINK DAVIS:
Al's 1503 *Johnny Be Good* . . . . ———
All Star 7171 *Bon Ton Rula* . . . . 4.00 - 7.00
Nucraft 2026 *Grasshopper Rock* . . . . 7.00 - 10.00
Okeh 7046 *Mama Say No* . . . . 7.00 - 10.00
18048 *Crawfish Crawl* . . . . 7.00 - 10.00
Sarg 136 *Cockroach* . . . . 8.00 - 12.00
Starday 235 *Sixteen Chicks* . . . . 10.00 - 15.00
242 *Grasshopper Rock* . . . . 10.00 - 15.00
255 *Don't Big Shot Me* . . . . 10.00 - 15.00
275 *Bayou Buffalo* . . . . 8.00 - 12.00
293 *Slippin' And Slidin' Sometimes* . . . . 10.00 - 15.00

LITTLE SAM DAVIS:
De Luxe 6025 *Goin' To New Orleans* . . . . 25.00 - 35.00
Rockin' 512 *1958 Blues* . . . . 30.00 - 40.00
519 *Goin' To New Orleans* . . . . 25.00 - 35.00

JIMMIE DAVISON:
Target 861 *Froggie Went A-Courtin'* . . . . 5.00 - 8.00

THE DAWNBREAKERS:
Century 600 *Deep In The Heart Of Texas* . . . . . ———

THE DAWNS:
Climax 104 *Why Did You Let Me Love You* . . . 5.00 - 8.00

JIMMY DAWSON (THE DIXIE DRIFTER):
K-Ark 774 *Mean Woman Blues* . . . . 10.00 - 15.00

RONNIE DAWSON:
Rockin' Records 1 *Rockin' Bones* . . . . 20.00 - 30.00

BING DAY:
Federal 12320 *Ponytail Partner* . . . . 15.00 - 20.00
Mercury 71446 *I Can't Help It* . . . . 5.00 - 9.00
71494 *How Do I Do It* . . . . 5.00 - 9.00
—*Poor Stagger Lee* . . . . ———

BOBBY DAY:
Class 211 *Little Bitty Pretty One* (78 rpm) . . . . . 15.00 - 25.00
229 *Rockin' Robin* (78 rpm) . . . . 20.00 - 30.00
(LP) 5002 *Rockin' With Robin* . . . . 50.00 - 80.00

DAVE (Y) (SONNY) DAY:
Fee-Bee 213 *Jelly Belly* . . . . 7.00 - 10.00
219 *Motorcycle Mike* . . . . 7.00 - 10.00

DAVE DIDDLE DAY:
Mercury 71114 *Blue Moon Baby* . . . . 10.00 - 15.00

JACK DAY:
Arcade 155 *Rattle Bone Boogie* . . . . 15.00 - 25.00

MARGIE DAY:
Cat 118 *Ho Ho* . . . . 5.00 - 7.00

THE DAYBREAKERS:
Aladdin 3434 *I Wonder Why* . . . . 5.00 - 8.00

THE DAYLIGHTERS:
Astra 1001 *This Heart Of Mine* . . . . 7.00 - 10.00
Bea & Baby 103 *You're Breaking My Heart* . . . . 8.0 - 12.00
Dot 16326 *On What A Way To Be Loved* . . . . 5.00 - 8.00
Tip Top 2002 *Baby I Love You* . . . . 7.00 - 10.00

THE DAZZLERS:
Lee—*Gee Whiz* . . . . ———

DEACON & THE ROCK AND ROLLERS:
Nau-Voo 804 *Rockin' On The Moon* . . . . 15.00 - 20.00

AL DEAN & HIS ALL STARS:
Warrior 506 *Fragile Heart* . . . . 15.00 - 20.00

BOBBY DEAN:
Chess 1673 *Just Go Wild Over Rock And Roll* . . 10.00 - 15.00
1710 *I'm Ready* . . . . 10.00 - 15.00
Profile 4006 *It's A Fad, Ma* . . . . 10.00 - 15.00

CHARLES DEAN:
Benton—*Train Whistle Boogie* . . . . ———

EDDIE DEAN:
Design (LP) 89 *Tribute To Hank Williams* . . . . . 8.00 - 12.00
Sage 226 *Rock & Roll Cowboy* . . . . 7.00 - 10.00

FRANK DEAN:
Trend 30-008 *Bubblin'* . . . . 4.00 - 7.00

JIMMY DEAN:
Columbia (LP) 1025 *Hour Of Prayer* . . . . 8.00 - 12.00

LENNY DEAN & THE ROCKIN' CHAIRS: (See ROCKIN' CHAIRS)

WALLY DEANE:
Artic 103 *Saddle Up A Satellite* . . . . 5.00 - 8.00
Globe 238 *Cool Cool Daddy* . . . . 7.00 - 10.00
—*Rockin' With Rosie* . . . . ———

THE DEANS:
Mohawk 126 *It's You* . . . . 5.00 - 8.00

FRANK DEATON & HIS MAD LADS:
Alta 2000 *Framed* . . . . 15.00 - 20.00
Bally 1042 *Just A Little Bit More* . . . . 15.00 - 20.00

JIMMY DEBERRY:
Sun 185 *Take A Little Chance* . . . . 75.00 - 100.00

THE DE'BONAIRS:
Ping 1001 *Say A Prayer For Me* . . . . 15.00 - 20.00

THE DEBONAIRES:
Combo 129 *As Other Lovers Are* . . . . 40.00 - 50.00
Dore 592 *Every Once In Awhile* . . . . 5.00 - 8.00

BUD DECKLEMAN & THE DAYDREAMERS:
Meteor 5014 *Daydreamin'* . . . . 15.00 - 20.00

THE DECOYS:
Aanko 1005 *I Want Only You* . . . . 10.00 - 15.00

THE DEDICATIONS:
C & A 506 *Shining Star* . . . . 10.00 - 15.00
Ramdrca 602 *Someone To Love* . . . . 7.00 - 10.00

DEE & PATTY:
D 1020 *Sweet Lovin' Baby* . . . . 10.00 - 15.00
Mercury 71252 *Our First Date* . . . . 4.00 - 7.00

FERN DEE:
Ember 1035 *You'll Never Know* . . . . 7.00 - 10.00

JIMMY DEE (& THE OFFBEATS):
Ace 627 *Wanda* . . . . 15.00 - 20.00
Dot 15664 *Henrietta* . . . . 5.00 - 8.00
15721 *You're Late Miss Kate* . . . . 10.00 - 15.00
TNT 148 *Henrietta* . . . . 8.00 - 12.00
152 *You're Late, Miss Kate* . . . . 10.00 - 15.00
161 *Rick Tick Tock* . . . . 40.00 - 60.00

JOE DEE:
Clix 811 *Satan's Angel* . . . . ———

JOHNNY DEE:
Colonial 430 *Sittin' In The Balcony* . . . . 3.00 - 5.00
430 *Sittin' In The Balcony* (78 rpm) . . . . 7.00 - 10.00
433 *Teenage Queen* . . . . 4.00 - 7.00
433 *Teenage Queen* (78 rpm) . . . . 7.00 - 10.00

MERCY DEE:
Flair 1073 *Romp And Stomp Blues*	10.00 -	15.00
1077 *Come Back Maybelline*	10.00 -	15.00
1078 *Stubborn Woman*	10.00 -	15.00
Rhythm 1774 *Trailing My Baby*	15.00 -	20.00
Specialty 458 *One Room Country Shack*	8.00 -	12.00
466 *Rent Man Blues*	8.00 -	12.00
481 *Dark Muddy Bottom*	8.00 -	12.00

RONNIE DEE:
Back Beat 522 *Action Packed*	7.00 -	10.00

THE DEE CALS:
Co-Ed 1960 *Stars In The Blue What Shall I Do*	10.00 -	15.00
Mayhams 1960 *Stars In The Blue What Shall I Do*	7.00 -	10.00

THE DEEJAYS:
SRC—*Love Me Baby*	75.00 -	100.00

THE DEEP RIVER BOYS:
Camden (LP) 303 *Presenting The Deep River Boys*	20.00 -	30.00
Jay-Dee 788 *Truthfully*	8.00 -	12.00
Que (LP) 104 *Midnight Magic*	30.00 -	50.00
RCA Victor 47-5268 *The Biggest Fool*	5.00 -	8.00
Vik 0205 *All My Love Belongs To You*	7.00 -	10.00
(LP) LXA-1019	30.00 -	50.00
Waldorf (LP) 108 (10") *Spiritual And Jubilees*	10.00 -	15.00
(LP) 120 (10") *Spirituals*	10.00 -	15.00

THE DEE-VINES:
Lano 2001 *I Believe*	5.00 -	8.00

THE DEFENDERS:
Parway 926 *I Laughed So Hard*	5.00 -	8.00

THE DELACARDOS:
Elgey 1001 *Letter To A School Girl*	7.00 -	10.00
Shell 308, 311	4.00 -	7.00

THE DEL-AIRS:
Delsey 302 *Mam Ma Marie*	7.00 -	10.00
M.R.S. 001 *While Walking*	5.00 -	8.00

THE DELATONES:
TNT 9027 *Little Jeanie*	10.00 -	15.00

THE DELCOS:
Ebony 01 *These Three Little Words*	7.00 -	10.00
Showcase 2501 *Arabia*	7.00 -	10.00

THE DELEGATES:
Vee Jay 212 *The Convention*	15.00 -	20.00
243 *Mother's Son*	15.00 -	20.00

THE DELICATES:
Unart 2017 *Black And White Thunderbird*	8.00 -	12.00

WAILIN' BILL DELL:
O.J. 1003 *You Gotta Be Loose*	15.00 -	20.00

JIMMY DELL:
RCA Victor 7194 *Cool It Baby*	7.00 -	10.00
7355 *I've Got A Dollar*	7.00 -	10.00

TONY DELL:
King 5766 *My Girl*	5.00 -	8.00

THE DEL LARKS:
East-West 116 *Lady Love*	8.00 -	12.00

THE DEL LOURDS:
Solar 1001 *All Alone*	4.00 -	7.00
1003 *Gloria*	7.00 -	10.00

THE DELLS:
Vee Jays 134 *Tell The World*	200.00 -	300.00
166 *Dreams Of Contentment*	20.00 -	30.00
204 *Oh What A Night*	7.00 -	10.00
230 *Movin' On*	8.00 -	12.00
236 *Why Do You Have To Go*	8.00 -	12.00
251 *A Distant Love*	10.00 -	15.00
258 *Pain In My Heart*	8.00 -	12.00
274 *The Springer*	5.00 -	8.00
292 *I'm Calling*	10.00 -	15.00
300 *My Best Girl*	10.00 -	15.00
(LP) 1010 *Oh What A Night* (black label)	8.00 -	12.00
(LP) 1010 (same, but maroon label)	75.00 -	100.00

THE DELL-VIKINGS (See THE DEL VIKINGS):

THE DELLWOODS:
Big Top 3137 *Don't Put Onions On Hamburgers*	7.00 -	10.00

THE DELMONICOS:
Acu 6318 *You Can Call*	5.00 -	8.00
Musictone 6122 *The World's Biggest Fool*	5.00 -	8.00

THE DELMORE BROTHERS:
King (LP) 589 *Sixteen Favorites*	8.00 -	12.00

ALTON DELMORE:
Linco 1315 *Good Times In Memphis*	5.00 -	8.00

THE DEL-PRADOS:
Lucky Four 1021 *Oh Baby*	10.00 -	15.00

THE DEL RAYS:
Carousel 213 *Girl In My Heart*	10.00 -	15.00
Chord 101 *Our Love Is True*	10.00 -	15.00
Future 7209 *When We're Alone*	6.00 -	10.00
Moon 110 *Have A Heart*	6.00 -	10.00

THE DEL RIOS:
Meteor 5038 *Alone On A Rainy Night*	15.00 -	20.00
Neptune 108 *I'm Crying*	7.00 -	10.00

THE DEL ROYALS:
Minit 610 *Who Will Be The One*	5.00 -	8.00

THE DEL-SATINS:
Laurie 3132 *Teardrops Follow Me*	4.00 -	7.00

THE DELTAIRS:
Ivy 101 *Lullaby Of The Bells* (yellow label)	10.00 -	15.00
105 *Standing At The Altar*	5.00 -	8.00

THE DELTA RHYTHM BOYS:
Camden (LP) 313 *The Delta Rhythm Boys*	20.00 -	30.00
Decca 29273, 29329	5.00 -	8.00
Elektra (LP) 138 *The Delta Rhythm Boys Sing*	15.00 -	20.00
Jubilee (LP) 1022 *The Delta Rhythm Boys In Sweden*	15.00 -	25.00
Mercury (LP) 25153 (10")	20.00 -	30.00
RCA Victor (LP) 3085 (10") *Dry Bones*	25.00 -	35.00
2828, 5094, 5217	5.00 -	8.00

THE DEL-TONES:
Oro-Ann 1001 *Best Wishes*	15.00 -	20.00

THE DEL-VICTORS:
Hi-Q 5028 *Baby Sitter*	———	

THE DEL VIKINGS (THE DEL VIKINGS):
Crown (LP) 5368 *The Del Vikings & The Sonnets*	10.00 -	15.00
Dot (LP) 1003 *The Best Of The Dell Vikings*	40.00 -	60.00
(EP) 1058 *Come Go With Us*	15.00 -	20.00
15538 *Come Go With Me* (78 rpm)	15.00 -	20.00
Fee Bee 205 *Come Go With Me*	10.00 -	15.00
211 *Whispering Bells*	10.00 -	15.00
218 *I'm Spinning*	7.00 -	10.00
221 *Willette*	7.00 -	10.00
902 *True Love*	7.00 -	10.00
Luniversee 106 *Somewhere Over The Rainbow*	10.00 -	15.00
(LP) 1000 *Come Go With The Del Vikings*	50.00 -	70.00
(Note: Luniverse 1000 has 8 songs.)		
Mercury (EP) 3362 *They Sing-They Swing*	10.00 -	15.00
(EP) 35 *The Del Vikings*	10.00 -	15.00
(LP) 20314 *They Sing-The Swing*	40.00 -	50.00
(LP) 20353 *Swinging Singing Record Session*	40.00 -	50.00
71132 *Cool Shake* (78 rpm)	8.00 -	12.00

JERRY DEMAR:
Ford 501 *Cross-Eyed Alley Cat*	20.00 -	30.00

THE DEMENS:
Teenage 1006 *You Broke My Heart*	7.00 -	10.00

THE DEMENSIONS:
Coral 62323 *Your Cheatin' Heart*	4.00 -	7.00
62359 *Fly Me To The Moon*	5.00 -	8.00
62392 *A Little White Gardenia*	7.00 -	10.00

THE DEMILLIES:
Laurie 3230 *Donna Lee*	4.00 -	7.00

THE DE MIRES:
Lunar 519 *Wheels Of Love*	8.00 -	12.00

THE DEMOLYRS:
V W R 900 *Rain*	———	

LITTLE JIMMY DEMPSEY:
Fox—*Bop Hop*	———	
—*Bouncing Back*	———	

GALEN DENNY:
Liberty 55164 *What Ya Gonna Do*	8.00 -	12.00

THE DENOTATIONS:
Lawn 253 *Lone Stranger*..................... 7.00 - 10.00
LEE DENSON:
Kent 306 *High School Bop*............ 15.00 - 20.00
Vik 0281 *New Shoes*................. 15.00 - 20.00
RAY DE PAUL:
ABC Paramount 9903 *Ready To Rip*......... 5.00 - 8.00
THE DERBYS:
Mercury 71437 *Night After Night*........... 7.00 - 10.00
TOMMY DEREK:
Flag 120 *Meet Me At The Hop*............. 15.00 - 20.00
ARNIE DERKSEN:
Decca 30906 *She Wanna Rock*........... 10.00 - 15.00
THE DERRINGERS:
Capitol 4532 *Sheree*................. 5.00 - 8.00
THE DESIRES:
Hull 730 *Let It Please Be You*......... 8.00 - 12.00
733 *Rendezvous With You*......... 8.00 - 12.00
THE DESTINATIONS:
Fortune 864 *Valley Of Tears*........... 7.00 - 10.00
DETROIT JUNIOR:
Bea & Baby 111 *Money Tree*........... 7.00 - 10.00
CJ 636, 637...................... 3.00 - 5.00
Foxy 002 *Christmas Day*.................. 5.00 - 8.00
USA 807, 814..................... 4.00 - 7.00
THE DE VILLES:
Aladdin 3423 *Kiss Me Again And Again*.... 6.00 - 10.00
Arrawak 201 *I Do Believe*............ 5.00 - 8.00
JAY DE VORE:
Bodark 004 *Doggone Mean*................. 5.00 - 8.00
THE DEVOTIONS:
Delta 1001 *Rip Van Winkle*............. 15.00 - 20.00
AL DEXTER:
Columbia (LP) 9005 (10") *Songs Of The Southwest* 15.00 - 20.00
Ekko 1020 *Pistol Packin' Mama*.............. 7.00 - 10.00
THE DIABLOS (See NOLAN STRONG & THE DIABLOS)
THE DIADEMS:
Star 514 *Why Don't You Believe Me*......... 7.00 - 10.00
THE DIALS:
Hilltop 219 *No Hard Feelings*........... 8.00 - 12.00
THE DIALTONES:
Goldisc 3005 *Till I Heard It From You*....... 5.00 - 8.00
THE DIAMONDS:
Atlantic 1003 *Two Loves Have I* (yellow label).. 20.00 - 30.00
1017 *Cherry* (yellow label)................. 15.00 - 20.00
Mercury (LP) 20309 *The Diamonds*....... 30.00 - 40.00
(LP) 20368 *The Diamonds Meet Pete Rugolo*. 20.00 - 30.00
70835, 70934, 71021, 71060 (maroon label)... 4.00 - 7.00
70835 *The Church Bells May Ring* (78 rpm).. 5.00 - 8.00
70934 *Ka-Ding Dong* (78rpm)............. 5.00 - 8.00
71021 *A Thousand Miles Away* (78 rpm)..... 5.00 - 8.00
71060 *Little Darlin'* (78 rpm)............ 10.00 - 15.00
71128 *Words Of Love* (78 rpm)........... 5.00 - 8.00
71165 *Zip Zip* (78 rpm)............. 5.00 - 8.00
71242 *The Stroll* (78 rpm)........... 10.00 - 15.00
Wing (LP) 12178 *Pop Hits*......... 15.00 - 20.00
THE DIATONES:
Bandera 2509 *Ruby Has Gone*.............. 15.00 - 20.00
(LITTLE) JIMMY DICKENS:
Columbia (LP) 1047 *Raisin' The Dickens*....... 15.00 - 20.00
(LP) 1545 *Big Songs By Little Jimmy Dickens*. 12.00 - 15.00
21206 *Rock Me*...................... 7.00 - 10.00
41173 *(I Got) A Hole In My Pocket*........ 5.00 - 8.00
DUKE DICKSON & THE JIVIN⁵:
Global—*Walkin' Shoes*................. ———
BO DIDDLEY:
Checker 814, *Bo Diddley*................. 5.00 - 8.00
819, 827, 832, 842, 850, 860.......... 4.00 - 6.00
878, 896, 931, 936, 942, 951, 1045.... 3.00 - 5.00
878 *Say! (Boss Man)* (78 rpm)......... 8.00 - 12.00
896 *Hush Your Mouth* (78 rpm)........... 7.00 - 10.00

924 *Crackin' Up* (78 rpm)................ 10.00 - 15.00
931 *Say Man* (78 rpm)................ 15.00 - 20.00
Chess (LP) 1431 *Bo Diddley* (black label)...... 25.00 - 35.00
(LP) 2974 *Have Guitar Will Travel*......... 20.00 - 30.00
ELROY DIETZEL:
Bo-Kay 101 *Teenage Ball*.................. 25.00 - 35.00
103 *Rock-N-Bones*................... 30.00 - 40.00
THE DIKES:
Federal 12249 *Light Me Up*............. 5.00 - 8.00
DANNY DILL:
ABC Paramount 9734 *I'm Hungry For Your Lovin'* 7.00 - 10.00
ARTIE DILLON:
Kandy Kane—*In My Teens*................. ———
ZIG DILLON:
"R" 501 *On Down The Line*......... 15.00 - 20.00
512 *Bird Song Boogie*................. 15.00 - 20.00
THE DING DONGS:
Brunswick 50073 *Early In The Morning*....... 10.00 - 15.00
MARK DINNING:
MG (LP) 3838 *Teen Angel*................. 20.00 - 30.00
ANDY DIO:
Johnson 114 *You Are My Sunshine*......... 12.00 - 18.00
Thor 104 *Rough And Bold*............ 15.00 - 20.00
DION & THE BELMONTS:
Laurie (LP) 1002 *Presenting Dion & The Belmonts* 20.00 - 30.00
DION & THE TIMBERLANES:
Mohawk 105 *The Chosen Few*............. 10.00 - 15.00
Jubilee 5294 *The Chosen Few*............ 10.00 - 15.00
THE DIPPERS:
Epic 9453 *Such A Fool Was I*......... 8.00 - 12.00
THE DISCIPLES:
Fortune 573 *I Found Out/12th Street*......... ———
DIXIE BLUES BOYS:
Flair 1072 *My Baby Left Town*........... 15.00 - 20.00
THE DIXIELANDERS:
Do-Ra-Me 1412 *Uncle John's Bongos*......... 7.00 - 10.00
BILLY DIXON & THE TOPICS:
Topix 6002 *I Am All Alone*......... 20.00 - 30.00
6008 *Lost Lullaby*................. 20.00 - 30.00
FLOYD DIXON:
Aladdin 3101 *Time And Place*............ 15.00 - 20.00
3121 *Bad Neighborhood*............. 15.00 - 20.00
3135 *Wine Wine Wine*................ 15.00 - 20.00
3144 *Red Cherries*.................. 15.00 - 20.00
3151 *Come Back Baby*............... 12.00 - 16.00
3166 *Broken Hearted Traveler*........ 10.00 - 15.00
3196 *Married Woman*................ 8.00 - 12.00
Cash 1057 *Oh Baby*.................. 5.00 - 8.00
Cat 106 *Moonshine*.................. 7.00 - 10.00
114 *Hey Bartender*................ 7.00 - 10.00
Checker 857 *Alarm Clock Blues*............ 5.00 - 8.00
Ebb 105 *Ooh Little Girl*............... 7.00 - 10.00
Kent 311 *Change Your Mind*............ 7.00 - 10.00
Specialty 468 *Hard Living Alone*.......... 7.00 - 10.00
477 *Hole In The Wall*............. 7.00 - 10.00
486 *Nose Trouble*................. 7.00 - 10.00
Swingin' 626 *Tight Skirts*............. 5.00 - 8.00
HELEN DIXON:
Vik 0212 *Roll Over Beethoven*......... 5.00 - 8.00
WEBB DIXON:
Astro 101 *Rock Awhile*............. 10.00 - 15.00
WILLIE DIXON:
Checker 822, 828, 851................ 4.00 - 7.00
Prestige (LP) 1003 *Blues*............. 15.00 - 20.00
CARL DOBKINS, JR.:
Decca (LP) 8938 *Carl Dobkins, Jr.*............ 15.00 - 20.00
LEROY DOBSON:
Ludwig 1006 *I Wannta Make Love*........... 7.00 - 10.00
CHUCK DOCKERY:
Dearborn—*Rock While We Ride*.............. ———
THE DODGERS:
Aladdin 3259 *You Make Me Happy*........... 15.00 - 20.00
3271 *Drip Drop*.................. 35.00 - 50.00

BILL DOGGETT:

King 4950 *Honky Tonk* (78 rpm)............	8.00 -	12.00

RAY DOGGETT:

Decca 30295 *It Hurts The One Who Loves You.*	8.00 -	12.00
Ken-Lee 101 *Beach Party*................	8.00 -	12.00
Kix 102 *Love Is Made Of This*..........	7.00 -	10.00
Pearl 716 *No Doubt About It*...........	8.00 -	12.00
Spade 1928 *Go Go Heart*...............	15.00 -	20.00
1932 *It Hurts The One Who Loves You*.....	15.00 -	20.00
TNT 159 *Whirlpool Of Love*............	8.00 -	12.00

ANDY DOLL:

———*Rolling Rhythm/Hey Ba Ba Re Bop*.....	———	
Starday 345 *You Can't Stop Me From Dreaming*	———	

THE DOLPHINS:

Shad 5020 *I Found True Love*..............	5.00 -	8.00

FATS DOMINO:

Imperial (EP) 127 *Fats Domino*...............	15.00 -	20.00
Imperial (EP) 138, 139, 140 *Rockin' & Rollin' with Fats Domino*.....................	8.00 -	12.00
Imperial (EP) 141, 142, 143 *Rock And Rollin'*...	8.00 -	12.00
Imperial (EP) 144, 145, 146 *This Is Fats Domino*	8.00 -	12.00
Imperial (EP) 147 *Here Comes Fats*..........	8.00 -	12.00
Imperial (EP) 148, 149, 150 *Here Stands Fats Domino*	8.00 -	12.00
Imperial (EP) 151 *Cookin' With Fats*........	8.00 -	12.00
Imperial (EP) 152 *Rockin' With Fats*........	8.00 -	12.00
Imperial 5180 *Reeling And Rocking*.........	20.00 -	30.00
5197 *Poor Poor Me*.................	20.00 -	30.00
5209 *How Long*....................	15.00 -	20.00
5209 *How Long* (red plastic).........	25.00 -	35.00
5220 *Cheatin'*....................	12.00 -	16.00
5220 *Cheatin'* (red plastic).........	25.00 -	35.00
5231 *Going To The River*............	12.00 -	16.00
5231 *Going To The River* (red plastic)......	25.00 -	35.00
5240 *Please Don't Leave Me*..........	8.00 -	12.00
5251 *Rose Marie*....................	8.00 -	12.00
5262 *Something's Wrong*.............	8.00 -	12.00
5272 *Little School Girl*...............	8.00 -	12.00
5283 *Baby Please*...................	8.00 -	12.00
5301 *I Lived My Life*...............	8.00 -	12.00
5313 *Love Me*.....................	7.00 -	10.00
5223 *Thinking Of You*...............	7.00 -	10.00
5348 *Ain't It A Shame*..............	5.00 -	8.00
Imperial 5357, 5369, 5375.............	5.00 -	8.00
Imperial 5586, 5396..................	4.00 -	6.00
Imperial 5407, 5417, 5428, 5442, 5454, 5477, 5492, 5515, 5526, 5537, 5553.............	3.00 -	6.00
Imperial 5407, 5417, 5428, 5442, 5454, 5477, (78 rpm).............................	8.00 -	12.00
Imperial 5492 *Don't You Know I Love You* (78 rpm)	8.00 -	12.00
5515 *Sick And Tired* (78 rpm).......	8.00 -	12.00
5526 *Little Mary* (78 rpm).........	8.00 -	12.00
5537 *Young School Girl* (78 rpm)...	8.00 -	12.00
5553 *Whole Lotta Lovin'* (78 rpm)...	10.00 -	15.00
5569 *Telling Lies* (78 rpm).........	10.00 -	15.00
Imperial (LP) 9004 *Rockin' And Rollin' With Fats Domino*..........................	30.00 -	40.00
Imperial (LP) 9000 *Rock And Rollin'*.........	30.00 -	40.00
Imperial (LP) 9028 *This Is Fats Domino*.......	20.00 -	30.00
Imperial (LP) 9038 *Here Stands Fats Domino*...	20.00 -	30.00
(LP) 9040 *This Is Fats*............	20.00 -	30.00
Imperial (LP) 9055 *The Fabulous Mr. Domino*..	15.00 -	20.00
Imperial (LP) 9062 *Fats Domino Swings*.......	15.00 -	20.00
Imperial (LP) 9065 *Let's Play Fats Domino*.....	15.00 -	20.00
Imperial (LP) 9103 *Fats Dommino Sings*.......	15.00 -	20.00
Imperial (LP) 9138 *A Lot Of Dominoes*.......	10.00 -	15.00

Note: LP's are all MONO. Early issues have maroon labels; later issues and reissues of early issues have multi-colored labels.

THE DOMINOES: (See also BILLY WARD)

Federal 12001 *Do Something For Me*.........	50.00 -	75.00
12010 *Harbor Lights*..............	100.00 -	200.00
12022 *Sixty Minute Man*............	30.00 -	40.00
12039 *Weeping Willow Blues*..........	40.00 -	60.00
12059 *That's What You're Doing To Me*.....	40.00 -	60.00
12068 *Have Mercy Baby*.............	35.00 -	50.00
12072 *Love Love Love*.............	40.00 -	60.00
12105 *I'll Be Satisfied*..............	25.00 -	35.00
12106 *Yours Forever*..............	25.00 -	35.00
12114 *The Bells*..................	30.00 -	40.00
12129 *These Foolish Things Remind Me Of You*	15.00 -	20.00

(Above have "gold top" labels)

CHARLIE DONALD:

ABC Paramount 9820 *Bop With Me, Baby*.....	7.00 -	10.00

THE DON CLAIRS:

Amp-3 1001 *I Lost My Job*................	8.00 -	12.00

DON & DEWEY:

Rush 1002 *Soul Motion*...............	5.00 -	8.00
Shade 1000 *My Heart Is Aching*.......	5.00 -	8.00
Spot 101 *Fiddlin' The Blues*.........	10.00 -	15.00

DON, DICK & JIMMY:

Dot (LP) 3152.....................	20.00 -	30.00

THE DON JUANS: (See also LITTLE EDDIE)

Fortune 824, 825....................	4.00 -	7.00
Jaguar 3020 *Kickin' My Hound Around*.......	———	

RAL DONNER:

Crown (LP) 5335 *Ral Donner & Ray Smith & Bobby Dale*...........................	10.00 -	15.00
Gone (LP) 2002 *Takin' Care Of Business*......	40.00 -	60.00

THE DOOTONES:

Dootone 366 *Teller Of Fortunes*.............	10.00 -	15.00
470, 471.......................	3.00 -	6.00

LEE DORSEY:

Fury (LP) 1002 *Ya Ya*................	20.00 -	30.00

MEL DORSEY (& CHUCK WAYNE):

Black Jack 103 *Little Lil*..............	7.00 -	10.00
Orbit 106 *Ain't Gonna Take It No More*......	5.00 -	8.00

SLIM DORTCH:

Eugenia—*Big Boy Rock*.................	———	

BOB DOSS:

Lynn 505 *I've Got You*................	8.00 -	12.00
Starday 265 *Somebody's Knocking*........	12.00 -	15.00

BUSTER DOSS:

Wizard 1640 *Messing Around*................	4.00 -	7.00

THE DOTS:

Caddy 101 *I Confess*................	7.00 -	10.00

JIMMY DOTSON (& THE BLUES BOYS):

Rocko 516 *I Need Your Love*..........	5.00 -	8.00
Zynn 511 *Looking For My Baby*.......	5.00 -	8.00

BIG BOB DOUGHERTY:

KCM 3701 *Dizzy Miss Lizzie*...............	———	

DAVEY DOUGLAS:

Ditto 110 *Shivers*...................	8.00 -	12.00
Liberty 55165 *Party Crashin'*.........	7.00 -	10.00

DICK DOUGLAS:

Northway 1005 *Rocket Ride*............	7.00 -	10.00

GLENN DOUGLAS:

Decca (LP) 8748 *Heartbreak*.............	15.00 -	20.00

K.C. DOUGLAS:

Cook (LP) 5002...................	20.00 -	30.00

MEL DOUGLAS:

San 1506 *Cadillac Boogie*.............	15.00 -	20.00

SHY GUY DOUGLAS:

Excello 2008 *Detroit Arrow*............	15.00 -	20.00
2024 *I'm Your Country Man*........	15.00 -	20.00
2032 *No Place Like Home*..........	15.00 -	20.00

JERRY DOVE & HIS STRING BUSTERS:

TNT 122, 144, 162, 173.............	4.00 -	6.00
141 *Pink Bow Tie*..............	20.00 -	30.00

LARRY DOWD (& THE ROCK-A-TONES):

Damion 6532 *Tell Me No Lies*...........	7.00 -	10.00
Spinning 6004 *Why Oh Why*...........	5.00 -	8.00
6009 *Pink Cadillac*.............	15.00 -	20.00

THE DOWLANDS:
Tollie 9002 *All My Loving*................. ————
THE DOWNBEATS: (See also O.S. GRANT; SONNY WOODS):
Sarg 168 *Darling Of Mine*................... 8.00 - 12.00
173 *I Need Your Love*.............. 10.00 - 15.00
186 *I Couldn't See*................. 7.00 - 10.00
197 *I Just Can't Understand*..... 7.00 - 10.00
("BIG") AL DOWNING:
Carlton 489, 507........................... 4.00 - 7.00
Challenge 59006 *Down On The Farm*........ 5.00 - 8.00
V-Tone 215 *Please Come Home*............ 5.00 - 8.00
White Rock 1111 *Down On The Farm*...... 15.00 - 20.00
1113 *Miss Lucy*............................ 20.00 - 30.00
THE DOZIER BOYS:
Fraternity 767 *Early Morning Blues*.......... 15.00 - 20.00
United 143 *I Keep Thinking Of You*.......... 20.00 - 30.00
RUSTY DRAPER:
Mercury 70921 *Pink Cadillac*................. 5.00 - 8.00
THE DREAMERS: (See also RICHARD BERRY)
Aladdin 3303 *Charles My Darling*............. 10.00 - 15.00
Cousins 1005 *Because Of You*............. 7.00 - 10.00
Flair 1052 *At Last*..................... 8.00 - 12.00
Goldisc 3015 *Teenage Vows Of Love*....... 5.00 - 8.00
Grand 131 *Tears In My Eyes*............. 10.00 - 15.00
Mercury 70019 *Please Don't Love Me*........ 8.00 - 12.00
Rollin 1001 *No Man Is An Island*........... 15.00 - 20.00
THE DREAM KINGS:
Checker 858 *MTYLTT*...................... 7.00 - 10.00
THE DREAMLOVERS:
Heritage 102 *When We Get Married*.......... 5.00 - 8.00
104 *Welcome Home*................... 5.00 - 8.00
V-Tone 229 *May I Kiss The Bride*........... 7.00 - 10.00
THE DREAMS:
Savoy 1130 *Darlene*...................... 15.00 - 20.00
1140 *Under The Willow*................. 15.00 - 20.00
1157 *I'll Be Faithful*................. 7.00 - 10.00
THE DREAMTONES:
Astra 551 *A Lover's Answer*.................. 7.00 - 10.00
Express 501 *Praying For A Miracle*........ 8.00 - 12.00
Klik 8505 *Love Me In The Afternoon*........ 15.00 - 20.00
THE DRIFTERS (featuring CLYDE McPHATTER):
Atlantic (EP) 534 *The Drifters Featuring Clyde McPhatter* .... 15.00 - 20.00
1006 *Money Honey*.................... 10.00 - 15.00
1019 *Such A Night*................... 7.00 - 10.00
1029 *Honey Love*..................... 7.00 - 10.00
1043 *Bip Bam*........................ 5.00 - 8.00
1048 *White Christmas*................ 5.00 - 8.00
1055 *Gone*........................... 5.00 - 8.00
1070 *Hot Ziggety*.................... 5.00 - 8.00
(Note: above are yellow label)
2025 *There Goes My Baby* (78 rpm)...... 15.00 - 20.00
(LP) 8003 *Clyde McPhatter & The Drifters*... 20.00 - 30.00
(LP) 8013 *The Good Life With The Drifters*.. 25.00 - 35.00
(LP) 8022 *Rockin' And Driftin'*............ 20.00 - 30.00
(above are black label)
(LP) 8059 *Save The Last Dance For Me*..... 12.00 - 18.00
Crown 108 *The World Is Changing*.......... 35.00 - 50.00
DRIFTING CHARLES:
Lanor 515 *Drifting Cloud*................. 5.00 - 8.00
DRINK SMALL & HIS GUITAR:
Sharp 101 *Cold Cold Rain*................. 10.00 - 15.00
THE DRIVERS:
Alton 252 *Doe Doe*....................... 5.00 - 8.00
De Luxe 6094 *Smooth, Slow And Easy*...... 7.00 - 10.00
6104 *My Lonely Prayer*............. 8.00 - 12.00
6117 *Dangerous Lips*............... 7.00 - 10.00
Drive 101 *No One For Me*................. ————
RCA Victor 7023 *Blue Moon*............... 5.00 - 8.00

THE DUALS:
Arc 4446 *Nearest To My Heart*............ 8.00 - 12.00
THE DUBS:
Gone 5002 *I Found Out*................... 7.00 - 10.00
5011 *Could This Be Magic*........... 5.00 - 8.00
5020 *Beside My Love*................ 5.00 - 8.00
Jose (LP) 4001 *The Dubs Meet The Shells*...... 30.00 - 40.00
Mark-X 8008 *Be Sure My Love*........... 7.00 - 10.00
DUCES OF RHYTHM & THE TEMPOS TOP-PERS (Lead, LITTLE RICHARD):
Peacock 1616 *Ain't That Good News*......... 8.00 - 12.00
THE DUDADS:
De Luxe 6083 *I Heard You Call Me Dear*...... 15.00 - 20.00
THE DU DROPPERS:
Groove 0001 *Laughing Blues*.............. 5.00 - 8.00
0013 *Just Whisper*................. 7.00 - 10.00
0036 *Boot 'Em Up*................. 5.00 - 8.00
0104 *Talk That Talk*.............. 5.00 - 8.00
0120 *You're Mine Already*........ 5.00 - 8.00
(LP) *—DuDroppin'*.................. 40.00 - 50.00
RCA Victor 5321 *I Found Out*........... 5.00 - 8.00
5425 *Whatever You're Doing*..... 5.00 - 8.00
5543 *The Note In The Bottle*..... 8.00 - 12.00
Red Robin 108 *Can't Do Sixty No More*...... 12.00 - 15.00
ARLIE DUFF:
Decca 29987 *Alligator Come Across*........ 8.00 - 12.00
Starday 302 *You've Done It Again*........... 7.00 - 10.00
TAM DUFFILL:
Groove 58-0004 *Cooly Dooly*............. 8.00 - 12.00
EDDIE DUGOSH:
Award 116 *One Mile*...................... 5.00 - 8.00
Sarg 135 *Strange Kinda Feeling*.............. 15.00 - 20.00
BILLY DUKE & HIS DUKES:
Casino 138 *Fun Lovin' Woman*............. 5.00 - 8.00
ROY DUKE:
Decca 29962 *Behave, Be Quiet, Or Be Gone*.... 10.00 - 15.00
30095 *Honky Tonk Queen*........... 10.00 - 15.00
30325 *I Mean, I'm Mean*............. 10.00 - 15.00
DUKE OF EARL (Gene Chandler):
Vee Jay (LP) 1040 *Duke Of Earl*........... 15.00 - 20.00
THE DUKES:
Imperial 5401 *Teardrop Eyes*............. 15.00 - 20.00
5451 *Baby Please*.............. 10.00 - 15.00
5480 *Loving You*................ 10.00 - 15.00
Specialty 543 *Oh Kay*................... 7.00 - 10.00
THE DU MAURIERS:
Fury 1011 *All Night Long*................. 8.00 - 12.00
SHELTON DUNAWAY:
Lyric 1010 *Shake 'Em Up*................. 5.00 - 8.00
BILL DUNCAN:
D B C 1232 *Whirlin' Twerlin' Rock*........... 20.00 - 30.00
DON DUNCAN:
Venture 111 *Somethin' Special*.............. 20.00 - 30.00
HERBIE DUNCAN:
Mar-Vel 1400 *Hot Lips Baby*............... 15.00 - 25.00
BILL DUNIVEN:
Vaden 306 *Knocking On The Backside (of Your Heart)*.................................. 15.00 - 20.00
GENE DUNLAP:
—Made In The Shade..................... ————
JOHN DUNN:
Spar 720 *If A Woman Answers*............. 5.00 - 8.00
WEBSTER DUNN, JR.:
Dunmar 101 *Go Go Baby*............... 15.00 - 25.00
THE DUPONTS:
Roulette 4060 *Half Past Nothing*........... 5.00 - 8.00
Royal Roost 627 *Somebody*............. 8.00 - 12.00
Winley 212 *Must Be Falling In Love*........ 7.00 - 10.00
CHAMPION JACK DUPREE: JACK DUPREE (& MR. BEAR):
Atlantic (LP) 8019 *Blues From The Gutter*..... 20.00 - 30.00
(LP) 8045 *Natural & Soulful Blues*.......... 12.00 - 16.00

(LP) 8056 *Champion Of The Blues*.........	12.00 - 16.00
Groove 0171 *Lonely Road Blues*..............	5.00 - 8.00
King (LP) 735 *Champion Jack Dupress Sings The*	
Blues..................	15.00 - 20.00
4633 *Tongue Tied Blues*...............	8.00 - 12.00
4651 *Please Tell Me Baby*..........	8.00 - 12.00
4695 *Walkin' Upside Your Head*........	8.00 - 12.00
4706 *Hard Feeling*.................	7.00 - 10.00
4779 *Two Below Zero*..............	7.00 - 10.00
4792 *Harelip Blues*................	7.00 - 10.00
Okeh (LP) 12103 *Cabbage Greens*.........	20.00 - 30.00
Red Robin 109 *Stumblin' Block Blues*.....	15.00 - 20.00
112 *Highway Blues*...............	15.00 - 20.00
130 *Shim Sham Shimmy*.........	15.00 - 20.00
Vik 0260, 0279, 0304...............	4.00 - 8.00

THE DUPREES:

Coed (LP) 905 *You Belong To Me*..........	35.00 - 50.00
(LP) 906 *Have You Heard*..........	35.00 - 50.00

NELDA DUPRY:

United 157 *Riding With The Blues*.......	7.00 - 10.00

TOMMY DURDEN:

Holiday 777 *A-Weepin' And A-Wailin'*........	7.00 - 10.00

PAUL DURHAM:

Sand Spur 15302 *She Lied*...............	————

THE DUSTERS:

Cuspid 5003 *She's Mine*...............	————

HUELYN DUVALL:

Challenge 1012 *Comin' Or Goin'*..........	10.00 - 15.00
59002 *Hum-Dinger*................	8.00 - 12.00
59014 *Three Months To Kill*........	8.00 - 12.00
59025 *Friday Night On A Dollar Bill*......	8.00 - 12.00
59069 *Pucker Paint*..............	7.00 - 10.00
Starfire 600 *It's No Wonder*............	7.00 - 10.00

THE DUVALS:

Boss 2117 *Cotton*...................	5.00 - 8.00

THE DWELLERS:

Howard—*Tell Me Why*...............	25.00 - 35.00
Oasis 101 *Oh Sweetie*...............	20.00 - 30.00

CONNIE DYCUS:

Mercury 71376 *Rock-A-Bye Baby Rock*.......	————

JERRY DYKE & THE VENDELLS:

Saturn—*Mean Woman Blues*..............	————

BOB DYLAN:

Columbia (LP) 1986 *The Freewheelin' Bob Dylan* (contains, cut 3 side, 1, *Let Me Die In My Footsteps*).................	50.00 - 75.00
42656 *Corrina Corrina*................	30.00 - 50.00
42856 *Blowin' In The Wind*..........	30.00 - 50.00
(Note: Prices on above are very speculative. Promotional copies of other 45s have premium value.)	

THE DYNAMICS:

Dynamic 1002 *Delsinia*.................	4.00 - 7.00
Emjay 1928 *This Love Of Ours*.............	8.00 - 12.00
Herald 569 *Betty My Own*............	5.00 - 8.00
Impala 501 *Moonlight*...............	12.00 - 18.00
LiBan 1006 *If I Give My Heart To You*......	8.00 - 12.00

JOHNNY EAGER (& HIS TRIO):

Design 818 *The Howl*...............	15.00 - 20.00
Sabre 100 *Please Mr. Doctor*............	20.00 - 30.00

THE EAGLES:

Mercury 70391 *Please, Please*.............	7.00 - 12.00
70464 *Such A Fool*.............	7.00 - 12.00
70524 *I Told Myself*............	7.00 - 12.00

FORD EAGLIN:

Imperial 5671, 5692, 5736, 5765, 5802, 5823, 5857, 5866, 5890, 5946..........	4.00 - 8.00

THE EARLS:

ABC Paramount 11109 *It's Been A Long Time Comin'*................	————
Old Town (LP) 104 *Remember Me Baby*.......	40.00 - 60.00
1141 *Look My Way*................	4.00 - 7.00

Rome 101 *Life Is But A Dream*.............	8.00 - 12.00
102 *Lookin' For My Baby*..............	8.00 - 12.00
5117 *My Heart's Desire*.............	8.00 - 12.00

JACK EARLS & THE JIMBOS:

Sun 240 *Slow Down*................	10.00 - 15.00

THE EARTHQUAKES:

Fortune 534, 538, 549...................	5.00 - 10.00

EDDIE EAY:

Echo 5911 *Dancin' Girl*.............	20.00 - 30.00

THE EBBTIDES:

Jan Lar 101 *Lonesome*...............	10.00 - 15.00
Marco 105 *Little Miss Blue*...........	5.00 - 8.00
Recorte 405 *Puppy Love*...............	7.00 - 10.00
Teen 121 *What Is Your Name, Dear?*........	————

THE EBBTONES:

Ebb 100 *I've Got A Feeling*..........	15.00 - 20.00
Million 2011 *Recess In Heaven*.............	15.00 - 20.00

THE EBONAIRES:

Aladdin 3211 *Three O'Clock In The Morning*...	20.00 - 30.00
Lena 1001 *Love Call*.................	10.00 - 15.00
Money 220 *The Very Best Luck In The World*..	15.00 - 20.00

THE EBONIERS:

Port 70013 *Hand In Hand*...............	4.00 - 7.00

THE EBONY MOODS:

Theron 108 *I've Got News For You*...........	————

THE ECHOES:

Andex 22102 *Dee-Dee-Di Oh*.............	5.00 - 8.00
Ascot 2188 *I Love Candy*.............	7.00 - 10.00
Combo 128 *My Little Honey*.............	15.00 - 20.00
Gee 1028 *Ding Dong*...............	8.00 - 12.00
Rockin' 523 *Please Say You're Mine*.....	30.00 - 40.00
Seg-Way 103, 106...................	3.00 - 5.00
Specialty 601 *Over The Rainbow*...........	8.00 - 12.00

THE ECHOTONES:

Dart 1009 *So In Love*.................	5.00 - 8.00

THE ECHO VALLEY BOYS:

Island 1/2 *Wash Machine Boogie*............	75.00 - 100.00

DUANE EDDY:

Jamie (EP) 100, 301, 302, 304.............	5.00 - 8.00
1104 *Rebel-'Rouser* (78 rpm)............	10.00 - 15.00

CORKY EDMINSTER:

Raynor 10820 *Chili Dippin' Baby*............	————

THE EDSELS:

Dub 2843 *Rama Lama Ding Dong*.............	6.00 - 9.00
Twin 700 *Rama Lama Ding Dong*.............	————

CHUCK EDWARDS (& THE FIVE CROWNS/ & HIS GUITAR):

Alanna 557 *If I Were King*.............	7.00 - 10.00
Duke 159, 163, 174..................	5.00 - 8.00

EDDIE ALVIS EDWARDS:

—*Real Gone Baby*.................	————

JIMMY EDWARDS:

Mercury 71209 *Love Bug Crawl*.............	7.00 - 10.00
71209 *Same, but 78 rpm*..........	8.00 - 12.00

JOHNNY EDWARDS & THE WHITE CAPS:

Northland 7002 *Rock 'N' Roll Saddles*.........	————

TIBBY EDWARDS:

Mercury 70591 *Flip Flop And Fly*...........	5.00 - 8.00

CHARLES EDWINS:

Duke 124 *I Got Loose*.................	7.00 - 10.00

WILLIE EGAN/EGANS; LITTLE WILLIE EGANS:

Dash 55001 *Rock & Roll Fever*.............	7.00 - 10.00
Mambo 102 *What A Shame*..............	7.00 - 10.00
111 *Come On*................	7.00 - 10.00
Spry 107 *Treat Me Right*.............	10.00 - 15.00
Vita 125 *Wear Your Black Dress*...........	7.00 - 10.00

COZY EGGLESTON:

States 133 *Big Heavy*.................	8.00 - 12.00

BOB EHRET:

Aladdin 3377 *Stop The Clock*...............	15.00 - 20.00

DONNIE ELBERT:
King (LP) 629 *The Sensational Donnie Elbert...* 40.00 - 60.00
THE EL CAPRIS:
Bullseye 102 *Oh, But She Did*............. 20.00 - 30.00
Fee Bee 216 *Your Star*.................... 15.00 - 20.00
Hi-Q 5006 *Girl Of Mine*.................. 8.00 - 12.00
Paris 525 *They're Always Laughin' At Me*..... 4.00 - 7.00
THE ELCHORDS, Featuring BUTCHY
     SAUNDERS:
Good 544 *Peppermint Stick*................ 5.00 - 8.00
THE EL DARADOS (See THE EL DORADOS)
THE EL DOMINGOS:
Chelsea 1609 *Lucky Me, I'm In Love*.......... 15.00 - 20.00
THE EL DORADOS: (See HAZEL
     McCOLLUM):
Vee Jay 115 *My Loving Baby*.............. 25.00 - 40.00
     127 *One More Chance*................... 25.00 - 40.00
     147 *At My Front Door*................ 7.00 - 10.00
     165 *I'll Be Forever Loving You*...... 8.00 - 12.00
     180 *Rock 'N' Roll's For Me*........... 8.00 - 12.00
     197 *Chop Ling Soon*.................. 15.00 - 20.00
     211 *Bim Bam Boom*.................... 10.00 - 15.00
     250 *Tears On My Pillow*.............. 10.00 - 15.00
     263 *Boom Diddle Boom*................ 8.00 - 12.00
     302 *Lights Are Low*.................. 8.00 - 12.00
Vee Jay (LP) 1001 *Crazy Little Mama* (maroon label) 50.00 - 80.00
     (LP) 1001 same, but black label............ 10.00 - 15.00
BILY ELDRIDGE:
Unart 2001 *Let's Go Baby*................. 10.00 - 15.00
Vulco 1580 *It's Over*..................... ————
THE ELEGANTS:
Apt 25005 *Little Star* (black label)............. 7.00 - 10.00
     25005 *Little Star* (78 rpm)................. 15.00 - 20.00
     25071, 25029.......................... 4.00 - 7.00
Hull 732 *Little Boy Blue*................... 8.00 - 12.00
Photo 2662 *A Dream Can Come True*........ 10.00 - 15.00
LES ELGART & HIS ORCHESTRA:
Columbia 40180 *Bandstand Boogie*........... 6.00 - 10.00
JOHNNY ELGIN:
Roulette 7005 *Sittin' At Home With The Blues*.. 5.00 - 8.00
THE ELGINS:
Congress 214 *Ritha Mae*.................... 7.00 - 10.00
Titan 1724 *My Illness*..................... 7.00 - 10.00
THE ELITES:
Chief 7040 *The Blues*..................... 10.00 - 15.00
THE ELLIS BROTHERS:
ABC Paramount 9954 *Sneaky Alligator*........ ————
REX ELLIS:
Rivermont 1160—.......................... ————
RAY ELLSWORTH:
Ellsworth 101 *Rock'N' Roll Show*............. 5.00 - 8.00
     101/102 *I Wanna Hold You Baby*........... 5.00 - 8.00
THE EL POLLOS:
Neptune 1001 *Why Treat Me This Way*....... 15.00 - 20.00
THE EL RAYS:
Checker 794 *Darling I Know*............... 15.00 - 20.00
M & M 104 *Till The End Of Time*........... 4.00 - 7.00
THE EL REYES:
Jade 501 *Mr. Moonglow*................... 15.00 - 20.00
THE EL TONES:
Cub 9011 *Little Mattie*.................... 5.00 - 8.00
THE EL TORROS:
Fraternity 811 *All The Tears Is Gone*......... 10.00 - 15.00
THE EL VENOS:
Groove 0170 *Geraldine*.................... 15.00 - 20.00
Vik 0305 *My Heart Beats Faster*............ 10.00 - 15.00
EMANON 4:
Flash 106 *Oh That Girl*................... 10.00 - 15.00
THE EMANONS:
ABC Paramount 9913 *We Teenagers*.......... 5.00 - 8.00
G.G.S. 443 *No I Miss You*................. ————

Josie 801 *Blue Moon*...................... 10.00 - 15.00
Winley 226 *We Teenagers*.................. 7.00 - 10.00
THE EMBERS:
Empress 101 *Solitaire*.................... 10.00 - 15.00
Herald 410 *Paradise Hill* (red plastic)......... 30.00 - 50.00
     401 *Paradise Hill* (black plastic)........... 15.00 - 20.00
THE EMBRACEABLES:
Sandy 1025 *From Someone Who Loves You*.... 7.00 - 10.00
TED EMBRY:
Ac'cent 1057 *New Shoes*.................. 10.00 - 15.00
THE EMCEES:
Cimarron 4044 *Wine, Wine, Wine*............ 10.00 - 15.00
THE EMERALDS: (See also LUTHER BOND)
Allied 10002 *Why Must I Wonder*............ 8.00 - 12.00
Bobbin 107 *That's The Way It's Got To Be*.... 15.00 - 20.00
     121 *Lover's Cry*....................... 15.00 - 20.00
Rex 1004 *All The Time*................... 8.00 - 12.00
     1013 *I Kneel At Your Throne*............ 8.00 - 12.00
Showboat 1501 *Gold Will Never Do*.......... 5.00 - 8.00
BILLY (THE KID) EMERSON:
Sun 195 *No Teasin' Around*................ 50.00 - 75.00
     214 *Move Baby Move*.................. 12.00 - 16.00
     219 *Red Hot*........................ 12.00 - 16.00
     233 *Something For Nothing*............. 8.00 - 12.00
THE EMERSONS:
Newport 7004 *Joannie Joannie*............. ————
THE EMOTIONS:
Fury 1010 *Candlelight*.................... 8.00 - 12.00
THE EMPERORS:
Haven 511 *Come Back, Come Back*.......... 50.00 - 80.00
THE EMPIRES:
Chavis 1026 *Love You So Bad*............. 10.00 - 15.00
Epic 9527 *Time And A Place*............... 5.00 - 8.00
Harlem 2333 *Magic Mirrow*................ 30.00 - 50.00
Whirlin' Disc 104 *Whispering Heart*.......... 10.00 - 15.00
Wing 90023 *Shirley*...................... 8.00 - 12.00
     90050 *By The Riverside*................ 8.00 - 12.00
     90080 *My First Discovery*.............. 8.00 - 12.00
THE ENCHANTERS:
Coral 61756 *True Love Gone*............... 5.00 - 8.00
     61832 *There Goes*.................... 5.00 - 8.00
     61916 *Bottle It Up And Go*............. 10.00 - 15.00
     62373 *The Day*...................... 5.00 - 8.00
Ep-Som—*I Need Your Love*............... 7.00 - 10.00
J.J. & M. 1562 *Oh Rosemarie*.............. 10.00 - 15.00
Mercer 992 *True Love Gone*............... 30.00 - 40.00
Musitron 1071/1072 *I Lied To My Heart*....... 7.00 - 10.00
Sharp 105 *We Make Mistakes*.............. 7.00 - 10.00
Stardust 102 *Spellbound By The Moon*........ 50.00 - 80.00
THE ENCHORDS:
Laurie 3089 *I Need You Baby*............... 5.00 - 8.00
THE ENCORES:
Checker 760 *When I Look At You*............ 125.00 - 200.00
THE ENDORSERS:
Moon 109 *Crying (Over You)*............... ————
SCOTT ENGEL:
Orbit 506 *Good For Nothin'*............... 6.00 - 9.00
BENNY ENGLAND:
Zenith 103 *Eloping*...................... 10.00 - 15.00
ENSENATORS:
Tar-X 101 *Just Like Before*................ ————
AL EPP:
Wildcat 0018 *Breaking My Heart*............ 8.00 - 12.00
DON EPPERSON:
Excell—*You're Gone Again*................ ————
EPICS:
Lifetime 1004 *Lonely*.................... 10.00 - 15.00
THE ERMINES:
Loma 701 *True Love*..................... 20.00 - 30.00
FRANKIE ERVIN with JOHNNY MOORE'S
     THREE BLAZERS:
Blaze 103 *Hot Rod*...................... 5.00 - 8.00

Hollywood 1031 *Johnny Ace's Last Letter*...... 8.00 - 12.00

ODIE ERVIN:
Big Town 111 *Note Pinned To My Bed*....... 15.00 - 20.00

THE ESCORTS:
Coral 62302 *Seven Wonders Of The World*..... 7.00 - 10.00
Premium 407 *Sorry*..................... 20.00 - 30.00
Scarlet 4005 *I Will Be Home Again*.......... 7.00 - 10.00

ESQUERITA:
Capitol (LP) 1186 *Esquerita*................. 75.00 - 100.00
(EP) 1186 *Esquerita*..................... 25.00 - 40.00
4007 *Oh Baby*...................... 10.00 - 15.00
4058 *Rockin' The Joint*.................. 10.00 - 15.00
4145 *Laid Off*...................... 10.00 - 15.00

THE ESQUIRE BOYS:
Guyden 705 *Rock-A-Beatin' Boogie*...... 7.00 - 10.00
705 *Rock-A-Beatin' Boogie (78 rpm)*...... 10.00 - 15.00

THE ESQUIRES:
Meridian—*Mission Bells*.................. 12.00 - 16.00
—*When I Fall In Love*.............. 12.00 - 16.00

THE ESSEX:
Roulette (LP) 25235 *A Walkin' Miracle*........ 15.00 - 20.00

SIDNEY ESTER & THE DREAMERS:
Dangold 2001 *Let Me Walk With You*........ 4.00 - 7.00

THE ETERNALS:
Hollywood 68/69, 70/71.................. 4.00 - 7.00

BILLY EUSTIS:
"R" 506 *I'm Sorry Your're Gone*............. 7.00 - 10.00

JIMMY EVANS (& THE JESTERS):
Shimmy 1054 *Messy Bessy*................. 8.00 - 12.00
Clearmont —*The Joint's Really Jumpin'*........ 35.00 - 50.00

MARK EVANS:
Tab 101 *It's Love*...................... 7.00 - 10.00

MARTY EVANS:
Coral 62192 *Poor Me*.................. 5.00 - 8.00

PAUL EVANS:
Guaranteed (LP) 1000 *Fabulous Teens*........ 25.00 - 40.00

RUSTY EVANS:
Brunswick 55103 *(Let The Midnight Special) Shine*
Its Light On Me...................... 5.00 - 8.00

BETTY EVERETT:
CJ 611 *Please Come Back*............... 5.00 - 8.00

BRACEY EVERETT:
Atlantic 2013 *The Lover's Curse*.............. 8.00 - 12.00

VINCE EVERETT:
ABC Paramount 10313 *Such A Night*......... 5.00 - 8.00
10360 *Ain't Gonna Be Your Low Down Dog.* 5.00 - 8.00
10472 *Baby Let's Play House*............ 5.00 - 8.00
10624 *Big Brother*.................. 4.00 - 7.00

THE EVERGREENS:
Chart 605 *Very Truly Yours*............... 20.00 - 30.00

THE EVERLY BROTHERS:
Cadence (EP) 104, 111, 118, 121, 134......... 8.00 - 12.00
(EP) 333 *Rockin' with The Everly Brothers*... 10.00 - 15.00
1315 *Bye Bye Love (78 rpm)*............. 15.00 - 20.00
1337 *Wake Up Little Susie (78 rpm)*........ 15.00 - 20.00
1342 *This Little Girl Of Mine (78 rpm)*...... 15.00 - 20.00
1348 *Claudette (78 rpm)*............. 15.00 - 20.00
1350 *Bird Dog (78 rpm)*.............. 20.00 - 30.00
1355 *Problems (78 rpm)*............. 15.00 - 20.00
(LP) 3003 *Everly Brothers*............. 20.00 - 30.00
(LP) 3016 *Songs Our Daddy Taught Us*...... 15.00 - 25.00
(LP) 3025 *Everly Brothers Best*......... 12.00 - 16.00
(LP) 3040 *The Fabulous Style Of...*......... 15.00 - 20.00
(LP) 3059 *Folk Songs*.............. 10.00 - 15.00
(LP) 3062 *15 Everly Hits*............. 10.00 - 15.00
Columbia 21496 *Keep A-Loving Me*......... 40.00 - 50.00

"EVERYBODY DIGS THE BOSS RECORD HOP":
Vinley (LP) 6001 *Paragons, Jesters, et al.*....... 15.00 - 20.00

THE EXCLUSIVES:
K&C—*It's Over*...................... 10.00 - 15.00

THE EXECS:
Fargo 1055 *Walking In The Rain*............. 10.00 - 15.00

DENNY EZBA:
Renner 213, 228, 238.................. 10.00 - 15.00
225 *Dirty Dirty Feeling*.................. 10.00 - 15.00
244 *Susie-Q*.................. 7.00 - 10.00

SHELLEY FABARES:
Colpix (LP) 431 *The Things We Did Last Summer* 15.00 - 20.00

FABIAN:
Chancellor (EP) 5003 *Hold That Tiger*......... 12.00 - 16.00
(LP) 5003 *Hold That Tiger*......... 20.00 - 30.00
(LP) 5005 *Fabulous Fabian*............... 15.00 - 25.00
(LP) 5009 *Fabian & Avalon—The Hit Makers* 20.00 - 30.00
(LP) 5012 *Good Old Summertime*......... 20.00 - 30.00
(LP) 5019 *Rockin' Hot*.......... 20.00 - 30.00
(LP) 5024 *16 Fabulous Hits*......... 15.00 - 20.00

THE FABULAIRES:
Main-Line 103 *While Walking*............. 8.00 - 12.00

THE FABULOUS ENCHANTERS:
Fine Arts 1007 *Why Are You Crying*......... 7.00 - 10.00

THE FABULOUS FABULIERS:
Angeltone 539 *She Is The Girl For Me*......... 8.00 - 12.00

THE FABULOUS FLAMES:
Bay-Tone 102 *Do You Remember*............. 10.00 - 15.00
105 *I'm So All Alone*.............. 10.00 - 15.00
Harlem 114 *So Long My Darling*......... 7.00 - 10.00
Rex—*My Joan*.............. 10.00 - 15.00

THE FABULOUS FOUR:
Chancellor 1078 *Why Do Fools Fall In Love*... 7.00 - 10.00
1085 *Betty Ann*............... 10.00 - 15.00
Melic 4114 *Welcome Me Home*............. 7.00 - 10.00

THE FABULOUS GARDENIAS:
Liz 1004 *It's You You You*.................. 7.00 - 10.00

THE FABULOUS PLAYBOYS:
Apollo 460 *Tears, Tears, Tears*.............. ————

THE FABULOUS THREE:
Hale 501 *Cross Every Mountain*.............. 5.00 - 8.00

THE FABULOUS TWILIGHTS:
Fortune 542 *My Little Darling*.............. 7.00 - 10.00

THE FABULOUS WINDS:
Celestial 111 *Rock & Roll Radio*............. 7.00 - 10.00

TOMMY FACENDA:
Legrande 1001 *High School U.S.A.*............. 10.00 - 15.00

DICK FAGAN & THE SCORES:
Sarg 160 *Nothing Really Shakes Me*......... 10.00 - 15.00

TOMMY FAILE:
Lawn 104 *That's All Right*............. 8.00 - 12.00
Silver Star 1001 *Long Gone*............. 8.00 - 12.00

WERLY FAIRBURN:
Capitol 2770, 2844, 2963............. 4.00 - 6.00
Columbia 21432, 21483................. 4.00 - 6.00
21528 *Everybody's Rockin'*......... 8.00 - 12.00
Savoy 1503 *All The Time*......... 5.00 - 8.00
1509 *Speak To Me Baby*............. 7.00 - 10.00
1521 *Telephone Baby*............. 7.00 - 10.00

JOHNNY FAIRE:
Surf 5019 *Bertha Lou*............. 10.00 - 15.00
5024 *Betcha I Getcha*............. 10.00 - 15.00

THE FAIRLANES:
Lucky Seven 102 *Seventeen Steps*............. 15.00 - 20.00
Radiant 101 *Baby Baby*............. 7.00 - 10.00

THE FALCONS:
Anna 1110 *This Heart Of Mine*.............. 8.00 - 12.00
Cash 1002 *I Miss You Darling*............. 40.00 - 60.00
Falcon 1006 *Now That It's Over*............. 15.00 - 20.00
Flick 001 *You're So Fine*............. 8.00 - 12.00
Mercury 70940 *Baby That's It*............. 5.00 - 8.00
Quality 1721 *My Only Love*............. 10.00 - 15.00
Savoy 843 *You're The Beating Of My Heart*.... 75.00 - 100.00
Silhouette 521 *Can This be Christmas*......... 7.00 - 10.00

THE FALLEN ANGELS:
Tollie 9049 *Up On The Mountain*............. 10.00 - 15.00

JOHNNY FALLIN:
Capitol 4216 *Party Kiss*............................ 8.00 - 12.00
JAY FANNING:
Acme 2032 *It's Love*........................... 10.00 - 15.00
THE FANTASTICS:
Copa 8005 *That One*........................... 5.00 - 8.00
RCA Victor 7572 *There Goes My Love*..... 5.00 - 8.00
THE FANTASYS:
Guyden 2029 *No One But You*............... 7.00 - 10.00
WAYNE FARMER & THE TEEN-BEATS:
Dodge 802 *Yeah! Yeah! My Baby*........... 4.00 - 7.00
THE FARMER BOYS:
Capitol 3077, 3162, 3246, 3322............. 3.00 - 5.00
3476 *My Baby Done Left Me*............. 7.00 - 10.00
3569 *Cool Down Mame*................... 8.00 - 12.00
LITTLE JOEY FARR:
Band Box 286 *Big White Cadillac*........... 10.00 - 15.00
BILLY FARRELL:
Imperial 7001 *Slippin' And Slidin'*.......... 7.00 - 10.00
MICKEY FARRELL & THE DYNAMICS:
Bethlehem 3080 *I'm Calling On You*........ 5.00 - 8.00
THE FASCINATIONS:
Sure 106 *Midnight*........................... 12.00 - 16.00
THE FASCINATORS:
Blue Lake 112 *Can't Stop*................... 75.00 - 100.00
Capitol 4053 *Chapel Bells*................... 10.00 - 15.00
4137 *Come To Paradise*................... 10.00 - 15.00
4247 *Oh Rosemarie*....................... 10.00 - 15.00
King 5119 *Tee Vee*......................... 8.00 - 12.00
Your Copy 1135 *The Bells Of My Heart*...... 80.00 - 120.00
1136 *Don't Give It Away*................. 80.00 - 120.00
JOHNNY FAY:
Dani 1539 *Sweet Linda Brown*.............. 10.00 - 15.00
THE FEATHERS:
Aladdin 3267 *Johnny Darling*............... 20.00 - 25.00
3277 *I Need A Girl*....................... 40.00 - 50.00
Show Time 1103 *Desert Winds*............. 20.00 - 30.00
1104 *Johnny Darling*..................... 20.00 - 30.00
1105 *Why Don't You Write Me*............ 20.00 - 30.00
1106 *Love Only You*..................... 20.00 - 30.00
CHARLIE FEATHERS:
Flip 503 *I've Been Deceived*................. 75.00 - 100.00
Holiday Inn 114 *Deep Elm Blues*........... 10.00 - 15.00
Kay 1001 *Why Don't You*................... 10.00 - 15.00
King 4971 *Everybody's Lovin' My Baby*..... 25.00 - 40.00
4997 *Bottle To The Baby*................. 40.00 - 60.00
5022 *Nobody's Woman*................... 20.00 - 30.00
5043 *When You Come Around*............ 20.00 - 30.00
Memphis 103 *Wild Wild Party*.............. 20.00 - 30.00
Meteor 5032 *Tongue-Tied Jill*.............. 75.00 - 100.00
Sun 231 *Defrost Your Heart*............... 75.00 - 100.00
503 *I've Been Deceived*................... 75.00 - 100.00
THE FEDERALS:
De Luxe 6112 *Come Go With Me*........... 10.00 - 15.00
Fury 1009 *Dear Loraine*.................... 10.00 - 15.00
DON FEGER:
Ebony 102 *Date On The Corner*............ 20.00 - 30.00
103 *Lookout Baby*....................... 20.00 - 30.00
TERRY FELL:
"X" 0114 *Mississippi River Shuffle*.......... 4.00 - 7.00
"X" 0149 *I'm Hot To Trot*.................. 5.00 - 8.00
DERRELL FELTS:
Dixie 2008 *Playmates*...................... ———
Okeh 7118 *Lookie Lookie Lookie*........... 8.00 - 12.00
NARVEL FELTS:
Mercury 71140 *Kiss-A-Me Baby*............. 4.00 - 7.00
Pink 701 *Cutie Baby*....................... 5.00 - 8.00
FREDDY FENDER:
Agro 5375 *A Man Can Cry*................. 4.00 - 6.00
Duncan 1000 *Mean Woman*................ 15.00 - 20.00
1001 *Wasted Days & Wasted Nights*...... 8.00 - 12.00
1002 *Wild Side Of Life*................... 5.00 - 8.00

1004 *Little Mama*.......................... 7.00 - 10.00
Imperial 5659, 5670.......................... 4.00 - 6.00
Norco 102, 104, 108......................... 4.00 - 6.00
103 *Going Out With The Tide*............ 5.00 - 8.00
107 *Bony Moronie*....................... 7.00 - 10.00
THE FENDERMEN:
Soma (LP) 1240 *Mule Skinner Blues*......... 30.00 - 50.00
FENTION & THE CASTLE ROCKERS:
Duke 190 *The Freeze*....................... 3.00 - 6.00
H BOMB FERGUSON & HIS MAD LADS:
Arc 9001 *Little Tiger*....................... ———
TROY FERGUSON:
Flame 101 *At The Jamboree*................ 7.00 - 10.00
AL FERRIER (& HIS BOPPIN' BILLIES):
Excello 2105 *Hey Baby*..................... 9.00 - 12.00
Goldband 1031 *No No Baby*................ 10.00 - 15.00
1035 *It's Too Late Now*.................. 8.00 - 10.00
1072 *Let's Go Boppin' Tonight*........... 10.00 - 15.00
Rocko 502 *Kiss Me Baby*................... 7.00 - 10.00
Zynn 510 *Chisholm Trail Rock*............. 7.00 - 10.00
1013 *Blues Stop Knockin'*................ 7.00 - 10.00
FERRIS & THE WHEELS:
United Artists 458 *Moments Like This*........ 10.00 - 15.00
THE FIDELITY'S:
Baton 252, 256.............................. 4.00 - 7.00
Sir 271, 276................................. 4.00 - 7.00
THE FIELD BROS.:
Carlton 475 *Time And Time Again*........... 5.00 - 8.00
THE FIESTAS:
Old Town 1062, 1069, 1080................. 3.00 - 5.00
1062 *So Fine* (78 rpm)................... 15.00 - 20.00
Vigor 712 *So Fine*......................... ———
HERBIE FIELDS:
Parrott 806 *Mr. Jump*...................... 5.00 - 8.00
LINCOLN FIG & THE DATES:
Worthy 1006 *Kiss Me Tenderly*.............. 8.00 - 12.00
BRIEN FISHER:
Spangle 2001 *Fingertips*.................... 7.00 - 10.00
United Artists 115 *It's Up To You*........... 7.00 - 10.00
SONNY FISHER:
Starday 179 *Rockin' Daddy*................. 20.00 - 30.00
190 *Sneaky Pete*......................... 35.00 - 50.00
207 *Rockin' & Rollin'*.................... 30.00 - 40.00
244 *Pink And Black*..................... 30.00 - 40.00
TOMMY FISHER:
B&D 1314 *Rock & Roll Robin Hood*......... 10.00 - 15.00
THE FI-TONES:
Angle Tone 525 *You'll Be The Last*.......... 8.00 - 12.00
Atlas 1050 *Foolish Dreams*................. 20.00 - 30.00
1051 *It Wasn't A Lie*.................... 20.00 - 30.00
1052 *I Call To You*...................... 15.00 - 20.00
Old Town 1042 *My Faith*................... 7.00 - 10.00
FIVE ARROWS:
Parrot 816 *Pretty Little Thing*.............. ———
THE FIVE BARS:
Money 224 *Story Weather*.................. ———
THE FIVE BILLS:
Brunswick—*Can't Wait For Tomorrow*....... 15.00 - 20.00
THE FIVE BLUE NOTES:
Onda 108 *My Special Prayer*............... 20.00 - 30.00
Sabre 103 *My Gal Is Gone*................. 60.00 - 80.00
108 *The Beat Of Our Hearts*............. 75.00 - 100.00
THE FIVE BUDDS:
Rama 1 *I Was Such A Fool*................. 30.00 - 40.00
2 *I Guess It's All Over Now*.............. 30.00 - 40.00
FIVE CAMPBELLS:
Music City 794 *Morrine*.................... 30.00 - 40.00
THE FIVE CHANCES:
Chance 1157 *I May Be Small*............... 100.00 - 125.00
Federal 12303 *My Days Are Blue*........... 15.00 - 20.00
States 156 *Gloria*.......................... 40.00 - 60.00

THE 5 CHANELS:
Deb 500 *The Reason* . . . . 5.00 - 8.00
THE FIVE CHORDS:
Cuca 1031 *Red Wine* . . . . 10.00 - 15.00
Jamie 1110 *Love Is Like Music* . . . . 8.00 - 12.00
THE FIVE CLASSICS:
Arc 4454 *My Imagination* . . . . 7.00 - 10.00
THE FIVE CROWNS:
Alanna 576 *If I Were King* . . . . 7.00 - 10.00
Caravan 15609 *I Can't Pretend* . . . . ————
Gee 1001 *God Bless You* . . . . 10.00 - 15.00
Old Town 790 *You Could Be My Love* . . . . . 125.00 - 175.00
  792 *Lullaby Of The Bells* . . . . 125.00 - 175.00
Rainbow 179 *A Star* (red plastic) . . . . 60.00 - 90.00
  184 *Who Can Be True* . . . . 50.00 - 75.00
  202 *Keep It A Secret* . . . . 90.00 - 125.00
  206 *Alone Again* . . . . 75.00 - 100.00
  335 *You Came To Me* . . . . 50.00 - 75.00
Riviera 990 *You Came To Me* . . . . 90.00 - 125.00
Transworld 717 *I Can't Pretend* . . . . 40.00 - 60.00
THE FIVE CRYSTALS:
Delcro—*Path Of Broken Hearts* . . . . 15.00 - 20.00
Kane 25592 *Hey Landlord* . . . . 5.00 - 8.00
THE FIVE C'S:
United 172 *Tell Me* . . . . 25.00 - 40.00
THE FIVE DAPPS:
Brax 207/208 *You're So Unfaithful* . . . . 30.00 - 40.00
THE FIVE DEBONAIRES:
Herald 509 *Whispering Blues* . . . . 15.00 - 20.00
THE FIVE DELIGHTS;
Newport 7002 *There'll Be No Goodbye* . . . . . 15.00 - 20.00
THE FIVE DIAMONDS:
Treat 501 *Ten Commandments Of Love* . . . . 40.00 - 60.00
THE FIVE DIPS:
Original 1005 *Teach Me Tonight* . . . . ————
FIVE DISCS:
Calo 202 *My Baby Loves Me* . . . . 10.00 - 15.00
Cheer 1000 *That Was The Time* . . . . 10.00 - 15.00
Dwain 803 *Roses* . . . . 20.00 - 30.00
Emge 1004 *I Remember* . . . . 25.00 - 35.00
Yale 243 *Come On Baby* . . . . 8.00 - 12.00
FIVE DOLLARS:
Fortune 821 *Harmony Of Love* . . . . 15.00 - 20.00
  830 *I Will Wait* . . . . 10.00 - 15.00
  833 *You Fool* . . . . 10.00 - 15.00
  845 *Yellow Moon* . . . . 10.00 - 15.00
  854 *That's The Way It Goes* . . . . . . 10.00 - 15.00
FIVE DOTS:
Note 1003 *I Just Love The Things She Does* . . . . 15.00 - 20.00
THE FIVE DUKES:
Atlas 1040 *I Cross My Fingers* . . . . 100.00 - 125.00
FIVE ECHOES/ECHOS:
Sabre 102 *Lonely Moon* (red plastic) . . . . 90.00 - 130.00
  105 *So Lonesome* . . . . 60.00 - 90.00
Vee Jay 129 *I Really Do* . . . . 40.00 - 60.00
  156 *Fool's Prayer* . . . . 25.00 - 35.00
FIVE EMERALDS:
S.R.C. 106 *I'll Beg* . . . . 75.00 - 100.00
  107 *Darling* . . . . 90.00 - 125.00
THE FIVE FLEETS:
Felsted 8513 *Oh What A Feeling* . . . . 8.00 - 12.00
FIVE FORTUNES:
Ranson—*Time Out For Love* . . . . 50.00 - 75.00
FIVE HEARTS:
Arcade 107 *Unbelieveable* . . . . ————
Flair 1026 *The Fine One* . . . . ————
THE FIVE JADES:
Duke 188 *Without Your Love* . . . . 8.00 - 12.00
FIVE JETS:
De Luxe 6018 *I Am In Love* . . . . 25.00 - 35.00
  6053 *I'm Stuck* . . . . 12.00 - 15.00

  6058 *Tell Me You're Mine* . . . . 12.00 - 15.00
  6064 *Crazy Chicken* . . . . 8.00 - 12.00
  6071 *Please Love Me Baby* . . . . 10.00 - 15.00
Fortune 833 *I'm Wanderin'* . . . . 10.00 - 15.00
THE FIVE KEYS:
Aladdin (LP) 806 *Best Of The Five Keys* (blue label) . . . 80.00 - 120.00
  3085 *With A Broken Heart* . . . . 90.00 - 125.00
  3099 *The Glory Of Love* . . . . 75.00 - 100.00
  3113 *It's Christmas* . . . . 75.00 - 100.00
  3118 *Yes, Sir, That's My Baby* . . . . . . 90.00 - 125.00
  3127 *Red Sails In The Sunset* . . . . . . 90.00 - 125.00
  3136 *I Hadn't Any One Til You* . . . . . 90.00 - 125.00
  3158 *I Cried For You* . . . . 90.00 - 125.00
  3167 *Can't Keep From Crying* . . . . . . 90.00 - 125.00
  3186 *I'll Always Be In Love With You* . . . 90.00 - 125.00
  3190 *These Foolish Things* . . . . 90.00 - 125.00
  3204 *Tear Drops In Your Eyes* . . . . . 75.00 - 100.00
  3214 *My Saddest Hour* . . . . 60.00 - 90.00
  3228 *Love My Loving* . . . . 60.00 - 90.00
  3245 *Deep In My Heart* . . . . 60.00 - 90.00
  3263 *Why, Oh Why* . . . . 50.00 - 75.00
  3312 *Story Of Love* . . . . 50.00 - 75.00
(Note: Above are to have blue labels; maroon label
  issues are worth somewhat less)
Capitol (EP) 828 *The Five Keys On Stage* . . . . . 12.00 - 15.00
  (LP) 828 *The Five Keys On Stage* . . . . . 40.00 - 60.00
  (LP) 1769 *The Fantastic Five Keys* . . . . 30.00 - 40.00
  3318 *You Broke The Rules* . . . . 5.00 - 8.00
Capitol (45 rpm—others) . . . . 3.00 - 5.00
King (LP) 688 *The Five Keys* . . . . 20.00 - 30.00
  (LP) 692 *Rhythm & Blues Hits—Past & Present* . . . 20.00 - 30.00
King (45 rpm) . . . . 3.00 - 5.00
Score (LP) 4003 *On The Town With The Five Keys* . . . 60.00 - 90.00
THE FIVE KIDS:
Maxwell 101 *Carolyn* . . . . ————
THE FIVE KINGS:
Columbia 43060 *Light Bulb* . . . . 10.00 - 15.00
Yvette 101 *Here Comes My Baby* . . . . 7.00 - 10.00
FIVE KNIGHTS:
Specialty 675 *Miracle* . . . . 10.00 - 15.00
FIVE LETTERS:
Ivy 102 *Hold My Baby* . . . . 20.00 - 30.00
THE FIVE LYRICS:
Music City 799 *I'm Traveling Light* . . . . ————
THE FIVE MASKS:
Jan 101 *Forever And A Day* . . . . 8.00 - 12.00
THE FIVE MASTERS:
Bumble Bee 502 *We Are Like One* . . . . 8.00 - 12.00
FIVE MEMBERS:
Gem 224 *Please Come Home* . . . . 35.00 - 50.00
FIVE NOTES:
Chess 1614 *Show Me The Way* . . . . 20.00 - 30.00
Jen-D— *You Are So Beautiful* . . . . ————
Josie 784 *You Are So Beautiful* . . . . 10.00 - 15.00
Specialty 461 *Thrill Me Baby* . . . . 50.00 - 75.00
FIVE OWLS:
Vulcan 303 *Pleading To You* . . . . 35.00 - 50.00
FIVE PEARLS:
Aladdin 3265 *Please Let Me Know* . . . . 25.00 - 35.00
FIVE PENNIES:
Savoy 1182 *Let It Rain* . . . . 7.00 - 10.00
  1190 *My Heart Trembles* . . . . 7.00 - 10.00
THE FIVE PLAYBOYS:
Fee Bee 213 *Pages Of My Scrapbook* . . . . ————
  232 *Angel Mine* . . . . ————
FIVE REASONS:
Cub 9006 *Three O'Clock Rock* . . . . 10.00 - 15.00
FIVE ROVERS:
Music City 798 *Down To The Sea* . . . . 15.00 - 20.00
FIVE ROYALES:
Apollo 441 *Courage To Love* (red plastic) . . . . 15.00 - 25.00

443 *Baby Don't Do It* (red plastic)............	15.00 -	20.00
(LP) 488 *The Rockin 5 Royales*................	50.00 -	75.00
Home of The Blues 112, 232, 234..............	4.00 -	8.00
King (LP) 580 *Dedicated To You*..............	35.00 -	50.00
(LP) 616 *Sing For You*.....................	25.00 -	35.00
(LP) 678 *Five Royales*.....................	20.00 -	30.00
4785 *How I Wonder*.....................	5.00 -	8.00
4830 *Someone Made You For Me*...........	5.00 -	8.00
King (others)..............................	4.00 -	7.00

FIVE SATINS:

Chancellor 1110 *Raining In My Heart*........	5.00 -	8.00
Cub 9090 *Can I Come Over Tonight*..........	4.00 -	7.00
Ember (EP) 101 *To The Aisle*...............	15.00 -	20.00
(EP) 102 *Our Anniversary*.................	15.00 -	20.00
(LP) 101 *The Five Satins Sing*.............	50.00 -	75.00
(LP) 401 *Five Satins Encore*..............	40.00 -	60.00
1005 *In The Still Of The Nite*.............	5.00 -	8.00
1005 *In The Still Of The Nite* (78 rpm)......	10.00 -	15.00
1014 *Our Love Is Forever*.................	5.00 -	8.00
1019 *To The Aisle*.......................	5.00 -	8.00
1019 *To The Aisle* (78 rpm)...............	10.00 -	15.00
1025 *Our Anniversary*....................	5.00 -	8.00
1028 *A Million To One*...................	5.00 -	8.00
1038 *A Night To Remember*................	5.00 -	8.00
1056 *Shadows*..........................	4.00 -	7.00
1061 *I'll Be Seeing You*..................	4.00 -	7.00
1070 *Wishing Ring*......................	5.00 -	8.00
Klik 7905 *She's Gone*.....................	15.00 -	20.00
Standard 1005 *In The Still Of The Night*......	50.00 -	75.00
5105 *All Mine*.........................	30.00 -	40.00

FIVE SCALDERS:

Drummond 3000 *If Only You Were Mine*......	60.00 -	80.00
3001 *Willow Blues*.......................	60.00 -	80.00

FIVE SCAMPS:

Okeh 7049 *With All My Heart*..............	20.00 -	30.00

FIVE SHARPS:

Jubilee 5104 *Stormy Weather*................	————	

Unknown in 45 rpm format. See Blues, etc. section
for listing and comments on 78 rpm issue.)

FIVE SHILLINGS:

Decca 30722 *Letter To An Angel*............	20.00 -	30.00

FIVE SOUNDS:

Aljon 115 *Tonight Must Live On*............	20.00 -	30.00

THE FIVE SPOTS:

Future 2201 *Get With It*....................	20.00 -	30.00

FIVE STARS:

Blues Boy Kingdom 106 *So Lonely Baby*.......	75.00 -	100.00
Hunt 318 *Dreaming*.......................	————	
Show Time 1102 *Walkin' And Talkin'*........	50.00 -	75.00
Treat 505 *We Danced In The Moonlight*.......	90.00 -	120.00

FIVE STRINGS: (See also SID KING)

Columbia 21361 *I Like It*...................	7.00 -	10.00
21403 *Drinking Wine Spoli Oli*.............	10.00 -	15.00

FIVE SWANS:

Music City 795 *Little Girl Of My Dreams*.....	15.00 -	20.00

FIVE THRILLS:

Parrot 796 *My Baby's Gone*.................	150.00 -	20.00
800 *Gloria*.............................	75.00 -	125.00

FIVE TINOS:

Sun 222 *Sitting By My Window*..............	90.00 -	110.00

FIVE TROJANS:

Edison International 410 *I Hear Those Bells*....	10.00 -	20.00
412 *Little Doll*..........................	10.00 -	20.00

FIVE VETS:

Allstar 713 *Right Now*.....................	10.00 -	15.00

FIVE WILLOWS:

Allen 1000 *My Dear Dearest Darling*.........	75.00 -	100.00
1002 *Dolores*...........................	75.00 -	100.00
1003 *White Cliffs Of Dover*...............	90.00 -	120.00
Herald 433 *Lay Your Head On My Shoulder*...	20.00 -	30.00
442 *Look Me In The Eyes*...............	15.00 -	20.00
Pee Dee 290 *Love Bells*...................	100.00 -	125.00

FIVE WINGS:

King 4778 *Johnny Has Gone*.................	30.00 -	50.00
4781 *Teardrops Are Falling*...............	30.00 -	50.00

BILL FLAGG:

MGM 12637 *Doin' My Time*.................	8.00 -	12.00
Tetra 4445 *Go Cat Go*....................	10.00 -	15.00
4448 *Guitar Rock*......................	10.00 -	15.00

SONNY FLAHERTY:

Spangle 2011 *My Baby's Casual*..............	7.00 -	10.00

FLAIRS: (See also SHIRLEY GUNTER; FATSO THEUS)

ABC Paramount 9740 *Steppin' Out*..........	5.00 -	8.00
Crown (LP) 5356 *The Flairs*...............	20.00 -	30.00
Epic 9447 *Shake Shake Sherry*.............	7.00 -	10.00
Flair 1012 *I Had A Love*.................	20.00 -	30.00
1028 *Love Me Girl*.....................	15.00 -	20.00
1044 *This Is The Night For Love*.........	15.00 -	20.00
Palms 726 *Roll Over Beethoven*............	————	

FLAMES:

Aladdin 3349 *So Alone*....................	20.00 -	30.00
G.M. 101 *Darling Jane*....................	7.00 -	10.00
7-11 2106 *Keep On Smiling*................	20.00 -	30.00
2107 *Together*.........................	20.00 -	30.00
2108 *Let's Talk It Over*.................	20.00 -	30.00
2109 *Sorrowful Heart*...................	20.00 -	30.00
2110 *I'll Hide My Tears*.................	20.00 -	30.00

FLAMINGOS:

Chance 1133 *If I Can't Have You* (red plastic)..	150.00 -	200.00
1140 *That's My Desire*...................	80.00 -	120.00
1145 *Golden Teardrops*..................	80.00 -	120.00
1149 *Plan For Love*.....................	80.00 -	120.00
1154 *Cross Over The Bridge*.............	80.00 -	120.00
1162 *Blues In A Letter*..................	80.00 -	120.00
Checker 815 *That's My Baby*..............	10.00 -	15.00
821 *Please*............................	10.00 -	15.00
830 *I'll Be Home*......................	8.00 -	12.00
837 *Get With It*.......................	7.00 -	10.00
846 *The Vow*..........................	7.00 -	10.00
853 *Would I Be Crying*.................	7.00 -	10.00
Chess (LP) 1433 *The Flamingos* (black label)....	50.00 -	75.00
End (LP) 205 *Flamingos*..................	10.00 -	15.00
(LP) 304 *Flamingo Serenade*.............	20.00 -	30.00
(LP) 307 *Flamingo Favorites*.............	20.00 -	30.00
(LP) 316 *Sound Of The Flamingos*..........	20.00 -	30.00
Decca 30335 *Ladder Of Love*..............	7.00 -	10.00
30454 *My Faith In You*.................	7.00 -	10.00
30948 *Jerri-Lee*.......................	7.00 -	10.00
Parrott 808 *Dream Of A Lifetime* (red plastic)...	75.00 -	100.00
811 *I Really Don't Want To Know*.........	very rare	
812 *I'm Yours* (red plastic).............	90.00 -	120.00
Vee Jay (LP) 1052 *Flamingos Meet The Moonglows*	20.00 -	30.00

FLARES:

Felsted 8604 *Loving You*...................	7.00 -	10.00
Press 2803 *Make It Be Me*.................	7.00 -	10.00

FLATT & SCRUGGS:

Columbia (LP) 1019 *Foggy Mountain Jamboree*.	10.00 -	15.00
Mercury (LP) 20358 *Country Music*..........	12.00 -	16.00

THE FLEETWOODS:

Dolton 2001 *Mr. Blue*....................	10.00 -	15.00

GEORGE FLEMING:

Fleming 501 *I'm Gonna Tell On You/The Shake*	————	

WADE FLEMONS:

Vee Jay (LP) 1011 *Wade Flemons*............	20.00 -	30.00

FLIPS:

Sapphire—*Why Should I*....................	20.00 -	30.00

FLORESCENTS:

Bethlehem 3079 *Being In Love*..............	5.00 -	8.00

PHIL FLOWERS:

Dot—*No Kissin' At The Hop*................	————	

BILL FLOYD:

Starday 663 *Hey Boy!*....................	7.00 -	10.00

Topic 8034 *I'll Huff And I'll Puff*............. 5.00 - 8.00

FRANK FLOYD:

F & L 100 *Rock A Little Baby*.............. ————

MERDELL FLOYD:

Erwin 100 *Juke Box Mama*................. 10.00 - 15.00

FLUORESCENTS:

Hanover 4520 *The Facts Of Love*........... 10.00 - 15.00

THE FLYERS:

Atco 6088 *My Only Desire*................. 7.00 - 10.00

RED FOLEY:

Decca (LP) 5303 (10") *Souvenir*.............. 10.00 - 15.00

(LP) 5338 (10") *Lift Up Your Voice*........ 10.00 - 15.00

(LP) 8294 *Souvenir Album*................. 10.00 - 15.00

(LP) 8296 *Beyond The Sunset*.............. 10.00 - 15.00

(LP) 8298 *...And Ernest Tubb*............. 10.00 - 15.00

(LP) 8767, 8806, 8847, 8903.............. 7.00 - 10.00

29517 *Plantation Boogie*................. 4.00 - 7.00

"FOLK FESTIVAL OF THE BLUES":

Argo (LP) 4031 *(various artists)*.......... *10.00 - 15.00*

EDDIE FONTAINE:

Argo 5309 *Nothing' Shakin'*............... 5.00 - 8.00

Chancellor 1018 *Goodness, It's Gladys*.... 7.00 - 10.00

Decca 30042, 30108.................... 3.00 - 6.00

30256 *Homesick Blues*................. 5.00 - 8.00

30446 *Honky Tonk Man*................. 5.00 - 8.00

Jalo 102 *It Ain't Gonna Happen No More*..... 10.00 - 15.00

Sunbeam 105 *Nothin' Shakin'*.......... 8.00 - 12.00

112 *Nobody Else Can Handle This Job*...... 5.00 - 8.00

Vik 0193 *Here 'Tis*...................... 4.00 - 6.00

FRANK FONTAINE:

MGM 12129 *Everybody Rock*.............. ————

EARLSON FORD:

Mercury 71108 *Ain't Nothin' Shakin'*.......... 8.00 - 12.00

TENNESSEE ERNIE FORD:

Capitol (LP) 888 *Ol' Rockin' Ern*............. 15.00 - 20.00

3262 *Sixteen Tons* (78 rpm)............. 5.00 - 8.00

(unnumbered) Special Commemorative Pressing celebrating artist's 20th anniversary (1949-1969) with Capitol Records. *Sixteen Tons/I've Got The Milk 'Em In The Mornin' Blues* (78rpm)..... ————

FRANKIE FORD:

Ace (LP) 1005 *On A Sea Cruise With Frankie Ford* 30.00 - 40.00

JIMMIE FORD:

Stylo 2102 *You're Gonna Be Sorry*............ 7.00 - 10.00

EARL FOREST/FORREST:

Duke 108 *Whoopin' And Hollerin'*......... 8.00 - 12.00

113 *53*............................. 8.00 - 12.00

121 *Out On A Party*................... 7.00 - 10.00

131 *Oh Ooh Wee*..................... 7.00 - 10.00

Meteor 5005 *I Wronged A Woman*....... 20.00 - 30.00

JESSIE FORTUNE:

U.S.A. 738, 747........................ 4.00 - 6.00

JOHNNY FORTUNE:

Park Avenue 130 *Dragster*............. ————

FORTUNES:

Checker 818 *Believe In Me*............. 15.00 - 20.00

Decca 30541 *Tarnished Angel*.......... 7.00 - 10.00

30688 *How Clever Of You*............. 7.00 - 10.00

Top Rank 2019 *Steady Vows*........... 7.00 - 10.00

THE FORTUNE TELLERS:

Sheryl 340 *Just A Little Bit Of Your Love*..... 4.00 - 6.00

THE FOSTER BROS.:

Hi Mi 3005 *Never Again*................ 7.00 - 10.00

Profile 4004 *Trust In Me*............... 7.00 - 10.00

CECIL FOSTER & THE AUDIOS:

Time 1 *Why Did You Do It To Me?*........ 8.00 - 12.00

Ultra 105 *Honest I Do*.................. 10.00 - 15.00

JERRY FOSTER & HIS BAND:

Back Beat 520 *What Would I Do*........ 5.00 - 8.00

LITTLE WILLIE FOSTER:

Blue Lake 113 *Falling Rain Blues*.......... 30.00 - 40.00

Cobra 5011 *Crying The Blues*................ 15.00 - 20.00

Parrot 813 *Falling Rain Blues*................ 30.00 - 40.00

FOUR ARCS:

Boulevard 102 *Life Of Ease*................. 35.00 - 50.00

FOUR BARS:

Josie 762 *Grief By Day, Grief By Night*........ 50.00 - 75.00

768 *If I Give My Heart To You*............ 25.00 - 40.00

783 *Why Treat Me This Way*............. 25.00 - 35.00

Republic 7101 *When Did You Leave Heaven*... 40.00 - 60.00

THE FOUR BELLS:

Gem 220 *My Tree*........................ ————

FOUR BLAZES:

United 114 *Mary Jo*...................... 7.00 - 10.00

125 *Rug Cutter*....................... 7.00 - 10.00

127 *Please Send Her Back To Me*........... 7.00 - 10.00

(Above are red plastic)

FOUR BROTHERS & A COUSIN:

Jaguar 3005 *Trust In Me*................... 50.00 - 75.00

FOUR BUDDIES/4 BUDDIES:

Club-51 105 *Look Out*.................... 40.00 - 60.00

Savoy 769 *I Will Wait*.................... 20.00 - 30.00

779 *Sweet Slumber*.................... 20.00 - 30.00

789 *My Summer's Gone*................. 40.00 - 60.00

817 *Heart And Soul*.................... 30.00 - 40.00

823 *Simply Say Goodbye*................ 50.00 - 80.00

845 *You're Part Of Me*................. 20.00 - 30.00

866 *What's The Matter With Me*........ 20.00 - 30.00

888 *My Mother's Eyes*................. 20.00 - 30.00

891 *I'd Climb The Highest Mountain*....... 10.00 - 15.00

FOUR CHICKADEES:

Checker 849 *Teenage Blues*............. 7.00 - 10.00

FOUR CLIPPERS:

Fox 960/961 *Rain*...................... 35.00 - 50.00

FOUR COUSINS:

20th Century 75020 *Time And Time Again*..... 35.00 - 50.00

THE FOUR CRUISERS:

Chess 1547 *On Account Of You*........... 50.00 - 80.00

FOUR DATES:

Chancellor 1014 *Eloise*.................. 3.00 - 5.00

1019 *I Say Babe*...................... 5.00 - 8.00

1027 *Feel Good*....................... 5.00 - 8.00

FOUR DEUCES:

Music City 790 *W-P-L-J* (maroon label)....... 10.00 - 15.00

(Above is found with various flip sides, and pressed of colored plastic)

796 *Down It Went*.................... 10.00 - 15.00

FOUR DOTS:

Bullseye 103 *Rita*...................... 15.00 - 25.00

104 *Peace Of Mind*.................... 10.00 - 15.00

Freedom 44002 *It's Heaven*.............. 8.00 - 12.00

FOUR DUKES:

Duke 116 *Crying In The Chapel*............. 25.00 - 35.00

FOUR ELDORADOS:

Academy 8138 *Little Susie*............... ————

FOUR EPICS:

Heritage 109 *When The Music Ends*......... 4.00 - 6.00

Laurie 3155 *Again*..................... 5.00 - 8.00

3183 *Dance, Jo-Ann*.................. 5.00 - 8.00

FOUR FELLOWS:

Glory 231 *Wish I Didn't Love You*........... 10.00 - 15.00

Glory 234, 236, 248.................... 4.00 - 7.00

Pop 0208 *That's Why I Pray*............. 5.00 - 8.00

FOUR GEMS:

Broadcast—*Outside Of Paradise*........... 10.00 - 15.00

FOUR GENTS:

Park 113 *On Bended Knee*................ 40.00 - 60.00

FOUR HAVEN KNIGHTS:

Atlas 1066 *In My Lonely Room*........... 20.00 - 30.00

Josie 824 *In My Lonely Room*............ 10.00 - 15.00

FOUR IMPERIALS:

Chant 101 *Teen Age Fool*	7.00 -	10.00
Dial 101 *Valley Of Tears*	5.00 -	8.00

4 J'S:

Impra 1267/1268 *Class Ring*	———	
Jamie 1267, 1274	4.00 -	7.00

FOUR J'S:

United Artist 125 *Rock & Roll Age*	6.00 -	9.00

FOUR JACKS:

Allen 21000 *I Challenge Your Kiss*	———	
Federal 12075 *You Met A Fool*	30.00 -	40.00
12087 *I'll Be Home Again*	30.00 -	40.00
Hollywood 1058 *Walking And Crying*	35.00 -	50.00
Pel 601 *I've Waited Long Enough*	———	
Rebel 1313 *I Can't Forget*	15.00 -	20.00

FOUR JOKERS:

Diamond 3004 *Transfusion*	7.00 -	10.00
Sue 703 *Written In The Stars*	7.00 -	10.00

FOUR KINGS:

Fortune 807 *Hurry Home Baby*	20.00 -	30.00
811 *You Don't Mean Me Right*	20.00 -	30.00
817 *Do-Li-Op*	20.00 -	30.00
Stomper Time 1163 *Walkin' Along*	———	

FOUR KNIGHTS:

Capitol (LP) 346 (10") *Spotlight Songs*	25.00 -	40.00
(LP) 346 *Spotlight Songs*	30.00 -	40.00
Coral (LP) 57221	25.00 -	35.00

FOUR LOVERS:

Epic 9255 *Pucker Up*	25.00 -	40.00
RCA (EP) 869 *The Four Lovers*	15.00 -	20.00
(EP) 871 *Joyride*	15.00 -	20.00
(LP) 1317 *Joy Ride*	75.00 -	100.00
6518 *The Girl In My Dreams*	6.00 -	9.00
6519 *Honey Love*	6.00 -	9.00
6646 *Lovey Dovey*	7.00 -	10.00
6648 *Never Never*	7.00 -	10.00
6812 *Shake A Hand*	8.00 -	12.00
Night Train (unissued?)	———	

RAY FOURNIA & ROCKING RELS:

Diamond Disk—*Settle Down*	———	

FOUR NOTES:

Blue Key—*I Didn't Mean To Be So Mean*	20.00 -	30.00

FOUR PALS:

Roulette 4127 *Yours To Possess*	5.00 -	8.00
Royal Roost 610 *If I Can't Have The One I Love*	8.00 -	12.00
616 *No One Ever Loved Me*	8.00 -	12.00

FOUR PENNIES:

Brunswick 55324 *'Tis The Season*	7.00 -	10.00

FOUR PHAROAHS:

Ransom 109 *Give Me Your Love*	8.00 -	12.00

FOUR PLAID THROATS:

Mercury 70143 *My Inspiration*	80.00 -	100.00

FOUR SEASONS:

Gone 5122 *Bermuda*	15.00 -	20.00
Vee Jay 576 *Peanuts*	10.00 -	15.00

THE FOUR SENSATIONS:

Rainbow 157 *Heaven Knows Why*	———	

FOUR SONS:

Linco 1316 *Little Rock*	7.00 -	10.00

FOUR SPEEDS:

De Luxe 6070 *I Need You Baby*	15.00 -	20.00

FOUR TEENS:

Challenge 59021 *Go Little Go Cat*	10.00 -	15.00

FOUR TOPS:

Chess 1623 *Could It Be You*	20.00 -	25.00
Riverside 4534 *Where You Are*	8.00 -	12.00

FOUR TROYS:

Freedom 40013 *In The Moonlight*	7.00 -	10.00

FOUR TUNES:

Jubilee (LP) 1039 *12 by 4*	15.00 -	25.00
5128, 5152, 5232, 5230	3.00 -	5.00

RCA Victor 3967 *Cool Water*	5.00 -	8.00
4102 *Wishing You Were Here Tonight*	5.00 -	8.00
4307 *Early In The Morning*	5.00 -	8.00
4427 *Tell Me Why*	5.00 -	8.00
4489 *Come What May*	5.00 -	8.00
4663 *I Wonder*	5.00 -	8.00
4828 *They Don't Understand*	5.00 -	8.00
4968 *Let's Give Love Another Chance*	5.00 -	8.00
5532 *Water Boy*	5.00 -	8.00
50-0008 *Careless Love*	20.00 -	30.00
50-0016 *My Last Affair*	20.00 -	30.00
50-0042 *The Lonesome Road*	20.00 -	30.00
(Above three are orange plastic)		
50-0085 *Old Fashioned Love*	8.00 -	12.00
50-0131 *May That Day Never Come*	8.00 -	12.00

THE FOUR VAGABONDS:

Lloyds 102 *P.S. I Love You*	———	

THE FOUR VOICES:

Mr. Peacock 106 *Lovely One*	———	

JIMMY FOWLER:

Dart 118 *Let's Rock & Roll*	———	

THE FOX:

RPM 420 *The Dream*	20.00 -	30.00

EUGENE FOX:

Checker 792 *Sinner's Dream*	15.00 -	20.00

NORMAN FOX & THE ROB-ROYS:

Back Beat 501 *Tell Me Why*	10.00 -	15.00
508 *My Dearest One*	10.00 -	15.00
Capitol 4128 *Pizza Pie*	15.00 -	20.00

ORVILLE FOX:

Ellis 101 *Don't Do Me This Way*	15.00 -	20.00

STEVE FRANCE:

Renown 110 *Dream Boy*	10.00 -	15.00

FRANKIE & JOHNNY:

Liberty 55271 *My First Love*	5.00 -	8.00

JOE FRANKLIN:

Renown 113 *Who Put The Pep In The Punch*	10.00 -	15.00

TILLMAN FRANKS:

Gotham 6412 *High Tone Poppa*	10.00 -	15.00
Pacemaker 1101 *Hayride Boogie*	10.00 -	15.00

CALVIN FRAZIER:

Checker 908 *Track Down*	5.00 -	8.00
JVB 86 *Have Blues Must Travel*	20.00 -	30.00
Savoy 858 *Little Baby Child*	7.00 -	10.00

RAY FRAZIER & THE MOONRAYS:

Excell 111 *Days*	5.00 -	8.00
112 *All My Love*	5.00 -	8.00

STAN FREBERG:

Capitol (EP) 496 *Any Requests?*	7.00 -	10.00
(LP) 777 *Child's Garden Of Freberg*	10.00 -	15.00
(LP) 1242 *With Original Cast*	10.00 -	15.00
2125, 2279, 2596, 2929	3.00 -	5.00

ALAN FREED:

Brunswick (LP) 54043 *The Alan Freed Rock & Roll Show*	30.00 -	40.00
Coral (LP) 57063 *Rock & Roll Dance Party*	15.00 -	25.00
(LP) 57115 *R & R Dance Party—Vol. 2*	15.00 -	25.00
(LP) 57177 *TV Record Hop*	20.00 -	30.00
(LP) 57213 *Rock Around The Block*	15.00 -	20.00
Coral 61626 *Right Now, Right Now*	7.00 -	10.00
61714 *Rock 'N' Roll Boogie*	7.00 -	10.00

BOBBY FREEMAN:

Jubilee (LP) 1086 *Do You Wanna Dance*	15.00 -	20.00

ERNIE FREEMAN:

Imperial 5474 *Raunchy* (78 rpm)	5.00 -	8.00
5486 *The Tuttle* (78 rpm)	5.00 -	8.00

DON FRENCH:

Lancer 104 *Lonely Saturday Night*	7.00 -	10.00
105 *Little Blond Girl*	7.00 -	10.00

LEFTY FRIZZELL:

Columbia (LP) 9019 *...Sings Jimmy Rodgers Songs*	15.00 -	20.00
(LP) 9021 *Listen To Lefty*	15.00 -	20.00

BOBBY FULLER:
Exeter 124 *I Fought The Law*............... 10.00 - 15.00
Yucca 140 *You're In Love*............... 7.00 - 10.00

JERRY FULLER:
Challenge 59085 *Anna From Louisiana*....... 4.00 - 6.00
LIN 5019 *Lipstick And Rouge*............ 10.00 - 15.00

JESSE FULLER:
Cavalier (LP) 5006 (10") *Frisco Bound*........ 25.00 - 40.00
   (LP) 6009 *Frisco Bound*............ 30.00 - 50.00

JOHNNIE FULLER:
Irma 110 *First Stage Of The Blues*........... 8.00 - 12.00

JOHNNY FULLER:
Aladdin 3278 *Johnny Ace's Last Letter*....... 15.00 - 20.00
Flair 1054 *Hard Times*............... 10.00 - 15.00
Hollywood 1043 *Train, Train Blues*....... 12.00 - 18.00
  1057 *Mean Old World*............ 10.00 - 15.00
  1063 *Roughest Place In Town*............ 10.00 - 15.00
  1077 *Too Late To Change*............ 7.00 - 12.00
  1084 *I Can't Succeed*................. 7.00 - 12.00
Money 206 *These Young Girls*............ 7.00 - 10.00
Rhythm 1767 *Fool's Paradise*............ 15.00 - 25.00
  1773 *Train, Train Blues*............ 15.00 - 20.00
  1777 *Lovin' Lovin' Man*............ 15.00 - 20.00
  1779 *Mean Old World*............ 15.00 - 20.00
  1782 *Johnny Ace's Last Letter*........ 15.00 - 20.00
Specialty 655 *Haunted House*............ 4.00 - 7.00

LOWELL FULSOM/FULSON:
Aladdin 3217 *Chuck With The Boys*......... 10.00 - 15.00
  3233 *You've Got To Reap*............ 10.00 - 15.00
Checker 804 *Reconsider Baby*............ 7.00 - 10.00
  812 *Check Yourself*................. 7.00 - 10.00
  820 *Lonely Hours*............... 7.00 - 10.00
  829 *Trouble Trouble*............ 7.00 - 10.00
  841, 854, 865, 882............ 5.00 - 8.00
  937, 952, 959, 972, 992, 1027, 1046......... 3.00 - 6.00
Hollywood 1029 *Guitar Shuffle*............ 10.00 - 15.00
Kent (LP) 5016 *Lowell Fulsom*............ 15.00 - 20.00
  (LP) 5020 *Lowell Fulsom*............ 15.00 - 20.00
Swing Time 289 *Best Wishes*............ 20.00 - 30.00
  295 *Guitar Shuffle*............ 20.00 - 30.00
  391 *The Highway Is My Home*............ 20.00 - 30.00
  308 *Black Widow Spider*............ 20.00 - 30.00
  315 *Raggedy Daddy Blues*............ 20.00 - 30.00
  320 *Good Party Shuffle*............ 15.00 - 20.00
  325 *Upstairs*................. 15.00 - 20.00
  330 *I Love My Baby*............ 12.00 - 16.00
  335 *Cash Box Boogie*............ 12.00 - 16.00
  338 *Juke Box Shuffle*............ 12.00 - 16.00

FURNESS BROTHERS:
Melmar 114 *Only Fate*............... 4.00 - 7.00
  116 *Please Don't Call Me Fool*............ 4.00 - 7.00

GADABOUTS:
Wing 90008 *Two Things I Have*............. ————

BOB GADDY:
Harlem 2330 *Slow Down Baby*............ 20.00 - 30.00
Jax 308 *Little Girl's Boogie*............... 15.00 - 20.00
Old Town 1031, 1039, 1050, 1057, 1064, 1070, 1077,
  1085............ 3.00 - 5.00

GAIL TONES:
Decca 30726 *Lover Boy*............ 8.00 - 12.00

EDDIE GAINES:
Summit—*Be Bop Battlin Ball*............ 20.00 - 30.00

ROY GAINES:
De Luxe 6119 *Gainesville*............ 7.00 - 10.00
  6132 *You're Right I'm Left*............ 7.00 - 10.00
Groove 0146 *Right Now Baby*............ 10.00 - 15.00

GENE GAITHER:
Astro 232 *Cute Little Chicky*............. ————

GALAXY'S:
Carthay 103 *A Lover's Prayer*............ 15.00 - 20.00

BARBARA GALE & THE LARKS:
Lloyds 111 *When You're Near*............. 20.00 - 30.00

GALES:
J.O.B. 3001 *Darling Patricia*............ 50.00 - 75.00
JVB 34 *My Eyes Keep Me In Trouble*............ 50.00 - 75.00
JVB 35 *Darling Patricia*............ 50.00 - 75.00

JAMES GALLAGHER:
Decca 29984 *Crazy Chicken*............ 8.00 - 12.00

BOB GALLION:
MGM 12195 *My Square Dancin' Mamma*...... 15.00 - 20.00

CECIL GANT:
Sound (LP) 601 *The Incomparable Cecil Gant*... 35.00 - 50.00

DAVE GARDNER:
OJ 1002 *White Silver Sands* (78 rpm)............ 7.00 - 10.00

CLARENCE (BON TON) GARLOW:
Aladdin 3179 *New Bon Ton Roula*............ 15.00 - 20.00
  3325 *I'm Hurt*............ 15.00 - 20.00
Feature 3005 *I Called You Up Daddy*............ 15.00 - 20.00
Flair 1021 *Crawfishin'*............ 10.00 - 15.00
Folk Star 1130 *Made Me Cry*............ 15.00 - 20.00
  1199 *No, No Baby*............ 15.00 - 20.00
Goldband 1043 *Sundown*............ 8.00 - 12.00
  1065 *Bon Ton Roule*............ 12.00 - 16.00

BILLY GARNER:
Mojo 2171 *Little Schoolgirl*............ 5.00 - 8.00

GABBY GARNER:
Erald 2052 *Smokin' Heart*............ 20.00 - 30.00

JOHNNY GARNER:
Imperial 5536 *Kiss Me Sweet*............ 15.00 - 20.00
  5548 *Didi Didi*............ 15.00 - 20.00

JIM GARNETT:
Manco 1029 *I Could Be Had*............ 7.00 - 10.00

BOBBY GARRETT:
E & M 1602 *Short Skirts*............ 5.00 - 8.00

ROBERT GARRETT:
Excello 2216 *Quit My Drinkin'*............ 5.00 - 8.00

GLEN GARRILSON (& THE NOTE KINGS):
Crest 1047 *Lovin' Lorene*............ 10.00 - 15.00
Lode 106 *Pony Tail Girl*............ 12.00 - 18.00

JIMMY GARTIN:
Hi-Q 5014 *Gonna Ride That Satellite*......... 8.00 - 12.00

GASSERS:
Cash 1035 *Tell Me*............ 10.00 - 15.00
Encino 1011 *Dody Mighty*............ ————

DAVE GATES & THE ACCENTS:
Robbins 1008 *Lovin' At Night*............ 10.00 - 15.00

DAVID GATES:
East West 123 *Real Swinging Baby Doll*....... 7.00 - 10.00
Mala 413 *What's This I Hear*............ 7.00 - 10.00

GATORVETTES:
Thunder 1001 *It It's Tonight*............ 10.00 - 15.00

DEE DEE GAUDET:
Dodge 805 *Where's The Law*............ 4.00 - 7.00

BOBBY GAY & THE SPARKLETONES:
Mida 104 *You're Nice*............ 7.00 - 10.00

GAY LARKS:
Music City 792 *Tell Me Darling*............ 10.00 - 15.00
  793 *Lil Dream Girl*............ 15.00 - 20.00
  809 *Church On The Hill*............ 20.00 - 30.00
  812 *Somewhere In This World*............ 15.00 - 20.00
  819 *Ivy League Clothes*............ 8.00 - 12.00

GAY NOTES:
Drexel 905 *For Only A Moment*............ 50.00 - 80.00
Post 2006 *Hear My Plea*............ 20.00 - 30.00

THE GAY POPPERS:
Savoy 1573 *I Need Your Love*............ 4.00 - 7.00

GAY TUNES:
Joyce 101 *I Love You*............ 10.00 - 15.00
Timely 1002 *Thrill OF Romance*............ 40.00 - 60.00

GAZELLES:
Gotham 315 *Honest*............ 30.00 - 40.00

THE G-GLEFS:
Pilgram 715 *Ka-Ding-Dong*	4.00 -	7.00
715 *Ka-Ding-Dong* (78 rpm)	10.00 -	15.00
Terrace 7503 *A Girl Has To Know*	4.00 -	7.00

GEMS:
Drexel 901 *Talk About The Weather* (red plastic)	90.00 -	125.00
903 *I Thought You'd Care*	125.00 -	175.00
904 *You're Tired Of Love*	150.00 -	200.00
915 *Till The Day I Die*	70.00 -	100.00
Recorte 407 *Please Change Your Mind*	8.00 -	12.00

GENE & EUNICE:
Combo 64 *Ko Ko Mo*	5.00 -	8.00
Score (LP) 4018 *Rock & Roll Sock Hop*	50.00 -	75.00

SONNY GENO:
Rip 130 *Rumble Rock*	8.00 -	12.00

J.C. GENT:
Marlo 1501 *Bad Gal Blues*	5.00 -	10.00

GENTLEMEN:
Apollo 464 *Tired Of You*	15.00 -	20.00
470 *Baby Don't Go*	15.00 -	20.00

BILL GENTRY:
Universal Artist 1001 *Baby What' Ya Say*	10.00 -	15.00

GEORGE & EARL:
Dixie—*Done Gone*	20.00 -	30.00
Mercury 70605 *Got Anything Good?*	4.00 -	7.00
70632 *Goin' Steady*	8.00 -	12.00
70683 *Don't Don't Don't*	5.00 -	8.00
70852 *Done Gone*	7.00 -	10.00

BARBARA GEORGE:
A.F.O. (LP) 5001 *I Know*	15.00 -	20.00

LLOYD GEORGE:
Imperial 5837 *Lucy Lee*	5.00 -	8.00
Post 1006 *Come On Train*	5.00 -	8.00

RAY GERDSEN:
—*Bye Bye Baby*	———	

GEORGIA GIBBS:
RCA Victor 7098 *Great Balls Of Fire*	4.00 -	7.00

DADDYO GIBSON:
Checker 848 *Night Train*	4.00 -	6.00

DON GIBSON:
MGM 12393 *I'm Gonna Fool Everybody*	5.00 -	8.00
12494 *I Ain't A-Studyin' You Baby*	7.00 -	10.00
RCA Victor (LP) 1743 *Lonesome Me*	10.00 -	15.00
(LP) 1918, 2038	7.00 -	10.00
48-0424 *Carolina Breakdown*	10.00 -	15.00

(Note: Above is made of translucent green plastic.)

GRANDDADDY GIBSON:
Bobbin 124 *I Don't Want No Woman*	8.00 -	12.00
127 *The Monkey Likes To Boogie*	8.00 -	12.00

JOE D. GIBSON:
Tetra 4450 *Good Morning Captain*	10.00 -	15.00

STEVE GIBSON & THE RED CAPS:
Jay Dee 796 *It Hurts Me But I Like It*	7.00 -	10.00
Mercury (LP) 25116 (10")	15.00 -	20.00
RCA Victor	3.00 -	5.00
Rose 5534 *I Miss You So*	3.00 -	5.00

DARLENE GILLESPIE:
Disneyland (LP) 3010 *Darlene Of The Teens*	10.00 -	15.00

MICKEY GILLEY:
Astro (LP) 101 *Lonely Wine*	50.00 -	75.00
102 *Down The Line*	10.00 -	15.00
104 *Susie Q.*	10.00 -	15.00
—*Breathless*	10.00 -	15.00
—*Is It Wrong*	10.00 -	15.00
Daryl 101 *What Have I Done*	5.00 -	8.00
Dot 15706 *Call Me Shorty*	30.00 -	40.00
Eric 7021 *Whole Lot Of Twistin' Goin On*	7.00 -	10.00
Khoury's 712 *Drive-In Movie*	20.00 -	30.00
Lynn 503 *Your Selfish Pride*	8.00 -	12.00
508 *My Baby's Been Cheating Again*	8.00 -	12.00
512 *Slippin' And Slidin'*	10.00 -	15.00
515 *My Babe*	10.00 -	15.00

Minor 106 *Ooh Wee Baby*	100.00 -	150.00
Potomac 901 *No Greater Love*	8.00 -	12.00
Princess 4004 *Drive In Movie*	8.00 -	12.00
4006, 4011, 4015	7.00 -	10.00
Sabra 518 *Valley Of Tears*	7.00 -	10.00
San 1513 *I Ain't No Bo Diddley*	8.00 -	12.00
Supreme 101 *Now That I Have You*	5.00 -	8.00
—*No One Will Ever Know*	———	

EARL GILLIAM:
Ivory 343 *Just You And I*	4.00 -	6.00
Sarg 128 *Nobody's Blues*	7.00 -	10.00
133 *Wrong Doing Woman*	7.00 -	10.00

JAZZ GILLUM:
Groove 5002 *Key To The Highway*	8.00 -	12.00
RCA Victor 50-0004 *Signifying Woman*	10.00 -	15.00
50-0017 *Look What You Are Today*	10.00 -	15.00
50-0035 *A Lie Is Dangerous*	10.00 -	15.00

(Note: Above are made of orange plastic)

LOU GIORDANO:
Brunswick 55115 *Stay Close To Me*	20.00 -	30.00

WILD CHILD GIPSON:
Hit 2002 *Uncle John*	10.00 -	15.00

THE GLADIOLAS:
Excello 2101 *Little Darlin'*	7.00 -	10.00
2120 *I Wanta Know*	7.00 -	10.00

GLAD RAGS:
Excello 2121 *My China Doll*	12.00 -	16.00

DICK GLASSER:
Argo 5279 *Crazy Love* (ship logo)	10.00 -	15.00
Columbia 41472 *Crazy Alligator*	8.00 -	12.00

BILLY GLASSER:
Ozark 1236 *I Left The Dance*	7.00 -	10.00

DARRELL GLENN:
Valley 105 *Crying In The Chapel*	7.00 -	10.00
109 *Only A Pastime*	3.00 -	5.00

GLEN GLENN:
Era 1061 *Everybody's Movin'*	7.00 -	10.00
1074 *One Cup Of Coffee*	5.00 -	8.00

THE G NOTES:
Tender 510 *Ronnie*	———	

THE GLENNS:
Rendezvous 118 *In The Chapel*	5.00 -	8.00

GO BOYS: (See also DUDLEY CALLICUTT)
"DC" 0418 *Flippin'*	10.00 -	15.00

THE GO-CARTS:
Hope 1003 *Rockin' Liza*	———	

"GO, JOHNNY, GO" (Soundtrack):
(with Chuck Berry, Eddie Cochran, Jimmy Clanton,
The Cadillacs, Richie Valens, et al. No designation of issuing record company) .... 100.00 up

GOLDEN GATE QUARTET:
Camden (LP) 308	15.00 -	20.00
Columbia (LP) 6102 (10")	15.00 -	20.00
Harmony (LP) 7018 *That Golden Chariot*	15.00 -	20.00
Mercury (LP) 25063 (10") *Look Up!*	15.00 -	25.00

GOLDEN RODS:
Vee Jay 307 *Wish I Was Back In School*	8.00 -	12.00

GOLDENTONES:
Hush 1002 *Little Island Girl*	8.00 -	12.00
—*Ocean Of Tears*	10.00 -	15.00
Jay-Dee 806 *The Meaning Of Love*	10.00 -	15.00
Lifetime 1004 *Stand By Me*	10.00 -	15.00
Samson 107 *I'm Wrong*	15.00 -	25.00

GOOD JELLY BESS:
Hermitage 775 *Come And Get It*	5.00 -	8.00

DICKIE GOODMAN:
Mark-X 8009 *The Touchables*	4.00 -	7.00
8010 *The Touchables In Brooklyn*	5.00 -	8.00
Rori (LP) 3301 *The Many Heads Of Dickie Goodman*	20.00 -	30.00
701 *Santa And The Touchables*	4.00 -	7.00

GOOD ROCKIN' BOB:
Goldband 1067 *Take It Easy Katy*	7.00 -	10.00

GOOD ROCKIN' SAMMY T.:
Junior 500 *Good Rockin' Mama*............ 10.00 - 15.00

HAL GOODSON:
Solo 108 *Who's Gonna Be The Next One Honey* 10.00 - 15.00

BILL GOODWIN:
Star—*Teenage Blues*........................ ———

THE GOOFERS:
Coral 61383 *Flip Flop And Fly*............. 7.00 - 10.00
   61650 *Tennessee Rock And Roll*........ 7.00 - 10.00
   61664 *I'm Gonna Rock & Roll Till I Die*..... 7.00 - 10.00

CURTIS GORDON:
Mercury 70861 *Mobile Alabama*.......... 20.00 - 30.00
   712097 *Sittin' On Top Of The World*....... 20.00 - 30.00
   71121 *Cry Cry (?)*...................... ———
RCA Victor 5356 *Rompin' And Stompin'*..... 10.00 - 15.00

MIKE GORDON & THE EL TEMPOS:
Cat 101 *Why Don't You Do Right?*.......... 4.00 - 7.00

ROSCO/ROSCOE GORDON:
Duke 109 *Too Many Women*............. 8.00 - 12.00
   114 *Ain't No Use*.................... 8.00 - 12.00
Flip 227 *Weeping Blues*................. 30.00 - 40.00
   237 *The Chicken*................... 4.00 - 6.00
RPM 350 *No More Doggin'*............. 12.00 - 16.00
   365 *Two Kinds Of Women*.......... 12.00 - 16.00
Sun 227 *Weeping Blues*................. 35.00 - 50.00

SONNY GORDON & THE ANGELS:
Grand 115 *Wedding Bells Are Ringing*........ 20.00 - 30.00

CHARLIE GORE:
Audio Lab (LP) 1526 *Country Gentleman*.... 10.00 - 15.00

JACKIE GOTROE:
Rhythm 111 *Raised On Rock & Roll*...... 30.00 - 50.00
Vortex 102 *Lobo Jones*................... 15.00 - 20.00

SAMMY GOWANS:
United Artists 114 *Rockin' And Rollin'*....... 15.00 - 20.00
   141 *Boogie Boogie Blues*.............. 15.00 - 20.00

CHARLIE GRACIE:
Cadillac—*No Sin In Rhythm*.............. ———
Cameo 105 *Butterfly* (78 rpm)............ 10.00 - 15.00
   111 *Wanderin' Eyes* (78 rpm)......... 10.00 - 15.00
   111, 118, 127...................... 5.00 - 8.00
Town & Country 5033 *My Baby Loves Me*..... 15.00 - 20.00
   5035 *Wildwood Boogie*.............. 15.00 - 20.00
20th Century 5033 *My Baby Loves Me*..... 15.00 - 20.00
   5035 *Wildwood Boogie*.............. 15.00 - 20.00

LOU GRAHAM:
Coral 61931 *Wee Willie Brown*.............. 7.00 - 10.00

BILLY GRAMMER:
Monument (LP) 40000 *Travelin' On*.......... 15.00 - 25.00

GERRY GRANAHAN:
Sunbeam 108 *Baby Wait*.................. 5.00 - 8.00

O.S. GRANT AND THE DOWNBEATS:
(See also DOWNBEATS)
Sarg 200 *You Did Me Wrong*............... 7.00 - 10.00

JUNIOR GRAVELY:
Velatone 796 *Take My Hands*............... 5.00 - 8.00

ARVELLA GRAY:
Gray 13, 14, 100..................... 4.00 - 6.00

BILLY GRAY:
Decca 29800 *Tennessee Toddy*.............. 5.00 - 8.00

PHIL GRAY:
Robbins 1002 *Somebody's Got My Baby*....... 8.00 - 12.00

RUDY GRAY:
Capitol 2946, 3044, 3149.............. 4.00 - 6.00

RUDY GRAYZELL:
Abbott 145, 147, 157................. 4.00 - 7.00
Starday 229 *The Moon Is Up*.............. 5.00 - 8.00
   241 *Duck Tail*.................... 15.00 - 20.00
   270 *Jig-Ga-Lee-Ga*................. 10.00 - 15.00
   321 *Let's Get Wild*................. 15.00 - 20.00
Sun 290 *Judy*...................... 5.00 - 8.00

"THE GREATEST ROCK & ROLL"
Atlantic (LP) 8001 (various artists).......... 8.00 - 12.00

"THE GREATEST WESTERN HITS"
Columbia (LP) 1257, 1408................. 8.00 - 12.00

BOBBY GREEN:
Oak 4429/4430 *Little Heart Attacks*....... 30.00 - 50.00

GEORGE GREEN:
Chance 1135 *Brand New Rockin' Chair*....... 15.00 - 20.00

LIL GREEN:
Groove 5004 *Why Don't You Do Right*...... 5.00 - 8.00

RUDY GREEN:
Excello 2074 *Cool Lovin' Mama*............. 12.00 - 16.00
   2090 *Teeny Weeny Baby*............. 12.00 - 16.00

(GUITAR) SLIM GREEN:
Canton 1789 *Shake 'Em Up*............ 8.00 - 12.00
Dig 142 *My Woman Done Quit Me*......... 7.00 - 10.00
Geenote 907 *Rock The Nation*.......... 8.00 - 12.00

VERNON GREEN & THE MEDALLIONS:
Dooto 446 *Magic Mountain*............. 8.00 - 12.00
Dootone 407 *Did You Have Fun?*........ 7.00 - 10.00

RUDY GREENE (& THE 4 BUDDIES):
Club 51 *103 You Mean Everything To Me*..... 40.00 - 60.00
Ember 1012 *Juicy Fruit*................. 10.00 - 15.00

LIL GREENWOOD (& THE FOUR JACKS):
Federal 12093 *Grandpa Can Boogie Too*....... 20.00 - 30.00
   12158 *I'll Go*.................... 10.00 - 15.00

**(BIG) JOHN GREER (& HIS RHYTHM
   ROCKERS):**
Groove 0119 *Come Back Maybelline*......... 5.00 - 8.00
RCA Victor 5375 *Rhythm In The Breeze*...... 4.00 - 6.00
   50-0007 *Drinkin' Wine, Spo-Dee-O-Dee*...... 10.00 - 15.00
   50-0029 *I Found A Dream*............. 7.00 - 10.00
   50-0051 *Rockin' Jenny Jones*.......... 10.00 - 15.00
   50-0096 *Cheatin'*.................. 7.00 - 10.00
(Note: Above are orange plastic)
   50-0108, 50-0113, 50-10125, 50-0137......... 4.00 - 7.00

CHUCK GREY & THE PANICS:
Fable 616 *Push The Panic Button*............ 10.00 - 15.00

BUCK GRIFFIN:
Holiday Inn 109 *Pretty Lou*.................. 5.00 - 8.00
Lin 1007 *Rollin' Tears*.................. 7.00 - 10.00
   1008 *Lookin' For The Green*........... 7.00 - 10.00
   1015 *Ballin' And Squallin'*.......... 25.00 - 40.00
Metro 20007 *The Party*.................. 7.00 - 10.00
MGM 12284 *Stutterin' Papa*.......... 20.00 - 30.00
   12439 *Bow My Back*................. 20.00 - 30.00
   12597 *Jessie Lee*.................. 20.00 - 30.00

CURLEY GRIFFIN:
Atomic 303 *You Gotta Play Fair*............ 15.00 - 20.00
   305 *Got Rockin' On My Mind*........... 20.00 - 30.00

GRIFFINS:
Mercury 70558 *I Swear By All The Stars Above*. 20.00 - 30.00
   70650 *Scheming*................... 20.00 - 30.00
   70913 *My Baby's Gone*.............. 15.00 - 20.00
Wing 90067 *Forever More*.............. 20.00 - 30.00

JOE GRIFFITH & HIS TEENAGE REBELS:
Reelfoot 1250 *Crazy Sack*.............. 7.00 - 10.00

PEGGY GRIFFITH:
Now 1008 *Rockin' The Blues*............. ———

SANDRA GRIMES:
Red Robin 129 *You Didn't*.............. ———

TINY GRIMES:
Red Robin 123 *Juicy Fruit*.............. 7.00 - 10.00

BIG GOY GROVES:
Spark 114 *I Gotta New Car*............. 8.00 - 12.00

CARL GROVES:
Musicale 116 *Canteen Baby*.............. ———

DON GUESS:
Brunswick 55101 *Shirl-Lee*............. 8.00 - 12.00

DANNY GUGLIELMI:
Encino 1001 *Hotrod*.................... ———

THE GUIDES:
Guyden 2023 *You Must Try*............. 4.00 - 6.00

GUITAR DAVE:
Central 291 *Zoro*.................... 4.00 - 6.00

GUITAR FRANK:
Bridges 2203/2204 *Wild Track*	15.00 -	20.00

GUITAR JR.:
Goldband 1076 *Now You Know*	5.00 -	8.00
Mercury 71602 *Knocks Me Out*	5.00 -	8.00

GUITAR SHORTY (with BOB TATE & HIS ORCH.):
Cobra 5017 *Irma Lee*	15.00 -	20.00
107 *I Never Thought*	7.00 -	10.00
Pull 301 *Hard Life*	7.00 -	10.00
302 *How Long Can It Last*	7.00 -	10.00

GUITAR SLIM:
Atco 6072, 6097, 6108, 6120	3.00 -	50.00
Diamond 204 *Broke And Lonely*	10.00 -	15.00
Imperial 5278 *Cryin' In The Mornin'*	10.00 -	15.00
5310 *Standin' At The Station*	10.00 -	15.00
Specialty 482, 490, 527, 536, 542, 551, 557, 569	4.00 -	7.00
(LP) 2120 *Things That I Used To Do*	25.00 -	35.00

THE GUM DROPS:
King 4963 *Chapel Of Hearts*	10.00 -	15.00

ARTHUR GUNTER:
Excello 2047 *Baby Let's Play House*	8.00 -	12.00
2053 *She's Mine All Mine*	5.00 -	8.00
2058 *Honey Babe*	10.00 -	15.00
2073 *Baby You Better Listen*	10.00 -	15.00
2084 *Love Has Got Me*	10.00 -	15.00
2125, 2137, 2147, 2164, 2191, 2201, 2204	4.00 -	8.00
(LP) 8017 *Black And Blues*	20.00 -	30.00

HARDROCK GUNTER:
Decca 46300 *Boogie Woogie On Saturday Night*	5.00 -	8.00
46350 *I've Done Gone Hog Wild*	5.00 -	8.00
46363 *Sixty Minute Man*	7.00 -	10.00
46367 *Dixieland Boogie*	5.00 -	8.00
King 1505 *I'll Give 'Em Rhythm*	5.00 -	8.00
Sun 201 *Gonna Dance All Night*	35.00 -	50.00

SHIRLEY GUNTER (& THE FLAIRS/QUEENS):
Flair 1050 *Ooop Shoop*	8.00 -	12.00
1060 *You're Mine*	7.00 -	10.00
1070 *That's The Way I Like It*	5.00 -	8.00
1076 *How Can I Tell You*	8.00 -	12.00
Modern 989 *Headin' Home*	5.00 -	8.00

BUDDY GUY (& HIS BAND):
Artistic 1501, 1503	4.00 -	6.00
Chess 1735, 1759, 1784, 1812, 1838, 1878	3.00 -	5.00

GUYTONES:
De Luxe 6114 *You Won't Let Me Go*	8.00 -	12.00
6159 *This Is Love*	8.00 -	12.00
6169 *Tell Me*	8.00 -	12.00

GYPSIES:
Atlas 1073 *Why*	15.00 -	20.00
Groove 0137 *Rockin' Pretty Baby*	5.00 -	8.00

WAYNE HAAS:
Choice 5607 *Betty Ann*	10.00 -	15.00

JIM HADLEY:
Buddy 117 *Midnight Train*	10.00 -	15.00

DON HAGER:
Oak 0357 *Bebop Boogie*	35.00 -	50.00
0358 *Little Liza Jane Bop*	35.00 -	50.00

JAY HAGGARD:
Daja 503 *Tom Cat*	8.00 -	12.00

MERLE HAGGARD:
Tally 155, 178, 179	4.00 -	8.00

JIMMY HAGGETT:
Caprock 107 *All I Have Is Love*	5.00 -	8.00
Sun 236 *They Call Our Love A Sin*	100.00 -	150.00

RONNIE HAIG:
ABC Paramount 9912 *Traveler Of Love*	8.00 -	12.00
Note 10014 *Rocking With Rhythm And Blues*	7.00 -	10.00

REX HALE:
Rhythm 303 *Down At The Big Mama's House*	———	

BILL HALEY AND/WITH (HIS/THE COMETS/SADDLEMEN):
Decca (EP) 2168 *Shake, Rattle And Roll*	10.00 -	15.00
(EP) 2209 *Dim, Dim The Lights*	10.00 -	15.00
(EP) 2322 *Rock 'N' Roll*	10.00 -	15.00
(EP) 2398, 2399, 2400 *He Digs Rock 'N' Roll*	10.00 -	15.00
(EP) 2416, 2417, 2418 *Rock 'N' Roll Stage Show*	10.00 -	15.00
(EP) 2532 *Rockin' The Oldies*	10.00 -	15.00
(EP) 2564 *Rockin' Around The World*	8.00 -	12.00
(EP) 2615, 2616 *Rockin' The Joint*	8.00 -	12.00
(EP) 2670 *Bill Haley & His Comets*	8.00 -	12.00
(EP) 2671 *Top Teen Hits*	8.00 -	12.00
(LP) 5260 *(10") Shake, Rattle And Roll*	35.00 -	50.00
(LP) 8225 *Rock Around The Clock*	15.00 -	20.00
(LP) 8315 *He Digs Rock 'N' Roll*	15.00 -	20.00
(LP) 8345 *Rock 'N' Roll Stage Show*	15.00 -	20.00
(LP) 8569 *Rockin' The Oldies*	15.00 -	20.00
(LP) 8655 *Let's Have A Party*	15.00 -	20.00
(LP) 8692 *Rockin' Around The World*	15.00 -	20.00
(LP) 8775 *Rockin' The Joint*	15.00 -	20.00
Essex (EP) 102 *Bill Haley's Dance Party*	20.00 -	30.00
(EP) 117, 118 *Rock With Bill Haley And The Comets*	15.00 -	25.00
(LP) 202 *Rock With Bill Haley And The Comets*	75.00 -	100.00
303 *Rock The Joint*	10.00 -	15.00
305 *Rocking Chair On The Moon*	10.00 -	15.00
310 *Real Rock Drive*	12.00 -	16.00
321 *Crazy Man Crazy*	10.00 -	15.00
327 *Fractured*	7.00 -	10.00
332 *Live It Up*	7.00 -	10.00
340 *I'll Be True*	7.00 -	10.00
348 *Straight Jacket*	8.00 -	12.00
374 *Sundown Boogie*	10.00 -	15.00
381 *Rocket 88*	10.00 -	15.00
399 *Rock The Joint*	5.00 -	10.00
Gone 5116 *War Paint*	4.00 -	7.00
Holiday 105 *Rocket 88*	75.00 -	100.00
108 *Green Tree Boogie*	75.00 -	100.00
110 *Pretty Baby*	75.00 -	100.00
111 *A Year Ago This Christmas*	60.00 -	90.00
113 *Jukebox Cannonball*	60.00 -	90.00
Somerset (LP) 4600 *Rock With Bill Haley*	20.00 -	30.00
Transworld (LP) 202	30.00 -	40.00
Transworld 718 *Yes Indeed*	7.00 -	10.00
Warner Bros. (LP) 1378 *Comets*	30.00 -	40.00

HALL BROTHERS:
Arc 4444 *My White Convertible*	15.00 -	20.00

BOBBY HALL & THE KINGS:
Harlem 2322 *Fire In My Heart* (red plastic)	80.00 -	120.00
2322 *Fire In My Heart* (black plastic)	50.00 -	75.00
Jax 314 *Why? Oh, Why?* (red plastic)	60.00 -	80.00
316 *You Made Me Cry*	50.00 -	70.00
320 *Sunday Kind Of Love*	40.00 -	60.00

FOX HALL:
Limelight 3003 *Do The Rock And Roll*	8.00 -	12.00

FREDDIE HALL (& THE NIGHT ROCKERS):
Abco 103 *Playin' Hard To Get*	10.00 -	15.00
Chance 1159 *Knock Me Out*	15.00 -	25.00
C.J. 601 *She's A Upsetter* (blue label)	10.00 -	15.00
610 *Love And Affection* (red label)	7.00 -	10.00

LARRY HALL:
Strand (LP) 1005 *Sandy*	20.00 -	30.00

ROY HALL (& HIS JUMPING CATS); ROY HALL'S ALLEY CATS:
Decca 29696 *Whole Lotta Shakin'*	15.00 -	25.00
29786 *See You Later, Alligator*	15.00 -	25.00
29820 *Blue Suede Shoes*	20.00 -	30.00
30060 *Three Alley Cats*	15.00 -	25.00
Fortune—*Goin' Down The Road Feelin' Bad*	———	
Hi-Q 5045 *Three Alley Cats*	5.00 -	8.00
5050 *Go Go Little Queenie*	5.00 -	8.00
Pierce—*One Monkey Can't Stop The Show*	———	

SONNY HALL:
D 1035 *The Day You Walked Away* . . . . 10.00 - 15.00

ROY HALLAWAY:
CM 12964 *I Received Your Letter* . . . . 7.00 - 10.00

THE HALLIQUINS:
Juanita 102 *Confession Of Love* . . . . ———

STUART HAMBLEN:
Coral (LP) 57254 *Remember Me* . . . . 12.00 - 16.00
Harmony (LP) 7009 *Hymns* . . . . 8.00 - 12.00
RCA Victor (LP) 1253 *It Is No Secret* . . . . 12.00 - 16.00
  (LP) 1436 *Grand Old Hymns* . . . . 10.00 - 15.00

GEORGE HAMILTON IV:
ABC Paramount (LP) 220, 251 . . . . 7.00 - 10.00
  9765 *If You Don't Know* (78 rpm) . . . . 10.00 - 15.00
Colonial 420 *If You Don't Know* . . . . 8.00 - 12.00

MACK HAMILTON:
Feature 1087 *I'm A Honky-Tonk Daddy* . . . . . . 7.00 - 10.00

WALTER HAMILTON:
Fortune 849 *Sherry Blues* . . . . 8.00 - 12.00

JACK HAMMER:
Milestone 2001 *Black Widow Spider Woman* . . . . ———

CURLEY HAMNER:
Fling 720 *Piano Tuner* . . . . 10.00 - 15.00

JOHN HAMPTON:
United 210 *Honey Hush* . . . . 15.00 - 20.00

PAUL HAMPTON:
Columbia 41037 *Play It Cool* . . . . 5.00 - 8.00
  41145 *Slam Bam Thank Ya Ma'ma* . . . . 5.00 - 8.00

WAYNE HANDY (& THE MELODY MASTERS):
Renown 102 *Say Yeah* . . . . 10.00 - 15.00
  104 *Betcha' Didn't Know* . . . . 10.00 - 15.00
Trend 30-006 *Betcha Didn't Know* . . . . 5.00 - 8.00
  30-015 *I Think You Oughta Look Again* . . . . . 5.00 - 8.00

MIKE HANKS & THE CONTOURS:
Braz 22 *Can I Be Your Lover Boy* . . . . 10.00 - 15.00

TYE TONGUE HANLEY:
JVB 88 *I'll Try To Understand* . . . . 20.00 - 30.00

KIRK HANSERD WITH BILL CARRIGAN'S TOP BOP BAND:
Dot 1281 *My Heart's Broke Baby* . . . . 7.00 - 10.00

DOUG HARDEN:
Liberty Bell 9006 *Dig That Ford* . . . . 10.00 - 15.00

JIM HARDIN:
Volcano 100 *High Stepping Woman* . . . . 15.00 - 20.00

PETE HARDIN:
Peach 748 *Baby Be My Chicadee* . . . . 15.00 - 20.00

BILL HARDY:
Rita 1001 *Rockin At The Zoo* . . . . 10.00 - 15.00

RON HARGRAVE:
MGM 12422 *Latch On* . . . . 10.00 - 15.00

FREDDIE HARKEY:
Hillcrest 1805 *Marooned On An Island* . . . . 8.00 - 12.00

BILLY HARLAN:
Brunswick 55066 *I Wanna Bop* . . . . 10.00 - 15.00

BOB HARMON:
Decca 29872 *Kentucky Home Boogie* . . . . 5.00 - 8.00

HARMONAIRES:
Holiday 2602 *Lorraine* . . . . 15.00 - 20.00

HARMONICA FATS:
Darcel 5000, 5003 . . . . 3.00 - 5.00

HARMONICA FRANK:
F & L 100 *Rock A Little Baby* . . . . 50.00 - 75.00
Sun 205 *Rockin' Chair Daddy* . . . . 75.00 - 100.00

HARMONICA JOE:
Skymac 1008 *Look Here Mama* . . . . 4.00 - 7.00

HARMONICA KID:
Nucraft 114 *Martha Lee* . . . . 7.00 - 10.00
  2022 *Jole Blon* . . . . 7.00 - 10.00

HARMONICA KING:
Lapel 103 *Hot Rolls* . . . . 5.00 - 8.00

HARMONICA SLIM:
Aladdin 3317 *Lonely Hours* . . . . 10.00 - 15.00
Cenco 1001 *I'll Take Love* . . . . 4.00 - 6.00
Spry 103 *Going Back Home* . . . . 10.00 - 15.00
Vita 138 *You Better Believe It* . . . . 7.00 - 10.00
  146 *Drop Anchor* . . . . 7.00 - 10.00

THE HARMONY BROTHERS:
Bobbin 109 *Baby, Tonight* . . . . 8.00 - 12.00
  116 *Saturday Night Bop* . . . . 8.00 - 12.00

BEN HARPER & THE CINCO'S:
Skylark 112 *Union Station Blues* . . . . 8.00 - 12.00
Talent 106 *Drive Way Blues* . . . . 5.00 - 8.00

BIG BUD HARPER WITH O.S. GRANT & THE DOWNBEATS:
Harlem 117 *Never Let Me Go* . . . . 4.00 - 7.00

SONNY HARPER:
Ball 1011 *Lonely Stranger* . . . . 5.00 - 8.00

SLIM HARPO:
Excello 2113 *I'm A King Bee* . . . . 7.00 - 10.00
  2138 *Strange Love* . . . . 7.00 - 10.00
  2162, 2171, 2184, 2194 . . . . 4.00 - 8.00
  (LP) 8003 *Raining In My Heart* . . . . 20.00 - 30.00
  (LP) 8005 *Baby Scratch My Back* . . . . 20.00 - 30.00

HARPTONES:
Andrea 100 *What Is Your Decision* . . . . 8.00 - 12.00
Bruce 101 *A Sunday Kind Of Love* . . . . 8.00 - 12.00
  102 *My Memories Of You* . . . . 8.00 - 12.00
  104 *I Depend On You* . . . . 7.00 - 10.00
  109 *Forever Mine* . . . . 10.00 - 15.00
  113 *Since I Fell For You* . . . . 7.00 - 10.00
  123 *Loving A Girl Like You* . . . . 7.00 - 10.00
  128 *I Almost Lost My Mind* . . . . 7.00 - 10.00
Cub 9097 *Your Love Is A Good Love* . . . . 4.00 - 7.00
Gee 1045 *Cry Like I Cried* . . . . 8.00 - 12.00
Paradise 101 *Life Is But A Dream* . . . . 8.00 - 12.00
  103 *It All Depends On You* . . . . 10.00 - 15.00
Rama 203 *Three Wishes* . . . . 8.00 - 12.00
  214 *On Sunday Afternoon* . . . . 8.00 - 12.00
  221 *The Shrine Of St. Cecilia* . . . . 8.00 - 12.00
Tip Top 401 *My Memories Of You* . . . . 10.00 - 15.00
Warwick 500 *I Remember* . . . . 4.00 - 7.00
  551 *No Greater Miracle* . . . . 4.00 - 7.00

HANK HARRAL:
Caprock 100 *Fabulous Oklahoma* . . . . 5.00 - 8.00
  102 *The D.J. Blues* . . . . 10.00 - 15.00
  104 *Tank Town Boogie* . . . . 15.00 - 20.00
  114 *Oklahoma Land* . . . . 5.00 - 8.00

BILL HARRIS:
Eagle 1002 *Danny Boy* . . . . 15.00 - 20.00

JOHNNY RAY HARRIS:
Ray's 100 *Cajun Weekend* . . . . ———

PEPPERMINT HARRIS:
Aladdin 3097 *I Got Loaded* . . . . 10.00 - 15.00
  Aladdin (others) . . . . 7.00 - 10.00
Dart 103 *You Got Me Wonderin'* . . . . 4.00 - 6.00
Duke 319 *Angel Child* . . . . 4.00 - 6.00
Money 214 *Cadillac Funeral* . . . . 8.00 - 12.00
"X" 0142 *Need Your Lovin'* . . . . 7.00 - 10.00

RAY HARRIS:
Sun 254 *Come On Little Mama* . . . . 15.00 - 20.00
  272 *Greenback Dollar* . . . . 7.00 - 10.00

THURSTON HARRIS:
Aladdin 3398 *Little Bitty Pretty One* (78 rpm) . . . 10.00 - 15.00
  3415, 3428 . . . . 5.00 - 8.00

WILLARD HARRIS:
Ekko 20001 *Talking Off The Wall* . . . . ———

WYNONIE HARRIS:
Atco 6081 *Destination Love* . . . . 5.00 - 8.00
King (EP) *Good Rockin' Tonight* . . . . 15.00 - 20.00
  4210 *Good Rockin' Tonight* . . . . 10.00 - 15.00
  4461 *Blood Shot Eyes* . . . . 8.00 - 12.00
  4485 *Loving Machine* . . . . 8.00 - 12.00

4526 *Keep On Churnin'*	10.00 -	15.00
4555 *Night Train*	10.00 -	15.00
4565 *Drinkin' Blues*	8.00 -	12.00
4592 *Rot-Gut*	8.00 -	12.00
4620 *Wasn't That Good?*	8.00 -	12.00
4685 *Quiet Whiskey*	8.00 -	12.00
4763 *Christina*	7.00 -	10.00
4774 *Git To Gettin' Baby*	7.00 -	10.00
4814 *Drinkin' Sherry Wine*	7.00 -	10.00
5050 *Big Old Country Fool*	7.00 -	10.00

(Note: Some distinction is made, with regard to the earliest numbers, between "original" and subsequent pressings which lack the suffixes "A" or "AA" after the catalog numbers, the later pressings bringing somewhat less.)

DANNY HARRISON:
Event 4273 *Rock-A-Billy Boogie* .... 8.00 - 12.00

JOHNNY HARRISON:
Starday 373 *I Don't Want A Sweetheart* .... ——

LEE HARRISON (Backed by THE KOUNTS):
Pearl 717 *So Unimportant* .... 10.00 - 15.00

WILBERT HARRISON:
De Luxe 6002 *The Letter*	8.00 -	12.00
6031 *Gin And Coconut Milk*	10.00 -	15.00
Fury 1023 *Kansas City* (78 rpm)	20.00 -	30.00
1028 *"1960"* (78 rpm)	20.00 -	30.00
Rockin' 526 *The Letter*	10.00 -	15.00
Savoy 1149 *Women And Whiskey*	5.00 -	8.00
1164 *Florida Special*	5.00 -	8.00
Savoy 1198, 1517, 1531, 1571	3.00 -	6.00
Sphere (LP) 7000 *Kansas City*	15.00 -	25.00

BILLY HART:
Roulette 4133 *Rock Bop-A-Lina* .... 8.00 - 12.00

CASEY HART:
Choice 14 *Blues For My Baby* .... 8.00 - 12.00

FREDDIE HART:
Columbia (LP) 1792 *The Spirited Freddie Hart* .. 15.00 - 20.00
21512, 21550, 41005 .... 5.00 - 8.00

LARRY HART:
Goldband 1070 *I'm Just A Mender* .... 10.00 - 15.00
Okeh 7077 *Looka Looka* .... 10.00 - 15.00

HARVEY (& THE MOONGLOWS):
Chess 1705, 1725, 1781 .... 4.00 - 6.00

WAYNE HASS (See HAAS)

SHIRLEY HAVEN & THE FOUR JACKS:
Federal 12092 *Troubles Of My Own* .... 15.00 - 25.00

"HAVING A BALL"
End (LP) 302 (The Chantels, The Dubs, et al) ... 15.00 - 20.00

HAWK:
Phillips 3559 *In The Mood* .... 5.00 - 8.00

HAWKETTES:
Chess 1591 *Your Time's Up* .... 30.00 - 40.00

DALE HAWKINS:
Checker 843 *See You Soon Baboon*	7.00 -	10.00
863, 876	5.00 -	8.00
863 *Susie-Q* (78 rpm)	15.00 -	20.00
900, 906, 913, 923, 929, 934, 940, 944, 962, 970	3.00 -	6.00
900 *La-Da-Dada* (78 rpm)	15.00 -	20.00
906 *My Babe* (78 rpm)	15.00 -	20.00
916 *Yeah Yeah* (78 rpm)	15.00 -	20.00
(LP) 1429 *Oh! Suzy-Q* (black label, yellow cover)	60.00 -	90.00
Tilt 781 *Money Honey*	4.00 -	7.00

HAWKSHAW HAWKINS:
King (LP) 587, 592 .... 8.00 - 12.00

SCREAMIN' JAY HAWKINS:
Epic (LP) 3448 *At Home With Screamin' Jay* ... 30.00 - 40.00

RONNIE HAWKINS (& THE HAWKS):
Roulette (LP) 25078 *Ronnie Hawkins* .... 20.00 - 30.00
(LP) 25102 *Mr. Dynamo* .... 20.00 - 30.00

ROY HAWKINS:
Rhythm 120 *I Hate To Be Alone* .... 7.00 - 10.00
RPM 440 *Is It Too Late* .... 7.00 - 10.00

HAWKS:
Imperial 5266 *Candy Girl*	20.00 -	30.00
5292 *It Ain't That Way*	15.00 -	20.00
5306 *Nobody But You*	12.00 -	18.00
Modern 990 *It's All Over*	15.00 -	20.00
Post 2004 *These Blues*	20.00 -	30.00

MICKEY HAWKS (With MOON MULLINS & HIS NIGHT RAIDERS):
Profile 4002 *Bip Bop Boom*	7.00 -	10.00
4007 *Hidi Hidi Hidi*	8.00 -	12.00
4010 *Screamin' Mimi Jeanie*	10.00 -	15.00

RON HAYDOCK:
Cha Cha 701 *99 Chicks* .... 35.00 - 50.00
1002 *Bop Hop* .... 35.00 - 50.00

JIMMY HAYES:
Happy Hearts 141 *Tom Cat Boogie* .... 10.00 - 15.00

LINDA HAYES & THE PLATTERS:
King 4752 *My Name Ain't Annie* .... *7.00 - 10.00*
4773 *Please Have Mercy* .... 5.00 - 8.00

DON HEAD:
Dub 2840 *Goin' Strong* .... 10.00 - 15.00

ROY HEAD & THE TRAITS: (See also THE TRAITS)
Suave 712 *Teen-Age Letter* .... 5.00 - 8.00
TNT (LP) 101 *Roy Head And The Traits* ..... 30.00 - 50.00

JIMMY HEAP:
Captiol 3156 *Sebbin Come Elebbin* .... 7.00 - 10.00
Fame 502 *Little Jewell* .... 15.00 - 25.00

BUDDY HEARD & HIS COMBO:
Red Top 501 *Let's Rock With Me* .... 10.00 - 15.00

HEARTBEATS:
Gee 1043 *When I Found You*	7.00 -	10.00
1047 *After New Year's Eve*	7.00 -	10.00
Guyden 2011 *One Million Tears*	5.00 -	8.00
Hull 711 *Crazy For You* (pink label)	15.00 -	20.00
713 *Darling How Long*	15.00 -	20.00
716 *People Are Talking*	15.00 -	20.00
720 *A Thousand Miles Away*	15.00 -	20.00
Network 71200 *Tormented*	8.00 -	12.00
Rama 216 *A Thousand Miles Away*	7.00 -	10.00
216 *A Thousand Miles Away* (78 rpm)	15.00 -	20.00
222 *Wedding Bells*	10.00 -	15.00
231 *Everybody's Somebody's Fool*	10.00 -	15.00
Roulette 4054 *Down On My Knees*	4.00 -	7.00
(LP) 25017 *A Thousand Miles Away*	40.00 -	60.00

HEARTBREAKERS:
RCA Victor 4327 *Heartbreaker*	75.00 -	100.00
4662 *Why Don't I*	50.00 -	75.00
4849 *There Is Time*	40.00 -	60.00
Vik 0261 *One, Two, I Love You*	25.00 -	30.00
0299 *My Love*	25.00 -	30.00

HEARTS: (See also LEE ANDREWS; BILLY AUSTIN)
Baton 208 *Lonely Nights*	5.00 -	10.00
211 *All My Love Belongs To You*	5.00 -	10.00
228 *I Had A Guy*	5.00 -	10.00

HEARTSPINNERS:
X-tra 109 *Oh So Much* .... ——

HEART-THROBS:
Lamp 2010 *So Glad* .... 15.00 - 20.00

BOBBY HELMS:
Decca (LP) 8638 *...Sings* .... 15.00 - 20.00
30423 *My Special Angel* (78 rpm) .... 15.00 - 20.00

BIG BERTHA HENDERSON:
Chance 1143 *Rock, Daddy, Rock* (red plastic) ... 20.00 - 30.00

JOCKO HENDERSON:
Wand 112 *Blast Off To Love* .... 8.00 - 12.00

R.D. HENDON:
——*Big Black Cat* .... ——

BOBBY HENDRICKS:
Sue 708 *Molly B. Good* .... 5.00 - 8.00

AL HENDRIX (With JOLLY JODY & HIS GO DADDIES):

ABC Paramount 9901 *Rhonda Lee*	7.00 -	10.00
Lagree 701 *Young And Wild*	10.00 -	15.00
Tally 119 *Rhonda Lee*	10.00 -	15.00

CLARENCE (FROGMAN) HENRY:

Argo (LP) 4009 *You Always Hurt The One You Love*	20.00 -	30.00
5259 *Ain't Got No Home* (78 rpm)	8.00 -	12.00

ROBERT HENRY:

King 4624 *Miss Anna B.*	35.00 -	50.00
4646 *Old Battle Ax*	35.00 -	50.00

GENE HENSLEE:

Imperial 8227 *Dig'n And Datin'*	10.00 -	15.00
8277 *Rockin' Baby*	10.00 -	15.00

HERALDS:

Herald 435 *Eternal Love*	30.00 -	40.00

HERBY JOE:

Abco 101 *Smokestack Lightning*	15.00 -	20.00

"HERE ARE THE HITS"

Fire (LP) 100 (The Scarlets, The Velvets, et al)	15.00 -	20.00

LITTLE JULIAN HERREA:

Dig 118 *Lonely Lonely Nights*	10.00 -	15.00
137 *Symbol Of Heaven*	15.00 -	20.00

DENNIS HERROLD:

Imperial 5482 *Hip Hip Baby*	15.00 -	20.00

BENNIE HESS:

Major 1001 *Wild Hog Hop*	40.00 -	60.00

BEN HEWITT:

Mercury 71413, 71472	4.00 -	6.00
71612 *Whirlwind Blues*	10.00 -	15.00

ERSEL HICKEY:

Epic 9263 *Hangin' Around*	8.00 -	12.00
9278 *Goin' Down That Road*	8.00 -	12.00
9298 *You Never Can Tell*	8.00 -	12.00
9309 *You Threw A Dart*	8.00 -	12.00
9357 *What Do You Want*	8.00 -	12.00

BOBBY HICKS:

Skyway 116 *Hassle It Jack*	————	

HIDE-A-WAYS:

MGM 55004 *Cherie*	50.00 -	80.00
Ronni 1000 *Can't Help Loving That Girl Of Mine*	rare	
(Note: Prices of up to $800.00 hve been quoted as the value of this record.)		

HI-FIDELITIES:

Fortune 528 *Last Night I Cried*	10.00 -	15.00

HIFIDELITY'S:

Hi-Q 5000 *Help, Murder, Police*	10.00 -	15.00

HI-FI'S:

Montel 1005 *I'm So Lonely*	————	

HI-FIVES:

Decca 30576 *My Friend*	8.00 -	12.00
30657 *A Shoulder To Cry On*	8.00 -	12.00
30744 *Lonely*	8.00 -	12.00

CHUCK HIGGINS:

Aladdin 3215 *Chuck-A-Buck*	7.00 -	10.00
Caddy 108 *The Blacksmith Blues*	————	
Combo 12 *Pachuko Hop*	7.00 -	10.00
144 *Long Long Time*	7.00 -	10.00
(LP) 300 *Pachuko Hop*	40.00 -	60.00
Dootone 387 *Gambling Woman*	5.00 -	8.00
Lucky 005 *Greasy Pig*	7.00 -	10.00
Money 214 *Rock And Roll*	8.00 -	12.00
Specialty 532 *Broke*	6.00 -	10.00

DONNA HIGHTOWER:

RPM 432 *Love Me Again*	8.00 -	12.00
481 *I Ain't Gonna Tell*	6.00 -	9.00

WILLIE HIGHTOWER:

Fury 5002 *If I Had A Hammer*	5.00 -	8.00

"HIGHWAY OF BLUES":

Audio Lab (LP) 1520 (Brownie McGhee, John Lee Hooker)	20.00 -	30.00

THE HI-LITERS:

Mercury 71342 *Dance Me To Death*	5.00 -	8.00

HILITES:

Okeh 7046 *I Found A Love*	30.00 -	40.00

HARVEY HILL, JR.:

SRC 104 *Boogie Woogie Woman*	20.00 -	30.00

HENRY HILL:

Federal 12030 *Sunday Morning Blues*	15.00 -	20.00
12037 *Hold Me Baby*	15.00 -	20.00
12044 *If You Love Me*	10.00 -	15.00
12053 *My Baby Is Back Home*	10.00 -	15.00

J.C. HILL:

Argo 5311 *Only True Love*	7.00 -	10.00

JAYCEE HILL:

Epic 9105 *Romp Stompin' Boogie*	————	

JOEL HILL:

Trans Amer. 519 *Little Lover*	25.00 -	35.00

"HILLBILLY JAMBOREE":

Starday (LP) 101 (various artists)	20.00 -	30.00

JOE HINTON:

Back Beat 519 *Ladder Of Prayer*	5.00 -	8.00

OTIS HINTON:

Timely 1003 *Walkin' Down Hill*	15.00 -	20.00

THE HI-TONES:

Fonsca 201 *Just For You*	5.00 -	8.00

CURTIS HOBECK:

Lu 508 *China Rock*	15.00 -	20.00

GARY HODGE:

Dolton 7 *Not For Love Or Money*	5.00 -	8.00

RALPH HODGES:

Whispering Pines 61 *Honey Talk*	7.00 -	10.00

SILAS HOGAN:

Excello 2221, 2231, 2241, 2251, 2255, 2266, 2270, 2271	4.00 -	8.00

SMOKEY/SMOKY HOGG:

Combo 4 *Bottle Up And Go*	15.00 -	20.00
9 *My Woman*	15.00 -	20.00
Crown (LP) 5226 *Smokey Hogg Sings The Blues*	10.00 -	15.00
Ebb 127 *Good Mornin' Baby*	7.00 -	10.00
Federal 12109 *Keep-A-Walkin'*	15.00 -	20.00
12117 *Your Little Wagon*	15.00 -	20.00
12127 *Gone, Gone, Gone*	15.00 -	20.00
Imperial 5269 *Tear Me Down*	15.00 -	20.00
5290 *Train Whistle*	15.00 -	20.00
Meteor 5021 *Dark Clouds*	15.00 -	20.00
Modern 924 *Can't Do Nothin'*	7.00 -	10.00
Show Time 1101 *No More Whiskey*	10.00 -	15.00

ROY HOGSED:

Capitol 1529 *Shuffleboard Shuffle*	7.00 -	10.00
1635 *Cocaine Blues*	7.00 -	10.00
1854 *The Snake Dance Boogie*	7.00 -	10.00
1987 *Mean Mean Woman*	7.00 -	10.00

THE HOLIDAYS:

Robbee 103 *Miss You*	5.00 -	8.00
Specialty 533 *Irene*	5.00 -	8.00

EDDIE HOLLAND:

Mercury 71290 *Little Miss Ruby*	7.00 -	10.00

THE HOLLY TWINS:

Liberty 55048 *I Want Elvis For Christmas*	————	

BUDDY HOLLY:

Coral (LP) 57210 *Buddy Holly* (maroon label)	35.00 -	50.00
(LP) 57279 *The Buddy Holly Story*	30.00 -	40.00
(LP) 57326 *The Buddy Holly Story Vol. 2*	35.00 -	50.00
(LP) 57426 *Reminiscing*	30.00 -	40.00
(EP) 81169 *Listen To Me*	15.00 -	25.00
(EP) 81182 *The Buddy Holly Story*	15.00 -	25.00
(EP) 81191 *Peggy Sue Got Married*	15.00 -	25.00
(EP) 81193 *Brown Eyed Handsome Man*	15.00 -	25.00
61852 *Words of Love*	15.00 -	20.00
61885 *Peggy Sue* (78 rpm)	20.00 -	30.00
61947, 61985, 62006, 62051, 62074	4.00 -	7.00
62210 *True Love Ways*	8.00 -	12.00

62369 *Reminiscing*	5.00 -	8.00
62369 *Wishing*	8.00 -	12.00
62390 *Rock Around With Ollie Vee*	15.00 -	20.00
62448 *Slippin And Slidin'*	8.00 -	12.00
62554 *Rave On*	8.00 -	12.00
Decca (EP) 2575 *That'll Be The Day*	15.00 -	25.00
29854 *Love Me*	30.00 -	40.00
30166 *Modern Don Juan*	15.00 -	25.00
30434 *That'll Be The Day*	20.00 -	30.00
30543 *Love Me*	10.00 -	15.00
30650 *Ting A Ling*	15.00 -	20.00
(LP) 86707 *That'll Be The Day*	75.00 -	100.00
(LP) 86707 same, but multi-colored label	20.00 -	35.00

HOLLYWOOD ARGYLES:

Lute (LP) 9001 *The Hollywood Argyles*	35.00 -	50.00

HOLLYWOOD ARIST-O-KATS:

Recorded In Hollywood 406 *I'll Be Home Again*	20.00 -	25.00

HOLLYWOOD FLAMES:

Atco 6155, 6164, 6171	3.00 -	5.00
Decca 29285 *Peggy*	15.00 -	20.00
48331 *I Know*	15.00 -	20.00
Ebb 119 *Buzz-Buzz-Buzz*	4.00 -	12.00
119 *Buzz-Buzz-Buzz* (78 rpm)	8.00 -	12.00
131 *Give Me Back My Heart*	6.00 -	9.00
144, 149, 153	4.00 -	7.00
Money 202 *Fare Thee Well*	30.00 -	50.00
Swing Time 345 *Let's Talk It Over*	60.00 -	80.00

HOLLYWOOD SAXONS:

Entra 1214 *Diamonds*	20.00 -	30.00

TOMMY HOLMES:

Cherry 112 *Wa-Chic-Ka-Noka*	*20.00 -*	*30.00*

DAVEY HOLT & THE HUBCAPS:

United Artist 110 *You Move Me*	———	

COUNTRY HOMES:

De Luxe 6036 *Come On And Put Me In The Alley*	20.00 -	30.00
6048 *It Can't Be*	20.00 -	30.00

HOMESICK JAMES:

Atomic H—*Johnnie Mae*	———	
Colt 632 *Set A Date*	7.00 -	10.00
U.S.A. 746 *Crossroads*	7.00 -	10.00

THE HONEY BEARS:

Spark 111 *I Shall Not Fail*	30.00 -	50.00

THE HONEY BEES:

Imperial 5400 *Endless*	7.00 -	10.00
5416 *What's To Become Of Me*	7.00 -	10.00

HONEYBOY:

Specialty 476 *Bloodstains On The Wall*	10.00 -	15.00

GLEN HONEYCUTT:

Sun 264 *I'll Be Around*	5.00 -	8.00

HONEYS:

Capitol 4952 *Shoot The Curls*	12.00 -	18.00
5034 *Pray For Surf*	10.00 -	15.00
5093 *The One You Can't Have*	10.00 -	15.00
Warner Bros. 5430 *He's A Doll*	15.00 -	20.00

EARL HOOKER (& HIS ROADMASTERS):

Age 29101, 29106, 29111, 29114	4.00 -	7.00
Bea & Baby 106 *Dynamite*	7.00 -	10.00
Chief 7016 *Blues In D Natural*	8.00 -	12.00
CJ 613 *Do The Chicken*	4.00 -	7.00
King 4600 *Race Track*	12.00 -	16.00
Rockin' 519 *Sweet Angel*	20.00 -	30.00

JOHN LEE HOOKER:

Atco (LP) 151 *Don't Turn Me From Your Door*	20.00 -	30.00
Chart 609 *Wobbling Baby*	8.00 -	12.00
614 *Misbelieving Baby*	8.00 -	12.00
Chess (LP) 1438 *House Of The Blues*	20.00 -	30.00
(LP) 1454 *Plays And Sings The Blues*	20.00 -	30.00
1505 *Union Station Blues*	12.00 -	15.00
1513 *Walkin' The Boogie*	12.00 -	15.00
Crown (LP) 5157 *The Blues*	15.00 -	20.00
(LP) 5232 *John Lee Hooker Sings The Blues*	10.00 -	15.00
(LP) 5295 *Folk Blues*	10.00 -	15.00

King (LP) 727 *John Lee Hooker Sings Blues*	20.00 -	30.00
Modern 835 *I'm In The Mood* (black label)	15.00 -	20.00
897 *It's Been A Long Time Baby*	8.00 -	12.00
901 *Ride Till I Die*	8.00 -	12.00
916 *Too Much Boogie*	7.00 -	10.00
923 *Down Child*	7.00 -	10.00
935 *Let't Talk It Over*	7.00 -	10.00
942, 948, 958, 966	6.00 -	9.00
Riverside (LP) 12-838 *Folk Blues*	15.00 -	20.00
Specialty 528 *I'm Mad*	7.00 -	10.00
Vee Jay 164, 188, 205, 233, 255, 265, 293	5.00 -	8.00
308, 319, 331, 349, 366	3.00 -	6.00
(LP) 1007 *I'm John Lee Hooker* (maroon label)	20.00 -	30.00
(LP) 1023 *Travelin'*	12.00 -	16.00
(LP) 1033 *The Folk Lore Of John Lee Hooker*	10.00 -	15.00

JESSE HOOPER:

Cherry—*All Messed Up*	———	
Meteor 5025 *All Messed Up*	80.00 -	100.00

EDDIE HOPE & THE MANISH BOYS:

Marlin 804 *Lost Child*	15.00 -	20.00

HOPELESS HOMER:

Goldband 1040 *New Way Of Rockin'*	15.00 -	20.00

LIGHTNIN'/LIGHTNING HOPKINS:

Bluesville (LP)1019 *Lightnin'*	15.00 -	20.00
(LP) 1057 *Walkin' This Road By Myself*	15.00 -	20.00
Candid (LP) 8010...*In New York* (mono)	15.00 -	20.00
Crown (LP) 5224...*Sings The Blues*	12.00 -	16.00
Decca 48306 *Happy New Year*	7.00 -	10.00
48312 *Highway Blues*	10.00 -	15.00
48321 *Bad Things On My Mind*	10.00 -	15.00
Herald 425 *Lightnin's Boogie*	8.00 -	12.00
428 *Lightnin's Special*	8.00 -	12.00
436 *Sick Feeling Blues*	8.00 -	12.00
443 *Early-Mornin' Boogie*	7.00 -	10.00
449 *They Wonder Who I Am*	7.00 -	10.00
456 *Don't Need No Job*	6.00 -	10.00
465 *Blues For My Cookie*	5.00 -	8.00
571 *Hopkins Sky Hop*	5.00 -	8.00
476 *Grandma's Boogie*	5.00 -	8.00
483 *That's All Right Baby*	5.00 -	8.00
490 *Shine On Moon*	5.00 -	8.00
497 *Remember Me*	5.00 -	8.00
Herald (higher numbers)	3.00 -	6.00
(LP) 1012 *Lightnin' Hopkins*	35.00 -	50.00
Imperial (LP) 9180 *On Stage*	30.00 -	40.00
(LP) 9186 *Lightning Hopkins Sings The Blues*	30.00 -	40.00
(LP) 9211 *Lightnin' Hopkins And The Blues*	20.00 -	30.00
Lightning 104 *Grieving Blues*	25.00 -	40.00
Score (LP) 4022 *Lightnin' Hopkins Strums The Blues*	40.00 -	60.00
TNT 8002 *Lightnin's Jump*	15.00 -	20.00
8003 *Leavin' Blues*	15.00 -	20.00
Tradition (LP) 1035 *Country Blues*	20.00 -	30.00
(LP) 1040 *Autobiography In Blues*	20.00 -	30.00

BIG JACK HORNER:

Trel 1001 *If I Can*	8.00 -	12.00

HORNETS:

Flash 125 *Crying Over You*	10.00 -	15.00
States 127 *I Can't Believe*	60.00 -	80.00

JOHNNY HORTON:

Columbia 21504, 21538, 40813, 40919, 40986, 41210	4.00 -	7.00
41043 *Lover's Rock*	7.00 -	10.00
41110 *Honky Tonk Hardwood Floor*	8.00 -	12.00
Dot (LP) 3221 *Johnny Horton*	15.00 -	20.00
Mercury 6418 *This Won't Be The First Time*	10.00 -	15.00
(LP) 20478 *The Fantastic Johnny Horton*	25.00 -	40.00
70100 *Tennessee Jive*	8.00 -	12.00
70156 *S.S. Lure-Line*	8.00 -	12.00
70198 *Red Lips And Warm Red Wine*	8.00 -	12.00
70227 *The Love Of A Girl*	7.00 -	10.00
70325 *Move Down The Line*	7.00 -	10.00
70462 *No True Love*	7.00 -	10.00
70636 *Ridin' The Sunshine Special*	8.00 -	12.00
Sesac (EP) 26 *Free 'N' Easy Songs*	5.00 -	8.00

SHAKEY (WALTER) HORTON:

Argo (LP) 4037 *The Soul Of Blues Harmonica*..	30.00 -	40.00
Chess 1529 *Walter's Boogie*.................	35.00 -	50.00
Cobra 5002 *Have A Good Time*.............	20.00 -	30.00

THE HOT-TODDYS:

Corsican 0056 *Shakin' And Stompin'*.........	————	
Shan-Todd 0056 *Shakin' And Stompin'*........	5.00 -	8.00

DAVID HOUSTON:

RCA Victor 6917 *Hackin' Around*...........	5.00 -	8.00

JOE HOUSTON:

Bayou 004 *Sabre Jet*.....................	————	
012 *Pig Tails*.......................	————	
017 *Landslide*......................	————	
Cash 1018 *Rockin' And Boppin'*...........	5.00 -	8.00
Crown (LP) 5006 *Rocks And Rolls All Night Long*	10.00 -	15.00

JOHNNY HOUSTON & THE CAPITALS:

East-West 100 *But It's Too Late*.............	————	

CAMILLE HOWARD:

Specialty 433 *Old Baldy Boogie*.............	8.00 -	12.00

CHUCK HOWARD:

ESV 1017 *Don't Let It Bother You*..........	7.00 -	10.00
Port 70002 *Crazy, Crazy Baby*.............	7.00 -	10.00

JOHNNY HOWARD:

De Luxe 6044 *Hastings Street Jump*........	50.00 -	75.00

VAN HOWARD:

ABC Paramount—*Maybe Baby*.............	————	
Hi-Q 3756 *Truck Driving Jack*.............	7.00 -	10.00

HOWIE & THE SAPPHIRES:

Okeh 7112 *More Than The Day Before*.......	5.00 -	8.00

HOWLIN' WOLF:

Chess (LP) 1434 *Moanin' In The Moonlight* (black label)	40.00 -	60.00
(LP) 1469 *Howlin' Wolf*...................	30.00 -	40.00
(LP) 1502 *The Real Folk Blues*.............	20.00 -	30.00
1510 *Mr. Highway Man*.................	15.00 -	25.00
1528 *My Last Affair*.................	15.00 -	25.00
1557 *All Night Boogie*.................	15.00 -	20.00
1566 *Rockin' Daddy*...................	15.00 -	20.00
1575 *Baby How Long*..................	10.00 -	15.00
1584 *Forty Four*.....................	10.00 -	15.00
1593 *Who Will Be Next*.................	10.00 -	15.00
1607 *Come To Me Baby*.................	10.00 -	15.00
1618 *Smoke Stack Lightning*.............	10.00 -	15.00
1632 *So Glad*.......................	8.00 -	12.00
1648 *My Life*.......................	8.00 -	12.00
1668 *Somebody In My Home*.............	8.00 -	12.00
1679 *Sitting On Top Of The World*........	8.00 -	12.00
1695, 1712, 1726, 1735, 1744, 1750, 1762, 1777, 1793, 1804, 1813, 1823, 1870, 1890, 1911...	5.00 -	8.00

JOE HUDGINS:

Robbins 1005 *Where'd You Stay Last Night*....	10.00 -	15.00

TOMMY HUDSON:

D 1073 *Band Stand Stomp*.................	8.00 -	12.00
White Rock 1110 *Rock-It*.................	8.00 -	12.00

JIMMY HUFF:

RPM 366 *She's My Baby*..................	15.00 -	20.00
RPM 390 *Big City Bound*.................	15.00 -	20.00

WILLIE HUFF:

Big Town 105 *Operator 209*...............	15.00 -	25.00
Rhythm 1770 *Beggar Man Blues*.............	20.00 -	30.00

PAUL HUFFMAN & THE REBEL COMBO:

Winston 1015 *She's Mine*.................	————	

JOE HUGHES:

Kangaroo 105/106 *Make Me Dance Little Ant*..	10.00 -	15.00

WALLY HUGHES:

Ember 1024 *Convertible Car*.............	5.00 -	8.00
1024 *Convertible Car* (78 rpm)..............	8.00 -	12.00

DENNIS HUNT & THE HUNTERS:

Say 11 *A Story Untold*.................	15.00 -	20.00

SLIM HUNT:

Excello 2055 *Welcome Home Baby*.........	15.00 -	20.00

FLUFFY HUNTER & JESSIE POWELL'S ORCHESTRA:

Federal 12056 *Love's A Fortune*.............	12.00 -	16.00

IVORY JOE HUNTER:

Atlantic 1049, 1066, 1086, 1095..............	4.00 -	8.00
(LP) 8008 *Rock And Roll* (black label).......	15.00 -	25.00
(LP) 8015 *Ivory Joe Hunter Sings The Old & The New*......	12.00 -	16.00
King (LP) 605 *16 Of His Greatest Hits*.........	10.00 -	15.00
MGM (EP) 1376, 1377, 1378.................	7.00 -	10.00
(LP) 3488 *I Get That Lonesome Feeling*......	20.00 -	30.00

LONG JOHN HUNTER:

Yucca 132 *Paso Rock*...................	8.00 -	12.00
138 *Ole Rattler*...................	8.00 -	12.00

TY HUNTER & THE VOICE MASTERS (See VOICE MASTERS) HURRICANES:

King 4817 *Poor Little Dancing Girl*..........	20.00 -	30.00
4867 *Maybe It's All For The Best*........	15.00 -	20.00
4898 *Raining In My Heart*..........	20.00 -	30.00
4926 *Your Promise To Me*..........	15.00 -	20.00
4947 *Dear Mother*.............	18.00 -	25.00
5018 *Fallen Angel*.............	18.00 -	25.00
5042 *Priceless*.............	18.00 -	25.00

HUSKIES:

Klik 205 *Sorry*.................	15.00 -	20.00

FERLIN HUSKY:

Capitol (LP) 718 *Ferlin Husky*...........	10.00 -	15.00
(LP) 880 *Boulevard Of Broken Dreams*.......	10.00 -	15.00
(LP) 976 *Sittin' On A Rainbow*...........	10.00 -	15.00
(LP) 1204 *Born To Lose*...........	10.00 -	15.00
(LP) 1280 *Ferlin's Favorites*...........	8.00 -	12.00
3310 *Slow Down, Brother*...........	5.00 -	8.00

HYTONES:

Hytone 121 *Let Me Hold Your Hand*........	————	

IDEALS:

Cool 108 *Do I Have The Right*.............	15.00 -	25.00
Paso 6401 *Together*.................	7.00 -	10.00
6402 *Magic*.................	8.00 -	12.00

I DIG ROCK AND ROLL:

Score (LP) 4002 (various artist).............	25.00 -	35.00

IMAGINATIONS:

Duel 507 *Guardian Angel*.................	5.00 -	8.00

IMPALAS:

Cub (LP) 8003 *Sorry (I Ran All The Way Home)*	30.00 -	40.00

IMPERIALS:

End 1091 *Traveling Stranger*.............	8.00 -	12.00
Great Lakes 1201 *Life Of Ease*.............	35.00 -	50.00
1212 *You'll Never Walk Alone*...........	75.00 -	100.00
Savoy 1104 *My Darling*.................	75.00 -	100.00

IMPLACABLES:

Kain 1004 *My Foolish Pride*.................	————	

IMPRESSIONS: (See also JERRY BUTLER):

Abner 1017 *Come Back My Love*.............	7.00 -	10.00
1017 *Come Back My Love* (78 rpm)...	10.00 -	15.00
1023 *The Gift Of Love*...........	7.00 -	10.00
1034 *A New Love*...........	7.00 -	10.00
Bandera 2504 *Listen To Me*.............	5.00 -	8.00
Swirl 107 *I Need Your Love*.............	————	
Vee Jay (LP) 1075 *For Your Precious Love*....	15.00 -	20.00

IMPRESSORS:

Cub 9010 *Do You Love Her*.............	8.00 -	12.00
Onyx 514 *Is It Too Late*.............	10.00 -	15.00

INDIVIDUALS:

Chase 1300 *Pillow Wet With Tears*..........	10.00 -	15.00
Music City 838 *Beverly My Darling*..........	10.00 -	15.00
Showtime 595 *Met Her At A Dance*.........	8.00 -	12.00
598 *Dear One*...........	8.00 -	12.00

INFATUATORS:

Destiny 504 *I Found My Love*.............	10.00 -	15.00

INK SPOTS:

King (LP) 535 *Something Old, Something New*..	30.00 -	40.00

(LP) 642 *Songs That Will Live Forever*......	15.00 -	20.00
1297 *Ebb Tide*............	10.00 -	15.00
1304 *Changing Partners*............	8.00 -	12.00
1336 *Melody Of Love*............	8.00 -	12.00
1378 *Yesterdays*............	8.00 -	12.00
1429 *There Is Something Missing*..........	10.00 -	15.00
1512 *Keep It Movin'*............	8.00 -	12.00
4670 *Here In My Lonely Room*............	15.00 -	25.00
4857 *I'll Walk A Country Mile*............	10.00 -	15.00
Waldorf (LP) 144 (10")............	20.00 -	30.00

AUTRY INMAN:

Decca 29936 *Be Bop Baby*............	10.00 -	15.00

INSPIRATIONS:

Apollo 494 *Raindrops*............	20.00 -	30.00
Jamie 1034 *Dry Your Eyes*............	8.00 -	12.00
Old Town 1053 *Starlight Tonight*............	15.00 -	20.00
Sultan 1 *The Feeling Of Her Kiss*............	5.00 -	8.00

INSPIRATORS:

Treat 502 *If Loving You Is Wrong*............	4.00 -	60.00

INTENTIONS:

Jamie 1253 *Summertime Angel*............	20.00 -	30.00

INTERIORS:

Worthy 1008 *Darling Little Angel*............	8.00 -	12.00

INTERVALS:

Apt 25019 *I Still Love That Man*............	5.00 -	8.0
Class 304 *Here's That Rainy Day*............	5.00 -	8.00

INVICTAS:

Jack Bee 1003 *Gone So Long*............	8.00 -	12.00

JERRY IRBY:

Daffan 108 *Clickety Clack*............	10.00 -	15.00
Jer-Ray 222 *Chantilly Lace*............	10.00 -	15.00

IRRIDESCENTS:

Hudson 8102 *Three Coins In The Fountain*.....	7.00 -	10.00

ROBERT A. IRVINE:

Presto 525 *Fastest Short In Town*............	————	

JIMMY ISLE:

Roulette 4065 *Goin' Wild*............	7.00 -	10.00

THE ISLEY BROTHERS:

RCA Victor (LP) 2156 *Shout!*............	15.00 -	20.00

IVAN:

Coral 62017 *Real Wild Child*............	8.00 -	12.00
62081 *Frankie Frankenstein*............	10.00 -	15.00
65607 *Real Wild Child*............	5.00 -	8.00

JIMMY IVES:

Comet 2141 *My Fumbling Heart*............	5.00 -	8.00

THE IVIES:

Brunswick 55112 *Sunshine*............	————	

IVORIES:

Jaguar 3023 *Alone*............	20.00 -	30.00
Mercury 71239 *Me And You*............	4.00 -	7.00

SONNY JOE IVY:

Jewel 738 *Ruby And The Gambler*............	5.00 -	8.00

IVY TONES:

Red-Top 105 *Oo Wee Baby* (blue label)........	7.00 -	10.00

J.B. & HIS BAYOU BOYS:

J.O.B. 1008 *The Moutain*............	40.00 -	60.00

J.B. & HIS HAWKS:

Chance 1155 *Combination Boogie*............	50.00 -	75.00
1160 *Pet Cream Man*............	60.00 -	80.00

JACK & JILL:

Caddy 110 *Party Time*............	5.00 -	8.00
Imperial 5464 *Record Hop*............	7.00 -	10.00

JACKIE & STARLITES:

Fire—*They Laughed At Me*............	————	
Fury—*The Laughed At Me*............	————	
1057 *I Found Out Too Late*............	————	

JACKS:

Crown (LP) 372 *The Jacks*............	10.00 -	15.00
(LP) 5021 *Jumpin' With The Jacks*............	20.00 -	25.00
RPM 428, 444, 467............	4.00 -	7.00
454 *How Soon*............	5.00 -	8.00
458 *Sugar Baby*............	5.00 -	8.00

JACKSON BROTHERS:

Atlantic 1034 *Love Me*............	7.00 -	10.00
RCA Victor 5005 *We're Gonna Rock This Joint*	7.00 -	10.00

BOBBY JACKSON:

Brunswick 55026 *Deep Elm Blues*............	7.00 -	10.00

BULL MOOSE JACKSON:

Audio Lab (LP) 1524 *Bull Moose Jackson*......	20.00 -	30.00
King (LP) 211, 261............	8.00 -	12.00
Encino 1004 *Watch My Signals*............	7.00 -	10.00

EDDIE JACKSON:

Fortune 186 *Rock 'N' Roll Baby*............	10.00 -	15.00

HANDY JACKSON:

Sun 177 *Got My Application Baby*............	100.00 -	150.00

LEE JACKSON:

Cobra 5007 *Fishin' In My Pond*............	10.00 -	15.00
Keyhole 115 *Please Baby*............	8.00 -	12.00

LIL/LITTLE SON JACKSON (& HIS ROCK & ROLLERS):

Imperial 5156 *Travelin' Woman*............	25.00 -	40.00
5165 *Upstairs Boogie*............	25.00 -	40.00
5175 *My Little Girl*............	25.00 -	40.00
5192 *Travelin' Alone*............	15.00 -	25.00
5204 *Journey Back Home*............	25.00 -	40.00
5218 *Black And Brown*............	20.00 -	30.00
5229 *Lonely Blues*............	20.00 -	30.00
5237 *Spending Money Blues*............	30.00 -	40.00
5248 *Confession*............	20.00 -	30.00
5259 *Dirty Work*............	20.00 -	30.00
5267 *Thrill Me Baby*............	20.00 -	30.00
5276 *Piggly Wiggly*............	15.00 -	25.00
5286 *Blues By The Hour*............	15.00 -	25.00
5300 *Let Me Down Easy*............	10.00 -	15.00
5312 *How Long*............	10.00 -	15.00
5319 *My Younger Days*............	8.00 -	12.00
5339 *Sugar Mama*............	8.00 -	12.00
5963 *Prison Bound*............	5.00 -	8.00
Imperial (LP) 9142 *Rockin' & Rollin'*.........	50.00 -	75.00
Post 2014 *Lonely Blues*............	10.00 -	15.00

WANDA JACKSON:

Capitol (LP) 1041 *Wanda Jackson*............	30.00 -	40.00
(LP) 1384 *Rockin' With Wanda*............	40.00 -	60.00
(LP) 1511 *There's A Party Goin' On*........	30.00 -	40.00
(LP) 1776 *Wonderful Wanda*............	15.00 -	20.00
3485, 3575, 3637, 3764, 3843, 3941, 4081, 4142, 4397, 4469, 4520............	4.00 -	8.00
(Note: 78 rpm issues of above numbers are worth somewhat more.)		
Decca 29253, 29514, 29627, 30153............	5.00 -	8.00

THE JAC-O-LACS:

Tampa 103 *Cindy Lou*............	————	

JIM JACONO & THE J'S:

Kay-Y 66783 *Take My Money*............	————	

JADES:

Ching (LP) 69 *So Tough!*............	————	
Nau-Voo 807 *Walking All Alone!*............	10.00 -	15.00

JAGUARS:

Aardell 0003 *I Wanted You*............	15.00 -	20.00
0006 *You Don't Believe Me*............	15.00 -	25.00
Ebb 129 *Hold Me Tonight*............	7.00 -	10.00
Original Sound 06 *Thinking Of You*..........	5.00 -	8.00
R-Dell 11 *The Way You Look Tonight* (red plastic)	50.00 -	80.00
11 same, but black plastic............	20.00 -	30.00
Rendezvous 159 *It Finally Happened*.........	10.00 -	15.00

"JAMBOREE!":

(Complete score of musical, with Jimmy Bowen, Fats Domino, Buddy Knox, Jerry Lee Lewis, et al.)	100 up
(Note: The price of this rare album is conjectural; a copy was recently offered at auction with a minimum bid of several hundred dollars.)	

BILL JAMES:

Mun Rab 104 *School's Out*............	7.00 -	10.00

BOBBIE JAMES & 4 BUDDIES:
Club 51 104 *I Need You So* . . . . 25.00 - 40.00

ELMER JAMES:
Trumpet 186 *Gonna Find My Baby* . . . . 15.00 - 25.00

ELMORE JAMES (& HIS BROOMDUSTERS):
Ace 508 *Dust My Broom* . . . . 15.00 - 20.00
Checker 777 *Country Boogie* . . . . 15.00 - 20.00
Chess 1756 *I Can't Hold Out* . . . . 7.00 - 10.00
Chief 7001 *The Twelve Year Old Boy* . . . . . . 10.00 - 15.00
    7004 *It Hurts Me Too* . . . . 10.00 - 15.00
    7006 *Cry For Me Baby* . . . . 10.00 - 15.00
    7020 *Knocking At Your Door* . . . . 8.00 - 12.00
Crown (LP) 5168 *Blues After Hours* . . . . 20.00 - 30.00
Enjoy 2015, 2020 . . . . 4.00 - 6.00
Fire 504, 1011, 1016, 1023, 1031, 1503 . . . . . . 3.00 - 6.00
Flair 1011 *Early In The Morning* . . . . 15.00 - 20.00
    1014 *Make A Little Love* . . . . 15.00 - 20.00
    1022 *Please Find My Baby* . . . . 15.00 - 20.00
    1031 *Hand In Hand* . . . . 15.00 - 20.00
    1039 *1839 Blues* . . . . 10.00 - 15.00
    1048 *Dark And Dreary* . . . . 10.00 - 15.00
    1057 *Sunny Land* . . . . 10.00 - 15.00
    1062 *Late Hours At Midnight* . . . . 10.00 - 15.00
    1069 *Happy Home* . . . . 10.00 - 15.00
    1074 *Dust My Blues* . . . . 10.00 - 15.00
    1079 *Blues Before Sunrise* . . . . 10.00 - 15.00
Kent (LP) 5022 *Original Folk Blues* . . . . 20.00 - 30.00
Meteor 5000 *I Believe* . . . . 15.00 - 20.00
    5003 *Sinful Woman* . . . . 15.00 - 20.00
Sphere Sound (LP) 7002 *The Sky Is Crying* . . . . 20.00 - 30.00
    (LP) 7008 *I Need You* . . . . 20.00 - 30.00
Trumpet 146 *Dust My Broom* . . . . 15.00 - 20.00
Vee Jay 249, 259, 260 . . . . 4.00 - 6.00

ETTA JAMES (& THE PEACHES):
Argo (LP) 4003 *At Last* . . . . 10.00 - 15.00
Modern (M) 947 *Roll With Me Henry* . . . . 10.00 - 15.00
    957 *Hey Henry* . . . . 7.00 - 10.00
    962 *Good Rockin' Daddy* . . . . 7.00 - 10.00
    972 *W-O-M-A-N* . . . . 7.00 - 10.00

JESSIE JAMES:
Kent 314 *Red Hot Rockin' Blues* . . . . 15.00 - 20.00

McKINLEY JAMES:
Tomahawk 737 *Ain't Gonna Pick No Cotton* . . . 15.00 - 20.00

SONNY JAMES:
Capitol (LP) 779 *Southern Gentleman* . . . . 10.00 - 15.00
    (LP) 867 *Sonny* . . . . 10.00 - 15.00
    (LP) 988 *Honey* . . . . 10.00 - 15.00
    (LP) 1178 *This Is Sonny James* . . . . 10.00 - 15.00
    3602 *Young Love* (78 rpm) . . . . 8.00 - 12.00
    3674 *First Date, First Kiss, First Love* (78 rpm) 7.00 - 10.00
    3840 *Uh-Huh-Mm* (78 rpm) . . . . 7.00 - 10.00

TOMMY JAMES (& THE SHONDELLS):
La Louisianne (LP) 109 *The Shondells At The Satur-*
    day Hop . . . . 30.00 - 40.00
Philco (Hip Pocket) HP 1 *I Think We're Alone Now* ———
    (Hip Picket) HP 2 *Hanky Panky* . . . . ———
(Above are 3-7/8 inches in diameter)
Red Fox 110 *Hanky Panky* . . . . ———
Snap 102 *Hanky Panky* . . . . 15.00 - 20.00

BOBBY JAMESON:
Talamo 1934 *I Wanna Love You* . . . . 5.00 - 8.00

JAN AND ARNIE:
Arwin 108 *Jennie Lee* (78 rpm) . . . . 15.00 - 20.00
    111, 113 . . . . 5.00 - 8.00
Dore 522 (DJ) *Baby Talk* . . . . 20.00 - 30.00

JAN & DEAN:
Challenge 9111 *Those Words* . . . . 7.00 - 10.00
J & D 401 *California Lullaby* . . . . 15.00 - 20.00
    402 *Like A Summer Rain* . . . . 15.00 - 20.00
Jan & Dean 10 *Hawaii* . . . . 8.00 - 12.00
    11 *Fan Tan* . . . . 8.00 - 12.00

JAN & THE RADIANTS:
Queen 24007 *Is It True* . . . . 4.00 - 7.00

JOHNNY JANIS:
ABC Paramount 9800 *I Played The Field* . . . . . . 5.00 - 8.00
    9840 *Later Baby* . . . . 5.00 - 8.00
Coral 61552 *Move It Or Lose It* . . . . 5.00 - 8.00

JOHNNY JANO:
Excello 2099 *Havin' A Whole Lot Of Fun* . . . . . 10.00 - 15.00
Hollywood 1087 *Mabel's Gone* . . . . 7.00 - 10.00

THE JARMELS:
Laurie 3083, 3124 . . . . 4.00 - 6.00

BOBBY JAY:
Imperial 5590 *Sweet Little Stranger* . . . . 10.00 - 15.00

DALE JAY:
Raven 001 *Shakin' All Over* . . . . 7.00 - 10.00

JOHNNY JAY:
Mercury 71232 *Sugar Doll* . . . . 5.00 - 8.00
    71232 *Sugar Doll* (78 rpm) . . . . 8.00 - 12.00
Play 1006 *That's What I Like About Love* . . . . . 10.00 - 15.00

P. JAY & THE HAYSTACKERS:
Oak 1202/1203 *High School Rock 'N' Roll* . . . . . 20.00 - 30.00

THE JAYES (Featuring BILL CURTISS):
Arc 4443 *Panic Stricken* . . . . 15.00 - 20.00

JAYHAWKS:
Aladdin 3379 *Johnny's House Party* . . . . 10.00 - 15.00
    3393 *Everyone Should Know* . . . . 15.00 - 20.00
Flash 105 *Counting My Teardops* . . . . 25.00 - 30.00
    109 *Stranded In The Jungle* . . . . 5.00 - 8.00
    111 *Love Train* . . . . 8.00 - 12.00

JAYTONES:
Brunswick 55087 *Gasoline* . . . . 15.00 - 20.00
Cub 9057 *My Only Love* . . . . 4.00 - 7.00

JIMMY JEFFERS & THE JOKERS:
Da-Mor 9220 *Raining Teardrops* . . . . 15.00 - 20.00
Fraternity 837 *Teardrops From My Eyes* . . . . . . ——

EDDIE JEFFERSON:
Checker 855 *Billie's Bounce* . . . . 5.00 - 8.00

WALLY JEFFERY:
Do-Re-Mi 1402 *Oh Yeah* . . . . 15.00 - 20.00

BOBBY JENKINS:
Hamilton 50001 *White Shorts And A Red Tee Shirt* 7.00 - 10.00

BO BO JENKINS:
Boxer 202 *Tell Me Who* . . . . ————
Chess 1565 *Democrat Blues* . . . . 40.00 - 60.00
Duchess 101 *Tell Me Who* . . . . ————
Fortune 838 *Ten Below Zero* . . . . 15.00 - 25.00

GUS JENKINS/JINKINS:
Flash 116, 123, 126, 128, 130, 131 . . . . 4.00 - 8.00

BABY BOY JENNINGS & THE SATELITES:
Savoy 1589 *Little Girl* . . . . 4.00 - 7.00

WAYLON JENNINGS:
Brunswick 55130 *Jole Blond* . . . . 25.00 - 40.00
Ramco 1989 *My Baby Walks All Over Me* . . . . . 7.00 - 10.00
Trend '63 106 *The Stage* . . . . 7.00 - 12.00

RALPH JEROME:
K.P. 1007 *Rockhouse* . . . . 7.00 - 10.00

JERRY & DEMAR:
Ford 501 *Cross-Eyed Alley Cat* . . . . 15.00 - 25.00

JESSE & BUZZY:
Savoy 1556 *Without Your Love* . . . . 4.00 - 7.00

JESSE & MARVIN:
Specialty 447 *Dream Girl* . . . . 7.00 - 10.00

JESSIE & THE SEQUINS:
Profile 4008 *Hold My Hand* . . . . 10.00 - 15.00

THE JESTERS:
Winley 218 *So Strange* . . . . 7.00 - 10.00
    248 *That's How It Goes* . . . . 7.00 - 10.00

JETS:
Gee 1020 *Heaven Above Me* . . . . 10.00 - 15.00

JEWELS:
Imperial 5351 *Hearts Can Be Broken* . . . . 8.00 - 12.00
    5362 *Please Return* . . . . 8.00 - 12.00

5377 *How*.................................	8.00	-	12.00
5387 *My Baby*...........................	8.00	-	12.00
R & B 1301 *Hearts Of Stone*..............	15.00	-	20.00
1303 *A Fool In Paradise*.................	20.00	-	25.00

JILL & RAY:

Le Cam 929 *Hey Paula*....................	15.00	-	20.00

JIMMY & DUANE:

Preston 212 *Soda Fountain Girl*..........	8.00	-	12.00

JIMMY & JOHNNY (& THE JADES):

Chess 4863 *Love Me*......................	15.00	-	20.00
D1004 *I Can't Find The Door Knob*........	10.00	-	15.00
D—*Don't Give Me That Look*..............	————		
Decca 29772 *Sweet Singing Daddy*..........	5.00	-	8.00
30061 *Sweet Love On My Mind*...........	15.00	-	20.00
TNT 184 *Don't Call Me, I'll Call You*........	7.00	-	10.00

JIMMY & WALTER:

Sun 180 *Before Long*.....................	75.00	-	100.00

GUS JINKINS (See GUS JENKINS)

THE JIVE-A-TONES:

Felsted 8506 *Flirty Gertie*...............	7.00	-	10.00

THE FIVE-A-TONES:

Fraternity 823 *The Wild Bird*.............	5.00	-	8.00

JIVE BOMBERS:

Savoy 1508 *Bad Boy*.....................	5.00	-	8.00
1513, 1515, 1535....................	3.00	-	5.00

JIVERS:

Aladdin 3329 *Cherie*....................	25.00	-	35.00
3347 *Ray Pearl*.....................	30.00	-	40.00

JIVETONES:

Apt 25020 *Geraldine*....................	7.00	-	10.00

JIVIN GENE:

Jin 109 *Going Out With The Tide*............	10.00	-	15.00

JODIMARS:

Capitol 3285 *Let's Rock*.................	7.00	-	10.00
3512 *Rattle Shakin' Daddy*..............	7.00	-	10.00
3588 *Clarabella!*.....................	4.00	-	7.00
3633 *Cloud 99*......................	4.00	-	7.00

JOEY & THE LEXINGTONS:

Dunes 2029 *Bobbie*.....................	8.00	-	12.00

JOHNNY & THE HURRICANES:

Big Top (LP) 1302 *The Big Sound Of*.........	20.00	-	30.00
Warwick (EP) 700 *Johnny & The Hurricanes*...	10.00	-	15.00
(LP) 2007 *Johnny & The Hurricanes*........	20.00	-	30.00
(LP) 2010 *Stormsville*....................	20.00	-	30.00

JOHNNY & THE JAMMERS:

Dart 131 *School Day Blues*................	10.00	-	15.00

JOHNNIE & JOE:

Chess 1654 *Over The Mountain Across The Sea.*	5.00	-	8.00
J & S 1630 *Warm Soft And Lovely*..........	7.00	-	10.00
1631 *False Love Has To Go*..............	7.00	-	10.00
1659 *There Goes My Heart*..............	7.00	-	10.00
1664 *Over The Mountain, Cross The Sea*.....	15.00	-	20.00

JOHNNY & THE JOKERS:

Harvard 804 *Do-Re-Mi Rock*..............	10.00	-	15.00

JOHNNIE & JONIE:

Challenge 59001 *Kee-Ro-Ryin'*............	5.00	-	8.00
59041 *Tijuana Jail*....................	4.00	-	6.00

AL JOHNSON:

Ric 956 *You Done Me Wrong*.............	5.00	-	8.00

(BIG) BILL JOHNSON:

——*My Hot Rod Car*.....................	————		

BUDDY JOHNSON:

Mercury (LP) 20209 *Rock 'N' Roll*.........	20.00	-	30.00

CLIFF JOHNSON:

Columbia 40865 *Go 'Way Hound Dog*.......	12.00	-	16.00

CURTIS JOHNSON:

Even 4268 *Baby Baby*....................	7.00	-	10.00

DEE JOHNSON:

Dixie 2022 *Back To School*..............	————		

HOYT JOHNSON:

Erwin 555 *Eenie Meenie Miney Moe*.........	15.00	-	25.00
Satellite 110 *I Just Can't Learn*...........	7.00	-	10.00

JIMMY JOHNSON:

Viv 3001 *Cat Daddy*.....................	10.00	-	15.00

LARRY JOHNSON:

Blue Soul 100 *Catfish Blues*...............	7.00	-	10.00

LONNIE JOHNSON:

King (EP) 267 *Tomorrow Night*.............	8.00	-	12.00
(LP) 520 *Lonesome Road*..................	20.00	-	30.00
4758 *Pleasing You*....................	7.00	-	10.00
Rama 9 *My Woman Is Gone*.............	10.00	-	15.00
14 *Will You Remember*..............	10.00	-	15.00
20 *This Love Of Mine*..............	10.00	-	15.00

MARV JOHNSON:

United Artist (LP) 3081 *Marvelous*.........	20.00	-	30.00

NEAL JOHNSON:

Specialty 688 *True To You Baby*............	8.00	-	12.00

RAY JOHNSON:

Demon 1502 *A Yellow Mellow Hardtop*.......	7.00	-	10.00

STAN JOHNSON:

Ruby 550 *Baby, Baby Doll*...............	10.00	-	15.00

THE JOKERS:

Lin 5027 *Dogfight*.......................	7.00	-	10.00

JOLLY JACKS:

Dasher 501 *Ugly Face*...................	10.00	-	20.00

JONES BOYS:(See also JIMMY JONES)

S-G 5007 *The Song Is Ended*...............	5.00	-	8.00

ALEX SNOOK JONES:

Blue Boy 1001 *Mean Old Greyhound*..........	7.00	-	10.00

CORKY JONES:

Pep 107 *Hot Dog*.......................	40.00	-	60.00

DEAN JONES:

MGM 12620 *Meet Me In The Study Hall*......	8.00	-	12.00

FLOYD JONES:

Chess 1527 *Early Morning*..................	35.00	-	50.00
J.O.B. 1013 *On The Road Again*............	50.00	-	75.00
Vee Jay 111 *Ain't Times Hard*............	40.00	-	60.00
126 *Floyd's Blues*....................	40.00	-	60.00

GEORGE JONES:

Mercury (LP) 20306 *...Sings*.............	12.00	-	18.00
(LP) 20477 *...Sings*.............	12.00	-	18.00
(LP) 20596 *...Salutes Hank Williams*.......	15.00	-	20.00
Starday 130 *No Money In This Deal*........	7.00	-	10.00
202 *Why Baby Why*.................	5.00	-	8.00
216 *Still Hurtin'*..................	5.00	-	8.00
234,247, 256, 264, 279................	4.00	-	7.00

GRANDPA JONES:

King (LP) 554 *Greatest Hits*................	8.00	-	12.00
(LP) 625 *Strictly Country Tunes*...........	10.00	-	15.00

JIMMY JONES & THE JONES BOYS:

Arrow 717 *Heaven In Your Eyes*............	20.00	-	30.00

LITTLE JOHNNY JONES (With THE CHICAGO HOUND DOGS):

Atlantic 1045 *Hoy Hoy*..................	10.00	-	15.00
Flair 1010 *I May Be Wrong*..............	10.00	-	15.00

RICKEY JONES:

Herald 498 *Hate To Say Goodbye*...........	5.00	-	8.00

LITTLE SONNY JONES:

Imperial 5275 *I Got Booted*...............	20.00	-	30.00

THUMPER JONES:

Starday 240 *Rock It*.....................	30.00	-	40.00

WILL JONES & THE CADETS (See THE CADETS)

JONESY'S COMBO:

Combo 79 *Ting, Ting Boom Scat*............	5.00	-	8.00

JORDAN & THE FASCINATIONS:

Carol 4116 *Once Upon A Time*..............	7.00	-	10.00

JOHNNY JORDAN:

Jolt 332 *Sweet Sweet Sweet*................	4.00	-	6.00

LOUIS JORDAN:

Aladdin 3223, 3227, 3243, 3246, 3249, 3264, 3270, 3279	4.00	-	8.00
Decca (LP) 8551 *Let The Good Times Roll*.....	20.00	-	30.00

Score (LP) 4007 *Go Blow Your Horn*.........	30.00 -	45.00
Wing (LP) 12126 *Somebody Up There Digs Me.*	15.00 -	20.00

BENNIE JOY:
Antler 4011 *Crash The Party*................	7.00 -	10.00
Dixie 2001 *Spin The Bottle*................	30.00 -	40.00
Ram 1001 *Ittie Bittie Everything*............	———	
Tri-Dec—*Spin The Bottle*...................	———	

JOYLARKS:
Snag 107 *Betty My Love*...................	20.00 -	30.00

JOYTONES:
Rama 202 *Is This Really The End?*..........	7.00 -	10.00

JUBALAIRES:
Capitol 821 *Blue Ribbon Gal*.............	15.00 -	20.00
845 *The Old Piano Roll Blues*..............	15.00 -	20.00

DON JULIAN & THE MEADOWLARKS:
Dooto (EP) 203....................	10.00 -	15.00
Dootone 359 *Heaven And Paradise*.........	8.00 -	12.00
367 *Always And Always*............	10.00 -	15.00
372 *This Must Be Paradise*.........	10.00 -	15.00
394 *Please Love A Fool*.........	15.00 -	20.00
405 *I'm A Believer*............	10.00 -	15.00
Magnum 716 *Lie*...................	7.00 -	10.00

JOHNNY JUMPER:
Vance—*Walking Talking/Worried Over You*....	———	

JUMPIN' JACKS:
Bruce 115 *Embraceable You*................	———	

JUMPIN' JAGUARS:
Decca 29938 *Shut The Door Baby*...........	———	

JUMPINTONES:
Raven 8004 *I Wonder*...................	7.00 -	10.00
8005 *That Angel Is You*.................	7.00 -	10.00

BILL JUSTIS:
Phillips 3519 *Raunchy* (78 rpm).............	15.00 -	20.00

KALIN TWINS:
Decca (LP) 8812 *The Kalin Twins*...........	15.00 -	20.00
30642 *When* (78 rpm).................	8.00 -	12.00

KASANDREA With THE MIDNIGHT RIDERS:
Sahara 101 *My Conscience Is Bothering Me*....	10.00 -	15.00

ANNE KAYE:
Gee 1015 *Every Fortune Teller Tells Me*.......	5.00 -	8.00

ERNIE K-DOE:
Minit (LP) 00002 *Mother-In-Law*.............	20.00 -	30.00

RAMSEY KEARNEY:
Jaxon 501 *Rock The Bop*..............	25.00 -	40.00

BILLY KEEN & THE TRADEWINDS:
Lesley 1922 *Don't Call Me*................	8.00 -	12.00

THE KELLY FOUR:
Silver 1001 *Strollin' Guitar*...................	———	
1006 *So, Fine, Be Mine!*..................	5.00 -	8.00

JIMMY KELLY:
Cobra 5028 *Little Chickie*.................	10.00 -	15.00

PAT KELLY & THE SHAMROCKS:
Chic 1009 *The Stranger Dressed In Black*......	5.00 -	8.00
——*Hey Doll Baby/Cloud 13*..........	———	

TINY KENNEDY:
Capitol 840 *Sister Flat Top*........	10.00 -	15.00

KENNY & THE CADETS:
Randy 422 *Barbie* (pink label with blue type)....	50.00 -	100.00

KENNY and DOOLITTLE:
Sims 123 *Kitty Kat*......................	10.00 -	15.00

KENNY AND THE KASUALS:
Mark (LP) 5000 *The Impract Sound Of Kenny And The Kasuals*......................	———	

(Note: High prices quoted for this album will undoubtedly be affected by a recent reissue.)

KENNY & MOE (THE BLUE BOYS):
De Luxe 6101, 6122, 6134, 6139, 6154........	5.00 -	8.00

HERB KENNY & THE COMETS:
Federal 12083 *Only You*..............	25.00 -	40.00

BOBBY KENT & THE KENTONES:
Bay State 82159 *Don't Go 'Way*...........	8.00 -	12.00

THE KENTS:
Argo 5299 *With All My Heart And Soul*.......	7.00 -	10.00
Dome 501 *I Love You So*..................	10.00 -	15.00

KEYNOTES:
Apollo 478 *Suddenly*.......................	15.00 -	20.00
484 *I Don't Know*....................	15.00 -	20.00
493 *Wish You Were Here*..............	20.00 -	25.00
498 *Now I Know*..................	15.00 -	20.00
503 *In The Evening*...............	20.00 -	25.00
513 *Now I Know*..................	15.00 -	20.00

KEYSTONES:
Epic 9187 *The Magic Kiss*..............	8.00 -	12.00
G&M—*The Magic Kiss*.............	20.00 -	30.00

KEYTONES:
Old Town 1041 *Seven Wonders Of The World*..	10.00 -	15.00

BILLY (THE) KIDD:
Jane 107 *Crazy Guitar*..................	7.00 -	10.00

KIDDS:
Imperial 5335 *Are You Forgetting Me*........	60.00 -	80.00
Post 2003 *You Broke My Heart*.............	35.00 -	50.00

KIDS FROM TEXAS:
Hanover 4500 *Long Legged Linda*............	———	

MERLE KILGORE:
Imperial 5379 *Teenagers Holiday*..............	15.00 -	20.00
5409 *Ernie*........................	15.00 -	20.00
5555 *Hang Doll*..................	10.00 -	15.00
8300 *Funny Feelin'*.................	10.00 -	15.00
Starday 469, 497..................	4.00 -	6.00

BILLY J. KILLEN:
Meridian 1510 *Georgia Boy*...............	———	

ALBERT KING:
Bobbin 114, 119, 126, 129, 135, 141, 143......	4.00 -	7.00
Coun-Tree 1006 *C.O.D.*....................	5.00 -	8.00
King (LP) 852 *The Big Blues*.............	15.00 -	20.00
5575, 5588, 5751...................	3.00 -	5.00
Parrot 798 *Bad Luck Blues*...............	10.00 -	15.00

B.B. (BLUES BOY) KING:
Crown (LP) 5020 *Singin' The Blues*...........	10.00 -	15.00
(LP) 5063 *The Blues*.................	10.00 -	15.00
(LP) 5115 *B.B. King Wails*.............	10.00 -	15.00
(LP) 5119 *B.B. King Sings Spirituals*.......	10.00 -	15.00
(LP) 5143 *The Great B.B. King*............	10.00 -	15.00
(LP) 5167 *King Of The Blues*.............	10.00 -	15.00
(LP) 5188 *My Kind Of Blues*............	10.00 -	15.00
Kent 301, 307, 315, 317, 319, 321, 327, 329, 330, 333, 346, 350, 351, 353, 358, 360, 362, 363..	3.00 -	6.00
RPM 380, 386, 391, 395, 403, 408, 411, 412, 416, 421, 425, 430....................	5.00 -	8.00
435, 437, 451, 457, 459, 468, 479, 486, 490, 492, 494, 498, 501.......................	4.00 -	8.00

CAROLE KING:
ABC Paramount 9921 *Goin' Wild*...........	10.00 -	15.00
9986 *Baby Sittin'*..................	10.00 -	15.00
Alpine 57 *Oh, Neil*.................	10.00 -	15.00
Companion 2000 *Nobody's Perfect*...........	10.00 -	15.00
Dimension 1009 *He's A Bad Boy*...........	5.00 -	10.00
RCA Victor 7560 *Queen Of The Beach*.......	10.00 -	15.00

EARL KING:
Ace 509 *Baby You Can Get Your Gun*........	8.00 -	12.00
514 *My Love Is Strong*..................	7.00 -	10.00
Specialty 531 *No One But Me*...............	5.00 -	8.00

EDDIE KING:
J.O.B. 1122 *Shakin' Inside*..............	20.00 -	30.00

FREDDY KING:
El-Bee 157 *Country Boy*....................	8.00 -	12.00
Federal 12384, 12401, 12415, 12428, 12432, 12443, 12450..........................	3.00 -	5.00
King (LP) 762 *Freddy King Sings*............	15.00 -	20.00
(LP) 773 *Let's Hide Away & Dance Away*....	15.00 -	20.00
(LP) 821 *Bossa Nova & The Blues*........	10.00 -	15.00

JACK KING:
4-Star 1725 *I Just Learned To Rock*...........	15.00 -	20.00

JIMMY KING:
Herald 535 *Knocking On Your Door* .... 7.00 - 10.00
KID KING'S COMBO:
Excello 2009, 2018, 2025, 2037, 2046, 2059, 2070,
2109 .... 4.00 - 8.00
PEE WEE KING & HIS BAND:
RCA Victor (LP) 1237 *Swing West* .... 20.00 - 30.00
   (LP) 3028 (10") .... 15.00 - 20.00
   (LP) 3071 (10") .... 15.00 - 20.00
   (LP) 3109 (10") *Waltzes* .... 15.00 - 20.00
   (LP) 3280 (10") *Swing West* .... 15.00 - 25.00
   6450 *Blue Suede Shoes* .... 8.00 - 12.00
RANDY KING:
TNT 9009 *Be Boppin' Baby/Whispering Wind*... ———
SID KING (& HIS FIVE STRINGS): (See also
   FIVE STRINGS)
Columbia 21361 *I Like It* .... 7.00 - 10.00
   21449 *Sag, Drag And Fall* .... 10.00 - 15.00
   21489 *Purr, Kitty, Purr* .... 10.00 - 15.00
   21505 *Blue Suede Shoes* .... 10.00 - 15.00
   21564 *Good Rockin' Baby* .... 10.00 - 15.00
   40680 *Oobie Doobie* .... 10.00 - 15.00
   40833 *When My Baby Left Me* .... 7.00 - 10.00
   41019 *I've Got The Blues* .... 7.00 - 10.00
SLEEPY KING:
Awake 852 *Rock Rock* .... 7.00 - 10.00
WILLIE KING with IKE TURNER'S BAND:
Vita 123 *Peg Leg Woman* .... 8.00 - 12.00
KING BEES with LLOYD PRICE'S
   ORCHESTRA:
Flip 323 *Puppy Love* .... 5.00 - 8.00
KRC 302 *Can't You Understand* .... 7.00 - 10.00
KING CROONERS:
Excello 2168 *Now That She's Gone* .... 10.00 - 15.00
   2187 *School Daze* .... 10.00 - 15.00
KING TOPPERS:
Josie 811 *Walkin' And Talkin' The Blues* .... 8.00 - 12.00
KING VICTOR:
Madison 110 *Boppin' Bobbie Jean* .... 7.00 - 10.00
THE KINGLETS with LEROY THOMAS:
Bobbin 104 *Pretty Please* .... 5.00 - 8.00
THE KINGS: (See also BOBBY HALL):
Baton 245 *Long, Lonely Nights* .... 10.00 - 15.00
Epic 9370 *I Want To Know* .... 7.00 - 10.00
Gotham 316 *God Made You Mine* .... 20.00 - 25.00
Jalo 203 *Angel* .... 7.00 - 10.00
Jay Wing 5805 *Surrender* .... 20.00 - 30.00
Specialty 497 *What Can I Do* .... 10.00 - 15.00
KINGS MEN:
Club-51 108 *Don't Say You're Sorry* .... 75.00 - 100.00
KINGSMEN:
Neil 102 *One Foolish Mistake* .... 8.00 - 12.00
KINKS:
Cameo 308 *Long Tall Sally* .... 20.00 - 30.00
   345 *Long Tall Sally* .... 15.00 - 20.00
   348 *You Still Want Me* (possibly unissued) .... ———
JIMMY KIRKLAND (With STAN GETZ &
   THE TOM CATS):
Fox 918/919 *Come On Baby* .... 10.00 - 15.00
Teen Life 918/919 *Come On Baby* .... 10.00 - 15.00
KLIXS:
Music City 823 *Elaine* .... 30.00 - 40.00
TOMMY KNACKIN:
Cascade—*Worry Worry Worry* .... ———
KNICKERBOCKERS:
Natural 3000 *You Must Know* .... 50.00 - 75.00
BAKER KNIGHT (& THE KNIGHTMARES):
Decca 30135 *Bring My Cadillac Back* .... 7.00 - 10.00
   30213 *Reelin' And Rockin'* .... 7.00 - 10.00
   30426 *Love-A Love-A Love-A* .... 7.00 - 10.00
GLADYS KNIGHT & THE PIPS:
Fury (LP) 1003 *Letter Full Of Tears* .... 25.00 - 35.00

JESSIE KNIGHT:
Checker 797 *Nothing But Money* .... 10.00 - 15.00
JOHNNY KNIGHT:
Morocoo 1005 *Snake Snake* .... 15.00 - 20.00
MARIE KNIGHT:
Mercury 70969 *Look At Me* .... 8.00 - 12.00
Wing 90069 *Tell Me Why* .... 5.00 - 8.00
SONNY KNIGHT:
Dot 15507 *Confidential* (78 rpm) .... 10.00 - 15.00
Eastman 787 *Lipstick Kisses* .... 4.00 - 7.00
   791 *Barbara* .... 4.00 - 7.00
Go Go 711 *Teenage Party* .... ———
Starla 10 *Once In A While* .... 5.00 - 8.00
Vita 137 *Confidential* .... 7.00 - 10.00
SUNNY KNIGHT:
Dot 15542 *Worthless And Lowdown* .... 7.00 - 10.00
KNOCKOUTS:
Shad 5013 *Darling Lorraine* .... 5.00 - 8.00
BUDDY KNOX (with THE (RHYTHM)
   ORCHIDS):
Blue Moon 402 *Party Doll* .... 50.00 - 75.00
Liberty (LP) 3251 *Golden Hits* .... 15.00 - 20.00
Roulette 4002, 4009, 4018, 4042, 4082 ...... 3.00 - 5.00
   4002 *Party Doll* (78 rpm) .... 10.00 - 15.00
   4009 *Rock Your Little Baby To Sleep* (78 rpm) 8.00 - 12.00
   4018 *Hula Love* (78 rpm) .... 8.00 - 12.00
   4042 *Swingin' Daddy* (78 rpm) .... 10.00 - 15.00
   4082 *C'mon Baby* (78 rpm) .... 10.00 - 15.00
   (LP) 25003 *Buddy Knox* .... 20.00 - 30.00
   (LP) 25048 *Buddy Knox And Jimmy Bowen*.. 30.00 - 40.00
Triple-D 797 *Party Doll* .... 35.00 - 50.00
KODAKS:
Fury 1007 *Teenagers Dream* .... 10.00 - 15.00
   1015 *Make Believe World* .... 8.00 - 12.00
   1019 *My Baby And Me* .... 8.00 - 12.00
   1020 *Guardian Angel* .... 8.00 - 12.00
J & S 1684 *Look Up To The Sky* .... 10.00 - 15.00
Sphere Sound (LP) 7005 *The Kodaks vs. The Starlites* 20.00 - 30.00
FREDDY KOENIG:
Lori 9548 *Hey Clarice!* .... 10.00 - 15.00
Valerie 225 *Hey Clarice!* .... ———
THE KO KOS:
Combo 141 *The First Day Of School* .... 5.00 - 8.00
KOOL GENTS:
Bethlehem 3061 *Picture On The Wall* .... 8.00 - 12.00
Vee Jay 173 *This Is The Night* .... 25.00 - 35.00
   207 *I Just Can't Help Myself* .... 25.00 - 35.00
PAUL KOSTY:
Fleet—*Don't Rock, Let's Roll* .... ———
KUF-LINX:
Challenge 1013 *So Tough* .... 5.00 - 10.00
   59004 *Eyeballin* .... 5.00 - 10.00
   59015 *All That's Good* .... 5.00 - 10.00
SLEEPY LA BEEF/LA BEFF:
Crescent 102 *Turn Me Loose* .... 20.00 - 30.00
Dixie (EP) 530 *Ballad Of A Teenage Queen*
   (*other cuts on this EP are by other artists; issued*
     without cardboard cover?) .... *25.00 - 40.00*
Gulf 62760 *Can't Get You Off My Mind* ...... 15.00 - 20.00
Mercury 71179 *All The Time* .... 15.00 - 20.00
Starday 292 *I'm Through* .... 20.00 - 30.00
TOMMY LA BEFF:
Wayside 1654 *Tore Up* .... 30.00 - 50.00
LABRADORS:
Chief 7009 *When Someone Loves You* .... 15.00 - 20.00
LENNY LACOUR:
Academy —*Rockin' Rosalie* .... ———
LADDERS:
Holiday 2611 *Counting The Stars* .... 10.00 - 15.00
Vest 826 *My Love Is Gone* .... 8.00 - 12.00
THE LADDINS:
Central 2602 *Now You're Gone* .... 7.00 - 10.00

Grey Cliff 721 *Light A Candle*	7.00 -	10.00
Theatre 111 *There Once Was A Time*	5.00 -	8.00
LA DELL SISTERS:		
Mercury 70888 *Rockin' Robert*	5.00 -	8.00
KENNY LAINE & HIS BULL DOGS:		
——*Columbus Stockade Blues*	———	
TOMMY LAM:		
Nabor 103 *Speed Limit*	10.00 -	15.00
GENE LAMARR:		
Flame 1102 *Just A Stranger*	10.00 -	15.00
Spry 113 *Moon Eyes*	20.00 -	30.00
JIMMY LAMBERTH:		
Meteor 5044 *Latch On To Your Baby*	20.00 -	30.00
TONY & JACKIE LAMIE:		
Sunset 706 *Wore To A Frazzell*	30.00 -	40.00
BILLY LAMONT:		
Okeh 7125 *Country Boy*	15.00 -	20.00
7131 *I'm Gonna Try*	5.00 -	8.00
TOMMY LAMPKIN:		
Ebb 110 *Three Minus One*	5.00 -	8.00
Imperial 5361 *Eternal Love*	20.00 -	30.00
LAMPLIGHTERS:		
Federal 12149 *Part Of Me*	20.00 -	25.00
12152 *Give Me*	10.00 -	15.00
12166 *I Can't Stand It*	15.00 -	20.00
12176 *Tell Me You Care*	10.00 -	15.00
12182 *Salty Dog*	10.00 -	15.00
12192 *Five Minutes Longer*	8.00 -	12.00
12197 *Yum Yum*	7.00 -	10.00
12206 *Believe In Me*	8.00 -	12.00
12212 *Love Rock And Thrill*	7.00 -	10.00
12242 *Hug A Little, Kiss A Little*	5.00 -	8.00
12255 *You Were Sent Down From Heaven* ...	5.00 -	8.00
12261 *Everything's All Right*	5.00 -	8.00
JERRY LANDIS:		
Amy 815 *The Lone Teen Ranger*	10.00 -	15.00
BUDDY LANDON:		
Jaguar 3026 *Raunchy Little Baby*	10.00 -	15.00
3028 *A Bolt Of Lightning*	10.00 -	15.00
LANE BROTHERS:		
RCA Victor 6900 *Uh Huh Honey*	5.00 -	8.00
HARRY LANE:		
RA-Q 602 *Gettin' Ready For Love*	7.00 -	10.00
JIMMY LANE & THE SUGARTONES:		
Time 6602 *Let Your Conscience Be Your Guide.*	7.00 -	10.00
RALPH LANE & THE WHITEY FOUR:		
Cowtown 811 *You Gotta Show Me*	12.00 -	16.00
LANES:		
Gee 1023 *Open Up Your Heart*	10.00 -	15.00
CURLEY LANGLEY:		
Arcadia 111 *She Wasn't Always Your Girl*	15.00 -	20.00
LOUISIANA LANNIS:		
Snowcap 1125 *Tongue Twister Boogie*	10.00 -	15.00
LARADOS:		
Fox—*Now The Parting Begins*	10.00 -	15.00
LARGOS:		
Dot 16292 *I Wonder Why*	7.00 -	10.00
Starmaker 1002 *Just A Picture*	———	
———*I Wonder Why*	———	
LARKS:		
Apollo 427 *Eyesight To The Blind*	150.00 -	250.00
429 *Hey Little Girl*	150.00 -	250.00
430 *I Don't Believe In Tomorrow*	150.00 -	250.00
435 *My Lost Love*	150.00 -	250.00
1184 *My Reverie*	100.00 -	150.00
1190 *In My Lonely Room*	125.00 -	200.00
1194 *I Live True To You*	150.00 -	250.00
(Note: Last three made of red-orange plastic)		
Jett 3001 *Love Me True*	8.00 -	12.00
Lloyds 110 *If It's A Crime*	40.00 -	70.00
112 *The World Is Waiting*	100.00 -	150.00

LARKTONES:		
Riki 140 *Why Are You Tearing Us Apart*	8.00 -	12.00
PAT LA ROCCA:		
Bella 4284 *Rowena*	10.00 -	15.00
LARRY & THE STANDARDS:		
Laurie 3119 *My Lucky Night*	7.00 -	10.00
ROC LA RUE & 3 PALS:		
Rama 226 *Teenage Blues*	15.00 -	20.00
ROGER LARUE & HIS PALS:		
Holland 7421 *I Don't Care If The Sun Don't Shine*	10.00 -	15.00
THE LATONS:		
Port 70030 *So In Love*	4.00 -	7.00
LAURELS:		
"X" 0143 *Truly, Truly*	30.00 -	40.00
ROD LAUREN:		
RCA Victor (LP) 2176 *I'm Rod Lauren*	15.00 -	20.00
CHARLES LAVERNE:		
Mark 117 *Hudson River Blues*	10.00 -	15.00
DALE LAVON:		
Cavalier—*The Rockin' Chair Roll*	———	
ART LAW:		
Gulfstream 1050 *Big Train*	10.00 -	20.00
BILL LAWRENCE:		
Freedom 44004 *Hey Baby!*	7.00 -	10.00
SYD LAWRENCE:		
Cosmic 1001 *The Answer To Flyer Saucer*	5.00 -	8.00
BOBBY LAWSON:		
Kyser 2122 *Burning Sensation*	10.00 -	15.00
M.R.C. 600 *Baby Don't Be That Way*	20.00 -	30.00
LAZY BILL & HIS BLUE RHYTHMS:		
Chance 1148 *She Got Me Walkin'*	40.00 -	60.00
LAZY LESTER:		
Excello 2095 *Lester's Stomp*	7.00 -	10.00
2107 *They Call Me Lazy*	5.00 -	8.00
2129 *Tell Me Pretty Baby*	5.00 -	8.00
Excello 2143, 2155, 2166, 2182, 2197	4.00 -	7.00
2206, 2219, 2230, 2235, 2243, 2274, 2277	3.00 -	6.00
(LP) 8006 *True Blues*	15.00 -	20.00
LEADBELLY:		
Allegro (LP) 4027 (10") *Sinful Songs*	20.00 -	30.00
Capitol (LP) 369 (10") *Leadbelly*	20.00 -	30.00
Folkways (LP) 4, 14, 24, 43 (10")	8.00 -	12.00
(LP) 241, 242 *Last Sessions*	8.00 -	12.00
Stinson (LP) 17 (10") *Memorial*	10.00 -	15.00
(LP) 19 (10") *Memorial Vol. 2*	10.00 -	15.00
(LP) 39 (10") *...Plays Parties*	10.00 -	15.00
(LP) 41 (10") *...Plays Parties, Vol. 2*	10.00 -	15.00
(LP) 48 (10") Memorial, Vol. 3	10.00 -	15.00
(LP) 51 (10") Memorial, Vol. 4	10.00 -	15.00
LEADERS:		
Glory 235 *Stormy Weather*	5.00 -	8.00
239 *Dearest Beloved Darling*	5.00 -	8.00
243 *Can't Help Loving That Girl Of Mine*	10.00 -	15.00
LEE & THE LEOPARDS:		
Gordy 7002 *Come Into My Palace*	5.00 -	8.00
"LITTLE" BRENDA LEE:		
Decca 30050 *Bigelow 6-200*	7.00 -	10.00
BOB LEE:		
Skyla 1117 *You Mostest Girl*	10.00 -	15.00
BOOKER LEE, JR.:		
Federal 12321 *Rockin' Blues*	10.00 -	15.00
BUDDY LEE:		
Brunswick 55228 *Ain't That Right*	5.00 -	8.00
DICKIE LEE (& THE COLLEGIATES):		
Sun 280 *Good Lovin'*	4.00 -	6.00
297 *Fool Fool Fool*	4.00 -	6.00
Tampa 131 *Stay True Baby*	10.00 -	15.00
FLOYD LEE:		
Enterprise 1233 *Go Boy*	10.00 -	15.00
HARRY LEE:		
Igloo 101 *Rockin' On A Reindeer*	10.00 -	15.00

JESSIE LEE With THE RHYTHMAIRES:
Mida 110 *Lonely Broken Heart* . . . . 7.00 - 10.00
JIMMY LEE:
Bandera 2506 *Chicago Jump* . . . . 10.00 - 15.00
JIMMY LEE AND JOHNNY MATHIS: (See also JIMMY & JOHNNY)
Chess 4865 *Love Me* . . . . 20.00 - 30.00
JOE LEE & HIS SEXTET With SCOTTY & BILL:
Fernwood 108 *Ethel Mae* . . . . 8.00 - 12.00
JOHN LEE:
Federal 12089 *Baby's Blues* . . . . 15.00 - 20.00
JOHNNY LEE:
De Luxe 6009 *I'm A Boogie Man* . . . . 15.00 - 20.00
JULIA LEE:
Capitol (LP) H-288 (10") *Party Time* . . . . 15.00 - 20.00
    (LP) T-288 *Party Time* . . . . 15.00 - 25.00
LEONARD LEE:
Lamp 8001 *Tryin' To Fool Me* . . . . 7.00 - 10.00
LONESOME LEE:
Bandera 2501 *Lonely Travelin'* . . . . 15.00 - 20.00
MABEL LEE:
Hull 712 *He's My Guy* . . . . 5.00 - 8.00
NANCY LEE:
Acme 711 *So They Say* . . . . 7.00 - 10.00
ROOSEVELT LEE:
Excello 2022 *Lazy Pete* . . . . 15.00 - 20.00
TOMMY LEE:
Delta 403 *Highway 80 Blues* . . . . 20.00 - 30.00
WALLY LEE With THE STORMS:
Sundown 122 *I Never Felt This Way* . . . . 15.00 - 20.00
LEFT HAND CHARLIE:
Folk Star 1131 *But You Thrill Me* . . . . 15.00 - 20.00
HANK LE GAULT:
Stardale 703/704 *I Knew* . . . . 30.00 - 50.00
LEGENDS:
Capitol (LP) 1925 *Legends Let Loose* . . . . 15.00 - 20.00
Hull 727 *The Legend Of Love* . . . . 8.00 - 12.00
Melba 109 *The Eyes Of An Angel* . . . . 8.00 - 12.00
Peacock 1694 *Goodbye Jesse* . . . . 7.00 - 10.00
PRICE LEGGS:
Glen Dell 101 *Jailbird Blues* . . . . ———
GARY LEMEL:
Rev. 3520 *Rockin' In The Halls* . . . . 10.00 - 15.00
J.B. LENOIR/LENORE (& HIS COMBO):
Checker 844 *If I Give My Love To You* . . . . 5.00 - 8.00
    856 *Don't Touch My Head* . . . . 5.00 - 8.00
    874 *Five Years* . . . . 5.00 - 8.00
    901 *She Don't Know* . . . . 5.00 - 8.00
J.O.B. 1008 *The Mountain* . . . . 20.00 - 30.00
    1012 *The Mojo* . . . . 30.00 - 50.00
    1016 *I Want My Baby* (red plastic) . . . . 50.00 - 75.00
    1102 *Play A Little While* . . . . 30.00 - 50.00
Parrot 802 *I'm In Korea/Eisenhower Blues* . . . . . 15.00 - 20.00
    802 *I'm In Korea/Tax Paying Blues* . . . . 15.00 - 20.00
(Note: Parrot 802 was issued with two different couplings.)
Parrot 809 *Mama, Talk To Your Daughter* . . . . . 15.00 - 20.00
    814 *What Have I Done* . . . . 15.00 - 20.00
    821 *I Lost My Baby* . . . . 15.00 - 20.00
Shad 5012 *Lou Ella* . . . . 5.00 - 8.00
Vee Jay 352 *Do What I Say* . . . . 5.00 - 8.00
LESLIE BROTHERS:
Columbia 40651 *Ready Ruby Rock & Roll* . . . . . ———
BOBBY LESTER & THE MOONGLOWS/MOONLIGHTERS:
Checker 806 *Shoo Doo-Be Doo* . . . . 7.00 - 10.00
    813 *Hug And A Kiss* . . . . 7.00 - 10.00
Chess (LP) 1471 *The Best Of Bobby Lester & The Moonglows* (black label) . . . . 30.00 - 40.00
BOBBY LEWIS:
Beltone (LP) *Tossin' And Turnin'* . . . . 15.00 - 20.00

Chess 1518 *Mumbles Blues* . . . . 20.00 - 30.00
Mercury 71245 *Mumbles Blues* . . . . 5.00 - 8.00
Spotlight 394 *Mumbles Blues* . . . . 7.00 - 10.00
GENE LEWIS:
Josie 819 *Too Young To Settle Down* . . . . 5.00 - 8.00
R-Dell 103 *Crazy Legs* . . . . 10.00 - 15.00
JACK LEWIS:
Imperial 5880 *Mop Top* . . . . 7.00 - 10.00
JERRY LEE LEWIS:
Sun (EP) 107, 108, 109, 110 . . . . 10.00 - 15.00
    259 *Crazy Arms* . . . . 7.00 - 10.00
    267 *Whole Lot Of Shakin' Going On* . . . . . . 5.00 - 8.00
(Note: 78 rpm issues of above command higher prices)
Sun 281 *Great Balls Of Fire* (78 rpm) . . . . 15.00 - 25.00
    288 *Breathless* (78 rpm) . . . . 10.00 - 15.00
    296 *High School Confidential* (78 rpm) . . . . . 15.00 - 20.00
    (LP) 1230 *Jerry Lee Lewis* . . . . 35.00 - 50.00
    (LP) 1265 *Jerry Lee's Greatest* . . . . 25.00 - 35.00
(Note: Promotional copies of Sun 45s, having white labels and Jerry Lee's picture stamped thereon, exist; their value is conjectural.)
JOHNNY LEWIS:
Rockin' 517 *She's Taking All My Money* . . . . 40.00 - 70.00
PETE (GUITAR) LEWIS:
Federal 12066 *Louisiana Hop* . . . . 15.00 - 25.00
    12076 *Harmonica Boogie* . . . . 15.00 - 25.00
    12103 *Scratchin' Boogie* . . . . 15.00 - 25.00
    12112 *The Blast* . . . . 15.00 - 25.00
Peacock 1624 *Goin' Crazy* . . . . 15.00 - 25.00
SAMMY LEWIS & WILLIE JOHNSON:
Sun 218 *I Feel So Worried* . . . . 10.00 - 15.00
SMILEY LEWIS:
Imperial 5194 *Bells Are Ringing* . . . . 15.00 - 20.00
    5208 *It's So Peaceful* . . . . 30.00 - 40.00
    5234 *Play Girl* . . . . 20.00 - 30.00
    5241 *Caldonia's Party* . . . . 20.00 - 30.00
    5252 *It's Music* . . . . 20.00 - 30.00
    5268 *Down The Road* . . . . 20.00 - 30.00
    5279 *I Love You For Sentimental Reasons* . . . 15.00 - 20.00
    5296 *Can't Stop Loving You* . . . . 15.00 - 20.00
    5316 *Too Many Drivers* . . . . 10.00 - 15.00
    5325 *Jailbird* . . . . 10.00 - 15.00
    5349 *Real Gone Lover* . . . . 10.00 - 15.00
    5356 *I Hear You Knocking* . . . . 7.00 - 10.00
    5372 *Queen Of Hearts* . . . . 7.00 - 10.00
    5380, 5389, 5404, 5418, 5431, 5531 . . . . . . 5.00 - 8.00
    (LP) 9141 *I Hear You Knocking* . . . . 90.00 - 125.00
Okeh 7146 *Tore Up* . . . . 15.00 - 20.00
TOMMY LEWIS:
Cenco 115 *Angel* . . . . 4.00 - 6.00
WALLY LEWIS:
Dot 15763 *I'm With You* . . . . 5.00 - 8.00
Liberty 55211 *Lover Boy* . . . . 7.00 - 10.00
Tally 117 *Kathleen* . . . . 7.00 - 10.00
RAY LIBERTO:
Dot 15848 *Wicked Wicked Woman* . . . . 5.00 - 8.00
TNT 156 *Wicked Wicked Woman* . . . . 8.00 - 12.00
    172 *I Want You To Love Me Tonight* . . . . . . 10.00 - 15.00
LICK, SLICK & SLIDE:
Savoy 1150 *I Got Drunk* . . . . 10.00 - 15.00
LIFEGUARDS:
ABC Paramount 10021 *Teenage Tango* . . . . 4.00 - 7.00
JIMMY LIGGINS:
Specialty 470 *Drunk* (red plastic) . . . . 10.00 - 15.00
JOE LIGGINS:
Specialty 338 *The Honeydripper* . . . . 10.00 - 15.00
    413 *Oh, How I Miss You* . . . . 7.00 - 10.00
    430 *Tanya* . . . . 7.00 - 10.00
    492 *Tears On My Pillow* . . . . 5.00 - 8.00
LIGHTCRUST DOUGHBOYS:
Audio Lab (LP) 1525 . . . . 15.00 - 20.00

PAPA LIGHTFOOT:

Aladdin 3171 *P.L. Blues*	25.00 -	35.00
3304 *Jumpin' With Jarvis*	15.00 -	20.00
Imperial 5289 *Mean Old Train*	25.00 -	35.00
Savoy 1161 *Mean Old Train*	10.00 -	15.00

LIGHTNIN' JR. & THE EMPIRES:

Haralem 2334 *Ragged And Hungry*	35.00 -	50.00

LIGHTNIN' LEON:

Rita 106 *Repossession Blues*	7.00 -	10.00

LIGHTNIN' SLIM:

Ace 505 *Bad Feeling Blues*	7.00 -	10.00
Excello 2066 *Lightnin' Blues*	7.00 -	10.00
2075 *Sugar Plum*	7.00 -	10.00
2080 *Goin' Home*	5.00 -	8.00
2096 *Bad Luck And Trouble*	5.00 -	8.00
2106, 2116, 2131, 2142, 2150, 2160, 2169, 2173, 2179, 2186, 2195	4.00 -	7.00
(higher numbers)	3.00 -	5.00
(LP) 8000 *Rooster Blues*	20.00 -	30.00
(LP) 8004 *Bell Ringer*	10.00 -	15.00
Feature 3006 *Rock Me Mama*	15.00 -	20.00
3008 *New Orleans Bound*	7.00 -	10.00
3012 *Ethel Mae*	7.00 -	10.00

LONNIE LILLIE:

Marathon 5003 *Truck Driver's Special*	30.00 -	50.00

LIMELIGHTERS:

Gilco 213 *This Lonely Boy*	20.00 -	30.00

LINCOLNS:

Atlas 1100 *Don't Let Me Shed Any More Tears.*	15.00 -	20.00
Bud 113 *Sometime Somewhere*	5.00 -	8.00

KATHY LINDEN:

Felsted 8510 *Billy* (78 rpm)	10.00 -	15.00

THE LINTONS:

Erica 005 *Lost Love*	4.00 -	6.00

RICKY LIST:

Roulette 4511 *The River*	4.00 -	7.00

"LISTEN TO OUR STORY":

Brunswick (LP) 59001 (10") (various artists)	20.00 -	30.00

LITTLE AL:

Excello 2098 *Little Lean Woman*	4.00 -	7.00
2128 *Easy Ridin' Buggy*	7.00 -	10.00

LITTLE ANTHONY & THE IMPERIALS:

End 1027 *Tears On My Pillow*	3.00 -	5.00
1027 *Tears On My Pillow*	15.00 -	20.00

LITTLE BEATS:

Mercury 71155 *Someone For Me*	10.00 -	15.00

LITTLE BUDDY:

N R C 010 *Let's Make Love*	5.00 -	8.00

LITTLE BUTCH & VELLS:

Angletone 535 *Over The Rainbow*	5.00 -	8.00

LITTLE CAESAR (& THE ROMANS):

Del-Fi (LP) 1218 *Memories Of These Oldies But Goodies*	20.00 -	30.00
Hollywood 234 *Long Time Baby*	8.00 -	12.00

LITTLE CLYDE & THE TEENS:

RPM 462 *A Casual Look*	10.00 -	15.00

LITTLE COOL BREEZES:

Ebony 1014 *Pack Your Bags And Go*	30.00 -	50.00
1015 *Won't You Come In*	30.00 -	50.00

LITTLE DANNY:

Sharp 112 *Mind On Loving*	7.00 -	10.00

LITTLE DENNY & THE TORKEYS:

Perry 1 *Rock And Roll Blues*	15.00 -	20.00
2 *She's Everybody's Darling*	10.00 -	15.00

LITTLE DOUG: (See also DOUG SAHM)

Sarg 113 *Rollin', Rollin'*	10.00 -	20.00

LITTLE EDDIE & THE DON JUANS:

Fortune 836 *This Is A Miracle*	4.00 -	7.00

LITTLE ESTHER (& THE DOMINOES/With LITTLE WILLIE/With BOBBY NUNN/& THE ROBINS):

Federal 12016 *The Deacon Moves In*	75.00 -	100.00
12042 *Cryin' And Singing' The Blues*	15.00 -	20.00
12055 *Ring A Ding Doo*	15.00 -	20.00
12063 *The Storm*	15.00 -	20.00
12065 *Better Beware*	15.00 -	20.00
12090 *Ramblin' Blues*	15.00 -	20.00
12108 *Last Laugh Blues*	10.00 -	15.00
12115 *Hollerin' And Screamin'*	10.00 -	15.00
12122 *You Took My Love Too Fast*	10.00 -	15.00
12126 *Hound Dog*	15.00 -	20.00
12142 *Cherry Wine*	10.00 -	15.00
King (LP) 622 *Melody Lane*	15.00 -	20.00
Savoy 731 *Double Crossing Blues*	15.00 -	20.00

LITTLE HUDSON'S RED DEVIL TRIO:

J.O.B. 1015 *Rough Treatment*	50.00 -	70.00

LITTLE IKE With JIMMY BECK ORCH:

Champion 1011 *She Can Rock*	5.00 -	8.00

LITTLE JAN & THE RADIANTS:

Goldisc 15 *If You Love Me*	8.00 -	12.00

LITTLE JOE:

House Of Sound 500 *Keep Your Arms Around Me*	20.00 -	30.00

LITTLE JOE BLUE:

Movin' 132 *Dirty Work Going On*	15.00 -	20.00

LITTLE JUNE & THE JANUARYS:

Profile 4009 *Oh What A Feeling*	10.00 -	15.00

LITTLE JUNIOR'S BLUE FLAMES:

Sun 187 *Feelin' Good*	15.00 -	20.00
192 *Mystery Train*	15.00 -	25.00

LITTLE LARRY:

Success 103 *Loretta*	5.00 -	8.00

LITTLE LINDA:

Coral 62279 *Hey Little Lover*	5.00 -	8.00

LITTLE LUTHER:

Apt 25060 *Ever Lovin' Baby*	5.00 -	8.00
Criss Cross 110 *Steppin' High*	5.00 -	8.00

LITTLE MAC/MACK:

Bea & Baby 109 *Don't Come Back*	7.00 -	10.00
118 *I'm Your Fool*	7.00 -	10.00
C.J. 606 *My Walking Blues* (blue label)	7.00 -	10.00
Checker 991 *I'm Happy Now*	5.00 -	8.00

LITTLE MILTON:

Bobbin 101 *I'm A Lonely Man*	5.00 -	8.00
103 *Long Distance Operator*	5.00 -	8.00
112, 120, 125	4.00 -	6.00
Checker (LP) 2995 *We're Gonna Make It*	10.00 -	15.00
Delta 403 *Little Milton's Boogie*	———	
Meteor 5040 *Let's Boogie Baby* (black label)	15.00 -	20.00
Sun 194 *Beggin' My Baby*	20.00 -	25.00
200 *Alone And Blue*	25.00 -	30.00
220 *Looking For My Baby*	12.00 -	16.00

LITTLE MOJO:

Indigo 139 *Mojo Theme*	4.00 -	7.00
Norman 505 *You Ain't The One*	4.00 -	7.00

LITTLE NAT:

Pik 1 *Do This, Do That*	4.00 -	6.00

LITTLE NATE & THE CHRYSLERS:

Johnson 318 *Someone Up There*	7.00 -	10.00

LITTLE NORMAN:

Decca 30353 *Drag Strip Baby*	———	

LITTLE PAPA JOE:

Blue Lake 116 *Easy Lovin'*	30.00 -	40.00

LITTLE RICHARD:

Camden (LP) 420 *Little Richard*	20.00 -	30.00
(EP) 446 *Little Richard Rocks*	15.00 -	20.00
Peacock 1658 *Little Richard's Boogie*	8.00 -	12.00
1673 *Maybe I'm Right*	10.00 -	15.00
RCA Victor 4582 *Get Rich Quick*	35.00 -	50.00
5025 *Please Have Mercy On Me*	35.00 -	50.00
Specialty (EP) 400, 401, 402 *Here's Little Richard*	10.00 -	15.00
(EP) 403, 404, 405 *Little Richard*	10.00 -	15.00
561 *Tutti-Frutti*	5.00 -	8.00
561 *Tutti-Frutti* (78 rpm)	10.00 -	15.00
572 *Long Tall Sally*	4.00 -	7.00

572 *Long Tall Sally* (78 rpm)	10.00 -	15.00
584 *Heeby-Jeebies*	4.00 -	7.00
584 *Heeby-Jeebies* (78 rpm)	10.00 -	15.00
591 *All Around The World*	4.00 -	7.00
591 *All Around The World* (78 rpm)	10.00 -	15.00
598 *Lucille*	4.00 -	7.00
598 *Lucille* (78 rpm)	10.00 -	15.00
606 *Jenny, Jenny*	4.00 -	7.00
606 *Jenny, Jenny* (78 rpm)	10.00 -	15.00
611 *Keep A Knockin'*	4.00 -	6.00
611 *Keep A Knockin'* (78 rpm)	10.00 -	15.00
624 *Good Golly, Miss Molly*	4.00 -	6.00
624 *Good Golly, Miss Molly* (78 rpm)	15.00 -	20.00
633, 652, 660	3.00 -	5.00
633 *True, Fine Mama* (78 rpm)	8.00 -	12.00
652 *She Knows How To Rock* (78 rpm)	8.00 -	12.00
660 *Wonderin'* (78 rpm)	10.00 -	15.00
(LP) 2100 *Here's Little Richard*	15.00 -	25.00
(LP) 2103 *Little Richard*	15.00 -	25.00
(LP) 21]4 *The Fabulous Little Richard*	15.00 -	20.00

LITTLE SAMMY:

Shade — *Can You Love Me*	15.00 -	20.00

LITTLE SHY GUY:

Calvert 107 *Let's Rock & Roll*	20.00 -	30.00

LITTLE SONNY:

Duke 186 *Hear My Woman Calling*	5.00 -	8.00
J.V.B. 5001 *I'll Love You Baby*	20.00 -	30.00

LITTLE TEMPLE & HIS "88":

Specialty 475 *I Ate The Wrong Part*	15.00 -	20.00

LITTLE VICTOR (& THE VISTAS):

Rendezvous 183 *No More*	4.00 -	6.00
Richland 2907 *Papa Lou and Gran*	15.00 -	20.00

LITTLE WALKING' WILLIE:

Jaguar 3012 *Clayhouse Blues*	10.00 -	15.00

LITTLE WALTER (& HIS JUKES/NIGHT CAPS):

Checker 758 *Juke*	20.00 -	30.00
764 *Mean Old World*	20.00 -	30.00
767 *Tonight With A Foolo*	20.00 -	30.00
770 *Off The Wall*	15.00 -	20.00
780 *Quarter To Twelve*	10.00 -	15.00
786 *Lights Out*	8.00 -	12.00
793 *Rocker*	10.00 -	15.00
799 *Blue Light*	7.00 -	10.00
805 *Mellow Down Easy*	7.00 -	10.00
811 *Thunder Bird*	7.00 -	10.00
817 *Roller Coaster*	7.00 -	10.00
825, 833, 838, 845, 852, 859, 867	5.00 -	8.00
890, 904, 930, 939, 955, 968, 986, 1043, 1081, 1117	3.00 -	6.00
Chess (LP) 1428 *The Best Of Little Walter* (black label)	40.00 -	60.00

LITTLE WALTER, JR.:

Lapel 101 *Don't Know*	8.00 -	12.00

LEE ROY LITTLE:

Cee Jay 578 *Your Evil Thoughts*	4.00 -	6.00

LITTLE WILLIE JOHN:

King (LP) 564 *Fever*	15.00 -	20.00
(LP) 496 *Talk To Me*	10.00 -	15.00
(LP) 603 *Mister Little Willie John*	10.00 -	15.00

LITTLE WILLIE LITTLEFIELD:

Argyle 1013 *Ruby Ruby*	5.00 -	8.00
Bullseye 1005 *Ruby Ruby*	8.00 -	12.00
Federal 12101 *Sticking On You Baby*	7.00 -	10.00
12110 *K. C. Loving*	7.00 -	10.00
12137 *My Best Wishes And Regards*	7.00 -	10.00
12148 *Miss K.C.'s Fine*	7.00 -	10.00
12163 *Don't Take My Heart Little Girl*	7.00 -	10.00
12174 *Goofy Dust Blues*	8.00 -	12.00
12221 *Jim Wilson's Boogie*	7.00 -	10.00
Rhythm 107 *Baby Shame*	15.00 -	20.00
108 *Ruby Ruby*	15.00 -	20.00
124 *Theresa*	8.00 -	12.00

JIMMY LLOYD:

Roulette 4062 *I Got A Rocket In My Pocket*	8.00 -	12.00
7001 *Where THe Rio De Rosa Flows*	10.00 -	15.00

ROBERT JR. LOCKWOOD:

J.O.B. 1107 *Sweet Woman From Maine*	40.00 -	60.00

WILLIE LOFTIN & THE DISCORDS:

Smoke 101 *Bad Habit*	5.00 -	8.00

LOGICS:

Everlast 5015 *One Love*	7.00 -	10.00

BOBBY LOLLAR:

Benton 101/102 *Bad Bad Boy*	10.00 -	15.00

LONESOME DRIFTER:

K 5812 *Eager Boy*	50.00 -	75.00
Ram 1738 *Honey Do You Love Me*	———	

LONESOME LEE (See LEE)

LONESOME SUNDOWN:

Excello 2092 *Lost Without Love*	7.00 -	10.00
2102 *My Home Is A Prison*	5.00 -	8.00
2117, 2132, 2145, 2154, 2163, 2174	4.00 -	7.00
2202, 2213, 2236, 2242, 2249, 2254, 2259, 2264	3.00 -	5.00

BUDDY LONG:

Demon 1517 *It's Nothin' To Me*	5.00 -	8.00

CURTIS LONG (& THE RHYTHM ROCKERS):

Linco 1314 *Hootchy Cootchy*	15.00 -	20.00
Stardale 55800/55801 *Goin' Out Of Town*	15.00 -	20.00

LONG JOHN:

Duke 122 *Crazy Girl*	10.00 -	15.00

LONG TALL LESTER:

Duke 197 *Working Man*	4.00 -	7.00

LONNIE & CRISIS:

Universal 103 *Bells In The Chapel*	7.00 -	10.00

LORD LUTHER:

Imperial 5596 *A Thinkin' Man's Girl*	7.00 -	10.00

BOBBY LORD:

Columbia 21339 *No More, No More, No More*	8.00 -	12.00
21498 *Pie Peachie Pie Pie*	8.00 -	12.00
21539 *Everybody's Rockin' But Me*	10.00 -	15.00
40666 *Beautiful Baby*	7.00 -	10.00
41352 *Party Pooper*	7.00 -	10.00
Harmony (LP) 7322 *The Best Of*	20.00 -	30.00

DICK LORY:

Columbia 41224 *Wild Blooded Woman*	8.00 -	12.00
Dot 15496 *Cool It Baby*	10.00 -	15.00

JOHN D. LOUDERMILK:

Columbia 41165 *Susie's House*	5.00 -	8.00

BOBBY LOUIS:

Capitol 4224 *Adult Western*	15.00 -	20.00
4272 *Call Of Love*	10.00 -	15.00

JOE HILL LOUIS:

Big Town 401 *Bad Woman Blues*	15.00 -	20.00
Checker 763 *Dorothy May*	30.00 -	50.00
Modern 839 *Big Legged Woman*	20.00 -	30.00
856 *Peace of Mind*	20.00 -	30.00

LESLIE LOUIS:

Rockin' 519 *Ridin' Home*	15.00 -	20.00

TOMMY LOUIS (& THE RHYTHM ROCKERS/With MARSHALL & THE VERSATILES):

Muriel 1001 *The Hurt Is On*	5.00 -	8.00
1002/1003 *Wail Baby Wail*	15.00 -	20.00

LOUISIANA RED:

Roulette (LP) 25200 *The Low Down Back Porch Blues*	15.00 -	20.00

THE LOUVIN BROTHERS:

Capitol (LP) 769 *Tragic Songs Of Life*	12.00 -	16.00
(LP) 825 *Nearer My God To Thee*	10.00 -	15.00
(LP) 910 *Ira & Charlie*	15.00 -	20.00

THE LOVE BROTHERS:

— *Baby, I'll Never Let You Go*	—	

BILLY LOVE:

Chess 1508 *Drop Top*	15.00 -	20.00
1516 *My Teddy Bear Baby*	15.00 -	20.00

HOT SHOT LOVE:
Sun 196 *Wolf Call Boogie*.................. 50.00 - 75.00
WILLIE LOVE & HIS THREE ACES:
Trumpet 172 *Fallin' Rain*................. 7.00 - 10.00
  173 *Vanity Dresser Boogie* .... 7.00 - 10.00
  174 *Shady Lane Blues*................. 7.00 - 10.00
  175 *V-8 Ford*.................... 7.00 - 10.00
  209 *Way Back*.................... 7.00 - 10.00
LOVE LARKS:
Mason's — *Diddle-Le-Bom*.............. 20.00 - 30.00
LOVE NOTES:
Holiday 2605 *United*................. 10.00 - 15.00
  2608 *If I Could Make You Mine*....... 8.00 - 12.00
Imperial 5254 *Surrender Your Heart*.......... 50.00 - 75.00
Premium 611 *A Love Like Yours*........... 10.00 - 15.00
Rainbow 266 *I'm Sorry*.............. 30.00 - 40.00
Riviera 970 *I'm Sorry*................. 50.00 - 75.00
  975 *Since I Fell For You*........ 100.00 - 150.00
Wilshire 200 *Our Songs Of Love*.......... 8.00 - 12.00
LOVETONES:
Plus 108 *Talk To An Angel*........... 8.00 - 12.00
BUDDY LOWE:
Crest 1049 *Ummmm-Kiss Me Goodnight*....... 7.00 - 10.00
JIM LOWE:
Dot (LP) 3051 *Songs They Sing Behind The Green Door*............... 20.00 - 30.00
  (LP) 3114 *Wicked Women*............... 20.00 - 30.00
  15456 *Blue Suede Shoes*................. 8.00 - 12.00
FRANKIE LOWERY:
Khoury's 716 *Kansas City Train*............. 8.00 - 12.00
JAY B. LOYD:
ABC Paramount 9922 *You're Just My Kind*.... 10.00 - 15.00
Hi 2017 *I'm So Lonely*................. 8.00 - 12.00
JIM LUCAS:
Republic 7123 *Tutti Frutti*............ 10.00 - 15.00
LUKE THE DRIFTER (See HANK WILLIAMS)
ROBIN LUKE:
Dot (DP) 1092 *Susie Darlin'*.......... 10.00 - 15.00
  15781 *Susie Darlin'* (78 rpm)......... 15.00 - 20.00
  15829 *Chica Chicka Honey*............ 5.00 - 8.00
  15899 *Strollin' Blues*.............. 5.00 - 8.00
  15959 *Who's Gonna Hold Your Hand*....... 5.00 - 8.00
International 206 *Susie Darlin'*................. 15.00 - 20.00
  208 *My Girl*.................... 8.00 - 12.00
  210 *You Can't Stop Me From Dreamin'*..... 10.00 - 15.00
  212 *Five Minutes More*.................. 8.00 - 12.00
BOB LUMAN:
Capitol 2972 *I Know My Baby Cares*......... 5.00 - 7.00
Imperial 5705 *Red Cadillac And A Black Moustache* 8.00 - 12.00
  8311 *Red Cadillac And A Black Moustache*... 10.00 - 15.00
  8315 *Make Up Your Mind*................. 7.00 - 10.00
(Note: above two are maroon label; black label later pressings command smaller premiums.)
LUMBERJACKS:
Hollywood 1040 *Lonely Blues*............... ——
KENNY LUNK & THE ROLLER COASTERS:
Holiday Inn 105 *Rip It Up Potatoe Chip*....... 8.00 - 12.00
NELLIE LUTCHER:
Capitol (LP) H-232 (10") *Real Gone*......... 20.00 - 30.00
  (LP) T-232 *Real Gone*.............. 20.00 - 30.00
Epic (LP) 1108 (10") *Whee! Nellie*............. 25.00 - 35.00
Liberty (LP) 3014 *Our New Nellie*............. 20.00 - 30.00
LY-DELLS:
Master 111 *Genie Of The Lamp*............ 8.00 - 12.00
  251 *Wizard Of Love*.................... 7.00 - 10.00
FRANKIE LYMON (& THE TEENAGERS): (See also TEENAGERS)
Gee 1018 *I Promise To Remember*........... 5.00 - 8.00
  1018 *I Promise To Remember* (78 rpm)...... 8.00 - 12.00
  1022 *The ABC's Of Love*................ 4.00 - 7.00
  1022 *The ABC's Of Love* (78 rpm)......... 8.00 - 12.00

  1026 *I'm Not A Juvenile Delinquent*........ 4.00 - 7.00
  1026 *I'm Not A Juvenile Delinquent* (78 rpm). 8.00 - 12.00
  1032, 1036, 1039................. 3.00 - 6.00
  1032 *Paper Castles* (78 rpm)........ 7.00 - 10.00
  1036 *Out In The Cold Again* (78 rpm)....... 7.00 - 10.00
  1039 *Goody Goody* (78 rpm)....... 8.00 - 12.00
Roulette (EP) *At The London Palladium*...... 7.00 - 10.00
  (LP) 25013 *Frankie Lymon At The London Palladium*................. 20.00 - 30.00
  25036 *Rock And Roll*................. 20.00 - 30.00
LEWIS LYMON & THE TEENCHORDS:
End 1003 *Too Young*..................... 8.00 - 12.00
  1007 *I Found Out Why*................ 8.00 - 12.00
Fury 1000 *I'm So Happy*............. 7.00 - 10.00
  1003 *Honey Honey*................ 7.00 - 10.00
  1006 *I'm Not Too Young To Fall In Love*... 7.00 - 10.00
Juanita 101 *Dance Girl*................ 5.00 - 8.00
JERRY LYNN:
D 1041 *Bugger Burns*................. 10.00 - 15.00
KATHY LYNN & HER PLAYBOYS:
Swan 4193 *I Got A Guy*................. 8.00 - 12.00
LORELEI LYNN:
Award 128 *Rock A Bop*................. 7.00 - 10.00
LORETTA LYNN:
Zero 107 *I'm A Honky Tonk Girl*............. 30.00 - 40.00
  110 *Heartaches Meet Mr. Blues*....... 30.00 - 40.00
  112 *The Darkest Day*.............. 30.00 - 40.00
JOE LYONS & THE ARROWS:
Hollywood 1065 *Honey Chile*............. 15.00 - 20.00
LYRES:
J & G — *Ship Of Love*............. 40.00 - 60.00
LYRICS:
Goldwax 101 *Darling*................. 5.00 - 8.00
Harlem 101 *Oh, Please Love Me*............. 20.00 - 30.00
  104 *The Beating Of My Heart*....... 15.00 - 20.00
Mid South 1500 *Crying Over You*........... 10.00 - 15.00
Rhythm 127 *Every Night*................ 35.00 - 50.00
Vee Jay 285 *Come On Home*............. 15.00 - 20.00
Wildcat 0028 *Oh, Please Love Me*........... 5.00 - 8.00
WILLIE MABON (& HIS COMBO):
Chess (LP) 1439 *Willie Mabon*............. 20.00 - 30.00
  1531 *Worry Blues*................. 7.00 - 10.00
  1538 *Night Latch*................. 7.00 - 10.00
  1548 *Monday Woman*............. 7.00 - 10.00
  1554, 1564, 1580, 1592, 1608, 1627............ 5.00 - 8.00
Federal 12306 *Light Up Your Lamp*........... 5.00 - 8.00
MAC & JAKE:
Meteor 5022 *Yakety Yak*................. 15.00 - 25.00
LOU MAC:
Blue Lake 119 *Move Me*............. 15.00 - 20.00
BILL MACK:
Imperial 8177 *Play My Boogie*.................. 15.00 - 25.00
  8212 *That's The Way I Like You*.......... 7.00 - 10.00
  8222 *That's How I Feel*................. 7.00 - 10.00
  8278 *Sue-Suzie Boogie*................. 10.00 - 15.00
Starday 231 *Kitty Kat*................. 20.00 - 30.00
  252 *Cat Just Got In Town*............ 20.00 - 30.00
  280 *It's Saturday Night*............ 15.00 - 25.00
  313 *Cheatin' On Your Mind*............ 10.00 - 15.00
  418 *Long, Long Train*............ 5.00 - 8.00
BILLY MACK:
Lewis Records 1001 *Tribute To Jerry Lee*..... 5.00 - 8.00
BOBBY MACK:
Tempus 1508 *She's My Little Baby*........... 5.00 - 8.00
LEON MACK:
Lavender 1554 *You Hurt Me So*........... 10.00 - 15.00
LONNIE MACK:
Fraternity (LP) 1014 *Wham Of The Memphis Man* 15.00 - 20.00
WARNER MACK:
Decca 30471, 30841................. 4.00 - 7.00
VINCENT MACREE & THE RHYTHM KINGS:
Gametime 103 *Teen-Age Talk*................. 4.00 - 7.00

JOHNNY MADARA:
Bamboo 511 *A Story Untold*................. 5.00 - 8.00

JIMMIE MADDIN:
American International 525 *Bird Dog*.... 7.00 - 10.00
542 *Tongue Tied*....................... 7.00 - 10.00
Freedom 44007 *I'm Studyin' You*........ 5.00 - 8.00
Imperial 5494 *Jeanie, Jeanie, Jeanie*.. 5.00 - 8.00
5496 *Shirley Purley*................... 5.00 - 8.00
Tampa 102 *Let 'Em Roll*................ 5.00 - 8.00

MADDOX BROTHERS (& ROSE):
Columbia 21559 *The Death Of Rock And Roll*.. 10.00 - 15.00
40836 *Ugly And Slouchy*................ 7.00 - 10.00
41020 *Stop Whistlin' Wolf*............. 7.00 - 10.00

ROSE MADDOX:
Capitol (LP) 1312 *One Rose*............ 15.00 - 20.00
(LP) 1548 *A Big Bouquet Of Roses*...... 12.00 - 16.00
21394 *Wild Wild Young Men*............. 5.00 - 8.00

MADDY BROTHERS:
Celestial 109 *Rockin' Party*........... 10.00 - 15.00

MADISON BROTHERS:
Sure — *Give Me Your Heart*............. 8.00 - 12.00
V-Tone 231 *Did We Go Steady Too Soon?*..... 5.00 - 8.00

THE MAGICS:
Debra 1003 *Chapel Bells*............... 5.00 - 8.00

MAGIC SAM:
Chief 7013 *Mr. Charlie*................ 7.00 - 10.00
7017 *Square Dance Rock*................ 7.00 - 10.00
7026 *Do The Camel Walk*................ 7.00 - 10.00
7033 *Blue Light Boogie*................ 7.00 - 10.00
Cobra 5013 *All Your Love*.............. 10.00 - 15.00
5021 *Look Watcha Done*................. 10.00 - 15.00
5025 *All Night Love*................... 8.00 - 12.00
5029 *Twenty One Days In Jail*.......... 8.00 - 12.00

THE MAGNETS:
Groove 0058 *You Just Say The Word*..... 15.00 - 25.00

THE MAGNIFICENT FOUR:
Blast 210 *The Closer You Are*.......... 7.00 - 10.00
Whale 506 *The Closer You Are*.......... —

MAGNIFICENTS:
Vee Jay 183 *Up On The Mountain*........ 10.00 - 15.00
208 *Caddy Bo*.......................... 7.00 - 10.00
235 *Off The Mountain*.................. 12.00 - 16.00
281 *Don't Leave Me*.................... 15.00 - 20.00

MAHARAJAHS:
Flip 332 *Why Don't You Answer?*........ 5.00 - 8.00

MOE MAHARREY:
Hi 2019 *I Cry For You*................. 5.00 - 8.00

SIDNEY MAIDEN:
Dig 138 *Hand Me Down Baby*............. 10.00 - 15.00
Flash 101 *Everything Is Wrong*......... 10.00 - 15.00
Imperial 5189 *Honey Bee Blues*......... 20.00 - 30.00

MAJESTICS:
Bim 1 *How Long Will It Last*........... 8.00 - 12.00
Chex 1006 *Lonely Heart*................ 7.00 - 10.00
Knight 105 *Pennies For A Beggar*....... 10.00 - 15.00
Linda 121 *Girl Of My Dreams*........... 7.00 - 10.00
Marlin 802 *Cave Man Rock*.............. 30.00 - 50.00

VINCENT MALOY:
Angle Tone 520 *Flying Home*............ ——
End 1019 *Hubba Hubba Ding Bing*........ 15.00 - 20.00

GENE MALTAIS:
Decca 30387 *Crazy Baby*................ 40.00 - 60.00
Lilac — *The Raging Sea*................ ——

MANDELLS:
Chess 1794 *Who, Me?*................... 8.00 - 12.00
Smart 323 *Darling I'm Home*............ 10.00 - 15.00
Smart — *Because I Love You*............ 10.00 - 15.00

MANHATTANS:
Carnival 506, 509, 512.................. 4.00 - 7.00
Ransom 787 *It Was A Night Like This*... 50.00 - 75.00

GEORGE MANIS:
Eclaire — *Hep, Two, Three*............. ——

BARRY MANN:
ABC Paramount (LP) 399 *Who Put The Bomp*.. 15.00 - 20.00

BILLY MANN:
Dig 120 *A Million Heartaches Ago*........... 8.00 - 12.00

CARL MANN (& THE KOOL KATS):
Jaxon 502 *Gonna Rock & Roll Tonight*........ 75.00 - 100.00
Phillips 3546 *Rockin' Love*................. 5.00 - 8.00
(LP) 1960 *Like, Mann*....................... 30.00 - 40.00

CHUCK MANN:
Leona 3699 *Little Miss Muffet*.............. 5.00 - 8.00

FRANKIE MANN & THE METEORS:
Apt 25024 *Toe To Toe*....................... 5.00 - 8.00

RED MANSEL & THE HILLBILLY BOYS:
Allstar 7160 *Johnny On The Spot*............ 5.00 - 8.00

JOE MAPHIS:
Columbia 21518 *Guitar Rock & Roll*......... 7.00 - 10.00
Republic 2006 *Water Baby Boogie*........... 7.00 - 10.00

MARATHONS:
Arvee (LP) 428 *Peanut Butter*............... 20.00 - 30.00

MARBLES:
Lucky 002 *Golden Girl*...................... ——

MARCELS:
Colpix (LP) 416 *Blue Moon*.................. 25.00 - 40.00

MARIGOLDS:
Excello 2057 *Rollin' Stone*................. 5.00 - 8.00
2061 *Two Strangers*......................... 5.00 - 8.00
2081 *It's You, Darling, It's You*........... 7.00 - 10.00

MARKEES:
Gone 5028 *Along Came Love*.................. 7.00 - 10.00

MORTY MARKER & THE IMPALAS:
Back Beat 521 *Tear Down The House*........ 7.00 - 10.00

MARK IV:
Cosmic 704 *45 RPM (78 rpm)*................. 10.00 - 15.00

ROOSEVELT MARKS ORCHESTRA With
CLAYTON LOVE:
Bobbin 102, 108............................. 4.00 - 7.00

MARQUEES:
Grand 141 *The Bells*........................ 8.00 - 12.00
Okeh 7096 *Wyatt Earp*....................... 8.00 - 12.00
Warner Bros. 5139 *Until I Die*.............. 7.00 - 10.00

MARSHALL BROTHERS:
Savoy 825 *Who Will Be The Fool*............ 80.00 - 100.00
828 *Just Because*........................... 80.00 - 100.00
833 *Why Make A Fool Out Of Me*.............. 80.00 - 100.00

PERCY MARSHALL:
Marshall 16481 *Give Me My Guitar and My Traveling Shoes*... 8.00 - 12.00

MARTELLS:
Cessna 477 *Forgotten Spring*................ 20.00 - 25.00

BILLY MARTIN:
Lucky 0009 *If It's Lovin' That You Want*...... 10.00 - 15.00

JANIS MARTIN:
RCA Victor (EP) 4093 *Just Squeeze Me*...... 25.00 - 35.00
6491 *Drugstore Rock & Roll*................. 7.00 - 10.00
6560 *Ooby Dooby*............................ 8.00 - 12.00
6652 *My Boy Elvis*.......................... 10.00 - 15.00
6744 *Let's Elope Baby*...................... 7.00 - 10.00
6832 *Love Me To Pieces*..................... 8.00 - 12.00
6983 *Love And Kisses*....................... 8.00 - 12.00
7104 *All Right Baby*........................ 10.00 - 15.00
7184 *Cracker Jack*.......................... 10.00 - 15.00
7318 *Bang Bang*............................. 10.00 - 15.00

JERRY MARTIN:
"R" 507 *Lover's Promise*.................... ——
"R" 510 *Deep In My Heart*................... ——

JIMMY MARTIN:
Jaxon 501 *Rock The Bop*..................... 30.00 - 40.00

RIC MARTIN:
Condor 101/102 *I Travel The Road*........... ——
103/104 *Warm One*.......................... ——

SONNY MARTIN:
Felsted 8507 *Rockabye Baby*................. 4.00 - 6.00

WINK MARTINDALE:

Dot (LP) 3245 *Deck Of Cards*................	15.00 -	20.00
OJ 1009 *Love's Got Me Thinkin'*............	5.00 -	8.00

MARTINIQUES:

Dance Land 770 *Broken Hearted Me*........	10.00 -	15.00
1002 *I Need Love*.......................	10.00 -	15.00

MARTY:

Novelty 701 *Marty On Planet Mars*.........	5.00 -	8.00
(Note: 78 rpm pressing exists.)		

MARVELIERS:

Cougar 1868 *Down*.......................	15.00 -	20.00

MARVELLOS:

Exodus 6214 *She Told Me Lies*.............	8.00 -	12.00
Theron 117 *Calypso Mama*.................	50.00 -	75.00

MARVELLS:

Magnet — *Did She Leave You*.............	20.00 -	30.00

MARVIN & THE CHIRPS:

Tip Top 202 *I'll Miss You This Christmas*.....	30.00 -	40.00

MARVIN & JOHNNY:

Crown (LP) 5381 *Marvin & Johnny*..........	10.00 -	15.00
Modern 968, 974.......................	4.00 -	7.00
Specialty 479 *Baby Doll*..................	5.00 -	8.00
530 *Flip*...........................	4.00 -	7.00
Swingin' 645 *Second Helping Of Cherry Pie*....	5.00 -	8.00

MARYLANDERS:

Jubilee 5079 *I'm A Sentimental Fool*.........	40.00 -	60.00
5091 *Make Me Thrill Again*..............	50.00 -	75.00
5114 *Good Old 99* (red plastic).........	25.00 -	40.00

THE MASCOTS:

Blast 206 *Once Upon A Love*..............	7.00 -	10.00
King 5377 *The Story Of My Heart*..........	7.00 -	10.00
5435 *Lonely Rain*......................	5.00 -	8.00
MGM 11959 *Please Have Mercy*..........	———	

JAMES MASK:

Bandera 1306 *Save Your Love*.............	5.00 -	8.00

MASQUERADES:

Boyd 1027 *Fanessa*.....................	———	

THE MASTERS:

Bingo 1008 *Lovely Way To Spend An Evening*..	7.00 -	10.00
Le Sage 714 *Crying My Heart Out*...........	15.00 -	20.00

SAMMY MASTERS:

4 Star 1696 *Pink Cadillac*................	10.00 -	15.00
1697 *Whop T Bop*....................	10.00 -	15.00
Calahad 526 *On Tour In Heaven*...........	4.00 -	7.00
Lode 108 *Rockin' Red Wing*..............	7.00 -	10.00

MASTER TONES:

Bruce 111 *Tell Me*.....................	——	

MATADORS:

Sue 700 *Vengeance*.....................	8.00 -	12.00
701 *Be Good To Me*...................	8.00 -	12.00

BILLY MATCH & STARFIRES:

Starfire 664 *I Want My Baby*.............	7.00 -	10.00

LITTLE ARTHUR MATHEWS:

Federal 12232 *I'm Gonna Whale On You*......	8.00 -	12.00

JOHNNY MATHIS:

Columbia 40851, 40093 (78 rpm)............	5.00 -	10.00

RAMON MAUPIN:

Fernwood 101 *Long Gone*.................	20.00 -	30.00
105 *Rockin' Rufus*.....................	20.00 -	30.00

ARTHUR LEE MAYE (& THE CROWNS):

Cash 1063 *Will You Be Mine*.............	20.00 -	30.00
1065 *All I Want Is Someone To Love*.......	20.00 -	30.00
Dig 124 *This Is The Night For Love*........	20.00 -	30.00
133 *A Fool's Prayer*...................	20.00 -	30.00
RPM 424 *Truly*.......................	15.00 -	20.00
429 *Love Me Always*..................	15.00 -	20.00
438 *Please Don't Leave Me*.............	25.00 -	35.00
Specialty 573 *Gloria*...................	7.00 -	10.00
Yvette 300 *Gloria*....................	10.00 -	15.00

NATHANIEL MAYER:

Fortune (LP) 8014 *Going Back To The Village Of Love*....	15.00 -	25.00

PERCY MAYFIELD:

Chess 1599 *Double Dealing*...............	5.00 -	8.00
Specialty 460 *Lost Mind*.................	7.00 -	10.00

MIKE McALISTER:

Hob Nob 441 *I Don't Dig It*..............	7.00 -	10.00

LEON McAULIFF:

ABC Paramount (LP) 394 *Cozy Inn*.........	15.00 -	20.00

DALE McBRIDE With GAYLON CHRISTIE & DOWNBEATS:

Fame 503 *It Might Have Been*.............	10.00 -	15.00
Kobb 1500 *If You See My Julie*...........	10.00 -	15.00

JERRY (BOOGIE) McCAIN (& HIS UPSTARTS):

Excello 2068 *Courtin' In A Cadillac*.........	6.00 -	9.00
2079 *If It Wasn't For My Baby*...........	4.00 -	7.00
2081, 2103, 2111.....................	4.00 -	7.00
2127 *The Jig's Up*....................	5.00 -	10.00
Trumpet 217 *Wine O-Wine*..............	8.00 -	12.00
231 *Stay Out Of Automobiles*...........	10.00 -	15.00

MAC McCLANAHAN:

Tiger 104 *That Nonsense Stuff*.............	———	

HAZEL McCOLLUM With THE EL DORADOS:

Vee Jay 118 *Annie's Answer*...............	20.00 -	30.00

JIMMY McCRACKLIN (& HIS BLUES BLASTERS):

Irma 102, 107, 109....................	5.00 -	8.00
Mercury 71516 *Georgia Slop*.............	5.00 -	8.00
Modern *Blues Blasters Boogie*............	8.00 -	12.00
934 *Darling Share Your Love*............	8.00 -	12.00
951 *Couldn't Be A Dream*..............	8.00 -	12.00
967 *That Ain't Right*.................	8.00 -	12.00
Peacock 1605 *She's Gone*...............	7.00 -	10.00
1615 *She Felt Too Good*..............	7.00 -	10.00
1634 *I Cried*.......................	4.00 -	7.00
1639 *My Story*......................	4.00 -	7.00

JIM McCRORY:

Key 5803 *Parking Lot*..................	7.00 -	10.00
5805 *Rock Ya Baby*..................	7.00 -	10.00

GENE McDANIELS:

Liberty (LP) 3146 *In Times Like These*.......	15.00 -	20.00

LUKE McDANIEL(S):

King 1247 *Drive On*...................	4.00 -	7.00
Trumpet 184 *No More*..................	7.00 -	10.00

JIM McDONALD:

KCM 3700 *Let's Have A Ball*..............	———	

SKEETS McDONALD:

Capitol (LP) 1040 *Goin' Steady*............	25.00 -	40.00
3461 *Heart Breakin' Mama*.............	15.00 -	20.00

BOB McFADDEN & DOR:

Brunswick (LP) 54056 *Songs Our Mummy Taught Us*	15.00 -	20.00

RUTH McFADDEN & THE SUPREMES (See THE SUPREMES) BROWNIE McGHEE (& HIS JOOK BLOCK BUSTERS):

Dot 1184 *Cheatin' And Lying*..............	8.00 -	12.00
Encore 102 *High Price Blues*.............	10.00 -	15.00
Folkways (LP) 2030 (10") *Blues*..........	———	
(LP) 2421 *Blues Of America*............	———	
(LP) 3557 *Blues*.....................	20.00 -	30.00
Harlem 2323 *Christina*.................	20.00 -	30.00
2329 *My Confession*..................	15.00 -	25.00
Jax 304 *Key To The Highway*............	15.00 -	25.00
310 *Dissatisfied Woman*...............	20.00 -	30.00
312 *Cherry Red*.....................	15.00 -	20.00
322 *Pawnshop Blues*..................	4.00 -	7.00
Old Town 1075 *She Loves So Easy*.........	15.00 -	20.00
Red Robin 111 *Don't Dog Your Woman*......	10.00 -	15.00
Savoy 835 *Diamond Ring*...............	10.00 -	15.00
844 *Bottom Blues*...................	10.00 -	15.00
872 *Tell Me Baby*...................	7.00 -	10.00
1177 *Anna Mae*.....................	7.00 -	10.00
1185 *When It's Love Time*..............		

1564 *Be My Friend*	5.00 -	8.00
(LP) 14019 *Back Country Blues* (with Sonny Terry)	15.00 -	25.00
Sharp (LP) 2003 *Brownie McGhee*	30.00 -	40.00

STICK McGHEE:

Atlantic 991 *New Found Love*	7.00 -	10.00
Essex 709 *My Little Rose*	10.00 -	15.00
Herald 553 *Money Fever*	4.00 -	7.00
King 4610 *Head Happy With Wine*	8.00 -	12.00
4628 *Whiskey, Women And Loaded Dice*	8.00 -	12.00
4672 *Jungle Juice*	8.00 -	12.00
4700 *I'm Doin' All The Time*	7.00 -	10.00
4783 *Double Crossin' Liquor*	7.00 -	10.00
4800 *Get Your Mind Out Of The Gutter*	7.00 -	10.00
Savoy 1148 *Things Have Changed*	5.00 -	8.00

WAYNE McGINNIS:

Meteor 5035 *Rock And Roll Rhythm*	20.00 -	30.00

MEL McGONNIGLE:

Rocket 101 *Rattle Shakin' Mama*	40.00 -	60.00

LOWELL McGUIRE:

Nasco 6007 *Leave My Girlie Alone*	5.00 -	8.00

CHESTER McINTYRE:

Sarg 180 *I'm Gonna Rock With My Baby Tonight*	7.00 -	10.00

L.C. McKINLEY (& HIS ORCHESTRA):

Bea & Baby 102 *Nit Wit*	8.00 -	12.00
States 135 *Weeping Willow Blues*	15.00 -	20.00
Vee Jay 133 *She's Five Feet Three*	10.00 -	15.00
159 *I'm So Satisfied*	7.00 -	10.00

GENE McKNOWN:

Aggie 101 *Rock-A-Billy Rhythm*	———	

BUTCH McLAREY:

Kliff 103 *Rockin' Hall*	30.00 -	50.00

OSCAR McLOLLIE (& THE HONEYJUMPERS):

Crown (LP) 5016 *Oscar McLollie & The Honeyjumpers*	15.00 -	20.00
Modern 970 *Convicted*	7.00 -	10.00

CECIL McNABB:

King 5116 *Clock Tickin' Rhythm*	20.00 -	30.00

BIG JAY McNEELY:

King (LP) 530...*In 3-D*	15.00 -	20.00
Savoy (LP) 15045 (10")	15.00 -	20.00

CLYDE McPHATTER (& THE DRIFTERS):

Atlantic (EP) 605 *Rock With Clyde McPhatter*	10.00 -	15.00
(EP) 618 *Clyde McPhatter*	10.00 -	15.00
1185 *Come What May* (78 rpm)	7.00 -	10.00
1199 *A Lover's Question* (78 rpm)	15.00 -	20.00
2028 *Since You've Been Gone* (78 rpm)	15.00 -	20.00
2038 *There You Go* (78 rpm)	15.00 -	20.00
(LP) 8003 *Clyde McPhatter & The Drifters* (black label)	30.00 -	40.00
(LP) 8024 *Love Ballads*	15.00 -	20.00
(LP) 8031 *Clyde*	15.00 -	20.00
King (LP) 559 *Clyde McPhatter With Billy Ward & His Dominoes*	40.00 -	60.00
(Note: This album exists as *Federal* 599, which is considerably rarer than the King issue.)		
MGM (LP) 3775 *Let's Start Over Again*	15.00 -	25.00

CARL McVOY:

Hi 2001 *Tootsie*	8.00 -	12.00
2002 *Little John's Gone*	7.00 -	10.00
Phillips 3526 *Tootsie*	4.00 -	6.00

MEADOWLARKS: (See also DON JULIAN)

RPM 399 *Love Only You*	20.00 -	30.00

MEDALLIONAIRES:

Mercury 71309 *Magic Moonlight*	10.00 -	15.00

MEDALLIONS:

Dooto (EP) 202	———	
Dootone 347 *Buick 59*	7.00 -	10.00
357 *The Telegram*	7.00 -	10.00
364 *Edna*	7.00 -	10.00
373 *My Pretty Baby*	8.00 -	12.00

379 *Dear Darling*	10.00 -	15.00
393 *I Want A Love*	10.00 -	15.00
400 *Shedding Tears For You*	10.00 -	15.00
407 *Did You Have Fun*	10.00 -	15.00
419 *For Better Or For Worse*	8.00 -	12.00
Essex 901 *I Know*	50.00 -	75.00
Sarg 191 *I Love You True*	7.00 -	10.00
194 *Lovin' Time*	7.00 -	10.00
Singular 1002 *A Broken Heart*	15.00 -	20.00

MELLO FELLOWS:

Lamp 8006 *My Friend Charlie*	7.00 -	10.00

MELLO HARPS:

Do Re Mi 203 *Love Is A Vow*	100.00 -	150.00
Tin Pan Alley	30.00 -	40.00

MELLO-KINGS:

Herald 502 *Tonite, Tonite*	4.00 -	7.00
502 *Tonite, Tonite* (78 rpm)	15.00 -	20.00
507 *Chapel On The Hill*	4.00 -	7.00
518 *Valerie*	5.00 -	8.00
536 *Running To You*	5.00 -	8.00
536 *Chip Chip* (actually *Down In Cuba* by THE ROYAL HOLIDAYS)	25.00 -	40.00
548 *Our Love Is Beautiful*	5.00 -	8.00
554 *I Promise*	5.00 -	8.00
561 *Till There Was You*	5.00 -	8.00
(LP)1013 *Tonight-Tonight*	35.00 -	50.00

MELLO-MOODS/MELLO MOODS:

Hollywood 396 *Song Of Love*	20.00 -	30.00
Prestige 799 *Call On Me*	100.00 -	130.00
856 *I'm Lost*	50.00 -	75.00
Recorded in Hollywood—*Beautiful Love*	15.00 -	20.00
Red Robin 104 *I Couldn't Sleep A Wink Last Night*	rare	
105 *How Could You*	———	

MELLO-TONES/MELLOTONES:

Decca (EP) 2399 *Mellotones*	12.00 -	15.00
48318 *Man Loves Woman*	50.00 -	75.00
Fascination 1001 *Rosie Lee*	10.00 -	15.00
—*Cassandra*	10.00 -	15.00
Gee 1037 *Rosie Lee*	7.00 -	10.00
1037 *Rosie Lee* (78 rpm)	10.00 -	15.00
Herald 502 *Tonite, Tonite*	15.00 -	20.00
Lee Tone 700 *Prayer Of Love* (blue label)	60.00 -	90.00

MELLOW KEYS:

Gee 1014 *I'm Not A Deceiver*	7.00 -	10.00

MELLOWS:

Candelight 1011 *You're Gone*	20.00 -	30.00
Jay Dee 793 *How Sentimental Can I Be*	8.00 -	12.00
801 *I Still Care*	8.00 -	12.00
807 *Yesterday's Memories*	8.00 -	12.00

MELODAIRES:

Flyright 915 *Now You Know*	7.00 -	10.00

THE MELODEERS:

Studio 9908 *Wishing Is For Fools*	———	

MEL-O-DOTS:

Apollo 1192 *Just How Long*	100.00 -	130.00

MELO GENTS:

Warner Bros. 5056 *Baby Be Mine*	10.00 -	15.00

MELOTONES (See MELLOTONES)

RAY MELTON:

Image 1005 *Boppin' Guitar*	15.00 -	20.00

MEMORIES:

Way-Lin 101 *Love Bells*	10.00 -	15.00

"MEMORY LANE HITS BY THE ORIGINAL GROUPS"

Fire (LP) 100	15.00 -	20.00

MEMPHIS MINNIE & HER COMBO/With LITTLE JOE & HIS BAND:

Checker 771 *Me And My Chauffeur*	15.00 -	20.00
J.O.B. 1101 *Kissing In The Dark*	25.00 -	40.00

MEMPHIS SLIM & HIS/THE HOUSE ROCKERS/ORCHESTRA:

Chess (LP) 1455 *Memphis Slim*	20.00 -	30.00

Folkways (LP) 3524 *The Real Boogie Woogie*...	———	
Money 212 *My Country Gal*................	7.00 -	10.00
United 138 *Back Alley*.....................	8.00 -	12.00
156, 166, 176, 182, 186, 189, 201........	5.00 -	8.00
Vee Jay 271, 294, 330, 343...............	4.00 -	6.00
(LP) 1012 *Memphis Slim At The Gate Of Horn*	15.00 -	25.00

MERCY BABY:

Ace 528 *Rock And Roll Blues*............	7.00 -	10.00
535 *Mercy's Blues*.....................	7.00 -	10.00
Mercy Baby 501 *You Ran Away*...........	10.00 -	15.00
502 *The Rock And Stomp*...............	10.00 -	15.00
Ric 995 *Don't Lie To Me*.................	5.00 -	8.00

MERCY DEE (See DEE):

MERRILL BROTHERS:

GM 102 *Mercy Blues*....................	8.00 -	12.00

BIG MACEO MERRIWEATHER:

Fortune (LP) 3002 *Big Maceo Merriweather & John Lee Hooker*...........................	20.00 -	30.00

METALLICS:

Baronet 2 *Need Your Love*................	5.00 -	8.00
14 *Get Lost*...........................	5.00 -	8.00

METRONOMES:

Specialty 472 *She's Gone*................	10.00 -	15.00
Strand (LP) *The Metronomes Sing The Standard Hits*	20.00 -	30.00

THE METROPOLITANS:

Junior 395 *So Much In Love*.............	7.00 -	10.00

METROS:

Just 1502 *All Of My Life*...............	7.00 -	10.00

THE METROTONES:

Reserve 114 *More And More*.............	40.00 -	60.00
116 *Please Come Back*.................	40.00 -	60.00
(above black label)		

LOUIE MEYERS (& THE ACES):

Abco 104 *Blusey*......................	15.00 -	20.00

JOEY MICHAELS:

Arcade 150 *Sixteen Cats*................	20.00 -	30.00

MICKEY & SYLVIA:

Groove (EP) 18 *Love Is Strange*............	15.00 -	20.00
Rainbow 316 *Se De Boom Run Dun*........	10.00 -	15.00
Vik (LP) 1102 *New Sounds*..............	30.00 -	40.00

ELMON MICKLE (& HIS RHYTHM ACES):

Elko 003 *Flat Foot Sam*.................	30.00 -	40.00
E.M. 132 *Lonesome Highway*.............	20.00 -	30.00
EM & EP 133 *Short 'N' Fat*.............	15.00 -	20.00
J Gems 1908 *Short 'N' Fat*.............	8.00 -	12.00

GARY MIDDLETON:

Harlem 102 *Don't Be Shy*...............	15.00 -	20.00

MIDNIGHTERS: (See also HAND BALLARD((::

Federal (EP) 333 *Midnighters Sing Their Greatest Hits*...............................	15.00 -	20.00
(LP) 541 *Midnighters Sing Their Greatest Hits*..	30.00 -	40.00
12169 *Work With Me Annie*.............	8.00 -	12.00
12185 *Sexy Ways*......................	7.00 -	10.00
12195 *Annie Had A Baby*.............	7.00 -	10.00
12202, 12205, 12210, 12220, 12224, 12227, 12230, 12240, 12243, 12251, 12260, 12270, 12285, 12293, 12299, 12305, 12317, 12339......	5.00 -	8.00
King (LP) 581...*Greatest Hits, Vol. 2*........	15.00 -	25.00
Sarg 187 *Rockin' Romance*...............	7.00 -	10.00

MIDNIGHTS:

Music City 746 *Hear My Plea*.............	10.00 -	15.00
762 *Cheating On Me*.................	10.00 -	15.00

MIKE & THE UTOPIANS:

Cee Jay 574 *I Wish*....................	10.00 -	15.00

BOBBY MILANO:

Challenge 59005 *Double Talking Baby*........	10.00 -	15.00

AMOS MILBURN:

Aladdin (LP) 704 (10") *Rockin' The Boogie*.....	75.00 -	100.00
(LP) 810 *Rockin' The Boogie*........	75.00 -	100.00
3125 *Boogie Woogie*.................	10.00 -	15.00
3124 *Trouble In Mind*...............	10.00 -	15.00

3125 *Flyin' Home*......................	10.00 -	15.00
3150 *Greyhound*......................	8.00 -	12.00
3159 *Rock Rock*......................	8.00 -	12.00
3164 *Let Me Go Home Whiskey*............	8.00 -	12.00
3168, 3197, 3218, 3226, 3240, 3248, 3253, 3269, 3293, 3320, 3332, 3363, 3383, 3420........	5.00 -	8.00
Score (LP) 4012 *Let's Have A Party*..........	40.00 -	60.00

MILLER SISTERS:

Flip 504 *I Knew You Would*.............	25.00 -	35.00
Sun 230 *There's No Right Way To Do Me Wrong*	20.00 -	30.00
255 *Ten Cats Down*..................	10.00 -	15.00
504 *I Knew You Would*...............	40.00 -	60.00

BOBBY MILLER:

Band Box 332 *Little Bo Beep*.............	5.00 -	8.00

BUDDY MILLER:

VEM 2226 *Teen Twist*..................	5.00 -	8.00

CARL MILLER:

Lu 503 *Rhythm Guitar*.................	15.00 -	25.00

CHUCK MILLER:

Mercury (LP) 20195 *After Hours*............	4.00 -	7.00

CLINT MILLER:

ABC Paramount 9878 *Bertha Lou*...........	5.00 -	8.00
9938 *Teenage Dance*.................	5.00 -	8.00

DICK MILLER & SOUTHERN RAMBLERS:

M & M— *Humpty Dumpty Love*.............	———

JODY MILLER:

Capitol (LP) 2349 *Queen Of The House*........	10.00 -	15.00

ROGER MILLER:

Starday 356 *Can't Stop Lovin' You*...........	———

TAL MILLER:

Goldband 1059 *Life's Journey*................	5.00 -	8.00
Hollywood 1094, 1097..................	5.00 -	8.00

WALTER MILLER With THE BARONS:

Meteor 5037 *My Last Mile*.............	20.00 -	30.00

WARREN MILLER:

United Artists 104 *Everybody's Got A Baby But Me*	7.00 -	10.00

LOU MILLET:

Republic 7130 *Slip Slip Slippin'*..............	25.00 -	35.00

BUDDY MILTON & THE TWILIGHTERS:

RPM 419 *Oo Wah*....................	20.00 -	30.00

LITTLE MILTON (See LITTLE)

ROY MILTON:

Dooto (LP) 223 *Rock 'N' Roll Vs. Rhythm 'N' Blues*	20.00 -	30.00
Dootone 363, 369....................	4.00 -	6.00
Specialty 429, 438, 464, 480, 538, 545....	4.00 -	7.00
(copies pressed of red vinyl command higher prices)		

SAL MINEO:

Epic (LP) 3404 *Dino*...................	15.00 -	20.00

JIMMY MINOR:

Mercury 71623 *So Doggone Lonesome*........	4.00 -	7.00

MINORBOPS:

Lamp 2012 *Need You Tonight*..............	10.00 -	15.00

THE MINOR CHORDS:

Lu Pine 112 *Many A Day*..................	———

MINORS:

Celeste 3007 *Jerry*....................	5.00 -	8.00

MINT JULEPS:

Herald 481 *Bells Of Love*..............	10.00 -	15.00

MINTS:

Lin 5001 *Busy Body Rock*.............	8.00 -	12.00
5007 *Night Air*.....................	8.00 -	12.00

MIRACLES:

Baton 210 *A Lover's Chant*................	8.00 -	12.00
Cash 1008 *You're An Angel*.............	20.00 -	30.00
End 1019 *Got A Job*.................	10.00 -	15.00
1029 *I Cry*........................	8.00 -	12.00
Fury 1002/1003 *Your Love*..............	50.00 -	75.00
Motown 1/2 *Bad Girl*.................	35.00 -	50.00
Tamla (LP) 220 *Hi, We're The Miracles*........	30.00 -	40.00
(LP) 223 *Cookin' With The Miracles*....	30.00 -	40.00
(LP) 224 *Shop Around*...........	30.00 -	40.00

Tamla 54028 *The Feeling Is So Fine*	8.00 -	12.00
54034 *Shop Around*	5.00 -	8.00
54034 *Shop Around* (Master number on label and in wax reads: H-55518A2)	15.00 -	25.00
54044 *Mighty Good Lovin'*	8.00 -	12.00
(Note: Above 45s, if original issues, will have the "striped" label design.)		

BILLY MIRANDA:

Checker 957 *Run Rose*	5.00 -	8.00

MISS PEACHES:

Groove 0009 *Calling Moody Field*	7.00 -	10.00

BILLY MITCHELL:

Atlantic 974 *Bald Head Woman*	15.00 -	20.00

BOBBY MITCHELL (& THE TOPPERS):

Imperial 5250 *One Friday Morning*	35.00 -	50.00
5270 *Baby's Gone*	15.00 -	20.00
5295 *Wedding Bells Are Ringing*	40.00 -	60.00
5326 *I Wish I Knew*	10.00 -	15.00
5346 *I Cried*	10.00 -	15.00
5378, 5392	5.00 -	8.00

FREDDIE MITCHELL:

Rock & Roll 609 *Three Strikes You're Out*	8.00 -	12.00

LEE MITCHELL:

Sharp 0862 *Rootie Tootie Baby*	10.00 -	15.00

MARLON MITCHELL:

Vena 0100 *Ice Cold Baby*	15.00 -	20.00

STANLEY MITCHELL & THE TORNADOS:

Chess 1649 *Four O'Clock In The Morning*	20.00 -	30.00

TOMMIE MITCHELL:

Mercury 70930 *Little Mama*	7.00 -	10.00

WILLIE MITCHELL:

Stomper Time 1160 *Tell It To Me Baby*	10.00 -	15.00

MIXERS:

Bold 101 *You Said You're Leaving Me*	50.00 -	75.00

HANK MIZELL:

King 5236 *Jungle Rock*	25.00 -	35.00

BOBBY MIZELL & LEE WAYNE:

20th Fox 160 *Same Thing*	5.00 -	8.00

RONNIE MOLLEEN:

King 5365 *Rockin' Up*	20.00 -	30.00

MONARCHS:

Neil 101 *In My Younger Days*	7.00 -	10.00
103 *Always Be Faithful*	8.00 -	12.00
Sound Stage 2502 *This Old Heart*	4.00 -	7.00
Wing 90040 *Angels In The Sky*	8.00 -	12.00

MONDELLOS:

Rhythm 105 *One Hundred Years From Today*	35.00 -	50.00

MONIQUES:

Centaur 105 *All The Way Now*	8.00 -	12.00

MONITORS:

Aladdin 3309 *Tonight's The Night*	10.00 -	15.00
Circus 219 *A Boy Friend's Prayer*	25.00 -	40.00
Specialty 595 *Our School Days*	10.00 -	15.00
622 *Closer To Heaven*	7.00 -	10.00
636 *Mama Linda*	5.00 -	8.00

MONOGRAMS:

Saga 1000 *My Baby Dearest Darling*	7.00 -	10.00

MONORAYS:

Nasco 6020 *It's Love Baby*	7.00 -	10.00
Red Rocket 476 *My Guardian Angel*	5.00 -	8.00
Tammy 1005 *My Guardian Angel*	5.00 -	8.00

MONOTONES:

Argo 5290 *Book Of Love*	5.00 -	8.00
5290 *Book Of Love* (78 rpm)	15.00 -	20.00
5301 *Tom Foolery*	7.00 -	10.00
5321 *The Legend Of Sleepy Hollow*	7.00 -	10.00
Hull 735 *Reading The Book Of Love*	10.00 -	15.00
Mascot 124 *Book Of Love*	15.00 -	25.00

MONTCLAIRS:

Audicon 111 *Good Night*	7.00 -	10.00
Hi-Q 5001 *Golden Angel*	8.00 -	12.00

Premium 404 *My Every Dream*	30.00 -	50.00
Rage 101 *Fools Fall In Love*	25.00 -	35.00
Sonic 104 *All I Want Is Love*	60.00 -	80.00

MONTEREYS:

Arwin 130 *Goodbye My Love*	8.00 -	12.00
Dominion 1019 *First Kiss*	15.00 -	20.00
East West 121 *I'll Love You Again*	5.00 -	8.00
Impala 213 *Without A Girl*	15.00 -	20.00
Nestor 15 *Someone Like You*	————	
Onyx 513 *Dearest One*	15.00 -	20.00
Teen Age 1001 *Someone Like You*	10.00 -	15.00

JOE MONTGOMERY:

Abbott 189 *Cool Cat*	————	

LITTLE BROTHER MONTGOMERY (& HIS BOGALUSA BOYS/VICKSBURGERS):

Ebony 1000 *Cow Cow Blues*	15.00 -	20.00
1002 *Fever*	15.00 -	20.00
1005 *Pinetop's Boogie*	15.00 -	20.00
1030 *Gonna Raise A Ruckus Tonight*	15.00 -	20.00

MOODS:

Kool 1029 *Opp-Sy-Do*	5.00 -	8.00
1032 *Only The Young*	5.00 -	8.00
Sarg 162 *Little Alice*	10.00 -	15.00
176 *Easy Going*	7.00 -	10.00
179 *Let Me Have Your Love*	10.00 -	15.00
184 *Rockin' Santa Claus*	7.00 -	10.00
185 *On The Move*	7.00 -	10.00
TNT 189 *It's Goodbye And Not Goodnight*	5.00 -	8.00

MOONBEAMS:

Great 100 *A Lover's Plea*	5.00 -	8.00
Sapphire 1003 *Cryin' The Blues*	15.00 -	20.00

GLEN MOONEY:

Fraternity 898 *Go Steady With Me*	7.00 -	10.00

MOONGLOWS:

Champagne 7500 *I Just Can't Tell No Lie*	80.00 -	120.00
Chance 1150 *Just A Lonely Christmas*	90.00 -	130.00
1152 *Secret Love*	70.00 -	100.00
1156 *I Was Wrong*	70.00 -	100.00
1161 *2:19 Train* (white label)	80.00 -	120.00
Chess (LP) 1430 *Look, It's The Moonglows* (black label)	50.00 -	75.00
1581 *Sincerely*	5.00 -	80.00
1589 *Most Of All*	5.00 -	8.00
1598 *Foolish Me*	7.00 -	10.00
1605 *Starlite*	8.00 -	12.00
1611 *In My Diary*	8.00 -	12.00
1619 *We Go Together*	5.00 -	8.00
1629, 1640, 1651, 1661, 1689	4.00 -	7.00
(Chess 1581 through 1669 are "silver top" label)		
(EP) 5123 *Look It's The Moonglows*	15.00 -	20.00
Vee Jay (LP) 1052 *The Moonglows Meet The Flamingos*	15.00 -	20.00

MOONLIGHTERS:

Josie 843 *Broken Heart*	5.00 -	8.00
Tara 100 *Glow Of Love*	20.00 -	30.00
Tara 102 *Rock-A-Bayou Baby*	20.00 -	30.00

CECIL MOORE:

Sarg 150 *Walkin' Fever*	8.00 -	12.00
165 *Kathy*	8.00 -	12.00
192 *My Money's Gone*	7.00 -	10.00
206 *Diamond Back*	4.00 -	6.00

DONNY LEE MOORE:

Shelley 1000 *I'm Buggin Out Little Baby*	10.00 -	15.00

JIMMY MOORE & THE TABS:

Nobel 720 *Oops!*	10.00 -	15.00

JOHNNY MOORE; JOHNNY MOORE'S COMBO/THREE BLAZERS; JOHNNY MOORE with JIMMY HAGGETT BAND:

Aladdin 3106 *Cloudy Skies*	10.00 -	15.00
Blaze 101 *Every Time*	4.00 -	7.00
110 *Run Sinner Run*	4.00 -	7.00

Vaden 111 *Country Girl*.................... 15.00 - 20.00
Modern 1002 *Lonesome Train*.................. 7.00 - 10.00
   1012 *Diesel Drive*........................ 7.00 - 10.00
   —*Dragnet Blues*........................ ——

LATTIE MOORE:
ARC 8005 *Pretty Woman Blues*.............. ——

MERRILL MOORE:
Capitol (EP) 608 *Merrill Moore*.............. 15.00 - 20.00
   2574 *House Of Blue Lights*................. 5.00 - 8.00
   2691, 2796, 2924, 3034, 3226, 3311, 3788.... 4.00 - 7.00

RUDY MOORE:
Federal 12253 *I'm Mad With You*............ 8.00 - 12.00
   12259 *Ring-A-Ling Dong*.................. 8.00 - 12.00
   12276 *Step It Up And Go*................. 8.00 - 12.00
   12280 *Robbie Dobbie*.................... 7.00 - 10.00

SCOTTY MOORE (TRIO):
Epic (LP) 24103 *The Guitar That Changed The*
   World............................ 15.00 - 20.00
Fernwood 107 *Have Guitar Will Travel*....... 8.00 - 12.00

SPARKLE MOORE:
Fraternity 751 *Rock-A-Bop*................. 10.00 - 15.00
   766 *Tiger*.............................. 10.00 - 15.00

MOOSE JOHN:
Ultra 102 *Wrong Doin' Woman*.............. 15.00 - 20.00

RICHARD MORELAND:
Picture 6969 *Please Don't Ask Me*........... ——
   7722 *Mailman Blues*..................... ——

CHARLIE MORGAN:
Walmay 101 *South Of Chicago*.............. 10.00 - 15.00

ROCKET MORGAN:
Zynn 502 *You're Humbuggin' Me*............ 15.00 - 25.00

JACKIE MORNINGSTAR:
Sandy 1018 *Rockin' In The Graveyard*........ 10.00 - 15.00

MOROCCANS:
Salem 1014 *Believe In Tomorrow*............ 50.00 - 70.00

MOROCCOS:
United 188 *Pardon My Tears*................ 20.00 - 30.00
   193 *Somewhere Over The Rainbow*........ 20.00 - 30.00
   204 *What Is A Teenager's Prayer*......... 25.00 - 35.00
   207 *Sad Sad Hours*..................... 20.00 - 30.00

TINY MORRIE:
Hurricane 6966 *Bernardine*................. ——

BOB MORRIS:
Cascade 5907 *Party Time*.................. 7.00 - 10.00

ELMORE MORRIS:
Peacock 1660, 1668........................ 4.00 - 7.00

GENE MORRIS:
Edmoral 1012 *Lovin' Honey*................ 20.00 - 30.00
Vik 0287 *Lovin' Honey*.................... 10.00 - 15.00
Winston 1046 *If You Need My Love*......... 15.00 - 20.00

LEO MORRIS:
Ivory 41465 *I Don't Need You*.............. 5.00 - 8.00

ROD MORRIS:
Ludwig 1002 *Ghost Of Casey Jones*.......... 7.00 - 10.00

BILL MORRISON:
TNT 9029 *Set Me Free*.................... 20.00 - 30.00
   9031 *Baby Be Good*..................... 20.00 - 30.00

ELLA MAE MORSE:
Capitol (LP) 513 *Barrelhouse, Boogie & Blues*... 20.00 - 30.00

ROY MOSS:
Fascination 1002 *Wiggle Walking Baby*....... 15.00 - 20.00
Mercury 70770 *You Nearly Lose Your Mind*... 20.00 - 30.00
   70858 *You Don't Know My Mind*......... 15.00 - 25.00

"MOUNTAIN FROLIC":
Brunswick (LP) 5900 (10") (various artists)...... 15.00 - 25.00

JUNE MOY (& THE FEATHERS:)
Showtime 1103 *Castle Of Dreams*............ 60.00 - 90.00

MUDDY WATERS:
Chess (LP) 1427 *The Best Of Muddy Waters*.... 40.00 - 60.00
(Note: Above LP has black label.)
Chess 1509 *Country Boy*................... 15.00 - 20.00

1514 *Please Have Mercy*.................. 15.00 - 20.00
1526 *Gone To Main Street*................ 15.00 - 20.00
1537 *Sad, Sad Day*...................... 15.00 - 20.00
1542 *Turn The Lamp Down Low*........... 15.00 - 20.00
1550 *Blow Wind Blow*.................... 10.00 - 15.00
1560 *She's So Pretty*..................... 10.00 - 15.00
1571 *Oh Yeah*.......................... 10.00 - 15.00
1579 *I'm Ready*......................... 10.00 - 15.00
1585 *Loving Man*........................ 10.00 - 15.00
1596 *I Want To Be Loved*................. 10.00 - 15.00
1602 *Young Fashioned Ways*............... 10.00 - 15.00
1612 *Sugar Sweet*....................... 10.00 - 15.00
1620 *All Aboard*......................... 8.00 - 12.00
1630 *Diamonds At Your Feet*.............. 8.00 - 12.00
1644, 1652, 1667, 1680, 1692, 1704, 1718, 1733,
   1739, 1748, 1758, 1765, 1774, 1796, 1819, 1827,
   1839, 1862............................. 5.00 - 10.00

MOON MULLICAN:
Coral (LP) 57235 *Moon Over Mullican*........ 80.00 - 120.00
   61994 *Jenny Lee*........................ 15.00 - 20.00
   62042 *Sweet Rockin' Music*............... 15.00 - 20.00
Dixie—*Good Times Gonna Roll Again*........ ——
King (LP) 555 *Moon Mullican Sings His All Time*
   Greatest Hits........................ 35.00 - 50.00
   (LP) 628 *16 Favorite Tunes*............... 20.00 - 30.00
   917 *I Was Sorta Wonderin'*............... 5.00 - 8.00
   947 *Without A Port Of Love*.............. 5.00 - 8.00
   965 *Cherokee Boogie*................... 8.00 - 12.00
   984 *Heartless Lover*.................... 5.00 - 8.00
   1043 *Shoot The Moon*................... 5.00 - 8.00
   1060 *Triflin' Woman Blues*............... 7.00 - 10.00
   1152 *A Thousand And One Sleepless Nights*.. 7.00 - 10.00
   1164 *Oogle, Oogle, Olglie*............... 7.00 - 10.00
   1198 *Rocket To The Moon*................ 7.00 - 10.00
   1244 *Grandpa Stole My Baby*............. 7.00 - 10.00
   1337 *Good Deal, Lucille*................. 7.00 - 10.00
   1366 *No Stranger*...................... 4.00 - 8.00
   1408 *You Got The Best Of Me*............ 4.00 - 8.00
   1467, 4894, 4915, 4979.................. 4.00 - 7.00

DEE MULLIN:
D 1066 *I've Really Got A Right To Cry*....... 7.00 - 10.00

GENE MUMFORD & THE SERENADERS:
Whiz— *Please Give Me One More Chance*..... 20.00 - 30.00

CHUCK MURPHY:
Columbia 21305 *Rhythm Hall*.............. 10.00 - 15.00

DON MURPHY:
Cosmopolitan 2264 *Mean Mama Blues*........ 10.00 - 15.00

JIMMY MURPHY:
Columbia 21486 *Here Kitty Kitty*............ 20.00 - 30.00
   21534 *Sixteen Tons Rock & Roll*.......... 20.00 - 30.00
   21569 *Baboon Boogie*.................. 25.00 - 35.00
Rev 3508 *I'm Gone Mama*................. 15.00 - 20.00

MUSKATEERS:
Swingtime 331 *Deep In My Heart*............ ——

MUSKETEERS:
Roxy 801 *Goodbye My Love*............... 50.00 - 75.00

SAMMY MYERS:
Ace 536 *Sleeping In The Ground*............ 5.00 - 8.00
Fury 1035 *Sad, Sad Lonesome Day*.......... 5.00 - 8.00

BIG BOY MYLES (& THE SHA-WEES):
Specialty 564 *That Girl I Married*........... 10.00 - 15.00
   590 *Hickory Dickory Dock*.............. 10.00 - 15.00

BILLY MYLES:
Ember 1026 *The Joker*.................... 4.00 - 7.00
   1026 *The Joker* (78 rpm).................. 15.00 - 20.00

THE MYSTICS:
Laurie 3038, 3047, 3104................... 4.00 - 7.00

CLIFF NASH:
Kim 1048 *This Little Boy's Gone Lookin'*...... 5.00 - 8.00

NATIVE BOYS:
Combo 113 *Strange Love*.................. 7.00 - 10.00

115 *Tears*	8.00 -	12.00
119 *Laughing Love*	15.00 -	20.00

JERRY NEAL:
Dot 15810 *I Hates Rabbits*	20.00 -	30.00

MEREDITH NEAL:
Blaze 101 *Gertrude*	20.00 -	30.00

FRED NEIL:
Look 1002 *Don't Put The Blame On Me*	7.00 -	10.00

FREDDY NEIL & FRIEND:
Brunswick 55177 *Listen Kitten*	8.00 -	12.00

JIMMY NELSON:
RPM 397 *Mean Poor Girl*	15.00 -	20.00

RICKY NELSON:
Imperial (EP) 153, 154, 155 *Ricky Nelson*	8.00 -	12.00
(EP) 156, 158, 159, 160, 161, 161, 162, 164	8.00 -	12.00
5463 *Be Bop Baby* (78 rpm)	15.00 -	20.00
5483 *Stood Up* (78 rpm)	15.00 -	20.00
5503 *Believe What You Say* (78 rpm)	15.00 -	25.00
5528 *Poor Little Fool* (78 rpm)	15.00 -	25.00
5545 *Lonesome Town* (78 rpm)	15.00 -	25.00
5565 *It's Late* (78 rpm)	15.00 -	25.00
(LP) 9048 *Ricky*	15.00 -	20.00
(LP) 9050 *Ricky Nelson*	15.00 -	20.00
(LP) 9059 *More Songs By Ricky*	12.00 -	16.00
(LP) 9061 *Ricky Sings Again*	12.00 -	16.00
(LP) 9082 *Songs By Ricky*	12.00 -	16.00
Verve (LP) 2083 *Teen Time*	35.00 -	50.00
10047 *Teenager's Romance* (78 rpm)	15.00 -	20.00
10070 *You're My One And Only Love* (78 rpm)	15.00 -	20.00

TOMMY NELSON:
Dixie 2014 *Hobo Bop*	15.00 -	20.00

WILLIE NELSON:
Bellair 107 *Night Life* (red plastic)	10.00 -	15.00
Betty 5702 *Misery Mansion* (red plastic)	8.00 -	12.00
5703 *Man With The Blues*	5.00 -	8.00

NEONS:
Tetra 4449 *Road To Romance*	7.00 -	10.00
—*Angel Face*	7.00 -	10.00

NERVOUS NORVUS:
Dot 15470 *Transfusion*	4.00 -	7.00
15485 *Ape Call*	5.00 -	8.00
15500 *The Fang*	7.00 -	10.00
Embee 177 *I Like Girls*	7.00 -	10.00

BILL NETTLES:
Starday 174 *Wine-O-Boogie*	10.00 -	15.00

JOE NETTLES & THE SATELLITES:
Circle 1174 *Oh Baby*	7.00 -	10.00

AARON NEVILLE:
Minit 618 *Show Me The Way*	7.00 -	10.00

CARL NEWMAN & HIS NIGHT HAWKS:
Trio 849 *Rockin' And A Boppin'*	————

JIMMY NEWMAN:
Dot 15766 *Carry On*	7.00 -	10.00

NEWPORT RHYTHMAIRES:
Newport 101 *Mornin' Blues*	7.00 -	10.00

THE NEWPORTS:
Kane 008 *If I Could Tonight*	5.00 -	8.00
Kent 380 *The Wonder Of Love*	5.00 -	8.00

NEW YORKERS (FIVE):
Danice 801 *Gloria My Darling*	20.00 -	30.00
Wall 547 *Dream A Little Dream*	8.00 -	12.00

BETTY NICKELL & THE ROCKETS:
Abbey 102 *Hot Dog*	————

ROCKY NIGHT WITH HIS NIGHT CATS:
Pearl 708 *Teen Age Bop*	15.00 -	20.00

NIGHT CAPS:
Vandan (LP) 8124 *Wine, Wine, Wine*	15.00 -	25.00

(Note: Original pressings of the above LP are quite scarce, but a reissue has been extensively distributed.)

ROBERT NIGHTHAWK & THE NIGHTHAWKS BAND:
States 131 *Maggie Campbell*	25.00 -	35.00

NIGHT OWLS:
Bethlehem 3087 *Bells Ring*	5.00 -	8.00
Cuca 1075 *Waitin' By The School*	10.00 -	15.00
NRC 015 *You Shouldn't Oughta Done It*	5.00 -	8.00

NIGHT RAIDERS (See MICKEY HAWKS)

NIPTONES:
Lorraine 1001 *Angie*	5.00 -	8.00

NITECAPS:
Groove 0134 *A Kiss And A Vow*	8.00 -	12.00
0147 *Sweet Thing*	10.00 -	15.00
0158 *You May Not Know*	10.00 -	15.00
0176 *In Each Corner Of My Heart*	10.00 -	15.00

NITE RIDERS:
Apollo 460 *Women And Cadillacs*	10.00 -	15.00
466 *Doctor Velvet*	10.00 -	15.00
MGM 12487 *Sittin' Sippin' Coffee*	5.00 -	8.00

FORD NIX & THE MOONSHINERS:
Clix 813 *Nine Times Out Of Ten*	————

HOYLE NIX:
Bo-Kay 110 *I Don't Lov-A Nobody*	5.00 -	8.00

WILLIE NIX:
Chance 1163 *Nervous Wreck*	30.00 -	40.00
Checker 756 *Truckin' Little Woman*	20.00 -	30.00
Sabre 104 *All By Myself*	35.00 -	50.00
Sun 179 *Baker Shop Boogie*	90.00 -	120.00

ELMORE NIXON:
Imperial 5388 *You Left Me*	8.00 -	12.00
Post 2008 *Don't Do It*	10.00 -	15.00

EDDIE NOACK:
D 1019 *Have Blues—Will Travel*	8.00 -	12.00
1037 *Walk 'Em Off*	8.00 -	12.00
1060 *A Thinking Man's Woman*	8.00 -	12.00
TNT 110 *Too Hot To Handle*	8.00 -	12.00

NOBELLS:
Mar 101 *Crying Over You*	8.00 -	12.00

EDDIE NOBLE:
Suite 16 *111 Mean Old Blues*	10.00 -	15.00

NOBLES:
Klik 305 *Poor Rock And Roll*	15.00 -	20.00
Sapphire 151 *Do You Love Me*	15.00 -	20.00

NOBLETONES:
C & M 182 *I Love You*	7.00 -	10.00
438 *I'm Crying*	7.00 -	10.00

SID NOEL:
Aladdin 3331 *Flying Saucer*	7.00 -	10.00

TERRY NOLAND:
Apt 25065 *Long Gone Baby*	5.00 -	8.00
Brunswick (LP) 54041 *Terry Noland*	50.00 -	75.00
55010 *Hypnotized*	4.00 -	7.00
55036 *Patty Baby*	5.00 -	8.00
55054 *Oh Baby Look At Me*	5.00 -	8.00
55069 *Crazy Dreams*	5.00 -	8.00
55092 *There Was A Fungus Among Us*	7.00 -	8.00
55122 *Guess I'm Gonna Fall*	7.00 -	10.00

LARRY NOLEN & HIS BANDITS:
Starday 668 *King Of The Ducktail Cats*	7.00 -	10.00

GENE NORMAN (& THE ROCKETS):
Snag 101 *Snaggle Tooth Ann*	10.00 -	15.00
Soma 1156 *No Help Wanted*	10.00 -	15.00

BOBBY NORRIS:
Capitol 5945 *I Went Rockin'*	————

CHUCK NORRIS:
Atlantic 994 *Let Me Know*	7.00 -	10.00

NOTATIONS:
Wonder 100 *What A Night For Love*	————

NOTE MAKERS:
Sotoplay 007 *It Hurts To Wonder*	25.00 -	40.00

NOTES:
Capitol 3332 *Don't Leave Me Now*	10.00 -	15.00
MGM 12338 *Trust In Me*	25.00 -	35.00
Sarg 117 *Little Girl*	5.00 -	8.00

NOTE TORIALS:
Impala— *My Valerie* .... ————
Sunbeam 119 *My Valerie* .... ————
ERNIE NOWLIN:
Missouri 640 *Tally Ho* .... 7.00 - 10.00
BOBBY NUNN & LITTLE ESTHER:
Federal 12100 *Mainliner* .... 15.00 - 20.00
NUTMEGS:
Herald 452 *Story Untold* .... 5.00 - 8.00
  459 *Ship Of Love* .... 7.00 - 10.00
  466 *Whispering Sorrows* .... 5.00 - 8.00
  475 *Key To The Kingdom* .... 10.00 - 15.00
  492 *A Love So True* .... 10.00 - 15.00
  538 *My Story* .... 8.00 - 12.00
Tel 1014 *A Dream Of Love* .... 7.00 - 10.00
NU-TONES/NUTONES:
Baton 260 *Remember The Night* .... 15.00 - 20.00
Hollywood Star 798 *Believe* .... 80.00 - 120.00
—*Goddess Of Love* .... 80.00 - 120.00
NU-TRENDS:
Lawn 216 *Together* .... ————
BOB OAKES & THE SULTANS:
Regent 7502 *You Gotta Rock And Roll* ...... 7.00 - 10.00
OCAPELLOS:
General 107 *The Stars* .... 15.00 - 20.00
OCTAVES:
Val 1001 *Mambo Carolyn* .... 5.00 - 8.00
DOYLE O'DELL & THE CASS COUNTY BOYS:
Era (LP) 20004 .... 15.00 - 20.00
LILLIAN OFFITT:
Chief 7012 *The Man Won't Work* ...... 8.00 - 12.00
  7015 *Oh Mama* .... 4.00 - 7.00
  7029 *Shine On* .... 4.00 - 7.00
Excello 2104, 2124, 2139 .... 3.00 - 5.00
LOUIS OGLETREE:
Parrot 822 *Tell It Like It Is* ...... 10.00 - 15.00
JOHNNY OLENN (& THE JOKERS):
Glenco 7001 *Sally Let Your Bangs Hang* ...... 5.00 - 8.00
Liberty (LP) 3029 *Just Rollin' With Johnny Olenn* ...... 50.00 - 75.00
TNT 1016 *Sally Let Your Bangs Hang Down* ... 10.00 - 15.00
  1018 *I Ain't Gonna Cry No More* ...... 10.00 - 15.00
OLE SONNY BOY:
Excello 2086 *Blues And Misery* ...... 15.00 - 20.00
BOBBY OLIVER:
Lucky Four 1004 *Where Do Dreams Go* ...... 4.00 - 7.00
  1006 *Lucille* .... 5.00 - 8.00
BIG DANNY OLIVER:
Trend 30-012 *Sapphire* .... 5.00 - 8.00
  30-016 *Blues For The 49* .... 4.00 - 7.00
ROCKY OLSON:
Chess 1723 *Kansas City* .... 4.00 - 7.00
OLYMPICS:
Arvee (LP) 423 *Doin' The Hully Gully* ...... 15.00 - 25.00
  (LP) 424 *Dance By The Light Of The Moon* .. 25.00 - 35.00
  (LP) 429 *Party Time* .... 20.00 - 30.00
Demon 1508 *Western Movies* (78 rpm) .... 25.00 - 35.00
SLIM O'MARY:
Mar-Vel 20 *Row, Boy, Sink Or Swim* ...... ————
ONTARIOS:
Big Town 121 *Memories Of You* .... 15.00 - 20.00
OPALS:
Apollo 462 *My Heart's Desire* .... 10.00 - 15.00
"OPRY STARS—JAMBOREE":
Mercury (LP) 20350 (various artists) ...... 10.00 - 15.00
ROY ORBISON (& THE TEEN KINGS & THE ROSES):
Monument (LP) 4002, 14002 *Lonely And Blue* .. 15.00 - 20.00
  (LP) 4007, 14007 *Crying* .... 15.00 - 20.00
RCA Victor 7381 *Sweet And Innocent* ...... 8.00 - 12.00
  7447 *Almost Eighteen* .... 8.00 - 12.00

Sun 242 *Ooby Dooby* .... 10.00 - 15.00
  251 *Rock House* .... 7.00 - 10.00
  265 *Devil Doll* .... 7.00 - 10.00
  284 *Chicken Hearted* .... 7.00 - 10.00
ORBITS:
Argo 5286 *Who Are You* .... 5.00 - 8.00
Flair-X 5000 *Message Of Love* .... 5.00 - 8.00
ORCHIDS:
King 4661 *Oh Why* .... 15.00 - 20.00
  4663 *Beginning To Miss You* ..... 15.00 - 20.00
Parrot 815 *You're Everything To Me* ...... 25.00 - 40.00
  819 *You Said You Loved Me* ...... 25.00 - 40.00
ORIGINAL CASUALS:
Back Beat (EP) 40 *Three Kisses Past Midnight* .. 10.00 - 15.00
  503 *So Tough* .... 5.00 - 8.00
  510 *Don't Pass Me By* .... 7.00 - 10.00
  514 *Three Kisses Past Midnight* ...... 7.00 - 10.00
THE ORIGINAL DELL-VIKINGS (See DEL-VIKINGS)
THE ORIGINALS (featuring TONY ALLEN):
Diamond 116 *You And I* .... 5.00 - 8.00
Original Sound 10 *Wishing Star* ..... 5.00 - 8.00
ORIOLES:
Abner 1016 *Sugar Girl* .... 20.00 - 30.00
Jubilee 5008 *I Challenge Your Kiss* ...... ————
(Above may not exist as 45 RPM)
  5016 *Forgive And Forget* .... 80.00 - 120.00
  5017 *What Are You Doing New Years Eve* .. 80.00 - 110.00
  5025 *At Night* .... 80.00 - 110.00
  5026 *Moonlight* .... 90.00 - 120.00
  5031 *I'd Rather Have You Under The Moon* . 90.00 - 120.00
  5040 *I Crossed My Fingers* ...... 90.00 - 120.00
  5045 *Oh Holy Night* .... 35.00 - 50.00
  5051 *I Miss You So* .... 60.00 - 80.00
  5061 *I'm Just A Fool In Love* ... 40.00 - 60.00
  5065 *Baby Please Don't Go* ...... 60.00 - 90.00
  5071 *When You're Not Around* .... 50.00 - 70.00
  5076 *Proud Of You* .... 80.00 - 110.00
  5084 *Gettin' Tired Tired Tired* . 35.00 - 50.00
  5092 *Don't Cry Baby* .... 60.00 - 80.00
  5102 *You Belong To Me* .... 50.00 - 70.00
  5107 *Till Then* (red plastic) ... 50.00 - 70.00
  5108 *Hold Me, Thrill Me, Kiss Me* (red plastic) .. 50.00 - 70.00
  5115 *Bad Little Girl* .... 25.00 - 35.00
  5120 *I Cover The Waterfront* (red plastic) .. 50.00 - 75.00
  5122 *Crying In The Chapel* ...... 5.00 - 8.00
  5127 *Write And Tell Me Why* ..... 8.00 - 12.00
  5134 *There's No One But You* .... 8.00 - 12.00
  5137 *Secret Love* .... 10.00 - 15.00
  5143 *Maybe You'll Be There* ..... 10.00 - 15.00
  5154 *In the Chapel In The Moonlight* ...... 8.00 - 12.00
  5161 *If You Believe* .... 8.00 - 12.00
  5172 *Runaround* .... 10.00 - 15.00
  5177 *I Love You Mostly* .... 8.00 - 12.00
  5189 *I Need You Baby* .... 10.00 - 15.00
  5221 *Moody Over You* .... 8.00 - 12.00
  5363 *Tell Me So* .... 7.00 - 10.00
Vee Jay 196 *Happy Till The Letter* .. 7.00 - 10.00
  228 *For All We Know* .... 5.00 - 8.00
  244 *Sugar Girl* .... 5.00 - 8.00
ORLANDOS:
Cindy 3006 *Cloudburst* .... 8.00 - 12.00
TONY ORLANDO & THE MILOS:
Milo 101 *Ding Dong* .... 10.00 - 15.00
J.D. ORR & THE LONESOME VALLEY BOYS:
Summit 105 *Hula Hoop Boogie* .... 50.00 - 80.00
DAVID ORRELL:
Felsted 8515 *You're The One* .... ————
THE OSBORNE BROTHERS & RED ALLEN:
MGM (LP) 3734 .... 12.00 - 18.00

MILT OSHINS:
Pelvis 169 *All About Elvis*................... 7.00 - 10.00
THE OSPREYS:
East West 110 *It's Good To Me*............ 5.00 - 8.00
JOHNNY OTIS:
Capitol (LP) 940 *The Johnny Otis Show*....... 35.00 - 50.00
   (EP) 1134 *Johnny Otis*................. 10.00 - 15.00
Dig (LP) 104 *Rock & Roll Hit Parade*........ 50.00 - 75.00
Peacock 1625, 1636.................... 5.00 - 8.00
"OUR BEST TO YOU":
Everlast (LP) 201 *(various artists)*............ 25.00 - 35.00
DANNY OVERBEA:
Apex 7751 *Stop*.................... 4.00 - 7.00
Checker 768 *Train, Train, Train*....... 15.00 - 20.00
   774 *40 Cups Of Coffee*................. 10.00 - 15.00
   796 *You're Mine*.................. 10.00 - 15.00
   808 *A Toast To Lovers*................. 7.00 - 10.00
   816 *Do You Love Me*................. 7.00 - 10.00
Federal 12324 *Candy Bar*................. 7.00 - 10.00
KENNY OWEN:
Poplar 106 *I Got The Bug*............ 7.00 - 10.00
BUCK OWENS: (See also CORKY JONES)
Newstar 6418 *Hot Dog*................. 25.00 - 35.00
Pep 105, 106, 109................. 5.00 - 8.00
PACERS:
Calico 101 *I Found A Dream*........... 5.00 - 8.00
Guyden 1064 *How Sweet*.................. ————
PACKARDS:
Paradise 105 *Dream Of Love*............ 20.00 - 30.00
Pla Bac 106 *Ladies*.................. 75.00 - 100.00
ALLEN PAGE & THE DELTONES:
Moon 301 *Honeysuckle*.................. 7.00 - 10.00
   302 *Dateless Night*................... 10.00 - 15.00
   303 *She's The One That Got It*........ 7.00 - 10.00
PAGEANTS:
Arlen 731 *Saturday Romance*............... 5.00 - 8.00
Du-Well 101 *Saturday Romance*............ 8.00 - 12.00
Goldisc 3013 *Happy Together*.......... 8.00 - 12.00
HAL PAIGE (& THE WAILERS):
Atlantic 1032 *Big Foot Mae*............ 10.00 - 15.00
Fury 1024 *After Hours Blues*.......... 8.00 - 12.00
J & S 1601 *Thunder Bird*.............. 10.00 - 15.00
"PAJAMA PARTY":
Roulette (LP) 20521 *(various artists)*....... 15.00 - 25.00
THE PALISADES:
Calico 113 *Close Your Eyes*............ 5.00 - 8.00
Debra 1003 *Chapel Bells*............... 5.00 - 8.00
TOMMY PALM:
Bob 101 *Stroll With Me Baby*.............. 7.00 - 10.00
CLARENCE PALMER & THE JIVE BOMBERS
   (See THE JIVE BOMBERS)
PALMS:
States 157 *Darling Patricia*.................. 15.00 - 20.00
PALS:
Guyden 2019 *My Baby Likes To Rock*....... 5.00 - 8.00
Turf 1000 *Summer Is Here*.............. 15.00 - 20.00
PAPA LIGHTFOOT (See LIGHTFOOT)
THE PARADONS:
Milestone 2003 *Diamonds and Pearls*.......... 3.00 - 5.00
Warner Bros. 5186 *Take All Of Me*.......... 4.00 - 7.00
PARAGONS:
Musicnotes (LP) 8001 *The Paragons Vs. The*
   Harptones.................... 15.00 - 20.00
Winley 215 *Florence*...................... 5.00 - 8.00
   220 *Let's Start All Over Again*........... 5.00 - 8.00
   223 *Two Hearts Are Better Than One*....... 7.00 - 10.00
   227 *Vows Of Love*................. 7.00 - 10.00
   240 *So You Will Know*............. 7.00 - 10.00
   250 *Kneel And Pray*............... 7.00 - 10.00
PARAKEETS:
Atlas 1071 *Teenage Rose*................ 10.00 - 15.00
Jubilee 5407 *Shangri-La*.................. 5.00 - 8.00

KENNY PARCHMAN:
Jaxon— *Don't You Know*............ 20.00 - 30.00
Lu— *Get It Off Your Mind*................ 15.00 - 25.00
PARIS BROTHERS:
Brunswick 55132 *This Is It*............... 5.00 - 8.00
Coral 62220 *Funny Feeling*.................. 4.00 - 6.00
(LITTLE) JUNIOR PARKER & HIS
   BAND/BLUE FLAMES/ORCHESTRA:
Duke (LP) 76 *Driving Wheel*............ 15.00 - 20.00
   120 *Dirty Friend Blues*.............. 7.00 - 10.00
   127 *Please Baby Blues*............. 7.00 - 10.00
   137, 147, 157, 164, 168, 177, 184, 193, 301, 324   4.00 - 7.00
   (See also LITTLE JUNIOR'S BLUE FLAMES)
TIM PARKER:
Emmons 1005 *That's Alright Mama*.......... ——
RAY PARKS & THE CANUCKS: (See THE
   CANUCKS with RAY PARKS)
FRED PARRIS & THE SATINS (See THE FIVE
   SATINS)
KENT PARRY & THE ROGUES:
Alton 600 *Stop Then Rock*.................. 8.00 - 12.00
DEAN PARRISH:
Warner Bros. 5436 *Come On Down*.......... 4.00 - 7.00
PARROTS:
Checker 772 *Please Don't Leave Me*.......... 90.00 - 120.00
AL PARSONS:
— *Wait For Me Baby/Memories Of Yesterday*.. ——
BILL PARSONS:
Starday 526 *Hot Red Volkswagen*............ 5.00 - 8.00
"PARTY AFTER HOURS"
Aladdin (LP) 705 (10") *(various artists)*........ 75.00 - 100.00
PASSIONS:
Audicon 102, 105, 106, 108, 112.......... 4.00 - 8.00
Capitol 3963 *My Aching Heart*............... 5.00 - 8.00
Diamond 146 *Sixteen Candles*............. 7.00 - 10.00
Octavia 8005 *I've Gotta Know*.............. 8.00 - 12.00
PASTELS:
United 196 *Put Your Arms Around Me*........ 15.00 - 20.00
PAT AND DEE:
Dixie 2006 *Gee Whiz*.................. 15.00 - 25.00
PRINCE PATRIDGE:
Big Moment 103/104 *Next Door Neighbors*..... 5.00 - 8.00
Crest 1006, 1022, 1009.............. 4.00 - 7.00
FRANK PATT & ORCHESTRA:
Flash 117 *Gonna Hold On*................. 5.00 - 8.00
JIMMY PATTON (with ANN JONES):
Moon (LP) 101 *Make Room For The Blues*..... 30.00 - 40.00
Sage 241 *Yah—I'm Movin' On*............ 20.00 - 30.00
Sims 103 *Guilty*.................. 5.00 - 8.00
   104 *Teen-Age Heart*.................... 10.00 - 15.00
   117 *Okie's In The Pokie*............... 25.00 - 40.00
   (LP) 127 *Blue Darlin'*................. 20.00 - 30.00
PAT PATTON:
King 4942 *Flip Kitten*................ ——
JERRY PAUL:
Holiday 1001 *Step Out*.................. 10.00 - 15.00
DUSTY PAYNE (& HIS RHYTHM ROCKERS):
Bakersfield 119 *Long Time Gone*............ 8.00 - 12.00
Fire 111 *I Want You*.................. 5.00 - 8.00
HAL PAYNE:
Starday— *Honky Tonk Stomp*............. 10.00 - 15.00
TOMMY PAYNE:
Felsted 8531 *I Go Ape*................ 7.00 - 10.00
XYZ 601 *Fire Engine Red Bandanna*......... 5.00 - 8.00
   603 *Cruisin' Around*................... 5.00 - 8.00
PEACHEROOS:
Excello 2044 *Be-Bop Baby*................. ——
PEACOCKS:
Nobel 711 *I Want You To Know*............ 40.00 - 60.00
PEAR DEVINES:
Alco— *So Lonely*.................. 20.00 - 30.00

PEARLS:

Atco 6057 *Shadow Of Love*	7.00 -	10.00
6066 *Bells Of Love*	9.00 -	12.00
On The Square 320 *Band Of Angels*	——	
Onyx 503 *Let's You And I Go Steady*	8.00 -	12.00
506 *Tree In The Meadow*	15.00 -	20.00
510 *Your Cheatin' Heart*	7.00 -	10.00
511 *Ice Cream Baby*	10.00 -	15.00
516 *The Wheel Of Love*	8.00 -	12.00

JIMMY PEARSON:

Dixie— *Nobody Cares/I'm Not Sure*	——	

RONNIE PEARSON:

500 *Hot Shot*	10.00 -	15.00
514 *She Bops A Lot*	10.00 -	15.00
516 *Flippin' Over You*	10.00 -	15.00

PAUL PEEK:

NRC 002 *Sweet Skinny Jenny*	5.00 -	8.00
008 *Olds-Mo-William*	5.00 -	8.00

CARROLL (WILD RED) PEGUES:

GM Record Co. 109 *Rhythm Feet*	10.00 -	15.00

DANNY PEIL & THE APOLLOS:

Raynard 602 *Jungle Jump*	5.00 -	8.00

MORRIS PEJOE:

Abco 106 *Maybe Blues*	15.00 -	20.00
Atomic H410/411 *You Gone Away*	10.00 -	15.00
Checker 766 *Gonna Buy Me A Telephone*	12.00 -	18.00
781 *Can't Get Along*	9.00 -	12.00
Vee Jay 148 *You Gonna Need Me*	8.00 -	12.00

PELICANS:

Class 209 *I Bow To You*	80.00 -	100.00
Imperial 5307 *Chimes*	80.00 -	100.00
Parrot 793 *Aurelia* (red plastic)	150.00 -	200.00

TRACY PENDARVIS:

Des Cant 1234 *First Love*	7.00 -	10.00
Scott 1202 *It Don't Pay*	7.00 -	10.00
1203 *All You Gotta Do*	7.00 -	10.00

PENGUINS:

Dooto (EP) 201 *The Penguins*	10.00 -	15.00
(EP) 241, 243, 244 *Cool Cool Penguins*	10.00 -	15.00
Dooto (LP) 242 *Cool Cool Penguins*	25.00 -	35.00
428 *That's How Much I Need You*	8.00 -	12.00
432 *Sweet Love*	8.00 -	12.00
435 *Do Not Pretend*	8.00 -	12.00
451 *To Keep Our Love*	8.00 -	12.00
345 *When I Am Gone*	8.00 -	12.00
348 *Earth Angel*	7.00 -	10.00
353 *Ookey Oook*	8.00 -	12.00
362 *Kiss A Fool Goodbye*	8.00 -	12.00
Mercury 70610 *Be Mine Or Be A Fool*	7.00 -	10.00
70654 *It Only Happens With You*	7.00 -	10.00
70703 *Devil That I See*	7.00 -	10.00
70762 *A Christmas Prayer*	10.00 -	15.00
70799 *My Troubles Are Not At An End*	7.00 -	10.00
70943 *Earth Angel*	10.00 -	15.00
71033 *Will You Be Mine*	10.00 -	15.00
Wing 90076 *Peace of Mind*	8.00 -	12.00

WILLIAM PENIX:

Daffan 116 *Dig That Crazy Driver*	15.00 -	20.00

LITTLE LAMBSIE PENN:

Atco 6082 *I Wanna Spend Christmas With Elvis*	7.00 -	10.00

TONY PENN:

P.R.I. 101 *Shake Rattle And Roll*	10.00 -	15.00

DICK PENNER:

Sun 282 *Cindy Lou*	5.00 -	8.00

RAY PENNINGTON:

Lee 502 *Boogie Woogie Country Girl*	15.00 -	25.00

HANK PENNY:

Decca 29926 *Rock Of Gibraltar*	4.00 -	7.00

JOE PENNY:

Federal 12322 *Bip A Little, Bop A Lot*	15.00 -	20.00
Sims 173 *Hatty Fatty*	7.00 -	10.00

CURLEY PENROD:

QQ 703 *There's A Leak*	8.00 -	12.00

THE PEPPERS:

Chess 1577 *Rocking Chair Baby*	8.00 -	12.00

THE PEREZ BROTHERS:

Wolfie 103 *Dream A Little Dream*	8.00 -	12.00

THE PERFORMERS:

Tip Top 402 *Give Me Your Heart*	5.00 -	10.00

CARL PERKINS:

Columbia (LP) 1234 *Whole Lotta Shakin'*	40.00 -	60.00
(EP) 12341 *Whole Lotta Shakin'*	15.00 -	20.00
41131 *Pink Pedal Pushers*	5.00 -	8.00
41207 *Levi Jacket*	5.00 -	8.00
41379 *Pointed Toe Shoes*	5.00 -	8.00
Flip 501 *Movie Magg*	75.00 -	100.00
Sun (DP) 115 *Dance Album*	20.00 -	30.00
224 *Gone, Gone, Gone*	15.00 -	20.00
234 *Blue Suede Shoes* (78 rpm)	5.00 -	8.00
235 *Tennessee/Sure To Fall*	Rare	

(Note: This record may not have been issued.)

243 *Boppin' The Blues*	5.00 -	8.00
249, 261, 274, 287	4.00 -	6.00

(Note: 78 RPM issues of above four records command somewhat higher premiums.)

JESSE PERKINS & THE BAD BOYS:

Savoy 1584 *Madly In Love*	5.00 -	8.00

LAURA LEE PERKINS:

Imperial 5493 *Kiss Me Baby*	10.00 -	15.00
5507 *Don't Wait Up*	10.00 -	15.00

REGGIE PERKINS:

Gem 1201 *Saturday Night Party*	10.00 -	15.00
Ray Note 9 *Date Bait Baby*	10.00 -	15.00

ROY PERKINS:

Meladee 111 *Bye Bye Baby*	10.00 -	15.00
Mercury 71278 *Drop Top*	4.00 -	7.00
Ram— *Drop Top*	4.00 -	7.00

IKE PERRY & THE LYRICS:

Courier 3614 *Don't Let It Get You Down*	5.00 -	8.00

PAUL PERRY:

—— *Got A Gal Named Dee*	5.00 -	8.00

THE PERSIANS:

Gold Eagle 1813 *Gee What A Girl*	3.00 -	6.00
Goldisc 1 *Vault Of Memories*	4.00 -	7.00
RSVP 111 *Tears Of Love*	4.00 -	7.00

PERSONALITIES:

Safari 1002 *Woe Woe Baby*	8.00 -	12.00

PETE & JIMMY & THE RHYTHM KNIGHTS:

Castle 504 *So Wild*	10.00 -	15.00

PETE PETERS:

—— *Rockin' In My Sweet Baby's Arms*	5.00 -	8.00

BOBBY PETERSON (QUINTET):

V-Tone 205, 214, 221	3.00 -	5.00

EARL PETERSON:

Columbia 21364 *Boogie Blues*	7.00 -	10.00
Sun 197 *Boogie Blues*	20.00 -	30.00

MIKE PETTIT & THE STAGS:

Anthem 601227 *It's A Reamer*	7.00 -	10.00

DARYL PETTY:

Hornet 502 *The Day I Die*	8.00 -	12.00

VI PETTY:

Nor-Va-Jak 1325 *True Love Ways*	10.00 -	15.00

PHANTOM:

Dot 16056 *Love Me*	15.00 -	20.00
Phantom 100 *I'm The Phantom*	15.00 -	20.00

THE PHARAOS:

Donna 1327 *The Tender Touch*	5.00 -	8.00

THE PHAROAHS:

Class 202 *Teenagers Love Song*	10.00 -	15.00

JOHNNY PHELPS:

Ski 5505 *Tom Katt*	8.00 -	12.00

THE PHILADELPHIANS:

Guyden 2093 *My Love, My Love*	5.00 -	8.00

THE PHILHARMONICS:
Future 2200 *Why Don't You Write Me*....... 8.00 - 12.00
"PHILLIP MORRIS COUNTRY MUSIC SHOW"
Columbia (LP) 1048 *(various artist)*.......... 10.00 - 15.00
BILL PHILLIPS:
Columbia 41218 *There's A Change In Me*...... 5.00 - 8.00
CARL PHILLIPS:
Bobbin 110 *Wigwam Willie*................. 15.00 - 20.00
EARL PHILLIPS:
Vee Jay 158 *Nothing But Love*.............. 8.00 - 12.00
MARVIN PHILLIPS:
Specialty 445 *Wine Woogie*................ 8.00 - 12.00
PHIL PHILLIPS with THE TWILIGHTS:
Clique 100 *Please Forgive Me*............. 5.00 - 8.00
Khoury's 711 *Sea Of Love*................ 30.00 - 40.00
LARRY PHILLIPSON:
Cinch 3858 *Bitter Feelings*................ 7.00 - 10.00
PIANO RED:
Checker 911 *So Worried*................. 5.00 - 8.00
Groove (EP) 3 *Jump Man Jump*........... 12.00 - 16.00
  (EP) 6 *Piano Red In Concert*............ 10.00 - 15.00
  (EP) 7 *Piano Red In Concert*............ 10.00 - 15.00
  (EP) 8 *Piano Red In Concert*............ 10.00 - 15.00
  0023 *Decatur Street Blues*............ 5.00 - 8.00
  0101 *Pay It No Mind*................ 5.00 - 8.00
  (LP) 0101 *Jump, Man, Jump*........... 35.00 - 50.00
  0118 *Six O'Clock Boogie*............ 8.00 - 12.00
  0126 *Red's Blues*.................. 7.00 - 10.00
  0136 *Jumpin' With Daddy*........... 7.00 - 10.00
  0145 *That's My Desire*.............. 7.00 - 10.00
  0169 *Woo-Ee*................... 7.00 - 10.00
  (LP) 1002 *Piano Red In Concert*........ 35.00 - 50.00
  5000 *Red's Boogie*................ 4.00 - 7.00
Jax 1000 *This Old World*............... 7.00 - 10.00
RCA Victor (EP) 587 *Rockin' With Red*....... 10.00 - 15.00
  4265 *Diggin' The Boogie*............ 8.00 - 12.00
  4380 *Hey Good Lookin'*............. 7.00 - 10.00
  4524 *Bouncin' With Red*............ 7.00 - 10.00
  4766 *The Sales Tax Boogie*.......... 7.00 - 10.00
  4957 *Daybreak*.................. 7.00 - 10.00
  5101 *Everybody's Boogie*........... 7.00 - 10.00
  5224 *She's Dynamite*.............. 7.00 - 10.00
  5337 *Decatur Street Boogie*.......... 7.00 - 10.00
  5544 *Right And Ready*............. 7.00 - 10.00
  6856 *Wild Fire*.................. 5.00 - 8.00
  6953 *Please Don't Talk About Me*...... 5.00 - 8.00
  7065 *South*.................... 5.00 - 8.00
  7217 *Comin' On*................. 7.00 - 10.00
  50-0099 *Rockin' With Red*........... 8.00 - 12.00
  50-0106 *My Gal Jo*............... 8.00 - 12.00
  50-0118 *Jumpin' The Boogie*.......... 7.00 - 10.00
  50-0130 *Layin' The Boogie*........... 7.00 - 10.00
LITTLE "GUITAR" PICKETT:
Jack 101 *The Buzzard*................ 5.00 - 8.00
PICO PETE:
Jet 100 *Hot Dog*.................... 8.00 - 12.00
WEEB PIERCE:
Decca 30045 *Teenage Boogie*............. 7.00 - 10.00
BILL PINKY & THE TURKS:
Phillips 3524 *After The Hop*............. 5.00 - 8.00
PIPES:
Dootone 388 *Be Fair*................. 10.00 - 15.00
  401 *You Are An Angel*............. 10.00 - 15.00
Jacy 001 *Baby Please Don't Go*.......... 15.00 - 20.00
PITCH PIKES:
Mercury 71099 *Zing Zing*.............. 5.00 - 8.00
AL (DR. HORSE) PITTMAN:
Clown 3008 *Woman! You Talk Too Much*..... 7.00 - 10.00
PLANTS: (See also BABY WASHINGTON)
J & S 248 *I Searched The Seven Seas*....... 10.00 - 15.00

  1602 *Dear I Swear*.................. 20.00 - 30.00
  1617 *From Me*.................. 20.00 - 30.00
PLATTERS (See also LINDA HAYES):
Federal (LP) 549 *The Platters*.......... 80.00 - 120.00
(Note: This album is the same as King 549 below. Copies have been found on the Federal label with King covers.)
  12153 *Give Thanks*.................. 40.00 - 60.00
  12164 *I'll Cry When You're Gone*......... 25.00 - 40.00
  12181 *Roses Of Picardy*............. 25.00 - 40.00
  12188 *Tell The World*.............. 20.00 - 30.00
  12198 *Voo-Vee-Ah-Bee*............. 12.00 - 16.00
  12204 *Take Me Back*.............. 15.00 - 20.00
  12244 *Only You*................. 20.00 - 30.00
  12250 *Tell The World*.............. 10.00 - 15.00
  12271 *Give Thanks*............... 10.00 - 15.00
King (EP) 378 *The Platters*............. 15.00 - 20.00
  (LP) 549 *The Platters*.............. 50.00 - 75.00
  (LP) 651 *The Platters*.............. 35.00 - 50.00
Mercury (EP) 3336, 3341................ 5.00 - 8.00
  (LP) 20146 *The Platters*............. 15.00 - 20.00
  (LP) 20216 *The Platters Vol. 2*......... 12.00 - 16.00
  (LP) 20298 *The Flying Platters*......... 10.00 - 15.00
  (LP) 20366 *Around The World*......... 8.00 - 12.00
  (LP) 20410 *Remember When*......... 8.00 - 12.00
  (LP) 20472 *Encore Of Golden Hits*....... 8.00 - 12.00
  70633 *Only You* (maroon label)......... 4.00 - 7.00
  70753 *The Great Pretender* (maroon label).... 4.00 - 7.00
  70819 *The Magic Touch* (maroon label)...... 4.00 - 7.00
  70893 *My Prayer* (maroon label)........... 4.00 - 7.00
  70948 *You'll Never Never Know* (maroon label) 4.00 - 7.00
  71011 *On My Word Of Honor* (maroon label). 4.00 - 7.00
(Note: 78 rpm issues of the last six titles usually command somewhat higher prices.)
PLAYBOYS:
Cat 108 *Tell Me*.................... 7.00 - 10.00
  115 *Good Golly Miss Molly*.............. 7.00 - 10.00
Tetra 4447 *One Question*............... 8.00 - 12.00
THE PLURALS:
Wanger 186 *Donna My Dear*............. 5.00 - 8.00
BOBBY POE:
White Rock 1112 *Rock & Roll Record Girl*..... 20.00 - 30.00
POETS:
Hade 1001 *I'll Never Let You Go*.......... 15.00 - 20.00
Imperial 5664 *I'm In Love*.............. 8.00 - 12.00
Pull 129 *Vowels Of Love*............... 12.00 - 16.00
BOBBY POORE:
Beta 1003 *Heartbreak Of Love*........... 4.00 - 7.00
(GROOVY) JOE POOVEY:
Dixie 733 *Careful Baby*................ 30.00 - 40.00
  2018 *Ten Long Fingers*.............. 35.00 - 50.00
POP CORN & THE MOHAWKS:
Motown 1002 *Shimmy Gully*............. 10.00 - 15.00
POPPA/POPPY HOP:
Ivory 127, 133, 134, 135................ 4.00 - 6.00
WALTER POPULIST & THE TRUETONES:
Flame 10152 *Come Back To Me*............ 8.00 - 12.00
BRUCE PORTER:
Lee— *Rattlesnake*.................. 15.00 - 20.00
ROCKY PORTER:
Stars 549(?) *First Sight*............... 15.00 - 20.00
ROYCE PORTER:
D 1026 *Lookin'*.................... 10.00 - 15.00
Look 1001 *Yes I Do*................. 25.00 - 40.00
Mercury 71314 *Good Time*............. 10.00 - 15.00
  — *Lookin'*.................... 8.00 - 12.00
Spade 1931 *A Woman Can Make You Blue*.... 40.00 - 60.00
SCHOOLBOY PORTER:
Chance 1114 *Rollin' Along*............. 8.00 - 12.00
THE POSSESSIONS:
Britton 1003/1004 *No More Love*......... 10.00 - 15.00

CURTIS POTTER:

Fox 409 *I'm A Real Glad Daddy*............. 35.00 - 50.00

AUSTIN POWELL & THE JAMES QUINTET:

Atlantic 968 *What More Can I Ask?*......... 50.00 - 75.00

CHRIS POWELL & THE BLUE FLAMES:

Okeh 6875 *Darn That Dream*................ 10.00 - 15.00

DOUG POWELL:

Tip Top 713 *Jeannie With The Dark Blue Eyes*. 15.00 - 25.00

JESSIE POWELL ORCHESTRA (See FLUFFY HUNTER)

JEFF POWERS:

Design 811 *Go, Girl, Go*.................. 12.00 - 16.00

JOHNNY POWERS (with STAN GETZ & THE TOM CATS/& HIS ROCKETS):

Fox 916/917 *Rock, Rock*................... 15.00 - 25.00

Fortune 199 *Honey, Let's Go*.............. 10.00 - 15.00

HI-Q 5044 *Honey, Let's Go*................ 8.00 - 12.00

Sun 327 *Be Mine, All Mine*................ 5.00 - 8.00

P.Q. ROCK & ROLL (See MILT OSHINS)

BILLY PRAGER:

Crystal 106 *Everybody's Rockin'*.......... 15.00 - 20.00

— *Do It Bop*............................. 15.00 - 20.00

LYNN PRATT:

Hornet 1000 *Tom Cat Boogie*.............. 10.00 - 15.00

1001 *I Don't Need*..................... 10.00 - 15.00

1002 *Come Here Mama*.................. 15.00 - 20.00

SCRAPPER PRATTS FALCONS:

Falcon 79492 *Guitar Man's Struggle*....... 15.00 - 20.00

THE PREACHERS:

Moonglow 5006 *Pain And Sorrow*.......... 15.00 - 20.00

PRECISIONS:

Highland 300 *Eight Reasons Why I Love*...... 8.00 - 12.00

PRELUDES:

Cub 9005 *Kingdom Of Love*............... 12.00 - 16.00

Empire 103 *Don't Fall In Love Too Soon*.... 10.00 - 15.00

PRELUDES FIVE:

Pik 230 *Straight*........................ 5.00 - 8.00

PREMEERS:

Herald 577 *Diary Of Our Love*............. 8.00 - 12.00

PREMIERS:

Alert 706 *Jolene*........................ 15.00 - 20.00

Cindy 3008 *China Doll*................... ——

Dig 113 *My Darling*..................... 10.00 - 15.00

F-M— *Magic Of Love*.................... 8.00 - 12.00

Ondex 1711 *Speaking Of You*.............. 15.00 - 20.00

ELVIS PRESLEY:

(Note: The collecting of Elvis' records and other Elvis collectibles involves intricacies beyond the scope of this book. Seemingly insignificant variations in labels or record jackets can mean wide price differences. Record sleeves may have values higher than the records themselves; the sleeves of records not listed here due to the minimal value of the records may be worth several dollars or more. The same is true of promotional copies of common records not otherwise worthy of inclusion herein. Also sought after are unofficial, "bootleg", and "fantasy" records — such as "Sun" records which were never originally produced by that company. Non-commercial issues, containing perhaps one track by Elvis, such as Armed Services radio transcriptions, are also in demand. Commercial issues which are often nothing more than repackagings of previously issued material, continue to proliferate with increasing emphasis on gimmickry such as colored vinyl and picture discs, and find a ready market, even at premium prices. Certain reissues, such as the higher-number maroon label EPs, command higher prices than their original issue counterparts. The listings below include only pre-1965 records issued commercially or promotionally; excluded are "bootleg" and spurious issues, foreign issues, recent reissues, etc.)

Rainbow— *The Truth About Me* (78 rpm)..... 35.00 - 50.00

(Above is a magazine insert record, often found affixed to another 78 RPM record to facilitate playing)

RCA Victor (EP-2 records) SPD-22 *Elvis Presley*. 100.00 up

(EP-3 records) SPD-23 *Elvis Presley*........ 150.00 up

(EP) 7-37 *Perfect For Parties*.............. 25.00 - 35.00

(Above were issued for promotional purposes)

(EP) 747 *Elvis Presley*................... 15.00 - 20.00

(EP) 821 *Heartbreak Hotel*............... 15.00 - 20.00

(EP) 830 *Elvis Presley*................... 15.00 - 20.00

(EP) 940 *The Real Elvis*.................. 15.00 - 20.00

(EP) 965 *Any Way You Want Me*.......... 15.00 - 20.00

(EP) 992 *Elvis Vol. 1*................... 10.00 - 15.00

(EP) 993 *Elvis Vol. 2*................... 10.00 - 15.00

(EP) 994 *Strictly Elvis*.................. 10.00 - 15.00

RCA Victor (LP) 1035 *Christmas Album*..... 80.00 - 120.00

(EP-2 Records) 1254 *Elvis Presley* (4 songs on each record)....................... 75.00 - 100.00

(EP-2 records) 1254 *Elvis Presley* (6 songs on each record)....................... 100.00 up

(EP) 1-1515 *Loving You*................. 8.00 - 12.00

(EP) 2-1515 *Loving You, Vol. 2*.......... 8.00 - 12.00

(LP) 1254 *Elvis Presley*................. 25.00 - 35.00

(LP) 1382 *Elvis*....................... 15.00 - 25.00

(LP) 1515 *Loving You*.................. 15.00 - 20.00

(LP) 1707 *Elvis' Golden Records*......... 20.00 - 30.00

(LP) 1884 *King Creole*.................. 15.00 - 20.00

(LP) 1951 *Elvis' Christmas Album*......... 15.00 - 20.00

(LP) 1990 *For LP Fans Only*............. 20.00 - 30.00

(LP) 2001 *A Date With Elvis*............. 15.00 - 20.00

Note: Double-pocket version of this album, with 1960 calendar on back cover commands higher premium.)

(LP) 2075 *50,000,000 Elvis Fans Can't Be Wrong* 15.00 - 25.00

(LP) 2697 *It Happened At The Worlds Fair*... 15.00 - 20.00

(LP) 3468 *Harum Scarum*................ 12.00 - 18.00

(LP) 3558 *Frankie And Johnny*............ 15.00 - 20.00

RCA Victor (LP) 3787 *Double Trouble*........ 20.00 - 30.00

(LP) 3893 *Clambake*.................... 25.00 - 35.00

(LP) 3921 *Elvis' Gold Records, Vol. 4*....... 30.00 - 50.00

(LP) 3989 *Speedway*.................... *100.00 up*

(Note: Foregoing EPs and LPs are all original MONO issues, with black labels having dog logo at top. Subsequent pressings, including Stereo issues, are worth substantially less.)

(EP) 4006 *Love Me Tender*.............. 10.00 - 15.00

(EP) 4041 *Just For You*................. 10.00 - 15.00

(EP) 4054 *Peace In The Valley*........... 10.00 - 15.00

(EP) 4108 *Elvis Sings Christmas Songs*...... 10.00 - 15.00

(EP) 4114 *Jailhouse Rock*................ 10.00 - 15.00

(EP) 4319 *King Creole, Vol. 1*............ 10.00 - 15.00

(EP) 4321 *King Creole, Vol. 2*............ 10.00 - 15.00

(EP) 4325 *Elvis Sails*.................. 15.00 - 20.00

(EP) 4340 *Christmas With Elvis*........... 10.00 - 15.00

(EP) 4368 *Follow That Dream*............ 10.00 - 15.00

(EP) 4371 *Kid Galahad*................. 10.00 - 15.00

(EP) 4382 *Viva Las Vegas*............... 10.00 - 15.00

(EP) 4283 *Tickle Me*................... 10.00 - 15.00

(EP) 4387 *Easy Come, Easy Go*........... 10.00 - 15.00

(EP) 5088 *A Touch Of Gold*.............. 20.00 - 30.00*

(EP) 5101 *A Touch Of Gold, Vol. 2*........ 20.00 - 30.00*

(EP) 5120 *The Real Elvis*................ 25.00 - 35.00*

(EP) 5121 *Peace In The Valley*............ 25.00 - 35.00*

(EP) 5122 *King Creole*.................. 25.00 - 35.00*

(EP) 5141 *A Touch Of Gold, Vol. 3*........ 20.00 - 30.00*

(EP) 5157 *Elvis Sails*.................. 25.00 - 35.00*

(*Note: Foregoing EPs are maroon label issues. Subsequent issues, with black or orange labels are worth only about $5.00 to $8.00 each.)

RCA Victor 6357 *Mystery Train*............. 5.00 - 10.00
  6357 *Mystery Train* (78 RPM)............. 15.00 - 25.00
  6380 *That's All Right*................... 7.00 - 12.00
  6380 *That's All Right* (78 RPM)........... 15.00 - 25.00
  6381 *Good Rockin' Tonight*............... 7.00 - 12.00
  6381 *Good Rockin' Tonight* (78 RPM)....... 15.00 - 25.00
  6382 *Milkcow Blues Boogie*............... 7.00 - 12.00
  6382 *Milkcow Blues Boogie* (78 RPM)....... 15.00 - 25.00
  6383 *Baby, Let's Play House*............. 5.00 - 10.00
  6383 *Baby, Let's Play House* (78 RPM)..... 15.00 - 25.00
  6420, 6540, 6604.................... 3.00 - 6.00
  6420 *Heartbreak Hotel* (78 RPM)......... 15.00 - 20.00
  6540 *I Want You, I Need You* (78 RPM).... 15.00 - 20.00
  6604 *Hound Dog* (78 RPM)............... 15.00 - 25.00
  6636 *Blue Suede Shoes*................. 7.00 - 12.00
  6636 *Blue Suede Shoes* (78 RPM)......... 20.00 - 30.00
  6637 *I Got A Woman*................... 8.00 - 14.00
  6637 *I Got A Woman* (78 RPM)........... 20.00 - 30.00
  6638 *I'll Never Let You Go*............. 8.00 - 14.00
  6638 *I'll Never Let You Go* (78 RPM)..... 20.00 - 30.00
  6639 *Tryin' To Get To You*............. 8.00 - 14.00
  6639 *Tryin' To Get To You* (78 RPM)..... 20.00 - 30.00
  6640 *Blue Moon*..................... 7.00 - 12.00
  6640 *Blue Moon* (78 RPM)............... 20.00 - 30.00
  6641 *Money Honey*.................... 8.00 - 14.00
  6641 *Money Honey* (78 RPM)............. 20.00 - 30.00
  6642 *Shake, Rattle And Roll*........... 8.00 - 14.00
  6642 *Shake, Rattle And Roll* (78 RPM)...... 20.00 - 30.00
  6643 *Love Me Tender*.................. 3.00 - 6.00
  6643 *Love Me Tender* (78 RPM)........... 15.00 - 20.00
RCA Victor 6800, 6870, 7000, 7035, 7150, 7240,
  7280, 7410........................ 3.00 - 5.00
  6800 *Too Much* (78 RPM)............... 15.00 - 20.00
  6870 *All Shook Up* (78 RPM)............. 15.00 - 25.00
  7000 *Teddy Bear* (78 RPM)............. 15.00 - 25.00
  7035 *Jailhouse Rock* (78 RPM).......... 15.00 - 30.00
  7150 *I Beg Of You* (78 RPM)............ 15.00 - 25.00
  7240 *Wear My Ring* (78 RPM)............ 15.00 - 25.00
  7280 *Hard Headed Woman* (78 RPM)....... 20.00 - 30.00
  7410 *I Got Stung* (78 RPM)............ 40.00 - 70.00
  (Note: The only copies seen of 7410 have come
  from jukebox operators.)
RCA Victor 37-7850 *Surrender* (7" 33⅓ RPM).. 30.00 - 50.00
  37-7880 *I Feel So Bad* (7" 33⅓ RPM)..... 30.00 - 50.00
  37-7908 *Little Sister* (7" 33⅓ RPM)......... 30.00 - 50.00
  37-7968 *Can't Help Falling In Love* (7" 33⅓ RPM) 40.00 - 60.00
  37-7992 *Good Luck Charm* (7" 33⅓ RPM)... 40.00 - 60.00
  37-8041 *She's Not You* (7" 33⅓ RPM)...... 40.00 - 60.00
  37-8100 *Return To Sender* (7" 33⅓ RPM).... 40.00 - 60.00
  (Note: Above issues should not be confused with
  the usual 45 RPM issues, which have corresponding catalog numbers; the 45s are of nominal value
  only. Note the "37" prefix to catalog numbers.)
  The 33⅓ RPM issues listed here command widely
  varying prices, which have been quoted as high
  as $50.00 to $100.00, particularly for the later
  issues. It is doubted that such high prices are
  actually realized; these issues should be regarded
  as highly speculative.)
RCA Victor 61-7704 *Stuck On You* (STEREO 45
  RPM) .... 30.00 - 50.00
  61-7777 *It's Now Or Never* (STEREO 45 RPM) 25.00 - 40.00
  61-7850 *Surrender* (STEREO 45 RPM)....... 35.00 - 50.00
  61-7880 *I Feel So Bad* (STEREO 45 RPM)... 35.00 - 50.00
  (Note: Above three issues should not be confused
  with the usual MONO 45 RPM issues, which
  have corresponding catalog numbers. Note the
  "61" prefix. The mono 45s have only nominal
  value.)
RCA Victor 68-7850 *Surrender* (7" STEREO 33⅓
  RPM)

  68-7880 *I Feel So Bad* (7" STEREO 33⅓ RPM)
  (Note: Above should not be confused with the
  usual 45 RPM records which have corresponding
  catalog numbers. Note the "68" prefix. Very high
  prices of $100.00 to $200.00 have been quoted
  for these records, but whether such prices might
  actually be realized is subject to doubt. These
  records should be regarded as highly speculative.)
RCA Victor G8-MW-8705 *TV Guide Presents Elvis
  Presley* .... - Rare -
  (Above is a special promotional record. Extreme-
  ly high prices have been quoted for it, particularly where it is accompanied by the original printed
  material.)
Sun 209 *That's All Right*.................. 90.00 - 130.00
  210 *Good Rockin' Tonight*................ 110.00 - 150.00
  215 *Milkcow Blues Boogie*............... 150.00 - 200.00
  217 *Baby, Let's Play House*.............. 80.00 - 110.00
  223 *Mystery Train*.................... 80.00 - 110.00

JOHNNY PRESTON:
Mercury (EP) 3397 *Johnny Preston*......... 10.00 - 15.00
  (LP) 20592 *Running Bear*................ 25.00 - 40.00
  (LP) 20609 *Come Rock With Me*.......... 25.00 - 40.00

PRESTOS:
Mercury 70747 *Til We Meet Again*......... 10.00 - 15.00

PRETENDERS:
Bethlehem 3050 *Ding Dong Bells*.......... 10.00 - 15.00
Central 2605 *Blue And Lonely*............ ——
Holiday 2610 *Tonight*................... 10.00 - 15.00
Power-Martin 1001 *Smile*................ 8.00 - 12.00
Rama 198 *Possessive Love*............... 10.00 - 15.00

PRETTY BOY:
Atlantic 1147 *Bip Bop Bip*............... 7.00 - 10.00
Big 617 *Rockin' The Mule*............... 7.00 - 10.00
Rhythm 1768 *Find My Baby*.............. 15.00 - 20.00

LLOYD PRICE:
ABC Paramount (LP) 277 *The Exciting Lloyd Price* 15.00 - 25.00
  (LP) 297 *Mr. Personality*................ 15.00 - 25.00
  (LP) 315 *Sings The Blues*................ 15.00 - 20.00
  9792 *Just Because* (78 RPM)............ 10.00 - 15.00
  9972 *Stagger Lee* (78 RPM)............. 20.00 - 30.00
  9997 *Is It Really Love?* (78 RPM).......... 10.00 - 15.00
KRC 303 *Hello Little Girl*................ 5.00 - 8.00
Specialty 428 *Lawdy Miss Clawdy*......... 8.00 - 12.00
Specialty 440 *Restless Heart*............. 5.00 - 8.00
  452 *Ain't It A Shame?*................. 5.00 - 8.00
  457 *So Long*....................... 5.00 - 8.00
  463 *Where You At?*................... 5.00 - 8.00
  483 *Too Late For Tears*................ 5.00 - 8.00
  494 *Walkin The Track*................. 5.00 - 8.00
  (Above are found pressed of red plastic; these command higher prices)
  535, 571, 582, 602................... 4.00 - 6.00
  (LP) 2105 *Lloyd Price*.................. 20.00 - 30.00

MEL PRICE:
Dixie 2016 *Little Dog Blues/Until*........... 20.00 - 30.00

RAY PRICE:
Columbia (LP) 1015 *Ray Price Sings Heart Songs* 15.00 - 20.00
  (LP) 1148 *Talk To Your Heart*............ 15.00 - 20.00

THE PRIMETTES:
LuPine 120 *Tears of Sorrow*.............. 10.00 - 15.00

BOBBY PRINCE:
Chance 1128 *Tell Me Why, Why, Why*....... 15.00 - 20.00

PRISONAIRES:
Sun 186 *Just Walkin' In The Rain*.......... 10.00 - 15.00
  191 *A Prisoner's Prayer*................ 15.00 - 20.00
  207 *There Is Love In You*............... 80.00 - 120.00

JIMMY PRITCHETT:
Crystal 503 *That's The Way I Feel*........... 10.00 - 15.00

PRODIGALS:
Abner 1015 *Won't You Believe*............ 15.00 - 20.00
Falcon 1011 *Marsha*................... 10.00 - 15.00

PROFESSOR LONGHAIR:

Atlantic 1020 *In The Night*	15.00 -	20.00
Ebb 101 *Cry Pretty Baby*	12.00 -	16.00
106 *Look What You're Doin'*	12.00 -	16.00
121 *Looka No Hair*	10.00 -	15.00
Ron 326 *Cuttin' Out*	6.00 -	10.00
329 *Go To The Mardi Gras*	6.00 -	10.00

PROPHETS:

Atco 6078 *Stormy*	8.00 -	12.00

PROWLERS:

Aragon 302 *Rock Me Baby*	10.00 -	15.00

RALPH PRUITT with HIS RHYTHM BOYS:

Meridian 1506/1507 *Hey Mr. Porter*	50.00 -	80.00

SNOOKY PRYOR:

J.O.B. 1014 *Cryin' Shame*	50.00 -	75.00
1126 *Boogie Twist*	25.00 -	40.00
Parrot 807 *Crosstown Blues*	15.00 -	20.00
Vee Jay 215 *Someone To Love Me*	10.00 -	15.00

RED PRYSOCK:

Mercury (LP) 20088 *Rock 'N' Roll*	15.00 -	25.00
(LP) 20211 *Fruit Boots*	15.00 -	20.00
(LP) 20307 *The Beat*	15.00 -	20.00

DENNIS PUCKETT:

Emerald— *Rockin' Teens*	15.00 -	20.00

WHITEY PULLEN:

Crown (LP) 332 *Country Music Star*	10.00 -	15.00
(LP) 5332 *Country Music Star*	15.00 -	20.00
Sage 274 *Walk My Way Back Home*	10.00 -	15.00
294 *Let's Go Wild Tonight*	15.00 -	20.00
313 *Tuscaloosa Lucy*	15.00 -	20.00

VERN PULLENS:

Spade 1927 *Bop Crazy Baby*	50.00 -	75.00
—— *Mama Don't Allow No Boppin'*	40.00 -	60.00

PYRAMIDS:

C-Note 1206 *Someday*	——	
Cub 9112 *Cryin'*	7.00 -	10.00
Davis— *Before It't Too Late*	5.00 -	8.00
— *At Any Cost*	5.00 -	8.00
Federal 12233 *Deep In My Heart For You*	20.00 -	30.00
Shell 711 *Ankle Bracelet*	5.00 -	8.00

QUADRELLS:

Whirlin Disc 103 *Come To Me*	10.00 -	15.00

QUAILS:

DeLuxe 6085 *Things She Used To Do*	20.00 -	30.00

QUAILTONES:

Josie 779 *Tears Of Love*	25.00 -	40.00

THE QUARTER NOTES:

DeLuxe 6129 *My Fantasy*	4.00 -	6.00
Dot 15685 *Like You Bug Me*	4.00 -	6.00
Fox 2 *Teen Age Blues*	7.00 -	10.00

DOUG QUATTLEBAUM:

Gotham 7519 *Don't Be Funny Baby*	30.00 -	50.00

QUEENS: (See also SHIRLEY GUNTER)

Flair 1050 *Oop Shoop*	5.00 -	8.00

? (QUESTION MARK) & THE MYSTERIANS:

Pa-Go-Go 102 *96 Tears*	20.00 -	30.00

QUESTION MARKS:

Swingtime 346 *Another Soldier Gone*	——	

ANDY QUINN:

Decca 30438 *Rock-A-Boogie*	8.00 -	12.00
30521 *Sweet Treat*	8.00 -	12.00

QUINNS:

Cyclone 111 *Oh Starlight*	7.00 -	10.00

EDDIE QUINTEROS:

Brent 7009 *Come Dance With Me*	4.00 -	7.00
7014 *Slow Down Sandy*	4.00 -	7.00

QUINTONES:

Hunt 322 *There'll Be No Sorrow*	4.00 -	7.00
Park 57-112 *More Than A Notion*	30.00 -	40.00

THE QUOTATIONS:

Verve 10245 *Imagination*	7.00 -	10.00

DON RADAR:

Strate 8 1507 *Rock & Roll Granpa*	7.00 -	10.00

THE RADIANTS:

Dootone 451 *I'm Betting My Heart*	7.00 -	10.00

RAINBOWS:

Dave 908 *I Know*	8.00 -	12.00
Pilgrim 703 *May Lee*	15.00 -	20.00
711 *Shirley*	12.00 -	16.00
Rama 209 *They Say*	25.00 -	35.00
Red Robin 134 *Mary Lee*	25.00 -	40.00

RAINDROPS:

Apollo 494 *Inspirations*	20.00 -	30.00
Sotoplay 0028 *I Still Love You*	——	
Spin It 104 *I Found Heaven In Love*	15.00 -	25.00
Vega— *Dim Those Lights*	15.00 -	20.00

CHRIS RANIER & THE ELRODS:

Red Head 1005 *Eleven O'Clock*	7.00 -	10.00

JERRY RAINES:

Drew-Blan 1001 *Dangerous Redhead*	4.00 -	7.00

MARVIN RAINWATER:

Crown (LP) 307 *Marvin Rainwater*	8.00 -	12.00
MGM (LP) 3534 *Songs By Marvin Rainwater*	15.00 -	20.00
(LP) 4046 *Gonna Find Me A Bluebird*	15.00 -	20.00
(LP) 3721 *Marvin Rainwater Sings With A Heart/A Beat*	20.00 -	30.00
12152 *Dem Low Down Blues*	8.00 -	12.00
12240 *Hot And Cold*	20.00 -	30.00
12412 *Gonna Find Me A Bluebird* (78 RPM)	7.00 -	10.00
12511 *My Brand Of Blues*	7.00 -	10.00
12609 *Baby, Don't Go*	8.00 -	12.00
12653 *Moanin' The Blues*	5.00 -	8.00
12665 *I Dig You Baby*	7.00 -	10.00

RAJAHS:

Klik 7805 *I Fell In Love*	15.00 -	20.00

RAMBLERS:

Jax 319 *Search My Heart* (red plastic)	50.00 -	75.00
MGM 11850 *Vadunt-Un-Vada Song*	30.00 -	50.00

RAMS:

Flair 1066 *Sweet Thing*	15.00 -	20.00

BILLY RANDALL:

Savoy 1570 *Rowena*	7.00 -	10.00

RANDY & THE RAINBOWS:

Rust 5059 *Denise*	4.00 -	7.00
5080 *Dry Your Eyes*	4.00 -	7.00

WAYNE RANEY:

Decca 30212 *Shake Baby Shake*	8.00 -	12.00
King (LP) 588 *Songs From The Hills*	20.00 -	30.00

RANNELS:

Boss 2122 *Boom Baby*	——	

RAVENS:

Argo 5255 *Kneel And Pray* (ship logo)	10.00 -	15.00
5261 *A Simple Prayer* (ship prayer)	8.00 -	12.00
5276 *Dear One* (ship logo)	8.00 -	12.00
5284 *Here Is My Heart*	7.00 -	10.00
Columbia 6-903 *Time Takes Care Of Everything*	35.00 -	50.00
6-925 *I'm So Crazy For Love*	35.00 -	50.00
39112 *You Don't Have To Drop A Heart*	40.00 -	60.00
Jubilee 5184 *Happy Go Lucky Baby*	4.00 -	7.00
5203 *Green Eyes*	4.00 -	7.00
King (EP) 310 *The Ravens*	40.00 -	60.00
Mercury 5800 *Begin The Beguine*	15.00 -	20.00
5853 *Chloe*	15.00 -	20.00
8291 *Write Me One Sweet Letter*	20.00 -	30.00
70060 *Don't Mention My Name*	20.00 -	30.00
70119 *Come A Little Bit Closer*	8.00 -	12.00
70307 *September Song*	15.00 -	20.00
70413 *Love Is No Dream*	35.00 -	40.00
70505 *White Christmas*	12.00 -	16.00
70554 *Old Man River*	20.00 -	25.00
National 9111 *Count Every Star*	100.00 -	150.00
Okeh 6825 *The Wiffenpoof Song*	40.00 -	60.00

6843 *Everything But You*	40.00 -	60.00
6888 *Mam'selle*	40.00 -	60.00
Regent (LP) 6062 *Write Me A Letter* (green label)	15.00 -	25.00

DANNY RAY:

Vin 1025 *Love Me*	7.00 -	10.00

DAVID RAY:

Kliff 101 *Lonesome Baby Blues*	30.00 -	50.00
102 *Jitter Buggin' Baby*	30.00 -	50.00

DON RAY:

Rodeo 129 *Rock 'N' Roll Blues*	15.00 -	25.00
130 *Imogene*	15.00 -	25.00

RAY-O-VACS:

Atco 6085 *Crying All Alone*	7.00 -	10.00
Decca 48162 *Besame Mucho*	7.00 -	10.00
Josie 781 *I Still Love You*	8.00 -	12.00

RAYS:

Argo 1074 *How Long Must I Wait*	6.00 -	10.00
Cameo 117 *Silhouettes* (78 RPM)	15.00 -	20.00
Chess 1613 *Tippity Top*	10.00 -	15.00
1678 *How Long Must I Wait*	8.00 -	12.00
(EP) 5120 *Tippity Top*	15.00 -	20.00
XYZ 102 *Silhouettes*	10.00 -	15.00
600 *Why Do You Look The Other Way*	7.00 -	10.00
605, 607	4.00 -	6.00

"RCA CAMDEN ROCKERS"

Camden (LP) 435 (various artists)	10.00 -	15.00

OTIS READ:

Nanc 1118/1119 *Come On Baby*	8.00 -	12.00

BILL READER:

Voll-Para 100 *There Was A Time*	7.00 -	10.00
— *Remember You're Mine*	——	

JIMMY REAGAN & THE RHYTHM ROCKERS:

G&G 128 *Lonely, Lonely Heart*	10.00 -	15.00

RICK REASON:

Mar-Vel 3300 *I Feel So Bad*	——	

PEARL REAVES & THE CONCORDS:

Harlem 2332 *I'm Not Ashamed*	30.00 -	40.00

JOHNNY REBB:

Bullseye 1027 *Rock On*	7.00 -	10.00
Flame 154 *My Body Can't Take It*	7.00 -	10.00

REBEL ROUSERS:

Memphis 107 *Thunder*	7.00 -	10.00
113 *Zombie Walks*	7.00 -	10.00

THE REBELS:

Marlee 009 *Wild Weekend*	8.00 -	12.00

JOHNNY REDD:

Corallen— *Rockin' With Ruby*	20.00 -	30.00

TEDDY REDELL:

Atco 6162 *Judy*	5.00 -	8.00
Hi 2024 *Pipeliner*	8.00 -	12.00
Vaden 110 *Knockin' On The Backside*	15.00 -	20.00
115 *Gold Dust*	8.00 -	12.00
116 *Judy*	10.00 -	15.00
301 *I Want To Hold You*	5.00 -	8.00

RED JACKS:

Apt 25006 *Big Brown Eyes*	5.00 -	8.00

TERRY REDMAN:

MGM 12735 *Come On Back*	5.00 -	8.00

RED TOPPERS:

Dan 3214 *I Never Had A Girl Like You*	5.00 -	8.00

REED BROTHERS & THE STINGERS:

Award 122/123 *Swamp Rock*	10.00 -	15.00

A. C. REED:

Age 29101 *This Little Voice*	4.00 -	7.00
29103 *I Wanna Be Free*	5.00 -	8.00
29112 *Mean Cop*	5.00 -	8.00
29123 *Lotta Lovin'*	5.00 -	8.00

AL REED:

Dot— *I Love Her So*	7.00 -	10.00
TNT— *I Love Her So*	10.00 -	15.00
Winner 700 *Top Notch Grade A*	7.00 -	10.00

BOB REED & HIS BAND:

Melatone 1003 *I'm Leaving You*	5.00 -	8.00

CHUCK REED:

Hit 101 *Talkin' No Trash*	7.00 -	10.00

EARL REED:

Cherokee 779 *Flat Foot Sam*	7.00 -	10.00

JAMES REED (& HIS BAND):

Big Town 117 *You Better Hold Me*	30.00 -	40.00
Flair 1034 *This Is The End*	15.00 -	20.00
1042 *You Better Hold Me*	15.00 -	20.00
Money 201 *My Love Is Real*	20.00 -	30.00
Rhythm 1775 *I Wanna Know*	20.00 -	30.00

JERRI REED:

Bango 500 *While You're Gone*	5.00 -	8.00

JERRY REED:

Capitol 3882 *Bessie Baby*	7.00 -	10.00

JIMMY REED:

Chance 1142 *High And Lonesome*	20.00 -	30.00
Vee Jay 100 *High And Lonesome* (red plastic)	35.00 -	50.00
105 *Jimmie's Boogie* (red plastic)	20.00 -	30.00
119 *Boogie In The Dark* (red plastic)	15.00 -	20.00
132 *Pretty Thing*	7.00 -	10.00
153 *I Don't Go For That*	7.00 -	10.00
168 *Ain't That Lovin' You Baby*	7.00 -	10.00
186, 203, 226, 237, 248, 253	4.00 -	7.00
270, 275, 287, 298, 304, 314, 326, 333, 347, 357	3.00 -	5.00
(LP) 1004 *I'm Jimmy Reed* (maroon label)	20.00 -	30.00
(LP) 1008 *Rockin' With Reed* (maroon label)	20.00 -	30.00
(LP) 1022 *Found Love*	15.00 -	20.00
(LP) 1025 *Now Appearing*	15.00 -	20.00
(LP) 1035 (2 records) *At Carnegie Hall*	15.00 -	20.00
(LP) 1039 *The Best Of Jimmy Reed*	10.00 -	15.00
(LP) 1050 *Just Jimmy Reed*	10.00 -	15.00
(LP) 1067, 1072, 1073	8.00 -	12.00

DANNY REEVES:

— *Bell Hop Blues/I'm A Hobo*	8.00 -	12.00

GLENN REEVES (& HIS ROCK-BILLYS/TOWN & COUNTRY PLAYBOYS):

Atco 6080 *Drinkin' Wine Spo-Dee-O-Dee*	10.00 -	15.00
Decca 30589 *Betty Bounce*	10.00 -	15.00
30780 *Tarzan*	10.00 -	15.00
Republic 7121 *That'll Be Love*	8.00 -	12.00
TNT 120 *I'm Johnny On The Spot*	10.00 -	15.00
129 *I Ain't Got Room To Rock*	10.00 -	15.00

JIM REEVES:

Abbott (LP) 5001 *Jim Reeves Sings*	35.00 -	50.00
RCA Victor (LP) 1256 *Singing Down The Lane*	20.00 -	30.00
(LP) 1410 *Bimbo*	15.00 -	20.00
(LP) 1576 *Jim Reeves*	10.00 -	15.00
(LP) 1685 *Girls I Have Known*	10.00 -	15.00

REGALS:

Aladdin 3266 *Run Pretty Baby*	25.00 -	35.00
Atlantic 1062 *I'm So Lonely*	8.00 -	12.00

REGENTS:

Cousins 1002 *Barbara-Ann*	20.00 -	30.00
Gee (LP) 706 *Barbara-Ann*	40.00 -	60.00
Kayo 101 *No Hard Feelings*	25.00 -	35.00

BILLY REINSFORD:

Hermitage 803 *Magnolia*	20.00 -	30.00

BOBBY RELF (& THE LAURELS):

Cash 1019 *Our Love*	10.00 -	15.00
Flair 1063 *Yours Alone*	8.00 -	12.00

REMINISCENTS:

Day 1000 *Oh Let Me Dream*	8.00 -	12.00

JOHNNY RENO:

Valley's Meadowlark 105-58 *Naughty Mama*	10.00 -	15.00

RE-VELS/REVELS:

Andie 5077 *Please*	5.00 -	8.00
Chess 1708 *False Alarm*	15.00 -	20.00
Sound 129 *You Lied To Me*	15.00 -	20.00
135 *Dream My Darling Dream*	10.00 -	15.00
Teen 122 *So In Love*	10.00 -	15.00

PAUL REVERE & THE RAIDERS:

Gardena 116 *Like Long Hair*............	4.00 -	7.00
(LP) 1000 *Like Long Hair*.............	30.00 -	50.00
Sande (LP) 1001 *Paul Revere & The Raiders*....	30.00 -	40.00

REVLONS:

Pet 802 *Dreams Are For Fools*.............	8.00 -	12.00

EDDIE REYNOLDS:

Dixie—*What Was It*...................	8.00 -	12.00

BIG JACK REYNOLDS & HIS BLUE MEN:

Hi-Q 5036 *I Had A Little Dog*............	7.00 -	10.00

JODY REYNOLDS:

Demon 1507 *Endless Sleep* (78 rpm).........	10.00 -	15.00
1515 *Beulah Lee*.................	7.00 -	10.00
1524 *Stone Cold*...............	8.00 -	12.00

WESLEY REYNOLDS:

Rose 108 *Trip To The Moon*...............	10.00 -	15.00
117 *Rag Mop*....................	8.00 -	12.00

JIMMY RHODES & THE SHUFFLES:

Cupid 5005 *I Wanna Go*...............	7.00 -	10.00

SLIM RHODES:

Sun 216 *Uncertain Love*................	15.00 -	20.00
225 *House Of Sin*...............	35.00 -	50.00
238 *Gonna Romp And Stomp*......	10.00 -	15.00
256 *Do What I Do*...............	5.00 -	8.00

TEXAS RED RHODES:

Echo 1001 *Go Cats Go*................	20.00 -	30.00

RHYTHM ACES:

Vee Jay 124 *I Wonder Why*.............	30.00 -	45.00
212 *Whisper To Me*...........	20.00 -	35.00
417 *Be Mine*.................	8.00 -	12.00

RHYTHM JESTERS:

Rama 213 *Rock Music*...............	7.00 -	10.00

RHYTHM MASTERS:

Flip 314 *Baby We Two*..............	10.00 -	15.00

RHYTHM ROCKERS:

Cross Country 524 *Fiddle Bop*........	15.00 -	20.00
Oasis 104 *Thinkin' About You*......	20.00 -	30.00
Sun 248 *Fiddle Bop*............	5.00 -	8.00

RHYTHM ROCKETS:

Gulfstream 6654 *My Shadow*...........	15.00 -	20.00

ELDON RICE:

El Rio 413 *Our Love Won't Die*............	10.00 -	15.00

CHARLIE RICH:

Groove 58-0025 *Big Boss Man*..........	5.00 -	8.00

DAVE RICH:

RCA Victor 7334 *Rosie Let's Get Cozy*.......	4.00 -	6.00

JAY RICHARDS & THE BLUES KINGS:

Goldband 1101 *Hear Love Knockin'*...........	7.00 -	10.00

JAPE RICHARDS: (See also BIG BOPPER)

D 1008 *Chantilly Lace*................	20.00 -	30.00
Mercury 71219, 71312.............	5.00 -	8.00
MGM 12421 *Crazy Blues*............	30.00 -	40.00

RICHIE (& THE ROYALS):

Rello 1 *And When I'm Near You*.............	8.00 -	12.00
3 *Be My Girl*..................	8.00 -	12.00

JIMMY RICKS (& THE RAVENS):

Baton 236 *I'm A Fool To Want You*......	4.00 -	6.00
Mercury 70213 *Who'll Be The Fool*.........	8.00 -	12.00
70307 *September Song*...........	5.00 -	8.00

TOMMY RIDGELY:

Atlantic 1039 *Jam Up*................	7.00 -	10.00

BILLY LEE RILEY:

Brunswick 55085 *Is That All To The Ball (Mr. Hall)?*	20.00 -	30.00
Home Of The Blues 223 *Flip, Flop And Fly*....	5.00 -	8.00
Sun 245 *Rock With Me Baby*.........	10.00 -	15.00
260 *Flying Saucer Rock & Roll*.....	8.00 -	12.00
277 *Red Hot*................	5.00 -	8.00
289 *Baby Please Don't Go*......	7.00 -	10.00
313 *Down By The Riverside*......	5.00 -	8.00
322 *Got The Water Boiling*......	15.00 -	20.00

BOB RILEY:

MGM 12612 *Wanda Jean*.............	10.00 -	15.00
York—*Big Dog*................	— — —	

OTIS RILEY:

Kappa 209 *Little Miss Bibbity Bobbity Boom*...	5.00 -	8.00

RINKY DINKS:

Atco 6121 *Early In The Morning* (78 RPM)....	15.00 -	20.00
6128 *Mighty Mighty Man* (78 RPM)........	15.00 -	20.00

CHUCK RIO:

Challenge 59019 *Denise*...................	5.00 -	8.00

RIP CHORDS:

Abco 105 *Let's Do The Razzle Dazzle*......	40.00 -	50.00

GEORGE RITCHIE:

Smart 321 *But In A Million Years*.........	10.00 -	15.00

THE RIVALS:

Darryl 722 *I Must See You Again*.........	5.00 -	8.00
Lu Pine 118 *It's Gonna Work Out*........	4.00 -	7.00

LITTLE BOBBY RIVERA (& THE HEMLOCKS):

Fury 1004 *Cora Lee*....................	7.00 -	10.00

RIVIERAS:

Algonquin 718 *A Night To Remember*........	5.00 -	8.00
Riviera (LP) 701 *Campus Party*...........	20.00 -	30.00

RIVILEERS:

Baton 200 *A Thousand Stars*............	10.00 -	15.00
201 *Forever*...................	20.00 -	30.00
205 *Eternal Love*...............	25.00 -	35.00
207 *For Sentimental Reasons*......	8.00 -	12.00
209 *Don't Ever Leave Me*.......	15.00 -	20.00
241 *A Thousand Stars*...........	8.00 -	12.00

THE RIVINGTONS:

Liberty (LP) 3282 *Doin' The Bird*.........	15.00 -	20.00
55610 *Cherry*...............	4.00 -	7.00

ROAMERS:

Savoy 1147 *I'll Never Get Over You*........	8.00 -	12.00
1149 *Women And Whiskey*...........	8.00 -	12.00
1156 *Chop Chop Ching-A-Ling*......	7.00 -	10.00

EDDIE ROBBINS:

David 1001 *Janice*................	5.00 -	8.00
Dot 15702 *A Girl Like You*...........	5.00 -	8.00
Power 214 *A Girl Like You*...........	8.00 -	12.00

MARTY ROBBINS:

Columbia (LP) 976 *The Song Of Robbins*......	15.00 -	20.00
(LP) 1087 *Song Of The Islands*.......	10.00 -	15.00
(LP) 1189 *Marty Robbins*.........	10.00 -	15.00
Columbia 2601 (LP) (10") *Rock'n Roll'n Robbins*	100.00 -	150.00
21351 *That's All Right*.........	7.00 -	10.00
21446 *Maybelline*...........	8.00 -	12.00
21461 *Pretty Mama*..........	7.00 -	10.00
21477 *Tennessee Toddy*......	7.00 -	10.00
40679 *Long Tall Sally*........	10.00 -	15.00
40706 *Respectfully Miss Brooks*...	5.00 -	8.00
40864 *A White Sport Coat* (78 RPM)...	10.00 -	15.00
41013 *The Story Of My Life* (78 RPM)......	10.00 -	15.00

MEL ROBBINS:

Argo 5340 *Save It*...................	10.00 -	15.00

ROBERT & JOHNNY:

Old Town 1052 *I Believe In You* (78 RPM)....	8.00 -	12.00

BOBBY ROBERTS with THE BAD HABITS:

Hut 881 *Hop Skip And Jump*..............	10.00 -	15.00
Sky—*Big Sandy*.....................	— — —	

DENNIS ROBERTS:

Yucca 133 *Come On*..................	5.00 -	8.00

DON "RED" ROBERTS:

Chart 643 *Don't Say Maybe*.............	— — —	
Rama 230 *Don't Say Maybe*.............	8.00 -	12.00

LANCE ROBERTS:

Decca 30955 *Gonna Have Myself A Ball*.....	7.00 -	10.00

WALTER ROBERTSON:

Flair 1053 *Sputterin' Blues*.............	20.00 -	30.00

ROBINS:

Arvee 5001 *Just Like That*.............	— — —	
Atco 6059 *Smokey Joe's Cafe*............	7.00 -	10.00
Crown 106 *I Made A Vow*............	35.00 -	50.00
120 *The Key To My Heart*...............	30.00 -	40.00

Knight 2008 *It's Never Too Late*.............	————	
Lavender 001 *White Cliffs Of Dover*.........	————	
RCA Victor 5175 *A Fool Such As I*.........	50.00 -	175.00
5271 *Oh Why*.................	25.00 -	40.00
5434 *How Would You Know*........	60.00 -	80.00
5489 *Empty Bottles*..............	20.00 -	30.00
5564 *Get It Off You Mind*.........	20.00 -	30.00
Spark 103 *Riot In Cell Block Number Nine*.....	10.00 -	15.00
107 *Framed*..................	10.00 -	15.00
110 *If Tear Drops Were Kisses*.......	15.00 -	25.00
113 *One Kiss*.................	10.00 -	15.00
116 *I Must Be Dreaming*..........	10.00 -	15.00
122 *Smokey Joe's Cafe*...........	20.00 -	30.00
Whippet 100 *Cherry Lips*.........	5.00 -	8.00
101 *Hurt Me*................	8.00 -	12.00
103 *That Old Black Magic*........	8.00 -	12.00
(LP) 703 *Rock & Roll With The Robins*......	40.00 -	60.00
BILL ROBINSON & THE QUAILS:		
De Luxe 6030 *Lonely Star*...........	35.00 -	50.00
6047 *I Know She's Gone*.........	35.00 -	50.00
6057 *Somewhere Somebody Cares*...	35.00 -	50.00
6059 *Heaven Is The Place*........	35.00 -	50.00
6074 *Oh Sugar*..............	40.00 -	60.00
FENTION/FENTON ROBINSON (& THE CAS- **TLE ROCKERS/HIS DUKES):**		
Duke 190, 191, 312, 329...........	4.00 -	6.00
Meteor 5041 *Crying Out Loud* (black label).....	25.00 -	40.00
U.S.A. 842 *From My Heart*..............	5.00 -	8.00
JIMMY LEE ROBINSON:		
Bandera 2510 *Twist It Baby*............	7.00 -	10.00
SUGAR CHILE ROBINSON:		
Captiol (LP) 589 *Boogie Woogie*.........	30.00 -	50.00
CARSON ROBINSON:		
MGM 12266 *Rockin' And Rollin' With Granmaw*	20.00 -	30.00
TOMMY ROCCO:		
Rozorback 102 *I'll Cry Awhile*..............	5.00 -	8.00
"ROCK & ROLL FOREVER":		
Atlantic (LP) 8010 (various artists)...........	15.00 -	20.00
(LP) 8021 Vol. 2 (various artists)...........	15.00 -	20.00
"ROCK & ROLL SOCK HOP":		
Score 4018 (various artists)............	20.00 -	30.00
"ROCK AND ROLL SPECTACULAR":		
Dawn (LP) 119 (various artists)...........	15.00 -	20.00
ROCK A TEENS:		
Doran 3515 *Woo-Hoo*............	10.00 -	15.00
Roulette (LP) 25109 *Woo-Hoo*...........	25.00 -	35.00
ROCKERS: (See also PAUL WINLEY):		
Carter 3029 *Count Every Star*...........	100.00 -	150.00
Federal 12267 *What Am I To Do*.......	8.00 -	12.00
12273 *Down In The Bottom*.......	8.00 -	12.00
Premium 401 *Angel Child*................	10.00 -	15.00
ROCKETONES:		
Melba 113 *Mexico*.......................	8.00 -	12.00
ROCKETS: (See also BILL BODAFORD)		
Modern 992 *Be Lovey Dovey*............	5.00 -	8.00
ROCKIN' BRADLEY:		
Fire 1007 *Look Out*................	10.00 -	15.00
ROCKIN' CHAIRS:		
Recorte 402 *Rockin' Chair Boogie*............	8.00 -	12.00
404 *Come On Baby*...................	8.00 -	12.00
ROCKIN' DUKES:		
OJ 1007 *My Baby Left Me*..............	20.00 -	30.00
"ROCKIN '50s"		
Atlantic (LP) 8037 (various artists)...........	10.00 -	15.00
ROCKING STOCKINGS:		
Sun 1960 *Rockin-Lang-Syne*............	8.00 -	12.00
ROCKIN' JESTERS:		
Oklahoma—*I Was Too Blind*...........	————	
ROCKIN' REBELS:		
Swan (LP) 509 *Wild Weekend*..........	25.00 -	35.00
ROCKIN' RONALD:		
End 1043 *Kansas City*...............	5.00 -	8.00

ROCKIN' R'S:		
Tempus 7541 *Crazy Baby*..................	7.00 -	10.00
ROCKIN' SAINTS:		
Decca 31144 *Cheat On Me Baby*.............	5.00 -	8.00
(COUNT) ROCKIN' SIDNEY/SYDNEY (& HIS **ALL STARS/DUKES):**		
Goldband 1158, 1159, 1162, 1170............	3.00 -	5.00
Jin 110 *My Little Girl*....................	10.00 -	15.00
156, 164, 168, 170, 174, 177...........	4.00 -	7.00
THE ROCK-ITS:		
Spangle 2010 *It's L-O-V-E*..................	15.00 -	20.00
"ROCK, ROCK, ROCK"		
Chess (LP) 1425 (black label) (From the motion pic- ture; with Flamingos, Moonglows).........	30.00 -	40.00
ROD & TERRY:		
Cuca 1206 *That's All Right*...............	10.00 -	15.00
BUCK RODGERS:		
Starday 245 *Little Rock Rock*...............	15.00 -	20.00
JIMMIE RODGERS:		
Roulette 4015 *Honeycomb* (78 RPM).........	15.00 -	20.00
4031 *Kisses Sweeter Than Wine* (78 RPM)...	15.00 -	20.00
4045 *Oh-Oh, I'm Falling In Love Again* (78 RPM)	15.00 -	20.00
4070 *Secretly* (78 RPM).............	10.00 -	15.00
4090 *Are You Really Mine* (78 RPM)......	10.00 -	15.00
4116 *Bimbombery* (78 RPM)...........	20.00 -	30.00
TOMMY ROE & BOBBY LEE TRAMMELL:		
Crown (LP) 5323 *Tommy Roe And Bobby Lee*..	15.00 -	25.00
JESSE ROGERS:		
Arcade 169 *Jump Cats Jump*.............	8.00 -	12.00
JIMMY ROGERS (& HIS ROCKING **FOUR/TRIO):**		
Chess 1506 *Back Door Friend*.............	25.00 -	40.00
1519 *The Last Time*.............	25.00 -	40.00
1543 *Act Like You Love Me*.......	15.00 -	20.00
1574 *Sloppy Drunk*.............	15.00 -	20.00
1616, 1643, 1659.............	5.00 -	8.00
1687, 1721.............	4.00 -	6.00
KENNY ROGERS:		
Ken-Lee 102 *Jole Blon*.................	5.00 -	8.00
Spade—*That Crazy Feeling*..................	————	
—*We'll Always Have Each Other*...........	————	
LELAN ROGERS:		
Lynn 502 *Hold, Part 1/Part 2*...............	8.00 -	12.00
ROY ROGERS:		
RCA Victor (LP) 1439 (& Dale Evans).........	15.00 -	20.00
(LP) 3041 (10") *Souvenir Album*...........	15.00 -	20.00
WELDON ROGERS:		
Imperial 5451 *So Long, Good Luck, And Goodbye*	20.00 -	30.00
Je-Wel 103 *This Song Is Just For You*.........	————	
104 *Women Drivers*...............	————	
105 *Heaven's Back Door*.............	————	
107 *If I Had One Day To Live*.........	————	
Peach 744 *If I Had One Day To Live*.........	————	
748 *I've Got The Yearning*.............	————	
ROLLING CREW:		
Aladdin 3301 *Home On Alcatraz*............	15.00 -	20.00
RICH ROMAN:		
CG 5003 *T.T.B.*.....................	7.00 -	10.00
ROMANCERS:		
Bay-Tone 101 *You Don't Understand*.........	8.00 -	12.00
Celebrity 701 *No Greater Love*.............	5.00 -	8.00
Dootone 381 *I Still Remember*.............	10.00 -	15.00
404 *This Is Goodbye*.............	10.00 -	15.00
Linda 119 *My Heart Cries*.............	4.00 -	7.00
Marquee 711 *Take Me To Paradise*........	5.00 -	8.00
Palette 5075 *It Only Happens With You*.......	————	
ROMANS:		
M.M.I. 1238 *Wild Ideas*.............	5.00 -	8.00
ROMEOS:		
Apollo 461 *I Beg You Please*.............	40.00 -	60.00
Atco 6107 *Fine Fine Baby*.............	8.00 -	12.00
Fox 748/749 *Let's Be Partners*.............	40.00 -	60.00
845/846 *Moments To Remeber*.............	20.00 -	30.00

RONETTES:

Colpix (LP) 486 *The Ronettes*	20.00 -	30.00
Phillies (LP) 4006 *Presenting The Fabulous Ronettes*	35.00 -	50.00
(Note: Some copies read "Ronnettes")		

RONNIE & MARLENE:
Westport 144 *Marlene*	5.00 -	8.00

THE ROOSTERS:
Epic 9487 *Let's Try Again*	5.00 -	8.00

ANDY ROSE:
Aamco 100 *Lov-A-Lov-A Love*	10.00 -	15.00

DANNY ROSS:
Minor 107 *Look At You Go*	15.00 -	20.00

DOCTOR/DR. ROSS (& HIS JUMP & JIVE BOYS/ORBITS):
Chess 1504 *Dr. Ross Boogie*	40.00 -	70.00
D.I.R. 101/102 *Industrial Boogie*	7.00 -	10.00
Fortune 538 *Sugar Mama*	8.00 -	12.00
857 *Cat Squirrel*	5.00 -	8.00
Hi-Q 5027 *Numbers Blues*	5.00 -	8.00
5033 *New York Breakdown*	5.00 -	8.00
Sun 193 *Come Back Baby*	50.00 -	80.00
212 *The Boogie Disease*	50.00 -	80.00

JERRY ROSS:
Murco 1016 *Ever'body's Tryin'*	15.00 -	20.00

LEE ROSS:
Liberty 55127 *Candy Lips*	5.00 -	8.00

PATTY ROSS:
Aardell 107 *Rock It Davy, Rock It*	————	

ROULETTES:
Ebb 124 *The Way You Carry On*	10.00 -	15.00

ROVERS:
Capitol 3078 *Why Oh-h*	5.00 -	8.00
Music City 750 *Why-Ohh* (red plastic)	25.00 -	40.00
780 *Salute To Johnny Ace*	25.00 -	40.00
792 *Whole Lot Of Love*	15.00 -	20.00

LYNN ROWE:
Hitt 181 *Red Rover*	8.00 -	12.00

PECK ROWELL:
Coin 101 *Take It Easy Greasy*	————	

ROYALE MONARCHS:
Dell 101 *Whole Lot Of Shakin' Goin' On*	————	

ROYAL HALOS:
Aladdin 3460 *My Love Is True*	5.00 -	8.00

ROYAL HAWK:
Flair 1013 *I Wonder Why*	10.00 -	15.00

ROYAL HOLIDAYS:
Penthouse 9357 *Margaret*	8.00 -	12.00

ROYAL JOKERS:
Atco 6052, 6077	5.00 -	8.00
Fortune 840 *Sweet Little Angel*	7.00 -	10.00
Hi-Q 5004 *September In The Rain*	5.00 -	8.00

ROYAL NOTES:
Kellit 7032 *Three Speed Girl*	12.00 -	16.00
7034 *You Are My Love*	12.00 -	16.00

ROYALS:
Federal 12064 *Every Beat Of My Heart*	50.00 -	75.00
12077 *Starting From Tonight*	70.00 -	90.00
12088 *Moonrise*	70.00 -	90.00
12113 *Are You Forgetting*	80.00 -	100.00
12121 *The Shrine Of St. Cecilia*	40.00 -	60.00
12133 *Get It*	20.00 -	30.00
12150 *Hello Miss Fine*	15.00 -	20.00
12160 *Someone Like You*	15.00 -	20.00
12169 *Work With Me Annie*	8.00 -	12.00

ROYAL TEENS:
ABC Paramount 9882 *Short Shorts* (78 RPM) . . .	15.00 -	20.00
Capitol 4261, 4335, 4402	3.00 -	6.00
Mighty 109, 111, 112	4.00 -	7.00
Power 113 *Sittin With My Baby*	————	
215 *Short Shorts*	10.00 -	15.00

ROYALTONES:
Old Town 1018 *Crazy Love*	10.00 -	15.00

DON RUBY:
Cub 9012 *Rockin' Piano, Outta Tune Guitar*	15.00 -	20.00

LAWSON RUDD:
Harvest 709 *Shake This Town*	10.00 -	15.00

RAY RUFF:
Bolo 741 *Pledge Of Love*	5.00 -	8.00
Lin 5034, 5035	3.00 -	5.00
Norman 503 *Half-Pint Baby*	5.00 -	8.00
524, 528	4.00 -	7.00

MISTER RUFFIN:
Spark 115 *Bring It On Back*	7.00 -	10.00

RIFF RUFFIN:
Cash 1023 *If I Can't Have You*	5.00 -	8.00

"RUMBLE"
Jubilee (LP) 1114 (various artists)	15.00 -	20.00

THE RUNAROUNDS/RUN-A-ROUNDS:
Felsted 8710 *Send Her Back*	————	
KC 116 *Unbelievable*	————	

OTIS RUSH (& HIS BAND):
Chess 1751, 1775	4.00 -	6.00
Cobra 5000, 5005, 5027, 5030, 5032	4.00 -	7.00
5010 *Groaning The Blues*	6.00 -	10.00
5015 *Jump Sister Bessie*	8.00 -	12.00
5023 *Three Times A Fool*	5.00 -	8.00

BOBBY RUSSELL & THE IMPOLLOS:
Felsted 8520 *She's Gonna Be Sorry*	4.00 -	8.00

MIKE RUSSO:
Crosley 218 *I'm Gonna Knock On Your Door* . .	7.00 -	10.00

CATHY RYAN & THE ADMIRALS:
King 4792 *It's A Sad, Sad Feeling*	10.00 -	15.00

CHARLEY RYAN:
Souvenir 101 *Hot Rod Lincoln*	20.00 -	30.00

JUNIOR RYDER AND THE PEACOCKS:
Duke 119 *Sad Story*	8.00 -	12.00

FORREST RYE:
Fortune 172 *Wild Cat Boogie*	7.00 -	10.00

RYTHM ROCKERS (See RHYTHM ROCKERS)

SABRES:
Cal-West 45847 *Always Forever*	20.00 -	30.00

THE SAFARIS:
Eldo 101 *Image Of A Girl*	5.00 -	8.00
110 *In The Still On The Night*	7.00 -	10.00

DOUG SAHM (& THE MARKAYS/ PHAROAHS/DELL-KINGS): (See also LITTLE DOUG)
Harlem 107 *Why, Why, Why*	7.00 -	10.00
108 Baby Tell Me	*10.00 -*	*15.00*
113 Slow Down	9.00 -	12.00
116 *Sapphire* (possibly unissued)	————	
Renner 212 *Big Hat*	5.00 -	8.00
215 *Crazy Crazy Feeling*	5.00 -	8.00
226 *Two Hearts In Love*	5.00 -	8.00
232 *Little Angel*	5.00 -	8.00
240 *Lucky Me*	5.00 -	8.00
247 *Mister Kool*	5.00 -	8.00
Satin 100 *Crazy Daisy*	15.00 -	20.00
Warrior 507 *Crazy Daisy*	15.00 -	25.00

SAIGONS:
Dootone 375 *You're Heavenly*	15.00 -	20.00

SAILOR BOY:
Dig 116 *Country Home*	7.00 -	10.00
126 *What Have I Done Wrong*	7.00 -	10.00

NICKY ST. CLAIR (See THE FIVE TROJANS)

ST. LOUIS JIMMY:
Duke 110 *Drinkin' Woman*	10.00 -	15.00
Herald 407 *Hard Luck Boogie*	20.00 -	30.00
Parrot 823 *Murder In The First Degree*	15.00 -	20.00

ST. LOUIS MAC:
Bea & Baby 113 *Broken Heart*	8.00 -	12.00

MAC SALES:
Meteor 5022 *A Gal Named Joe* (red label)	15.00 -	25.00

SAM THE SHAM & THE PHAROAHS:
XL 906 *Wooly Bully* . . . . 10.00 - 15.00

SAMMY & THE DEL-LARKS:
En-Jay 100 *I Never Will Forget* . . . . 10.00 - 15.00

CLARENCE SAMUELS:
Apt 25028 *We're Going To The Hop* . . . . 5.00 - 8.00
Excello 2093 *Chicken Hearted Woman* . . . . 7.00 - 10.00
Lamp 8004 *Crazy With The Heart* . . . . 7.00 - 10.00
     8005 *Lightnin' Struck Me* . . . . 7.00 - 10.00

CURLEY SANDERS (& THE SANTONES):
Concept—*Walking Blues* . . . . ————
Jamboree 509 *Brand New Rock & Roll* . . . . 8.00 - 12.00

HANK SANDERS:
Crest 1039 *How Much How Much* . . . . 10.00 - 15.00

SLIM SANDERS:
V-M 612 *All My Love* . . . . 10.00 - 15.00

WILLIS SANDERS & THE EMBERS:
Juno 215 *I'll Be With You* . . . . ————
Jupiter 213 *Taking A Chance On You* . . . . 10.00 - 15.00

SANDMEN: (See also CHUCK WILLIS)
Okeh 7052 *Somebody To Love* . . . . 10.00 - 15.00

TOMMY SANDS:
RCA Victor 5435 *Love Pains* . . . . 7.00 - 10.00
     5800 *Don't Drop It* . . . . 5.00 - 8.00

FRANK SANDY & THE JACKALS:
MGM 12678 *Let's Go Rock 'N' Roll* . . . . ————

RALPH SANFORD:
King 1403 *Oo-Ee-Baby* . . . . 7.00 - 10.00

JOHNNY SARDO:
Chock Full Of Hits 104 *Romance In The Dark* . . 15.00 - 20.00
     —*Hip Hop Take A Ride With Me* . . . . ————
Warner Bros. 5014 *I Wanna Rock* . . . . 4.00 - 7.00

SATELLITES:
Class 234 *Heavenly Angel* . . . . 8.00 - 12.00
Malynn 234 *Heavenly Angel* . . . . ————

SATINTONES:
Motown 1000 *My Beloved* . . . . 10.00 - 15.00
     1006 *A Love That Can Never Be* . . . . 8.00 - 12.00
     1020 *Zing Went The Strings Of My Heart* . . . . 10.00 - 15.00

SATISFACTIONS:
Chesapeake—*We Will Walk Together* . . . . 8.00 - 12.00

SAUCERS:
Felco 104 *Why Do I Dream* . . . . 8.00 - 12.00
Kick 100 *Hi-Oom* . . . . 15.00 - 20.00
Lynne 101 *Hello Darling* . . . . 30.00 - 40.00

LITTLE BUTCHIE SAUNDERS & HIS
     BUDDIES:
Herald 485, 491 . . . . 7.00 - 10.00

DUKE SAVAGE & ARRIBINS:
Argo 5346 *Your Love* . . . . 5.00 - 8.00

ASHTON SAVOY & HIS COMBO:
Hollywood 1081 *Juke Joint* . . . . 8.00 - 12.00

SAVOYS:
Combo 75 *Darling Stay With Me* . . . . 25.00 - 35.00
     81 *Evil Ways* . . . . 15.00 - 25.00
Combo 90 *Chip Chop Boom* . . . . 15.00 - 25.00
Savoy 1188 *Say You're Mine* . . . . 7.00 - 10.00
Tip Top 1008 *Sweetheart Darling* . . . . 60.00 - 90.00

HENRY SAWYER & THE JUPITERS:
Planet-X 9621 *It Takes Two* . . . . ————

RAY SAWYER:
Sandy 1030 *Rockin' Satellite* . . . . 10.00 - 15.00

SAXONS:
Contender 1313 *Is It True* . . . . 10.00 - 15.00
Tampa 139 *My Love Is True* . . . . 10.00 - 15.00

ALONZO SCALES:
Wing 90020 *My Baby Likes To Shuffle* . . . . 15.00 - 25.00
     90049 *Hard Luck Child* . . . . 15.00 - 25.00

SCALE-TONES:
Jay-Dee 810 *Everlasting Love* . . . . 10.00 - 15.00

SCAMPS:
Peacock 1655 *Yes, My Baby* . . . . 8.00 - 12.00

SCARLETS:
Cine Vista 1001 *Joannie* . . . . 8.00 - 12.00
Fury 1036 *Truly Yours* . . . . 5.00 - 8.00
Klilk 7905 *She's Gone* . . . . 10.00 - 15.00
Red Robin 128 *Dear One* . . . . 25.00 - 35.00
     133 *Love Doll* . . . . 30.00 - 40.00
     135 *True Love* . . . . 30.00 - 40.00
     138 *Kiss Me* . . . . 35.00 - 50.00

MURRAY SCHAFF'S ARISTOCRATS:
Essex 366 *Believe Me* . . . . ————
Sound 101 *Believe Me* . . . . ————

STEVE SCHICKEL:
Mercury 70999 *Leave My Sideburns Be* . . . . 8.00 - 12.00

TYRONE SCHMIDLING:
Andex 4022 *Honey Don't* . . . . 15.00 - 25.00

THE SCHOLARS:
Imperial 5449 *Beloved* . . . . 5.00 - 8.00

SCHOOLBOY CLEVE:
Feature 3013 *Strange Letter Blues* . . . . 10.00 - 15.00

SCHOOLBOYS:
Juanita 103 *Angel Of Love* . . . . 8.00 - 12.00
Okeh 7076 *Shirley* . . . . 5.00 - 8.00
     7085 *Mary* . . . . 5.00 - 8.00
     7090 *Pearl* . . . . 6.00 - 9.00

DUANE SCHURB:
Enterprise 1226 *Rolly Polly* . . . . 10.00 - 15.00

STEVE SCHULTE:
Felsted 8502 *Too Blue To Cry* . . . . 5.00 - 8.00

HOYT SCOGGINS:
Starday—*Tennesse Rock* . . . . 10.00 - 15.00

SCOOTERS:
Dawn 224 *Someday We'll Meet Again* . . . . 15.00 - 20.00

SCOTT BROTHERS:
Fabor 117 *Yuggi Duggi* . . . . 5.00 - 8.00

JACK SCOTT:
ABC Paramount 9818 *Baby She's Gone* . . . . 15.00 - 20.00
     9860 *Two Timin' Woman* . . . . 15.00 - 20.00
Capitol (LP) 2035 *Burning Bridges* . . . . 20.00 - 30.00
Carlton (LP) 107 *Jack Scott* . . . . 35.00 - 50.00
     (LP) 122 *What Am I Living For* . . . . 35.00 - 50.00
     462, 483, 504, 514, 519 . . . . 3.00 - 5.00
     (EP) 1070, 1071 *Presenting Jack Scott* . . . . . . 12.00 - 16.00
     (EP) 1072 *Jack Scott Sings* . . . . 12.00 - 16.00
Groove 58-0031, 58-0037, 58-0042 . . . . 4.00 - 7.00
Guaranteed 211 *Go Wild Little Sadie* . . . . 4.00 - 7.00
Jubilee 5606 *My Special Angel* . . . . 4.00 - 7.00
Sesac (LP) 4201/4202 *Soul Stirring* . . . . ————
Top Rank (LP) 319, 619 *I Remember Hank Williams* 25.00 - 40.00
Top Rank (LP) 326, 626 *What In The World's Come*
     Over You . . . . 25.00 - 40.00
     2055, 2075, 2093 . . . . 3.00 - 6.00

MABEL SCOTT:
Parrot 780 *Mabel's Blues* (red plastic) . . . . 15.00 - 20.00

RAY SCOTT (& THE SHADES):
Erwin 700 *Boppin' Wigwam Willie* . . . . ————
Satellite 104 *You Drive Me Crazy* . . . . 50.00 - 80.00
Stomper Time—*High Heel Sneakers* . . . . ————
     1161 *Boy Meets Girl* . . . . 30.00 - 50.00
Tri Ess 1001 *We Need Love* . . . . 4.00 - 7.00

RODNEY SCOTT:
Canon 225 *Granny Went Rockin'* . . . . 10.00 - 15.00
     231 *You're So Square* . . . . 10.00 - 15.00

SANDY SCOTT:
Choice 5606 *Shake It Up* . . . . 7.00 - 10.00

TOMMY SCOTT:
Federal 10003 *Rockin' And Rollin'* . . . . 7.00 - 10.00
     10011 *Tennessee* . . . . 7.00 - 10.00

LEVI SEABURY:
Blues Boy Kingdom 101 *Boogie Beat* . . . . 10.00 - 15.00

EDDIE SEACREST:
KRC 5001 *Shakin' With A Flavor* . . . . 15.00 - 20.00

KELLY SEARS:
Quintet 104 *Barnyard Rock*.................. 5.00 - 8.00

DICK SEATON:
K-Ark—*Juke Box Rock*...................... 15.00 - 20.00

SEBASTIAN:
Take 30 2002 *Darling I Do*................. 7.00 - 10.00

SECRETS:
Decca 30350 *See You Next Year*............ 5.00 - 8.00

NEIL SEDAKA:
Decca 30520 *Laura Lee*.................... 10.00 - 15.00
Guyden 2004 *Ring-A-Rockin'*.............. 7.00 - 10.00
Legion 133 *Ring-A-Rockin'*............... 10.00 - 15.00

ALVIE SELF:
Don-Ray 5960 *Let's Go Wild*.............. 8.00 - 12.00

JIMMY SELF:
Coral 62009 *Oh Babe*..................... ————

RONNIE SELF:
ABC Paramount 9714 *Pretty Bad Blues*....... 25.00 - 35.00
  9768 *Sweet Love*..................... 25.00 - 35.00
Columbia (EP) 2149 *Ain't I'm A Dog*..... 50.00 - 75.00
  40875 *Big Fool*...................... 8.00 - 12.00
  40989 *Ain't I'm A Dog*............... 8.00 - 12.00
  41101 *Bop-A-Lena*.................... 8.00 - 12.00
  41166 *Date Bate*..................... 8.00 - 12.00
  41241 *Petrified*..................... 8.00 - 12.00
Decca 30958, 31131...................... 3.00 - 5.00

STEWART SELF:
Starrett 5709 *Mary Ellen*................ 5.00 - 8.00

SENATORS:
Golden Crest 514 *Loretta*............... *7.00 - 10.00*
Winn 1917 *Wedding Bells*................. 15.00 - 20.00

SENIORS:
Interlude 163 *It's Been A Long Time*......... ————
Tetra 4446 *Evening Shadows Falling*......... 15.00 - 20.00

CHARLES SENNS:
OJ 1014 *Gee Whiz Liz*.................... 15.00 - 20.00

SENSATIONS:
Argo (LP) 4022 *Let Me In*............... 20.00 - 30.00
Atco 6056 *Yes Sir That's My Baby*....... 5.00 - 8.00
  6090 *You Made Me Love You*............ 5.00 - 8.00

SENTIMENTALS:
Mint 802 *Wedding Bells*.................. 4.00 - 7.00

SEQUINS:
Red Robin 140 *Don't Fall In Love*............ 30.00 - 40.00

SERENADERS:
Chock-Full-Of-Hits— *I Wrote A Letter*........ ————
De Luxe 6022 *Please, Please Forgive Me*....... 50.00 - 75.00
J-V-B 2001 *Tomorrow Night*............... 75.00 - 100.00
MGM 12623 *Never Let Me Go*............... 15.00 - 20.00
Teen Life 9 *Gates Of Gold*.............. 50.00 - 75.00

JOANNA SEVILLE:
Ace 654 *There Was A Boy*................ ————

SEVILLES:
J-C 116 *Charlena*....................... 7.00 - 10.00

SHADOWS:
Decca 48307 *Tell Her*................... 15.00 - 20.00
Del-Fi 4109 *Under Stars Of Love*......... 5.00 - 8.00
Delta 1509 *There Stands The Glass*.......... 30.00 - 40.00

SHAKEY JAKE:
Artistic 1502 *Roll Your Money Maker*........ 7.00 - 10.00
The Blues 303 *Respect Me Baby*............ 7.00 - 10.00

DEL SHANNON:
Big Top (LP) 1303 *Runaway*............... 20.00 - 30.00
  (LP) 1308 *Little Town Flirt*......... 20.00 - 30.00

SHANTONS:
Jay-Mar 164 *Lover's March*.............. 15.00 - 20.00
  241 *Lucille*........................ 15.00 - 20.00
Pam 112 *Why Don't You Believe Me*........ 15.00 - 20.00

SHARPS:
Aladdin 3401 *What Will I Gain*............ 8.00 - 12.00
Chess 1690 *6 Months, Three Weeks*......... ————

Combo 146 *All My Love*................... 10.00 - 15.00
Dot 15806 *All My Love*.................. 7.00 - 10.00
Jamie 1040 *Come On*..................... 5.00 - 8.00
  1108 *Look At Me*.................... 5.00 - 8.00
  1114 *Here's My Heart*............... 5.00 - 8.00
Lamp 2007 *Lock My Heart*................ 10.00 - 15.00
2 Mikes— *Heaven Only Knows*............. 100.00 up
Vik 0264 *Come On*....................... 7.00 - 10.00

LAWRENCE SHAUL:
Reed 1049 *Tutti Frutti*.................. 15.00 - 20.00

SHA-WEEZ:
Aladdin 3170 *No One To Love Me*.......... 100.00 - 150.00

THE SH-BOOMS:
Cat 117 *Could It Be*.................... 5.00 - 8.00

JERRY SHEELY & THE VERSATILES:
Star 220 *Love Only Me*.................. ————

THE SHEIKS (See SHIEKS) JIM SHELBY:
Barton 409 *I'm A Long Gone Daddy*......... 10.00 - 15.00

THE SHELLS:
Johnson 104 *Baby Oh Baby*............... 5.00 - 8.00
  107 *Explain It To Me*............... 7.00 - 10.00
  109 *Better Forget Him*.............. 5.00 - 8.00
  110 *In The Dim Light Of Dark*....... 7.00 - 10.00
  119 *Deep In My Heart*............... 5.00 - 8.00

GARY SHELTON:
Mercury 71310 *Kissin' At The Drive-In*....... 5.00 - 8.00

ROSCOE SHELTON:
Excello 2146, 2167, 2170, 2176, 2181, 2192, 2198   3.00 - 5.00
  (LP) 8002 *Roscoe Shelton*............. *15.00 - 20.00*

THE SHEPPARDS:
Apex 7750 *Never Felt This Way Before*........ 7.00 - 10.00
  7760 *Just Like You*................. 7.00 - 10.00
  7762 *Tragic*........................ 7.00 - 10.00
Theron 112 *Love*....................... 50.00 - 75.00
United 198 *Sherry*...................... 25.00 - 35.00
Wes 7750 *The Glitter In Your Eyes*........... ————

TONY SHERIDAN & THE BEAT BROTHERS:
Decca 31382 *My Bonnie/The Saints*.......... 100.00-up
(Note: Prices as high as $1000.00 have been quoted
  for this Beatle record! Promotional copies are com-
  moner than regular commercial copies.)

SHERIFF & REVELS:
Vee Jay 306 *Shambalor*.................. 10.00 - 15.00

BILL(Y) SHERRELL/SHERRILL:
Mercury 71679 *Like Makin' Love*.......... 5.00 - 8.00
Tyme 102 *Cadillac Baby*................. 10.00 - 15.00
  104 *Kool Kat*....................... 10.00 - 15.00
  106 *Rock On Baby*................... 10.00 - 15.00

SHERWOODS:
Magnifico 105 *Happy Holiday*............. 7.00 - 10.00

SHIEKS:
Cat 116 *Walk That Walk*................. 7.00 - 10.00
Ef-N-De 100 *Baby Please Don't Cry* (red label).. 80.00 - 120.00
Federal 12237 *Sentimental Heart*......... 15.00 - 20.00
  12355 *Sentimental Heart*............ 8.00 - 12.00

SHIELDS:
Dot 15856 *I'm Sorry Now*................ 7.00 - 10.00
Falcon 100 *You'll Be Coming Home Soon*...... ————
Tender 513 *You Cheated*................. 10.00 - 15.00

THE SHINDIGS:
Mustang 3003 *Wolfman*................... ————

REESE SHIPLEY:
Valley 106 *Catfish Boogie*.............. 5.00 - 8.00

SHIRELLES:
Decca 30669 *My Love Is A Charm*.......... 7.00 - 10.00
  30761 *I Got The Message*............. 7.00 - 10.00
Scepter (LP) 501 *Tonight's The Night*......... 20.00 - 30.00
  (LP) 504 *Baby It's You*............. 20.00 - 30.00
  1208 *Tonight's The Night* (pink & black label). 8.00 - 12.00
  1211, 1212.......................... 4.00 - 7.00

SHIRLEY & LEE:
Aladdin 3153 *I'm Gone*.................... 15.00 - 20.00
   3173 *Baby*....................... 12.00 - 16.00
   3192 *So In Love*................ 10.00 - 15.00
   3205 *The Proposal*........... 10.00 - 15.00
   3222 *Lee Goofed*.............. 8.00 - 12.00
   3244 *Confessin'*............... 7.00 - 10.00
   3289 *Feel So Good*........... 5.00 - 8.00
   3302 *Lee's Dream*............ 5.00 - 8.00
   3318, 3325, 3338, 3362, 3369, 3380, 3390.... 3.00 - 6.00
  Imperial (LP) 9179 *Let The Good Times Roll*... 40.00 - 50.00
  Score (LP) 4023 *Let The Good Times Roll*..... 60.00 - 90.00
  Warwick (LP) 2028 *Let The Good Times Roll*... 20.00 - 30.00
TROY SHONDELL:
Gold Crest 161 *This Time*............... 7.00 - 10.00
THE SHONDELLS (See TOMMY JAMES):
SHOWCASES:
Galaxy 732 *This Love Is Real*............... ———
HAROLD SHUTTERS:
Golden Rod 204 *Rock 'N' Roll Mr. Moon*...... 30.00 - 40.00
   300 *Bunny Honey*.................... ———
SHYTANS:
Bruce 110 *Skokiann*................. 7.00 - 10.00
JERRY SIEFERT:
Note 10018 *Dirty White Bucks And The Tight Peg
Pants*........................ 10.00 - 15.00
SILHOUETTES:
Ember 1029, 1032, 1027.................. 4.00 - 7.00
   1029 *Get A Job* (78 RPM)............ 15.00 - 25.00
   1032 *Headin' For The Poorhouse* (78 RPM).. 7.00 - 10.00
  Junior 396 *I Sold My Heart To The Junkman*.. 15.00 - 20.00
   400 *Evelyn*...................... 15.00 - 20.00
   593 *Get A Job*..................... 30.00 - 40.00
(Note: Above should have brown label.)
  20th Fox 240 *Never*................... 10.00 - 15.00
BOB SILVA:
Monarch— *Weepin' And Wailin'*............. ———
THE SILVA-TONES (See SYLVA-TONES)
SID SILVER:
Bakersfield 510 *Bumble Rumble*............. 8.00 - 12.00
JOHNNIE SILVERS:
Sims 111 *Tuff Stuff* (blue label)........... 10.00 - 15.00
SILVERTONES:
Joey 302 *Canadian Sunset*................. 10.00 - 15.00
AL SIMMONS:
Dig 138 *Old Folks Boogie*............. 7.00 - 10.00
   142 *You Ain't Too Old*............... 7.00 - 10.00
GENE SIMMONS:
Sun 299 *Drinkin' Wine*.................... 30.00 - 50.00
MACK SIMMONS & HIS BOYS:
C.J. 607 *Jumping At The Cadillac*........... 5.00 - 8.00
FRANK SIMON:
4 Star 1647 *Sugar Plum Boogie*............. 8.00 - 12.00
DONALD SIMPSON & THE ROCKENETTES:
Major 1002 *Save Me Your Love*........ 25.00 - 35.00
CHUCK SIMS:
Trend 30-000 *Little Pigeon*................. 7.00 - 10.00
FRANKIE LEE SIMS:
Ace 524, 527, 539.................... 4.00 - 7.00
Speciality 459 *Lucy Mae Blues*............. 6.00 - 10.00
   478 *I'm Long Gone*............... 6.00 - 10.00
   487 *I'll Get Along Somehow*........ 6.00 - 10.00
   (LP) 2124 *Lucy Mae Blues*......... 20.00 - 30.00
Vin 1006 *Well Goodbye Baby*........... 5.00 - 8.00
MAC SIMS:
Pacer 1201 *Drivin' Wheel*.............. 8.00 - 12.00
BEAD SINGLETON & THE NOTES:
Stentor 101 *Shrine Of Echoes*........... 15.00 - 20.00
EDDIE SINGLETON & THE CHROMATICS:
Brunswick 55080 *Too Late*................. 15.00 - 25.00

BOBBY SISCO:
Chess 1650 *Go, Go, Go*.................... 20.00 - 30.00
Mar-Vel 111 *Honky Tonkin Rhythm*......... 15.00 - 20.00
GENE SISCO:
Dess 7001 *Grandma Rock And Roll*.......... 15.00 - 25.00
SIX TEENS:
Flip 315, 322, 326................... 3.00 - 5.00
   315 *Casual Look* (78 RPM)............. 10.00 - 15.00
SKEE BROTHERS:
Epic 9275 *Big Deal*.................... 10.00 - 15.00
Okeh 7108 *That's All She Wrote*........... 15.00 - 20.00
EDDIE SKELTON:
Dixie 2011 *Keep It Swinging*.............. 25.00 - 35.00
Starday 924 *My Heart Gets Lonely*......... 15.00 - 25.00
   315 *That's Love*.................... 15.00 - 25.00
BILL SKIDMORE III:
Crest 1040 *Date Bait*................... 10.00 - 15.00
MACY SKIPPER:
Light 2020 *Who Put The Squeeze*............ 10.00 - 15.00
NORM SKYLAR:
Crest 104 *Rock 'N' Roll Blues*............. 15.00 - 20.00
SKYLARKS:
Decca 48241 *You And I*................ 30.00 - 40.00
THE SKYLINERS:
Calico 103, 109, 117................. 3.00 - 5.00
   (LP) 3000 *The Skyliners*................ 30.00 - 40.00
Colpix 188 *I'll Close My Eyes*............. 5.00 - 8.00
THE SKYSCRAPERS:
Mercury 70795 *I Thought You'd Care*........ 12.00 - 16.00
FREDDIE SLACK:
Wing (LP) 60003 *Boogie Woogie On The 88*.... 15.00 - 20.00
SLADES:
Domino 500 *You Cheated*............... 7.00 - 10.00
   800 *You Gambled*.................. 5.00 - 8.00
   901 *Just You*..................... 5.00 - 8.00
Liberty 55118 *Baby*.................. 4.00 - 6.00
SLICK SLAVIN:
Imperial 5540 *Speed Crazy*................. 8.00 - 12.00
SLIM HARPO (See HARPO)
SLY FOX:
Spark 108 *Hoo-Doo Say*.................... 15.00 - 20.00
   112 *My Four Women*................. 15.00 - 20.00
SMART TONES:
Hearld 529 *Bob-O-Link*............... 10.00 - 15.00
AL SMITH:
Goldband 1092 *If I Don't See You*............ 4.00 - 7.00
ARTHUR SMITH:
MGM (LP) 236 (10") *Foolish Questions*....... 15.00 - 20.00
   (LP) 533 (10") *Fingers On Fire*............. 20.00 - 30.00
   (LP) 3301 (10") *Specials*............... 20.00 - 30.00
   (LP) 3525 *Fingers On Fire*............. 20.00 - 30.00
   12544 *Teen-Aged Rebel*............. 7.00 - 10.00
BILLY SMITH:
Red Head— *Tell Me Baby*.................. ———
BOBBY SMITH:
Fox 104 *She's Gone From Me*.............. 15.00 - 20.00
CARL SMITH:
Columbia (LP) 959 *Sunny Down South*........ 12.00 - 18.00
   (LP) 1022 *Smith's The Name*........ 12.00 - 18.00
   (LP) 1172 *Let's Live A Little*......... 10.00 - 15.00
   (LP) 2579 (10")................. 15.00 - 20.00
   (LP) 9025 (10") *Sentimental Songs*........... 15.00 - 20.00
   (EP) 9591, 10222.................. 4.00 - 7.00
CHESTER SMITH:
Decca 30603 *You Gotta Move*.............. 5.00 - 8.00
DAYTON SMITH:
Warrior 501 *What Will The Answer Be*........ 10.00 - 15.00
FLOYD SMITH & THE MONTCLAIRS:
Fortune 540 *This Is A Miracle*.............. 5.00 - 8.00
GENE SMITH:
Rem 458 *I'm Gone*....................... 15.00 - 20.00

(LITTLE) GEORGE SMITH (& HIS HARMONICA):

Carolyn 1420 *Nobody Knows*	7.00 -	10.00
J&M 001 *Go Ahead On Women*	25.00 -	35.00
RPM 434 *Telephone Blues*	7.00 -	10.00
442 *Blues Stay Away*	7.00 -	10.00
456 *Love Life*	7.00 -	10.00
478 *You Don't Love Me*	5.00 -	8.00

HENRY SMITH:

Dot 1220 *Good Rocking Mama*	10.00 -	15.00

HUEY (PIANO) SMITH & HIS CLOWNS:

Ace (EP) 104 *Having Fun With Huey Smith*	10.00 -	15.00
530 *Rocking Pneumonia & The Boogie Woogie Flu* (78 RPM)	15.00 -	20.00
538 *Just A Lonely Clown* (78 RPM)	8.00 -	12.00
(LP) 1004 *Having A Good Time*	20.00 -	25.00
(LP) 1015 *For Dancing*	20.00 -	25.00
(LP) 1027 *'Twas The Night Before Christmas*	15.00 -	25.00
8008 *Quiet As It's Kept*	———	

KENNY SMITH:

Rural Rhythm 507 *Walkin' By My Lonesome*	15.00 -	20.00

LENDON SMITH with THE JESTERS:

Meteor 5030 *Lost Love*	15.00 -	20.00

MACK ALLEN SMITH:

Statue 602 *Such A Night*	5.00 -	8.00
607 *Mean Old Frisco*	4.00 -	7.00

RAY SMITH: (See also PAT CUPP)

Infinity 007 *Let Yourself Go*	5.00 -	8.00
Judd (LP) 701 *Travelin' With Ray*	75.00 -	100.00
Sun 298 *Right Behind You Baby*	5.00 -	8.00
308 *Why Why Why*	5.00 -	8.00
319 *Rockin' Bandit*	4.00 -	7.00
372 *Travelin' Salesman*	5.00 -	8.00
375 *Candy Doll*	4.00 -	7.00
Tollie 9029 *Did We Have A Party*	8.00 -	12.00

ROBERT CURTIS SMITH:

Bluesville (LP) 1064 *Clarksville Blues*	———	

RONNIE/RONNY SMITH:

Brunswick 55137 *Lookie, Lookie, Lookie*	5.00 -	8.00
Hamilton 50003 *My Babe*	4.00 -	7.00
Imperial 5667 *Long Time No Love*	5.00 -	8.00
5679 *I Hear You Knocking*	4.00 -	7.00

SAMMY SMITH:

Wee Rebel 102 *Alaska Rock*	15.00 -	20.00

SHELBY SMITH:

Rebel 728 *Rockin' Mama*	20.00 -	30.00

WARREN SMITH:

Sun 239 *Rock 'N' Roll Ruby*	8.00 -	12.00
250 *Ubangi Stomp*	8.00 -	12.00
268 *Miss Froggie*	5.00 -	8.00
286 *I've Got Love If You Want It*	7.00 -	10.00
314 *Sweet Sweet Girl*	5.00 -	8.00

LONNIE SMITHSON:

Starday 330 *Me And The Blues*	10.00 -	15.00

SMOKEY JOE:

Flip 228 *Signifying Monkey*	15.00 -	20.00
Sun 228 *Signifying Monkey*	25.00 -	40.00

SMOOTHTONES:

Jem 412 *Bring Back Your Love To Me*	10.00 -	15.00

SMOKEY SMOTHERS:

Federal 12385, 12395, 12405, 12420, 12441, 12466, 12488, 12503	3.00 -	5.00
King (LP) 779	15.00 -	20.00

THE SNAPPERS:

20th Fox 148 *If There Were*	7.00 -	10.00

LESLIE SNEED:

Cascade 103 *Oh, Baby Doll*	7.00 -	10.00

EDDIE SNOW:

Sun 226 *Ain't That Right*	40.00 -	60.00

HANK SNOW:

RCA Victor (LP) 1113 *Just Keep A-Movin'*	15.00 -	20.00
(LP) 1156 *Old Doc Brown*	15.00 -	20.00
(LP) 1233 *Country Classics*	15.00 -	20.00
(LP) 1419 *Country & Western Jamboree*	15.00 -	20.00
(LP) 1435 *Country Guitar, Vol. 2*	15.00 -	20.00
(LP) 3026 (10") *Hank Snow*	20.00 -	30.00
(LP) 3070 (10") *Hank Snow Sings*	15.00 -	25.00
(LP) 3131 (10") *Hank Snow Salutes Jimmy Rodgers*	20.00 -	30.00
(LP) 3267 (10") *Country Guitar*	15.00 -	25.00

THE SOLATAIRES/SOLITAIRES:

Argo 5316 *Please Kiss This Letter*	5.00 -	8.00
Old Town 1000 *Blue Valentine*	10.00 -	15.00
1006 *Please Remember My Heart*	15.00 -	20.00
1006/1007 *Please Remember My Heart*	20.00 -	30.00
(Note: Later issues have #1006 on both sides)		
Old Town 1008 *Lonely*	35.00 -	50.00
1010 *I Don't Stand A Ghost Of A Chance*	30.00 -	40.00
1012 *My Dear*	8.00 -	12.00
1014 *The Wedding*	7.00 -	10.00
1015 *Magic Rose*	7.00 -	10.00
1019 *The Honeymoon*	7.00 -	10.00
1026 *The Angels Song*	7.00 -	10.00
1032 *Give Me One More Chance*	7.00 -	10.00
1034 *Walking Along*	5.00 -	8.00
1044 *No More Sorrows*	5.00 -	8.00
1049, 1066, 1071, 1096	4.00 -	7.00

KING SOLOMON:

Big Town 102 *Mean Train*	15.00 -	20.00

SOLOTONES:

Excello 2060 *Front Page Blues*	20.00 -	30.00

SONICS:

Checker 922 *You Made Me Cry*	7.00 -	10.00
Groove 0112 *As I Live On*	15.00 -	20.00
Harvard 801 *This Broken Heart*	10.00 -	15.00
X-Tra— *Once In A Lifetime*	15.00 -	20.00

SONNY GUITAR:

Yucca 136 *Betty Lou*	8.00 -	12.00

SONS OF THE PIONEERS:

Camden (LP) 413 *Wagons West*	8.00 -	12.00
RCA Victor (LP) 1130 *Favorites*	10.00 -	15.00
(LP) 1431 *How Great Thou Art*	10.00 -	15.00
(LP) 1483 *One Man's Songs*	10.00 -	15.00
(LP) 3032 (10")	15.00 -	20.00
(LP) 3095 (10")	15.00 -	20.00
(LP) 3162 (10") *Western Classics*	15.00 -	20.00

SOOTHERS:

Part 70041 *I Believe In You*	5.00 -	8.00

THE SOPHOMORES:

Dawn 216 *Cool Cool Baby*	5.00 -	8.00
218 *I Get A Thrill*	5.00 -	8.00
Epic 9259 *Charade*	—	

THE SOUL STIRRERS featuring SAM COOKE:

Specialty (LP) 2106	15.00 -	25.00

SOUNDS:

Modern 981 *Sweet Sixteen*	8.00 -	12.00
Sarg 172 *Life*	10.00 -	15.00
181 *My Pillow Of Dreams*	10.00 -	15.00

SOUVENIERS:

Inferno 2001 *I Could Have Danced All Night*	8.00 -	12.00

RED SOVINE:

Decca 30239 *Juke Joint Johnny*	5.00 -	8.00

BOB B. SOXX & THE BLUE JEANS:

Philles (LP) 1002 *Zip-A-Dee Doo Dah* (blue label)	25.00 -	35.00

SPADES:

Major 1007 *Close To You*	15.00 -	20.00

DICK SPAIN:

Oasis 1001 *Straw Broom Boogie*	25.00 -	35.00

SPANIELS:

Chance 1141 *Baby It's You* (red plastic)	75.00 -	100.00
Neptune 125 *For Sentimental Reasons*	7.00 -	10.00
Vee Jay 101 *Baby It's You* (red plastic)	100.00 -	150.00
103 *The Bells Ring Out*	20.00 -	30.00

107 *Goodnite Sweetheart, Goodnite*	15.00 -	20.00
107 same, but red plastic	35.00 -	50.00
116 *Let's Make Up* (red plastic)	35.00 -	50.00
116 *Let's Make Up* (black plastic)	15.00 -	20.00
131 *Don'cha Go*	15.00 -	20.00
154 *You Painted Pictures*	8.00 -	12.00
178 *False Love*	10.00 -	15.00
189 *Dear Heart*	10.00 -	15.00
202 *Since I Fell For You*	15.00 -	20.00
229 *You Gave Me Peace Of Mind*	10.00 -	15.00
246 *I.O.U.*	5.00 -	8.00
257 *I Need Your Kisses*	8.00 -	12.00
264 *I Lost You*	8.00 -	12.00
278 *Tina*	8.00 -	12.00
290 *Stormy Weather*	7.00 -	10.00
301 *Heart And Soul*	10.00 -	15.00
310 *Trees*	8.00 -	12.00
328 *100 Years From Today*	8.00 -	12.00
342 *People Will Say We're In Love*	8.00 -	12.00
350 *Bus Fare Home*	5.00 -	8.00
(LP) 1002 *Goodnight, It's Time To Go* (maroon label)	40.00 -	60.00
(LP) 1024 *The Spaniels*	35.00 -	60.00

OTIS SPANN:
Checker 807 *It Must Have Been The Devil*	5.00 -	8.00

SPARKS:
Hull 723 *Danny Boy*	15.00 -	20.00
724 *Adreann*	8.00 -	12.00
RPM 417 *Make A Little Love*	20.00 -	30.00

SPARKS OF RHYTHM:
Apollo 479 *Don't Love You Any More*	10.00 -	15.00
— *Stars Are In The Sky*	10.00 -	15.00
541 *Everybody Rock And Go*	7.00 -	10.00

JERRY SPARKS:
Fidelity 4058 *My Tears*	4.00 -	7.00

SPARROWS:
Davis 456-45 *Love Me Tender*	15.00 -	25.00
Jay Dee 783 *Tell Me Baby*	25.00 -	35.00
790 *I'll Be Lovin' You*	25.00 -	35.00

MERLE SPEARS:
Whit 711 *Gonna Move*	7.00 -	10.00

SPECK & DOYLE:
Syrup Bucket 1000 *Big Noise, Bright Lights*	35.00 -	50.00

RONNIE SPEEKS & THE ELRODS:
King 5548 *What Is Your Technique*	4.00 -	7.00

SPELLBINDERS:
Date 1556 *Since I Don't Have You*	5.00 -	8.00

JIMMY SPELLMAN:
Dot 15607 *Doggonit*	7.00 -	10.00
Viv 1005 *Lover Man*	10.00 -	15.00

SPENCER & SPENCER:
Gone 5053 *Stagger Lawrence*	4.00 -	7.00

SONNY SPENCER:
Memo 17984 *Gilee*	5.00 -	8.00

SPIDERS:
Imperial 5365 *I Didn't Want To Do It*	18.00 -	20.00
5280 *I'll Stop Crying*	12.00 -	18.00
5291 *I'm Slippin' In*	15.00 -	20.00
(above are blue label with script letters)		
Imperial 5305 *The Real Thing*	10.00 -	15.00
5318 *She Keeps Me Wondering*	12.00 -	18.00
5331 *That's Enough*	8.00 -	12.00
5344 *Am I The One*	8.00 -	12.00
5354 *Bells In My Heart*	8.00 -	12.00
5366, 5376, 5393, 5405, 5423, 5714	5.00 -	10.00
(LP) 9140 *I Didn't Want To Do It*	60.00 -	90.00

SPIEDELS:
Crosley 201 *Dear Joan*	5.00 -	8.00

SPINNERS:
Capitol 3955 *Lovers Prayer*	4.00 -	7.00
Rhythm 125 *My Love And Your Love*	30.00 -	40.00
Tri-Phi 1001 *That's What Girls Are Made For*	5.00 -	8.00

SPLENDORS:
Taurus 10 *The Golden Years*	7.00 -	10.00

SPOTLIGHTERS:
Aladdin 3436 *Whisper*	10.00 -	15.00
Imperial 5342 *It's Cold*	10.00 -	15.00

SPROUTS:
Spangle 2002 *Teen Billy Baby*	10.00 -	15.00

TOMMY SPURLIN:
Art 109 *One Eyed Sam*	25.00 -	40.00
Perfect 109 *Hang Loose*	30.00 -	50.00

THE SPUTNIKS:
Class 217 *My Love Is Gone*	7.00 -	10.00

SPYDELS:
Addit 1220 *We're In Love*	5.00 -	8.00
MZ 009 *No More Teasing*	—	

SQUIRES:
Aladdin 3360 *Dreamy Eyes*	10.00 -	15.00
Boss 2120 *It's Time*	—	
Congress 223 *Joyce*	8.00 -	12.00
Dice 478 *Every Word Of This Song*	7.00 -	10.00
Mambo 105 *Sindy*	15.00 -	20.00
Vita 113 *Me And My Deal*	15.00 -	20.00
116 *Heavenly Angel*	12.00 -	18.00
128 *Breath Of Air*	12.00 -	18.00

SONNY STAFFORD:
Blue Moon 476 *Record Hop Blues*	15.00 -	20.00

JOHNNY STANDLEY:
Magnolia 1003 *Rock & Roll Must Go*	7.00 -	10.00

DOUG STANFORD:
D 1034 *Won't You Tell On Me*	7.00 -	10.00

RAY STANLEY:
Argo 5280 *Over A Coke* (ship logo label)	8.00 -	12.00
Zephyr 011 *Pushin'*	7.00 -	10.00
022 *My Lovin' Baby*	8.00 -	12.00

STAR COMBO:
Skippy 102 *Mr. Rock And Roll*	5.00 -	8.00

JOHNNY STARK:
Crystalette 709 *Roll Baby Roll*	10.00 -	15.00
713 *Cold Coffee*	10.00 -	15.00
715 *Rockin' Billy*	10.00 -	15.00

DOC STARKES:
Linda 109 *Rockin' To School*	15.00 -	25.00

STARLIGHTERS:
Hi-Q 5016 *Zoom*	8.00 -	12.00
Irma 101 *Love Cry*	—	
Sun Coast 1001 *Until You Return*	35.00 -	50.00

STARLINGS:
Dawn 212 *I'm Just A Crying Fool*	—	
Josie 760 *My Plea For Love*	40.00 -	60.00

STARLITES: (See also JACKIE & THE STARLITES)
Combo 73 *Arline*	30.00 -	40.00
Ember 1011 *They Call Me A Dreamer*	10.00 -	15.00
Fury 1034 *Valarie*	8.00 -	12.00
1045 *Silver Lining*	8.00 -	12.00
Peak 5000 *Missing You*	15.00 -	20.00

ANDY STARR:
Arcade 115 *I Love My Baby*	—	
MGM 12263 *Rockin' Rollin' Stone*	20.00 -	30.00
12315 *She's A-Goin' Jessie*	20.00 -	30.00
12364 *Round And Round*	20.00 -	30.00
12421 *No Room For Your Kind*	20.00 -	30.00

BILLY STARR:
Imperial 8186 *Hound Dog*	10.00 -	15.00

FRANK STARR:
Holiday Inn 104 *Knees Shakin'*	10.00 -	15.00
Lin 5009 *Dig Them Squeaky Shoes*	15.00 -	20.00
5013 *Tell Me Why*	7.00 -	10.00
5033 *Me & The Fool*	5.00 -	8.00

JIMMY STARR:
Debbie 101 *Oooh Crazy*	4.00 -	7.00

JIMMY STAYTON:
Blue Hen 220 *Hot Hot Mama*............... 50.00 - 80.00

SONNY STEELE:
Republic 2020 *Mine Mine Mine*............ 4.00 - 7.00

PAUL STEFEN & THE ROYAL LANCERS:
Citation 5004 *Say Mama*................... 4.00 - 7.00

N.A. STEPHENSON:
Westwood 201 *Boogie Woogie Country Girl*.... 35.00 - 50.00

RAY STEVENS:
Capitol 4030 *Cat Pants*................... 7.00 - 10.00

FRANKLIN STEWART:
Lu 501 *That Long Black Train*............. 15.00 - 20.00

GENE STEWART:
King 5124 *Oh Baby, Dance With Me*......... 7.00 - 10.00

VERNON STEWART:
Peach 751 *Mean Mean Baby*................. 15.00 - 20.00

WYNN STEWART:
Jackpot 48005 *Come On*................... 5.00 - 8.00

ARBEE STIDHAM:
Abco 100 *Meet Me Halfway*............... 15.00 - 20.00
   107 *When I Find My Baby*............. 15.00 - 20.00
Checker 778 *I Don't Play*............... 12.00 - 16.00
RCA Victor 47-4951 *I Found Out For Myself*.. 10.00 - 15.00
   50-0003 *I Found Out For Myself*.......... 15.00 - 20.00
   50-0024 *Falling Blues*............... 15.00 - 20.00
   50-0037 *Barbecue Lounge*............. 15.00 - 20.00
   50-0083 *Any Time Ring My Bell*........ 15.00 - 20.00
   50-0093 *Squeeze Me Baby*............. 15.00 - 20.00
   50-0101 *You'll Be Sorry*............. 15.00 - 20.00
   (Note: #50-0003 through 50-0101 are orange plastic.)
States 164 *I Stayed Away Too Long*...... 15.00 - 20.00

TINY STOKES:
Big T 235 *Blackfoot Boogie*............. 10.00 - 15.00

THE STOMPERS:
Landa 684 *Foolish One*................... 5.00 - 8.00

DOUG STONE:
Cee Dee 101 *Memphis Yodel Blues*........... 7.00 - 10.00

JEFF STONE:
Sarg 151 *Everybody Rock*................. 15.00 - 20.00

JERRY STONE with THE FOUR DOTS:
Freedom 44002 *My Baby (She Loves Me)*...... 5.00 - 8.00

LAWRENCE STONE:
Dig 130 *Everytime*....................... 7.00 - 10.00

BILLY STORM: (See also THE VALIANTS)
Barbary Coast 1001 *The Way To My Heart*.... 7.00 - 10.00

WARREN STORM:
Nasco 6015 *Mama Mama Mama* (78 RPM)..... 10.00 - 15.00
   6025 *Troubles, Troubles*................. 5.00 - 8.00
Rocko 512 *Oh Oh Baby*................... 5.00 - 8.00

STORMY HERMAN & HIS MIDNIGHT RAMBLERS:
Dooto 358 *Bad Luck*..................... 5.00 - 8.00

CARL STORY:
Columbia 21250 *Step It Up And Go*........ 5.00 - 8.00

JIMMY STRANGE & FLAHERTY'S CARAVAN:
Jenn 101 *Real Gone Daddy*................. 20.00 - 30.00

STRANGERS:
King 4697 *I've Got Eyes*................. 20.00 - 30.00
   4079 *Blue Flowers*..................... 20.00 - 30.00
   4745 *Get It One More Time*............. 20.00 - 30.00
   4821 *Without A Friend*............... 20.00 - 30.00
Titan 1702, 1702, 1704.................. 4.00 - 7.00

JOHNNIE STRICKLAND:
Roulette 4119 *She's Mine*................ 10.00 - 15.00
   4147, 4335............................. 3.00 - 5.00

STRIDERS:
Apollo 480 *Hesitating Fool*............. 20.00 - 30.00

BOBBY STRIGO:
Renown 109 *The Pad*.................... 10.00 - 15.00

STRIKES:
Imperial 5443 *If You Can't Rock Me*......... 8.00 - 12.00

   5446 *Rockin'*.......................... 7.00 - 10.00
Lin 5006 *If You Can't Rock Me*............ 10.00 - 15.00

STROLLERS:
States 163 *In Your Dreams*.................. 15.00 - 20.00

BARRETT STRONG:
Anna 1111 *Money* (78 RPM)................ 50.00 up
   (Note: The existence of this very late 78 RPM issue has been verified.)

NOLAN STRONG & THE DIABLOS:
Fortune 509, 510, 511, 514, 516, 518, 519, 522. 5.00 - 8.00
   536 *Since You're Gone*................ 8.00 - 12.00
   841 *Harriet*......................... 7.00 - 10.00
   (LP) 8012 *Fortune Of Hits*............. 15.00 - 20.00
   (LP) 8015 *Mind Over Matter*........... 15.00 - 20.00

STUDENTS:
Checker 902 *I'm So Young*............. 5.00 - 8.00
   1004 *My Vow To You*................. 5.00 - 8.00
Note 10012 *I'm So Young*............... 15.00 - 20.00
   10019 *My Vow To You*............... 15.00 - 20.00

GENE STUMP & BILL SWAIN:
Clix 830 *Stream Of Love*............. —

THE SUADES:
Spinning 6011 *Wrong Yo-Yo*............. 10.00 - 15.00

SUBURBANS: (See also ANN COLE)
Baton 227 *TV Baby*..................... 7.00 - 10.00

SUGAR BOY:
Checker 795 *I Bowed On My Knees*........... 8.00 - 12.00

SUGARCANE & HIS VIOLIN:
Eldo 103 *They Say You Never Can Miss*...... 5.00 - 8.00

SUGARTONES:
Cannon 391 *How Can I Pretend*............ 10.00 - 15.00
   392 *How Can You Forget So Soon*......... 10.00 - 15.00

BRAD SUGGS:
Meteor 5034 *Bop, Baby, Bop* (black label)..... 15.00 - 25.00

JERRY SULLIVAN:
Vee 100 *Ella Mae*....................... 8.00 - 12.00

SULTANS:
DeCade 101 *God Made An Angel*............ 5.00 - 8.00
Duke 125 *How Deep Is The Ocean*........ 12.00 - 16.00
   133 *I Cried My Heart Out*............. 12.00 - 16.00
   135 *What Makes Me Feel This Way*....... 8.00 - 12.00
   178 *If I Could Tell*................. 6.00 - 10.00
Jam 103 *Toss In My Sleep*............. 10.00 - 15.00
Jubilee 5054 *You Captured My Heart*...... 80.00 - 120.00
   5077 *Don't Be Angry*............... 70.00 - 100.00
Tilt 782 *It'll Be Easy*............... 8.00 - 12.00

GENE SUMMERS:
Capri 507 *Alabama Shake*............... 10.00 - 15.00
Jan 100 *School Of Rock 'N' Roll*........ 10.00 - 15.00
   102 *Gotta Lotta That*............... 15.00 - 20.00
   106 *Twixteen*..................... 15.00 - 20.00

SUNBEAMS:
Acme 109 *Please Say You'll Be Mine*......... 25.00 - 40.00
Herald 451 *Tell Me Why*................ 20.00 - 30.00

THE SUNDOWNERS featuring WILBUR MARTIN:
T.R.C. 2839 *Live It Up*.................. 15.00 - 20.00

SUNNYLAND SLIM (TRIO) (& HIS BOYS/PLAYBOYS):
Blue Lake 105 *Going Back To Memphis*....... 35.00 - 50.00
   107 *Shake It Baby*................. 35.00 - 50.00
Club 51 106 *Be Mine Alone*............. 40.00 - 60.00
Cobra 5006 *Highway 61*............... 15.00 - 20.00
J.O.B. 1003 *Leaving Your Town*......... —
   1105 *Shake It Baby*................. 30.00 - 50.00
   1108 *Four Day Bounce*............... 30.00 - 50.00

SUNRAYS:
Sun 293 *Lonely Hours*................ 5.00 - 10.00

SUNSETS:
Petal 1040 *Lydia*..................... 10.00 - 15.00

SUPERBS:
- Heritage 103 *Rainbow Of Love*.............. 5.00 - 8.00
- Melmar— *My Love For You*.............. 10.00 - 15.00

SUPERIORS:
- Main Line 104 *Lost Love*.................. 8.00 - 12.00
- Verve 10370 *What Would I Do*............ 5.00 - 8.00

SUPREMES:
- Ace 534 *Just For You And I*.............. 15.00 - 20.00
- Kitten 6969 *Could This Be You*............ —
- Motown (LP) 606 *Meet The Supremes* (cover shows girls sitting on stools)............ 30.00 - 40.00
- Old Town 1017 *Darling Listen To The Words*... 15.00 - 20.00
- 1024 *Tonight*.......................... 25.00 - 35.00

SURFARIS:
- DFS 11/12 *Wipe-Out*.................... 15.00 - 20.00

SURF RIDERS:
- Nasco 6008 *Rocko Socko*................. 10.00 - 15.00

SURVIVORS:
- Capitol 5102 *Pamela Jean*................ *10.00 - 20.00*

DEL SWADE:
- Production 65216 *Better Get Ready, Betty*..... 10.00 - 15.00

SWALLOWS:
- After Hours 104 *My Baby*.............. 150.00 - 200.00
- *Federal 12319 Angel Baby*............ 10.00 - 15.00
- 12328 *We Want To Rock*.............. 8.00 - 12.00
- 12329 *Beside You*.................. 8.00 - 12.00
- 12333 *Itchy Twitchy Feeling*.......... 8.00 - 12.00
- King 4458 *Dearest*.................. 100.00 - 150.00
- 4466 *Since You've Been Gone Away*..... 150.00 - 200.00
- 4501 *Eternally*.................... 80.00 - 100.00
- 4515 *Roll Roll Pretty Baby*.......... 50.00 - 80.00
- 4525 *Beside You*.................. 50.00 - 80.00
- 4533 *I Only Have Eyes For You*........ 80.00 - 100.00
- 4579 *Please Baby Please*............ 50.00 - 70.00
- 4612 *Laugh (Though You Want To Cry)*..... 40.00 - 60.00
- 4632 *Nobody's Lovin' Me*.............. 30.00 - 40.00
- 4656 *Trust Me*.................... 25.00 - 35.00
- 4676 *I'll Be Waiting*.............. 40.00 - 60.00

JIMMY SWAN:
- MGM 12226 *Hey, Baby, Baby*............ 7.00 - 10.00
- 12348 *Country Cattin'*.............. 7.00 - 10.00
- Trumpet 176 *Juke Joint Mama*.......... 10.00 - 15.00
- 177 *Triflin' On Me*.................. 7.00 - 10.00
- 197 *Losers Weepers*................ 7.00 - 10.00
- 198 *Lonesome Daddy Blues*.......... 7.00 - 10.00

SWANNEE & THE ROCKABILLIES:
- Clix 825 *Thrill Happy*................ —

SWANS:
- Rainbow 233 *My True Love*............ 75.00 - 100.00

BOBBY SWANSON & THE SONICS:
- Igloo 1003 *Rockin' Little Eskimo*............ 15.00 - 20.00

HANK SWATLEY:
- Aaron 101 *Oakie Boogie*................. 25.00 - 35.00

AL SWEATT:
- Keen 289 *Little Red Wagon*............ 20.00 - 30.00

JIM SWEENEY:
- Date 1001 *The Midnight Hour*.......... 5.00 - 8.00

SWINGING HEARTS:
- Diamond 162 *Please Say It Isn't So*...... 8.00 - 12.00
- Lucky Four 1011 *Please Say It Isn't So*........ 4.00 - 7.00
- Magic Touch 2001 *You Speak Of Love*....... 7.00 - 10.00

HAWARD/HOWARD SWORDS WITH THE BLUE LIGHT BOYS:
- Meteor 5019 *You Will Have To Pay*.......... 12.00 - 16.00

THE SYCAMORES:
- Groove 0121 *I'll Be Waiting*.............. —

BOBBY SYKES:
- Decca 30573 *Touch Of Loving*.......... 7.00 - 10.00

ROOSEVELT SYKES (& HIS HONEYDRIPPERS):
- Crown (LP) 5287 *Roosevelt Sykes Sings The Blues* 15.00 - 20.00

- House Of Sound 505 *She's Jail Bait*.......... 7.00 - 10.00
- Imperial 5347 *Sweet Old Chicago*............ 8.00 - 12.00
- 5367 *Crazy Fox*............ 7.00 - 10.00
- Kent 384, 434.................. 3.00 - 5.00
- RCA Victor 50-0025 *Stop Her Papa*.......... 15.00 - 20.00
- 50-0040 *My Baby Is Gone*............ 15.00 - 20.00
- (Note: Above two are made of orange plastic.)
- United 129 *Security Blues*.................. 15.00 - 20.00
- 139 *Four O'Clock Blues*............ 10.00 - 15.00
- 152 *Tell Me True*.............. 8.00 - 12.00

THE SYLVA-TONES:
- Argo 5281 *Roses Are Blooming*.............. 8.00 - 12.00

SYLVIA & MICKEY:
- Cat 102 *Speed Life*............ 5.00 - 8.00

BOBBY SYSOM:
- Blue Moon 304 *Big Time Mama*.............. 20.00 - 30.00

TABBYS:
- Time 1008 *My Darling*.............. 8.00 - 12.00

TABS:
- Noble 719 *Never Forget*.............. 7.00 - 10.00
- 720 *Oops*......................... 7.00 - 10.00

DICK TACKER:
- Kingston— *Rock All Night With Me*.......... —

THE TADS:
- Dot 15518 *You Reason*.................... 5.00 - 8.00

TOM TALL:
- Crest 1038 *Stack-A-Records*.................. 20.00 - 30.00
- 1051 *High School Dance*.......... 7.00 - 10.00
- Fabor 132 *Hot Rod Is Her Name*.......... 8.00 - 12.00

JOHNNY T. TALLEY:
- Mercury 70902 *Lonesome Train*.............. 8.00 - 12.00

TAMPA RED:
- RCA Victor 4275 *Boogie Woogie Woman*...... 10.00 - 15.00
- 4898 *True Love*.................. 10.00 - 15.00
- 5134 *Too Late, Too Long*.......... 8.00 - 12.00
- 50-0019 *Come On, If You're Coming*.... 12.00 - 18.00
- 50-0027 *It's A Brand New Boogie*......... 12.00 - 18.00
- 50-0041 *That's Her Own Business*.... 12.00 - 18.00
- 50-0056 *It's Too Late Now*.......... 12.00 - 18.00
- 50-0084 *1950 Blues*.............. 12.00 - 18.00
- (Note: Last five records are made of orange plastic.)

ROY TAN:
- Dot 15551 *I Don't Like It*.............. 4.00 - 7.00
- 15551 *I Don't Like It* (78 RPM)........ 10.00 - 15.00
- 15595 *Hot Rod Queen*.......... 7.00 - 10.00

TANGENTS:
- Fresh 1 *I Can't Live Alone*.............. 4.00 - 7.00

TANGIERS:
- A-J 905 *The Plea*.................... —
- Decca 29603 *Tabarin*................. 25.00 - 40.00
- 29971 *Oh, Baby!*.............. 15.00 - 25.00
- Strand 25039 *Don't Stop The Music*......... 10.00 - 15.00

ROY TANN (See ROY TAN)

TANTONES:
- Lamp 2002 *I Love You Really I Do*.......... 15.00 - 20.00
- 2008 *So Afraid*.................. 15.00 - 20.00

TARHEEL SLIM (& LITTLE ANN):
- Fire 1000, 1009.................. 4.00 - 8.00
- (Note: 78 RPM issues of above exist.)
- Fury 1016 *Number 9 Train*.................. 8.00 - 12.00

FRANKIE TARO:
- G&G 111 *Susy Ann*.......... 25.00 - 40.00

BILL TAYLOR (& THE CYCLONES/& SMOKEY JO):
- Flip 502 *Split Personality*.......... 40.00 - 60.00
- Trophy 500 *Nelda Jane*.......... 7.00 - 10.00
- — *Wombie Zomie/I'm Young*.............. —

WILD BILL TAYLOR:
- Fame 502 *Little Jewel*.......... 10.00 - 15.00

BOB TAYLOR:
- Yucca 110 *Don't Be Unfair*.......... 10.00 - 15.00

TAYLOR

CARMEN TAYLOR & THE BOLEROS:
Atlantic 1041 *Freddie* . . . . 15.00 - 20.00

EDDIE TAYLOR:
Vee Jay 149 *E.T. Blues* . . . . 10.00 - 15.00
   185 *Big Town Playboy* . . . . 8.00 - 12.00
   206 *Don't Knock At My Door* . . . . 8.00 - 12.00
   267 *Lookin' For Trouble* . . . . 8.00 - 12.00
Vivid 104 *I'm Sitting Here* . . . . 4.00 - 7.00

FAITH TAYLOR & THE SWEET TEENS:
Bea & Baby, 104, 105 . . . . 4.00 - 7.00

HOUND DOG TAYLOR:
Bea & Baby 112 *My Baby's Coming Home* . . . . . 8.00 - 12.00
Firma 626 *Alley Music* . . . . 4.00 - 6.00

KIRK TAYLOR & THE MAJESTICS:
Bandera 2507 *From Out Of This World* . . . . 4.00 - 6.00

KOKO TAYLOR:
Checker 1092 *I Got What It Takes* . . . . 5.00 - 8.00
   1135, 1148 . . . . 3.00 - 6.00
U.S.A. 745 *Honkey Tonky* . . . . 4.00 - 7.00

MORRIS TAYLOR:
Key 5718 *Look-A-What* . . . . 7.00 - 10.00

R. DEAN TAYLOR:
Mala 444 *Long Way To St. Louis* . . . . 5.00 - 8.00

RAY TAYLOR with THE ALABAMA PALS:
Clix 801 *Clockin' My Card* . . . . —
   802 *Connie Lou* . . . . 50.00 - 75.00

TRUE TAYLOR:
Big 614 *True Or False* . . . . 8.00 - 12.00

VERNON TAYLOR:
Dot 15632 *I've Got The Blues* . . . . 5.00 - 8.00

WILLIAM TELL TAYLOR with JIMMY HEAP & THE MELODY MASTERS:
D 1051 *I Like It* . . . . 8.00 - 12.00

TEARDROPS:
Josie 766 *The Stars Are Out Tonight* . . . . 25.00 - 40.00
King 5037 *Don't Be Afraid To Love* . . . . 8.00 - 12.00
Sampson 634 *Come Back To Me* . . . . 50.00 - 75.00
Saxony 1007 *That's Why I'll Get By* . . . . —

THE TEARS:
Astronaut 5001 *She's Mine* . . . . 7.00 - 10.00
Dig 112 *Until The Day I Die* . . . . 5.00 - 8.00

TEASERS:
Checker 800 *How Could You Hurt Me So* . . . . . 75.00 - 100.00

TED AND JOHNNY:
Peach 0566 *Teenage Party* . . . . 25.00 - 40.00

TEDDY & THE CONTINENTALS:
Richie 445 *Do You* . . . . 10.00 - 15.00

THE TEDDY BEARS:
Imperial 5562 *I Don't Need You Anymore* . . . . . 7.00 - 10.00
   5594 *Don't Go Away* . . . . 5.00 - 8.00

TEENAGE MOONLIGHTERS:
Mark 134 *I Want To Cry* . . . . 10.00 - 15.00

"TEENAGE PARTY"
Gee (LP) 702 (The Crows, Cleftones, et al.) . . . . . 15.00 - 20.00

THE TEENAGE (featuring FRANKIE LYMON):
Gee (EP) 601 *The Teenagers Go Rockin'* . . . . 8.00 - 12.00
   (EP) 602 *The Teenagers Go Romantic* . . . . . . 7.00 - 10.00
   (LP) 701 *The Teenagers featuring Frankie Lymon*
   (mono) . . . . 30.00 - 40.00
   1002, 1012 . . . . 3.00 - 6.00
   1002 *Why Do Fools Fall In Love* (78 RPM) . . 10.00 - 15.00
   1012 *I Want You To Be My Girl* (78 RPM) . . 10.00 - 15.00

TEENANGELS:
Sun 388 (DJ) *Tell Me My Love* . . . . 12.00 - 16.00

TEENCHORDS (See FRANKIE LYMON)
TEEN KINGS; TEEN KINGS (Vocal, Roy Orbison):
Bee 1114 *Tell Me If You Know* . . . . —
Je-Wel 101 *Ooby Dooby* . . . . 100.00 up
(Note: This record has supposedly been sold for as much as $500.00 at auction; no transaction at such a lofty figure or anything close to it has been verified.)

TERRY

TEENOS:
Dub 2839 *Love Only One* . . . . 4.00 - 7.00

TEEN QUEENS:
Crown (LP) 373 *Teen Queens* . . . . 10.00 - 15.00
   (LP) 5022 *Eddie My Love* . . . . 15.00 - 20.00
Kent 348 *Eddie My Love* . . . . 3.00 - 5.00
RPM 453 *Eddie My Love* . . . . 4.00 - 7.00
   453 *Eddie My Love* (78 RPM) . . . . 7.00 - 10.00
   460, 464, 470, 484 . . . . 3.00 - 5.00

TELLERS:
Fire 1038 *Tears Fell From My Eyes* . . . . 7.00 - 10.00

BOB TEMPLE:
King 4958 *Come Back Come Back* . . . . 5.00 - 8.00

TEMPO MENTALS:
Ebb 112 *Dearest* . . . . —

TEMPOS:
Kapp 213 *I Got A Job* . . . . 4.00 - 6.00

TEMPO TONES:
Acme 713 *Ride Along* . . . . 10.00 - 15.00
   715 *In My Dreams* . . . . 10.00 - 15.00
   718 *Come Into My Heart* . . . . 10.00 - 15.00

TEMPO TOPPERS: (See also DUCES OF RHYTHM)
Peacock 1628 *Always* . . . . 15.00 - 20.00

TENDERFOOTS:
Federal 12214 *Kissing Bug* . . . . 8.00 - 12.00
   12219 *My Confession* . . . . 10.00 - 15.00
   12225 *Those Golden Bells* . . . . 15.00 - 20.00
   12228 *Sindy* . . . . 15.00 - 20.00

TENDER SLIM:
Herald 571 *Don't Cut Out On Me* . . . . 7.00 - 10.00

TENNESSEE JIM:
Choise 852 *My Baby She's Rockin'* . . . . 15.00 - 20.00

TERMITES:
Bee— *Give My Your Heart* . . . . 20.00 - 30.00

TERRACE TONES:
Apt 25016 *Words Of Wisdom* . . . . 7.00 - 10.00

TERRANS:
Graham 801 *Moonrise* . . . . 8.00 - 12.00

CLYDE TERRELL:
Excello 2151 *Poor Folk* . . . . 5.00 - 8.00

SISTER O.M. TERRELL:
Columbia 21092 *The Gambling Man* . . . . 7.00 - 10.00

DON TERRY:
Lin 5018 *Knees Shakin'* . . . . 15.00 - 20.00

FLASH TERRY:
Suncoast 1003 *She's My Baby* . . . . 12.00 - 18.00

GENE TERRY & HIS DOWN BEATS:
Savoy 1559 *Fine—Fine* . . . . 5.00 - 8.00

GORDON TERRY:
RCA Victor 7428, 7632 . . . . 4.00 - 6.00

MARK TERRY:
Kem 2746 *Nobody's Darling* . . . . —

SONNY TERRY (with BROWNIE McGHEE): (See also BROWNIE McGHEE)
Elektra (LP) 14 (10") *Folk Blues* . . . . 20.00 - 30.00
Everest (LP) 206 *Sonny Terry* . . . . 20.00 - 30.00
Fantasy (LP) 3254 *Sonny Terry* . . . . 20.00 - 30.00
Folkways (LP) 35 (10") *Harmonica* . . . . —
   (LP) 2006 (10") *Washboard Band* . . . . —
   (LP) 2035 (10") *Harmonica* . . . . —
   (LP) 2327 *(10") Blues & Folksongs* . . . . —
Gotham 517 *Four O'Clock Blues* . . . . 15.00 - 20.00
   518 *Lonesome Room* . . . . 12.00 - 16.00
Gramercy 1004 *Hootin' Blues* (red plastic) . . . . . 15.00 - 20.00
Groove 0015 *Louise* . . . . 7.00 - 10.00
   0135 *Hootin' Blues No. 2* . . . . 5.00 - 8.00
Harlem 2327 *Dangerous Woman* . . . . 20.00 - 30.00
Jax 305 *I Don't Worry* . . . . 12.00 - 16.00
Josie 828 *Fast Freight Blues* . . . . 5.00 - 8.00
Old Town 1023 *Uncle Bud* . . . . 7.00 - 10.00

RCA Victor 5492 *Hootin' And Jumpin'*......	8.00 -	12.00
5577 *I'm Gonna Rock My Wig*......	8.00 -	12.00
Red Robin 110 *Harmonica Hop*......	15.00 -	20.00
Riverside (LP) 12-644...*And His Mouth Harp*...	20.00 -	30.00
Roulette (LP) 25074 *Folk Songs*............	15.00 -	20.00
Stinson (LP) 55 (10") *Blues*............	—	

THE TEXANS:
Gothic 001 *Rockin' Johnny Home*........	5.00 -	8.00
Infinity 001 *Green Grass Of Texas*.......	5.00 -	8.00

TEXAS MATADORS:
IMA— *Flower Blossom*............	7.00 -	10.00

TEXAS RED (& JIMMY):
Bullseye 1009 *Coming Home*............	8.00 -	12.00
Checker 879 *Black Snake Blues*..........	5.00 -	8.00

JOHN TEXIERA:
G & G 100 *Strike It Rich*............	10.00 -	15.00

RUDY THACKER:
Lucky 0012 *Black Train*............	10.00 -	15.00

SISTER ROSETTA THARPE:
Promenade (LP) 2234 *Spirituals In Rhythm*.....	15.00 -	20.00

FRANK THAYER:
Outlaw 1 *Evening Shadows*............	7.00 -	10.00

THEMES (with JACK SNOW):
Excello 2152 *The Magic Of You*........	8.00 -	12.00
Stork 001 *There's No Moon Out Tonight*......	4.00 -	7.00

JOE THERRIEN, JR. (& THE ROCKETS/SULLY TRIO):
Brunswick 55005 *Hey Babe, Let's Go Down Town*	10.00 -	15.00
Jat 101 *I Ain't Gonna Be Around*............	20.00 -	30.00

FATSO THEUS & THE FLAIRS:
Aladdin 3324 *Be Cool My Heart*............	25.00 -	35.00

THE 13TH FLOOR ELEVATORS:
International Artists (LP) 1 *The Psychedelic Sound Of*...	40.00 -	50.00
(LP) 9 *Bull Of The Woods*............	35.00 -	50.00
111, 113, 126............	4.00 -	8.00

ALEXANDER "MUDCAT" THOMAS:
NRC 062 *Step It Up And Go*............	5.00 -	8.00

B.J. THOMAS:
Pacemaker (LP) 3001 *So Lonesome I Could Cry*.	20.00 -	25.00

BILLY THOMAS:
Play Back 0037 *I Must Be Crazy*............	8.00 -	12.00

JERRY THOMAS:
Orchid 274 *Jungle Dan*............	10.00 -	15.00

JESSE THOMAS:
Elko 107 *Another Fool Like Me*............	30.00 -	40.00
Hollywood 1072 *Cook Kind Lover*............	7.00 -	10.00

KID THOMAS:
Federal 12298 *The Wolf Pack*............	15.00 -	20.00
T.R.C. 1012 *Rockin' This Joint Tonight*........	10.00 -	20.00

LAFAYETTE THOMAS:
Savoy 1574 *Lafayette's A-Comin'*............	10.00 -	15.00

MULE THOMAS:
Hollywood 1091 *Blow My Baby Back Home*....	10.00 -	15.00

RUFUS THOMAS (JR.):
Chess 1517 *Juanita*............	30.00 -	50.00
Sun 181 *Bear Cat*............	25.00 -	35.00
188 *Tiger Man*............	25.00 -	35.00

TAB(BY) THOMAS:
Delta 416 *Thinking Blues*............	15.00 -	20.00
Excello 2212, 2222, 2281............	3.00 -	5.00
Feature 3007 *Tomorrow*............	8.00 -	12.00
Rocko 511 *Too Late Blues*............	5.00 -	8.00
Zynn 1002 *My Baby's Got It*............	5.00 -	8.00

BUDDY THOMPSON:
Atco 6095 *This Is The Night*............	5.00 -	8.00

FRED THOMPSON:
Jim Dandy 4501 *Please Be Fair*............	5.00 -	8.00

HANK THOMPSON:
Capitol (LP) 418 (10") *Brazos Valley Songs*.....	12.00 -	16.00
(LP) 418 *Brazos Valley Songs*............	15.00 -	20.00
(LP) 618 *North Of The Rio Grande*........	15.00 -	20.00
(LP) 729 *All Time Hits*............	12.00 -	16.00
(LP) 826 *Hank*............	12.00 -	16.00
(LP) 975 *Dance Ranch*............	12.00 -	16.00
(LP) 1246 *Songs For Rounders*............	10.00 -	15.00
3623 *Rockin' In The Congo*............	3.00 -	6.00

HAYDEN THOMPSON:
Phillips 3517 *Love My Baby*............	10.00 -	15.00
Profile 4015 *Whatcha Gonna Do*............	12.00 -	18.00

JUNIOR THOMPSON:
Meteor 5029 *Mama's Little Baby* (red label).....	25.00 -	35.00
Tune (unnumbered) *How Come You Do Me?*...	35.00 -	50.00

KID GUITAR THOMPSON:
Dore 581 *My Baby Done Me Wrong*.........	7.00 -	10.00

LORETTA THOMPSON:
Skoop 1050............		
United 214 *Hi De Ho Rock And Roll*........	15.00 -	20.00

WILLIE MAE ("BIG MAMA") THORNTON:
Bay Tone 107 *Big Mama's Blues*............	5.00 -	8.00
Kent 424 *Before Day*............	3.00 -	5.00
Peacock 1567 *All Fed Up*............	5.00 -	8.00
1587 *Let Your Tears Fall Baby*............	5.00 -	8.00
1603 *Michievous Boogie*............	7.00 -	10.00
1612 *Hound Dog*............	10.00 -	15.00
1621 *Cotton Picking Blues*............	5.00 -	8.00
1626 *The Big Change*............	5.00 -	8.00
1632 *I Smell A Rat*............	5.00 -	8.00
1642 *Stop Hoppin' On Me*............	5.00 -	8.00
1647 *Walking Blues*............	5.00 -	8.00
Peacock 1650, 1654, 1681............	4.00 -	7.00

CHUCK THORP:
Jaro 79029 *Long Long Ponytail*............	10.00 -	15.00

"THOSE GOOD OLD MEMORIES"
Capitol (LP) 1414 (various artists)............	15.00 -	25.00

THRASHERS:
Mason's 178 *Jeannie*............	20.00 -	30.00
178 *Jeannie* (red plastic)............	10.00 -	15.00

THREE CHUCKLES:
Boulevard 100 *Run Around*............	10.00 -	15.00
Vik (LP) 1067............	30.00 -	40.00

THREE D'S:
Paris 511 *Crazy Little Woman*............	5.00 -	8.00
514 *Jumpin' Jack*............	5.00 -	8.00

3 DOTS AND A DASH:
Imperial 5115 *Don't Cry Baby*............	30.00 -	50.00
5164 *Let's Do It*............	25.00 -	35.00

THE THREE HONEYDROPS:
Music City 814 *Rockin' Satellite*............	—	

THRILLERS:
Big Town 109 *The Drunkard*............	40.00 -	60.00
Herald 432 *Lizabeth*............	20.00 -	30.00
Thriller 3530 *I'm Gonna Live My Life Alone*...	75.00 -	100.00

THUNDERBIRDS:
De Luxe 6075 *Baby Let's Play House*.........	15.00 -	20.00
G.G. 103 *Love Is A Problem*............	15.00 -	20.00

THE TIDES:
"620" 1007 *Who Told You*............	4.00 -	7.00

TIFANOS:
Tifco 822 *It's Raining*............	8.00 -	12.00

SONNY TIL (See ORIOLES)

BIG SON TILLIS & D.C. BENDER:
Elko 821 *Rocks Is My Pillow*............	25.00 -	35.00
822 *Ten Long Years*............	25.00 -	35.00
823 *Dayton Stomp*............	20.00 -	35.00

CLYDE TILLIS:
Cash 1054 *It Makes No Difference Now*.......	7.00 -	10.00

MEL TILLIS:
Columbia 40944 *Juke Box Man*............	5.00 -	8.00
41026 *Hearts Of Stone*............	5.00 -	8.00
41115 *Teen Age Wedding*............	5.00 -	8.00

TIM TAM & THE TURN-ONS:
Palmer 5006 *Kimberly*............	15.00 -	20.00

TINO & REVLONS:
Dearborns 525 *Rave On* .... 5.00 - 8.00
TITANS:
Specialty 614 *Sweet Peach* .... 4.00 - 7.00
   625 *Don't You Just Know It* .... 4.00 - 7.00
   632 *Arlene* .... 4.00 - 7.00
Vita 148 *So Hard To Laugh, So Easy To Cry* ... 15.00 - 20.00
BUD TITUS:
Sage 244 *Hocus Pocus* .... 10.00 - 15.00
"TODAY'S HITS"
Philles (LP) 4004 (various artists) .... 30.00 - 50.00
JOHNNY TODD:
Modern 1003 *Pink Cadillac* .... 10.00 - 15.00
TOKENS:
Gary 1006 *Doom-Long* .... —
Melba 104 *I Love My Baby* .... 5.00 - 8.00
RCA Victor (LP) 2514 *The Lion Sleeps Tonight.* 15.00 - 20.00
TOM & JERRY:
Big 613 *Hey, Schoolgirl* .... 8.00 - 12.00
   616 *Our Song* .... 8.00 - 12.00
   618 *That's My Story* .... 7.00 - 10.00
   621 *Baby Talk* .... 10.00 - 15.00
Hunt 319 *That's My Story* .... 15.00 - 20.00
KENNY TOMERLIN:
Teen Ager 1001 *Crazy Little Teen* .... 5.00 - 8.00
TONY & THE MASQUINS:
Ruthie 1000 *My Angel Eyes* .... 10.00 - 15.00
TONY & THE RAINDROPS:
Chesapeake 609 *While Walking* .... 5.00 - 8.00
TONY & THE TECHNICS:
Chex 1010 *Ha Ha He Told On You* .... 4.00 - 7.00
TONY & THE TWILIGHTERS:
Jalynne 106 *Did You Make Up Your Mind* .... —
JACKSON TOOMBS:
Excello 2083 *Kiss-A-Me-Quick* .... 10.00 - 15.00
TOPICS:
Perri 1007 *The Girl In My Dreams* .... 12.00 - 18.00
THE TOP NOTES:
Atlantic 2080 *Warm Your Heart* .... —
TOPPERS: (See also BOBBY MITCHELL)
Jubilee 5136 *Baby Let Me Bang Your Box* ..... 10.00 - 15.00
TOPPS:
Red Robin 126 *Tippin'* .... 15.00 - 25.00
THE TOPS:
Singular 712 *An Innocent Kiss* .... —
THE TOREADORS:
Midas 1001 *Do You Remember?* .... 15.00 - 20.00
THE TORNADOS:
Bumble Bee 503 *Love In Your Life* .... 5.00 - 8.00
JACKIE TORRELL:
Dude— *I'm Gonna Look* .... —
"TOWN HALL PARTY"
Columbia (LP) CL-1072 (various artists) .... 15.00 - 20.00
TOWN THREE: (See also WES VOIGHT)
De Luxe 6176 *Another Guy's Line* .... 10.00 - 15.00
   6180 *I Want A Lover* .... 10.00 - 15.00
THE TOYS:
Dyno Voice (LP) 9002...*Sing A Lover's Concerto* 20.00 - 30.00
BUCK TRAIL:
Trail 100 *Knocked Out Joint On Mars* .... 15.00 - 25.00
TRAILBLAZERS:
Watson— *Grandpa's Rock* .... —
TRAITS: (See also ROY HEAD)
Renner 221 *Little Mama* .... 10.00 - 15.00
   229 *Got My Mojo Working* .... 10.00 - 15.00
TNT 164 *One More Time* .... 10.00 - 15.00
   175 *Live It Up* .... 15.00 - 20.00
   185 *Night Time Blues* .... 15.00 - 20.00
BOBBY LEE TRAMMELL:
ABC Paramount 9890 *Shirley Lee* .... 8.00 - 12.00
Alley 1004 *Come On Baby* .... 8.00 - 12.00

Atlanta 1501 *Sally Twist* .... 5.00 - 8.00
  (LP) 1503 *Arkansas Twist* .... 30.00 - 40.00
Fabor 127 *You Mostest Girl* .... 5.00 - 8.00
Radio 102 *You Mostest Girl* .... 4.00 - 6.00
Sims 183 *New Dance In France* .... 4.00 - 7.00
Souncot 1113 *You Mostest Girl* .... 7.00 - 10.00
Vaden 304 *Been A-Walking* .... 10.00 - 15.00
Warrior 1554 *Woe Is Me* .... 15.00 - 20.00
CARL TRANTHAM & RHYTHM ALL STARS:
Starday 361 *Deedle Deedle Dum* .... 10.00 - 15.00
TRAVELERS:
Atlas 1086 *Lenora* .... 8.00 - 12.00
TRAVIS & BOB:
Sandy 1019 *Little Bitty Johnny* .... —
MERLE TRAVIS:
Capitol (LP) 891 *Back Home* .... 25.00 - 35.00
TREBLE CHORDS:
Decca 31015 *Teresa* .... 10.00 - 15.00
TREND TONES:
Superb 100 *Never Again* .... 10.00 - 15.00
TREMAINES:
Cash 100 *Jingle Jingle* .... 75.00 - 100.00
Old Town 1051 *Jingle Jingle* .... 7.00 - 10.00
Val 101 *Jingle Jingle* .... 15.00 - 20.00
V-Tone 107 *Heavenly* .... 7.00 - 10.00
TOMMY TREMBLE & THE SHADOWS:
Sound Tex 641013 *She Said* .... 7.00 - 10.00
THE TREMONTS:
Brunswick 55217 *Legend Of Love* .... —
THE TREN-DELLS:
Jan 111 *Tough Little Buggy* .... 10.00 - 15.00
GRAY TREXLER:
Rev 3507 *Teen Baby* .... 10.00 - 15.00
TREYS:
Bella— *Come To Me* .... 8.00 - 12.00
TRIDELLS:
San Dee 1009 *Land Of Love* .... 8.00 - 12.00
TRI-LADS:
Bullseye 1003 *Cherry Pie* .... 7.00 - 10.00
FRANK TRIOLO:
Flagship 106 *Ice Cream Baby* .... 25.00 - 35.00
DELBERT TROILINDER:
Mist 1012 *So We Walked* .... —
TROJANS:
Tender 516 *Alone In This World* .... 12.00 - 16.00
TROOPERS:
Lamp 2009 *My Resolution* .... 15.00 - 25.00
TROPHIES:
Challenge 9133 *Desire* .... 8.00 - 12.00
TROUPERS:
Red Top— *Peter, Pumpkin Eater* .... 8.00 - 12.00
TRUETONES:
Felsted 8625 *Singing Waters* .... 8.00 - 12.00
Monument 4501 *Honey Honey* .... 30.00 - 40.00
THE TRUMPETEERS:
Grand (LP) 7701 *The Last Supper* .... —
Score (LP) 4021 *Milky White Way* .... 35.00 - 50.00
TRU-TONES:
Chart 634 *Tears In My Eyes* .... 30.00 - 40.00
ERNEST TUBB:
Decca (LP) 5301 (10") *Favorites* .... 10.00 - 15.00
  (LP) 5344 (10") *The Old Rugged Cross* .... 10.00 - 15.00
  (LP) 5336 (10") ...*Sings Jimmy Rodgers Songs*. 15.00 - 25.00
  (LP) 8291 *Favorites* .... 12.00 - 18.00
  (LP) 8553 *Daddy Of 'Em All* .... 15.00 - 20.00
JUSTIN TUBB:
Decca 30606 *Rock It On Down To My House* . 5.00 - 8.00
ANITA TUCKER:
Capitol 3277 *Let's Make Love* .... 10.00 - 15.00
BILLY JOE TUCKER:
Maha 103 *Boogie Woogie Bill* .... —

ERNEST TUCKER:
Jubilee 5340 *Mirror, Mirror On The Wall*...... 5.00 - 8.00
ORRIN TUCKER:
White Rock 1115 *Been Lookin' For Love*..... 5.00 - 8.00
RICK TUCKER & THE TURKS:
Veeda 4005 *I'll Be There*.................. 5.00 - 8.00
LEE TULLY:
Flair-X 3007 *Elwood Pretzel*.............. 7.00 - 10.00
TUNE BLENDERS:
Federal 12201 *Oh Yes I Know*............. 15.00 - 20.00
TUNEMASTERS:
Mark 7002 *Sending This Letter*............. 15.00 - 25.00
TUNE ROCKERS:
Pet— *No Stoppin' This Boppin'*.............. —
United Artists 139 *The Green Mosquito* (78 RPM)
 (Note: The existence of this record in 78 RPM form
 has not been verified: foreign 78s do exist.)
THE TUNE WEAVERS:
Casa Grande 101 *Little Boy*............... 10.00 - 15.00
 4038 *This Can't Be Love*.............. 8.00 - 12.00
 4040 *There Stands My Love*.......... 8.00 - 12.00
Checker 872 *Happy, Happy Birthday Baby*..... 5.00 - 8.00
 872 *Happy, Happy Birthday Baby* (78 RPM).. 10.00 - 15.00
 (Checker 872 occurs with two different flip sides)
TURBANS:
Herald 458, 469, 478, 486, 495, 510.......... 4.00 - 8.00
 458 *When You Dance* (78 RPM).......... 10.00 - 15.00
Imperial 5807, 5828, 5847................. 4.00 - 7.00
Money 209 *No No Cherry*................ 10.00 - 15.00
 211 *When I Return*.................... 10.00 - 15.00
 (Note: flip side of Money 211 is by THE TURKS)
Roulette 4281, 4326....................... 3.00 - 5.00
TURKS: (See also RICK TUCKER)
Bally 1017 *This Heart Of Mine*............. 8.00 - 12.00
Cash 1042 *It Can't Be True*.............. 8.00 - 12.00
Money 211 *Emily*........................ 10.00 - 15.00
 215 *I've Been Accused*.................. 10.00 - 15.00
RICHARD TURLEY:
Fraternity 845 *Makin' Love To My Baby*...... 10.00 - 15.00
IKE TURNER & KINGS OF RHYTHM:
Cobra 5033 *Walking Down The Aisle*........ 8.00 - 12.00
JACK TURNER:
Hickory 1050 *Everybody's Rockin' But Me*..... 8.00 - 12.00
JESSIE LEE TURNER:
Carlton 509 *Baby Please Don't Tease*....... 5.00 - 8.00
Imperial 5649 *I'm The Little Space Girl's Father*. 7.00 - 10.00
Sudden 105 *The Elopers*.................. 4.00 - 7.00
(BIG)JOE TURNER:
Atlantic (EP) 536 *Joe Turner Sings*....... 10.00 - 15.00
 (EP) 565 *Joe Turner*.................. 10.00 - 15.00
 (EP) 606 *Rock With Joe Turner*....... 15.00 - 20.00
 982 *Still In Love*.................. 8.00 - 12.00
 1001 *Honey Hush*.................. 8.00 - 12.00
 1016 *TV Mama*.................. 7.00 - 10.00
 1026 *Shake, Rattle & Roll*.......... 7.00 - 10.00
 1040 *Well All Right*.................. 5.00 - 8.00
 1053 *Flip, Flop And Fly*.............. 5.00 - 8.00
 1069 *Midnight Cannonball*............ 5.00 - 8.00
 1080 *The Chicken And The Hawk*........ 5.00 - 8.00
 (LP) 1234 *Boss Of The Blues*......... 20.00 - 30.00
 (LP) 1243 *Joe Turner Sings Kansas City Jazz* (black
 label).......... 20.00 - 30.00
 (LP) 1332 *Big Joe Rides Again*........ 20.00 - 30.00
 (LP) 8005 *Joe Turner* (black label)......... 20.00 - 30.00
 (LP) 8023 *Rockin' The Blues*.......... 20.00 - 30.00
 (LP) 8033 *Big Joe Is Here*.......... 20.00 - 30.00
Crown (LP) 5295 *Joe Turner With Red Nelson*. 15.00 - 20.00
Decca 29711 *Piney Brown Blues*........ 8.00 - 12.00
 29924 *Corrine, Corrina*............... 8.00 - 12.00
Savoy (LP) 14012 *...And The Blues*.......... 15.00 - 20.00
 (LP) 14016 *Careless Love*........... 15.00 - 20.00

TU TONES:
Lin 5021 *Saccharin Sally*................. 5.00 - 8.00
TV SLIM: (See also OSCAR WILLS)
Checker 870 *Flat Foot Sam*............... 4.00 - 7.00
 1029 *The Big Fight*............... 4.00 - 7.00
Clif 103 *Flat Foot Sam*............... 15.00 - 20.00
Speed 704 *Flat Foot Sam Meets Jim Dandy*.... 7.00 - 10.00
 705 *My Ship Is Sinking*........... 5.00 - 8.00
 706 *My Baby Is Gone*........... 7.00 - 10.00
 711 *Don't Reach 'Cross My Plate*........ 5.00 - 8.00
 714, 715, 803, 807, 810.......... 4.00 - 7.00
 6865 *To Prove My Love*.......... 7.00 - 10.00
"TWELVE FLIP HITS"
Flip (LP) 1001 (various artists)............... 20.00 - 30.00
TWILIGHTERS (& DONALD RICHARDS):
Bubble 1334 *My Silent Prayer*............ 10.00 - 20.00
Cholly 712 *Let There Be Love*......... 15.00 - 20.00
Ebb 117 *Live Like A King*............ 8.00 - 12.00
Groove 0154 *Sittin' In A Corner*......... 15.00 - 20.00
J-V-B 83 *How Many Times*............ 50.00 - 80.00
Marshall 702 *Please Tell me You're Mine* (red plastic) 80.00 - 120.00
MGM 55011 *Little Did I Dream*......... 20.00 - 30.00
 55014 *Half Angel*................. 20.00 - 30.00
Paloma 100 *You Better Make It*......... —
Pico 2801 *Eternally*................. —
Specialty 548 *It's True*............. 10.00 - 15.00
Spin 1 *Yes You Are*............ 30.00 - 50.00
Super— *Please Come Home*......... 10.00 - 15.00
TWILIGHTS:
Finesse 1717 *My Heart Belongs Only To You*... 5.00 - 8.00
Six Star 1002 *Little Richard*................. 8.00 - 12.00
TWILITERS (See TWILIGHTERS)
CONWAY TWITTY:
Mercury 71086 *I Need Your Lovin'* (maroon label) 8.00 - 12.00
 71148 *Shake It Up*......... 10.00 - 15.00
 71384 *Double Talk Baby*......... 8.00 - 12.00
Metro (LP) 512 *It's Only Make Believe*........ 12.00 - 18.00
MGM (LP) 3744 *Conway Twitty Sings*........ 15.00 - 20.00
 (LP) 3786 *Saturday Night*........ 15.00 - 25.00
 (LP) 3818 *Lonely Blue Boy*........ 15.00 - 20.00
BIG "T" TYLER:
Aladdin 3384 *King Kong*............. 5.00 - 8.00
FRANKIE TYLER:
Okeh 7103 *I Go Ape*............. 15.00 - 20.00
JOHNNY TYLER:
Ekko 1000 *Devil's Hot Rod* (red plastic)........ 15.00 - 20.00
Rural Rhythm 515 *Lie To Me Baby* (red plastic) 15.00 - 20.00
Starday 263 *Lie To Me Baby*........ 10.00 - 15.00
KIP TYLER (& HIS FLIPS):
Challenge 1014 *She Got Eyes*........... 8.00 - 12.00
 59008 *Ooh Yeah Baby*............ 8.00 - 12.00
Ebb 154 *She's My Witch*......... 7.00 - 10.00
 156 *Oh Linda*............... 4.00 - 7.00
Starla 003 *Let's Monkey Around*......... 7.00 - 10.00
RUCKUS TYLER:
Fabor 135 *Rollin' And A-Rockin'*........... 15.00 - 25.00
TYMES:
Parkway (LP) 7032 *So Much In Love*....... 15.00 - 20.00
UNIQUES:
End 1012 *Tell The Angels*............ 12.00 - 16.00
Lucky Four 1024 *Silver Moon*......... 15.00 - 20.00
Peacock 1695 *Picture Of My Baby*......... 5.00 - 8.00
Tee Kay 112 *A Million Miles Away*...... 8.00 - 12.00
UNIQUE TEENS:
Dynamic 110 *Whatcha Know Now*.......... 7.00 - 10.00
UNIVERSALS:
Cora-Lee 101 *The Pictures*........... 10.00 - 15.00
Mark-X 7004 *Again*................. 15.00 - 20.00
Shepherd— *A Love Only You Can Give*...... 7.00 - 10.00
UPFRONTS:
Lummtone 103 *It Took Time*........... 7.00 - 10.00

UPSETTERS:

Little Star 123 *Every Night About This Time*...	8.00 -	12.00
128 *Valley Of Tears*.....................	8.00 -	12.00

UPSTARTS:

Apollo 468 *Feed Me Baby*................	15.00 -	20.00

AL URBAN:

Sarg 148 *Lookin' For Money*.............	10.00 -	15.00
158 *Won't Tell You Her Name*...........	10.00 -	15.00

VAL-CHORDS:

Gametime 104 *Candy Store Love*............	7.00 -	10.00

BLACKIE VALE:

Hurricane 100 *If I Had Me A Woman*........	—	

RITCHIE VALENS:

Del-Fi (LP) PR-1 *Ritchie Valens*...........	8.00 -	12.00
(LP) 1201 *Ritchie Valens*................	20.00 -	30.00
(LP) 1206 *Ritchie*..................	15.00 -	25.00
(LP) 1214—*In Concert At Pacoima Jr. High*..	30.00 -	40.00
(LP) 1225 *His Greatest Hits*...........	15.00 -	25.00
(LP) 1247 *His Greatest Hits, Vol. 2*.......	20.00 -	30.00

VALENTINES:

Old Town 1009 *Tonight Kathleen*............	30.00 -	40.00
Rama 171 *Lily Maebelle*.................	7.00 -	10.00
181 *I Love You Darling*.................	10.00 -	15.00
186 *Christmas Prayer*.................	20.00 -	30.00
196 *The Woo Woo Train*..............	8.00 -	12.00
201 *I'll Never Let You Go*...........	8.00 -	12.00
208 *Nature's Creation*.................	8.00 -	12.00
228 *Don't Say Goodnight*.............	8.00 -	12.00

THE VALETS:

Jon 4219 *You And You Alone*..............	5.00 -	8.00

VALIANTS:

Ensign 4035 *Walkin' Girl*..................	5.00 -	8.00
Keen 34004 *This Is The Night*.............	4.00 -	7.00
3-4007 *Walkin' Girl*.................	4.00 -	7.00
3-4026 *Please Wait My Love*...........	4.00 -	7.00

FRANKIE VALLE/VALLEY/VALLI/VALLY (& THE ROMANS/THE TRAVELLERS):

Cindy 3012 *Real*........................	15.00 -	20.00
Corona 1234 *My Mother's Eyes*...........	25.00 -	40.00
Decca 30994 *Please Take A Chance*..........	15.00 -	20.00
Mercury 70381 *Forgive And Forget* (maroon label)	25.00 -	40.00

VALQUINS:

Gaity 161 *Falling Star*.................	—	

AL VANCE:

Goldwax 116 *Every Woman I Know*.........	7.00 -	10.00

VAN DYKES:

Decca 30654 *The Fixer*...................	7.00 -	10.00
De Luxe 6193 *The Bells Are Ringing*........	5.00 -	8.00

VARIETEERS:

Hickory 1025 *Call My Gal, Miss Jones*........	—	

VARNELLS:

Arnold 1003 *Who Created Love*.............	7.00 -	10.00
1006 *All Because*.................	7.00 -	10.00

BOBBY VAUGHN:

Whiz 503 *Good Good Lovin'*.............	7.00 -	10.00

DALE VAUGHN:

Von 480 *High Steppin'*.................	75.00 -	100.00

DELL VAUGHN with THE FORTUNE AIRES:

Fortune— *Rock The Universe*..........	8.00 -	12.00
Hi-Q 5044 *Rock The Universe*..........	8.00 -	12.00

VECTORS:

Standard 700 *One Day*.................	—	

RUSS VEERS:

Trend 30010 *Warm As Toast*............	10.00 -	15.00

VELAIRES:

Jamie 1198 *Roll Over Beethoven*............	5.00 -	8.00
1203 *Sticks And Stones*............	7.00 -	10.00
1211 *Ubangi Stomp*.................	7.00 -	10.00

GENE VELL:

Whiz 9001 *I Done Got Over*............	8.00 -	12.00

VELOURS:

Cub 9001 *Remember*..................	4.00 -	7.00

Onyx 501 *My Love Come Back*..............	15.00 -	20.00
Onyx 508 *Romeo*.....................	10.00 -	15.00
512 *Can I Come Over Tonight*...........	7.00 -	10.00
515 *This Could Be The Night*...........	10.00 -	15.00
Onyx 520 *Remember*.................	10.00 -	15.00
Orbit 9001 *Remember*.................	12.00 -	18.00

VELS:

Trebco 16 *Please Be Mine*...............	20.00 -	30.00

VELVETEERS:

Spitfire 15 *Tell Me You're Mine*..............	75.00 -	100.00

VELVETONES:

Aladdin 3372 *The Glory Of Love*............	20.00 -	30.00
3391 *I Found My Love*.............	20.00 -	30.00
Ascot 2117 *I Want Him So Bad*.............	4.00 -	7.00
D 1049 *Penalty Of Love*.............	15.00 -	20.00
1072 *Worried Over You*.............	10.00 -	15.00
Deb 1008 *Stars Of Wonder*.............	5.00 -	8.00
Imperial 5878 *The Glory Of Love*............	5.00 -	8.00
Milmart 113 *A Prayer At Gettysburg*.........	—	

THE VELVETS:

Fury 1012 *I-I-I (Love You So-So-So)*..........	7.00 -	10.00
Red Robin 120 *They Tried*..............	25.00 -	35.00
122 *I*.....................	20.00 -	30.00
127 *I Cried*.................	20.00 -	30.00
20th Fox 165 *If I Could Be With You*.......	—	

THE VELVITONES (See VELVETONES)

NICK VENET:

Imperial 5522 *Love In Be Bop Time*.........	5.00 -	8.00
RCA Victor (EP) 4100 *Flippin'*..............	7.00 -	10.00

VENTURES:

Blue Horizon 100 *Cookies And Cake*.........	—	

VERNALLS:

Ru Lu 6753 *Raindrops*...................	30.00 -	40.00

LARRY VERNE:

Era (LP) 104 *Mister Larry Verne*............	20.00 -	30.00

VERNON & CLIFF:

Dootone 443 *You Came Along*.............	5.00 -	8.00

RAY VERNON:

Rumble 1349 *Evil Angel*.................	8.00 -	12.00

THE VERSATILES: (See also JERRY SHEELY):

Atlantic 2004 *Passing By*.............	7.00 -	10.00
Coaster 800 *In The Garden Of Love*.........	8.00 -	12.00
Peacock 1910 *The White Cliffs Of Dover*.....	8.00 -	12.00
Rocal 1002 *Lundee Dundee*.............	8.00 -	12.00

VERSATONES:

All Star 501 *Tight Skirt And Sweater*.........	8.00 -	12.00

THE VESTELLES:

Decca 30733 *Ditta Wa Do*..............	7.00 -	10.00

THE VETS:

Swami 551 *Wipe The Tears From Your Eyes.*—		

VIBES:

Allied 10006 *What's Her Name*.............	10.00 -	15.00
Chariot 105 *Stop Torturing Me*.............	75.00 -	100.00

VIBRAHARPS:

Atco 6134 *It Must Be Magic*.............	7.00 -	10.00
Beech 713 *Walk Beside Me*.............	10.00 -	15.00

VIBRANAIRES:

After Hours 103 *Doll Face* (red plastic).......	150.00 -	200.00
Chariot 103 *Doll Face*.............	80.00 -	120.00

MAC VICKERY:

Abco 502 *Bell Bottom Jeans*.............	—	

RAY VICT & THE BOP ROCKERS:

Goldband 1042 *Bop Stop Rock*.............	8.00 -	12.00

VICTORIANS:

Selma 1002 *Wedding Bells*.............	15.00 -	20.00

VIDALTONES:

Josie 900 *Forever*......................	7.00 -	10.00

VIDELS:

JDS 5004 *Mister Lonely*.............	8.00 -	12.00
5005 *She's Not Coming Home*.............	8.00 -	12.00
Rhody 2000 *Be My Girl*.............	7.00 -	10.00

THE VIDEOS:
Casino 102 *Moonglow You Know*............ 5.00 - 8.00
DARRYL VINCENT:
Sandy 1016 *Daddy's Gone Batty*............ 15.00 - 20.00
  1020 *Wild Wild Party*................. 15.00 - 20.00
GENE VINCENT & THE BLUE CAPS:
Capitol (EP) 764 *Bluejean Bop!*.......... 15.00 - 25.00
  (Note: The EP is actually three, together compris-
  ing the LP following. Although the EP catalog
  numbers have prefixes 1-, 2-, and 3-designating
  parts 1, 2, and 3, these prefixes are omitted here
  and in the case of other EPs in series.)
Capitol (LP) 764 *Bluejean Bop!*............ 50.00 - 75.00
  (EP) 811 *Gene Vincent And The Blue Caps (3
  parts)*.................................. 15.00 - 25.00
  (LP) 811 *Gene Vincent And The Blues Caps*.. 50.00 - 75.00
  (EP) 970 *Gene Vincent Rocks And The Blue Caps
  Roll* (3 parts).......................... 15.00 - 20.00
  (LP) 970 *Gene Vincent Rocks And The Blues Caps
  Roll*.................................... 50.00 - 75.00
  (EP) 985 *Hot Rod Gang*.................. 15.00 - 20.00
  (EP) 1059 *A Gene Vincent Record Date (3 parts)*.. 15.00 - 20.00
  (LP) 1059 *A Gene Vincent Record Date*..... 50.00 - 75.00
  (LP) 1207 *Sounds Like Gene Vincent*....... 40.00 - 60.00
  (LP) 1342 *Crazy Times*................. 40.00 - 60.00
  3450, 3530, 3558, 3617, 3678, 3763......... 3.00 - 5.00
  (Note: 78 RPM issues command higher premiums.)
Capitol 3874, 3959, 4010, 4105, 4153, 4237, 4313,
  4442, 4525................................ 4.00 - 8.00
Challenge 59365 *Hurtin' For You Baby*....... 4.00 - 7.00
VINES:
Cee-Jay 582 *I Must See You Again*......... 7.00 - 10.00
DOT VINSON:
MGM 12734 *Livin' With The Blues*......... 5.00 - 8.00
EDDIE "CLEANHEAD" VINSON:
Aamco (LP) 74 *Clean Head's Back In Town*.... 15.00 - 20.00
VISCOUNTS:
Amy (LP) 8008 *Harlem Nocturne*........... 20.00 - 30.00
Madison (LP) 1001 *The Viscounts*......... 20.00 - 30.00
Mercury 71073 *My Girl*................. 5.00 - 8.00
Star-Fax 1002 *Wondering*................. —
THE VISIONS:
Big Top 3092 *Tell Me You're Mine*......... 7.00 - 10.00
R & R 3002 *It's You I Love*.............. —
VISUALS:
Poplar 115 *Submarine Race*.............. 7.00 - 10.00
  117 *My Juanita*....................... 7.00 - 10.00
  121 *Please Don't Be Mad At Me*........... 10.00 - 15.00
THE VOCALEERS:
Paradise 113 *I Need Your Love So Bad*....... 4.00 - 7.00
Red Robin 113 *Be True*................. —
  114 *Is It A Dream*.................... 30.00 - 40.00
  119 *I Walk Alone*..................... 35.00 - 50.00
  125 *Love You*....................... 35.00 - 50.00
  132 *Angel Face*...................... 25.00 - 35.00
Twistime 45-T-11 *A Golden Tear*.......... 4.00 - 7.00
Vest 832 *Hear My Plea*................. 5.00 - 8.00
VOCALTONES:
Apollo 488 *My Girl*................... 15.00 - 20.00
  492 *Darling*........................ 20.00 - 25.00
  497 *My Version Of Love*................ 20.00 - 25.00
Cindy 3004 *Walkin' By Baby*.............. —
VOICE MASTERS:
Anna 102 *Needed*..................... 10.00 - 15.00
  123 *Everytime*....................... 7.00 - 10.00
VOICES:
Cash 1011 *Why*...................... 10.00 - 15.00
  1016 *Santa Claus Boogie*................ 8.00 - 12.00
VOICES FIVE:
Craft 116 *For Sentimental Reasons*......... 5.00 - 8.00
WES VOIGHT: (See also TOWN THREE)
King 5211 *I'm Movin' In*................ 15.00 - 20.00

VOILINAIRES:
Drummond 4000 *Another Soldier Gone*...... —
VOLTONES:
Dynamic 107 *If She Should Call*........... 40.00 - 60.00
VOLUMES:
Chex 1002 *I Love You*.................. 5.00 - 8.00
Ivy 104 *In My Heart*.................. 8.00 - 12.00
Jaguar 3004 *I Won't Tell A Soul*.......... 20.00 - 30.00
  3006 *So Disappointed With Love*.......... 20.00 - 30.00
Jubilee 5446 *Teenage Paradise*........... 4.00 - 7.00
VONDELLS:
Marvello— *Valentino*.................. 10.00 - 15.00
THE VOWS:
Tamara 760 *Dottie*................... 4.00 - 7.00
THE VOXPOPPERS:
Mercury 71315 *Ping Pong Baby*........... 3.00 - 5.00
WADE & DICK:
Sun 269 *Bop Bop Baby*................ 4.00 - 6.00
DON WADE:
San 206 *Gone, Gone, Gone*.............. 15.00 - 20.00
RONNIE WADE:
King 5061 *Gotta Make Her Mine*.......... 7.00 - 10.00
  5078 *I Know But I'll Never Tell*.......... 5.00 - 8.00
  5112 *All I Want*..................... 5.00 - 8.00
CHARLIE WAGGONER:
Linco 503 *One Eyed Sam*................ 15.00 - 20.00
PORTER WAGONER:
RCA Victor (LP) 1358 *Satisfied Man*........ 15.00 - 20.00
THE WAILERS:
Golden Crest (LP) 3075 *The Fabulous Wailers*.. 20.00 - 30.00
JACKIE WALKER:
Imperial 5473 *Peggy Sue*............... 10.00 - 15.00
Imperial 5490 *Only Teenagers Allowed*....... 10.00 - 15.00
LANIE WALKER:
—— *Eenie Meenie Miney Mo/No Use Knocking* ——
T-BONE WALKER:
Atlantic 1065 *T-Bone Shuffle*............ 5.00 - 8.00
  1074 *Play On Little Girl*................ 5.00 - 8.00
  (LP) 8020 *T Bone Blues*................ 25.00 - 35.00
Capitol (LP) 370 *T-Bone Walker (10")*....... 25.00 - 35.00
  (LP) 1958 *The Great Blues Vocals & Guitar Of
  T-Bone Walker*.......................... 15.00 - 20.00
Imperial 5171 *Cold Cold Boogie* (blue label)..... 30.00 - 40.00
  5202 *Street Walking Woman*.............. 20.00 - 30.00
  5216 *Blue Mood*..................... 15.00 - 20.00
  5228 *Long Distance Blues*............... 12.00 - 16.00
  5239 *Party Girl*..................... 12.00 - 16.00
  5284 *Wanderin' Heart*................. 8.00 - 12.00
  5311 *High Society*................... 7.00 - 10.00
  (LP) 9098 *T-Bone Walker Sings The Blues*.... 30.00 - 40.00
  (LP) 9116 *Singing The Blues*............ 30.00 - 40.00
  (LP) 9146 *I Get So Weary*.............. 20.00 - 30.00
WAYNE WALKER:
Brunswick 55133 *You've Got Me*.......... 4.00 - 7.00
SHADY WALL:
Decca 30539 *The New Raunchy*........... 4.00 - 7.00
BILLY WALLACE (& THE BAMA DRIFTERS):
Deb 1003 *Don't Flirt With My Baby*........ 7.00 - 10.00
Mercury 70876 *That's My Reward*......... 10.00 - 15.00
  70957 *Burning Wind*.................. 7.00 - 10.00
JOE WALLACE & THE OWLS:
Moon 304 *Leopard Man*................ 10.00 - 15.00
VANN WALLS & THE ROCKETS:
Atlantic 988 *Open The Door*............. —
JAMES WALTON & HIS BLUES KINGS:
Hi-Q 5029 *Miss Jessie James*............ 4.00 - 7.00
SQUARE WALTON:
RCA Victor 5493 *Gimme Your Bank Roll*..... 10.00 - 15.00
  5584 *Bad Hangover*.................. 10.00 - 15.00
WANDERERS:
Cub 9023, 9094....................... 4.00 - 7.00
Kent 356 *Everybody's Somebody's Fool*....... 10.00 - 15.00

Onyx 518 *Thinking Of You*................	10.00 -	15.00
Savoy 1109 *We Could Find Happiness*.......	15.00 -	25.00

BILLY WARD & HIS DOMINOES:

Decca (EP) 2549 *Billy Ward & The Dominoes*...	10.00 -	15.00
(LP) 8621 *Billy Ward & The Dominoes*......	40.00 -	50.00
29933, 30043, 30149.................	4.00 -	7.00
30420 *To Each His Own*..............	5.00 -	8.00
Federal (LP) 548 *Billy Ward & His Dominoes*...	50.00 -	80.00
12139 *You Can't Keep A Good Man Down*..	8.00 -	12.00
12162 *Until The Real Thing Comes Along*....	7.00 -	10.00
12178 *Tootsie Roll*.................	7.00 -	10.00
12184 *Handwriting On The Wall*.......	7.00 -	10.00
12193 *Above Jacob's Ladder*.........	7.00 -	10.00
12209 *Can't Do Sixty No More*.......	7.00 -	10.00
12218 *Cave Man*.................	5.00 -	8.00
12263 *Bobby Sox Baby*.............	5.00 -	8.00
12301 *One Moment With You*..........	5.00 -	8.00
12308 *Have Mercy Baby*............	5.00 -	8.00
Jubilee 5163 *Come To Me Baby*..........	6.00 -	10.00
5213 *Take Me Back To Heaven*.......	6.00 -	10.00
King (LP) 548 *Billy Ward & His Dominoes with Clyde McPhatter*..................	35.00 -	50.00
(King 548 is a repackaging of Federal 548, above)		
(LP) 733 *Billy Ward And His Dominoes*......	20.00 -	30.00
1280 *Rags To Riches*..............	5.00 -	8.00
1281 *Christmas In Heaven*.........	5.00 -	8.00
1342 *Tenderly*.................	7.00 -	10.00
1364 *Three Coins In The Fountain*......	5.00 -	8.00
1365 *Little Things Mean A Lot*.......	7.00 -	10.00
1492 *Learnin' The Blues*...........	7.00 -	10.00
1502 *Give Me You*..............	7.00 -	10.00
5463 *Lay In On The Line*..........	5.00 -	8.00
Liberty (LP) 3056 *Sea Of Glass*.........	15.00 -	20.00

WILLIE WARD:

Fee-Bee 233 *I'm A Madman*.................	15.00 -	20.00

EDDIE WARE & HIS BAND:

States 130 *Lonely Broken Heart*...........	10.00 -	15.00

BABY BOY WARREN:

Blue Lake 106 *Santa Fe* (red plastic).......	35.00 -	50.00
Drummond 3003 *Stop Breakin' Down*........	40.00 -	60.00

DOUG WARREN & THE RAYS:

Image 1011 *Around Midnight*............	5.00 -	8.00

JOEY WARREN:

Superior 3305 *Goatee*.................	4.00 -	7.00

WASHBOARD SAM:

Chess 1545 *Diggin' My Potatoes*........	15.00 -	20.00
RCA Victor 50-0023 *I'm Just Tired*.........	15.00 -	20.00
50-0048 *Market Street Swing*.......	15.00 -	20.00
50-0090 *Motherless Child Blues*.......	15.00 -	20.00
(Note: Above RCA Victor records are made of orange plastic.)		

BABY WASHINGTON & THE PLANTS:

J & S 1632 *I Hate To See You Go*........	7.00 -	10.00

LEROY WASHINGTON:

Excello 2144 *Wild Cherry*............	8.00 -	12.00

BILL WATKINS:

Tip-Toe 14321 *I Got Troubles*.........	15.00 -	20.00

KATIE WATKINS:

Checker 879 *Snake Blues*........	5.00 -	8.00

GENE WATSON & THE ROCKETS:

Tri-Dex— *My Rockin' Baby*.........	—	

JIMMY WATSON:

Brunswick 55079 *Daisy*.................	5.00 -	8.00

YOUNG JOHN WATSON:

Federal 12120 *Highway 60*...........	15.00 -	20.00
12131 *Motor Head Baby*...........	15.00 -	20.00
12143 *I Got Eyes*.............	12.00 -	16.00
12157 *What's Going On*.........	10.00 -	15.00
12175 *Space Guitar*............	10.00 -	15.00

JOHNNY WATSON:

Cactus— *I'm Not Crazy*...........	15.00 -	20.00

JOHNNY "GUITAR" WATSON:

Class 246 *One More Kiss*.................	3.00 -	5.00
Goth 101 *Rat Now*.................	4.00 -	7.00
Jowat 118 *Baby Don't Leave*...........	5.00 -	8.00
King (LP) 857 *Johnny "Guitar" Watson*........	15.00 -	25.00
RPM 455 *Three Hours Past Midnight*......	8.00 -	12.00

HUNTER WATTS:

Hammond 103 *Wild Man Rock*..............	15.00 -	20.00

ALVIS WAYNE:

Westport 132 *Swing Bop Boogie*.........	20.00 -	30.00
138 *Don't Mean Maybe, Baby*.........	20.00 -	30.00
140 *You Are The One*.........	8.00 -	12.00

BILLY WAYNE:

Hillcrest 778 *I Love My Baby*.........	10.00 -	15.00

BOBBY WAYNE:

Mercury 71070 *Gone*.................	7.00 -	10.00

GAYLON WAYNE:

Universal Artist 52071 *High School's On Fire*...	7.00 -	10.00

LITTLE JACKIE WAYNE:

Rem 306 *White Felt Hat*.............	—	

JAMES WAYNE:

Aladdin 3234 *Crying In Vain*.............	10.00 -	15.00
Imperial 5258 *Sweet Little Woman*.......	10.00 -	15.00
Peacock 1672 *Please Be Mine*...........	7.00 -	10.00

ROY WAYNE:

Clif 101 *Honey Won't You Listen*.............	20.00 -	30.00

SCOTTY WAYNE:

Talen Scout 1008 *Only One*.............	5.00 -	8.00
1011 *Roobie Doobie*.................	7.00 -	10.00

THOMAS WAYNE:

Mercury 71287 *You're The One That Done It*..	10.00 -	15.00
—*Boppin' The Blues*.........	—	

WEE WILLIE WAYNE:

Imperial 5355 *Travelin' Mood*.............	5.00 -	8.00
5368 *Good News*.................	5.00 -	8.00
5737 *I Got To Be Careful*.............	3.00 -	5.00
(LP) 9144 *Travelin' Mood*.................	20.00 -	30.00

JOE WEAVER & THE BLUENOTES/DON JUANS:

Fortune 825 *Baby, I Love You So*...........	8.00 -	12.00
Jaguar 3011 *Lazy Susan*.................	15.00 -	20.00

BOBBY WEBB (& THE JETS):

Jazzmar 1 *Feel The Same*.............	10.00 -	15.00
Webb 429 *Tears Over You*.............	5.00 -	8.00

BOOGIE BILL WEBB:

Imperial 5257 *Bad Dog*.................	20.00 -	30.00

DON WEBB:

Brunswick 55158 *I'll Be Back Home*........	4.00 -	6.00

WEBS:

Sotoplay 660 *Let Me Take You Home*........	25.00 -	40.00

KATIE WEBSTER:

Action 1000 *Close To My Heart*.............	4.00 -	6.00
Rocko 503, 513.......................	3.00 -	5.00
U.S.A. 736, 742.......................	3.00 -	5.00
Zynn 505 *Hoowee, Sweet Daddy*.............	10.00 -	15.00

THE WEBTONES:

MGM 12724 *My Lost Love*.............	7.00 -	10.00

RUSTY WELLINGTON (& HIS BLUE RANGERS):

Arcade 124 *I Want A Little Lovin'*.............	7.00 -	10.00
MGM 12581 *Rocking Chair On The Moon*.....	7.00 -	10.00

ARDIS WELLS:

Azalea 132 *Baby Doll*.............	5.00 -	8.00

GLENN WELLS & THE BLENDS:

Jin 122 *Lesson In Love*.............	7.00 -	10.00

JUNIOR WELLS (& HIS EAGLE ROCKERS):

Chief 7005 *Two Headed Woman*.............	7.00 -	10.00
Chief 7016, 7021, 7034, 7035, 7038, 7048...	7.00 -	10.00
Profile 4005 *I Could Cry*.............	5.00 -	8.00
4011 *Come On In This House*.............	5.00 -	8.00
4013 *You Don't Care*.............	5.00 -	8.00

Shad 5010 *So Tired*............................	4.00 -	6.00
States 122 *Cut That Out* (red plastic).........	30.00 -	40.00
134 *Junior's Wail*....................	30.00 -	40.00
139 *'Bout The Break Of Day*...........	25.00 -	35.00
143 *So All Alone*....................	25.00 -	35.00
COY WERLEY:		
Sundown 122 *Black Jack*...................	15.00 -	20.00
JIMMY WERT:		
Skyline 752 *Bingo Blues*...................	10.00 -	15.00
JOE WEST:		
Bandbox 276 *Maybe You're The One*.........	7.00 -	10.00
SONNEE WEST:		
Nor Va Jak 1956 *Rock Ola Ruby*.............	75.00 -	125.00
SONNY WEST:		
Atlantic 1174 *Rave On*.....................	10.00 -	15.00
SPEEDY WEST:		
Capitol (LP) 1341 *Steel Guitar*..............	15.00 -	20.00
KENT WESTBERRY:		
Art 172 *My Baby Don't Rock Me*............	—	
WALT WESTBROOK:		
Bobbin 106, 119...........................	4.00 -	7.00
GEORGE WESTON:		
Jackpot 48013 *Hey Little Car Hop*...........	5.00 -	8.00
48017 *Shelley Shelley*................	6.00 -	10.00
Talley 118 *Hold Still Baby*..............	8.00 -	12.00
ONE WHEELER:		
Columbia 21371, 21418, 21454, 21500, 21523, 40787, 40917............................	3.00 -	6.00
K-Ark 671 *Too Hot To Handle*............	7.00 -	10.00
Okeh 18022 *Run 'Em Off*.................	5.00 -	8.00
18049 *Little Mama*...................	7.00 -	10.00
WHEELERS:		
Cenco 107 *Once I Had A Girl*.............	7.00 -	10.00
WHEELS:		
Premium 405 *My Heart's Desire*.............	8.00 -	12.00
408 *Teasin' Heart*....................	8.00 -	12.00
THE WHIPS:		
Flair 1025 *Pleading Heart*..................	—	
WHIRLERS:		
Port 70025 *Magic Mirror*...................	4.00 -	7.00
Whirlin Disc 108 *Magic Mirror*............	15.00 -	20.00
THE WHIRLWINDS:		
Guyden 2052 *Angel Love*..................	5.00 -	8.00
WHISPERS:		
Gotham 7309 *Fool Heart*..................	15.00 -	20.00
7312 *Are You Sorry*..................	30.00 -	40.00
DONNIE WHITE:		
King 5122 *That's My Doll*................	8.00 -	12.00
FLOYD WHITE & THE DEALERS:		
Criterion 1 *Cinderella*.....................	—	
JOSH WHITE:		
Decca (LP) 5082 (10") *Ballads*...........	15.00 -	25.00
(LP) 5247 (10") *Ballads, Vol. 2*......	15.00 -	25.00
(LP) 8665 *Josh White*..............	15.00 -	25.00
Elektra (LP) 102 *Josh At Midnight*..........	20.00 -	30.00
(LP) 114 *Josh*...................	20.00 -	30.00
(LP) 123 *25th Anniversary Album*.........	20.00 -	30.00
(LP) 158 *Chain Gang Songs*.......	15.00 -	25.00
London (LP) 338 (10")...................	15.00 -	20.00
(LP) 1341 *Josh White Program*.......	20.00 -	30.00
Mercury (LP) 25014 (10") *Josh White Sings*.....	15.00 -	20.00
(LP) 20203 *Josh White's Blues*.......	20.00 -	30.00
Period (LP) 1209 *(And Big Bill Broonzy)*.......	20.00 -	30.00
Stinson (LP) 14 (10") *Blues*..............	—	
(LP) 15 (10") *Folk Songs*............	—	
WILBUR WHITFIELD & THE PLEASERS:		
Aladdin 3381 *P. B. Baby*..................	8.00 -	12.00
RAY WHITLEY:		
Vee Jay 433 *Yessirree-Yessirree*.............	7.00 -	10.00
SLIM WHITMAN:		
Imperial (DP) 131 *Songs By Slim Whitman*.....	10.00 -	15.00

(EP) 137 *Songs By Slim Whitman*..........	10.00 -	15.00
8134 *My Love Is Growing Stale*...........	10.00 -	15.00
8144 *Bandera Waltz*....................	10.00 -	15.00
8156 *China Doll*.......................	10.00 -	15.00
8163 *By The Waters Of The Minnetonka*...	8.00 -	12.00
8169 *Keep It A Secret*..................	8.00 -	12.00
8180 *How Can I Tell?*..................	10.00 -	15.00
8189 *Restless Heart*....................	8.00 -	12.00
8201 *Danny Boy*.......................	7.00 -	10.00
8208 *Darlin' Don't Cry*.................	7.00 -	10.00
8220 *Stairway To Heaven*...............	7.00 -	10.00
8223 *Secret Love*......................	7.00 -	10.00
8236 *We Stood At The Altar*.............	7.00 -	10.00
(above are blue label with script lettering; following are red label with script lettering)		
Imperial 8257 *Beautiful Dreamer*.............	7.00 -	10.00
8267 *The Singing Hills*	7.00 -	10.00
8281 *Cattle Call*......................	7.00 -	10.00
8290 *Roll On, Silvery Moon*.............	7.00 -	10.00
8298 *I'll Never Stop Loving You*.........	7.00 -	10.00
8299 *You Have My Heart*..............	7.00 -	10.00
8304, 8305, 8307, 8308, 8309, 9310, 8312, 8316, 8317, 8318, 8319, 8320, 8321, 8322, 8323, 8326, 8327, 8328, 8329......................	5.00 -	10.00
5731, 5746, 5766, 5778, 5791, 5821, 5859, 5871, 5900, 5919, 5938, 5966...................	4.00 -	7.00
(LP) 9003 *Slim Whitman Favorites* (maroon label)	20.00 -	30.00
(LP) 9026 *Slim Whitman Sings*............	20.00 -	30.00
(LP) 9056 *Slim Whitman*................	15.00 -	25.00
(LP) 9064 *Country Favorites*.............	15.00 -	25.00
RCA Victor (LP) 3217 (10") *Sings & Yodels*....	40.00 -	60.00
48-0145 *Birmingham Jail*...............	15.00 -	20.00
(Above is pressed of translucent green plastic)		
WHOOPING CRANES:		
El Ray 1000 *Heart And Soul*.............	5.00 -	8.00
"WHOOPERS":		
Jubilee (LP) 1119 *(The Dominoes, Orioles, et al.)*.	15.00 -	20.00
JOHNNY WICK:		
United 116 *Jockey Jack Boogie*..............	10.00 -	15.00
COYE WILCOX:		
Azalea 124 *Zippy, Hippy, Dippy*.............	—	
CHUCK WILEY:		
United Artists 113 *Tear It Up*...............	15.00 -	20.00
JESS WILLARD:		
Ekko 1018 *Don't Hold Her So Close*.........	5.00 -	8.00
SLIM WILLETT:		
Audio Lab (LP) 1542......................	—	
WALLY WILLETTE:		
Flag— *Eenie Meenie*....................	10.00 -	15.00
AL WILLIAMS & THE BARDS:		
Dawn 208 *I'm A Winedrinker*..............	10.00 -	15.00
ANDRE WILLIAMS (& THE DON JUANS):		
Epic 9196 *Bacon Fat*....................	5.00 -	8.00
Fortune 824 *Pulling Time*.................	5.00 -	8.00
834 *Mean Jean*......................	5.00 -	8.00
837 *Jail Bait*......................	5.00 -	8.00
Ronald 1001 *Please Give Me A Chance*.......	8.00 -	12.00
BERNIE WILLIAMS:		
Imperial 5360 *Don't Tease Me*..............	7.00 -	10.00
BILLY WILLIAMS:		
Coral (LP) 57251 *Half Sweet, Half Beat*........	15.00 -	25.00
61363 *Smoke From Your Cigarette*.......	4.00 -	7.00
Mercury (LP) 20317 *Oh Yeah*	15.00 -	20.00
BOB WILLIAMS: (See also THE CYCLONES)		
Debonair 161 *My Goose Is Cooked*..........	4.00 -	7.00
BUZZ WILLIAMS:		
Worthmore (DP) 185 *Blue Suede Shoes; Heartbreak Hotel* other cuts by other artist of no interest)	4.00 -	7.00
CORA WILLIAMS with THE FOUR JACKS:		
Federal 12079 *Sure Cure For The Blues*........	15.00 -	25.00
EDDIE WILLIAMS:		
Excello 2158 *You Broke Your Vows*..........	7.00 -	10.00

WILLIAMS

FLETCHER WILLIAMS:

Bullseye 1001 *Mary Lou*	5.00 -	8.00

HANK WILLIAMS:

MGM (LP) 107 (10") *Hank William Sings*	40.00 -	60.00
(LP) 168 (10") *Moanin' The Blues*	35.00 -	50.00
(LP) 202 (10") *Memorial Album*	35.00 -	50.00
(LP) 203 (10") *Hank Williams As Luke The Drifter*	40.00 -	70.00
(LP) 242 (10") *Honky Tonkin'*	35.00 -	50.00
(LP) 243 (10") *I Saw The Light*	40.00 -	60.00
(LP) 291 (10") *Ramblin' Man*	10.00 -	15.00
(EP) 1014 *Crazy Heart*	10.00 -	15.00
(EP) 1076 *Move It On Over*	10.00 -	15.00
(EP) 1082 *There'll Be No Teardrops Tonight*	10.00 -	15.00
(EP) 1101, 1102 *Hank Williams Sings*	10.00 -	15.00
(EP) 1135, 1136 *Ramblin' Man*	10.00 -	15.00
(EP) 1165 *Luke The Drifter*	10.00 -	15.00
(EP) 1215, 1216, 1217 *Moanin' The Blues*	10.00 -	15.00
(EP) 1218 *I Saw The Light*	10.00 -	15.00
(EP) 1317, 1318, 1319 *Honky Tonkin'*	10.00 -	15.00
(EP) 1491, 1492, 1493 *Sing Me A Blue Song*	10.00 -	15.00
(EP) 1554, 1555, 1556 *The Immortal Hank Williams*	8.00 -	12.00
(LP) 3219 *Ramblin' Man*	40.00 -	70.00
(LP) 3267 *Hank Williams As Luke The Drifter*	50.00 -	80.00
(LP) 3272 *Memorial Album*	35.00 -	60.00
(LP) 3330 *Moanin' The Blues*	35.00 -	60.00
(LP) 3331 *I Saw The Light*	40.00 -	70.00
(LP) 3412 *Honky Tonkin'*	35.00 -	50.00
(LP) 3560 *Sing Me A Blue Song*	35.00 -	50.00
(LP) 3605 *The Immortal Hank Williams*	35.00 -	50.00
(LP) 3733 *The Unforgettable*	25.00 -	35.00
(LP) 3803 *The Lonesome Sound Of*	20.00 -	30.00

(Note: Above must have original yellow and black labels.)

MGM 30751, 30752, 30753, 30754 together comprise 45 RPM album set #202, *Hank Williams Memorial Album*	30.00 -	40.00
30755, 30756, 30757, 30758 together comprise 45 RPM album set #203, *Hank Williams As Luke The Drifter*	30.00 -	50.00

JIM(MIE) WILLIAMS:

Dub 2842 *You're Always Late*	8.00 -	12.00
Sun 270 *That Depends On You*	4.00 -	6.00

JODY WILLIAMS:

Argo 5274 *Lucky Lou*	5.00 -	8.00

PO' JOE WILLIAMS:

Atomic H (unnumbered) *Rock 'N' Roll Boogie*	10.00 -	15.00

LARRY WILLIAMS:

Specialty 608 *Short Fat Fannie*	4.00 -	6.00
608 *Short Fat Fannie* (78 RPM)	10.00 -	15.00
615 *Bony Moronie*	4.00 -	6.00
615 *Bony Moronie* (78 RPM)	10.00 -	15.00
626 *Dizzy, Miss Lizzy*	4.00 -	6.00
626 *Dizzy, Miss Lizzy* 78 RPM	10.00 -	15.00
634 *Hootchy-Koo*	3.00 -	5.00
634 *Hootchy-Koo* (78 RPM)	7.00 -	10.00
647 *I Was A Fool*	3.00 -	5.00
647 *I Was A Fool* (78 RPM)	8.00 -	12.00
(LP) 2109 *Here's Larry Williams*	20.00 -	30.00

LESTER WILLIAMS:

Duke 123 *Let's Do It*	7.00 -	10.00
131 *Crazy 'Bout My Baby*	5.00 -	8.00
Imperial 5402 *McDonald's Daughter*	10.00 -	15.00

LEW WILLIAMS:

Imperial 5411 *Bop Bop Ba Doo Bop*	15.00 -	20.00
5429 *Centipede*	10.00 -	15.00
8306 *I'll Play Your Game*	10.00 -	15.00

MAURICE WILLIAMS & THE ZODIACS:

Herald (LP) 1014 *Stay*	25.00 -	35.00

MEL WILLIAMS (& THE MONTCLAIRS):

Decca 29370 *Lessons In Love*	5.00 -	8.00

Dig (LP) 103 *All Through The Night*	20.00 -	30.00
107 *Here At My Phone*	5.00 -	8.00
114 *Hold Me*	5.00 -	8.00
123 *Don't Cry Baby*	5.00 -	8.00
128 *All Through The Night*	5.00 -	8.00

MORRY WILLIAMS & THE KIDS:

Tee Vee 301 *Are You My Girl Friends*	8.00 -	12.00

OTIS WILLIAMS & HIS CHARMS/NEW GROUP:

De Luxe 6088, 6090, 6091, 6095, 6097, 6098, 6105, 6115, 6130, 6137, 6138, 6149, 6158, 6165, 6174	3.00 -	6.00
6093 *Ivory Tower* (78 RPM)	5.00 -	8.00
King (LP) 560 *Otis Williams & His Charms Sing All Time Hits*	30.00 -	40.00
(LP) 614 *This is Otis Williams & The Charms*	25.00 -	35.00

PO' JO WILLIAMS (See JOE WILLIAMS)

REBECCA WILLIAMS:

Lamp 2011 *Please Give Me A Match*	7.00 -	10.00

ROBERT WILLIAMS & THE GROOVERS:

Tip Top 730 *Cranberry Blues*	5.00 -	8.00

RON WILLIAMS (& THE CUSTOMS):

Imperial 5729 *On Top Of Old Smokey*	5.00 -	8.00
5800 *Don't Tell Me Maybe*	5.00 -	8.00
Pastel 404 *Hey Little Pearl*	7.00 -	10.00
Ty-Tex 100 *Sue Sue Baby*	8.00 -	12.00

SONNY BOY WILLIAMS:

Duplex 9005 *Alice Mae Blues*	10.00 -	15.00

SUGAR BOY WILLIAMS:

Herald 555 *Five Long Years*	7.00 -	10.00

TONY WILLIAMS (See PLATTERS)

WAYNE WILLIAMS & THE SURE SHOTS:

Sure 1001 *Red Hot Mama*	80.00 -	120.00

JAMES WILLIAMSON:

Chance 1131 *The Woman I Love*	20.00 -	30.00

SONNY BOY WILLIAMSON:

Act 511 *Boppin' With Sonny*	7.00 -	10.00
Checker 824 *Don't Start Me To Talkin'*	8.00 -	12.00
834 *Let Me Explain*	7.00 -	10.00
847 *The Key To Your Door*	5.00 -	8.00
864 *Fattening Frogs For Snakes*	5.00 -	8.00
883, 894, 910, 927, 943, 956, 963, 975, 1003, 1036, 1065, 1080, 1134	3.00 -	6.00
(LP) 1437 *Sonny Boy Williamson* (black label)	35.00 -	50.00
RAM 2501 *Mailman, Mailman*	3.00 -	6.00
RCA Victor 50-0005 *Little Girl* (orange plastic)	15.00 -	20.00
50-0030 *Southern Dream* (orange plastic)	15.00 -	20.00
Trumpet 145 *Pontiac Blues*	10.00 -	15.00
166 *Nine Below Zero*	8.00 -	12.00
168 *Stop Now Baby*	6.00 -	10.00
212 *Cat Hop*	7.00 -	10.00
215 *Gettin' Out Of Town*	7.00 -	10.00
216 *Red Hot Kisses*	10.00 -	15.00
228 *Empty Bedroom*	12.00 -	16.00

CHUCK WILLIS (with THE ROYALS/& THE SANDMEN):

Atlantic (EP) 591 *It's Too Late*	10.00 -	15.00
(EP) 608, 609, *Rock With Chuck Willis*	10.00 -	15.00
1130, 1168, 1179, 1192, 2029	3.00 -	5.00

(Note: 78 RPM issues command somewhat higher premiums.)

Atlantic (LP) 8018 *The King Of The Stroll* (black label)	30.00 -	40.00
Epic (LP) 3425 *Chuck Willis Wails The Blues*	40.00 -	50.00
Okeh 6985 *I've Been Treated Wrong Too Long*	8.00 -	12.00
7015 *You're Still My Baby*	5.00 -	8.00
7041 *Change My Mind*	5.00 -	8.00
7051 *Lawdy Miss Mary*	5.00 -	8.00
7055 *I Can Tell*	8.00 -	12.00
7067 *It Were You*	5.00 -	8.00

DON WILLIS:

Satellite 101 *Boppin' High School Baby*	75.00 -	100.00

HAL WILLIS:

Athens 704 *Walkin' Dream*	7.00 -	10.00
Atlantic 1114 *My Pink Cadillac*	10.00 -	15.00

LITTLE SON WILLIS:

Swing Time 304 *Operator Blues*	25.00 -	40.00
305 *Harlem Blues*	25.00 -	40.00
306 *Nothing But The Blues*	25.00 -	40.00
341 *Roll Me Over Slow*	20.00 -	30.00

RAY WILLIS:

Jane 103 *Whatta You Do*	10.00 -	15.00

ROD WILLIS:

Chic 1010 *Somebody's Been Rocking My Baby*	5.00 -	8.00

SLIM WILLIS:

C. J. 622, 627, 635	4.00 -	6.00

WILLOWS:

Club 1014 *This Is The End*	15.00 -	20.00
Eldorado 508 *The First Taste Of Love*	8.00 -	12.00
Heidi 107 *Sit By The Fire*	7.00 -	10.00
Melba (LP) 102 *Church Bells May Ring*	50.00 -	80.00
102 *Church Bells Are Ringing*	20.00 -	30.00
102 *Church Bells May Ring*	5.00 -	8.00
106 *My Angel*	7.00 -	10.00

BILLY JACK WILLS:

MGM 11966 *There's Good Rocking Tonight*	10.00 -	15.00

BOB WILLS (& HIS TEXAS PLAYBOYS)

Columbia (LP) 9003 *Round Up*	20.00 -	30.00
Harmony (LP) 7036 *Bob Wills Special*	12.00 -	16.00
MGM (LP) 91 (10") *Ranch House Favorites*	20.00 -	30.00

OSCAR WILLS: (See also TV SLIM)

Argo 5277 *Flatfoot Sam* (ship logo label)	5.00 -	8.00

WILLY & RUTH:

Spark 105 *Love Me*	—	

ANDY WILSON:

Athens 700 *Little Mama*	4.00 -	7.00
Back Beat 518 *Too Much Of Not Enough*	4.00 -	7.00
Bullseye 1012 *Teenage Martha*	5.00 -	8.00
1020 *Worry Worry*	5.00 -	8.00
1023 *Little Boy Blue*	3.00 -	6.00
Dot 1127 *Hillbilly Boogie*	5.00 -	8.00

DALLAS WILSON:

Rodeo 127 *High Steppin' Daddy*	10.00 -	15.00

DOYLE WILSON:

Lamp 2015 *Hey Hey*	—	

EASY DEAL WILSON:

Sims 112 *Gotta Have You*	8.00 -	12.00

HENRY WILSON & THE BLUENOTES:

Dot 15692 *Mighty Low*	8.00 -	12.00

HOP WILSON (& HIS TWO BUDDIES):

Goldband 1071 *Chicken Stuff*	6.00 -	10.00
1078 *Broke And Hungry*	6.00 -	10.00

J. FRANK WILSON:

Josie (LP) 4006 *Last Kiss*	15.00 -	25.00
Le Cam 722 *Last Kiss*	10.00 -	15.00
Tamara 761 *Last Kiss*	7.00 -	10.00

JACKIE WILSON:

Brunswick (LP) 54042 *He's So Fine*	20.00 -	30.00
(LP) 54045 *Lonely Teardrops*	20.00 -	30.00
55105 *Lonely Teardrops* (78 RPM)	30.00 -	50.00

JIMMY WILSON (& THE BLUES BLASTERS):

Big Town 101 *Tin Pan Alley*	7.00 -	10.00
107 *Blues At Sundown*	5.00 -	8.00
113 *Mountain Climber*	10.00 -	15.00
115 *Trouble In My House*	10.00 -	15.00
123 *I've Found Out*	10.00 -	15.00
Chart 610 *Alley Blues*	10.00 -	15.00
629 *Send Me The Key*	10.00 -	15.00
Goldband 1974 *Big Wheel Rolling*	5.00 -	8.00
Irma 108 *Blues In The Alley*	7.00 -	10.00
Rhythm 1765 *Strangest Blues*	15.00 -	20.00
7-11 2104 *Ethel Mae*	15.00 -	20.00
2105 *Crying Like A Baby Child*	15.00 -	20.00

PEANUTS WILSON:

Brunswick 55039 *Cast Iron Arm*	50.00 -	75.00

TOM WILSON:

Crest 1007 *Can You Bop?*	—	

MAGGIE SUE SIMBERLEY:

Sun 229 *How Long*	15.00 -	20.00

DANNY WINCHELL:

Recorte 406, 410, 415	4.00 -	7.00

PAUL WINLEY & THE ROCKERS:

Premium 401 *Angel Child*	10.00 -	15.00

WINNERS:

Rainbow 331 *Can This Be Love*	—	

JACK WINSTON:

Jay Bee— *It's Rock 'N' Roll*	15.00 -	20.00

JOHNNY WINTER (& THE CRYSTALIERS):

Frolic 501 *That's What Love Does*	10.00 -	15.00
503 *Ease My Pain*	10.00 -	15.00
509 *Gangster Of Love*	10.00 -	15.00
512 *I Won't Believe It*	10.00 -	15.00
KRCO 106 *Creepy*	10.00 -	15.00
107 *One Night Of Love*	10.00 -	15.00
Sonobeat 107 *Rollin' And Tumblin'*	5.00 -	8.00

DON WINTERS:

Coin 102 *Pretty Moon*	—	

MAC WISEMAN:

Dot 15544 *Step It Up And Go*	5.00 -	8.00

NORMAN WITCHER:

Poor Boy 102 *Somebody's Been Rocking My Boat*	20.00 -	30.00

JIMMY WITHERSPOON:

Checker 798 *Big Daddy*	7.00 -	10.00
810 *Waiting For Your Return*	5.00 -	8.00
826 *It Ain't No Sedan*	5.00 -	8.00
Crown (LP) 5156 *Jimmy Witherspoon*	10.00 -	15.00
(LP) 5192 *Jimmy Witherspoon Sings The Blues*	10.00 -	15.00
Federal 12095 *Foolish Prayer*	8.00 -	12.00
12099 *Lucille*	8.00 -	12.00
12107 *Corn Whiskey*	8.00 -	12.00
12118 *Jay's Blues*	8.00 -	12.00
12138 *East Mile*	8.00 -	12.00
12155 *Miss Mistreater*	8.00 -	12.00
12156 *Sad Life*	10.00 -	15.00
12173 *Just For You*	6.00 -	10.00
12188 *Highway To Happiness*	5.00 -	8.00
12189 *I Done Told You*	5.00 -	8.00
HI Firecord (LP) 421 *At Monterey*	10.00 -	15.00
King (LP) 634 *Jimmy Witherspoon*	15.00 -	20.00
Pacific Jazz (LP) 1267 *Singin' The Blues*	15.00 -	20.00
RCA Victor (LP) 1639 *Goin' To Kansas City Blues*	15.00 -	20.00
6977 *Who Baby Who*	4.00 -	7.00

DANNY WOLFE:

Dot 15571 *Pretty Blue Jean Baby*	5.00 -	8.00
15667 *Let's Flat Get It*	7.00 -	10.00
15715 *Pucker Point*	5.00 -	8.00

JIMMY WOLFORD:

4 Star 1714 *My Name Is Jimmy*	15.00 -	20.00

BOBBY WOOD:

Pen 113 *Everybody's Searchin'*	10.00 -	15.00

NORMAN WOOD:

Tamm 2015 *Black Lake Boogie*	—	

TOMMY WOOD:

D 1000 *Can't Play Hookey*	15.00 -	20.00

JERRY WOODWARD:

RCA Victor 7616 *Who's Gonna Rock My Baby*	5.00 -	8.00
Reed 1017 *Who's Gonna Rock My Baby*	10.00 -	15.00

BILL WOODS:

Bakersfield— *Phone Me, Baby*	10.00 -	15.00
Fire 100 *Go Crazy Man*	8.00 -	12.00

BOB WOODS:

Kingsport 100 *Greasy Corner Boogie*	—	
110 *Sunshine Boogie*	—	

DONALD WOODS & THE VEL-AIRES:

Flip 306 *Death Of An Angel*	5.00 -	8.00

DONALD WOODS & THE YEL-AIRES:
Flip 306 *Death of an Angel*................ 5.00 - 8.00

JOHNNY WOODS & FAMOUS RHYTHM ACES:
Bo-Kay 113 *Valley Of The Blues*............ —

SONNY WOODS (& THE DOWNBEATS/with THE TWIGS):
Hollywood 1015 *Chapel Of Memories*........ 10.00 - 15.00
Peacock 1679 *So Many Tears*................ 7.00 - 10.00
  1689 *Someday She'll Come Along*.......... 7.00 - 10.00

DON WOODY:
Decca 30277 *Bird Dog*..................... 15.00 - 25.00

SHEB WOOLEY:
MGM (EP) 1188, 1189, 1190 *Sheb Wooley*..... 8.00 - 12.00
  (EP) 1607 *Purple People Eater Plays Earth Music* 10.00 - 15.00
  (EP) 1607 *The Purple People Eater*......... 10.00 - 15.00
  (LP) 3299 *Sheb Wooley*................... 15.00 - 20.00

JIMMY WORK:
All 502 *Tennessee Border*.................. —

WAYNE WORLEY:
Brent 7024 *Red Headed Woman*.............. 7.00 - 10.00
Elbridge 11016 *Red Headed Woman*.......... 20.00 - 30.00

JOHN WORTHAN:
Peach 722 *Write You A Letter*.............. 15.00 - 20.00

DOUG WRAY:
Epic 9322 *Goose Bumps*.................... —

LINK WRAY (& HIS WRAYMEN):
Cadence 1347 *Rumble* (78 RPM).............. 10.00 - 15.00
Epic (LP) 3661 *Link Wray And His Wraymen*.. 25.00 - 35.00
Swan (LP) 510 *Jack The Ripper*............ 15.00 - 25.00

LUCKY WRAY:
Starday 552 *It's Music She Says*........... 10.00 - 15.00
  575 *Got Another Baby*.................... 10.00 - 15.00
  608 *Teenage Cutie*...................... 10.00 - 15.00

WRENS:
Rama 65 *Come Back My Love*................ 50.00 - 75.00
  174 *Serenade Of The Bells*............... 50.00 - 75.00
  175 *Betty Jean*......................... 50.00 - 75.00
  184 *I Won't Come To Your Wedding*....... 70.00 - 100.00
  194 *C'est La Vie*....................... 40.00 - 60.00

DALE WRIGHT (& THE WRIGHT GUYS):
Fraternity 804, 818, 831, 837.............. 4.00 - 7.00

JOHNNY WRIGHT with IKE TURNER:
RPM 443 *Suffocate* (red label)............. 8.00 - 12.00

STEVE WRIGHT:
Lin 5022 *Wild Wild Woman*................. 10.00 - 15.00

GENE WYATT:
Ebb 123 *Love Fever* .... 10.00 - 15.00

JIMMY YANCEY:
Atlantic (LP) 103 (10") *Yancy Special*..... 15.00 - 20.00
  (LP) 130 *Jimmy & Mama Yancey*........... 20.00 - 30.00
  (LP) 134 *Jimmy & Mama Yancey*........... 20.00 - 30.00
  (Note: Abvoe two are 10" LPs.)
  (LP) 1231 *Pure Blues/Jimmy & Mama Yancey* 20.00 - 30.00

LAFAYETTE YARBOROUGH:
Bart (?)— *Comic Book Crazy*............... 4.00 - 7.00

MALCOLM YELVINGTON:
Sun 211 *Drinkin' Wine Spodee-O-Dee*....... 30.00 - 40.00
  246 *Rocking With My Baby*............... 15.00 - 20.00

RUSTY YORK:
Chess 1730 *Sugaree*....................... 4.00 - 7.00
King 5103 *Shake 'Em Up Baby*.............. 10.00 - 15.00
  5511, 5587.............................. 4.00 - 7.00
Note 10021 *Sugaree*....................... 7.00 - 10.00
P.J. 100 *Sugaree*......................... 7.00 - 10.00
Sage— *Sadie Mae*......................... 8.00 - 12.00

DONNIE YOUNG:
Decca 31077 *Shakin' The Blues*............ 8.00 - 12.00

FARON YOUNG:
Capitol (LP) 778 *Sweethearts Or Strangers*...... 15.00 - 20.00
  (LP) 1004 *The Object Of My Affection*...... 12.00 - 16.00
  (LP) 1096 *This Is Faron Young*............ 12.00 - 16.00
  (LP) 1185 *My Garden Of Prayer*........... 12.00 - 16.00
  (LP) 1245 *Talk About Hits*............... 10.00 - 15.00

GEORGE YOUNG:
Mercury 71259 *Can't Stop Me*.............. 10.00 - 15.00

MIGHTY JOE YOUNG:
Fire 1033 *Empty Arms*..................... 7.00 - 10.00

LENNY YOUNG & THE JAY BIRDS:
Jackpot 48006 *Lovable*.................... 4.00 - 7.00

NELSON YOUNG:
Lucky 0002 *Rock Old Sputnick*............. 7.00 - 10.00

ROY YOUNG:
Can. Hall (?)— *Big Fat Mama/Just Keep It Up*.. —

YOUNG LADS:
Felice 712 *Night After Night*............. 10.00 - 15.00
Neil 100 *Moonlight*....................... 10.00 - 15.00

YOUNGSTERS:
Empire 104 *Shattered Dreams*.............. 8.00 - 12.00
  109 *Dreamy Eyes*........................ 7.00 - 10.00

YOUNGTONES:
Brunswick 55089 *Oh Tell Me*............... 15.00 - 20.00
X-Tra 104 *You I Adore*.................... 15.00 - 20.00
  110 *Patricia*........................... 15.00 - 20.00
  120/121 *Can I Come Over*................ 10.00 - 15.00

"YOUR FAVORITE SINGING GROUPS":
Hull (LP) 1002 (various artists)........... 20.00 - 35.00

"YOUR OLD FAVORITES":
Old Town (LP) 101 (various artists)............ 20.00 - 30.00

EDDIE ZACK (& COUSIN RICHIE):
Columbia 21387 *Rocky Road Blues*.......... 5.00 - 8.00
  21441 *I'm Gonna Roll And Rock*.......... 7.00 - 10.00

FRANCIS ZAMBON:
Vamalco 503 *Our Love Will Last*........... 7.00 - 10.00

REX ZARIO:
Arcade 163 *Jukebox Cannonball*............ 10.00 - 15.00
Skyrocket 1001 *Go Man Go, Get Gone*....... 10.00 - 15.00

ZEBULONS:
Cub 9069 *Falling Water*................... 8.00 - 12.00

DANNY ZELLA (& THE LARADOS/HIS ZELL ROCKS):
Dial 100 *Sapphire*........................ 10.00 - 15.00
Fox 10056/10057 *Wicked Ruby*.............. 7.00 - 10.00

BEN JOE ZEPPA:
Era 1042 *Topsy Turvy*..................... 5.00 - 8.00
Metrol 9001 *Shame On You Miss Lindy*....... 5.00 - 8.00

ZIRCONS:
Heigh Ho 607 *Where's There's A Will*........ 5.00 - 8.00
  608/609 *I Couldn't Stop Crying*........... 5.00 - 8.00
MelloMood 1000 *Lonely Way*................ 5.00 - 8.00

BIBLIOGRAPHY

Steven C. Barr, THE (ALMOST) COMPLETE 78RPM RECORD DATING GUIDE, Toronto, Canada, published by the author, 1979, 1980. (The first and second editions are out-of-print; a third edition is anticipated in 1985.)

Brian Case & Stan Britt, THE ILLUSTRATED ENCYCLOPEDIA OF JAZZ, Harmony Books, New York, 1978. (Contains selective discography of albums, photos of album jackets, short biographies of over 400 jazz artists.)

Robert Dixon & John Godrich, RECORDING THE BLUES, Stein and Day, New York, 1970. (The story of recording companies; how and where they recorded the artists they recorded; many interesting reproductions and illustrations of record labels and record company promotional materials.)

Ken Clee, THE DIRECTORY OF AMERICAN 45 R.P.M. RECORDS, privately published by Stak-O-Wax, P.O. Box 11412, Philadelphia, Pennsylvania 19111. (Four volumes, loose-leaf format. Discography, or more properly, a collection of artist and label discographies. Records listed in order of release with titles of both sides. Volumes are available individually or as a set.)

John Godrich & Robert Dixon, BLUES & GOSPEL RECORDS, 1902-1943, Third Edition, Storyville Publications & Co., Ltd., 66 Fairfax Drive, Chigwell, Essex IG7 6HS, England. (A massive discography, arranged alphabetically by artist, providing 78 rpm issue numbers, all songs recorded by each artist in chronological order, including unissued titles; recording dates, accompaniment personnels, recording locations, master numbers, "take" numbers. Prefatory material includes information about "race" labels and recording "field trips.")

Roger D. Kinkle, THE COMPLETE ENCYCLOPEDIA OF POPULAR MUSIC AND JAZZ, 1900-1950, Arlington House, New Rochelle, New York, 1974. (Four volumes, 2642 pages. Data on movie musicals; performers, with biographies; singers; composers; bandleaders; musicians; listings of 100 to 200 songs, most popular, for each year; representative recordings for each year; Broadway musicals; numerical listings of 9 major labels.)

Mike Leadbitter & Neil Slaven, BLUES RECORDS 1943-1966, Oak Publications, New York, 1968. (Discography, containing the recorded work of over 1,000 artists. Recording dates, records issued, personnels, recording locations.)

Dan Mahoney, THE COLUMBIA 13/14000-D SERIES — A Numerical Listing, Walter C. Allen, Stanhope, New Jersey, 1961. (Interesting, in-depth treatment of the Columbia "Race" series, Artists, Song titles, master numbers, dates, and even quantities of records ordered.)

Bill C. Malone, COUNTRY MUSIC U.S.A., University of Texas Press, Austin, Texas, 1968.

Oliver Read & Walter L. Welch, FROM TIN FOIL TO STEREO: Evolution of the Phonograph, Howard W. Sams, Inc., Indianapolis, Indiana, 1976. (In addition to detailed and scholarly treatment of its main subject, contains information about record companies and their corporate genealogy.)

Brian Rust, THE AMERICAN DANCE BAND DISCOGRAPHY, 1917-1942, Arlington House Publishers, New Rochelle, New York, 1975. (Two volumes, 2066 Pages. Discography, providing 78 rpm issues numbers, all songs recorded by each artist/band in chronological order, including unissued titles; recording dates; personnels; recording locations; master numbers; "takes".)

(Note: the above set is out-of-print, but is expected to be republished by Storyville Publications & Co., Ltd., in 1985.)

Brian Rust, THE AMERICAN RECORD LABEL BOOK, DaCapo Press, Inc., 233 Spring Street, New York, New York, 10013. (Information about, and in most cases, photographs of, many American and some British labels up to about 1942.)

Brian Rust, THE COMPLETE ENTERTAINMENT DISCOGRAPHY, FROM THE MID-1890s TO 1942, DaCapo Press, Inc., 233 Spring Street, New York, New York 10013. (Covers the recorded output of celebrities and personalities. Includes brief biographies of artists, details of their 78 rpm record issues; unissued recordings; recording dates, locations, accompanying personnels.)

Brian Rust, JAZZ RECORDS, 1897-1942, Fifth Edition, Storyville Publications & Co., Ltd., 66 Fairfax Drive, Chigwell, Essex IG7 6HS, England. (Two massive volumes covering virtually all known 78 rpm records of jazz interest. In addition to the usual thorough discographical data, this set includes a song index. This, and the other discographies by Rust, above, cannot be praised too highly!)

Nick Toches, COUNTRY–THE BIGGEST MUSIC IN AMERICA, Stein and Day, New York, 1977 (Animated, knowledgeable treatment of the subject and more; rockabilly, blues, etc.)

PUBLICATIONS

BLUES UNLIMITED
   38A Sackville road, Bexhill-On-Sea, Sussex, England (Blues, Rhythm & Blues)

BUYGONE RECORD SALES (Magazine)
   30, Radcliffe Road, West Bridgford, Nottingham, NG2 5HH, England. (Primarily a marketplace for Rock 'n' Roll, Rhythm & Blues, Rockabilly.)

GOLDMINE
   700 East State Street, Iola, Wisconsin 54990. Phone: (715) 445-2214. (Large bi-weekly publication featuring articles, discographical data, reviews and an extensive advertising/auction section offering mainly Rock 'n' Roll, Rhythm & Blues, Rockabilly, etc. of the 1950s and later. Has lately undertaken to broaden its coverage to include recordings of other styles and periods: jazz, classical and country.)

THE GROOVEYARD:
   P.O. Box 05-0978, Tice, Florida 33905-0978. (Small monthly magazine dealing with various types of records and related memorabilia.)

I.A.J.R.C. JOURNAL
   Quarterly publication of the International Association of Jazz Record Collectors. Sent to members. Yearly dues: $15.00. Write to: Gene Miller, Secretary, 90 Prince George Drive, Islington, Ontario, Canada M9B 2X8. (Articles, research and an excellent source of information on available reissues of jazz; the club itself offers to members low-priced LP reissues of its own.)

J.E.M.F. Quarterly
   Publication of The John Edwards Memorial Foundation, Folklore & Mythology Center, University of California, Los Angeles, California 90024 (Hillbilly, Country/Western, primarily)

JOSLIN'S JAZZ JOURNAL
   Box 213, Parsons, Kansas 67357. (Attractively produced quarterly tabloid, primarily of interest to collectors of jazz and dance band 78s and LPs. Contains articles, research and reviews, in addition to advertisements and auctions.)

LIVING BLUES
   2615 N. Wilton Ave., Chicago, Illinois 60614 (Covers all aspects of the blues: historical, contemporary; interviews, record and book reviews, blues-related news, articles, photos.)

NEW AMBEROLA GRAPHIC
   37 Caledonia St., St. Johnsbury, Vermont 05819 (Concerned largely with artists/recordings of very early days of recording-cylinders as well as discs.)

NEW KOMMOTION
   Adam Komorowski, 3 Bowrons Avenue, Wembley, Middx., England HA0 4QS (Rock 'n' Roll, Rockabilly primarily.)

NOT FADE AWAY
   Neil Foster, 16 Coniston Avenue, Prescot, Merseyside, England L34 25W (Rock 'n' Roll, Rockabilly primarily)

R.A.T.E.
   The Record and Tape Exchange Program of the Big Bands Collectors Club, P.O. Box 3171, Pismo Beach, California 93449. (Sent four times a year to members. A vehicle for buying, selling and trading recordings; exchange of information and ideas. Dues are $5.00 for the calendar year.)

R.P.M. (RECORD PROFILE MAGAZINE)
   24361 Greenfield, Suite 201, Southfield, Michigan 48075 (Bi-monthly magazine dealing primarily with 1950s and later Rock 'n' Roll, Rhythm & Blues, but tending like Goldmine, to broaden its scope. Includes ads, auctions, articles and research. Graphically and substantively satisfying, especially in view of its recent origin – August, 1983.)

RECORD AUCTION MONTHLY
   P.O. Box 758, Utica, Michigan 48087. (Primarily concerned with music of the 1950s and later, this recently started publication contains auctions, advertisements and articles.)

RECORD MART
   16, London Hill, Rayleigh, Essex, England SS6 7HP. (A quarterly trading vehicle for collectors of rock 'n' roll, rockabilly, rhythm & blues, and other music of the 1950s and later. Most offerings are 45s and LPs; few 78s.)

RED HOT
   Tony Scott, Editor, 90 Wordworth Street, Hove, Sussex, England BN3 5BH (Rock 'n' Roll, Rockabilly, primarily.)

RECORD RESEARCH
   65 Grand Avenue, Brooklyn, New York 11205 (Much discographical information; primarily of interest of 78 collectors, jazz, dance bands, blues, country. "Blues Research" is a subsidiary publication, appearing irregularly, sometimes as part of the parent publication; it deals with post-war blues and rhythm and blues.)

STORYVILLE

Storyville Publications & Co., Ltd., 66 Fairview Drive, Chigwell, Essex IG7 6HS, England (also publishers of discographies; see Bibliography, preceding.) (Bi-monthly magazine covering vintage jazz and blues with articles, extensive research and reviews.)

TIME BARRIER EXPRESS

P.O. Box 206, Yonkers, New York 10710. (Primarily of interest to Rhythm and Blues collectors)

VINTAGE JAZZ MART

4 Hillcrest Gardens, Dollis Hill, London NW2 6HZ, England. (Primarily a marketplace for collectors of jazz and blues 78s and LPs, consisting mostly of offerings at auction, but including set sale offerings as well. Frequency of appearance is only five issues in two years. The infrequency is understandable when each prodigious issue arrives. U.S.A./Canadian subscription agent is: Dan Allen, Walter C. Allen of Canada, Box 929, Adelaide Station, Toronto, Ontario, Canada ONT M5C 2K3.)

WHISKEY, WOMEN AND --- The Rhythm and Blues Jubilee

Dan Kochakian, Editor, 39 Pine Avenue, Haverhill, Massachusetts 01830. ("Dedicated to Blues & Rhythm Music from then to now.")

Belshaw, George & His K.F.A.B. Orch	52	Bill and Slim	140	Blasers, The	258
Belltones, The	256	Billings, Bud and Joe	199	Blattner, Jules	258
Bellus, Tony	256	Bills, Dick	257	Blazer Boy	258
Beltones, The	256	Billy and Jesse	140	Bledsoe, Blazer Boy Steve	258
Bellus, Tony	256	Billy Bird	257	Blendairs, The	258
Belvederes	256	Billy Boy	140	Blenders, The	258
Belvideers	257	Billy Guitar	258	Blends, The	258
Belvin, Jessie	257	Billy The Kid	258	Blendtones, The	258
Ben's Bad Boys	52	Binder, Long Man	258	Blevins, Frank	200
Benbow, Baby	139	Bine, Doug	199	Blevins, Rubye	200
Bennett, Boyd	257	Bing Bones	258	Bilhove, Marv	258
Bennett, Eloise	52	Binkley Brothers	199	Blind Andy	200
Bennett, Will	139	Binney, Jack	53	Blind Arthur	141
Bennett's Swamplanders	52	Bird, Connie	258	Blind Blake	141
Benson, Joe	257	Bird, Elmer, Happy/String Band	199	Blind Gary	141
Benson Orch. of Chicago	52	Bird, Louis	199	Blind Mack	141
Benson's Orch, Benny	52	Bird, Nat	199	Blind Norris	141
Bentley Boys	199	Bird's Kentucky Corn Crackers	199	Blind Percy	141
Bentley, Gladys	139	Birdson, Larry	258	Blind Sammie	141
Benton, Brook	257	Birkhead, L.O.	200	Blind Willie	141
Benton, Buster	257	Birmingham Bluetette	53	Blockbusters, The	258
Benton, Merve	257	Birmingham Five	53	Bloom, Rube	53
Benton, Walt	257	Birmingham Jug Band	53	Blu-Disc Orchestra, The	53
Bergeron, Shirley	257	Birmingham Quartet	140	Blue Angels, The	258
Berigan, Bunny	52	Birmingham, Sam	140	Blue Belle	141
Bernard, Glory	139	Birmingham, Serenaders	53	Blue Belles, The	258
Bernard, Rod	257	Bisbee, Jasper	200	Blue Bill	141
Bernie, Ben	52	Bishop, Billy	200	Blue Boy	141
Berry, Chu	257	Bivens, Lester Pete	200	Blue Boys	141, 200
Berry, Chuck	52	Black Ace	140	Blue, Bud	200
Berry Cups	257	Blackbirds of Paradise	53	Blue Charlie	258
Berry Kids	257	Black Brothers	200	Blue Chips	258
Berry, Lou	257	Black Boy Shine	140	Blue Diamonds, The	258
Berry, Mike	257	Black Diamond	140	Blue Dots	258
Berry, Red & The Bell Raves	257	Black Diamond Orchestra	53	Blue Flames (see Little Jr.)	258
Berry, Richard	257	Black Diamond Serenaders	141	Blue Grass Footwarmers	53
Berton, Vic	52	Black Dominoes, The	141	Blue Harmony Boys	141
Bertrand, Jimmy	52	Black, Frankie	141	Blue Jay Boys	53
Bessemer Melody Boys	140	Black Ivory King	140	Blue Jacks, The	141
The Best of Rhythm and Blues	257	Black, Jimmie	140	Blue Moon Melody Boys	53, 200
Beverly Hill Billies	199	Black Kids of Harmony	200	Blue Notes, The	258
Biagini, Henry & His Orch.	53	Black, Lewis	141	Blue Rhythm Band/Boys	53
Biddleville Quintette	140	Black Pirates, The	141	Blue Rhythm Orchestra	53
Big Aces, The	53	Black Spider Dumplin	141	Blue Ridge Cornshuckers	200
Big Bill et al	140	Black Swan Dance Orch.	53	Blue Ribbon Boys/Band	53
Big Bloke	140	Blackard, Dad	200	Blue Ribbon Syncopators	53
Big Bopper	257	Blackburn, Mamie	141	Blue Ridge Duo	200
Big Chief	140	Blackwell, Francis Scrapper	141	Blue Ridge Highballers	200
Big Connie	257	Blackwell, Otis	258	Blue Ridge Hillbillies	200
Big Daddy	257	Blackwell, Willie '61'	141	Blue Ridge Mountaineer	200
Big Ed	257	Blackwells, The	258	Blue Ridge Mountaineers	200
Big Five	257	Blair, Sunny	141	Blue Ridge Mountain Entertainers	200
Big Four	257	Blake, Charley	141	Blue Ridge Mountain Girls	200
Big Jeff and the Radio Playboys	199	Blake, Curley	200	Blue Ridge Mountain Singers	200
Big Joe And His Rhythm Washboard Band	140	Blake, Eubie	200	Blue Ridge Playboys	200
Big John	140	Blake, Tommy	53	Blue Sky Boys Trio	200
Big Mac	257	Blakeley, Cliff	258	Blue Smitty	141
Big Maceo	140, 257	Blakeley, Jimmy	258	Blue Tones, The	258
Big Maybelle	257	Blakeley, Wellington	258	Bluebirds, The	53
Big Memphis Ma Rainey	140, 257	Blakeman, Guy	258	Blues Birdhead	141
Big Oscar	140	Blalock and Yates	200	Blues Chasers, The	53
Big Richard	140	Blanchard, Dan	200	Blues King, The	141
Big Sister	140	Blanchard, Jackie	258	Blues, Man The	141
Big Trio	140	Bland, Billy	258	Blues Rockers, The	141, 258
Big Walter	257	Bland, Bobbie Blue	258	Blues Slim	258
Big Willie	140	Bland, Glen	258	Blues, The	258
Bigard, Barney	53	Bland, Jack	53	Blues Toppers, The	258
Bigeou, Esther	140	Blakenship Brothers	258	Bluie, Louie	141
Bilbro, D. H.	140	Blankenship Family	200	Blythe's Blue Boys	53
				Blythe's Sinful Five	53

James, Bobbie	294
James, Corky	82
James, Elmer	160, 294
James, Elmo/Elmore	160, 294
James, Etta	294
James, Frank	160
James, Harry & His Orch	82
James, Jeanette	82
James, Jelly	82
James, Jesse	294
James, Madelyn	83
James, McKinley	294
James, Pauline	160
James, Sadie	160
James, Skip	160
James, Sonny	294
James, Springback	161
James, Sunny	161
James, Tommy	294
James, Ulysses	161
James, W. Lawrence	161
Jameson, Bobby	294
Jammin Jim	161
Jan & Arnie	294
Jan & Dean	294
Jan & Radiants	294
Janis, Johnny	294
Jano, Johnny	294
Jarmels	294
Jarrell, Ben	220
Jarrett, Art	83
Jarvis & Justice	220
Jaxon, Frankie "Half Pint"	83
Jay, Bobby	294
Jay, Dale	294
Jay, Johnny	294
Jay, P. & The Haystackers	294
The Jayes	294
Jayhawks	294
Jaytones	294
The Jazz Harmonists	83
The Jazz-O-Harmonists	83
The Jazzopators	83
Jazzbo, Tommy	161
Jefferies, Speed	83
Jeffers, Jimmy	294
Jefferson, Eddie	294
Jefferson, George	161
Jefferson, Blind Lemon	161
Jeffery, Wally	294
Jelly Belly & Slim Seward	161
The Jelly Whippers	83
Jenkins, Blind Andrew	220
Jenkins, Bobby	294
Jenkins, Bo Bo	294
Jenkins, Frank	220
Jenkins, Freddy	83
Jenkins, Gooby	220
Jenkins, Gus	294
Jenkins, Hazekia	161
Jenkins & Jenkins	161
Jenkins, Oscar Mountaineers	220
Jenkins, Robert	161
Jenney, Jack	83
Jennings Brothers	220
Jennings, Baby Boy	294
Jennings, Herb	220
Jennings, Waylon	294
Jerome, Ralph	294
Jerry & Demar	294

Jesse & Buzzy	294
Jesse & Marvin	294
Jessie & the Sequins	294
Jesse's String Five	220
Jesters	294
Jets	294
Jeter-Pillar Orch	83
Jewels	294
Jill & Ray	295
The Jim Dandies	83
Jim Jam	161
Jimmies' Blue Melody Boys	83
Jimmies' Joys	83
Jimmy & Duane	295
Jimmy & Johnny & The Jades	295
Jimmy & Walter	161,295
Jinkins, Gus	295
Jiv-A-Tones	295
Jive Bombers	295
Jivers	295
Jivetones	295
Jivin Gene	295
Jodimars	295
Joe & His Rhythm Orch	83
Joe Joe	161
Joe's Hot Babies	83
Joey & The Lexingtons	295
Johnnie & Joe	295
Johnnie & Jonie	295
Johnny & The Hurricanes	295
Johnny & The Jammers	295
Johnny & The Jokers	295
Johnny & Slim	220
Johns, Whitey	220
Johnson, Al	295
Johnson, Alec	161
Johnson, Babe	161
Johnson, Bert	83
Johnson, Bessie	161
Johnson, Big Bill	161,295
Johnson, Biliken, Addams & Roberts	161
Johnson, Bill (Louisiana Jug Band)	83
Johnson, Blanche	83
Johnson Boys	83, 161
Johnson Brothers	220
Johnson, Bud	161
Johnson, Buddy	295
Johnson, Bunk	83
Johnson, Buster	161
Johnson, Caroline	83
Johnson, Charlie	83
Johnson, Cliff	295
Johnson, Conrad	161
Johnson, Curtis	295
Johnson, Dee	295
Johnson, Earl	220
Johnson, Easy Papa	161
Johnson, Eddie	83, 161
Johnson, Edity (North)	162
Johnson, Edna	162
Johnson, Edward	220
Johnson, Elizabeth	162
Johnson, Elnora	162
Johnson, Elvira	162
Johnson, Fannie	162
Johnson, Frank	162
Johnson, Gene	220
Johnson, Gladys	162
Johnson, Graveyard	83
Johnson, Harry "Slick"	162

Johnson and Harvy	220
Johnson, Haven	83
Johnson, Hoyt	295
Johnson, JC	83
Johnson and Jackson	161
Johnson, James	83, 220
Johnson, James "Steadyroll"	162
Johnson, James "Stump" and his Piano	162
Johnson, Jellyroll	162
Johnson, Jess	220
Johnson, Jesse	162
Johnson, Jimmy	295
Johnson, Jimmy's String Band	220
Johnson, Johnny	84
Johnson, Julia	162
Johnson, Julia and Leon Hyatt	220
Johnson, Ki Ki	162
Johnson, Larry	295
Johnson, Leroy Country	162
Johnson, Lil	162
Johnson, Lonnie	295
Johnson, Lonnie and Blind Willie Dunn	162
Johnson, Louise	163
Johnson, Margaret	163
Johnson, Martha	163
Johnson, Mary	163
Johnson, Maw	295
Johnson, Merlin	163
Johnson, Neal	295
Johnson, Nelson-Porkchops	161
Johnson, Paul (and Charlie)	220
Johnson, Pete	84
Johnson, Porkchop	163
Johnson, Ray	163,295
Johnson, Red	163
Johnson, Robert	163
Johnson, Rockheart	163
Johnson, Ruth	163
Johnson, Sam (Suitcase)	163
Johnson, Sara	163
Johnson, Sherman and His Clouds of Joy	163
Johnson, Smilin Tubby	220
Johnson and Smith	161
Johnson, Sonny Boy and His Blue Blazers	163
Johnson Stan	295
Johnson, Stove	295
Johnson, Stovepipe	163
Johnson, Stump	163
Johnson, T.C. "Blue Coat" Tom Nelson	163
Johnson, Tillie	163
Johnson, Tommy	163
Johnson's Henry	73
Johnson's Jazzers	83
Johnson's Plantation Serenaders	83
Johnson's Roy Happy Pals	84
Johnston, Merle & His Ceco Coxuriers	84
Jolly Jacks	295
Jolly Jivers	163
Jolly Jug Band	163
Jolly Three	84
Jones, Alberta (Trio) and Her Red Peppers	163
Jones, Alex "Snook"	295
Jones, Anna	164
Jones, Bessie	164
Jones, Bo	164
Jones, Bobby and His Orch	84
Jones Boys	295
Jones Brothers	220
Jones, Buddy	220
Jones, Carl	220

Shindigs	322	Six Men And A Girl	119	Smith, Kate	119
Shines, Johnny	180	Six Teens	323	Smith, Kenny	324
Shippee, Uncle Joe	241	Sizzlers, The	119	Smith, Laura	182
Shipley, Reese	322	Sizemore, Asher	241	Smith, Lendon	324
Shirelles	322	Skee Brothers	323	Smith, Leroy	119
Shirkey, Earl & Roy Harper	241	Skeet's Charley Orch	119	Smith, Little George & His Harmonica	324
Shirley, Chesley	241	Skelton, Eddie	323	Smith, Mack Allen	324
Shirley & Lee	323	Skidmore III, Bill	241, 323	Smith, Mamie	182
Shoe Shine Johnny	180	Skiles, Bob	241	Smith, Mandy	182
Shondell, Troy	323	Skiles, Dude	119	Smith, Marshall	242
Shondells	323	Skillet Dick & Frying Pans	119	Smith, Merritt & Keith Pooser	242
Shores, Bill	241	Skipper, Macy	323	Smith, Merritt & Leo Boswell	242
Shores Southern Trio	241	Skoodle Dum Doo & Shetfield	180	Smith, Pine Top	182
Short Brothers	241	Skyland & Scottie	241	Smith, R.B. & S.J. Allgood	242
Short Creek Trio	241	Skylar, Norm	323	Smith, Ray	324
Short, Jaydee	180	Skylarks	323	Smith, Robert	182
Short, Jelly Jaw	180	Skyliners	323	Smith, Robert Curtis	324
Shorty George	180	Skyscrapers	323	Smith, Ronnie	324
Shreveport Home Wreckers	180	Slack, Freddie	323	Smith, Ruby	182
Shreveport Sizzlers	118	Slades	323	Smith, Sammy	324
Shufflin Sam & His Rhythm	180	Slavin, Slack	323	Smith, Shelby	324
Shunatona, Chief	241	Sleepy Joe & His Washboard Band	180	Smith, Six Cylinder	182
Shutters, Harold	323	Slim Harpo	323	Smith, Slim	242
Shytans	323	Slim & His Hot Boys	119	Smith, Spark Plug	182
Sides, Connie	241	Slim & Slam	119	Smith, Stuff	119
Siefert, Jerry	323	Sloane & Threadgill	241	Smith, Susie	182
Siegel, Al	118	Sloke & Ike	180	Smith, Thunder	183
Sigler's Birmingham Merrymakers	118	Sluefoot Joe	180	Smith, Travelin J.	241
Signorelli, Frank	118	Sly Fox	323	Smith, Trixie	183
Silhouettes	323	Smallwood, Lester	241	Smith, Walter	242
Silva, Bob	323	Smart Tones	323	Smith, Warren	324
Silva Tones	323	Smith, Al	323	Smith, Willie The Lion	119
Silver Slipper Orch	118	Smith, Anne	180	Smith & Woodlieff	241
Silver, Sid	323	Smith, Arthur	241, 323	Smith's Garage Fiddle Band	241
Silvers, Johnnie	323	Smith, Bessie	180	Smith's Hoss Hair Pullers	241
Silvertones	323	Smith, Bessie Mae	181	Smith's Ike (Chicago Boys)	182
Silvester, Johnny & His Orch	118	Smith, Billy	323	Smith's, Kid (Family)	241
Simeon, Omer	118	Smith, Blaine & Cal	241	Smith's, Lloyd (Gut Bucketeers)	119
Simmons, Al	323	Smith, Bobby	323	Smith's, Sammy (Stompers)	119
Simmons, Bill	241	Smith, Carl	323	Smith's, Ted (Rhythm Aces)	119
Simmons, Gene	323	Smith, Charles B.	241	Smithson, Lonnie	324
Simmons, Lester	118	Smith, Chester	323	Smokehouse Charley	183
Simmons, Mack	323	Smith, Clara	181	Smokey Joe	183, 324
Simmons, Matt	241	Smith, Clementine	181	Smokey Mountain Boys	242
Simms, Howard	118	Smith, Dayton	323	Smokey Mountain Fiddler Trio	242
Simon, Frank	323	Smith, Elizabeth	181	Smokey Mountain Ramblers	242
Simpkins, Joseph	118	Smith, Eilliam & Versey	183	Smokey Smothers	324
Simpson, Bill	180	Smith, Ethel	181	Smolev, Marvin	119
Simpson, Coletha	180	Smith, Fats & Rhythm Kings	119	Smoothtones	324
Simpson, Donald & Rockenetts	323	Smith, Flossie & Red Hot Twins	181	Smyth's County Ramblers	242
Sims, Arthur	118	Smith, Floyd & The Montclairs	323	Snappers	324
Sims, Chuck	323	Smith, Fred & His Society Orch	119	Sneed, Jack & His Sneezers	120
Sims, Frankie Lee	180, 323	Smith, Funny Paper	181	Sneed, Leslie	324
Sims, Henry	180	Smith, Gene	323	Snooks & His Memphis Ramblers	120
Sims, Joe & Clarence Williams	180	Smith, Grace	181	Snooky & Moody	183
Sims, Mac	323	Smith, Guy	182	Snow, Eddie	183, 324
Sims, Oliver	241	Smith, Hank	241	Snow, Hank	324
Singing Boys, The	118	Smith, Harl & His Orch	119	Snow, Hattie	183
Singleton, Bead & the Notes	323	Smith & Harper	180	Snowden, Q. Roscoe	183
Singleton, Eddie	323	Smith, Harry	241	Snyder, Bob	120
Sioux City Six	118	Smith, Hazel	182	Sodjas', Joe (Swingtette)	120
Sisco, Bobby	323	Smith, Henry	182, 324	Soileau, Leo & Lafleur (Moise) Robin	242
Sisco, Gene	323	Smith, Horace	182	Solataires	324
Sissle, Noble	118	Smith, Huey & His Clowns	324	Solomon & Hughes	242
Sisson, Allen	241	Smith, Ivy	182	Solomon, King	324
Six Black Diamonds	119	Smith, Jabbo	119	Solotones	324
Six Hottentots, The	119	Smith, Jane	182	Sonics	324
Six Jolly Jesters	119	Smith, Jimmie	241	Sonny Boy & Lonnie	183
Six Jumping Jacks	119	Smith, Joe	119, 241	Sonny Boy & Sam	183
		Smith, Julia	182	Sonny Guitar	324

Tharpe, Sister Rosetta		329	"Those Good Old Memories" (LP)	329	Tony & The Masquins	330
Thayer, Frank		329	Thrashers	329	Tony & Raindrops	330
Theard, Sam		187	Three Baccer Tags, The	245	Tony & Technics	330
Them Birmingham Night Owls		123	Three Barbers, The	124	Tony & Twilighters	330
Themes		329	Three Black Diamonds	124	Too Bad Boys, The	188
Therrien, Joe Jr.		329	Three Blue Chasers	124	Too Tight Henry	188
Theus, Fatso & The Flairs		329	Three Boswell Sisters, The	124	Toombs, Jack	246
Thies, Henry & His Orch		123	Three Chuckles	329	Toombs, Jackson	330
Thirteenth Floor Elevators		329	Three D's	329	Toomey, Welby	246
Thomas, Alexander Mudcat		329	Three Deuces, The	124	Toon, George	246
Thomas, Al "Fats"		187	Three Dots & A Dash	329	Top Notes	330
Thomas, Andrew		187	Three Fifteen & His Squares	124	Topics	330
Thomas, Andy		187	Three Georgia Crackers	245	Toppers	330
Thomas, B.J.		329	Three Happy Dandies	124	Topps	330
Thomas, Bessie		187	Three Honeydrops	329	Tops	330
Thomas, Billy		329	Three Hot Eskimos	124	Toreadors	330
Thomas, Bud		187	Three Howard Boys	246	Torey, George	188
Thomas, Earl		187	Three Jacks, The	124	Tornados	330
Thomas, Elvie		187	Three Jolly Miners	124	Torok, Mitchell	246
Thomas, F.T.		187	Three Kentucky Serenaders	246	Torrell, Jackie	330
Thomas, George		187, 245	Three Keys, The	124	Towel, Jim	188
Thomas, Grayson		245	Three Monkey Chasers	124	"Town Hall Party"	330
Thomas, Henry		188	Three Muskateers	246	Town Three	330
Thomas, Hersal		124	Three Old Cronies	246	Townsend, Henry	188
Thomas, Hociel		124	Three Peppers, The	124	Townsend, Jessie	188
Thomas, Howard		124	Three Stripped Gears	246	Townsend, Sam	188
Thomas, Jerry		329	Three T's, The	124	Toys	330
Thomas, Jesse		188, 329	Three Tobacco Tags	246	Trail, Buck	330
Thomas, Josephine		188	Three Tweedy Boys	246	Trailblazers	330
Thomas, Kid		329	Three Virginians	246	Traits	330
Thomas, L.J.		188	Three Williamsons	246	Tram, Bix & Eddie	125
Thomas, Lafayette		329	Three's A Crowd	124	Tram, Bix & Lang	125
Thomas, Millard G.		124	Thrillers	329	Trammell, Bobby Lee	330
Thomas, Mule		329	The Thrillers	188	Trantham, Carl	330
Thomas, Ramblin		188	Thunderbirds	329	Travelers	125, 246, 330
Thomas, Rambling		188	Thruston, Bud	124	Travers, Vincent & His Orch	125
Thomas, Rufus		188, 329	Tibbs, Andy	188	Travis & Bob	330
Thomas, Sippie		188	Tibbs, Leroy	124	Travis-Carlton Orch	125
Thomas, Tabby		329	Tides	329	Travis, Merle	330
Thomas's Collegians, Eddie		124	Tifanos	329	Traymore Orch, The	125
Thomas' Devils		124	Til, Sonny	329	Treble Chords	330
Thomas' Muscle Shoals Devils		124	Tillis, Big Son & D.C. Bender	329	Tremaine, Paul	125
Thomas, Washington		188	Tillis, Clyde	329	Tremaines	330
Thompkins, Jed		246	Tillis, Mel	329	Tremble, Tommy & Shadows	330
Thompkins, Jim		188	Tim Tam & The Turn-Ons	329	Tremer, George H.	125
Thompson, Bud		245	Timonty, Tim	124	Tremonts	330
Thompson, Buddy		329	Tin Pan Paraders, The	124	Tren-Dells	330
Thompson, Cranford & Miles		245	Tindull's, Klien (Paramount Serenaders)	124	Trend Tones	330
Thompson, Edward		188	Tino & Revlons	330	Trent, Aplhonse	125
Thompson, Ernest		245	Tinsley, Slim	188	Trent, Jo	125
Thompson, Ernest E.		245	Tinsley's Washboard Band	125	Trexle-Gray	330
Thompson, Evelyn		188	Tisdom, James	188	Treys	330
Thompson, Floyd		245	Titans	330	Tri-Lads	330
Thompson, Fred		329	Titus, Bud	330	Triangle Harmony Boys	125
Thompson, George		124	Tobacco Tags	246	Triangle Quartette	188
Thompson, Georgia		245	Tobier, Ben	125	Trice, Rich	188
Thompson, Hank		245, 329	Tobins, Midnight Serenaders	125	Trice, Welly	188
Thompson, Hayden		329	"Todays' Hits" (LP)	330	Tridells	330
Thompson, Hugh		245	Todd, Johnny	330	Trimble, Carl	246
Thompson, Johnny		124	Tokens	330	Triolo, Frank	330
Thompson, Junior		329	Tolbert, Skeets & His Gentlemen Of Swing	125	Triolinder, Delbert	330
Thompson, Kay & Her Boys/Orch		124	Tom and Chuck	246	Trojans	330
Thompson, Kid Guitar		329	Tom & Jerry	125, 330	Trombone Red	125
Thompson, Loretta		329	Tom & Roy	246	Troopers	330
Thompson, Uncle Jimmie		245	Tomerlin, Kenny	330	Trophies	330
Thompson & Miles (Red Fox Chasers)		245	Tomlin, Kingfish Bill	188	Troupers	330
Thornhill, Claude		124	Tomlin, Pinky	125	Troutts, Charlie (Melody Artists)	125
Thornton, Margaret		188	Tommie & Willie	246	Troy Harmonists, The	125
Thornton, Willie Mae		188, 329	Tommy and Jimmy	188	Trowbridge, Dorethea	188
Thorp, Chuck		329	Tompkins, Tommy Red	125	Tru-Tones	330